THE ORTHODOX PATRISTIC WITNESS
CONCERNING CATHOLICISM

Ὁ ἍΓΙΟΣ   ΦΩΤΙΟΣ
ΚΠΟΛΕΩΟ

Saint Photios the Great

THE ORTHODOX PATRISTIC WITNESS CONCERNING CATHOLICISM

Testimony from the Lives and Writings of the Saints and Elders, Decisions of the Ecumenical Councils and Other Authoritative Sources

An Orthodox Ethos Publication

Uncut Mountain Press

THE ORTHODOX PATRISTIC WITNESS
CONCERNING CATHOLICISM
Testimony from the Lives and Writings of the Saints and Elders,
Decisions of the Ecumenical Councils and
Other Authoritative Sources

© 2024
Uncut Mountain Press

uncutmountainpress.com

Special Thanks to Our Volunteer Translators: The Very Rev. Hieromonk Polycarpos (Strosnider), Gregory Heers, Nicholas Nelson, Kira Rogozhina, Ellaina Chiru, Pascu Nicolae, Simeon Nachev.

The Orthodox Ethos Team.
The Orthodox Patristic Witness Concerning Catholicism—1st ed.

ISBN (Hardcover): 978-1-63941-026-2
ISBN (Softcover): 978-1-63941-025-5

I. Orthodox Christian Theology
II. Orthodox Christian Ecclesiology

This Volume is dedicated to
all the zealous confessors of the Faith
who are bravely standing against
the false embrace of the Latin Papists.

Saint Justin Popović

"According to the true Church of Christ, that has existed since the advent of Christ the Theanthropos into this world as His theanthropic Body, the dogma of the infallibility of the Pope is not only a heresy, but the ultimate heresy. No other heresy has so radically and so comprehensively risen against Christ the Theanthropos and His Church as Papism has through the dogma of the infallibility of the Pope, a man. This is undoubtedly the heresy above all heresies. It is the horror above all horrors. It is an unseen rebellion against Christ the God-Man. It is, alas, the most dreadful banishment of the Lord Christ from the earth. It is the repeated betrayal of Christ, the repeated crucifixion of the Lord Christ, not on a wooden cross this time but on the golden cross of papist humanism. All this is hell thrice over for the wretched earthly being called man."[1]

— *Saint Justin Popović*

---

1   Saint Justin Popović, *The Orthodox Church and Ecumenism*, trans. Benjamin Emmanuel Stanley (Birmingham: Lazarica Press, 2000), 148-149.

SUMMARY OF CONTENTS

DETAILED CONTENTS

PART II
Historical Struggles Against the Latins

PART IV
Other Authoritative Texts

PART VI
Clerics, Monastics, & Distinguished Lay Confessors

PART VII
Analysis of Major and Recent Errors

APPENDIX

Saint Gregory Palamas
Fresco • Pantokratoros Monastery, Chapel of Timi Prodromos • 1819

INTRODUCTION

What is the position of the Orthodox Church with regard to Catholicism? Who are the ultimate authorities to inform us of this? Without hesitation, every Orthodox Christian looks to the Saints and the patristic consensus to answer this question. It is the diachronic voice of Holy Tradition as presented by the Saints individually and collectively in council. All contemporaries who would claim to represent the Church and provide answers to the above questions must be in agreement with, and give voice to, the choir of Holy Fathers gone before us.

Herein lies the great value of the book which you, O dear and pious reader, hold in your hands: it is the most extensive collection of lives of saints and of their writings with regard to Catholicism ever published, in any language. Herein you will find the very most authoritative answers to the foregoing questions. You will find the lives of many saints who suffered at the hands of the Latins or Latin-minded in defense of the Orthodox Faith. You will read the conclusions, decisions and proclamations of the most authoritative councils, decrees of Holy Synods, encyclicals of holy Patriarchs, and liturgical texts definitively setting forth the confession of faith of the Church vis-a-vis the cacodoxy of Papal Protestantism. Lastly, you will be introduced to the writings of our contemporary elders and other distinguished theologians from Greece, Russia, and around the world, who followed the saints and stood for Holy Orthodoxy against the soul-damaging teachings which the West, tragically, came to embrace.

A few points of clarification are in order regarding 1) historic strategies used by Papism and 2) the use of the name "Roman":

1) Over the past millennium, from the separation of the papacy from the communion of the Church until today, a variety of methods have been employed to draw Orthodox Christians into submission to the Pope.

Initially, the Papacy relied on both diplomatic pressure and militaristic intimidation to seek Orthodox reunion under papal terms. For example, see Part II, Sections A-F.

After the fall of Constantinople and Roman Empire in 1453, the Papacy continued diplomatic pressures through the Ottoman Turks, along with ambassadors representing Western governments. After the founding of the Jesuit order, around the time of the Council of Trent (1545), "missionary" work among the Orthodox began in earnest. Deceitful proselytism was very effective in devastating Orthodox communities, even to the point of threatening the very existence of several of the eastern patriarchates.[2] It was a sad, but not uncommon

---

2   Metropolitan Kallistos Ware, Eustratios Argenti: A Study of the Greek Church

occurrence for many bishops, and even patriarchs, to submit to Rome secretly, or sometimes even publicly.

This was the time of the rise of Uniatism (12th-19th centuries). The strategy of Uniatism eventually became one where the Latins let Orthodox dioceses and parishes operate entirely unchanged except for recognition and proclamation of the Pope as their head. This method worked to diminish Orthodox numbers all over the world. Examples of this are found in this book, in Part II, Section H and Part VI, Section B, 6.

At the Second Vatican Council (1962-65), Ecumenism became the chosen strategy of the Vatican. Ecumenism sought to erase borders through popularizing principles which diminish the identifying marks between Orthodoxy and heresy; i.e., they developed a new ecclesiology to effectively replace the once-universally attested "exclusivist" patristic ecclesiology. See Part VI, Section B, 9. This has since morphed into a global perennialist paradigm which seeks not only to blur the boundaries between truth and heresy but all religions. Fr. Seraphim Rose's "religion of the future" has become the religion of the present.

2) In this book (excluding quotations), we refer to the inhabitants of the "Byzantine Empire" as Romans or East Romans. We often deny this name to the "Roman Catholics" because, according to Orthodox primary sources and apologists they are neither truly "Roman" nor "Catholic". Old Rome is sometimes a term for the city itself. Rather than "Roman," many Orthodox historians (especially Greek) referred to them as "Franks" (since that was the barbarian tribe that became dominant in the West after the fall of the Western Empire) or "Latin" (referring to their language), or "papal" (being the heart of their heresy). In this way, the language of the book aligns with and follows the tradition of the Fathers before us who never used a changing or confusing terminology.

A brief historic explanation of how these terms became so confused in the West would be appropriate here. After the conversion of the Roman Empire to the Christian Faith and during the time of the Ecumenical Councils, the Roman identity became deeply intertwined with the Orthodox Faith while the term "Greek" referred to the pagans. This became firmly understood across the world. Charlemagne, in an attempt to bolster legitimacy by discrediting authentic Roman authority in Constantinople, called a council in Frankfurt in the year A.D. 794. Here, he established a diplomatic policy towards the East Romans which identified them with Greeks[3] (for accepting the Seventh

---

Under Turkish Rule (London: Oxford University Press, 1964), 54.

3   Han Lamers, *Greece Reinvented: Transformations of Byzantine Hellenism in Renaissance Italy* (Leiden: Koninklijke Brill NV), 2015, 65. This act made use

Ecumenical Council) and therefore idolaters.[4] Thus, he usurped the name Roman when declaring himself a Roman Emperor and (curiously) the historic barbarian lands outside the old Western Roman Empire now became the "Holy Roman Empire" of the Middle Ages. In the East, the Romans continued to call themselves Roman, as did their Muslim neighbors. Political conversation did not buy into Charlemagne's "lie" and continued to call them Franks.[5] When the Eastern Roman Empire fell to the Ottoman Turks, the Ottomans continued to call their conquered people "Romans." The term "Byzantine" was invented roughly one hundred years after the fall of the Empire by the German historian Hieronymus Wolf in his *Corpus Historiæ Byzantinæ.*[6] When the modern state of Greece emerged in freedom with the overthrow of its Turkish captors, the name "Byzantine" became more popular in the West to avoid confusion with the term "Greek" (referring to Charlemagne's lie) in the new socio-political creation of the modern Greek state with modern, "European" Greek people. This became official policy for Western powers with the London Protocol of January 31, 1836.[7]

We have intentionally kept our editorial comments to a minimum throughout. We believe history, a developed dogmatic consciousness on behalf of the reader, but most especially our Saints speak for themselves as to how the Orthodox Church and each Orthodox Christian ought to relate to Catholicism. May these texts guide you and many others into the patristic consensus of the Holy Orthodox Church with respect to Catholicism, so that "you may be able to withstand in the evil day, and having done all, to stand."[8]

---

of the historiographical concept of *translatio imperii* which, obviously was not recognized by New Rome (Constantinople).

4   Giovanni Domenico Mansi, *Sacrorum Conciliorum nova et amplissima collectio,* Volume 17. 493-496.

5   Although this desired recognition on the part of the Franks did provide diplomatic leverage that the East Romans did sometimes use.

6   John McLean, "Western Civilization," Lumen, accessed February 5th, 2024, https://courses.lumenlearning.com/atd-herkimer-westerncivilization/chapter/naming-of-the-byzantine-empire/.

7   Great Britain. Foreign and Commonwealth Office, "British and Foreign State Papers 1836-1837," *The Foreign Office*, vol. 25 (London, James Ridgway and Sons, Piccadilly), 1853, 729 [In French].

8   Ephesians 6:13

OI AΓΙOI AΓOPEI - TAI O CIOMAPTYPS ΕΠΙ ΠΑΡΙΑΡΧΥ
BEKKΥ ΤΥ ΛΑΤΙ ΝΟΦΡΟΝΟC
MA PTY P'CANTEC

The Holy Venerable Athonite Martyrs
Under The Latin-Minded Patriarch Bekkos

PART I

THE LIVES OF MARTYRS AND CONFESSORS AGAINST THE LATINS

Icon of the Yearly Menaion

A. MENAION

September 4th: New Hieromartyr GORAZD Bishop of SLOVAKIA and the CZECH LANDS[9]

This Holy New Martyr was born in 1879 in Moravia and named Matthew Pavlik. As a Roman Catholic priest, he became interested in Slav Christian origins, and the mission of Saints Constantine and Methodius in Moravia and he was among the leaders of a movement for reform within the Roman Catholic Church. When Czechoslovakia was established as a state after the First World War (1919), he was a member of a delegation sent to Rome to ask for autonomous status for the local Church and for the use of the Czech language to be permitted in the Liturgy. The Roman See turned down these proposals, whereupon about 800,000 Christians, Fr. Matthew Pavlik and other priests among them approached Bishop Dositheus of the Orthodox Patriarchate of Serbia, who was very active among Carpatho-Russians formerly united to Rome, with the request that he receive them also into the Orthodox Church. Following a visit of Bishop Dositheus to Prague in 1920, Father Matthew was converted to Orthodoxy, and a year later was consecrated Bishop for the Orthodox of Moravia and Silesia by Patriarch Demetrius

---

9   Hieromonk Makarios of Simonos Petra, The Synaxarion: *The Lives of the Saints of the Orthodox Church, Volume One, September-October,* trans. Christopher Hookway (Ormylia: Holy Convent of the Annunciation of Our Lady, 1999), 37-39.

of Serbia, receiving the name of Gorazd, a holy disciple of Saint Methodius (27 July). Taking these great missionaries as a pattern of pastoral labours, Bishop Gorazd did a great deal to restore Orthodoxy in Czechoslovakia, despite the turning back of some of those who had been leaders of the reform movement but who found demands of the Orthodox Church too "burdensome." Bishop Gorazd patiently bore criticism, false accusations, trials and tribulations of all kinds. He set up several parishes in Moravia and Bohemia and made a Czech translation of the Divine Services, which was used in the eleven Churches he founded. He published a prayer that was for the people, a Book of Needs (*Trebnik*) for the use of priests, a catechism and various devotional works in Czech. He enjoyed the confidence and respect of the Patriarch of Serbia and sent a large number of young men to prepare for the priesthood there.

During the Second World War, seven members of the Czech resistance who, after the assassination of the representative of the Reich, had taken refuge in the crypt of the Orthodox cathedral in Prague, were captured and executed. The two priests of the cathedral were arrested and the Nazi authorities were planning reprisals against the whole Orthodox Church. Bishop Gorazd gave himself up to the Nazis to save his priests' and accepted full responsibility for what had occurred. He was arrested on the 25th of June 1942, tortured, and shot on the 4th of September, and thus he sealed the foundation of the autonomous Church of Slovakia and Czech Lands with his blood. Despite his voluntary sacrifice, the Orthodox Church was subjected to retaliation. The Churches were closed, and the priests sent to concentration camps in Germany.

September 5th: Hieromartyr ATHANASIUS, Abbot of the Monastery of St. Symeon the Stylite at BREST-LITOVSK

St. Athanasius, a staunch defender of Orthodoxy and opponent of the Roman Catholic effort to convert the Orthodox, was born in 1596 which coincided with the year of the false union of Brest-Litovsk arranged between Rome and some Russian bishops for those Orthodox living under Polish rule in Lithuania to come under the ecclesiastical jurisdiction of Rome. Born to a Lithuanian nobleman of limited wealth, he was a tutor in his early life to wealthy Polish families. He understood the Polish, Latin, Greek and Russian languages, and read many theological writings in addition to the holy fathers.

In 1627, recognizing the futility of this vain, earthly world, he became a monk at the Monastery of Khutyn near Orsha in Little Russia. This monastery, along with several others, were located on the private lands of noble families and leaders, and so were independent of the influence of the Polish occupying forces. By tradition, the monastery was "deeply committed to the preservation of Orthodoxy, so that it was able to offer a great encouragement to the Orthodox people in the face of Roman Catholic propaganda"[10] in order to "resist the onslaught of heretical, Latin teachings."[11]

He was sent to several other monasteries, being ordained to the priesthood at Vilna. He wound up at the Kupyatitsk Monastery, a monastery in need of restoration, as deputy. Metropolitan Peter Moghila tasked him with restoring the monastery and after a divine revelation from the Mother of God, St. Athanasius set out on a journey to receive support from the Tsar for rebuilding the Orthodox church, which he obtained. Two years later, following the death of the igumen of the monastery of St. Symeon the Stylite in Brest-Litovsk, he was appointed Abbot there. "From then on, he was to be a resolute and tireless fighter against Roman proselytism, clothed in Orthodox rites and customs known as the *Unia*. For the next eight years, by prayer, preaching and through his writings, the Saint devoted all his strength to refuting the false Union, and to bringing back to the holy sheepfold of Christ those who had strayed."[12] First, he republished all the documents regarding the false union and the anathemas and writings which opposed it. He personally presented the apologetics in the churches. He immersed his

---

10 Hieromonk Makarios of Simonos Petra, The Synaxarion: *The Lives of the Saints of the Orthodox Church, Volume One, September-October*, trans. Christopher Hookway (Ormylia: Holy Convent of the Annunciation of Our Lady, 1999), 45.

11 Holy Trinity Monastery, "The Holy New Martyr, St. Athanasius of Brest," *Orthodox Life 23*, no. 4 (Jul-Aug 1973): 6.

12 Hieromonk Makarios of Simonos Petra, The Synaxarion: *The Lives of the Saints of the Orthodox Church, Volume One, September-October*, trans. Christopher Hookway (Ormylia: Holy Convent of the Annunciation of Our Lady, 1999), 45.

flock in Orthodox doctrine and published educational materials including the writings of the holy Fathers.

The Orthodox population were being harshly persecuted by the Polish occupational forces, Jesuits, and Polish colonizers to convert the Orthodox and St. Athanasius petitioned the King of Poland, Vladislav IV, for relief. The king issued a decree, however, enforcement of it was ignored. Even worse, some of the Orthodox leaders, fearful of their own safety, sought to limit his efforts.

"It is difficult for us to express the conditions under which Orthodox Christians suffered in *Uniate* territory. And to a great measure, the minds and senses of the Orthodox were stunned with disbelief at the actions of the Latins, for the atrocities which they wrought against the faithful were truly beyond the comprehension of the Orthodox....

"Western notions of human vengeance and earthly punishments in connection with the Church are utterly alien to Orthodoxy. All these things were rendered the more shocking because those committing the atrocities professed the name Christian. The Orthodox were slaughtered indiscriminately at times and it was not uncommon that, while it was crowded with worshippers on a feast day, the doors of an Orthodox church would be barricaded from the outside and the building set fire, recalling the ancient martyrdoms under the first pagan Rome."[13]

As time progressed, a dearth of clergy and a lack of spiritual education among the younger priests created a vacuum of spiritual ministry. In addition, some of the wealthier Orthodox "sold themselves to the *Unia* for financial and social advantages."[14] Faced with increasing opposition and a lack of similar-minded courageous faithful, he prayed to the Mother of God before the wonder-working icon of Kupyatitsk and when he said the words "free us from all troubles," he heard the response "Oh, Athanasius! Complain to the Seim[15] through My icon and Kupyatitsk cross and demand of the king that the irreligious *Unia* be forever

---

13 Holy Trinity Monastery, "The Holy New Martyr, St. Athanasius of Brest," *Orthodox Life 23*, no. 4 (Jul-Aug 1973): 8-9.

14 Ibid., 9.

15 *Seim/Sejm*: The Governmental Polish State Council of the Period.

abolished and the Orthodox Church be left in peace. And warn them that otherwise God's wrath is inevitable."[16]

In 1643, he went again to the Seim to appeal for relief from the persecution of the Orthodox. The king was moved and granted elementary human rights to them. But St. Athanasius was attacked by Orthodox leaders and accused of insanity, as their financial and social interests were in jeopardy. He was deprived of his abbotship, defrocked from the priesthood and taken to Kiev for mental examination where he was found to be of sound mind. Thus being vindicated, he returned to the Brest-Simeonov Monastery to his abbotship and priesthood, resuming his ecclesiastical duties.

While the Latin persecution had abated for a short while, it resumed, so he petitioned the king again but was imprisoned, although he managed to submit another petition to the Seim while still incarcerated in 1645. During this time, Metropolitan Peter Moghila,[17] his ardent supporter, reposed. He was released in 1647 and returned to St. Simeon Monastery, but in 1648 the Latin *Unia* redoubled their persecutions with such brute force and bloodshed that it resulted in a rebellion led by the Cossack Hetman Bogdan Khmelnitsky. It was quickly quelled by Polish forces with political leaders being arrested and by the Unia's Jesuit troops arresting Orthodox Christian Church leaders.

Arrested and imprisoned, St. Athanasius was charged with undermining the Union of Brest-Litovsk, inciting rebellion, opposing state-church educational initiatives, etc. but none of the legal charges were sustained. It was decided to detain him until a suitable charge could be made. From the day of his incarceration on July 1st until September 5th, 1648, he endured both physical and mental tortures by his captors and the Roman Catholic authorities but "he never ceased to cry 'Anathema to the Union.'"[18] Tortured with hot coals, flogged and burnt, he was fi-

---

16 Holy Trinity Monastery, "The Holy New Martyr, St. Athanasius of Brest," *Orthodox Life 23*, no. 4 (Jul-Aug 1973): 9.

17 Peter Moghila is justly condemned for introducing or allowing to be introduced, a whole flood of Latin notions and theology into Russia. But he also was a staunch defender of the physical integrity of the Russian Church, and he strove with zeal to preserve the parishes and monasteries intact. (Footnote Taken From *Orthodox Life 23*, no. 4 (Jul-Aug 1973), 10).

18 Hieromonk Makarios of Simonos Petra, *The Synaxarion: The Lives of the Saints*

nally shot to death by his executioners, then decapitated and thrown into a pit. His incorrupt body, discovered some time later and brought to the monastery in which the saint had served, was found to work miracles and healings.

September 6th:
New Hieromartyr MAXIMUS Sandovich[19]

St. Maximus Sandovich was born in 1886 in the village of Zhdenia on the present frontier of Poland with Slovakia, in territory which was part of the Austro-Hungarian Empire at the time. His piety was evident from his early years. As a schoolboy, he would get up early to read the services and sing the canticles of the church in his room. He wanted to become a priest or monk and so, at the end of his secondary education, he entered a *Uniate* monastery of the region as a novice. But the life of this establishment soon disappointed him, and he left after three months for the Monastery of Pochaev in Ukraine (see 28 Oct.), as much renowned for the strictness of its typicon and for the spiritual life of the fathers, as for its witness to the Orthodox tradition. When Maximus was still a novice, Metropolitan Antony Khrapovitsky (1863-1936), visited the monastery and asked the Abbot to let him take a novice with him who could be put to study in his Seminary, with a view to ordination to serve the Ukrainian communities in the Carpathian region, that had returned to Orthodoxy from the Unia. Maximus was chosen so he had to give up his heart's desire for the monastic life and follow the Bishop. When he had finished his studies at the Seminary in Zhitomir, he married a Byelorussian wife and was ordained by the Metropolitan in 1911.

His pastoral ministry began in the town of Grab, not far from his native village, where he served the first Orthodox Liturgy since the Carpatho-Russians yielded to Uniatism in the eighteenth century. He was arrested on a visit to his family home, sentenced to eight days imprison-

---

of the Orthodox Church, Volume One, September-October, trans. Christopher Hookway (Ormylia: Holy Convent of the Annunciation of Our Lady, 1999), 46.

19   Hieromonk Makarios of Simonos Petra, The Synaxarion: *The Lives of the Saints of the Orthodox Church, Volume One, September-October*, trans. Christopher Hookway (Ormylia: Holy Convent of the Annunciation of Our Lady, 1999), 50-52.

ment and heavily fined. Father Maximus was unshaken by this and continued to serve the divine Liturgy in the surrounding villages, despite the penalties imposed by the courts upon himself and those who assisted him. In March 1912, he was remanded in custody at Lvov, charged with being Orthodox, using Church books written in Russian and of collaborating with the enemy, for so Russia was regarded by the Austro-Hungarian authorities. Despite the lying accusations heaped up against him, and the ill-treatment and harassment of all kinds that he endured, when he and his companions came to trial in June 1914, they were acquitted. In poor health, he was able to return to Zhdenia. But, on the outbreak of the First World War in August, he was again arrested, together with his pregnant wife, his father and the Orthodox of his village. They were imprisoned at Gorlice, the county town. On 6 September 1914, Father Maximus was brought out of his cell before a judge who summarily informed him that he was condemned to death. He was shot in the prison yard before the eyes of the assembled Orthodox prisoners. As he fell, Christ's valiant Martyr cried out, "Long live Holy Orthodoxy!" whereupon one of the executioners, seized with anger, rushed forward and stabbed him. It was not until 1922 that his body could be taken to Zhdenia, where it was laid to rest near the Church. From then on, pilgrims flocked to his tomb. Veneration of Saint Maximus, as the very image of their ethnic and religious identity, grew among the Carpatho-Russian Orthodox, especially during the years of their deportation.

See pages 518 and 540 for some liturgical hymns to him.

September 7th: Monk and Martyr MACARIUS, Archimandrite of KANEV

"St. Macarius came from the province of Volhynia in the northwest of Ukraine, when the Orthodox were experiencing aggressive attempts at proselytism by the Roman Catholics."[20] "Born in 1605 in Ovruch,

---

20 Hieromonk Makarios of Simonos Petra, *The Synaxarion: The Lives of the Saints of the Orthodox Church, Volume One, Introduction/September-October*, trans. Christopher Hookway (Ormylia: Holy Convent of the Annunciation of Our Lady, 1999), 56.

Volhynia, to a family known for their zeal for Orthodoxy, from 1614-1620 Macarius Tokarevsky studied at the Assumption Ovruch Monastery and upon the death of his parents became a novice there. In 1625, Monk Macarius received a blessing to be assigned to the Kupyatichi Pinsk Monastery where in 1630 he became a hierodeacon and subsequently a hieromonk in 1632. He became well known for the example of his monastic life.

"In 1637 while presenting money to Peter Mohyla, Metropolitan of Kiev which had been collected by the brothers for the reconstruction of the St. Sophia Church in Kiev and asking for help with the construction and renovation of the Kupyatichi Pinsk Monastery church, the Metropolitan was impressed with his devoutness and gave him a universal list for collecting donations. In 1638 the Metropolitan appointed him abbot of the Kamenets Resurrection Monastery. This monastery was robbed and seized by the Uniates in 1642. St. Macarius was called back to the Kupyatichi Monastery to be hegumen until 1656. From 1656-1659, he was hegumen of the Pinsk monastery and in 1660 became archimandrite and head of the Assumption Ovruch Monastery. There were constant problems with the Latin Poles for over a decade. The Dominicans seized land, robbed the monasteries and beat the brethren but the brethren were steadfast and would not abandon the monastery. In 1671 when Ovruch was demolished by the Tatars and no brethren remained, Archimandrite Macarius went to the Kiev-Pechersk Lavra. Metropolitan Joseph (Nelyubovich-Tukalsky) appointed him abbot of the Kanev monastery, where he was needed as a defender of Orthodoxy, after thirty years of standing up for the faith against the *Uniates*.

"Hetman Korolenko who had petitioned Metropolitan Joseph for the appointment of St. Macarius to the Kanev Monastery visited often and in 1675 with the blessing of Macarius, renounced his Turkish citizenship and became a Russian citizen. The Turkish authorities sent troops and on September 4th, 1678, they broke into the monastery. St. Macarius was waiting for them with a cross in his hands on the porch of the temple. The invaders demanded the monastic treasures to which the saint replied that his treasures were in heaven whereupon being frustrated by his answer, they hung him by his hands and feet between the two pillars. On September 7th, 1678, they cut his head off. The witnesses to the martyrdom carried his body into the monastery church where they barricaded themselves. The Turks returned and burned the temple, lighting it with firewood. The surviving townspeople, upon going through the rubble, found only one body still intact and as if it was still alive, with a cross on his chest and another cross in his hand. This was the body of the martyred Macarius. They buried him under the altar on September 8th.

"In 1688 during the temple renovation, the coffin was opened, and his incorrupt body was discovered. Due to the danger of an attack on the Kanev monastery May 13th, 1688, the holy relics were transferred to the Perevaslav Regimental Resurrection Church. His copy of the book *Conversations of John Chrysostom on the 14 Epistles of St. Paul the Apostle* with his handwritten notes in it was also transferred there. In 1713, his relics were moved again, this time to the newly constructed St. Michael's Pereyalavl Monastery and when that closed, they went to Pereyaslavl Ascension Monastery on August 4th, 1786. In 1942 the relics were transferred again, this time to the Trinity Church of Cherkassy and finally in 1965 they went to the temple in honor of the Nativity of the Blessed Virgin Mary in Cherkassy. His feast day is on September 7th, the day of his repose, and on May 13th, the day of the transfer of his holy relics."[21]

September 13th: JOHN of PRISLOP[22]

Our holy Father John most probably lived in the first half of the seventeenth century at the Monastery of Prislop situated at the foot of the Parin and Prishop range of hills in Transylvania. This monastery had been founded by Saint Nicodemus of Tismana (26 Dec.) on the site of an ancient hermitage, and was to play an important part in the defence of Orthodoxy against the proselytizing efforts of the *Uniates* in Transyl-

21 "Martyr Macarius of Kanevsky" Russian Orthodox Church, Official Website of the Moscow Patriarchate, accessed November 11th, 2022, http://www.patriarchia.ru/db/text/913570.html [In Russian.]

22 Hieromonk Makarios of Simonos Petra, *The Synaxarion: The Lives of the Saints of the Orthodox Church, Volume One, Introduction/September-October*, trans. Christopher Hookway (Ormylia: Holy Convent of the Annunciation of Our Lady, 1999), 100.

vania, until its destruction by the Austrian authorities in the middle of the eighteenth century.

September 22nd: TWENTY-SIX MONKS and MARTYRS of ZOGRAPHOU Monastery (Mount Athos)[23]

Even after the Schism of 1054, there were attempts at reunification of Rome and Byzantium. It was the Fourth Crusade (1204) that marked the final separation of the two sees. The next two centuries witnessed very many attempts to restore communion, but developments such as Latin domination of Byzantium by the Crusaders, papal centralization, scholastic theology, and the dogmatization of the *filioque* at the Second Council of Lyons complicated reconciliation. The period of Latin dominion had left behind deep scars on the Byzantine body politic.

The truth is that political more than religious considerations motivated the negotiations during the Komnenian and Palaiologan periods. The Palaiologos Dynasty particularly needed military aid to fight the Turks and others. The papacy, utilizing this threat to their advantage, demanded the total ecclesiastical submission of the Orthodox Church in return for military aid from the West. Unionist attempts failed, as the unions of Lyons and Ferrara-Florence patently showed. Lyons was an excellent example of the limitations of Byzantine imperial influence over religious policy, and of the unrelenting rigidity of papal diplomacy. In the end, both councils only served to widen the separation.

Our account opens with Emperor Michael VIII Palaiologos (r. 1259-1282) who came to power by dubious means. He usurped the throne of Emperor Theodore II Laskaris who died in 1258. Michael joined an aristocratic conspiracy to murder George Mousalon, regent for the child emperor John IV Laskaris. Michael succeeded Mousalon as regent and was crowned co-emperor in 1259. He further secured his position after the recovery of Constantinople from the Latins when he soon received a

---

23   Holy Apostles Convent & Dormition Skete, *The Great Synaxaristes of the Orthodox Church, September*, trans. Holy Apostles Convent and Dormition Skete (Buena Vista: Holy Apostles Convent & Dormition Skete, 2003), 559-568.

second coronation. He ordered the blinding of his co-emperor John IV (1261), thus becoming sole emperor. He was excommunicated by Patriarch Arsenios (1254-1260, 1261-1265). The position of Byzantium was extremely precarious. Michael hoped to win over Pope Clement IV, who wished to eliminate the "Greek Schism."

In 1271, the Italian Gregory X was elected pope. He was an enthusiastic supporter of movements for a Crusade and ecclesiastical reunion. The union with the "Greek Church" formed the center of his policy in the East. This pope was not satisfied with the vague promises of union with which Michael VIII had already beguiled Rome for more than a decade. He gave Emperor Michael an ultimatum: either the Greek Church was to submit, in which case he guaranteed the full support of the Roman Catholic powers, or else he could no longer restrain the persistent demands of Charles of Anjou, king of Naples and Sicily (1265-1285), who made no secret of his projected plans to attack Constantinople. Despite the obstinate position of the Byzantine clergy, Michael VIII came to terms with the papal legate in Constantinople. Ultimately, Michael was able to persuade a section of the clergy to accept the union. The historic act was concluded at the Council of Lyons on the 6th of July, 1274. In the name of the emperor, the Grand Logothete George Acropolites swore to acknowledge not only the papal primacy but also the Roman faith. The ecclesiastical members of the Byzantine legation, the former Patriarch Germanos and Metropolitan Theophanes of Nicaea also signed the imperial declaration. With union now realized, papal pressure on Charles of Anjou obliged him to abandon his projected conquest of Byzantium. Michael VIII betrayed the Faith so that he might secure his throne. But his thirty pieces of silver purchased him a severe internal crisis. The Byzantine people and the majority of the clergy repudiated the union and offered bitter opposition to Michael VIII. His relations with the Church had already deteriorated after the blinding of the young John Laskaris. Michael deposed Patriarch Arsenios, but had been granted a dispensation by his successor, Patriarch Joseph I (1266-1275). When Michael VIII submitted to the pope and demanded that the Orthodox should recognize papal supremacy, a storm broke throughout the populace. Patriarch Joseph refused to accept the union, so Michael made another drastic change in ecclesiastical leadership. He chose John Vekkos.

John Vekkos was chartophylax[24] of Hagia Sophia (1263-1275). He served twice as Michael VIII's ambassador: first, to Stefan Uroš I in Serbia (1268), and then to Louis IX in Tunis (1270). Initially, he opposed the plans for the union of Orthodoxy with Roman Catholicism, and was imprisoned (1273). After further study of the Latin doctors, he changed his views, was released from prison, and went on to become head of the Unionist party. Soon thereafter, John XI Vekkos was chosen Patriarch of Constantinople (1275-1282). Throughout his patriarchate, he supported Michael VIII.

The emperor ignored the protests of his subjects and adhered to the union. Cruel persecutions followed against subjects of both high and low degree. The prisons were crowded with both clergy and laity, commoners and nobility, for the schism affected all sections of the population, and the imperial family itself was divided. With the death of Pope Gregory X (1276), Nicholas III (1277-1280) tried to uphold his conception of a universal Church. In 1281, another papal election put the Frenchman Martin IV on the papal throne. He condemned the Byzantine emperor as schismatic and deposed him. No Catholic sovereign was allowed to communicate with Michael VIII. Thus, the union collapsed, abandoned by Rome herself. The Western powers united against Byzantium. The Balkan rulers joined the anti-Byzantine front and, in cooperation with Charles Anjou, John of Thessaly and the new Serbian King Milutin (1282-1321), invaded Macedonia in 1282. Yet, the tide of fortune temporarily changed, and a terrible catastrophe overwhelmed Charles of Anjou when Michael helped the king of Aragon, Peter III, to attack Charles.

Michael VIII, at his death (d. 1282), was refused burial by the Orthodox Church. Patriarch John Vekkos was deposed after Michael's death. In 1283, at a synod meeting at Constantinople, he was formally

---

24 "Chartophylax was an ecclesiastical office of Constantinople and the provinces, usually a deacon... By the 11th century, the importance of his functions far exceeded his rank in the hierarchy. He was also intermediary between the patriarch and clergy. In the patriarch's absence, he represented him and presided over a synod." *The Oxford Dictionary of Byzantium*, s.v. "Chartophylax." Footnote in Ibid., 561.

charged with heresy and banished to Prusa. Once more, he was condemned at the Synod of Vlachernai (1285), and imprisoned. The office of Patriarch (1282-1283) was once again bestowed on Joseph, who had been deposed after the Council of Lyons.

Now during Michael's reign, Mount Athos was exercising a growing influence on the spiritual life of the entire empire. While the state was disintegrating, the Patriarchate of Constantinople remained the center of the Orthodox world. The Church remained the most stable element in the Byzantine Empire. The Athonite fathers, comprised of Greeks, Georgians, Serbians, Bulgarians, and Russians, addressed an epistle to the apostate Michael VIII, declaring that they abhorred the union. They neither recognized the pope's primacy nor considered his name worthy of commemoration. They refused to use unleavened bread and to change the Symbol of Faith by adding the *filioque*, that is, "and from the Son," with regard to the procession of the Holy Spirit. They declared the emperor a heretic, unless he forsook the papal union and innovations. The emperor, by royal decree (1278), imposed the union by any and all means. The papacy still did not trust Michael, even though he placed his own family in irons and paraded them before the papal envoys. It was during this period that the Latins came to the Holy Mountain Athos, having been invited by Michael to come to the East and crush the Bulgarians, who were laying waste to his provinces. The Catholic sovereigns agreed to help, not because they viewed Michael as a brother in Christ, but rather so that they might destroy him.

The Latins came to the Athonite peninsula and systematically terrorized the Great Lavra, Iveron, and Vatopedi, leaving behind some forced or frightened converts, but also a company of Orthodox martyrs and confessors in the ruins. The Latins then went north of Konstamonitou, in the interior of the Athos peninsula, to the Monastery of the holy Great-martyr George, known as Zographou. The monastery lies on top of a rise, tucked into a woody fold, hidden from the sea. From the 13th [century] onward, the monastery was under the control of Bulgarian monks.

At that time, the hegumen of Zographou was Abbot Thomas. He became aware of the Latin marauders seeking Orthodox souls, as told in the following moving account. There was a certain virtuous and aged monk who lived in Zographou's vineyard, being about one-half hour's walk to the southwest. His rule of prayer was to recite the Akathist Hymn to our most holy Lady, the Theotokos. He pronounced the Akathist daily before her icon, wherein she is depicted holding the Christ Child in a Directress-type icon.[25] One day, as he was reciting his customary rule, and was at that part were the Archangel Gabriel greets the Virgin Mary, saying, "Rejoice," the elder suddenly heard from the sacred icon the following words, "Rejoice thou also, O elder of God!" The old monk began to tremble. He then heard the Mother of God's voice coming from the icon, saying to him, "Cease fearing, but go quickly to the monastery, and announce to the brothers and to the abbot that enemies of both my Son and I are approaching. Whosoever, therefore, is weak in spirit, in patience let him hide until the temptation passes. All those who desire martyric crowns, let them stay and lock themselves within the monastery. Go, therefore, quickly." The old monk fell before the icon, asking, "How, O Lady, shall I leave thee, my protectress, in this place?" She replied, "Concern not thyself for me, but hasten to the monastery."

The elder obeyed the voice and will of our all-immaculate Lady. He left his cell, hastening as much as possible to the monastery, that each one might be granted time to consider which way he might choose. As soon as the elder came to the monastery gate, he beheld the very same icon of the Mother of God before which he recited the Akathist Hymn in his cell. By divine power, the icon was born aloft and went on before the elder to the monastery gate. The old monk fell down and venerated the icon. He then entered and related the warning given by the Theotokos. The monks, seeing the icon and hearing the miracle, gave glory to God and His compassionate Mother. At the news that the heretic Latins were approaching, each man was stirred at the coming peril.

The abbot exhorted those who remained behind, quoting from Saint Paul's Epistle to the Romans, saying, "As many as are led by the Spirit of God, these are sons of God. For ye did not receive a spirit of bondage again to fear, but ye received a Spirit of adoption, whereby we cry, 'Abba, Father.' The Spirit Himself beareth witness with our spirit, that we are children of God: And if children, also heirs – on the one

---

25 This notable miracle-working icon of Zographou, is surnamed *Akathistos*. Footnotes from Ibid., 563.

hand heirs of God, on the other hand joint-heirs of Christ, if indeed we suffer with Him, in order that we might also be glorified together. For I reckon that the sufferings of the present time are not worthy in comparison to the future glory to be revealed in us [Rom. 8:14-18]." Abbot Thomas urged them to keep their faith unhypocritically, and that they rekindle the gracious gift of God, for "God gave us not a spirit of cowardice, but of power, and of love, and of a sound mind. Therefore," says Saint Paul to Saint Timothy, "do thou not become ashamed of the testimony of our Lord, nor me His prisoner, but suffer hardship with the Gospel, according to God's power [2 Tim. 1:8]." He then looked upon the brotherhood and told those that feared torture to conceal them-selves, and added, "Let them take the precious things of the church with them." The weaker among the brethren took themselves away, conceal-ing themselves in the mountains and caves. Twenty-two of the monks, including Abbot Thomas, stood their ground with four laymen. The ab-bot then took those that remained and ascended the monastery's tower. They took with them the icon from which the aged monk received the warning. They remained within, expecting both the enemies and their martyric crowns for confessing the Faith.

In a short while the Latins, together with the Latin-minded, arrived. "Open up unto us," they demanded. The abbot answered, "Even if an an-gel from out of heaven should preach a gospel besides what Gospel has been preached to us, let such a one be anathema [cf. Gal. 1:8]. Declare your teaching. If it is not from God, begone!"

With all their might, the Latins employed every rhetorical tech-nique that their western learning afforded them to madden or move the Orthodox to their way of thinking and interpretation of Scripture. The papists demanded that those of Zographou open the monastery tower and acknowledge the headship of the pope over the œcumenical Church. In a wily manner, they spoke of the *filioque*, unleavened bread, shaved beards, and priests as bridegrooms of the Church. If the Orthodox com-plied, they promised, the pope's clemency and plenty of gold would be theirs. If they refused, they could expect destruction and death. The ven-erable monks made a reply to the Latin innovations. They quoted holy writ and the words of our Saviour Himself, Who said, "Whenever the Paraclete should come, Whom I shall send to you from the Father, the

Spirit of the truth Who proceedeth from the Father [John 15:26]." The fathers also recited other passages in the Gospel of Saint John: "I will ask the Father, and He shall send you another Paraclete [Jn. 14:16]"; and, "The Paraclete, the Holy Spirit, Whom the Father will send in My name, that One shall teach you all things [Jn. 14:26]." The fathers, from their tower on high, also gave the example of the Forerunner who "beheld the Spirit descending out of heaven as a dove, and abode upon Christ [cf. Jn. 1:32]. Then there came to be a voice out of the heavens, 'Thou art My Son,' and the rest [cf. Mk. 1:11; Mt. 3:17]." The fathers then concluded this portion, saying, "Thus, it is evident that it is from the Father alone that the Spirit proceeds."

The monks then warned the Latins not to blaspheme, saying, "Christ says that every sin and blasphemy shall be forgiven to men, but the blasphemy against the Spirit shall not be forgiven. Whosoever shall speak a word against the Son of Man, it shall be forgiven him; but whosoever shall speak against the Holy Spirit, it shall not be forgiven him, neither in this age nor in the coming one [Mt. 12:31, 32]." They added, "No synod or council has stated that the Holy Spirit proceeds from the Father and the Son. What canon has been enacted by the holy Fathers that we ought to use unleavened bread or shave our beards? You are filled with seven evil spirits that contradict the seven OEcumenical Synods. You do not preach the Gospel, but the presumptions of Antichrist, even as Mohammed.

"We do not offer unleavened bread as the Jews. The bread at the Mystical Supper was leavened."[26] We do not shave the hairs of our beard; for there is no decree on this matter in the Scriptures or oecumenical synods. Trim not your beards but your tongues. The things which proceed out of the mouth come forth from the heart, and those defile the man. We do not cut our beards, but rather strive against those things that defile a man, that is, evil thoughts, murders, adulteries, fornications, thefts, false testimonies, and blasphemies [cf. Mt. 15:19, 20].

---

26 Unleavened wafers are an innovation; for from the time of Christ down to the year 1053 the Church of the Westerners was conducting mass with leavened bread. It was during that year that Leo IX became the first inventor of unleavened wafers. Footnote from Ibid., 566.

"Moreover, there are not many bridegrooms, but one Bridegroom, Jesus. And you tell us that your pope is the head of the Church? From what place do you derive such a teaching? For us, Christ is the Head of the Church! We say to you, therefore, accept Orthodoxy, for neither your violence nor your tyranny shall convert us. We will not pollute our souls nor defile this sacred place. We will not open the gates of the monastery. Depart from this place!" The Latins, greatly maddened, shouted up at them, "Indeed, since you wish it, what remains is for you to die."

The Latins then busied themselves gathering wood, which they placed around the tower and put to the torch. The mighty conflagration reached a great height. None of the monks or laymen consigned to the flames enveloping the tower withdrew. All conducted themselves with a steady and manly bearing, glorifying and blessing the Lord. After they prayed on behalf of their enemies, they surrendered their souls into the hands of God, to Whom is due glory and dominion to the ages of the ages. Amen.

A voice was then heard from on high, "Be rejoicing and be exceedingly glad, for your reward is great in the heavens [Mt. 5:12]." Though the terrified Latins heard the voice, they did not come to repentance. They left and continued their path of destruction. The concealed brethren returned to a devasted monastery. In the ruins of the tower, the icon was found undamaged. It is generally believed that those who suffered martyrdom departed to their much beloved Lord in 1276.[27] The names of the laymen have not been left to us, but the twenty-two martyred monks and confessors are as follows: Abbot Thomas, Barsanuphios, Kyril, Micah (or Michael), Simon, Hilarion, Iakovos, Job, Cyprian, Savvas, Iakovos, Martinian, Kosmas, Sergios, Menas, Joseph, Ioannikios, Paul, Anthony, Efthymios, Dometian, and Parthenios the ecclesiarch. Parthenios, however, did not repose quickly. The heretics did not notice that his dashed body was still conscious. When the brethren returned to Zographou, they found him among the immolated remains of those val-

---

27   There appears to be disagreement about the year of their martyrdom. According to Slavonic records on the Holy Mountain, the year given is 1276, but according to Greek sources, 1280. The Athonite Monastery of Iveron, however, published a book (1659) entitled *Noetic Paradise* (pp.19-34), giving the year as 1276. Footnote from Ibid., 567.

iant martyrs. Before he reposed on the 10th of November, he recounted the events of his co-sufferers and confessors.

The surviving brothers took up the icon of the Virgin Mary and deposited it within the Church of the Dormition. An everburning vigil lamp is maintained before this Icon of the Akathist. The monastery was speedily rebuilt through grants of the Palaiologan emperors, particularly, Andronikos II Palaiologos (r. 1282-1328) and John V Palaiologos (r. 1341-1391), and with the assistance of many rulers of the lower Danube countries. In the third *Typikon* of Mount Athos (1394), Zographou occupied tenth place in the monasterial hierarchy. Although the monastery flourished to some extent in the 14th [century], gradually the situation deteriorated, leaving the monastery nearly deserted. The rulers of Hungro-Wallachia were forthcoming with assistance, including Stephen VI the Good, who was markedly generous (1502). The only 18th [century] building at Zographou is the southeast wing (1716). Between 1862 and 1896, the northern and western ranges, the refectory, and the guest cells were renovated and the imposing portico constructed. The situation of the monastery improved in the 18th and 19th centuries. Zographou, at the beginning of the 18th [century], was the home of many monks of Bulgarian, Serbian, and Greek extraction. Services were conducted in both Greek and Bulgarian. In 1845, Bulgarian supremacy was confirmed, and the house is still Bulgarian today.

Until 1873, a portion of the tower remained, but was in danger of utterly collapsing. During new construction to rebuild the monastery, the remnants of the tower barred completion of the northern wing. When it was deemed necessary to remove the remains of the tower, it was resolved that a monument be erected to commemorate the very spot of the martyrs' sacrifice. The cenotaph was finished in the same year. On the day of the consecration of the memorial, at midnight during the all-night vigil, when the lives and sufferings of these martyrs were read during Orthros, a slight sound could be heard in the church. Concurrently, a pillar of fire hovered over the *katholikon* (main church), illuminating Zographou and the environs on that moonless night. The pillar stood for a few minutes, then formed a ring over the memorial, as though crowning it. This miraculous sign occurred for one-quarter of an hour before many witnesses. All glorified God, Who is wondrous in these saints, who cut down the heresy of the Latins and reproved the vainglorious emperor with his mindless patriarch, Vekkos. Thus, because they offered themselves as sacrifices to the Lord, their memory abides forever. Through the intercessions of Thy Saints, O Christ God, have mercy on us. Amen.

See page 462 for patristic commentary.
See page 520 for some liturgical hymns to them.

September 24th: PETER the ALEUT[28]

The holy martyr Peter Tchounagnak was an Aleut Indian converted to Orthodoxy in the late 18th or 19th century by Russian Orthodox missionaries. He departed this life in San Francisco, California, on Sept. 8, 1815, martyred for refusing to become Roman Catholic at the hands of Padre Abella at Dolores Mission. Little or no public interest was accorded him until quite recently. How is it that he has attracted the public's attention, and why so late? When the Russian Orthodox Church began to compile information on the first missionaries sent to Alaska, and particularly when considering canonization of St. Herman of Alaska, an account by one of Peter's fellow prisoners was found among the notes of St. Herman's devoted spiritual son, Simeon Yanovsky (who was later to become Schema-monk Sergei), which relates the Aleut martyr's death. Yanovsky, in turn, told Father Herman in 1819, at St. Paul's Harbor on Kodiak Island, later relating their conversation in writing as follows:

> "Once I told him how the Spaniards in California had taken fourteen of our Aleuts captives, and how the Jesuits had tortured one Aleut to death, trying to force them all to accept the Catholic faith, to which the Aleuts did by no means consent, answering: 'We are Christians, we have been baptized;' showing them the crosses on their necks. But the Jesuits retorted: 'No, you are heretics and schismatics, and if you do not agree to accept the Catholic faith, we will torture you to death.' And they

---

28 Holy Trinity Monastery, "The Historical Background of the Martyrdom of St. Peter the Aleut," *Orthodox Life,* no. 1 (January-February 1981): 12-22.

left them in the prison until evening, two to a cell, to think it over. In the evening they came with lanterns and lighted candles and began again trying to persuade them to accept the Catholic faith. But the Aleuts, permeated with Divine grace, firmly and decisively answered that they were Christians and would not change their faith. Then these fanatics began to torture them: at first one, with the other as witness. At first, they cut off one joint of his toes, one toe at a time, then the next joint; he endured everything and kept on saying: 'I am a Christian, and will not change my faith.' Then they cut off one joint from each of his fingers, then the next joint; then they chopped off his hands, then his feet — the blood flowed. But the martyr endured to the end and repeated unchangingly this one phrase. He died from loss of blood."

The next day they wanted to torture others, but that same night an order came from Monterey that all the captive Russian Aleuts be sent at once under guard to Monterey; and so, on the next day all, except the deceased, were sent off. This was told to me by an Aleut who was an eyewitness, a comrade of the martyred one; he later escaped captivity by fleeing. Upon hearing this I reported it to the Central Administration in St. Petersburg.

When I finished relating this to Father Herman, he asked me: 'And what was the name of the martyred Aleut?' I answered, 'Peter, but I don't remember his last name.' Then he got up and stood before the icons, piously crossed himself and pronounced these words: 'Holy New Martyr Peter, pray to God for us!'"

The only other information given about Peter was Yanovsky's introduction:

The Russian-American Company founded Fort Ross, not far from San Francisco, in 1812. There climate and soil favored agriculture, stock raising, a vegetable garden, and the like; all this was to be of use to the Company. This required manual labor. Some Russians and Aleuts, coming from northern regions to work, were settled there. But the new colony of Russians, being situated at the border of California, which then belonged to Spain, aroused suspicion in the Spaniards concerning the aims of the Russian-American Company. Fearing that the Russians meant to take possession of the town of San Francisco, the Spanish government began to demand that they abandon Fort Ross, and it began to cause various unpleasant incidents. Finally, in 1815 the Spanish arrested some twenty or thirty Russian Orthodox Aleuts. Some of those arrested were held in San Francisco, while others were deported to other places. They were forced to labor and were badly treated. It is unknown how fourteen Russian Orthodox Aleuts ended up in prison in San Francisco and for some reason fell into the hands of Jesuits.

It was not hitherto known during which raid Peter was captured. Examining Yanovsky's account and research contained in a doctoral thesis by Michael George Kovach (University of Pittsburgh), we can deduce that he was among the second group of Aleuts and Russians taken prisoner, and suffered an undeserved, cruel and bloody death about one year later, in 1815. Why did he die so tragically? Possibly the answer lies in Spanish attitudes towards foreigners classified as heretics, the general pattern of missionary work carried out among Indians by California's Spanish missionaries, and the atmosphere at Francisco de Asis Mission itself. The missionary techniques employed in Spanish California must also be explained by Spanish attitudes toward Indians of all types. They were generally viewed as pathetic, savage, primitive and barbarous people incapable of any intelligence above that of children and so were treated with paternal condescension. The basic tactics of the Spanish Franciscans' missionary work can be described as follows:

> By gifts of trinkets, food and clothing they attracted the simple people, whose timidity they overcame by making a display of the friendliness of other Indians they had brought along for that purpose. When necessary, even a double portion of food was offered to those willing to accept the little understood but apparently harmless rite of conversion. And surely the soft-voiced kindly padre would do no harm by speaking strange words while sprinkling a few drops of water on the heads of their wonder-

ing children... In return for the favors, the gullible natives gave vent to their gratitude by joining in the construction of the settlement... Only after the rude chapel, barracks, and dwellings became enclosed within a stockade did it dawn on the trusting natives that they had built themselves a prison, walled and guarded. Once a convert, always a convert, even though the confinement was mitigated by the benevolence of their captors... In time, the poor natives discovered there was no legal escape from their new homes, for every enterprising runaway was caught and severely punished.

Each time a mission was built, so was a presidio, or fort, to billet three to five soldiers to catch runaways and protect the padres, whose only protection, other than a cross and breviary, was a deerskin mantle, scant protection from flying arrows. Unaccustomed to "civilized" life which demanded continual work, many mission Indians longed for their past of free nomadic hunting and fishing, while others simply longed for their families. After several months, many Indians grew fretful and thin, gazing constantly with sadness toward their homes which were visible in the distance. Those who could be trusted were permitted to return to visit their tribes for a short while once each year, but due to a high escape rate few were granted this permission. Usually, the only change in their daily environment occurred when they worked at the pueblos or presidios nearby, work for which they were not paid, since the "fathers took it for the benefit of the community, so it was said, although we do not know what part of these products reached the community." Of the Indians that did escape, most were recaptured in short order and punished. On account of the enmities between the different tribes, fugitives were never given refuge in any other tribe but their own, and thus it was not easy for them to resist for long the armed soldiers who pursued them, knowing exactly where to find them.

Punishments were brutally calculated to inflict smarting pain and embarrassing humiliation rather than any long-term privation or permanent injury. They consisted of working shackled, imprisonment in chains, or sitting in stocks. For grave offences or sins the condemned was tied to a cannon or post to receive twenty-five or more lashes. If the culprit pleaded for pardon, the severity of the blows might be lessened, but never the number. Men were punished in public as an example, while women were punished in private, so as not to excite the men to revolt. The most painful punishment of all, however, was called "a la ley de Bayone," where a musket was passed under the knees so that the feet and hands could be tied around it. All such punishments were inflicted by the padres, though at times they were compelled to call upon the aid of the soldiers who acted as escorts, or three Indian magistrates, referred to as "caciques" by the people. These magistrates, or "caciques," had no choice but to fulfill the will of their superiors blindly and passively, both when it came to administering lashes and in maintaining orderly conduct among their fellow Indians in church. If faults were especially serious, the priest had to investigate the case, arrest the culprit, and inform the presidio commandant of the fort who handled the case. The missions had no qualms about administering these punishments because they believed that they were acting in the Indians' best interests as "wise and prudent fathers," which to their minds implied that authority possessed by all parents to educate their children by exhorting, rebuking and chastising them when necessary. Thus, they justified their guardianship over the Indians, which they felt had devolved upon them because they had baptized them.

Corporal punishments are inflicted on Indians of both sexes who neglect pious exercises, and for several sins, the punishment, of which in Europe is reserved only to divine justice, are punished with chains or stocks. In a word... from the moment a new convert is baptized, he becomes the same as if he had pronounced eternal vows if he makes his escape for the purpose of returning to his relations in the independent villages, they cause him to be summoned to return three times; and if he refuses, they claim the authority of the governor, who sends soldiers to force him away from the midst of his family and conduct him to the missions, where he is sentenced, to receive a certain number of lashes of the whip [...] and this custom, against which reason so forcible objects, is mentioned because theologians have decided that baptism could not in conscience be administered to men so fickle unless the government in some measure, become responsible for their perseverance, but officiating as god-father.

When they were not dealing with discipline problems, the padres' principal duties were to oversee the neophytes' morals, to instruct them in the basics of the Roman Catholic faith, as well as to civilize them by teaching them useful trades. Most men worked as laborers in the fields, but some were trained as mechanics, stonemasons, cattle, horse, and sheep herders, butchers, shoemakers and blacksmiths. Generally, the women were trained as weavers, cooks and seamstresses. In addition to the regular cleaning, they were under obligation to fulfill duties in various mission buildings. Strictly enforced segregation of both sexes was maintained, and girls and widows in particular were put to work under lock and key to protect them from any sort of "mischief." Only marriage allowed a couple the freedom to live in a separate house within the mission walls or on a rancho, and to cook their own meals. All other unmarried mission inhabitants over the age of 9 or 10 ate their meals in the community kitchen. Sundays and certain prescribed holidays were the only days of rest from their appointed tasks, such rest commencing after fulfillment of the mass obligation, since no age group was exempt from church worship. The best-treated Indian boys (those either born to converts or who had been kidnapped by Spanish soldiers at an early age to be raised as house servants) were usually the ones privileged to learn to read, sing and play musical instruments so as to keep up the interest of their newly-converted tribal peers and elders in a service that was virtually unintelligible to them.

While this formed the general pattern of Californian Franciscan missionary work, Peter's death must also be understood within the context of the historical atmosphere peculiar to the Mission of Francisco de Asis at which he died in 1815, for this Mission was quite different from all others in California, because it had one of the lowest records for baptisms and one of the highest for runaways. Cruelty was part of its early heritage, bequeathed by such persons as Father Dani, Father Landeta, the useless and unbalanced Fernandez, the violently demented Antonio Horra of San Miguel, Governor Borica, and Ensign Moraga. Its reputation further suffered because epidemics took high tolls, as did venereal disease. In the face of all these problems, together with the lack of agricultural security, it is no wonder that sheer force was employed in attempts to replenish lost numbers and to hold the few it still had.

"It is by means of their noise that they endeavor to stir the imagination of the Indians and to make men of these savages. It is, indeed, the only means of producing an effect on them. When the drums begin to beat, they fall on the ground as if they were half-dead, no one dares to move; all remain stretched upon the ground without making the slightest movement until the end of the service, and even then, it is necessary to tell them several times that the mass is finished. Armed soldiers are stationed at each corner of the church. After the mass, the superior delivers a sermon in Latin to his flock."

What a contrast to Spanish ways was the Russian philosophy of missionary work and the Russian pattern of missionary activities in Alaska! Although native peoples everywhere were regarded as mere children in need of conversion, protection and guidance, Russian missionaries never extended the idea of guardianship to any legal or civil areas which would adopt people and confine them to any specific place to live, nor did they use soldiers for protection or to bring back the lapsed. If generalizations could be made, one could say that Spanish monks subscribed ideologically to "conversion by force or sword," while Russian monks subscribed ideologically to the theory of "conversion by example." In fact, the precept "save your own soul first, and thousands will be saved around you" early formed the basis for all missionary activity undertaken by the Orthodox Church. This in turn kept conversion figures low, causing many people to chastise the Russian Orthodox Church in particular for "failures" in evangelizing the non-Christian world.

Yet when one reflects on the fact that Siberia, the abode of wild pagan tribes, was only first crossed in 1582, it is a real credit that by 1817, approximately 70% of all people living within Russia's borders were Orthodox Christians! Primarily this was achieved by monks in search of places suitable for ascetic endeavor, who went into forests and settled near rivers and lakes, using hollow trees, mud huts, or cabins as habitations while struggling in unceasing prayer, fasting and manual labor to save their souls. In the process, the surrounding heathens were not only gradually enlightened spiritually but also in a "civilized fashion," being transformed from nomads to settlers. When conditions were favorable, these early individual habitations grew into monasteries with settlements around them which grew into towns. Under less favorable circumstances these habitations remained small churches. The monks that left the Monastery of Valaam on Lake Ladoga in Russia to convert the Aleuts and other Indian tribes in Alaska began to establish Christianity using the time-tested Russian method of incipient monastic foundations. Some went on to teach the Aleuts trades, to establish churches and schools, and to instruct them in their native language and in Russian; and although this carefully laid groundwork did not result in the foundation of monasteries, the life of these first monastic missionaries, examples of evangelical simplicity and holiness, were seeds which yielded a bountiful harvest of those converted to faith in Christ, as Peter's life bears' witness. The site of St. Peter's grave is not known, for the bodies of most Indians at Dolores Mission were cast into unmarked graves. Thus, we are deprived of his relics, unless an act of God reveals them.

October 13th: MELETIUS I (Pigas), Patriarch of ALEXANDRIA[29]

[Saint Meletius I] was offered a promising career as a professor of theology. He refused, in order not to have to accept the decisions of the Council of Florence and returned to his fatherland... [and] agreed to direct the Greek School of Candia. Not contenting himself with teaching, he also inspired his pupils and the whole people with his preaching and ardent attachment to the Orthodox faith, which was being threatened by the proselytism of the Latin occupiers. He was elected abbot of the monastery (1569), but his zeal for the defence of Orthodoxy quickly exposed him to the hatred of the Latin clergy, who managed to remove him [...] despite his discouragement at the situation in the Church, oppressed by the Turks and internally corrupted by unworthy clergy, he set to work, mainly through preaching, to confirm the faithful in the Faith and the principles of Christian morality. He also exerted himself in vain to bring the non-Chalcedonian Copts [Monophysites] to Orthodoxy.

---

29 Hieromonk Makarios of Simonos Petra, *The Synaxarion: The Lives of the Saints of the Orthodox Church, Volume Seven, Appendix-General Index*, trans. Mother Maria Rule (Athens: Indiktos Publishing Company, 2008), 39-42.

At first, open to the coming-together of the Churches in the hope of union, he was quickly confronted with the proselytism of the Latins, who founded schools and charitable institutions to attract the Orthodox under trial. Meletius then began to write treatises against their theological deviations (the *Filioque* and Papal primacy) and their attempts to impose the Gregorian calendar. He pursued more friendly relations with the Reformed Churches, without ever making any doctrinal concession, and maintained a theological correspondence with the theologians of Tübingen, which gave hope of a closer relationship. He even considered travelling to Russia and Poland to combat the Jesuits and Uniatism, but, being stopped by his obligations, he sent Cyril Lukaris, who became his successor on the Alexandrian throne and future Patriarch of Constantinople (1572-1638). He contented himself with sending letters to these Churches, encouraging them to found schools and publishing houses in order to stand against Latin propaganda. Like Saint Basil and the great Confessors of former times, he had the care of all the Churches, which were being tested in many different ways.

Meletius only agreed to govern the Church as 'guardian of the throne of Alexandria' (*epitiritis*) in the hope that one of his two friends and fellow-workers, Gabriel Severus and Maximus Margourios, would finally be elected, although he had often reprimanded the latter for his unionist tendencies. During the two years that he fulfilled this charge (1597-8), he succeeded in re-establishing the Church's economic situation, giving it healthy management, and showed the same zeal in confronting simony among the clergy and restoring Christian practices while striving for the defence of Orthodoxy. Having completed his work and wanting to return to Alexandria, he went via Chios for one last battle against the Latins, and he was sick and worn out with such labours for the well-being of the Church that he gave his valiant soul into God's hands at the age of only fifty-two, on 13 September 1601. A worthy successor to the great Confessors of the Faith of the Patristic age, Saint Meletius was outstanding in his constancy in the true Faith and his zeal for the maintaining of the Church's life during a period of dark slavery, and he is seen as one of the most brilliant of the Greek Patriarchs under the Turkish occupation.

October 21st:
Confessors and New Martyrs of ROMANIA:
BESSARION, SOPHRONIUS, and OPREA.[30]

Christ's holy confessor and Martyr Bessarion Sarai was born in 1714 at Madian in Bosnia and received the baptismal name of Nicolas. From childhood, he was attracted to the life of solitude and prayer. When he was eighteen, he went on a pilgrimage to the Holy Land and became a monk at the monastery of St. Sabas, with the name of Bessarion. He visited Mount Athos in the course of his return journey and, back in his own country, entered the Monastery of Pakrou in Slavonia. He served as a deacon there for seven years and was ordained priest. His love for the place where our Saviour lived and preached took him once more to the Holy Land, whence he returned again to his own countrymen to bear witness among them to Christ crucified and risen.

The Orthodox people held Bessarion in high regard for his holy life and outstanding gift as a preacher of the word of God. At that time the Orthodox of the Balkans, particularly in the territory of the Austro-Hungarian monarchy, had much to suffer from Uniate propaganda. Indeed, the Roman Catholics did their utmost to prevail upon the Orthodox to deny the faith of their Fathers and submit to the Pope of Rome. This pressure was particularly felt in Banat and in Transylvania during the reign of Maria Theresa (1741-80). Earlier, the Calvinists had used violent means to propagate their beliefs, but the Serbian and Romanian Orthodox had remained firm in their faith.

In about the year 1742, the Serbian Patriarch Arsenius IV, well aware of Bessarion's ability as a preacher and of his stature as a Confessor of the Orthodox faith, sent him to the Banat and Transylvania to sustain the people. The situation was critical because some Orthodox, under the influence of various kinds of pressure exerted by the political and ecclesiastical authorities, had begun to conform to the Union. Saint Bessarion saw his task as a God-given mission, and zealously defended

---

30 Hieromonk Makarios of Simonos Petra, *The Synaxarion: The Lives of the Saints of the Orthodox Church, Volume One, September-October*, trans. Christopher Hookway (Ormylia: Holy Convent of the Annunciation of Our Lady, 1999), 450-452.

the faith and the Orthodox people in the threatened provinces. He went from village to village, urging the people to remain true to their Orthodox inheritance. The faithful, who felt the strength and divine grace that flowed forth in this preaching, would often attend his coming in procession, candles and censers in hand, and their parish-church bells ringing out. But the devil, the enemy of mankind, accomplished the imprisonment and torture of Saint Bessarion by the Hapsburgs. He was transferred from one prison to another and finally incarcerated at Kufstein in the mountains of Tyrol. There he died, worn out by the sufferings and torments he endured for Christ. His holy name and his confessions of the faith were venerated by the Orthodox people during his lifetime, and, after his Martyr's death, they immediately regarded him as a Saint.

Saint Sophronius was born at Ciorara, near Alba Julia in Romania. He became a monk in Wallachia but returned to his own part of the country and about the year 1755 founded a little skete there. He was visited by many Orthodox Christians whom he sustained in their faith and encouraged not to give way to Uniate propaganda. The Roman Catholics destroyed the skete, therefore, and forced Sophronius to leave those parts. From that moment, he went among the people, preaching fidelity to the traditions of the Fathers. Nine times was the Saint arrested and persecuted, but the Grace of God protected him. He organized meetings, including clergy and laity, the most well-known being that held at Alba Julia in 1761, which successfully petitioned the Viennese authorities to allow the Orthodox to have their own bishops. After that, Saint Sophronius retired to the Monastery of Curtea-de-Arges, where he fell asleep in the peace of the Lord.

The Holy Martyr Oprea Milaouch was born of peasant stock at Saliste near Sibiu. He was married and the father of a family. Persecution of the Orthodox, and the resulting exodus of not a few among them to Wallachia, led him to make a stand for the defence of Orthodoxy. Orthodox orphans were oppressed in various ways, and he took up their case with the authorities. In 1752, he went to Vienna to seek freedom of religion for the Orthodox of Arad. For this, he was arrested and condemned to hard labour for life in the prison at Kufstein. On 24 July 1784, Oprea's wife, Stana, petitioned the Emperor Joseph II for the release of her husband, who had been a prisoner for thirty-two years. The

Austrian prison directorate replied that it had no record of a convict of his name, so it appears that the Holy Confessor had already ended his contest and received the crown of martyrdom from Christ.

October 21st: Priest-Confessors JOHN of GALES and MOSES Macinic of SIBIEL in ROMANIA[31]

Saint Moses Macinic was ordained a priest by Neophytus, the Metropolitan of Hungro-Wallachia in 1746. He stood out valiantly against the Uniate policy of the Austrian government that aimed at imposing Roman Catholicism upon the Orthodox people of Transylvania. He was, therefore, arrested and held in prison at Sibiu for seventeen months. He was released on condition of no longer exercising the priestly ministry and lived for some time as a simple villager. In 1752, the faithful commissioned him to go to Vienna with Saint Oprea Milaouch of Saliste to present a petition to the Empress Maria Theresa, asking for justice and protection for the Orthodox Church in the southern part of Transylvania. The Empress responded by ordering their incarceration in the fortress of Kufstein. In the years that followed, representatives of the clergy and people of Transylvania repeatedly asked for the release of the holy Confessors, but in vain. It appears that both Saints ended their days in the dungeons of Kufstein, preserving unsullied their Orthodox faith and receiving from Heaven the Martyrs' glorious crown.

Saint John of Gales was ordained at Bucharest (or Riminic) because there was no Orthodox bishop in Transylvania. He was one of the valiant confessors of the Orthodox faith, who stood out against the Uniate policy of the Austrian government. On one occasion, gendarmes[32] burst into his house in the village of Gales, at dead of night, to arrest him. As Father John was away, they tied up his wife and began to torture her. The neighbours heard her cries and ran to the house, and one of them was killed by a pistol shot. In 1752, Father John and other faithful people

---

31 Hieromonk Makarios of Simonos Petra, *The Synaxarion: The Lives of the Saints of the Orthodox Church, Volume One, September-October*, trans. Christopher Hookway (Ormylia: Holy Convent of the Annunciation of Our Lady, 1999), 452-454.

32 *Gendarme*: An armed police officer in France and other European nations.

went to Banat, where they put into the hands of the holy confessors Moses Macinic and Oprea, a schedule of misdeeds of the Uniates against the Orthodox Christians in the west of Transylvania, to take as a petition to the Court of Vienna. On returning home, Saint John continued to struggle for the preservation of the Orthodox tradition. He was arrested in May 1756 and taken in chains to Sibiu. He was condemned to perpetual imprisonment and transferred to the prison of Deva and, a year later, to Graz in Austria. Some merchants from Brasox, on business in Graz, visited him in prison there in 1776. They found Father John as steadfast as he had been twenty years before. 'I would rather die in prison', he told them, 'than renounce my glorious faith!' He was afterwards transferred to the fortress of Kufstein. Sometime after 1780, he ended his days there amid inexpressible sufferings, as did the other Transylvanian confessors of the Orthodox faith.

October 26th: Martyr EUPRAXIA of PSKOV[33]

Saint Eupraxia came of a princely family. She married the Prince of Pskov, Yaroslav Vladimirovich, who, urged by some Latin bishops, repudiated her because of her Orthodox faith, and married a German. The Princess then took the veil in the Monastery of the Holy Forerunner that she had founded in Pskov and became the Abbess. In 1243, she was summoned by her former husband and assassinated by one of his henchmen. Her body was laid to rest in her monastery where it soon became a source of miracles.

October 28th: ATHANASIOS I, Patriarch of CONSTANTINOPLE

"The Holy Patriarch Athanasios I, Patriarch of Constantinople from 1289-1293 and 1303-1309, was born in Andrianople between 1230-

---

33 Hieromonk Makarios of Simonos Petra, *The Synaxarion: The Lives of the Saints of the Orthodox Church, Volume One, September-October,* trans. Christopher Hookway (Ormylia: Holy Convent of the Annunciation of Our Lady, 1999), 402.

1235. He discovered his calling to the monastic life at a young age and pursued the monastic life in his teenage years. Saint Athanasios first went to the Holy Monastery of Esphigmenou on Mount Athos where he grew up in the ascetic life and then eventually travelled to the Holy Land where he spent time in the monastic communities there. Eventually he returned to the empire where he spent time in various monasteries on the Aegean coast before finally settling down in the Holy Monastery of St. Lazarus on Mount Galesion near Ephesus. In 1278 he left for Mount Athos but soon returned because of the persecution of the Athonite Fathers by the Latin Unionist sympathizer Patriarch John XI Bekkos. Saint Athanasios "went to the holy mountain of Ganos in Thrace. Here he founded a monastery called Νέα Μονή for the disciples who by now were flocking to his side, attracted by his reputation for piety and asceticism and his opposition to the Unionist policy of Bekkos."[34]

Saint Athanasios was known by Saint Gregory of Palamas as the forerunner of hesychasm because of his life of strict asceticism and the pure form of Orthodox Monasticism he followed which was characteristic of the Hesychast movement that was to come.[35] He lived during a tumultuous time in Byzantine history in which the Church was still not entirely recovered from the schism produced by the Union of Lyons in 1274, and simultaneously which was in the midst of another controversy concerning the rabid dispute between supporters of Patriarch Arsenius and Patriarch Joseph. Saint Athanasios, who for the majority of his life lived in the manner of a hesychast, was consecrated Patriarch on October 14th, 1289. The new Byzantine Emperor Andronicus favored Athanasios as he was a pious and simple monk who he thought would be an acceptable middle ground among the two warring political sides of the Arsenites and Josephites.

However, during the periods of his patriarchal reign, Saint Athanasios attempted to bring change to the Church and the moral corruption that was heavily entrenched within the ranks of the clergy and monastics. His demands of the clergy to uphold the highest standards of moral conduct and asceticism that the Church has always expected out of

---

34 Alice-Mary Maffry Talbot, "Patriarch Athanasius (1289-1293; 1303-1309) and the Church," in *Dumbarton Oak Papers*, 27 (1973), 16.

35 Ibid., 16.

its monastics and clergy largely upset the more powerful and politically connected clergy and he was forced to resign from his see in October 1293. In 1303 after more political maneuvering on all sides, Saint Athanasios was reinstated as the rightful Patriarch. However, this revived the tension between him and those clergy who, rather than living ascetic lives of monastics, were steeped in the life and luxuries of the capital city.

During the reign of Emperor Michael VIII, Saint Athanasios had been the subject of persecution for his staunch position against the pro-unionist imperial policy. During this period the unionists were not in a position to maintain much of a threat, due to the fact that most of them were either dead, imprisoned, or exiled from the empire. Even so, the unionists that did remain attempted to affect a false union with the Latin papists and the Orthodox, not only by endeavoring to influence the emperor, but also the patriarch. "Unionist propaganda; for example, the Dominican Simon of Constantinople, who returned to Pera in 1299, addressed four dogmatic letters to [Emperor] Andronicus and court officials. In one of his letters Athanasius threatened to resign because certain people were pressuring him to celebrate the liturgy in accordance with the Roman ritual."[36]

The saintly patriarch, however, vigorously countered papist influence from poisoning the Orthodox flock. In 1305, to protect the Orthodox faithful against the soul-destroying heresies of the papists he expelled a group of "Franciscans who had founded a monastery in the capital."[37] In 1303-1304, Saint Athanasios in a letter to the emperor referred to Catalan Company leader Roger de Flor, attesting that he accompanied members of the Orthodox Church when he was in the Aegean islands, out of concern that de Flor would try to force the Orthodox Greeks to submit to the heretical doctrine of Papal Supremacy.[38]

During the second patriarchate of Saint Athanasios in 1309 he was forced to resign again by his political and religious enemies because of his unyielding position on the Arsenite schism that was plaguing the empire since his first patriarchate, as well as his desire to "impose upon

---

36   Alice-Mary Maffry Talbot, "Patriarch Athanasius (1289-1293; 1303-1309) and the Church," in *Dumbarton Oak Papers*, 27 (1973), 20.

37   Ibid., 20.

38   Ibid., 20.

everyone [clergy/monastic] the ascetic discipline which he had prac-ticed as a monk and continued even as a patriarch."[39] Saint Athanasios the forerunner to the Hesychasts, defender of the monastic tradition, and confessor against the Latin heresies, retired to the Holy Monastery of Xerolophos where disciples flocked to the monastery to learn the true ascetic life of this saintly patriarch until his repose in 1310.

See page 346 for some of his letters.

October 28th: JOB of POCHAEV

St. Job's Reaction Toward the Unia

St. Job was abbot of the Monastery of the Holy Cross at Dubno around the year 1582 until the first years of the 17th century during the time of the Union of Brest in 1596 which resulted in the persecution of the Orthodox faith and Russian nationalism in the area of Volhynia, Po-dolia and the Ukraine. Under the rule of Prince Constantine of Ostrog, St. Job did not directly experience the oppression of the *Unia*, but the evil which it caused affected him greatly both in the feeling of his heart and in the activities of his life.

The Saint's Monastic Life and His Aid to the Orthodox

He practiced a strict asceticism, which was only magnified by his ob-servance of the cruelties the Jesuits and Uniates perpetrated upon Or-thodoxy. He devoted himself to the appropriate activities which would educate and strengthen the Orthodox faithful, including instructing them in living a moral life. He also increased his own asceticism. Prince Constantine was a great defender of the Orthodox faith at that time. King Sigismund III of Poland respected and feared him and he also had the respect of Pope Clement VIII of Rome. In addition, the peo-ple feared whoever Prince Constantine respected and supported and for

---

39   Ibid., 15.

this reason the Jesuits and Uniates feared Job. The prince was a god-fearing ruler who observed the Orthodox customs and fasts and enjoyed
visiting the monastery to spend time in prayer and with the pious Job,
supporting St. Job's efforts at the monastery for the faithful. Through
the means of the prince's support, including financial, St. Job was able to
take steps against the enemies of the Orthodox.

He devoted much time to distributing ecclesiastical books, which
were the only support to the Orthodox against the teachings of Papism
and the Unia. As he instructed them to do, his large brotherhood studied and translated the writings of the holy fathers in order to publish
and distribute them to the Orthodox brethren. At the same time, Prince
Constantine published the first bible in the Slavonic language, the Os-
trozhsky Bible (1581-1588). It was of great spiritual help to the Russians
to read this in their native language, particularly during the time when
Catholic teachings were being promoted by the Latins and Uniates. It is
most likely he would not have accomplished this task without the blessing of his spiritual father, St. Job, and it is also likely that his spiritual
father would have been directly involved in it.

His Relationship with Prince Constantine of Ostrog

The struggle against the Latins and Jesuits was difficult; even the
son of Prince Constantine, Janusz, had succumbed to their efforts and
turned to Catholicism during his father's lifetime. While Prince Constantine staunchly supported Orthodoxy against the efforts of Catholics
and Protestants, he "often used the weapons of the enemies of Orthodoxy for Orthodox ends and thus became suspect of being inclined, at
times toward Socinianism,[40] at times toward Catholicism. It is also well
known that the Prince of Ostrog took quite an active part in meetings
between the Orthodox and Protestants, with the view of uniting the interests of both parties."[41] In 1599 he invited Orthodox clergy and also

40 *Socinianism*: A heretical theology from the 16th and 17th century founded by
    Italian Renaissance Humanists Lelio Sozzini and Fausto Sozzini which professed
    a belief in God and adherence to the Christian scriptures but denied the divinity
    of Christ and consequently denied the Orthodox doctrine of the Holy Trinity.

41 Saint Job of Pochaev. *St. Job of Pochaev: Life, Liturgical Service and Akathist*

the *Uniate* Abbot Isaacius of the Holy Savior Monastery in Dubno to attend a gathering in Vilno with him but was met with opposition to this gathering from St. Job.

They might have also had disagreements with monasticism as the Prince desired to reorganize the monasteries under the rule of Saint Basil the Great similar to Western monastics so as not to incur the criticism of the heterodox who accused the Orthodox hermits of living as "cattle and wild beasts."[42] In 1592, he introduced the Monastery of the Holy Savior in Dubno, a monastic community following the rule of Saint Basil the Great, and intended to organize a convent and re-organize St. Job's Monastery of the Exaltation of the Holy Cross similarly. The reorganization would implement skete-style monasticism instead of coenobitic, mirroring the Catholic Monasteries and eventually allowed for the Catholic and Uniates to turn them into monasteries of the Latin Order of Basil the Great. With these changes to monasticism around the same time that the Jesuits launched secret persecutions and the appearance of the first False Dimitry, St. Job secretly left the Dubno Monastery (circa 1600) and went to Mount Pochaev.

AT THE MONASTERY OF POCHAEV

Based on his arrival time, he most likely was the first abbot of the newly coenobitic Monastery of Pochaev, as the archives of the Pochaev Lavra contain no information about a previous abbot. "For truly," Dositheus notes, "the all-holy Virgin Mary, the Theotokos, wished to have in her monastery, which is like unto heaven, such an exceeding ascetical and skilled guardian."[43] At that time the enemies of Orthodoxy were concentrating on destroying the Orthodox monasteries and churches in Volhynia. When St. Job had been in Dubno, there were no remaining Orthodox churches in Lutsk, the main city of Volhynia. Initially they

---

Hymn, trans. Reader Isaac E. Lambertsen (Liberty: St. John of Kronstadt Press, 1997), 10.

42   Ibid., 11.

43   Saint Job of Pochaev. *St. Job of Pochaev: Life, Liturgical Service and Akathist Hymn*, trans. Reader Isaac E. Lambertsen (Liberty: St. John of Kronstadt Press, 1997), 14.

were converted into taverns and then destroyed completely. In 1630, Prince Nicholas Czartoryski, whose father had converted to Catholicism in 1598, gave the Jesuits the city and monastery of Peresopnitsa. In the early 17th century, Volhynia had lost two of the great defenders of Orthodoxy: Bishop Gideon of L'vov and Prince Constantine of Ostrog. Following their deaths, the two best schools of those towns were closed. Upon Constantine's death his son, who was in apostasy, confiscated many Orthodox churches and converted them to Latin churches, leading many Orthodox into the Unia and Latin Rite. His niece, Anna Aloysia Chodkiewicz, daughter of Prince Alexander Constantinovich of Ostrog, also promoted the Catholic faith to the Orthodox.

In 1612, Bishop Michael Kopystensky of Lutsk and Ostrog, the last remaining Orthodox bishop in Volhynia, reposed and the Orthodox had no one to ordain their priests. In addition, Hypatius Pociej, the Uniate Bishop of Vladimir, with other Uniate authorities in Volhynia, arrived with soldiers, and prevented the Orthodox to gather for prayer, closed the Orthodox churches and committed many other persecutions of the faithful.

The Pochaev Printing Press Under St. Job

Upon St. Job's arrival at the Pochaev Monastery, the printing press there was already established. Due to the persecution, most of the established printing presses of Volhynia, including the ones at Ostrog, Kremenets, Rakhmanovsk, and others, ceased publishing by the first half of the 17th century. The Pochaev press printed leaflets containing the order of the proskomedia, letters and epistles of the Orthodox hierarchs, prayers, etc. and by that same timeframe was the only press still in existence, which supported the Orthodox Church despite the continuing persecution by the Latins. In addition to these publications, in St. Job's manuscript are teachings and extracts of writings against the non-Orthodox: Jews, Catholics and Protestants.

St. Job at the Council of Kiev in 1628

In 1620, Job Beretsky was consecrated as Metropolitan of Kiev, replacing the apostate Michael Rogoza. Patriarch Theophanes also ordained Bishop Isaacius Boriskovich to the Diocese of Lutsk, to which the Monastery of Pochaev belonged. Meletius Smotritsky, who had been consecrated as archbishop of the Diocese of Polotsk, Vitebsk and Moghilev, had previously championed for the Orthodox Church but defected to the Latins, shortly after the murder of Josaphat Kuntsevich, Uniate bishop of Vitebsk in 1623. Meletius was accused by the Uniates and Jesuits of being involved in his death. He spent three years in Greece, hoping the accusations would die down. The king ordered the murderers to be executed and Meletius, rather than facing execution, acquiesced by writing against the Orthodox Church.

Upon hearing of Meletius' writing against Orthodoxy, Metropolitan Job Boretsky convened an ecclesiastical Council in Kiev in 1628, calling all the Orthodox bishops, archimandrites and abbots of Western Russia to attend on August 15th of which St. Job was in attendance. On that day, in a service in the Church in the Church of the Dormition of the All-holy Theotokos, the main church of the Lavra of the Kiev Caves, Meletius renounced the Unia and his own Apologia writing, and pronounced anathema upon Archimandrite Cassian Sakovich who had published his Uniate writings, (although he subsequently apostasized from Orthodoxy).[44] The day after that, the Council signed a conciliary declaration where everyone affirmed by signing that they "were all standing firmly in the Eastern Orthodox Faith, were not considering defecting to the Unia, and promised under oath not to give it up, but to urge all the Orthodox people to adhere to it."[45] In addition to Bishop Isaacius of Lutsk, and Peter Moghila, St. Job of Pochaev signed his name 'John Zhelezo, Abbot of Pochaev.'

---

44 Boris Mouravieff, *A History of the Church of Russia*, trans. R.W. Blackmore (London: Rivington & Co, 1842), 179.

45 Saint Job of Pochaev. *St. Job of Pochaev: Life, Liturgical Service and Akathist Hymn*, trans. Reader Isaac E. Lambertsen (Liberty: St. John of Kronstadt Press, 1997), 31.

The Saint's Successor and the Fate of the Monastery

In 1649, the venerable Job turned ninety-eight and began to think about who would be worthy to succeed him as the next abbot of the monastery. For more than 50 years, the Unia had been establishing itself in south-western Russia. Almost all of the Orthodox monasteries and churches in Volhynia were destroyed, and many Russian Orthodox families had converted to Latinism. Volhynia was almost entirely controlled by the Jesuits and [Uniate] Basilians. The Poles accepted the demand of Khmelnitsky (24 February 1649) that the Unia be abolished, and Orthodoxy be safe from persecution, the king did not sanction this, and it was clear that the law would not uphold it. It was clear that the Uniates with a few steps would be able to gain control of the Monastery of Pochaev, which due to the efforts of St. Job, had remained as the sole safeguard of Orthodoxy in Volhynia. The Latins did not dare to take over the monastery in his lifetime. The Hieromonk Samuel Dobryansky was chosen as his replacement, although in a few decades the Monastery of Pochaev would come under control of the Latin Uniates.

See page 543 for some liturgical hymns to him.

October 30th: JOSEPH I, Patriarch of CONSTANTINOPLE[46]

Saint Joseph had been a married priest. On the death of his wife, he became a monk at Mount Galesion in Asia Minor and then Abbot there. His meekness and love for the poor were well-known. He was strict in his ascesis, without guile and utterly innocent of the 'sciences,' falsely so called, of this world. He was the spiritual father of the Emperor Michael VIII Palaeologus (1259-1282), during whose reign, on 28 December 1266, he was elevated to the Patriarchal dignity. At his first

---

46 Hieromonk Makarios of Simonos Petra, *The Synaxarion: The Lives of the Saints of the Orthodox Church, Volume One, September-October*, trans. Christopher Hookway (Ormylia: Holy Convent of the Annunciation of Our Lady, 1999), 528.

Liturgy, he insisted on the Emperor publicly confessing before the holy altar his two grievous sins of perjury and of blinding John IV Lascaris, the rightful heir to the throne, and only then would he admit him to holy communion. His affection for Michael Palaeologus did not prevent him from fiercely opposing the Emperor's policy of union with the Church of Rome, which was based on expediency without regard for the primacy of the truth. Joseph was deposed, therefore, in 1274 and obliged to retire to the Monastery of the Peribleptos. He was replaced as Patriarch by John XI Bekkos (1274-82), the Latinizing persecutor of the Orthodox. Joseph was restored to the Patriarchal throne in December 1282. But he was old, in poor health and he grieved for the Church, torn by the Arsenite and Josephite factions. He soon fell ill and was unable to take part in the Council that assembled to condemn Bekkos. He died three months later on 23 March 1283.

See page 336 for an excerpt from his writings.

October 30th: MILUTIN, King of SERBIA[47]

Saint Milutin (known as Saint Stephen Urosh II) was the son of King Stephen Urosh I (who at the end of his life entered a monastery, taking the name Symeon) and Queen Helen (who after her repose was canonized a saint). Saint Milutin ascended to the throne after his older brother Dragutin abdicated (he is also canonized a saint). When the Emperor Michael VIII Palaeologus (1259-82) attempted to force the Orthodox Church of the Balkans and the Athonite monks into union with the Latin church due to political concerns, Saint Milutin and his people fought to oppose this heretical union. Because of his unceasing prayer and faith in God, Saint Milutin emerged victorious. When he had taken the throne, he promised to build as many churches as the number of years he reigned. As his reign lasted forty-two years, he built forty-two churches, both within his Kingdom (such as in Grachanitsa, Studenitsa,

---

47 Hieromonk Makarios of Simonos Petra, *The Synaxarion: The Lives of the Saints of the Orthodox Church, Volume One, September-October*, trans. Christopher Hookway (Ormylia: Holy Convent of the Annunciation of Our Lady, 1999), 529-530.

Stro-Nagorichino) and outside of it (such as in Constantinople, Thessalonica, Sofia, Jerusalem, Mount Sinai and on Mount Athos.) Adjacent to the churches, he established hospices for the poor. Despite his incredible wealth, he was known to dress as a poor man, going out at night with one or two servants in order to see how the poor were suffering in order that he might better aid them. He reposed on 29 October 1321. His holy, uncorrupt, and miracle-working relics rest in Sofia.

November 4th: Holy and Pious Emperor
JOHN III DOUKAS VATATZES the MERCIFUL[48]

This pious, Christ-loving emperor came of the illustrious Doukas family. After the Latin crusaders had taken Constantinople in 1204, the Byzantine Empire was divided into four rival kingdoms: the Latin Empire of Constantinople, the Empire of Nicaea in Asia Minor (to which the lawful Emperor and the Ecumenical Patriarch withdrew), the Despotate of Epirus in Western Greece and the Bulgarian Kingdom of John II Asen. In 1222, John III succeeded his uncle Theodore Lascaris, who died childless. Theodore was an able statesman who had managed to recognize the forces of the Empire of Nicaea on the traditional Byzantine model. In political ability John was one of the most outstanding of all the Byzantine Emperors, and the greatest ruler of the Empire of Nicaea. Thanks to a series of brilliant military victories and to a well-thought-out system of alliances, he secured control of Asia Minor after some years and regained most of the territories that were in the hands of the Latins. He even took Adrianople, within reach of Constantinople, so that on his death in 1254, the Empire of Nicaea was in possession of almost all the territory of the Byzantine Empire before the Latin conquest. It only remained to regain the Imperial City, which John's successor, Michael Palaeologus, accomplished in 1261.

The pious Emperor John, zealous for the good of the Church, and wanting to promote the union of the Churches, supported a number of

---

48 Hieromonk Makarios of Simonos Petra, *The Synaxarion: The Lives of the Saints of the Orthodox Church, Volume Two, November-December*, trans. Christopher Hookway (Ormylia: Holy Convent of the Annunciation of Our Lady, 1999), 35-37.

theological discussions with Gregory IX, the Pope of Rome. In 1232, a council met at Nymphaion, the capital of the Empire of Nicaea, at which both Churches were represented. Patriarch Germanus II (1222-40) and the renowned Nicephorus Blemmydes (1197-1272) who were the leaders on the Orthodox side, took a conciliatory point of view in the controversy about the procession of the Holy Spirit, and they accepted, as a compromise, the formula proceeding from the Father through the Son. But all was in vain, because the Pope persisted in supporting the Latin Empire of Constantinople. The discussions continued under his successor, Pope Innocent IV, who seemed ready to give up his claims on Constantinople. Union of the Churches appeared close, but never came about because Patriarch Germanus firmly opposed it on doctrinal grounds.

November 12th: Martyrs and Confessors ATANASIE TODORAN from BICHIGIU, VASILE from MOCOD, GRIGORE from ZAGRA, and VASILE from TELCIU

ONE ACCOUNT[49]

The Holy Martyr Athanasius Todoran was born in Bichigiu village, Sălăuța valley, Năsăud region of Transylvania, to a family of Orthodox Christians. Few things are known about his childhood; it is only known that he was an outstanding person in his community, an educated person, who has been administrator and tax collector in the communes on Bichigiu and Sălăuța valleys.

---

49 "St. John the Merciful, Patriarch of Alexandria; Martyrs and Confessors of Nasaud: Athanasius, Basil, Gregory and Basil; St. Nilus the Faster of Sinai," Official News Agency, Basilica.ro, The Romanian Orthodox Church, accessed October 20th, 2022, https://basilica.ro/en/st-john-the-merciful-patriarch-of-alexandria-martyrs-and-confessors-of-nasaud-athanasius-basil-gregory-and-basil-st-nilus-the-faster-of-sinai/

Given his virtues and courage he was a member of a military regiment of the empire from Vienna ever since his youth. Hence, as his retirement was postponed, he left the army of his masters, who had a different faith, and went back home. Followed by the people of the empire, he took refuge in Ţibleş Mountains, in Maramureş and Chioaru land. While in this exile, he always prayed [to] God for him[self] and for his fellow human beings who were suffering and in all kind of humiliations.

His pains grew when the ones of other faiths caught and imprisoned him for a few years in the Hoopers' Tower, in Bistriţa citadel. Once released from prison, he went back to Bichigiu village, where the Orthodox faith of his forerunners was threatened by uniatism. Thus, because the village had no Orthodox priest, he firmly refused to confess to and take Holy Communion from a uniate priest.

General Bukov sent by the Court of Vienna to survey and accelerate the conversion of the Romanians to Catholicism in Transylvania, came to attend the swearing in of the frontier guards of Năsăud and the blessing of the flag, accompanied by the uniate bishop. At that time of hard trials for the Orthodox Christians, when the militaries were prepared to swear in, "old Tănase Todoran", aged 104 at the time, came in front of the crowd riding a horse and delivered a speech for the Romanian frontier guards. He said: "We have been frontier guards for two years and we have not received papers from the empress to confirm we were free people, as we were promised!

So, we shall not bear arms to see our holy faith mocked! Let down your arms!" The passionate words of the pious old man bore fruits in the hearts of his listeners and so the soldiers who were about to swear in the oath of faith to Vienna took Athanasius' side and put down their arms.

Soon afterwards, the authorities undertook investigations in order to punish the Saint confessors. Thus, on 12 November 1763, the supporters of the centuries old faith and of the freedoms of the Romanian people were tortured on the same plateau of Salva. The bones of the righteous martyr Athanasius were broken with a wheel from head to toes and his head was tied to a wheel, "because he hindered the people to convert to uniatism and join the frontier guard...". Three other faithful died a martyr's death together with him: Basil from Mocod, Gregory from Zagra and Basil from Telciu. Nineteen other Orthodox Christians were whipped, many of them to death. The heads of the martyr saints were put on pillars at the gates of the houses where they had lived and pieces of their bodies cut to pieces were laid at crossroads. This was the martyr's death of the worthy Holy Martyr Athanasius, who shed his blood for the faith of the forefathers and for the rights of his Romanian brothers from Transylvania. His suffering and that of those who died together with him have been always honoured in the souls of the Orthodox faithful of Năsăud area.

ANOTHER ACCOUNT[50]

The Nasăuden saints Atanasie Todoran from Bichigiu, Vasile Dumitru from Mocod, Marin Grigore from Zagra and Vasile Oichi from Telciu suffered martyrdom on November 12, 1763. They were defenders of the ancestral faith and the Romanian nation. This holy martyr of our nation, Atanasie Todoran, was born in Bichigiu, a village on the Sălăuței Valley, in a family of free peasants, related to the family of priests Coșbuc from Hordou, ancestors of the poet George Coșbuc. There is quite a bit of information about his life. A leader in the commune, well-read, he had been a county and tax collector in the communes of Valea Bichigiului and Sălăutai.

It seems that from his youth he was part of a regiment which was stationed somewhere near Vienna, and, his release still being delayed, he deserted and returned home. Pursued by the people of the kingdom, he took refuge in the Țibleșului Mountains, in Maramureș and in Șara Chioarului. He arrived in Moldova, where he served for many years, as evidenced by the fragment of a document issued by ruler Mihai Racoviță, from which it appears that Atanasie, aged 74, was released from the army, after serving 13 years as a captain, and that he is raised to the rank of a rasaz. For the old desertion, he was imprisoned for several years in the Dogarilor Tower in the Bistriței citadel. After he was released, he returned to Bichigiu. There being no Orthodox priest in the village, he

---

50 "The Lives of the Holy Martyrs and Confessors of Năsăud," Moldova & Bucovina, Romanian Orthodox Church Metropolia, accessed October 20th, 2022, https://doxologia.ro/liturgica/vietile-sfintilor/viata-sfintilor-martiri-marturisitori-nasaudeni [In Romanian].

fiercely opposed his son's communion with unleavened bread, as well as his confession by a uniate priest. The old man buried his boy in the rite of the ancestral faith; his daughter had also died years before, when he was a fugitive in the mountains.

In the years 1761-1762, he negotiated with the government in Vienna, together with other leaders, the militarization of 21 communes on Valea Bichigiului, Sălăuţei and Someșului Mare. He himself was in Vienna, together with other Romanians, where the pact with the government was concluded and they were given assurances that, after entering the border regiment, the Romanians from the Năsăud region would benefit from facilities. However, he requested that, through the establishment of the border regiment, the Romanians would not be forced to renounce their faith, because for decades the Transylvanian Orthodox faced the imposition, almost by any means, of the united faith. Returning home and waiting for the fruits of the agreement, Atanasie realized that the wishes of the Romanians had not been taken into account and he began to face the militarization process. The people of Năsăuden clearly saw that the frontier system aimed to convert them to Catholicism and then, that the promise of the abolition of serfdom did not apply to them.

On May 10, 1763, in Salva, on the plateau called "La Mocirla", the consecration of battle flags and the taking of oaths by nine companies of the newly established Border Regiment was organized. General Bukow, sent by the Vienna Court to follow and promote the conversion to Catholicism in Transylvania, came to receive the oath of the border guards from Nasuand and to consecrate their flag. When the soldiers were ready to take the oath, "old man Tănase Todoran", 104 years old, came out on horseback and gave a speech to the border guards. Among other things, he told them: "For two years we have been border guards and we have not received a letter from the high empress that we are free people! — and then we will not bear arms so that the holy faith may mock us! Down with the weapons!" The old man's fiery words paid off. The soldiers who were to take the oath of allegiance to Vienna went over to the side of Athanasius, throwing down their weapons, as a sign of protest and disobedience.

Soon after, inquiries were made so that the culprits could be punished. On November 12, 1763, on the same plateau in Slava, the execution of those found guilty of the May revolt took place. Atanasie Todoran was crushed with the wheel from top to bottom, and his head was tied to a wheel, "for holding people back from uniting and enlisting in the border military status..." — as stated in the sentencing. Along with Atanasie, Vasile Dumitru from Mocod, Grigore Manu from Zagra and Vasile Oichi from Telciu were martyred by hanging, "for the same fault", nineteen other people were beaten with rods; many of those beaten died under the blows. The heads of the martyred were raised on stakes at the gates of the houses in which they had lived, and pieces of the dismembered bodies were placed at the crossroads. Receiving a martyr's death, Athanasius shed his blood for the ancestral faith and for the rights of Transylvanian Romanians. From then until today, the honoring of his memory is done continuously in the consciences of the Orthodox people of Năsăuden, and the testimonies of the time place the three who suffered together with him.

See page 524 for a troparion to St. Atanasie Todoran.

November 14th: GREGORY PALAMAS, Archbishop of Thessaloniki

His Life[51]

"[Saint] Gregory's father was an eminent official at the court of Emperor Andronicus II Palaeologus. The gifted Gregory, completing his secular studies, did not want to enter the service of the imperial court, but withdrew to the Holy Mountain and was tonsured a monk. He lived a life of asceticism in the Monastery of Vatopedi and the Great Lavra. He led the struggle against the heretic Barlaam and finally defeated him. He was consecrated as Metropolitan of Thessalonica in the year 1347. He is glorified as an ascetic, a theologian, a hierarch and a miracle-worker. St. Gregory authored many important works including *In Defense of*

---

51   Saint Nikolai Velimirović, The *Prologue of Ohrid, Volume Two, July to December,* trans. Father T. Timothy Tepsić (Vrnjačka Banja: Sebastian Press - Western American Diocese of the Serbian Orthodox Church, 2002), 543-544.

Those Who Devoutly Practice a Life of Stillness defending the hesychastic life as well as *Apodictic Treatises on the Procession of the Holy Spirit* against the Latin teaching that the Holy Spirit proceeds not from the Father alone but from the Father *and the Son* (*Filioque*). St. Gregory's teachings on hesychasm and the essence and energies of God were upheld as the teachings of the Church at the Ninth Ecumenical Council. The Most-holy Theotokos, St. John the Theologian, St. Demetrius, St. Anthony the Great, St. John Chrysostom and angels of God appeared to him at different times. He governed the Church in Thessalonica for thirteen years, of which he spent one year in slavery under the Saracens in Asia. He entered peacefully into rest in the year 1360, and took up his habitation in the Kingdom of Christ. His relics repose in Thessalonica, where a beautiful church is dedicated to him."

His Struggle Against
the Heresies of Barlaam of Calabria[52]

At that time, Barlaam, a monk from Calabria, won a great name for himself as a speculative thinker in Constantinople. He was particularly fond of expounding the mystical writings of Saint Dionysius the Areopagite (3 Oct.), which he interpreted in an entirely philosophical way, making knowledge of God the object of cold reason and not of experience. When this refined humanist learned of the methods of prayer of some simple monks of his acquaintance, who allowed a place to the sensory element in spiritual life, he was scandalized. He took occasion to calumniate them and to accuse them of heresy. The hesychast monks appealed to Gregory who then wrote several polemical treatises in which he answered the accusations of Barlaam by locating monastic spirituality in a dogmatic synthesis. He showed that ascesis and prayer are the outcome of the whole mystery of Redemption, and are the way for each person to make the grace given at Baptism blossom within himself. He also defended the authenticity of the methods which the Hesychasts

---

52 Hieromonk Makarios of Simonos Petra, *The Synaxarion: The Lives of the Saints of the Orthodox Church, Volume Two, November-December*, trans. Christopher Hookway (Ormylia: Holy Convent of the Annunciation of Our Lady, 1999), 136-138.

used to fix the intellect in the heart; for since the Incarnation we have to seek the grace of the Holy Spirit in our bodies, which are sanctified by the Sacraments and grafted by the Eucharist into the Body of Christ. This uncreated grace is the very glory of God which, as it sprang forth from the body of Christ on the day of the Transfiguration, overwhelmed the disciples (see Matt. 17). Shining now in the heart purified from the passions, it truly unites us to God, illumines us, deifies us and gives us a pledge of that same glory which will shine on the bodies of the Saints after the general Resurrection. In thus affirming the full reality of deifi-cation, Gregory was far from denying the absolute transcendence and unknowableness of God in His essence. Following the ancient Fathers, but in a more precise manner, he made a distinction between God's im-participable essence and the eternal, creative and providential energies by which the Lord enables created beings to participate in His being, His life and His light — without, however, introducing any division into the unity of the divine Nature. God is not a philosophical concept for Saint Gregory: He is Love, He is Living Person and *consuming fire*, as Scripture teaches (Deut. 4:24), Who does everything to make us God-like. Saint Gregory's brilliant answer to Barlaam was first accepted by the authorities of Mount Athos in the Hagiorite Tome and then adopted by the Church, which condemned Barlaam (and with him the philo-sophical humanism that would soon inspire the European Renaissance), during the course of two Councils at the Church of St. Sophia in 1341.

Barlaam's condemnation and his departure for Italy did not bring the controversy to an end. No sooner had Gregory returned to his Athonite hermitage from Thessalonica — where he had been writing his treatise in seclusion — than Akindynos, an old friend of his, restated the substance of Barlaam's arguments and condemned Gregory's distinction between essence and energies as an innovation. Akindynos, who at first aspired to be an umpire between Barlaam and Gregory, was the kind of rigid conservative who does no more than repeat set phrases without seeing to enter into the spirit of the tradition. At the same time, a dread-ful civil war broke out as a result of the rivalry between the Duke Alexis Apokaukos and Saint Gregory's friend, John Cantacuzenus (1341-7). The Patriarch, John Calecas, sided with Apokaukos and encouraged Akindynos to bring a charge of heresy against Gregory — which led to the excommunication and imprisonment of the Saint. During the four years of Gregory's confinement, there was no slackening of activity. He carried on a huge correspondence, and wrote an important work against Akindynos. When John Cantacuzenus gained the upper hand in 1346, the Regent, Ann of Savoy, came to the defence of the Saint and deposed the Patriarch on the eve of Cantacuzenus' triumphal entry into the City. He nominated Isidore as Patriarch (1347-50), and summoned a new Council to vindicate the Hesychasts. The controversy was not finally resolved until 1351, at a third Council which condemned the humanist Nicephorus Gregoras. In the Synodal Tome the doctrine of Saint Gregory on the uncreated energies and on the nature of grace was recognized as the rule of faith of the Orthodox Church.

Among Isidore's new episcopal appointments, Gregory was named Archbishop of Thessalonica in 1347; but he was unable to take possession of his see as the city was in the hands of the Zealots, the party opposed to Cantacuzenus. After finding shelter for a while at Lemnos, where he showed heroic devotion during an epidemic, Gregory was eventually able to enter the city, acclaimed as if Christ Himself were coming in triumph, with the chanting of the Easter hymns....

See page 348 for some of his writings against the Latins.
See page 524 for some liturgical hymns to him.

November 23rd: Grand Prince ALEXANDER NEVSKY

HIS LIFE[53]

Alexander was the son of Prince Yaroslav. From childhood, his heart was directed to God. He defeated the Swedes on the river Neva on July 15, 1240, for which he received the appellation "Nevsky" ["of the Neva"]. On that occasion, Saints Boris and Gleb appeared to one of

---

53   Saint Nikolai Velimirović, *The Prologue of Ohrid, Volume Two, July to December*, trans. Father T. Timothy Tepsić (Vrnjačka Banja: Sebastian Press - Western American Diocese of the Serbian Orthodox Church, 2002), 577.

Alexander's commanders and promised their help to the great prince, who was their kinsman. Once, among the Golden Horde of the Tartars, he refused to bow down to idols or to pass through fire. Because of his wisdom, physical strength and beauty, even the Tartar Khan respected him. He built many churches and performed countless works of mercy. He entered into rest on November 14, 1263 at the age of forty-three. On this day, November 23, the translation of his relics to the town of Vladimir is commemorated.

HIS STRUGGLE AGAINST THE LATINS[54]

In 1252 [...] At the same time, Alexander was faced with continuous threats from the West. He dealt firmly with the missionaries that Innocent IV, the Pope of Rome, sent to the Russian principalities to convert the Orthodox people to the Latin faith. He dismissed doctrines foreign to the apostolic tradition which the Russian people had received from Constantinople; and the Roman Catholic powers responded by launching a veritable crusade against the holy Prince. In 1256, an alliance of Swedes, Danes, Finns and Teutonic Knights advanced towards Novgorod but were thrown back by Alexander, who even occupied Finland.

December 5th: Monks and Confessors of ATHOS, COSMAS the PROTOS and his COMPANIONS[55]

Determined to impose the union of the Churches—accepted under pressure at the Council of Lyons (1274) to secure Papal support for the Byzantine Empire—Michael VIII Palaeologus sent troops to Mount Athos, the stronghold of Orthodoxy and center of opposition to his pol-

---

54 Hieromonk Makarios of Simonos Petra, *The Synaxarion: The Lives of the Saints of the Orthodox Church, Volume Two, November-December*, trans. Christopher Hookway (Ormylia: Holy Convent of the Annunciation of Our Lady, 1999), 217-218.

55 Hieromonk Makarios of Simonos Petra, *The Synaxarion: The Lives of the Saints of the Orthodox Church, Volume Two, November-December*, trans. Christopher Hookway (Ormylia: Holy Convent of the Annunciation of Our Lady, 1999), 329.

icy, with orders to take sanguinary measures against monks who would not recognize the false union.

When the Emperor's soldiers reached Karyes, the capital of Athos, which was organized as a lavra in those days, they seized the Protos of Athos, who had been an example to all of what a steadfast monk should be. They put him to the sword together with many other fathers there, and in their fury ransacked and fired the Church and monastic buildings, leaving rack and ruin behind them. Emerging from the wild places and thick forests where they had taken refuge, the Orthodox monks buried the holy Martyrs at the entrance to the Church of the Protaton. Through the centuries, generations of monks piously lit the lamp each day above the "tomb of the Protos"; but it was not until 5 December 1981 that his relics were solemnly taken from the earth, and that a service was held in his honour in the presence of a great crowd.

December 13th: DOSITHEUS, Metropolitan of MOLDAVIA[56]

He was born in 1624, in Suceava, today's Romania and passed into eternal life in 1693, Żółkiew (Jovkva), Poland—today's Ukraine. He was Metropolitan of Moldavia (1671 -1673, 1675-1686), a scholar, a fine poet, a good translator and a witness to the Orthodox faith. For his missionary work, in 2005 the Romanian Orthodox Church proclaimed him a saint. Saint Dositheus was born in 1624 in Suceava in a faithful family named Barilă. His parents Leontie and Misira were Romanians refugees. They came from Transylvania, and they had relatives in the neighbouring country, Poland. The little baby was baptized as Demetrius, because he was born around the 26th of October when in the Eastern Church is celebrated, St. Demetrius.

---

56 "Holy Hierarch Dositheus, Metropolitan of Moldavia; Martyrs Eustratius, Auxentius, Euguene, Mardarius and Orestes at Sebaste; Virgin-martyr Lucy of Syracuse," Official News Agency, Basilica.ro, The Romanian Orthodox Church, accessed October 20th, 2022, https://basilica.ro/en/%E2%80%A0-holy-hierarch-dositheus-metropolitan-of-moldavia-%E2%80%A0-martyrs-eustratius-auxentius-eugene-mardarius-and-orestes-at-sebaste-virgin-martyr-lucy-of-syracuse/

The young Demetrius went to the best schools of his time in Moldova and after that, at the school of the Orthodox Brotherhood from the Monastery of the Dormition of Theotokos, from Lviv, at that time in Poland. In his times he proved to be a talented child in translating the Holy Text of the Scriptures and the writings of the Church fathers, and that happened because he knew many languages, as Greek, Latin, Church Slavonic, Polish and Ukrainian. In addition to these teachings, he learned at Probota monastery, near Suceava (the Capital of Moldova), also the spiritual teaching, being from his youth very familiar with the exercise of prayer, obedience and ascetic labours. In 1649, he was tonsured as a monk, being named Dosoftei (the Slavonic form of the Greek name Dositheos). Because of his prestige as a scholar and of his virtues, Dositheus was named bishop of Huşi in 1658, and after a year, he went to the seat of Romania. In 1671 he was elected as metropolitan of Moldova. As the highest Hierarch of the Principate, he remained gentle and humble with everyone, and amazed all by the wisdom he had.

Historian Ion Neculce, in his Chronicle of Moldavia describes him as follows: "This metropolitan Dositheus was not a simple man by his nature. And he was from mazâl [refugee] ancestry. Very learned, he knew several languages: Hellenic, Slavonic, and other books of wisdom. He was a devout monk and gentle as a lamb. In our country, at that time was no man alike. And the people say about him that he was a saint."

His hierarchical mission happened to meet a difficult social and political time in Moldova, with many changes of the princes, because of the Polish and Turk interference in the country's business. But even like that, he accomplished his mission in a special way, through translating the liturgical service books into the Romanian language, known by the people. His first published books were the Psalms versified in Romanian and the Akathistos of the Mother of God (a prayer similar to the Rosarium, both in 1673). He proved to understand very deeply the sense of the Psalms and he succeeded to put them in verse in Romanian, which is something special because nobody did it before in this land. His language is very beautiful, being used until today. Also, he was a theological authority and revised the Romanian translation of the Old Testament made by Nicolae Milescu, this text being included into the first Romanian Bible, in 1688. Because of the political situation and of his anti-Turk convictions, he was pushed to leave the country and to find refuge in Poland. In 1674 he was replaced in the Metropolitan Seat from Iaşi (the new capital city) with St. Theodosius, the bishop of Roman. In the following year, he came back as Metropolitan and Theodosius withdrew to the monastery of Bogdana, receiving after a little while a martyr's death.

After the recovery of the printing machine in Iaşi, St. Dositheus printed new books in Romanian: *The Holy Liturgy* (1679 and 1683), *The Explained Book of Psalms* (1680) with parallel text in Romanian and Slavonic, the *Moliftfelnic* (Book of the Sacred Services, 1681). Between 1682-1686 he translated from different Greek and Slavic sources and printed in Romanian *The Life and the Passing Over of the Saints*, in four volumes. The work remained unfinished, due to the forced departure to Poland. This book is particularly necessary for the Church's mission, being another great gift of Metropolitan Dosoftei to the Romanian believers. He speaks for the first time about the local saints, such as Daniel of Voroneţ,... Rafail from Agapia, Chiriac from Bisericani Chiriac from Tazlău, Epifanie from Voroneţ, Partenie from Agapia, Ioan from Râşca, and Inochentie from Pobrata, all the saints being officially canonized only in the 20th century.

In 1686, the Polish King Jan Sobieski, being into an anti-Ottoman campaign, came to Moldova to attract on his side the prince Constantin Cantemir. Being forced to withdraw, the Poles [robbed] Moldova and [took] Dositheus as a hostage along with some spiritual treasures, as the relics of St. John the New. Metropolitan Dosoftei lived the last years of his life away from the country, but he continued his scholarly work and was in touch with the Orthodox hierarchs in Moscow and Kyiv. So, he helped to settle the theological conflicts about the Eucharistic prayer, by translating from Greek to Church-Slavonic several works of John Chrysostom, Ephrem the Syrian, Germanus, Patriarch of Constantinople, and Simeon of Thessalonica, about this topic. Despite the pressures made against him by the Polish authorities, he refused the Uniatism and remained as Orthodox bishop until he passed away, on December 13, 1693. Saint Dositheus was buried in the Nativity church in Jolkiew, today in Ukraine. Today his relics are settled in the Metropolitan Cathedral in Iaşi, Romania.

December 20th: DANIEL II,
Archbishop of SERBIA[57]

The son of rich and pious parents, Daniel was placed in the service of King Milutin (1282-1321, 30 Oct.) but, eager to follow the example of the great monastic Fathers, he fled from court and became a monk at the monastery of Konchulsk. From there, he was appointed Abbot of Chilandar, the Serbian monastery on Mount Athos. He was deeply grieved by the civil war in the Byzantine Empire, as well as by that between Milutin and Dragutin in Serbia. In addition, he had to endure the incursion of the bloodthirsty Catalans who ravaged the Holy Mountain in 1309 and massacred many of the monks (see 5 Dec.). He resigned as Abbot of Chilandar and withdrew to the Typikarion, the hesychast cell founded by Saint Sabas (14 Jan.) near Karyes. He was able to enjoy the peace and quiet there for only a short time because he was recalled by Milutin and appointed Bishop of Banya in 1316. He subsequently became Bishop of Hom and Archbishop of the Serbian Church in 1325. Saint Daniel was an austere ascetic who, through his contests and his humility, obtained the gift of spiritual tears from God. He reconciled Milutin and his son Stephen Dushan, strove against the Latin and Bogomil heretics, founded the monasteries of Banya and Dechani, and built many churches. He is also the author of a famous chronicle of the Princes and Archbishops of Serbia. He fell asleep in peace on 20 December 1338.

---

57 Hieromonk Makarios of Simonos Petra, *The Synaxarion: The Lives of the Saints of the Orthodox Church, Volume Two, November-December*, trans. Christopher Hookway (Ormylia: Holy Convent of the Annunciation of Our Lady, 1999), 502-503.

January 4th: EFTHYMIOS, Hegumen of the Athonite Monastery of VATOPEDI and the TWELVE MONKS and MARTYRS of VATOPEDI[58]

Efthymios, the venerable martyr, and those holy fathers with him, flourished in 1280 when the Latin-minded Emperor Michael VIII Palaiologos (r. 1259-1282) and Patriarch John XI Vekkos (1275-1282) dispatched troops and surrounded the Holy Mountain Athos. The purpose of their mission was to enjoin the monks to follow them on their erroneous path of union with the papacy. Since the holy Athonite fathers refused such a union, many were made to suffer hardships and atrocities which led to their martyric deaths. When the soldiers came to Vatopedi, one of the larger monasteries atop a green slope built above a small inlet on the northeast side of the peninsula, the fathers rejected union with Rome. Some resisted, but many fled for refuge elsewhere. Those who were captured included the holy Prohegumen Efthymios and twelve other monks. After the tyrants subjected them to diverse torments, the Unionists sought vengeance against the monks who defied them, by hanging them. They could not be persuaded to embrace strange and unorthodox doctrines, which were unacceptable to the Orthodox Church.

When the Latinizers began their hostilities at the Lavra, some of the monks, terrified at being condemned to death, accepted the Unionists. They handed over to them many holy vessels, including chalices, gospels, censers, and other such sacred articles of the monastery. Thus, the monastery was looted, and those monks agreed to commune with the Latin-minded. At their repose, their miserable bodies remained as solid as wood and blackened all over, emitting a foul smell, so that they could not be buried in the cemetery of the brethren, but instead were placed in an underground cave, which needed to be fenced off. Thus, they died as foreigners and strangers to the holy Orthodox Church and her right believing doctrines.

---

58 Holy Apostles Convent & Dormition Skete, *The Great Synaxaristes of the Orthodox Church, January*, trans. Holy Apostles Convent and Dormition Skete (Buena Vista: Holy Apostles Convent & Dormition Skete, 2003), 135-136.

January 8th: MACARIUS MAKRES, Abbot of the PANTOKRATOR Monastery on ATHOS[59]

Saint Macarius was born in 1383, and at the age of eighteen he became a monk at the Monastery of Vatopedi (Mt Athos). For ten years, under the guidance of a wonderful elder named Armenopoulos, he advanced in secular studies as well as in the ascetic virtues. He was on several occasions rapt in ecstasy by God. He wrote a eulogy of Saint Maximus the Kavsokalyvite (13 Jan.) and in all things sought to imitate the way of life of that angel in the flesh.

On the death of his spiritual father, he put himself under the direction of David of Thessalonica, another holy elder. After his ordination to the priesthood, Macarius felt drawn to the hesychast life, but was not able to fulfill his desire since the Emperor Manuel II Palaeologus summoned him and his Elder David to Constantinople. He made David his counsellor and confessor but could not for long restrain the desire of the two monks for the hesychast life. However shortly after their return to Athos, Elder David gave back his soul to God (1422) and Macarius, under constant pressure from the Emperor, had again to forgo silence and undistracted prayer and make his way back to Constantinople. Having refused the abbacy of the Stoudion, he was appointed to direct the Monastery of the Pantokrator, then in decline. Giving unstintingly of himself, he travelled to Serbia and Russia, and thanks to the support of King Stephen of Serbia and of Metropolitan Photius of Moscow, he was able to re-animate his Monastery and gather a community. Appointed concurrently protosyncellus of the Patriarchate and confessor to the Emperor, he took an active and magnanimous part in negotiations between the Greeks and Latins, but without the least compromise of the sacred principles of Orthodoxy.

In 1429 he led a delegation to Pope Martin V in Rome to prepare for a council of church union. On the eve of a second mission to Rome he fell ill of the plague and withdrew to the island of Halki, where he

---

59 Hieromonk Makarios of Simonos Petra, *The Synaxarion: The Lives of the Saints of the Orthodox Church, Volume Three, January-February*, trans. Christopher Hookaway (Ormylia: Holy Convent of the Annunciation of Our Lady, 2001), 87-88.

gave back his soul to God on 7 January 1431. Besides numerous Lives of the Saints and homilies for the feasts, he wrote dogmatic treatises on the differences between the Orthodox and the Latins.

January 8th: Hieromartyr ISIDORE of YURYEV and his SEVENTY-TWO COMPANIONS

"The city of Yuryev (now Tartu in Estonia) to the west of Pskov had been conquered by the Teutonic Knights at the beginning of the thirteenth century and its population converted by force to Roman Catholicism. By 1472, the Orthodox community amounted to no more than seventy-two people with the Priest Isidore at their head. They were all thrown into the River Oneg during the service of blessing the water at Theophany. A year later, their bodies were found incorrupt on the riverbank at some distance from the town, and they were buried in the Church of Saint Nicolas."[60]

"In the year 1030, the pious Great Prince Yaroslav the Wise (who was named George in holy baptism), the son of the Great Prince St. Vladimir, Equal to the Apostles, subjected to his authority an alien tribe which lived in the hinterlands of Novgorod and Pskov. Afterwards, he founded a city on the River Omovzha (or Embakh), and constructed in it a church dedicated to St. George the Great-martyr. This city was called Yuriev. From the mid-1100's on, German Catholics began to penetrate this land by sea, and settled there. Having grown strong, they brought it under their control, since at that time internal strife and discord reigned in the Russian land. Having enslaved the local pagan inhabitants, the Germans, more by force than by consent, converted them to the Latin faith which they themselves professed, and, at the same time, began to oppress those Orthodox Christians that lived in their midst.

In the days of Great Prince Ivan III Vasilievich of Moscow, the Orthodox Christians subject to the Germans had two churches in the Russian quarter of the city of Yuriev — one dedicated to St. Nicholas the Wonderworker, and the other to the Great-martyr St. George. Two priests served in these churches — one by the name of Ivan, surnamed

---

60 Ibid., 91.

Shestnik (i.e. stranger), was from Muscovy; the other was called Isidore. When the Germans — at first with promises, later with threats — began to lure the Orthodox inhabitants of the city into Latinism, the priest Ivan, who had dwelt in Yuriev all of two and a half years, left for Pskov. Soon thereafter he received the monastic tonsure with the name Jonah, and founded the Pskov-Caves Monastery on the border of Pskov and Livonia. Having dwelt there in a holy manner, he was accounted worthy of a blessed repose in the Lord. But Isidore remained in the City of Yuriev and had great disputes with the Germans on the Orthodox faith. Not infrequently he reproached the heterodox, exhorting them to abandon the Latin faith (Roman Catholicism) and embrace Holy Orthodoxy.

In 1472, the Latins took up arms against the divinely-protected City of Pskov and the Orthodox populace subject to it, in order to plant in its midst, the Latin faith confirmed principally by the canons of the pseudo-council of Florence, at which it had been decided to reinstate so-called Christian unity by force. Meanwhile, the priest Isidore served blamelessly at the Church of Saint Nicholas the Wonderworker as a star shining forth amongst the Christians of his flock. And it came to pass that the elder of the city of Yuriev, a German by the name of Yuri Tryasigolov, rose up against Isidore and against the Orthodox Christians and complained about them before the Latin bishop Andrew and the city rulers saying that he had heard from this Russian and his whole flock blasphemy against the Latin faith and the use of unleavened bread, and praise for the Greek faith alone.

Thus, did he stir up wrath amongst the bishop and the nobles; thenceforth the Latins sought to torment the Orthodox Christians of the City of Yuriev. The holy Feast of the Theophany of our Lord fell on January 6, 1472. The priest Isidore with all the Orthodox duly went forth to the river Omovzha with the precious cross to sanctify the water. There on the waters of the Holy Theophany, Germans who had been sent by their bishop Andrew and the above mentioned elder, laid hold of Isidore the Christian teacher and those men and women and, like fierce wolves, dragged them before their bishop and the civil judges.

Great was the torment the mighty warriors of Christ endured in the judgment hall for their faith, which the Germans sought to force them to renounce. Saint Isidore, however, and all the Orthodox confessors with him, as it were with one mouth, replied turning first to the bishop, then to all their judges: 'God forbid, O ye enemies of the Truth, that we Orthodox renounce the True Christ and the Orthodox faith! We will not spare our bodies for Christ God, however much you torment us. We beseech you, wretched ones: Spare your own souls for the Lord's sake, for ye are God's creation.' Then with great boldness did Saint Isidore unmask the false wisdom of the Latins and their apostasy from true Christianity. The enraged Latin bishop ordered the Orthodox cast into prison and summoned all the local rulers from the surrounding castles, as though to put the Orthodox on trial. As soon as the Orthodox Christians had come together, Saint Isidore instructed his flock in prison.

Afterwards the holy Isidore with his companions stood in the prison facing east and began to sing and to pray with tears and heartfelt sighs. He partook of the reserved Gifts of the Holy and Life-creating Mysteries and communed all the men, women and children who were with him. All were filled with spiritual joy, and the devout priest instructed them again concerning the reward of eternal blessings for good deeds and of eternal torments for deeds of darkness. 'Let not one of us,' he said to his companions, 'from the least to the greatest, fear either the threats or the tortures themselves. For if we suffer well for the Son of God, Our Lord Jesus Christ, we will receive the reward of our suffering on the day of judgment.' And with one spirit, with a loud voice, they chanted a hymn in honor of the martyrs: 'O holy Martyrs, who have endured suffering and have been crowned, beseech ye the Lord, that He will have mercy on our souls.'

Messengers from the Latin bishop and civil judges arrived at the prison and, leading the Orthodox Christians forth, delivered them to the place of judgment at the town hall for a short trial before the bishop and all the Latins that had assembled for the spectacle. As the sun amongst the stars, so stood the confessor Saint Isidore with his companions before them. At first the bishop strove with unctuous words to incline the confessors of Orthodoxy toward his own faith. Turning to Saint Isidore, as the leader and guide of the flock, but afterwards to all those under his care, the bishop said: 'You need but to obey me and the governors of this city in the presence of these many Germans who have come together from the surrounding castles of my realm. Accept our precious faith (which is truly one with yours) and the use of unleavened bread, and do not destroy yourselves. Be true brethren unto us and partakers of our riches. If you so desire, hold to your own faith again; only confess your guilt now before me and the judges and Germans.' But the confessors replied to the bishop: 'Why do you try to persuade us with false and lying words? You cannot dissuade us from the true Christian faith. Do with us as you wish, for behold, we stand before thee and repeat to thee that which we have said previously.'

Then, like serpents, consumed with rage against the Orthodox, the stern bishop and the other judges ordered all of them driven into the river Omovzha in whatever clothing they had on. Saint Isidore, still vested as a priest, was cast into the very hole in the ice through which, through Orthodox prayers, the water had been sanctified earlier on the Feast of Theophany. Thus, did they deal with them as with criminals, executing them in a cruel manner for their Orthodox faith in Christ. Seventy-two suffered who considered Saint Isidore their instructor. They surrendered their pure souls into the hands of the living God and were crowned with crowns that fade not away. There was at the time of their martyrdom a most wondrous sight. Among the Orthodox was to be seen a young mother who had in her arms a three-year-old child, most beautiful and comely of countenance. The wicked Germans wrested the infant from his mother's arms and cast her into the river. Beholding his mother drowned with the blessed martyrs, the child began to weep in the arms of the tormentors, and however much they tried to calm him, he struggled all the more, scratching their faces.

Then the cruel tormentors cast him down beside the hole in the ice. The lad, creeping up to the hole itself, crossed himself thrice, and facing the people, exclaimed: 'I also am a Christian. I believe in the Lord and wish to die, as did our teacher Isidore and my mother.' And thus saying, he cast himself beneath the ice. Thus, did a child suffer for the truth. Spring arrived and the river Omovzha overflowed its banks. Then did the relics of all the confessors of Christ appear almost three miles upstream from the City of Yuriev, under a tree near a mountain. They were all incorrupt and lay facing the east, as though arranged by human hands. The priest Saint Isidore lay in their midst in all his priestly raiment. Thus, did the Lord glorify His holy saints. Then the Orthodox merchants of the city of Yuriev took up the relics of those who had suffered and buried them in the city around the Church of Saint Nicholas the wonderworker where they shall rest until the Second Coming of Christ."[61]

January 14th: SAVA, First Archbishop of SERBIA and founder of HILANDER Monastery on Mount Athos[62]

In the year 1204, when the Crusaders plotted to assassinate Emperor Alexios V Doukas Mourtzouphlos (1204), they failed. After planning another assault on the city, on the 12th of April, both Crusader and Venetian forces attacked the sea walls of Constantinople on the side facing the harbor of the Golden Horn. The Byzantine defenders successfully beat them back, but the Latins returned. After they had scaled the walls, they entered the city and cruelly sacked it. Thousands of Orthodox were slain or taken captive; thousands more fled the capital. A Latin emperor was crowned Baldwin of Flanders (1204-1205). Then, in 1205, a young Byzantine nobleman, Theodore I Laskaris, the son-in-law of the former Emperor Alexios III Angelos, rallied the remnants of Constantinopolitan aristocracy and the hierarchy. He organized a government-in-exile across the straits of Nicaea. After the Latin takeover of Constantinople, Theodore, circa 1208, was crowned as "Emperor of the Rhomaioi (Romans)," in order to perpetuate the Byzantine monarchy.

After the fall of the city, the protos of Athos sent the blessed Sava and the heads of the monasteries to Laskaris, the founder of the empire of Nicaea and its emperor, with regard to the necessary matter facing the Holy Mountain Athos. Though the precise nature of these matters is unclear, more than likely, the inroads made by the Latins were necessarily a main topic. This is because Boniface of Montferrat, and now marquis of Thessalonike, pressured the monks to accept papal authority and prac-

---

61   Holy Trinity Monastery, "The Suffering of The Holy Hieromartyr Isidore the Priest and The Seventy-Two Martyred with Him in Yuriev of Livonia," *Orthodox Life*, 28, no. 1 (January-February 1978), 3-7.

62   Holy Apostles Convent & Dormition Skete, *The Great Synaxaristes of the Orthodox Church, January*, trans. Holy Apostles Convent and Dormition Skete (Buena Vista: Holy Apostles Convent & Dormition Skete, 2003), 418-427.

tices of the Latin Church. In the summer of 1205, Cardinal Benedict, Innocent III's legate at Constantinople, placed the monasteries under the jurisdiction of the Latin bishop of Sebasteia. Then, after he had built himself a castle (Frangokastro) on Athonite territory, he pillaged and terrorized the monks with the help of Frankish barons. Unarmed monks were tortured in the hope of uncovering monastery treasures.

The emperor, with the entire senate, and even the patriarch and the body of priests, were then situated in Nicaea, the new capital of Byzantine power. When Saint Sava arrived in Nicaea and met with Laskaris, his kinsman through marriage, the emperor desired not so much to meet Saint Sava due to their kinship, as because he was extremely desirous to behold this preeminently virtuous man. Therefore, he rejoiced exceedingly upon beholding the holy Sava, whom he rendered great attention. As Laskaris conversed with the holy elder, marvelling at his virtue, he regarded him with profound reverence.

Despite the Athonite embassy to Nicaea, the Athonites were made to endure four years of unconscionable spoliation and injury by the Latins. Saint Sava tells us that the Latins "even invaded us and that holy place; and there was great turmoil." Only after the joint action of Innocent III (1198-1216) and the Latin emperor Henry of Flanders was the Bishop of Sebasteia deposed and exiled for the enormity of this crimes against the Athonites. In 1213, the Athonite monasteries even appealed to the pope for protection. Though it was no more than an administrative formality, the Mountain was granted the protection of both Innocent III and Emperor Henry, until their deaths in 1216. Afterward, the Athonites looked to Nicaea for protection, much to the dissatisfaction of the new pope, Honorius III (1216-1227).

During this time, Stefan [Sava's brother] divorced his first wife, Evdokia. For reasons of state, he later married the fanatical Roman Catholic Anna, the granddaughter of the Venetian Doge Enrico Dandolo (d. 1205), who played a leading role in the conquest of Constantinople in 1204. Prompted by his new bride to be a crowned king, and surrounded by antagonistic Latin kingdoms of Constantinople, Hungary and Bulgaria, the grand župan agreed to be crowned by Pope Honorius III. Thus, in 1217, Pope Honorius III sent a special delegation with royal insignia and crown that he might confer upon Stefan the title of king. Sava strived to prevent his brother's coronation by papal legate. He understood that his sister-in-law, Anna, planned to have her husband crowned a Roman Catholic king and, thereby, hoped to convert the Serbs to Roman Catholicism. Though it is not clear, it appears that, in protest, Sava departed. When he left Serbian soil for Hilandar, the miraculous and healing myrrh of Saint Symeon ceased to flow. Not much time passed before Stefan sent a letter to Sava at Hilander requesting his return; for he believed only then would the myrrh continue flowing. Saint Sava responded by writing an epistle that was to be opened and read over the tomb of Saint Symeon at Studenica. It was only then that the myrrh resumed flowing.

Next, Stefan wrote Sava another letter expressing his aim toward the independence of the Serbian Church. A Latin patriarch was set up in Constantinople, and another was in Bulgaria during the reign of Kalojan (1197-1207). After the Fourth Crusade, Boniface of Montferrat became marquis of Thessalonike. His territory encompassed Macedonia and western Thrace, and he had interests as distant as the Peloponnesos. Moreover, after this crusade, Greece was easily conquered by the Franks. The following Frankish states were established: the principality of Achaia (Morea), the duchy of the Archipelago, the lordship of Athens and Thebes, and Evia (Euboea, Negroponte). Serbia was surrounded, because the Vatican ofttimes incited her northern neighbors to conquest and latinize her. The Serbs needed their own independent Orthodox Church, especially since the oecumenical patriarch was living in exile at Nicaea. Stefan needed strong Church backing.

After much prayer, Sava, with a group from Hilandar, entered a ship and sailed to Nicaea to see Emperor Theodore Laskaris and Patriarch Manuel I Sarantenos (1215-1222). The Byzantines, meanwhile, were combating the crusaders on one side and the Seljuk Turks on the other.... When Saint Sava and the emperor met again... Sava spoke to him about the Serbian people and their need for an independent church and their own archbishop.... the two of them [Serbian patriarch and emperor] decided that the holy Sava should be Archbishop of Serbia... Finally compelled to do as they wished, Sava was ordained by the patriarch. Archbishop Sava [...] instructed his flock daily, teaching them the word of the Gospel and a life according to Christ. The Orthodox faithful were strengthened by his sermons and the example of his virtue. Many heretics, by the grace and sweetness of his teachings, turned from their heresy to piety. Thus, in but a little while, the unbelievers and heretics of his see became Orthodox. All revered Saint Sava as their only shepherd and teacher. With determination and subtlety, he defended the autocephalous Serbian Church against papal claims.

Afterward the saint left the holy land and entered a ship bound for Nicaea. Emperor Theodore and Patriarch Michael had reposed. The new emperor, Theodore's son-in-law, was John Doukas Vatatzes (1222-1254). When John succeeded him to the imperial throne, he was an ardent protector of all victims of wrongdoing, a bastion of justice, and a fount of mercy, so that he was surnamed "the merciful." Likewise, he was a zealot of piety and Orthodoxy, and was the cause of many Jews receiving holy Baptism during his reign. Having a desire to unite east and west, he called for a dialogue. Pope Gregory IX (1227-1241) sent legates to a meeting presided over by Germanos the New, Patriarch of Constantinople (1223-1240). Peace between the groups was thwarted when the westerners refused to remove the addition of the *Filioque* from the Symbol of Faith.

[Saint Sava] shepherded the flock in a God-pleasing fashion. He illuminated all of Serbia with the bright beams of his virtues and his divine teachings. He preserved and kept them unharmed from the noetic wolves, wisely directing them into the heavenly sheepfold. However, since that area of the Balkans was so riddled with heresies, the saint entered into other provinces where he taught them apostolically. Going from place to place, he led both the heretics and impious to true piety.

January 18th: MAXIM, Archbishop of WALLACHIA

Saint Maxim, Archbishop of Wallachia was born in 1462 to the ruler Stefan the Blind Branković and given the name George. His father died in exile when he was 23 years old and he was left to rule the Serbs in Srem. Those times under Turkish occupation were difficult for the Serbs. His rule was benefitted greatly from the contacts he had made with the western European rulers while he was prince as he was able to secure food and supplies to the Turkish-persecuted Serbs. He strengthened their faith by reminding them to "remain faithful to the Orthodox faith in Jesus Christ as delivered through God's enlightened St. Sava." The Hungarian King Matthew, in return for his support to the persecuted Serbs, pressured Despot [ruler] George by offering his daughter, Princess Isabella, for marriage with the stipulation that he convert to Roman Catholicism, with the marriage arranged to solidify Serbo-Hungarian political ties. "Holy Despot George refused this offer, being very pious and truly a monastic in spirit. He also felt obligated, as the oldest son, to care for his aging mother, Queen Angelina. George also explained to King Matthew of Hungary that he would never depart from the Orthodox faith in favor of the Latin heresy, that he would never abandon the faith of St. Sava, the same faith for which his loyal Serbian people were now suffering. He replied with the famous saying: *I would rather remain under the Ottoman yoke than acquiesce to the heretical Latin faith*. And, as time passed, after many conversations with Princess Isabella, Holy Despot George was able to convince her to devote her life to Christ. In the end, she too became a monastic."[63]

January 19th: MELETIUS the Confessor of MOUNT GALESION[64]

"How can I," the narrator [said], "recount the rest of this narrative without tears? I say this because, at that time, even as a cloud full of hailstones threatens injury and harm, in like manner the Latin-minded in favor of union rained down persecutions upon the Church of Christ. The devil, the prince of evil, after much warfare directed against the flock of Christ, also advanced this last attack, the change of the Symbol of Faith, that is, the Creed. Thus, the Church of Old Rome was taken into captivity by the enemy, which caused the other Churches to weep and lament for the departure of the first among sisters from the Faith, for which loss

---

63 Fr. Daniel Rogich, *Serbian Patericon: Saints of the Serbian Orthodox Church – Volume One*, (Canton: Hesychia Press, 2023), 73-74.

64 Holy Apostles Convent & Dormition Skete, *The Great Synaxaristes of the Orthodox Church, January*, trans. Holy Apostles Convent and Dormition Skete (Buena Vista: Holy Apostles Convent & Dormition Skete, 2003), 671-676.

even the angels, the guardians of the Church, mourned. The devil, however, rejoiced at the division and separation of the Christians.

Now, from the time of the sack of Constantinople during the Fourth Crusade (1204), the Latin Empire had established itself in the city. Attempts were made to bring the Orthodox to submit to the papacy. Therefore, there was urgent need for the saint to lend his assistance to the Orthodox in the capital. The true Faith was being compromised by Emperor Michael VII Palaiologos (1259-1282) in order to extract promises from the Latins. The *Filioque* and other cacodox dogma pervaded the west and arrived in the east when Emperor Michael, called "the azymite," reigned, who tyrannized the Eastern Church for years.

In the summer of 1261, Constantinople reverted from Latin rule to Orthodox hands. But on Feast of the Nativity, in 1262, Emperor Michael blinded the rightful heir to the throne. He then had the youth imprisoned, which act brought upon Michael the excommunication of Patriarch Arsenios Autoreianos (1254-1260; 1261-1265). The emperor subsequently deposed the patriarch and had his father confessor, Joseph I, a monk of Mount Galesios, installed as patriarch (1266-1275, 1282, 1283). This action divided the Orthodox, since many faithful chose to remain with the unjustly deposed Arsenios. Joseph was deemed a usurper. While this division took place among the Orthodox, Emperor Michael attempted to impose his policy of Unia with Rome in order to advance his political agenda. Persecutions then arose against the opponents of the union. Soldiers of Christ, on behalf of the truth, were not missing in this struggle. Father Meletius took up spiritual arms and went to defend Orthodoxy in the midst of the embattled Church. He decided to seek not his own benefit, but rather that of his neighbor. He left his solitude and went all about the province of Bithynia, strengthening and supporting the Christians in Orthodoxy. He bade them to guard and preserve piety. He exhorted them to diligently distance themselves from this novel and perverse dogma, which was named Latinismos or Latinism.

In 1275, the Unia of Lyons was proclaimed. After some initial wavering, Patriarch Joseph denounced the Unia, and this act resulted in his deposition. Thereupon, John XI Vekkos was installed (1275-1282). Together with the emperor, he championed the union and persecuted the anti-unionists. Vekkos ordered the commemoration of Pope Gregory (1271-1276), so that at his services could be heard, "Gregory, the supreme pontiff of the apostolic see and universal pope." As for the Filioque, the addition of the blasphemous words, "and from the Son" was introduced not only into the Creed, but also into liturgical exclamations, so that one could hear, "And to Thee do we send up glory, to the Father and to the Son and to Him Who proceedeth from Both, the Holy Spirit."

Now when Emperor Michael the azymite presented corrupted Latin dogmas to the Great Church and sought the union between the Eastern Church and that of the west, he needed to expel the Orthodox patriarch from his throne. As we said, he appointed John Vekkos, who would champion the cause of union. Thereupon, the Orthodox were imprisoned, ill-treated, and subjected to manifold torments. It was then that the blessed Meletius thought to speak to Emperor Michael. Father Meletius mentioned this to the divine Galaction, a certain priest-monk with whom he struggled in the ascetic life on Mount Galesios. Father Galaction was expressive with language, at the summit of virtue, and worthy of respect. The two monks went together to Constantinople, where they gained an audience before Emperor Michael. They confessed the Orthodox faith boldly. They declared themselves defenders of the Faith and said that they would suffer no intercommunion with the heresy of *Latinismos*, which had been censured and rebuked by the divine fathers. They explained that the holy oecumenical synods confessed to, and upheld, that article of the Symbol of the Faith which pronounces that the Holy Spirit proceeds from the Father. Those who dared to alter the Creed with either additions or subtractions of even the tiniest detail were subject to excommunication. After saying this and many other edifying explanations, they added, "Why then dost thou, O emperor, look askance at the words of Christ, which are recorded in the holy Gospel [Jn. 15:26], as is attested to by both the holy apostles [Gal. 4:6; Eph. 1:17] and fathers, and the sacred canons of the universal Church? Why has thou given thyself over to deception and error? Why hast thou sought to displace the apostolic traditions? It is impossible that this should happen. Do not then undertake to move the immovable. For it is better that we should lose our lives than lose our Orthodoxy."

This boldness of the two confessors was deemed as a pointed and personal insult by the emperor. He delivered both men up to prison. These valiant soldiers of Christ endured the hardships of prison with joy. After a few days of confinement, the command came that they be removed from their prison cell and brought before the emperor. Michael was hoping that the sufferings and ills of prison life would have undermined the resolve of the monks. He was thinking that as wax, they might have melted from the fire of temptation. Nevertheless, these holy men had not softened their position. On the contrary, their resolve was hardened as iron, being fired by the warmth of their faith. Therefore, like iron hammers, they pounded the cacodox. At this second examination, they displayed even more courage and daring than at the first. The emperor waxed hot with anger. He sentenced the two holy monks to banishment on the island of Skyros, off the coast of Evia in the Aegean. This island, however, was under the metropolitanate of Athens. From Skyros, Father Meletius was remanded to Rome in chains for the purpose of entering into discourse with the pope's theologians. The pope consigned Father Meletius to bonds and a dungeon for seven long years. The holy confessor was then returned to Skyros, according to an imperial command, where he was incarcerated with the goodly Galaction.

The dungeon where the saints were detained was as the land of "darkness and the shadow of death [Ps. 106:10]." They were put to the test with many days of hunger, for by starvation had the authorities on Skyros determined to put the confessors to death. But those venerable fathers, and especially the divine Meletius, decided to keep a fast. This brought [to] Meletius' remembrance his old custom of fasting for many days. He therefore utilized this doleful torture as another occasion to mount the ladder to Paradise, by keeping a strict fast for forty days. Now the warden of the prison observed their abstinence and greatly marvelled, so that he mentioned the matter to his wife, saying, "O woman, we are lost, fighting against God. I say this because those two imprisoned monks possess such virtue that they appear to be angels rather than men." He then recounted to her their many days of fasting and their frequent prayers and vigils throughout the night. His wife was brought to a state of astonishment and wonder at these feats. In the morning, the warden's wife took their only daughter and went to see the holy prisoners. She entered and prostrated herself before their feet, asking for the blessings.

The saints, though they were found in the midst of such a terrible hardship, nonetheless rejoiced in their tribulations, they were giving glory to God at all times and in every place. The emperor had a mania to spread Latinismos. To do so, he drew many to him, not only by employing threats and punishments, but also be bestowing offices and dignities. Whatever might advance his position, even if it meant utilizing treacherous and fraudulent means against what was just and true, he perpetrated. Some became his friends and followers of the moment and accepted Latinismos. All the Orthodox whom the emperor could not persuade, were either exiled or put to death. By employing such tyrannical ways of achieving his goals, he removed from his presence those who would not consent to his Latin way of thinking, for he believed that by such methods of disposal he would overcome all. He then at some point summoned his nobles and assumed a pleasant tone with them, saying, "It seems to me that the Church now has great peace, which gift profits the patriarch, because there is nothing to trouble the world." After hearing these words of the emperor, some of those present, seeking to ingratiate themselves with him, had one among them speak for the rest. He said, "Sire there are those who have been banished to Skyros, who are reputed to be more discerning and knowledgeable than the rest, but who resist they sovereignty and rule." The emperor inquired, "And who are these persons?" The nobleman answered, "Meletius and Galaction, the Galesiots." The pronouncement of these names wounded the emperor's heart, because these men were renowned for their virtue.

Straightway, a royal ship was fitted out. The emperor's men were dispatched to bring the two Galesiots to Constantinople. They were brought to the capital and placed in the prison known as Noumeron. In the meantime, many days passed. The emperor gave pretexts against hearing their case, saying that other matters of great import demanded his attention rather than to hear some churchmen. Thus, their examination before the emperor kept being postponed. But evil hierarchs and especially the patriarch slandered the saints persistently within the palace walls. O just and long-suffering God, how was this to be endured? These evil men used every means to persuade the godly Meletius and Galaction to subscribe to Latinismos, for death was the only other option. At length, by imperial command, the stout-hearted ones were taken from the prison and made to appear before the emperor. Once again, they demonstrated boldness and valor, but to a greater degree than before. The saints this time were subjected to greater punishments than those administered previously. Forthwith, they were submitted to a long and cruel thrashing with staves, until their bodies lay prone upon the ground, barely showing life and breath. Afterwards, when they came to themselves, the sacred Galaction was cast into prison. The divine Meletius was suspended from ropes and a piece of wood. Then — behold, the miracle! — straightway, that wood blossomed forth and was covered with leaves.

The emperor heard of this miracle and changed his mind regarding his dealings with the two prisoners. By the mediation of others, the emperor conversed with the blessed man. He asked Father Meletius to have communion with Latinismos. The saint, having disdained the imperial request, then took flight as an eagle to the clouds, not to be caught or vanquished by the snares and machinations of these evil men. The emperor was in a state of wonderment. He knew not how to react to the fathers. Since he could not overcome their resolve, he thought to subject their bodies to tortures. The emperor had his executioners blind Galaction and sever the tongue of Meletius. He chose those particular mutilations so that neither could Galaction serve or liturgize again, nor could Meletius speak on the theology of the Holy Trinity. But no matter how the emperor contrived to disable them, his will did not prevail. The divine Meletius, even with the cutting of his tongue, spoke clearly and distinctly. Galaction, when peace was established in the Church, returned to liturgize and celebrate the bloodless sacrifice. In 1282, Michael Palaiologos died, under excommunication by Patriarch Arsenios. Michael was also under excommunication by Pope Martin IV (1281-1285) for being "the protector of the schismatic and heretical Greeks." Among his countrymen, he was unpopular for his subservience to Rome and persecution of the Orthodox. His son and heir did not give him a funeral, but rather had his body buried by night in a secret manner in the corner of a provincial monastery. Thereupon, pious Andronikos II (1282-1328) became emperor of the Romans. He repudiated all efforts toward union with Rome. The transgressor and lawless one, Vekkos, retired to a monastery [...] Both Fathers Meletius and Galaction were removed from prison, together with many others who had refused to espouse Latinismos.

See page 337 for the first part of his list against the Latins.

See page 337 for the first part of his list against the Latins.

January 19th: MARK EUGENIKOS, Metropolitan of EPHESUS[65]

This luminary of the Orthodox faith enlightened the dark days in which the Byzantine empire, on the verge of economic collapse and hard-pressed on all sides by the Turks, was struggling for its life, and faced the dolorous alternative of falling into the hands of the infidel and ceasing to exist as a Christian state, or of submitting to the haughty dominion of the Latin heretics, who were not disposed to lend their financial and military support at a lesser price than union of the Churches, or rather, of submission of Orthodoxy to the Papacy.

Despite his desire to remain withdrawn from the world, his knowledge and his virtue won him the regard of the Emperor John VIII Palaeologus (1425-48), who was making preparations for a great council of union with the Roman Church in the hope of obtaining support of the Pope and of the Western European princes. It was out of obedience to the Emperor that Mark, the devout hesychast monk, agreed to ascend the pulpit of the Church, to be consecrated Metropolitan of Ephesus and to join the Byzantine delegation as substitute for the Patriarchs of Jerusalem, Antioch and Alexandria and as their exarch at the Council.

The Greek delegation, consisting of the Emperor, the Patriarch Joseph II (1416-39), twenty-five bishops and a staff of about seven hundred, embarked for Italy in a burst of enthusiasm. Everyone was sure that the union longed for by all Christians would soon be established. Saint Mark too, far from being a narrow anti-Latin fanatic as he is often portrayed, shared the same hope while firmly taking his stand on the rock

---

65 Hieromonk Makarios of Simonos Petra, *The Synaxarion: The Lives of the Saints of the Orthodox Church, Volume Three, January-February*, trans. Christopher Hookaway (Ormylia: Holy Convent of the Annunciation of Our Lady, 2001), 216-221.

of the Faith. For him, as for most of the Greeks, the only possible union was in the return of the Roman Church to unity in the charity which she had broken through her innovations. But as soon as they arrived at Ferrara, it was clear that Pope Eugenius and his theologians had quite another disposition. This was made evident, first of all, in matters of protocol; then it became increasingly apparent that the Byzantine delegates were being treated as virtual prisoners, prevented from leaving the city, and having the promised grants towards their living expenses so long withheld that some of the bishops were reduced to selling their personal effects in order to buy food.

The following were the topics on the agenda: (i) the dogma of the Procession of the Holy Spirit and the question of the addition of *Filioque* (the phrase "and from the Son") to the Nicene Creed, (ii) the question of the existence of Purgatory, (iii) the use by the Latins of unleavened bread (azyme) for the Eucharist, and the question of the consecration of the holy Gifts by the sole words of Institution (according to the Latins) or by invocation of the Holy Spirit (*epiclesis*) (iv) the primacy of the Pope. Since the Latins were in overwhelming majority and their opinions on the question of dogma were clearly going to be carried whenever it came to a vote, the Emperor and the Patriarch delayed the opening of debates on the fundamental issues until there was agreement on another method of balloting. In the meantime, it was decided to discuss the secondary question of Purgatory. Saint Mark responded in the name of the Orthodox Church to the arguments of the Latin theologians. The souls of the departed can indeed benefit to their "advancement," and even the damned to a relative "relief" of their lot, thanks to the prayers of the Church and through the infinite mercy of God; but the notion of a punishment prior to the Last Judgement and of a purification through a material fire is altogether foreign to the tradition of the Church.

It was soon obvious to the better-informed that two worlds were confronting one another, and that all discussion of doctrine would inevitably lead to an impasse. The weeks went by without any progress. Discussion of Purgatory having been broken off because of the plague, they went on to consider the burning question of the arbitrary addition of *Filioque* to the Latin version of the creed. Saint Mark once again firmly gave voice to the conscience of the Church.

The Symbol of the Faith must be preserved inviolate, as at its origin. Since all the holy doctors of the Church, all the Councils and all the Scriptures put us on our guard against heterodoxy, how dare I, in spite of these authorities, follow those who urge us to unity in a deceitful semblance of union — those who have corrupted the holy and divine Symbol of Faith and brought in the Son as second cause of the Holy Spirit.

At the end of seven months of disappointed hopes and empty talking, Pope Eugenius had the council transferred to Florence. Once assembled there, it was decided to deal finally with the question of dogma. Having his spirit ever fixed in God and purified by prayer, Saint Mark was able to set forth with lucid sobriety the teaching of Scripture and of the holy Fathers on the Procession of the Holy Spirit. When the Latin theologians took up the word, they bombarded the participants through endless sessions with subtle arguments supported by a whole rational apparatus and by many quotations from the Fathers taken out of context or misunderstood. The contest was like that of David against Goliath. As time went on, Bessarion, the Metropolitan of Nicaea, and Isidore, the Metropolitan of Kiev, emerged as determined advocates of Union — whether because of personal ambition or because of the ingrained hostility of their humanist tendency to the hesychast and monastic traditions represented by Mark. Behind the scenes, they did all they could to persuade the other bishops that the Latins had not strayed from the truth and that their doctrine of the Holy Spirit was not heretical but that they had done no more than develop the traditional teaching in their own language.

Frustrated by the idleness of the proceedings, by their lack of funds and by the haughtiness of the Latins; concerned too for the future of the threatened City and feeling caught in a trap, the bishops gradually let themselves be won over to adopt a compromise Union, as the Emperor and Patriarch did not cease to urge on them. The doctrinal debate like all the other discussions having reached a dead end, the Greeks wanted to be done with the council, leave and disavow their consent once they had returned home. But despite pressure and insults from his opponents, Saint Mark would not give way: "It is not permissible to make compromises in matters of faith," he declared. He had perceived the futility of seeing to argue against the sophistries of the Latins and, as dissension grew apace among the Greeks, he decided to withdraw from the struggle and make plain his disapproval by suffering in silence. The Latins then became all the bolder; they too would have no compromise, and they began to demand that the Greeks accept the *Filioque* and adopt certain of their liturgical customs. Suppressing their remaining qualms of conscience all the Greeks, on the Emperor's orders, finally signed the decree of false Union. There was in fact no Union to speak of, since, although the decree was read in both languages at the solemn liturgy celebrated on 6 July 1439 in the presence of the Pope and the whole council, not one Greek took communion, and the two delegations seated on either side of the altar did not even exchange the kiss of peace.

Only Saint Mark had refused to sign. When Pope Eugenius was told, he exclaimed: "The bishop of Ephesus has not signed, so we have achieved nothing!" He summoned the Saint and wanted to have him condemned as a heretic; but thanks to the protection of the Emperor, he was able to return to Constantinople with the rest of the delegation.

On their arrival in the City, the makers of the false Union were received with contempt and public reprobation. The assembly of the believers — the holy people, the royal priesthood (1 Pet. 2:9) — which is the bearer of the fulness of the truth and the final arbiter of the validity of councils, unanimously rejected the pseudo-Council of Florence and deserted the churches of those in communion with the Unionists, while it greeted Saint Mark as a second Moses, a confessor of the Faith and a pillar of the Church. Breaking his silence, the Saint then set out on a campaign against the Union, or rather to re-establish the unity of the Orthodox Church by his preachings and writings, and also by his tears and his prayers. "I am convinced," he said, "that inasmuch as I distance myself from them (the Unionists) I draw near to God and to all the Saints, and to the extent that I separate myself from them I am the more united to the truth." He had to flee from Constantinople on the election of Metrophanes, the new Patriarch, to avoid concelebrating with him, and he made his way to his diocese of Ephesus. But he clashed with the Unionists there and left, hoping to find refuge on Mount Athos. He was arrested on the way and sent by order of the Emperor to force residence on the island of Lemnos. Freed in 1442, he returned to this monastery where he continued the struggle to his last breath (23 June 1444). On his deathbed, Saint Mark handed on the torch of Orthodoxy to his former pupil George Scholarios, who had succumbed for a short time to the false union but repented of it. He became an ardent defender of the Faith and, taking the name of Gennadios, was the first Patriarch of Constantinople after the fall of the City.

With the defeat at Varna (10 Nov. 1444) of the crusade organized by the Pope, there was no further obstacle to the Turkish offensive. In December 1452 the Union was officially proclaimed in Constantinople in the forlorn hope of obtaining vital aid from the West, but none was forthcoming. In the end, with the fall of Constantinople on 29 May 1453, the false union of the Churches vanished amid the rubble and ashes of the earthly city, leaving the Orthodox Faith alive and intact for the salvation of the Christian people.

See page 366 for writings from him.

January 19th: MAKARIOS Kalogeras of PATMOS

St. Makarios Kalogeras, the Teacher-of-the-Nation was born into a wealthy family on Patmos in 1688. Later in life he went to Constantinople to continue his education and came into contact with noteworthy families and clerics of the capital city. After many years of study, he was ordained a deacon and served in the Metropolitanate of Nikomedia. As St. Makarios placed great significance on the teaching and raising of the Greeks under oppression of the Turks, he returned to Patmos and in 1713 he founded the Patmias School where the lessons were offered free to all students. In the beginning St. Makarios taught by himself, however after a few years the best students were selected as teachers of the school. These students were from Patmos and other areas under the Ottoman empire oppressors.

His chief co-workers were Monk Kosmas from Lemnos and St. Gerasimos the Byzantine. The number of students increased to around one-hundred and because of this there was a need to create more buildings, which came to fruition through the help of generous gifts from benefactors in Constantinople. The Patmias School became one of the most significant schools of Hellenism in the 18th century and was a key contributor in maintaining the true Orthodox position on the Latin heresies. Patriarch Cyril V the Confessor of Orthodoxy against the Latins was once a student of St. Makarios Kalogeras prior to his ascension to the patriarchal throne. St. Makarios was the teacher for many of the Orthodox figures during this time and a confessor of true Orthodox Christian ecclesiology, teaching his students the oneness of the Orthodox faith, and himself being a major promulgator of the Orthodox teaching of receiving papists and other heretics strictly by Baptism.[66] After being weakened by an infection, he fell asleep in the Lord on the island of Patmos in 1737.

January 21st: MAXIMUS the Greek[67]

[St. Maximus the Greek] was sent to Russia, in response to the request of Grand Prince Basil Ivanovich, with the task of translating the scholarly works of the holy Fathers on the Psalter and other Church books into Slavonic, to provide arguments with which to counter the heresy of Judaism. In spite of much opposition Maximus completed his task with such success that he was constrained to remain in Russia to correct their poor translations from the Greek, of the Scriptures and liturgical books, and to enlighten the people through his preaching.

The Tzar, wishing to assemble a Council to refute Matthew Baskin, who had brought the Calvinist heresy into Russia, appealed to Saint Maximus for help; and he, with all his strength gone and unable to travel, sent an admirable refutation of the heresy to the Council. It was the last work for the Church of this Confessor of the Orthodox faith [...] Opposed with good reason to the infiltration of western humanism, he conveyed the treasures of the Byzantine spirit and literature to the Rus-

---

66   Vassa Kontouma, "Concilum Constantinopolitanum 1755-1756," in *The Great Councils of the Orthodox Churches Decisions and Synodika: From Constantinople 861 to Constantinople 1872, Volume I*. ed. Giuseppe Alberigo & Alberto Melloni (Bologna: Brepols Publishers, 2016), 348.

67   Hieromonk Makarios of Simonos Petra, *The Synaxarion: The Lives of the Saints of the Orthodox Church, Volume Three, January-February*, trans. Christopher Hookaway (Ormylia: Holy Convent of the Annunciation of Our Lady, 2001), 250-252.

sian people. Soon after his decease, he was recognized and venerated as a holy Martyr and Enlightener of Russia.

January 27th: DANILO (Jakšić) the Confessor, Bishop of UPPER KARLOVAC AND PLAŠKI[68]

Born Gorski Kotar on the Feast of the Nativity of Christ in 1715 to pious parents, the young St. Danilo attended the feast days at the Gomirje Monastery with his family. At age 19 he was ordained a hierodeacon and then later a hieromonk. During the time when the Uniate Roman Catholic Bishop Teofil (Pašić) "worked fiendishly to convert Serbs to Roman Catholicism" Hieromonk Danilo served as a parish priest and defended the Orthodox faith. Eventually he became archimandrite of the monastery, building up its library, creating a vestment shop and iconography school, and improving the buildings. The land around the monastery was given to Serbian refugees by the Hungarians, freeing them from persecution by the Turks, but opening them up to other persecution. During his latter reign, the Roman Catholic Church placed Žumberak in the Unia and forbid St. Danilo from entering that region and then unjustly accused him of abandoning his flock. The last remaining Orthodox deacon in Žumberak died in prison rather than join the Unia. The Court of Vienna denied St. Danilo's consecration as the Metropolitan of Sremski Karlovac in 1770. Many priests who spoke out against this were imprisoned.

February 5th: THEODOSIUS, Archbishop of CHERNIGOV[69]

St. Theodosius, Archbishop of Chernigov, was born to a noble family from Uglich which had distinguished itself in the defense of that city during the Time of Troubles... The father of St. Theodosius was a priest

68 Fr. Daniel Rogich, *Serbian Patericon: Saints of the Serbian Orthodox Church – Volume One*, (Canton: Hesychia Press, 2023), 91-94.

69 Holy Trinity Monastery, "The Life of Our Holy Father Theodosius, Archbishop of Chernigov," *Orthodox Life*, no. 1 (January-February 1979): 2-13.

named Nikita; his mother's name was Maria. At the home of his parents — Godly people, devout and meek — Theodosius received his first lessons in the fear of God and Christian piety, and under their influence he was, while yet a child, endowed with inclinations towards that piety with which he was adorned all the rest of his life. By nature, meek, obedient and impressionable, Theodosius burned with the love of God and with zeal for His Church from his youth [...] he was sent by his father to the Theophany School of the Kiev Brotherhood for further education [...] There he grew and was strengthened spiritually in the knowledge of the truth of the Orthodox faith, and there in particular the unwavering intention to consecrate his whole life to God and to the podvigs of piety was born in him [...] in the hours in which he was not occupied with his studies, Theodosius lovingly devoted himself to prayer, pious thoughts and the reading of the word of God. By his Christian piety, good behavior and submissiveness, the holy one attracted the attention of Lazarus Baranovich, the solicitous head of the school, who later, in one of his letters, wrote of the young saint as "a lamb of Christ's flock that hath learned the submissiveness of an obedient sheep." Now the Theophany School of the Kiev Brotherhood, which had been founded for the preservation and protection of the Orthodox faith then under attack by the Polish Catholic clergy and the Jesuits in particular, conducted all instruction in a strictly Orthodox spirit which penetrated the souls of its pupils; under the guidance of the school's instructors, many of whom were true luminaries of Orthodox spiritual enlightenment, St. Theodosius doubtless received the best education possible at that time. The experienced wisdom and spiritual foresight of Lazarus Baranovich even then beheld in the youth a future great hierarch of the Church.

After the completion of his training in the Theophany School, St. Theodosius did not long remain in the world. Making haste to forsake all the "beauty" of this world and to receive the monastic habit. Yet no matter how far away the learned, pious and energetic monk hid himself from the world, he was unable to escape the notice of the higher spiritual authorities [and he was] appointed to the position of abbot of the famous Vydubitsky Monastery in Kiev. Founded in 1070 by Great Prince Vsevolod I at that site on the banks of the River Dnieper where the inhabitants of Kiev received Holy Baptism during the reign of St.

Vladimir, the monastery had fallen under the control of the Uniates and Polish Catholics at the beginning of the seventeenth century and had been brought to the brink of ruin under their administration. The monastery was returned to the Orthodox in 1637, but was in such a state of dilapidation that little could be done to make it habitable. The majority of the brethren had abandoned the decaying buildings, and many of the monastic estates had been illegally alienated from it.

The saintly hierarch labored much during his governing of the Chernigov diocese and concerned himself with the state of Orthodoxy in Little Russia in general, availing himself of every opportunity to counteract the pernicious influence of the Polish Uniate Catholics by preaching the true faith with zeal and by fostering a Russian national consciousness among his flock and a spirit of loyalty to the Muscovite sovereign. In this respect, St. Theodosius demonstrated the advantages not only of the Orthodox Church, but of an Orthodox government as well; and the fruits of his activity, his patriotic fervor and moral influence are apparent from the fact that even inhabitants of the Polish-dominated segment of Little Russia often sought consolation and comfort from the holy ascetic, despite threats and intimidations from the Polish authorities. Thus, in January of 1694, one of the military governors of Smolensk, Dominic Polybensky, wrote to the saintly archpastor: "The ancestral faith of my forebears which was extinguished in them during the battle between the Lithuanians and the Poles, the Russian faith of the Holy Eastern Church, serves as a reason for me to place myself in subjection to the tsar of the Muscovites, who is its protector. To this end do my ancestors summon me, arousing within me love for that faith and loathing for the infamous activities of the adherents of the Roman faith, both secular and clerical — activities so abominable that it is not only difficult for me to write of them, but even to speak of them. The wise benevolence of the tsars [i.e. of Ivan V and Peter I Alexievich] towards their subjects is known throughout the whole world. Since here [in Poland] the return of anyone to the faith of our forefathers is forbidden by the constitution under pain of death and confiscation of property, it is now an opportune time to place ourselves in subjection to the tsars." This letter greatly gladdened the heart of St. Theodosius, and in his reply to Polybensky he urged him not to abandon this good intention. The latter soon came to Chernigov, embraced the Orthodox faith, married and was made ataman of the city.

February 6th: PHOTIOS the Great, Patriarch of CONSTANTINOPLE

HIS LIFE

Our Holy God-bearing Father, Photios, was a brilliant luminary of the Church. He came from the East Roman nobility, being a relative of the emperor and grandson of the famous Patriarch Tarasius who presided over the Seventh Ecumenical Council. St. Photios was a layman, whom the people loved and respected; a layman faithful and dedicated to the Church; a layman who was a fervent preacher of the Gospel. Against his will, with the affection of the people and the respect of the officials, he was seized and made Patriarch. In six days he became a monk, subdeacon, deacon, priest, and on Christmas Day in 857 he was ordained a bishop and undertook the duties of Patriarch. The hatred of those who could not see his glory was ignited. They fought against him and accused him everywhere. A great synod was convened, in which representatives of the Pope also participated, examined the accusations of his enemies and affirmed him. Photios remained on the throne. Satan however, envied this glory of the Church. Another king was enthroned and removed Photios by force, sending him into exile. An unlawful synod condemned him. He suffered much in exile but he returned to the throne. The people, seeing Photios on the throne again, rejoiced. Photios began to preach Orthodoxy with new vigor and enthusiasm. Saint Photios took measures when the Pope sent men to Bulgaria to preach and turn the people away from Orthodoxy and to obey the Pope. He asked the papists to leave Bulgaria and leave the people in peace. They did not leave, however, and continued to plant weeds in the souls of the people with their heretical teachings. Then Photios convened a great Council, which condemned the heretical teachings and excommunicated the Pope. This was the Eighth Ecumenical Council in A.D. 879. St. Photios was a prolific writer; one of his most significant and well known is against the *filioque* entitled *On the Mystagogy of the Holy Spirit*. St. Photios reposed in the Lord in A.D. 891.

His Struggles in Defense of the Faith[70]

In 857 Bardas, the uncle of the Emperor Michael III, assumed power with the title of Caesar. He forced the resignation of the holy Patriarch Ignatius (23 Oct.) who had denounced his immoral behaviour, and prevailed on the clergy to elect the wise and pious Photius as his successor. Photius held out against his election strongly as he could, since he regarded death itself as preferable to that perilous office in those troubled times; but, in the fact of injunctions and threats he at last gave way, and agreed to give up the peace of his study and philosophical discussions with like-minded friends. He was consecrated Patriarch of Constantinople on 25 December 858, having been raised through all the degrees of the priesthood in the previous six days. In a letter to Caesar Bardas, he wrote: 'Our promotion has not been willed by us and we are enthroned as a prisoner...' The more extreme supporters of Ignatius then used every means to oppose and discredit the new hierarch, alleging the irregularity of his sudden elevation from layman to Patriarch. Photius sought to avoid confrontation and did all in his power to re-establish unity and peace in the Church by strengthening her in love, the bond of perfection. He took firm action against the remaining Manichean and iconoclast heretics, took in hand the restoration of the many churches, monasteries and charitable foundations damaged by the iconoclasts, and took an especial interest in missions to spread the Gospel among the barbarians. But his attempts to appease the supporters of Ignatius failed; and while expressing disapproval of the violent measures taken against them by the government, he was obliged to summon a Council in 859, which confirmed the deposition of Ignatius and exiled him to Mytilene and then to Terebinthus. Agitation against Photius continued however and, in 861, another Council, known as the 'First-Second', assembled in the

---

70 Hieromonk Makarios of Simonos Petra, *The Synaxarion: The Lives of the Saints of the Orthodox Church, Volume Three, January-February*, trans. Christopher Hookaway (Ormylia: Holy Convent of the Annunciation of Our Lady, 2001), 422-429.

Church of the Holy Apostles with the official purpose of approving the restoration of Orthodoxy and of pronouncing the definitive condemnation of iconoclasm. In addition, the Council recognized the validity of the nomination of Photius, with the full agreement of the papal legates there present, who, although acting contrary to the Pope's instructions, thought that they had thus achieved the triumph of papal authority.

The arrogant and ambitious Pope Nicolas I (858-68), who supported Ignatius, took the opportunity of the controversy to assert openly for the first time the pretension of the Popes of Rome to jurisdiction 'over the whole earth and over the universal Church.' To the primacy of honour of the Roman Church and her authority as arbiter in matters of dogma, which had always been acknowledged by the other Churches — especially when the Arian, Monothelite and iconoclast heresies were being promoted by Emperors in Constantinople — the Papacy now ascribed to itself the hegemonic claims which the Frankish Empire, after the death of Charlemagne and the Treaty of Verdun (843), could no longer sustain. On the initiative of authoritarian Popes, the Papacy sought to exercise a supremacy over the whole Church that was supposed to have been granted by Christ Himself and to have given the Popes the right to intervene in the domestic affairs of the other Churches, and to impose on them all the usages of the Roman Church, such as clerical celibacy, Saturday fasting and unleavened bread for the Eucharist.

The opposition of Pope Nicolas I and his interference in the internal affairs of the Byzantine Church, when he had only requested to pronounce decisively on iconoclasm, drove Saint Photius to condemn the novel usages of the Roman Church. 'Abolition of small things which have been received through tradition' he wrote, 'will lead to complete contempt for dogmas.' Incensed by this response, the Pope wrote to all the bishops of the East accusing Photius of adultery as being in illicit possession of another's see, and he decreed on his own initiative the deposition of the Patriarch of Constantinople — a thing never before heard of. Moreover, asserting the right of Popes to judge Councils, he declared that the decisions of the 'First-Second' were invalid. Nor did he stop there, but summoned to Rome a Council of Western bishops, which declared Photius deposed and excommunicated all the clergy ordained by him. When the Emperor Michael III objected to these proceedings, the Pope informed him (in 865) that he derived his supremacy over the universal Church from Christ Himself. Then, in successive letters, he subjected Photius to a litany of insults, to which that true disciple of the Saviour made no reply.

The holy Patriarch did not allow these conflicts and cares to hamper his apostolic activity. With the support of the Emperor, he promoted the evangelization of the Slav peoples, engaging his learned friend and colleague Constantine (whom we venerate as Saint Cyril) and his brother Methodius, an ascent from Mount Olympus to undertake a preliminary mission to the Khazars of Southern Russia in 860. Three years later, at the request of the Prince of Moravia, he sent the two brothers on that great missionary endeavor which marked the beginning of the conversion of the Slav peoples of the Balkans.

At about the same time, Boris (Michael) the Khan of Bulgaria, who had recently been baptized by Photius with the Emperor Michael as his godfather, bringing his whole nation into the Christian fold, turned away from Constantinople, which had refused to grant him a patriarch, and looked to Rome for support (866). Seizing his opportunity, the Pope immediately sent Latin missionaries to Bulgaria with instructions to spread their innovations in this young Church which the Byzantines had evangelized, especially the addition of the *Filioque* to the Creed.[71] Seeing the peril of an innovation which touched on the doctrine of the Holy Trinity, Saint Photius estimated that it was time *for the meek to become a warrior* (Joel 4:9 LXX) and that he would have to break his silence and issue a rejoinder. He addressed an *Encyclical Letter* to all the bishops of the East in which he vigorously condemned the errors of the Latins, especially the *Filioque*. He summoned a great Council to Constantinople, which in 867 proclaimed the victory of Orthodox doctrine over all the heresies, and anathematized Pope Nicolas and his mission-

---

71 The erroneous doctrine of the procession of the Holy Spirit "from the Father and the Son," and not from the Father alone as Holy Scripture teaches, was first propounded by St. Augustine as a personal opinion, and would have caused no real difficulty had it not been taken up by Frankish theologians desirous of establishing a doctrinal distinction from the Greek Church, and finally by the Roman Church herself as a handle for the ambition of the Popes to dominate the universal Church.

aries in Bulgaria. The two Churches were thus separated by a formal schism, which was a precursor of the final break in 1054.

Michael III was assassinated at the end of 867 and Basil I, the founder of the Macedonian dynasty, became Emperor. He immediately deposed Saint Photius, whom he imprisoned in the Monastery of the Protection, and recalled Saint Ignatius. In spite of the irenic efforts of Ignatius, the enemies of Photius then began a regular persecution of all the clergy ordained by him. In view of the continuing disturbance, the Emperor decided to refer the case of the two claimants to the Patriarchal throne to Rome for judgement, which was a godsend for the Papacy. Hadrian II, Nicolas's successor, assembled a Council in 869, which once again condemned Photius, declared the Council of 867 invalid, publically burnt its *Acts* and ordered that a new Council should meet in Constantinople. The bishops, few in number, who attended this false Council—called the 'Eighth Ecumenical Council' (870) by the Latins—were overawed by the Emperor and, in their cowardice, condemned the Beacon of the Church and exiled his supporters to the boundaries of the Empire. More than 200 bishops were then deposed and many priests were deprived of their orders. Hailed like a criminal before the synod and summoned to answer the accusations made against him, Saint Photius, after a long silence, replied: 'God hears the voice of him who keeps silent. For Jesus Himself by keeping silent did not escape condemnation.' As they insisted that he answer, he replied: 'My justification is not of this world.' As a worthy imitator of the Passion of the meek and long-suffering Jesus, Saint Photius, in spite of illness, bore for three years the pain of harsh imprisonment, deprivation of books and company without a word of complaint. Imputing no responsibility to the blameless Ignatius for these cruelties, he encouraged his suffering friends by letter and prayed for the Emperor and his persecutors.

Meanwhile, the bishops took cognizance of the fact that their cowardly opportunism had led them to submit their Church to the dictates of Rome; and they persuaded the Emperor to declare invalid the decrees of the Council of 870 and to release Photius. The Saint was then received at court with great honour, and Basil appointed him as his children's tutor. Photius lost no time in making his peace with Ignatius. The two Saints, victims of the rivalry of contrary parties which had made use of their names, embraced warmly, and Photius gave his entire support to the aged and infirm Patriarch, whom he visited daily. On the death of Saint Ignatius on 23 October 877, the Church unanimously placed Photius once again on the Patriarchal throne. Veneration of the memory of Saint Ignatius was introduced not long after by Photius himself, and the Church thus befittingly eulogizes them together in the Synodikon read on the Sunday of Orthodoxy: Eternal memory to the very blessed, very Orthodox and very illustrious Patriarchs Ignatius and Photius! A Council was convoked at Constantinople in 879-80 attended by 383 Fathers under the presidency of Photius and in the presence of legates from the Pope. The Council confirmed the rehabilitation of Photius, annulled the Council of 870 and restored communion between the two Churches, anathematizing all innovation and especially the heretical addition to the Symbol of Faith. With the restoration of peace and unity in the Church, the greatest desire of the hierarch was fulfilled. He immediately set about the task of peacemaking, seeking reconciliation with his enemies and showing a fatherly care devoid of bitterness for the former partisans of Ignatius.

When Leo VI (886-912) succeeded his father Basil I, he summarily deposed the holy Patriarch, holding him indirectly responsible for making known to his father a plot which Leo had hatched against him. Saint Photius was imprisoned as an evildoer in the Monastery of the Armenians and was confined there for five years, lacking all human consolation but shining like gold tried in the furnace of manifold temptations (1 Pet. 6-7). This was the period in which, without books of his own, he wrote the *Mystagogy of the Holy Spirit* — a systematic refutation of the *Filioque* heresy, in which he shows that the Holy Spirit proceeds eternally from the Person of the Father, the Source of the Divinity, and is sent to us by the Son in order to make us partakers of the divine nature (2 Pet. 1:4). Leaving this treatise as his testament to [the] Holy Church in view of the conflicts to come, he departed to join the choir of holy Fathers and Doctors on 6 February 893. The miracles which soon took place in plenty at his tomb helped to convert even his inveterate enemies.[72]

---

72 The calumnies spread about St. Photius by the extreme partisans of St. Ignatius, accepted for centuries by historians and Western apologists alike without serious examination, made him responsible for all the discord and division which paved

Humble, serene and long-suffering in tribulations, this true confessor of
the Faith, unjustly called a fanatic by his enemies, remains one of the
great luminaries of Orthodoxy and a wholly trustworthy witness of the
spirit of the Gospel.

See page 295 for some of his writings.
See page 530 for the Akathist service to him.

February 10th: CONSTANTINE (Ostrozhskii), Prince of OSTROG

OPPOSED THE "UNION OF BREST-LITOVSK," RELICS BURNED BY THE LATINS[73]

Saint Constantine of Ostrog lived in the sixteenth century, during
the time of the domination of the Belarussian, Ukrainian and western
Russian people under the Kingdom of Poland and the Grand Duchy of
Lithuania. The most powerful man among the nobility in Vollynia, he
was sometimes called "the uncrowned King" of the region. He is remembered principally for his opposition to the so-called "Union of Brest-Litovsk" in which Orthodox congregations in the regions controlled by the
Poles were brought, mostly by coercion, into communion with the Pope
of Rome. As Metropolitan Kallistos of Diokleia wrote, the authors of
that Union, "began by using deceit, and ended by resorting to violence."
Orthodox churches and monasteries were seized by force and given to
those favoring the Union, while those wishing to remain Orthodox were
severely persecuted. Saint Constantine sought, with others among the

---

the way for the great schism of 1054. Fortunately, the research of modern Roman
Catholic historians (notably F. Dvornik, *The Photian Schism*, Cambridge, 1970)
have re-established the facts of the matter, which in all respects corroborate the
tradition of the Orthodox Church.

73 Protopresbyter James Thornton, *Pious Kings and Right-Believing Queens: An
Encyclopedia of the Royal and Imperial Saints of the Orthodox Church* (Belmont:
Institute for Byzantine and Modern Greek Studies, 2013), 104.

right-believing nobility, to prevent the obliteration of Orthodoxy and to protect the Orthodox Faith and culture.

He is remembered for his sponsorship of an academy at Ostrog, "modeled on the Graeco-Byzantine pattern," to educate Orthodox clergy and other spokesmen for the Church. He is remembered as well for his sponsorship of the publication of the famed Ostrog Bible, a translation from the Greek Septuagint into Old Church Slavonic. Father Georges Florovsky (1893-1979) writes of this Bible that it "remains a landmark in Slavonic Bible history" and calls it "a magnificent achievement" and "a monument of scholarship, literature and theology." At his death in 1608, the Saint was buried at the Kiev Caves Monastery. His Relics were later burned by the Latins. Saint Constantine Ostrozhskii, Prince of Ostrog is commemorated on February 10.

February 13th: GREGORY, Archbishop of MOGILEV[74]

In 1755, he was consecrated Bishop of Mogilev on the Dnieper, with jurisdiction over Belarus, which then belonged to the Kingdom of Poland and where the Orthodox were submitted to pressure from the Catholics, both Latin and Uniate. Having been present at the coronation of Catherine II in 1762, he presented the Empress with a request for the protection of the Orthodox in the Kingdom of Poland, and travelled to Moscow and St. Petersburg in support of their cause. He won his petition, and it was under the protection of Russian troops that he returned to Poland and presented a Memorandum to the King in 1767 concerning the situation of the Orthodox of Poland and Lithuania. He even made use of Russian military support to have certain Polish Catholic bishops deported and replace them with Orthodox ones. But in the face of the Poles' opposition, he had to withdraw to Smolensk, where, during his four-year stay there, he wrote a manual with Bishop Parthe-

---

74 Hieromonk Makarios of Simonos Petra, *The Synaxarion: The Lives of the Saints of the Orthodox Church, Volume Seven, Appendix-General Index,* trans. Mother Maria (Thessaloniki: Indiktos Publishing Company, 2008), 127-128.

nius for the parish clergy, which became a classic and ran to twenty-five editions.

After the annexation of Belarus by Russia in 1772, he was able to return to his diocese, and invested great energy in restoring ecclesiastical life and making a stand against injustice. Through his ardent preaching, he succeeded in bringing more than a hundred and twelve thousand Uniates back to Orthodoxy in two years. He also obtained the creation of a Diocese in Sluc for the Orthodox who remained in the Kingdom of Poland.

February 17th: Hieromartyr HERMOGENES, Patriarch of MOSCOW and ALL RUSSIA[75, 76]

Born in 1530, Hieromartyr Hermogenes, Patriarch of Moscow and All Russia, came from the Don Cossacks. He was raised in a small monastery dedicated to the Transfiguration and founded by Saint Barsanuphius of Tver. According to the Patriarch himself, he was a priest in the city of Kazan at the Kazan Gostinodvorskaya Church in the name of St. Nicholas (December 6 and May 9). After the death of his wife, he became a monk and from 1582 he was archimandrite of the Transfiguration Monastery in Kazan. On May 13, 1589, he was consecrated bishop and became the first Metropolitan of Kazan.

During the service of His Holiness the Patriarch in Kazan in 1579, he witnessed the appearance of the miraculous Kazan Icon of the Mother of God appeared. While still a priest, he, with the blessing of the then Kazan Bishop Jeremiah, transferred the newly-appeared icon from the place of its acquisition to the church in the name of St. Nicholas. Possessing an uncommon literary talent, the saint himself composed in

---

75   "Hieromartyr Hermogenes, Patriarch of Moscow and All Rus" Russian Orthodox Church, Official Website of the Moscow Patriarchate, accessed November 11th, 2022, http://www.patriarchia.ru/db/text/909261.html

76   Hieromonk Makarios of Simonos Petra, *The Synaxarion: The Lives of the Saints of the Orthodox Church, Volume Three, January-February,* trans. Christopher Hookaway (Ormylia: Holy Convent of the Annunciation of Our Lady, 2001), 544-547.

1594 a legend about the appearance of the miraculous icon and the miracles performed from it.

In 1591, the saint gathered the newly baptized Tatars[77] to the cathedral and instructed them in the faith for several days. In 1592, the relics of St. Herman, the second Kazan Archbishop (commemorated 25 September, 6 November, 23 June) who died in Moscow on November 6, 1567 during a pestilence, were transferred and buried near the church in the name of St. Nicholas. With the blessing of Patriarch Job (1589-1605), Saint Hermogenes performed the burial at the Sviyazhsky Dormition Monastery.

On January 9, 1592, Saint Hermogenes sent a letter to Patriarch Job, in which he informed him that in Kazan there was no special commemoration of Orthodox soldiers who laid down their lives for the faith and the Fatherland near Kazan, and asked to establish a specific day of memory. At the same time, he reported on three martyrs who suffered in Kazan for the faith of Christ, of which one was Russian, named John (commemorated 24 January), originally from Nizhny Novgorod, captured by the Tatars, and the other two, Stefan and Peter (commemorated 24 March), newly converted Tatars. The saint expressed regret that these martyrs were not inscribed in the Synod, which was read on the Sunday of Orthodoxy and that memory eternal was not sung to them.

In response to St. Hermogenes, the Patriarch sent a decree dated February 25th, which prescribed "for all Orthodox soldiers killed near Kazan and within Kazan, to perform a memorial service in Kazan and throughout the Kazan Metropolis on the Sabbath day after the Intercession of the Most Holy Theotokos and enter them in a large synodik, read on the Sunday of Orthodoxy," it was commanded to enter the three martyrs of Kazan in the same Synod, and the day of their memory was entrusted to the Holy Hierarch Hermogenes. The saint announced a patriarchal decree for his diocese, adding that liturgies and memorial services for the three Kazan martyrs would be served in all churches and monasteries and they would be commemorated at litias and at liturgies

---

77 *Tartars*: A member of several different Turkic-speaking peoples that collectively numbered more than 5 million in the late 20th century and lived mainly in west-central Russia along the central course of the Volga River, the Kama River and east to the Ural Mountains.

on January 24th. Saint Hermogenes showed zeal for the faith and firmness in observing Church traditions, and cared about enlightening the
Kazan Tatars with the faith of Christ.

In 1595, with the active participation of the saint, discovery of the
relics of the Kazan wonderworkers took place: Saints Guriy, the first
Archbishop of Kazan (commemorated October 4, December 5, June
20), and Barsanuphius, Bishop of Tver (commemorated October 4,
April 11). Tsar Theodore Ioannovich (1584-1598) ordered the construction of a new stone Church in the Kazan Spaso-Preobrazhensky
Monastery on the site of the former one, where the saints were buried.
When the coffins of the saints were found, Saint Hermogenes came with
a council of clergy, ordered the coffins to be opened, and seeing the incorruptible relics and clothes of the saints, informed the Patriarch and
the Tsar. With the blessing of Patriarch Job and by order of the king,
the relics of the newly-appeared miracle workers were placed in a new
temple. Saint Hermogenes himself compiled the lives of Saints Gurias
and Barsanuphius.

For outstanding Archpastoral qualities, Metropolitan Hermogenes
was elected to the primatial see, and on July 3rd, 1606, he was elevated
by the cathedral of saints to the Patriarchal throne in the Moscow Dormition Cathedral. Metropolitan Isidore presented the Patriarch with
the staff of St. Peter the Wonderworker of Moscow (commemorated
October 5, December 21, August 24), and the Tsar presented the new
Patriarch with a Panagia adorned with precious stones, a white klobuk
and a staff. According to the ancient order, Patriarch Hermogenes made
a procession on a donkey.

The activities of Patriarch Hermogenes coincided with a difficult period for the Russian State — the invasion of the impostor false Dmitry
and the [Papist] Polish King Sigismund III. The Primate devoted all his
strength to serving the Church and the Fatherland. In this feat, Patriarch
Hermogenes was not alone; he was imitated and helped by selfless compatriots. With special inspiration, His Holiness the Patriarch opposed
the traitors and enemies of the Fatherland, who wanted to introduce
Uniatism and Latin Papism in Russia and eradicate Orthodoxy by enslaving the Russian people.

When the impostor approached Moscow and settled in Tushino, Patriarch Hermogenes sent two messages to the rebellious traitors. In one of them, he wrote, "You forgot the vows of our Orthodox faith, in which we were born, baptized, brought up and raised, violated the kiss of the cross and the oath to stand to death for the house of the Most Holy Theotokos and for the Muscovite state but have fallen for your false would be tsarlet. My soul hurts, my heart aches, and all my insides are tormented, all my structures are trembling; I weep and cry out with sobbing; have mercy, have mercy, brethren and children, my souls and my parents, departed and alive. Look at how our Fatherland is being plundered and ruined by strangers, how the Holy Icons and Churches are desecrated,[78] how the blood of the innocent is shed, crying out to God. Remember against whom you take up arms: is it not against God who created you? Is it not your own brothers? Are you ruining your Fatherland? I beseech you in the Name of God, leave your undertaking behind, while there is time, so that you do not perish to the end." In another letter, the Primate called: "For God's sake, know yourself and convert, please your parents, their wives and children, and all of us; and we will pray to God for you."

Soon, the righteous judgment of God also happened on the Tushinsky thief. He suffered the same sad and inglorious fate as his predecessor; he was killed by his own associates on December 11th, 1610. But Moscow continued to be in danger, as it contained Poles and traitorous boyars[79] loyal to Sigismund III. Letters sent by Patriarch Hermogenes to towns and villages excited the Russian people to liberate Moscow from enemies and elect a legitimate Russian Tsar. Muscovites raised an uprising, in response to which the Poles set fire to the city, while they themselves took refuge in the Kremlin. Together with the Russian traitors, they forcibly removed the Holy Patriarch Hermogenes from the Patriarchal throne and imprisoned him in the Miracle Monastery.

---

78 During the invasion of Russia from 1610-1612 by Sigismund III, the Papist King of Poland, it was the desire of the Latin Poles to convert all of Russia to Latin Papism. During this period of Latin occupation the Papist Poles desecrated Orthodox Christian Churches, people, and other holy things.

79 *Boyars*: A member of the old Aristocracy in Russia, next in rank to a prince.

On Bright Monday in 1611, the Russian militia approached Moscow and began the siege of the Kremlin, which lasted several months. The Poles [Latin Papists], besieged in the Kremlin, more than once sent ambassadors to the Patriarch demanding that he order the Russian militias to move away from the city, threatening the death penalty. The saint answered firmly: "Why are you threatening me? I'm afraid of God alone. If all of you, Lithuanian people, leave the Muscovite state, I will bless the Russian militia to go from Moscow, if you stay here, I will bless everyone to stand against you and die for the Orthodox Faith." Already from captivity, Hieromartyr Hermogenes delivered his last message to the Russian people, blessing the liberation war against the conquerors. He said "If you suffer for the Faith, God will pardon you, and will forgive your sins in this life and the next." The Russian governors did not show consistency; therefore, they could not take the Kremlin and release their Primate.

The liberation of Russia, for which Saint Hermogenes stood with such indestructible valour, was successfully concluded by the Russian nation. However, as the Russian forces drew closer to Moscow, the conditions of his imprisonment became harsher and he was deprived of food and water, dying on February 17th, 1611, only ten days before the city was liberated. The body of the Priest-martyr Hermogenes was buried in the Chudov monastery, but in 1654 was transferred to the Moscow Dormition (Uspensky) cathedral. The glorification of Patriarch Hermogenes into the rank of Sainted-Hierarchs occurred on the 12th of May 1913.

See page 527 for liturgical hymns to him.

February 26th:
Monk SYMEON the Myrrh-streaming[80]

Nemanja, the initiator and beginner of eight centuries of Serbian history was also a great sufferer [...] three-fold sufferer: for Christ his God, for his people, and for his soul. As a result, he also became a great victor and immortal.

A miraculous man: he had two baptisms, two names, two callings in his life, and after death, two graves. First, he was baptized a Catholic, and later after he grew up, he renounced his Latin baptism and was baptized according to the Orthodox rite. As a ruler he was called Nemanja after the biblical name Nehemiah, and later as a monk he was called Simeon. He was a ruler and a sword-bearer, and in old age a monk and cross-bearer. His first grave was at Hilander Monastery, the second at Studenica Monastery. He was a Theodule — a servant of God — both as a sword-bearer and as a cross-bearer, as Nemanja the ruler and as Simeon the monk. And even after death, as a myrrh-flowing saint, he remained a servant of God and a helper of his people.

Nemanja was a lord: he was also a captive. He waged war against his brothers and non-brothers. He fought with Orthodox and heretics. He had a traitor among his own natural brothers. Against the Orthodox Greeks he waged war in defense of his country and his national identity, i.e., in defense of the Serbian name, which the Greeks wanted to drown in Hellenism because of the sameness of faith. Against the Latins and Bogomil heresies he fought in defense of the true and pure faith.

Nemanja led his people on general courses against two powerful forces — the panhellenism of Constantinople and the pan-theocracy of Rome. He, perhaps, unconsciously, spontaneously, and semi-consciously, only traced the path for the future of his people. By becoming a monk in his old age, the mighty Nemanja set a seal on his choice of the heavenly kingdom. He directed the spirit of his descendants towards heaven, and by his own example bequeathed a moral to his whole people: throughout this earthly life one must prepare himself for eternal life.

---

80   Bishop Nikolai Velimirovich, *A Treasury of Serbian Orthodox Spirituality,* trans. Fr. Theodore Micka and Fr. Steven Scott (Grayslake: The Free Serbian Orthodox Diocese of the United States of America and Canada, 1988), 12-15, 29.

March 24th: IRINEJ (Ćirić) the Confessor, Bishop of BAČKA[81]

Born on April 19, 1884 with the name Ivan, he was orphaned at the age of 10 when both of his parents died of tuberculosis, and went to live with his uncle, Fr. Milan Ćirić. At age 18 he enrolled in the Moscow Theological Academy studying religion and secular subjects and then receiving his Doctorate at the University of Vienna in Austria in Semitic Studies. Realizing his soul's calling to dedicate his life to the church, he petitioned his bishop to become a monk and received the name Irinej.

"In the early years of the twentieth century there was a growing movement among the Rusyn[82] people away from the Greek Catholic Church to their ancestral Orthodox Faith. This Greek Catholic or Uniate Church was formed from a document signed in 1646 (Union of Uzhorod)[83] which allowed the Orthodox people to keep their liturgical life when they accepted the authority of the pope. This union with Rome was forced upon the people by the Austro-Hungarian authorities with the approval of many Orthodox clergy who desired the higher standard of living they would receive as Uniate Catholic priests. Any attempt to maintain the Orthodox Faith was met with arrests, persecution, and violence. With the end of WWI and the breakup of the Austro-Hungarian Empire, the persecution eased and the Orthodox Faith revived among the people. Many priests and bishops, especially from Serbia, aided in this flowering of Orthodoxy in the Carpathians. And Bishop Irinej was at the forefront, becoming the head of this new Orthodox Church of

---

81 Fr. Daniel Rogich, *Serbian Patericon: Saints of the Serbian Orthodox Church – Volume One*, (Canton: Hesychia Press, 2023), 193-199.

82 Rusyn, Rusyn ruskyi, also called Ruthenian, Carpatho-Rusyn, Lemko, or Rusnak, any of several East Slavic peoples (modern-day Belarusians, Ukrainians, and Carpatho-Rusyns) and their languages. The name Rusyn is derived from Rus (Ruthenia), the name of the territory that they inhabited.

83 The false Union of Uzhhorod (Uzhgorod) in 1646 brought many Ruthenians (or Rusyns) into the Latin Papist Confession when sixty-three Ruthenian Orthodox priests, who represented Ruthenians living under papist rule, betrayed Holy Orthodoxy, apostatizing, and accepting the authority of the Pope of Rome while being allowed to maintain their outward byzantine liturgics and becoming another faction of the *uniates*.

Carpatho-Russia in 1927.... Not only in Slovakia and the Ukraine, but Bishop Irinej used all of his talents in the service of the Lord and His Orthodox Church in representing the Serbian Orthodox Church in inter-Christian affairs... At all times, Irinej defended the true Orthodox faith, calling all Christians, just as he had done in Slovakia, to come back to the Mother Church of Orthodox Christianity. He would never compromise the Orthodox Faith and became a Defender of Orthodoxy."[84] In 1955, he reposed on the eve of the Feast of the Annunciation.

April 6th: GREGORY the SINAITE[85]

During this period, there was an effort to reunify the Churches of Byzantium and Rome. This history of restoration of communion is littered with many attempts. Latin domination of Byzantium by the crusaders of the Fourth Crusade (1204), papal centralization, scholastic theology, and the dogmatization of the *Filioque* at the Second Council of Lyons, together with cultural and political differences, resulted in the maintenance of the breach. Emperor Michael VIII moved to have a union of the Churches of Constantinople and Rome. He wished to forestall the projected invasion of the empire by Charles I of Anjou. He explained that this was his motive for agreeing to the Union of the Churches at Lyon (1274). His Unionist policy alienated his subject and the majority of the clergy. Let us now return to a synopsis of Elder Gregory's disciples.

The second disciple of Elder Gregory was Joseph, a fellow countryman and companion of Gerasimos. This ascetic's struggles, on behalf of the Orthodox Faith, were borne by him with genuine magnanimity. He mightily opposed the Latins and extricated many from their ill-conceived beliefs; so that, by the grace of God, he converted them to Orthodoxy. No one else, even among those who were well-known and progres-

---

84   Fr. Daniel Rogich, *Serbian Patericon: Saints of the Serbian Orthodox Church – Volume One*, (Canton: Hesychia Press, 2023), 196.

85   Holy Apostles Convent & Dormition Skete, *The Great Synaxaristes of the Orthodox Church, April*, trans. Holy Apostles Convent and Dormition Skete (Buena Vista: Holy Apostles Convent & Dormition Skete, 2003), 187-189.

sives in secular wisdom, was able to contend and bring the Latin-minded to Orthodoxy as well as Father Joseph.

Another disciple, the wonderful Abba Nicholas. He originally came from Athens. He was elderly, about eighty years of age, and worthy of reverence. The old man was conspicuous for his prudence, self-control, and modest manners. For the sake of Orthodoxy, he endured, with greatness of spirit, much ill treatment under the Latin-minded emperor, Michael VIII Palaeologus. Abba Nicholas was forced into exile. His belongings were confiscated. Ofttimes he was hurled into dark prison cells. This came about when he was preaching the word of God in his homeland. He exhorted the people to preserve their Orthodox Faith and not to accept the unsound and ruinous doctrines of the Latins. The emperor dispatched his minions, of like mind with him, who were harsh and even savage. They inflicted many punishments upon the holy man. By order of the emperor, Abba Nicholas was bound with ropes and chains to his neck and his hands. The Latinophiles then plucked at his honorable beard, in order to shame him. In an inhuman manner, they beat him with rods and kicked him with their feet. With no pity, they dragged him through the public roads that they might make a spectacle of him. The vain-minded ones, however, did not realize that, on account of the malice and wickedness they exhibited, they made themselves only a spectacle. As for Abba Nicholas, he earned great glory and respect among the faithful.

April 24th: SAVA (Branković), Metropolitan of ARDEAL [86]

Under Ottoman rule, religious life came to a standstill in practically all Orthodox countries. Many Orthodox leaders and theologians received their training in the West. As a result, heresy entered the Orthodox Church from high ecclesiastical positions. For example, Cyril Loukaris, the Ecumenical Patriarch of Constantinople, in 1620 wrote a *Confession of Faith* which was totally Calvinistic both in spirit and con-

---

86   Fr. Daniel Rogich, *Serbian Patericon: Saints of the Serbian Orthodox Church – Volume One*, (Canton: Hesychia Press, 2023), 279-283.

tent. Therefore, the encroachments of Uniatism, coupled with the Turkish and Hungarian problems, spelled for the Serbian and Romanian Orthodox most difficult, confusing and even frightening times. Yet it was the context which our Holy Father Sava used in order to show himself a pillar of Orthodoxy and divine flower of spiritual regeneration....

Bishop Sava's episcopal service was plagued by the missionary activities of the Calvinists who tried to convert the Orthodox, and who were supported by the Prince of Transylvania (Michael I Apafi). In addition, frequent wars threatened the stability of the area during his first years as metropolitan. Sava, however, proved equal to the task, being a faithful Defender of the Church. He always showed little interest in yielding to the demands of the political authority to establish Calvinism among the ranks of the Orthodox, let alone unity with the Roman Catholics.

April 24th: New Hieromartyr BRONKO (Dobrosavljević) of VELJUN[87]

The Independent State of Croatia (NDH) was founded on March 19, 1941, after the invasion of Yugoslavia by the Axis powers. The NDH consisted of the present-day Republic of Croatia and modern-day Bosnia and Hercegovina together with Syrmia in modern-day Serbia.... Its day-to-day administration was comprised almost exclusively of Croatians, including monks and nuns, under the leadership of the Ustaše. Before the war, the Ustaše were an ultranationalist, fascist, racist, and terrorist organization, fighting for an independent Croatia... [they] were virulently anti-Serb and anti-semitic.... Those who were not of Croatian blood (i.e., Serbs and Jews) would not have any political role in the future Croat state.... The Ustaše regime promulgated race laws taking the *Nuremberg Race Laws*[88] as their model. These laws were formally direct-

---

87   Fr. Daniel Rogich, "*Serbian Patericon: Saints of the Serbian Orthodox Church – Volume One*," (Canton: Hesychia Press, 2023), 285-289.

88   On September 15th, 1935, the National Socialist German Workers' Party (Nationalsozialistische Deutsche Arbeiterpartei), primarily known as the Nazi Party announced two new laws related to race: The Reich Citizenship Law and The Law for the Protection of German Blood and German Honor. These laws informally became known as the Nuremberg Laws or Nuremberg Race Laws. This

ed against Serbs, Jews, and Gypsies, yet their main targets were Serbs, Orthodoxy, and the Orthodox worldview. On April 4, 1941, the day of the capitulation of Yugoslavia, the *Decree for the Protection of the People and the State* was passed. It imposed the death penalty for threatening the interests of the Croatian people or the existence of the Independent State of Croatia... On April 22, 1941, the Ustaše Government passed a resolution declaring the Serbian Orthodox Church on the territory of Independent Croatia as *illegal*.... Serbs, Jews, and Gypsies became state property, like cattle. Ante Pavelić was uncompromising: *For the final solution to the Croatian Question, one third of the Serbs are to be killed, one third to be forcibly converted to Catholicism, and one third to be expelled.* On April 22, Pavelić jointly with the Minister of Education and Cults Mmile Bodak adopted the Religious Conversion Law that obliged the Orthodox to convert to Catholicism. Mile Budak echoed Pavelić's sentiments during his speech in Gospić on June 9: *We shall slaughter one third of the Serbs, deport another third, and force the last third into Roman Catholicism and thus make them Croats. We shall destroy every trace of theirs, and all that will be left will be a bad memory of them. For Serbs, Jews, and Gypsies, we have three million bullets!*[89]

Fr. Branko, born on January 4, 1886, was a priest awarded the *Order of Saint Sava*[90] and the *Order of the Yugoslav Crown of the Fifth Degree*[91]

---

is because they were first announced at a Nazi Party rally held in the German City of Nuremberg.

89 Fr. Daniel Rogich, *Serbian Patericon: Saints of the Serbian Orthodox Church – Volume One*, (Canton: Hesychia Press, 2023), 285-287.

90 *Order of Saint Sava*: The decoration was founded in 1883 as a Serbian Order. It became a Yugoslavian Order after World War I and was abolished with the proclamation of the People's Federated Republic of Yugoslavia, November 29th, 1945. The order was created as a civil merit decoration to be given for services in the fields of religion, education, science, and the arts as well as for relief and social work. The decoration was given to persons whose services were appropriate to the purposes of the Order. It was given to military as well as civilians and to nationals and foreigners alike.

91 King Aleksandar I Karađorđević instituted the Order on April 5th, 1930, to commemorate the change of the official name of the Realm from Kingdom of the Serbs, Croats, and Slovenes to the Kingdom of Yugoslavia. The Order was organized in five classes, and was awarded to Yugoslavian citizens who forwarded national unity and cooperation, or for merit towards the Crown, State and Nation

for his service to his parishioners. Along with his son and 520 other Serbs, he was arrested by the Ustaše on the Feast of St. George the Great Martyr, April 23, 1941, "for being Orthodox, not willing to be converts to Catholicism and unwilling to leave Croatia. They were locked up at the police station... severely tortured... brought to the woods... three miles from their parish church... taken to a ditch, forced to dig their own graves and then hacked to death with axes. Fr. Branko and his son were left for last. Fr. Branko was then forced to recite the funeral prayer as his son was chopped to pieces. Then Fr. Branko was tortured: his hair and beard were torn off, ears cut off and eyes gouged out before he was skinned alive."

Roman Catholic Archbishop Aloysius (Stepinac) of Zagreb claimed that he either did not know about the horrific crimes or actively struggled against his clergy participating in them. Neither version holds water. Stepinac was a well-informed man and too power-hungry not to have control of his own diocese. As to the allegation that Stepinac *struggled against the clergy who were subordinate to him*, there is no evidence of any reprimand or struggle against them. As the leader of the military clergy in Croatia, Stepinac did nothing to prevent those under his authority from committing these heinous crimes. More than that, he awarded murderers with icons and crosses instead of excommunicating them. He supported the Poglavnik (the Ustaše leader Ante Pavelić) and his program.

See page 528 for his Kontakion.

April 29th: BASIL (Jovanović) of OSTROG[92]

St. Basil of Ostrog was born on December 28, 1610, to poor but devout parents Petar and Anastasia in Mrkonjic in Popovo Polje. Given the name Stojan at baptism, he was raised at home to honor and respect

---

in public service, as well as to the foreign nationals for diplomatic merit. The Order of the Yugoslav Crown was senior to Order of St. Sava.

92 "Saint Vasilije Ostroski," Svetosavlje Orthodox Christianity of Serbian Style and Experience, accessed March 26th, 2023, https://svetosavlje.org/sveti-vasilije-ostroski/

the things of God more than the fleeting things of this life. He attended Liturgy regularly, prostrating to the ground and kissing it as he entered the Church, and was equally pious as he worshipped during the service. Although his family was poor, he would share what little bread he had with the other boys who helped him watch the sheep when he was a shepherd.

In their hatred towards his parents, Muslim neighbors who had apostasized from Christianity persecuted Stojan. His parents decided to send him to the monastery of Zavala where the abbot was his uncle Seraphim. He was steadfast in reading holy books and scripture, and af- ter reading the writings of the holy fathers and yearning for their ascetic life, he decided to become a monk and was given the name Basil. After his tonsuring, he was ordained to the diaconate and then the priesthood, and served with Metropolitan Mardarius of Tsetinye.

During that time, the Roman Pope sent clerics (the Jesuits) to the areas of Primorie, Montenegro and Herzegovina to proselytize and con- vert the Orthodox to their Latin heresy and bring them under papal authority. When Metropolitan Mardarius was made aware of this pro- paganda, he was indifferent. Only due to the faith and devotion of the Orthodox people and the zealous efforts of St. Basil against the union, the propaganda did not serve to convert the faithful. St. Basil advised the Metropolitan to remain steadfast in Orthodoxy and fight against the papal heretics, but the Metropolitan did not heed his advice and slandered St. Basil in front of people. Due to the devout life of the saint which the people had witnessed, they were not duped by the Metropol- itan's slanderous accusations. Wishing to flee from the Metropolitan's scheming ways, St. Basil returned back to his monastery Tyrdos where he continued to advise the people to be steadfast in the faith and earned the name of zealot of Orthodoxy by the faithful. He continued to fight against the Uniate propaganda and the Turks, visiting the people in their homes in the villages to preach unto their salvation, as did Saint Sava before him, and performing the holy mysteries and services. The Turks gave him the name 'Mantis of Paradise'. His ministry work agitated the local Turks and incited them to attempt to kill him. He fled to Russia to escape, returning after a while with gifts, books, and vestments for the churches in need, and money for the poor.

The hatred against him by the Uniates and Muslims had not abated, and he was forced to leave again this time to a pilgrimage to Mount Athos. On his way, he went to Pec and spoke with the holy patriarch Paisij Janievac about the oppression of the Orthodox Serbs in Herzegovina by the Turks and the threat to the faithful of the Latin propaganda. The patriarch blessed his travel to the Holy Mountain, but recognizing his holiness, he advised him to return to him in Pec after his visit to Athos with the intention of having him be the spiritual leader of the Orthodox people in the Zahum region. St. Basil spent most of his time on Mount Athos in Hilandar, the Serbian monastery. True to his word, he returned to Pec to meet with the patriarch who, on the feast of the Transfiguration, consecrated St. Basil as a bishop and appointed him the Metropolitan of Trebinje with his seat at the Tyrdos Monastery. Upon his return to Tyrdos, the people welcomed him, and he continued his apostolic endeavors, despite the dangers which had resumed. He was able to continue through the power of his prayer which, by the grace and blessing of God, allowed him to heal and perform miracles. Even while he was still alive, people considered him a saint because of his devout life and prayers. He traveled to minister to the people, and they also came to him at the monastery to receive guidance, prayers and alms. He encouraged the people to give alms and restore churches and monasteries, including the Tyrdos monastery.

When the Turks killed the Metropolitan of Eastern Herzegovina, Paisi Trebiesanin, whose seat was in Onogost, the Serbian Patriarch St. Gavrilo Rajic appointed St. Basil to be Metropolitan. He remained at Tyrdos initially and then moved to Onogost. The Turks persecuted the Serbian people more cruelly, robbing homes, looting churches and monasteries, and enslaving the Orthodox. Although he lived in the monastery of St. Luke and had restored the monastery of St. Dimitri, St. Basil was forced to move to a cave in Piesivci. The people, upon hearing this, advised him to move to the Ostrog monastery with its pious abbot, Elder Isaiah, and the virtuous ascetic life there. St. Basil settled in the cave of Isaiah and ruled his metropolis from this monastery for 15 years. He attracted other monks and ascetics and rebuilt the Church of the Presentation of the Blessed Virgin Mary. Later, he built the church of the Holy and Life-giving Cross. He strove to make his monastery a center of spiritual life for the faithful and when the monastery grew larger, he appointed Isaiah, grandson of the venerable Isaiah, as the abbot. St. Basil increased his asceticism, fasting and prayer, while also building churches and cells for his flock, even carrying some of the stones himself. Again, he ministered to the people from his monastery where they sought him since they considered him a saint. He wrote: "I am writing to confirm the truth so that Christians know that I spent some time in Ostrog in the desert, and I devoted all my hard work and all my possessions there, and spared nothing for God's sake and for the sake of the Holy Mother of God. And with some brothers, with the help of God, I restored there what can be seen in the work itself. And many did mischief to me, but God was my helper in every good deed. And I am writing this so that the church ministers who after me will serve God and the Holy Mother of God in Ostrog, in the cold rock of heat for God's sake know, so that you and the Christians who will be after me know too."

Prince Raich with his six sons persecuted the saint and the monastery. St. Basil considered moving, particularly to Mount Athos, but he ascertained that the evil was the work of a demon in order to hinder his virtue. Neighboring Bielopavlics and their priest begged him not to leave them without his help and the Saint decided to stay. He made a trip to the blessed Patriarch Maximus in Pec to apprise him of the situation. The Patriarch wrote a letter to the prince and the people, admonishing the people to help protect the monastery, and cursing anyone who harmed the saint and monks. Saint Basil prophesied to the prince that because of the harm they were committing against the monastery, all his sons would die. The prince did not abate until all of his sons did indeed die, and then he went to St. Basil who comforted him and told him to repent. He again prophesied, this time that God would comfort him and bless him with a male offspring. This prophecy also came true, in addition to many other prophecies, and miracles which occurred by his prayers. On April 29, 1671, peacefully in his cell in the Ostroka hermitage, St. Basil reposed in the Lord and was buried in a grave under the church of the Holy Presentation of the Mother of God. His grave was the site of countless miracles which continue to this day. Seven years after his death, a vision of St. Basil came to the abbot to open his grave. When they did so, they found his incorrupt relics which now reside in a coffin at the Church of the Presentation of the Blessed Virgin Mary and are also the source of many miracles.

May 2nd: BORIS-MICHAEL, Tsar of BULGARIA[93]

Born and brought up a pagan, the glorious Prince Boris was instructed in the Christian faith through the influence of his sister and one of his uncles, Enrabot (Boyan) who suffered martyrdom during the persecution unleashed by his predecessor Malomir. When he took power, the Prince turned first of all to the Latin missionaries, at the time of an alliance with the Franks against the King of Moravia; but, becoming aware of the religious and cultural pre-eminence of Byzantium, he asked the Emperor Michael III for Baptism for himself and his people. He was baptized with great solemnity in 864, by a bishop sent especially from Byzantium, and received the name of his sponsor, the Emperor Michael. Following his example, a great number of the people — boyars and people of all classes — were converted *en masse*. The Patriarch of Constantinople, Saint Photios (6 Feb.), sent the Tsar a letter setting out the duties of a Christian ruler, and then sent missionaries to Bulgaria. Boris made great efforts to organize his young Church after the Byzantine model, but nurtured the hope of autonomy. Finding Constantinople ill-disposed, he turned to the Pope of Rome, who sent missionaries to Bulgaria with the task of disseminating the particular liturgical practices of the Latin Church and its erroneous concept of the Procession of the Holy Spirit. The Tsar, quickly becoming aware of the danger of an allegiance that was not only ecclesiastical but political, drove the Latin missionaries out of his kingdom.

In March 870, a Council placed the Bulgarian Church under Constantinople's protection, and an archbishop from Byzantium, assisted by ten bishops, settled in Preslav to direct the Bulgarian Church. Patriarch Ignatius later sent priests to Bulgaria to instruct the local clergy; and,

---

93 Hieromonk Makarios of Simonos Petra, *The Synaxarion: The Lives of the Saints of the Orthodox Church, Volume Three, January-February*, trans. Christopher Hookaway (Ormylia: Holy Convent of the Annunciation of Our Lady, 2001), 23-24.

from 885 onwards, the five disciples of Saints Cyril and Methodius, the 'Five from Ochrid': Clement, Nahum, Angelarius, Gorazd and Sabas, were entrusted with the mission, preaching the Faith in the Slav language. They progressively baptized the rest of the people; so that soon, through the Tsar's support, the territory of Bulgaria was covered with churches in which God's praises were sung in Slavonic.

In 888, the sovereign renounced the throne and retired to the Monastery of St. Panteleimon. But when his son Vladimir (888-93) set himself to destroy his father's work by turning once more to the Latins and persecuting the Orthodox clergy, Michael laid aside his monastic garments and put on a soldier's uniform once more. He drove Vladimir from the throne and installed his younger son Symeon. Having restored order, he then put on his monastic habit again and spent the rest of his life in ascesis, silence and prayer. He fell asleep in peace on 2 May 907.

May 3rd: THEODOSIUS (FEODOSIJ), Superior of the LAVRA CAVES Monastery[94]

One day the pious great prince Izjaslav, son of Jaroslav and grandson of Volodimer, came to our holy Feodosij, the superior of the Caves Monastery, and said to him, "Father, tell me about the faith of the Varangians." Our venerable father Feodosij said, "Listen, pious prince, to what your highness has asked of our humility. Their faith is evil and their law impure. They have adopted the faith of Sabellius and many other heretical beliefs, and have defiled the entire land. You must guard against them, pious autocrat. Their heresies are as follows: first, they do not kiss the icons; second, they do not kiss the relics of saints; third, they draw a cross on the ground, kiss it, then get up and trample on it; fourth, they eat meat during Lent; fifth, they celebrate [the Eucharist] with unleavened bread; and sixth, their priests baptize with one immersion, whereas we do so with three, and we anoint the newly baptized person with oil and perfume, while they sprinkle the mouth with salt. They do not christen with the names of the saints, but with those of the parents. Therefore,

---

94   Muriel Heppell, *The Paterik of the Kievan Caves Monastery*, trans. Muriel Heppell (Cambridge: Harvard University Press, 1989), 211-214.

it is good to shun the Latins' faith, and not to observe their customs, nor receive communion with them, nor listen to anything they say, since their beliefs are wrong and their life unclean. They eat with dogs and cats and drink their own urine — this is vile and wicked — and they eat tortoises, wild horses, asses, animals that have been strangled, and the flesh of bears and beavers. On the Tuesday of the first week in Lent they allow meat to be eaten; their monks eat lard and fast on Sundays.

Christians should not give their daughters to them in marriage, nor receive them into their own homes, nor swear any oath of brotherhood with them, nor have them as godparents, nor exchange kisses with them, nor eat with them, nor drink from any single vessel. If one of them should ask you for anything, give him something to eat for God's sake, but in his own dish; if he has no dish, give him something in your dish, then wash it and say a prayer. They do not ask forgiveness of their sins from God, but from their priests, according to the gifts [which they give]. Their priests do not marry legal wives, but commit fornication with their servants. They celebrate the Liturgy, but think that they commit no sin in doing so. Their bishops keep concubines, go to war, and wear rings on their fingers. They bury their dead with their feet to the west, their heads to the east, their arms alongside their bodies, and their eyes, ears, and nose sealed with wax. They take their nieces in marriage. They celebrate with a dead substance, thinking that the Lord is dead, while we celebrate the Liturgy with a living body and see the Lord Himself sitting on the right hand of the Father, Who will come again to judge the living and the dead. They [use] dead Latin substances and perform a Liturgy in which there is no life, while we, who bring to the living God a pure and undefiled sacrifice, will attain eternal life. Thus, it is written, 'He shall reward every man according to his words.'

It is not good to take their loaves, since there are many evil and unrighteous things in them. Their faith is perverted and leads to destruction; they do things that even the Jews do not do. Many of them have followed the heresy of Sabellius. They are the most pagan and evil nation, because it is impossible to protect oneself against them, but one can against the pagans. The Latins have the Gospel, the Apostle, and the holy icons. They go to church, but their faith and their law are unclean. They have dishonored the whole land with the multitude of their heresies, because there are Varangians throughout the land. Orthodox Christians who live among them in the same place suffer much repression at their hands. Whoever preserves himself from them and keeps his faith pure will stand rejoicing at the right hand of God, but whoever willfully draws close to them will stand weeping bitterly with them on the left. For there is no eternal life for those living in the faith of the Latins or the Saracens, nor will they share the lot of the saints in the world to come. It is not fitting to praise their faith; anyone who does brings reproach upon himself. Or if he begins to praise continually the faiths of others and to deny Orthodox Christianity, he will appear as a man of double faith, close to heresy. You must guard against such actions, my son, and have nothing to do with them. Rather flee from them, continually praise your own faith, and, as far as you can, exercise yourself in it with good deeds.

Be merciful, Christ-lover, not only to the members of your own household, but also to strangers. If you see anyone naked, clothe him; if he is hungry or weighed down by poverty, be merciful to him. Even if he is a heretic of some other faith and a Latin, show mercy to all men and deliver them from misfortune. You will not lose your reward from the Lord, for God nourishes all men, pagans as well as Christians. Pagans and the heterodox are under God's care, but the recompense of the blessed will be different in the next world. We who live in the true faith are watched over by God here and will be saved in the life to come by our Lord Jesus Christ. If someone who professes this holy faith dies for God's sake, he will not with confidence lose the true faith, but will die for Christ. For it is said that the saints died for their faith, so that they might live in Christ.

If, my son, you find the heterodox disputing with true Christians and trying to entice them away from the Orthodox faith, since you truly know this Orthodoxy, do not hide within yourself, but help the Orthodox against those whose faith is evil. If you help them, you will deliver your sheep from the lion's mouth, like a good shepherd. But if you keep silent, it is as though they were snatched away from Christ and handed over to Satan, and you must answer for it on the Day of Judgment. If anyone should say to you, 'God has given this faith and that one,' then say to him, 'Who are you, you heretic? Do you think that God has two faiths? Have you not heard, accursed and perverted as you are by an evil faith, that which is written: "Thus saith the Lord, one Lord, one faith, one baptism." The Lord also said, "It becometh us to fulfill all righteousness." Having completed all these things, He sent His disciples to preach to the ends of the earth, and then ascended into heaven.'

Thus you, one of evil faith, after holding to the Orthodox faith for so many years, have turned away to an evil faith and to Satan's teaching. Have you not heard [the words of] the Apostle Paul, saying, 'There are some that trouble you and would pervert the gospel of Christ, but though an angel from heaven preach any other gospel unto you than that which we have preached unto you, let him be accursed.' You have renounced the preaching of the apostles and the edification of the holy fathers, and you have accepted a faith based on error and a perverted dogma leading to perdition. Therefore, you have been torn away from us and set apart, so that it is not fitting that we should share in the holy Mysteries, nor receive communion together, nor admit you to our Divine Liturgy, because there are many heresies among you."

May 4th: NICEPHORUS the Hesychast of MOUNT ATHOS[95]

Nikiphoros the Monk, often known as Nikiphoros the Hesychast or the Athonite, lived in the second half of the thirteenth century. He was born in Italy, so St. Gregory Palamas tells us, and was originally Roman Catholic. But, rejecting what Palamas terms the "kakodoxy" of the Latin West, he travelled to the Byzantine Empire, where he embraced the Orthodox faith, becoming a monk on the Holy Mountain of Athos. Here he dwelt in "quietness and stillness", according to Palamas—presumably this means that he lived in a small hermitage, not in a fully-organized cenobium—and eventually he withdrew to the 'most isolated parts' of the mountain. Like Theoleptos of Philadelphia, he was fiercely opposed to the unionist policy of Michael VIII, and he has himself left an ac-

---

95   St. Nikodemos of the Holy Mountain and St. Makarios of Corinth, *The Philokalia: The Complete Text Volume IV*, trans. G.E.H. Palmer, Phillip Sherrard and Kallistos Ware (London: Faber and Faber, Ltd., 1995), 192.

count of the imprisonment and exile that he suffered in consequence during 1276-7.

May 7th: ALEXIS (Toth) of WILKES-BARRE, Pennsylvania[96]

Born in 1854 of a Carpatho-Russian clerical family belonging to the Greek-Catholic (Uniate) Church [...] Appointed secretary to the Uniate bishop of Presov [...] He was sent to the USA in 1889, to serve in the parish in Minneapolis, Minnesota. Having taken up his charge, he went to report to the Roman Catholic archbishop who, being opposed to the existence of national communities in America, received him with open hostility and refused to recognize his credentials. Father Toth opposed this unjust decision, but he had to face the united policy of the Catholic bishops, who were afraid that the Uniate communities would be opposed to the emigrants' assimilation into American culture. In expectation of expulsion, Father Alexis explained the situation to his parishioners, who refused any sort of servile submission and advised him to approach the Russian Orthodox bishop in San Francisco.

After several visits to each other, Bishop Vladimir received Father Alexis and 361 of his parishioners into the communion of the Holy Orthodox Church (1891); and sometime later, the parish was incorporated into the Diocese of Alaska and the Aleutian Islands. This example gave encouragement to hundreds of other immigrants from Eastern Europe, and Father Alexis's ardent sermons about the Orthodox Church persuaded them to return to the Church of their forefathers. Although inflexible in matters of faith, Father Alexis always exhorted his parishioners to avoid all condemnation of others and intolerance towards the heterodox. At the cost of great toil, he published many writings on the Orthodox faith and of pastoral teaching for the newly converted.

His conversion, however, brought him many enemies, and he was accused of selling his compatriots to the "Muscovites" for financial gain

---

96 Hieromonk Makarios of Simonos Petra, *The Synaxarion: The Lives of the Saints of the Orthodox Church, Volume Five, May-June*, trans. Christopher Hookway (Ormylia: Holy Convent of the Annunciation of Our Lady, 1999), 85-86.

— he who was forced to work in a bakery until he received a salary from the Russian Church; he who, despite his meagre resources, never failed in almsgiving and who shared his money with other, poorer, priests. Father Alexis sought only the Kingdom of God and His righteousness (Matt. 6:33), and bore all affliction with joy.

The Orthodox bishops in America recognized his talents and virtues, and often sent him to preach to the Orthodox Slavs dispersed around the country. He also visited many Uniate parishes, explaining the difference between the Orthodox and the Catholics, the Uniates and the Protestants, and thus played his part in the return of seventeen American parishes to the bosom of Orthodoxy. When he came to the end of his labours, thousands of Carpatho-Russians and Galicians had returned to the Church, providing the leaven for the expansion of Orthodoxy in the New World.

May 13th: Monks and Martyrs of the Monastery of IVIRON[97, 98]

Georgian monks began to settle on Mt. Athos in the middle of the 10th century, and a Georgian monastery, Iveron, was founded there not long after. At that time foreign armies were constantly invading Mt. Athos. In the 13th century the Crusaders stormed through the region, and between 1259 and 1306 the pope's private army devastated Mt. Athos several times. Monks of Zographou and Vatopedi monasteries and the Protaton were martyred for the Orthodox Faith, and the monks of the Iveron Monastery eventually met the same fate. During this period Georgian and Greek ascetics labored together at the Iveron Monastery, and many young ascetics of the new generation began to arrive from Georgia.

---

97 Hieromonk Makarios of Simonos Petra, *The Synaxarion: The Lives of the Saints of the Orthodox Church, Volume Five, May-June*, trans. Christopher Hookway (Ormylia: Holy Convent of the Annunciation of Our Lady, 1999), 148.

98 Archpriest Zakaria Machitadze, *Lives of the Georgian Saints*, trans. David Ninoshvili, Lauren Elizabeth Ninoshvili (Platina: Saint Herman of Alaska Brotherhood, 2006), 197-198.

The Crusaders demanded that the Iveron monks convert to Catholicism and acknowledge the primacy of the Roman pope. But the monks condemned their fallacies and anathematized the doctrine of the Catholics. According to the Patericon of Athos, the Iveron monks were forcibly expelled from their monastery. Nearly two hundred elderly monks were goaded like animals onto a ship that was subsequently sunk in the depths of the sea. The younger, healthier monks were deported to Italy and sold as slaves to the Jews. Some sources claim this tragedy took place in the year 1259, while others record that the Georgian monks of the Holy Mountain were subject to the Latin persecutions over the course of four years, from 1276 to 1280.

May 14th: LEONTIOS, Patriarch of JERUSALEM

His Life [99]

St. Leontios was born in Stromnitsa (formerly known as Tieriopolis) and in childhood was educated in the Holy Scriptures and diligently read the Lives of the Saints. After the repose of his father, he was ordained to the holy priesthood. Leontios was tonsured a monk in Constantinople and afterwards, in obedience to his elder, went to reside at the Monastery of St. John the Theologian on Patmos. When the abbot of the monastery became ill, God enlightened the abbot to leave behind a written order appointing Leontios as his successor. God revealed to Leontios that he would be consecrated a bishop and was eventually consecrated Patriarch of Jerusalem where he served from 1170 until his repose in 1190. Patriarch Leontios was greatly loved by the people and widely revered for his miracles and his gift of clairvoyance.

---

99 Holy Apostles Convent & Dormition Skete, *The Great Synaxaristes of the Orthodox Church, May*, trans. Holy Apostles Convent and Dormition Skete (Buena Vista: Holy Apostles Convent & Dormition Skete, 2003), 693-722.

The Latins Attempt to Murder St. Leontios in Jerusalem[100]

"The holy Leontios arrived in Jerusalem at night. He entered the Church of the Holy Resurrection, where he worshipped alone at the sepulcher of our Savior. He took it for granted that his presence would go completely unnoticed, but such was not the case; for, by the miracles that he performed, he was well known to all. At that time, Jerusalem was stricken by drought, and the Christians of the city had need of another Prophet Elias to rescue them from their plight. For this, God sent the great Leontios. By the prayers of the man of God, it rained so heavily that the cisterns overflowed and the parched farms received ample water. Not less interesting, and vastly more important, was that the hopes of all were revived that they would have an abundant crop of wheat, wine, and the other blessings of the Lord. The wondrous Leontios was extolled and praised by all. The lips of all exclaimed that this saint of God had come to their land to liberate them from the threat of destruction. (Let us, too, fall at his feet, that we may have him as our helper!)

"When the more fanatical Latins of Jerusalem learned of this wonder, they became envious, especially their bishop, who was overcome by hatred. It was he who plotted to murder the saint who, of course, had never harmed him. At night, therefore, the Latin hierarch dispatched men to the saint's chambers in order to murder him. Upon approaching, they detected a light in the saint's lodgings. They tried to enter, but when they searched for the door they were unable to find it. God, moreover, preserved Leontios; for it was He Who blinded the assassins. All night long they tried to find the entrance. After accepting their failure, they returned to the Latin bishop. They insisted that Leontios was guarded by God and that no one could harm him! This remarkable event was recounted everywhere, to the amazement of all. Indeed, the fame of the holy man reached even the queen of cities, Constantinople."

---

100 Ibid., 714-715.

May 16th: Hieroschemamonk PAISIOS from the PUTNA Hermitage

"This hieroschemamonk was the last abbot of Sihăstria Putnei. Disciple of the same abbot, Sila, Venerable Paisios pastored this skete between 1783 and 1790, after which the skete remained deserted and ruined for almost two centuries, due to the Austro-Hungarian occupation and the harsh times of our days.

The pious abbot Paisios had a holy life, like his predecessors, spending the years of his life only in prayer, fasting and spiritual contemplation. When the Orthodox Bukovina from Northern Moldova came under Catholic occupation and most of the monasteries in these parts were closed down, the Catholics made great efforts to convert the Romanian Orthodox villages and towns to Catholicism. That is why Venerable Paisios made great efforts to defend Orthodoxy in Northern Bukovina, in the face of Catholic persecution.

Going from place to place, the hieroschemamonk Paisios urged the Orthodox people to keep the true faith with sanctity and not to be afraid to confess Christ with both words and acts. Reaching the end of his days, he gave his soul peacefully in the hands of God, being buried near the nave, on whose tombstone it is written: "Here rest the bones of the servant of God, Paisios the hieroschemamonk, and he passed away in 1790." His holy relics are yellow and fragrant, with a powerful divine grace, and are kept in the altar of the church, completely renovated in recent years, being consecrated on September 29, 1996. Lord, Jesus Christ, Son of God, count among your saints the pious fathers Sila, Nathan and Paisios, together with all the pious and the righteous of the Romanian people."[101]

"In conjunction with the 500th anniversary of the founding of the Putnei Monastery, during their meeting held June 6-7, 2016, the Holy Synod of the Romanian Orthodox Church decided to number among

---

101 "Hieromonk Paisios Defender of Orthodoxy in Northern Bucovina," Romanian Orthodox Metropolia of Moldova & Bucovina, accessed October 20th, 2022, https://doxologia.ro/pateric/ieroschimonahul-paisie-aparatorul-ortodoxiei-bucovina-de-nord

the Saints of Venerables, Silas, Paisios and Nathan with their feast day being on May 16th."[102]

May 19th: Thirteen Martyrs of the Monastery of KANTARA on Cyprus: Abbot JOHN, CONON, BARNABAS, GENNADIUS, GERASIMUS, THEOCTISTUS, JEREMIAH, JOSEPH, MARK, CYRIL, THEOGNOSTIUS and MAXIMUS[103, 104]

In about 1228, John and Conon, two ascetics from the Holy Mountain of Athos, arrived on Cyprus, which was then under Latin occupation. After having stayed in the famous monasteries of Machaira and Chrysostom, they settled in the isolated Monastery of the Mother of God of Kantara. Their virtues and ascetic strivings quickly became known by the people, who hurried to them as to a spring of living water capable of re-invigorating their threatened faith. The Latin Archbishop Eustorgius of Leucosia,[105] fearful that this fame would upset his plans, then sent two envoys to the monastery in order to subdue the holy monks. When he attempted to convince them that the Divine Liturgy must be celebrated with unleavened bread (azymes), John proposed that each party

102 "Venerable Theodore the Sanctified: Ven. Silas, Paisios and Nathan from Sihastria Putnei," Official News Agency, Basilica.ro, The Romanian Orthodox Church, accessed October 20th, 2022, https://basilica.ro/en/venerable-theodore-the-sanctified-%E2%80%A0-ven-silas-paisios-and-nathan-from-sihastria-putnei/

103 These saints are unknown in the Synaxarion, they are only venerated in Cyprus. According to other sources the thirteen saints were from Mount Athos.

104 Hieromonk Makarios of Simonos Petra, *The Synaxarion: The Lives of the Saints of the Orthodox Church, Volume Five, May-June*, trans. Christopher Hookway (Ormylia: Holy Convent of the Annunciation of Our Lady, 1999), 204-206.

105 In 1191, Richard Coeur de Lion took possession of Cyprus and not knowing what to do with it, gave it to the Templars. He had been preceded by the adventurer Renaud de Chatillon who had carried out many cruel acts, especially against the Orthodox clergy. Later, the Frankish clergy reduced the number of Orthodox Bishops from fourteen to four, constraining them to be nothing more than stewards of the Latin bishops. They built many churches and tried in every way to steal the people to their faith and traditions. This Latin occupation, with its deplorable consequences, lasted until 1571.

celebrate the Liturgy separately and then go into a furnace, for the fire to indicate which is the true Faith; but the Latins refused the proposition and left the monastery. The thirteen fathers spent the following night in prayers of thanksgiving, and, in the morning, they set out for Leucosia. On the way, the people rushed in a mass towards the holy confessors to receive their blessing. Having immediately been warned of the monks' arrival, Eustorgius had them summoned to his magnificent court. John, Conon and their companions refuted the arguments of the Latins with the words of the Holy Fathers.

The furious [Papist] archbishop, finding no reply to them, had them flogged and thrown into prison. For three years, they endured harsh incarceration in a dark, dank and stinking prison with constancy and trust in God, given moldy bread to eat, constantly insulted by their jailers and frequently put to torture. But they remained inflexible in the face of all the proposals put by the archbishop's envoys; and, appearing before him at the beginning of the second year, they replied to him with yet greater valor. They were then given over to the executioners. Theognostus was the first of them to receive the crown of martyrdom, after which his body was given to the flames. In the third year (1231), the holy fathers were again summoned before Eustorgius' assistant, the inquisitor Andrew, who had been ordered to make an end of these rebels.

They answered him with one voice that they were proud, at the risk of their lives, to confess the Orthodox faith that the prophets had proclaimed, the apostles had preached, and the fathers and councils had defined. Three days later, they were summoned again, in the presence of Eric I, the Latin King of Cyprus (1218-54), who gave Andrew license to castigate them as he wished. The executioners then tied them by the feet behind twelve horses which they set galloping along the streets of the city, in order to terrorize the Orthodox Christians. They finally untied their almost-dead bodies and threw them onto a ready-prepared pyre. While John was standing in prayer in the midst of the flames, one of those present hit him on the head with a cudgel, but the Saint, in falling, extinguished the fire. The executioners then lit a second brazier, onto which they threw the bodies of the saints and the bones of animals pell-mell, then they scattered the ashes. A little later, Andrew, having become

Bishop of Avila in Spain, was burned alive while he was sleeping at his fireside.

May 20th: DOVMONT-TIMOTHY, Duke of UTENA and Prince of PSKOV[106]

Saint Dovmont-Timothy, Prince of Pskov, was born (1240 AD) in Lithuania to a family of pagan nobility. Inasmuch as Lithuania suffered at the time from ongoing internal strife among the Princely families, in 1265 the Saint departed his native land and, along with three hundred followers, settled in Pskov, an ancient Russian city located close to the present Estonian frontier. Shortly after his arrival, he and his retinue were converted to Orthodox Christianity, the Prince himself being given the baptismal name of "Timothy." Not long thereafter, the Saint was elected sovereign Prince of the city, chosen because of his exemplary virtue and courage. He ruled the city and region for thirty-three years. Embracing the Orthodox Christian faith, Saint Dovmont-Timothy embraced it fully, carefully observing the fasts praying, continuously, and faithfully attending the Divine Services. In addition to his personal piety, he quickly established a reputation for great charity towards the poor and generosity to the Church establishing new church buildings and monasteries.

Saint Dovmont-Timothy married Princess Maria Dmitrivna, the daughter of Dmitri of Pereyaslavl and granddaughter of Saint Alexander Nevsky. After the Saint's death, she entered the monastic life and is known as "Righteous Schema-Nun Martha of Pskov." Saint Dovmont-Timothy was charged as a ruler with the defense of his new motherland, an obligation he took most seriously. As a result, the walls and defenses of Pskov were made virtually impregnable. In February 1268, when the Teutonic Knights of Lithuanian again invaded Russian lands, the Saint met them in battle. He was at that time allied with Grand Prince Yaroslave of Tver, with whose army he combined his forces to counter the threat. The

---

106 Protopresbyter James Thornton, *Pious Kings and Right-Believing Queens: An Encyclopedia of the Royal and Imperial Saints of the Orthodox Church* (Belmont: Institute for Byzantine and Modern Greek Studies, 2013), 133-135.

Russian armies encountered the Lithuanians and Germans at the Battle of Rakovor (sometimes called "the Battle of Wesenberg"), delivering a humiliating defeat to the invaders. It is said that before the great battle, Saint Dovmont-Timothy had entered a Church to pray. Placing his sword, scabbard, and sword belt on the steps of the Amvon, the Priest then blessed him, and blessed his sword, and then solemnly fastened the sword-belt around the Warrior-Saint. In thanksgiving for his victory, the Saint built the still-extant Cathedral of the Holy Trinity in Pskov.

In the year following the victory at the Battle of Rakovor, the Teutonic Knights moved against Pskov, besieging the town. However, Saint Dovmont-Timothy drove them off, defeating them so soundly that they would not renew their attacks in that region for another three decades, giving the Saint's realm a long period of peace. However, in 1299, the Germans and Lithuanians finally gathered sufficient courage to attempt another invasion. Attacking Pskov, they could not break through the tremendous walls. Yet, since they found the monasteries Snetnogorsk and Mirozhsk outside the city walls undefended, they burned both monasteries and martyred Saints Joasaph, founder of Snetnogorsk, and Vasilii, Hegumen of Mirozhsk, along with seventeen other monks (commemorated on March 4). The attack on the monasteries and on unarmed monks is evidence of the hatred that the Knights — themselves supposedly Christians of the papal religion — felt towards the Orthodox Church. Outraged at this murder of helpless civilian monks, Saint Dovmont-Timothy led his army in a counterattack that drove the foreigners from Russia. Several months after what would be his final military victory, the Saint fell ill and reposed in the Lord. He is entombed at the Holy Trinity cathedral in Pskov and is commemorated on May 20th.

August 5th: EUGENIUS of AITOLIA[107]

[St. Eugenius of Aitolia] was ordained priest by Patriarch Cyril Lukaris, who greatly admired his virtue and culture (1619)... Suffering

---

107 Hieromonk Makarios of Simonos Petra, *The Synaxarion: The Lives of the Saints of the Orthodox Church, Volume Six, July-August*, trans. Mother Maria Rule and Mother Joanna Burton (Ormylia: Holy Convent of the Annunciation of Our Lady, 2008), 382-384.

from the persecutions inflicted on Cyril Lukaris, which culminated in the Patriarch's execution (1638), and distressed at seeing the Church torn apart by politics and subject to foreign influence, Eugenius decided to devote his life to the defence of Orthodoxy. This attitude drew on him the hatred of the new pro-Latin Patriarch, Cyril Kondaris, who had a search made in his house to find the Office that Eugenius had composed in honor of Cyril Lukaris, who he saw as a martyr. Taken to the Patriarchate, he defended the memory of his benefactor before the Patriarch, who, fulminating with anger, deposed him and had him driven away.

See page 385 for writings from him.

August 11th: NIPHON, Patriarch of CONSTANTINOPLE[108]

Saint Niphon was born in the Peloponnese of noble and virtuous parents. From his earliest childhood, the saint forsook play to apply himself to the study of the Holy Scriptures and our God-bearing Fathers [...] Having heard that a wise and virtuous Athonite monk called Zachariah had settled in the town of Arta, he hurried to his retreat and asked him to teach him the practices and way of life of the Holy Mountain.

However, the troubles brought about in the Church by the false union concluded at the Council of Florence (1439) did not allow the monks to enjoy the hesychia that they desired, and Saint Niphon followed his Elder to the regions of Ascalon and Krogia (in Albania) to confirm the people in the Orthodox faith. [Saint Niphon] finally withdrew to the Monastery of Dionysiou, where he received the Great Habit [...] His fame spread [...] so that when Metropolitan Parthenius of Thessalonica died, the clergy and people chose Niphon to succeed him [...] Immediately after his consecration (1482), he undertook the preaching of the Orthodox faith to set aright the errors introduced by the Council

---

108 Hieromonk Makarios of Simonos Petra, *The Synaxarion: The Lives of the Saints of the Orthodox Church, Volume Six, July-August*, trans. Mother Maria Rule and Mother Joanna Burton (Ormylia: Holy Convent of the Annunciation of Our Lady, 2008), 436-438.

of Florence, and made himself the consoler of the Christian people in their affliction under the Ottoman yoke. He encouraged the faithful to submit to the decrees of Providence, in the hope of future blessings, and urged them to persevere in the practice of the evangelical virtues. He also went at night to the houses of the poorest to give them assistance, and succeeded by his patient exhortations in converting many pagans.

August 15th: MACARIUS the ROMAN and Wonderworker of NOVGOROD[109]

This great luminary of Orthodoxy saw the light of day in Rome at the end of the fifteenth century. The son of a devout and affluent family, he was brought up in the fear of God and received a full education in the sciences of the time. A promising future was opening to the young man, but his heart secretly thirsted to drink at the fount of eternal life, living a life dedicated to prayer. As the years passed, he renounced little by little the distractions and affairs of worldly life to devote himself to meditation on the Holy Scriptures. Dreaming of imitating the lives of the Fathers, whose exploits he read of with eagerness, he was however tormented by the spectacle offered by Rome and the whole of Italy, given over to the violent torrent of a godless humanism, wrongly called the Renaissance but which was nothing but a return to classical paganism.

Meditating on the causes of this decadence and ascertaining that it had its origins in the schism that had separated the Christian West from the venerable tradition of the holy Fathers, he begged Christ with tears to show him the way back. The Lord opened his spiritual eyes and showed him that the Eastern Orthodox Church had remained unchanging in its doctrine and offered its faithful the authentic means of following the example of the saints. Like his contemporary, Saint Maximus the Greek (21 Jan.), he decided to leave for distant Russia, which was at the time the only country in which Orthodoxy was freely practiced. He gave all his possessions to the poor and, clad in an old habit, set off on his travels.

---

109 Hieromonk Makarios of Simonos Petra, *The Synaxarion: The Lives of the Saints of the Orthodox Church, Volume Six, July-August*, trans. Mother Maria Rule and Mother Joanna Burton (Ormylia: Holy Convent of the Annunciation of Our Lady, 2008), 488-489.

August 16th: NILUS of ERIKOUSSA, Restorer of the Monastery of GIROMERION[110]

Saint Nilus was the nephew of Emperor Theodore I Lascaris (1204-22), who reigned in Nicaea after the taking of Constantinople by the Crusaders. In order to escape pressure from the Latins, Nilus became a monk in the Monastery of Akoimetoi, where he lived until the Byzantines re-took possession of Constantinople (1261) through the victories of Saint John Vatatzes the Merciful (4 Nov.). Nilus then undertook a pilgrimage to the Holy Places, and, on his return, after having been away six years, he went with a holy elder to reproach Emperor Michael VIII Palaeologus (1259-82) for his pro-Latin policy. They were arrested and set adrift in a boat in the open sea, without either rudder or pilot; and, buffeted by the waves during the storm, landed after forty days at the Monastery of Iviron on the Holy Mountain of Athos. Putting themselves in the hands of Providence, Nilus remained there three years as a simple doorkeeper.

August 25th: GENNADIOS II SCHOLARIOS, Patriarch of CONSTANTINOPLE[111]

Saint Gennadios II Scholarios, given the name George Scholarios, was born in Constantinople in the year 1400. There is very little known of his early childhood. He lived during the period in which the false Council of Florence was well under way. During this false council, Saint Gennadios was still a layman. However, his vast knowledge of the Holy Orthodox Tradition, the Latin language, and his increasing knowledge of post-Schism heretical Papist theology would eventually draw him

---

110 Hieromonk Makarios of Simonos Petra, *The Synaxarion: The Lives of the Saints of the Orthodox Church, Volume Six, July-August*, trans. Mother Maria Rule and Mother Joanna Burton (Ormylia: Holy Convent of the Annunciation of Our Lady, 2008), 498-499.

111 St. Gennadios II Scholarios, *From Ashes and Ruin: Selection from the Writings of St. Gennadios Scholarios*, trans. Dr. John Palmer (Columbia: Newrome Press, 2022), 16-24.

into the debate and would put him on the side of the anti-unionist confessors of the Orthodox Faith, against the heretical Latins. Saint Mark of Ephesus during the end of his life passed the defense of Holy Orthodoxy against the Latin Papist to Saint Gennadios and is quoted as saying:

> I speak now of the dignitary Scholarios, whom I knew from his early youth, to him I am well disposed, and for whom I have a great love, as for my own son and friend. In my intercourse and conversation with him even to the present time, I have conceived a clear picture of his exceptional prudence and wisdom and power with words, and therefore I believe that he is the only one to be found at the present time who is able to extend a helping hand to the Orthodox Church, which is agitated by the attacks of those [Latin supporting unionists] who would destroy the perfection of the dogmas, and likewise, with the help of God, to correct the Church and affirm Orthodoxy. [...] And I myself lay upon him this battle, so that he would be defender of the Church and leader of sound teaching and champion of right doctrines and the Truth in my place, having support in God and in the Truth itself, about which the very battle is being waged; so that being a participant in this with the Holy Teachers and God-bearing Fathers, the great theologians, he would receive his reward from the Just Judge when He declares victorious all those who fought for Piety.

After the fall of Constantinople in May 1453, Gennadios was captured by the Turks and sent into slavery for a brief period before being released by the commanding Turks. He was eventually chosen by the newly convened Synod of Constantinople to be the new leader of the Orthodox in the City and was ordained a deacon, priest, bishop, and enthroned as Patriarch of Constantinople. In August 1454 he announced his resignation as the Patriarch of Constantinople and travelled to Holy Mount Athos, where he settled at the Holy Monastery of Vatopedi until his repose in 1472. Saint Gennadios was believed to be canonized by the Ecumenical Patriarchate in 1484. This was later confirmed by The Holy Metropolis of Serres. The memory of Saint Gennadios II Scholarios is celebrated on August 25th.

See page 383 for a writing from him.

August 27th: Greatmartyr PHANOURIOS the Newly-Manifest[112]

At that time the isle of Crete had no Orthodox hierarch, but a Latin bishop, for it was ruled then by the Venetians, who had shrewdly refused to permit an Orthodox hierarch to be consecrated whenever one died. This they did with evil intent, thinking that with time they could thus convert the Orthodox to the papist dogmas. If Orthodox men wished to obtain ordination, they had to go to Cythera.

---

112 Holy Trinity Monastery, "The Holy and Glorious Greatmartyr Phanourios the Newly-manifest," *Orthodox Life*, no. 3 (May-June 1981): 36.

Synaxis of Romanian Saints

B. MOVEABLE FEASTS

First Sunday of Great Lent:
Holy New Martyr THEODORE Sladić[113]

St. Theodore was born in the mid-eighteenth century in the village of Kukurzari near the town of Komogovina. Not much is known about his early life but the times he lived in were marked by persecution of the Serbian Orthodox in the Balkans by the Uniate movement of the Roman Catholic Church with the fear that the Serbs might succumb to Roman Catholicism. In 1766 the Turkish Sultan Mustapha III decreed that the Patriarchate of Peć was officially abolished, thereby making the Serbian Church subjugated to the Ecumenical Patriarchate. Many Serbs left the church, and the order, culture and education it provided, and reverted to pre-Christian customs and practices. Eager to avoid both the Turkish yoke and the Roman heresy, this made them vulnerable to succumb to the ideas of the Enlightenment. Serbian monasteries were closed resulting in a lack of clerical education.

Theodore was approached by both the propagandists of the Latin Unia and by Serbians under the spell of Western rationalism to abandon the Church teachings and embrace their modern ways of thinking. "Venerable Theodore was an ardent Orthodox and, due to his love for liturgical ritual and the vision of the doctrines of the Church, he became

113 Fr. Daniel Rogich, *Serbian Patericon: Saints of the Serbian Orthodox Church – Volume One*, (Canton: Hesychia Press, 2023), 165-169.

an outspoken proponent against the Latin Unia and the rationalistic innovations of Western Europe. He felt that the Unia would never add to the true Orthodox faith, and that attachment to the papacy was nothing more than an economic ploy on the part of Rome."[114]

He and 150 followers were arrested during the first week of Great Lent in 1788 by the Turkish authorities on the charge of political and religious treason. By refusing to participate in the evil tax system imposed on the Church, they were martyred by the Turkish authorities by being burned to death.

Second Sunday after Pentecost:
Synaxis of All Romanian Saints[115]
Venerable Hieromonk PAHOMIE (PACHOMIUS)
Abbot of Peri Monastery[116]

This venerable abbot of Peri Monastery, from northern Maramureș, was born in Țara Oașului (Oaș Country), a relative of Dragoș Vodă, the first dismounter (founder) of Moldavia. Beginning the ascetic monastic life as a young man, at one of the existing sketes in his area, he became worthy of the gift of priesthood in a short time and was full of zeal for the confession of Christ and for the defense of the Orthodox faith. Becoming well known in all the villages of M Maramures, Venerable Pachomius becomes a counselor and spiritual father to the Romanians from Maramureș, whom he would visit and guide them on the path of salvation.

In the second half of the 14th century, when the sons of Saș Vodă (Sas of Moldavia), Baliță and Drag, founded the monastery in Peri with the patron Saint Michael the Archangel, the venerable Pachomius was named abbot of this monastery. And in 1391, when the Peri monas-

---

114 Fr. Daniel Rogich, *Serbian Patericon: Saints of the Serbian Orthodox Church – Volume One*, (Canton: Hesychia Press, 2023), 166.

115 This is the feast day for the following two Romanian saints. Very little information is available on them.

116 Archimandrite Ioanichie Bălan, *Patericul Românesc* (Sihăstria: Mănăstirea Editura, 2005), 92-93.

tery became a stavropegial (owed canonical allegiance to the Patriarch of Constantinople), the abbot Pachomius was appointed by Patriarch Anthony of Constantinople as patriarchal exarch over all the Romanian Orthodox villages in the north of Transylvania. In this role, abbot Pachomius had the right to supervise the priests and Orthodox believers from Maramureş, Ugocea, Bărcău, Arva, Sălaj, Almaş, Ciceu, Unguraş and Valea Bistriţei.

Thus, Venerable Pachomius walked from village to village, consecrating new churches, appointing priests, judging ecclesiastical misunderstandings, raising the morale of the peasants, teaching and defending the Orthodox faith. He was also the spiritual leader of the Ieud, Bârsana and Peri Monasteries in Maramureş, where dozens of monks were leading ascetic lives, good servants of the Church of Christ, spiritual fathers for the faithful, confessors and defenders of the Orthodox faith. Thus, Venerable Pachomius of Peri makes out of the monks, fathers and apologists of our ancestral Orthodoxy, and from the monasteries of Maramureş makes true Orthodox strongholds of resistance and defense, in the north of Transylvania, always hit by [Roman] Catholic proselytism.[117] In the course of the first decades of the 15th century, Venerable Pachomius of Peri, the father of the Orthodox Romanians from Maramures, fell asleep unto the Lord in peace, leaving behind numerous monks and priests serving in the villages.

Metropolitan IOSIF (JOSEPH) Muşat, First Hierarch of MOLDAVIA[118]

The first known metropolitan of Moldavia was [...] Metropolitan Joseph Muşat. He was from the Muşat family, the ruling dynasty at that time, being a close relative of Petru (Peter) Muşat (1375-1391) and Alexander the Good (1400-1432). From his youth he dedicated his life to Christ in the community of Neamţ Monastery, where he learned to fear

---

117 *Proselytize*: To induce someone to convert to one's own faith. (i.e., Latins converting Orthodox Christians to Papalism).

118 Archimandrite Ioanichie Bălan, *Patericul Românesc* (Sihăstria: Mănăstirea Editura, 2005), 93-95.

God and the asceticism of the spiritual life from the devout monks here. Then, becoming a priest, he became abbot of Neamț Monastery. At the proposal of the lord Petru Mușat, he was ordained bishop of Cetatea Albă (modern day Bilhorod-Dnistrovskyi) by Metropolitan Anthony of Halici. But he does not stay here for long and is called to be Metropolitan of Moldavia. But the Ecumenical Patriarchate refusing to recognize him and causing a great disturbance in the Church, the humble Metropolitan Joseph retired from his chair at the Neamț Monastery and then at Bistrița. Later, he settled in "a monastery, in Boistea, near Targu Neamț, where the cell of bishop Joseph was and where there are nuns". From here, the wise metropolitan courageously supported the hard-tested Moldavian Church, taught and defended the True faith against [Roman] Catholic proselytism, ordained priests, advised the ruler, and was a spiritual father to all. It was said about him that he even took part in the anointing as ruler of Alexander the Good, in the fortress of Suceava, in the year 1400.

On July 26, 1401, with the will of God and the perseverance of the good lord Alexander I Mușat, Metropolitan Joseph was recognized by the Patriarchate of Constantinople as father and head of the See of the Metropolitanate of Moldavia. For almost 15 years, he herded Christ's flock in peace, well organizing the spiritual matters and managing the ecclesiastical matters with skill, like a good treasurer of God's house. His first task was to advise Alexander the Good, his nephew, to bring the relics of the Holy Martyr John the New from Cetatea Albă to Suceava, as a protector of the country and comforter of the pious folk. Then, the metropolitan himself went with a large procession, with priests and a lot of people, led by the voivode himself, to meet the holy relics south of Iași, at the place called "Poiana Vlădicăi" (Bishop's Glade) and placed them with great honor in the Mirăuți church from the capital of Moldavia.

In those years also, the pious Metropolitan Joseph renewed almost entirely the church settlements his parents founded in the Neamț Monastery, to which he dedicated his most precious belonging, the miracle-working icon of the Theotokos, which he had received as a gift from Byzantium. He also advised the Voivode to rebuild two beautiful monasteries, Bistrița (1402) and Moldovița, as a place of prayer and eternal rest.[119] On January 7, 1407, Metropolitan Joseph unites the two voivode-ship monasteries, Neamț and Bistrița, and appoints his disciple, Archi-mandrite Dometian, abbot over them, "so that these monasteries are not separated from each other, because they both belong to my bishopric." Also at his prompting, Abbot Dometian wrote the famous Diptychs of the Bistrița Monastery, which still exists today. He appointed worthy ab-bots at the monasteries of Probea, Bogdana, and Moldovia and spiritu-ally ministered to everyone. He fell asleep in the Lord in old age in 1415 and was buried at Bistrița Monastery. His gravesite was re-discovered in 1975 as some work was being done in the church.

---

119 *Voivode*: The title denoting a military leader.

Harold Godwinson,
the last Orthodox king of England, killed in the Battle of Hastings (1066)

PART II

HISTORICAL STRUGGLES
AGAINST THE LATINS

A. THE NORMAN INVASION
OF ENGLAND (1066)

Scholars have begun to realize in the last few decades a phenomenon which fits perfectly with Orthodox ecclesiological traditions. To be specific, around the time of 1054 A.D., those places which had the Christian Faith established and where the Papal-sanctioned armies had not devastated and enslaved these already existing Christian populations were retaining connections with the Eastern and surviving part of the Roman Empire. Instead of making alliances with barbaric and heretical powers (e.g., the Germanic Carolingian Franks), usually the Western kingdoms who held to the Orthodox Faith preserved some contact with Romans in the East, and, by extension, the Orthodox Christian Faith in the heart of New Rome (i.e., the Orthodox city of Constantinople). Over the recent decades much research has uncovered a variety of evidence for this.[120]

The West fell into Roman Catholicism gradually as these barbaric tribes sought to control the Papacy on one hand and sought to forcibly replace Orthodox bishops throughout the Western Empire on the other. On the European continent, Fr. John Romanides discusses this and documents the evidence for this.[121] Ireland's conquest is explained in some detail below. The Normans are among those heretical and barbaric tribes which moved to improve their status by allying with a heretical Pope. The Normans' conquest of England is when we see Papal heresy come to En-

---

120 For examples, see Fr. Gregory Telepneff, *The Egyptian Desert in the Irish Bog*s, 17. See also Moss, *The Fall of Orthodox England* (footnote 28).

121 Romanides, "Do Forced Replacements of their Orthodox Predecessors have Apostolic Succession?" See page 785.

gland with force. The interesting thing about the Norman Conquest is how well it is documented. We explore a little of this.

William the Conqueror was given the blessing of Pope Alexander II to force the English Church into submission to Rome. William landed in Hastings in October of 1066 under the Pope's banners and, in the battle there, his knights brutally killed the English king, Harold II (Godwinson).[122] William was crowned king the following Christmas Day in London, after which the Norman invaders set London ablaze and persecuted the local English while King William followed this up with a heavy tax on its residents.[123] The last holdout of the English occurred in 1071 on the Isle of Ely. William went personally to see the English finally subjugated, but the English continued to successfully hold off the Normans. Eventually the Normans conquered the monastery but not after King William had called for a witch and had her mounted on a tower to curse the English armies.[124]

Reforms were forced on the English Church and many desecrations and sacrileges were done during these changes. Orthodox bishops we imprisoned and killed there or starved. These are extensively cataloged in many primary sources of the time. When reading them, one will find that the very language used was changed from English to Latin in one instance of primary source material: i.e., *The Anglo-Saxon Chronicle* (indicating the grandiosity of the cultural shift taking place, away from the English Church and toward the papal religion).[125] Monks were killed also;[126] sacred places were profaned with a "marked disrespect for pre-Conquest saints";[127] and the behavior of "Christian" conquerors rivaled or surpassed the atrocities of even pagans.[128]

---

122 Vladimir Moss, *The Fall of Orthodox England*, Mayford, Woking, Surrey, United Kingdom: OrthodoxChristianBooks.com, 2011, accessed November 3rd, 2017, https://www.orthodoxchristianbooks.com/downloads/910_THE_FALL_OF_ORTHODOX_ENGLAND.pdf. See pages 69-70.

123 Ibid, 72.

124 Ibid, 76.

125 Ibid, 83

126 Ibid, 80, footnote 178.

127 Ibid, 82.

128 Ibid, 78-84.

B. INVASION OF IRELAND BY HENRY II OF ENGLAND (1169-1171)

We see a similar operation happen again with the Normans but now against the Irish about 100 years later.

Laudabiliter, some believe, was a bull issued in 1155 by Pope Adrian IV. Its existence is questioned by scholars. There is no question, however, that the Anglo-Norman invaders of Ireland believed such a papal bull gave the Pope's blessing to enforce the claim of the Norman King of England, Henry the II, "as a true Catholic prince should, to enlarge the boundaries of the Church, to reveal the truth of the Christian faith to peoples still untaught and barbarous, and to root out the weeds of vice from the Lord's field"[129] as the bull states.

The invasion began in May of 1169, when Anglo-Norman mercenaries were used to overthrow one Irish king after another. The Normans and Irish fought each other over the course of a few years with the Norman armies holding territory while also expanding. This culminated in Henry II arriving to Ireland in October 1171 to finish the war and assert control of Ireland personally. "It was at this time [Christmas of 1171] that the archers laid violent hands on the trees planted by the hands of the saints in old times round the cemetery at Finglass, and were carried off by a new sort of pestilence..."[130] The author of these historical annals saw fit to point out this sacrilege to indicate the impiety of the conquer-

---

129 Sebastian Lidbetter, "Hadrian IV (1154-1159) and the 'Bull' Laudabiliter: A Historiographical Review," Wilfrid Laurier University, 2019, accessed August 24th, 2023, https://scholars.wlu.ca/etd/2221. See page 106.

130 Thomas Wright, *The Historical Works of Giraldus Cambrensis*, 232.

ors towards the established church and life in Ireland. The profaning of sacred sites thus shows the irreverence characteristic of papal armies in acquiring a hold of Ireland and forcing its church into heresy.

The Synod of Cashel is the tool which brought about this transition from Orthodoxy to Papalism. After the murder or forcible submission of political and ecclesiastic leaders from much of Ireland, this synod was convened by the authority of King Henry II. The Synod was "recounted and carefully reduced to writing under the seal of the bishop of Lismore, who, as the Pope's legate, presided at the synod."[131] A constitution was put forward with decrees "reforming" the Irish Church and in its final decree stated "That divine offices shall be henceforth celebrated in every part of Ireland according to the forms and usages of the church of England. For it is right and just that, as by divine Providence Ireland has received her lord and king from England, she should also submit to a reformation from the same source. Indeed both the realm and church of Ireland are indebted to this mighty king for whatever they enjoy of the blessings of peace and the growth of religion; as before his coming to Ireland all sorts of wickedness had prevailed among this people for a long series of years, which now, by his authority and care of the administration, are abolished." We can surmise that at this point (at the latest) the *filioque* entered the Creed, leavened bread used for the Eucharist was replaced with unleavened bread, commemorating the heretical Pope, and all other abuses and innovations from the Pope found their way into Ireland.

---

131 Ibid. 232.

C. THE SACK, OCCUPATION, & RECAPTURE OF CONSTANTINOPLE (1204-1261)

THE STATE

The pillage and overthrow of Constantinople with the Fourth Crusade in 1204 resulted in renewed efforts at a union of churches by the Latins on the Orthodox east by coercion. The papacy desired this union in order to gain ecclesiastical authority over the Orthodox Christian Church. For the exiled Emperor in Nicea, the primary goal was to regain his throne in Constantinople, in addition to ensuring Latin help against Turkish attacks or future Latin crusades; a task which could only be accomplished with either the assistance or neutrality of the Pope. During that era, the emperors used the potential of a union as an enticement to garner papal support or neutrality.

With the downfall of Constantinople, the political landscapes of the east and west were in constant change. The Latin Empire of the east (known to the Latins as Romania) was formed by the remnants of the Eastern Roman Empire in Constantinople and various areas where eastern imperial rivals were exiled. The Franks and Venetians, the two major forces responsible for the crusade's success, met to elect a new Emperor. Emperor Baldwin I was chosen as the weaker candidate instead of Boniface, the Margrave of Montferrat, whose ambitions caused fear to the Venetians.

Enthroned in Hagia Sophia on May 16, 1204, as the Latin Emperor of Constantinople, Baldwin replaced the East Roman imperial system with a Frankish feudal system, rewarding his knights with distribution of lands seized from the Roman nobility. Constantinople itself was divided, with 3/8 being Venetian, awarded to Enrico Dandolo the Doge who had backed the conquest, and 5/8 for the Latin Emperor. Dandolo was exempt from any feudal monetary obligation and the Venetians also came away from the conquest with control of all the sea routes from their city-state to Constantinople. With so many areas under different authorities, this feudal structure weakened the Latin Empire.

Boniface was given lands in Asia Minor but also managed to secure lands in Thessaloniki, Athens, Thebes, all of Thessaly and Macedonia, since the lords in these kingdoms were indebted to him for militarily securing their positions. Although not chosen by the Venetians as Emperor for fear of his power, he had still managed to become a threat. The Latins refused to allow the Bulgarians in Thrace to retain their lands, violating a previous agreement. Around that time, the Bulgarian Tsar who had at first recognized the papacy, returned to the Orthodox Church and offered exile to Patriarch John X at the time of the sacking of Constantinople. When the revolt in Thrace occurred, Kaloyan aided the Bulgarian people against the Latins. Baldwin was taken prisoner in the Battle of Adrianoupolis in spring 1205 and executed. The Latin Empire suffered losses with the death of Baldwin, the loss in Thrace and the retreat of Latins from Asia Minor. However, Baldwin's successor, his brother Henry, managed to recapture much of Thrace and endeared himself to all his citizens as he was a more diplomatic ruler.

His death after 10 years of rule created a decline in power and unity in the empire as he left no male heirs and subsequent rulers did not have similar leadership skills. In 1217, Peter of Courtenay, his brother-in-law, was the first to succeed him. Married to Yolande, sister of both of the first two Emperors of "Romania," he was taken prisoner on his way from Rome to Constantinople and was probably executed around the year 1219 during his imprisonment. His wife ruled until her death in 1219, at which time her son Robert inherited the throne as his older brother refused it. He was a weak ruler, marrying the daughter of the exiled emperor in Nicea who laid claim to the throne of the East Romans. He died fleeing from Constantinople when his subjects revolted. His reign saw the ceding of some Latin lands to the Greek despots in exile. This gave power to efforts by the exiled nobles to regain East Roman lands and these changes only increased the chaos in the Latin kingdoms of the east with ever-weakening rulers.

The Latin throne then transferred to Robert's younger brother Baldwin II, who was a minor. Considering the good relations with the Bulgarians, it was arranged that Baldwin would be betrothed to the daughter of the Bulgarian Tsar John and the Tsar would become the acting imperial regent. The Latins decided to give control of the Empire to the king of one of the ruled states created by the Crusaders, John of Jerusalem, who was eighty. He was crowned co-Emperor with Baldwin in 1231 and ruled until his death in 1237. Before John's death, Baldwin traveled on two trips selling religious artifacts, including pieces of the True Cross of Christ, in order to obtain funds for his kingdom. By the end of his reign in 1261, the Latin Empire had been reduced to the confines of the city of Constantinople. When the city was recaptured in July 1261, Baldwin the last Emperor of Romania, escaped to the West and died in 1273.

The Orthodox were no less removed from the chaos brought about by the downfall of Constantinople with power struggles between the East Romans in exile and changing loyalties which accounts for why they did not attempt to take back Constantinople sooner and makes it an incredible feat that they managed to restore their empire. In analyzing the political powers that influenced the restoration of the Roman Empire, there were three main kingdoms: Trebizond, which was established almost at the same time as the sack of Constantinople and ruled by members of the Comnenos family who had fallen from power, also Epirus, then also Nicea which were established as a result of the fleeing of the refugees and were ruled by exiled nobles of the Eastern Roman Empire. Grandson Alexios Comnenos was Emperor of the city of Trebizond, a fertile land located several hundred miles from the Latins where maritime and caravan routes met and traded, making the city flourish. His younger brother David started an expedition westward and when the Latins heard of it, they made an agreement to support him against rival imperial claimants. This agreement came to an end in 1214 when the Emperors of Nicea and Constantinople signed a treaty defining and recognizing each other's territorial boundaries.

After 1214, Nicea advanced into Trebizond, but the Turks intervened when they got to Sinope. David was killed immediately but Alexios was captured and became a servant of the Turks to save himself and Trebizond. The kingdom had no real further influence on Romanity after this.

The Kingdom of Epirus was founded by Michael Angelos Dukas (Michael I) who originally desired a position with the Latins in Constantinople, but when this did not come to fruition, forced his cousin Alexios III to proclaim him a lord. He developed a strong military and made Epirus "a center for Byzantine resistance, ensuring that the Latinization of the Byzantines in exile would not come about by some simple process of political or cultural assimilation. It became, over time, the express aim and purpose of Michael and those under his influence to overthrow the Latins and to restore the Byzantine monarchy and its cultural, political and social heritage."[132]

His brother Theodore succeeded him in 1215, expanding the empire in Macedonia and around the Adriatic and also including Thessaloniki. This expansion coupled with the capture and execution of the Latin Emperor Peter was a large detriment to the Latin Empire. Crowned by the Serbian Archbishop of Ohrid, he took the title of Roman Emperor upon entering Thessaloniki, asserting his threat to the Latins.

He successfully took over Andrianopoulos on his way towards Constantinople, but was captured at the Battle of Klokotnitsa by the forces of John Asen II who had a pact with the Nicene Empire. He was blinded but released and Thessaloniki was removed from Epirus and ruled by two emperors, Theodore's brother Manuel (1230-1237) and then his son John (1237-1242). In 1242, John entered into a treaty with the Empire of Nicea in order to receive the title of lord, and dropping his claim to the imperial throne. In 1246, Nicea took Thessaloniki and John was imprisoned while his blind father was retired to a small estate. Epirus went to the illegitimate son, Michael II, of the illegitimate Michael I who, in attempting to take over parts of Macedonia broke a treaty with Nicea for which Theodore was imprisoned and Michael was brought

---

132 Archbishop Chrysostomos (González de Iturriaga Alexopoulos) of Etna, *Orthodox and Roman Catholic Relations* (Etna: Center for Traditionalist Orthodox Studies, 2001), 104.

into submission. Epirus survived as a kingdom but for several centuries did not play a significant role in the Empire.

The Empire of Nicea, unlike Epirus and Trebizond, was fertile, geographically close to Constantinople, well populated and had been the site of two Ecumenical Councils. Theodore Lascaris, son-in-law of Emperor Alexios II Angelos, had fled Constantinople to Brusa and then Nicea and avoided the Fourth Crusade. He successfully fought the Turks and nobles of Trebizond, and conquered the Anatolian coasts, establishing himself as the Emperor in 1208 by a newly-elected Patriarch in exile, which gave him legitimacy over rivals. In 1214, he signed an agreement with the Latins, defining the territories of the two states and therefore enabling him to concentrate on his rivalry with Trebizond. He married his third wife Maria, daughter of Yolande, regent of the empire and widow of Emperor Peter. In 1219, he initiated a failed attempt at having the Pope dissolve Romania by offering ecclesial unity. In the same year, he established commercial contracts with the Venetians which were economically beneficial.

In addition to limiting the power of the Latins and Empire of Trebizond, he also defeated the Turks, killing the Sultan in 1211 which secured the eastern side of his empire. He died in 1221 and was succeeded by his son-in-law, John III Dukas Vatatzes. Theodore's brothers attempted to overthrow Emperor John with the help of the Latins. The brothers were both captured and blinded in 1223. In 1225, after defeating the Latin soldiers who had supported the brothers, John signed a treaty in which the Latin Empire gave up almost all of its land in Asia Minor. Emperor John found an ally in the Bulgarian Tsar John Asen and in 1235, the Nicaean and Bulgarian forces set out to capture Constantinople. Asen turned around though, and joined with the Latins to take over Tzurulum, a city in Thrace. An epidemic broke out in which Asen lost his wife, son and the Bulgarian Patriarch and caused him to believe this was a divine judgment against his betrayal to Vatatzes. He made peace with Emperor John but after his death in 1241 and the invasion of the Mongols, the Bulgarian power was dissipated.

Emperor John conquered Thessaloniki in 1246 and gained influence in the Roman Empire with his marriage to the sister of the Emperor Frederick II, Constance (Anna), who converted to Orthodoxy.

His efforts were crucial to the restoration of the Roman Empire to Constantinople. During his reign, he increased the power and reputation of Nicea, and found favor with the citizens through increased education, the building of hospitals, and his merciful rule. He died in 1254 and was canonized 500 years later, Emperor John the Merciful.

John's successor was his son, Theodore II Lascaris, who was not well liked by the eastern nobility. His reign marked the end of the Roman stance of ecclesiastical compromise to the Latin Church for political reasons. He died of epilepsy after reigning for only four years. His seven-year-old son succeeded him to the throne under the regency of George Mazulon, Theodore's personal advisor. Mazulon was slain days after the death of the emperor and the regency passed to Michael Palaeologos, a man whom Theodore had no trust in. After defeating an attack on Nicea by Epirus, Sicily, and Latin rulers of some of the East Roman kingdoms, Michael set his sights on Constantinople. Realizing that the Venetians were a viable threat to this, he signed a treaty in 1261 with the Genoese, competitors of the Venetians, to give them maritime supremacy in the Mediterranean in return for protection against Venetian attack. With this in place, on June 25, 1261, the Nicene army overtook the city of Constantinople for the Byzantine Empire. Michael VIII was crowned Emperor in Hagia Sophia by the Patriarch. John IV Lascaris was blinded and imprisoned and Palaelogos became the last ruling family of the Eastern Roman Empire.

THE CHURCH

The Latin conquest of Constantinople during the Fourth Crusade resulted in the division of the Orthodox Church. There were the faithful who existed under the rule of the Latin Empire (Frankokratia), and those who were in exile. Those under the Latins were united to the papacy through forced conversion. They fell under a Latin Patriarch, Thomas Morosini, who was not at first authorized by Pope Innocent, but was eventually recognized and supported by him. While it is true that the Orthodox capitulated to this by the sheer reason of having been conquered and as a mechanism for self-preservation, a lesser understood reason is that those Orthodox under the Latin rule acted within certain theological and ecclesiological principles. Their capitulation to the Latins was administrative and did not change the spiritual experience of the Church, which was on a higher level and not based in external aspects of Church governance. "Papal attempts to impose Roman [i.e., Latin] standards and practice often resulted in compromise and concession. And yet, the living unity of Orthodoxy remained strong. Superficial submission for fear of retaliation did not mean surrender."[133]

Professor Geanopoulos writes that, "After the Fourth Crusade of 1204 many of the Greek clergy had been dispossessed of their ecclesiastical properties and the people forced to accept the supremacy of the Roman [i.e., Latin] Church... In addition, certain feudal practices characteristic of the Latin church had been imposed upon the Greek clergy, such as the taking of a compulsory personal oath recognizing papal authority through the clasping of one's hands within those of a Latin superior. Finally, a papal legate had even been dispatched to Constantinople to dictate ecclesiastical decisions, and in effect influence political decisions. Eloquent testimony of the deep Greek resentment towards their Latin conquerors is... [the fact that] ... the Greeks were accustomed to purify their altars following each use by the Latins, and to rebaptize their children after performance of the equivalent Latin rite."[134]

"Even in the very deference of the Orthodox to the Latins, and still more so in encounters such as the one described by Professor Vryonis, we see in essence the problem of the divergent ways in which the Byzantines and Westerners understood Church authority. Not only in the categorical Orthodox rejection of a Latin system of liturgics imposed on them by the supposed primacy of the Roman Church and of its customs and patterns of worship, but in their failure to grasp the very idea that prerogatives of an office or See could contain within them spiritual authority of a personal sort, one can easily perceive why the Orthodox Byzantines failed to come into union with the Latins and

---

133 Archbishop Chrysostomos (González de Iturriaga Alexopoulos) of Etna, *Orthodox and Roman Catholic Relations* (Etna: Center for Traditionalist Orthodox Studies, 2001), 114.

134 Ibid., 115.

why hope for reconciliation was impeded, not so much by external animosity, as by the ecclesial consciousness of the Orthodox."[135]

For the Orthodox, ecclesiastical authority is neither legalistic nor is it attached to a person in a specific office, but is derived from historical succession which does not preclude fallibility, and pays obedience to those in spiritual authority through spiritual illumination. "*Ex oriente lux, ex occidente lex*," "light from the East, law from the West" aptly describes the two churches. The Eastern Church, while uniform in dogma and doctrine, was able to assimilate diverse liturgical traditions in rubrics and language. It was able to accept the idea of the papacy as a temporal authority over the Church as long as that authority did not extend to spiritual matters.

"Remarkably, even when the Orthodox were inclined to recognize their new political Latin masters, recognition of the existing ecclesiastical situation was resisted. In 1207, after the death of patriarch John X Camaterus in exile, and before the promotion of his successor..., the clergy and monks of Constantinople actually petitioned the Latin emperor Henry of Flanders to elect a new Patriarch. Although they had resolved to accept his authority as legitimate, they were unwilling to accept Morosini's or Innocent's.... All in all, Byzantium's 'catholic' grasp of primacy, directly possessed by each local church, in all its sacramental and hierarchical fullness, ...helps to explain why the unionist policy imposed on the East by the papacy in 1204 met with such stiff resistance. There was no way by which the East could have accommodated its own ecclesiology into Rome's centralism and absolutism. As a result, papal religious unity by compulsion never took root. It did not take long for the Orthodox to realize that Rome's transformation of its primacy and moral authority into direct dictatorial power was a threat to their own ecclesial integrity and identity. Their underground activity, frequent open opposition, hostility, and recalcitrance, were evidence of this intuition."[136]

---

135 Archbishop Chrysostomos (González de Iturriaga Alexopoulos) of Etna, *Orthodox and Roman Catholic Relations*, (Etna: Center for Traditionalist Studies, 2001), 116.

136 Ibid., 119.

The East Romans were willing to give the Pope primacy of honor, but only if there was ecclesiological unity with the papists abandoning the doctrinal and liturgical innovations that had been introduced into the Latin church. Policies instituted against the Orthodox were varied. Pope Innocent III, wanting to win over the Orthodox faithful, declared the Mount Athos properties protected. The Greek priests in the Latin lands were allowed to keep the Churches in areas that were inhabited mostly by Greeks, but in mixed areas, the bishops were made to be Latins. Some Greek priests defied Latin ecclesiastical orders and kept contact with Greek clergy in non-Latin areas. Greek clergy who conformed to papal directives often were removed by Latin bishops who wanted to take over all the bishoprics. The diocese was restructured according to economic or political value, further giving incentive to the Latin bishops to desire the financially healthier sees under the Greek bishops. Most Latin bishops, not having a deep religious life, viewed the Greek parishioners as schismatics. Innocent III mandated rebaptism and reordination for Orthodox who joined the Westerners. Instead of a unified *Romania*, the changes resulted in a heterogeneous mix tending towards the mistreatment of Greek traditions and customs.

The Orthodox in exile lands struggled with the geographical and political divisions. With the death of Emperor Alexios III in 1206, the Latins would not allow the election of a new Greek Orthodox Patriarch in Constantinople. The exiled Orthodox turned to the exiled states and Theodore Lascaris directed the Orthodox ecclesiastical authorities in Constantinople to convene in Nicea and elect a new Patriarch. Michael IV Autorianos, well-educated and an ecclesiastical finance minister, was selected and he crowned Lascaris in 1208, making Nicea the new political and ecclesiastical hub of Orthodoxy, although Lascaris was not recognized by Innocent III and other bishops in exile such as the Despots in Epirus did not recognize him. Their local synod of Bishops acted independently of Nicea, attempting to progress to the establishment of an autocephalous Church that would also encompass Serbia. To counter this, Nicea established a Serbian Archbishopric under Sava. In 1232, Epirus was brought back into canonical union with Nicea when it was forced to surrender its claims to the throne.

The Eastern Empire also struggled in conflicts with the Bulgarians. After prolonged fighting led by Emperor Isaac II, a peace treaty was signed which founded the Archbishopric of Turnovo, with a self-proclaimed primacy. In 1190 and 1194, despite the peace treaty, the Romans invaded Bulgaria but were defeated. In 1195, Alexios III usurped the throne in Constantinople and had his brother Isaac II, who was leading offensives against Bulgaria, blinded, which ended the assaults on Bulgaria. In 1207, Tsar Kaloyan accepted his crown from a Cardinal sent to Bulgaria by the Pope and appointed the Archbishop of Turnovo the primate of the Bulgarian Church. Kaloyan's successor Tsar Asen reneged on the alliance with Rome, paving way in 1235 to align with Nicaea, whereupon the Nicaean Church and state granted the establishment of the Bulgarian Patriarchate underneath Constantinople. With all rivals to the ecclesiastical claims taken care of, Nicea had established itself as the Roman seat of Orthodoxy, paving the way for its return to Constantinople.

Throughout the time of Latin occupation of Constantinople, various meetings between the Orthodox Church and the Papists were held. In the initial meeting in 1204 with Cardinal Peter Capuano, he demanded the immediate Orthodox obedience to the Latin Patriarch and Pope. The Orthodox response was that they did not believe in papal supremacy and John X, living in exile, was still their ecclesiastical Patriarch. In 1206, Cardinal Benedict traveled through Greece after his appointment to Constantinople in 1205. His conversations with the Greeks led him to believe they could be persuaded to accept the primacy of the Pope. When he arrived for three meetings in Constantinople, the Orthodox representatives, Monk John and Deacon Nicholas Mesarites, rejected union as Christ is the head of the Church and not the Pope. Patriarch John had died recently, but they made it clear that they were loyal to the Patriarchate in Nicea. A request for the Pope to elect an Orthodox Patriarch of Constantinople was denied, and a year later the Patriarchate in exile was established in Nicea. Many clergy from Constantinople fled to the Church in Nicea, preferring rule under the Turks than not remaining true to the Orthodox faith.

In 1214 after the appointment of Cardinal Pelagius as Papal Legate in Constantinople, another meeting between the Latins and Orthodox was held in Constantinople and Nicea. The Cardinal felt the need to make an effort at accord as the elected Patriarch in Nicaea, Theodore II Irenicos, was anti-Latin and encouraging the Orthodox to resist Latinization. The meeting in Constantinople concentrated on Latin demands for the Orthodox to submit to papal supremacy. The talks were not fruitful. In Nicea, the talks concerned papism but also the *filioque* which had been inserted into the Western Creed. This meeting did not end in agreement either.

In 1215, the Latins held the Fourth Lateral Council where the innovated parallel Latin Papist Patriarchates of Constantinople, Antioch and Jerusalem who were founded when these cities fell to the Crusaders were in attendance.[137] The main topics of discussion concerned the Papists, and the issue of the Orthodox in the Latin Empire was raised but was not a large concern. The notion that this was a "union council" was rejected since no Orthodox Christian representatives were invited as Pope Innocent considered the Orthodox to be part of the papal faith by virtue of their being conquered.[138] This council granted Constantinople the place of second in honor to Rome in the fifth canon, although the Fourth Ecumenical Council in 451 had already declared Constantinople Patriarchal status second only to Rome in honor but at the time without the approval of the Roman Church. The fourth constitution from the Forth Lateran Council notes that, "The Greeks [Orthodox Christians] even had the temerity to rebaptize those baptized by the Latins; and some, as we are told, still do not fear to do

---

137 *Latin Patriarchates*: The Latin Patriarchates were the anti-canonical and anti-ecclesiastical innovations of the Latin Papists when they invaded the ecclesiastical territory of Orthodox Christians during the Frankish Invastions (called "Crusades" in the West). These Latin Patriarchates were created in Antioch (1098), Alexandria (1219), Constantinople (1204), and Jerusalem (1099) and expelled the canonical Orthodox Christian Patriarchs of these ancient sees. The Papists maintained these anti-Orthodox, Latin Patriarchates of Antioch, Alexandria, and Constantinople for 760 years until their final abolishment by Pope Paul VI in 1964. The so-called Latin Patriarchate of Jerusalem is still in existence and is located in the Church of the Holy Sepulchre in Jerusalem.

138 *Fourth Lateran Council:* The Fourth Council of the Lateran took place in Rome in 1215 and is considered by the Papists to be the "12th Ecumenical Council" of the twenty-one so-called "Ecumenical Councils" recognized by the Latin confession.

this"[139] which attests to the Orthodox Christian adherence to the Church's teaching that there are no mysteries (baptism, chrismation, eucharist, etc.) outside of the Holy Orthodox Church.

In 1219, Emperor Theodore I Lascaris married as his third wife Maria, daughter of Yolande, regent of the Empire. He attempted to convince the Orthodox Patriarchs of Constantinople (in Nicaean exile), Alexandria, Antioch and Jerusalem to convene a synod in order to unite with the Church of Rome. Lascaris' motivations were clearly politically motivated and not at all concerned with theological matters. On account of his marriage, the Greeks in Epirus accused him of disloyalty and John, the ruling bishop of Nafpaktos suggested that the reclaiming of Constantinople could not occur with a union with the papacy. As he realized the restoration of the Eastern Romans in Constantinople was a true possibility, he did not fight against the anti-union stance of the Patriarchs.

As most Roman emperors of the times, Emperor John Vatatzes had similar political motivations for a union, with one of the stipulations being the surrender of the Latin Empire. Like Lascaris, John had also married the daughter of a Latin ruler, Emperor Frederick II. However, as the Latins no longer were in a powerful position, the East Romans did not have to make large concessions. Germanos II, Patriarch of Nicea, in 1232 sent a request to Pope Gregory IX to re-open dialogue between the Orthodox churches and the Papists resulting in a period of discourse from 1236-1256. In the first two meetings in 1234, the Pope sent a delegation of monks to Nicaea where the *filioque* and use of leavened or unleavened bread was discussed. While the meeting began in a conciliatory fashion, it devolved into a shouting match, each side accusing the other of being the heretics.

Pope Innocent IV's reign from 1243-1254 witnessed numerous meetings of the Latins and Orthodox. He was particularly focused on promoting positive interaction between Constantinople and Nicea and was concerned with the relation of Frederick II and John Vatatzes. Negotiations stopped in 1254 with the deaths of Emperor John and

---

139 "Fourth Lateran Council: 1215, 4th Constitution, On the pride of the Greeks towards the Latins," Papal Encyclicals Online, accessed December 16th, 2022, https://www.papalencyclicals.net/councils/ecum12-2.htm#4

Pope Innocent, but no agreement had been reached prior to that as Emperor John no longer needed papal support to attempt to regain Constantinople. John's son, Emperor Theodore II Lascaris, succeeded him to the throne and negotiations with the Pope's successor, Alexander IV, were unsuccessful as Theodore wanted many theological and political changes in order to achieve union and Alexander could not give the city to the Emperor.

The history of this time period demonstrates that the Roman Emperors' goal of restoring the Roman Empire to Constantinople shaped their interactions with the Latins in order to gain political aid or neutrality to accomplish this. The presupposition for a union between the two churches was always the same: For the Orthodox, the Latins needed to reject *Romanity*. Similarly, the papacy offered military aid or neutrality if the Orthodox only would acknowledge the supremacy of the See of Old Rome. Both sides had reason for enmity against the other; the Orthodox against the Latins as their conquerors and as theological innovators; and for the Latins, the Orthodox being so-called "schismatics" and unwilling to recognize their heretical Latin doctrine of papal supremacy.

While the Emperors were willing to use union of the Orthodox Church with Old Rome to restore Eastern Romans to Constantinople, they did not disavow the Orthodox faith itself. This is evident in the Bulgarian and Serbian rulers returning to the Orthodox Church once their powers were consolidated and also when it was obvious that the return of Romanity to Constantinople was possible, that the ecclesiastical dialogues were tapered off. Towards the end of the era when the East Romans were able to envision their return to Constantinople and were not negotiating from a position of desperation, the negotiations moved away from the issue of papal primacy only and included concerns of theology — the *filioque* and use of leavened and unleavened bread — signifying a genuine interest in reconciliation. On a personal level, there were interactions that were amiable such as when five stranded Franciscan monks returning from Turkish captivity were offered help by the Nicene Empire.

"Force and conquest during the era of the Empire of Romania helped to shape the psychologies and ecclesiologies of the East and

West, and especially the collision between the realities of the Orthodox struggle for political and cultural survival and the rise of Papism; more importantly, in affording us the opportunity to isolate these elements, the experiences of the period of the Latin yoke help us, in turn, to develop a better understanding of why later contact between the East and West were doomed to fail at achieving Church unity."[140]

140 Archbishop Chrysostomos (González de Iturriaga Alexopoulos) of Etna, *Orthodox and Roman Catholic Relations* (Etna: Center for Traditionalist Orthodox Studies, 2001), 136.

D. EYEWITNESS ACCOUNT OF 1204 BY NIKETAS CHONIATES (1155-1217)[141]

How shall I begin to tell of the deeds wrought by these nefarious men! Alas, the images, which ought to have been adored, were trodden under foot! Alas, the relics of the holy martyrs were thrown into unclean places! Then was seen what one shudders to hear, namely, the divine body and blood of Christ was spilled upon the ground or thrown about. They snatched the precious reliquaries, thrust into their bosoms the ornaments which these contained, and used the broken remnants for pans and drinking cups, precursors of Antichrist, authors and heralds of his nefarious deeds which we momentarily expect. Manifestly, indeed, by that race then, just as formerly, Christ was robbed and insulted and His garments were divided by lot; only one thing was lacking, that His side, pierced by a spear, should pour rivers of divine blood on the ground.

Nor can the violation of the Great Church be listened to with equanimity. For the sacred altar, formed of all kinds of precious materials and admired by the whole world, was broken into bits and distributed among the soldiers, as was all the other sacred wealth of so great and infinite splendor. When the sacred vases and utensils of unsurpassable art and grace and rare material, and the fine silver, wrought with gold, which

141 University of Pennsylvania Press, "The Sack of Constantinople: Accounts of the Sack by Niketas Choniates," in *Translations and Reprints from the Original Sources of European History, Volume III* (Philadelphia: University of Pennsylvania Press, 1912), 15-16.

encircled the screen of the tribunal and the ambo, of admirable work-manship, and the door and many other ornaments, were to be borne away as booty, mules and saddled horses were led to the very sanctuary of the temple. Some of these which were unable to keep their footing on the splendid and slippery pavement, were stabbed when they fell, so that the sacred pavement was polluted with blood and filth.

Nay more, a certain harlot, a sharer in their guilt, a minister of the furies, a servant of the demons, a worker of incantations and poisonings, insulting Christ, sat in the patriarch's seat, singing an obscene song and dancing frequently. Nor, indeed, were these crimes committed and others left undone, on the ground that these were of lesser guilt, the others of greater. But with one consent all the most heinous sins and crimes were committed by all with equal zeal. Could those, who showed so great madness against God Himself, have spared the honorable matrons and maidens or the virgins consecrated to God?

Nothing was more difficult and laborious than to soften by prayers, to render benevolent, these wrathful barbarians, vomiting forth bile at every unpleasing word, so that nothing failed to inflame their fury. Whoever attempted it was derided as insane and a man of intemperate language. Often, they drew their daggers against anyone who opposed them at all or hindered their demands.

No one was without a share in the grief. In the alleys, in the streets, in the temples, complaints, weeping, lamentations, grief, the groaning of men, the shrieks of women, wounds, rape, captivity, the separation of those most closely united. Nobles wandered about ignominiously, those of venerable age in tears, the rich in poverty. Thus it was in the streets, on the corners, in the temple, in the dens, for no place remained unassailed or defended the suppliants. All places everywhere were filled full of all kinds of crime. Oh, immortal God, how great the afflictions of the men, how great the distress!

E. CAPTURE OF DYRRACHION & THESSALONIKI[142]

INHUMANITY OF THE LATIN CONQUERORS & SACRILEGE AGAINST ORTHODOXY[143]

What evil was left undone by this Roman-hater who had stored up such animosity against every Hellene, which not even the serpent, the ancient plotter against the human race, had once conceived and born? Because the most accursed Latins liken to true paradise the land which is our allotted portion to inhabit, and to reap the fruits thereof, and because they are madly in love with our blessings, they are always hostile to our race, and are forever the engineers of evil. Though they may dissemble friendship, adapting to the circumstances, they hate us as their worst enemies, and though their words are affable and softer than oil flowing without sound, yet they are darts and thus sharper than a double-edged sword. Between us and them the greatest chasm of divergence has been established; our way of thinking is incompatible with theirs; and we are

---

142 Alicia Simpson, Niketas Choniates: *A Historiographical Study* (Oxford: Oxford University Press, 2013), 319-320.

143 The historian Niketas Choniates (1155-1217) is giving his own brief report of the capture of Dyrrachion & Thessaloniki during the Latin conquest and sack of the East Roman Empire in 1204. Choniates, like many other Romans, believe that this illegal conquest by the Latin Papists was done out of envy of the beauty and riches of East Roman lands and that their enmity is masked by pseudo-friendship when it suited their needs; and that there was a true hatred for the Orthodox Church and the Roman people.

separated at great length from each other even though we come into physical contact and often happen to share the same dwelling. Carrying their heads high most of the time and standing upright because of their pretentious haughtiness, the Latins observe our steps closely so that they are ready to bruise us and probe thoroughly the softness of our character and our humility, which is due to the modesty of our spirit. We, on the other hand, despise their arrogance, boastfulness, and pride, and the mucus discharged from their noses that keeps their head held high. We proceed against their pride and annihilate them with the help of Christ, who gives us the power to trample on serpents and scorpions and grants us protection from all harm and wrongdoing.

F. EPITAPHIOS FOR
JOHN MESARITES (1206)[144]

Introductory Note[145]: Nikolaos Mesarites was an ecclesiastical writer in Constantinople who, along with his brother John resisted the uncanonical appointment of a new patriarch over Constantinople by the Latins shortly after the start of the *Frankokratia* (rule of the Latins following their conquest of the City in 1204). After his brother's death, Nikolaos composed an honorific and lengthy epitaph for his brother which details the intense argumentation between a Latin Cardinal, Benedict (representing the false Latin Patriarch), and the Orthodox monks of the city (believed to be represented by John Mesarites, himself). After his brother's death in 1207, Nikolaos left Constantinople for the Empire of Nicaea and became the Metropolitan of Ephesus. What follows is an excerpt of the *Epitaphios* which records the dialogue between the Cardinal Benedict and the Orthodox monks of Constantinople.

---

144 Nikolaos Mesaritēs, *Nicholas Mesarites: His Life and Works (in Translation)*, ed. Michael Angold (Liverpool: Liverpool University Press, 2017), 175-184. Footnotes from the original text.

145 Introductory note from The Orthodox Ethos team.

Friday 29 September Indiction X 6715 [A.D. 1206][146]

Cardinal Benedict[147] and the Latin patriarch Thomas,[148] [who had been] sent out by the Roman pontiff, summoned the monks residing on the Marmora islands and on Mount Auxentios, who assembled in the Thomaites hall,[149] where they found the prelates ready to receive them. They listened to what the latter had to say, After the cardinal had made his normal verbose peroration, he addressed the following words to the monks: "How Greeks, do you have the effrontery not to submit to your patriarch sent to you by the pope? Why do you refuse to recognise him as patriarch and to record him in your sacred diptychs? For the pope is head of all churches and has the authority to act as he likes in churches the world over. You well know that if you fail to do as he requires, you run the severe risk of incurring our indignation [not only] because [you are] contumacious, but also because you [are ignoring] the injunction of the Apostle Paul to submit to the prevailing powers" (Colossians 1:16).

The monks:[150] "We, your lordship, are neither contumacious nor do we oppose the traditions established by the apostles and the synods. If we have so far failed to record in our sacred diptychs the patriarch sent by the pope, it is because we had a patriarch, whom we always remembered in our prayers. While he was numbered among the living, we could not remember any other [patriarch] in our prayers. Following his recent departure[151] to our Lord we have not nor would we have been able to remember any other patriarch in our prayers, since we are still

146 The heading reads as follows in cod. Mosqu. Syn gr. 393(214) and cod. Athous Iberon 382: 'In the year 6715 debate of Cardinal Benedict with the monks [resident] in the city, recorded by Mersarios on Thursday 29 Sepmteber of the first indiction.'

147 Of Sta Susanna.

148 See *Oxford Dictionary of Byzantium III*, sub Thomas Morosini.

149 See K. Dark and J. Kostenec, 'The patriarchal palace at Constantinople in the seventh century: Locating the Thomaites and the Makron', *JOB*, 64 (2014), 33-40.

150 A marginal note adds: 'That is to say the *hieromonachos* John Mesarites.'

151 The patriarch John X Kamateros died on 26 May 1206.

without a patriarch. According to the prevailing usage we remember the whole Orthodox episcopate in the place of a patriarch."

The cardinal: "You have done well not to remember any other patriarch, while yours was still alive. Since he has now paid his eternal debt, you are obliged to submit to the patriarch sent by the pope and to remember him in your prayers. I have been sent specifically to install him in office."

The monks: "It is our task, your lordship, to tell you that in accordance with apostolic and canonical traditions we did not remember another in our prayers, while he was living; nor following his death are we able to remember any other patriarch until we have another patriarch established according to the holy and sacred canons and according to the ancient custom prevailing among us."

The cardinal: "This man is your patriarch and no other having been sent to you from the apostolic throne, which has the power of binding and loosing whatever it chooses in the manner of Peter, the first of the apostles, and the power of ordaining whomsoever it pleases to churches throughout the whole world. To Peter alone among the apostles did Christ give the keys of the kingdom of Heaven."

The monks: "If this is the truth, your lordship, that the throne of Rome possesses canonical authority to ordain a patriarch for this [see], show us and we shall remain silent and accept it."

And the cardinal: "Is the throne of Peter, the first of the apostles, not Rome?"

The monks: "No, your lordship. The twelve apostles were sent by our Saviour Christ, as ecumenical teachers to the whole world, for which reason they did not have thrones peculiar to each of them. How was it possible for each to preside in a particular place, when they were sent to teach the whole world the message of salvation? Consequently, each built upon the teaching of the other and taught those who had received instruction from another, [which means that] there is no difference of status among them. After bishops were everywhere established in cities the present hierarchy was instituted to prevent one bishop interfering in the diocese of another unless requested to by the bishop of the diocese."

The cardinal: "What you say is not true! We have demonstrated to you that the twelve apostles had thrones peculiar to themselves. For example, James, being one of the twelve, had as his personal throne the church of Jerusalem, as Peter had Rome and so on."

The monks: "You are getting confused, your lordship, by identical names, for the James who was an adornment to the church of Jerusalem was not one of the twelve."

The cardinal: "He certainly was one of the twelve, for the Apostle Paul says, 'But other of the apostles saw I none, save James, the Lord's brother' (Gal. 1:19). Is Paul lying?"

The monks: "By the mouth of our Lord, your lordship, Paul does not lie. James, the brother of our Lord, was an apostle, but not one of the twelve, being numbered among the seventy."

All the Latins asserted that he was of the twelve, while the monks said this was not the case. There was uproar and the Latins had a New Testament brought in, so that the passage in question could be read out: "These are the names of the apostles..." And when they reached "James the son of Alphaeus" (Mat. 10:3) the Latins all raised their voices [in triumph] as though condemning the monks.

The monks told the [Latins] that the son of Alphaeus and the brother of God were separate individuals. They explained who the son of Alphaeus was and who the brother of God was. Having thus dumbfounded the [Latins] they began once again to demonstrate that Rome was not the throne of the Apostle Peter. "For if Rome was the throne of Peter how is it that the first bishop of Rome was Linos, one of the seventy, and after him the second was Xystos, while the Apostle Peter ordained Clement as the third bishop of Rome? And how was it that one of the seventy had precedence over the Apostle Peter, the first of the twelve [apostles], so that it was the former who was the first to reign as bishop of the then first and Queen of cities? It is not [as you would have it]! But as we said, the seventy – together with other bishops – had different cities as their particular thrones, in contrast to the twelve apostles, who were teachers to the whole ecumene. It was for this reason that Peter did not depart for Rome as bishop, but wandered as far as Rome in pursuit of Simon Magus with the aim of confounding his teachings. There he confronted Simon Magus and encompassed his death by admonishing the demons, who carried him through the air to stop carrying him, but let him fall to earth at the spot over which he was being carried. Peter met his blessed end at the order of Nero on the grounds of causing the murder of, as Nero thought, such a great and godlike man."

These words halted them in their tracks, so they tried another tack.

The cardinal: "Well now, just as you say, is Rome not the head of all churches?"

The monks: "Who is it, your lordship, who says that Rome is not the head or the first [of all the churches]? It is head, but of all the churches under it, just as following apostolic and conciliar canons the church of Alexandria [is head] of those under it and the church of Antioch of those under it and the church of Jerusalem of those under it and the church of Constantinople of all the churches under it. Rome is first among the churches, not because it is the oldest—the first and mother of churches is the church of Jerusalem—but because it is the highest-ranking throne. For which reason the bishop of Rome only [has the right to be] called the bishop of the highest-ranking throne, not the senior high priest, nor the first; not the great high priest nor the pinnacle of high priests, nothing of that sort, but only the bishop of the highest-ranking throne. It is and is called the highest-ranking throne because after conversion to Christianity [Rome] happened to be the seat of Empire and senate. For [much the same] reason the church of Constantinople was given precedence over the church of Alexandria and equal honours with the first and older Rome and was called New Rome."

The cardinal: "And does not the bishop of Rome possess the authority to judge all bishops?"

The monks: "Not at all, your lordship! According to the canons clergy are all judged by their own bishops, the bishops by their metropolitans, the metropolitans by the synod and their patriarchs, whom they recognize as their heads and by whom they were ordained. The expulsion of a patriarch by his own synod is not a problem as long as he accepts the judgment of his own synod. If, however, he finds fault with it, he has the right, as long as they are in communion, to resort to the judgment of the pope. So, when wrongfully expelled from his own church, the great Athanasios[152] resorted to the then bishop of Rome, just as at the same time, when Paul the Confessor,[153] bishop of Constantinople, was similarly driven from his church by Constantius,[154] the son of Constantine the Great, acting with his fellow Arians, he too resorted to Rome. Both men recovered their particular thrones as a result of the council called on the order of the two brother emperors at Serdica,[155] now called Triaditza, to examine the fury directed by the Arians against the council of Nicaea. It also issued canons dealing with appeals to the pope, who comes first in both the prayers of remembrance and in ecclesiastical ranking, but only when he is in communion with the other patriarchs. The above-mentioned canons do not give him the right to appoint a bishop or a patriarch for regions that are not subject to him and so it has been from the beginning."

The cardinal: "And on what basis are you able to demonstrate that the pope does not have the authority to make bishops and patriarchs wherever he pleases and that he is not able to examine all patriarchs and bishops?"

---

152 *Oxford Dictionary of Byzantium* I, sub Athanasios.

153 *Oxford Dictionary of Byzantium* III, sub Paul I.

154 *Oxford Dictionary of Byzantium* I, sub Constantius II.

155 *Oxford Dictionary of Byzantium* III, sub Serdica, Local Council of. [Editor: often spelled "Sardica."]

The monks: "From these apostolic and conciliar canons." Adduced in evidence were the thirty-fourth canon of the Holy Apostles[156] and the thirty-fifth and -sixth canon of the first ecumenical council,[157] and then the third canon of the second ecumenical council[158] and the sixteenth of the synod held in the renowned church of the Wisdom of God the Word, which validated the seventh ecumenical council.[159] On the basis of these the monks were able to show that the bishop of Rome had no authority to ordain bishops or a patriarch anywhere except in cities that from the beginning were subject to him; furthermore, that the bishop of Rome was not superior to the bishop of Constantinople, except only in so far that it preceded it in time and in hierarchical standing, perhaps too in so far that it supervised appeals from other [patriarchates]. "We have no difficulty in demonstrating these things. The immense difficulty, not to say the impossibility, lies in your refusal to accept them. Even if it were our intention, we do not have to show proof—following the precedent set by the seven ecumenical councils—that [we have] an emperor, who is our co-religionist, as a condition of the validity of what we have demonstrated canonically."

A mischief-maker, reckoned by the Latins to be one of their learned men, failed to catch the words "who is our co-religionist" at the end of the phrase "for we do not have an emperor, who is our co-religionist." He therefore took to task the monk who was delivering the speech, [accusing him] of opposing imperial authority and saying "we do not have an emperor." Uproar ensued: the Latins cheered on their fellow-countryman and denied that the words 'who is our co-religionist' had been littered, while the Constantinopolitans insisted that they had been. With a gesture of his hand the monk who had been speaking stopped the noise

---

156 See *Oxford Dictionary of the Christian Church*, sub Apostolic Constitutions.

157 First Council of Nicaea (325).

158 First Council of Constantinople (381).

159 The Council of Constantinople (879-880). See Fr. George Dragas, "The Eighth Ecumenical Council: Constantinople IV (879/880) and the Condemnation of the Filioque Addition and Doctrine" (*The Greek Orthodox Theological Review*, Vol. 44, Nos. 1-4, 1999), 357-369. https://web.archive.org/web/20050817074822/ http://www.geocities.com/trvalentine/orthodox/dragas_eighth.html

both sides were making and requested that the interpreter say as loudly as possible how he had heard the words and how he had translated it. And under no compulsion the interpreter confessed the truth: that the monk had said, "Not having an emperor, who is a co-religionist," not just that he did not have an emperor.

When the interpreter said these things, the cardinal broke off from a properly conducted debate and began a vituperative attack on patriarchs, bishops, emperors, dignitaries and the whole people as contumacious. He called them Pharisees and accused them of slandering the Latins by stigmatizing them as so-called azymites[160] and as *pneumatomachoi*.[161] He even went so far as to accuse them of being heretics and other things besides.

He heard in reply the monks saying the following: "It is not right to blame others for what was done by others, particularly, if it is a matter of coarse types lacking education and refinement saying and doing inappropriate things, for which the educated are blamed. It is for this reason, your lordship, that, when we see disgusting acts carried out by your rabble, it does not cross our mind to blame the bishops of such people on the grounds that they act and think like them. To take one example, the holy icons are treated shamefully by your people, but would it be correct to suspect that your teachers [encouraged such behavior]? Of course, it wouldn't!"

So fuming with rage was the cardinal that he was unable to say anything in reply to these [words]. Abandoning dialogue, he spoke to the monks as follows.

The cardinal: "Too much talk leads nowhere, so tell me in a word whether or not you accept as your patriarch the patriarch, who was sent by the pope. Yes or no!"

The monks: "We, your lordship, are not able to think or say other than what has been passed down and taught to us. If you are able to prove that the canons are false, prove it!"

---

160 I.e. those that communicated with unleavened bread.

161 I.e. those that refused to accept the divinity of the Holy Spirit.

The cardinal: "You have until Monday to think over what you have been asked. This coming Monday you must say whether you will accept or will refuse to accept the patriarch as your patriarch." With that he rose and left in a fury.

MONDAY 2 OCTOBER, X INDICTION, 6715 (1206)

After again giving his usual verbose sermon, the cardinal spoke as follows to the monks: 'Answer, monks. Do you recognize the patriarch seated here as your patriarch?'

The monks: "While our patriarch lived, your lordship, we had no need of another patriarch. Now that he has come to the end of his human life, we seek another patriarch, but [he must be chosen] according to what is pleasing to God, according to the sacred and holy canons and according to the ancient custom that has prevailed among us for 870 years. If the prelate seated here was made patriarch in such wise, we shall recognize him and accept him. If, however, it was done in defiance of these [rules], how can we accept a state of affairs that threatens to separate us from God and is subject to anathema, since it goes counter to what we traditionally think and say?"

The cardinal: "I was sent by the pope with the express purpose of installing in his church, as your patriarch, one canonically ordained by [the pope]."

The monks: "Prove, your lordship, that he was canonically ordained according to the ancient custom that prevails among us and that will be sufficient."

The cardinal: "And how can you prove that what the pope does is not according to the canons?"

The monks: "From these canons!" And in the hearing of all there were read out the aforementioned canons, for in the first session only the chapter headings had been rehearsed. The cardinal listened to the canons without interruption and claimed not to know the canons.

The monks: "And what are we to do, your lordship, if you don't have the canons?"

The cardinal: "You have no right to say that the pope does not think and act correctly, for the Roman Church has never been guilty of wrong belief. All the heresies came from you Constantinopolitans: the heresies of Arius, Macedonius, Nestorius, and Eutyches,[162] and so on. But no heresy has ever had its origins with us."

The monks: "How can you say this, your lordship? Was not your bishop Honorius bishop of Rome? Was it not he who was dismissed and anathematized by the sixth ecumenical council[163] held in the reign of Constantine Poganates?"[164]

The cardinal: "You will not find any account of this written in the official record, but on a separate parchment"; thus casting aspersions on our official records.

The monks: "You will not find this account only in our records, your lordship, but in those of all other Christian peoples written in whatever language they speak. How then? Are their copies also suspect?"

The cardinal: "Forget about your quibbling! Say whether or not you will have the man sitting here as patriarch!"

The monks: "Listen patiently, your lordship, to what we propose over the matter under discussion and you will understand from what we are about to say what we think about the prelate who is present and more to the point what the canons enjoin. If we were to go back to for-

---

162 Fourth-and-fifth-century heretics: see *Oxford Dictionary of the Christian Church*, sub Arianism, Arius, Eutyches, Macedonius, Nestorius.

163 *Oxford Dictionary of Byzantium* I, sub Constantinople, Councils of: Constantinople III.

164 *Oxford Dictionary of Byzantium* I, sub Constantine IV.

mer times and it so happened that our patriarch had died or had rightly
or wrongly been expelled with the result that the church of Constantinople was without a bishop, a cleric of the Church of Constantinople
would depart with a suitable escort to see whoever was then pope of
Rome, as long as he was in communion with us. If having been ordained
by him bishop of Constantinople he was sent back, it would have been
our opinion that both ordinant and ordained should be dismissed, because both have acted against canon law and the ancient custom that
prevails among us. If it has been our intention to conform to canon law
over these matters, what do you imagine that we think both over the
question under discussion and over the prelate sitting next to you, when
he is a foreigner speaking a different tongue [from us] and when we do
not even know who he is or where he comes from?"

The cardinal had nothing to say in reply. For quite some time he
bowed his head and then raising it said to all the gathered monks and
laity, "Do you share the position set out by the monk[165] who is acting as
your spokesman or do you disagree? Speak!"

And all with one voice shouted out in ringing tones: "We are all of
one mind." For a moment the resounding reply of people united in voice
and soul disconcerted the cardinal and those with him.[166] [Eventually]
the cardinal [retorted], "I see that you are all contumacious, obstinate,
and impudent and display no signs of humility with the result that you
have no idea of what is good for you."

The monks: "Listen patiently, your lordship! We, whom you see
here assembled, are neither contumacious nor impudent, but every moment have been and still are being terribly humiliated by you. If we were
as refractory as you say we are, we would, along with other Constantinopolitans, have departed for the lands of Emperor Theodore Komnenos
Laskaris and for those of Lord David Komnenos and for those of the
barbarians, who share our faith, even for those of the Turks, as many
have done fleeing from the constant hardships and daily murders, which
you inflict upon us. However, we have not done so, making the correct

---

165 A marginal note adds: 'who was Mesarites.'

166 A marginal note adds: 'And right away the whole body of Italians asked whether
there was any other monk from among them, who would stand up.'

estimation, as we see it, that it is pleasing to God that we do not flee from you, [because] you have been sent by God to chastise and discipline us, but [rather] submit to the painful things that He has inflicted upon us for our sins, but certainly not for our bad faith. It is for this reason that we every day endure a myriad of evils suffered at the hands of your people and rejoice in Holy God, who has thus seen fit to wipe away our sins, [even though] we lack [our] daily sustenance. We may have been deprived of all possession, but we will have one source of wealth - our hallowed and orthodox faith, which you cannot take away from us, however much pain you contrive to inflict upon us. While we breathe, we shall never appear as traitors to our hallowed faith. It will not happen, even with the threat of death [hanging] over us."

Hearing this the cardinal once again bowed his head and calmed down a little, as though stupefied. He got up and taking the patriarch, who was sitting beside him, left the assembly, with orders to everybody not to break up the meeting but to await their return. After a little he resumed his feat, but without saying anything to the patriarch made way for the latter to take up the debate.

The patriarch: "The right thing for you to do, all you Greeks assembled here, is to show obedience both to the apostolic throne and to us, having been ordained and sent here on its behalf. Since you refuse to do so, after due deliberation we shall do what we consider is right for you." With these words he arose with the cardinal. It was in this way that the meeting broke up.

G. THE RECEPTION OF
THE COUNCIL OF FLORENCE
IN MOSCOW[167]

When the Metropolitan Photius died in 1431, Grand Prince Basil had a candidate ready for the vacant see in the person of Bishop Iona of Riazan', and Iona actually entered upon the duties of metropolitan-designate. In Constantinople, however, the metropolitanate was conferred on a rival candidate of the Grand Prince of Lithuania. Even the death of the Lithuanian metropolitan in 1435 did not advance Basil's plan; a Greek national appointee of the patriarch, Isidore, arrived in Moscow early in 1437. Some years later, Basil wrote to Patriarch Mitrophanes: "We do not know for what reason you did not accept our petition, or pay attention to our letters and our envoy [...] nor why you did not place Bishop Iona on the metropolitan see [...] but sent us one for whom we did not ask, namely, Isidore." The Grand Prince, however, was not forced to tolerate the company of the new metropolitan [for] very long, for Isidore left Moscow on his way to Ferrara on September 8, 1437.

After very active participation in favor of the Union, Isidore returned to Russia in 1440. For half a year, he stayed in Kiev, proclaiming the Union but provoking very little reaction in Southwest Russia. The Metropolitan entered Moscow on March 19, 1441. He entered the city, the chronicle tells us, as a papal legate, with a Latin cross carried be-

---

167 Michael Cherniavsky, "The Reception of the Council of Florence in Church History," *Church History: Studies in Christianity and Culture*, 24, no. 4. (December 1955): 347-359.

fore him, and at Mass in the cathedral he revealed his position: Instead of starting in the diptychs with the name of the oecumenical patriarch, he first intoned the name of the Roman Pope, Eugene; then, after the end of the service "Isidore ordered the proclamation of the decisions of this apostate eighth council. That is, of the sugar-coated falsities of the Latins; all this in order to remove Christendom from the Divine Revelation." Hearing all this, according to the chronicle, the Grand Prince understood the heresy of the "wolf-like" Isidore, would not accept the latter's benediction, and shortly decreed his deposition and removal from the metropolitan see. Isidore was arrested and imprisoned in the Chudov monastery, and Basil ordered him to be tried by a synod of archbishops and bishops. The metropolitan did not choose to wait for his trial; he escaped from the monastery, perhaps with the knowledge of the Russian authorities, and made his way finally to Rome.

So much, then, for the bare historical facts, presented with the bias of the Russian chronicles. It is my task to examine the reception of the proposed Church Union in Moscow, the immediate reaction in Russia to the news that the great schism within Christianity had been healed. What I have chosen to regard as "immediate" is the reaction that took place in the period between 1441, the year of Isidore's return to Moscow, and 1461, the year in which appeared the last Russian account of the council written by a participant. This chronological arbitrariness presents us with certain advantages — for 1461 is the last year in the reign of Grand Prince Basil II, the Dark, under whom all the events connected with the Council take place and all the eyewitness accounts are written. The long reign of his great son Ivan III may be regarded as the beginning of the intellectual exploitation of the Council, when the many implications of the events are realized, carried to their logical and illogical conclusions, and then made to serve as foundations for new ideological structures.

The sources important for our purpose all derive from the eyewitness account of Simeon [a companion of Isidore at Florence] and do not differ significantly in important details or in their ideological premises; these premises or biases are shown by Simeon from the very beginning. His opposition to the Union and to Isidore was so great that he actually ran away from the metropolitan's party on its way back, and after a short period of confinement in a monastery by the suspicious government, emerged as the anti-Union authority on the Council. Accordingly, it is possible to use all the sources almost indiscriminately in examining the Russian reaction to the Council.

The story of this reaction begins shortly after Isidore's arrival in Moscow, before he left for Italy, when, according to the chronicle, he "impudently began to discuss the journey to the Council." The Russian stand was established even before the Council met, and the developing myth, as it should, gained consistency and continuity. Thus, even before the prelates assembled at Ferrara, the Grand Prince showed his opposition to the very idea of an Eighth Oecumenical Council and of an Orthodox Union with the Latins whose heresies concerning both the bread and the wine of the Communion, and the procession of the Holy Spirit, were quite unacceptable; Greek teachers had done their work well in the preceding four and a half centuries. As to the idea of a Council, Basil, we are told, reminded the metropolitan of the "Commandments of the Holy Fathers who had accomplished the work of the Seventh Council, had included in their holy canons all of the divine law of the holy apostles and had sealed the holy Orthodox faith with the proclamation [...] of the divine Trinity; while they had cursed those contemplating an Eighth Council." Nevertheless, when the metropolitan insisted, Basil gave him permission to go, with a final injunction: "you are going to the Eighth Council, which should never take place according to the rules of the holy fathers; when you return from it, bring us back our ancient Orthodoxy which we have received from our ancestor Vladimir." From the beginning the Russian Grand Prince, defensor fidei, rejected both the Council itself and its purpose — the union of the two churches. In Russian eyes, no union was possible between Orthodoxy and heresy, no compromise; unless Rome turned Orthodox, the only possible results was the betrayal of Orthodoxy, betrayal of salvation of mankind. Also, within this concept, we find a change in the meaning of Orthodoxy, for Isidore was required to preserve the Orthodoxy of St. Vladimir rather than the one of Constantine and the Greeks; the ancient Russian faith and dogma became the standard of true Orthodoxy and of salvation; the myth was extended further and further back in time.

[When] the sessions began, and the Russian monk [Simeon] saw the outcome in very simple terms — the Byzantine Emperor, his patriarch and his metropolitans were bought by the papacy. The Greeks sold their faith for gold, or, like Isidore and others, for honours — a cardinal's hat, papal favour, bishoprics — and this becomes the only explanation then current in Russia. Isidore himself emerged as one of the most active participants, and Simeon's second redaction presents him as most instrumental in success of the Council, but, at least in the beginning, Isidore owed the high regard in which he was held to his being the Russian representative [a function of the respect given to Grand Prince Basil]. He was appointed to serve as the vicar of the Patriarch of Antioch because, Simeon wrote, "in Russia there was such high and Orthodox Christianity."

The only high Eastern cleric to escape Russian disapproval was St. Mark, the metropolitan of Ephesus, acting also as the vicar of the Patriarch of Alexandria. Mark was the defender of Orthodoxy, the confuser of his Latin enemies, the conscience of the emperor and patriarch; all the other Greek prelates went over to the Roman cause. However, though silent, the Russian delegation, headed by the Bishop of Suzdal, also remained faithful to the cause of salvation. Abraham the Bishop was, in fact, placed under arrest by Isidore to force him to sign the articles of Union, and the rest of the delegation was also threatened into acquiescence, but the fidelity to Orthodoxy of the Russians at Florence was taken for granted.

On his return Isidore, as we have seen, revealed his intentions; he entered Moscow as a papal legate intent on serving the Pope. He had already done so in Kiev and Smolensk, in the presence of Orthodox princes; the latter could not object, however, since they were vassals of a Polish Catholic king and therefore, the chronicle informs us, did not dare argue with Isidore. In Moscow, the metropolitan faced a different situation, for there ruled the "Faithful, Christ-loving, pious and truly Orthodox Grand Prince Vasilii Vasilievich, the white tsar of All Russia." The Grand Prince perceived the abominable heresy of Isidore before any of the Russian bishops did, and on his own authority deposed and imprisoned the metropolitan. Basil was young and ignorant, but he was strong in the faith, Simeon wrote, "burning with the flame of piety," and because of this he equalled in his actions the apostle-like Emperor Constantine, who had established Orthodoxy, and his own ancestor St. Vladimir, who had baptized Russia. Again, the Byzantine emperor in his shameful role at Florence is compared with the Russian ruler, and the author calls Basil the "New Constantine," the "Great, Sovereign, God-crowned Russian Tsar."

Two conclusions can be drawn: It was the Grand Prince himself who by exposing heresy saved Orthodoxy in Russia; and it was Russia which was the only Orthodox country left in the world. Basil II, therefore, not only fulfilled the highest function of rule in Russia, but became the instrument of salvation for the world as a whole: the tragedy of Florence became the great triumph of the Grand Prince of Moscow. So, it was, certainly, in the eyes of Simeon: through his marvelous intelligence and piety the Grand Prince has preserved Orthodoxy, exposed a heresy which was unnoticed by all the Russian bishops, and thwarted the infidels. The Grand Prince is the joy and hope of all the clergy, all the princes and all Christians in general.

The glory of the Russian prince is the more striking, however, against the background of the betrayal of Orthodoxy which took place at the Council; the significance of this betrayal in politico-theological terms was brought out by the author of the Selections; he first addressed the Byzantine emperor: "Oh great sovereign Emperor; why did you go to them? What were you thinking of? What have you done? You have exchanged light for darkness; instead of the Divine Law you have received the Latin faith; instead of truth and righteousness, you have loved flattery and falsity. Formerly you were the agent of piety, now you are the sower of evil seeds; formerly you were haloed by the light of the Heavenly spirit, now you are clothed in the darkness of unbelief." The Christian Emperor has betrayed his highest duty while the Grand Prince had fulfilled his own; completing the contrast, the Russian writer then addresses Russia: "It is fitting for you to rejoice in a people truly Orthodox in the universe, lighted by the rays of the sun. You are clothed with the light of true faith, having God's many coloured cloak of HIS great favour and benevolence. Rejoice in the sovereignty over you of the God-chosen, beloved-of-God, enlightened-of-God, glorified-of-God, wise-in-God seeker of the Holy Law, supreme mediator for the faith, beautified-of-God, greatly sovereign pious Grand Prince Vasilii Vasiliev-ich, God-crowned tsar of Orthodoxy and of all Russia."

The conclusions reached by Simeon are summarized once more by the writer — the divine election of the Russian people as bearers of true Orthodoxy, the controlling role in this Orthodoxy of the Grand Prince, and the equation which could derive out of it: the Grand Prince of Russia is the Orthodox emperor.

Finally, there was a change more directly related to the effects of the Union. For nine centuries the Church of Hagia Sophia in Constantinople had been the spiritual center of the world for Eastern Christianity; it embodied Orthodoxy and supremacy. Its antitype on the local level, during the early centuries of Christianity in Russia, had been St. Sophia in Kiev. Now, in the decade of the 1450's, the centers, both universal and local, shifted. Hagia Sophia had succumbed to heresy and then had been conquered and desecrated by the Turks, while Kiev had long since sunk to the status of border settlement. The new center was the cathedral of the Virgin in Moscow, with the tombs of the patron saints of Moscow, metropolitans Peter and Alexius. So in 1459, Russian bishops expressing the new, Moscow-centered ecclesiolatry, swore to be ever faithful to the "holy cathedral Church of the Holy Virgin in Moscow." If all these developments cannot be proven to derive directly from the reception in Russia of the Florentine Council, they can at least serve to reveal the mood of the times; and this general mood may help us to understand the form Russian reaction to the Union of Florence had taken. According to the weight of evidence, then, at no time were the Russians willing to entertain the idea of Union, or even of a Council. Yet the Union meant to them the disappearance of the hitherto acknowledged supreme source of Orthodoxy and authority. Into the vacuum stepped the Grand Prince of Moscow. One other consideration remains; the intellectual repercussions concerning the Union continued for a century in Russia but already at this stage the writings showed a programmatic harmony portentous for the future. They all draw certain conclusions from the ecclesiastical supremacy of the Grand Prince of Moscow, in juxtaposition with the uniqueness of Russian Orthodoxy after 1441. The intentions and the view of Simeon and his contemporaries may become clearer if one recalls the year 1393 when the patriarch of Constantinople, Antonios, wrote to the Grand Prince Basil I his famous letter, reproaching him for his disrespect toward the patriarch and particularly toward the emperor: "you forbid the metropolitan to intone the divine name of the emperor in the diptychs ... you say 'we have the Church but do not have the emperor...' The sacred emperor occupies a high place in the Church; he is not like other local princes and sovereigns ... from the beginning he had confirmed and established Orthodoxy in the universe ... he is created emperor and autocrat of the Romans, that is, of all Christians.... It is impossible for Christians to have the Church but not to have the emperor." The defender of Orthodoxy is the Universal Christian Emperor. This was taught to the Russians by Constantinople, and they remembered their lesson well. In history, as we know, everything is well prepared by preceding events; in preparing for the translation of this Byzantine lesson into a programme, Simeon condensed the intellectual and even emotional reaction of his age to the Council of Florence in a sonorous hymn at the end of his *Tale [of Isidore's Council]*:

"Rejoice, Orthodox Prince Vasilii, you have stifled the Latin heresy and would not let it grow amongst Orthodox Christians.

Rejoice, Orthodox Prince Vasilii, the confirmer of Orthodoxy and of all the Russian lands, the joy and happiness of the Divine Church and of all Orthodox Christians."

H. THE VATICAN AND RUSSIA: THE UNIATE QUESTION[168]

There is a great deal of controversy over this question. We will first add that the Soviet authorities must be censured for victimizing the Uniates as they should be censured for subjecting other confessions to similar victimization. Nevertheless, this does not mean that the Russian Orthodox people must have a guilt complex over this, something which is insistently being instilled in their hearts and souls by various means of public opinion. When similar pressure comes out of emigre newspapers which have lost completely all feeling of nationality it is indeed a sad occurrence, but one which we are already accustomed to. What is even more sad and utterly unacceptable is when a pastor gives in to temptation, placing in the forefront of his thinking the notorious so-called "human rights" and the battle with the "personality cult" [which are empty catch phrases inapplicable here].

In connection with the Uniate question, the conditions and the setting within which the Unia of 1595-96 and the following years was imposed must be firmly brought to mind. Six hierarch-apostates, headed by Mikhail Ragoza, started a purely clerical movement, totally separated from the people, without any regard for tradition [and therefore illegal]. Let us also not forget the flagrant lawlessness and persecution which confessors from among the people, organized into the famous brotherhoods, were subjected to. We must also not lose sight of the fact that

---

168 Deacon Herman Ivanov-Treenadzaty, *The Vatican & Russia* (Jordanville: Holy Trinity Monastery, 1990) 9-13.

the "Greek Faith" [Orthodoxy], existing on the territory of the Polish
Lithuanian State was not recognized as lawful, and judging by the facts,
was outside the law. This allowed the pany (Polish lords) the right to
[unlawfully] dispose of Orthodox property with impunity, to give their
churches and cathedrals to the Uniates or even to lease them to the Jews!

In other words, it should be clear that if the Uniates are now
suffering, it is because of their guilt of four centuries ago, connected
with the false council of 1595 and the "initiative group" of 1946. In
the past it was the Catholic authorities and Polish lords who persecuted the Orthodox who did not recognize the Unia, and now the Soviet
authorities persecute the Uniates who do not abide by the decisions of
the Lvov Council of 1946. It is not the Orthodox who persecute the
Uniates but the Godless Communists. This should, however, not prevent us from rejoicing that a majority of the faithful, who were once
pulled away from the fold, have now returned. Today for some reason,
repentance is insistently demanded of Orthodox in conjunction with
the liquidation of Uniatism in Soviet Russia. But we ask, when did any
of the Roman popes express their regret concerning encroachment on
the rights of the Orthodox, and all the crimes committed against them
by Uniatism? None of the Popes ever expressed their regret, including
the present John Paul II, who does not let an occasion pass in order to
praise the monster Josaphat Kuntsevich, considered by the Vatican to be
a hieromartyr.

The very memory of this most evil of personalities is inconceivably scandalous. To recall his last name is in itself a "casus belli." Just
before his "martyr's end," which occurred on November 12, 1623, in
Vitebsk, Kuntsevich ordered the disposal of dead Orthodox by having
their corpses exhumed and thrown to dogs. In all of his Polotsky diocese,
both in Mogilyov and in Orsha, he pillaged and terrorized the Orthodox, closing and burning churches. Eloquent complaints were sent to
judges and to the Polish Sejm. The most convincing condemnation of
Kuntsevich's character is found in a letter dated March 12, 1622, one
and a half years before his death, from the Lithuanian chancellor Leo
Sapiega, clearly a Roman Catholic, the representative of the Polish king
himself: "By thoughtless violence you oppress the Russian people and
urge them on to revolt. You are aware of the censure of the simple peo-

ple, that it would be better to be in Turkish captivity than to endure such persecutions for faith and piety. You write that you freely drown the Orthodox, chop off their heads, and profane their churches. You seal their churches so the people, without piety and Christian rites, are buried like non-Christians. In place of joy, your cunning Uniatism has brought us only woe, unrest, and conflict. We would prefer to be without it. These are the fruits of your Uniatism." Let us remember that these words are not the fantasies or the slanders of a fanatically-tempered Orthodox, but the contents of a historical letter from the head of a Roman Catholic state, the Chancellor of the Grand Duchy of Lithuania, written on behalf of the Polish King to a turbulent Uniate bishop. In the very same letter and with much foresight Leo Sapiega writes, "It would have been better not to have given us nationwide strife and hatred, and instead to have preserved us from nationwide condemnation."

Arriving in Vitebsk on the 12th of November 1623, with a band of his cohorts, Kuntsevich proceeded to knock down the tents where the Orthodox secretly held divine services. One of Kuntsevich's deacons attacked an Orthodox priest. The crowd, which had run out of patience, then turned on Kuntsevich, who was personally leading this pogrom, and with sticks and stones beat him to death. His maimed body was placed in a sack and tossed into the Diva River. Such was the inglorious end of the earthly life of this alleged "apostle of unity" as none other than Pope John Paul II shamelessly dares to call him. Before John Paul II, Pius IX on June 29, 1867, already glorified Josaphat Kuntsevich as a saint. In 1923, on the occasion of the 300th anniversary of Kuntsevich's death, Pius XI published an encyclical *Ecclesiam Dei (The Church of God)* in which Kuntsevich is named "hieromartyr," a "righteous person," and where it is said that such an example of "holy life" should aid in unifying all Christians.

On November 25, 1963, during the rule of Paul VI, Kuntsevich's remains were brought to Rome to the papal basilica of St. Peter, where they now "rest" under the altar of St. Basil the Great, near the relics of Sts. Gregory the Theologian and John Chrysostom. Without any remorse and at the same time scorning historical truth in order to satisfy his petty interests in a struggle with Orthodoxy, John Paul II is not afraid to speak about the "noble personality" of Josaphat, "whose spilled blood has forever fortified the great work of the Unia." In his message to his Ukrainian flock, *Magnum Baptismi Donum (The Great Gift of Baptism)*, published on April 19, 1988, not a single word rectifies the now established [false] representation of Uniatism and the actions of Kuntsevich. At the same time, the Roman Catholic community continues to demand from the Orthodox certain acts of repentance and apologies for damages carried out against them, as well as for unfriendly and unchristian relations.

I. THE PERSECUTION OF
THE ORTHODOX IN
THE REPUBLIC OF POLAND
(1918-1939)

The territory known as the Second Polish Republic (at the time called the Republic of Poland) existed during the years 1918-1939. During this era the government, in order to build a national Polish state, implemented policies that decreased the number of Orthodox churches and monasteries, confiscated their property ceding them to the state or Roman Catholic Church, closed Orthodox churches and forcibly converted the faithful to Roman Catholicism.

The first transfers occurred from 1918-1924 when 400 Orthodox church buildings were confiscated, some being transferred to the Uniates, and the remaining taken over by the Roman Catholic Church. Orthodox Churches in major Polish cities were demolished. The greatest loss was the Suprail Monastery. Many of the churches did not continue to have a religious function; for example, in Ostrolgka one became a junkyard, in Skierniewice a grain warehouse, in Staszów another a cinema. In most cases, no furnishings were removed, and the altar and icons left in place, which was regarded by the Orthodox faithful as profaning the holy and an affront to the Orthodox faith.

In areas with an Orthodox majority, the number of churches was purposely limited. The policy of the state was for the eastern regions comprised of non-Polish inhabitants to be assimilated into a national, cultural and religious homogeny. This first transfer period of forced transfers caused a public outcry and social conflict, instead of uniting the people of Poland. The second period of transfers in 1929 occurred when the Supreme Court canceled the expiration of claims for returning property lost during the previous period. Thirty-two lawsuits against the state and 109 against other institutions and private individuals were filed. Roman Catholic bishops demanded the return of Orthodox Churches, parish buildings and properties which belonged to Roman and "Greek" Catholics. Many of these lawsuits concerned churches in places where no Roman Catholics lived. The Catholics also demanded the return of Orthodox monasteries, and cathedrals totaling 1/3 of the Orthodox Church property in their claims. Bishop Henryk Przezdziecki of Podlachia demanded the court turn over 248 churches in his diocese. The Roman Catholics were demanding over 100 Orthodox churches which were never under the jurisdiction of Catholic bishops. This new set of transfers through the lawsuits compromised the Orthodox Church's ability to function in the majority of Poland. The Roman Catholic bishops were aware what effect their actions had on the Orthodox Church's ministry.

An Orthodox synod of bishops in 1930 created diocesan committees comprised of clergy and laity to gather evidence for the trials in defending the Orthodox Church properties. Bishop Vitaly of the Russian Orthodox Church-in-exile sent a complaint to the League of Nations in 1929: "the religious discrimination and oppression which have been used since the beginning of the new Polish Republic. (...) The demolition of Orthodox churches, closure of Orthodox cemeteries, expulsion of Orthodox bishops from their parishes, removing the Orthodox patriarch from the position of the head of the Orthodox Church, renaming the Orthodox Church as the "Polish Orthodox Church" — all are acts that breach the essential rights of the Orthodox Russian minority in Poland, guaranteed by the Versailles Treaty of 28 June 1919."

While statements by Roman Catholic Bishops stated they just wanted churches taken by force to be returned, due to the lawsuits, no one was convinced. The Greek-Catholic hierarchs believed that the lawsuits should be considered a dissolution of the union. The papal nuncio, Francesco Marmaggi, supported the Roman Catholic bishops.

The Concordat of 1925 with the Holy See which gave the Catholic Church favored religious status made it difficult for the state to define the legal position of the Orthodox Church and would cause more conflict. These transfer cases took place until the end of 1933 and on January 16, 1934, the Supreme Court decided in the case of 69 churches that the transfers were improper because they were administrated by state authorities. Lower courts then refused to bring the cases to court and carry out the 1919 decisions concerning the transfer of former Catholic churches taken over by the Orthodox. However, as a result of earlier transfers, the Orthodox Church had lost a large number of parishes. Since its organizational structure was still in place, new churches were built, and attempts were made to reactivate the old. Compared to data from 1922, the number of parishes and clergy increased.

While Orthodox Churches were demolished in both the first and second stages along with other forms of church persecution, in the third transfer stage which took place from 1937-1939 the activity was mostly the demolition of Orthodox churches. Emphasis was on churches that were symbolic of the Tsar's reign with the official reason being that the churches were not necessary, were in need of repair or had been built as a result of Russification. The real reason was to weaken the Belarusan and Ukrainian movement by eliminating active Orthodox churches. The army and police persecuted the Orthodox Church and people in order to convert them to Roman Catholicism to propagate Polish values and traditions. Orthodox in the Lublin region resisted the missionary activities. In 1938 due to Catholic protests which were fueled by the press being notified in advance in order to publicize, resolutions were passed that demanded the demolition of closed Orthodox churches. From May until July 1938, the demolitions took place by local administration and committees with help from the army police. Coercion methods including blackmail and threats were used to pressure the Orthodox while their churches, which served thousands of faithful, were destroyed. In most cases, the Orthodox made no physical attempt to resist the demolitions, and only prayed and protested.

These property transfers and demolitions weakened the Orthodox Church presence and priestly activities in Poland, creating conditions which were ripe for transfer, which was the intent of the state's policies. When the Orthodox no longer had Orthodox Churches to attend, they started attending Roman Catholic Churches. However, the persecution served to unite the Orthodox faithful, clergy, and church hierarchy, and anti-government/anti-Polish sentiment grew within the Orthodox community. The fruit of this was witnessed in the Khelm, Podlachia, and Volhynia regions during the Second World War.

J. THE SERBIAN ORTHODOX NEW MARTYRS (1941-1945)

1. "The Genocide of the Serbs in the Twentieth Century Incurred More Deaths Than the Spanish Inquisition" by Edmond Paris[169]

"It is with reason that the Serbian Orthodox Bishop, Dr. Nikolaj Velimirović, so well-known to the Anglo-Saxon world, compared what happened in Croatia, on such a large scale, with the darkest days of the Middle Ages. In an article published in 1954 by the ecclesiastical review Svecanik, the Bishop wrote: "The Spanish Inquisition is noted for its atrocities. The head inquisitor, named by the Pope, was the Dominican Monk Thomas de Torquemada, who is remembered with such sinister bitterness. During the eighteen-year period of his mandate, 10,220 persons were burned at the stake while 114,401 (according to the historian Motley) perished from hunger and torture in their prisons, which meant 125,000 people within a period of eighteen years. This record is frightful enough, but the inquisition of the Serbian Orthodox was much more terrible, for 750,000 Serbs were killed in just four years."

It would be difficult to find a parallel of such ferocious persecution in all history. Even the Duke of Albe, that sinister representative of the Spanish King (Philippe II), to the Low Countries, seemed quite moder-

169 Edmond Paris, *Genocide in Satellite Croatia, 1941-1945: A Record of Racial and Religious Persecutions and Massacres* (Chicago: The American Institute for Balkan Affairs, 1961), 4-5.

ate in comparison, having tortured and killed some 18,000 Protestants within six years.

In France, the massacre of St. Bartholomew on August 24, 1572, so justifiably stigmatized by the historians, resulted in only 100,000 victims. The twentieth century, however, was doomed to witness in Europe, in the name of racial purity and religion such a genocide[170] as the past has never known, in which the Orthodox Serbs in Croatia barely escaped complete extermination. Yet this gigantic holocaust, which took place only a few years ago and which was witnessed by the present generation, has given rise to the most fantastic stories, accompanied by an intense propaganda that still continues a tireless effort to "cleanse" the guilty of any sense of responsibility. All kinds of printed matter, written under the guise of the "greatest objectivity," and published largely by the Croatian and Vatican printing presses, is being circulated throughout the world.

In order to re-establish a truthful record concerning this tragedy, with its causes and the roles played by those who never hesitated profiting by this expansion of religious and national imperialism, while defying all humanity, I have undertaken the gathering of numerous testimonies printed by the Croatian and Catholic press during those tragic times. Here also are records of Yugoslav and foreign documents which appeared after the war, and testimonies, published in authentic sources, from some of the persecuted who escaped the inferno.

Unfortunately, I have been obliged to choose only a limited number of these significant texts which are numerous enough to fill an entire library. But these selected testimonies will amply suffice as a record of actual events, and thus serve in throwing light upon those responsible for this drama. It is difficult for the world to believe that a whole people could be doomed to extermination by a government and a religious hierarchy of the twentieth century, just because it happened to belong to another ethnical and racial group, and which had inherited the Christianity of Byzantium rather than that of Rome.

---

170 *Genocide*: Any acts committed with intent to destroy, in whole or in part, a national, ethnical, racial or religious group as such [...] a crime under international law, contrary to the spirit and aims of the United Nations and condemned by the civilized world.

May I add that far from desiring to stir up hard feelings, I have been motivated by the desire to divulge the truth concerning the frightful tragedy that took place, and to show what a shameful racial and religious recession has resulted from such fanaticism. May the disaster of the recent past serve as a lesson for future generations!

2. "On the Serbian Orthodox New Martyrs of the Second World War" by Joachim Wertz[171]

The twentieth century has seen the crowning of a multitude of martyrs. Holy Russia, from the time of the Bolshevik revolution to the present, has given us millions of new heavenly intercessors, champions of the faith. This is well known to the entire Orthodox Church. Unfortunately, many Orthodox Christians are ignorant of the sufferings of the nearly 750,000 Orthodox Serbian Christians who gave their lives in the defense and confession of the faith during the time of the last world war in the so-called "Independent State of Croatia" and in other parts of German-occupied Yugoslavia at the hands of the Croatian nationalists and other enemies of the Orthodox Church, at the instigation of and with the open participation of the Latin clergy. This persecution was aimed at the complete elimination of the Orthodox Church in these areas. Attempts at forced conversion to Catholicism were joined to a systematic and completely overt destruction of every trace of Orthodoxy. All of this was done in such a fierce and inconceivably brutal manner and in such a short span of time and relatively small geographic area that it is difficult even to imagine. Indeed, the characteristics of this recent persecution are unprecedented in the history of the Church after the persecutions of the first centuries. The sacrifice and memory of these martyrs must not be allowed to remain hidden, known only to their fellow Orthodox countrymen, but should be published and commemorated for the edification of all Orthodox Christians.

Briefly, several points should be kept in mind concerning the history of Serbia and of Yugoslavia between the two world wars. After World

---

171 Holy Trinity Monastery, "On the Serbian Orthodox New Martyrs of the Second World War," *Orthodox Life 33*, no. 1 (January-February 1983): 15-22.

War I the Kingdom of Serbs, Croats and Slovenes (later to become the Kingdom of Yugoslavia) was created by the victorious allies out of the former kingdoms of Serbia and Montenegro as well as virtually all of the territory of the former Austro-Hungarian Empire inhabited by the South Slavic peoples. This included Slovenia and Croatia, both predominantly Roman Catholic, as well as Dalmatia, Bosnia and Herzegovina, areas of mixed Roman Catholic, Orthodox and Moslem populations. Bosnia, Herzegovina and Dalmatia, as well as parts of Slovenia (the area of north-central Yugoslavia between the historic Croatian and Serbian lands), acquired large permanent Serbian populations during the centuries of Turkish rule. The Serbs in these regions, in the main, settled there after fleeing Turkish oppression, and were granted land and privileges in return for military service in defense of the Austro-Hungarian borders against the Turks. Historically, in these areas the Serbs lived peacefully alongside their Croatian neighbors. They lived, however, in a state of constant harassment on the part of the Austrians, sometimes subdued and at other times violent in character. The Austrians from time to time attempted to impose the Unia on the Serbs.

These efforts, for the most part, met with little success, though this did produce several martyrs and heroic confessors of the Orthodox faith. But Austrian and Vatican policy considered it potentially more profitable to devote the full force of the Uniate movement to the western Ukrainian lands. In Slovenia there was no Orthodox populace. Although Roman Catholics, the Slovenes have always been friendly to the Serbs and valued their political union with Serbia in the Yugoslavian kingdom. One must bear in mind that, although Yugoslavia was politically based and founded on the Serbian kingdom, this was not something brought about by Serbian imperialism. It was an arrangement devised by the major world powers after the First World War, and accepted by Serbia and the Serbian king in a spirit of duty and friendship in the hope that the South Slavic peoples could live in peace after many centuries of occupation and oppression. In fact, since the 18th century, this "Yugoslav idea" based on a strong Serbian state was always popular among the Croats and championed by their intellectuals.

Nevertheless, in the 19th century hatred for the Serbs began to be cultivated as part of the policy of the growing Croatian nationalist movement. This hatred, which previously had been more or less confined to the Croatian clergy, Austrian Jesuits and the Austro-Hungarian government, began to infect certain elements of the populace with the rise of various political figures such as Ante Starcevic who claimed that "the Serbs are a breed fit only for the slaughterhouse." In World War I, the policy of the Austrians was to sow as much discord between the Croats and Serbs living in the Dual Monarchy as possible, since Austria was at war with the two Serbian kingdoms of Serbia and Montenegro. One of the causes of this war, of course, was Austrian attempts to prevent a unified Serbian kingdom which would naturally include the largely Serbian portions of Bosnia and Herzegovina. It must also be remembered that one of Austria's allies in that war was Bulgaria, which, though an Orthodox kingdom, was a traditional enemy of Serbia and was certainly not favorable to a large unified Serbian state on its borders. Also, Austrian policy historically sought to keep Serbia and Bulgaria enemies and to damage any fraternal relations between them.

With this policy of Austria in mind, we see that in 1884 a movement was begun in Croatia, founded by a certain Josip Frank, a Jewish convert to Catholicism, called the Pravasi or the Frankovci. This was an ultra-nationalist Croatian Movement created to foster hatred towards Serbs among Croatians. It was composed of some wealthy residents of Zagreb, clergy, small-townsmen, and certain undesirables of Croatian society who organized local gangs of terrorists. One of its members in the early 20th century was Ante Pavelic, later to become the head of the so-called "Independent State of Croatia." These Frankovci were used by the Austrians for terrorizing the Serbian inhabitants of Bosnia, where they succeeded in murdering quite a few Serbian clergy.

In the 1930's, after the creation of Yugoslavia, this movement was secretly revived in the form of the notorious terrorist organization known as the Ustasi led by Ante Pavelic, who busied himself training his followers in Italy and Hungary.[172] At the same time anti-Serbian and anti-monarchist terrorist groups were formed across the border from Yugoslavian

---

172 *Ustasi*: A Croatian fascist and ultra-nationalist political organization active between 1929 and 1945. The ideology of the movement was a blend of fascism, Roman Catholicism and Croatian ultra-nationalism. This movement persecuted Orthodox Christianity and was responsible for the murdering of Serbian Orthodox faithful and the forced conversion to Latin Papism of many others.

Macedonia in Bulgaria. Some of these groups allied themselves with Pavelic's Ustasi. Also, in 1934, a camp for terrorists at Janka Puszta in Hungary was founded to train potential assassins of King Alexander of Yugoslavia, while enjoying the protection of the Horthy government in Budapest. On October 9, 1934, King Alexander was indeed assassinated in Marseilles, France. He suffered a martyr-like death at the hands of a Bulgarian-Macedonian terrorist working in collaboration with the fanatical Ustasi. His murder was a very fortunate occurrence for the enemies of the Serbs and Yugoslavia, since there was no one to take his place as leader of the Serbs and unifier of Yugoslavia.

King Alexander died leaving as his heir his young son Peter. Peter was in his teens and thus a regency was established according to King Alexander's will, headed by his cousin Prince Paul. Prince Paul was not well liked, and he himself felt out of place in Yugoslavia, favoring as he did Western European culture. During the regency two notorious and extremely unwise policies were worked out, the first by the regent and his prime minister, Stojadinovic, a man who earlier advocated the recognition of the Soviet Union. These two agreements, extremely unpopular among the Serbs, were the Concordat with the Vatican, and the Sporazum, creating a virtually autonomous Croatia in a highly preferred position. The Concordat was an attempt by the leader of the Slovene Clerical Party to settle the Croatian problem by appealing to the more conservative Croats and at the same time to gain autonomy for Slovenia. In effect it would have virtually established the Roman Catholic Church in Yugoslavia and granted it privileges denied to the Orthodox Church.

The Serbs felt this to be an attack on the Orthodox Church, and the Church together with virtually all the Serbian people mounted unprecedented resistance to the proposed agreement. In the midst of the crisis Patriarch Varnava died. His health had suffered under the strain of the controversy, and it was even rumored that he had been poisoned. The concordat was passed by the parliament on the very day the patriarch died and was immediately followed by the excommunication of those Serbian deputies who voted in favor of it. There was also a demonstration organized by the Church and headed by bishops and clergy that set out from the cathedral in Belgrade and was violently broken up by the police. The prime minister had a serious crisis on his hands and withdrew the proposal. The Sporazum of 1939 was negotiated by Premier Cvetkovic, who replaced the extremely unpopular Stojadinovic, and the Croatian political leaders. It created an internally autonomous Banovina of Croatia. But most importantly, the Banovina included the territory of the historic Croatian kingdom, including even areas where the majority of the population was Serbian. Even this did not satisfy the demands of the Croats, and the Serbs feared that Srem and all of Bosnia would be given away. Within a week after the Sporazum was signed, war broke out in Europe.

On August 25, 1939, Prince Paul's government, bowing to German pressure, signed the Three-Power Pact with Germany and Italy. Intense indignation arose in Serbia. Two days later a coup d'etat was carried out by a group of officers, who in noble Serbian tradition preferred destruction and martyrdom to treachery and dishonor. King Peter was declared of age, and Prince Paul fled the country. One week later, on Palm Sunday morning, German planes bombed Belgrade. The war had now come to Yugoslavia.

On April 10, as the German troops were being welcomed into Zagreb, the independent state of Croatia was proclaimed. Many Croats, blinded by chauvinism, enlisted in the service of the invading armies. Croatian militia units joined the Ustasi in attacks on isolated Yugoslavian army units, after which they handed over the Serbian officers and soldiers to the Germans.

Yugoslavia formally capitulated on April 18, and the country was immediately carved up. The provinces of Slavonia, Bosnia-Herzegovina and Srem were given to the Croatian state. During the first days of the occupation, the most prominent Serbs, at the head of whom stood the patriarch, Gavrilo, and the renowned bishop of Zica, Nikolai (Velimirovich), both of whom had sought refuge in the monastery of Ostrog in Montenegro, were arrested. They were later taken to the concentration camp of Dachau in Germany, where they were interned until the end of the war, and where they suffered and endured much abuse and indignities. Later, after their arrests, Bishop Irinej (Djordjevic) of Dalmatia another prominent hierarch, was seized by the Italians and imprisoned in a camp in Italy until the end of the war.

Very revealing as to the utter fanaticism that gripped the Roman Catholic Church in Croatia during these early days of the war and the infant Croatian state, is this excerpt from the diocesan newspaper of the archdiocese of Sarajevo: "Until now, God spoke through papal encyclicals. And? They closed their ears... Now God has decided to use other methods. He will prepare missions. European missions. World missions. They will be upheld not by priests, but by army commanders. The sermons will be heard with the help of cannons, machine guns, tanks and bombers." The Ustasi were known to have publicly taken oaths in the Catholic churches, pledging to work for the eradication of the Serbs and Orthodoxy. Especially militant and very prominent in the Ustasi were members of the Franciscan Order. Immediately after the proclamation of the Ustasi state, the Croatian primate, Archbishop Alojzije Stepinac of Zagreb, gave his blessing in the name of the Roman Church to the Croatian state and established "close collaboration." (It should be pointed out, however, that the Croatian Catholic Church was, at least officially, speaking for itself at that time. The procedure for obtaining recognition by the Vatican was in full progress, but officially the Vatican still recognized the Kingdom of Yugoslavia and had diplomatic relations with the government-in-exile. In short, the Vatican gave de facto recognition to the Ustasi regime, together will full diplomatic protocol at state occasions, though never official recognition.)

The massacres of Orthodox Serbs began shortly after the creation of the Croatian state. In the Serbian villages in the Bjelovar region 250 people were buried alive. In the village of Otecac some 331 Serbs were slain together with their priest who was tortured to death. In Kosinj the Ustasi assembled about 600 Serbs and slaughtered them. In a similar manner in these first months alone hundreds were massacred and forced to undergo horrible tortures, both physical and psychological, in scores of villages. Soon both the private and public use of the Cyrillic alphabet was prohibited, and the Serbs were required to wear the letter "P" (for Pravoslavac — Orthodox) on their arms.

The Ustasi plan called for the extermination of one portion of the Serbian population and for the forced conversion to Roman Catholicism of the other. In either case, the Serbs, as an Orthodox people, had no place in the Catholic Croatian state. This shows that in spite of the presence of widespread National Socialist "Aryan" racist propaganda in Croatia, the hatred for the Serbs was based on their being Orthodox. One Catholic periodical in lauding the head of the Ustasi state, Pavelic, praises the Ustasi "Crusader" (Krizar) organization as "Raised in the spirit of radical Catholicism, which knows no compromises so far as principles are concerned, that never knew what it meant to give in and abandon any part of the program of Croatian nationalism." Thus, the program of Serbian conversion and/or liquidation, can be viewed as being in the tradition of the medieval crusades which were launched to stamp out the enemies of the Roman church. Archbishop Stepinac saw the Serbs as being schismatics and an evil "almost greater than Protestantism." Croatia was viewed as a bastion of Roman Catholicism in the Balkans. In 1944 a Berlin newspaper wrote: "An extraordinary ecclesiastical struggle is going on in Croatia. The Ustasi government is persecuting the Orthodox Church and is trying to convert as many Orthodox people as possible to Catholicism by means of intimidation and all kinds of devices. At the opening of the so-called Croat Assembly, Pavelic said that religious freedom did exist in principle, but it did not include the Orthodox Church. Apart from nationalistic reasons, Pavelic endeavored to represent himself as a missionary by virtue of his work on behalf of the church, thus desiring to acquire greater prestige. We still recall his visit to the pope at the time when he was just organizing his 'State.'"

On May 8, 1941, the infamous martyrdom of the Serbs of the Glina region began. The Ustasi began by killing seven Serbs. In the short time that followed, they arrested and murdered 560 people from that region. Then on May 11 a train carrying 120 Serbs stopped at Glina. They were then removed to the courtyard of a local Jewish merchant, where a number of them were killed, and the rest taken to an unknown destination.

On May 4, the Orthodox bishop of Banja Luka, Platon, was ordered by the Ustasi to leave town immediately. He then appealed to the local Catholic bishop to intercede with the authorities to grant him several days to prepare. The Catholic bishop gave him his word, but during the night six Ustasi terrorists came and arrested the hierarch. Then, together with Father Dugan Subotic, he was led some six kilometers away to the village of Vrbanja, where they were all killed. Their bodies revealed how they had been tortured. They were shaved with a blunt knife, their eyes were put out, their ears and noses cut off, and fires were lit on their chests. Their remains were found in the Vrbanja river on May 23.

A few days later the eighty-year-old Metropolitan of Bosnia, Peter (Zimonjic), was arrested by an Ustasi cleric. He was ordered to forbid the use of the Cyrillic alphabet, and when he refused, he was taken to Zagreb and later to the infamous concentration camp of Jasenovac, where he perished.

On May 21, Bishop Sava (Trlajic) of Karlovac was arrested at his home. He was taken, together with three priests and thirteen other Orthodox Serbs, in a truck to Ogulin. There they were locked in a stable, beaten and tortured, and then taken to Gospic, from where on August 15, they were sent together with 2,000 other Serbs to the Adriatic island of Pag, where they were all killed.

The metropolitan of Zagreb, Dositej, is also numbered with those who suffered martyrdom, having been beaten and tortured before his death. The martyrdom of these hierarchs and other clergy, the imprisonment of others, as well as the conditions of the occupation in general, caused the disintegration of all Orthodox ecclesiastical administration and open Church life in the territories of Croatia, Bosnia-Herzegovina, and the Vojvodina from 1941 to 1945.

In many villages the massacres followed a certain pattern: The Ustasi would arrive and assemble all the Serbs. They would then order them to convert to Catholicism. Those who refused, as the majority did, were told to assemble in their local Orthodox parish church. They would then lock them in the church and set it ablaze. In this manner many Orthodox men, women and children perished in scores of Serbian settlements.

In the area between Gospic and Velebit, where the terrain is rocky with many canyons and ravines, the Ustasi would take their Orthodox Serbian prisoners in long convoys on foot, two-by-two and all linked by a long chain, to the edge of a cliff, where they would kill them and then throw their bodies into the ravine. Thousands were killed in this manner in that area alone. Even more horrible, in the same general area, in village after village, children were found impaled on stakes, all the rest of the inhabitants having been already slaughtered.

On August 3, 1941, all Orthodox between the ages of sixteen and sixty from the villages of Vrginmost and Cemernica were assembled to be forcibly proselytized. There were about 3000 in all. But instead of Croatian clerics, trucks arrived, and the Serbs were herded into them and taken to Glina, where they were told that a priest was waiting to convert them to Catholicism, after which they would be returned home. In Glina they were joined by Serbs from Topusko. But instead of being converted they were put in jail, from which every night a thousand of them were taken to the local Orthodox church and there stabbed one-by-one. In this manner 2000 were put to death in the Glina church, while the last group of a thousand was burned to death, together with the church itself and its pastor, Father Bogdan Opacic.

Massacres of the Serbian Orthodox population were also carried out in the Vojvodina, a region under Hungarian occupation. In the town of Curug, Serbs were rounded up and gunned down on the Feast of the Nativity of Christ in 1942. But the most numerous massacres occurred in Novi Sad from January 21-23 of the same year, when nearly a thousand Serbs were martyred. Some of them were even thrown into the ice-covered river while still alive.

As the tide of the war began to turn, and the Ustasi regime began to lose control of the mountainous regions, it became more difficult to continue to carry out village massacres. The Ustasi were afraid to enter certain areas without the support of the German army, and the Germans could not spare the troops to help in this kind of madness. Therefore, the regime began to put all their efforts into centralized concentration camps. These camps became nothing less than slaughterhouses for Orthodox Serbs. The camps began to multiply rapidly. There were many but for brevity we will discuss only the most infamous, that of Jasenovac. In all, hundreds of thousands perished in these camps.

Jasenovac was made up of wooden huts built on damp marshy land on the banks of the river Sava. The conditions were unsanitary, and it was plagued by famine. In all, during 1941 and 1942 about 200,000 people died or were killed there. The commander-in-chief of the Croatian concentration camps boasted with pride: "We have slaughtered here at Jasenovac more people than the Ottoman empire was able to do during its occupation of Europe." In 1942 alone some 12,000 children were murdered at Jasenovac. Most of those who survived the camp later perished from weakened health. Utterly indescribable tortures have been reported by foreign observers as having been inflicted on Serbian women and children at Jasenovac. Most are too terrible to recount. The Ustasi even killed, in a horrible fashion, babies just about to be born, right in the very wombs of their mothers.

An example of the character of the fanatically clever thinking of the Ustasi is provided in this quote from a communication of a Franciscan to the Ustasi commander at the village of Derventa, from whence 500 Serbs were deported to the camps: "There are 500 widows in the five villages who could marry Catholics, for there are no more Serbian Orthodox. This would be an excellent chance to indoctrinate them, and they in turn would indoctrinate their families with Catholicism and Croatism." The fanatics would stop at literally nothing to erase all traces of the Orthodox Serbs and at the same time increase the numbers of Croatian Catholics.

It should be emphasized that the Ustasi program was a total one of either the extermination or complete assimilation of the Orthodox. Thus, for the most part the Unia, which existed in Croatia, did not seriously enter into their considerations. This was still too "eastern" for them and too much of a reminder of Orthodoxy. The regime, if it could, would probably have decreed its complete Latinization. But the Unia was too valuable an institution to the Vatican for its own purposes for this to have been attempted.

It must also be pointed out that of those Serbs who were coerced into accepting Catholicism and who survived the war, most did in fact return to Orthodoxy after the war. However, during the persecutions, many Serbian children were taken from their parents or "rescued" from the camps. Many of these orphans still remain unaccounted for. They were taken to be raised as Catholics, and no doubt they grew up as Catholics, not knowing their true identity or their original faith.

After the surrender of Italy, the Ustasi regime's days were numbered. In May 1945 Pavelic, his deputies and about 500 clerics fled to Austria after entrusting what was left of the government and their wealth stolen from their victims to Archbishop Stepinac.

During the time of the persecution, nearly 300 Orthodox churches in the territory of the Croatian state were destroyed. In the diocese of Karlovac 173 out of 189 temples were demolished. Others were desecrated by being turned into slaughterhouses, stables and latrines. Still others were given over to the Roman Catholics, as were several of the historic Orthodox monasteries. Many of the damaged churches have been restored by the Serbian Church since the war. Others are still to be repaired and can be seen crumbling and abandoned in Yugoslavia today.

The new Serbian martyrs of World War II included five bishops and at least 177 other clergy martyrs. In all, both clergy and lay, they number about 750,000. The late Bishop Nikolai (Velimirovich), over a quarter of a century ago, inscribed into the Church calendar by his own hand the following notation for the date August 31 (O. S.): "The 700,000 who suffered for the Orthodox faith at the hands of the Roman crusaders and Ustasi during the time of the Second World War. These are the New Serbian Martyrs."

Through their prayers may all the Orthodox be saved and strengthened in the defence of the Faith! Amen.

K. THE EXCOMMUNICATED CORPSES OF MOUNT ATHOS

ON THE UNION OF THE CHURCHES
AND ON THE EXCOMMUNICATED[173]

Determined to unify the Latins and the Orthodox through the agreement at the Council of Lyons (1274), Emperor Michael VIII Paleologos with the support of Patriarch John Bekkos brought the Latins to the Holy Mountain to concelebrate with the Orthodox monks. The monks of Zographou and Iveron refused to concelebrate and the accounts of their martyrdom were written above. The monks of the monastery of monasteries of Xeropotamou and the Great Lavra, however, welcomed the Latins to their monastery to concelebrate, the latter even ringing the bells. This modern-day testimony below confirms God's displeasure toward these concelebrations of the Orthodox with the Latins. Monk Lazarus Dionysiates writes the following:

---

173 Monk Lazarus Dionysiates, "On the Union of the Churches and on the Excommunicated", *Hagiorite Library*, year 28, issue 5, ed. Sotirios N. Skhinas (Volos, 1963). And see Monk Lazarus Dionysiates, "Ἡ ἑνωτικὴ κίνησις καὶ τὸ Ἅγιον Ὄρος: Λατινόφρονες ἐπὶ αἰῶνος τυμπανιαῖοι [The Unionist Movement and the Holy Mountain: Latin-Minded Bloated for Centuries]," *Typos Hellenikos-Orthodoxos* (Athens, Greece), December 1963. And see Holy Apostles Convent & Dormition Skete, *The Great Synaxaristes of the Orthodox Church, January*, trans. Holy Apostles Convent and Dormition Skete (Buena Vista: Holy Apostles Convent & Dormition Skete, 2007), 136.

216

Seeing that from the beginning of the year of our Lord 1960, the newly established Pope John has proclaimed throughout the world that he intends to convoke in Rome an Ecumenical Council, the subject of which would be the union of the churches, and that many of our own, both clergymen and laymen, scientists and theologians, have received this message with joy and defend such a union with zeal, writing pieces in various journals—and for this reason we saw last year His All-Holiness Patriarch Athenagoras of Constantinople visiting the Orthodox Patriarchates of the East, and also Patriarch Alexei of Russia himself with company having visited His Beatitude Archbishop Theocletus of Athens and all Hellas and also the Patriarchates of the East, for the exchange of views and discussion of this serious topic—for this reason, we thought it good to note down, touching only on the surface of the matter, and remind [the readers] of certain events, which took place on this Mountain of Athos after the return of Emperor Michael Palaeologus and Patriarch Beccus from Italy with the aim of forcing even the Athonite fathers, who were exercising asceticism in the holy monasteries, the sketes, and the cells, to accept their uniate intentions.

[He then proceeds to recount the witness and martyrdom of the holy martyrs of the monasteries of Zographou, Vatopedi, and Iviron, and also of the skete of Karyes, for which see pages 34, 74, 79, and 133 in this present volume. Then he says:]

...So this is what happened to those that did not accept but rather reproved these Latinizing uniates. Now let us see what followed for those that received them as friends and concelebrated with them. In the Monastery of Xeropotamou, during the Liturgy, there was a fire and a great resounding, roaring earthquake, which brought down the temple, and buried the priests of shame that were therein, and overthrew the walls of the monastery, leaving only one leaning over at one point. When the Emperor and those with him saw these things, they departed in great disgrace, while the fungus (mushroom) of forty branches that used to sprout under the holy altar on the feast of the holy Forty Martyrs sprouted no more, since the sanctuary had been defiled.

Let us also see what happened at the Great Lavra, where they welcomed them with bell-tolls. There too we see that the things which followed were even more fearful, brimming with horror and terror. Hear the account, as the truthful tradition has preserved and handed it down to our days:

The hierodeacon of the Lavra who coöfficiated in this Liturgy was overtaken by divine wrath and measured out his life, consumed like a candle burnt by the fire, whereas the seven or, according to others, eleven concelebrant priestmonks were found after death to be undissolved, bloated, excommunicated. Their remains could still be seen in public view inside the narthex of the cemetery church of the Holy Apostles as late as the end of the nineteenth century, both for the instruction and chastisement of coming generations and furthermore so that those that saw them be moved to compassion and pray for them, that the Lord forgive them and dissolve their bloated bodies into the earth whence they were taken. I forgot to mention that the wall-paintings of the church were also blackened, and were later renovated in the year 1544 by the renowned painter Theophanes.

In connection with the aforementioned bloated (excommunicated) bodies, a small incident has been preserved and is to this day recounted. Once, when the muleteers were merry with drunkeness, they made a bet with a great monetary reward: whoever had the courage and the composure to take an excommunicated corpse and carry it thither where they were feasting would win the money; and indeed, one daring man was found, who went, with pistol in hand, carried such an abominable relic, and won the bet and the promised monetary award. Tradition also preserves the following: a certain pilgrim, being particularly sensitive, when he drew near and saw the pitch-black bloated bodies, with the hair, with the long, curved nails, with their mouths open, where the mice were freely going in and out, was so frightened that he died on the spot from a heart attack. This became the cause for their removal from the monastery, and they took them to the shores of the Rumanian Skete and shut them into a cave precipitous and hard to climb; but since even there the curious would not cease visiting them, looking at them, and photographing them, therefore now recently they completely blocked the gate of the cave with built stones, and this cave became completely unrecognizable, which contains these excommunicated uniate Latin-minded Lavriotes. When, in the year 1925, I was sailing through the upper parts in a boat heading for Orphanion of Pangaion, the brothers Pachomius and Andronicus who had the boat showed me this cave.

Our brother Christodulus told me that when he was in Karyes in the year 1935, he saw a Rumanian layman who had a photograph of three such excommunicated bodies, and he was very much frightened at their sight. These things we note for the sake of historical truth; let him that understandeth understand, and let him hear that hath ears to hear. It is not impossible even now, or after a few years, for such tragic cases and incidents to be repeated, wherefore there is need of watchfulness and preparation, for the safeguarding of our Orthodox Faith from the tentacles and delusions of the Latinizing Papists, Masons, etc.

I was writing on the 5th of April 1963.
Monk Lazarus Dionysiates

A TERRIFYING MEETING[174]

Elder Gabriel, the Spiritual Father

A brother used to hear of the excommunicated at the Lavra of Athos, who had received and concelebrated with John Beccus, the Latin-minded Patriarch of Constantinople; yet he doubted the truth of these accounts and would always investigate and ask if there was any eyewitness that had seen them with his own eyes, in order to put to rest his doubts which gnawed at him.

Eventually, he was told that the Spiritual Father had

174 Monk Moses the Athonite, Μέγα Γεροντικὸ ἐναρέτων Ἁγιορειτῶν τοῦ Εἰκοστοῦ Αἰῶνος [Great Gerontikon of Virtuous Athonites of the Twentieth Century], Vol. 2: 1956-1983 (Thessaloniki: Mygdonia Publishing, 2011), 731.

seen them; so he came and asked me if I knew anything about this and whether I saw them with my own eyes. I informed him that I had seen them and that these accounts are most certainly true, because I had come to the Holy Mountain in 1885, at twenty years of age...

Two years after my arrival, it chanced that we took wheat from the Monastery of Konstamonitou, weighing about 1200 okes, and for this reason, we were going by sea in our boat to get it. At the time I was 22 years old and the month was September, two days after the Feast of the Precious Cross.

In the evening we stopped at the haven of the Great Lavra, planning to continue our journey in the morning, as indeed we did. A little while, however, after we had left the Lavra behind, my elder, the monk Meletius, says to me:

"Gabriel, my child, farther ahead is the place of the excommunicated, those who received the Latin-minded in the Great Lavra and coöfficiated with John Beccus and those with him. I have seen them before, but because you are young and one day there may be talk about this and some may say that all this is a lie and there is nothing really, no excommunicated bodies, but these are only stories said to scare people, for this reason, let us go so that you can see them with your own eyes, so that whatever others may tell you later in contradiction, you may not believe them; for the Holy Writ says that the eye is more reliable than the ear."

As my Elder was saying these words, we arrived at a sheer cliff, which was frightening only to look at, and he says to me:

"Here they are."

I was scrutinizing the area trying to see something and I responded: "Are you playing with me?"

He laughed then and says to me:

"What do you think they are, some cross or perhaps icons, for people to look at them and cross themselves?[175] Whereas they have the devil's form. This you will see and believe..."

Then we came very near to that sheer ravine and with great effort we managed to get out [of our boat] and using all hands and feet, so to speak, we managed to climb five or six metres; and then I saw a cave. We entered and a miserable sight greeted my eyes:

---

175 I.e., they should be set up prominently so as to be visible to those sailing below.

Three men were placed against the rock, upright, with their clothes, the outer and the inner cassocks, their eyes open, the hair and the beard of all three deeply white and very long, their faces the colour of fumes [black], and likewise the lower parts of their hands, their fingers turned a bit inwards; their fingernails were two to four centimetres long, while their toenails could not be seen as they were covered by their socks and shoes.

I even wished to handle them, to see if their bodies were indeed soft or just dry skin and bones; but my elder would not let me, saying, "Put not your hand upon the wrath of God."

In every other respect, however, I examined them with great care; only touch them I did not. At the time, looking at them did not scare me; now, however, when I recall them, my soul is shaken and I can neither sleep, for days on end, nor eat, for two or even three days in a row, although when I saw them I had no thoughts soever.

I am writing this with my own hand on the 2nd of March 1964 in the Holy Monastery of Xenophon.

Priestmonk Gabriel the Spiritual Father of the Iverian Cell
"Birth of the Honourable Forerunner and Baptist John",
also known as "Malaki".

Icon of the Eighth Ecumenical Council,
St. Stephen's Monastery, Meteora, Greece

PART III

CONFESSIONS AND TEXTS FROM OUR HOLY FATHERS

Icon of the First Ecumenical Council

A. ECUMENICAL COUNCILS

1. Introduction to the Ecumenical Councils[176]

In this section we present to you the united voice of Christendom in the Great and Holy Ecumenical Councils which declare the Creed: the one true statement of Faith. It can be said conclusively that present day Latins do not belong to the Church of the first millennium as they do not pass the straightforward test set out by their own church as well as all of Christendom: i.e., to believe and state the Nicene Creed without addition or alteration. By departing from it they are no longer part of the original Church that Christ referred to when He said "I will build my church" (Mt. 16:18).

The Fathers of the Great and Holy Ecumenical Councils did not discuss their own interpretations of the Bible as the Protestants do; neither did they ask the Pope to define the dogma of the Church due to his inherent infallibility as the Latins do; they did something entirely different. They discussed what they had received. They understood their role to be as witnesses of Tradition, not interpreters or logicians. They

---

176 For a full treatment of the Ecumenical Councils in the context of the uniqueness of Orthodox spirituality, a necessary read is the chapter "The Divinely Inspired Theology of the Fathers" from on Ecumenical Councils from Metropolitan Hierotheos Vlachos, *Empirical Dogmatics, Volume 1* (Levadia: Birth of the Theotokos Monastery, 2013), 222-234. Then see "Councils of the Church" from Metropolitan Hierotheos Vlachos, Empirical Dogmatics (Levadia: Birth of the Theotokos Monastery, 2013), 388-407.

never asked what they thought the Bible meant, but what was handed down to them. When in the Fourth Ecumenical Council they examined the Tome of Pope St. Leo, they did not ask if it matched with scripture, but if it was the traditional faith of the Church. It was not the teaching of the Pope of the 5th century, but of Peter in the first that they wanted to believe. Thus, after studying the Tome they cried; "This is the faith of the Fathers! This is the faith of the Apostles! ...Peter has spoken by Leo! The Apostles thus taught! Cyril thus taught!"

2. The Divine Math of the Ecumenical Councils

The true, One, Holy, Catholic, and Apostolic Church was founded by Christ. This Church has preserved that deposit of faith in the Orthodox Liturgy, the Holy Bible, and the teachings of the Holy Fathers. "That good thing which was committed unto thee keep by the Holy Ghost which dwelleth in us" (II Tim. 1:14). The central theology of the Orthodox Church has been codified in the primary statement of belief, the Nicene Creed. This short text is so central to Orthodox theology that it was called "the holy *mathema*," that is, the holy lesson, both because all Christians ought to learn it and because it taught the dogmas of the faith. The word "mathematics" comes from that same Greek word for lesson, "*mathema*" and indeed, the theology of the Orthodox Church is like math ina way. Students cannot make up their own math or teach a different math. Either a student is mathematical, accepting the true math, or he is a-mathematical, outside of math. Students who change even one symbol on one side of a math equation convert a true equation into a-mathematical nonsense. This is why the entire church declared through the great Ecumenical Councils for over a thousand years that those who add to or subtract from the creed "even one word" are anathema.

The creed was written at the First Ecumenical Council. The Second Ecumenical Council added to it and also set forth that it is now complete and cannot be added to. The Third, Fourth, Fifth, Sixth, Seventh, and Eighth Ecumenical Councils reaffirmed that they believe, teach, and baptize only with this Creed. They also

anathematize any who would add to the Creed even by one syllable. Each of the first Seven Ecumenical Councils have been accepted
by the entire church including the Church of Rome. Each Council
does not declare itself a "Great and Holy" Ecumenical Council, but
only declares that about the Councils which came before. The 8th
Ecumenical Council specifically responds to the filioque addition
to the Creed by the West and recognizes the Seventh Ecumenical
Council as being a Great and Holy Ecumenical Council.

As stated among the canons of the Fifth Ecumenical Council:
"We know only one symbol of faith, that which the holy fathers of
Nice[a] set forth and handed down. This also the three holy Synods
handed down. Into this we were baptized, and into this we baptize..."

3. First Ecumenical Council (Nicea, A.D. 325)

"We believe in one God, the Father Almighty, maker of all things
visible and invisible; and in one Lord Jesus Christ, the Son of God, the
only-begotten of his Father, of the substance of the Father, God of God,
Light of Light, very God of very God, begotten, not made, being of one
essence with the Father. By whom all things were made, both which be in
heaven and in earth. Who for us men and for our salvation came down
[from heaven] was incarnate and was made man. He suffered and the
third day he rose again, and ascended into heaven. And he shall come
again to judge both the living and the dead. And [we believe] in the
Holy Spirit. And whosoever shall say that there was a time when the Son
of God was not, or that before he was begotten he was not, or that he
was made of things that were not, or that he is of a different substance
or essence [from the Father] or that he is a creature, or subject to change
or conversion all that so say, the Catholic and Apostolic Church anath-
ematizes them."[177]

---

177 The First Ecumenical Council, "The Nicene Creed," in *Nicene and Post-Nicene
Fathers: The Seven Ecumenical Councils, Volume 14*, ed. Philip Schaff & Henry
Wace (Peabody: Hendrickson Publications, 1999), 3.

4. Second Ecumenical Council
(Constantinople, A.D. 381)

"We believe in one God, the Father Almighty, maker of heaven and earth and of all things visible and invisible. And in one Lord Jesus Christ, the only begotten Son of God, begotten of his Father before all worlds, Light of Light, very God of very God, begotten not made, being of one substance with the Father, by whom all things were made. Who for us men and for our salvation came down from heaven and was incarnate by the Holy Spirit and the Virgin Mary, and was made man, and was crucified also for us under Pontius Pilate. He suffered and was buried, and the third day he rose again according to the Scriptures, and ascended into heaven, and sitteth at the Right Hand of the Father. And he shall come again with glory to judge both the quick and the dead. Whose kingdom shall have no end.

"And in the Holy Spirit, the Lord and Giver-of-Life, who proceedeth from the Father, who with the Father and the Son together is worshipped and glorified, who spake by the prophets. And in one, holy, Catholic and Apostolic Church. We acknowledge one Baptism for the remission of sins, we look for the resurrection of the dead and the life of the world to come. Amen."[178]

5. Third Ecumenical Council
(Ephesus, A.D. 431)

a. Introduction

The canon presented below from the Third Ecumenical Council is the chiefest and most frequently referenced violation in regards to the Creed which the Pope and the West commit. By adding the heresy, even only the word *"filioque"* alone to the Creed, they fall under this condem-

---

178 The Second Ecumenical Council, "The Holy Creed Which the 150 Holy Fathers Set Forth, Which is Consonant with the Holy and Great Synod of Nice," in *Nicene and Post-Nicene Fathers: The Seven Ecumenical Councils, Volume 14*, ed. Philip Schaff & Henry Wace (Peabody: Hendrickson Publications, 1999), 163.

nation of the Ecumenical Councils which reaffirmed this canon many times over subsequent centuries, including by Popes and the churches in the West.

b. Canon VII[179]

When these things had been read, the holy Synod decreed that it is unlawful for any man to bring forward, or to write, or to compose a different (ἑτέραν) Faith as a rival to that established by the holy Fathers assembled with the Holy Ghost in Nicæa. But those who shall dare to compose a different faith, or to introduce or offer it to persons desiring to turn to the acknowledgment of the truth, whether from Heathenism or from Judaism, or from any heresy whatsoever, shall be deposed, if they be bishops or clergymen; bishops from the episcopate and clergymen from the clergy; and if they be laymen, they shall be anathematized.

And in like manner, if any, whether bishops, clergymen, or laymen, should be discovered to hold or teach the doctrines contained in the Exposition introduced by the Presbyter Charisius concerning the Incarnation of the Only-Begotten Son of God, or the abominable and profane doctrines of Nestorius, which are subjoined, they shall be subjected to the sentence of this holy and ecumenical Synod. So that, if it be a bishop, he shall be removed from his bishopric and degraded; if it be a clergyman, he shall likewise be stricken from the clergy; and if it be a layman, he shall be anathematized, as has been aforesaid.

c. Interpretation of Canon VII by Saint Nikodemos of the Holy Mountain[180]

In view of the fact that at this holy and Ecumenical Council's meeting there were read both the Creed of the holy and Ecumenical First Council held in Nicaea, and the Creed of Jewish-minded Nestorius, in which his unholy dogmas were set forth and which Charisius the pres-

---

179 The Third Ecumenical Council, "The Canons of the Two Hundred Holy and Blessed Fathers Who Met at Ephesus: Canon VII," in *Nicene and Post-Nicene Fathers: The Seven Ecumenical Councils, Volume 14*, ed. Philip Schaff & Henry Wace (Peabody: Hendrickson Publications, 1999), 231.

180 Saint Nikodemos, Hieromonk Agapios, *The Rudder (Pedalion): Of the Metaphorical Ship of the One Holy, Catholic, and Apostolic Church of Orthodox Christians*, trans. D. Cummings (Athens: Kesisoglou the Caesarian, 1908), 230.

byter of Philadelphia brought to the Council, after they had been read, this holy Council issued this Canon decreeing that it is not permissible for anyone to compose and write, or to offer to those converted from any other faith to Orthodoxy another Creed than the Symbol of the Faith defined and decreed by the Holy Fathers who assembled in the city of Nicaea and were enlightened by the Holy Spirit. As for those persons who shall dare to compose any other symbol of faith (or creed), or to present it openly, and to offer it to any of the Greeks and Jews and heretics turning away from faith to recognition and knowledge of the truth, such persons, if they be bishops and clergymen, are to be expelled from their episcopate and clericate, respectively, but if laymen they shall be anathematized. Similarly: too, all those who are discovered to be thinking to themselves or to be teaching others the unholy and heretical dogmas of Nestorius concerning the incarnation of the only-begotten Son of God, contained in the exposition of faith composed by him, but brought to this Council by the presbyter named Charisius, these persons also, I say, if they be bishops and clergymen, are to stand deposed, and expelled from their episcopate and clericate, respectively; but if they be laymen, they are to be anathematized, as we said before.

6. Fourth Ecumenical Council (Chalcedon, A.D. 451)

"Aetius, the reverend deacon of Constantinople read from a book [the creed of the 150 fathers.]

"The holy faith which the 150 fathers set forth as consonant to the holy and great Synod of Nice. 'We believe in one God,' etc."[181]

"Concerning the Virgin Mother of God, we thus think and speak; and of the man-net of the Incarnation of the Only Begotten Son of God, necessarily, not by way of addition but for the sake of certainty, as we have received from the beginning from the divine Scriptures and from

181 The Fourth Ecumenical Council, "Extracts from the Acts, Session II," in *Nicene and Post-Nicene Fathers: The Seven Ecumenical Councils, Volume 14*, ed. Philip Schaff & Henry Wace (Peabody: Hendrickson Publications, 1999), 249.

the tradition of the holy fathers, we will speak briefly, adding nothing whatever to the Faith set forth by the holy Fathers in Nice."[182]

"And we will allow the defined Faith, the symbol of the Faith set forth by our holy Fathers who assembled some time ago at Nice, to be shaken by no one. Nor would we permit ourselves or others, to alter a single word of those set forth, or to add one syllable, remembering the saying: 'Remove not the ancient landmark which thy fathers have set,' for it was not they who spoke but the Spirit himself of God and the Father, who proceedeth also from him, and is not alien from the Son, according to his essence."[183]

7. Fifth Ecumenical Council (Constantinople, A.D. 553)

"Therefore, being gathered together, before all things we have briefly confessed that we hold that faith which our Lord Jesus Christ, the true God, delivered to his holy Apostles, and through them to the holy churches, and which they who after them were holy fathers and doctors, handed down to the people credited to them.

"We confessed that we hold, preserve, and declare to the holy churches that confession of faith which the 318 holy Fathers more at length set forth, who were gathered together at Nice, who handed down the holy mathema or creed. Moreover, the 150 gathered together at Constantinople set forth our faith, who followed that same confession of faith and explained it. And the consent of fire 200 holy fathers gathered for the same faith in the first Council of Ephesus. And what things were defined by the 630 gathered at Chalcedon for the one and the same faith, which they both followed and taught. And all those wile from time to time have been condemned or anathematized by the Catholic Church,

---

182 The Fourth Ecumenical Council, "The Letter of Cyril to John of Antioch," in *Nicene and Post-Nicene Fathers: The Seven Ecumenical Councils, Volume 14*, ed. Philip Schaff & Henry Wace (Peabody: Hendrickson Publications, 1999), 251.

183 Ibid., 253.

and by the aforesaid four Councils, we confessed that we hold them condemned and anathematized."[184]

8. Sixth Ecumenical Council
(Constantinople, A.D. 680-681)

"The holy and Ecumenical Synod further says, this pious and orthodox Creed of the Divine grace would be sufficient for the full knowledge and confirmation of the orthodox faith."[185]

9. Seventh Ecumenical Council
(Nicea, A.D. 787)

Canon 1: "Now if the word of prophesy bids us keep the testimonies of God forever and to live by them, it is evident that they must abide unshaken and without change. Therefore Moses, the prophet of God, speaketh after this manner: 'To them nothing is to be added, and from them nothing is to be taken away.' And the divine Apostle glorying in them cries out, 'which things the angels desire to look into,' and, 'if an angel preach to you anything besides that which ye have received, let him be anathema.' Seeing these things are so, being thus well-testified unto us, we rejoice over them as he that hath found great spoil, and press to our bosom with gladness the divine canons, holding fast all the precepts of the same, complete and without change, whether they have been set forth by the holy trumpets of the Spirit, the renowned Apostles, or by the Six Ecumenical Councils, or by Councils locally assembled for promulgating the decrees of the said Ecumenical Councils, or by our holy Fathers. For all these, being illumined by the same Spirit, defined such things as were expedient. Accordingly those whom they placed un-

---

184 The Fifth Ecumenical Council, "The Sentence of the Synod," in *Nicene and Post-Nicene Fathers: The Seven Ecumenical Councils, Volume 14*, ed. Philip Schaff & Henry Wace (Peabody: Hendrickson Publications, 1999), 307.

185 The Sixth Ecumenical Council, "The Definition of Faith," in *Nicene and Post-Nicene Fathers: The Seven Ecumenical Councils, Volume 14*, ed. Philip Schaff & Henry Wace (Peabody: Hendrickson Publications, 1999), 344.

der anathema, we likewise anathematize; those whom they deposed, we also depose; those whom they excommunicated, we also excommunicate; and those whom they delivered over to punishment, we subject to the same penalty."[186]

10. Eighth Ecumenical Council (Constantinople A.D. 879)[187]

a. Introduction

In 879, in Constantinople, 383 bishops convened to handle the schism between Old Rome and the East caused by the dismissal of St. Photios in 869-870 from his position of Patriarch of Constantinople. Among all these bishops included representatives of all the Patriarchs and of the Pope of Old Rome. The decisions of Constantinople, 879 were accepted unanimously by all these representatives, including those from the West. Pope John VIII accepted the decisions of his representatives and the West continued recognizing the authority of this council for, approximately, another 200 years.[188] Many later councils and Fathers have admitted this council has all the attributes of an Ecumenical Council, while some explicitly referred to it as the Eighth Ecumenical Council.

---

186 The Seventh Ecumenical Council, "The Canons of the Holy and Ecumenical Seventh Council," in *Nicene and Post-Nicene Fathers: The Seven Ecumenical Councils, Volume 14*, ed. Philip Schaff & Henry Wace (Peabody: Hendrickson Publications, 1999), 555.

187 See the upcoming publication of the Minutes for this Council from Uncut Mountain Press.

188 For more information, see Alexander Kazhdan, Alice Mary Talbot, ed., "Council of 879-80," in *The Oxford Dictionary of Byzantium*, Volume I (Oxford: Oxford University Press, 1991), 513.

b. *Oros*[189]

Jointly sanctifying and preserving intact the venerable and divine teaching of our Lord and Savior Jesus Christ, which has been established in the bosom of our mind, with unhesitating resolve and purity of faith, as well as the sacred ordinances and canonical stipulations of his holy disciples and Apostles with an unwavering judgement, and indeed also the preaching of the seven holy and ecumenical Councils which were directed and actualized by the inspiration of the one and the same Holy Spirit, and honouring and jointly preserving with a most sincere and unshakable resolve the canonical institutions inviolate and unfalsified, we expel those whom they removed from the Church, but we embrace and regard worthy of reception those whom they declared as deserving honor and sacred respect as being men of the same faith or even teachers of piety. Thus believing and thus declaring regarding these things, we embrace with mind and tongue and declare to all people with a loud voice the Definition of the most pure faith of the Christians which has come down even to us from the beginning through the Fathers, subtracting nothing, adding nothing, changing nothing, falsifying nothing; for subtraction and addition, when no heresy is stirred up by the ingenious fabrications of the evil one, introduces condemnation of the uncondemnable and an inexcusable assault on the Fathers, but to change with falsified words the definitions of the Fathers is much worse than the foregoing. Therefore this holy and ecumenical Council, embracing with divine longing and uprightness of mind the definition of the Faith that was from the beginning and considering it divine, therein also founding and erecting the firmament of salvation, is of this mind and cries out to all to proclaim:

I believe in one God, Father Almighty, Creator of heaven and earth, and of all things visible and invisible.

And in one Lord Jesus Christ, the only-begotten Son of God, begotten of the Father before all ages; Light of Light, true God of

---

189 Πατριάρχης Ἱεροσολύμων Δοσίθεος Β΄ (Νοταρᾶς), "Πρακτικὰ τῆς Συνελθούσης ἐν Κωνσταντινουπόλι Συνόδου τοῦ Φωτίου, Γράφει ὁ Ἰγνάτιος ἀπὸ τὸ Πατριαρχεῖο," στὸν Τόμο Χαρᾶς. Μεταφρασμένο ἀπὸ τὸν Ἱερομόναχο Πολύκαρπο (Strosnider). Ἐπεξεργασία ἀπὸ τὸν Κωνσταντῖνο Σιαμάκη καὶ τὸν Γρηγόριο Χῖρς. (Θεσσαλονίκη: Ρηγοπούλου, 1985), 379-381.

true God, begotten, not created, of one essence with the Father through Whom all things were made. Who for us men and for our salvation came down from heaven and was incarnate of the Holy Spirit and the Virgin Mary and became man. He was crucified for us under Pontius Pilate, and suffered and was buried; And He rose on the third day, according to the Scriptures. He ascended into heaven and is seated at the right hand of the Father; And He will come again with glory to judge the living and dead. His kingdom shall have no end.

And in the Holy Spirit, the Lord, the Creator of life, Who proceeds from the Father, Who together with the Father and the Son is worshipped and glorified, Who spoke through the prophets.

In one, holy, catholic, and apostolic Church.

I confess one baptism for the forgiveness of sins.

I look for the resurrection of the dead, and the life of the age to come.

Amen.

Thus we believe; into this confession of the Faith were we baptised; through it the word of truth has shown every heresy to be shattered and destroyed. Those who are of this mind we call brothers and fathers and fellow-heirs of the heavenly commonwealth. But should someone dare to compose another exposition besides this sacred Symbol, which has come down even to us from our blessed and sacred fathers, and call it a Definition of faith, and thus steal for himself the dignity of the confession of those divine men and enfold it with his own inventions, and set it forth as a common lesson to the faithful or even to those returning from some heresy, and be so audacious as to utterly adulterate with spurious words or additions or subtractions the antiquity of this sacred and venerable Definition, in accordance with the decree that has been declared already before us by the holy and ecumenical Councils, if he be one of the clergymen, we subject him to complete defrocking, and if he be of the laymen, we defer him to the anathema.

After the reading, the present sacred concourse cried out, "Thus are we all minded, thus do we believe, into this confession were we baptised and vouchsafed the priestly rank. Them who are otherwise minded, in violation of these things, we regard as enemies of God and of the truth.

Should someone dare to compose and set up another Symbol besides this one or to add or subtract, and be so bold as to declare it a Definition, he is condemned and cast away from all Christian confession. For to subtract or to add is to portray as imperfect the confession to the holy and consubstantial and undivided Trinity, which has been from the beginning to this very day. It convicts the apostolic tradition and the doctrine of the fathers. Should therefore someone arrive at such an end of mindlessness as to dare, as has been said above, to set up another Symbol and call it a Definition, or to make either an addition or a subtraction in the one handed down to us from the holy and ecumenical first great Council in Nicea, let him be anathema."

11. Ninth Ecumenical Council (Constantinople, A.D. 1341, 1347, and 1351)[190]

The Ninth Ecumenical Council was convened in the years 1341, 1347, and 1351 A.D., in the city of Constantinople. This Council upheld the Orthodox Faith as taught by St. Gregory Palamas and condemned the philosophical teachings (having heretical Western influences) of Barlaam of Calabria. Emperor Andronicus III Palaeologus initially presided over the Council. Later Councils had co-Emperor John Cantacuzenus also presiding.

The Councils recognized the practice of *hesychasm* as the authentic life in Christ. Other doctrinal points were dogmatized too: the distinction of the essence and energy of God, that the energies of God (the light on Mt. Tabor) is an uncreated and not a created light, and that the Jesus Prayer is a useful tool in Orthodox life. Barlaam denied all these teachings during the Council in 1341 and taught errors born out of Augustinian and Thomistic speculations, rather than divine revelation. It

---

190 The Synodal Tome of the Council of Constantinople of 1341 can be found throughout the public domain in Greek and in English. However, we have cited the work of Jaroslav Pelikan, an American scholar in the History of Christianity, as the source for this historical Orthodox Christian synodal decree because he was a convert to the Holy Orthodox Church, and we wish to bring attention to his outstanding scholarship.

follows then, he also believed we could use the rational mind to know God in His essence, which was also condemned.

In 1347, these councils condemned those (particularly Akindynos) who continued the teachings of Barlaam.

The Councils in 1351 further refuted the enemies of St. Gregory and clarified his Orthodoxy. This included the correct and incorrect understandings of the Council of 1341, a defense of icons, reiterating that God's essence and energies are both distinct and yet both are uncreated, the reading of various patristic witnesses across Church history, and a reading of the acts of the Sixth Ecumenical Council that showed agreement with St. Gregory. Shortly after the Council, the teachings of St. Gregory Palamas were added to the Synodikon of Orthodoxy as dogmatic teachings of the Orthodox Church.

The Ninth Ecumencial Council relates to Catholicism not in as direct a way to other condemnations of Catholicism. The issue is with St. Augustine's reception throughout the West. Recent and valuable scholarship by many Orthodox teachers has demonstrated how the speculations and errors of Augustine made their way into Western thought to eventually form scholasticism. Augustine's errors allowed for a rogue "Christian" philosophy to mature in the West (and as Fr. John Romanides argues, this was intentionally done by the Franks to set them apart from the "Greeks," thus allowing them to condemn the Orthodox Church as heretics[191]). Barlaam was under those influences of the West. Papademetriou explains it succinctly:

> Augustine himself had not been personally attacked by the Hesychasts of the fourteenth century but Augustinian theology was condemned in the person of Barlaam, who caused the controversy. This resulted in the ultimate condemnation of western Augustinianism as presented to the East by the Calabrian monk, Barlaam, in the Councils of the fourteenth century.

> Palamas, the Orthodox protagonist, wrote numerous treatises against the *filioque* and the basic theological philosophical presuppositions of Latin theology. Saint Gregory Palamas followed

---

191 See Fr. John Romanides' argument in his text *Franks, Romans, Feudalism, and Doctrine.*

the Cappadocian theological presuppositions and maintained that God's essence is totally transcendent and supported the evidence of personal participation in the uncreated energies. That is, he opposed the identity of the essence with the attributes in God. It was the conflict of the theology of revelation based on Augustine, which came from the West through Barlaam, that was reacted against. Revelation for Palamas is directly experienced in the divine energies and is opposed to the conceptualization of revelation. The Augustinian view of revelation by created symbols and illumined vision is rejected. For Augustine, the vision of God is an intellectual experience. This is not acceptable to Palamas. The Palamite emphasis was that creatures, including humans and angles, cannot know or comprehend God's essence.

In the person of Barlaam, the East rejected Augustinian theology. The East perceived that Augustine accepts the neo-Platonic presupposition that the saint is able to have vision of the divine essence as the archetype of all beings. Barlaam contended under the influence of neo-Platonism that through *ekstasis*, the reason going out of the body when it functions in a pure way, one has a vision of the divine archetype. Palamas calls this the Greek pagan error and maintained that man attains *theosis* through participation in the divine energies. [192]

Therefore, in the Ninth Ecumenical Council, while the West was not explicitly condemned as heretical, the ideas which had flourished in the West were condemned through Barlaam.

See Appendix I for two tomes, one for the Council in 1341 and another for the Council in 1351.

---

192 Rev. Dr. George C. Papdemetriou, "Saint Augustine in the Greek Orthodox Tradition," Greek Orthodox Archdiocese of America, accessed January 24th, 2024, https://www.goarch.org/-/saint-augustine-greek-orthodox-tradition

Icon of the Ninth Ecumenical Council,
St. Stephen's Monastery, Meteora, Greece

A liturgy in Hagia Sophia

B. LOCAL COUNCILS

1. Council of Constantinople in 867

The history of the Council of Constantinople in 867 follows the conversion of the Bulgars (Bulgarians) to the Orthodox Christian Faith which began with the baptism of Boris, later named Michael, the first ruler of the Bulgarian Empire from 852-889. "Boris was baptized and given the name Michael after the Byzantine emperor who stood as his sponsor (godfather)...."[193] Although, Boris-Michael was baptized by the Eastern Romans into the Eastern Orthodox Church, he "remained undecided between Rome and Constantinople" for political reasons.[194] In 866 Boris-Michael wrote to the German Emperor Louis II and "asked him to send a bishop and priest to Bulgaria. At the same time, he requested a bishop from Rome. Pope Nicholas I decided to make the most of the opportunity offered by Boris' request. Immediately, he sent as papal legates two bishops, Paul of Populania and Formosus of Porto."[195] Obviously, to the Eastern Romans this was a threat to the situation in Constantinople as the armies of the Bulgars could turn on the East Romans and invade the borders of the Eastern Empire at any time. They

---

193 Despina Stratoudaki White, *Patriarch Photios of Constantinople: His Life, Scholarly Contributions, and Correspondence Together with a Translation of Fifty-Two of His Letters* (Boston: Holy Cross Press, 1981), 30.

194 Ibid., 30.

195 Ibid., 30.

felt that it was necessary for them to win the Bulgarians back to the side of the East.

"The Greek missionaries, who had been forced to leave Bulgaria, had made complaints about certain innovations which their Western rivals were introducing in Bulgaria. The Latins, for instance, allowed the Bulgars to drink milk and eat cheese during lent, a practice forbidden by the Eastern Church. The Western Church forbade their priests to be married, while in the east a priest could get married before his ordination. What was even more serious, the Latins taught that the Holy Spirit proceeded not only from the Father, as was stated in the Nicene Creed, but also from the Son. The procession of the Holy Spirit had occupied the Fathers of the Eastern and Western Churches from the early centuries of Christianity. The first Ecumenical Synod in Nicaea (325) in composing the creed, simply stated: 'And in the Holy Spirit, the Lord and Giver of Life, who proceeds from the Father, who together with the Father and Son is worshipped and glorified.' The Third Ecumenical Synod at Ephesus (431) and the Fourth in Chalcedon (451) forbade any additions or alterations to the Nicaean-Constantinopolitan Creed. The Eastern Church has retained the creed unaltered since then."[196]

"The Eastern Church has continued to abide by the decrees of the ecumenical synods and by the teachings of the Cappadocian Fathers and Athanasios the Great, especially as to the consubstantiality of the Spirit with the Father and the Son.... Patriarch Photios, with the consent of Emperor Michael III and his co-emperor Basil, sent an encyclical letter to the Patriarchs of Antioch, Alexandria and Jerusalem summoning a general synod in the summer of 867 in Constantinople. The purpose of this synod was to examine and condemn the above-mentioned practices of the Latins in Bulgaria, as well as the doctrine of the procession of the Holy Spirit from the Son as well as the Father. Unfortunately, very little of what occurred at this synod has reached us, and the meager information we have comes exclusively from anti-Photian sources. What can be inferred with certainty is that the synod did take place and was attended by many bishops. Pope Nicholas was condemned for the Latin practices in Bulgaria; the Roman doctrine of the procession of the Holy Spirit from the Father and the Son [filioque] was rejected as heretical

---

196 Ibid., 31.

and Roman interference in the affairs of the Byzantine Church was pronounced unlawful; iconoclasm was condemned once more, and Louis II was recognized as emperor of the West at the closing of the synod. Patriarch Photios for many years occupied himself with the *filioque* question. Consequently, in 883 he sent the famous letter to the metropolitan of Aquileia, in which at great length he defended the position of the Eastern Church on this issue. Very upset, the patriarch wrote:

> It has come to our ears that some of those who live in the West, either because they have not been fully satisfied with the Lord's utterance [John 15:26] or, because they have no understanding of the definitions and dogmas of both the Fathers and Synods, or because they overlook the precisions therefrom, or because they have minds that are insensible to such matters, not knowing how else one would state it; nevertheless, surreptitiously introduce the teachings (would that they had not) that the Divine and all-Holy Spirit proceeds not only from God, that is, the Father, but also from the Son, and through such utterance produce extensive harm to those who believe it.

"Again in 885 he wrote the long treatise *On the Mystagogy of the Holy Spirit*. Pope Nicholas died on 13 November 867 without hearing the sentence passed on him by the Eastern bishops and was succeeded by Adrian II."[197] During this same time, on the 24th of September in 867, the political climate had changed with the murder of Emperor Michael III by his so-called friend Basil. Basil was then elevated to power as the Emperor and became the founder of the Macedonian Dynasty. Due to Basil's grievous sin of murder against Emperor Michael III, Saint Photios refused Holy Communion to the new Emperor. This act of excommunicating the murderous emperor eventually led to the deposing of Saint Photios and replacing him with the former Patriarch of Constantinople, Ignatios. Emissaries from Constantinople were eventually sent to Rome in the spring of 869 to inform the Latins of the decisions of the Council of Constantinople in 867.

"The Byzantine embassy was received by the pope at the Church of Santa Maria Maggiore, where the acts of the Synod of 867 were read.

---

197 Ibid., 32-35.

Subsequently, a synod took place, probably at the beginning of June, since a letter sent by the pope to the emperor referring to the findings is dated 10 June 869. The synod condemned and anathematized Photios, including all his acts and all the bishops and churches that he had consecrated. At the end of the meeting, the acts of the Synod of [Constantinople] 867 were burned in front of St. Peter's Cathedral in Rome in the pouring rain. In his letter to the emperor the pope asked that the minutes of the Synod of 867 be burned also in Constantinople."[198] Unfortunately, because of the various religious and political hostilities which occurred on both sides of the empire, most (if not all) of the minutes of the Council in 867 were burned and these texts are lost to history.

2. Council of Constantinople in 1170

Makarios of Ancyra is documented to have described this council by writing: "They took counsel totally to cut off with a total severance the Pope and all those with him... but they did not hand them over to a total anathema, as with the other heresies, uttering the apostolic expression, 'A man that is a heretic after the first and second admonition reject, knowing that he that is such is subverted, and sinneth, being condemned of himself.'"[199]

3. Council of Constantinople in 1285

The Council of Constantinople in 1285 is often called the Council of Blachernae. It convened in 1285 in the Blachernae Palace in Constantinople. The council's session presidents were Gregory II (Patriarch of Constantinople), Athanasius III (Patriarch of Alexandria), and Emperor Andronicus II Palaeologus.

---

198 Ibid., 34-35.

199 Archim. Andronicus Demetracopoulos, Ἱστορία τοῦ Σχίσματος τῆς Λατινικῆς Ἐκκλησίας Ἀπὸ τῆς Ὀρθοδόξου Ἑλληνικῆς [A History of the Schism of the Latin Church from the Greek Orthodox Church], (Leipzig: Otto Wigand, 1867), 32-33. Translated by Daniel Houlis in On Common Prayer with the Heterodox, (Uncut Mountain Press, 2022), 18. The Scriptural reference is Titus 3:10-11.

This council was a response to the papal Council of Lyons held 11 years earlier (1274) in the city of Lyons, in what is now modern day France. Pope Gregory X had declared that the Orthodox Church would be incorporated under Papal rule. Indulgences had been approved for forgiveness of sins for those who participated in a planned crusade, the filioque heresy was reaffirmed with several orthodox clerics made to recite the heretical addition three times. Despite brutal repression of Orthodox laypeople, clergy, and hierarchs who opposed the Council of Lyons, the vast majority of Orthodox did not accept its rulings.

The Council of Constantinople in 1285 was chiefly concerned with John XI (Beccus), who was an earlier patriarch. John Beccus was an unrepentant pro-unionist continuing the papal agenda towards the Church established in the Council of Lyons. The Church condemned with this Council of 1285.

"The council, then, was held sometime after mid-January 1285, after the emperor had returned, when sufficient time had passed to allow the necessary preparations to be made... the deliberations began on the first day of Lent, which would have been 5 February 1285... the final, fifth session was held six months later... It is after these five session were held that the synodal decree, the *Tomus*, was written, for none had been drawn up during the actual debates.... The Council of Blachernae, then, had two quite separate phases. The first, in February, included four sessions and was given over to a hearing of both parties, although neither side managed to convince the other. The second, in August, was for the most part formal, and included the deposition of the unionist Theoctistus of Adrianople, a public and solemn reading of the text of the *Tomus*, and the signing ceremony that followed....

"The truth is, the Council of 1285 was anything but a self-contained debate dealing with verbal formulas. On the contrary, its focus was exclusively Trinitarian, and dealt with two major approaches to the Trinity – the Augustinian and the Cappadocian – which, in the course of the Middle Ages, had established themselves in East and West. Suffice it to say, the Byzantines were duty-bound to defend their own biblical and Cappadocian approach to the Trinity, when challenged in the aftermath of Lyons with the doctrine of the eternal personal procession of the Holy Spirit from the Father and the Son, as from one single principle... the two paths [i.e., Eastern versus Western Trinitarian approaches] involved not only what may be called 'theological method,' but also basic differences in the doctrine of God." [200]

"In 1285, the members of the Council of Blachernae formally commissioned Patriarch Gregory II of Cyprus to draw up an official document of its decisions. A text had not been penned during the actual course of the council's discussion from February to August 1285. The result was the *Tomus* of 1285—possibly the single most important conciliar decision of the entire thirteenth century.... Essentially, what the synod requested was a formal statement of its decision, or a record of its 'resolutions and judgement,' as the eleven anathemas of the text clearly indicate. The document of 1285 is, in fact, a synodal sentence of deposition and a unanimous condemnation, not only of Beccus and his lieutenants George Metochites and Constantine Meliteniotes, but of unionism and the Council of Lyons as well. The text was finally read from the pulpit of the Hagia Sophia at a solemn gathering of the faithful. A signing ceremony followed shortly after. Besides being a condemnation, however, the *Tomus* is a mature and creative exposition of the Orthodox case— that is, a theological rebuttal of unionism and the foreign and 'strange doctrine' of Lyons."[201]

TOMUS OF THE COUNCIL[202]

By the most holy and ecumenical patriarch, Lord Gregory of Cyprus, who was attacked by certain individuals, and for whom this vigorous reply was given. The disturbance and storm, which occurred in the Church a short while ago, had, as it were, for its father and leader, the

---

200 Aristeides Papadakis, *Crisis in Byzantium: The Filioque Controversy in the Patriarchate of Gregory II of Cyprus (1283-1289)* (New York: Fordham University Press, 1983), 62-63.

201 Aristeides Papadakis, *Crisis in Byzantium: The Filioque Controversy in the Patriarchate of Gregory II of Cyprus (1283-1289)* (New York: Fordham University Press, 1983), 153.

202 Aristeides Papadakis, *Crisis in Byzantium: The Filioque Controversy in the Patriarchate of Gregory II of Cyprus (1283-1289)* (New York: Fordham University Press, 1983), 155-165. The following footnotes are from the original text.

Adversary himself, who is forever stricken with envy of man's salvation, and who is always seeking to do that which would prevent it. Even so, he also had individuals who, although they were, at first, not the major leaders at fault, but only worked as so many servants and instruments, by preference, did for the disturbance whatever he wanted done. But, since from the beginning, the union [of 1274], the certain harmless accommodation, and the alleged benefit to us were not, in reality, what they claimed, their actual intention was made clear by their actions. And this was proposed as a bait, drawing men's souls to that which was hidden; it was, further, proposed with promises, with the most terrible imprecations, and with solemn oaths, to the effect that they had nothing else in mind other than that which these very things signified — harmlessness, safety, that is, irreproachability. Shortly afterward, however, these imprecations and oaths were forgotten, as if they had been made for some purpose other than that for which they were intended. And the union and accommodation, and their hitherto seemingly important undertaking, are, as it were, cast down, while the words and the deeds of evil are raised up. And someone[203] dares to declare in our midst that the Spirit also proceeds from the Son, just as it does, indeed, from the Father, and that the only-begotten Son — like the Father, who begets the Son — is its cause. This, then, is how the disturbance begins, how the great struggle against the Church is rekindled.

Almost everyone knows (there is no need to explain it again) that this alien doctrine, which disturbed us lately, was not a recent development, but had its genesis with others, not with us. All the same, it was brought here like a foreign plague, and flourished for quite some time. And it was John Beccus who gave it the strength to grow so much and he accepted it and became the suitable ground, as it were, for its growth; and he nourished it, in my opinion, from the rivers of evil and lawlessness, or, as he falsely said, from Holy Scriptures, interpreting it wrong-

---

203 This "someone" is clearly John Beccus. The account here is historically accurate, and refers to the fact that initially the Union of Lyons, as sponsored by Michael VIII, was grounded on the principle of οἰκονομία. However, Beccus' attempt to justify the *filioque* theologically, shortly after his accession, transferred the issue from the plane of accommodation to that of theology. What was being threatened was the integrity of Byzantine theological tradition and custom, which Michael had promised to retain undisturbed.

ly, spreading babble from there, and committing sacrilege, while, at the same time robbing the meaning of Scripture, and the sense of those who listened superficially or of those who had an eye on his wealth. Yet, this evil man was almost in his eighth year of office and residence in this city; for this is how long he had been established on the patriarchal throne, the prize for a bad crop. And all this time God allowed the Church to suffer and endure the worst because of the multitude of the sins of everyone, by which we alone provoke the anger of Him who is without passion.[204]

Eventually, however, God pitied us, his servants, and looked upon us with mercy and raised up an emperor — who seems to live only for the purpose of doing his bidding — and the Church, just as, in the past, He had raised David's fallen and ruined tabernacle through him.[205] And the man who had accepted and nourished the evil and discord was removed from our midst, and the true doctrine concerning the Spirit is expressed with confidence, and those who wish to change the life dearest to God are, in the future, free to build on the foundation of faith. It is, likewise, commendable, and truly salutary, and the work of superior planning to attend to the future safety of the Church and, in every way, to secure its stability so that if someone hateful to God should again attempt to disturb it, he will be shown to be acting in vain, because he will be repelled by the unshakable words of our faith. This could be accomplished satisfactorily if we do two things. We should first define our belief clearly, that is, the Orthodox faith, and raise it as a permanent monument to our sublime faith; seen, thus, from a distance — being visible to all — it will attract to itself the spiritual eyes of everyone. Secondly, we must make this evil, destructive and alien teaching known, so that when this has been exposed, we will all turn away from it and despise it and quickly escape from its danger.

Accordingly, the faith which we acknowledge and believe in our heart is as follows. We believe as we have been taught from the beginning and from the Fathers. We have been taught and we believe in one God, the Father almighty, creator of heaven and earth, and of all things visible and invisible, who, being without principle (ἄναρχος), unbegot-

---

204 Beccus' Patriarchate: 26 May 1275 to 26 December 1282.

205 Acts 15:16.

ten, and without cause, is the natural principle and cause of the Son and of the Spirit. We also believe in His only begotten Son, who, being consubstantial with Him, was begotten eternally and without change from Him, through whom all things were made. We believe in the all-Holy Spirit, which proceeds from the same Father, which, with the Father and the Son together, is worshipped as coeternal, co-equal, co-essential, co-equal in glory, and as joint-creator of the world. We believe that the only-begotten Word of the supersubstantial and life-giving Trinity came down from heaven for us men and for our salvation, was incarnate by the Holy Spirit and the Virgin Mary and became man; that is, He became perfect man while remaining God and in no way altered or transformed the divine nature by His contact with the flesh, but assumed humanity without change. And He, who is passionless according to His divine nature, suffered the passion and the cross and, on the third day, rose from the dead and ascended into heaven and sat at the right hand of God the Father. We believe in accordance with God, holy tradition and teaching in one holy, catholic, and apostolic Church. We acknowledge one baptism for the remission of sins, we look for the resurrection of the dead, and the life of the age to come.

Additionally, we acknowledge a single hypostasis of the incarnate Word, and we believe the same Christ to be one, and we proclaim and know Him after the Incarnation, as redeeming with two natures, from which, and in which, and which He is. Consequently, we believe in two energies and two wills of the same Christ, each nature having its own will and its own saving action. We venerate, but not absolutely and without adoration, the holy and sacred images of Christ, of the immaculate Mother of God, and of all the saints, because the honor we show them passes over to the original. We reject the recently established union [of Lyons] which provoked God's hostility toward us.[206] For this union divided and ravaged the Church, under the pretense of harmless accommodation, persuading it, by their stupidity and deception, to establish their glory, but not God's,[207] and to turn from Orthodoxy and the sound teaching of the Fathers, and to fall down the precipice of heresy and blas-

---

206 Cf. Rom. 8:7.
207 Rom. 10:3.

phemy.[208] We also render void their dangerous doctrine concerning the procession of the Holy Spirit. We have been taught from God, the Word Himself, that the all-Holy Spirit proceeds from the Father; and we confess that it has its existence from the Father, and that it prides itself — exactly as the Son Himself does — in the fact that the same [Father] is essentially the cause of its being. And we know and believe that the Son is from the Father, being enriched in having the Father as His cause and natural principle, and in being consubstantial and of one nature with the Spirit, which is from the Father. Even so, He is not, either separately or with the Father, the cause of the Spirit; for the all-Holy Spirit's existence is not "through the Son" and "from the Son" as they who hasten toward their destruction and separation from God understand and teach.[209] We shun and cut off from our communion those who do not correctly uphold the sound faith but blaspheme blatantly, and think and speak perversely and perpetuate what is most alarming and unbearable to hear.[210]

They were originally members of our nation and of our doctrine and belonged to the Church, and yet they rebelled against it and put it aside — the Church which had spiritually given them birth and had nourished them. And they placed the Church in ultimate danger and showed themselves blameworthy children, estranged sons, who had veered from their paths. You did not repay well — evil and perverse generation — either the Lord God or Mother Church. One should be willing to endure every danger — even death itself should not be rejected — on behalf of the Church and its doctrines.[211] And yet, their behavior toward the Church was worse than that of natural enemies, for they were openly emotionally disturbed and had altogether lost the ability of distinguishing between friend and foe. The first among them, as we said, was John

---

208 The word "blasphemy" is used repeatedly by Gregory to describe Beccus' doctrine concerning the procession of the Spirit. To be sure, the deeply biblical nuance of the word in Scripture and in patristic literature did not escape him. In the New Testament, the word indicates violation of the power and majesty of God (Mark 2:7; Luke 5:2 1). In the early patristic period, opposing theological views were stigmatized as blasphemy. See especially G. Kittel, ed., *Theological Dictionary of the New Testament, I* (Grand Rapids-London, 1964), 621-25.

209 Psalm 73:27.

210 Acts 20:30.

211 Matt. 17:17.

Beccus who (because Christ had visited his own Church, and moved against him and his evil associates, and proceeded clearly forward with the result that he was going to be justly punished for his endless chatter), after appearing to repent for the mischief he had caused when he went raving mad, and, after composing a pious statement and giving it to the synod handling his case, had hardly tasted leniency and escaped condemnation, when he turned back to his own vomit of blasphemy.[212]

Indeed, this statement should be made known so that all who hear it may judge if he was justly condemned. The verbatim text was as follows:[213]

> Because of my attempt to promote the precarious accommodation of the supposed ecclesiastical union, and to bring everyone around to agree to it, it happened that I spoke and wrote on Church doctrine; certain things which I had said, however, were found to be of a dubious nature and at variance with sacred and holy doctrine and this being so, the synod had them condemned. I said, for example, that the Holy Spirit has, as cause of its personal existence, the Father and the Son, and that this doctrine was in harmony with the formula which declares that the 'Spirit proceeds from the Father through the Son.' In the final analysis, this means that the Spirit has two causes, and that both the direct and the remote principles of causation were implied. That is, the Son is as much the cause of the existence of the Spirit as the meaning of the preposition "through" allows. And since all these doctrines are found in my own writings and speeches, they are mine, for no one else had thought and written these. Additionally, I said that the Father and the Son [together] constitute a single cause of the Spirit from whom, as from one principle and source, the Spirit has its being. All this and anything else that may lead to such dogmatic absurdity — before God, his awesome angels, and before the holy and sacred synod — from the bottom of my heart, without deceit, without

---

212 2 Peter 2:22.

213 This passage indicates that the text was intended for those who had assembled to "hear" the *Tomus* read from the pulpit of the Hagia Sophia.

hiding one thing and saying another, I turn away from, I reject, and I cast out because they lead to the ultimate destruction of the soul. I confess with heart and tongue and I believe as does the holy Catholic Church from the beginning in the Holy Trinity, the one God, thus: that the Father does not have His being either from another or from Himself, but is without beginning and without cause that the only-begotten Son of God has His existence by generation from the Father and has the Father as His cause; I confess and believe that the Holy Spirit has — by procession — its existence from God the Father; and that the Father, according to the voices of the holy teachers, is the cause of the Son and of the Spirit; that the formula 'the Spirit proceeds through the Son' in no way renders the Son, either separately or with the Father, the cause of the Spirit because, according to the dubious and absurd view of certain individuals, the Son and the Father constitute the one cause and unique principle of the Spirit. These, then, are the doctrines that I confess. I hope it will be these and all the doctrines of the holy catholic Church of God, according to this written confession, that I shall be found confessing unto my last breath. Everyone who, now or in the future, does not confess thus I dissociate myself from, and I cast out far from the Orthodox faith of Christians. This is the statement of my confession and faith, by which I acknowledge and witness to everyone, and by which I indicate clearly that I hold to the faith concerning God, and that I am entirely devoted to the evangelical, apostolic, and patristic doctrine and teaching. Because of my boldness, by which I precariously attempted to delve into certain of the above-mentioned doctrines, I was deposed from the episcopate by the most holy [Joseph], lord and ecumenical patriarch, and by his holy and sacred synod, in which the most holy [Athanasius] pope and patriarch of Alexandria was also present. As such, I approve this lawfully and canonically rendered sentence of deposition, and I accept this resolution as justifiable and lawful. I shall never try to regain the priesthood.

Nevertheless, once this confession which he wrote and signed with his own hand was published, he annulled it immediately as soon as the ecclesiastical court had given him a reprieve. And he again composes books and blasphemies, and he again adds spurious doctrines and the opinions of others which our fathers did not know. And he obstinately tries to prove himself superior to these "errors" of this evil, whereas, of course, he should have done this solely by repentance and by the suppression of all that he had written. By ignoring the way,[214] he veered from the straight path and was given to a mind even more reprobate than before.[215] We imagine that the spirit of error left him for a while, but attacked him again with greater force, having brought along not seven, but a whole legion of spirits, and that it took possession of his soul and filled it.[216] Therefore, he is again summoned and asked to account for this change from good to evil. And who summons him but the emperor [Andronicus] who is jealous of God, the God of hosts,[217] and who has become as the hand of the Most High himself in the restoration of the Church and the faith, whom I happily call a new Moses, God's excellent servant,[218] who rescued the present-day people of Israel not from that ancient material bondage of Egypt, but from another one that is far worse. Because of this service, the emperor has been drawn by the hand of God, whose books contain his name.[219] We, therefore, need not write a great deal about him.

And Beccus was asked by the emperor and by the holy synod to state the reasons for which he turned back (after he had obtained the grace of a commendable repentance, and had put — to speak scripturally — his hand to the plow,[220] and had agreed to follow the Church's order), and lost all ability to gain the kingdom of heaven, preferring blasphemy to truth. However, it became clear from his words (he did not say anything that is true), and from his actions (he made no attempt to hide his wickedness), that he is so closely united with heterodoxy that no words

---

214 2 Peter 2:15.

215 Rom. 1:28.

216 Cf. Matt. 12:43-45.

217 1 Kings 19:10.

218 Heb. 3:5.

219 Cf. Phil. 4:3; Apoc. 17:8.

220 Luke 9:62.

would convince him to renounce his position. Accordingly, the entire assembly of the faithful, inspired by the righteous zeal against him and those who share his views, render this decision like the ancient priests pronouncing against their own kin, the sons of Israel, who had broken the law.

1. To John Beccus and to those who follow him, to Constantine Mel-iteniotes and George Metochites, who were born of us,[221] and who were reared in our customs and doctrines, but who did not abide in them despite the fact that these were their own and of the Fa-thers, and had been established with the passage of time ever since the Christian faith began to be preached in these parts. But these, against which not even the gates of hell have prevailed nor shall pre-vail[222]—they have despised, and I do not know why they condemn them, or why they refuse to praise them. But then they introduced instead a belief that was entirely unknown to its authors, for they re-spect neither the text's antiquity nor those who revealed these truths, namely, the ones who spoke of the things of the Spirit not for any other reason but because they were filled with the Spirit. To these men because they were so corrupt that they held beliefs both strange and alien to our traditions to the detriment and destruction of the Church; and, sometime later, they renounced this madness and de-clared by word and in writing before countless eyes and ears that they would be accursed if, in the future, they should not be found in full possession of the traditional faith, but drawn to a belief alien to the Church; and because they did not abide by their own written statement concerning this repentance, but changed their mind and opinion and again turned to their previous apostasy, as if possessed of a rebellious nature and a faithlessness toward ancestral doctrines, to these, because they wickedly turned away and preferred this sepa-ration from their own Church, we pronounce the resolution which they have pronounced upon themselves (or in the case of those who, in the future, will dare to do so), we cut them off (since they hold such views) from the membership of the Orthodox, and we banish them from the flock of the Church of God.

---

221 Cf. 1 John 2:19.

222 Matt. 16:18.

2. To the same [John Beccus], and to those who along with him were rash enough to introduce into the apostolic faith matters which the teachers of the Church did not hand down and which we have not received through them, we pronounce the above-recorded resolution and judgment, we cut them off from the membership of the Orthodox, and we banish them from the flock of the Church of God.

3. To the same, who say that the Father is, through the Son, the cause of the Spirit, and who cannot conceive the Father as the cause of the hypostasis of the Spirit—giving it existence and being—except through the Son; thus, according to them the Son is united to the Father as joint-cause and contributor to the Spirit's existence. This, they say, is supported by the phrase of Saint John of Damascus, "the Father is the projector through the Son of the manifesting Spirit." "He Himself [the Father], then, is mind, the depth of reason, begetter of the Word, and, through the Word, projector of the manifesting Spirit." This, however, can never mean what they say, inasmuch as it clearly denotes the manifestation—through the intermediary of the Son—of the Spirit, whose existence is from the Father. For the same John of Damascus would not have said—in the exact same chapter—that the only cause in the Trinity is God the Father, thus denying, by the use of the word "only," the causative principle to the remaining two hypostases.[223] Nor would he have, again, said elsewhere, "and we speak, likewise, of the Holy Spirit as the 'Spirit of the Son,' yet we do not speak of the Spirit as from the Son."[224] For both of these views to be true is impossible. To those who have not accepted the interpretation given to these testimonia by the Fathers, but, on the contrary, perceive them in a manner altogether forbidden by them, we pronounce the above recorded resolution and judgment, we cut them off from the membership of the Orthodox, and we banish them from the flock of the Church of God.

4. To the same, who affirm that the Paraclete, which is from the Father, has its existence through the Son and from the Son, and who again propose as proof the phrase "the Spirit exists through the Son and from the Son." In certain texts [of the Fathers], the phrase denotes the Spirit's shining forth and manifestation. Indeed, the very Para-

---

223 John of Damascus, De fide orthodoxa, in *Kotter, Die Schriften des Johannes von Damaskos II*, 36 (= PG 94.849B).

224 Ibid.

clete shines from and is manifest eternally through the Son, in the same way that light shines forth and is manifest through the intermediary of the sun's rays; it further denotes the bestowing, giving, and sending of the Spirit to us. It does not, however, mean that it subsists through the Son and from the Son, and that it receives its being through Him and from Him. For this would mean that the Spirit has the Son as cause and source (exactly as it has the Father), not to say that it has its cause and source more so from the Son than from the Father; for it is said that that from which existence is derived likewise is believed to enrich the source and to be the cause of being. To those who believe and say such things, we pronounce the above resolution and judgment, we cut them off from the membership of the Orthodox, and we banish them from the flock of the Church of God.

5. To the same, who say that the preposition "through" everywhere in theology is identical to the preposition "from" and, as a result, maintain that there is no difference in saying that the Spirit proceeds "through the Son" from saying that it proceeds "from the Son" — whence, undoubtedly, the origin of their idea that the existence and essence of the Spirit is from the Son. And they either infer a double or a single procession of origin, and join the Son to the Father according to this explanation of "cause," both of which are beyond all blasphemy. For there is no other hypostasis in the Trinity except the Father's, from which the existence and essence of the consubstantial [Son and Holy Spirit] is derived. According to the common mind of the Church and the aforementioned saints, the Father is the foundation and the source of the Son and the Spirit, the only source of divinity, and the only cause. If, in fact, it is also said by some of the saints that the Spirit proceeds "through the Son," what is meant here is the eternal manifestation of the Spirit by the Son, not the purely [personal] emanation into being of the Spirit, which has its existence from the Father. Otherwise, this would deprive the Father from being the only cause and the only source of divinity, and would expose the theologian [Gregory of Nazianzus] who says "everything the Father is said to possess, the Son, likewise, possesses except causality."[225] To these who speak thus, we pronounce the above-recorded resolution and judgment, we cut them off from the

---

225 Gregory of Nazianzus, Oratio 34, PG 36.252A.

membership of the Orthodox, and we banish them from the flock of the Church of God.

6. To the same, who contend that the unique essence and divinity of the Father and the Son is the cause of the Spirit's existence — an idea which no one who has ever had it in his mind has either expressed or considered making public. For the common essence and nature is not the cause of the hypostasis; nor does this common essence ever generate or project that which is undivided; on the other hand, the essence which is accompanied by individual characteristics does, and this, according to the great Maximus, denotes the hypostasis.[226] But also, according to the great Basil, because he too defines the hypostasis as that which describes and brings to mind what in each thing is common, and which cannot be described by means of individual characteristics which appear in it (Basil, locus incognitus). Because of this, the indivisible essence always projects something indivisible (or generates the indivisible that generates), in order that the created may be [simultaneously] the projector as well as the projected; the essence of the Father and the Son, however, is one, and is not, on the whole, indivisible.[227] To these, who absurdly blaspheme thus, we pronounce the above-recorded resolution and judgment, we cut them off from the membership of the Orthodox, and we banish them from the flock of the Church of God.

7. To the same, who teach that the Father and the Son — not as two principles and two causes — share in the causality of the Spirit, and that the Son is as much a participant with the Father as is implied in the preposition "through." According to the distinction and strength of these prepositions, they introduce a distinction in the Spirit's cause, with the result that sometimes they believe and say that the Father is cause, and sometimes the Son. This being so, they introduce a plurality and a multitude of causes in the procession of the Spirit, even though this was prohibited on countless occasions. As such, we pronounce the above-recorded resolution and judgment, we cut them off from the membership of the Orthodox, and we banish them from the flock of the Church of God.

---

226 Cf. Maximus the Confessor, Letter 7: To John the Presbyter, PG 91.436A.

227 On this section, cf. John of Damascus, De fide orthodoxa, in Kotter, Die Schriften des Johannes von Damaskos, II, 27 (= PG 94.825A-B).

8. To the same, who stoutly maintain that the Father by virtue of the
    nature — not by virtue of the hypostasis — is the Holy Spirit's cause;
    the result is that they necessarily proclaim the Son as cause of the
    Spirit, since the Son has the same nature as the Father. At the same
    time, they fail to see the absurdity that results from this. For it is
    necessary first that the Spirit be the cause of someone, for the simple
    reason that it has the same nature as the Father. Secondly, the num-
    ber of the cause increases, since as many hypostases as share in nature
    must, likewise, share in causality. Thirdly, the common essence and
    nature is transformed into the cause of the hypostasis, which all log-
    ic — and, along with this, nature itself — prohibits. To these, who
    believe in such things strange and alien to truth, we pronounce the
    above-recorded resolution and judgment, we cut them off from the
    membership of the Orthodox, and we banish them from the flock
    of the Church of God.

9. To the same, who state that, in reference to the creation of the world,
    the phrase "through the Son" denotes the immediate cause, Imme-
    diate or primordial cause,[228] as well as the fact that it denies the Son
    the right to be creator and cause of things made "through Him."
    That is to say, in theology proper [the study of the Trinity in itself],
    even if the Father is called the initial cause of the Son and the Spirit,
    He is also, "through the Son," the cause of the Spirit. Accordingly,
    the Son cannot be separated from the Father in the procession of
    the Spirit. By saying such things, they irrationally join the Son to
    the Father in the causation of the Spirit. In reality, even if the Son,
    like the Father, is creator of all things made "through Him," it does
    not follow that He is also the Spirit's cause, because the Father is the
    projector of the Spirit through Him; nor, again, does it follow that,
    because the Father is the Spirit's projector "through the Son," He
    is, through Him, the cause of the Spirit. For the formula "through
    the Son" here denotes the manifestation and illumination [of the
    Spirit by the Son], and not the emanation of the Spirit into being.
    If this was not so, it would be difficult, indeed, even to enumerate
    the theological absurdities that follow. To these, who irrationally ex-
    press such views, and ascribe them to the writings of the saints, and
    from these stir up a multitude of blasphemies, we pronounce the
    above-recorded resolution and judgment, we cut them off from the

---

228 προκαταρκτικὴ αἰτία; cf. Basil, On the Holy Spirit, PG 32.136B.

membership of the Orthodox, and we banish them from the flock of the Church of God.

10. To the same, who declare that the Son is said to be the fountain of life in the same way that the Virgin Mother of God is said to be the fountain of life.[229] The Virgin is so called because she lent living flesh to the only-begotten Word with a rational and intellectual soul, and became the cause of mankind born according to Christ. Similarly, those who understand life to be in the Holy Spirit will think of the Son as the fountain of life in terms of cause. Hence, their argument — from conclusions drawn of incongruous comparisons and examples — for the participation of the Son with the Father in the procession of the Spirit. And yet, it is not because the Virgin is said to be the fountain of life that the only-begotten Word of God is called the fountain of life. For she is so called because it is from her that real life came, for the same Word of God and true God was born according to His humanity, and she became the cause of His holy flesh. As for the Son, He is the fountain of life because He became the cause of life for us who were dead to sin; because he became as an overflowing river to everyone; and because, for those who believe in the Son, the Spirit is bestowed as from this fountain and through Him. This grace of the Spirit is poured forth, and it is neither novel nor alien to Scripture were it to be called by the same name as Holy Spirit. For, sometimes, an act (ἐνέργεια) is identified by the name of the one who acts, since frequently we do not refuse to call "sun" the sun's own luster and light.[230] To these, whose ambition is to draw such conclusions, and to reconcile what by nature cannot at all be reconciled, we pronounce the above-recorded resolution and judgment, we cut them off from the membership of the Orthodox, and we banish them from the flock of the Church of God.

11. To the same, who do not receive the writings of the saints in the correct manner intended by the Church, nor do they honor what appears to be the closest [interpretation] according to the patristic

---

229 For the use of the phrase in patristic literature, sec G. W H. Lampe, *A Patristic Greek Lexicon* (Oxford, 1961-1968), fasc. 4, 1080.

230 Cf. Patriarch Philotheus' words in Against Gregoras, PG 151.916D: "And this divine splendor and grace, this energy and gift of the all-Holy Spirit, is called Holy Spirit by Scripture ... for we call 'sun' not only the solar disk, but the splendor and energy sent forth from there."

traditions and the common beliefs about God and things divine, but distort the meaning of these writings so as to set them at variance with the prescribed dogmas, or adhere to the mere word and, from this, bring forth strange doctrine, we pronounce the above-recorded resolution and judgment, we cut them off from the membership of the Orthodox, and we banish them from the flock of the Church of God.

Certainly, the doctrines of the above-listed and already expelled individuals are filled with blasphemy, malice, and fall short of all ecclesiastical prudence. Even if Beccus, the father of these doctrines — or someone among his zealous supporters — confidently affirms that these teachings are the thoughts of the saints, in reality, we must suppose him a slanderer and blasphemer of the saints. For where have the God-bearing Fathers said that God the Father is, through the Son, the cause of the Spirit? Where do they say that the Paraclete has its existence from the Son and through the Son? Again, where do they say that the same Paraclete has its existence from the Father and from the Son? In what text do they teach that the one essence and divinity of the Father and the Son is the cause of the Holy Spirit's existence? Who, and in which of his works, ever prohibited anyone from saying that the hypostasis of the Father is the unique cause of being of the Son and the Spirit? Who among those who believe that the Father is the cause of the Spirit has taught that this is by virtue of the nature, not by virtue of the hypostasis? And who has failed to maintain this as the characteristic that distinguishes the Father from the other two hypostases? Finally, who says that those other teachings, about which he has lied by insulting the Fathers, belong to the Fathers? He abstains from neither evil. For at some places, he alters their own words, and, even when he uses the words without distortion, he does not adhere to their true meaning. Neither does he look at the aim that the author had in mind, but arrogantly passes over the purpose and the desire, and even the express intent of the author's statement, and adheres to the word and, having obtained the shadow instead of the body, composes books. And this is like saying that he twists ropes of sand and builds houses therefrom to make I do not know what, unless it is a monument and a memorial — the former, an advertisement of his folly the latter, a declaration of the struggle he undertook against his own salvation. This being so, we condemn the doctrines themselves together with their authors, and judge that their memory, like the expelled, be eliminated from the Church with a resounding noise.

They are like thorns and thistles which, by divine permission, have grown within the life-giving precincts of the Church, or like evil weeds which the enemy has sown among the authentic wheat of the gospel.[231] For he found an opportunity for his wickedness in the forebearance of the avenging God. They are a death-bearing brood of vipers[232] (if you prefer something that has a greater resemblance to evil) and, according to Scripture, descendants of serpents bringing death to every soul that approaches them; and they are worth preserving so long as they do not need to be born at all and men do not know of them. They should be destroyed with fire, and with iron, and with every possible means — a task the Church should undertake — and they should be given over to non-being and to ultimate destruction. Indeed, we counsel all the sons of our Church to avoid them with great care, and not even to listen to them in a cursory manner.

But we cannot stop with admonition alone but must supplement this with both threat and fear for the sake of the security of the future.[233] But what does this threat consist of? Is it because the act [of Lyons] which occurred a short while back — I know not why they called it "accommodation" and union, when it deserves a completely different name — confused the Church and finally ravaged it? Indeed, this act introduced precariously and very dangerously the aforementioned and unreasonable doctrines, which had John Beccus as their protector. Thus, we define our position very clearly for everyone, should any individual — living now or in the future — ever dare to revive that act which has been

---

231 Cf. Matt. 13:24-30.

232 Luke 3:7.

233 This section, beginning with "But we cannot" and continuing to the end of the *Tomus*, is quoted verbatim by Gennadios Scholarios in his Second Treatise on the Procession of the Holy Spirit; see L. Petit et al. (edd.), Œuvres complètes de Gennade Scholarios, II (Paris, 1929), 424-26. The patriarch here draws the threads of his argument together, and summarizes the reasons for the rejection of the Union of Lyons. Gennadios was particularly anxious to show that the Church had indeed solemnly and formally rejected the decision of 1274 and the dogmatization of the *Filioque*. Hence his lengthy quotation.

wisely abolished, or attempt to impose doctrines on our Church which have been already profitably condemned, or suggest them either secretly and maliciously, or introduce a proposal in favor of believing or approving these doctrines, or strive for their free acceptance among us, and thus scorn the genuine doctrines of the early Church and its present decrees against the spurious and alien and, indeed, against the accommodation and act by which they crept into the Church to its detriment. This Beccus, and anyone who agrees ever to receive those members of the Roman Church who remain intransigent concerning those doctrines for which they were from the beginning accused by our Church and for which the schism occurred, and who agree to receive them more openly than we were accustomed, that is, prior to this misleading accommodation and worthless union [of Lyons] hostile to the good — this man, besides expelling him from the Church, cutting him off, and removing him from the assembly and society of the faithful, we subject to the terrible penalty of anathema. For he should not even be forgiven by men, he who did not learn not to dare such things (after such an experience of the preceding evil, or after the recent condemnation), and who did not understand not to contrive against the accepted formulations of the Fathers, nor to remain forever a disciple and subject of the Church.

And we proclaim and do these things, as we said, for the sake of remaining spiritually unharmed, for the mutual benefit of everyone, for those who now belong to our devout Church, and for those who after this shall continue to do so. Remain steadfast, true [followers] of God, by avoiding and loathing those other doctrines that are opposed to the truth, and those fabrications of Beccus. Avoid not only him, but those individuals mentioned above by name who together with him spew out blasphemies which, till now, they have made their own, and which they accept unrepentantly. By so doing, the Paraclete will abide in you, and will preserve you not only from the plague of such error, but from the greater plague of the passions for the participation in the eternal benefits and the blessedness prepared for the just. And may you be and remain so.

The recorded resolution and decision has now been issued by the Church against those who have rebelled and repudiated the Church. In a short while it will be proclaimed by the supreme judge, unless, before the arrival of His great and manifest day,[234] they set themselves free by repentance, tears and mourning beyond endurance. For if they repent and look again at the light of Mother Church with the pure eyes of the soul, they will be like those who, in coming to Christ, will not be turned out. To the contrary, Christ will approach the returning one and will embrace him, even if he is a prodigal son who has wasted his inherited portion,[235] or a lost sheep which had abandoned its sheepfold, or an individual who has removed himself from grace. So, it is with the Church which in like manner shall gather them together and reckon as its own and forthwith establish them among the ranks and company of its children, provided they lament one day and experience what we experience now. And although we excommunicate them, separate them from the Church of the devout, impose on them the awesome and great judgment of separation and estrangement from the Orthodox, we do not do it because we wish to exult over their misfortune or to rejoice over their rejection. On the contrary, we grieve and bear their isolation with loathing. But why do we need to act in this fashion? Mainly for two reasons: the first being that their unhappiness and bitterness will cause them, after they have realized their folly, to return repentant and save themselves in the Church. Secondly, others will henceforth be chastened and disciplined so as not to attempt anything similar, or attack that which is holy, or behave willfully against that which is sacred; lest, if they show such audacity, they receive the same rewards in accordance with the example that has been set.

Some Manuscripts Add the Following Paragraph.

Whereas the Son is the living and enhypostatic wisdom of God the Father, the Holy Spirit which proceeds ineffably and eternally from God the Father alone as Scripture affirms, is likewise the light and self-subsistent life of the inaccessible and eternal light. Whosoever is of a different mind we cut them off from the membership of the Orthodox, and we banish them from the flock of the Church of God.

---

234 Acts 2:21.

235 Luke 15:11-32.

4. Council of Constantinople in 1450[236]

[Arriving back in Constantinople from the Union Council in Florence,] the inhabitants of Constantinople assailed the Bishops with questions: "How did the Council end? Have we gained the victory?" Those who had been forced to the union, or had joined it from interested motives, but had not as yet lost all conscience of their crime, did not conceal the truth. Feeling themselves now at liberty in their native land, amidst their Orthodox brethren, they answered with heartfelt sorrow: "We have sold our faith, we have exchanged Orthodoxy for heterodoxy, and losing our former pure faith have become azymites [Papists]. May our hands, which signed the unjust decree be cut off! May our tongues which have spoken consent with the Latins be plucked out!" These were the first words of the good but weak Pastors — Anthony of Heraclea, the oldest members of the Council, and others. Such news made a terrible impression on the Orthodox townspeople. Everyone avoided the new arrivers, and those who had anything to do with them. The clergy who had remained in Constantinople would not even agree to officiate with those, who, repenting of their consent to the union, declared that they were forced to it. [...] The Bishops and clergy of Constantinople demanded that the Ecumenical Council should be held in Constantinople itself to terminate all the evil caused by the adherents of the union. But the Emperor John [Palaiologos] died (Oct. 31, 1448) before he had the time to satisfy these demands; at all events before his death, he rejected all union with the Church of Rome. At last, the innermost wishes of the Orthodox pastors and people were fulfilled. A year and a half after Constantine's accession to the throne of Byzantium, three Eastern Patriarchs in whose name, though without their consent, the Florentine unorthodox "decree" was signed, viz., Philotheus of Alexandria, Dorotheus of Antioch and Theophanes of Jerusalem, assembled in Constantinople with many Metropolitans and Bishops to quiet the disturbed Church. Assembling a Council in the Church of St. Sophia in Constantinople, they deprived Gregory Mamma of his patriarchal throne and appointed the Orthodox Athanasius in his place, and then in the name of all the

---

236 Ivan N. Ostroumoff, *The History of the Council of Florence*, trans. Basil Popoff (Boston: Holy Transfiguration Monastery, 1971), 164-177.

Eastern Church rejected the decree of the Council of Florence which they convicted as having acted contrary to the Orthodox faith, and accused the Church of Rome of many digressions from the ancient rules and rites of the Church Ecumenical.

5. Council of Constantinople in 1484[237]

a. Introduction

The Council of Constantinople in 1484 "defines the nature of the gathering by a common profession of faith which excludes the *Filioque*," the heretical addition to the Nicaean creed which is characteristic of Latin Christianity. This council references that the creed cannot be changed as stated by the First Canon of the Second Ecumenical Council in 381 *(The Faith of the Three Hundred and Eighteen Fathers assembled at Nice in Bithynia shall not be set aside, but shall remain firm).*[238] This council also refused the heretical decisions made at the Council of Ferrara-Florence (1438-1439) and upheld the theological positions put forth by Saint Photios the Great at the Eight Ecumenical Council (879) and those of the Council of Constantinople in 1285. Furthermore, this council of 1484 rejected the *Filioque* on the basis of Saint Dionysius the Areopagite and Saint Gregory of Nazianzus, establishing the rejection of the heretical Latin doctrine for future generations of Orthodox Christians. This holy synod declared invalid the false union of 1439, recognized the existence of the schismatic Latin church as separated from Orthodoxy, and set forth a service for accepting those coming from the Latins to renounce their false doctrines and to be Chrismated into Holy

---

237 Symeon Paschalidis, "Concilum Constantinopolitanum 1484," *The Great Councils of the Orthodox Churches Decisions and Synodika: From Constantinople 861 to Constantinople 1872, Volume I*, ed. Giuseppe Alberigo & Alberto Melloni (Bologna: Brepols Publishers, 2016), 218-227.

238 Second Ecumenical Council, "Canons of the One Hundred and Fifty Fathers who assembled at Constantinople, Canon I," in *Nicene and Post-Nicene Fathers, The Seven Ecumenical Councils, Volume 14*, ed. Philip Schaff & Henry Wace (Peabody: Hendrickson Publishers, 1999), 172.

266 The Orthodox Patristic Witness Concerning Catholicism

Orthodoxy.[239] However, it should be noted that the *Oros* of 1755 was signed by Patriarch Cyril V of Constantinople, Patriarch Matthew of Alexandria, and Patriarch Parthenios of Jerusalem, which decreed that all converts coming from Papal heresy to be received by the One True Baptism of the Holy Eastern Orthodox Church (*See Oros of 1755* on page 277).

b. Decree of the Holy and Ecumenical Council Which Assembled for the Overturning of the Council in Florence[240]

This holy and ecumenical council, which assembled in the divine and all-venerable temple of the most holy Theotokos the All-Blessed [Pammakaristos] by the approval and grace of God and by the concourse of the blessed and most holy patriarchs of the queen of cities, the City of Constantine that is, of that memorable, already departed Sir Maximus and of the one now directing the helm of the catholic Church, Sir Symeon, decreed the following:

---

239 Prior to St. Mark of Ephesus and following the 1484 Council, baptism was the means by which Latins were received into the Orthodox Church. As to why the Latins were said to be received by chrismation by St. Mark of Ephesus and the 1484 Council, St. Nikodemos the Hagiorite and St. Athanasios Parios explained that at this time the Orthodox had become very weak under the force of the Ottomans while the Pope was in authority over all of the kings and militaries of Europe. Had it been decreed at that time that the Latins must be received by baptism, this would have led "the Pope to rouse the Latin races against the Eastern, take them prisoners, kill them, and inflict innumerable barbarities upon them." (Agapios and Nicodemus, *The Rudder*, Footnote 66 of the 85 Canons of the Holy Apostles). St. Nikodemos and St. Athanasios Parios said that reception of the Latins by chrismation at that time was due to the Latin viciousness against the Orthodox. However, by their time (the 18th century) this threat had passed and (of great importance) the Latins had abandoned the apostolic form of three immersions; therefore, 'the season of economia has passed' (St. Athanasios Parios, quoted in Metallinos, *I Confess One Baptism*, p. 91) and the Latins must now be received by baptism as was decreed at the 1755 Council of the Three Patriarchs. For more on this see *On the Reception of the Heterodox into the Orthodox Church: The Patristic Consensus and Criteria*, Chapters 10 and 15.

240 Machi Paizi Apostolopoulou, "Concilum Constantinopolitanum 1484," in *The Great Councils of the Orthodox Churches Decisions and Synodika: From Constantinople 861 to Constantinople 1872, Volume I*, ed. by Giusepper Alberigo & Alberto Melloni, trans. Gregory Heers (Bologna: Prepols Publisher, 2016), 223-228.

> We believe in one God, the Father Almighty, Maker of heaven and earth, and of all things visible and invisible; and in one Lord Jesus Christ, the Son of God, the Only-begotten, begotten of the Father before all ages; Light of Light, true God of true God, begotten, not made; being of one essence with the Father, by Whom all things were made; Who for us men and for our salvation came down from the Heavens, and was incarnate of the Holy Spirit and the Virgin Mary, and became man; and was crucified for us under Pontius Pilate, suffered and was buried; and arose again on the third day according to the Scriptures; and ascended into the Heavens, and sitteth at the right hand of the Father; and shall come again, with glory, to judge the living and the dead; Whose Kingdom shall have no end; and in the Holy Spirit, the Lord, the Giver of life; Who proceedeth from the Father; Who with the Father and the Son together is worshipped and glorified; Who spake by the prophets; in one, Holy, Catholic, and Apostolic Church; we confess one baptism for the remission of sins; we look for the resurrection of the dead, and the life of the age to come. Amen.

This venerable and holy symbol of the Faith, lying thus unmoved, was sufficient for the knowledge and confirmation of piety; for it both perfectly teaches concerning Father and Son and Holy Spirit and clearly presents the incarnate economy of God the Word, and no one should have arrived at so great impudence and daring as to add or subtract something from it. Yet because the inventor of wickedness and foe of the human race from the beginning, always and daily inventing novelties and swaggering against piety, was ever seeing that the sacred initiators of the churches of various times were waging war against his resolutions and his devices, and were, by the grace of God, conciliarly bringing down his engines of war, as many as he cunningly contrived against the holy ones, he judged that it was necessary to place even this ultimate blasphemy in the race of the Italians and through this race to vomit forth, thoughtlessly and very dangerously, that the all-Holy Spirit, Who is of one essence and of one honour and co-eternal with Father and Son, proceeds also from the Son and has existence from Him, just as also from the Father of course, that is, with respect to that ineffable and beginningless progression, and to make an addition in the Symbol, seeing that hence many and blasphemous things follow after this position and it is gathered that in the Holy Trinity the origins of the Holy Spirit are two and His value and authority are thus belittled; and that on this point not a small number of past heresies begin to come back to life again, while the decisions of the ecumenical councils are annulled in this part, all of which dogmatised that the Holy Spirit proceeds from the Father; or rather, even before the councils, the theology of our Lord Jesus Christ is set at naught, Who said, "When the Comforter is come, even the Spirit of truth, which proceedeth from the Father, he shall testify of me."

Yet our blessed fathers did not leave this inexamined or unhealed. Therefore, there was need of an ecumenical council, which indeed assembled in the Queen of Cities under the blessed Photius, the president of Constantinople, and subjected to everlasting anathema those who babble that the worshipful and all-holy Spirit has existence also from the Son and who would add perhaps a word to the Symbol. So also, not a few years later, the great council that assembled against Bekkos declared similar things against such men.

Neither so, however, did the inventor of wickedness learn to keep quiet; but through the pretense of a supposedly ecumenical council, which convened not long ago in Florence of Italy, he did not neglect to renew once more this forementioned and already departed heresy, along with some other strange things. Therefore, since then and till now, seeing that the Church is thus troubled and tossed on the waves due to the fact that many, even of our own pupils of the Church, have accepted such heresies and endeavour to hold them fast in opposition to the divine will, this holy and ecumenical council of hierarchs and patriarchs, through its present decree, judged, regarding the things that were badly and thoughtlessly done and dogmatised conciliarly in Florence, being spurious dogmas and foreign to the Catholic Church, that it is necessary to trample upon them, and to relegate what has to do with Florence to obscurity, and for the Church of Christ to become of one mind with the ecumenical councils, and to unite her with them rightly.

Wherefore we believe with both soul and intellect, and with tongue we preach and confess, that the almighty and Holy Spirit, in respect of that ineffable and everlasting progression, according to the Lord's words, proceeds from God the Father, that is, only from the paternal hypostasis according to His essence, while the Son does at all contribute anything or mediate in respect of the Spirit's procession, lest there be thought to be two causes in the Trinity and two origins in the uncreated Divinity; seeing that the power to beget and to originate are properties not of essence but of hypostasis, and this therefore can be only the paternal hypostasis. Therefore we also acknowledge God the Father as the only source and cause of Them that are from Him, following rightly the theology of the Lord and the decisions of the sacred and great theologians of the Church: the blessed Dionysius the Areopagite, who says that the Father is the only source of the superessential divinity and that "from the immaterial and indivisible Good the interior rays of Its goodness have their being;"[241] and Gregory the Theologian who said, "The Father and the Son and the Holy Spirit have in common the divinity and that They did not come into being, whereas the Son and the Holy Spirit have in common that They are from the Father," and Gregory of the Nyssans, who says, "There is one and the same person, the Father, from whom precisely the Son is begotten and the Holy Spirit proceeds,"[242] as well as the declarations of many other saints, which direct the mind toward this point; and it is our prayer that we remain in this belief [doxa] of piety unshaken to the end. But as for those who believe or also preach otherwise regarding the procession of the Holy Spirit or, as we said, opine and innovate contrarily to the truth, we turn away from them as from heretics and subject them to the anathema.

Furthermore, by this present conciliar tome, we overturn both the council that assembled in Florence and the very chapters which are contained in the decree published by that council, and we declare it henceforth to be null and inefficacious, and we consider and hold it as having never even assembled at all to begin with, since it dogmatised things not in harmony with, and hostile toward, the holy eight ecumenical councils

---

241 Saint Dionysius the Areopagite, "On Mystical Theology," in *Patrologia Graeca, Vol. 3*, trans. Jacques Paul Migne (1857-1866) & Gregory Heers (2022) (Paris: Imprimerie Catholique, 1857), 1033.

242 Saint Gregory of Nyssa, "That When We Speak of Three Person in the Godhead We Do Not Speak of Three Gods: To the Greeks, from the Common Notions," in *Patrologia Graeca, Vol. 45*, trans. Jacques Paul Migne (1857-1866) (Paris: Imprimerie Catholique, 1857), 180.

before it as regards the matter of the procession of the Holy Spirit and the rest. Furthermore, we also turn away from the sacrifice performed through unleavened bread and the rest, the very things which in Florence were embraced and which are contained in the decree that was made there, as we already said; and we are in harmony, in all dogmas and customs of the Church, both written and unwritten, with the forementioned holy and ecumenical councils; and we both wish and pray that what was dogmatised by them and by us in this present tome be harmoniously preserved unfalsified and unshaken forever, by the protection and help of the holy and uncreated and consubstantial Trinity, the one Master and God of all; for to Him is due the glory, the honour, and the magnificence unto the endless ages. Amen.

6. Council of Constantinople in 1583

In his *Church History*, Metropolitan Meletios of Athens writes: "In 1583, during the reign of Patriarch Jeremiah, a Synod of Metropolitans was convened in Constantinople, with Patriarch Sylvester of Alexandria also in attendance. This Synod condemned the innovation in the Calendar introduced by Gregory of Rome and refused to comply with the request of the Latins that they accept it."[243] The surviving documents of that council are no longer extant and efforts to preserve the written record of it are riddled with forgeries from a "Monk Iakovos" of New Skete, Athos.

7. Council of Constantinople in 1587

Athanasios Comnenos Hypselantes is the author of the book *Τὰ Μετὰ τὴν Ἅλωσιν [The Aftermath of the Fall of Constantinople]*. He writes that in "the year of salvation 1587...a second Synod was held in Constantinople, in the presence of the Ecumenical Patriarch Jeremiah, Meletios Pegas of Alexandria [representing Patriarch Sylvester], and Patriarch Sophronios [IV] of Jerusalem, and those present synodally rejected

243 Metropolitan Meletios of Athens, Ἐκκλησιαστικὴ Ἱστορία [Church History], §9 Vol. III (Vienna: 1784), 402.

the correction of the date of Holy Pascha made by Pope Gregory XIII as parlous, unnecessary, and the cause of many scandals to all Christian nations."[244] This is corroborated by Patriarch Dositheos of Jerusalem.[245]

8. Council of Constantinople in 1593

Also in the *Δωδεκάβιβλος* from Patriarch Dositheos of Jerusalem, he mentions there was a council in Constantinople in 1593 which again condemned the Pope's calendar innovation. They resolved in that council "that Pascha should occur as determined by the First Synod [i.e., the First Ecumenical Council in Nicea in 325] and that the calendar concocted by the Latins should be anathematized."[246]

9. Council of Constantinople in 1722

In 1722, a need arose to convene a Synod in Constantinople provoked primarily by the constant missionary work and proselytization toward Orthodox Christians in Syria by Papists. The patriarchs Athanasios of Antioch (+1724) and Chrysanthos of Jerusalem (1707-1731) participated. They synodically decided that Latins converting to Holy Orthodoxy would be baptized. Chrysanthos of Jerusalem wrote a "Confession of Faith" condemning Catholicism, which in part stated, "keep away from the innovations and reforms of the Latins, who did not leave any dogma or mystery or tradition of the Church incorrupt and unadulterated."[247] The other patriarchs in attendance signed this Confession. The persistent trial for the Church in those years from Papist missionaries eventually became the catalyst for another Council in Constantinople in 1755 or 1756.

---

244 Athanasios Comnenos Hypselantes,.*Τὰ Μετὰ τὴν Ἅλωσιν [The Aftermath of the Fall of Constantinople]* (Constantinople: 1870), 113.

245 Dositheos of Jerusalem, *Δωδεκάβιβλος* (Bucharest: 1715), 1169.

246 Ibid., 232.

247 For complete information, see: I.N. Karmiris, Τὰ Δογματικὰ καί Συμβολικὰ Μνημεῖα τῆς Ὀρθοδόξου Ἐκκλησίας (Athens: 1953), 822-859 [In Greek].

10. Council of Constantinople in 1755[248]

Early eighteenth-century Greece was a turbulent time that had multiple conflicts occurring simultaneously such as the rise of the Holy Kollyvades Fathers with their defense of the Holy Orthodox faith against innovations, as well as the political climate which was filled with persecution from both the Ottomans in the east and the constant interference from Protestants and Papists from the west. "At this same time, Greek Orthodoxy was undergoing a period of profound expansion. On the one side, the Phanariot families which had established strong ties with the Ottoman powers found themselves at the heads of networks controlling the political and economic affairs at numerous levels. On the other side, thanks to the commitment of high ecclesiastical dignitaries a century earlier, centers of Greek higher education multiplied and flourished. After the successes secured by the New Patriarchal Academy of Constantinople, established by [Patriarch] Nektarios of Jerusalem (1661-1669) in 1662 or the Phrontisterion established by Sebastos Kymitetes (c.1632-1702) in Trebizond in 1682, a new type of school emerged among the monastic communities. For example, the Patmias, which was established by [St] Makarios Kalogeras at the Monastery of Saint John the Theologian in 1713."[249]

These schools were responsible for the new renaissance of the Greek language and culture that had been suppressed by the Ottoman Empire for over 300 years as well as the heretical Papist and Protestant doctrines that were invading traditional Orthodox Christian lands.[250] During this

---

248 Some date the year this Council took place as 1756.

249 Vassa Kontouma, "Concilum Constantinopolitanum 1755-1756," in *The Great Councils of the Orthodox Churches Decisions and Synodika: From Constantinople 861 to Constantinople 1872, Volume I*, ed.by Giuseppe Alberigo & Alberto Melloni. (Bologna: Brepols Publishers, 2016), 348.

250 Ibid., 348.

period there was an intellectual climate that affected the succession of patriarchs. This climate essentially created two different parties among the Greek Orthodox population. On the one side were those close to the establishment of the Phanar and the Phanariots who preferred so-called moderate theology which allowed them to enjoy wider ranging support among the heterodox governmental powers such as the Papist King of France. However, on the other side was the smaller traditional Ortho-dox Christian party of Patriarch Cyril, the lower-level clergy and the holy monastics, all who were trying to maintain a traditional Orthodox life free from the new heretical western influences and expansions.[251] What also helped the cause of Patriarch Cyril was his effort to protect his Orthodox Christian flock from the threat of Papist Uniatism.[252]

Between 1750-1757 there arose again a controversy concerning the reception of converts from the Latin heresy and how they should be re-ceived into the Holy Orthodox Church. According to the historical wit-nesses there were Papists from Pera who, wishing to come into Holy Or-thodoxy, approached the priests of the region about conversion. These priests reached out to Patriarch Cyril for his patriarchal guidance re-garding how to proceed with receiving these heretics into the Church.[253] In response to the priests' question, Patriarch Cyril instructed them to maintain the akriveia (ἀκρίβεια) of the Church and to baptize them for the reason that outside of the canonical Holy Eastern Orthodox Church there is no mysteriological grace within Papalism.[254]

Patriarch Cyril's decision to maintain the akriveia of the Church caused a negative reaction from the Phanariots of his own synod, the intellectual class of Greeks, the Uniates, those families who had entered into mixed marriages with Latin Papists, and the "staff of Western em-bassies who thought that the situation was rapidly moving out of their control. The result of the events was the deposition of Cyril in May/

---

251 Ibid., 348.

252 Ibid., 349.

253 Ibid., 349.

254 Akriveia (ἀκρίβεια): Defined as Exactitude. In Orthodox Christian theology *akriveia* is maintaining the strict observance of exactitude to the Gospel as laid down by the Holy Apostles and followed by the Holy Fathers..

June 1751."²⁵⁵ "After the usual bribery and intrigue, Cyril's Orthodox and Latin opponents succeeded in expelling him from the Patriarchal throne"²⁵⁶ in the anti-canonical deposition by heterodox western governments in cooperation with the Ottoman Turks. They then installed a new Patriarch named Paisios II who already had been installed as the Patriarch of Constantinople three different times prior but did not take any sides concerning the controversy of baptizing papal heretics.

Although the newly installed Paisios II was considered a "moderate" on the grounds that he did not adopt a position in the so-called baptismal controversy, the situation continued to be a point of contention because of a little-known holy monastic, Saint Auxentius, "who seems to have been the main inspirer of the popular anti-Western feeling"²⁵⁷ according to Georges Florovsky. Father Auxentius was a monk from Katirli and was considered to be as the saints of old, who held the purity of Orthodoxy above all else and was believed to be a miracle worker among the Orthodox Christian people.²⁵⁸ St. Auxentius preached constantly against the heretical baptism of the Latins among the faithful and for that he was persecuted by the Phanariot bishops who were under the extreme influence of Papist governments (embassies) within Constantinople. St. Auxentius, beloved by the Orthodox people but causing a stir with his preaching of Holy Orthodoxy against the polluted waters of the Latin baptism, was eventually arrested by the Turkish government.²⁵⁹

However, this arrest of the holy monastic was not without consequence for the Turks. On September 6th, 1752, a large crowd of the holy father's supporters gathered at the Phanar in Constantinople and

---

255 Vassa Kontouma, "Concilum Constantinopolitanum 1755-1756," in The Great Councils of the Orthodox Churches Decisions and Synodika: From Constantinople 861 to Constantinople 1872, Volume I, ed. by Giuseppe Alberigo & Alberto Melloni. (Bologna: Brepols Publishers, 2016), 350.

256 Metropolitan Kallistos Ware, Eustratios Argenti: A Study of the Greek Church Under Turkish Rule (London: Oxford University Press, 1964), 71.

257 George Florovsky, "Review of 'Studies and Documents Relating to the History of the Greek Church and People Under Turkish Domination' by Theodore H. Papadopoulos, M. A.," Church History 23, no. 1 (March 1954), 90-92.

258 Metropolitan Kallistos Ware, Eustratios Argenti: A Study of the Greek Church Under Turkish Rule (London: Oxford University Press, 1964), 71.

259 Ibid., 72.

forced their way inside attempting to seize the Patriarch Paisios whilst accusing him of being a Frank for not supporting the baptism of Latins converting to Orthodoxy and dragging him through the marketplace. Fortunately for Patriarch Paisios he was saved by a contingent of Turkish troops. The Turkish government, never having dealt with a riot of this magnitude, asked the people what they wanted so that order might be restored to which the people demanded the return of Patriarch Cyril, the rightful Patriarch of Constantinople. "The French Ambassador Comte Dessalleux, says that there were more than ten thousand in the mob: an insurrection of this sort among the Greeks — something unparalleled, so they say, since the capture of Constantinople — caused such terror in the Seraglio, that the Sultan sent message after message to the Grand Vizier telling him to pacify the riot at any price."[260]

This struggle between the righteous Patriarch Cyril and the overtly papist sympathizers on the synod raged on and culminated with the synod publishing a synodical decree in 1755, without the Patriarch himself. In the decree the synod condemned a book written by Christopher the Aetolian opposing the Latin's baptism. This action of the synod was a direct challenge to Patriarch Cyril. Then in the same year, Patriarch Cyril produced two formal pronouncements which anathematized the Synodal Decree of the papal-influenced synod and all those who supported the recognition of heretical baptism. Patriarch Cyril states in his anathema:

> May they be cut off from the Lord God Almighty, and accursed and without forgiveness, and may their corpses remain undissolved and swollen. Rocks and iron shall be dissolved, but not they. May they inherit the leprosy of Gehazi and the noose of Judas; may they lament and tremble upon earth, as Cain did; may the wrath of God be upon their heads and their portion with the traitor Judas and the Jews who fought against God; may the earth gape apart and swallow them up, as once it swallowed Dathan and Abiram; may the Angel of the Lord persecute them with the sword all of the days of their life; may they be subject to all the Patriarchal and Synodal curses, and under judgement of

---

260 Ibid., 73.

the eternal Anathema, and condemned to the fire of Gehenna. Amen.[261]

In July of 1755 Patriarch Cyril issued an *Oros* entitled "A Definition of the Holy Church of Christ Defending the Holy Baptism Given from God, and Spitting Upon the Baptism of the Heretics Which are Otherwise Administered." This weighty *Oros* issued by the canonical Patriarch of Constantinople was signed not only by himself but also by Patriarch Matthew of the Alexandrian Patriarchate and Patriarch Parthenios of the Jerusalem Patriarchate. Patriarch Cyril approached the Patriarch of Antioch to sign the *Oros* as well. Although he agreed with all three Patriarchs in their ecclesiology he did not sign because Patriarch Cyril did not have the support of his Metropolitans.[262] Another factor preventing his signing is that he had "been on an alms-seeking visit to Russia and had his throne [had] been snatched in his absence by a usurper."[263] In 1933, the Holy Synod of the Patriarchate of Antioch issued a formal decree that all converts received in its jurisdiction should be received by baptism, thereby also adopting policy expressed in the 1755 Encyclical.[264]

After the issuance of the anathema and patriarchal *Oros* signed by the three Orthodox Patriarchs, the episcopal Latin sympathizers continued to fight against this true doctrine of the Orthodox Church. Eventually, Patriarch Cyril had the Latin sympathizing bishops of the synod forcibly removed to their home diocese and out of the capital where they had taken up permanent residence to the detriment of their flocks. However, some of these Metropolitans escaped the removal back to their assigned diocese with the help of the Latin Papists in Constantinople. One of these figures was Callinicus of Proilabos who fled from his diocese and

---

261 Metropolitan Kallistos Ware, *Eustratios Argenti: A Study of the Greek Church Under Turkish Rule* (London: Oxford University Press, 1964), 74.

262 Metropolitan Kallistos Ware, *Eustratios Argenti: A Study of the Greek Church Under Turkish Rule* (London: Oxford University Press, 1964), 73-76.

263 Steven Runciman, *The Great Church in Captivity: A Study of The Patriarchate of Constantinople from the Eve of the Turkish Conquest to the Greek War of Independence.* 1st ed., (Cambridge: University Printing Press, 1968), 358.

264 See *Echos d'Orient*, vol. xxxiii, (Paris: 1934), 99. Quoted in Ware, Eustratios Argenti, 106.

found a refuge in the French embassy for many months while he plotted to replace Patriarch Cyril with the help of the French Papist government.[265] It was in July 1757 that the righteous Patriarch Cyril was again deposed and replaced with Callinicus who the Orthodox people believed to be a traitor to Holy Orthodoxy and a secret papist.[266] The synod of the Ecumenical Patriarchate of that period never sided with the righteous Cyril, largely because they had been compromised and under the influence of the papist governments that were operating in Constantinople. However, the weight of the Oros of 1755 signed by the three Holy Patriarchs of Constantinople, Alexandria, and Jerusalem, although not always used, has remained in force and has never been revoked to the present day.[267]

THE OROS OF THE GREAT CHURCH IN 1755 CONCERNING THE RECEPTION OF HERETICS[268]

Many are the means by which we attain our salvation. And these, so to speak, in a ladderlike fashion are interlinked and interconnected, all aiming at one and the same end. First of all, then, is the baptism which God delivered to the sacred Apostles, such being the case that without it the rest are ineffectual. For it says: "Unless one is born of water and spirit, he cannot enter the kingdom of heaven." The first manner of generation brought man into this mortal existence. It was therefore imperative, and necessarily so, that another, more mystical manner of generation be found, neither beginning in corruption nor terminating therein, whereby it would be possible for us to imitate the author of our salvation, Jesus Christ. For the baptismal water in the font takes the place of a womb,

265 Vassa Kontouma, "Concilum Constantinopolitanum 1755-1756," *The Great Councils of the Orthodox Churches Decisions and Synodika: From Constantinople 861 to Constantinople 1872, Volume I*, ed. by Giuseppe Alberigo & Alberto Melloni (Bologna: Brepols Publishers, 2016), 349.

266 Metropolitan Kallistos Ware, *Eustratios Argenti: A Study of the Greek Church Under Turkish Rule* (London: Oxford University Press, 1964), 78.

267 Ibid., 78.

268 Protopresbyter George D. Metallinos, *I Confess One Baptism*, trans. Hieromonk Seraphim (Daphne: St. Paul's Monastery, 1994), 133-136.

and there is birth for him who is born, as Chrysostom says; while the Spirit which descends on the water has the place of God who fashions the embryo. And just as He was placed in the tomb and on the third day returned to life, so likewise they who believe, going under the water instead of under the earth, in three immersions depict in themselves the three-day grace of the Resurrection, the water being sanctified by the descent of the All-holy Spirit, so that the body might be illumined by the water which is visible, and the soul might receive sanctification by the Spirit which is invisible. For just as water in a cauldron partakes of the heat of the fire, so the water in the font is likewise transmuted, by the action of the Spirit, into divine power. It cleanses those who are thus baptized and makes them worthy of adoption as sons. Not so, however, with those who are initiated in a different manner. Instead of cleansing and adoption, it renders them impure and sons of darkness.

Just three years ago, the question arose: When heretics come over to us, are their baptisms acceptable, given that these are administered contrary to the tradition of the holy Apostles and divine Fathers, and contrary to the custom and ordinance of the catholic and Apostolic Church? We, who by divine mercy were raised in the Orthodox Church, and who adhere to the canons of the sacred Apostles and divine Fathers, recognize only one Church, our holy, catholic, and Apostolic Church. It is her Mysteries [i.e., sacraments], and consequently her baptism, that we accept. On the other hand, we abhor, by common resolve, all rites not administered as the Holy Spirit commanded the sacred Apostles, and as the Church of Christ performs to this day. For they are the inventions of depraved men, and we regard them as strange and foreign to the whole Apostolic tradition. Therefore, we receive those who come over to us from them as unholy and unbaptized. In this we follow our Lord Jesus Christ who commanded His disciples to baptize "in the name of the Father, and the Son, and the Holy Spirit"; we follow the sacred and divine Apostles who order us to baptize aspirants with three immersions and emersions, and in each immersion to say one name of the Holy Trinity; we follow the sacred Dionysios, peer of the Apostles, who tells us "to dip the aspirant, stripped of every garment, three times in a font containing sanctified water and oil, having loudly proclaimed the threefold hypostasis of the divine Blessedness, and straightway to seal the newly baptized with the most divinely potent myron [i.e. chrism], and thereafter to make him a participant in the super-sacramental Eucharist" and we follow the Second and Penthekte Holy Ecumenical Councils, which order us to receive as unbaptized those aspirants to Orthodoxy who were not baptized with three immersions and emersions, and in each immersion did not loudly invoke one of the divine hypostases, but were baptized in some other fashion.

We too, therefore, adhere to these divine and sacred decrees, and we reject and abhor baptisms belonging to heretics. For they disagree with and are alien to the divine Apostolic dictate. They are useless waters, as Sts. Ambrose and Athanasios the Great said. They give no sanctification to such as receive them, nor avail at all to the washing away of sins. We receive those who come over to the Orthodox faith, who were baptized without being baptized, as being unbaptized, and without danger we baptize them in accordance with the Apostolic and synodal Canons, upon which Christ's holy and Apostolic and catholic Church, the common Mother of us all, firmly relies.

Together with this joint resolve and declaration of ours, we seal this our Oros, being as it is in agreement with the Apostolic and synodal dictates, and we certify it by our signatures.

In the year of salvation 1755,

+ CYRIL, by God's mercy Archbishop of Constantinople New Rome, and Ecumenical Patriarch

+ MATTHEW, by God's mercy Pope and Patriarch of the great city of Alexandria, and Judge of the Ecumene

+ PARTHENIOS, by God's mercy Patriarch of the holy city of Jerusalem and all Palestine

11. Council of Constantinople in 1838[269]

Let us guard the genuine children of the Eastern Church from the blasphemies of Papism... from the chasms of heresies and from the soul-destroying precipices of their papal delusion... that ye may learn how great the difference is between us the Orthodox and the Catholics, so that ye be not deceived henceforth by the sophistries and innovations of these heretics... of this ill-conceived and satanic heresy of theirs.

12. Council of Constantinople in 1895[270]

There are substantial differences which concern the God-given dogmas of our faith and the God-established canonical regiment of the administration of the Churches... The Papist Church... not only refuses to return to the canons and the terms of the ecumenical councils, but at the end of the 19th century broadened the existing chasm, officially proclaiming infallibility... The current Roman Church is a church of innovations, of adulteration of the writings of the Fathers, of misinterpretation of Scripture and the terms of the ecumenical councils. Therefore, it was reasonably and justly denounced and is still denounced, as long as it remains in its delusion.

In a praiseworthy book published by the Holy Monastery of Gregoriou, the perspectives of a plethora of Saints and Teachers of our Church — more than 40 persons — are recorded, who denounced the heretical papal innovations. Indeed, some of them gave even their blood for the Orthodox Faith. Moreover, besides the ecumenical councils, theologian Panagiotis Simatis also cites many Local Councils of our Orthodox Church after the Schism which condemn the heretical teachings of

---

269 For complete information, see I.N. Karmiris, *Τὰ Δογματικὰ καὶ Συμβολικὰ Μνημεῖα τῆς Ὀρθοδόξου Ἐκκλησίας. [The Dogmatic and Symbolic Monuments of the Orthodox Church]* (Athens: 1953), 894-902 [In Greek]. Excerpt from Gotsopoulos, *On Common Prayer with the Heterodox*, 18-19.

270 For complete information, see I.N. Karmiris, *Τὰ Δογματικὰ καὶ Συμβολικὰ Μνημεῖα τῆς Ὀρθοδόξου Ἐκκλησίας. [The Dogmatic and Symbolic Monuments of the Orthodox Church]* (Athens: 1953), 932-946 [In Greek]. Excerpt from Gotsopoulos, *On Common Prayer with the Heterodox*, 19-22.

Papism: 1089, 1233, 1273, 1274, 1282, 1285, 1341, 1351, 1441, 1443, 1484, 1642, 1672, 1722, 1727, 1755, 1838, 1848, 1895, 1948.

Some, in their effort to characterize Papism as a mere schism, argue that it is not a heresy since it has not been condemned by an ecumenical council. They wish to forget the express condemnation formulated at the Council of 879, held in Constantinople. The idea that only the Seven Ecumenical Councils (the last occurring in 787) delineate what is heresy is foreign to Orthodox theology. The 15th canon of the First-Second Council speaks of "some heresy condemned by the holy councils [author's note: not just the Ecumenical ones], or Fathers," whereas the ecclesiastical author Vincent of Lerins (5th c.) is entirely clear: "if some new question should arise on which no such decision has been given, they should then have recourse to the opinions of the holy Fathers, of those at least, who, each in his own time and place, remaining in the unity of communion and of the faith, were accepted as approved masters; and whatsoever these may be found to have held, with one mind and with one consent, this ought to be accounted the true and Catholic doctrine of the Church, without any doubt or scruple." Furthermore, this notion is especially dangerous from an ecclesiological perspective. Is it being implied that perhaps from A.D. 787 the Orthodox Church ceased to be self-defined and to contrast Herself with delusion, falsehood, and heresy? Does this view not steer immediately to a self-negation of Orthodox Ecclesiology?

What would happen if this rationale — that since no ecumenical council has pronounced judgment regarding Papism (which appeared in the 9th century), therefore no Orthodox, and especially no responsible shepherd, has the right to call it a heresy — were extended to other heresies? I wonder about the Jehovah's Witnesses, the Mormons, the Pentecostals, televangelists, etc. Which ecumenical council has pronounced judgment regarding them? Or are they perhaps not heretics? Of course, they are heretics, in other words outside of the "One, Holy Catholic and Apostolic Church," since (a) they self-identify as non-Orthodox and (b) they deny the experience and tradition of our Church, in other words, Orthodox Theology, as it has been recorded in the decisions of the Ecumenical and Local Councils, in the texts of the Fathers (consensus Patrum) and in her liturgical life. But is this not exactly what the Roman Catholics are doing? Do they not believe contrary to those things that the ecumenical councils have decreed (mainly the Second, but also the Third, Fourth, Sixth and Seventh)? Do they not believe contrary to what our Orthodox Church teaches and lives? Do they not identify themselves as non-Orthodox, as they do not accept our faith?

It is moreover for this reason — and I ask that we carefully consider this point — that we do not have merely "a group of Orthodox that consider Roman Catholics and Protestants to be heretics" or "only pronouncements by particular ecclesiastical writers," as some erroneously contend, but the totality of the Saints of our Church who dealt with this issue unanimously conclude that Papism is heresy. There is not one Saint of our Church — no, not one — who contends that Papism is not a heresy. If someone — whoever he may be — does not accept the clear and fixed teaching of our Church and the unanimous opinion of our saints that Papism is heresy, that is a matter of his own personal choice and responsibility. Perhaps he knows better than the Saints, perhaps he is higher than the Councils, or has some private revelation, which grants him the right to decide *ex cathedra*, "infallibly" but also arbitrarily! Notwithstanding, even if the Papists were merely schismatics, common prayer with them would still be prohibited according to the canons!

Mosaic of the Mother of God in the Hagia Sophia, Constantinople

Ὁ ἍΓΙΟΣ   ΜΕΛΕΤΙΟΣ
Ὁ ΝΕΟΣ

Saint Meletius the Confessor of Mount Galesion

C. THE BYZANTINE LISTS

1. Introduction

As early as the 9th century in the Eastern Roman Empire, Orthodox ecclesiastical authorities took note of major theological heresies, religious aberrations, and other cultural differences growing out of the West (primarily among the Franks). The breadth of concerns among Orthodox Romans for the Western Latins demonstrated that these two worlds were becoming remarkably different from one another. A different spirit was becoming evident. The growing points of concern in both dogma and practice eventually developed into various lists we now label the "Byzantine Lists." Tia Kolbaba[271] has provided us with probably the best research of any academic in analyzing these various lists. Her book *The Byzantine Lists: Errors of the Latins* is an essential resource when analyzing the texts. She describes them as "represent[ing] these differences as self-evidently heinous and heretical, asserting — or at least implying — that merely to know that Latins do these things is to recognize them as heretics."[272]

We are grateful for Tia Kolbaba's work. She brought an increased level of seriousness to these texts (some of which are authored by sig-

---

271 Tia Kolbaba is an accomplished scholar specializing in Early Christianity and Byzantine Studies and is the Chair of the Department of Religion at Rutgers University. Her doctorate and masters work focused on Medival Studies.

272 Tia Kolbaba, *The Byzantine Lists: Errors of the Latins* (Chicago: University of Illinois Press, 2000), 3.

nificant saints of the Orthodox Church) that did not exist before. She writes:

> Those who study religion concentrate on theology and ecclesi-ology, not on the sort of issues raised by the lists—issues which they label adiaphora, matters of indifference to the faith. Those who study other aspects of the conflict between East and West tend to study the lists only superficially, if at all, and to conclude that the lists simply prove their point. In other words, the items in the lists are so clearly trivial that they must be masks for some deeper conflict.
>
> When I began studying the lists, I shared some of these assump-tions about their triviality, but was nevertheless intrigued by them. At the very least, I thought, it would be worthwhile to figure out what they said and what they meant.... [273]

The Byzantine Lists originate from different authors and periods of time within Eastern Christian history, the lists are almost a genre (but not exactly since the Greek language used in the lists is sometimes high aristocratic Greek, sometime poetic, and sometimes very common to the point of bordering on "illiteracy"[274]). Some of these lists are the basis for other lists and some are entirely original compositions. The authors' vo-cations vary greatly: bishops, monastics, educators, unknown (concern-ing details of their lives), and anonymous (concerning their identity).

2. Sources and Texts[275]

In the ranks of our Fathers among the Saints who wrote such lists critical of the Latins, we have at least the following:

Saint Photios the Great wrote an Encyclical to the Eastern Patri-archs (867). See page 104 for his life and page 295 for his Encyclical.

---

273 Ibid. 4-5

274 Ibid., 179.

275 Ibid., 174-183.

Saint Theophylact of Ochrid wrote a letter "Concerning Those Who Accuse the Latins" (1090). See page 317 for his life and the text of his letter.

Saint Meletius the Confessor of Mount Galesion wrote a Poem Against the Latins. Currently, only the section of his poem is available in English. Read it on page 337. Read his life on page 89.

Saint John II, Metropolitan of Kiev wrote a letter to Pope Clement (i.e., Anti-Pope Clement III of Old Rome). See page 310 for his letter.

Other significant texts which list errors of the Latins from those not recognized as saints in the Church are the following:

Patriarch Michael Cerularius of Constantinople penned a letter to Patriarch Peter II of Antioch in 1054. This is the same Patriarch that in the same year anathematized Pope Leo IX and Cardinal Humbert for the latter's brazen actions in Constantinople. Many of the lists are born out of this list from Patriarch Michael. See page 637 for his letter.

Additional lists referenced below have not yet been translated into English.

John of Claudiopolis wrote "On Azymes" which documents the historical development of Latin errors then identifies eighteen specific points of difference between the Orthodox and the "Azymites."

Niketas Seides wrote "On the Many Differences regarding the Law" in preparation for his dialogue with Latins when representatives of the Pope came to Constantinople.

Unknown author of *Opusculum contra Francos*.

Konstantinos Stilbes wrote "The Faults of the Latin Church—Dogma, the Scriptures, and Many Other Matters" which is the longest list containing seventy-five paragraphs. It was written shortly after the Fourth Crusade.

"Pseudo-Athanasius II of Alexandria" is the name given to the text "Letter to All Christians" but probably written by monks. This is the position of Kolbaba, but the academic rationale for this seems weak based on Orthodox histography. While Kolbaba states the "claims to be from Patriarch Athanasios II" and dated "January 1276," this puts the letter in the time of the reign of Patriarch Athanasios III over Alexandria, who chaired the Church's condemnation of the false union with the Synod of Lyon, and who spent the last part of his life in a monastery.[276]

Two Anonymous texts are also of historical significance.

The more common points of contention which appear in the Byzantine lists include the anti-canonical insertion of the *Filioque* heresy into the Nicene Creed by the Latins; their non-canonical use of azymes (Jewish Matzah) or unleavened bread in the eucharist; prohibition of clerical marriage; baptizing by single immersion; making the sign of the cross incorrectly (left to right); failure to revere the holy icons; irreverence for the Theotokos by refusing to call her the Theotokos; celebrating more than one divine liturgy per day, per altar, per Church, and per priest; bishops and priests fighting in war and killing or being killed; allowing marriages within forbidden degrees (such as immediate family or godchildren); clergy shaving their beards; wearing improper clerical clothing during liturgies and for everyday dress; insufficient reverence for the holy altar; and monastics eating lard and other meats.[277]

3. Reputation of the "Byzantine Lists"

Met. Hierotheos (Vlachos) summarizes the teaching of Fr. John Romanides regarding the different traditions of patristic theology and western theology by stating the following:

> When one studies the whole course of Christianity through the ages, one sees that two trends of theological thinking and life developed.
>
> The first trend began at Pentecost, when the Prophets were united with the Apostles, and they share the same point of reference and the same experience. The difference lies in the fact that the Prophets share in the unincarnate Word, and were subject to the power of death, whereas the Apostles shared in the incarnate

---

276 "Previous Patriarchs Archives - Page 3 of 7." Πατριαρχείο Αλεξανδρείας, accessed January 21st, 2024, https://www.patriarchateofalexandria.com/patriarch_category/previous-patriarchs/page/3/?lang=en

277 Ibid., 32-72.

Word and transcended death. There is the same experience and often the same confession, with some exceptions.

However, from the second until the fourth century the Fathers were under pressure from heretics, and, in order to confront them, they used the terminology of that era, without altering their empirical knowledge... This task was upheld by the Ecumenical councils.... Thus the Fathers of the Ecumenical Councils Christianised Hellenism, whereas the heretics (Arians, Monophysites, Monothelites), who were expelled from the Church, Hellenised Christianity.

The second trend began in the West, mainly in the ninth century, with pre-scholasticism and scholasticism proper. Essentially it developed the tradition of the ancient heretics and used ancient Greek philosophy, particularly Blessed Augustine's Neoplatonism and speculation, upon which the ancient heretics relied. From scholastic theology the West moved on to the Reformation, the Renaissance, the Enlightenment and the modern philosophical, psychological, existential and social currents that now predominate....

The encounter between Western and Russian theology gave rise to what is described as post-patristic theology.... post-patristic theology is an attempt to give a new interpretation to patristic texts, which should be detached from the atmosphere and terminology of the era in which they were written, and should be rewritten for our own era. [278]

Academic analysis of the "Byzantine Lists" are excellent exhibits for this phenomenon of studies through a post-patristic theological lens. When reading academic resources concerning the "Byzantine Lists," from an Orthodox point of view, one is made aware that their purpose is to protect the faithful from delusion and heresy and bring the heretics to repentance and awareness of their loss of grace and need to return to Christ. However, when reading these same resources inside the world

---

278 Metropolitan Hierotheos (Vlachos), *Patristic and Scholastic Theology in Perspective* (Levadia: Birth of the Theotokos Monastery, 2023), 566-567.

of academia, the most charitable explanation found for reading them is to learn the characteristics of papal and Orthodox polemics and discover the general nature of those exchanges. However, this latter academic approach is exactly post-patristic theological work. Even the name "Byzantine Lists" builds off an academic invention of a nomenclature with no historic basis.[279] The former view is spiritual therapy in approaching these writings. The latter view is a fruitless intellectual exercise.

Since the Western *phronema* is dominant globally, few are left unscathed by its influence. It follows, then, that many readers of these lists will see the accusations and then assume they are minor details critical of the Latins that are immoderate, trivial, or even fanatical (to use some common public descriptions of them). A casual reader may be confused why such complaints might be valuable to raise in the first place. The reason for this perplexity among many of today's readers is twofold:

1. Our contemporary culture has inherited a dominating nominalist spirit from the West. The dichotomy between nominalism and an ancient (and Orthodox) phronema that gave importance to symbols in everyone's life is very easily seen in the controversy regarding unleavened bread (azymes) and leavened bread. This controversy far exceeds the scope of the present summary, but suffice to say the use of azymes by the Papists is seemingly an inconsequential practice but in reality has many significant implications. To have bread without yeast or any rising agent as a cause for violent hostility between cultures may seem ridiculous to a nominalist spirit. In brief, here is how a single change (apparently miniscule) from leavened bread to unleavened bread goes against the Faith:

    •   Scholarship generally admits the use of unleavened bread in the West is not of apostolic origin (Cf. Reginald Wooley, The Bread of the Eucharist and Edward Martin, "The Bread of the Eucharist"). By enforcing this stance all over the West, they show themselves to have turned their back on that which was given to them from the Apostles. This demonstrates a hostile stance to the received tradition of their Fathers and disobedience to the Apostles.

---

279 See the introduction to this book on page 19.

- To say the Eucharistic bread is unleavened rather than leavened is to disregard the reading of Scripture. The word for unleavened bread in Greek is ἄζυμος. The word for leavened bread is ἄρτος. The passages where they are relevant for the Mystical Supper are Mt. 26:26; Mk. 14:22; Lk. 22:19; 24:30, 35; 1 Cor. 10:16, 17 (twice); and 11:26, 27, 28. In all these places, the writers never say Jesus took ἄζυμος and blessed it, they write that Jesus took ἄρτος, common ordinary leavened bread.

- Probably the most serious consequence of this change is that to argue the Lord's Mystical Supper in the upper room consisted of azymes is to argue that the Lord and His disciples were eating a Passover meal. The implication of this is that Christ is not the Pascha Lamb which was sacrificed for our salvation. To take this position is to essentially undermine Christ's salvation and annihilate some of the most important prophesies and typologies which pointed to Christ from the Old Testament. The controversy here is the understanding of Jewish custom regarding the "first day of unleavened bread." Both the Papists and the Orthodox have interpretations justifying themselves; however, only the Orthodox interpretation keeps the integrity of Church praxis whole and consistent with history, Scripture, and patristic teachings.

- Eucharistic typology in the Old Testament is destroyed by azymes. The Eucharist is, literally, a thanksgiving, from the Greek word meaning "gratitude." And according to the Hebraic Law, the thanksgiving sacrifices, unlike the others, were specifically to include leavened bread. The other offering which is brought with leaven is the offering of first fruits: "You shall bring from your dwellings two loaves of bread to be waved, made of two tenths of an ephah; they shall be of fine flour, they shall be baked with leaven, as first fruits to the Lord" (Lev. 23:17). Following the offering of first fruits, Christ Himself is called the first fruits, "But in fact Christ has been raised from the dead, the first fruits of those who have fallen asleep" (I Cor. 15:20). For the Orthodox, the Paschal celebration centers upon that resurrection of our Lord, more so than upon His death. Note also that unleavened bread is called the "bread of affliction" (Deut. 16:3) - it could be argued that this is not really appropriate for the resurrectional and "Eucharistic" celebration of the Lord's Day.

- St. Nikolai Velimirovich writes: "According to the Bible, unleavened bread was the bread of slaves while leavened bread was for free men, God's children. So for that reason the Orthodox Church uses leavened bread at Holy Communion."[280]

Now one should see that to make the change from leavened to unleavened bread is, in fact, no small problem. For the Papists to stop use of leavened bread and begin use of unleavened bread was, in a symbolic way, a confession of all these aforementioned points (and therefore a major error). By such a change, the Papists suggest to the rest of the Church they are departing from the Faith. Regarding the many other seemingly small changes one may read in the lists, these are likely to have other similar implications behind it. Some grievances may not be as serious as the use of azymes; nevertheless, our Fathers still see these deviations as unacceptable departures from the Faith and praxis that the Church received from the Apostles.

2. Even among the writings of the saints, we see a listing of errors grouped into more serious errors while some are deemed as lesser errors. A hierarchy of priority seems implicit in the patristic mind. The issue of the *filioque* is a Trinitarian heresy and therefore often seen as most urgent for the Papacy to correct; it is enough to estrange the West from the Church. Others errors are listed as being of serious concern, usually if any violation of the canons occurs. Other customs are mentioned as a matter of concern but sometimes with an understanding that they exist after the more heretical issues. This is seen clearly and in a pastoral way in the closing statement in the letter of St. John II of Kiev. The temptation certainly exists, especially among academics, to dismiss some of these minor complaints as petty grievances. However, to not burden the papists with complaints, if some authors focus on more major issues than others this does not

---

280 Saint Nikolai Velimirovich, "Woman as a Symbol of Christ," *Orthodox Life*, no. 6 (November-December 1951): 8-9.

imply (nor is there any evidence to suggest) the minor issues were not of some importance and in need of correction along with those underlying errors.

These lists of grievances by Orthodox ecclesiastical figures regarding the Franko-Latins include many more than have been presented. However, those which have been mentioned should provide some insight into how far the West had already departed from an Orthodox Christian dogmatic consciousness, even during the centuries surrounding the popularly provided year of 1054 for the Great Schism. These would not include egregious heresies that continued to develop later among the Latins, such as papal infallibility, created grace, the immaculate conception, purgatory, etc. The heresies, liturgical abuses, and any of the departures from the West's Orthodox Christian roots are only a small part of why ecumenical dialogue between the Latins and Orthodox has proved futile. These lists spanning five centuries do not take into account the further departure and falling into heresy by the Latin Papists in more recent centuries as witnessed to and denounced by the contemporary Saints and Fathers of the Eastern Orthodox Church.

Saint Photios the Great
Iconostasis of the Church of the Holy Trinity, Halki, Constantinople.

D. CONFESSIONS AND OTHER PATRISTIC TEXTS

1. St. Photios the Great, Patriarch of Constantinople (+893)[281]

THE ENCYCLICAL LETTER TO THE BISHOPS OF THE EAST IN 866 BY ST. PHOTIOS THE GREAT [282]

1. So, the evil one evidently had not had enough of his wicked deeds, nor did he cease from the devices and schemes which from the beginning he had endeavored to stir up against the human race. He led mankind on with innumerable deceits before the coming of our Lord in the flesh, herding us astray into foreign and lawless practices, by which he also secured his tyranny over mankind with all his might. After the incarnation also he did not cease to trip up and carry away those who trusted in him with innumerable traps and snares. Thence the Simons and Marcions, Montanuses and Manis, and the other heretics multiplied their varied and diverse battles against God. Thence Arius arose, and Macedonius and Nestorius,

---

281 See page 104 for an account of his life.

282 Saint Photios the Great, "The Encyclical Letter to the Bishops of the East in 866 by St. Photios the Great," in *Creeds & Confessions of the Faith in the Christian Tradition*, ed. Jaroslav Pelikan & Valerie Hotchkiss (New Haven: Yale University Press, 2003), 298-308.

Eutyches and Dioscorus, and the remaining company of impiety, against which the seven holy ecumenical councils were organized, and the local conferences of reverend and inspired men gathered, mowing down the evil weeds from the roots with the sword of the Spirit and preparing the wheat field of the church to grow up clean.

2. But when these heretics were gone and relegated to silence and oblivion, the pious were nourishing a good and profound hope that no inventors of newer impious schemes would ever arise after all the devices which the evil one had attempted, since his plots had turned against him. They hoped also that no new defenders and champions would appear for the heresies which had already received conciliar condemnation, since these had been checked by the destruction and punishment of their originators and the followers who were striving to imitate them. With these hopes pious theology was relaxing from its efforts, especially in the imperial city, in which, by God's cooperation, many undesirable trends have been straightened out, and many tongues which formerly spat out abominations have been taught to praise with us the common Maker and Creator of all. The imperial city gushes forth the springs of orthodoxy as if from some lofty and elevated hill, pours the pure streams of piety unto the ends of the inhabited world, and waters with doctrine like rivers the souls there. Although those souls for a long time were parched by the heat of impiety and idiosyncratic worship and dried up into barren deserts, nevertheless when they receive the rain of doctrine as the field of Christ, they bear fruit in abundance. In particular, the inhabitants of Armenia were entangled in the heresy of the Jacobites and boldly rejected the right proclamation of orthodoxy, yet after that well-attended holy council of our fathers assembled at Chalcedon, where your prayers came to our aid, they were enabled to reject that long-standing error. Today the region of the Armenians worships in a pure and orthodox manner the worship of Christians, joining the catholic church in loathing Eutyches, Severus, Dioscorus, and those others who threw stones at piety, Peter and Julian of Halicarnassus and all their scattered offspring, and in subjecting them to the unbreakable bonds of anathema.

3. The Bulgarian nation also, barbaric and Christ-hating as they were, turned to such docility and knowledge of God that they departed from their ancestral demonic rites, put off the error of idolatry and superstition, and were grafted unexpectedly into the Christian faith.

4. But what wicked, evil-eyed, godless counsel and action [followed]! Such a story, with the gospel as its theme, is converted into dejection; joy and gladness is turned into grief and tears. For that nation had not yet been honoring the true religion of Christians for two years when impious and ill-omened men (for what else could one of the pious call them?) arising from the darkness (for they sprang from the Western regions) alas — how shall I narrate the rest? These men fell upon the nation newly established in piety and newly formed, like lightning or earthquake or a hailstorm, or rather, to speak more appropriately, like a solitary wild beast, and with feet and teeth, that is with the pressure of a shameful way of life and corrupt doctrine, ravaged and violated (as far as depended on their own audacity) the vineyard of the Lord, beloved and newly planted. For they wickedly dared to corrupt them and draw them away from the orthodox and pure doctrines and the blameless faith of Christians.

5. First, they shifted them unlawfully into fasting on Saturday; for a little disregard of the things that have been handed down by tradition often leads into a complete disdain for doctrine. Then they cut off the first week of the fast from the rest of Lent and drew them into milk-drinking, consumption of cheese, and other similar pleasant eating. And then, to widen the road of transgression for them and to turn them aside from the straight and royal highway, these very men who were making many brides into husbandless wives and mothers of fatherless children, these same men induced the Bulgarians to loathe and reject the presbyters adorned with lawful marriage (those who were truly priests of God). They scattered the seeds of Mani's farming among them and defiled with a second sowing of tares the souls who were just beginning to sprout the seeds of piety.

6. Furthermore, proclaiming themselves bishops, they did not shudder to re-anoint those who were chrismated with myron by presbyters,

and maintained the fantastic claim that the chrismation of presbyters is useless and is celebrated in vain.

7. Has anyone heard such madness as these crazy men dared without
    hesitation to anoint again those once anointed with myron, and to
    subject the sublime and divine mysteries of Christians to persistent
    laughter and widespread ridicule? And theirs is the wisdom of the
    truly uninitiated: for they say that priests may not sanctify with
    myron those who are being consecrated, but it is reserved to high-
    priests only. Whence comes this law? Who is the lawgiver? Which
    of the apostles? Or of the fathers? Or was it one of the councils?
    Where and when did it meet? Whose votes prevailed? May a priest
    not seal with myron those who are being baptized? Then he may
    not baptize at all, nor perform any priestly functions — so that if
    the priest is not to be cut in half but complete, he would have to be
    returned to a lay status. He consecrates the lordly body and blood of
    Christ, and with them he sanctifies those who have previously been
    initiated; why can he not sanctify by anointing with myron those
    now being initiated? The priest baptizes, solemnizing a purifying
    gift for the one being baptized; how will you take away from him
    the guard and seal of the purification which he himself administers?
    Are you taking away the seal? Do not entrust him with administer-
    ing the gift, nor with using it to consecrate anyone, lest your priest,
    being set apart by empty words, show you to be leader and bishop of
    the same vain chorus with himself.

8. Not only in this matter did they come to transgress the law, but also,
    they attained what must be the summit of evils. Besides the afore-
    mentioned nonsense, they even attempted to adulterate with bas-
    tard ideas and interpolated words (O scheme of the devil!) the holy
    and sacred creed, which holds its undisputed force from the decrees
    of all the ecumenical councils; they make the novel assertion that
    the Holy Spirit proceeds not from the Father alone but also from
    the Son.

9. Who ever heard such a sound burst forth from those who commit-
    ted heresy at any time? What kind of crooked serpent disgorged this
    into their hearts? Who ever of those enrolled among the Christians

would dare to introduce two causes in the Holy Trinity, saying that the Father is cause of the Son and the Spirit, and of the Spirit the son is an additional cause? He would dissolve the divine monarchy into ditheism, and no less than the pagan mythology, he would tear up the theology of Christians, and do violence to the postulate of the supersubstantial and monarchic Trinity. For if the procession from the Father is perfect (it is perfect, because perfect God proceeds from perfect God), what is the procession from the Son? And what is its purpose? It would be excessive and pointless.

10. Again, if the Spirit proceeds from the Son, just as from the Father, why is not the Son begotten from the Spirit, just as from the Father? Thus, everything would be heretical for the heretics, both their ideas and their words, and there would be nothing left for them to dare.

11. Consider this also. If the particularity of the Spirit is recognized in that he proceeds from the Father, just as the particularity of the Son is recognized in that he is begotten from the Father, and if (according to their nonsense) the Spirit also proceeds from the Son, then the Spirit is distinguished from the Father by more particularities than the Son is. For common to the Father and the Son would be the production of the Spirit from them, but particular to the Spirit would be his procession both from the Father and from the Son. But if the Spirit is distinguished by more differences than the Son, the Son would be closer to the Father's essence than the Spirit would be. And thus, Macedonius's bold attack against the Spirit will emerge again, and their drama will again be put on stage.

12. Furthermore, if everything which is common to the Father and the Son is assuredly common to the Spirit as well (like "King," "Lord," "Creator," "All-Ruler," "supersubstantial," "simple", "formless," "bodiless," "invisible," and all the rest), and if the production of the Spirit is common to the Father and the Son, then it follows that the Spirit will proceed from himself, and will himself be the source of himself, and both cause and effect; which not even the myths of the pagans invented.

13. Besides, if it is characteristic of the Spirit alone to be referred to different sources, how is it not characteristic of the Spirit alone to have a polytheistic source?

14. Again, if they divide the Spirit from the other two by inventing a new kind of sharing between the Father and the Son, and if the Father is joined to the Son in sharing of essence but not in some sharing of their particularities, then they separate the Spirit from being related to them in essence.

15. Do you see how vainly, or rather in how blatant an appeal to the multitude, they have applied the name of Christians to themselves? "The Spirit proceeds from the Son." Where did you hear this? From which of the evangelists do you have this saying? Of what council is this blasphemous word?

16. The Lord our God says: "The Spirit, who proceeds from the Father." Who will not close his ears to the excess of their blasphemy? This opposes the Gospels. It resists the holy councils. It cancels the blessed and holy fathers: the great Athanasius; Gregory preeminent in theology; the great Basil, the royal robe of the church; John who is truly called Chrysostom, the golden mouth of the inhabited world, the sea of wisdom. But why do I mention one or another? This blasphemous and godless expression takes up arms against all of the holy prophets together, the apostles, the hierarchs, the martyrs, and the Lord's own words.

17. The Holy Spirit proceeds from the Son? By the same procession or antithetical to his procession from the Father? For if he proceeds by the same procession, would not this make common the distinguishing properties by which alone the Trinity is characterized to be and to be worshiped as Trinity? But if he proceeds by an antithetical procession, does not this expression reveal new Manis and Marcions stretching out again their godless tongue against the Father and the Son?

18. Besides what has been said, if the Son is begotten from the Father, but the spirit proceeds from both the Father and the Son, since the Spirit is referred to two causes, he could not avoid being compound.

19. Again, if the Son is begotten from the Father, but the Spirit proceeds from the Father and the Son, what is different about the Spirit, that something else does not proceed from him? So, their godless opinion would imply not three but four hypostases, or rather an unlimited number, as the fourth produces another, and that one again another, until they descend into a pagan multiplicity.

20. Besides what has been said, one should also consider this: if the procession of the Spirit from the Father results in his existence, what will the procession from the Son contribute to the Spirit, if the paternal procession is sufficient for his existence? For no one would dare to say that it results in some other part of what has to do with the essence, since all doubleness and composition are completely excluded from that blessed and divine nature.

21. Besides what has been said, if everything which is not common to the all-powerful, consubstantial, and sublime Trinity must belong to just one of the three, and if the production of the Spirit is not common to the three, it must therefore belong to only one of the three. Then (on one hand) will they say that the Spirit proceeds from the Father? And if they do, how can they keep from renouncing the new mystical doctrine which is so dear to them? But if from the Son, why did they not presume from the beginning to reveal their whole attack on God, namely that they were not only adding the Son as a producer of the Spirit, but were also removing this role from the Father? Following this line of reasoning, indeed they could transfer also the begetting with the production, so that they would not even say that the Son is begotten from the Father, but would make the fantastic assertion that the Father is begotten from the Son. Thus, they would be the leaders not only of heretics but also of madmen.

22. See from this how their impious and mindless counsel is made manifest. For since everything which appears and is named in the all holy, connatural, and consubstantial Trinity either is common to all, or else belongs to just one of the three; but the production of the Spirit is neither common nor, according to them, of some one alone (may he be merciful to us, and turn the blasphemy onto their heads) —

then there is no production of the Spirit at all in the life-creating and all-perfect Trinity.

23. One could add innumerable arguments to the measure of what has been said, refuting their godless opinion, which the genre of a letter does not permit now to include nor to mention. Therefore, these matters have been reported in an elementary manner and in outline; the individual refutation and the broad teaching are stored up until our common meeting, if God grants.

24. Those bishops of darkness (for they called themselves bishops) sowed this heresy with their other unlawful practices into that simple and newly established nation of the Bulgarians. The report of these matters came to our hearing; we were struck through our bowels a grievous blow, as if one saw the offspring of his womb torn and dismembered before his eyes by serpents and wild beasts. We who expended toils, pains, and sweat for their regeneration and perfection experienced similar unbearable grief and misfortune when our children were perishing.

25. For we mourned as much at the event which occurred and their suffering, as we had been filled with joy when we saw them released from their former error.

26. But we mourned them and are still mourning, and to raise them from their calamity we will not give sleep to our eyes nor closing to our eyelids until we bring them back (as far as we are able) into the tabernacle of the Lord.

27. By a conciliar and divine decree, we have condemned these deceivers and enemies of God, the new forerunners of apostasy, the servants of the adversary, those deserving of innumerable deaths, the common corrupters, those who so grievously mangled that tender nation newly established in piety. We are not now defining their apostasy, but from the existing canons of the councils and the apostles we are revealing the previously defined judgment against them and making it clear again to all.

28. It is human nature not so much to be kept on the right track by the memory of past punishments as to be taught self-control by the sight

of punishments in the present. And those punishments which have gone past are confirmed by the agreement of those which are present. Therefore, we have excluded from every Christian flock these men who persevere in their manifold error. The sixtyfourth [sixty-sixth] canon of the holy apostles says we should drive out those who practice fasting on Saturdays, as follows:

29. "If any clergyman is found fasting on the Lord's day or on Saturday, except only the one [before Pascha], let him be defrocked; but if he is a layman, let him be excommunicated." Yes, indeed, and the fifty-fifth canon of the sixth holy ecumenical council makes this declaration:

30. "Whereas we have learned that those who live in the city of the Romans are fasting on the Saturdays of the holy forty days' fast, contrary to the traditional ecclesiastical order; the holy council has decreed that for the church of the Romans also the canon should be valid unshakably which says: 'If any clergyman is found fasting on the holy day of the Lord, or on the Sabbath, except the one and only, let him be defrocked, but if he is a layman, let him be excommunicated.'"

31. Furthermore, the fourth canon of the Synod of Gangra concerning those who abominate marriage says this: "If anyone should judge that one ought not partake of the offering when a married presbyter is celebrating, let him be anathema." Likewise the sixth council also agrees in bearing witness against them, writing in this manner: "Whereas we have learned that it is handed down in the church of the Romans in the form of a canon, that those who are about to be granted the honor of ordination as deacon or presbyter must declare that they are no longer joined to their wives; for our part, therefore, following the strict order of the ancient apostolic canon, we wish the lawful marriages of ordained men to flourish from now on, by no means dissolving their union with their wives or depriving them of intercourse with each other at the proper time. So if anyone is granted the honor of ordination as deacon or subdeacon, let him by no means be prevented from approaching such a rank, because he lives with a lawful wife; nor let him be asked to declare at the time

of ordination that he will abstain from the lawful intercourse with his own wife, lest by doing this we be compelled to despise marriage which was validated and blessed by God with his own presence, as the voice of the Gospel cries out: 'Those whom God has joined together, let no man put asunder,' and the apostle teaches, 'Marriage is honorable among all and the marriage-bed undefiled,' and 'Are you bound to a wife? Do not seek to be free.' So, if anyone dares, acting against the apostolic canons, to deprive any ordained man, a presbyter, we mean, or a deacon or subdeacon, of the union and fellowship with his lawful wife, let him be defrocked. Likewise, if any presbyter or deacon puts away his wife on the pretext of piety, let him be excommunicated; but if he persists, let him be defrocked."

32. But the mitigation of the first week and the rechrismation of those who have already been baptized and chrismated will not need, I suppose, any canons for their condemnation; it is self evident from the description alone that they surpass every excess of impiety.

33. Not only so, but also the equally excessive blasphemy against the Spirit (or rather against the Holy Trinity as a whole), even if they had ventured no other of the audacities which have been mentioned, is sufficient even alone to subject them to innumerable anathemas.

34. We thought it right to bring the knowledge and awareness of these matters to Your Brotherhood in Christ according to the ancient custom of the church; we advise and beg you to become eager allies in combating these impious and godless assertions. Do not depart from the traditional order, which our forefathers, by their deeds, handed over to us to keep; but with great zeal and eagerness choose and send representatives on your behalf, men bearing your authority, adorned with piety and priestliness in word and life. Thus, we may remove from the midst of the church the new gangrene of this heresy, and pull up by the very roots those mad enough to introduce such an admixture of wickedness into the newly founded and established nation. Because of their common apostasy let us commit them to the fire which according to the Lord's words will receive those who are accursed.

35. For thus, when heresy is driven out and piety prevails, we have good hope that we can return the newly catechized and newly enlightened community of the Bulgarians to the faith which was delivered to them. And indeed, not only this nation exchanged the faith in Christ for their former impiety, but also that nation called Rus of whom many people often speak and consider second to none for cruelty and bloodthirstiness, who indeed raised their hands even against the Roman empire, when they had enslaved those around them, and from that were filled with presumption. Nevertheless, these also have now accepted the pure and unadulterated worship of Christians in exchange for the pagan and godless belief in which they were held before, establishing themselves voluntarily in a position of subjects and allies, instead of their recent audacious brigandage against us. And to such a point the desire and zeal for the faith kindled them (Paul again exclaims, "Blessed is God forever!") that they even accepted a bishop and shepherd, and are embracing the rites of Christians with great honor and zeal and diligence.

36. While these are renouncing their former beliefs and are taking in exchange for them the pure faith of Christians, by the grace of the loving God who desires all men to be saved and to come to the knowledge of truth, if Your Brotherhood also should cooperate eagerly in cutting out and burning the weeds, we trust in the Lord Jesus Christ our true God that his sheepfold will be increased still more and the saying will be fulfilled that "all shall know me, from the least of them to the greatest" and "to all the earth has gone out the voice" of the apostolic teachings "and their words to the ends of the inhabited world."

37. Therefore, those who are sent by you in your place, representing your reverend and holy person, must be entrusted with the authority that has been allotted to you in the Holy Spirit. Thus, they may be ready to speak and free to act with the authority of an apostolic throne concerning these topics and others similar to them. And indeed, also a synodical letter has reached us from the regions of Italy, filled with unspeakable accusations which the inhabitants of Italy have sent against their own bishop himself with much condemnation and innumerable oaths, begging us not to overlook them as they are so

pitiably perishing and oppressed by such a heavy tyranny, and as the laws of the priesthood are being violated and all ecclesiastical regulations are being overturned. These matters were already brought to the ears of all earlier by monks and presbyters coming up from there (it was Basil and Zosimas and Metrophanes and others with them, who were bitterly lamenting this great tyranny, and were calling in tears for the vindication of the churches). But now also, as I said before, various letters from various sources have arrived from there, filled with the whole tragedy and innumerable laments. We have attached to this letter of ours copies of these according to their request and petition (for they entreated with terrible oaths and supplications that these should be distributed to all the archiepiscopal and apostolic thrones, as the letters themselves will show when they are read.) Thus, when the holy and ecumenical council is gathered in Christ, a common vote may confirm that which is acceptable to God and the conciliar canons in regard to these matters, and deep peace may take hold of the churches of Christ.

38. We call not only upon Your Blessedness for this, but indeed also upon the representatives of the other archiepiscopal and apostolic thrones, of whom some are already present, others are expected to arrive in a short time.

39. Let not Your Brotherhood in the Lord make your brothers wait too long with delay and extension of time, knowing that if anything insufficient or inappropriate is accomplished because of your procrastination, you will not draw the condemnation upon any other than yourself.

40. We thought we should add this also to the letter, to be transmitted to every community of the church under you, that the seventh holy ecumenical council should be listed and numbered with the six holy ecumenical councils. A report has come to us that some churches under your apostolic throne number ecumenical councils up to the sixth but do not know the seventh. What was ratified in it they hold with as much zeal and reverence as anything else, but they have not yet learned to proclaim it in the church along with the others, although it preserves everywhere equal honor to theirs.

41. For this council, like the others, defeated a very great heresy, having representatives of the four high-priestly thrones as participants and voting members, Thomas the priest-monk and his companions were present, as is clear, from your apostolic throne of Alexandria; from Jerusalem and Antioch, John and his companions; and from the presbyterate of Rome, Peter the most pious protopresbyter and another Peter a presbyter, monk and abbot of the holy monastery of Saint Sabba at Rome.

42. When all these had come together, along with our father in God the most holy and thrice-blessed man Tarasius archbishop of Constantinople, the seventh great ecumenical council was assembled, triumphantly defeating the heresy of the icon-fighters or rather Christ-fighters. Since the barbarian and foreign nation of the Arabs had occupied the countryside, perhaps it was not easy for the proceedings of this council to be conveyed to you. For this reason, the decisions made there, even if by many they are honored and followed, nevertheless are not known, as they say, to be decisions of this council.

43. We ought therefore to proclaim this council as great, holy, and ecumenical, as I said before, along with the six before it. Not to accomplish and do this is, in the first place, to wrong the church of Christ, overlooking such a great council, and to such an extent breaking and dissolving its bond of unity. In the second place, it gives credence to the allegations of the iconoclasts (whom I know well that you abominate no less than the other heretics), when they say that their heresy was not condemned by an ecumenical council but that they are being penalized by the judgment of one throne, using this excuse for talking nonsense.

44. Because of all this, we request and advise as brothers to brothers, proposing what is fitting, that both in your synodical letters and in all the other synodical and ecclesiastical narratives and discussions you number and count this council with the six holy ecumenical councils, reckoning it seventh after them.

45. May Christ our true God, the first and great high priest, who voluntarily made himself a good-omened sacrifice for us and shed his own

blood as a ransom for us, grant that your high priestly and honorable head may be shown stronger than the barbarian nations which surround you; may he grant you to complete a calm and gentle course of life; may he grant you to attain also the inheritance above in ineffable joy and gladness, where all the blessed ones reside, and from which all pain and sighing and sadness are removed, in Christ our true God; to whom be glory and power unto the ages of ages. Amen.

We pray for you as the holiness requires which you have inherited from your fathers. Do you yourselves likewise not fail to remember Our Mediocrity.

ST. PHOTIOS OF CONSTANTINOPLE:
ON THE MYSTAGOGY OF THE HOLY SPIRIT[283]

87. Are you ignorant of ancient things? Do you fear your fathers? Do you truly examine their doctrine? Recently (the second generation has not yet passed), Leo [III, pope of [Old] Rome, 795-816], another renowned man who was adorned with miracles, removed all pretext for heresy from everyone. Because the Latin language, frequently used by our holy Fathers, has inadequate meanings which do not translate the Greek language purely and exactly, and often render false notions of the doctrines of the Faith, and because it is not supplied with as many words that can interpret the meaning of a Greek word in its exact sense, that God-inspired man conceived an idea (the idea being conceived not only because of what we have just said, but also because of that heresy [the *Filioque*] now openly proclaimed without restraint, but then only being hinted at in the city of [Old] Rome). He decreed that the people of [Old] Rome should recite the sacred Symbol of Faith in the Greek tongue. Through these divinely inspired plans, he supplemented and redressed the inadequacy of the Latin tongue and expelled from the pious the suspicion of a difference in faith, pulling up by the roots the pollution then growing in the provinces of [Old] Rome. In the city of [Old] Rome, he posted notices and decrees that the sacred Symbol of

283 Saint Photios, *The Mystagogy of the Holy Spirit*, trans. Joseph P. Farrell (Brookline: Holy Cross Orthodox Press, 1987), 103-105.

Faith be recited in the same Greek tongue with which it had been first proclaimed according to the authoritative utterance of the Synods, even by those who used Latin in the mystical and sacred rites. Not only for [Old] Rome did he decree it, but also throughout the provinces which deferred to the high priesthood and rule of [Old] Rome. He sent sermons and synodical letters that everyone think and do the same, and he ensured the immutability of the doctrine by anathemas....

89. Thus, these men shone with piety, attesting that the Spirit proceeds from the Father, as did my John [Pope John VIII, 872-882, who signed the decrees of the Eighth Ecumenical Synod that met in Constantinople, 879-880 and agreed to prohibit the *Filioque* from the Symbol of Faith, ending the schism] — he is mine because, besides other reasons, he was more in harmony with others who are our Fathers. Our John, being courageous in mind as well as piety, and courageous because he abhors and casts down unrighteousness and every manner of impiety, was able to prevail in both the sacred and the civil laws and to transform disorder into order. This man, favoured amongst the Roman archbishops by his more-than-illustrious and God-serving legates Paul, Eugene and Peter (bishops and priests of God), who were with us in the synod [the Eighth Ecumenical Synod that met at Constantinople, 879-880], this grace-filled bishop of [Old] Rome accepted the Symbol of the Faith of the Catholic Church of God, as the bishops of [Old] Rome had done before him. He both confirmed and subscribed to it with wondrous and notable sayings, with sacred tongue and hand through those very illustrious and admirable men aforementioned. Yes, and after that, the holy Hadrian, his successor, sent us a synodical letter according to the prescription of ancient custom, sending us the same doctrine, testifying for the same theology, namely, that the Spirit proceeds from the Father. Consequently, those sacred and blessed bishops of [Old] Rome both believed and taught thus throughout their life, and they remained in the same confession until they passed from this perishable life to the imperishable. Which of these bishops of [Old] Rome, by life, thought or teaching, altered the profession of immortal life by saying the heretical and diseased word [*filioque*]? Can those diseased with heretical sickness claim they drank the deadly poison of so great an impiety from any of

the aforementioned without immediately becoming adversaries of those who triumphantly illumined Western lands with Orthodoxy?

2. St. John II, Metropolitan of KIEV (+1089)

HIS LIFE,
WHICH WE COMMEMORATE ON THE 31ST OF AUGUST.

"John was a Bulgarian by birth. He came to Kiev in the year 1080 and immediately attained such esteem that he was soon elevated to the throne of the Metropolitan. John governed the Church for eight years. He wrote an epistle to Pope Clement, in which he reprimanded him for the innovations that had been introduced by the Roman Church. He died peacefully in the year 1089."[284]

He "earned general profound respect. The Ven. Nestor, his contemporary, says the following about him: 'this man is an expert in books, skillful in teaching, merciful to the needy and the widows, kind to everyone, rich and poor, humble and meek.' ... the following are famous [writings]: 'Message of Metropolitan John to Clement, Pope of Old Rome' and 'Church Canons', written for Monk James with his explanation of the Canons of the universal (catholic) Church in their application for the Russian Church."[285]

HIS LETTER TO CLEMENT, POPE OF OLD ROME[286]

1. I have received your love in Christ, O true man of God, worthy of the apostolic see and calling; for although seated far from our mean-

---

284 Saint Nikolai Velimirović, *The Prologue of Ohrid, Volume Two*, July to December, trans. Father T. Timothy Tepsić (Vrnjačka Banja: Sebastian Press - Western American Diocese of the Serbian Orthodox Church, 2002), 233.

285 "St. John, Metropolitan of Kiev (1089)," Today's Scripture Readings, accessed December 9th, 2023, https://www.holytrinityorthodox.com/calendar/los/August/31-04.htm.

286 Andrei Nikolaevich Pavlov, *Kriticeskie opyty po istopie drev-nejse] Greko-Russkoj polemiki protev Patenjan*, (St. Petersburg, 1878), trans. Nicholas Nelson, 169-186.

ness and lowliness, by the wings of love you reach even unto us, and
you cordially and genuinely address us and spiritually pray for our
sakes and wholly accept and adore the teachings of our Orthodox
and blameless Faith, as that holy and in every way honourable man,
the virtuous bishop of Your Holiness, related to us and clearly articulated. Since, therefore, these things are so and you were put forth
as such a hierarch for us from God and are not like those distorters
and forgerers of the truth who served as hierarchs a little earlier, for
this reason I, also, the least in all, address you, the holy head, and noetically kiss you in return. May you ever rejoice exceedingly and be
always sheltered by the heavenly, most high, and almighty hand, and
may the compassionate and placable and merciful God grant that
during your tenure and in your days the scandals and impediments
to the way of God that have arisen (I know not whence or how) between you and us may be corrected. Why and how is it that to this
day these things have not been corrected? I am greatly bewildered. I
do not know what spiteful and jealous demon, enemy of truth and
of piety, has brought about these things, and has torn your brotherly
love and concord away from the whole Christian company—I do
not mean entirely, for we know you to be Christians by the grace of
God on high, and on many matters we very much do accept you, but
in certain things you are going off into schism.

2. Now consider the following. The Holy and Œcumenical Councils
   are seven in total; this is acknowledged by all. By these councils the
   pious and Orthodox Faith of us Christians was both studied and
   taught and from them it unequivocally and clearly received confirmation and authority with all certainty and proof. These are the sev-
   en pillars of the Wisdom of God the Word, upon which He built
   well His own holy house, the Catholic and Œcumenical Church.
   All the presidents and successors of the See of Peter, the chief of
   the holy and all-praised Apostles, like-mindedly followed after these
   holy and sacred seven Œcumenical Councils and with one accord
   agreed with them, some being personally present and agreeing with
   the proceedings and voting in support of what was being said, while
   others sent out those most familiar to them and of the same faith
   as themselves and cooperated and in a word, from your apostolic
   and divine throne they surely confirmed all things. Thus, at the First
   Œcumenical Council, Silvester agreed; at the Second, Damasus; at

the Third, Celestine; while the blessed and ever-memorable Pope Leo was the support of the Fourth Holy and Œcumenical Council, and his most wise and holy epistle, which he sent to Flavian, was widely regarded as a pillar of Orthodoxy by all those that were shining forth in the council at that time. At the Fifth Council, Virgil was present. At the Sixth, Agathon agreed, an honorable man, wise in divine matters. In the Seventh Holy and Œcumenical Council, the most holy Pope Hadrian agreed and joined in the discussion through the holy and God-bearing men sent by him, the archpriest Peter of the most holy Church of Rome and the priest Peter, abbot of the Monastery of Saint Sabbas in Rome.

3. Therefore, since this is how things were, how did this division and schism between us come about? Who was it that planted such and so many weeds in Rome? Of the many things which you dare to do in violation of the Divine and Holy Canons, we write but a few to your love. Firstly, you fast on Saturdays, outside of the norm. In addition, you cut out and separate the first week of the [Great] Fast from the rest of the fast and drag down the peoples to the eating of cheese and the drinking of milk and to similar gluttony. You also loathe and turn away from those priests who are lawfully married and living with their wives. Those who were already sealed with myrrh by priests you dare to anoint again, as if it were not possible for priests but only for bishops to do this. I will not mention the issue of unleavened bread, something which is so obviously of the Jewish faith and worship. But there is something that is the summit of these evils, and to this you have ascended: for in addition to the forementioned offences, even the Sacred and Holy Creed, which has been proclaimed by all of these sacred and holy councils, that which no one has the power to defy and overrule, even this did you try to adulterate, introducing the innovation that the Holy Spirit proceeds not only from the Father but also from the Son.

4. Those things, among many others, need much attention and correction; and for this reason it is necessary for your holiness to write and send a letter to your brother in spirit, the most holy Patriarch of Constantinople, and to spare no effort, so that these scandals may be solved, and that we may be unified and in spiritual agreement, as the blessed Paul requests of us, saying, "Now I beseech you, brethren, by the name of our Lord Jesus Christ, that ye all speak the same thing,

and that there be no divisions among you; but that ye be perfectly joined together in the same mind and in the same judgment" (1 Cor. 1:10). Thus, since these crimes are six (for of all the ones we have heard, we have only pointed out so many in the letter that we sent you), if you accept them meekly and reasonably, we will afterwards write to you about the others also. If things are indeed as we have heard, O holy Pope, then know full well and be convinced that you are violating the Canons of the holy Apostles and again of the Holy Œcumenical Councils, which the ancient patriarchs of Old Rome accepted, as we shall immediately elaborate below.

5. First of all, let us examine the sin of fasting on Saturdays; for indeed Canon 64 of the Holy Apostles strictly censures those that fast on Saturdays and casts them out of the Church, as seen here: "If any of the clergy be found fasting on the Lord's day, or on the Sabbath, excepting the one only, let him be deposed. If a layman, let him be excommunicated."

6. Yet the second accusation is also characteristic of the Jacobite and the Armenian heresies, something completely unacceptable for Orthodox Christians; I am referring to the eating of cheese, the sucking of eggs, and the drinking of milk during Holy and Great Lent. For what Christian would dare do such a thing or even think of it? For this is unacceptable for the pious. Be made aware, therefore, of Canon 56 of the Sixth Holy and Œcumenical Council. Your own Pope Agathon agreed with this council. Now hear what this canon says: "Likewise we have learned that in the country of the Armenians and in other regions on the Saturdays and on the Sundays of holy Lent some persons eat eggs and cheese. It has therefore seemed best to decree also this, that the Church of God throughout the inhabited earth, carefully following a single procedure, shall carry out fasting, and abstain, precisely as from every kind of thing sacrificed, so and especially from eggs and cheese, which are fruit and produce from which we have to abstain. As for those who fail to observe this rule, if they are Clergymen, let them be deposed from office; but if they are laymen, let them be excommunicated."

7. The third crime is that you loathe to receive communion from the hands of priests that are married. Hear, then, what is said about this in the holy and pious council which was convened in Gangra by the holy and God-bearing fathers. The relevant decision is contained in

the fourth Canon that they instituted, thus: "If any one shall maintain, concerning a married presbyter, that it is not lawful to partake of the oblation when he offers it, let him be anathema." And likewise the Sixth Council [in Canon 13] says, "If any Presbyter or Deacon, or any of the ecclesiastical roll, expel his own wife on the pretext of reverence, let him be excommunicated; and if he persist, let him be deposed from office."

8. The fourth sin is the re-anointing of those already baptized and anointed. How is this not also an absurdity, given that the sacred Symbol of Faith is always and everywhere and by each one of the faithful read aloud and spoken thus: "I confess one baptism for the remission of sins"? So if we have one baptism, then we also have one holy myrrh pertaining to the same baptism, not separately and at another time, but at the same time, together with the holy baptism, performed by the priests as well as by the bishops.

9. Your fifth transgression is that of the unleavened bread [azymes]. This has its roots and its origins in very many heresies, as we intend to prove. However, because this issue requires many scriptural proofs and references, we shall write to you further about this at another time. At this time, however, the only thing we shall say is that the Jews make use of unleavened bread in memory of the flight from Egypt. We, however, are the sons of Christians, and never at any time were we subject to the Egyptian tyrant; rather, we are commanded to scorn all of these Jewish practices and habits, the sabbath, unleavened bread, and circumcision. And whoever keeps one of these, as the divine Apostle writes, he is a debtor to fulfill the whole Jewish law (Gal. 5:3). Regarding this, the Apostle Paul says once more, "Brethren, I have received of the Lord that which also I delivered unto you, that the Lord Jesus the same night in which he was betrayed took bread, blessed it, brake it, sanctified it, and gave it to his holy disciples and apostles, saying, Take, eat" (cf. 1 Cor. 11:22-23). Note this phrase: he did not say, "He took unleavened bread [ἄζυμον]" but rather leavened bread [ἄρτον], for at that time [Holy Thursday] neither was there unleavened bread nor was the Passover being celebrated, for Him to have given unleavened bread to his disciples. It also becomes clear from the following: whereas the Jewish Passover was celebrated standing up, the scriptures state that "He sat down with the twelve" (Mat. 26, 20) and regarding the one disciple,

"which also leaned on his breast at supper, " (Jn. 21, 20). He Himself said, "With desire I have desired to eat this passover with you" (Lk. 22:15). To what is He referring? To the handing down of the new mystery. For indeed they had shared every Jewish passover together many times, He and His disciples. How, therefore, did He desire this passover which He was eating? And why did he say "this"? For in saying "this", He made it clear that "this" was something different from "that", the Jewish passover. And again, "Do this in remembrance of me" (Lk. 22:19). He did not say, "Do that," the unleavened bread of the Jews, but "do this," the regular bread, "which I have given you." For this was truly leavened bread, and not unleavened, as has been clearly proven. And then regarding Judas, He says, "He it is, to whom I shall give a sop, when I have dipped it, that betrayeth me" (Jn. 13:26). If you are saying, though, that these things are to be done with unleavened bread for the sake of the purity of the Godhead and His unmixedness with anything material, then you are in error, falling into the ancient heresy of Valentinus, Manes, and also Apollinarius of Laodicea and Paul the Syrian of Samosata, Eutyches, Dioscorus, Severus, and the Monothelites that appeared at the time of the holy Sixth Council, Sergius, Pyrrhus, Paul, and those with them. All of these men were similarly inspired by the devil, and all their heresies are almost as one, since they deny the perfect incarnation and hypostatic union of the one Saviour Christ, our True God.

10. But about all of these things, as we have said, and if you so desire and it is the will of God, we can have a more lengthy discussion another time, if the Giver of life grants us to live upon this earth. Now, therefore, let us come also to the sixth chapter. This was the blasphemy regarding the Holy Spirit. For you say, "We believe in the Father, in the Son, and in the Holy Spirit, who proceeds from the Father and the Son." It is truly amazing, or better put, frightful, how you could dare to adulterate the faith of the very three hundred and eighteen holy fathers and of the later holy Œcumenical Councils, the faith which is sung throughout the earth and to the ends of the inhabited world in all the Christian Churches with one voice thus: "We believe... in the Holy Spirit, the Lord, the Giver of Life, who proceedeth from the Father, who with the Father and the Son together is worshiped and glorified." Why then do you not also say it as do all Christians? Instead, you thought to add to it, and indeed you are introducing new teachings, even though the Apostle says, "if any man preach any

other gospel unto you than that ye have received, let him be anathema" (Gal. 1:9). May you never hear that word. It is truly a dreadful thing to change one jot or one tittle, or one syllable, of the Holy Scriptures. Or do you not realize what a great scandal this is? For you thus seem to be introducing two causes and two origins of the Holy Spirit, degrading His value and deposing the Holy Spirit from His rightful place, and in so doing you are in danger of falling into the heresy of Macedonius and the Pneumatomachi. May you not do so. I therefore plead with you and fall down before your holy feet; I beg of you, awaken regarding all of the above, especially regarding the unleavened bread as well as the present issue, for the one endangers Holy Communion, while the other, the right Faith.

11. I wanted to write to you also about the strangled and unclean animals and regarding the monks that consume meat, but these things and their like are for later, if God allows for it and corrects the greater issues first. Forgive me, for the Lord's sake; out of great love I wrote you these things. If it is true, as we have heard, that you do these things, "search the scriptures" and you will find that all these things are in need of correction.

12. I entreat your love in the Lord above all else, if you will, to write unto our most holy patriarch of Constantinople and to his holy Metropolitans, who hold forth the word of life, shining as lights in the world (Phil. 2:16, 15). By the grace of God, they are able to discuss these matters with you and bring about correction. And afterwards, if it pleases you, write also to me, the least of all. I, John, the least Metropolitan of Russia, bid farewell to you and to all those in your flock, both the clergy and the people. All our most holy and God-beloved bishops and abbots and all the pious clergy and people with us also bid farewell unto you. May the grace of the All-Holy Spirit be with you and all of yours. Amen.

3. St. Theophylact of Bulgaria (+1107)

HIS LIFE,
WHICH WE COMMEMORATE ON THE 31ST OF DECEMBER.

Theophylact was born on the island of Euripos and educated in Constantinople by the most eminent teachers of that time. As a priest of the Great Church, he was chosen bishop and sent, against his will, to Ohrid, where he remained about twenty-five years (from about 1082 to 1108 A.D.). Chromatianus of Ohrid calls him "the wisest archbishop." A man of enormous learning, both secular and theological, of refined Byzantine tastes, melancholy and sensitive, Theophylact felt among the Slavs in Ohrid like an exile among barbarians. He wrote commentaries on the Four Gospels and other books of the New Testament. These are the best works of their kind after that of St. Chrysostom, and are read even today with great benefit. His other known works include his Letters and the Life of St. Clement of Ohrid. In old age, St. Theophylact withdrew from Ohrid to Thessaloniki, where it is thought he finished his earthly life and took up his habitation in blessed eternity.

REGARDING THE CHARGES AGAINST THE LATINS[287]

Your request was presented before me,[288] my most pious son in the Lord, and I saw this as good and suitable for the eyes of a hierarch, who, at the present time, is cast out like the gatekeeper of some cruel and ungrateful master.[289] You requested of us to dispute briefly, as much as this is possible, the ecclesiastical errors of the Latins, which you claimed to be

---

287 Saint Theophylact of Ohrid, "Concerning Those Who Accuse the Latins," in *Patrologia Graeca, Vol. 126*, Jacques Paul Migne (1857-1866), translated into English by & Bogomil Sabtchev (Philosophia, 2020) (Paris: Imprimerie Catholique, 1857), 221-254.

288 Ps 118:170.

289 Most likely, blessed Theophylact is referring to the period of being an archbishop of Ochrid, Bulgaria with some bitterness since he did not want to be away from Constantinople.

many and to exert no little force in dividing the churches. And we know that the others, almost all of them, think in such a way. We, however, do not think so: for we have neither known the errors to be many, nor are they able to divide the churches. Since none of the charges brought forth pertains to the very essence of our faith, we hesitate to oppose so many and to disturb easily agitated souls, lest our love grows cold.[290] This coldness, as we have already heard, has been first of all dealt on me in this present time which abounds in inequity.[291] For we do not receive in a brotherly manner what has been presented by our brothers, but stand against them in opposition and each one of us strives to appear as one elbowing and pushing back his rival who is ahead of him; and we believe to be deemed wise in the presence of many and that it would be the ultimate divine doctrine if we should attach to our neighbors some heresy and to be men of vision if we should expose the dark-gleaming Lucifer. Therefore, on account of these things, it seems to me that this time is to be passed over in silence, as the old prophecy instructs.[292] Nevertheless, I understand the loyalty of your love, not deeming it right to be hurt by the bad practices of others. For I let the Egyptians, on the one hand, be delayed by the palpable darkness[293] and encounter blood in the waters, and on the other hand, I gladly see every Israelite enjoy the light for their work and the water for their salvation. Simply put, I'm glad to see the divine miracles be to the former, a punishment, but to the latter, salvation.

Thus, as I was saying, the Latins seem to be erroneous in many things: they use unleavened bread in their offering, fast on Saturdays, and calculate differently the period of the fast before the Passion; and while, on the one hand, they forbid the marriages of clergy, on the other hand they allow those of the laity indiscriminately and without any limits. Moreover, if you're able to hold your laughter, I would add that they shave their beards—both the laity and those in priestly offices, whose hands are flashing with golden rings and their priestly robes are woven from silken yarn and they dress in multi-colored fabrics. Moreover, the meat-eating monks, when they stretch forth their hands to worship

---

290 Matt 24:12.

291 Referring again to his 'exile'.

292 Eccl 3:7.

293 Exod 10:21.

the Lord, are dragged down to the earth.[294] Thus, they all sin together. But should you see bandits feasting on the meat of strangled animals, would you detest the church of the Romans for teaching such things? It is possible that one of those who are extremely faithful, of great fervor, and zealous for orthodoxy, would rise up and would not only accuse us of ignorance and confusion regarding the divine or of coldness and the betrayal of our own customs but would also enumerate many more accusations than those already mentioned. I think that some of these do not need any correction while others need one that is moderate and fitting. If such a correction succeeds, the church gains a little and if it fails no harm would be brought about. It seems to me that having communion with the Latins is to some inadequate and if this is not corrected it would inflict a great harm upon the inheritance of the Son, which He took from among the nations; this I will both show and prove to you inasmuch as this is possible. If this discourse doesn't seem too long to us, we will also examine in moderation some of the other matters.

Now, their greatest error, which in Solomon's words makes one fall into the trap of hell,[295] is the innovation in the Symbol of Faith, which was added by those who proclaim that the Spirit proceeds from the Father and the Son. It is necessary that the Symbol of the faithful is a Symbol which is free from every adulteration; for even the axe-bearers of whom Ezekiel speaks are not to spare the marked, unless the sign appears to them genuine.[296] How then shall we answer to this innovation? Simply, plainly, and completely, as it befits the disciples of the fishermen. For if we had chosen to follow another teacher, we would have persuaded the disciples and defenders of contrary opinions using his own words. Since those who were eyewitnesses and ministers of the Word from the very beginning[297] handed down to us this same Word, saying that the Spirit is the Spirit of Truth and proceeds from the Father,[298] then our ar-

---

294 Eastern monks do not consume meat, imitating the angelic state and the state of Adam before the fall. The assumption is that meat-eating is inappropriate in the strict ascetic life and weighs down the soul.

295 Prov 9:18.

296 Ezek 9:2–4.

297 Luke 1:2.

298 John 15:26.

gument is simple: either bring forth the other teacher who speaks more clearly than the Word and more wisely than the Wisdom, from whom you have taken this new dogma which is so exceedingly dear to you, or if you don't have such a teacher, accept our one teacher, Christ, Who teaches concerning His kindred Spirit, from Whom and how He has His existence and Who testifies with His own testimony that the Spirit proceeds from the Father. If indeed, as you think, He proceeds also from the Son, what would have prevented Him from saying: 'The One who proceeds from the Father and Me?' Thus, you have been found not following Christ, the Bearer of good news to the poor,[299] even though you claim to have taken up your cross.[300] But if you have been persuaded of this by some of the approved fathers,[301] show us this father and that would be sufficient for us. But if you're not able to show us, despite your many labors, then either the approved father did not say that, or the one who has said it has not been approved.

And even if we concede to you in this argument, still, we shall not make the exception into a rule—a principle to which you yourselves adhere. For while countless theologians talk about the Holy Spirit, no one is saying such a thing, except that the Spirit has appeared through the Son and that He is from God through the Son. Should one or two be found to teach the opposite, this is an agreement not with these fathers, but with those who are full of the spirit of deception: 'But it has been written:', he would say, 'the Spirit of the Son'[302] and 'the Spirit of Christ'.[303] And I affirm this, since He has also been called 'the Spirit of Truth and 'the Spirit of Life'[304] for the Son is both Truth and Life[305] and

---

299 Luke 4:18.

300 Mark 8:34.

301 The greatest church fathers, whose teachings have been approved by synods as dogmas and doctrines of the Church.

302 Gal 4:6.

303 Rom 8:9.

304 Rom 8:2.

305 John 14:6.

I would also add 'of Wisdom'[306] and 'of Power'[307] for the Son is these as well; but this is not because the Spirit originates from Him but because He is related to Him, a kindred Spirit and not alien, and as One Who rests in Him,[308] and is sent through Him,[309] and bestowed, and imparted to the worthy.[310]

It is great that this discourse has advanced and reached the most important point. It seems to me, oh you, who are considering the things above[311] that you do not err so much due to an evil intention as you do so out of ignorance of what is correct. For you think that the procession is equal to the bestowing and imparting; since the Spirit happens to be sent and bestowed and imparted the Son, you suppose that there is no offense even if you declare that He also proceeds from the Son. However, this is not the case. How so? We affirm that these differ utterly and completely from each other. For the precession is indicative of how the Spirit is. For just as the Son is from the Father, begotten and not by any other manner, so the Spirit also is from the same source, I mean from the Father, and not begotten, for there are not two Sons, but proceeding. Therefore, the procession is the manner by which the Spirit has His being from the Father and by which His uniqueness is made known. But the sending, bestowing, and imparting are not indicative of how the Spirit has His being, but rather through them some richness is revealed and likewise an abundance of goodness, which has its existence from the Father and is poured upon the worthy by the Son, to whom the Spirit is also said to have been revealed through the Son, for it is to those who receive the Word, and not to those who are ignorant of Him, that the Spirit manifests Himself; and of His divinity which was not previously known by anyone, we have learned clearly through the Son, when He associated Himself with the Father in the deifying baptism.

---

306 Eph 1:17.

307 Isa 11:2.

308 Isa 11:2, 1Pet 4:14.

309 John 16:7.

310 Gal 3:5.

311 Col 3:2.

Thus, it is also said that the Lord breathed the Spirit[312] into the disciples after the Resurrection but not as His originator—for, if I may say so, the inbreathing of the Spirit is not an act of origination, especially because He is not given in His entirety then, but only one of His gifts, that of the forgiveness of sins. For the fullness of the Spirit had been appointed for the time of Pentecost, to be given by Him, Who has Him in essence whenever He wishes, and to whomever He wishes, and as He wishes, that is to some in the form of one gift, to others in the form of many, and to others the entire 'other Comforter'[313] Himself. Let us stop, then, reconciling the irreconcilable—the bestowing and the procession, and interweaving the incompatible.

Moreover, if on the one hand, you should say that this is known by you—that the Father is the cause of being to the Spirit in the manner of generation, just as He is to the Son in the manner of birth and, on the other hand, you say that the Spirit is from the Son, not according to this meaning, but according to the outpouring and imparting and having a sound mind, you are constrained in this by the poverty of words and the shallowness of the Latin language, then I shall show you the blessed poverty, blessed by the Spirit[314] and the brotherly acceptance[315] and you yourself shall detest the impurity of the haughty heart[316] and thus, in one spirit, believing the same, we shall glorify in one accord the Father and the Son and the Holy Spirit, the first as begetting and sending forth, the second as being begotten, and the third as proceeding. For, if you are indeed poor in words and the richness of the language causes you confusion in thoughts and words and because of this you are not able to distinguish the pouring forth of the Spirit from the Son, or the imparting, or whatever else you may wish to call it, from the procession, in which the being of the Spirit is from the Father alone, then, elsewhere, I shall allow your use of these as your language allows you, and I mean in the communal talks and, if you wish, in ecclesiastical sermons but on the following condition in this matter—that you do not disregard those

---

312 John 20:22.

313 John 14:16.

314 Matt 5:3.

315 Rom 15:7.

316 Prov 16:5.

who hear in one word two meanings. However, in the Symbol of Faith, the procession from the Father only is proclaimed, for herein is for us the confession of faith, which must be pure and radiant and simple—for such are also the objects of belief, and it contains in itself nothing confused or dark or convoluted. Just such is also the exposition of our faith, being a proclamation of the prevailing Spirit in the second council; it is also the inspiration and the concord of the fathers regarding Him and is kept by all the churches, which you cannot look down upon as inferior in rank, for the rank is equal, while in numbers and victories they are greater.

Reflect with me also upon the following matter. If the bestowing of the Spirit by the Son is not different than the procession from the Father, then we come to one of two conclusions: either the Son also is the cause of the Spirit's being, or the Father also is a bestower, just as the Son is. But if the Son also is the cause, then we have two sources of the One. For one who owes his existence to many is either greater, or equal, or lesser than the one who has his being from one source, but he could not be equal, for then he, too, would have been from one source. Hence, what remain is that he is either greater or lesser, and then, the Spirit would either be greater than the Son—and behold what an impious innovation, for no one yet from those impudently disposed against the Son ever dared to say such a thing, or, on the other hand, he would be lesser, in which case Macedonius would return to life. And if He is bestowed also by the Father just as by the Son, He is either without a source—but what would happen then to the position of the Father? How has then His unique mode of being been made common? Or we shall search for a different cause of His being and then a tetrad of persons will be presented to us and a pair of divinities—one of the trinity and another of the external fourth person, who has come to us from your marvelous innovation.

Moreover, if the procession was identical to the bestowing, I would seek a different word that may show the manner, in which the Spirit is from the Father. Again, if the Father is greater than the Son with regards to the cause of being, He would also be greater than the Spirit in the same respect. But if the Son was the cause of being for the Spirit, He would thus be also greater than Him. And where have you encountered the saying that the Son is greater than the Spirit? Furthermore, if indeed, the inbreathing of the Lord to His disciples reveals, according to you, the procession of the Spirit from Him, namely of the whole Spirit and not just of one gift, then He gave them the Comforter but where, then, would go the saying: 'If I do not go away, He will not come to you.'[317] Moreover, if the Comforter Himself, rather than the gift of the forgiveness of sins, was given then through the inbreathing—for the Word was in the habit of calling also the gifts spirits, then the arrival at Pentecost was either of this same Spirit and superfluous or of another spirit, Who that was, we must seek to find out.

The summary, thus, of what we have said is that the Spirit proceeds only from the Father but not 'and from the Son'. Other arguments of ancient wise men[318] could also be presented, but we have made use of none of them in this present discourse, taking into consideration what was said by Paul—not to build upon another man's foundation[319] and to boast of work already done[320] but as much as possible to take pride in what is wholly ours, provided that our weakness has at least something good which is our own, even though it may not be the fullness of grace.

I also hear that some write voluminous books at present about this dogma and perhaps they have contributed gold, precious stones, and purple cloth to God's tabernacle. But accept now the skins of flesh presented by me, if for no other reason than their having the red color from the Word who took on flesh for my sake and shed His blood, in order to initiate me into the mysteries, and especially those of the Spirit and show me to be royal and anointed, by sealing and anointing[321] me through His blood and the Spirit.

And many have a zeal regarding the offering of unleavened bread, which is great and hotter even than fire, that is, they would rather give up their soul than put an end to that opinion of theirs, but if some give in to their own lust, this is what Paul considers the condemnation and

---

317 John 16:7.

318 Usually, referring to the prophets, apostles, and fathers.

319 Rom 15: 20.

320 2Cor 10:16.

321 2Cor. 1:21–22.

the snare of the devil.[322] And what must be said to them, we shall say later, chastising the excessiveness of the zeal of some and to others showing as humble what they consider not to be humble at all. But we shall not misinterpret the 'the first day of the feast of unleavened bread'[323] by saying to the Latins that it was the tenth day on which the lamb was consumed. For we have seen the law which calls the fifteenth day[324] 'the first day of the feast of unleavened bread' in which the night dawns upon the partaking of the Pascha. Thus, a certain holy father of ours, explaining the day which is called by the evangelist 'the first of the feast of unleavened bread' states that for Matthew the first day is called the day before the feast, knowing to which day the law has assigned this name and yet indicating that what is said by the evangelist is something new. But we shall not present the Lord either as not observing the lawful Pascha and thus demonstrating that He did not partake of the unleavened bread or as observing it, but before the time that removes the leaven, so that leavened bread was also present. Such things some of the zealots have already dared to say. And so I shall not put up myself with anyone of those who speak in such a way; for the tradition is not so eager as to build the mysteries of truth on a lie. But if Christ is the way and the truth, I shall neither voluntarily stray from the way, nor shall I be deceived by the lack of truth.

What then is my argument? On the one hand, the Lord at the right time and when the hour had come ate the Paschal meal, when it was prepared for Him by the disciples and the owner of the house,[325] clearly according to the custom and not otherwise—or else, the Gospel would have indicated the innovation, just as it did with the other things which He made use of in order to surpass the law, and not only He, but also the disciples—namely, the making of clay on a Saturday,[326] the command to

---

322 1 Tim 3:6–7.

323 Mark 14:12, Mt 26:17.

324 Exod 12:18.

325 Luke 22:11.

326 John 9:6.

The Orthodox Patristic Witness Concerning Catholicism

take up the bed,[327] the rubbing of the heads of grain,[328] the eating of bread with unwashed hands.[329] On the other hand, he ate the lawful meal first, and then He transmitted to the disciples the mystery of His own Pascha, clearly from the bread found around them, and, at that time, what was to be found was unleavened bread. But just because that bread was unleavened, because the necessity of the law made it so, doesn't mean that we, who fully enjoy the freedom in Christ, shall make unleavened bread out of necessity and throw away the leavened. Or consider the following, for there's no harm in so being concerned with the contents of the law in yet another way: because that bread was fitting, and rather more than fitting, and which happened to be frugal and made of barley flour—for neither the host, nor the guests were accustomed to luxurious living but were companions with the true frugality of life and were accustomed to barley loaves of bread, with which thousands were fed by them, so that you might learn the poverty which works wonders, what then prevents us from demanding such unleavened bread and banishing from the alter the available bread made of fine wheat flour, as if, even now, we would hear the Lord saying: 'if you should bring me wheat bread, it would be futile!'

We could say the same also about the cup. For that, which was present then, would have been a watery and sour wine, in accordance with God's earthly humility, but now a wine of fine bouquet is often offered. Should we then reject this precious wine and accept the one which smells of poverty? Or should we consider worthy only such and such a Palestinian wine made from the field, from which was also filled the Lord's cup, which was also, if we should continue this nonsense, made of the same clay? That would truly be befitting to a great poverty of mind. Would you, also, after a meal, partake of the mystery and reclining at the table and being in the upstairs dining room ask for all the other things which were then carried out as demanded by the times, but now they are transformed into another type ordained to us by piety and faith. And, perhaps, whoever hears the book of Acts calling to mind in many places

---

327 John 5:8.

328 Luke 6:1.

329 Matt 15:2.

the breaking of bread[330] and finding the same thing in Paul[331] also, he would conclude that what was broken then mystically was of the same kind as what was served for a regular meal. And what was eaten was by no means the unleavened bread, for the latter had been allotted for certain prescribed days and sacrifices. But if these arguments are not compelling, then the scale of balance shall favor the other side, and yet to me it measures the greater part, for which victory is granted, for a runner wins the wreath even if he gets an advantage by a single step.

Besides, let the multitude of eastern servants of God and the reputation of the Church of Jerusalem, from which, as from a spring streams the fountain of faith and apostolic tradition, and which also offers leavened loaves, persuade you. Why do I tell you about the easterners, among whom you would also count the Indians and Ethiopians? Do me a favor and look towards Egypt and the parts of Libya which are near Cyrene[332] and its deserts and you shall see that all are concerned for only one thing, abiding by the same rule about the loaves of bread of the mystical offering. But examine also the bread of the Church of the Corinthians, which you would not describe as one that does not hold fast to the traditions, for the one who established the tradition[333] praised it as holding fast to it and whenever opposed, as prevailing over every kind of, let's say, arrogance, so that I may not offend anyone by saying impiety. I know that you hear the Sardinians too witnessing against you concerning the offering of unleavened bread, but you pretend to be deaf. I, however, hear them clearly—both the old proverb which proclaims 'a witness from home'[334] and the one which gives me the white stone tablet.[335]

Why then by contradicting the many and, I would say, those of great importance, do you think that you don't sin at all and by behaving against the tradition of the churches you raise your eyebrows? It is

---

330 Acts 20:7.

331 1Cor 10:16.

332 Acts 2:10.

333 1Cor 10: 16–17.

334 'Οἴκοθεν ὁ μάρτυς' – proverb about a person lying and being exposed by some of his own people, whom he thought would be his accomplices.

335 Rev 2:17.

necessary that you concede, but you still try hard to subject us to your
views and accuse us, who, had we wished, could have accused you more
justly. But we are careful not to cause trouble for you on account of this
and not to arouse further ambitious and contentious feelings, but you
do not know how to show consideration to those who are considerate.
Otherwise, if we should wish to examine harshly your fasting on Saturdays, we would show that it follows neither apostolic nor patristic teachings. For those who fast on Sunday or Saturday, with one exception,[336]
are condemned by the apostles, the laity with excommunication and the
clergy with deposition. And, perhaps, you shall not judge as illegally
added those canons which the 6th council respected, for the delegates
of your Agatho[337] were present there for the formulation of dogmas and
the instigator Basil[338] was present for the establishment of laws. Thus,
they were so many, that the place was filled by the whole synod of yours.
But also the fathers in Laodicea, to whom the 6th council showed total
respect, said that it was not necessary to offer bread[339] during the forty
days of Lent, except on Saturday and Sunday. They would not have laid
down that law, had they accepted Saturday as a day of fasting. We do not
overlook that this is the case also with the birthdays of the martyrs, that
is, their commemorations, which they ordained not to be celebrated
during Great Lent except on Saturdays and Sundays; for they pertain to
celebration and not to affliction which the fast signifies to us. But what
is brighter than the memory of the martyrs? Would you like me to show
you also a royal[340] decree? That Basil, whose power in words and spirit
extended over all the earth, and by which powers he spoke about fasting
to the beautiful and great church of Caesarea, which became such because of him, reckons the fast to be five days and shows your calculation
of six days to be an interpolation. He would have suitably employed to-

336 A reference to the appointed fast in the Orthodox Church on Great and Holy
Saturday.

337 Agatho, Pope of Rome (c. 577 – January 10, 681).

338 Archbishop Basil of Gortyna – papal legate in Crete.

339 Reference to the celebration of the Eucharist.

340 βασιλικὸν (play on words with Βασίλειος, the name of St. Basil the Great)

wards you the words of Isiah: 'Not such is the fast that I choose, says the Lord.'[341]

And so, what was necessary to be said to the westerners, by the student and teacher of the truth concerning the unleavened bread and the fasting on Saturdays has been said by us according to our ability. Someone might have considered also worthy of a discourse the topic of marriages, which seems to them as something wrongful, but I don't have the free time to move Kamarina[342] other than to say that the marriage of our ordained priests is criticized by them and not just the marriage, but also other innumerable things as they say. For, this resembles the contentiousness which makes one blind to reality but clear-sighted to what does not exist, the former being the virtues and the latter being the vices. When, indeed, the time comes to defend ourselves against the charges brought against us, then it would also be time to speak about marriage, for it has been wronged either by them or by us or has been treated agreeably by both sides in regards to the purpose of marriage which we all uphold.

It remains to admonish also many of our own people—those who are zealous, but not according to knowledge, and those who, even more terribly, out of self-love tear apart the body of Christ. First of all, I shall speak to the former, those who are simple-minded.

Not all things are required of all people, my brothers, just as not to everyone all things should be conceded, but only those things are demanded, which if not cast down, will bring damage to what is vital, to which one should cling with both hands and feet. That removal would be like a certain tax which is exacted by necessity, knowing that its contribution would bring no small advantage wherever it is utilized. On the other hand, there are things which do no great harm but their removal by force causes the greatest damage—these should be discarded of, as does a reasonable man, who knows the rules of business and is willing to barter the small things for the greater, but never the greatest for the most insignificant. Thus, I observe also the doctors making judgements

---

341 Isa 58:4.

342 'Καμάριναν κινεῖν', lit. to move Kamarina – a lagoon providing a defense to the ancient city of Kamarina in Sicily, which was drained out of superstition, proving to be an unnecessary task that weakened the city's defenses.

in the treatments of bodies: they bring in total attention to the ways of eating and medication of those who suffer from brain or heart or liver disorders. But there is a time when the teaching of the profession accomplishes nothing and they turn to natural antidotes and barbarously utter spells and tie rubbish of various materials on the one who suffers and they do not only hang these things on the sick person but also become attached themselves to the help of these trinkets. And if the doctors see some insignificant part of the body harmed from this treatment, they care for it little or not at all and certainly they pray that this part of the body is perfect and healthy, but if both are not possible, they chose the less harmful over what is more harmful; at the first symptoms of sickness in these insignificant parts the doctors stick to their treatment plan even though one of those insignificant parts is suffering, but if, as they treat the patient, they discover that some of the vital organs has fared ill, then they do cease the treatment.

That same principle must also be observed in the beautiful body of the Church by those who care for it, who, and I consider this praiseworthy, when the faith and the dogmas are suffering badly, utilize great speed for their healing and by words and deeds stand against the causes of sickness and by using their own remedies, or rather even before that, they ask for the true antidote from above and use the charm which prevails over all, which is the calling upon the name of the Lord Jesus Christ, Who lifted up our weaknesses and took away our sicknesses, and healed every depravity, Who is the Word of God, and the Wisdom, and the Power,[343] and the right hand and the arm and all the other names of divine knowledge and power. But if such therapy is not successful on account of the stubbornness and malignancy of the disease, which Paul calls gangrene,[344] then it is necessary to accept the steel of excommunication or anathema or the burning or the performance of surgical cutting, so that the evil teaching would not spread and attack those who are healthy. In such a way, that skilled doctor treated what he called gangrenes: some he handed over to Satan so they would learn not to blaspheme,[345] and oth-

---

343 Matt 8:17.

344 2Tim 2:17.

345 1Tim 1:20.

ers who preached against his teaching he subjected to anathema,[346] even if they had been well-recognized and possessing a higher rank - for this is what the angel that was introduced by the epistle of Paul signifies.[347]

And now let us address the westerners. If something concerning a dogma is wrong, then it shakes up the faith of the fathers. And this is certainly the case with the addition to the symbol of faith regarding the Holy Spirit. And there the danger is the greatest, for by considering this as not being worthy of correction, the one who forgives remains unforgiven, even though his teachings are uttered from the throne which the haughty have set forth high, even though they put forward the confession of Peter, even though they boast of its blessing, even though they dangle the keys to the Kingdom at us, which the more they consider him to have honored, the more they disgrace themselves, for the things he established they destroy and they pull out the foundations from underneath the church, which he is believed to have upheld. But here, you, for my sake, must become a fighter, who in other respects are meek, gird yourself with the sword of the spirit, proclaim through the word of God which separates flesh from spirit,[348] worldly delusion from divine mysteries, and which is able to discern the human and the perilous thoughts. Pierce, then, as a Levite and a servant of God those who make into idols the creations of their own delusions and who bow down their heads in worship and who require everyone to prostrate before the high rank of that wicked power.

But if that dogma of theirs is rejected by them and the innovation gives way to the older traditions, then the matters of unleavened bread and the fasts would be accepted and overlooked by us who would ask in the spirit of gentleness that in these things also there would be oneness of mind. Thus, become like Paul in this matter who appears to those under the law as one under the law and with those who have made a vow he purifies himself, and shaves, and spends money for the offerings of purification and circumcises Timothy, who regards the righteousness in the law as rubbish, who shows how Christ and the name of the faith in

---

346 Gal 1: 8–9.

347 Ibid.

348 Heb 4:12.

Him might be useless to the circumcised Galatians[349] and stops the flow of his preaching being provoked by an apparent disagreement. Likewise, do also the helmsmen who loosen the foot of the sail, so that they could empty the submerged sail and so that the ship would be saved together with the crew.

He would demand this from your steering as well: to not always keep the sail tight and especially where the spirit of delusion and ethnic conceit abounds but to loosen it knowledgeably and to make the journey life-saving by means of slowness rather than deadly by means of speed and to safeguard the journey by means of slackening rather than cause shipwreck by means of unyielding. It would be best if the body of the faithful were perfect in all its members, with beautiful hair and nails, as the body of the daughter of a king, the bride of Christ, Who is beautiful in appearance, surpassing the sons of men, and Who fully, and perfectly, and gladly joins what is of His own kind. It would be good also if none of the members of the body were missing and especially the eyes, by which we see the sun of the Trinity and therefore also all the other senses which we need for the acquisition of the Spirit. However, this body's hair and nails do not correspond to the beauty of the other parts, for the hair, on the one hand, is not quite as black and not like that of king David who was ruddy and with beautiful eyes, or like that of the shining and fiery brother of the bride,[350] and the nails, likewise, are either too long, or too short, so that even the small straws either cannot be grasped at all or can be grasped but very clumsily.

Therefore, you shall not despise the rest of the body, on account of those things, but, on the contrary, you shall not even notice them, being enamored by the others and having your eyes fixed upon the beauty of some of the members in order not to incline in a different direction. Thus, you might, all the more, warm the spirit and might serve the Lord[351] with the service of a good and faithful person, should you appear concerned for the Lord's house. But you would be concerned if you cannot tolerate when it suffers a loss. And it suffers a loss, when its fullness is diminished. It is diminished when we drive out our co-ser-

349 Gal 5:2–6.

350 Song 5:10.

351 Rom 12:11.

vants. We drive them out when we are hardened towards them. We are hardened towards them, when we do not condescend. Let us therefore condescend, so that we would not appear harsh. For when we are not harsh, we shall extend a welcome. When we extend a welcome, we shall fill the house of the Lord. And filling it, we shall make it richer. And from this good will, we shall be attested as good and faithful servants, and because of this we shall be led into the joy of the Lord. Do you see where this condescension takes us and exalts us? Hence, we shall not be hardened either about the unleavened bread or about the fasts by exercising the rigid thinking of the pagans: for this is like gluing earthenware with earthenware without inserting something of a more pliable nature, which would likely become the glue.

It is not necessary to argue much about the rest of the enumerated things which they themselves acknowledge to keep, except for the devouring of strangled animals, for not even the name of this practice is tolerable for the reasonable Latins, just as the name of robbery or fornication is not tolerable for us, even though the wild and beastlike men would practice these. So, the remaining charges seem to many to be unpardonably wrong, but this is not the case, according to the reasoning of a man, who I suppose, is well-instructed in the ecclesiastical histories and who has learnt that not every custom is able to divide the churches but only the one that leads to the corruption of dogma. And certainly, the very errors of those illustrious judges are such customs as well: some are out of piety, such as the offering of salutations to the holy pavements[352] —we shall not really accept that satanic slander, that the veneration of icons is not acceptable to the Latins, others are out of economy, which pardons the weakness, perhaps even of the soul, but surely that of the body, as when the monks eat meat when they are sick and they do that in a disciplined manner and indeed spiritually. But if some abuse this practice on account of their carelessness, then the argument towards them should be different, but not to the former who make reasonable arrangements. There are other issues according to other principles which are implemented by the Western churches, but none of them is able to tear us asunder, even if the critics had the supporting evidence of being followers of the canons of the fathers.

---

352 Likely a reference to statues, made of similar materials as the pavements.

And if my address had not become too long and hadn't gotten close to being a history, I would have shown you thousands upon thousands of customs which were overlooked by the ancient fathers for the sake of saving the souls of their brothers. For they had known well not to please themselves, and they knew that each of them should please his neighbor for his own good and build him up.[353] But now, woe to our swelling burden and we ask 'who is my neighbor?'[354] Thus, we strike down countless people who are standing up so that we might raise up our own will, and we raise it up, not so that it simply stands, but so that it is able to bury others into oblivion. We transform and transpose all things in order to give substance to what is non-existent and to form the formless. And if we come to the point to utter some word, even though it might appear most ridiculous, we shall hasten to prove that is the voice of God, worthy of the hearing of Moses and Aaron, for it would be too lowly to say the hearing of Ithamar and Eleazar, and even more lowly to say the multitudes of Israel, even though they had been cleansed three days in advance.[355] And we do not realize that we behave indecently twice: by defaming the authority and by continuing to argue. For blessed is he who does not sin in word, as someone has declared; but praised is also he who, after having sinned, finds the sin and knows it and abhors it as something detestable, just as some monster, which is born in the night, but then in the day it is seen, and abhorred, and therefore rejected.

Shall we not imitate the humility of the Lord, Who did not please Himself[356] but us, who are many, and Who was bound as an outcast, in order that He might bind us to Himself and each other in the bond of peace, and Who shed His blood, in order that He might bring together into one the children of God, who had been scattered, and so that one flock might be formed from all the sheep, being tended by one shepherd[357] and avoiding the distraction in front of wolves, which no less contributes for their dispersion, but rather it enables them to cause the scattering of the flock. What caused the Pharisees to be blamed?

---

353 Rom 15:1–2.

354 Luke 10:21.

355 Exod 19:10–11.

356 Rom 15:3.

357 John 10:16.

Wasn't it the coveting of honor and of being first and the desiring to be called 'rabbi' by other men? Didn't that very thing make those miserable people God-killers? What is the smoke of the wrath of the Lord, I seek to learn, and Isaiah[358] answers me that the expression 'do not touch me' was said by the proud, whom the Lord opposes.[359] I will also show you a Pharisee worthy of emulation, Gamaliel, who suggested nothing pharisaic against the apostles, but everything which was in opposition he piously and devoutly exposed in defense of the apostles. And I do not know whether we, who are obliged to exceed in righteousness[360] the important Pharisees, since in no other way can we enter the kingdom, into which we believe to have been invited and for which to have been destined more than the Pharisees, shall exclude our brothers from the church or whether we shall exclude ourselves from the kingdom.

Don't you see Paul who overpowers the critics of his preaching who were associated with Peter? Don't you see Peter being reproved by him and bearing the reproaches in meekness? But you yourself, unless you see everyone cower before the thunder of your word and bow their head to the ground before its lightning, as did the disciples when on Mount Tabor the Lord led them to experience the radiance of the revealed divinity, time and again you dig out and present the Simons and Marcions, whom time has done well to bury and conceal, and the mud of the gnostics is stirred up, and the illusion of Samellius is formed anew, and the madness of Arius and the dark Photinus and the rest of the group of the sons of perdition... but lest I defile this discourse, I shall not enumerate all of them by name. And will you attach these heresies to your brother? Oh, what blindness! To that same brother you attribute the heresies of those who do not agree even among themselves. You bind him with those as if with some long ropes in order to seize the one who is running away and you don't do this to him alone, but you also take hold of other accomplices, whom you challenge under the pretense of piety. However, often times you do not know what is piety, but desire to make a name for yourselves by the condemnation of your brother. Oh, the machinations of the wicked one, who makes even now the idols into gods, who records

358 Isa 65:5.

359 1Pet 5:5.

360 Matt 5:20.

the vice as virtue and who succeeds to be venerated and respected! But not so for us, servants of Christ, and friends, and brothers, let us not thus alienate ourselves from God, who draws all people on account of his goodness. Let us not drive away almost everyone on account of our arrogance. Let us not make our thrones a foundation of evil, nor the height of our office, a tower of triviality—for this is to me a situation created on account of ambition and conceit. But as long as we are strong, let us support the weak, or if we are doctors, let us heal the afflicted. But if we afflict them, even though I don't want to say it, I shall say it: this is the work of thieves and not doctors!

These things I am saying to you and against the conceited and the scoffers, who will not accomplish anything, as the Holy Spirit says. But you are like the banker who receives the talent from me. Be careful then to return the interest in time, which in my opinion is the criterion which adds to whatever the Spirit gives to the industrious person. Empowered by the grace of the Spirit, may we purely and without adulteration proclaim Him, according to the patristic definitions and teach others the same, in God the Father, Who teaches knowledge to the human person and in Christ Jesus, our Lord, to Whom belongs the glory unto the ages. Amen.

4. St. Joseph I,
Patriarch of Constantinople (+1283)[361]

Do Not Pray in Common with The Latins Who Blaspheme the Holy Spirit and are Joined to the Devil[362]

Therefore, the Italians have no good excuse for their delusion. They themselves have become delusion and perdition for themselves. And not only do they blaspheme against the Holy Spirit, but they practice every manner of impiety [...]. Let us therefore not pray in common with

---

361 See page 63 for an account of his life.

362 Protopresbyter Anastasios K. Gotsopoulos, *On Common Prayer with the Heterodox*, (Uncut Mountain Press, 2022), 16.

them... so that we may not also become joined to the devil [...]. For how can there be union for us when myriads of dogmas come between us?

5. St. Meletius the Confessor of Mount Galesion (+1286)[363]

INTRODUCTION

St. Meletius Galesiotes lived from 1209-1286. He is called "*Homologetes*" (the Confessor) because of the sufferings he underwent in his steadfast resistance to the church union between Constantinople and Rome through the work of Michael VIII Palaiologos at the Second Council of Lyons (1272-1274).

During the course of his ascetic struggles Christ appeared to the Saint and commanded him to go to Constantinople to defend the true Orthodox faith against false union.[364] St. Meletius did so and compared the Emperor to Julian the Apostate and, like St. Maximus the Confessor, was imprisoned, exiled and had his tongue cut out. When the Saint was departing to the Lord his face shone like the sun and after his death his holy body remained incorrupt and became the source of many miracles.

Before this, between 1276 and 1280 he wrote a poem that was intended to present all of the essentials of the Orthodox faith in a single "gathering." Below are translated excerpts of this work of which, only "Logos I" has been translated into English. The other divisions are not in English, and a suspicion that St. Meletius never finished the latter section of the poem, since they are not extant.[365] The divisions of this poem are as follows:

---

363 See page 89 for an account of his life.

364 Hieromonk Makarios of Simonos Petra, *The Synaxarion: The Lives of the Saints of the Orthodox Church, Volume Three, January-February*, trans. Christopher Hookaway (Ormylia: Holy Convent of the Annunciation of Our Lady, 2001), 215.

365 Tia M. Kolbaba, "Meletios Homologetes On the Customs of the Italians", *Revue des études byzantines*, tome 55 (1997): 139.

1. On the customs of the Italians.

2. On the procession of the Holy Spirit.

3. On the meaning of the formula:
    "the Spirit from the Son".

4. On the formula "from the Son" (εκ του Υἱοῦ)
    when used by the Orthodox Fathers.

5. On the expression "Spirit of the Son"
    and on how the Spirit manifests itself.

6. On presumption as the primary cause of heresy
    and on the danger of ignorance of the Scriptures.

7. On azymes (unleavened bread in the eucharist).

8. On the danger of being in communion with
    heretics; therefore, on the danger of being in
    communion with Latins.

9. On those pastors who are responsible for today's
    heresies and evils (i.e. a denunciation of orthodox
    churchmen who support [this] church union.

10. That one must never be silent about the truth.

    Epilogue: call to combat and invitation to martyrdom.

Logos I:
Concerning the Customs of the Italians[366]

1. The greatest and most terrible fault is the one
in their teaching about God, that addition [the
filioque] which they shamelessly dare to add to the
revered Creed, contrary to sacred Scripture. This is the
first and principal act of lawlessness among them,

---

366 Kolbaba Tia M. Meletios Homologetes *On the Customs of the Italians*. In: Revue
des études byzantines, tome 55, 1997. 137-168.

whence they earn Synodical anathema, removing
themselves far from Orthodox people, for they were
anathematized by the second Synod. Also, they have
the later [Synods] which anathematize them and
throw them out of the Church of Christ. For the later
Synods agree with the earlier and you will find one
harmony in all of them.

2. You should know their second evil is the offering
of azymes which the sixty-second canon of the
Apostles chases from the assembly of the faithful,
condemning all those who accept this [offering]
after the divine grace [i.e., after the Incarnation] on
the grounds that they worship shadow and type.

And in the catechetical discourse, they are convicted
of no small number of other errors; they [the authors
of the discourse] also receive the anathema of those
Armenians on the grounds that they offer azymes.
For the anathema is addressed to all those who do
not use leavened bread in the offerings, but rather
sacrifice animals. For just as the terrible Apollinarios
foolishly babbled that the body of the Lord was
without a soul and without a mind, so also these
[azymites] uphold the blasphemy in their deeds.
What he accomplished with words, they accomplish
with deeds.

3. Their priests are defiled with bloodshed and wars.
They audaciously carry swords; they fight in battles.
But the sixth [canon] of the Apostles and the eighth
of the illustrious Synod in Sardica discipline those
who engage in such wicked practices with
excommunication and complete deposition. Again,
another canon of the Apostles, the twentieth, deposes
likewise all those who strike others, whether they dare

to strike believers or unbelievers. In addition, the
twenty-third canon of the Synod which met by divine
grace in Ankyra says that everyone who commits
involuntary homicides remains eight years in penance,
even with respect to robbers, as the reverend Basil
teaches when he explains well the canon of which
we have been speaking.

For this [principle], on the one hand, [applies] among
lay people. For matters of killing bring all priests to
deposition, even if someone does this involuntarily.
But the one who kills willingly, I do not know under
what conditions he will pay a suitable penalty. And
this is so even if in these matters the popes, the first
among bishops, imitate the enemies of the Lord, show
themselves to be admirers of those who killed Christ,
commit murder, and bring about the death of both
souls and bodies.

4. They like to fast often on Sabbaths, even if one
of the great feasts happens to fall on the Sabbath;
but the fifty-first canon of the Apostles, and also the
sixty-first of them, and along with these absolutely
all of the holy Synods, impose on them
excommunication with deposition.

5. During Cheesefare Week, they eat meat even on
Wednesday. They eat meat during the first week
of the fasts. They do not observe the sacred forty
days, and on account of these things the sixty-sixth
canon of the divine Apostles sentences them
to anathema.

6. They nourish themselves on things killed by wild
beasts, strangled things, and things which died of
natural causes. Regarding these things, the sixty-third

[canon] of the divine Apostles imposes upon the Italians the weight of excommunication.

7. Priests abstain from lawful marriage, while they fearlessly fornicate, defile themselves with adulteries, and take mistresses openly and knowingly. Thus they fittingly incur the excommunication of the sixtieth and fifth apostolic canons. Again, the fourth canon of the Synod in Gangra anathematized likewise all those who do these things, should someone say that the priests come to the sacrifices offering their household affairs instead of offerings.

8. They associate with heretics, especially Armenians, for like, as they say, gathers with like and, according to the proverb, birds of a feather stick together. Also, in this regard, the tenth canon of the Apostles and the third canon of the Synod in Laodicea subject them to excommunication and deposition.

9. They baptize infants in one immersion; instead of oil they lawlessly use saliva in addition, they offer salt during baptism. And on account of these things the second Synod, as you know, and with it the one that came after it, as you well know, anathematized them as transgressors.

10. They were wholly ignorant of the presanctified. Thus the sixth Synod of God condemned them in its fifty-second canon, and the Synod after it was in harmony with it regarding these matters.

11. They form crosses in the churches on the surface of the earth and after they kiss these they then walk upon them. They make the holy icons into chairs and beds; like the children of Mani, they burn them to

ashes, and that they are again anathematized on
account of this you know from the yearly synodical
saying.

12. To those Gentiles who were about to convert,
the Apostles forbade polluted things, strangled
things, and fornication. But the Italians continue
these things as if [such behavior were] lawful.

13. The place of the sacrifices is open, accessible
to all. Among them, sacred things are not distinct
from profane. Therefore the sixty-ninth canon of
the sixth Ecumenical Synod considers them
excommunicated, for it scarcely encourages entrance
to the all-holy sanctuary even at the right time and
then for the emperors alone.

14. Another canon in this Council, the fifty-fifth,
if they do not do all things in accord with us —
even the smallest thing — justly imposes
upon them the weight of excommunication.

But now they have not even a remnant of piety,
and why should I uselessly and vainly prolong
the argument? For if someone were about to explain
each of their customs — what sort of evils and
illegitimacies each is filled with, what chastisement
and what sort of condemnation each deserves —
perhaps there would not be enough time for the
narrative. Therefore, I leave off recording the canons
which condemn them and which they transgress,
and I touch synoptically upon only the chief matters
and these very truly are few out of many.

15. They say "in one Lord of us," but not "of us all."
For they reveal this when they have produced

something in addition to us [i.e., the Filioque].
But if indeed they simply confess "one Lord," they
have shown that they would leave "us all" out.

16. They do not call the Theotokos Theotokos.

17. Except for the crucifixion alone, they do not
make other representations, nor do they form the
revered icons as drawings or paintings. But they have
even the crucifixions sculpted, not drawn on a flat
surface, and [thus] practice a barbaric custom.

18. In a single church they sacrifice three times
in the same day, and indeed wherever they may
happen to be they celebrate the liturgy fearlessly.

19. They make the sign [of the cross] crookedly,
with the thumb, and they do not at all form the
cross straight.

20. Their priests do purifications and aspersions
remaining completely in the customs of the Jews.

21. Those who are convicted of errors, they anoint
with oil for the remission of sins, for the forgiveness
of errors.

22. From the fourth day of the revered first week
[of Lent] until holy Pascha they do not say the
Alleluia, for they consider Christ to be in the desert.

23. They hide the cross in those days, secreting
it until Pascha comes. Then, when they have brought
it forth as if from some grave, they make the invisible
visible to all before it.

24. They say that the Divine should not be praised in any other tongue than that of the Italians, that of the Hellenes, and, with these two, that of the Hebrews.

25. The priests and the bishops wear stoles not of wool, but rather of silk.

26. During the awesome eucharistic celebration they converse fearlessly, they sit without fear, and they hardly rise or keep silence at the time of the elevation.

27. They say, "Take, Eat." But their celebrants present a kiss instead of the communion.

28. During Lent, they do not all fast equally, but some observe even more weeks than we do, as many as eight or more; others, on the other hand, observe only six weeks, fewer than we do.

29. In those [days], children eat eggs and cheese, and the weak eat meat, even if their illness is brief.

30. If a monk becomes a bishop he may often eat meat both if he is sick and if he is walking on the road. He eats pig's fat any time and any place.

31. They always eat meat on Wednesday, just as they eat eggs and cheese on Friday.

32. Again, on Pascha they sacrifice a lamb with unleavened bread, which the Hebrews do, just like the Armenians.

33. During the time when the very holy Virgin gave

birth, if they find some icon of her in the churches, they take it far away, they throw it far off.

34. On Friday and on the Sabbath of the Holy Days, in the corners of the churches, in hidden places, they search for Christ with bare feet.

35. They leave their dead bishops unburied, observing eight days after their death. Then they bury them with their hands stretched out upon their thighs. They also close up all their senses with wax. What madness!

36. They consecrate four months, in the four seasons of the year, offering them as first fruits; in those times they also do ordinations. But in the other eight months they are utterly idle.

37. They take sisters of brothers-in-law as brides. They fearlessly commit incest; they perform illicit marriages.

38. They openly eat every unclean thing, even beavers. They do not have any discretion in these matters.

39. They say that all sinners receive purification in the purifying fire of Purgatory, and they learned this from the terrible Origen.

40. Very many others of the most barbaric customs they hold as if they were pious and follow as if they were laws. They do not take heed of the Synods, nor do they observe the canons. They do not accept the traditions of the holy fathers. They consider themselves, and themselves alone, to be everything.

They have cardinals instead of the Apostles, and
fill the place of the twelve [Apostles] with twelve
[cardinals]. [They have] nine orders of monks as if
they were the nine orders of angels [lit., incorporeal
beings]. In addition, they propose both five patriarchs
and an emperor greater than the other emperors,
and under them counts, princes, and kings, as if these
were all and everything were in these. Those who
submit to them acquiesce in all these things. But
we reject them, and likewise these [customs],
guarding the holy traditions of the Fathers and
observing the laws of our Church.

6. St. Athanasios I, Patriarch of Constantinople (+1310)[367]

LETTER TO THE BISHOPS[368]

Since each of the most holy bishops must soon go to his assigned see,
and since there are certain matters which require a joint supplication to
the ruler, such as the question of the Latins and the rumor that they are
teaching with impunity,[369] and are corrupting many of wavering faith,

---

367 See page 55 for an account of his life.

368 S. Athanasii I Patriarchae Constantinopolitani, "Epistula XXIII ad Episcopos,"
in *Epistulae CXV Ad Imperatorem Andronicum II, Eiusque Propinquos Necnon
Officiales Missae*, trans. Alice-Mary Maffry Talbot (Washingtoniae, D.C.:
Dumbarton Oaks, 1975), 53.

369 Saint Athanasius was concerned about a group of Franciscan friars residing within
the City of Constantinople who was spreading their heretical Latin teachings
among the Orthodox Christian faithful. These friars had started a monastery
in the center of Constantinople and within the market-place where Orthodox
Christians frequented. George Pachymeres, a Byzantine Greek historian of the
period, says that Athanasius was apoplectic at the presence of the Franciscan friars
within the Orthodox Christian city and forced Emperor Andronicus to confiscate
their property and expel the friars from the Holy City of Constantinople in order
to protect the Orthodox faithful.

we should not go away without attending to this. There is also the issue of the Jews and Armenians [Monophysites] that they should leave the capital, and other such God-pleasing acts which require a joint supplication, and the factor of the oppressive summer weather.[370] Wherefore, if you please after our meal on Sunday let us assemble and go together to the emperor. For I do not think that he will fail to see the advantage of the proposal. Therefore, for the sake of the Lord, let no one be absent through hesitancy. If you judge it fitting, let us assemble at Chora, and from there go together to meet with the emperors.

LETTER TO THE EMPEROR ANDRONICUS[371]

Wherefore, I ask your majesty that without delay you make more frequent inspection tours, especially in the vicinity of the walls and gates of the city, both within and without, nor let us make excuses on account of the paucity of your retinue or personal safety, and entrust to this man or that those matters which God has entrusted to you; for eyes are more trustworthy than ears. Order what is just, that no one, especially the Latins should enter the city bearing arms.

LETTER TO THE EMPEROR ANDRONICUS[372]

Therefore, to adopt an imperial usage, I entreat, I entreat, I entreat, that your divine majesty entrust to him the responsibility for this worthy undertaking, for it will contribute much to the incomparable blessing of

---

370 This letter also refers to the concern of Saint Athanasius regarding the Jews and Armenian Monophysites spreading their heretical confession among the Orthodox Christian population.

371 S. Athanasii I Patriarchae Constantinopolitani, "Epistola XVII ad Andronicum Imperatorem," in *Epistulae CXV Ad Imperatorem Andronicum II, Eiusque Propinquos Necnon Officiales Missae*, trans. Alice-Mary Maffry Talbot (Washingtoniae, D.C.: Dumbarton Oaks, 1975), 43.

372 S. Athanasii I Patriarchae Constantinopolitani, "Epistola XVII ad Andronicum Imperatorem," in *Epistulae CXV Ad Imperatorem Andronicum II, Eiusque Propinquos Necnon Officiales Missae*, trans. Alice-Mary Maffry Talbot (Washingtoniae, D.C.: Dumbarton Oaks, 1975), 245.

good order. For the state is suffering great harm from the famine, since the Romans' fortune, both gold and silver, has almost all ended up in the hands of the Latins. But the worst is their arrogance as they laugh at us haughtily, and despise us so much that they boast of receiving favors from the wives of citizens in payment for grain (may this not happen!). For this reason, I ask that your divine majesty see to it that they not gloat anymore in such undertakings, but that He Who upsets the counsels of the nations may cover them eternally with confusion as with a mantle.

7. St. Gregory Palamas (+1359)[373]

ST. GREGORY PALAMAS FIGHTS AGAINST LATIN SCHOLASTIC HERESY[374]

During the years 1333-1334, discussions were held in Constantinople concerning the union of the Churches between the representatives of the Pope and the Patriarchate. The head of the Orthodox delegation, Barlaam the Calabrian, while supporting the eastern view, employed in both his oral conversations and his written essay the paradoxical reasoning that claim of the Latin (viz. that the Spirit proceeds also from the Son) is not on logic, since the divine is incomprehensible and unprovable [anapodiction]. Since apparently this position, being in harmony with the physiological presuppositions of Barlaam, undermined the foundations of Orthodox dogma, Saint Gregory composed works of his own.

1. Apodictic Treatises on the Procession of the Holy Spirit
Following a direction opposite to that of Barlaam, he emphasizes that there is proof [apodeixis] in the case of God, but it is different from the logical constructions of men and is founded on the faith, enlightenment, and Tradition. Afterward, on the basis of ancient writings, he

---

373 See page 70 for an account of his life.

374 Saint Gregory Palamas, *Apodictic Treatises on the Procession of the Holy Spirit*, trans. Fr. Christopher C. Moody and Gregory Heers (Florence: Uncut Mountain Press, 2022), 20-21.

explicates the dogma concerning the procession from the Father and the pouring forth through (or from) the Son. These two treaties were written in 1335 and are among the first works of Saint Gregory.

2. Counter-Epigraphs

These were directed at the Epigraphs of Bekkos. The Latin-minded Patriarch had made a philological anthology of passages from the Fathers in order to show the Latin dogma is in harmony with the patristic teaching, which Saint Gregory refutes with this work. They had been composed at this time along with the previous, but in all likelihood, they were revised around 1340, because he also classifies Akindynos with the "irreverent" Barlaam.

THE FILIOQUE IS A CACODOXY[375]

Into these absurdities the race of the Latins would have also fallen manifestly; had we not stripped away the greatest part of the cacodoxy by contradicting this novel dogma [*filioque*].

THE LATINS DOGMATIZE AGAINST THE TRUTH[376]

But I think that no one among those with a sound mind and not with them [sc. the Latins], will dispute that they not only speak things contrary to us but also think contrary to us. Nor will such a man dispute the fact that they dogmatize not only against us but also against the very word of truth itself, which has been preserved among us undiminished, and without increase, and entirely unaltered.

---

375 Saint Gregory Palamas, *Apodictic Treatises on the Procession of the Holy Spirit*, trans. Fr. Christopher C. Moody and Gregory Heers (Florence: Uncut Mountain Press, 2022), 59.

376 Ibid., 59.

THE FILIOQUE IS AN ALIEN ADDITION TO THE FAITH[377]

But to the point of our present treatise, this addition [the Filioque] which of course has not been uttered by those who boldly proclaimed the truth; which the Spirit did not announce, although He announced all Truth; to which the Savior did not bear witness or make known, although He had made known to His beloved as many thing as he heard from the Father and came for that very reason, to bear witness to the truth: how was it that you, then, have the audacity to speak it, innovatively introducing an alien addition into the boundary of the Faith? The chosen Fathers, when they convened together, having been moved by the Spirit, composed this and handed it down to be a Symbol free from false belief in the Father and the Son and the Holy Spirit, to be a sincere touchstone of genuine knowledge of God and a sure Confession for all those who have chosen to rightly divide the word of truth.

THERE IS NOT ONE ORIGIN OF THE DIVINITY OF THE ONE SPIRIT IN THE CASE OF THE LATIN FILIOQUE[378]

The Latins have two alternatives: either let them say that the Spirit is only from the Son and thus that he is from one origin (which, however, would not be the same origin as the one from which the Son is, and therefore again there will be two origins for the divinity and the Father will no longer be greater than the Son in cause, since He [the Son] will likewise be a cause of Divinity), or let them instead say that He [the Holy Spirit] is only from the Father and thus reverently grant one origin to the Spirit, just as to the Son. For, as long as they say that he is from the Son or from both, but not only from the Father, there cannot possibly be one origin of the divinity of the one Spirit.

---

377 Saint Gregory Palamas, *Apodictic Treatises on the Procession of the Holy Spirit,* trans. Fr. Christopher C. Moody and Gregory Heers (Florence: Uncut Mountain Press, 2022), 65.

378 Ibid., 95.

In the Latin Filioque There are Two Origins of the One Divinity[379]

For as with all creation that came forth from both, each is the origin of all, so also, according to those who think like the Latins, when the Spirit proceeds from both, each will be an origin of the Spirit, and on this basis, there will be two origins of the one divinity. For if the Son contributes something in this case, too, just as in that case also He doubtlessly co-creates, He, too, is admittedly a cause of the Spirit. If, however, He does not contribute anything, He has been assumed in vain, and so as with a geometric proof the Latin theologians are genuinely proven vain; for they cannot say that 'just as with created things, although each divine person exists as an origin, nonetheless the origin is one, so here, too, it is one, even if it is spoken of as from both.'" Of course [this cannot stand, since] just as we have said, in the former case, the creative power is actually natural, not hypostatic, and because of this the creative power is one and in both. In the latter case, however, the generative capacity is not in both.

The Latins Blaspheme in Describing the Procession of the Holy Spirit[380]

Now the Latins — O the simultaneous senselessness and madness! — they actually despise the reverend and confessed order in God. And those things which Basil the Great and Gregory the Theologian confess to be beyond their own knowledge, as being ineffable and transcending us, these things the Latins boast that they understand. Yet they innovate regarding the inexpressible and incomprehensible procession of the Holy Spirit, or, to speak more bluntly, they blaspheme, when they say that the procession is both indirect and direct, both proximate and far, by which they risk degrading the Holy Spirit into a creature. Therefore, the Holy Spirit is not by necessity nor is He always placed after the Son by divinely inspired Scripture.

---

379 Ibid., 127.
380 Ibid., 139.

LATIN WRITINGS NOT IN AGREEMENT WITH
COMMON CONFESSION CANNOT BE RECEIVED[381]

But writings not so familiar are suspicious, and especially as they are produced by the Latins, who through their addition have plotted even against the conspicuous Symbol of Faith. For having invented and audaciously ventured an addition into a text that is in the mouths of all true Christians, and which is proclaimed many times every day, what else would they not have done in the text's unknown to the masses? Therefore, writings which are not common nor familiar are held in suspicion, for fear lest an evil man have sown tares among them. These very writings, if in fact they agree with the common confession, must be received, but if they do not, they cannot be received.

8. St. Nicholas Cabasilas (+1392)

HIS LIFE,
WHICH WE COMMEMORATE ON THE 20TH OF JUNE.

"Nicholas Cabasilas was born in Thessalonica in 1322 or 1323. He received an excellent education, first in his home city and then in Constantinople. There he entered the imperial service, and for a decade was prominent as an official and friend of the emperor John VI Cantacuzenos, who entrusted him with various important missions, including a very difficult one to his home city, which was torn by social upheaval and party strife. When John VI was deposed in 1354 and retired to monastic life, Nicholas retired from political life and devoted himself to philosophy and theology.

"It is in this latter period that we find him entering upon an ecclesiastical career. It used to be thought that Nicholas, like his uncle Nilus Cabasilas, became bishop of his native city. This has now been shown to be unlikely. The records of the see know nothing of him in that capacity.

---

381 Saint Gregory Palamas, *Apodictic Treatises on the Procession of the Holy Spirit*, trans. Fr. Christopher C. Moody and Gregory Heers (Florence: Uncut Mountain Press, 2022), 157.

Nor on the other hand, as has been more recently maintained did he remain a layman. It has now been established that he entered the Manganon monastery near Constantinople, and that he probably became a priest.

"This was also the period of his greatest literary activity [notably *The Life in Christ* and *A Commentary on the Divine Liturgy*]. Nothing is certain about the date of his death, though he appears to have continued his activity past the tragic fall of his native Thessalonica to the Turks in 1387."[382]

"In 1351, during a council which condemned Akindynos and proclaimed Hesychasm as the official doctrine of the Church, Cabasilas openly took the side of Palamite theology and declared himself favourable to the project of a Council of Union with the Latin Church, but without doctrinal compromise."[383]

See page 236 for general information on the Council of 1351 along with information regarding its related councils in 1341 and 1347; see page 918 in Appendix I for its Synodal Tome.

The Criticisms Certain Latins Made of Us, and a Refutation of These[384]

Certain Latins attack us thus: They claim that after the words of the Lord; "Take and eat" and what follows there is no need of any further prayer to consecrate the offerings, since they are already consecrated by the Lord's word. They maintain that to pronounce these words of Christ and then to speak of bread and wine and to pray for their consecration as if they had not already been consecrated, is not only impious but futile and unnecessary. Moreover, they say that the blessed Chrysostom is wit-

---

382 St. Nicholas Cabasilas, "Translator's Foreword," *The Life in Christ*, trans. Carmino J. DeCatanzaro (Crestwood: St. Vladimir's Seminary Press, 1974), 10.

383 Hieromonk Makarios of Simonos Petra, *The Synaxarion: The Lives of the Saints of the Orthodox Church, Volume Five, May-June*, trans. Christopher Hookway (Ormylia: Holy Convent of the Annunciation of Our Lady, 1999), 564.

384 St. Nicholas Cabasilas, A *Commentary on the Divine Liturgy*, trans. J.M. Hussey and P.A. McNulty (London: SPCK, 1983), 71-76.

ness that these words consecrate the offerings when he said in the same way that the words of the Creator, "Be fruitful and multiply", spoken on a single occasion by God, continue to take effect, so the words once spoken by the Saviour are also operative forever. Those who rely more on their own prayer than on God's word are in the first place implying that his words lack effectiveness. They show that they put more trust in themselves, and in the third place they make the holy sacrament dependent on something uncertain, namely, human prayer, and in so doing they represent so great a mystery in which the most steadfast faith must be shown as something full of uncertainty. For it does not follow that he who prays will necessarily be heard, even if he has the virtue of Paul.

It is not difficult to refute all these arguments. Take first the works of divine John on which they rely and consider whether the words of Christ can be compared to the words of the Creator. God said: "Be fruitful and multiply." What then? After these words do we need nothing more to achieve this, and is nothing else necessary for the increase of the human race? Is not marriage and conjugal union essential, and all the other cares which go with marriage, and without which it would be impossible for mankind to exist and develop? We consider marriage, therefore, necessary for the procreation of children, and after marriage we still pray towards this end, and without seeming to despise the Creator's command, being well aware that it is the primary cause of procreation, but through the medium of marriage, provision for nourishment and so on. And in the same way, here in the liturgy we believe that the Lord's words do indeed accomplish the mystery, but through the medium of the priest, his invocation, and his prayer. These words do not take effect simply in themselves or under any circumstances, but there are many essential conditions, and without these they do not achieve their end. Who does not know that it is the death of Christ alone which has brought remission of sins to the world? But we also know that even after his death faith, penitence, confession, and the prayer of the priest are necessary, and a man cannot receive remission of sins unless he has first been through these processes. What then? Are we to dishonour his death and to claim that it is of no effect, by believing that its results are inadequate unless we ourselves add our contribution? By no means.

It is unreasonable to address reproaches like these to those who pray for the consecration of the offerings. Their confidence in their prayer is not confidence in self, but in God who has promised to grant what they are seeking. It is indeed the very contrary which is fundamental to the conception of prayer. For suppliants perform the act of prayer because they fail to trust themselves in the matters about which they pray, and they believe that they can obtain their requests from God alone. In throwing himself upon God, the man who prays admits that he recognizes his own helplessness and that he is dependent on God for everything. This is not my affair, he says, nor within my own powers, but it had need of you, Lord, and I trust it all to you. These principles have an even more wonderful application when we are forced to ask things which are above nature and beyond all understanding, as the sacraments are. Then it is absolutely essential that those who make prayer should rely on God alone. For man could not even have imagined these things if God had not taught him of them; he could not have conceived the desire for them to receive it if he had not received the hope of it from him who is the Truth. He would not even have dared to pray for those things if God had not clearly shown him that it was according to his will that they should be sought for, and that he is ready to grant them to those who ask. As a result, the prayer is neither uncertain nor the result unsure, as the Lord of the gift has in every way made known his desire to grant it. This is why we believe that the sanctification of the mysteries is in the prayer of the priest, certainly not relying on any human power, but on the power of God. We are assured of the result, not by reason of man who prays, but by reason of God who hears; not because man has made a supplication, but because the Truth has promised to grant it.

There is no need to speak of the way in which Christ has shown his desire ever to grant this grace. This is why he came into the world, why he was made a sacrifice, why he died. This is why altars and priests and every purification and all the commandments, the teaching and the exhortations exist: This is why the Saviour declared that he desired to keep the Passover, for it was then that he was going to give the true Passover to his disciples. This is why he commanded them "Do this in remembrance of me", for he wished this mystery to be performed among us always.

How then could those who pray have any doubt about the object of their prayer, if he intended that those things which they seek to have should be received by them, and he himself wishes to grant them who alone has the power to give? Therefore, those who believe that the offerings are consecrated by prayer are neither scorning the words of the Saviour, not trusting in themselves, nor yet causing dependence on something uncertain, such as human prayer, as the Latins vainly reproach us.

A further proof is that the all-holy Chrism, stated by the blessed Dionysius to be in the same category as Holy Communion, is also consecrated and sanctified by prayer. And the faithful have no doubt that this prayer is efficacious and consecrates. In the same way the ordination of priests, and that of bishops as well, is effected by prayer. He who is ordaining lays on his hands and then says to the clergy: "Let us pray for him, that the grace of the Holy Spirit may come upon him." Similarly in the Latin Church the bishop ordaining priests anoints the head of the candidate with oil and prays that he may be richly endowed with the grace of the Holy Spirit. And it is through prayer that the priest gives absolution from sins to penitents. In the last sacrament of Unction, it is equally the prayer of the priests which confers it: this sacrament has the power to give healing from bodily illness and the remission of sins to those on whom it is performed, as is confirmed by Apostolic tradition: "Is there any sick among you? Let him call for the elders of the church; and let them pray over him, anointing him with oil in the name of the Lord; and the prayer of faith shall save the sick, and the Lord shall raise him up; and if he have committed sins they shall be forgiven him."

How can those who condemn the prayer in the sacraments answer all these arguments?

If, as they say, the result of prayer is uncertain it would be equally uncertain whether the priest is truly of that holy office whose name he bears, or whether the Chrism has the power to consecrate, and therefore it would be impossible for the sacrament of holy communion to exist, since there would be neither priest nor altar. For our critics would hardly maintain that the words of the Lord would be effective if they were spoken by just anyone, and perhaps even without an altar. And indeed, the altar upon which the bread must be placed is in fact itself consecrated with the Chrism which in turn is consecrated by prayer. And further, who can give us sure remission of sins if there is doubt about the priests and their supplications?

To follow the innovations of these men would indeed inevitably mean the total destruction of all Christianity. It is therefore clear that for those who hold such doctrines the very foundations of their virtue are in question, and there is indeed great danger for those who fabricate innovations of this kind, alien to the tradition of the Fathers and undermining the security which this tradition guarantees. For God himself has said that he answers prayer and grants the Holy Spirit to those who ask, and nothing is impossible to those who pray in faith, and his assurance cannot be untrue. It is nowhere stated that this will happen to those who simply speak this or that word. It is the tradition of the Fathers who received this teaching from the Apostles and from their successors, that the sacraments are rendered effective through prayer; all the sacraments, as I have said, and particularly the Holy Eucharist. Basil the Great and John Chrysostom, the great teachers of the Church, affirmed his, as so many others had already done. Those who deny such authorities deserve no consideration from those who believe in right doctrine. The words of the Lord about the holy mysteries were spoken in a narrative manner. None of the Apostles or teachers of the Church has ever appeared to say that they are sufficient to consecrate the offerings of sacraments. The blessed John himself said that, spoken once by Christ, and having actually been said by him, they are always effective, just as the word of the Creator is. But it is nowhere taught that now, spoken by the priest, and by reason of being said by him, they have that efficacy. In the same way the Creator's word is not effective because it is spoken by a man, applied to each particular case, but only because it was once spoken by the Lord.

9. St. Symeon, Archbishop of Thessaloniki (+1429)

"Our holy Father Symeon was from Constantinople. After completing his education in secular learning and divinity, he cultivated the virtues of the angelic life: humility, meekness, self-control and prayer, before succeeding Gabriel (d. 1416 or 1418) on the episcopal throne of Thessalonica. In those difficult days, when the capital of Macedonia was about to pass under the Turkish yoke, Symeon proved an incomparable shepherd. In spite of poor health and frequent illness, he fed his flock unfailingly with the honey of his words, renewing their courage in the difficulties that beset them, and exhorting them to place all their hope in God. He had great trials to endure from those who were tempted to surrender the city either to the Turks or to the Venetians. He expended the little strength that illness left him in preaching fidelity to the Orthodox faith and to the Emperor, and in exhorting the people to have confidence in the aid of Saint Demetrius. During the Venetian occupation (1423-30), he encouraged the people to bear with it in order to delay the Turkish invasion for as long as possible. Six months before the city fell to Murad II on 29 March 1430, Saint Symeon dreamt that he was in a richly decorated house and heard a voice telling him not to tarry there admiring its beauties but to get out quickly before it fell to the ground. So, he fell asleep in peace, spared the sad sight of the fall of his beloved city. The inhabitants of Thessalonica, whatever their race or religion, whether Orthodox, Latins or Jews, bewailed the loss of the father of them all, the good shepherd who had wholeheartedly given his life for his sheep. "Saint Symeon was one of the last disciples of Saint Gregory Palamas (14 Nov.). Firmly established upon the rock of the faith, he clearly set forth Orthodox doctrine against every heresy, and illustrated it above all in his liturgical works. He brought to the conduct of divine service in the Church of Saint Sophia in Thessalonica a splendour similar to that of the Great Church of Constantinople. He composed many hymns and prayers, and compiled a vast spiritual commentary on all the rites and ceremonies of the Byzantine Church, so that these treasures are not lost to us, even though the Christian Empire is no more. Saint Symeon died more than five hundred years ago, but it was not until 1981 that his veneration received the formal recognition of the Ecumenical Patriarchate."[385]

---

385 Hieromonk Makarios of Simonos Petra, *The Synaxarion: The Lives of the Saints of the Orthodox Church, Volume One, Introduction/September-October*, trans. Christopher Hookway (Ormylia: Holy Convent of the Annunciation of Our

St. Symeon Responding to a Latin[386]

I remember, brother, some such thing that I had said in Constantinople to a man of the Latin party. For when this man approached me wishing to discuss, in response to his words I said as much as God had given me to say from His saints in defence of Him and of His divine dogmas. Finally, he asked, "And why do you grant communion to the Eastern hierarchs, the so-called patriarchs, and commemorate them in church, although they are barbarous and do not even know what Christianity is, but do not accept the Pope, who is wise, and those learned men that surround him?"

To which I said, "We do not turn away from the pope at all, nor are we out of communion with him; rather, we are one with him just as also with Christ, and consider him our father and shepherd." Then, since he was at a loss and asking how this could be, since we not only are not in communion with their pope but even call him a heretic, I replied to him saying, "With Pope Peter and Linus and Clement and Steven and Hippolytus and Silvester, Innocent and Leo and Agapetus, Martin and Agatho, and with the popes and patriarchs that are like unto them, we have unbroken communion and union in Christ, and no cause will divide us from them. This is clear from the fact that we celebrate them all, considering them teachers and fathers and keeping their sacred memories and calling them patriarchs and fathers, seeing that we carry the Symbol [Nicene Creed] of their faith spotless, and were baptised as they were baptised, and were consecrated as they were consecrated, and as they surrendered their souls to Christ in the Symbol, so do we, too, surrender them.

"Therefore, if there be one like unto them in the Symbol of Faith and in his life and in the customs of Orthodoxy, this father is in communion with us, and we hold him as we hold Peter, and the bonds of our union will remain for a long time and unto the ages of ages, just as Orthodoxy remained with those holy men even to a thousand years and their Or-

---

Lady, 1999), 108-110.

386 St. Symeon, Archbishop of Thessaloniki, "Against All Heresies," in *Patrologia Graeca, Vol. 155*, trans. Jacques Paul Migne (1857-1866) & Gregory Heers (2022) (Paris: Imprimerie Catholique, 1857), 120-121.

thodox Faith remains with us. For it is clear that they confessed the divine Symbol just as we do, and this is witnessed by the decrees [ὅροι] of all the Ecumenical Councils, but more clearly by those of the Sixth and Seventh. Ever since the innovation [filioque] regarding the divine Symbol, however, we can no longer find the pope nor the apostolic man and father, seeing that it is also not possible to find the current so-called popes agreeing with the apostle Peter's faith and confession, but only with his denial. And just as Peter is not Peter, nor an apostle, nor first, when he has denied Christ, so the so-called pope will never be a pope if he does not hold the faith of Peter, which Peter sealed by his triple confession of love, since he had thrice denied. Nor will he be a successor if he is not rich in the matters pertaining to the good confession of the divine Peter and of his successors, which confession the Father revealed from above." As we were saying these things, our interlocutor fell silent.

"ON THE SACRED LITURGY" IN THE LITURGICAL COMMENTARIES[387]

The bread is four-sided, and not round and unleavened, as that sacrificed by the Latins, because, as we said, it is fully complete since God took on a fully complete human nature, with a soul and the four elements; and because all the world is four-part and the Word itself is the creator of the world; and because the body which Christ took on is made of four elements, and because the incarnate Word sanctified all the ends of the world, both the heavenly and the earthly, and because the shape of this typifies the cross, having been crucified and died on which, He restored us and the whole world. But the Latins say that the roundness signifies both the being without beginning and the being without end of the divinity. And what do we, the Orthodox, say reflecting on this? It is not the qualities of God that we are dealing with now. The mystery of the incarnation and the passion are being proclaimed here, as well as matters regarding His becoming human and the crucifixion, which are

---

387 St. Symeon of Thessaloniki, "On the Sacred Liturgy," in *The Liturgical Commentaries*, trans. Steven Hawkes-Teeples (Toronto: Pontifical Institute of Mediaeval Studies, 2011), 189-203.

being typified. Still the divine form was neither set aside nor left behind; rather, it is seen in the seal.

And it is necessary, rather, that what concerns the fulfillment of the Savior's economy of salvation be contemplated in the bread in its four-part form, while what concerns His divinity is contemplated in the seal of the bread, which is round, and in the middle of the seal the cross or the Savior Himself is depicted, all showing together that the incarnate Word is without beginning and without end, that He is God, has appeared among us, was truly incarnate and suffered, and that, being God in substance, he became a man in substance. Therefore, it is necessary not only to depict what concerns His divinity, but also what concerns His humanity, so that it not seem, as some of the heretics maintain, that what was related to His humanity disappeared and that He was wholly God, as those holding to one nature [monophysites] say. But it did not occur in this way, nor have we received any such teaching, but He remains complete in each nature, His divinity having been completely united to His humanity.

For He deified His whole humanity, and made it equally God by the ultimate union. He maintained, however, His own nature, and is complete man, just as He is also complete God, both in a given place and everywhere and above all things, and yet He bears the qualities of the body. For, because of this, after His rising and according to His incorruption, He was both seen and touched, and He entered closed doors. Do you see that He was incorruptible and preserved His own qualities? That He is uncreated and created? And that He is of two natures, even if He is perfectly one in His hypostasis? Therefore, follow Orthodoxy, and do not offer either dead or inanimate things; do not renew the customs of the Jews, or introduce Jewish law, or celebrate with unleavened bread. But, the Latin claims, Paul says to offer unleavened bread. He says, "Let us, therefore, celebrate the festival, not with the old leaven, but with the unleavened bread of sincerity and truth." Oh, what stupidity! So, we who live by Orthodoxy say. Is this what you believe the herald of God means? He says this, O man, to overturn the root and cause of sin.

Therefore, he says, "not in the old leaven of malice and fornication." And, in fact, he speaks truly. Renounce this leaven, the fornication of the one who had fornicated in Corinth, and every other impurity, because the whole purpose of this passage is about this impurity, and his reasoning is about that fornicator, saying, "Cast out such a person. Do you not know that a little leaven leavens all the dough?" For thus malice, like a ruinous disease, having started from one, infects the rest. Therefore, he says, "Cast out the old leaven, so that you be new dough," mixed in Christ, as new and sinless as Christ is, for Christ is also the new Adam. And through Him, you are "unleavened bread," that is, having no share in sin by baptism and chrism. "For Christ our Pascha was also sacrificed for us," transporting us out of the Egypt of sin. This is the meaning and statement of Paul. And, in accordance with this, overturn and drive out the leaven of sin, and have no share in this at all.

But do not shake off the leaven of incorruption, to which the kingdom of heaven is likened, because it brings together, and unites to itself and changes in itself those obeying the divine proclamation. Indeed, "a woman," that is, the Church of the supercelestial Bridegroom, "mixed it with three measures of wheat flour," that is, the three orders of the saved — the slaves, the salaried workers and the sons, both those who are moderate in marriage and also virgins —"until it was entirely leavened" and made worthy in the Resurrection of God's kingdom, which gathered together in grace the just who lived prior to the law and those who lived in accordance with the law, which the grace of the Gospel has completed.

For the Savior Himself, the truly divine and most pure leaven, the bread of life, who is also eternal king, by being incarnate and coming into the world, saved both those who lived before the law and those who live in the law, having snatched away their bonds; and He united them to those who believe in Him. In yet another perspective, He is mixed as a pure and living leaven, allotted proportionally in three to His rational creation in its present state, that is to say, to the angels, to the departed saints, and to us the living who believe in Him, until the whole is completely leavened, all having risen through Him and all having become one, when both the nature of His angels and our own nature partake of His glory.

So be leavened in the Lord and be eager to be part of the leaven of the kingdom of heaven, and do not seek to share in the Jewish law's unleavened bread, because the law is a shadow, a lifeless image and not living. And for this reason, Paul regarded the unleavened loaves as dead and shadowy, and they are not called simply "bread," but "unleavened bread," having only the name "bread" by participation. And be a partner in the great sacrifice of Melchizedek, a sacrifice of bread — not unleavened bread — and wine, a prelude to the new sacrifice of Melchizedek, of the true and eternal Melchizedek and only high priest Jesus Christ, about whom it is written, "You are a priest forever, according to the order of Melchizedek."

If you are unwilling, then perhaps along with unleavened bread you will sacrifice an irrational lamb, and will partake according to Jewish custom, or even concelebrate with them; and you will receive the unleavened bread as a friendly gift from foreigners, which my fathers were forbidden to do, or you will even be circumcised and keep the Jewish sabbath, for that follows, since nothing is abominable to you. For you often partake of the table among the Jews, and there is little difference between you and these God-slayers and atheists.

We, on the other hand, have nothing in common with them. "The old has passed away; behold, everything has become new," cries out Paul. We have baptism instead of circumcision, the lamb of God instead of the sacrifice of an irrational animal, and instead of unleavened bread the leavened bread of the kingdom of Christ, who is "the living bread, come down from heaven" in place of the manna. "The one eating it will not die," as He said. And if you still dispute, as is your custom, and continue vigorously to argue this and say that the offering then was unleavened, because the Pascha of the Jewish law was performed by means of unleavened bread, there are many perfectly truthful accounts of greater and divine men shattering your arrogance and ignorance that the Savior did not take leavened bread when He handed on the mysteries.

And the Gospel witnesses to this, teaching that it was not the day of the feast of the unleavened bread when Christ offered himself in the sacred service, but it was before the feast of the unleavened bread. It says, "Before the feast of the Pascha, Jesus knowing" and He handed on the sacrifice when He had the supper. And it was then when He also completed the washing of the apostles' feet. And these things occurred before the Jewish Pascha. See what it says on the day of the passion. "And they did not go into the praetorium, so that they might not be contaminated, but might eat the Pascha." And again, at the crucifixion it says, "Since it was the day of preparation, for that day of the sabbath was a great day." And about this the Gospel again says, "He took bread." And it does not add "unleavened bread." Also, what the Lord said: "I have earnestly desired to eat this Pascha with you before I suffer," teaches this quite clearly. For He was not desiring to partake of the Jewish Pascha, which He had often performed. But He came putting an end to the shadow.

Besides, even if He performed the Pascha of the Jewish law, He had done it earlier, and later He handed on His own Pascha. And He desired to pass this on before He suffered, so that He would remain with us, so that it would truly be as He said: "The one who eats my flesh and who drinks my blood remains in me, and I remain in him." Therefore, He was not fulfilling all the Jewish law's requirements at that supper, but He finished the washing of the apostles' feet and was reclining; He was having not only roasted meat, but also a dish in which Judas dipped. Because it was not yet the time for the Pascha of the Jews, He did not perform only the Jewish Pascha then, but especially His own, about which He also said, "Do this in my memory," and "My flesh is truly food, and my blood is truly drink."

And that the old usage has ceased, He witnesses once again, saying, "The law and the prophets until John." So, it is true that He did not give and was not content then with the Pascha of the Jews, that of an unreasoning lamb and of animal blood, but He desired to hand on to His disciples His own Pascha, and He handed on to them the very thing which He did then once, and commanded to be done forever. Even if, then, all these things and what the fathers say do not ward off your folly, and even if what was offered then by the Savior was unleavened, these contemporary times would require you to do something more complete, just as indeed we received the teaching that we should do the rest above and beyond the law, and that our justice should greatly "exceed that of the scribes and Pharisees."

But also, we are free from the law by the blood of Jesus Christ. For, Paul says, Christ freed us from the curse of the law; and we have no part in the servitude of the law. For if we again perform the works of the law, Paul says again, "Christ will be of no use to us." For Christ, having fulfilled all things for us, set us free. For He was circumcised, but we are not circumcised; we are baptized in the Spirit. And we do not eat meat and blood that have been sacrificed, but His flesh and blood.

So, it is quite clear that His sacrifice of the awe-inspiring bread and chalice was the tradition handed down and not the Pascha of the Jewish law, because He says, "This is the new covenant in my blood," and "This is my blood, the blood of the new covenant." Just as earlier, giving us His flesh for food, He said, "Take, eat; this is my body," which you cannot imitate. You have been won over to such an extent by the unleavened bread. And you are unable to cut and share the body, just as you cannot share the blood, even though He says this, "Drink of this everyone; this is my blood." But you do not do even this. For you do not share the chalice with those coming forward to receive communion; you have innovated to such an extent.

But we do the sacred service in Christ according to Him. We break the bread, as He broke it; and we eat it, as He said, and distribute it to the faithful, and we offer complete bread since He was a complete man, even to the extent of abrogating the sacrifice of the law, since it ended when the truth appeared.

And we believe that the Savior did the sacred service using complete leavened bread for the Pascha which He desired to do, even if He had carried out the Pascha of the law earlier. Since He was reclining and had a dish in which Judas dipped a piece of bread, it does not appear that he was performing the Pascha of the law at that time. For the law says that everything there is to be roasted on a fire, and not boiled in water. So, it is likely that He carried out the Pascha of the law at another time, and at that time He carried out His own Pascha, which He desired.

And I often say this: I myself desire always in Him to taste of this living Pascha through His mercy now and also in the age to come, and I pray for this to come to pass always for me and for all the brothers. And consecrating the sacred chalice in the sacred service in Christ Himself, our God, the One who has offered Himself for us, we present it in love to all the brothers to drink of it, as we were commanded. We become one as He prayed, and we are one with Him together with the Father and the Spirit, as He said. But enough about this; we have said more than we set out to say in brief, being forced to do so by the subject.

10. St. Mark Eugenikos, Metropolitan of Ephesus (+1444)[388]

THOSE IN UNION WITH THE PAPISTS ARE SUBJECT TO ANATHEMAS[389]

They (who had accepted union with the papists) have dishonored and corrupted the Church by making her mingle with those putrid members that have been cut off from her for many years and are subject to countless anathemas, and through communion with them they have besmirched the spotless Bride of Christ.

ENCYCLICAL LETTER OF ST. MARK OF EPHESUS[390]

The many writings of St. Mark occasioned by the false Union of Florence are an important source material for all who wish to understand the position of the Church of Christ as against the heresies of the Roman Church, as well as against the pseudo-Orthodoxy that proclaims that "nothing separates us" precisely where the Fathers have pronounced anathema. The present Letter was written probably in July of 1440 as an answer to the promulgation in Constantinople of the false Union.

TO ALL ORTHODOX CHRISTIANS ON THE MAINLAND AND IN THE ISLANDS: FROM MARK, BISHOP OF THE METROPOLY OF EPHESUS: REJOICE IN CHRIST!

Those who have ensnared us in an evil captivity and desire to lead us away into the Babylon of Latin rites and dogmas could not, of course,

---

388 See page 95 for an account of his life.

389 Ἅγιος Μάρκος Ἐφέσου, «Ἐπιστολὴ πρὸς Ἱερομόναχο Θεοφάνη.» Στὸ Ὀρθόδοξος Ἑλλάς, ἤτοι, περὶ τῶν Ἑλλήνων τῶν γραψάντων κατὰ Λατίνων καὶ περὶ τῶν συγγραμμάτων αὐτῶν (Λειψία: Τύποις Μέτζγερ καὶ Βίττιγ, 1872), 106.

390 Orthodox Christian Books & Icons, "Encyclical Letter of St. Mark of Ephesus," *Orthodox Word 3*, no. 2 (March-April-May 1967): 53-59.

completely accomplish this, seeing immediately that there was little chance of it, in fact that it was simply impossible; but having stopped somewhere in the middle, both they and those who followed after them, they neither remained any longer what they were, nor became they anything else. For having quit Jerusalem, a firm and unwavering faith, but being in no condition and not wishing to become and to be called Babylonians, they thus called themselves, as if by right, "Greco-Latins," and among the people are called "Latinizers." And so these split people, like the mythical centaurs, confess together with the Latins that the Holy Spirit proceeds from the Son and has the Son as Cause of His existence, and yet together with us confess that He proceeds from the Father. And they say together with them that the addition of the Creed (of the Filioque) was done canonically and with blessing, and yet together with us do not permit it to be uttered. (Besides, who would turn away from what was canonical and blessed?!) And they say together with them that unleavened bread is the Body of Christ, and yet together with us do not dare to accept it. Is this not sufficient to reveal their spirit, and how that it was not in quest of the Truth (which, having in their hands, they betrayed) that they came together with the Latins, but from a desire to enrich themselves and to conclude not a true, but a false Union.

II

But one should examine in what manner they have united with them; for everything that is united to something different is naturally united by means of some middle point between them. And thus, they imagined to unite with them by means of some judgement concerning the Holy Spirit, together with them expressing the opinion that He has existence also from the Son, but everything else between them is divergent, and there is among them neither any middle point nor anything in common. Just as before two divergent Creeds are uttered; likewise there are celebrated two Liturgies, divergent and discordant one with the other: one with leavened bread, the other with unleavened bread; divergent also are baptisms: one performed with triple immersion, the other with pouring over the head from above, and one with anointing with chrism, the other completely without; and all rites are in everything divergent and discordant one with the other, and likewise the fasts and church usages and other like things. What kind of unity is this, when there is no apparent and clear sign of it? And in what manner have they united with them, desiring also to preserve their own (for in this they were unanimous) and at the same time not following the traditions of the Fathers?

III

But what is their own "wise" opinion? "Never," they say, "has the Greek Church said that the Holy Spirit proceeds only from the Father; she has said simply that He proceeds from the Father, thus not excluding the participation of the Son in the Procession of the Holy Spirit. Therefore (they say) both before and now we exhibit unity."

Alas, what absurdity! Alas, what blindness! If the Greek Church, having received it from Christ Himself and the Holy Apostles and Fathers, has said that the Spirit proceeds from the Father, but has never said (for she has received this from no one) that the Holy Spirit proceeds from the Son, then what else does this signify than that she affirms that the Holy Spirit proceeds only from the Father? For if He is not from the Son, evidently, He is only from the Father.

Do you know what is said concerning the Generation? "Begotten of the Father before all ages." Would anyone add here "only of the Father"? Yet it is precisely thus and in no other way that we understand it, and, if need be, will express it. For we have been taught that the Son is begotten of none else, but only of the Father. Therefore, too John Damascene says, on behalf of the whole Church and all Christians: "We do not say that the Holy Spirit is from the Son." And if we do not say that the Spirit is also from the Son, then it is apparent that we thus say that the Spirit is only from the Father; therefore, a little before this he says: "We do not call the Son Cause." And in the next chapter: "The sole Cause is the Father."

IV

What more? "Never," they say, "have we considered Latins heretics, but only schismatics." But this too they have taken from them (the Latins), for the latter, having nothing with which to accuse us in our doctrine, call us schismatics because we have turned away from the obedience to them which, as they think, we should have. But let us examine the matter. Will it be just for us likewise to show them kindness and place no blame on them in matters of the Faith?

It was they who gave the grounds for the schism by openly making the addition (the Filioque), which until then they had spoken in secret; while we were the first to separate ourselves from them, or rather, to separate and cut them off from the common Body of the Church. Why, may I ask? Because they have the right Faith or have made the addition (to the Creed) in an Orthodox fashion? Surely whoever would begin to talk like that would not be right in the head. But rather because they have an absurd and impious opinion and for no reason at all made the addition. And so we have turned away from them as from heretics and have shunned them.

What more is necessary? The pious canons speak thus: "He is a heretic and subject to the canons against heretics who even slightly departs from the Orthodox Faith." If, then, the Latins do not at all depart from the correct Faith, we have evidently cut them off unjustly: but if they have thoroughly departed (from the Faith) — and that in connection with the theology of the Holy Spirit, blasphemy against Whom is the greatest of all perils — then it is clear that they are heretics, and we have cut them off as heretics.

Why do we anoint with chrism those of them who come to us? Is it not clear that it is because they are heretics? For the seventh canon of the Second Ecumenical Council states:

> As for those heretics who betake themselves to Orthodoxy, and to the lot of those being saved, we accept them in accordance with the subjoined sequence and custom: Arians, and Macedonians, and Sabbatians, and Novatians, those calling themselves *Cathari* ("Puritans") and *Aristeri* ("Best"), and the Quarto-

decimans, otherwise known as Tetradites, and Apollinarians we accept when they offer *libelli* (recantations in writing) and anathematize every heresy that does not hold the same beliefs as the Catholic and Apostolic Church of God, and are sealed first with holy chrism on their forehead and their eyes, and nose, and mouth, and ears; and in sealing them we say: 'The seal of the gift of the Holy Spirit.'

Do you see with whom we number those who come from the Latins? If all those (enumerated in the canon) are heretics, then it is clear that these (the Latins) are the same. And what does the most wise Patriarch of Antioch, Theodore Balsamon, say of this in reply to the Most Holy Patriarch of Alexandria, Mark? "Imprisoned Latins and others coming to our Catholic churches request communion of the Divine Sacraments. We desire to know: is this permissible?" (Answer:) *"He that is not with Me is against Me; and he that gathereth not with Me scattereth abroad* (St. Matt. 12:30; St. Luke 11:23). Because many years ago the celebrated Roman Church was separated from communion with the other four Most Holy Patriarchs, having apostasized into customs and doctrines foreign to the Catholic Church and not Orthodox (it was for this reason that the Pope was not deemed worthy of sharing in the commemoration of the names of the Eastern Patriarchs at Divine Services), — therefore we must not sanctify one of Latin race through the Divine and most pure Gifts (given) by priestly hands, unless he shall first resolve to depart from Latin dogmas and customs and shall be catechized and joined to those of Orthodoxy."

Do you hear, how they have departed not only in customs, but also in dogmas foreign to those of Orthodoxy (and what is foreign to Orthodox dogma is, of course, heretical teaching), and that, according to the canons, they must be catechized and united to Orthodoxy? And if it is necessary to catechize, then clearly it is necessary to anoint with chrism. How have they suddenly presented themselves to us as Orthodox, they who for so long and according to the judgement of such great Fathers and Teachers have been considered heretics? Who has so easily "made" them Orthodox? — It is gold, if you desire to acknowledge the truth, and your own thirst for gain; or, to express it better: it did not make them Orthodox, but made you like them and carried you into the camp of heretics.

V

"But if," they say, "we had devised some middle ground (compromise) between dogmas, then thanks to this we would have united with them and accomplished our business superbly, without at all having been forced to say anything except what corresponds to custom and has been handed down (by the Fathers)." This is precisely the means by which many, from of old, have been deceived and persuaded to follow those who have led them off to the steep precipice of impiety; believing that there is some kind of middle ground between two teachings that can reconcile obvious contradictions, they have been exposed to peril.

If the Latin dogma is true that the Holy Spirit proceeds also from the Son, then ours is false that states that the Holy Spirit proceeds from the Father (and this is precisely the reason for which we separated from them); and if ours is true then without doubt theirs is false. What kind of middle ground can there be between two such judgments? There can be none, unless it were some kind of judgment suitable to both the one and the other, like a boot that fits both feet. And will this unite us?

VI

But someone will say, how shall we regard those moderate Greco-Latins who, maintaining a middle ground, openly favor some of the Latin rites and dogmas, favor but do not wish to accept others, and entirely disapprove of still others? One must flee from them as one flees from a snake, as from the Latins themselves, or, it may be, from those who are even worse than they — as from buyers and sellers of Christ. For they, as the Apostle says, suppose that gain is godliness (I Tim. 6:5), of whom he adds: flee these (I Tim. 6:11), for they go over to them (the Latins) not in order to learn, but for gain. *What communion hath light with darkness? And what concord hath Christ with Belial? Or what part hath he that believeth with an infidel?* (II Cor. 6:14-15).

Behold how we, together with Damascene and all the Fathers, do not say that the Spirit proceeds from the Son, while they, together with the Latins, say that the Spirit proceeds from the Son. And we, together with the divine Dionysios, say that the Father is the sole Source of the supernatural Divinity, while they say together with the Latins that the Son also is the Source of the Holy Spirit, by this clearly excluding the Spirit from the Divinity. And we, together with Gregory the Theologian, distinguish the Father from the Son in His capacity of being Cause, while they together with the Latins unite Them into one in the capacity of being cause. And we, together with St. Maximus and the Romans of that time and the Western Fathers, "do not make the Son the Cause of the Spirit", while they, in their Conciliar Decree (Act of Union), proclaim the Son "in Greek, Cause, and in Latin, Principle" of the Spirit. And we, together with the Philosopher and Martyr Justin affirm, "As the Son is from the Father, so is the Spirit from the Father"; while they say together with the Latins that the Son proceeds from the Father immediately, and the Spirit from the Father mediately. And we, together with Damascene and all the Fathers, confess that it is not known to us in what consists the difference between generation and procession; while they, together with Thomas (Aquinas) and the Latins, say that the difference consists in this, that generation is immediate, and procession mediate. And we affirm, in agreement with the Fathers, that the Will and Energy of the Uncreated and Divine Nature are uncreated; while they, together with the Latins and Thomas, say that Will is identical with Nature, but that the Divine Energy is created, whether it be called Divinity, or the Divine and Immaterial Light, or the Holy Spirit, or something else of this nature, and in some fashion these poor creatures "worship" the created "Divinity" and the created "Divine Light" and the created "Holy Spirit." And we say that neither do the Saints receive the Kingdom and the unutterable blessings already prepared for them, nor are sinners already sent to hell, but both await their fate which will be received in the future age after the resurrection and Judgement; while they, together with Latins, desire immediately after death to receive according to their merits, and for those in an intermediate condition, who have died in repentance, they give a purgatorial fire (which is not identical with that of hell) so that, as they say, having purified their soul by it after death, they also together with the righteous will enjoy the Kingdom (of Heaven); this is contained in their Conciliar Decree (Act of Union). And we, obeying the Apostles, who have prohibited it, shun Jewish unleavened bread; while they, in the same Act of Union, proclaim that what is used in the services of the Latins is the Body of Christ. And we say that the addition to the Creed arose uncanonically and anticanonically and contrary to the Fathers; while they affirm that it is canonical and blessed — to such an extent are they unaware how to conform to the Truth and to themselves! And for us the Pope is as one of the Patriarchs, and that only if he be Orthodox; while they with great gravity proclaim him Vicar of Christ, Father and Teacher of all Christians. May they be more fortunate than their Father, who are also like him: for he does not greatly prosper, having an antipope who is the cause of sufficient unpleasantness; and they are not happy to imitate him.

VII

And so, brethren, flee from them and from communion with them; for they are false apostles, deceitful workers, transforming themselves into the Apostles of Christ. And no marvel; for Satan himself is transformed into an angel of light. Therefore, it is no great thing if his ministers also be transformed as the ministers of righteousness; whose end shall be according to their works (II Cor. 11:13-15). And in another place the same Apostle says of them: For they that are such serve not our Lord Jesus Christ, but their own belly; and by good words and fair speeches deceive the hearts of the simple. Nevertheless, the foundation of God standeth sure, having this seal (Rom. 16:18, II Tim 2:19). And in another place: Beware of dogs, beware of evil workers, beware of concision (Philippians 3:2). And then, in another place: But though we, or an angel from heaven, preach any other gospel unto you than that which we have preached unto you, let him be accursed (Gal. 1:8). See what has been prophetically foretold, that "though an angel from heaven" — so that no one could cite in justification of himself an especially high position. And the beloved Disciple speaks thus: If there come any unto you, and bring not this doctrine, receive him not into your house, and give him no greeting; for he that giveth him greeting is partaker in his evil deeds (II John 10-11).

Therefore, in so far as this is what has been commanded you by the Holy Apostles, — stand aright, hold firmly to the traditions which you have received, both written and by word of mouth, that you be not deprived of your firmness if you become led away by the delusions of the lawless. May God, Who is All-powerful, make them also to know their delusion; having delivered us from them as from evil tares, may He gather us into His granaries like pure and useful wheat, in Jesus Christ our Lord, to Whom belongs all glory, honor, and worship, with His Father Who is without beginning, and His All-holy and Good and Life-giving Spirit, now and ever and unto the ages of ages. Amen.

ADDRESS OF ST. MARK OF EPHESUS ON THE DAY OF HIS DEATH[391]

Introductory Note[392]: On the final day of his earthly life, the last thoughts of St. Mark were not for himself, but for Orthodoxy, to which he had devoted his whole life. Appealing to his followers to stand firm in the battle for Orthodoxy, he turned especially to one man in whom he hoped to find a successor to himself as leader in this battle. This hope was richly fulfilled in the person of George Scholarios, who became an ardent champion of Orthodoxy and, as first Patriarch of Constantinople after the fall of Byzantium, was instrumental in freeing the Church from the yoke of the false Union. He was subsequently canonized under his monastic name of Gennadios and is commemorated on August 31.

I WISH TO EXPRESS MY OPINION in more detail, especially now that my death is approaching, so as to be consistent with myself from beginning to end, and lest anyone should think that I have said one thing and concealed another in my thoughts, for which it would be just to shame me in this hour of my death.

---

391 Orthodox Christian Books & Icons, "Address of St. Mark of Ephesus on the Day of His Death," *Orthodox Word* 3, no. 3 (June-July 1967): 103-106.

392 Introduction from the *Orthodox Word*.

Concerning the Patriarch I shall say this, lest it should perhaps occur to him to show me a certain respect at the burial of this my humble body, or to send to my grave any of his hierarchs or clergy or in general any of those in communion with him in order to take part in prayer or to join the priests invited to it from amongst us, thinking that at some time, or perhaps secretly, I had allowed communion with him. And lest my silence give occasion to those who do not know my views well and fully to suspect some kind of conciliation, I hereby state and testify before the many worthy men here present that I do not desire, in any manner and absolutely, and do not accept communion with him or with those who are with him, not in this life nor after my death, just as (I accept) neither the Union nor Latin dogmas, which he and his adherents have accepted, and for the enforcement of which he has occupied this presiding place, with the aim of overturning the true dogmas of the Church. I am absolutely convinced that the farther I stand from him and those like him, the nearer I am to God and all the saints; and to the degree that I separate myself from them am I in union with the Truth and with the Holy Fathers, the Theologians of the Church; and I am likewise convinced that those who count themselves with them stand far away from the Truth and from the blessed Teachers of the Church. And for this reason I say: just as in the course of my whole life I was separated from them, so at the time of my departure, yea and after my death, I turn away from intercourse and communion with them and vow and command that none (of them) shall approach either my burial or my grave, and likewise anyone else from our side, with the aim of attempting to join and concelebrate in our Divine services; for this would be to mix what cannot be mixed. But it befits them to be absolutely separated from us until such time as God shall grant correction and peace to His Church.

THEN, TURNING TO THE DIGNITARY SCHOLARIOS, HE SAID: I speak now of the dignitary Scholarios, whom I knew from his early youth, to whom I am well-disposed, and for whom I have great love, as for my own son and friend... In my intercourse and conversation with him even to the present time, I have conceived a clear picture of his exceptional prudence and wisdom and power with words, and therefore I believe that he is the only one to be found at the present time who is able to extend a helping hand to the Orthodox Church, which is agitated by the attacks of those who would destroy the perfection of the dogmas, and likewise, with the help of God, to correct the Church and affirm Orthodoxy, if only he will not wish himself to retreat from the deed and hide his candlestick under a bushel. But I am thoroughly convinced that he will not act thus and, seeing the Church in distress from the waves and the Faith in dependence upon infirm man (I speak according to human standards), and knowing that it is possible for him to help her, he will not to such a degree disobey his conscience as not to hasten with all speed and readiness to enter the battle; for being wise, he is not at all unaware that the destruction of the Orthodox Faith would be the general perdition.

It is true that in the past, considering that the battle which was being conducted by others, especially by me, was sufficient, he did not reveal himself as an open champion of the Truth, being compelled, it may be, by counsels or by individuals. But I too at an earlier time carried nothing or quite little into the battle, having sufficiency neither of strength nor of zeal; and now I have already become nothing: and is there anything less than nothing? And so if then he likewise supposed that we ourselves could set something right, and he considered it superfluous for himself to do what others could do, as well as what, with his completely insignificant help, would be harmful to others, as he often explained to me, asking pardon — then at the present time, when I am departing from hence, I see no other equal to him who could take my place in the Church and the Faith and in the dogmas of Orthodoxy. Therefore, I consider him worthy, being called or rather compelled by the times, to reveal the spark of piety hidden in him and fight for the Church and sound doctrine; so that what I could not accomplish, he might set right, with the help of God. For by the grace of God he can do this, with the mind he has been given and his power of words, if he will only desire to use these at the propitious time.

And he is equally obliged in his relation to God and Faith and Church to fight faithfully and purely for the Faith. And I myself lay upon him this battle, so that he would be defender of the Church and leader of sound teaching and champion of right doctrines and the Truth in my place, having support in God and in the Truth itself, about which the very battle is being waged; so that being a participant in this with the

Holy Teachers and God.bearing Fathers, the great theologians, he would receive his reward from the Just Judge when He declares victorious all those who fought for Piety. But he himself must with all his strength exert zeal for the well-being of the right doctrines of the Church, as being obliged to give an answer for this on the Judgment Day to God and to me, who have entrusted this to him and have likewise reckoned upon bringing into the Good Land these words with over a hundredfold fruits to come from them. Let him answer me concerning this, so that departing the present life I might have perfect confidence, and that I might not die in sorrow, despairing over the correction of the Church.

THE REPLY OF LORD SCHOLARIOS: I, your Holy Eminence, first of all thank your great holiness for the praises which you have spoken of me; for, having desired to show me favor, you have testified of me such great things as I do not possess, and I am convinced that this is not even near to me. But this proceeds from the height of goodness and virtue and wisdom of your great holiness, in which I myself, seeing it from the beginning, have not ceased to delight even to the present time, as is indeed owing in relation to your great holiness, as a father and teacher and preceptor; and being directed, as by a rule, by your perfect understanding of the dogmas and the justness of the judgments which you have accepted and with which I am in accord, and likewise rejecting without doubt what is not in accord with your judgment, I have never refused to fulfill my duty as a son and disciple in relation to your great holiness. You, your great holiness, are yourself a witness to this. You know that I have always acted thus toward you, and revealing the deeper feelings of my convictions, I have given you these vows.

Concerning the fact that earlier I did not step out openly into the battle which your great holiness was waging, but kept silent, no one knows better the reason for this than your great holiness, for I often confided my arguments to you and sincerely opened my heart concerning this and begged forgiveness, and I was not deprived of it. But now, with God's help, I have come to despise this, and have made myself a sincere and open defender of the Truth, in order fearlessly to proclaim the dogmas of my Fathers and the perfection of Orthodoxy, in accordance with the view of your greatest holiness. I say this not because I see you already taken from hence, for we have not abandoned our last hopes, but we hope in God that you will recover from your infirmity and will be with us and will labor together in this. If, however, by the judgments known to God, you will depart from hence to that place of rest which you have prepared for yourself, and if by reason also of our unworthiness you will go there where you are worthy to dwell, — then, affirming absolutely, I say to you before God and the Holy Angels who now stand invisibly before us, and before the many and worthy men here present, that in everything I shall be in place of you and in place of your tongue, and of that with which you burned and which you handed down with love, I myself, both defending and offering to all, will betray absolutely nothing, but will fight for it to the end, at the risk of blood and death. And although my experience and strength are small, I am nonetheless convinced that your great holiness will fill in my insufficiency with the God-pleasing prayers characteristic of you, both now when you are here with us, and when you shall have departed.

LETTER OF SAINT MARK OF EPHESUS TO MONK THEOPHANES[393]

Most honorable and deeply beloved in the Lord, reverend father and brother among hieromonks,

Know that after we had returned to Constantinople, one of the Latin-minded who had signed came up to the patriarchate and gave us trouble, and so I left for my church. Yet finding no peace there, and falling seriously ill and being harmed and afflicted by the impious and attacked as lacking proper authorization, I left that place also, intending to head to the Holy Mountain. So, having crossed over to Callipolis and passing through Lemnos, I was detained and confined there by the emperor. Nevertheless, the Word of God and the power of truth are not bound; they rather run swiftly and succeed prosperously; and the majority of our brethren, taking heart at my exile, attacked with reproofs those wicked individuals and transgressors of the true faith and of the laws of the Fathers, and they drove them away

---

393 Saint Mark of Ephesus, "Confession of Faith: Letter of Lord Mark of Ephesus to Theophanes," in *Patrologia Graeca, Vol. 160*, trans. Jacques Paul Migne (1857-1866) & Gregory Heers (2023) (Paris: Imprimerie Catholique, 1857), 1095-1100.

from all sides as impure and rejected ones, not suffering to concelebrate with them, nor to commemorate them as Christians at all.

Now I learn that some young boy, an attendant of the bishop of Monembasia, has been ordained metropolitan of Athens by the Latin-minded, and that, living there, he concelebrates with the Latins indiscriminately and unlawfully ordains as many as he finds, of whatever sort they may be.

I therefore beseech your holiness to take up the zeal of God as a man of God and friend of the truth and trueborn disciple of Saint Isidore, and to encourage God's priests to avoid in every way any communion with him and neither concelebrate with him nor commemorate his name at all, and to consider him not a high priest but rather a wolf and a hireling, nor to celebrate in the Latin churches at all, so that the wrath of God that came upon Constantinople for the transgressions committed there may not also come upon you.

Know also that the false union, by God's grace and power, will be dissolved almost immediately, while the doctrine of the Latins, far from being confirmed by the false council, which was ever their striving, has been even more overturned and refuted and decried everywhere as blasphemous and impious, and those who confirmed it do not dare even open their mouths in its defense. So, the 'elder' of this your hireling, not shepherd, the mindless bishop of Monembasia, who received from the Emperor the abbey of the Forerunner, is not even commemorated by his own monks, nor is he censed as a Christian at all. Instead, they consider him only as someone responsible for material affairs, like some sort of governor. When the Emperor learned of this, he did not say a word, but even openly admitted to repenting for the things that were done and transferred the blame onto those who agreed and signed.

Therefore, you also, my brethren, flee from communion with the uncommunicate, and from commemorating those who should not be commemorated. Behold, I, the sinful Mark, tell you that anyone who commemorates the Pope as an Orthodox hierarch is bound to fulfill all the practices of the Latins, even up to the shaving of the beard, and the Latin-minded man will be judged along with the Latins and considered a transgressor of the Faith.

May your holy prayers be with us. To the blessed prince Constantine Contipetri, and to all other princes who received us as guests, may there be repentance and the blessing from God.

Mark, Bishop of Ephesus. June 16.

LETTER FROM LORD MARK OF EPHESUS TO LORD GEORGE SCHOLARIUS[394, 395]

Most distinguished, wisest, most learned, and dearly beloved brother and spiritual son, Sir George, I pray to God that you may be sound in soul and body and prosper in all things. By God's mercy, I am moderately well in body myself.

You had brought us so much pleasure and joy when you embraced the right belief, the pious and ancestral mindset, and undertook the defense of truth when it had been condemned by the unjust judges. Nevertheless, we are now filled with as much sorrow and sadness as we hear that you have once again moved to the other side and believe and speak the contrary, and have come together with the evil stewards to seek compromises and dispensations. Are these good things, worthy of a philosopher's spirit? And yet I was already planning to sing your praises and had in mind the great Gregory, the namesake of theology, who, when

---

394 Saint Mark of Ephesus, "Confession of Faith: Letter of Lord Mark of Ephesus to Lord George Scholarius," in Patrologia Graeca, Vol. 160. trans. Jacques Paul Migne (1857-1866) & Gregory Heers (2023) (Paris: Imprimerie Catholique, 1857), 1091-1096.

395 This letter of St. Mark of Ephesus was to the Lord George Scholarios, in fact, the future St. Gennadios Scholarios. In addition to the Orthodox clergy who would be present at this Council in Florence, the Emperor brought with him a number of laymen, one of which was George Scholarios. Even if they have not come down to us in their original form, Scholarios' speeches, as the Latins themselves avow, contained exhortations for peace to be founded not on any interested motives but on truth. Albeit, for a period of time during this false council Scholarios was under pressure from the Emperor to ensure the success of the council because of the political ramifications. It was during this time and for a brief period that Scholarios inclined towards the Latin way of thinking. However, Saint Mark of Ephesus, who was Scholarios' teacher, wrote this scathing letter to him in order to help the future saint correct course, after which Scholarios became one of the Church's most zealous defenders against the Latin heresies.

praising a certain philosopher Heron who was persisting in the error of the Arians, said, "His beautiful body having been torn to pieces by claws, he was sent out into exile." But you, having experienced no harm yourself, were dismayed, as it seems, only by threats, or easily persuaded by promises of gifts and honors, and have betrayed (so easily!) the truth once again. Who will give water to my head and a fountain of tears to my eyes, that I may mourn for the daughter of Sion, I mean the soul of the philosopher, which is being blown away and moved about like the chaff from a summer threshing floor? But you may say perhaps, "There has been no change to the contrary beliefs; rather, we are considering a sort of middle way and economy."

Never, my friend, have ecclesiastical matters been corrected through a middle way. There is no middle way between truth and falsehood. Just as one who goes out of the light necessarily becomes covered by darkness, so we could truly say that whoever deviates even slightly from the truth is subjected to falsehood. And though it is possible to speak of a middle ground between light and darkness, what is called grey dawn or twilight, no one can even conceive of a middle ground between truth and falsehood, as hard as he may try. Listen to how Gregory the great theologian extols a council that sought the middle ground: "That council ought to be called either Tower of Chalana [i.e. Babel], which beautifully divided the languages (would that such a division could take place in our case also, since the agreement is for evil), or assembly of Caiaphas, in which Christ was condemned, or some other such thing, since it has overturned and confused everything, destroying the pious and ancient doctrine and the equal honour of the Trinity, so as to set up camp and cast down by their engines of war the consubstantiality, opening the gates to impiety through the middleness of what they wrote; for they became wise in acting wickedly, but they knew not how to do good."

Cannot these things be applied to our council? Yes, and very much so, I would certainly say. Yet even though it may have wanted it very much, it could not use middleness and duplicity, as it was restrained by those who offered him payment. Therefore, as it pleased them, it vomited blasphemy, and indeed, to use the prophet's words, they have laid eggs of asps and woven the web of spiders; and truly, what they have skillfully crafted and called a definition is indeed the web of a spider. So, let us not be deceived again by those who once more resort to deceit and duplicity. They are the assembly of Caiaphas, as long as the union made by them casts its shadow over the Church.

How long, wretched one, will the nobility and honor of your soul be engrossed with empty things? How long will you dream? Be zealous for the truth, too, some time! Flee from Egypt without turning about, flee from Sodom and Gomorrah! Preserve yourself on the mountain, lest you be caught together with them. But you are captivated by a little empty glory, deceitful riches, adorned splendid garments, and the other things that constitute the happiness of this world. Alas for the unphilosophical mind of the philosopher! Look around you at those who have been tested before you with similar honors. Tomorrow, you too will descend into the underworld, leaving everything behind on the earth; and indeed, the most exact account of your deeds on earth will be demanded of you, just as the blood of lost souls will be demanded from the false council, the blood of those who were made to stumble in the mystery of the Faith, who accepted in their souls the intolerable and *unforgivable blasphemy, a blasphemy against the Holy Spirit, and dared to refer His existence to two origins*[396], those who engaged in the impious and absurd Latin customs, those who brought upon their own heads the curses and anathemas against the innovation of the Faith.

"But this union that came to pass will be for the protection and growth of our race." Indeed, very true! Do you not see the enemies of the Cross fleeing, with one of ours pursuing a thousand, and two putting ten thousand to flight? In fact, we see the very opposite. Except the Lord build our empire, in vain do they labor that build it. Except the

---

396 St. Mark of Ephesus is referring to the heretical trinitarian doctrine of the *filioque*. St. Mark is making abundantly clear to Scholarios that this innovative Latin doctrine is an unforgiveable blasphemy against the Holy Spirit which cannot be accepted within the doctrine of the Orthodox Church. This position of St. Mark stands staunchly against there being a difference of linguistics or any other misunderstanding as has recently been promulgated by the Assembly of Canonical Orthodox Bishops, 2003 Agreed Statement of the North American Orthodox-Catholic Theological Consultations' paper entitled "The Filioque: A Church Dividing Issue" which recommends in its document that Orthodox and Catholics refrain from labeling as heretical the traditions of the other side on the subject of the procession of the Holy Spirit."

Lord guard our city, in vain do they watch that guard her with the Pope's golden coins.

Therefore, come now and at this time, transform yourself completely. Leave the dead to bury their own dead. Leave to Caesar, what belongs to Caesar. Render to God the soul which He created and adorned. Consider how great a debtor you are to Him; repay His kindness. Yea, I beseech you, my dearest and most learned friend, make me rejoice in you; grant me to give glory to God. May He keep you safe from every grievous encounter.

Mark, the humble Metropolitan of Ephesus and all Asia.

11. St. Gennadios II Scholarios, Patriarch of Constantinople (+1473)[397]

UNION WITH LATINS CAUSES DIVISION FROM GOD AND ETERNAL DISGRACE[398]

If ye will be thus united with the Latins, ye will be both divided from God and submitted to unending disgrace.

12. St. Barlaam, Metropolitan of Moldavia (+1657)

HIS LIFE, WHICH IS CELEBRATED ON THE 30TH OF AUGUST[399]

"Varlaam was Metropolitan of Moldova and adviser of Ruler Vasile Lupu for decades. Varlaam was born in a family of free peasants from

---

397 See page 143 for an account of his life.

398 Protopresbyter Anastasios K. Gotsopoulos, *On Common Prayer with the Heterodox*, (Uncut Mountain Press, 2022), 17.

399 "Metropolitan Varlaam, great scholar, theologist, architect of Moldova's national Church," Moldpres, accessed November 17th, 2023, https://www.moldpres.md/en/news/2021/01/22/21000425

Bolotesti, Putna county, in 1580. From an early age, he showed a special interest in monasteries and spiritual life. As of the age of ten years, he was often a guest of the Neamt Monastery and then he took knowledge of the lifestyle of the hermits from the Secu Monastery, where he learned the Greek and Slav languages. He became a monk at Secu and in 1610 he became superior of the monastery for more than two decades. The purity of soul and his strength prompted the election of Varlaam as Metropolitan of Moldova in 1632– the first son of a peasant in this position....

"Less mentioned in history was the moment when Varlaam, through the international recognition of his achievements, was one of the three candidates to the Patriarchal See of Constantinople. Sources of the archives from the Constantinople Patriarchy confirm that Varlaam lost the Patriarchal See of Constantinople by just one vote.

"After Ruler Vasile Lupe had lost his throne, Varlaam retired to the Secu Monastery, where he died in 1667. He was buried near the wall of the Monastery's church. The Synod of the Romanian Orthodox Church put Varlaam forward for canonization, which was actually accomplished on 30 August 2007."

DEFENDED ORTHODOXY BY
TRANSLATING ORTHODOX CONFESSION OF FAITH[400]

Former abbot of the Monastery of Seku in Moldavia, Saint Barlaam (Moutsok) became Metropolitan of Moldavia. In order to refute the Confession of Faith by Patriarch Cyril Lukaris (1629) — that professed all the major doctrines of Calvinism — a synod was convened in Jassy in 1642, under the initiative of Basil Lupu, Voivode of Moldavia, and Metropolitan Barlaam.[401] In response to Lukaris, the Synod adopted the Or-

---

400 Hieromonk Makarios of Simonos Petra, *The Synaxarion: The Lives of the Saints of the Orthodox Church, Volume Six, July-August*, trans. Mother Maria Rule and Mother Joanna Burton (Ormylia: Holy Convent of the Annunciation of Our Lady, 2008), 673.

401 In 1629 in Geneva the document A Confession of Faith was published under the name of Patriarch Cyril Lukaris, who was well-known for his Orthodox stance against the Unia. As this document was written with Calvinistic leanings and the entire rest of the body of writings of the Patriarch staunchly defend Orthodox

thodox Confession of Faith of Peter Moghila, Metropolitan of Kiev (15 Dec.), that had been translated by Saint Barlaam, and largely cleansed of its Latin elements by the theologian Meletius Syrigos. In addition, the Jassy Synod, which had recently been convened to deal with Lukaris' Confession, took measures to limit the influence of local Protestant propaganda. Saint Barlaam, who had greatly contributed to the success of this assembly, dedicated the rest of his life to the defence of Orthodoxy in Moldavia (+1657).

13. St. Eugenios Aitolos (fl. 17th century)[402]

Westerners Act Contrary to the Tradition of the Church in Making Statues and Setting Them Up in Their Churches[403]

The Orthodox Church not only does not venerate statues, but does not even make them, for many reasons: (1) Why in the present definition of Hers does this Synod say that Icons are to be made from paints, from tesserae and from other appropriate material...? She did not mention making statues, but nonetheless this definition of Hers excludes statues. (2) Because neither the letters that the Patriarchs wrote to each other and to kings, nor the letters of Pope Gregory to Germanos nor of Pope Adrian to the present Synod, nor the pronouncements and lectures that the Bishops and monks delivered in all eight acts of the present Synod, make any mention whatsoever of statues.... But even the

---

teachings, the authorship of this work has been called in to question as an attempt of the Jesuits to discredit the Orthodoxy of Lukaris in order to jeopardize his anti-Latin stance in the eyes of the faithful. Patriarch Lukaris verbally denied authorship of the Confession but there is no written confirmation. See: Fr. Josiah Trenham, *Rock and Sand: An Orthodox Appraisal of the Protestant Reformers and Their Teachings* (Columbia: Newrome Press: 2018), 92-93.

402 See page 140 for an account of his life.

403 Constantine Cavarnos, *The Question of Union: A Forthright Discussion of the Possibility of Union of the Eastern Orthodox Church and Roman Catholicism*, trans. Hieromonk Patapios (Etna: Center for Traditionalist Orthodox Studies, 2006), 30.

synods that took place among the Iconoclasts... mention paintings and pictures, never statues, about which the Iconoclasts, had statues existed, would not have kept silent, but would have written against for the greater condemnation of the Orthodox.... Some say that for this reason the Church of Christ rejected statues, in order to avoid completely the similarity to idols. Idols were carved statues that were palpable on all sides.... Hence, from all that has been said, it is proved that the Westerners act contrary to the Tradition of the Church in making statues and setting them up in their churches.

THE POPE WISHES TO BE BOTH HIERARCH AND KING[404]

Power and authority are divided in two. One is worldly — God entrusted this to kings and rulers; the other is spiritual — God put this into the hands of the Hierarchs and stewards of souls. The one is contrary to the other: for the one is earthly, while the other is Heavenly. The one wears the sword and puts to death, while the other meekly forgives and bestows life.... The king is entrusted with bodies, the Priest with souls.... The former compels, the latter entreats. The former has perceptible weapons, the latter spiritual weapons. The same absurdity ensues if by chance a king should dare to set foot on the Holy Bema, or the Hierarch should dare to be king, and gird himself with a saber, as did the twin-horned giant of Rome — I mean the Pope —, who, besides being inwardly and spiritually a hierarch, wants to be outwardly and physically a king; he wants to bless and to put to death, to hold the pastoral staff and the murderous sword. A mixture of things unmixable and a grotesque monster!

The Eighty-third Apostolic Canon states "A Bishop, or Presbyter, or Deacon... who wishes to hold both things, Roman [i.e., civil] and Priestly office, let him be deposed. For the things of Caesar belong to Caesar, and those of God to God."

---

404 Constantine Cavarnos, *The Question of Union: A Forthright Discussion of the Possibility of Union of the Eastern Orthodox Church and Roman Catholicism*, trans. Hieromonk Patapios (Etna: Center for Traditionalist Orthodox Studies, 2006), 30.

14. St. Cosmas Aitolos, Equal-to-the-Apostles (+1779)

His life,
which is celebrated on the 24ᵀᴴ of August[405]

The Hieromartyr, Equal to the Apostles, enlightener to a nation en-slaved by the Turks, Cosmas was born in the village of Mega Dendron in Aitolia in 1714. He first studied in the Monastery of Panagia Segditsa in Parnassidos and in Lampotina Nafpaktia, after which he attended the fa-mous school Vrangianon Agrafon where he taught classes in philosophy, ancient Greek, theology, mathematics, medicine and other subjects. He then studied at the Athoniada School on the Holy Mountain of Athos, after which he went to Philotheou Monastery where he was tonsured a monk. While at Philotheou, he was burdened by the thought of his people who, under the Turks, were losing both the Greek language and the Orthodox faith and becoming vulnerable to the temptation to apos-tatize to Islam on other heresies. After much prayer, he sought a blessing from his elders to return to his people to preach, to strengthen them in the Orthodox faith and help preserve them from apostasy. After receiv-ing a blessing, he left Athos and went to the Patriarch of Constantinople who gave him written permission to preach throughout Greece. St. Cos-mas travelled far and wide, giving fiery sermons which attracted large gatherings. He made prayer ropes that he would distribute to encourage the faithful to pray the Jesus Prayer ceaselessly. Wherever he went, he established schools for the strengthening of the faithful and instructed priests to build large fonts to ensure all Orthodox are baptized in three full immersions. When he spoke out against the Jews for persecuting Christians and forcing them to work on Sundays, the angry Jews slan-dered him to the Turkish authorities and gave a large sum of money to Ahmet Kurt Pasha of Berat to put him to death. St. Cosmas foreknew his death and radiated with joy when arrested. He was hung from a tree

---

405 Monk Moses the Athonite, "Hieromartyr Kosmas the Aitolos (+1779),"
trans. John Sanidopoulos, accessed November 5th, 2023, https://www.
johnsanidopoulos.com/2014/08/hieromartyr-kosmas-aitolos-1779-1-of-2.html

and his holy relics were thrown into the Apsos River. His martyrdom took place on August 24, 1779. St. Cosmas left behind many edifying writings and prophecies concerning the Last Days.

DIVINE ECONOMY ALLOWED THE ORTHODOX TO FALL UNDER THE TURKS RATHER THAN THE LATINS[406]

Two Antichrists (the Pope & Mohammed): And by examining and searching the Scriptures and the holy Gospel, my brethren, we find that the prophet Elias has come and the antichrist has also come and killed the prophet Elias; and now we await neither prophet Elias nor antichrist. The antichrist is — the one is the Pope and the other is the one that's over our head, without me saying his name (Pseudo-Prophet Mohammed). You understand, but it grieves me to tell you this, because these antichrists are in perdition, as it is. We have continence; they, perdition. We fast; they overeat. We keep virginity; they, fornication: we, righteousness; they, unrighteousness.

And Bishop Augustine Kantiotes comments: "The Saint speaks thus concerning the Pope because he feared his plots against the Orthodox Church, and along with other eminent teachers of our race, he believed that it was by some divine economy that our race fell into the power of the Turks and not into the power of the western peoples, because the westerners, the Franks, having become masters, would have launched a furious attack on the Orthodox and would have forced them to recognise and bow down before the Pope, just as they succeeded in doing in some places during the years of the Venetocracy [Venetian occupation of many islands]. Viewed from this angle, the Pope is condemned as being antichrist, as seeking to impose his delusions through force and plots and to become the sole ruler of the entire Christian world."

---

406 Metropolitan Augustinos Kantiotes, *St. Kosmas of Aetolia* (Athens: Orthodox Missionary Brotherhood, 2014), 258-259.

PROPHECY ABOUT THE POPE[407]

A prophecy: "Curse the Pope, because he will be the cause." The cause of what? For the sake of context: This prophecy is found among many others, some which refer to the fulfillment of the longing (i.e. freedom), to a time of fantastic novelties ("You will see in the field a carriage without horses running faster than a hare," or "Out of the schools will come things that your mind cannot imagine"), but mostly of great difficulties, e.g. "Many will be dying of famine," "Many towns will be destroyed; three countries will become one," "So much will happen that the mothers will give birth prematurely out of their fear," or "A handful of gold for a handful of flour."

15. St. Paisius Velichkovsky (+1794)

HIS LIFE,
WHICH IS CELEBRATED ON THE 15TH OF NOVEMBER[408]

This great luminary, St. Paisius, was born in Poltava on December 21, 1722, of very pious parents, his father being a priest in the city cathedral. Being orphaned of his father, he was sent by his mother to study at the Moghila Academy in Kiev 1735. After four years of studies his soul did not find rest in the world but instead felt himself called to monastic asceticism.

After three years of spiritual asceticism in Moldavia, in 1746 and at the age of 24 years, he departed for the Holy Mountain. When he arrived on Mt. Athos, he traveled through all the monasteries and hermitages to find a skilled guide. Not finding a spiritual father according to his

---

407 Ibid., 314.

408 Saint Paisius Monastery, "St. Paisius (Velichkovsky): A Brief Summary of His Life, Compiled by the Sisters of St. Paisius Monastery," accessed November 1st, 2023, https://stpaisiusmonastery.org/about-the-monastery/life-of-st-paisius/a-brief-life/a-brief-life-english/. See also his life *Blessed Paisius Velichkovsky: The Man Behind the Philokalia*, translated by Fr. Seraphim Rose from St. Herman of Alaska Press.

desire, he retired to the desert, where he labored in asceticism alone for four years, in much want and toil, in prayer and the reading of the Holy Fathers, and in tears and vigil day and night.

In 1750 Elder Basil visited Athos and tonsured the desert-dweller a monk, giving him the name of Paisius, and afterwards Paisius was ordained to the priesthood. The renown and love which Paisius enjoyed was so great that monks came to him from all over the Holy Mountain. The blessed abbot himself labored during the day making spoons, and at night in reading and transcribing the books of the Holy Fathers, sacrificing only three hours to sleep.

St. Paisius keenly perceived that spiritual life must be grounded in the study of the patristic ascetic texts. He therefore began his life-long labors of translating these precious texts, an enterprise inexpressibly difficult.

In the summer of 1763, due to the ever-increasing number of brothers and the material difficulties of their life on Mt. Athos, Abbot Paisius came to Moldavia with sixty-four disciples and was given Dragomirna Monastery. There he lived for twelve years, gathering a community of 350 monks. Here he organized a veritable school of monks to correct, translate and duplicate the patristic and ascetic texts. Already at Dragomirna there was achieved a Romanian Philokalia: a voluminous collection of texts, whose main theme was the Jesus Prayer. Thus, the first Philokalia in a vernacular language was born.

In the autumn of 1775 Elder Paisius went to Secu Monastery, accompanied by two hundred monks; and in the summer of 1779 he moved for the last time to the great lavra of Moldavia, Neamts Monastery, where he lived for fifteen years, the most fruitful years of his life. There he translated numerous works of the Holy Fathers.

On Wednesday, November 15, 1794, at the age of seventy-two, this great beacon, Elder of elders, St. Paisius Velichkovsky, passed to eternal rest, leaving behind him over one-thousand monks: Romanians, Russians, Serbs, Bulgarians, and Greeks. As has been said of him, he was truly a rekindler of the light of eldership, a replenisher of the common life and a bridge to the Holy Fathers.

After St. Paisius' repose, many of his Russian disciples went back to Russia, bringing with them and disseminating, very vigorously, this Paisian transmission. These were holy men, strikingly reminiscent of the ancient desert ascetics, and they were the chief cause of the 19th-century flowering of sanctity in Russia.

In Romania, Elder Paisius' relics continued to work miracles. Here, his legacy flourished in the forests and mountains of Moldavia, which were filled with anchorites of Paisian inspiration. Hundreds of hesychastic ascetics, likewise at times attaining the sanctity of the great desert saints of ancient times, were nurtured under the grace-filled influence of elder Paisius.

To a Uniate Priest, on the Procession of the Holy Spirit: A certain Uniate priest by the name of John came to doubt the truth of his confession and appealed to Elder Paisius with the entreaty that he clear up his perplexity. The main part of the Elder's reply is given here:

"The Holy Spirit Himself, who proceeds from the Father and reposes in the Son, has inspired you by His grace to appeal with this question to a humble and sinful, but Orthodox, son of the Eastern Church [...] The first and most important error of the *Uniates* is the teaching, which they have taken from the Romans, that the Holy Spirit proceeds from the Father and from the Son [*Filioque*]. This is the first and most important of all the heresies, for it includes in itself an incorrect judgment, contrary to the Sacred Scripture, about God, who is One in the Holy Trinity. He who confesses that the Holy Spirit proceeds from the Father and from the Son supposes in God two principles: one of the Father, another of the Son. But we Orthodox confess in the Trinity one principle of the Father, as our Lord Jesus Christ Himself taught us in the holy Gospel, when He said that the Holy Spirit proceeds from the Father alone. He said: When the Comforter is come, Whom I will send unto you from the Father, the Spirit of truth, Who proceedeth from the Father (John 15:26). And the Apostle says: *Every good gift and every perfect gift is from above, coming from the Father of lights* (James 1:17). Do you see? He says "the Father of lights"; that is, the Father is the root and fount of Divinity; and the two lights, the Son and the Spirit from the single light, the Father, have their pre-eternal being, the Son in being begotten and the Holy Spirit in procession.

The Divine Prophet David says: *By the word of the Lord were the heavens established, and all the might of them by the Spirit of His mouth* (Psalm 32:6). Do you see? He called the Father Lord, but he calls the Son Word, as pre-eternally begotten of Him; and he calls the Holy Spirit the Spirit of His (and not "Their") lips, as proceeding from the Father alone. One could search out many other testimonies also from the Old and New Testaments, which show more clearly than the sun that the Holy Spirit proceeds from the Father alone and reposes in the Son, as was disclosed also in the Baptism of the Lord.

Further, all the holy ecumenical teachers who have interpreted the Scripture as if with one mouth say that the Holy Spirit proceeds from the Father, and nowhere have they written that He proceeds from the Son also. Thus, if the Uniates think exactly like the Romans in such a serious heresy, what hope do they have for salvation, unless they openly renounce this Spirit-fighting heresy and become united again with the Holy Orthodox Eastern Church?

Spare neither property nor relatives if they do not wish to listen to you, but by all means save your own soul from perdition; because there is nothing more needful for you than the soul for which Christ died. But in fleeing, it is better for you to remain in poverty than to blaspheme the Holy Spirit as the Romans blaspheme Him. Depart and flee from the Unia as speedily as possible, lest death overtake you in it and you be numbered among the heretics and not among the Christians. And not only go away yourself, but advise others to go away also, if in your conscience you know that they will hear you. And if they will not hear you, then at least depart yourself from the nets of the enemy and be united in soul and heart with the Holy Orthodox Church, and thus, together with all [the faithful] holding the inviolate faith and fulfilling the commandments of Christ, you will be able to be saved."[409]

---

409 Orthodox Christian Books & Icons, "The Life and Ascetic Labors of Elder Paisius Velichkovsky Part Fifteen: The Letters of Elder Paisius from Niamets," *Orthodox Word 11*, no. 5 (September-October 1975): 202-203, 210.

PERSECUTION BY THE UNIATES AND PAISIUS GOES TO KIEV[410]

While he was laboring thus in the monastery in peace and quiet, by God's permission a persecution was raised in the Ukraine against the Orthodox faith by the evil-opinioned Uniates, who strove to convert the Orthodox Christians to their impiety. Some of the terrors of the Uniate rule in the Ukraine at this time are described by Archbishop Philaret of Chernigov in his Church History: "It is difficult to imagine all the cruelties to which the Orthodox were subjected at that time, Orthodox priests were tied to pillars, beaten with whips, placed in prison, tortured with hunger, their fingers were cut off with swords, their arms and legs broken. Whoever then remained alive but did not desire the Unia was chased out of his house. Attacks were made on monasteries in broad daylight, they were pillaged and burned, the monks were tortured and often killed. The residents of villages and small towns were tortured with inhuman tortures in order to make them Uniates. The Orthodox people were chased like sheep into the Latin and Uniat[e] churches. During the very reading of the Gospel in an Orthodox church, an official would enter, beat the people with a whip and chase them like cattle from their stalls. Many suffered the destruction of their homes, terrible beatings, and some death.

Because of the Uniate persecution there was great disturbance and anger in the monastery, and when the fathers who were living there saw that the Uniates kept the church locked and sealed for more than a month, some of them began to leave, each going wherever he wished. Paisius went with some of the brethren who were going to Kiev, inasmuch as for fear of the Poles it was impossible for them to go to Moldavia. This was clearly by God's Providence, so that His faithful servant would find out about his mother. Coming into Kiev, he was accepted into the Kiev Caves Lavra and assigned to the printshop under the reverend Hieromonk Macarius, in order to learn how to make engravings. And while the Blessed one was staying in the Lavra, there came from Poltava to Kiev to venerate the holy places his relative, the wife of his

---

410 Schema-monk Metrophanes, *Blessed Paisius Velichkovsky: The Man Behind the Philokalia* (Platina: St. Herman of Alaska Brotherhood, 1994), 38-39.

deceased brother the Archpriest John, and meeting him she began to tell him concerning his mother.

SAINT PAISIUS RECALLS THE STORY OF THE MARTYRDOM OF AN ORTHODOX CHRISTIAN BY THE HANDS OF A PAPIST[411]

Leaving that little hermitage, we made our way with great difficulty to the high ground where there was a great level plain, and the air there was quite salubrious. Forthwith I began to feel my illness abating, and little by little I grew stronger in body and could walk with greater ease and comfort. With all my soul I rendered thanks for God's goodness, which had not forsaken me utterly. But as the monks and I made our way, beginning at noon the sky grew dimmer and dimmer with very dark and gloomy clouds, and seeing this the others hurried greatly on their way in order to escape the rain. Since I was unable to go so quickly with them, however, I was left alone, and soon a great cloud came over-head with the frightful noise of hail, and a great rain poured down with frightful lightning and thunder. Hail the size of small nuts fell and cov-ered the field to a depth of nearly four inches, and I was so completely soaked that water dripped from my clothes. With great difficulty I made my way through the hail, and it was very late in the night when I reached the village where my companions were. Having spent the night in the house of a certain man, I found them in the morning in a school, where a certain cantor had given them lodging; and seeing me they rejoiced greatly. Then they began enquiring of the cantor which road led to Mol-davia, telling him that it was their intention to go thither. But he began telling them, "O holy fathers, I advise you not to go there at this time, for there is great fear on the road. Soldiers are on patrol everywhere on account of the fear of brigands, and I fear lest you fall into the hands of these merciless soldiers who, if for no other reason, simply because of their hatred of the Orthodox faith, may do you the utmost harm.[412] For

---

411 St. Paisius (Velichkovsky), "A Young Orthodox Martyr," in *The Life of Paisij Velyčkovs'kj*, trans. J.M.E. Featherstone (Cambridge: Harvard University Press, 1989), 39-41.

412 The cantor is referring to soldiers of the [Papist] Polish-Lithuanian Commonwealth.

not long ago in this our village the following happened. There was in this Church before me a cantor of blessed memory who feared denunciation by the persecutors of the Orthodox faith, and when during the liturgy he read the Creed, that is, 'I believe in one God,' and came to the part, 'And in the Holy Ghost,' he would read it thus: 'the Lord, the Giver of life, which proceedeth from the Father *true*.'[413] Reading the Creed in this manner, he escaped denunciation by the enemies of the Orthodox faith. But in time he was denounced to the administrator of the village by the blasphemers of the holy faith for not reading the Creed in accordance with their blasphemy: not 'the Holy Ghost which proceedeth from the Father and the Son,' but only, 'from the Father true.'

Hearing this the administrator was greatly enraged, and taking several soldiers he came with them to the church a little before the reading of the Creed. When that blessed cantor began to read the Creed, forthwith the other drew near him to listen diligently to his reading of it. The cantor understood why the other had drawn near, and he read loudly and slowly, with boldness. When he got to the words, 'And in the Holy Ghost,' he was filled with the Holy Ghost and pronounced loudly, 'And in the Holy Ghost, the Lord, the Giver of life, which proceedeth from the Father,' omitting the addition of the word true, which he had included out of fear. Hearing this the administrator forthwith shouted like a wild beast and set upon him; and seizing him by the hair he threw him upon the ground and kicked him mercilessly with his feet. He ordered him to be dragged from the church and to be beaten mercilessly with rods. Whilst this was being done, someone went quickly to call his mother, telling her also the reason why her son was being beaten. She ran to him with tears and exhorted him not to lose heart in his struggle: calling upon God for help, he ought not shrink from giving his life over to death for the Orthodox faith.

Kissing his head, she said to him, 'O dearly beloved son of mine, be not afraid of this brief torment which you suffer for your confession of the Orthodox faith: persevere as a valiant soldier of Christ for His sake even unto death, that you may be deemed worthy by Him of a martyr's crown in His heavenly Kingdom.' Said he to his mother, 'O dearly beloved mother of mine, have no doubt about me, for I am ready, God

---

413 I.e., *istina* ("true," masc. sing. gen.), which sounds very much like *i syna* (= *filioque*).

strengthening me, to suffer not only this beating, but ten thousand of the most cruel deaths for the Orthodox faith. Even as God, glorified and worshipped in the holy Trinity, is one, and there is no God but Him, so the holy faith of the holy Eastern church, in which alone is certain hope of salvation through good deeds, is one, and there is no other but it. How, therefore, can I not fervently desire to suffer the most cruel of deaths for its sake?' Hearing this his mother rejoiced with inexpressible joy and, raising her hands to heaven, thanked Christ God that she had been deemed worthy to give birth to such a sufferer for His sake. When that tormentor saw and heard this, he became yet more wroth, and shouted to the soldiers to beat him more harshly. The sufferer for Christ's sake endured this cruel beating with joy and thus refuting the impiety of the Westerners and glorifying the Orthodox faith by his confession of it, he committed his soul into the hands of God."

16. St. Nikodemos of the Holy Mountain (+1809)

HIS LIFE

WHICH IS CELEBRATED ON THE 14TH OF JULY[414]

St. Nikodemos was born in 1749 on the Greek island of Naxos to pious and devout parents. From a young age he gave himself over to reading and was blessed by God with an extraordinary memory whereby he could quickly and easily recall and quote anything he had read. While in Naxos, he met several Athonite fathers who had left the Holy Mountain during the Kollyvades controversy, the conflict over whether memorial prayers for the departed were permitted to be performed on Sundays. Through this encounter was kindled in St. Nikodemos a desire for monasticism and for the defense and proclamation of the Orthodox faith among those struggling under the Turkish occupation. St. Nikodemos was introduced to St. Macarios the Metropolitan of Corinth who was

---

414 Hieromonk Makarios of Simonos Petra, "St. Nicodemus of the Holy Mountain – Bright Star of the Church," adapted by Sretensky Monastery Press, trans. Maria Stepanova, accessed November 5th, 2023, https://orthochristian.com/155098.html

of one mind with him and in 1775 he set out for the Holy Mountain. It was there that St. Macarios entrusted him with editing the *Philokalia*. St. Nikodemos immersed himself in the practice of the Jesus Prayer and lived hesychastically while working on compiling and producing many important patristic texts including *The Evergetinos, Concerning Frequent Communion, and Exomologetarion (A Manual of Confession)*. While on Athos, Hieromonk Agapius of Peloponnese recruited St. Nikodemos to revise and translate his collection of Church canons and rules and to provide detailed commentaries based on the writings of the Holy Fathers. This resulted in the publication of the *Rudder* or *Pedalion*, which remains to this day the most authoritative and comprehensive collection and patristic commentary on the Holy Canons of the Church. The *Rudder* was endorsed by the Patriarch of Constantinople and instructed to be distributed throughout the Orthodox world. The saint produced an abundance of texts for the edification of the Orthodox faithful and was seen as a sure and reliable guide who embodied and clearly conveyed Orthodox patristic teaching on a multitude of topics. He reposed on July 14, 1809.

ON THE SO-CALLED BAPTISM OF THE HERETICAL LATINS[415]

So, following what has been said, since the form of the Apostolical Canon demands it, we declare that the baptism of the Latins is one which falsely is called baptism, and for this reason it is not acceptable or recognizable either on grounds of exactitude or on grounds of economy. It is not acceptable on grounds of exactitude: (1st) because they are heretics. That the Latins are heretics there is no need of our producing any proof for the present. The very fact that we have entertained so much hatred and aversion against them for so many centuries is a plain proof that we loathe them as heretics, in the same way, that is to say, as we do Arians, or Sabellians, or Spirit denying and Spirit-defying Macedoniacs.

---

415 Saint Nikodemos, Hieromonk Agapios, *The Rudder (Pedalion): Of the Metaphorical Ship of the One Holy, Catholic, and Apostolic Church of Orthodox Christians*, trans. D. Cummings (Athens: Kesisoglou the Caesarian, 1908), 72.

The Latin Heretics[416]

Enough was said concerning them by St. Mark of Ephesus in Florence (at the twenty-fifth general assembly), who spoke frankly as follows: "We have split ourselves off from the Latins for no other reason than the fact that they are not only schismatics but also heretics." Wherefore we must not even think of uniting with them.

Since the Latins Are Heretics, Therefore They Are Unbaptized[417]

Even the great ecclesiarch Silvester (Section 9, Chapter 5) said: 'The difference of the Latins is a heresy, and our predecessors also held it to be such.' So, it being admitted that the Latins are heretics of long standing, it is evident in the very first place from this fact that they are unbaptized, in accordance with the assertions of St. Basil the Great above cited, and of the saints preceding him named Cyprian and Firmilian.

Latins Are Unbaptized As They Do Not Observe the Three Immersions[418]

Because, having become laymen as a result of their having been cut off from the Orthodox Church, they no longer have with them the grace of the Holy Spirit with which Orthodox priests perform the mysteries. This is one argument that is as strong and indisputable as the Canons of St. Basil the Great are strong and indisputable, and the words of St. Cyprian the ecclesiastic martyr, seeing that they have received and retain the sanction of the holy Sixth Ecumenical Council. (2nd). The Latins are unbaptized because they do not observe the three immersions which have to be administered to the one being baptized, as the Orthodox Church has received instructions from the Holy Apostles from the beginning.

---

416 Ibid., 72.

417 Ibid., 72.

418 Ibid., 72-73.

BAPTIZING IN THE NAME OF THE HOLY TRINITY INEFFECTIVE WHEN DONE BY HERETICS[419]

The earlier Latins, being the first to innovate with regard to the Apostolical Baptism, began using affusion, which means the process of pouring a little water on the head of the child, a practice which is in vogue in some regions; but the most of them take a bundle of hog hairs and sprinkle a few drops of water three times on the infant's forehead. In other parts of the earth, however, as we have been informed by one who has returned thence, they merely take a little cotton (everyone knows how much water cotton absorbs), and, dipping it into water, they wipe the child with it and call it baptized. So, the Latins are unbaptized because they do not perform the three immersions and emersions, in accordance with the Apostolic tradition. As touching these three immersions, we do not say how necessary and indispensable they are to the celebration of Baptism. Whoever wishes may read about it, but as for any need there may be, let him read the manual of the highly educated and most learned Eustratius of Argent. But we too shall say in connection with Apostolic Canon L whatever is now needed on this head. If, however, anyone among the Latins or the Latin-minded [Orthodox] should put forward a claim to the three invocations of the Holy Trinity, he must not pretend to have forgotten those things which he was told further above by divine Firmilian and by Athanasios the Great: to wit, that those supergodly names are quite clearly ineffective when pronounced by the mouth of heretics. For, unless this be the case, we must most certainly believe that wicked old women actually do miracles by simply repeating the divine names in incantations.

LATINS CANNOT PERFORM BAPTISM AS THEY ARE HERETICS[420]

So, the Latins, because they are heretics, cannot perform a baptism, having lost the perfective grace, adding to their iniquities the overthrow of the Apostolic Baptism of three immersions. And so, I say, let those

---

419 Ibid., 73.
420 Ibid., 312.

who accept the Latins' sprinkling reflect on what have they to say in a reply to the authority of the present Apostolic Canon, and further in reply to the following Canon XLVII. I know what the immediate defenders of the Latin pseudo-baptism argue. They argue that our Church became accustomed to accepting converts from the Latins with chrism, and there is, in fact, some formulation to be found in which the terms are specified under which we do allow them in.

LATINS ARE CHRISMATED BUT THEY OUGHT TO BE BAPTIZED[421]

With regard to all this we reply in simple and just words, that it is enough that you admit that she used to receive them in chrism (alone). So, they are heretics. For why the chrism if they were not heretics? So, they being admittedly heretics, it is not probable that the Orthodox and Apostolic Church would deliberately disregard these Apostolical Canons and the Synodical Canons which we have noted in the preceding pages. But, as it seems and as it is proper for us to believe, the Church wished to employ some great economy with respect to the Latins, having as an example conducive to her purpose that great and holy Second Ecumenical Council. For the fact is that the Second Council, as we have said, employed economy and accepted the baptism of Arians and of Macedoniacs with the aim and hope of their returning to the faith and receiving full understanding of it, and also in order to prevent their becoming yet more savage wild beasts against the Church, since they were also a very great multitude and strong in respect of outward things. And, as a matter of fact, they accomplished this purpose and realized this hope.

For, thanks to this economy those men became more gentle towards the Orthodox Christians and returned so far to piety that within the space of a few years they either disappeared completely or very few of them remained. So those preceding us also employed economy and accepted the baptism of the Latins, especially when performed in the second manner, because Papism, or Popery, was then in its prime and had all the forces and powers of the kings of Europe in its hands, while on the other hand, our own kingdom was breathing its last gasps. Hence it

---

421 Ibid., 73-74.

would have become necessary, if that economy had not been employed, for the Pope to rouse the Latin races against the Eastern, take them prisoners, kill them, and inflict innumerable barbarities upon them. But now that they are no longer able to inflict such woes upon us, as a result of the fact that divine Providence has lent us such a guardian that he has at last beaten down their brow, now I say, that the fury of Papism (otherwise known as Roman Catholicism, or Popery) is of no avail against us, what need is there any longer of economy? For there is a limit to economy, and it is not perpetual and indefinite.

That is why Theophylactus of Bulgaria says: "He who does anything as a matter of economy, does it, not as simply something good, but as something needed for the time being" (commentary on Gal. 5:11). "We have employed economy enough," says St. Gregory the Theologian in his eulogy of Athanasius, "without either adopting what is alien or corrupting what is our own which if we were to do, makes us really bad economists (or poor managers of economy)." That is what I say too. It is certainly bad economy when it does not serve to convert the Latins and forces us to transgress the strictness of the holy Canons and to accept the pseudo-baptism of heretics. "For economy is to be employed where there is no necessity of transgressing the laws," says divine Chrysostom.

The fact that the configuration was made economically is plainly evident from this that until then the Easterners had been baptizing the returning Westerners, as is attested by the regional synod in the Lateran of Rome, held in the year 1211 after Christ. For it says in its fourth canon that the Easterners would not hold services wherever Westerners had been holding services unless they first purified the place by the ceremony of sanctification. And afterwards it says that the Easterners themselves re-baptized [meaning "baptized"] those joining the Eastern Church on the ground that they had not had a holy Apostolic baptism. (See Dositheus, pages 8-24 of the Dodecabiblus). So when it is taken into account that up to that time, according to the testimonies of the same enemies, the Easterners had been baptizing them, it is plain that it was for the sake of a great economy that they later employed the expedient of chrism simply because our race could not afford, in the plight in which it then was in, to excite further the mania of Popery; and in addition there is such evidence in the fact that they then abrogated and invalidated all that had been wrongly done in Florence, and there was great excitement [rage] among the Latins on this account. Now the need of economy having passed away, rigorism and the Apostolical Canons must have their place.

CONCERNING AN "EMERGENCY BAPTISM" BY A LATIN PRIEST[422]

Those that have been baptized without there being any emergency by an unholy layman [referring to a Latin Priest] pretending to be a priest, are not to be commemorated after they die, for it is asserted that they are un-baptized. Note moreover that we do not say that we re-baptize the Latins, but that we baptize them. For their baptism belies its name, and is not in any way a baptism, but merely a light sprinkle.

AGAINST THE SO-CALLED BAPTISM OF THE HERETICAL LATINS[423]

St. John Damascene: "The three immersions of Baptism serve to represent the three days that the Lord was buried." But why should I be citing the old Fathers of ours in testimony with a view to showing the necessity of the immersions in Baptism? Let anyone who desires read the wise man and theologian of the Latins named Corderius, and he will see, in his discourse concerning Baptism how he refutes the wicked opinion of Thomas Aquinas (the Latin theologist of the thirteenth century) who holds that it is a matter of indifference whether baptism is performed with three immersions or not, and how he decides to have the three immersions and emersions duly observed in accordance with the ordinance of Baptism of our Eastern Church

In the Dictionary of Franciscus of Pivat, it is written that St. Otto baptized with three immersions. Fearing, he says, lest the Latins disregard the Apostolic ordinances applying to Baptism and subject them to insult, he ordered baptismal fonts to be constructed of marble and to be fixed to the churches, and to project from the ground up to knee high, in order that infants being baptized in them might have room enough to

---

422 Ibid., 76.
423 Ibid., 83-84.

be totally immersed. Hence it is that in the church of St. Mark in Venice such a baptismal font has been in existence down to this day, to the disgrace of the Papists. Yet the fact is that even Pope Pelagius agreed in asserting that three immersions are necessarily needed for holy Baptism. From all that has been said here, then what conclusion follows?

That three immersions and emersions are necessary in Baptism to symbolize the three days' and nights' death and burial, and Resurrection of the Savior, wherein salvation, emission and reconciliation are given by God to all mankind. It is therefore logical to conclude that the Latin sprinkling, being destitute of immersions and emersions, is consequently destitute also of the form, or type, of the three days' death, and burial, and resurrection of the Lord. From these facts it's plainly evident that it is also destitute and admittedly void of all grace and sanctification and remission of sins.

If the Latins nevertheless insist that their sprinkling is able to afford sanctification and grace through invocations of the Holy Trinity, let them learn that Baptism is not consummated by invocations of the Holy Trinity alone, but that the ceremonial form of the Lord's death and burial and resurrection is also requisite. Since a belief in the Trinity alone cannot save the one being baptized, but a belief in the death of the Messiah is also necessary, thus it is by means of both that he is placed within reach of salvation and bliss. For "with three immersions" (for it is well to repeat St. Basil's statement), "and an equal number of invocations the mystery is completed, that form of death may be symbolized and we who are being baptized may be illuminated in our souls by having theognosy [i.e., knowledge of God] conferred upon us."

Please note, however, that just as we assert that the baptism offered by the Latins is heretical and unacceptable, on account of the reasons stated here, we Orthodox Christians must also be careful in regard concerning our own baptism and see that it is not performed in basins and troughs in which only a small part of the legs of the infants being baptized is actually dipped under the surface of the water. And I leave out of account the fact that on numerous occasions those troughs tip over and the holy water is spilled. Hence, when we criticize the Latins for setting aside the Apostolic Baptism, then we, on the contrary, must see that we keep ours safe and irreproachable. Accordingly, as concerning this and with regard to all the other things, the cares and obligations devolve upon the pastors of the souls. We are only so far doing what we can to point out the goal of the work and cry out so as to give notice of it; let them look after their part, as they shall have to give an account of themselves. We add further this observation, that perhaps, in agreement with what great Gregory of Thessalonica says, the Lord, after first disclosing to us his descent into and ascent out of Hades through the process of baptizing believers in accordance with His directions, actually delivered this process to us as a means toward salvation (Sermon 2, concerning Baptism).

Since the Orthodox Baptism is not only a ceremonial form of only the burial of the Lord's body, as the Apostle and the other Fathers have said, but also of the descent of His soul into Hades, as St. Basil and St. Chrysostom asserted in the foregoing, in order that through the ceremonial form of Christ's burial, on the one hand — according to Gregory himself again — the body of the one being baptized may be theurgically affected while, on the other hand, through the ceremonial form of the descent into Hades his soul may be deified; it appears that just as seeds and plants unless sown deeply into the ground and not left on the surface, cannot sprout and bear fruit, but will either wither or are trodden underfoot or are picked up and eaten by birds, so and in like manner the unfortunate Latins, since they are not "planted together," as the Apostle says, that is to say, they are not planted together with Christ like plants in the process of Baptism. That is what is meant by the expression "planted together" according to St. Basil who says: "Having been buried with Christ, we are incapable of being corrupted as a result of deadness, but, instead, we are merely simulating burial precisely like a planting of seeds."

And again: "Having been planted in the likeness of death, we shall also rise up together in all events. For such is the result which is bound to follow as a consequence of the planting" (Sermon 1, concerning Baptism, p. 656 of Vol. II). This is corroborated also by the fact that by means of the plant and seed of wheat the Lord alluded to Himself, and to His burial by means of the illustration of planting wheat, when He said, "If a grain of wheat fall into the ground and die,' (John 12:24), 'it brings forth much fruit." Thus, I say that inasmuch as the Latins are not planted together with the double-natured grain of Christ in the water of Baptism, neither their body nor their soul is theurgically affected, to put the matter more plainly, they simply cannot sprout salvation, but inevitably wither and go to destruction.

LATIN PAPISTS ARE ENTIRELY DEVOID OF DIVINE GRACE IN THEIR SO-CALLED MYSTERIES[424]

That is why Balsamon [...] says that if any heretical priest or deacon is baptized (or anointed with chrism), his former priesthood is to be considered as a depravity and as not being real. But if thereafter he is found worthy, he may become both a priest and a prelate. Hence it follows as a matter of logical inference that since, according to the present Apostolical Canon, heretics have no Holy Orders, whatever ministrations they may perform are banalities and devoid of grace and sanctity. Consequently, it also follows in keeping herewith that the unleavened wafers and the sacraments of Latin heretics are also banalities and not holy in accordance with Apostolic Canon XLVI. This is perfectly true in spite of the fact that Demetrios Chomateinos [...] and John of Kitros [...] said that we were making no mistake if we deemed the sacraments of the Latins holy.

For they said this out of regard for the fact that they were then accepting Latins as duly baptized, since the latter had not yet set aside the law requiring three immersions and three emersions in baptism. Note also that these same writers who said these things added nevertheless that we ought not to allow any Orthodox Christian to receive communion from the Latins. It is with this tenor that we also ought to understand also that which Bryennius wrote concerning them in his letter to Nicetas: "Moreover, even five hundred years ago and earlier the Easterners regarded the rites of the Westerners as common." That explains why wherever the Latins had held any church services, the Easterners first went through the ceremony of sanctification for the purpose of purifying the premises, and afterwards held services. See also the Canon of the Council held in Laodicea in the footnote to Apostolic Canon XLVI.

---

424 Ibid., 121.

CONCERNING THE JEWISH AZYMES OF THE LATIN HERETICS[425]

This shows how blameworthy and reprehensible the Latins are being guilty of introducing innovations into the mystery of the divine Eucharist and of celebrating it with Jewish unleavened wafers. The fact that unleavened wafers are an innovation is patent. For from the time of Christ down to the year 1053 the Church of the Westerners was conducting mass with leavened bread; for it was during that year that [Pope] Leo IX became the first inventor of the use unleavened wafers in connection therewith. The contention of the Latins that the Lord celebrated the Mystical Supper with unleavened bread has been proved to be utterly false, first of all because of the fact that leavened bread has been found which was the very bread that the Lord handed to his disciples. For Nicholas of Hydrous in his argument against unleavened wafers says that when the Franks (i.e. the Western Europeans) captured Constantinople, they found in the imperial storeroom pieces of the precious Wood, the crown of thorns, and the sandals of the Savior, along with one nail; but they also found in one of the vessels stored there and ornamented with gold and gems and pearls, a loaf of bread of which the Lord had given pieces to the Apostles.

REJECT THE LATIN HERESIES BUT DO NOT ABHOR WHAT LITTLE ORTHODOXY THEY HAVE RETAINED[426]

We must hate and abhor the erroneous beliefs and illicit customs of the Latins and other heretics. However, should we find anything in them which they have understood correctly, and which accords with the canons of the Holy Councils, then we ought not hate and abhor this.

---

425 Ibid., 128-129.

426 St. Nikodemus the Hagiorite, Ἑορτοδρόμιον, ἤτοι Ἑρμηνεία εἰς τοὺς ᾀσματικοὺς κανόνας τῶν Δεσποτικῶν καὶ Θεομητορικῶν ἑορτῶν [Heortodromion: Interpretation of the Canons of the Feasts of our Lord and of our Lady], (Venice: Nicholas Glykys, 1836), 584 [In Greek]. Quoted in Protopresbyter Theodore Zisis, Following the Holy Fathers: Timeless Guides of Authentic Christianity (Columbia: Newrome Press, 2017), 271.

17. St. Athanasios of Paros (+1813)

His life,
which is celebrated on the 24th of June[427]

St. Athanasios was born in 1722 in the village of Kostos in Paros to pious parents. In 1745 he went to Smyrna and enrolled there in the famous "Evangelical School" where he became distinguished for his mastery of foreign languages, his intelligence and purity of life. In 1752, he went to the Holy Mountain and enrolled in the Athoniada Academy for further study. Athanasios' reputation spread far and wide and he eventually became the director of the Athoniada Academy. While on the Holy Mountain the Anti-Kollyvades movement began, and as a defender of the Orthodox teaching that memorial prayers for the departed should be performed on Saturdays and not Sundays, he was pressured to leave the Holy Mountain. When the Russo-Turkish War erupted, he traveled to Chios where he established a university and wrote many volumes of books for the enlightenment of the Orthodox faithful who were struggling under Turkish occupation. St. Athanasios is remembered for his holy life, as one of the greatest defenders of the faith in the 18th-19th centuries, a great light among the Kollyvades Fathers, and a bright luminary for the faithful. He reposed on June 24, 1813.

We Speak Against the Filioque, a Pernicious Heresy, so the Orthodox Will Not be Led Astray[428]

So the heresy of the *Pneumatomachi*[429] blasphemed against the Holy Spirit with respect to what He is, saying that He was not at all a creator

---

427 Archimandrite Nicholas Arkas, "Saint Athanasios Parios (1722-1813)," trans. Hugh Cyril Donohoe, accessed November 5th, 2023, https://www.johnsanidopoulos.com/2013/06/saint-athanasios-parios-1722-1813.html

428 St. Athanasios of Paros, "That the Holy Spirit Proceeds from the Father Alone," in *Compendium or Collection of the Divine Doctrines of the Faith (Ἐπιτομὴ εἴτε Συλλογὴ τῶν Θείων τῆς Πίστεως Δογμάτων)*, trans. Gregory Heers (Leipzig: Breitkopf & Härtel, 1806), 164-177.

429 *Pneumatomachi*: A heretical sect which flourished in the region adjacent to

and classifying Him among the creatures instead, while the derangement of the Latins, although confessing Him to be the third person of the Holy Trinity and true God along with all pious, is curious after the manner of His existence, which is ineffable and beyond unknown for every created nature, and, thinking that they know hidden things better than the God-Man Word, the one of the Trinity, they dogmatize the opposites of what He handed over. For He on the one hand declares through His own most truthful mouth saying, "The Spirit of truth, which proceedeth from the Father," but they add, "and from the Son," as if the Only-Begotten had explained the manner of the incomprehensible existence of the Spirit imperfectly.

Since, therefore, this most pernicious heresy (for a heresy it is, since it blasphemes in many ways against the eighth article of faith through its addition of "from the Son") is still alive for us and does not cease to grieve and trouble our holy Church (although now more moderately than in the former years, due to the indifference ushered in with the rise of the atheists), for this cause our treatment of this, or against this, seems consequent and necessary, not so as to persuade the Latins now, after almost a millennium, to learn the truth properly (for I consider this impossible), but so as to secure our own men, so that they may not be led astray into perdition by their usual sophistries and pseudo-explanations.

THE HERETICAL LATIN FILIOQUE INNOVATION CREATED SCHISM[430]

The haughty race of Latins, reckoning as worthless the piety of the Divine teachers, dared first to say with their lips that the Holy Spirit proceeds also from the Son, which many of our teachers have proved very clearly to be the source of fearful absurdities and blasphemous con-

---

Hellespont (Dardanelles/ Δαρδανέλλια) during the latter half of the fourth, and the beginning of the fifth century. They denied the divinity of the Holy Spirit, hence the name *Pneumatomachi* or combaters against the Spirit.

430 St. Athanasios Parios, *Epitome or Collection of the Divine Dogmas of the Faith* [in Greek] (Leipzig: 1806), 163-164, 172-176. Quoted in Constantine Cavarnos, *The Question of Union: A Forthright Discussion of the Possibility of Union of the Eastern Orthodox Church and Roman Catholicism*, trans. Hieromonk Patapios (Etna: Center for Traditionalist Orthodox Studies, 2006), 24.

clusions. Secondly, they had the impudence to add this very innovation of faith to the Holy Symbol, stirring up a great and unspeakable quarrel in the Church of Christ, such that this one Church was divided into two Churches opposing — alas! — and warring against each other up to this day... This most evil heresy is alive in our day and does not cease to grieve and disturb our Holy Church, although now more moderately than in earlier times, on account of the indifference forced upon us by the atheists.

PAPISTS HAVE STRAYED FROM THE DIVINE BAPTISM AND ARE UNBAPTIZED[431]

Alas, the truth about the innovation-loving Papists! Into what a state they have strayed, annulling the truly Divine, Holy and Apostolic Baptism, and devising certain affusions, and very short ones at that, on the head alone, and sprinklings on the forehead with hogs' bristles, so that they are, and are agreed to be, completely unbaptized and worse than Eunomians. If the latter did not baptize with three immersions, according to the order of the Apostles, at the very least they baptized with one.

18. St. John of Moldavia (+1843)

THE MONK PARTHENIUS IN HIS DESCRIPTION OF HIS TRAVELS, RELATES THE FOLLOWING OF THE DISCIPLES OF THE GREAT ELDER PAISIUS VELICHKOVSKY[432]

The great Elder Paisius was so wary of all heresies and schisms that he baptized all converts, both from among schismatics and those from the heresies of the Latin West, which practice is kept even unto this day

---

431 Ibid. 350. Quoted in Constantine Cavarnos, *The Question of Union: A Forthright Discussion of the Possibility of Union of the Eastern Orthodox Church and Roman Catholicism*, trans. Hieromonk Patapios (Etna: Center for Traditionalist Orthodox Studies, 2006), 27.

432 Holy Trinity Monastery, "Schemamonk John of Moldavia," *Orthodox Life 29*, no. 6 (November-December 1979).

in the Church of Moldavia. He displayed his manifest zeal for piety when he lived with his brethren in the Dragomir Monastery: after a certain period of war his monastery together with Bukovina passed under the sovereignty of the Austrians. He abandoned his monastery and all its possessions, movable and immovable, and went to Moldavia, saying to his brethren, 'Fathers and brethren! Whosoever desireth to obey and follow his elder, the sinful Paisius, let him come with me; I do not give my blessing for anyone to remain in Dragomir, for it is impossible to live in a courtyard of heretics and escape their heresy. The Pope of Rome roareth like a lion in other kingdoms as well, seeking whom he might devour; even the Turkish empire he leaveth not in peace, but ever troubleth and grieveth the Holy Eastern Church; and therefore, all the more will he swallow up those who live in the Austrian kingdom.' And thus, he departed for Moldavia with all his flock. The Moldavian suzereign, seeing his zeal for piety, bestowed upon him two monasteries instead of one: Sekoul, dedicated to St. John the Forerunner, and afterwards Niamets, dedicated to the Ascension of the Lord. The Elder Paisius always taught the brethren to guard themselves from heresies and schisms, to submit themselves in all things to the most holy Ecumenical Patriarchs, and to honor the zealots of piety: the most holy Photius, Patriarch of Constantinople, and the blessed Mark, Metropolitan of Ephesus, who both struggled against the Pope of Rome. However, I took pleasure in his sweet teachings but for a short time, only two years.

ADDRESS TO POPE EUGENIUS IV[433]

Once we spoke entirely alike, and there was no schism between us and then we, both sides (Orthodox and Latins), were in agreement with the Fathers; but now, when we do not speak alike, how can we be together? Now too we (Orthodox) speak exactly the same as we did then, and we are in agreement both with ourselves and with the Fathers — both ours and yours — if you wish to acknowledge what is true. But you, having introduced innovation, by this necessarily reveal that you are in

---

433 Orthodox Christian Books & Icons, "St. Mark of Ephesus and the False Union of Florence," *Orthodox Word* 3, no. 1 (January-February 1967): 2.

disagreement first of all with yourselves, and then with the Fathers we have in common and finally with us.

19. St. Ignatius Brianchaninov (+1867)

HIS LIFE,
WHICH IS CELEBRATED ON THE 30TH OF APRIL[434]

The future St. Ignatius was born on April 15/28, 1807, in the village of Pokrovskoye in the Vologda region of Russia. His given name at birth was Dimitry Alexandrovitch Brianchaninov. Of noble birth, his father was a wealthy provincial landowner. In due course, the young Dimitry was sent to study at the Pioneer Military Academy in St. Petersburg to be educated as a military officer. Even before entering the academy, Dimitry had aspired to the monastic life, but his family did not support those plans. Nevertheless, as a student he was able to find some time to devote to prayer and the inner life, and to find other students with similar aspirations. Remaining obedient to his parents, he remained diligent in his studies, winning the praise of his teachers and coming to the attention of the Grand Duke Nicholas Pavlovich, the future Tsar Nicholas I.

After graduating from the academy, he took up his first commission in the army but soon became seriously ill. This made it possible for him to request an honorable discharge and, having made a full recovery, to at last embrace the monastic life. He was tonsured as a monk in 1831 and given the name Ignatius. His spiritual father was the revered elder, Leonid of Optina. Shortly after his tonsure he was ordained as a priest. Meanwhile, his absence from the army had come to the attention of Tsar Nicholas. As soon as he was able to locate Father Ignatius in his small monastery near Vologda, he ordered him back to the capital. So, at the age of only twenty-six, Father Ignatius was made an archimandrite and appointed as head of the St. Sergius Monastery in St. Petersburg. He served faithfully in that capacity for the next twenty-four years.

---

434 Bishop Ignatius Brianchaninov, *The Arena*, trans. Archimandrite Lazarus (Jordanville: Holy Trinity Publications, 2012), 239.

In 1857 he was ordained to the episcopacy, serving as bishop of Stavropol and the Caucasus. This period of his life lasted for only four years, after which he withdrew into seclusion at the Nicolo-Babaevsky Monastery in the Kostroma region of Russia. Here he was able to devote the remaining six years of his life to spiritual writing and correspondence with his numerous spiritual children. He composed five volumes of Ascetical Works.... Bishop Ignatius reposed on April 30/May 13, 1867. The Russian Orthodox Church canonized him at its local council in 1988 and his relics now reside at the Toga Monastery in the Yaroslavl region of Russia.

Heresy is a Hidden Rejection of Christianity[435]

When men began to abandon idolatry, in its obvious absurdity, and to come to the knowledge and confession of the Redeemer, when all the efforts of the devil to maintain idolatry between people remained in vain, then he invented *"heresies"*, and through heresy, preserving for the people holding on to it the name and some appearance of Christians, not only took away Christianity from them, but also replaced it with blasphemy.

What does Arianism mean? "This is a denial of Christ and Christianity," a denial of God. If the Son is a creature, as Arius claimed, then there is no true God in the Three Persons. If the Son is not God, where is the incarnation of God? Where is the sacrament of human nature to the nature of God (2 Pet. 1:4) acquired for human beings by the incarnation of God? Where is the salvation? Where is Christianity? *"Do not believe in the Son nor the Father"* (1 John 2:23), says the Word of God. Arianism is both atheism and blasphemy.

"What is Nestorianism? — rejection of the incarnation of the God of the Word. If a simple person was born of a Virgin, then where is the conception of the Holy Spirit (Matthew 1:18) — where is the event of the words of Scripture: *"The word is flesh"* (John 1:14)? Where is the birth of the Son of God (Luke 1:31)? Where is Christianity? The heresy is repeated by Nestorius of Ariev, but under a different guise: the essence

---

435 Bishop Ignatius Brianchaninov, *The Arena*, trans. Archimandrite Lazarus (Jordanville: Holy Trinity Publications, 2012), 239.

of these heresies is one — the rejection of Christ, and through the rejection of Christ — rejection of God.

Eutychius and the Monothelites do the same: by merging in the God-man the two natures and the two wills together, and by affirming that in Christ mankind has disappeared into the Godhead like a drop of wine in a vast sea, they come to the same goal, though on the other hand, to which Arius and Nestorius came: because by rejecting the presence of human nature in the incarnate Son of God, they necessarily reject all that the Lord has endured as a man, and therefore reject the redemption of mankind by the suffering and death of the Lord, and reject all of Christianity.

Iconoclasts are also striving. By rejecting the possibility of depicting Christ with painting, they implicitly reject the coming of the Son of God in human flesh. If the Son of God was endowed with flesh, then there is a full possibility of depicting Him, ineffable by the Divine nature, as a man. If it is possible to depict Him, then Images of Him should be especially revered. We revere the images of our parents, kings, chiefs, benefactors, put them in places of honor: all the more the icon of our Savior should be respected, and according to it the icons of the Mother of God and all the saints.

The same is intensified to commit Papism; this is the name of the heresy that embraced the West, from which various Protestant teachings descended, like from the tree of a branch. Papism appropriates to the pope the attributes of Christ, and thereby rejects Christ. Some Western writers have almost explicitly uttered this denial, saying that it is far less a sin to deny Christ than the sin of denying the pope. The Pope is an idol of the Papists; he is their deity. Because of this terrible error, the grace of God departed from the Papists; they are devoted to themselves and to Satan, to the inventor and father of all heresies, including Papism. In this state of darkness, they distorted some dogmas and sacraments, and deprived it of its essential significance, throwing out of it the invocation of the Holy Spirit and the blessing of the offered bread and wine, in which they are transformed into the Body and Blood of Christ. This essential part of the Liturgy was in all the Liturgies celebrated by the Apostles of Christ throughout the universe, and was also in the original Liturgy of Rome. No heresy expresses so openly and brazenly excessive pride in its own, harsh contempt for people and hatred for them. Papism invented the most terrible torture, the most terrible executions for humanity. Countless thousands of people died in stuffy dungeons, burned at the stake, tortured in various ways. And this terrible, murder-breathing, bloodthirsty savagery is called the one true Christianity, and with frenzied jealousy seeks to draw the entire universe into its heresy. "*From their fruit thou shalt know them*," the Savior said of their teachers and their teachings (Matthew 7:16). In its fruits, Papism comes very close to Mohammedanism: both of these heresies recognize as an act of faith and the highest virtue all the atrocities and all the murders committed by them in every society of people of a different faith.

The Protestants rebelled against the errors of the Papists, or rather rebelled against the ugly authority and divinity of the popes; but since they acted on the impulse of passions, drowning in debauchery, and not with the direct purpose of striving for the Holy Truth, and not as Cornelius the Centurion sought it, they were not worthy to see it. "*Whoever does evil, hates the Light, and does not come to the Light*" (John 3:20). The Protestants, of all the errors of the Papists, rejected only their wicked opinion of the Pope; they followed other errors of the Papists, strengthened many errors, and added many new ones to the old errors and mistakes. For example, they rejected all the ordinances, the priesthood itself; rejected the Liturgy altogether; rejected all church traditions and left it to each of their followers to explain the Holy Scriptures arbitrarily, while it, when uttered by the Holy Spirit, can only be explained by the Holy Spirit (2 Pet. 1:21).

Heresies should also include the doctrine that, without touching either dogmas or sacraments, rejects residence according to the commandments of Christ, and allows Christians to live paganly. This teaching, which on the surface seems as if not hostile to Christianity, is in fact quite hostile to it: it is a denial of Christ. The Lord Himself said, "*Not every one that saith unto me, Lord, Lord, shall enter into the kingdom of heaven; but he that doeth the will of my Father which is in heaven.... And then will I profess unto them, I never knew you: depart from me, ye that work iniquity.*" (Matthew 7:21, 23). Faith can only be alive in works of faith; without them, she is dead (James 2:26). However, the most correct concept of Christian dogma is lost from non-Christian life. Even at a time when idolatry was very strong, heretics were living pagan lives. Saint Athanasius the Great makes this remark about the Arians, who indulged in the amusements of idolaters and resembled them in morality. In modern times, pagan life appeared initially in the depths of Papism; the pagan feeling and taste of the Papists are manifested with particular brightness in the application of arts to objects of religion, in the pictorial and sculpted images of saints, in their church singing and music, in their religious poetry. All their schools bear the imprint of sinful passions, especially voluptuousness; there is no sense of chastity and decency, no sense of simplicity, no sense of purity and spirituality. Such is their church music and singing. Their poet, describing the liberation of Jerusalem and the Holy Sepulcher, does not stop to invoke the muse; he sings Zion along with Helicon, from the Muse passes to the Archangel Gabriel. The infallible popes, these new idols of Rome, are examples of debauchery, tyranny, atheism, blasphemy over all that is holy. Pagan life, with its comedy and tragedy, with its dances, with its rejection of shame and decency, with its fornication and adultery and other customs of idolaters, firstly, was resurrected in Rome under the shadow of its gods — the popes, from there it spread throughout Europe. Through heresies, and finally through pagan life, all pagans who once converted to Christianity, abandoned and are leaving Christianity, returning to their former utter ignorance of God and to serving demons, though no longer in the form of idolatry.[436]

CONCERNING THE IMPOSSIBILITY OF SALVATION FOR THE HETERODOX AND HERETICS[437]

You say that "heretics are Christians none the less." Where did you get that from? Do you mean to say that people who call themselves Christians without knowing anything about Christ, due to their extreme ignorance, would decide to call themselves the same kind of Christians as

---

436 Святой Игнатий (Брянчанинов), *Полное собрание творений святителя Игнатия Брянчанинова*, Том 4, Эдитед бы Александр Николаевич Стрижев (Москва: Издательство Паломник, 2001), 447-472.

437 Holy Trinity Monastery, "Concerning the Impossibility of Salvation for the Heterodox and Heretics," *Orthodox Life*, no. 3 (January-February 1991): 12-14.

the heretics, those same heretics who are cut off from the Holy Christian faith because of their blasphemous heresy? Do true Christians actually reason this way? A multitude of saints chose a martyr's crown, preferring the worst and prolonged tortures, imprisonment and exile, rather than to take part with heretics in their blasphemous teachings. The Orthodox Church has always considered heresy to be a mortal sin, and the person infected with the terrible illness of heresy to be spiritually dead, foreign to grace and salvation, in communion with the devil and his pernicious state. Heresy is a sin of the mind. Heresy is more of a demonic than human sin. It is the devil's daughter, his inheritance, his impiety, nearly idol worship. The fathers usually call idol worship impiety and heresy wickedness. In idol worship the devil received the worship due to God from blinded humans, in heresies he makes blinded humanity the cohort in his main sin, blasphemy. If one read the Acts of the Councils with attention one is easily convinced that the character of heretics is satanistic.

One reads of their horrible hypocrisy, immeasurable pride; one sees their behavior motivated by continual lies. One notes that they are the prey to base passions. Whenever possible they commit the worst crimes and most horrible atrocities. Their uncompromising hatred towards the members of the Orthodox Church is especially noticeable. Heresy is accompanied by a hardening of the heart, a terrible, darkening damage to the mind, a stubborn desire of the soul to remain infected and difficulty in healing the person sick with this malady. Every heresy is blasphemy against the Holy Spirit. It either blasphemes the dogma of the Holy Spirit or His activity, but blaspheme the Holy Spirit it must. The essence of all heresy is blasphemy....

The heresy of Eutichios [Eutyches] consisted in that he did not confess two natures in Christ after His incarnation as the Church does; he allowed for only one nature, the divine. You say, "Only that? We read the reaction of a certain person in power to the Patriarch of Constantinople about the Arian heresy. The reaction is amusing due to its lack of knowledge and pitiful in its essence. This person advises the Patriarch to preserve peace, to create no disturbances which are so abhorrent to the spirit of Christianity, just over a few words. He writes that he finds nothing wrong in the teaching of Arius, the difference is only in the turn of a phrase. Only! The historian Flery notes that in these so-called harmless phrases, the divinity of our Lord Jesus Christ is denied. Only! It is the denial of the whole Christian faith! All ancient heresies under various guises strove toward one goal: they denied the divinity of the Word and distorted the dogma of the incarnation.

The more recent heresies strive to deny the activity of the Holy Spirit. With great blasphemy they reject the divine liturgy, all the mysteries, all those places where the Orthodox Church always recognized the activity of the Holy Spirit. They called it a purely human statute, superstition, a mistake... the audacity. Perhaps this is the only reason why you do not consider heresy a sin. Here the heretics reject the Son of God, here they reject and blaspheme the Holy Spirit... and is that all? Those who accept blasphemous teachings and blaspheme are not hooligans, they do not steal and even do good deeds (of our fallen nature), they are wonderful people! How could God refuse them salvation... the whole basis for your lack of understanding is a deep ignorance of Christianity. Do not think that such ignorance is unimportant. No! The results can be disastrous especially now when so many booklets are spreading around with Christian titles and satanic contents.

Being ignorant of true Christian teaching one might accept a false, blasphemous thought for a true one and in accepting it be lost forever. Blasphemers are not saved! Those doubts which you expressed in your letter already point a finger at you and your salvation. The essence of your quandaries is separation from Christ. Do not play with your salvation, do not risk it! Otherwise you will weep for eternity. Study the New Testament and the Holy Fathers of the Orthodox Church (and please not the Theresas, not the Francis and other western madmen which the heretical church gives out for saints). Study the Holy Fathers of the Orthodox Church in order to correctly understand the Scriptures, how to live properly, think and feel as a Christian should. Before the terrible hour comes, in which you will have to stand in judgment before God, earn that justification which is freely given by God to all people by means of Christianity.

St Ignatius Referring to Francis of Assisi when discussing Spiritual Delusion in the Orthodox Monastic Life[438]

Saint John of the Ladder remarks that those who are prone to conceit and self-confidence and to other passions of the soul should on no account choose life of a solitary for themselves, but should remain among the brethren and save themselves by the practice of the commandments, because every kind of life, whether in the desert or in a community when it is in accordance with the will of God and when its aim is to please God is rich in blessing.

From premature reclusion stems diabolic delusion, not only obvious delusion, but also that which is invisible outwardly. Mental and moral delusion is incomparably more dangerous than the former as it is extremely difficult to cure, and is often insusceptible to treatment. This kind of delusion, which is based on pride or self-confidence, is called by the holy Fathers opinion. It consists in this: an ascetic receives false ideas about spiritual objects or about himself, but he takes them for true ones. False ideas and visions, through the natural sympathy and co-operation of the mind with the heart and of the heart with the mind, are invariably accompanied by deceptive pleasurable sensations of the heart. These are no other than the action of refined sensuality and vainglory. Those who are infected by this delusion become preachers of a false ascetical teaching, and sometimes become heresiarchs for the eternal destruction of themselves and their neighbours.

St. Isaac the Syrian in his 55th Word says that a certain Malpas lived in solitude a strict ascetic life with the object of attaining a high spiritual state. But he fell into pride and obvious delusion by demons and became the inventor and leader of the heresy of the Euchites.[439]

As an example of a book written in the state of delusion called opinion, we cite the following:

---

438 Bishop Ignatius Brianchaninov, *The Arena*, trans. Archimandrite Lazarus (Jordanville: Printshop of St. Job of Pochaev, 1997), 39-40.

439 *Euchites*: A heretical Christian sect from Mesopotamia in the late 4th century who were synodally anathematized as heretics in 383 AD and were condemned as heretical by Saint John Damascene in the 7th century.

"When Francis [of Assisi] was caught up to heaven," says a writer of his life, "God the Father, on seeing him, was for a moment in doubt to as to whom to give the preference, to His Son by nature or to His son by grace — Francis." What can be more frightful or madder than this blasphemy, what can be sadder than this delusion!

20. St. Theophan the Recluse (+1894)

HIS LIFE,
WHICH IS CELEBRATED ON THE 10TH OF JANUARY[440]

This modern-day Church Father was born in Chernavsk in central Russia. The son of a priest, he entered seminary at a young age, then completed the four-year course in theology at the Academy of Kiev. Though he distinguished himself as a student, his heart turned increasingly toward the monastic life, and he was tonsured a monk and ordained a priest upon completion of his studies. During his time at the Academy he often visited the Lavra of the Caves, and there became a spiritual child of Elder Parthenius (March 25).

His desire for monastic life was not fulfilled immediately, for the Church felt need of his intellectual gifts. He served as a professor at the Theological Academy in St. Petersburg, then worked for seven years in the Russian Mission to the Near East, mostly in Palestine. During this time he gained a perfect mastery of Greek and studied the works of the Church Fathers in the original languages. Returning to Russia, he was soon consecrated a bishop; but after seven years of episcopal service, he at last achieved his heart's desire, resigning as bishop and retiring to a small monastery at Yvschen, where he spent the rest of his days.

After taking full part in the liturgical and communal life of the monastery for several years, he took up the life of a recluse in 1872. He lived

---

440 "St. Theophan the Recluse, Bishop of Tambov (1894)," Holy Trinity Russian Orthodox Church, accessed November 5th, 2023, https://www. holytrinityorthodox.com/htc/orthodox-calendar/?year=2023&today=23&month=1&trp=0

in two small rooms, subsisting almost entirely on bread and tea, visited only by his confessor and the abbot of the monastery. He celebrated the Divine Liturgy every day in his cell. All of his time not taken up by inner prayer was devoted to translating the works of the Fathers into Russian and, increasingly, to writings of his own. Most importantly, he prepared a Russian-language edition of the Philokalia which had a deep impact upon Russian spiritual life.

Though he received no visitors, St Theophan entered into correspondence with many who sought his counsel, and so in time became the spiritual father of many believers throughout Russia. He reposed in peace in 1894.

In addition to the Philokalia, St. Theophan produced (among other works): a Spiritual Psalter of selections from St. Ephraim the Syrian; The Path to Salvation, an exposition of Orthodox Spirituality written in clear, plain language for those living in the world; collections of his letters to spiritual children; and Unseen Warfare, a treatise on prayer and the ascetical life.

HOMILY, DECEMBER 29, 1863,
SUNDAY AFTER CHRIST'S BIRTH[441]

It reached my ears that, as it seems, you consider my sermons very strict and believe that today no one should think this way, no one should be living this way and therefore, no one should be teaching this way. "Times have changed!" How glad I was to hear this. This means that you listen carefully to what I say, and not only do you listen, but you are also willing to abide by it. What more could we hope for, we who preach as we were ordered and as much as we were ordered? Despite all this, in no way can I agree with your opinion. I even consider it my duty to comment on it and to correct it, since — even though it perhaps goes against your desire and conviction — it comes from something sinful, as though Christianity could alter its doctrines, its canons, its sanctifying ceremonies to answer to the spirit of each age and adjust itself to the

---

441 "Why Christianity Should Not Change with the Times," Holy Monastery of Pantokrator (Melissochori), accessed October 19th, 2022, https://www.impantokratoros.gr/saint_theophan_christianity.en.aspx

changing tastes of the sons of this century, as though it could add or subtract something.

Yet, it is not so. Christianity must remain eternally unchanging, in no way being dependent on or guided by the spirit of each age. Instead, Christianity is meant to govern and direct the spirit of the age for anyone who obeys its teachings. To convince you of this, I will put forward some thoughts for you to consider. Some said that my teaching is strict. First of all, my teaching is not my own, nor it should be. In this sacred office nobody should, nor even can, preach his own teaching. If I or someone else ever dare to do so, you can put us outside the Church. We preach the teachings of our Lord, God and Saviour Jesus Christ, of the holy Apostles, and the Holy Church, which is guided by the Holy Spirit. At the same time, we make sure to do everything possible to keep these teachings whole and inviolate in your minds and hearts. Every thought we present and every word we use, we do so very carefully, so as not to overshadow this brilliant and divine teaching in any way. Nobody can act differently.

Such a law that calls for each man's preaching in the Church to be "God-sent," was established at the creation of the world, and should thus remain valid until the end of the world. The Prophet Moses, after the delivery of the commandments from God Himself to the people of Israel, concluded: "You shall not add to the word which I am commanding you, nor take away from it, that you may keep the commandments of the Lord your God, which I command you." (Deut. 4:2) This law of constancy is so unalterable that the Lord and Savior Himself, when He was teaching the people on the mountain, said: "Do not think that I came to abolish the Law or the Prophets; I did not come to abolish but to fulfill. For truly I say to you, until heaven and earth pass away, not the smallest letter or stroke shall pass from the Law until all is accomplished." (Math. 5:17-18) Then He gave the same validity to his teaching, before interpreting the commandments in the spirit of the gospel, by adding: "Whoever then annuls one of the least of these commandments, and teaches others to do the same, shall be called least in the kingdom of heaven." (Math. 5:19)

This means that anyone who wrongly interprets the commandments of God and lessens their validity, will be an outcast in the future life.

This is what He said at the beginning of His preaching. He assured the same thing to Saint John the Theologian, the beholder of ineffable revelations, to whom He described the final judgement of the world and the Church, indicating in the Apocalypse (Book of Revelations): "I testify to everyone who hears the words of the prophecy of this book: if anyone adds to them, God will add to him the plagues which are written in this book; and if anyone takes away from the words of the book of this prophecy, God will take away his part from the tree of life and from the holy city, which are written in this book." (Apoc. 22:18-19)

From the time of His first appearance in the world until the Second Coming, Christ has given the Holy Apostles and their successors the following law: "Go therefore and make disciples of all the nations... teaching them to observe all that I commanded you." (Math. 28:19-20) That means "for you to teach, not what anyone else could possibly imagine, but what I ordered, and this to the end of the world." And He adds: "And lo, I am with you always, even to the end of the age. Amen." (Math. 28:20) The Apostles received this law and sacrificed their lives in order to keep it. And to those who wanted to keep them from preaching what it was they preached under the threat of punishment and death, they replied: "Whether it is right in the sight of God to give heed to you rather than to God, you be the judge; for we cannot stop speaking about what we have seen and heard." (Acts 4:19-20) This clear law was delivered by the apostles to their successors, was accepted by them, and has timeless effect in the Church of God. Because of this law, the Church is the pillar and the ground of truth. Can you see then what an inviolable steadfastness it has? After that, who would be so bold as to stubbornly disturb or move anything in Christian doctrine and law?

Next listen to what is said of the Prophet Ezekiel who for seven days was in the ecstasy of prayer and after seven days heard the word of the Lord: "Son of man, I have made you a watchman to the house of Israel: therefore, hear the word at my mouth" (Ezek. 3:17), and he declared to the people: Here is the law for you! If you see a wicked person committing iniquity and you do not tell him: leave your iniquity and change your way, "that wicked person shall die for his iniquity, but his blood I will require at your hand." (Ezek. 3:18) Conversely, "if you warn the wicked, and he does not turn from his wickedness, or from his wicked way, he shall die for his iniquity, but you will have delivered your soul. Again, if a righteous person turns from his righteousness and commits injustice, and I lay a stumbling block before him, he shall die. Because you have not warned him, he shall die for his sin, and his righteous deeds that he has done shall not be remembered, but his blood I will require at your hand. But if you warn the righteous person not to sin, and he does not sin, he shall surely live, because he took warning, and you will have delivered your soul." (Ezek. 3:19-21)

What a strict law! And though it sounds in the consciences of all pastors during their election and consecration, when a heavy yoke is put on them, namely the instruction of the flock of Christ that He entrusted to them, big or small, not only to guide it but also to preserve it. How could anyone be so bold, to pervert everything in the law of Christ, when this involves the destruction of both pastors and flock? If the saving power of this teaching depended on our opinion of it and our consent to it, it would make sense for someone to imagine rebuilding Christianity according to human weaknesses or the claims of the age and adapt it according to the sinful desires of his heart. But the saving power of Christian law does not at all depend on us, but on the will of God, by the fact that God Himself established precisely the exact path of salvation. Beyond this there is no other way, nor could it exist. Therefore, anyone who teaches in any other way, is deviating from the true path and is destroying himself and you. What logic is there in that?

Notice how strict judgment was mentioned when something similar happened to the nation of Israel during the difficult years of their captivity. Some prophets, out of pity for the suffering and sick talked to the people, not as the Lord had ordered, but as their heart dictated. Concerning them the Lord gave the following commands to Ezekiel: "And you, son of man, set your face against the daughters of your people, who prophesy out of their own minds. Prophesy against them and say, Thus says the Lord God: Woe to the women who sew magic bands upon all wrists, and make veils for the heads of persons of every stature, in the hunt for souls." (Ezek. 13:17-18)

This means: Woe to those who order any kind of special treatment and suggest such leniency, so no one feels the slightest displeasure, either from those on top or those at the bottom, not caring whether this is for their salvation or destruction, whether it is pleasing to God, or repulsive. Woe to them, because "thus says the Lord God...your pillows and veils," namely your candied and comforting teaching, "upon which there you are perverting souls, I will tear from your arms and I will let their souls that you are perverting, go away." (Ezek. 13:20-21) from this teaching of yours and I will destroy you corrupters. This is the benefit of this special treatment and leniency, such as you want to hear from preachers! When you put all this deep in your heart, it is not right for you to want us to make any concessions in Christian doctrine, having the wrong desire to be pleased by us. On the contrary, you are obliged to persistently demand from us to remain true to doctrine, as strictly and firmly as possible.

Have you ever heard of the indulgences of the Pope of Rome? Here is what they are: special treatment and leniency, which he gives defying the law of Christ. And what is the result? From all of this, the West is corrupt in faith and in their way of life, and is now getting lost in its disbelief and in the unrestrained life with its indulgences. The Pope changed many doctrines, spoiled all the sacraments, nullified the canons concerning the regulation of the Church and the correction of morals. Everything has begun going contrary to the will of the Lord, and has become worse and worse.

Then came along Luther, a smart man, but stubborn. He said, "The Pope changed everything as he wanted, why shouldn't I do the same?" He started to modify and re-modify everything in his own way, and in this way established the new Lutheran faith, which only slightly resembles what the Lord had commanded, and the Holy Apostles delivered to us.

After Luther came the philosophers. And they in turn said, "Luther has established himself a new faith, supposedly based on the Gospel, though in reality based on his own way of thinking. Why, then, don't we also compose doctrines based on our own way of thinking, completely ignoring the Gospel?" They then started rationalizing, and speculating about God, the world, and man, each in his own way. And they mixed up so many doctrines, that one gets dizzy just counting them.

Now the Westerners have the following views: Believe what you think best, live as you like, satisfy whatever captivates your soul. This is why they do not recognize any law or restriction and they do not abide by God's word. Their road is wide, all obstacles displaced. Their way is broad, all the obstacles taken out. But the broad road leads to perdition, according to what the Lord says. This is where leniency in teaching has led!

Lord, save us from this broad way! But it is better to love each difficulty that the Lord has appointed for our salvation. Let us love Christian doctrines and let us compel our mind with them, pushing it not to think otherwise. Let us love Christian morals and let us compel our will in them, forcing it to lift the light yoke of the Lord humbly and patiently. Let us love all Christian rituals and services which guide us, correct us, and sanctify us. Let us compel our heart with them, encouraging it to convey its desires from the earthly and perishable, to the heavenly and imperishable.

Let us confine ourselves as though in a cage. Or better, let us drag ourselves, as if we were passing through a narrow passage. Let it be narrow, so no one can deviate neither to the right, nor the left. Yet undoubtedly, through this narrow way we will obtain the kingdom of the heavens in return. For as you know, this kingdom is the kingdom of the Lord. The Lord laid this narrow way and said, "Follow exactly this route and you will obtain the kingdom of heaven." Could anyone then doubt whether the traveler will get to his destination? And what mind would one have who starts wanting all kinds of annulment of the commandments, when by doing this he would immediately lose his way and be lost?

Once you have fully understood this assertion, do not worry if something in our teaching seems to be strict. The only thing you should strive for is to carefully make sure if it is from the Lord. And after you have made sure it is from the Lord, accept it with all your heart, no matter how strict or obliging it may be. And not only avoid wanting special treatment and leniency with doctrine and the ethics, but even flee from all these, as though fleeing from the fire of Gehenna. Those who cannot escape from this are those who think up such things and with them lure those who are spiritually weak to follow them. Amen.

21. St. John of Kronstadt (+1908/1909)

HIS LIFE,
WHICH IS CELEBRATED ON THE 20TH OF DECEMBER[442]

On October 19, 1829, in the far north of Russia, a weak and sickly child, named John (Ioann), was born in the family of Ilia Sergiyev, church reader in the village of Sura in the Archangelsk province. From his earliest years he went with his father to their poor and humble church, served in the altar, loved the service books, became very pious. His favorite book was the Holy Gospel. All of this became a firm religious foundation for the boy in his later long and glorious life in Christ. Learning came very hard to Vanya in his childhood, which sorrowed him greatly, but also served to spur him on to especially fervent prayers to God for help. And a miracle occurred! Once, during his sojourn in his religious school, after a fervent prayer during the night, the boy experienced a sudden shiver all over his body, and it was as though a curtain fell from his eyes, as though his mental sight opened up, and he experienced lightness and joy in his soul. After that night the boy immediately began reading with great ease, began to comprehend and memorize everything with the greatest facility. He finished his school at the top of his class, graduated from the Archangelsk Seminary in first place, and entered the St. Petersburg Religious Academy.

After graduating from the academy in 1855, St. John was ordained a priest and spent the rest of his life and pastoral activity in Kronstadt. As a married priest in the world, he nevertheless gave himself up to strict fasting and ceaseless prayer, the daily serving of the divine liturgy, and care for the poor and destitute. For his way of life, St. John was often mocked, abused, maligned, and persecuted, but his patience and love overcame everything. His gift of miracle-working and clairvoyance became known throughout Russia. Thousands of people from all ends of Russia daily arrived in Kronstadt, seeking help from St. John and even more sent him letters and telegrams. St. John reposed on December 20,

---

442 Bishop Nikon, "The Life of the Pastor of Kronstadt," Orthodox Christianity, accessed November 7th, 2023, https://orthochristian.com/43914.html

1908, having foretold the day of his death. Tens of thousands of people attended his funeral, and a multitude of miracles occurred at his tomb, both then and in the times that followed.

Life in Unfailing Union with the Church
The Indispensability of Belonging to the One True Orthodox Church[443]

Thus, it is indispensable to belong to Christ's Church, the Head of which is the Almighty Tsar, the Conqueror of hades, Jesus Christ Himself. His kingdom is the Church which wars with principalities, powers, the world-rulers of the darkness of this age, with spirits of wickedness in high places, spirits who compose a skillfully organized kingdom, and do combat in an extremely experienced, intelligent, well-directed and powerful manner with all men, having well studied all their passions and inclinations. Here no man by himself on the battlefield can be a combatant; and even a great community which is not Orthodox, and is without the Head — Christ — can do nothing against such cunning, subtle, constantly vigilant enemies, who are so skilled in the science of their warfare. For Orthodox Christians, a mighty support is necessary from on high, from God, from Christ's holy warriors who have defeated the enemies of salvation by the power of the grace of Christ, from pastors and teachers, and then from common prayer and the Mysteries. Behold, precisely such a helper in the struggle with our invisible and visible enemies is the Church of Christ, to Which, through God's mercies, we belong. The Catholics have invented a new head, having demoted the one true Head of the Church — Christ. The Lutherans fell away and remained without a head. The Anglicans likewise. There is no Church among them; the union with the Head is broken; there is no Almighty help and Belial wages war with all his power and cunning, and holds them all in his delusion and perdition. A multitude perish in atheism and depravity.

By creating man in His own image and Likeness, the Creator placed a close bond between Himself and His creation, that is, man. Man was obliged to maintain this blessed union through scrupulous submission

---

443 Holy Trinity Monastery, "The Church — The Treasury of Salvation," *Orthodox Life*, no. 4 (July-August 1970): 23-29.

to his Creator, through fulfillment of His holy, wise, and life-giving commandments; as a summary of these commandments, the commandment not to taste of the fruits of the tree of the knowledge of good and evil was given to him. This commandment was to have strengthened his will in its agreement with the will of God, so that God's will should be one with the will of man, — as the will of one of the Persons of the Trinity is in complete accord with the will of the second and third Persons: "As Thou, Father, art in Me, and I in Thee, that they also may be one in Us" (John 17:21). But by his disobedience, man audaciously broke his union with God and thus fell away from God and His life. And since the wages of sin is death, man was subjected to temporal and eternal death, and to all the innumerable, pernicious consequences of sin — illnesses, calamities, griefs, sorrows, corruption, every sort of deformity, and every kind of slavery to sin. Other than the Son of God no one could reestablish this lost union, and He, in His measureless goodness and condescension towards fallen man, most wisely and wonderfully restored it; and intelligent and chosen men have utilized this marvelously good restoration. But by what means was this union re-established? By the Son of God's assumption of human nature without sin, fulfilling all God's righteousness with human nature, taking upon Himself our curse, suffering and dying for us, and, having conquered death, by rising from the dead and giving resurrection to us — incorruption to us. He established one Church upon the earth with Himself as the Head and under the direction of the Holy Spirit. Within the Church, He granted all the means for the restoration of the broken union with God through the Mysteries and teaching, through the guidance of the pastors; He gave Baptism, Chrismation, Repentance, Divine Service, constant instruction in the Word of God. Now, whoever wishes to live in holy union with God, be thou in union with the Church which instructs — which holds Divine Service unto holiness and truth and the Kingdom of God — and thou shalt be saved.

"He that is not with Me is against Me: and he that gathered not with Me scattereth" (Luke 11:23). He who is not with the Church is against the Church; he who is not within the Church is against the Church; he who has not the faith is against the faith; he who does not do the works of repentance, the works of virtue, is against virtue. It is but a small thing to be named a Christian: one must do the works and fulfill the commandments which Christ decreed; unceasing repentance is necessary, unceasing attention to oneself in the spirit of faith, unceasing prayer, unceasing correction, unceasing forcing of oneself ahead, unceasing self-perfection, and with this goal — unceasing self-examination: are we in the faith? do we live according to the faith? are we with the Church? do we go to church? do we love the Church? do we fulfil the dictates of the Church? or the commandments of Christ preached by Her? Behold then how Christ God teaches. Therefore, he who does not repent, who does not attend church, and instead of church goes to the theater and various spectacles and worldly gatherings, disdaining the Church — such a one is not a Christian.

God has bound the Orthodox faithful to Himself by means of the one Holy Spirit and the one Church, by one faith, by the unity of the law, the Mysteries, and the hierarchy, for the general good of His rational creation. One must hold on to this bond through holiness of life and submission to one another.

Christian man! While there is still time, strive to appropriate God and His Saints to thyself here upon the earth through faith and piety; be churchly, nourish in thyself the spirit of churchliness; the spirit of repentance, holiness, peace, thoughts of God, the spirit of love, meekness, humility, patience, submissiveness to good, salvation. Lift not thine head, and scorn not thy Mother the Church which saves thee; — attend church often during Divine Service, stand with humility, listen, reflect, or read and chant. If thou dost not gain Her here — and through Her, God — thou shalt remain foreign to Her and to God, and after death, God shall not take thee, and all His Saints shall renounce thee as someone foreign to them in spirit and in disposition of heart and thoughts. Thou shalt be driven into a strange country, into the gloomy and fiery place of the fallen spirits and unrepentant souls of men. Be wise, therefore, in order to escape the craftiness of the devil, and attain thy great calling.

Thou belongest to the Church of God, that is, the community of those who believe in Christ; this Church is the one Body of Christ, God is the Head. Art thou a worthy member, dost thou live in holiness, dost thou always repent, dost thou correct thine heart and life, dost thou cor-

rect thy morals, thoughts, feelings, intentions, yearnings, thy whole behavior? Art thou a living member, or dead? Will the Saints receive thee
when thou departest from this temporal life into the eternal one? Will
they not renounce thee as a putrid member reeking, worthless? Will not
thy fate be in common with those who are reprobate from God? Hasten
to set this matter right, to correct thine entire behavior. For this thou art
granted time.

The work of the salvation of our souls is the greatest and most wise
work, and to learn this work, this art, it is necessary to have recourse to
those to whom this work is known, and who have completed it. This
work of salvation, this work of repentance, is especially known to the
Saints, since they have especially endeavored to concern themselves with
it, and have carried it in a surpassing manner, one saving for their souls
and pleasing to God. Indeed, the Saints have left this spiritual inheritance, this art of repentance and salvation, to the Orthodox Church,
having laid up in Her, as in a secure treasure house, all their understanding, their instruction, their zeal, their art, their experiences. Let us therefore learn repentance and salvation from Her. We all have come and do
come to the church services for Sundays, holidays, ordinary days, and
the Great Fast. All these services teach us repentance and salvation. Have
you heard the Great Canon of St. Andrew of Crete? Heard the prayer
of St. Ephrem the Syrian? Heard the troparia and canons for the Great
Fast? What a spirit of repentance is in them! What a compunction, what
contrition for the sins of sinful mankind! What a thirst for salvation
and pardon from God! What wails and tears of sinners repenting! Behold and learn repentance and propitiation of the Lord from the holy
Church. Attend well, reflect, comprehend your sins, have contrition, repent, vaunt not yourselves, do the works of mercy: for the merciful shall
obtain mercy.

It fell to the lot of fallen man, after the measureless compassion of
God and the unsearchable wisdom and justice of God, to have the hon-
or of confessing the name of God before unbelievers and of suffering
for this Name, the Name of the Lord God Who is glorified and worshipped in Trinity. The Apostles, martyrs, hierarchs, monastic saints,
and the righteous have been deemed worthy of this honor in particular.
All those who now struggle for the Orthodox Christian faith and for

virtue — those who firmly defend the holy Orthodox faith and Church and undergo slander and torment at the hands of Her enemies — are also found worthy of this honor.

The Holy men of God would not betray the faith by even so much as a word, and if it did happen that, because of the cunning of the persecutors, they unawares betrayed it by either word or deed, they were ready to erase their sin by means of the tortures. See how strictly the Saints held to the right confession! And of what sort are present-day Christians? "Reeds shaken with the wind" (Matth. 11:7).

"Receiving the end of your faith, even the salvation of your souls" (I Peter 1:9). Behold the end and goal of the Orthodox Christian faith — the salvation of the soul of every believer. How invaluable is our faith; how holy, true, God-pleasing, powerful, saving! How necessary it is to love Her, worthily to esteem Her, constantly to utilize Her for one's own salvation and that of others. O Lord, save the race of Orthodox Christians, and convert all the non-orthodox to Orthodoxy, as to the one faith which saves, established by Thee, glorified by Thee, and to be eternally glorified by Thee! Thou art holy and righteous — and Thy faith is holy and righteous.

What does the rite of conversion from different beliefs and confessions and of being united to the Orthodox Church show forth? The indispensability of the rejection of false beliefs and confessions, of the renunciation of errors, of the confession of the true faith, and — of repentance for all former sins and of the promise to God to keep and firmly confess the blameless faith, to guard against sins, and to live in virtue.

The beginning of all false teachings, heresies, sects, and schisms is in the serpent who deceives the whole world. The first, most pernicious false teaching was preached by the serpent to Eve in paradise and then to Adam, then Cain, to whom the primordial manslayer — the devil — falsely whispered against Abel that he stood in Cain's way, went against him, did not think, did not feel, did not live as he did; that he supposedly mocked him, reviled him. From hence arise all heresies, sects, and schisms. They wish to be teachers, not from God but rather from themselves and according to their passions. From hence arise the followers of Tolstoy, the Pashkovtsy, the Stundists, and others.[444]

---

444 The *Stundists*: were another heretical Protestant Evangelical sect that emerged

"Suppose ye that I am come to give peace on the earth? I tell you, nay; but rather division: for from henceforth there shall be five in one house (the Church of Christ) divided, three against two, and two against three" (Luke 12:51-52). Catholics, Reformed, Lutherans, Old Believers, sectarians. A hatred of Orthodoxy, fanaticism against Orthodoxy, persecution of the Orthodox, and even killings, run like a crimson thread through all the ages of Catholicism's existence. "By their fruits ye shall know them." Was such a spirit commanded to us by Christ? It is always possible to say to Catholics, Lutherans, and Reformed: "Ye know not what manner of spirit ye are of" (Luke 9:55).

The cause of all the errors of the Roman Catholic Church is pride and the acknowledgment of the pope as the real head of the church, and what is more — that he is infallible. From hence all the oppression on the part of the western church arises. The oppression of thought and faith, the deprivation of true freedom both in faith and life, in all things upon which the pope has placed his heavy hand; from hence come the false dogmas, from hence the duplicity and slyness in thought, word, and deed; from hence — the various false rules and regulations for the confession of sins; from hence indulgences; from hence the distortion of dogmas; from hence the fabrication of the saints of the western church and of non-existent relics, not glorified by God; from hence — "the exalting against the knowledge of God" (II Cor. 10:5), and every sort of opposition to God under the appearance of piety and zeal for the greater glory of God.

The pope and the papists have become so proud and have so exalted themselves that they have thought to criticize Christ Himself, the Hypostatic Wisdom of God Himself, and have extended their pride to the point that they have distorted some of His words, commandments, and ordinances which should not be altered to the end of this age: for example, His statement concerning the Holy Spirit, His commandment concerning the cup of His all-immaculate Blood, of Which they have

---

among Ukrainian peasants in present day Ukraine around the last half of the 19th century. The creation of this sect was largely influenced by German Baptists, Pietists and Mennonites who had settled into the southern parts of the Russian Empire and were believed to have been "trained as enemies of Russia and accomplices of Protestant Germany." See: Heather J. Coleman, Russian Baptists and Spiritual Revolution, 1905-1929 (Indianapolis: Indiana University Press, 2005).

deprived the layman, setting at naught the words of the Apostle Paul: "For as often as ye eat this bread, and drink this cup, ye do shew the Lord's death till He come" (I Cor. 11:26); instead of leavened bread in the liturgy, they use wafers.

I thank the Lord Who has heard and hears my prayers in the presence of the most saving and dread sacrifice (the Body and Blood of Christ) for the great communities which have gone astray in their faith, which though named Christian are in reality apostate — the Catholic, Lutheran, Anglican, and others; also, that all peoples may be drawn to the true faith, as also our Old Believers.

Count L. Tolstoy infringed upon the truth of the Gospel and the whole of Sacred Scriptures and perverted the thought of the Gospel, which is indisputably most important and invaluable for the people of all ages. He rejected the belief in Christ as the Son of God, the Redeemer and Saviour of the world, and led astray many who followed in his footsteps, and destroyed them; he renounced the Church, founded by Christ, trampled upon the grace of Baptism, Chrismation, Repentance, Communion and all the Mysteries; because of his self-conceit he accounts himself to be the judge of the Word of God and his own supreme criterion, and does not verify himself by It. But woe unto them that are wise in their own eyes and in their own sight! (Esaias 5:21).

22. St. Raphael (Hawaweeny) of Brooklyn (+1915)

HIS LIFE,
WHICH IS CELEBRATED THE SATURDAY BEFORE
THE SYNAXIS OF THE BODILESS POWERS OF HEAVEN
ON 8ᵀᴴ OF NOVEMBER

Born on November 20, 1860, in Beirut, Lebanon, to devout parents Michael and Mariam Hawaweeny (his mother was the daughter of a priest), Saint Raphael grew up in Damascus, Syria. Their parish priest, the New Hieromartyr Joseph of Damascus, and hundreds of their neighbors were martyred several months before he was born so the family had fled to Beirut, but later returned to Damascus where he attended parochial school for his primary and secondary education.

He was tonsured a monk in 1879 by Patriarch Hierotheos of Antioch and served as his cell attendant. The Patriarch of Constantinople offered a scholarship to Halki Seminary in Constantinople to one Syrian student and Saint Raphael was selected to attend. There he was ordained as a deacon December 20, 1885. When he graduated and returned to Damascus, he accompanied Patriarch Gerasimus of Antioch on his visitations and sometimes preached to the faithful when the Patriarch was unable. He was sent to the Theological Academy in Kiev to further his theological studies, ordained a priest on June 16, 1889, in Kiev, Russia, and an Archimandrite July 28, 1889, in Moscow where he served in the Patriarchate of Antioch's church there.

He spoke out against the replacement of Patriarch Germanus by Patriarch Spyridon who was a Cypriot as he had preferred an Arabic-speaking hierarch to replace him. When Patriarch Spyridon was appointed, St. Raphael was suspended from priestly duties. He used that time to write about the Arabization of the See of Antioch both in journals and in books. Eventually he apologized to the Patriarch, they were reconciled, and he was able to resume his priestly ministry.

There had been a large influx of Orthodox immigrants from the Middle East in North America in the last decades of the 19th century. Although it is not known how the Arab immigrants learned of this pious Syrian priest's existence in Russia, in 1895 he was invited by the Benevolent Society of Syrian Orthodox of New York to go there as the community had no priest or place of worship. Within two weeks of arriving in New York, he had managed to secure a small church which he dedicated to Saint Nicholas and he began preaching and celebrating the divine services. While he had remediated the problem in New York, he was concerned about the Arab Christian immigrants throughout the rest of North America who also needed a priest and community and therefore were in danger of either succumbing to the heterodox religions or abandoning religion altogether. He began to travel to the scattered faithful and preached the word of God, performed marriages and baptisms, received confessions and served Divine Liturgies, sometimes in homes when no Orthodox Church was available in the area. In 1898 he published the first Orthodox prayer book in Arabic in North America which was a treasure for the faithful, particularly if they had no clergy.

In 1898, he requested from Bishop Nicolas, who led the Patriarchate of Moscow's mission, to provide Arabic-speaking priests for the churches he had founded and was approved to send to Syria for clergy. In 1899, St. Raphael started traveling in earnest and went to forty-three cities over seven months ministering to various Orthodox — either Greek, Russian or Arab — who were dependent on the Russian Mission. After Patriarch Meletius, an Arab, was elected to the see of Antioch after 168 years of not having an Arab as primate, there were various proposals to assign Saint Raphael to a see in Syria. He consistently declined to leave his flock in the United States in order to do so. In 1901, he bought an existing church in Brooklyn on Pacific Street, had it remodeled to Orthodox architecture, and then it was consecrated by Saint Tikhon as the Cathedral of St. Nicholas. St. Tikhon, realizing that he was unable to regularly visit all of the increasing number of American communities and recognizing the special pastoral qualities possessed by St. Raphael, requested from the Holy Synod in Russia to transfer his see from San Francisco to New York and to consecrate Father Raphael as his vicar-bishop of the Arab communities. After this request was granted, when St. Raphael was made bishop February 29, 1904, in New York by Archbishop Tikhon and Bishop Innocent, it was as the first Orthodox Christian hierarch consecrated in North America.

St. Raphael continued his work of ordaining priests for the new parishes he had created and supporting the faith. In the beginning of 1905 the first edition of Al-Kalimat (The Word), a journal for the Arab faithful, was published in order to disseminate the Church teachings and increase contact among the communities which were widespread. He translated Greek liturgical books into the Arabic language and sent these to Arabic communities in the Middle East and immigrants in North and South America, Africa and Australasia in order to support the Orthodox faith. In July 1905, St. Raphael went to Pennsylvania to bless the grounds of the Monastery of St. Tikhon, the first Orthodox monastery in the new world, and the orphanage of South Canaan. Desiring to further the Orthodox education of the children, he created night schools in New York. He also facilitated the use of a translation into English of the services.

He fell asleep in the Lord on February 27, 1915, after suffering from heart disease during his last years. His earthly accomplishments were many; among other things, at the time of his death he was overseeing thirty churches with 25,000 parishioners, he had authored or translated fourteen books (including the Small and Great Euchologion) and many writings including "An Historical View of the Errors of the Papal Church, and A Refutation of the Proclamation of Pope Leo XIII" and created The Word journal in which he authored many articles. Greater than these accomplishments was the way in which he was a true shepherd by his unceasing selflessness and dedication in leading people to Christ and the Church; the thousands of faithful who attended his funeral were a testimony to this.

EXCERPTED RESPONSE TO AN EPISTLE OF POPE LEO XIII ON THE PRESERVATION OF EASTERN RITES[445]

...It follows from all this that the chief object of all such papal encyclics and epistles is not the union of churches or the preservation of rites and dogmas, but simply the subjection and enslavement of all Christian peoples to the Pope of Rome, And in the eyes of the Popes, neither rites nor dogmas are of such importance as the recognition of the dogma of the Pope's supremacy. Let any community, though it be downright heretical one, recognize that, and it will be considered a member of the Roman Catholic Church. That this is really so, is sufficiently shown by the contradictory and even heretical doctrines found among many Christian communities in Syria, which, notwithstanding, are "united" with the Roman Church. Thus for instance, some of them (the Jacobites, Armenians, Copts), hold the false doctrine of Jesus Christ's single nature; others recognize two natures in Him; some confess two wills in Christ, others (the Maronites), only one; some hold to the Nestorian doctrine on Christ (the Chaldeans); others repudiate it; some again accept the addition Filioque ("and from the Son") in the Creed, while others reject it; some (the Armenians), admit the use of unleavened bread in the Sacrament of the Eucharist, while others condemn it; some approve

---

445 Russian Orthodox North American Mission, *Russian Orthodox American Messenger*, no. 9 (March 1899).

the marriage of priests; others forbid it; others again turn their churches facing the East – or the West, – or indiscriminately, North or South, etc. etc... And in spite of all these contradictions in rite and dogma, all these communities are accounted members of the Church of Rome, because they acknowledge the supremacy of the Pope over them! What is this, if not a patent proof that the Popes of Rome think nothing either of church rites or of the fundamental Christian dogmas, in comparison with the dogma of their own supremacy, invented by themselves?

Then let the Popes write and publish as many encyclics and epistles as they please – they never will be able by such means to bring the Eastern Orthodox Church into subjection to their authority. The Orthodox Church was, is, and will be for all time the One Catholic, Holy, Apostolic Church, against which not only the Pope's scheming, but not the gates of hell itself, shall prevail.

THE TRUE SIGNIFICANCE OF SACRED TRADITION AND ITS GREAT WORTH[446]

This is St. Raphael's thesis written in Greek at the Theological School at Halki. It was submitted on May 1, 1886. Its purpose is a defense of the Orthodox Faith in his time of aggressive proselytizing by the Papists and Protestants.

"Sacred Tradition and Holy Scripture are [...] very closely tied to one another, so that each by necessity requires the other, and the absence of one in these important points is detrimental to the other. In this way, when Holy Scripture is disregarded, Sacred Tradition runs the danger of distortion because then the human can be mixed up easily with the divine, the profane with the holy, and truth with falsehood. On the other hand, when Sacred Tradition is removed, Holy Scripture is subject to many misinterpretations because when Holy Scripture is left to each one's free understanding and interpretation, a certain strange diversity within the one and same Christian teaching can hence result.

---

446 Saint Raphael (Hawaweeny), *The True Significance of Sacred Tradition and Its Great Worth*, trans. Fr. Patrick Demetrios Viscuso (DeKalb: Northern Illinois University Press, 2016), 45-84.

Let us now examine the more modern and at the same time more important of the two aforesaid one-sided heresies: I speak of the Papists and the Protestants. Whereas the Orthodox Christian who freely searches the scriptures subjects his individual precarious interpretation to the certain judgment of the universal Church, "taking captive," according to divine Paul, "every thought to the obedience of Christ" (2 Cor. 10:5), on the other hand the Papist who is prevented from the free search of the scriptures blindly follows Papist traditions in many fables, so resting his conscience upon the so-called infallible judgments of the Roman Pontifex as the supreme interpreter of Holy Scripture, and the Protestant who, basing himself only on his individual conscience, interprets the Scriptures in a completely arbitrary way. Thus papism, which centers in this manner all ecclesiastical life in one sole person, the Pope, established in Rome a religious, so to speak, oracle, in whom the Apostolic Traditions, distorted in many ways and confused with human nonsense, are presented as incontestable writ of divine origin! The Protestant, who also rejected Sacred Tradition along with this Papist prattle, was deprived of any firm basis in the interpretation of Holy Scripture and so, one-sidedly following Scripture, dismembered the one Church into so many parts.

Because Papism, thus impelled by an uncivilized spirit and centralization, mixes the human with the divine for the attainment of this very aim and so distorts and falsifies sacred Traditions, Protestantism, spurred on by a tendency to struggle against these arrogant claims of Papism, stumbled into the opposite excess of indiscipline and decentralization, completely rejecting Sacred Traditions as human writ. On account of this, come, let us discuss certain brief points concerning Sacred Tradition, demonstrating on the one hand its true significance against the Papists who distort it, and on the other hand its great worth against the Protestants who reject it...."

"Human tradition is what was handed over by men. It is distinguished into apostolic, ecclesiastical, and purely human. The first of these has its origin from the Apostles themselves, who are viewed not as heralds of divine laws or as stewards of Holy Mysteries, but as shepherds of the faithful and bishops of the Churches. [...] apostolic traditions are Holy and great Lent and in general all the remaining regulations of which the Apostolic Canons treat. [...] Ecclesiastical tradition is that which has its source from the successors of the Apostles and afterward [...] the sign of the cross, prayer toward the East, [and] generally the tradition concerning all ecclesiastical ceremony, order and teaching, as well as all commonly received customs [...]. Finally, human tradition is clearly that which men handed over having neither mission nor authority in the Church. Such are, for example the teaching concerning the primacy of the pope and generally all the innovations of the papal Church and other heretical, erroneous beliefs...."

"To this day, the Orthodox Church also recognizes this alone as a universal symbol [Nicene Creed], rejecting the two other symbols falsely viewed by both the Papists and Protestants as likewise universal, the so-called Apostolic, concerning which very correctly Mark Eugenikos answered the Latins in Florence, saying, "We neither have, nor do we know a symbol of the Apostles" [...] and the false Athanasian [...] which is just an obscure work of the Papist church...."

"Deciding whether a certain tradition is or is not in accord with scripture is neither proper for one, as the Papist church is asserting, or for many, because everyone is subject to error, but to the Holy Church in general, which the Holy Spirit itself "guides to all truth" and which Paul calls "a pillar and bulwark of truth" (Jn. 16:13, 1Tim. 3:15), and for which reason all those who reject the Councils of the Fathers and their traditions that are in harmony with divine revelation and piously preserved by the Orthodox Church are excommunicated from the Orthodox Church...."

"It remains for us to examine which of the two churches already divided and in conflict, I speak of the eastern and the western, is the true treasury and certain protection of Sacred Traditions. The Papist church, which is separated from the One, Holy Catholic, and Apostolic Orthodox Church of Christ through condemnations, which the Lord knows, confidently asserts that the apostolic church of Rome is a true treasury of the truly Apostolic Traditions; the infallible representative of Christ on earth, the key-keeping Pope, is the faithful guardian of them!

Whereas the ancient Roman Church viewed the bishop of Rome as simply a spiritual and only an administrative leader of the west, the Papist church views him as both an absolute spiritual and worldly leader of Christianity as a whole, contrary to the Scripture [...] and Tradition. Whereas the ancient Roman Church viewed the hierarch of Rome as *primus inter pares* (first among equals) and as subject to the decisions of the ecumenical councils, to which also the Apostle Peter submitted himself (Gal. 2:11), the Papist church views him as *summus pontifex* (supreme hierarch) and, when placed above the councils, honors and venerates him as the infallible (oh the folly!) representative! of God upon earth, contrary to both Scripture [...] and Tradition [...] Whereas the Orthodox Roman Church taught that the Holy Spirit proceeds from the Father while anathematizing any addition or subtraction in the Symbol of Faith, the Papist church not only teaches the *Filioque* (from the Son), but also adds it in the Symbol of Faith [...] contrary to Scripture [...] and Tradition.

Whereas the Orthodox Roman Church celebrated baptism by triple immersion, the papist one introduced infusion and sprinkling, contrary to both scripture [...] and tradition. Whereas the Orthodox Roman Church immediately after Holy Baptism celebrated the Mystery of Chrismation, the Papist one celebrates it not just by the bishop alone, but also after the child reaches seven to twelve years of age calling it confirmation [...] contrary to both Scripture [...] and Tradition [...] Whereas the orthodox Roman Church celebrated the divine Eucharist with leavened bread, the papist one celebrates it with unleavened, contrary both to Scripture [...] and Tradition [...] Whereas the Orthodox Roman Church invoked God that He might hallow the offered gifts when blessing them with the Sign of the Cross, the Papist one recites simply and historically the words of institution ("this is My body" and "this is My blood"), being of the opinion that by them and by only displaying the holy gifts, they are hallowed and *transubstantiated*, contrary clearly to apostolic and divine tradition.

Finally, whereas the Orthodox Roman Church provided this fearful mystery to all faithful without exception and under both species, the papist one not only deprived small children of it contrary to apostolic Tradition [...] but also dared to exclude all the laity from communion of the precious blood of Christ, contrary both to Scripture [...] and Tradition [...] Whereas the Orthodox Roman Church viewed the penances imposed in the mystery of repentance as having a simple correcting effect on the one repenting, the Papist one, misunderstanding the true meaning of this mystery, not only subdivided it into three, namely, into *contritionem* (contrition), *confessionem* (confession), and *satisfactionem* (satisfaction), but also views the penances as having an effect propitiatory of the divine justice that is offended by the sin of the one repenting, and as if this did not suffice, it added, on the one hand, that by virtue of the authority given to it from God to bind and loose, it can release from these penances the one repenting through pardoning absolutions, which are bestowed from the inexhaustible treasury that it possesses of excess merits earned not only by Christ, but also the saints; and on the other hand, that these absolutions work even after death to emancipate the one who happened to die under the burden of penances from the punishment of purifying fire. The Papist church teaches all these things contrary both to Scripture [...] and Tradition [...] Whereas the Orthodox Roman Church prescribed celibacy as obligatory only for bishops... the papist one imposed it on all clergy in general, both great and small, contrary both to Scripture [...] and Tradition [...] Whereas the Orthodox Roman Church permitted the dissolution of marriage in the case of spousal infidelity, the papist one views it as completely indissoluble, contrary both to Scripture [...] and Tradition [...] Whereas the Orthodox Roman Church celebrated unction both by priests and for any sick whatsoever, the Papist one celebrates it only by the bishop and only for those who are dying as a last anointing (extrema unctio), contrary both to Scripture [...] and Tradition [...]

But after these doctrines and mysteries had finally undergone such change and alteration in the Papist church, what must one understand regarding the other apostolic and church customs? Perhaps Papism left these undisturbed? Not at all, because whereas the Orthodox Church of Rome forbade fasting or kneeling on the Sabbath, breaking the fast on Wednesday or Friday, eating blood or clotted blood or any other impure thing, using any musical instrument whatsoever in the churches, venerating statues or unwritten images, ordaining more than one priest during one and the same liturgy, offering every day more than one sacrifice on the same altar, shaving hair or the beard and much more the mustache — whereas, I say, all these things and many such others, on account of good order and decorum, the ancient Orthodox Church of Rome forbade, as identically the Orthodox Eastern Church does up to the present day, on the other hand, the Papist church does not only simply allow all these things, but imposes strictly many of them, completely contrary to the purely apostolic and church tradition of which was decreed, "Let the ancient customs prevail" (First Ecumenical Council, canon 6).

Consequently, after also explaining such things of Papism, let any impartial man tell us which of the two said churches is the true treasury and certain protection of Sacred Traditions, or as Irenaeus said, "the rich storehouse in which the Apostles have deposited all things of truth" the Papist church, which innovated so much and greatly from 1054 until the present day, or the Orthodox Eastern Church, which neither added nor subtracted nor altered a jot or tittle from the divine deposit handed over to it from apostolic times until the present day?

While the great pontiffs of Rome who draw their inspiration from the soul-corrupting love of power subverted both divine and human doctrines and so, deviating altogether from the royal road, dragged with themselves during the gloomy darkness of the Middle Ages all the peoples of the west into the dreadful abyss of most impious innovations, suddenly, as from a light of the renaissance of letters that began to shine in the west already during the fifteenth century, some, being enlightened, observed both with fear and trembling that they were being brought to a precipice; therefore, also immediately after discontinuing their destructive march, they decided that, if possible, with the leaders who seduced them they would return with all speed to that royal road from which they deviated. But their mischievous guides, the haughty pontiffs of Rome, becoming intoxicated with much conceit, could no longer regain their senses from their lethargy, but every day constructing new paths, they fabricated new claims, which they had received from supposed ancient traditions, and so increased day by day the power of despotism and tyranny, hastening their march to the abyss of spiritual destruction. Hence those wretched servants of revived letters, finally seeing that thus they cried vainly when protesting against the excessive Papist claims, shook off the burdensome yoke of Papist tyranny and in this manner decided that they would alone return to that ancient royal road. But the infants! Instead of joining among themselves to seek what leads without confusion to the royal road, on the contrary, while taking the road completely opposite to the spiritual despotism of Rome, they went to the other extreme of spiritual anarchy and religious mob rule. Consequently, these Protestants who discarded all tradition and church legislation submit scripture as the sole source of Christian faith all the same when each of them interprets arbitrarily, without Sacred Tradition, he is basing his religious conviction upon his individual conscience. Thus, when utterly destroying any unity in faith, they surpassed the Papists...."

23. St. Nektarios of Aegina, Metropolitan of Pentapolis (+1920)

His life
WHICH IS CELEBRATED ON THE 9ᵀᴴ OF NOVEMBER

St. Nektarios of Pentapolis and Aegina was born Anastasios Kephalas on October 1st, 1846, in Selyvria, Thrace. Anastasios left for the City of Constantinople at the age of 14 in order to support his poor family. Around the age of 19, the future Saint Nektarios left Constantinople for the Island of Chios where he entered into the monastic life and later was called to serve in the Greek Orthodox Patriarchate of Alexandria. While Saint Nektarios was working at the Patriarchate, Patriarch Sophronios became very fond of him and sent him to the University of Athens in Greece to complete his education. Upon graduating, he returned to Alexandria. He was ordained a priest and was assigned as a preacher among the Orthodox Christians in Cairo, Egypt. He was later consecrated a bishop by the Alexandrian Patriarchate. Saint Nektarios was beloved by the people who were under his pastoral care, and it was believed that he was going to be elected the next Patriarch of Alexandria. However, due to jealousy because of this widespread belief, he began to be subjected to slander and persecution by his fellow clergymen within the Patriarchate of Alexandria.

These clergymen who had set out to slander the holy bishop were eventually successful in gaining the ear of Patriarch Sophronios and convincing him that Saint Nektarios was plotting to overthrow him and take his Patriarchal throne. With the mind of the Patriarch successfully convinced by the slanderers, Patriarch Sophronios exiled Saint Nektarios from the Patriarchate, and succeeded in taking away his position and meager salary which supported him, thereby casting him into homelessness, and requesting him to leave Egypt. Saint Nektarios, not wanting to cause any scandal or any offense to his spiritual father, Patriarch Sophronios, left for Greece despite the protest of the laity for the injustice that was done to him. He arrived in Athens, where he tried to support himself by any means that he could, all the while continually being persecuted and slandered from rumors coming out of the Patriarchate of Alexandria and being sent to Greece. He carried his cross in saint-like fashion and eventually, through the will of God, found himself appointed as the Dean of the Rizarios Theological School in Athens in 1894. Saint Nektarios served as the dean of the theological school for many years before retiring from his position and becoming the spiritual father to a group of pious female monastics on the small island of Aegina and founding the Monastery of the Holy Trinity in 1910.

During his years at the monastery, many faithful flocked to Aegina to participate in the divine services celebrated by the holy hierarch, listen to his homilies, receive his arch-pastoral blessing, and be healed of their various illnesses by his intercessions. Saint Nektarios, known for his extreme humility and love for his flock, is numbered among the Holy Kollyvades Fathers for his staunch confession of ecclesiological boundaries of the Orthodox Church. He died on November 9th, 1920, and was buried in a chapel at the Monastery in Aegina. Thirty-three years after his blessed repose, his relics were exhumed from his grave and they gave off a heavenly fragrance as a sign of his true sanctity.

Saint Nektarios was officially canonized by the Ecumenical Patriarchate of Constantinople in 1961. In 1998, seventy-eight years after his repose and thirty-seven years after his official canonization by the Ecumenical Patriarchate, the Greek Orthodox Patriarchate of Alexandria issued a public posthumous apology to Saint Nektarios for the slander and lies that their forefathers committed against this Righteous saint of our century.

St. Nektarios of Aegina on the Papal Heresies[447]

St. Nektarios to the Readers: "I've composed this present work which bears the approval of the Holy Synod of the Church of Greece for the following reasons: A) in order to explain those things concerning the Holy Priesthood, concerning the primacy of the blessed Peter, and concerning the true equality of the bishops according to the spirit of the Orthodox Church, and B) in order to give assistance to the sacred clergy for the enrichment of their knowledge."[448]

"Regarding the primacy of the Apostle Peter, not only do the Apostles say nothing but neither do the Apostolic Fathers. If not a single word regarding the privileges of the Apostolic Peter nor of his successors the Bishops of Rome is found recounted in their writings [...] then no mention will be found regarding the privilege of the Apostle Peter and his successors, the bishops of Rome. And although the whole divine Apostolic Tradition is preserved most accurately in their writings, nothing mentions the hegemonic primacy of Peter and his successors.

Nor is there preserved in unwritten tradition anything concerning the primacy of Peter and his successors. The majority of this unwritten tradition is preserved in the liturgical books and in the literature of the Fathers of the second century. And in them, we encounter not a single testimony confirming the much-discussed absolute primacy and privileges of the Apostle Peter over the other Apostles, nor of the successors of Peter over the other bishops of the Catholic Church. Nor from the writing of the Apologist does anyone say anything concerning the primacy of Peter. If you go through the writings of: Justin Martyr, Athenagoras, Tatian, Theophilus of Antioch, Codratus, Aristeides, and the other writers of the second and third centuries in detail, you will not find a single hint about the primacy and privileges of the Apostle Peter and his successors in Rome. And while many of them speak about order in the

---

447 Saint Nektarios of Aegina wrote extensively against the heresy of Papal Primacy and Supremacy in the Church. In his book "*The Priesthood*," he refutes these heresies in the chapters entitled: "On the Primacy in the Hierarchy" and "On Equality of the Hierarchy."

448 Saint Nektarios (Kefalas), *The Priesthood, Volume 4*, trans. Nun Christina & Anna Skoubourdis (Jerusalem: Virgin Mary of Australia and Oceania, 2021), 11.

Christian Church, about its governance, about the persecuted bishops, about the true and Christian Orthodoxy, none mention the supreme authority of the Popes upon the whole Catholic Church. History teaches these things, and Holy Tradition, the Holy Scriptures and their correct interpretation also convince us of these things."[449]

ON THE WRITINGS OF ST. NEKTARIOS BY JOHN MAVROS, GRADUATE OF THE THEOLOGICAL SCHOOL, UNIVERSITY OF ATHENS

"His Study Concerning the Causes of Schism is considered to be a thorough refutation of the Papist errors in such matters as Papal infallibility.... In one of the last works of his life, the Manual for Priests, St. Nektarios examines the question of the primacy of the Bishop of Rome, using a calm and clear historical judgement, from a thoroughly Orthodox point of view. He notes:

"Concerning the Evangelist John, the familiar friend of Christ, the Virgin and Theologian, what shall I say first and last? Which laud and hymn shall I bring forth? Who has heard such praise as the Evangelist has had? In the Lauds he is called the "sweetness of the Trinity," after receiving all other praises. And yet, through the primacy of Peter and because of their succession to his privileges, St. John comes after and was obliged to be subordinated while living to [those] such as Linus, Anicitus, and Clement, the successors of Peter (if indeed they were), and through them to receive the dogmatic truths!! (1907 ed., p. 81.) Truly an excellent reply, imposing silence on the nonsense of Papal primacy."[450]

---

449 Saint Nektarios (Kefalas), *The Priesthood, Volume 4*, trans. Nun Christina & Anna Skoubourdis (Jerusalem: Virgin Mary of Australia and Oceania, 2021), 100-101.

450 Orthodox Christian Books & Icons. "On the Writings of Saint Nektarios," *Orthodox Word 2*, no. 2 (April-May-June 1966): 59-61.

Primacy of the Pope is the Dogmatic Difference Which Caused the Schism[451]

The most important dogmatic difference [between the Orthodox and Latins] is the dogma of the primacy of the Pope. In this dogma, observes Saint Nectarios, "lies the reason for the schism, which is truly the greatest, because it overturns the spirit of the Gospel, and the most important dogmatic reason, being a denial of the principles of the Gospel. The remaining dogmatic reasons, although very important, can be regarded as secondary and as a consequence of this first reason."

Primacy of the Pope Gave Birth to So Many Heresies[452]

In saying that he is the head of the Church, the Pope banished Christ from the Western Church... This excessive arrogance of the Pope, this obsession of his with supreme power gave birth to so many heresies.

The Church Has Recognized Only Herself Alone in the Totality of Her Bishops as Infallible and Sinless

"His Beatitude the Pope sinned greatly when he proclaimed himself infallible and sinless.... Infallibility abrogates Synods, takes away from them significance, importance, and authority, and proclaims them incompetent, disturbing the confidence of the Faithful in them. The proclamation of the infallibility of the Pope disturbed the foundations of the Western Church; because it provided ground for suspicion about the authority of the Synods, and secondly it made her depend on the intellectual and spiritual development of a single person, the Pope....

451 Saint Nectarios [Kefalas] of Pentapolis, *Historical Studies on the Causes of the Schism*, Vol. 1, 2nd edition (Athens: 2000), 69. Quoted in Constantine Cavarnos, *The Question of Union: A Forthright Discussion of the Possibility of Union of the Eastern Orthodox Church and Roman Catholicism*, trans. Hieromonk Patapios (Etna: Center for Traditionalist Orthodox Studies, 2006), 18.

452 St. Nectarios of Pentapolis, *Historical Studies on the Causes of the Schism*, 84. Quoted in Protopresbyter Anastasios K. Gotsopoulos, *On Common Prayer with the Heterodox*, (Uncut Mountain Press, 2022), 15.

Since every Pope judges concerning what is right as it seems to him, and interprets Scripture as he wills, and lays down the law as he considers right, in what respect is he different from the multifarious dogmatists of the Protestant Church? Perhaps in that in the case of Protestants each individual constitutes a Church, while in the Western Church one individual constitutes the entire Church, not always the same individual, but ever a different one."[453]

"From the convocation of the Oecumenical Synods, we are taught [writes Saint Nectarios further down] that the One, Holy, Catholic, and Apostolic Church has recognized no one else as sinless and infallible than Herself alone in the totality of Her Bishops. In vain, then, do those around the Pope of Rome struggle to prove that he is infallible or does not err when he makes dogmatic pronouncements *ex cathedra* ['from the chair'], because the Oecumenical Synods stand protesting with stentorian voices against such an impious appropriation by the Bishop of Rome. That which the One, Holy, Catholic, and Apostolic Church for nineteen entire centuries believed and professed, it is impossible for Her to annul and deny, in order to accept and profess the new dogma of the Roman Church concerning infallibility. If the Bishop of Rome were infallible when he makes dogmatic pronouncements *ex cathedra*, this would need to have been confessed by the Church from the first centuries; but not only is it not confessed, but it is also proven false, because the local, provincial, and Oecumenical Synods confess the complete opposite. If the Church did recognize such an attribute in the Pope, she would have confessed this through deeds, seeking from him the solution of questions that were being presented, and She would not have resorted to Synods, and indeed oecumenical ones, for the solution of dogmatic questions. The convocation of the Oecumenical Synods denies the Pope such a Divine charisma. The Oecumenical Synods not only did not concede such a prerogative to the Pope, but actually fought against such an

---

453 St. Nectarios of Pentapolis, *The Seven Oecumenical Synods* [in Greek] (Athens: 1892), 22-23,27. Quoted in Constantine Cavarnos, *The Question of Union: A Forthright Discussion of the Possibility of Union of the Eastern Orthodox Church and Roman Catholicism*, trans. Hieromonk Patapios (Etna: Center for Traditionalist Orthodox Studies, 2006), 21.

arrangement and the attempt to lay claim to such a thing, and through canons made the great Pontiff equal to the other Bishops."[454]

POPES BOTH SIN AND ARE PUNISHED, PERHAPS EVEN ETERNALLY DUE TO THEIR EVILS[455]

Saint Nektarios enumerates ten Popes who had been proven to be "heretics and in error" in addition to others. He states this of the Pope responsible for the Fourth Crusade which caused the downfall of the city of Constantinople and the pillaging of Churches by the Franks in the year 1204: "Men of great virtues were convinced that Innocent III had fallen into great errors. Hence the Popes both sin and are punished, perhaps even eternally, on account of the evils they did to the Greek Church, their false unions, and their impious and anti-Christian decrees."

RESOLUTION OF LATIN SYNOD OF CONSTANCE PROCLAIMS COMMANDMENT OF JESUS HERETICAL

The Latin Synod at its fourteenth synod in Constance, Switzerland (1414-1418), "Forbade the imparting of the Divine Eucharist under both species to the laity. The resolution of this Synod is as follows: "In some places in the world, certain people impudently maintain that the Christian laity should partake of the Divine Eucharist under both species, in the bread and the wine, and that the laypeople truly commune in this way... The present Synod of Constance declares and resolves that, although Jesus Christ enjoined them to commune under both species..., although in the ancient Church all the faithful communed under both

---

454 St. Nectarios [Kefalas] of Pentapolis, *Historical Study Concerning the Causes of the Schism*, Vol. I, 2nd edition (Athens: 2000), 94. Quoted in Constantine Cavarnos, *The Question of Union: A Forthright Discussion of the Possibility of Union of the Eastern Orthodox Church and Roman Catholicism*, trans. Hieromonk Patapios (Etna: Center for Traditionalist Orthodox Studies, 2006), 22.

455 Constantine Cavarnos, *The Question of Union: A Forthright Discussion of the Possibility of Union of the Eastern Orthodox Church and Roman Catholicism*, trans. Hieromonk Patapios (Etna: Center for Traditionalist Orthodox Studies, 2006), 22-23.

species.... nonetheless, in order to avoid certain dangers and scandals, custom has prudently established that only the celebrants should commune under both species, while the laity should commune only the kind of bread.... Since this custom was rightly established by the Church, and has been observed for a long time, it is necessary that it be established as law... Those, then, who obstinately maintain the contrary, must be chastised as heretics and severely punished by the bishops of the province, and by the inquisitors." The conclusion we deduce from this resolution that the Synod is correcting(!) the Saviour Jesus Christ, who gave the commandment, and also the Ancient Church, which it proclaims heretical and worthy of the punishments of the Holy Inquisition. Such as the decisions of the Western Synods, which were convened not in the Holy Spirit, but in a human spirit, self-serving at that and based on ulterior motives."[456]

PERSECUTIONS BY THE CHRISTIANITY OF THE WEST INSTIGATED BY THE POPES

The combining of worldly and spiritual powers has resulted in bloody and fatal religious campaigns including the Crusades and the Holy Inquisition. Not only did this result in loss of life, but also the looting of the Orthodox Church's Holy Relics, Icons, Crosses, Vessels and profaning of the Sacred Altars. Saint Nectarios asserted that the Fourth Crusade could be considered the work of Pope Innocent III because he "thought it his duty to enjoin princes to undertake a campaign against the heretics (that is, the Orthodox), because, he said, the swords were entrusted to princes by the Most High for the defense of the faithful and for the retribution of the evil-doers.... The capture of Constantinople by the wild and Vandal-like Crusaders of the West set the seal on the Schism. The Crusaders showed in deed and word that the Christianity

---

456 Saint Nectarios [Kefalas] of Pentapolis, *Historical Studies on the Causes of the Schism*, Vol. 2, 2nd edition (Athens: 2000), 179-180. Quoted in Constantine Cavarnos, *The Question of Union: A Forthright Discussion of the Possibility of Union of the Eastern Orthodox Church and Roman Catholicism*, trans. Hieromonk Patapios (Etna: Center for Traditionalist Orthodox Studies, 2006), 28-29.

of the West was a monstrosity, while Pope Innocent III testified that he was their true shepherd and guide."

The Pope "not only wrote to the Latin grandees who held sway over the East, 'that they should force the Greeks into union in every way,' but also sent a crowd of bishops, priests and monks throughout the East to compel the Greeks to accept the union.... After taking possession of the Eastern regions, they drove the Orthodox hierarchs from their own Thrones, persecuted the clergy who were not subject to them and the Pope, and seized their Thrones and places. The deeds perpetrated by the Latins at the same time in Thessalonica are so inhuman, cruel, and shameful, that even just to hear them causes horror.... Behold the things that truly remove the Greeks from the Latins. The Eastern Church strongly detests such principles, such thoughts, such ideas. Since they offend the spirit of the Gospel, even the very principles of the Gospel, they are truly evil and heretical principles, and are rejected by the Greek Church."[457]

PAPISTS DEFINE VIRTUES AND SINS BASED UPON THEIR FURTHERANCE OF PAPAL AGENDA, NOT THE GOSPEL[458]

The historical development of the Schism made clearly known to us the manifold means and the various activities of the Popes of the Roman Episcopal See towards their enslavement and the oppression of the Church to and by them. The unbridled love of power and ambition contrived and accomplished everything to render the Popes rulers of the Church and tyrants of the world. Their love of power exceeded every limit; the program was drawn up and its application was sought after

---

457 Saint Nectarios [Kefalas] of Pentapolis, *Historical Studies on the Causes of the Schism*, Vol. 2, 2nd edition (Athens: 2000), 946, 99-102. Quoted in *The Question of Union: A Forthright Discussion of the Possibility of Union of the Eastern Orthodox Church and Roman Catholicism*, trans. Hieromonk Patapios (Etna: Center for Traditionalist Orthodox Studies, 2006), 33-34.

458 Saint Nectarios [Kefalas] of Pentapolis, *Historical Studies on the Causes of the Schism*, Vol. 1, 2nd edition (Athens: 2000), 207-209. Quoted in Constantine Cavarnos, *The Question of Union: A Forthright Discussion of the Possibility of Union of the Eastern Orthodox Church and Roman Catholicism*, trans. Hieromonk Patapios (Etna: Center for Traditionalist Orthodox Studies, 2006), 35.

with all strength. Every obstacle had to be removed, every hindrance destroyed. Everything that prevented the development of the program was condemned as deadly sin. And the moral principles concerning sin and righteousness were overturned... Sins were characterized not in accordance with the moral principles of the Sacred Gospel, but in accordance with the principles of the Papal program. *The Evangelical virtues could be characterized as deadly sins* that collided with the program, while deadly sins according to the Gospel could be characterized as very great virtues that served the program.

ON THE CAUSE OF THE GREAT SCHISM

"The most important causes are (a) the arrogant and anticanonical claims concerning the primacy of the Popes of Rome, which are opposed to the spirit of the one Holy Universal (Katholike) and Apostolic Church that is expressed in the Holy Scriptures and guarded by the seven Holy Œcumenical Synods (b) the innovations that have been made through which the Roman church has gone away from the Orthodox Universal and Apostolic Church; and (c) annulling the validity of the Holy Synods, which alone are able to possess the truth of the Church."[459]

"It was the Roman Church, concludes the Holy Father [Nektarios], which 'opened the chasm of separation, by changing the nature of the Church' through the institution of the primacy of the Pope. The separation 'was completed at the time of Photios,' who refused to recognize such primacy, 'since the Church ran the danger of ceasing to be one Universal and Apostolic Church and becoming a Roman church, or rather a Papal church, no longer teaching the doctrines of the Holy Apostles, but teaching instead those of the Popes.'"[460]

"Conditions for the union are such that they render union impossible. Because each Church asks of the other neither more nor less than the negation of itself, the negation of the fundamental principles on which the whole structure of the Church rests. For the western church is

459 Father Constantine Cavarnos, "Life of Saint Nectarios," in *The Modern Orthodox Saints*, (Belmont: Institute for Byzantine Studies, 1981), 67-68.
460 Ibid., 68.

based on the primacy of the Pope, while the Eastern Church rests on the Œcumenical Synods."[461]

SEPARATION OF THE CHURCHES CAUSED BY CATHOLIC CHURCH PROFESSING DOGMAS OF THE POPES NOT THE APOSTLES

"Thenceforth the separation of the Churches began, which came into completion quite rightly under Photios, since the Church was in danger of going away from the One, Catholic, and Apostolic Church to become a Roman Church, or rather a papist Church, professing no longer the dogmas of the holy Apostles, but those of the popes."[462]

24. St. Hilarion Troitsky (+1929)

HIS LIFE
WHICH IS CELEBRATED ON THE 15TH OF DECEMBER[463]

One of the most eminent figures of the Russian Orthodox Church in the 1920s was Archbishop Hilarion of Verey, an outstanding theologian and bishop. Throughout his life he burned with great love for the Church of Christ, right up to his martyric death for her sake. His literary works are distinguished by their strictly ecclesiastical content and his tireless struggle against scholasticism, specifically Latinism, which had been influencing the Russian Church from the time of Metropolitan Peter Moghila [of Kiev]. His ideal was ecclesiastical purity for theological schools and theological studies. His continual reminder was: There is no

---

461 Ibid., 69.

462 Μητροπολίτου Πενταπόλεως Νεκταρίου (Κεφαλᾶ), *Μελέτη Ἱστορικὴ περὶ τῶν Αἰτιῶν τοῦ Σχίσματος, περὶ τῆς Διαιωνήσεως αὐτοῦ καὶ περὶ τοῦ Δυνατοῦ ἢ Ἀδυνάτου τῆς Ἑνώσεως τῶν Δύο Ἐκκλησιῶν, τῆς Ἀνατολικῆς καὶ Δυτικῆς*, Τόμος Α΄ (Ἀθήναις: Ἐκ τοῦ Τυπογραφείου Παρασκευᾶ Λεώνη, 1911), 10-11.

463 Metropolitan John (Snychev) of St. Petersburg and Ladoga, "The Life of Holy Hieromartyr Hilarion (Troitsky), Archbishop of Verey," trans. Nun Cornelia, *Orthodox Word*, Issue 264-265, Vol 45, nos. 1 & 2 (Jan.-Apr. 2009).

454   The Orthodox Patristic Witness Concerning Catholicism

salvation outside the Church, and there are no Sacraments outside the Church.

Archbishop Hilarion born on September 13, 1886, to a priest's family in the village of Lipitsa, in the Kashira district of Tula Province. After completing seminary, he entered the Moscow Theological Academy, and graduated with honors in 1910 with a Candidate degree in Theology. He remained at the Academy with a professorial scholarship. He was an excellent student and always earned the highest marks in all subjects. In 1913, he received his master's degree in theology for his fundamental work, On the Dogma of the Church. He wrote many other words on dogma and ecclesiology including The Church on Unity & the World Conference of Christian Communities.

On March 28, 1913, in the Skete of the Paraclete of the Holy Trinity–St. Sergius Lavra, he received the monastic tonsure. About two months later, on June 2, he was ordained a hieromonk, and on July 5 of the same year, raised to the rank of Archimandrite. On May 11/24, 1920, Archimandrite Hilarion was elected, and on the next day, consecrated as Bishop of Verey, a vicariate of the Moscow diocese, and later was raised to the rank of Archbishop. After the Bolshevik Revolution, Archbishop Hilarion spent many years in different prisons in terrible conditions, and reposed overtaken by illness a prison in Leningrad on December 15/28, 1929.

On the So-called "Ecumenism" of St. Philaret of Moscow[464]

It is no use quoting from some Russian theologian's or hierarch's words to the effect that the partitions separating the Christian churches do not reach the heavens: the fact of the West's falling away from the Church in 1054 is for the Orthodox believer a present fact of religious experience... [Y]ou adduce the viewpoint of the famous Metropolitan of Moscow, Philaret, who wrote in one of his early treatises: "No church which believes Jesus to be the Christ will I dare call false." But there are

---

464 Saint Hilarion Troitsky, *The Church on Unity & the World Conference of Christian Communities*, trans. Margaret Jerinec Acton (Montreal: Monastery Press, 1975), 24.

quite a few obstacles to recognizing as valid Metropolitan Philaret's reasoning that churches can be either pure truth or impure truth. A church of impure truth seems to me to be evidently a false one, and there cannot be a false church; such a church ceases to be a church, becoming an extra-ecclesial community. For Metropolitan Philaret did not partake of the Eucharist with the Latins; and neither do other theologians of ours, who occasionally show too much zeal in defending the unacceptable doctrine of the unity the Church, according to which the one Church may embrace local churches that have for centuries been out of communion with each other. And this looks inconsistent to me. Why then shouldn't one celebrate the mass or partake of the eucharist with a priest of the local Roman Church? No, the falling away of Rome from the Church (or of the East from Rome) is a fact on hand, which should not be hushed up and reduced to zero.

ON THE LATINISM OF THE ROMAN PAPISTS[465]

The Latins were admitted to the Church through baptism, like the heathens, or through the mystery of anointing with chrism, just as the ancient Church used to admit the Arians, Macedonians, Apollinarians, and similar heretics. We have an anti-Latin mission in our theological schools there are also chairs for the exposure of Latinism. The Latins use violence, fraud (Uniate Churches) and propaganda to convert the Orthodox to Papism. The Pope proclaims indulgences to anyone who for a certain number of days will offer prayers for conversion of Eastern schismatics. The Latins convened councils, acknowledging them as Oecumenical; in the centuries past they have invented new dogmas never heard of in the ancient Church. The Eastern Church has condemned as heresies the new dogmas of Latinism. Let us take a comparatively recent example. Pope Pius IX, in his missive of January 6, 1848, addressed to the Easterners, defends all the falsehoods of Latinism and calls upon the Orthodox to return to the true Church. Four months later, on May 5, 1848, four Eastern patriarchs and all the bishops comprising the synods

---

465 Saint Hilarion Troitsky, *The Church on Unity & the World Conference of Christian Communities*, trans. Margaret Jerinec Acton (Montreal: Monastery Press, 1975), 21-22.

of Constantinople, Antioch, and Jerusalem issued a "circular letter of the One, Holy, Catholic and Apostolic Church to all Orthodox Christians."

Along with a refutation and condemnation of the papal missive, the patriarchs speak of a return of the separated churches to the body of the One, Holy, Catholic and Apostolic Church. This missive also condemns the *filioque* clause in resolute words: "The One, Holy, Catholic and Apostolic Church, following in the footsteps of the holy Fathers of both the East and the West, now proclaims — as it did in the old times of our forefathers — this belief, recently introduced, that the Holy Spirit proceeds from the Father and from the Son, to be a downright heresy, and its adherents whosoever they may be — to be heretics; the communities made up of them are heretical societies, and any spiritual or ecclesiastical intercourse with them constitutes a grave transgression for the Orthodox flock of the Catholic Church."

St. Hilarion on the Latin Lack of Patristic Phronema[466]

I am convinced that the contemporary Latin is incapable of understanding the thought of the ancient Church concerning the life of grace.

25. St. Sebastian Dabovich (+1940)

His life
which is celebrated on the 30ᵗʰ of November

Born Jovan Dabovich in San Francisco June 9, 1863 to Serbian immigrants, St. Sebastian is known as the Father of Serbian Orthodoxy in America. He attended the Kiev and St. Petersburg Theological Academies. While at St. Petersburg in 1887, he became the first native-born American to be tonsured as an Orthodox monk. Subsequently he was ordained as a Hierodeacon. After completing his studies, he returned to San Francisco serving at Saint Alexander Nevsky Church. In 1892 he

---

466 Saint Hilarion Troitsky, *The Church on Unity & the World Conference of Christian Communities*, trans. Margaret Jerinec Acton (Montreal: Monastery Press, 1975), 42.

was ordained as a Hieromonk by Bishop Nicholas (Ziorov), becoming the first person in the US to be ordained as an Orthodox priest. The bishop sent him to Minneapolis to replace Saint Alexis Toth at St. Mary's Church. His work with the saint allowed him to help Uniate converts adopt the Orthodox way of life, and to catechize Episcopalians into the Orthodox Church.

He built many Serbian churches in the New World, including St. Savva in Jackson, CA in 1894 which is the first church he ever built and the first Serbian Church in the Western Hemisphere. Under Bishop Nicholas in the OCA, he ministered, preached and taught in Washington, California and Minneapolis. Afterwards, he worked in the administration of the ROCOR North American Mission under Saint Tikhon (Belavin). His love of Christ was evident in his deep knowledge of the faith and his commitment to imparting the correct teachings of the Church. He was dedicated to evangelization and educational ministries. It is said that Fr. Sebastian baptized more people than any other Serbian priest of the Western Hemisphere. He compiled one of the first English translations of the Divine Liturgy, and wrote and published (without any outside funding) some of the first Orthodox catechism books in English. A large number of his inspiring sermons given in the Russian Orthodox Cathedral in San Francisco were published.

He spread the Orthodox faith everywhere, to different ethnic backgrounds, traveled across America and to Alaska, Russia, Japan, and the areas around the Adriatic and Baltic Seas. He helped across all Orthodox jurisdictions whether Russian, Serbian, Bulgarian, Greek, Syrian, or Arab. In 1905, St. Sebastian was appointed as Dean of Serbian churches and the Synod also appointed him the head of the Serbian mission. Archbishop Tikhon requested him to be in charge of a Serbian Mission in the North American diocese and elevated him to the rank of Archimandrite for his work in the Church. In 1910, he went to Serbia to serve as a chaplain in the Serbian Army during both the Second Balkan War and World War I. From 1936 until his repose on November 17/30, 1940, he lived in retirement at the Saint Savva of Serbia Monastery in Žiča.

St. Nikolai [Velimirović] of Serbia, who buried Fr. Sebastian, called him "a viceless man" and also "the greatest Serbian missionary of modern times." Ten years after his repose, St. Nikolai wrote of him: "Here is a man who indebted all the Serbian race, especially all the Serbs and all the Serbian organizations in America. Should that man remain without a monument or any sign of honor on American soil? He does not need it. He did not wish it. All he wished to his last breath was the Kingdom of Heaven, which I believe he has obtained by the grace of his Lord. But his people need it; his posterity needs it. The Serbian people always cultivated the noble virtue of gratitude. Let them express their traditional gratitude to this remarkable Serbian — Father Sebastian Dabovich." In 2007, Saint Sebastian's remains were unearthed from his grave in Serbia and transferred to the St. Savva Church in Jackson, CA.

THE TRUE CHURCH OF CHRIST[467]

We have learned that the true confession of faith by itself is not sufficient for salvation. Of necessity another condition is required: to belong to the Orthodox Church, and that is the recognition of a lawful hierarchy or priesthood, the reception of the Sacraments from the same hierarchy, and obedience to it in matters concerning salvation. In a community of Christians in which there is no lawful bishop, who is the dispenser of the gifts of saving grace, there are no sacramental gifts of the Holy Spirit, there can be no Mystery of the Body and Blood of Christ; and where the Holy Spirit and Christ are not present, who sacramentally abide in Christians, there can be, of course, no Church. Sacred Scriptures testifies to this very decidedly.

Which hierarchy is the true and lawful one? It is the priesthood which has retained and continues to follow these conditions:

1. In the first place such a hierarchy is true, which has received the grace of the Holy Spirit from the Apostles themselves in an unbroken line of succession from one to another. If, for instance, in a certain locality bishops and priests were found to be wanting, the succession being broken, and in their absence the laity elected new ones

---

467 Orthodox Christian Books & Icons, "The True Church of Christ," *Orthodox Word 1*, no. 5 (September-October 1965): 184-187.

and laid their hands upon them and proclaimed them to be bishops and presbyters, such a hierarchy would be unlawful and without grace, as the laity cannot transmit that which they do not possess themselves — the grace of the priesthood. In the time when the erring Church of Rome spawned Protestant sects, the Protestants commenced to elect and establish presbyters themselves, and these ministers not only baptize, but they officiate at a so-called "communion service," which of course is not a valid sacrament, as the ministers have no apostolic ordination and are not presbyters. As we learn from history, only that hierarchy is authentic, which received the grace of the Priesthood from the Lord Jesus Christ's Apostles themselves, through an unbroken succession of the lawful heirs of this Sacrament. And this is necessary. As the inclination to sin is transmitted successively from one to another by inheritance in the conception and birth of the body, thus also grace, that is the power of God, which wipes away sin and gives strength in struggle with it, being bestowed, is transmitted uninterruptedly by the laying on of episcopal hands in the Priesthood, by anointing all Christians with the Holy Chrism, and also through sacred acts and visible forms in other Sacraments.

2. Secondly, an authentic hierarchy is such, which confesses all the truths of holy religion, for there are heresies which entirely deprive bishops and priests of their ministerial grace.

3. Thirdly, a Priesthood to be lawful must administer the Sacraments orderly, according to the rules of the Holy Church Catholic, not changing essential actions, as there are acts and conditions in the rites of Mysteries that are essential, without which a certain Sacrament may not be valid. Should a sacred minister violate an essential rule he is subject to degradation, if the violation has been intentional, or at least, the Mystery is void of power. The seventh rule of the Apostolic Canon enjoins: "Should anyone, bishop or presbyter, administer not three immersions in Baptism in commemoration of the death of the Lord, but one, let him be cast out." And those who were baptized by one immersion, it was ordered that they should be rebaptized. If a priest should consecrate chrism himself, and anoint the newly-baptized with it, such an act would not be the Mystery of unction with chrism, because it would be the usurpation of the

rights and power of a bishop, and such a thing is forbidden presbyters by the sixth rule of the Council of Carthage. Should a bishop or priest use only water in place of wine in the Mystery of communion, as some heretics do, such an offering would not be a true Sacrament.

4. Fourthly, to be a lawful and true hierarchy, the same must be governed and govern its spiritual charge according to the rules of the Holy Apostles, the Seven Ecumenical Councils, and other laws which are accepted by the Orthodox Church in general. Having apostasized from these universal or catholic regulations, the Roman Church invented a doctrine concerning the supremacy of the Bishop of Rome overall. This has been one of the chief causes of the Roman schism or separation from the Orthodox Catholic Church.

5. A fifth condition necessary for proving the lawfulness of the Priesthood is its unity with the Orthodox Church in the spirit of peace and love. Whoever destroys this unity, except for a genuine and important cause, and bishops and priests together with Christians who follow them, that separate themselves from the higher Church authorities, are excommunicated from the Church, according to the rules of the Apostles and the canons of the Councils. The Orthodox Church, which is one, is one spiritual body, animated only by the Holy Spirit, having only One Head — the Lord Jesus Christ. The Orthodox Church is holy, not having spots, or wrinkle, or any such thing (Ephes. 5:27). She sanctifies sinners by her teaching and sacraments.

The Orthodox Church is catholic, because she was organized by the Lord Jesus Christ for the salvation of all people in the whole world, and she is the gathering of all true believers in all places, times, and peoples. The Orthodox Church will continue on earth until the Second Coming of Christ, "imperishable and not conquered by the powers of hell." In regard to holy doctrine, she is blameless and will ever remain unchangeable, as she has abiding in her the Holy Spirit, the Spirit of Truth. Therefore, she is, according to the Apostle, *the pillar and foundation of the Truth* (I Tim. 3:15). The existence of the lawful hierarchy and the administration of the Holy Mysteries will never cease in the Church.

The Lord Jesus Christ Himself said: *I will build My Church, and the gates of hell shall not prevail against her, and again: Behold I am with you always, even unto the end of the world.* Therefore, it is the duty of Christians to obey the Church, for outside of her there is no salvation. *If thy brother neglects to hear the Church, let him be to thee as a heathen man and a publican* (St. Math. 18:17) saith the Lord. May God, who is glorified in the Trinity, help us by His grace to become, through our membership in the Church Militant on earth, members of the Church Triumphant in heaven, that we may glorify His All-honorable and majestic Name with the angels and saints forever, without end. Amen.

26. St. Nikolai Velimirovich, Bishop of Zhicha and Ochrid (+1956)

HIS LIFE
WHICH IS CELEBRATED ON THE 5ᵀᴴ OF MARCH[468]

He was also the inspirer of a popular religious movement which promoted the practice of prayer, frequent Communion and the translation or composition of hymns and prayers in the Serbian language (not in Church Slavonic), the adherents of which breathed a spirit of enthusiasm and an evangelical freshness into the Serbian Church at that time. Bishop Nicolas' influence, in the midst of his people, was such that every one of his words, whether written or spoken, was considered worthy of being among the maxims of the Desert Fathers. Beyond the care he had for the flock that God had confided to him, he extended his concern to the whole Church. He showed himself to be a man of peace and reconciliation, and worked at maintaining good relations with the Orthodox Greeks and Bulgarians. In 1930, he took part in the Pan-Orthodox Pre-Conciliary Council in the Monastery of Vatopedi on Mount Athos, where he became the voice of Orthodoxy against the adapting of the Church's traditions to the present times. He was also the principal architect of the denunciation of the concordat with the Vatican that Yu-

468 Hieromonk Makarios of Simonos Petra, The Synaxarion: *The Lives of the Saints of the Orthodox Church, Volume Seven, Appendix-General Index*, trans. Mother Maria (Rule) (Athens: Indiktos Publishing Company, 2008), 142.

goslavia was ready to conclude in 1937, which would have turned the country into a mission field for the Roman Catholic Church. The holy Bishop had long foreseen that all-powerful Europe would crumble into dust if its Christian foundation were overthrown. He wrote prophetically about this: "Christ has withdrawn from Europe as He once did from the country of the Gadarenes, at the request of its inhabitants."

MIRACLE OF THE FEAST OF THE ZOGRAPHOU MARTYRS[469]

Once, during the celebration of the Feast of the twenty-six martyrs of Zographou, on October 10th, 1873, there was a great all-night vigil. It was a moonless night. In the middle of the night, while the monks were chanting and reading the lives of the holy martyrs in the church, a noise was suddenly heard, and over the church a fiery pillar appeared, extending from earth to heaven. It was so bright that things at a distance could be seen as though it were midday. This wondrous manifestation lasted for about a quarter of an hour and then disappeared.

HYMN OF PRAISE FOR THE HOLY MARTYRS OF ZOGRAPHOU[470]

Heroes of Zographou, knights of truth,
Sacrificed themselves for the Orthodox Faith,
And shamed the proud, shameless Latins,
As their souls rose up to the Kingdom of God.
The tower's flames mounted up to heaven,
As the monks in the fire sent up praise to God!
Heaven with its angels beheld that spectacle,
As the criminals crawled about like worms below the tower.
In the flames, Abbot Thomas, a true parent,
Encouraged his brethren, and began the Psalms:

---

469 Saint Nikolai Velimirović, *The Prologue of Ohrid, Volume Two, July to December,* trans. Father T. Timothy Tepsić (Vrnjačka Banja: Sebastian Press - Western American Diocese of the Serbian Orthodox Church, 2008), 389.

470 Ibid., 389.

He who glorifies the Lord does not fear death,
And he who dies for God will not perish.
The sacrifice is offered, and the altar of oblation remains:
The bodies were burned, the souls flew off,
And by that sacrifice, Zographou increased in glory
With magnificence eternal and true.
St. George the knight, cherishes his knights
As the Mother of God cherishes all heavenly citizens.
In these knights of righteousness, the Church rejoices:
They are her children, her fruitful branches.

THEOCRACY OF ROME WAS A BITTER PERSECUTOR[471]

Serbian magnanimity has often led to weakness, even to a great and fatal weakness —servility. The Serbs displayed this weakness during the Turkish and Austrian period as refugees in Russia and Romania. For in the course of time and in several waves, as many of the Serbian people emigrated to Russia and Romania as remained on that dreadful Balkan battlefield during that period.

On this dreadful Balkan battlefield there are today eight million Serbs. There ought to be just as many in Southern Russia and Romania. But there are none in Russia, for they all flowed into the melting pot and were recast into something else. And in Romania which, like Croatia, is half Serbian by blood, only a handful of Serbs remain, like a rear guard of a defeated army. A brother is a brother, and they are Orthodox, and we are Orthodox, so let us go and call ourselves Russians and Romanians! If such a thought had not been conceived, there would have been a million Serbs in Southern Russia today and in Romania as well.

This unbelievable weakness, this Achilles' heel, also manifested it-self during the era of Catholic-Orthodox Yugoslavia. The Catholics are our brothers, we were told, religion does not matter, the main thing is blood and language [...] and history, and the gallery of our glorious

---

471 Bishop Nikolai Velimirovich, *A Treasury of Serbian Orthodox Spirituality*, trans. Fr. Theodore Micka and Fr. Steven Scott (Grayslake: The Free Serbian Orthodox Diocese of the United States of America and Canada, 1988), 77-79.

Christ-loving tsars and kings, and the field of Kosovo, and the Uprising, and Kumanovo and Kajmakcalan, and the many millions of Serbs
who fought for the venerable cross and golden freedom, and the Serbian
banner-bearers — that all means nothing. We shall demolish and raze
all these lofty heights and conform them so that we may all be identical.
This is the language of the politicians and historians in Belgrade.

And thus, we shall decorate our most bitter persecutors, the servants
of the theocracy of Rom[e] and the autocracy of Vienna with the Star
of Karageorge, with swords and the Order of St. Sava Nemanjic. And
furthermore, we shall set the greatest betrayers of the Slavs and Orthodoxy and even Croatian-hood itself, the pretended kings Tomislav and
Zvonimir, on an equal footing with Tsar Dushan, King Milutin, and
Karageorge.

The nationalism of the Balkan peoples can be easily toned down by
a greater Christian consciousness. The greater this Christian consciousness becomes — and this means becoming conscious of the truth of God
— the more the rough edges of nationalism will be rounded off; not for
the purpose of eradicating it altogether, but for the purpose of toning
it down to patriotism and giving it dignity through faith in Christ and
service to Christ.

LETTER TO A LEARNED ORTHODOX MAN WHO ASKS WHY ORTHODOXY DOES NOT HAVE A POPE (LETTER 48)[472]

Orthodoxy does have its own pope, older than all of the popes and
patriarchs in the world. It had Him from the beginning and it will have
Him to the end of time. That is the same pope whom all the Apostles of
Christ called upon. The Holy Spirit. The Spirit of wisdom and reason,
the Spirit of comfort and power of God — He is the true pope of Christ's
Church always and forever and without a substitution or replacement,
without dispute or choice, without a predecessor and successor. And
that the Apostles recognized the Holy Spirit as their highest leader and
pope is attested by a document written by their own hands at the First

472 Saint Nikolai Velimirovich, *Missionary Letters of Saint Nikolai Velimirovich –
Volume 1*, trans. Hierodeacon Serafim (Baltic) (Grayslake: Joe Buley Memorial
Library/New Gracanica Monastery, 2008), 86-87.

Apostolic Council in Jerusalem which says these important words: *For it seemed good to the Holy Ghost, and to us* (Acts: 15:28). It is apparent that the Apostles placed the Holy Spirit before and above themselves. Before this and every meeting they prayed to Him, called upon Him, submitted themselves completely to Him. Do not all the elders of the Orthodox Church do this to this day?

Whenever the councils meet, they first remember their infallible pope: the Holy Spirit. They call upon Him with fear and trembling before beginning any work and they completely submit themselves to Him. This is not only done by Church elders but also by government officials in Orthodox countries, ministers and senators, who would always first call the Holy Spirit and would then begin their work in the counsels or senates. The school's elders have also always done the same. Do you know that at the beginning of the school day they call upon the Holy Spirit together with their students? And the All-Good, All-Powerful and All-Wise Holy Spirit guides everything, strengthens everything, inspires everything: The Church, the state and the education system. And He governs everyone in everything, but not through force like earthly dictators but rather like a father, with wisdom and love. He is our father through the baptism we were baptized with. And you know that the Greek word pope means father. So, by the true, historical and moral meaning the Holy Spirit is our father, our pope. Then why would the Orthodox Church need another father or pope? Did the Lord Christ not warn us to be wary of earthly popes and fathers? He commanded 19 centuries ago: *And call no man your father (pope) upon the earth: for one is your Father, which is in heaven.* (Matt. 23:9)

Peace and health from God to you.

27. St. Joseph the Hesychast (+1959)

His life
WHICH IS CELEBRATED ON THE 16TH OF AUGUST[473]

Saint Joseph was born on the Greek island of Paros on February 12, 1897, to simple but pious parents. Because of their extreme poverty, he left home at the age of seventeen to work in Piraeus as a merchant to support his large family and eventually he was engaged to be married. One day he beheld a wondrous vision of two angels in the form of palace guards, leading him to serve the heavenly king. After this vision, he became pensive and lost all interest in worldly things; he spent his time reading the lives of saints, especially those of the great ascetic Fathers, which ignited in his heart the desire to become a monk. He then called off his engagement, and in preparation for his life on the Holy Mountain, he started conditioning himself to ascetic struggles by fasting and praying in the countryside of Athens.

In 1921, after two years of living ascetically in the world, he finally made his way to the Holy Mountain, his heart longing for a God-bearing spiritual guide to teach him the art of noetic prayer, and he began traversing the crags and caves in search of one. After searching for some time without success, he decided to join the brotherhood of St. Daniel of Katounakia. But St. Daniel, seeing his desire for a more austere life, gave him a blessing to live in greater seclusion with a co-struggler, Father Arsenios, with whom he labored single-mindedly to acquire ceaseless prayer.

St. Joseph was tonsured a monk on Sunday, August 31, 1925, the commemoration day of the deposition of the precious sash of the Theotokos, and soon after began to acquire a brotherhood. He was sought after as a skilled and clairvoyant spiritual guide and an experienced teacher of noetic prayer. A few months before his death, St. Joseph was visited by the Theotokos, whom he held in special reverence, and was promised by

---

473 "St. Joseph the Hesychast (1897-1959)," Saint Anthony's Greek Orthodox Monastery, accessed November 7th, 2023, https://stanthonysmonastery.org/pages/st-joseph-the-hesychast

her, that she would take him on her feast day. Thus the saint fell asleep in the Lord on August 15, 1959, the day the Orthodox Church celebrates the Dormition of the Theotokos. Saint Joseph's legacy has been carried on by his disciples, who have reestablished the practice of noetic prayer and watchfulness on the Holy Mountain, brought Athonite monasticism to the United States and Canada through the labors of Geronda Ephraim of Arizona, and encouraged many Orthodox faithful through the publishing of his life and letters.

CONCERNING CATHOLICS AND OTHER HETERODOX[474]

This is how you should speak to the Lord:

"O my beloved, sweetest Jesus Christ, who was it that entreated Thee on my behalf, and who prayed for me to come into the world, and to be born by good and faithful Christian parents? While so many others are born to Turks, Catholics, Masons, Jews, pagans, and the rest[475], who do not believe, but are as if they have not been completely born and end up being punished eternally. So how much must I love Thee and thank Thee for such a great gift and kindness which Thou hast bestowed upon me. And even if I were to shed my blood, I would not be able to thank Thee enough.

"And furthermore, whose prayers made Thee, my sweetest Savior, patient with me for so many years – for I have sinned since my youth – and not grow tired of seeing me acting unjustly, stealing, getting angry, being gluttonous, greedy, envious, jealous, and full of every evil, and insulting Thee my God with my deeds?

"But Thou, my Lord, didst not send death upon me to seize me in my sins, but readily Thou wast patient with me. If I had died, I would have been punished eternally! How good art Thou, O Lord!

---

474 Saint Anthony's Greek Orthodox Monastery, *Monastic Wisdom: The Letters of Elder Joseph the Hesychast* (Florence: Saint Anthony's Greek Orthodox Monastery Press, 1998), 343-344.

475 In essence, what the Elder is teaching here is that we be thankful that God has brought us to a position where we can partake of the salvific life of the Orthodox Church.

"And who entreated Thee to bring me to repentance and confession, and to clothe me with the great and angelic schema? How magnificent art Thou, O Lord! How awesome is Thy great dispensation! How abundant are Thy gifts, O Master! How inexhaustible are Thine indescribable wonders! Who will not shudder, marveling at Thy goodness? Who will not be amazed, beholding Thine abundant mercy? I shudder, O Master, when I speak of Thine abundant gifts.

"My Master and Lord is crucified to save the crucifiers. With my sins, I crucify my Creator, and He Who fashioned me frees me! O sweet love of Jesus, how much am I indebted to Thee! Not only because of the eternal life which Thou hast promised to give me should I love Thee, not only because Thou wilt give my Thy grace, not even because of paradise, but I am obligated to love Thee because Thou hast freed me from the slavery of sin and passions."

28. St. John (Maximovitch) of Shanghai and San Francisco (+1966)

The Holy Hierarch John Maximovitch was born in the Kharkov region in 1896 and reposed in San Francisco in 1966. In 1921, during the Russian Civil War, his family fled to Belgrade, joining the ranks of Russian exiles in Serbia, where he later became a monk and was ordained priest. In 1934 he was made Bishop of Shanghai, where he served until the Communists came to power. Thereafter he ministered in Europe, serving as Bishop first in Paris then in Brussels, until he became Archbishop of San Francisco in 1962. Throughout his life he was revered as a strict ascetic, a devoted man of prayer, and a truly wondrous unmercenary healer of all manner of afflictions and woes. He served the Divine Liturgy daily, slept little more than an hour a day, and kept a strict fast until the evening. It is doubtful that any one man gave so much protec-

476 Holy Transfiguration Monastery, *The Great Horologion* (Boston: Holy Transfiguration Monastery, 1997), 515.

tion and comfort as he to the Russian Orthodox people in exile after the Revolution of 1917; he was an unwearying and watchful shepherd of his sheep in China, the Philippines, Europe, and America. Through his missionary labours he also brought into the Church many who had not been "of this fold." While serving as a bishop in Europe and then America, he labored to increase the knowledge and veneration of Pre-Schism Orthodox saints of the West for the Orthodox residing in Western lands. Since his repose in 1966, he has been especially glorified by God through signs and miracles, and his body has remained incorrupt. In addition to his published homilies which have been translated into several languages, St. John also authored the book The Orthodox Veneration of Mary the Birthgiver of God which explains the Orthodox view of the Theotokos and how Orthodox teachings differ from Latin teachings concerning her.

Severe Judgment for Those Who are Outwardly Orthodox but Surreptitiously Work to Make Russia Catholic or Protestant [477]

In the future life the judgment will be most severe for those Russians who, being educated in superb colleges, become the fiercest enemies of Russia. One is forced to foresee already that in the future the Diaspora will give many conscious workers against Orthodox Russia, who will strive to make it Catholic or spread various sects and likewise those who, while remaining outwardly Orthodox and Russian, will secretly work against Russia.

Prince Alexander Nevsky Preserved the Russian Spiritual Might Against the Catholic Swedes [478]

Prince Vladimir gave the Russian people a new meaning of life and a new vitality. Calamities, failures and defeats are powerless before the

---

477 Orthodox Christian Books & Icons, "The Meaning of the Russian Diaspora," Orthodox Word 9, no. 3 (May-June 1973): 93.

478 Saint John (Maximovich), "The Faithfulness to the Russian Path of Righteousness," Pravoslavnaja Rus, no. 11 (June: 1994): 1-3.

main force of life, powerless before spiritual life. The Kingdom of God, the spiritual joy of participating in it remain untouched. The terrible storm passes, and again a man lives. Thus, during the most cruel tortures, the martyrs rejoiced, sensing God's grace.

This is the source of Russia's vitality. Calamities do not strike her heart. The Tartars burned the whole of Russia. Kiev fell, and in the same year Novgorod arose; and that great commander and leader of the Russian people, the Right-believing Prince Alexander Nevsky, roused the Russian people for a struggle, not with the Tartars, who had racked Russia's body, but with the Catholic Swedes, who, taking advantage of Russia's misfortune, wanted to seize the soul of the Russian people and kill the spiritual might of the Russian nation and Russia. For Alexander Nevsky it was necessary above all to preserve that spiritual might.

The Corruption by the Latins, in the Newly-invented Dogma of the "Immaculate Conception," of the True Veneration of the Most Holy Mother of God and Ever-Virgin Mary[479]

When those who censured the immaculate life of the Most Holy Virgin had been accused, as well as those who denied Her Ever-virginity, those who denied Her dignity as the Mother of God, and those who disdained Her icons — then, when the glory of the Mother of God had illuminated the whole universe, there appeared a teaching which seemingly exalted highly the Virgin Mary, but in reality denied all Her virtues.

This teaching is called that of the Immaculate Conception of the Virgin Mary, and it was accepted by the followers of the Papal throne of Rome. The teaching is this: that "the All-blessed Virgin Mary in the first instant of Her Conception, by the special grace of Almighty God and by a special privilege, for the sake of the future merits of Jesus Christ, Saviour of the human race, was preserved exempt from all stain of original sin" (Bull of Pope Pius IX concerning the new dogma). In other words, the Mother of God at Her very Conception was preserved from original

---

479 Saint John (Maximovitch), *The Orthodox Veneration of the Mother of God* (Platina: Saint Herman of Alaska Brotherhood, 1976), 35-47.

sin and, by the grace of God, was placed in a state where it was impossible for Her to have personal sins.

Christians had not heard of this before the ninth century, when for the first time the Abbot of Corvey, Paschasius Radbertus, expressed the opinion that the Holy Virgin was conceived without original sin. Beginning from the 12th century, this idea begins to spread among the clergy and flock of the Western church, which had already fallen away from the Universal Church and thereby lost the grace of the Holy Spirit.

However, by no means all of the members of the Roman church agreed with the new teaching. There was a difference of opinion even among the most renowned theologians of the West, the pillars, so to speak, of the Latin church. Thomas Aquinas and Bernard of Clairvaux decisively censured it, while Duns Scotus defended it. From the teachers this division carried over to their disciples: the Latin Dominican monks, after their teacher Thomas Aquinas, preached against the teaching of the Immaculate Conception, while the followers of Duns Scotus, the Franciscans, strove to implant it everywhere. The battle between these two currents continued for the course of several centuries. Both on the one and on the other side there were those who were considered among the Catholics as the greatest authorities.

There was no help in deciding the question in the fact that several people declared that they had had a revelation from above concerning it. The nun Bridget, renowned in the 14th century among the Catholics spoke in her writings about the appearances to her of the Mother of God, Who Herself told her that She had been conceived immaculately, without original sin. But her contemporary, the yet more renowned ascetic Catherine of Sienna, affirmed that in Her conception the Holy Virgin participated in original sin, concerning which she had received a revelation from Christ Himself. (See the book of Archpriest A. Lebedev, *Differences in the Teaching on the Most Holy Mother of God in the Churches of East and West.*)

Thus, neither on the foundation of theological writings, nor on the foundation of miraculous manifestations which contradicted each other, could the Latin flock distinguish for a long time where the truth was. Roman Popes until Sixtus IV (end of the 15th century) remained apart from these disputes, and only this Pope in 1475 approved a service in which the teaching of the Immaculate Conception was clearly expressed; and several years later he forbade a condemnation of those who believed in the Immaculate Conception. However, even Sixtus IV did not yet decide to affirm that such was the unwavering teaching of the church; and therefore, having forbidden the condemnation of those who believed in the Immaculate Conception, he also did not condemn those who believed otherwise.

Meanwhile, the teaching of the Immaculate Conception obtained more and more partisans among the members of the Roman-Papist church. The reason for this was the fact that it seemed more pious and pleasing to the Mother of God to give Her as much glory as possible. The striving of the people to glorify the Heavenly Intercessor, on the one hand, and on the other hand, the deviation of Western theologians into abstract speculations which led only to a seeming truth (Scholasticism), and finally, the patronage of the Roman Popes after Sixtus IV — all this led to the fact that the opinion concerning the Immaculate Conception which had been expressed by the Paschasius Radbertus in the 9th century was already the general belief of the Latin church in the 19th century. There remained only to proclaim this definitely as the church's teaching, which was done by the Roman Pope Pius IX during a solemn service on December 8, 1854, when he declared that the Immaculate Conception of the Most Holy Virgin was a dogma of the Roman Church.

Thus, the Roman Church added yet another deviation from the teaching which it had confessed while it was a member of the Catholic, Apostolic Church, which faith has been held up to now unaltered and unchanged by the Orthodox Church. The proclamation of the new dogma satisfied the broad masses of people who belonged to the Roman church, who in simplicity of heart thought that the proclamation of the new teaching in the church would serve for the greater glory of the Mother of God, to Whom by this they were making a gift, as it were. There was also satisfied the vainglory of the Western theologians who had defended and worked it out. But most of all the proclamation of the new dogma was profitable for the Roman throne itself, since, having proclaimed the new dogma by his own authority, even though he did listen to the opinions of the bishops of the Catholic church, the Roman Pope by this very fact openly appropriated to himself the right to change the teaching of the Roman church and placed his own voice above the testimony of Sacred Scripture and Tradition. A direct deduction from this was the fact that the Roman Popes were infallible in matters of faith, which indeed this very same Pope Pius IX likewise proclaimed as a dogma of the Catholic church in 1870.

Thus was the teaching of the Western church changed after it had fallen away from communion with the True Church. It has introduced into itself newer and newer teachings, thinking by this to glorify the Truth yet more, but in reality, distorting it. While the Orthodox Church humbly confesses what it has received from Christ and the Apostles, the Roman church dares to add to it, sometimes from "zeal not according to knowledge" (Rom. 10:2), and sometimes by deviating into superstitions and into the "contradictions of knowledge falsely so-called" (1 Tim. 6:20). It could not be otherwise. That "the gates of hell shall not prevail" against the Church (Matt. 16:18) is promised only to the True, Universal Church; but upon those who have fallen away from it are fulfilled the words, "As the branch cannot bear fruit of itself, except it abide in the vine; so, neither can ye, except ye abide in Me." (John 15:4)

It is true that in the very definition of the new dogma it is said that a new teaching is not being established, but that there is only being proclaimed as the church's that which always existed in the church, and which has been held by many Holy Fathers, excerpts from whose writings are cited. However, all the cited references speak only of the exalted sanctity of the Virgin Mary and of Her immaculateness, and give Her various names which define Her purity and spiritual might; but nowhere is there any word of the immaculateness of Her Conception. Meanwhile, these same Holy Fathers in other places say that only Jesus Christ is completely pure of every sin, while all men, being born of Adam, have borne a flesh subject to the law of sin. None of the ancient Holy Fathers say that God in miraculous fashion purified the Virgin Mary while yet in the womb; and many directly indicate that the Virgin Mary, just as all men, endured a battle with sinfulness, but was victorious over temptations and was saved by Her Divine Son.

Commentators of the Latin confession likewise say that the Virgin Mary was saved by Christ. But they understand this in the sense that Mary was preserved from the taint of original sin in view of the future merits of Christ (Bull on the Dogma of the Immaculate Conception). The Virgin Mary, according to their teaching, received in advance, as it were, the gift which Christ brought to men by His sufferings and death on the Cross. Moreover, speaking of the torments of the Mother of God which She endured standing at the Cross of Her Beloved Son, and in general of the sorrows with which the life of the Mother of God was filled, they consider them an addition to the sufferings of Christ and consider Mary to be our Co-Redemptress. According to the commentary of the Latin theologians, "Mary is an associate with our Redeemer as a Co-Redemptress" (see Lebedev, op.cit., p. 273). "In the act of Redemption, She, in a certain way, helped Christ" (Catechism of Dr. Weimar). "The Mother of God," writes Dr. Lentz, "bore the burden of Her martyrdom not merely courageously, but also joyful, even though with a broken heart" (Mariology of Dr. Lentz). For this reason, She is "a complement of the Holy Trinity," and "just as Her Son is the only Intermediary chosen by God between His offended majesty and sinful men, so also, precisely, the chief Mediatress placed by Him between His Son and us is the Blessed Virgin." "In three respects — as Daughter, as Mother, and as Spouse of God — the Holy Virgin is exalted to a certain equality with the Father, to a certain superiority over the Son, to a certain nearness to the Holy Spirit" ("The Immaculate Conception," Malou, Bishop of Brouges).

Thus, according to the teaching of the representatives of Latin theology, the Virgin Mary in the work of Redemption is placed side by side with Christ Himself and is exalted to an *equality with God*. One cannot go farther than this. If all this has not been definitively formulated as a dogma of the Roman church as yet, still the Roman Pope Pius IX, having made the first step in this direction, has shown the direction for the further development of the generally recognized teaching of his church, and has indirectly confirmed the above-cited teaching about the Virgin Mary.

Thus, the Roman church, in its strivings to exalt the Most Holy Virgin, is going on the path of complete *deification* of Her. And if even now its authorities call Mary a complement of the Holy Trinity, one may soon expect that the Virgin will be revered like God. There have entered on this same path a group of thinkers who for the time being belong to the

Orthodox Church, but who are building a new theological system having as its foundation the philosophical teaching of Sophia, Wisdom, as a special power binding the Divinity and the creation. Likewise developing the teaching of the dignity of the Mother of God, they wish to see in Her an essence which is some kind of mid-point between God and man. In some questions they are more moderate than the Latin theologians, but in others, if you please, they have already left them behind. While denying the teaching of the Immaculate Conception and the freedom from original sin, they still teach Her full freedom from any personal sins, seeing in Her in Intermediary between men and God, like Christ: in the person of Christ there has appeared on earth the Second Person of the Holy Trinity, the Pre-eternal Word, the Son of God, while the Holy Spirit is manifest through the Virgin Mary.

In the words of one of the representatives of this tendency, when the Holy Spirit came to dwell in the Virgin Mary, she acquired "a dyadic life, human and divine: that is, She was completely deified, because in Her hypostatic being was manifest the living, creative revelation of the Holy Spirit" (Archpriest Sergei Bulgakov, *The Unburnt Bush*, 1927, p.154). "She is a perfect manifestation of the Third Hypostasis" (Ibid., p.175), "a creature, but also no longer a creature" (p. 191). This striving towards the deification of the Mother of God is to be observed primarily in the West, where at the same time, on the other hand, various sects of a Protestant character are having great success, together with the chief branches of Protestantism, Lutheranism and Calvinism, which in general deny the veneration of the Mother of God and the calling upon Her in prayer.

But we can say with the words of St. Epiphanius of Cyprus: "There is an equal harm in both these heresies, both when men demean the Virgin and when, on the contrary, they glorify Her beyond what is proper" (*Panarion*, "Against the Collyridians"). This Holy Father accuses those who give Her an almost divine worship: "Let Mary be in honor, but let *worship* be given to the Lord" (same source). "Although Mary is a chosen vessel, still She was a woman by nature, not to be distinguished at all from others. Although the history of Mary and Tradition relate that it was said to Her father Joachim in the desert, 'Thy wife hath conceived,' still this was done not without marital union and not without the seed of man" (same source). "One should not revere the saints above what is proper, but should revere their Master. Mary is not God, and did not receive a body from heaven, but from the joining of man and woman; and according to the promise, like Isaac, She was prepared to take part in the Divine Economy. But, on the other hand, let none dare foolishly to offend the Holy Virgin" (St. Epiphanius, "Against the Antidikomarionites").

The Orthodox Church, highly exalting the Mother of God in its hymns of praise, does not dare to ascribe to Her that which has not been communicated about Her by Sacred Scripture or Tradition. "Truth is foreign to all overstatements as well as to all understatements. It gives to everything a fitting measure and fitting place" (Bishop Ignatius Brianchaninov). Glorifying the immaculateness of the Virgin Mary and the manful bearing of sorrows in Her earthly life, the Fathers of the Church, on the other hand, reject the idea that She was an intermediary between God and men in the sense of the joint Redemption by Them of the human race. Speaking of Her preparedness to die together with the renowned Father of the Western Church, Saint Ambrose, Bishop of Milan, adds: "But the sufferings of Christ did not need any help, as the Lord Himself prophesied concerning this long before: *I looked about, and there was none to help; I sought and there was none to give aid* (Is. 63:5)" (St. Ambrose, "Concerning the Upbringing of the Virgin and the Ever-Virginity of Holy Mary," ch. 7).

The same Holy Father teaches concerning the universality of original sin, from which Christ alone is an exception. "Of all those born of women, there is not a single one who is perfectly holy, apart from the Lord Jesus Christ, Who in a special new way of immaculate birth-giving, did not experience earthly taint" (St. Ambrose, *Commentary on Luke*, ch. 2). "God alone is without sin. All born in the usual manner of woman and man, that is, of fleshly union, become guilty of sin. Consequently, He Who does not have sin was not conceived in this manner" (St. Ambrose, Ap. Aug. "Concerning Marriage and Conception"). "One Man alone, the Intermediary between God and man, is free from the bonds of sinful birth, because He was born of a Virgin, and because in being born He did not experience the touch of sin" (St. Ambrose, *Against Julian*, Book 2).

Another renowned teacher of the Church, especially revered in the West, Blessed Augustine, writes: "As for other men, excluding Him Who is the cornerstone, I do not see for them any other means to become temples of God and to be dwellings for God apart from spiritual rebirth, which must absolutely be preceded by fleshly birth. Thus, no matter how much we might think about children who are in the womb of the mother, and even though the word of the holy Evangelist who says of John the Baptist that he leaped for joy in the womb of his mother (which occurred not otherwise than by the action of the Holy Spirit), or the word of the Lord Himself spoken to Jeremiah: *I have sanctified thee before thou didst leave the womb of thy mother* — no matter how much these might or might not give us a basis for thinking that children in this condition are capable of a certain sanctification, still in any case it cannot be doubted that the sanctification by which all of us together and each of us separately become the temple of God is possibly only for those who are reborn, and rebirth always presupposes birth. Only those who have already been born can be united with Christ and be in union with this Divine Body which makes His Church the living temple of the majesty of God" (Blessed Augustine, Letter 187).

The above-cited works of the ancient teachers of the Church testify that in the West itself the teaching which is now spread there was earlier rejected there. Even after the falling away of the Western church, Bernard, who is acknowledged there as a great authority, wrote, "I am frightened now, seeing that certain of you have desired to change the condition of important matters, introducing a new festival unknown to the Church, unapproved by the reason, unjustified by ancient tradition. Are we really more learned and more pious than our fathers? You will say, 'One must glorify the Mother of God as much as possible.' This is true; but the glorification given to the Queen of Heaven demands discernment. The Royal Virgin does not have need of false glorifications, possessing as She does true crowns of glory and signs of dignity. Glorify the purity of her flesh and the sanctity of Her life. Marvel at the abundance of the gifts of this Virgin; venerate Her Divine Son; exalt Her Who conceived without knowing concupiscence and gave birth without knowing pain. But what does one yet need to add to these dignities? People say that one must revere the conception which preceded the glorious birth-giving; for if the conception had not preceded, the birth-giving also would not have been glorious. But what would one say if anyone for the same reason should demand the same kind of veneration of the father and mother of Holy Mary? One might equally demand the same for Her grandparents and great-grandparents, to infinity. Moreover, how can there not be sin in the place where there was concupiscence? All the more, let one not say that the Holy Virgin was conceived of the Holy Spirit and not of man. I say decisively that the Holy Spirit descended upon Her, but not that He came with Her."

"I say that the Virgin Mary could not be sanctified before Her conception, inasmuch as She did not exist. If, all the more, She could not be sanctified in the moment of Her conception by reason of the sin which is inseparable from conception, then it remains to believe that She was sanctified after She was conceived in the womb of her mother. This sanctification, if it annihilates sin, makes holy Her birth, but not Her conception. No one is given the right to be conceived in sanctity; only the Lord Christ was conceived of the Holy Spirit, and He alone is holy from His very conception. Excluding Him, it is to all the descendants of Adam that must be referred that which one of them says of himself, both out of a feeling of humility and in acknowledgement of the truth: *Behold I was conceived in iniquities* (Ps. 50:7). How can one demand that this conception be holy, when it was not the work of the Holy Spirit, not to mention that it came from concupiscence? The Holy Virgin, of course, rejects that glory in spite of the teaching of the Church, a novelty which is the mother of imprudence, the sister of unbelief, and the daughter of lightmindedness." (Bernard, Epistle 174; cited, as were the references from Bl. Augustine, from Lebedev.) The above-cited words clearly reveal both the novelty and the absurdity of the new dogma of the Roman church.

The teaching of the complete sinlessness of the Mother of God (1) does not correspond to Sacred Scripture, where there is repeatedly mentioned the sinlessness of the "One Mediator between God and man, the man Jesus Christ" (1 Tim. 2:5); "and in Him is no sin" (1 John 3:5); "Who did no sin, neither was guile found in His mouth." (1 Peter 2:22); "One that hath been in all points tempted like as we are, yet without sin" (Heb. 4:15); "Him Who knew no sin, He made to be sin on our behalf"

(II Cor. 5:21). But concerning the rest of men it is said, *Who is pure of defilement? No one who has lived a single day of his life on earth* (Job 14:4). *God commendeth His own love toward us in that, while we were yet sinners, Christ died for us... If, while we were enemies, we were reconciled to God through the death of His Son, much more, being reconciled, shall we be saved by His life* (Rom. 5:8-10).

(2) This teaching contradicts also *Sacred Tradition*, which is contained in numerous patristic writings, where there is mentioned the exalted sanctity of the Virgin Mary from Her very birth, as well as Her cleansing by the Holy Spirit at Her conception of Christ, but not at Her own conception by Anna. "There is none without stain before Thee, even though his life be but a day, save Thou alone, Jesus Christ our God, Who didst appear on earth without sin, and through Whom we all trust to obtain mercy and the remission of sins." (St. Basil the Great, Third Prayer of Vespers of Pentecost.) "But when Christ came through a pure, virginal, unwedded, God-fearing, undefiled Mother without wedlock and without father, and inasmuch as it befitted Him to be born, He purified the female nature, rejected the bitter Eve and overthrew the laws of the flesh" (St. Gregory the Theologian, "In Praise of Virginity"). However, even then, as Sts. Basil the Great and John Chrysostom speak of this, She was not placed in the state of being unable to sin, but continued to take care of Her salvation and overcame all temptations (St. John Chrysostom, *Commentary on John*, Homily 85; St. Basil the Great, Epistle 160).

(3) The teaching that the Mother of God was purified before Her birth, so that from Her might be born the Pure Christ, is meaningless; because if the Pure Christ could be born only if the Virgin might be born pure, it would be necessary that Her parents also should be pure of original sin, and they again would have to be born of purified parents, and going further in this way, one would have to come to the conclusion that Christ could not have become incarnate unless all His ancestors in the flesh, right up to Adam inclusive, had been purified beforehand of original sin. But then there would not have been any need for the very Incarnation of Christ, since Christ came down to earth in order to annihilate sin.

(4) The teaching that the Mother of God was preserved from original sin, as likewise the teaching that She was preserved by God's grace from personal sins, *makes God unmerciful and unjust*; because if God could preserve Mary from sin and purify Her before Her birth, then why does He not purify other men before their birth, but rather leaves them in sin? It follows likewise that God saves men apart from their will, predetermining certain ones before their birth to salvation.

(5) This teaching, which seemingly has the aim of exalting the Mother of God, in reality completely *denies all Her virtues*. After all, if Mary, even in the womb of Her mother, when She could not even desire anything either good or evil, was preserved by God's grace from every impurity, and then by that grace was preserved from sin even after Her birth, then in what does Her merit consist? If She could have been placed in the state of being unable to sin, and did not sin, then for what did God glorify Her? If She, without any effort, and without having any kind of impulses to sin, remained pure, then why is She crowned more than everyone else? There is no victory without an adversary.

The righteousness and sanctity of the Virgin Mary were manifested in the fact that She, being "human with passions like us," so loved God and gave Herself over to Him, that by Her purity She was exalted high above the rest of the human race. For this, having been foreknown and forechosen, She was vouchsafed to the purified by the Holy Spirit Who came upon Her, and to conceive of Him the very Saviour of the world. The teaching of the grace-given sinlessness of the Virgin Mary denies Her victory over temptations; from a victor who is worthy to be crowned with crowns of glory, this makes Her a blind instrument of God's Providence.

It is not an exaltation and greater glory, but a *belittlement* of Her, this "gift" which was given Her by Pope Pius IX and all the rest who think they can glorify the Mother of God by seeking out new truths. The Most Holy Mary has been so much glorified by God Himself, so exalted is Her life on earth and Her glory in heaven, that human inventions cannot add anything to Her honor and glory. That which people themselves invent only obscures Her Face from their eyes. *Brethren, take heed lest there shall be anyone that maketh spoil of you through philosophy and vain deceit, after the tradition of men, after the rudiments of the world, and not after Christ*, wrote the Apostle Paul by the Holy Spirit (Col. 2:18).

Such a "vain deceit" is the teaching of the Immaculate Conception by Anna of the Virgin Mary, which at first sight exalts, but in actual fact belittles Her. Like every lie, it is a seed of the "father of lies" (John 8:44), the devil, who has succeeded by it in deceiving many who do not understand that they blaspheme the Virgin Mary. Together with it there should also be rejected all the other teachings which have come from it or are akin to it. The striving to exalt the Most Holy Virgin to an equality with Christ ascribing to Her maternal tortures at the Cross an equal significance with the sufferings of Christ, so that the Redeemer and "Co-Redemptress" suffered equally, according to the teaching of the Papists, or that "the human nature of the Mother of God in heaven together with the God-Man Jesus jointly reveal the full image of man" (Archpriest S. Bulgakov, *The Unburnt Bush*, p. 141) — is likewise a vain deceit and seduction of philosophy. In Christ Jesus *there is neither male nor female* (Gal. 3:28), and Christ has redeemed the whole human race; therefore, at His Resurrection equally did "Adam dance for joy and Eve rejoice" (Sunday Kontakia of the First and Third Tones), and by his Ascension did the Lord raise up the whole of human nature.

Likewise, that the Mother of God is a "complement of the Holy Trinity" or a "fourth hypostasis"; that "the Son and the Mother are a revelation of the Father through the Second and Third Hypostases"; that the Virgin Mary is "a creature, but also no longer a creature" — all this is the fruit of vain, false wisdom which is not satisfied with what the Church has held from the time of the Apostles, but strives to glorify the Holy Virgin more than God has glorified Her.

Thus are the words of St. Epiphanius of Cyprus fulfilled: "Certain senseless ones in their opinion about the Holy Ever-Virgin have striven and are striving to put Her in place of God" (St. Epiphanius, "Against the Antidikomarionites"). But that which is offered to the Virgin in senselessness, instead of praise of Her turns out to be blasphemy; and the All-Immaculate one rejects the lie, being the Mother of Truth (John 14:6).

29. St. Justin (Popović) of Tjelije (+1979)[480]

His life,
which is celebrated on the 1st of June[481]

St. Justin was born on March 25, 1894, in the southern Serbian town of Vranje. He was baptized Evangelos with the surname Popović. In 1914, St. Justin graduated from the School of St. Sava in Belgrade. After serving in the Serbian army, he was tonsured a monk on January 1, 1916, and given the name of St. Justin the martyr and philosopher. Later, he went to study in Athens and received his doctorate in Patristic Studies in 1926, after which he returned to Serbia. With the establishment of the new leadership in Yugoslavia in 1945, Father Justin was expelled from the University of Belgrade along with 200 professors. He was then arrested in southern Serbia and imprisoned. He completed his days confined to the Ćelije [or Tjelije] Monastery, Valievo and reposed in the Lord on March 25, 1979, the day of the Annunciation and the day of his birth. St. Justin is venerated as a contemporary Holy Father for his defense of the faith and his fidelity to the Holy Fathers who came before him. He wrote many important Orthodox dogmatic works including three volumes on *Orthodox Dogmatic Theology, The Orthodox Church and Ecumenism, and Orthodox Faith and Life in Christ.* St. Justin was a staunch defender of Orthodox ecclesiology and an outspoken critic of those who sought to blur the boundaries of the Church and mix truth with falsehood in the contemporary Ecumenical Movement.

---

480 See page 528 for the Apolytikion to him.

481 "Memory of Saint Justin Popović," *Orthodox Times*, accessed November 5th, 2023, https://orthodoxtimes.com/memory-of-saint-justin-popovic-2/

Orthodox Dogma Replaced by the Latin Heretical Dogma[482]

Orthodox dogma, the universal dogma of the Church, has been rejected and replaced by the Latin heretical and universal dogma of the primacy and later the infallibility of the Pope, a man. This universal heresy has engendered other heresies: the Filioque, the removal of the epiclesis, the introduction of material grace, unleavened bread, purgatory, a repository of surplus deeds, a mechanical teaching on salvation and, thereby, a mechanical teaching on life, on papo-centrism, on the Holy Inquisition, indulgences, the killing of sinners because of their sin, jesuitics, scholastics, casuistics, monarchistics, social humanism and so forth.

Papism is the Most Radical Protestantism[483]

Papism has determinedly and persistently worked at replacing the God-Man by a man, until it has replaced Him forever with the ephemeral "infallible" man, with the dogma of papal infallibility. By this dogma, the Pope was clearly and decisively pronounced to be not only somewhat higher than a man, but also higher than the holy apostles, the holy fathers and the holy Ecumenical Councils. With such distancing from the Theanthropos, from the universal Church as a theanthropic organism, Papism has outdone Luther, the creator of Protestantism. In fact, the first, radical protest in the name of humanism against Christ the God-Man and His theanthropic organism, the Church, can be traced to Papism, not Lutheranism. Papism is actually the first and earliest Protestantism.

Make no mistake: Papism is the most radical Protestantism, for it has transferred the foundations of Christianity from the eternal God-Man to ephemeral man. It has proclaimed this as its central dogma, as the highest truth, the highest value, the highest norm for all beings and things in all worlds. The Protestants only accepted the essence of this

---

482 Saint Justin Popović, *The Orthodox Church and Ecumenism*, trans. Benjamin Emmanuel Stanley (Birmingham: Lazarica Press, 2000), 153.

483 Ibid., 119-120.

dogma and worked it out to a fearsome extent and in fearsome detail. In fact, Protestantism is nothing other than generally-applied Papism, for in Protestantism every man individually lives out the main principle of Papism. Following the example of the infallible man in Rome, every Protestant is an infallible man, for he pretends to personal infallibility in matters of faith. It could be said that Protestantism is vulgarized Papism, devoid of mysticism, authority and power.

INFALLIBILITY OF THE POPE HAS BECOME THE UNIVERSAL DOGMA OF PAPISM[484]

By the appropriating, through the dogma of infallibility, of all the power and rights belonging solely to Christ the God-Man, the Pope, a man, has, in fact, by this act, proclaimed himself a church within the papist Church and has become all-powerful in it. He has become his own version of the "upholder of all things". For this reason, the dogma of the infallibility of the Pope has become the universal dogma of Papism. The Pope cannot give it up at any price, as long as he is the Pope of humanistic Papism.

PAPISM IS THE PINNACLE OF NIHILISM[485]

What is the core of the dogma of the infallibility of the Pope, a man? The de-theanthropising of man. All the humanisms are working on it, even the religious ones. They all return man to atheism, to paganism, to a twofold death: spiritual and physical. By distancing itself from the God-Man, every humanism gradually turns into nihilism. The present breakdown of all humanisms headed by Papism (which is both an indirect and a direct, an involuntary and a voluntary, parent of all European humanisms), illustrates this. The catastrophic breakdown of Papism lies in the dogma of the infallibility of the Pope. This dogma is the pinnacle of nihilism. European man has thereby, in a dogmatically determined way, proclaimed the dogma of the autarchy of European man, and has

---

484 Ibid., 144.

485 Ibid., 148-149.

thus finally revealed that he does not need the God-Man, that there is no place on earth for Him; *Vicarius Christi* replaces Him completely. Every European humanism lives by this dogma, upholds it and stubbornly confesses it.

INFALLIBILITY OF THE POPE IS THE ULTIMATE HERESY[486]

According to the true Church of Christ, that has existed since the advent of Christ the Theanthropos into this world as His theanthropic Body, the dogma of the infallibility of the Pope is not only a heresy, but the ultimate heresy. No other heresy has so radically and so comprehensively risen against Christ the Theanthropos and His Church as Papism has through the dogma of the infallibility of the Pope, a man. This is undoubtedly the heresy above all heresies. It is the horror above all horrors. It is an unseen rebellion against Christ the God-Man. It is, alas, the most dreadful banishment of the Lord Christ from the earth. It is the repeated betrayal of Christ, the repeated crucifixion of the Lord Christ, not on a wooden cross this time but on the golden cross of papist humanism. All this is hell thrice over for the wretched earthly being called man.

DEFENDING ORTHODOXY AGAINST THE CONCORDAT[487]

Wherever he went, and on all who came to seek his advice, he left a profound impression: that of a man who lived only for God and for the defence of the truth of the Gospel. Taking the Prophets and the Fathers of the Church as models, he steadfastly asserted that, in Orthodoxy, all is according to the Gospel: faith, prayer, ascesis, the Divine Office, the Holy Mysteries and the holy virtues. The whole of the Church's Tradition is nothing other than the living gospel. In the turmoil that preceded the Second World War, he refused to take part in the game of political passions, proclaiming evangelical truth with no fear of human pressure. It was thus that he unambiguously defended the cause of Orthodoxy,

---

486 Ibid., 149-150.

487 Hieromonk Makarios of Simonos Petra, *The Synaxarion: The Lives of the Saints of the Orthodox Church, Volume Seven, Appendix-General Index*, trans. Mother Maria (Rule) (Athens: Indiktos Publishing Company, 2008), 156-158.

when the Vatican was seeking to impose Catholicism as the state religion in Yugoslavia in the form of a Concordat (1937).

During the sixties, although some Orthodox were taken up with the path of ecclesiological relativism, going as far as denying the uniqueness of the Church of Christ in the name of Christian charity, Father Justin once more made himself the mouthpiece of the Church's conscience to denounce the dangers threatening Orthodoxy. If, in his writings, he radically condemned heterodox dogmas much in the manner of the Old Testament prophets, he had in fact great sensitivity towards people, and a ready compassion for human misery.

ONLY ORTHODOXY IS THE VESSEL OF GOD-HUMAN CHRIST, NOT ROMAN CATHOLICISM OR PROTESTANTISM[488]

And today only Orthodox ascetic efforts and virtues can bring about sanctity in every soul, in the soul of all our people — seeing that the God-human objective of the Church is unalterable, and its means are likewise so, since Christ is indeed the same, yesterday and today and unto all ages (Heb. 13:8). Herein lies the difference between the world of men and the one in Christ: the human world is transient and time-bound, whilst that of Christ is as ever whole, for ever more. Orthodoxy, as the single vessel and guardian of the perfect and radiant Person of God-human Christ, is brought about exclusively by this exertion of virtues by grace, through entirely God-human Orthodox means, not borrowings from Roman Catholicism or Protestantism because the latter are forms of Christianity after the pattern of the proud European being, and not of the humble God-human being.

PAPACY REPLACES THE GOD-MAN WITH AN INFALLIBLE MAN[489]

In the European West, Christianity gradually became transformed into humanism. For several centuries the God-man became more and

---

488 Father (St.) Justin Popovich, *Orthodox Faith and Life in Christ*, trans. Fr. Asterios Gerostergios (Belmont: Institute for Byzantine and Modern Greek Studies, 2020), 29-30.

489 Ibid., 89-91.

more limited and confined to His humanity, eventually becoming the infallible man of Rome and Berlin. Thus, on the one hand there appeared a western Christian humanistic maximalism (the papacy) which took everything away from Christ, and on the other hand a western Christian humanistic minimalism (Protestantism) which sought very little if anything from Christ. In both man takes the place of God-man as that which is of most value and is the measure of all things. Thus, a most grievous correction of the God-man, His work, and His teaching was accomplished!

The Papacy persistently and continuously tried to replace the God-man with man, until finally when the dogma of the infallibility of man supplanted the God-man with an infallible man. With this dogma, man (the Pope) was proclaimed decisively and clearly to be something not only greater than man, but greater than the holy Apostles, the holy Fathers, and the Oecumenical Synods. With this rebellion against the God-man and the catholic-ecumenical Church, papal maximalism surpassed even Luther himself, the founder of Protestant minimalism. Indeed, the first fundamental protest against the one, holy, catholic, and apostolic Church is to be found in the Papacy and not in Lutheranism. Yet it is precisely in this protest that one finds the origins of Protestantism.

We must not be mistaken. Western Christian humanistic maximalism, i.e., the Papacy, is fundamentally Protestantism since it removed the foundation of Christianity from the eternal God-man and placed it in finite man claiming this to be the measure and criterion of all. Protestantism did nothing more than to simply accept this dogma and to develop it to a point where it has reached horrendous proportions and particulars. Truly, then, Protestantism is nothing other than an abstract papism being applied to everything, that is, the basic principle of the infallibility of one man has been applied to every individual human being. According to the example of the infallible man of Rome, every Protestant becomes infallible since he claims personal infallibility in matters of faith. From this it can be said that Protestantism is a popularized Papism lacking however a mystical dimension, authority, and power.

Christianity, with all its infinite theanthropic truths, was confined in the West to the human individual with the result that western Christianity was transformed into humanism. This may seem paradoxical, but it is true. The historical reality of this is shown in an indisputable way. In its essence, western Christianity is fundamentally humanistic since it has declared man infallible, thus transforming the theanthropic religion into a humanistic one. Proof of this is found in the fact that the Roman Church transported the God-man back to heaven and in His place put a substitute: *Vicarius Christi*... What a tragic absurdity: to appoint a substitute representative for the all-present Lord and God! It is, however, a fact that this absurdity was realized in western Christianity.

Thus, the de-incarnation of the incarnate God, the de-incarnation of the God-man, was somehow accomplished. Western Christian humanism proclaimed that the all-present God-man was not present in Rome and thus appointed His substitute in the person of an infallible man. It is as if this humanism were saying to the God-man: Depart from this world and go to the next since we have your representative who infallibly represents you in everything.

This replacement of the God-man with a human person is reflected in the replacement of a Christian theanthropic methodology by a human one. From this replacement has emerged the primacy of Aristotelian philosophy in Scholasticism, the causative method and the holy inquisition in morality, papal diplomacy in the international arena, the papal state, forgiveness of sins through both indulgences and the radio and finally the Jesuit movement in its various forms. All this leads to the following conclusion: Humanistic Christianity constitutes the most decisive protest against the God-man and His role as the criterion of all things.

Infallibility of the Pope is the Rebirth of Idolatry[490]

All the European humanisms strive consciously or unconsciously, but they strive unceasingly, for one result: to replace faith in the God-man with a belief in man, to replace the Gospel of the God-man with a gospel according to man, to replace the philosophy of the God-man with a philosophy according to man, to replace the culture of the God-man with a culture according to man. In brief, they seek to replace life according to the God-man with life according to man.

---

490 Ibid., 101-102.

This has been developing for centuries until in the last century, in 1870 at the First Vatican Council, all these efforts achieved their pinnacle in the dogma of the infallibility of the Pope. This dogma subsequently became the central dogma of the papacy. In our own times, during the Second Vatican Council, this doctrine was discussed so persistently and so skillfully that the notion of its inviolability and inalterability was strongly reinforced. This doctrine has an overwhelming significance for the fate of the European civilization, and for the apocalyptic times into which it has brought itself. Through this dogma all European humanisms have built their ideals and their idol: man has been declared the supreme godhead, the ultimate godhead.

The dogma concerning the infallibility of the 20th century pope is nothing other than the rebirth of idolatry and polytheism, the rebirth of idolatrous value judgments and criteria. Through the dogma of infallibility, the pope usurped for himself, that is for man, the entire jurisdiction and all the prerogatives which belong only to the Lord God-man. He effectively proclaimed himself as the Church, the papal church, and he has become in her the be-all and end-all, the self-proclaimed ruler of everything. In this way the dogma of the infallibility of the pope has been elevated to the central dogma (*svedogmat*) of the papacy.

The Fall of the Pope is the Consequence of the Desire to Substitute Man for the God-Man[491]

In the history of the human race there have been three principal falls: that of Adam, that of Judas, and that of the pope. The principal characteristic of falling into sin is always the same: wanting to be good for one's own sake; wanting to be perfect for one's own sake; wanting to be God for one's own sake. In this manner, however, man unconsciously equates himself to the devil, because the devil also wanted to become God for his own sake, to put himself in the place of God. And in this self-elevation he instantly became devil, completely separated from God, and always in opposition to him. Therefore, the essence of sin, of every sin (*svegreha*), consists of this arrogant self-aggrandizement. This is the very essence of the devil himself, of Satan. It is nothing other than

---

491 Ibid., 105-106.

one's wanting to remain within one's own being, wanting nothing within oneself other than oneself. The entire devil is found here: in the desire to exclude God, in the desire to always be by himself, to always belong only to himself, to be entirely within himself and always for himself, to be forever hermetically sealed in opposition to God and everything that belongs to God.

And what is this? It is egotism and self-love embraced in all eternity, that is to say: it is hell. For that is essentially what the humanist is — entirely within himself, by himself, for himself, always spitefully closed in opposition to God. Here lies every humanism, every hominism. The culmination of such satanically oriented humanism is the desire to become good for the sake of evil, to become God for the sake of the devil. It proceeds from the promise of the devil to our forefathers in Paradise — that with his help, "they would become as gods" (Gen. 3:5). Man was created with theanthropic potential by God who loves mankind, so that he might voluntarily direct himself, through God, toward becoming God-man, based on the divinity of his nature. Man, however, with his free will sought sinlessness through sin, sought God through the devil. And assuredly, following this road, he would have become identical with the devil had God not interceded in His immeasurable love of mankind and in His great mercy. By becoming man, that is to say God-man, he redirected man toward the God-man. He introduced him to the Church, which is His body, to the reward (podvig) of theosis through the holy mysteries and the blessed virtues. And in this manner, he gave man the strength to become "a perfect man, in the measure of the fullness of Christ" (Eph. 4:13), to achieve, that is, the Divine destiny, to voluntarily become God-man by grace. The fall of the pope is a consequence of the desire to substitute man for the God-man.

PAPAL INFALLIBILITY EXTERMINATES MAN AS A SPIRITUAL AND PHYSICAL ENTITY[492]

The Second Vatican Council resulted in the rebirth of all European humanisms, the rebirth of cadavers. Since Christ the God-man is present

---

492 Saint Justin Popović, *The Orthodox Church and Ecumenism*, trans. Benjamin Emmanuel Stanley (Birmingham: Lazarica Press, 2000), 109-110.

in this terrestrial world, each and every humanism is a cadaver. Matters reached this stage because the Council persisted in maintaining the dogma concerning the infallibility of the pope (= the man). Examined from the vantage point of the eternally living God-man, the historic Lord Jesus, all humanisms resemble criminal utopias to a greater or lesser extent. In the name of man, they find various ways to murder man, to exterminate him as a spiritual and physical entity. All the humanisms arrive at one tragic, irrational result: they strain at a gnat, and they swallow a camel. In the matter of papal infallibility, the notion has been elevated to dogma. And it is a horror, a horror in the extreme. Why? It is because the very dogma regarding the infallibility of man is nothing other than the shuddering funeral of every humanism, from the ideas that the Vatican has established as dogma to the satanic humanism of Sartre. In the humanistic pantheon of Europe all the gods are dead, with European Zeus at the forefront. Dead, until such time as there arises in their withered hearts a complete, self-denying repentance, accompanied by the lightning and thunder of Golgotha, with its resurrectional earthquakes and transformations, and with its richly yielding storms and ascensions. And then? Then, their doxologies to the living, eternal, wondrous God-man, the only lover of mankind in all the worlds, will be unending.

PAPACY IS THE FIRST PROTESTANTISM[493]

What is at the core of the dogma regarding papal (man's) infallibility? It is the de-theanthropization of man. This is sought by all humanisms, even the religious ones. All return man to idolatry, to polytheism, to the dual death, spiritual as well as physical. Distancing itself from the God-man, every humanism by degrees becomes nihilism. This reveals the simultaneous bankruptcy of all humanisms, led by that of the papacy which, directly or indirectly, voluntarily or involuntarily, is the father of all European humanisms. The resulting bankruptcy, the disastrous bankruptcy of the papacy lies in the dogma of papal infallibility. It is precisely this dogma of nihilism that is uppermost. For this, European man in a doctrinaire and determined manner has proclaimed the dogma of self-sufficiency, and in this way has asserted that the God-man is

---
493 Ibid., 110.

not needed. There is no place for him on earth... the dogma concerning infallibility of the pope has led to the proclamation of the general infallibility of man. And from this followed the innumerable popes of all European cultures, of the Vatican, and of Protestantism. The papacy is the first Protestantism.

DOGMA OF THE POPE IS THE HERESY OF HERESIES[494]

With respect to the dogma concerning papal infallibility, as a practical matter the pope has been proclaimed to be the Church, and the pope — a man — has usurped the place of the God-man. This is the ultimate triumph of humanism and simultaneously "the second death" (Rev. 20:14, 21:8) of the papacy, and through it and after it the death of every humanism. However, the dogma of papal infallibility is not only a heresy but the greatest heresy against the True Church of Christ, which has existed in our terrestrial world as a theanthropic body ever since the appearance of the God-man. No other heresy has revolted so violently and so completely against the God-man Christ and His Church as has the papacy with the dogma of the pope-man's infallibility. There is no doubt about it. This dogma is the heresy of heresies, a revolt without precedent against the God-man Christ on this earth, a new betrayal of Christ, a new crucifixion of the Lord, this time not on wood but on the golden cross of papal humanism. And these things are hell, damnation for the wretched earthly being called man.

PAPISM IS A PAN-HERESY[495]

Ecumenism is the common name for the pseudo-Christianity of the pseudo-Churches of Western Europe. Within it is the heart of European humanism, with Papism as its head. All of pseudo-Christianity, all of those pseudo-Churches, are nothing more than one heresy after an-

---

494 Saint Justin Popović, *The Orthodox Church and Ecumenism,* trans. Benjamin Emmanuel Stanley (Birmingham: Lazarica Press, 2000), 111-112.

495 Father (St.) Justin Popovich, *Orthodox Faith and Life in Christ*, trans. Fr. Asterios Gerostergios (Belmont: Institute for Byzantine and Modern Greek Studies, 2020), 169.

other. Their common evangelical name is Pan-heresy. Why? This is because through the course of history various heresies denied or deformed certain aspects of the God-man and Lord Jesus Christ; these European heresies remove Him altogether and put European man in His place. In this there is no essential difference between Papism, Protestantism, Ecumenism, and other heresies, whose name is "Legion."

Orthodox dogma, that is to say the overriding dogma of the Church, is rejected by them and replaced by the Latin heretical overriding dogma of the primacy and infallibility of the Pope, that is to say of man. From this pan-heresy heresies were born and continue to be born: the Filioque, the rejection of the invocation of the Holy Spirit, unleavened bread, the introduction of created grace, cleansing fire, superfluous works of the saints, mechanized teachings about salvation, and from this sprang mechanized teachings about life, Papocaesarism[496], the Inquisition, indulgences, the murder of sinners because of their sins, Jesuitism, the scholastics, the casuists, Monarchianism, and social individualism of different kinds.

There Are No Mysteries Outside of the Orthodox Church; True Sacraments Are Only Received Through Repentance and Return to the Orthodox Church of Christ[497]

The teaching of the Orthodox Church of the God-Man Christ, formulated the following about heretics through the Holy Apostles, the Holy Fathers, and the Holy Synods: heresies are not a Church, nor can they be a Church. Therefore, they cannot have Holy Mysteries, especially the Sacrament of the Eucharist, the Sacrament of Sacraments. Precisely because the Holy Eucharist is everything and all in the Church: even the God-man Lord Jesus Christ and the Church itself and everything in general of the God-man.

---

496 *Papocaesarism*: A government in which the religious authority is the secular authority, such as the Vatican city-state and the role of the Pope as a Head of State.

497 Father (St.) Justin Popovich, *Orthodox Faith and Life in Christ*, trans. Fr. Asterios Gerostergios (Belmont, MA: Institute for Byzantine and Modern Greek Studies, 2020), 172-174.

Intercommunion, that is to say participating with heretics in the Holy Sacraments, and especially in the Holy Eucharist, is the most shameless betrayal of our Lord Jesus Christ, Judas' betrayal. It is especially the betrayal of the whole of the one and unique Church of Christ, of the Holy Tradition of the Church. One would have to rid oneself of one's Christ-like way of thinking and one's conscience before the various sacraments, before their holy meanings, and the holy commandments in order to do this.

First of all, we would have to ask ourselves on what Ecclesiology and on what Theology of the Church is "intercommunion" based? This is because all of Orthodox Theology is not founded on or based on "inter-communion," but upon the theanthropic reality of communion, that is to say upon theanthropic Communion itself. (cf. 1 Cor. 1:9, 10:16-17; 2 Cor. 13:13; Heb. 2:14; 3:14; John 1:3) The idea of inter-communion is contradictory in itself and totally inconceivable for the Orthodox Catholic conscience.

The second fact, indeed a sacred fact of Orthodox faith, is the following: In Orthodox teaching about the Church and the Sacraments, the single most unique mystery is the Church itself, the Body of the God-man Christ, so that she is the only source and the content of all divine Sacraments. Outside of this theanthropic and inclusive Mystery of the Church, the Pan Mystery itself, there are no and cannot be any "mysteries"; therefore, there can be no inter-communion of Mysteries. Consequently, we can only speak about Mysteries within the context of this unique Pan-Mystery which is the Church. That is because the Orthodox Church, as the Body of Christ, is the source and foundation of the Sacraments and not the other way around. The Mysteries, or Sacraments cannot be elevated above the Church, or examined outside the Body of the Church.

Because of this, in accordance with the mind of the Catholic Church of Christ, and in accordance with the whole of Orthodox Tradition, the Orthodox Church does not recognize the existence of other mysteries or sacraments outside of itself, neither does it recognize them as being mysteries, and one cannot receive the sacraments until one comes away from the heretical "Churches," that is to say the pseudo-Churches, through repentance to the Orthodox Church of Christ. Until then one remains outside the Church, un-united with it through repentance, and is as far as the Church is concerned, a heretic and consequently outside of the saving communion. This is because *"what fellowship hath righteousness with unrighteousness and what communion hath light with darkness?"* (2 Cor. 6:14)"

PAPAL QUEST FOR INFALLIBLE POWER PRODUCES REBELLION AGAINST CHURCH & GOD, LACK OF REPENTANCE, ALLIANCE WITH THE DEVIL[498]

The apostolic sorrow of the holy Bishop then asks: What is Europe?

It is the desire and the longing for power and pleasure and knowledge. All of which is human: firstly, human desire and longing, and secondly human knowledge. And the two are personified by the Pope and Luther. What then is Europe? Europe is the Pope and Luther, human desire to the extreme and human knowledge to the extreme. The European Pope is the human desire for authority. The European Luther is the obstinate decision of man that everything must be explained by the mind, the Pope as the ruler of the world and the scientist as the sovereign of the world. This is Europe in a nutshell, ontologically and historically. The one means the surrender of mankind into the fire and the other means surrender of mankind into the water. And both mean: the separation of man from God because the one means the rejection of faith and the other the rejection of the Church of Christ. For the spirit of evil has been working in this way on the body of Europe for a few centuries now. And who can expel this evil spirit from Europe? No one, except the One Whose name has been marked in red in the history of the human race as the only One Who expels demons from people. You already know who I mean. I mean the Lord Jesus Christ, the Messiah, and Savior of the world, Who was born of the Virgin, killed by the Jews, resurrected by God, witnessed by the centuries, justified by heaven, glorified by the Angels, confessed by the saints, and accepted by our forefathers.

According to human desire, every nation and every person seeks power, pleasure, and glory, imitating the Pope of Rome. According to human wisdom, every nation and every person finds that he or she is wis-

---

498 Ibid., 183-191.

496 The Orthodox Patristic Witness Concerning Catholicism

er than everyone else and that he or she deserves all earthly things. How then can there not be wars between people and nations? How then can there not be foolishness and wilderness in people? How then can there not be sicknesses and terrible diseases, drought and floods, insurrections and wars? For just as pus has to seep out of a pus-filled wound, and a stench has to come out of a place filled with filth, this has to happen.

Papism uses politics because this is the only way it can get power. Lutheranism uses philosophy and science because it believes that this is the only way to obtain wisdom. And so desire declared war against knowledge and knowledge against desire. This is the new Tower of Babel, this is Europe. But in our time, however, there came a new generation of European, a generation that married desire to knowledge through atheism and rejected both the Pope and Luther. Now neither desire is hidden, nor wisdom praised. Human desire and human wisdom are joined in our ties and thus a marriage has taken place which is neither Roman Catholic nor Lutheran, but obviously and publicly satanic. Today's Europe is neither Papist nor Lutheran. It is above and outside of them both. It is totally earthly, without even the desire to ascend to heaven, either with the passport of the infallibility of the Pope or by the ladder of Protestant wisdom. It totally denies the journey from this world. It wants to stay here. It wants the grave as its cradle. It does not know about the other world. It doesn't smell the heavenly fragrance. It does not see the Angels and the Saints in its dreams. It does not want to hear about the Theotokos. Debauchery makes it hate virginity. The whole square which is Europe is sunk now in darkness. All of the candles are out. Oh! the awful darkness. Brother plunges the sword into his brother's breast, thinking that he is the enemy. Fathers reject their sons, sons their fathers. And the wolf is a far more loyal friend to man than man is.

Oh, my brothers! Do you not see all this? Have you not felt the darkness and the wrongdoing of un-Christian Europe on your bodies? Do you prefer Europe to Christ, death to life? Moses offered these two choices to his people. And we also put these two choices before you. You have to know that Europe is death, Christ is life. Choose life and live forever. And here is the shocking lament of the Bishop who is equal to the Apostles for Europe:

Oh my brothers! The 18th century is the father of the 19th century, and the 19th century is the father of the 20th. The father fell into great debt. And the son paid the debts of the father in full, but he became even more indebted, and his debt was passed on to the grandson. The father was ill with a very serious sickness, the son did not cure himself of this disgraceful sickness of the father, but allowed it to spread even further and so it was transmitted to the grandson three times stronger. The grandson is the 20th century, the century we are living in.

The 18th century signifies the rebellion of the Roman Pontiff against the Church and the clergy. The 19th century signifies the rebellion against God. The 20th century signifies the alliance with the Devil. The debts have increased, and the sickness has gotten worse. The Lord said that he will visit the sins of the fathers unto the third and fourth generations. Do you not see that the Lord is visiting upon the grandchildren the sins of its European fathers? Do you not see the whip upon the backs of the grandchildren because of the unpaid debts of the grandfathers? The anti-Christ king is the beginning of the 19th century. The Pope, the anti-Christ, is the middle of the same century. The philosophers of Europe, the anti-Christs (from the lunatic asylum) are in the end of that century.

Are these the victors of the 19th century? No, they are the carriers of the dreaded sickness which was inherited from the 18th century. The sickest people, Caesar, the Pope, and the philosopher... these are not the winners but the losers. When Bonaparte laughed in front of the holy churches of the Kremlin, when Pius was declared infallible, and when Nietzsche publicly announced his worship of the anti-Christ, then the sun darkened the sky. And if there were a thousand suns, they would all have been darkened for shame and sorrow because of this amazing thing that the world has never seen before: an atheist king, an atheist pontifix, and an atheist philosopher.

Who is the victor then, if it is not the kaiser, the pontifex, and the philosopher of the Europe that rejected Christianity? The winner is the Balkan peasant and the Russian moujik according to the word of Christ: *"for the least among you is the greatest."* (Luke 9:48) Who was the most unknown, meaningless, and least person of the 19th century, the century of the great Napoleon, of the infallible Pius, and of the unapproachable Nietzche? Who if it was not the Russian moujik pilgrim "to the Holy Places," and the Balkan peasant fighter against the crescent, the liberator of the Balkans?

A satanic plan of battle, a satanic clergy, and satanic wisdom, this is what the kaiser, the Pope, and the philosopher of the 19th century were [...] What did God reveal to these simple peasants? He revealed bravery, the heavenly light, and divine wisdom. In other words, He revealed all that was opposite to the Western kaiser, Pope, and philosopher; it was like night and day. [...] The ambitious and haughty people of Europe do not recognize their own faults. They have lost an awareness of sin, of sin and repentance. For them, someone else is always to blame for every evil in this world, never themselves. Then how is it possible for them to commit a sin, since they have sat upon the throne of God and proclaimed themselves infallible! Their religious leader, the Pope was the first to declare himself this. The leaders and the kings of the West then followed his example. Everyone declared himself infallible, those who wore the cross and those who brought the sword.

EXCERPT FROM "ON THE SUMMONING OF THE 'GREAT COUNCIL' OF THE ORTHODOX CHURCH"[499]

This is an excerpt of a letter from May 7th, 1977, regarding a future "Great Council," which occurred in 2016 and which is referenced in the resolutions of the "First Pre-Conciliar Conference" from 1976. This letter was written from then-Archimandrite Justin Popovich to Bishop Jovan of Sabac and the Serbian hierarchs, to be given to the Holy Synod and the Council of Bishops of the Serbian Orthodox Church. The truths he writes about at that time still ring true in our day.

I bow in reverence before the age-old achievements of the Great Church of Constantinople, and before her present cross, which is neither small nor easy, which according to the nature of things, is the cross of the entire Church — for, as the Apostle says, "When one member

---

499 Saint Justin (Popović), *The Life and Writings of Blessed Justin Popovich: The Conscience of the Serbian Church* (New South Wales: Holy Dormition Sisterhood, 2003), 53-59.

suffers, the whole body suffers." Moreover, I acknowledge the canonical rank and first place in honour of Constantinople among the local Orthodox Churches, which are equal in honour and rights. But it would not be in keeping with the Gospel if Constantinople, on account of the difficulties in which she now finds herself, were allowed to bring the whole of Orthodoxy to the brink of the abyss, as once occurred at the pseudo-council of Florence, or to canonize and dogmatise particular historical forms which, at a given moment might transform themselves from wings into heavy chains, binding the Church and her transfiguring presence in the world. Let us be frank: the conduct of the representatives of Constantinople in the last decades has been characterized by the same unhealthy restlessness, by the same spiritually ill condition as that which brought the Church to the betrayal and disgrace of Florence in the 15th Century. (Nor was the conduct of the same Church under the Turkish yoke an example for all times. Both the Florentine and the Turkish yokes were dangerous for Orthodoxy.) With the difference that today the situation is even more ominous: formerly Constantinople was a living organism with millions of faithful — she was able to overcome without delay the crisis brought about by external courses as well as the temptation to sacrifice the faith and the Kingdom of God for the goods of this world. Today, however, she has only metropolitans without faithful, bishops who have no one to lead (i.e. without dioceses), who nonetheless wish to control the destinies of the entire Church. Today there must not, there cannot be a new Florence! Nor can the present situation be compared with the difficulties of the Turkish yoke. The same reasoning applies to the Moscow Patriarchate. Are its difficulties or the difficulties of other local Churches under godless communism to be allowed to determine the future of Orthodoxy?

The fate of the Church neither is nor can be any longer in the hands of the Byzantine emperor or any other sovereign. It is not in the control of a patriarch or of any of the mighty of this world, not even in that of the "Pentarchy" or of the "autocephalies" (understood in the narrow sense). By the power of God, the Church has grown up into a multitude of local Churches with millions of faithful, many of whom in our days have sealed their apostolic succession and faithfulness to the Lamb with their blood. And new local Churches appear to be rising on the horizon, such as the Japanese, the African and the American, and their freedom in the Lord must not be removed by any "super-Church" of the papal type (cf. Canon 8, III Ecumenical Council), for this would signify an attack on the very essence of the Church. Without their concurrence the solution of any ecclesiastical question of ecumenical significance is inconceivable, not to mention the solutions to questions that immediately concern them, i.e., the problem of the diaspora. The age-long struggle of Orthodoxy against Roman absolutism was a struggle for just such freedom of the local Church as catholic and conciliar, complete and whole in itself. Are we today to travel the road of the first and fallen Rome, or of some "second" or "third" similar to it? Are we to believe that Constantinople, which in the persons of its holy and great hierarchs, its clergy and its people, so boldly opposed for centuries past the Roman protectionism and absolutism, is today preparing to ignore the conciliar traditions of Orthodoxy and to exchange them for the neo-papal surrogate of a "second," "third" or other sort of Rome?

My conscience once more obliges me to turn with insistence and beseeching to the Holy Council of Bishops of the martyred Serbian Church: let our Serbian Church abstain from participating in the preparations for the "ecumenical council," indeed from participating in the council itself. For should this council, God forbid, actually come to pass, only one kind of result can be expected from it: schisms, heresies and the loss of many souls. Considering the question from the point of view of the apostolic and patristic and historical experience of the Church, such a council, instead of healing, will but open up new wounds in the body of the Church and inflict upon her new problems and misfortunes.

I recommend myself to the holy and apostolic prayers of the Fathers of the Holy Council of Bishops of the Serbian Orthodox Church.

The unworthy Archimandrite Justin
(Spiritual father of the Monastery of Chelije [Tjelije])
Eve of the Feast of Saint George, 1977
Monastery of Chelije, Valjevo (Yugoslavia)

30. St. Iakovos of Evia (+1991)

HIS LIFE,
WHICH IS CELEBRATED ON THE 22ND OF NOVEMBER

Saint Iakovos (Tsalikis) of Evia, a truly grace-filled elder who was a dwelling-place of the Holy Spirit and among one of the holiest saints of modern Greece, was born in Livisi, Asia Minor on November 5th, 1920. Born to Stavros and Theodora, he was one of nine children. He lived through the Greek and Turkish population exchanges in 1923 after which the Tsalikis family settled in the village of Saint George in Amifisa for a brief period of time and then relocated again, this time to Farakla in Northern Greece in 1925. As a child, Saint Iakovos was educated at the ecclesiastical school of Saint Paraskevi and it was during this early period of his life that he expressed a great inclination for the monastic life, frequently keeping his rule of prayer and fasting. During his teen years the Second World War broke out in Greece, and he was drafted into the Greek Army in 1947 and eventually discharged from military service in 1949. The young Saint Iakovos decided in 1951 to enter the monastic life and went to the Holy Monastery of Saint David in Evia which at the time was occupied only by a handful of monastics. He was tonsured into the monastic life November 31st, 1952, and on December 17th he was ordained a Hierodeacon. After many years of ascetic struggle, he was chosen to be the Abbot of the Monastery of Saint David's in 1975. Prior to becoming the Abbot of the monastery, Geronda Iakovos was sought out by the faithful of Evia who would frequently visit the monastery to see him for his pastoral guidance, to have their confessions heard and to attend the divine services.

Saint Iakovos during his earthly life was a great ascetic, a struggler for Christ, and was a successful exorcist who was known for banishing many demons from the faithful who were possessed. It was for this reason that he was constantly under the physical assault of the demons. A contemporary of Saint Porphyrios of Kafsokalyvia (+December 1991), he reposed in the Lord in November of 1991. In November of 2017, twenty-six years after the repose of the Holy Elder, Saint Iakovos was canonized by the Holy Synod of the Ecumenical Patriarchate of Constantinople.

ON THE BAPTISM OF LATINS[500]

The entire wondrous life of Elder Iakovos, with his spiritual bodily struggles, was based on his Orthodox faith. Particular events and practices of the wise and discerning Elder confirm the precise observance of the dogmatic teaching of the Church. The Elder taught in practice. Let's refer to one of the many such examples. When an adherent of Catholicism expressed a desire to become Orthodox, he told him 'what prevents you to be baptized' (Acts 8:36). Out of respect to the ecclesiastical hierarchy he counseled us to go to the bishop of the area and to announce the man's decision. 'You will go to the bishop who, immediately upon hearing of your decision, will rise from his throne and embrace you, my child, out of joy that you want to become Orthodox.' In saying this he was actually describing his own spiritual state and desire. To our great surprise, we were not able to even see the face of the Bishop! Through his Deacon, he communicated to us that, according to the decision of the Holy Synod [of the Church of Greece], the baptism of Latins is valid and does not need to be repeated. He simply needs to sign a written confession and the Mystery of Chrismation is to be performed.

When we informed the Elder of this, he said: I don't know what the Holy Synod decided I know what the Gospel says: 'He that believeth and is baptized shall be saved' (Mark 16:16). He said this and went and brought a large baptismal font, appropriate for adults, from nearby Limni, Euboea. In the chapel of St. Haralambos, which was the cell of Saint David of Euboea, the Holy Elder performed the Mystery of Baptism with great splendour, and also the Mystery of Chrismation according to the Orthodox typicon, with help of the Archimandrite Father Paul Ioannou, his spiritual child, who later became the Metropolitan of Siatista. I, who write these words, was the Godfather (sponsor).

---

500 Dr. Nicholas Baldimtsis, *Life and Witness of St. Iakovos of Evia* (Florence: Uncut Mountain Press, 2023), 66-67.

31. St. Porphyrios of Kavsokalyvia (+1991)

HIS LIFE,
WHICH IS CELEBRATED ON THE 2ND OF DECEMBER[501]

Our Venerable Father Porphyrios was born into a pious family of poor farmers on the island of Evia, Greece in AD 1906. He was greatly influenced by the life of St. John the Hut-dweller (commemorated January 15th), and wanted to follow his example. At about the age of fifteen, he went to Mt. Athos. En route, he met his two future spiritual fathers, Hieromonks Panteleimon and Ioannikios, who took him to live in the hut of St. George at Kavsokalyvia. Porphyrios was obedient, filled with the joy of Christ, and embraced the monastic life with great zeal. He slept little, went barefoot, and did many prostrations. He learned the prayers, hymns, and Gospel by heart, and because of his love and labors for Christ, he acquired the gift of clairvoyance, which he called "spiritual television."

But his severe ascetic struggles wore him down, and he developed pleurisy and was forced to move back to the world to regain his health. He went to the monastery of St. Haralampos on Evia and was ordained to the priesthood. He became a father confessor to many and saved souls from the evil traps of the devil. With the outbreak of World War II, he became the hospital chaplain for the Polyclinic in Athens, ministering to the sick and suffering. He remained there thirty-three years. Though uneducated, through the Holy Spirit he was able to diagnose illnesses and advise doctors as to how they should treat specific medical cases. His remarkable gift of clairvoyance became known throughout the world and he was visited by Latins and other non-Orthodox who perceived the work of the Holy Spirit in him in a way that was unheard of in their own traditions. After 1984, St. Porphyrios finally moved back to St. George's hut on Mt. Athos where he reposed in 1991.

---

501 "A Life of Saint Porphyrios of Kavsokalyvia," *God is Wonderful in His Saints: Book of Akathists* (Wenatchee: Three Hierarchs Publishing, 2015), 451.

Through the Existence of Uniates, Papists Demonstrate They Want the Orthodox to Recognize the Pope[502]

Our holy Elder Porphyrios understands the devices of Papism quite well. "Do not be afraid," he would say, "the attitude of the Pope has always been to subject the Orthodox Church and the day will come when the dialogue will be called off. Nothing will happen. Furthermore, by the existence of the Uniates, this Trojan Horse, they show plain as day that they are interested in having the Orthodox recognize the Pope as their head and nothing more.

St. Porphyrios Does Not Accept Any Religion Other Than Orthodoxy[503]

They call me from all over the world, so that it might be known that I too am a free spirit and accept all religions? No, I do not accept this! No matter who might tell me this, even if it were an angel... No, I will say, you speak lies, you are not a good spirit. You are an evil spirit and say such things. This is what I would say to the angel. I will not believe him. Take the proper measures yourselves.

32. St. Sophrony of Essex (+1993)

His life,
which is celebrated on the 11ᵗʜ of July

Born into a Russian Orthodox family in Moscow on September 22nd, 1896, Archimandrite Sophrony attended the Moscow School of

---

502 Hieromonk Savas of the Holy Mountain, *Healing the Soul: Saint Porphyrios of Kafsokalyvia as a Model for Our Lives*, trans. Sisterhood of the Saint John Chrysostomos Greek Orthodox Monastery (Pleasant Prairie: St. John Chrysostomos Monastery, 2021), 100-101.

503 Hieromonk Savas of the Holy Mountain, *Healing the Soul: Saint Porphyrios of Kafsokalyvia as a Model for Our Lives*, trans. Sisterhood of the Saint John Chrysostomos Greek Orthodox Monastery (Pleasant Prairie: St. John Chrysostomos Monastery, 2021), 102.

Fine Art. After the October Revolution, he moved to Paris where he was a successful painter. He strayed from his childhood faith when he engaged with the Eastern religions for a time, but he repented of this foray and returned to Orthodoxy. After a brief period of theological study in Paris at the St. Sergius Institute, in 1925 he left to become a monk on Mount Athos in Greece. Ordained a deacon by St. Nikolai (Velimirovich) in 1930, it was at this same time that he met Staretz Silouan who became his spiritual father. It was under the guidance of Saint Silouan that Fr. Sophrony experienced divine illumination, knowing God. He spent fifteen years in a monastery and when Staretz Silouan died in 1938, he left the monastery and spent seven years as a hermit 'in the desert' on Athos. In 1941 he was ordained a priest and shortly after was elected to be the spiritual confessor for a few of the monastic communities on Mount Athos. He returned to France in 1947, editing and publishing the writings of St. Silouan. Unable to return to the Holy Mountain due to a serious illness, he moved to England in 1959 and founded the Monastery of Saint John the Baptist at Tolleshunt Knights where he lived until his repose on July 11th, 1993.

THERE IS ONE UNIQUE AND TRUE CHURCH WHICH CHRIST FOUNDED WHICH MAINTAINS UNSPOILED THE TEACHING OF CHRIST AND POSSESSES THE FULNESS OF KNOWLEDGE AND GRACE AND INFALLIBILITY[504]

At the present time a significant part of the Christian world tends to accept one of the most dangerous heresies [ecumenism]. What it consists of is people saying that in our days there is not one Church which has kept fully the true teaching of Christ; or which possesses complete knowledge of the mystery of the holy, grace-filled Christian life on the ethical and ascetic level. Supposedly, many of the churches which are nominally Christian have equal grace, and because of that we should proceed towards the union of the churches on the basis of some common program. One of the most frequent questions which one comes across is the question of who will be saved and who will not be saved.

---

504 Saint Sophrony (Sakharov), *Striving for Knowledge of God* (Essex: Stavropegic Monastery of St. John the Baptist, 2016), 144-146.

These people usually think that it is not only the Orthodox who will be saved (according to Orthodox teaching), not only the Catholics (according to Catholic teaching), but all virtuous people in general who believe in Christ. This viewpoint has passed from the Protestants to the faithful of other churches. There are many among the Orthodox who hold this opinion.

Some people think that no single one of the existing churches can receive the fulness of knowledge and grace, because each one of them in one or another degree has deviated from the truth. They think that only now 'at the end of the ages' they (these sages) have fully grasped the spirit of the teaching of Christ, and that the entire Christian world has been led astray for many centuries until now. That now the time has come when we must unite all the separated parts into one universal and apostolic Church, which will have the fulness of truth in all its aspects, even though this union will only embrace what is common to all the churches. What is even worse, some of them are pondering in their hearts a certain high, supra-ecclesial, mystical, understanding of Christian religion, which... I won't say more about this.

I digressed into discussing this for one reason only: to tell you that I very much want you (and I pray to God for this) not to be deceived by all that, but to be convinced firmly in your heart and mind that on this earth there is one unique and true Church which Christ founded; that this Church maintains unspoiled the teaching of Christ, that she in her totality (and not in her individual members) possesses the fulness of knowledge and grace and infallibility. [I want you to be convinced] that what for several people seems to be incompleteness in her teaching is none other than the potential for some scholarly elaboration of her inexhaustible and infinite riches—this, however, does not contradict in any measure what I said above about her possessing the fulness of knowledge.

The definitive form of expression of the Church's teaching at the Ecumenical Councils cannot be subjected to any change. All future academic work must obligatorily concur with what was given in divine revelation and in the teaching of the Ecumenical Councils of the Church. The same is true in connection with grace: only the one and unique Church can have the fulness of grace.

SOME OF THE ERRORS OF CATHOLICISM
ACCORDING TO ST. SOPHRONY[505]

But in Roman Catholicism (as compared to Orthodoxy) there are many basic errors, both from the dogmatic point of view as well as from the point of view of the (spiritual) church life. The [Roman Catholic] point of view about repentance and the practice of Confession is not in accord with the spirit of Christ (as I understand it), and this is connected with an incorrect vision of the work of man's redemption. There is a certain "worldly", "juridical", approach to resolving these questions. Anomalies and even frankly crude delusions in the moral-ascetic life are accepted as grace-given, and taken as criteria of holiness (for example the phenomenon of the stigmata.) And at the same time, the spiritual practices of the Orthodox ascetics are trampled on, ridiculed, and repudiated. Several of the holy Fathers who were more advanced in this noetic activity of inner prayer are treated as particularly inveterate heretics (for example, St. Gregory Palamas).

33. St. Paisios the Athonite (+1994)

HIS LIFE,
WHICH IS CELEBRATED ON THE 12TH OF JULY

Saint Paisios of the Holy Mountain, was born Arsenios Ezepnidis in Cappadocia, Asia Minor on July 25th, 1924, on the feast of Saint Anna in the village of Farasa, which has given birth to many other Holy Orthodox Saints. His godfather was Saint Arsenios the Cappadocian. During Saint Paisios' early years, the family settled in Epirus, Greece. During his young adult years and during the civil war, Arsenios joined the Greek military to fulfil his national duty and became a radio operator, an assignment which he executed fearlessly. After his time in the world as a young man, he finally became a monastic in 1950 at the Holy Monastery of Koutloumousiou Monastery on Mount Athos. He worked to preserve his silence and to progress spiritually in the Hesychastic life

---

505 Ibid., 60.

on Mount Athos. He was spiritually enriched by reading the lives of the saints, the Gerontikon, and other spiritual writings of the Holy Orthodox Church. He felt that his spiritual failings were the cause of the ills of the world. It was at the hermitage of Panagouda where the elder became widely known for his God-given spiritual gifts. Every day he would receive the sick, suffering, and sorrowful all day and then would dedicate his entire night to further prayer and spiritual labors. However, after many years of this very strict hesychastic lifestyle, he began to have physical health issues which he never complained about or made known to most people. Despite his constant struggles, he was always grace-filled. Throughout his monastic life, he received various visits from the Theotokos, the Saints, such as the Three Hierarchs — Sts. Basil, Gregory the Theologian, and John Chrysostom. Toward the later stages of his life, he was diagnosed with cancer. However, regardless of his condition he still regularly received people and gave them spiritual counsel and comfort. Saint Paisios died in a state of sanctifying grace on July 12th, 1994, at the Holy Monastery of Souroti, where he is buried today.

THE EUROPEAN SPIRIT HAS INFILTRATED THE CATHOLICS[506]

Have you seen what happened to the Catholics? I remember years ago, when I was at the Stomion Monastery in Konitsa, someone brought me an article from a newspaper. It said: "Three hundred nuns protested for not being allowed to watch movies and for having to wear their habits at full length and not up to the knee." I found it outrageous, and I wondered, "Why, then, did you become nuns?" The article said that eventually they got rid of their habits. Given the way they were thinking, they had already thrown them away! Another time, I saw a Catholic nun who did not differ at all from a laywoman. She was supposedly performing missionary work but looked no different from those very secular young women involved in various charities. We should not allow this European spirit to come into our lives. We should never reach this point.

---

506 Saint Paisios (Ezepnidis) of Mount Athos, *Spiritual Counsels Volume I: With Pain and Love for Contemporary Man*, trans. Cornelia A. Tsakiridou & Maria Spanou (Thessaloniki: Holy Monastery Evangelist John the Theologian, 2011), 87-88.

ORTHODOX AND CATHOLICS CANNOT PRAY TOGETHER SINCE WE DON'T AGREE ON DOCTRINE[507]

He was also visited by heretics who wanted to entrap him, but the discerning elder readily recognized them and treated them accordingly. Once, two Catholics visited him. One was a journalist and the other, a secretary at the Vatican. They asked him to recite the Our Father with them. "In order for us to say the Our Father together," he replied, "we must agree on the doctrine, which we don't, since between us and you, there is a great gulf fixed."

CATHOLICS HAVE GOTTEN RID OF THE HOLY SPIRIT AND PUT LOGIC IN ITS PLACE[508]

"Geronda, what is the place of reason and logic in the spiritual life?"

"Which logic are you talking about? If you mean secular logic, then yes, this kind of logic has no place at all in the spiritual life. Angels and saints enter through our windows; we can see them, talk with them, and then they leave [...] There is no way that one can explain this logically. Today, with the increase in all kinds of knowledge, our trust only in logic has unfortunately shaken our faith to its foundations and filled our souls with question marks and doubts. This is why we are deprived of miracles, because a miracle cannot be explained logically, it can only be experienced. In contrast, faith in God can bring divine power down from Heaven and overturn all human conclusions; it can perform miracles, resurrect the dead and astonish science. From the outside, all things pertaining to the spiritual life seem upside down. If we don't abandon our own secular frame of mind in favor of a spiritual one, it will be impossible to become acquainted with the mysteries of God that appear so strange or upside down, to us now. Those who believe that they can come

---

507 Saint Paisios (Ezepnidis) of Mount Athos, *Saint Paisios the Athonite*, trans. Fr. Peter Chamberas (Thessaloniki: Holy Hesychasterion "Evangelist John the Theologian," 2018), 484-485.

508 Saint Paisios (Ezepnidis) of Mount Athos, *Spiritual Counsels Volume I: With Pain and Love for Contemporary Man*, trans. Cornelia A. Tsakiridou & Maria Spanou (Thessaloniki: Holy Monastery Evangelist John the Theologian, 2011), 252-254.

to know the mysteries of God through mere scientific theory resemble a fool who thinks he can look through a telescope and see Paradise.

"Logic is very harmful when we use it to scrutinize the divine, the mysteries and miracles. Logic drove the Roman Catholics, as I have heard, to put the Holy Communion through chemical tests to determine if it is the actual Body and Blood of Christ! But the saints had so much faith that they often saw flesh and blood on the Holy Communion Spoon. Pretty soon, they will be putting the saints through an X-ray machine to establish their sainthood! What the Catholics have done is to get rid of the Holy Spirit and put logic in His place. And now they spend their time with 'white magic.'"[509]

CATHOLIC RATIONALISM LIMITS THE POWER OF GOD[510]

A Catholic man with a good disposition came to see me, he was in tears. I said to him, "Among the most important differences that we have with you is that you put the mind first, whereas we put the faith first. You have developed rationalism; and, in general, you stress the human factor. With your rationalism, you limit the power of God, because you put divine Grace aside. You put a preservative in Holy Water (Aghiasmos) to keep it from spoiling. We, on the other hand, pour Holy Water on spoiled things, and they become fresh again. We believe in the Grace that sanctifies, and for this reason Holy Water remains unspoiled for two hundred years, five hundred years; it never spoils."

MANY CATHOLICS ARE DISAPPOINTED WITH PAPISM AND ARE RETURNING TO ORTHODOXY[511]

Once a man complained to me, "There isn't a single Orthodox person to represent Orthodoxy in conferences abroad." He went on and on,

---

509 *White Magic*: The practice of this magic produces favourable results which appear both miraculous and mysterious, but are actually caused by natural causes.

510 Saint Paisios (Ezpenidis) of Mount Athos, *Spiritual Counsels Volume I: With Pain and Love for Contemporary Man*, trans. Cornelia A. Tsakiridou & Maria Spanou (Thessaloniki: Holy Monastery Evangelist John the Theologian, 2011), 252-254.

511 Ibid., 234-235.

as if it were the end of the world. I said to him, "When God asked Prophet Elijah, 'What are you doing here on Horeb, Elijah?' he answered, 'I am the only one left and they seek my life...' And God replied, 'There are seven thousand people in Israel who have not bowed to worship Baal.' There were seven thousand faithful people, and the Prophet Elijah was saying that he was all alone! You, likewise, are in despair despite the existence of so many faithful. Who do you think our own Pantocrator is? Is He like the Icon of the Pantocrator on the dome of a Church that has been damaged by an earthquake and needs to be restored by the Archaeological Service?" "In America," the man replied, "there is no one." I answered, "But I have got to know many faithful people from America." "Yes," he answered, "but the Catholics are always plotting against us." "What I know is that many Catholics are disappointed with Papism, and are returning to Orthodoxy," I said. "Isn't it true that when Patriarch Demetrios visited the United States, many Catholics were saying, 'The Patriarch is a true Christian while the Pope is a merchant'? Weren't they speaking out in indignation? Are you saying that Catholics are always plotting to enter Orthodoxy in order to adulterate it? Where is God in all this? Can the devil ever prosper?"

CATHOLICISM IS NOW FULL OF THE ATHEISTIC SPIRIT[512]

You have theologians who advise people not to receive Holy Communion because they might catch AIDS! They were probably admitted to the School of Theology by default (because the computer gave them an admission score)! This kind of theology does not know God. In the old days they used to say, "The child has learned the sacred letters," because education was then a sacred thing. Now you see a professor of Theology who does not believe in God and insults the Prophets in front of the students. And yet he is not dismissed. Can you tell me, my good man, what are you doing in a Theology Department? What kind of theologians will you prepare for graduation? This is the result of the influence of Protestants and Catholics! Catholicism is now full of the

---

512 Saint Paisios (Ezpenidis) of Mount Athos, *Spiritual Counsels Volume I: With Pain and Love for Contemporary Man*, trans. Cornelia A. Tsakiridou & Maria Spanou (Thessaloniki: Holy Monastery Evangelist John the Theologian, 2011), 336-337.

atheistic spirit! Catholics are even trying to cut out the saints. "Saint Catherine," they claim, "was not really that great; her father was only a small and unimportant king. Saint Nicholas was not a major saint, either. Saint George was actually a mythical person. The Archangel Michael does not exist; he is a manifestation of God. And so was the Archangel Gabriel." Pretty soon they will be claiming, "Christ is not God; He was only a great teacher." Then they will go even further, "God is only a force." In the end, they will claim: "God is nature!" There are Orthodox today who go for this nonsense, even though there is so much tangible evidence, so many Prophets and prophecies, and so many living miracles.

GOD ENLIGHTENS THE ORTHODOX SPIRIT WHERE THERE IS A FIRST AMONG EQUALS BUT NOT SO FOR THE PAPIST SPIRIT WHICH HAS NO CONCILIARITY[513]

The Administration of the Church. The Orthodox Church has always been administered by Synods. It is in the Orthodox spirit for the Church to be administered by Synods, and for Monasteries by the Assembly of Elders. Decisions are reached jointly by the archbishop and the Synod, and by the abbot or abbess and the Assembly of Senior monastics. The archbishop is first among equals. And the Patriarch is not a Pope; he and the other hierarchs have the same rank. The Pope's rank is different — he sits up high and others kiss his feet! But the Patriarch sits together with all the other hierarchs and his work is to coordinate. This is also the relationship between an abbot or abbess and the members of the Assembly of Elders; the abbot or abbess is first among equals.

An archbishop or an abbot cannot do whatever he wants. God enlightens a hierarch or an Elder on one issue; He enlightens one about the other. You see, this is like the four Evangelists, who complemented each other. Here, too, (in the Assembly of Elders), each person will state his opinion, and if someone disagrees, his dissent will be recorded in the minutes. Especially in cases where a decision is contrary to the commandments of the Gospel, those who disagree should have their dissent

---

513 Saint Paisios (Ezpenidis) of Mount Athos, *Spiritual Counsels Volume I: With Pain and Love for Contemporary Man*, trans. Cornelia A. Tsakiridou & Maria Spanou (Thessaloniki: Holy Monastery Evangelist John the Theologian, 2011), 373-374.

recorded. Otherwise, it will appear as if the decision was unanimous. If this person signs the document without recording his objection, he has actually done wrong and stands to blame. But if he makes his opinion public, even if the majority disagrees, he will be in good standing with God. When the Synod or the Assembly of Elders does not function well, then we may say that we have the Orthodox spirit, but it is the Papist spirit that is at work. The Orthodox spirit says that each and every person has the right to speak and register his mind; no one should refrain from speaking out of fear in order to flatter a superior or because he wants to be on good terms with the archbishop or the abbot.

St. Paisios on the Graceless "Priesthood" of the Latin Papist[514]

The elder also related to the following story: once a priest came to the skete. When I first saw him, I was not told anything about him [by God]. As we talked, I realized that he was a Catholic [Papist]. I told him sternly, put your biretta on first, and then go and visit monasteries. I found out later that he was a Catholic priest named Bonaventure, and wherever he went he dressed to fit in, to fool people; with Greek Orthodox clergy he dressed like a Greek Orthodox priest, with Russian Orthodox clergy, like a Russian Orthodox priest, and so on. The Elder saw before him a man with long hair, beard, and a cassock; but he wasn't fooled by appearances. Divine Grace gave witness within him that this apparent priest did not really have the priesthood. In the words of scripture, he *"needed not that any should testify of man: for he knew what was in man."*

---

514 Hieromonk Isaac (Atallah), *Saint Paisios of Mount Athos*, trans. Hieromonk Alexis (Trader) & Fr. Peter Heers (Chalkidiki: Holy Monastery of Saint Arsenios the Cappadocian, 2009), 158.

Johannes Climacus: The Ladder to Paradise
Russia, ca. 1560

PART IV

OTHER AUTHORITATIVE TEXTS

New Hieromartyr Maxim Sandovich

A. LITURGICAL TEXTS

The liturgical texts of the Church used in honor of various saints and feasts express how the Church understands the holy people and sacred events that are being commemorated. In the case of saints who defended the Orthodox Faith against the Latin heresies, the liturgical texts used in their honor commemorate them specifically for their defense of the Faith and struggle against heresy, for their wise shepherding of their spiritual flocks, and for their role as teachers and enlighteners of the faithful. The Church venerates such saints not merely for the purity of life, their ceaseless prayer, and ascetical struggles, but also explicitly for contending against heresy and boldly proclaiming the truth of Orthodoxy. The liturgical texts give the Church's reasons for such saints and feasts to be publicly and universally commemorated when She worships in "spirit and truth."

1. Select Liturgical Texts from the Menaion in Reference to the Papists

a. Holy New Hieromartyr Maximus Sandovich

LITTLE VESPERS

On "Lord, I have cried," 4 stichera,
in Tone 1: Spec. Mel.: "Joy of the ranks of heaven"

O holy Martyr Maximus, as thou didst receive the grace to confront death with bravery and to confess the Holy Faith in the face of the heretics, entreat Christ, we pray, that He make us steadfast in Orthodoxy. Having proclaimed the sanctity of the Orthodox Faith, when thou wast felled by the weaponry of the cruel heretics thou didst surrender thy soul into the hands of the Savior.

Glory..., in Tone VI

O wondrous hieromartyr, persecuted and imprisoned for the sake of Orthodoxy, thou didst provide an example for all by meekness, love and humility, and the Holy Spirit taught thee what to say while the heretics slew thy body.

GREAT VESPERS

Spurning the heresy of the Latins, thou didst flee to Mount Pochaev, the bastion of pure Orthodoxy; and with the holy hierarch Anthony as thy teacher, thou didst study the doctrines of piety and the dogmas of truth. And after thine ordination to the priesthood, thou didst return to thy native land, where thou didst nurture thy pious flock in the pastures of righteousness. Pray thou, that we all be saved.

And 4 stichera, idiomela, in Tone VI

Now is the village of Zhdynya glad, for it witnessed the birth of the holy hieromartyr, a beacon leading his people, who were languishing in error, to the True Faith! The city of Zhitomir is exalted, for therein the holy hieromartyr Maximus studied diligently the commandments of the Lord, the writings of the holy fathers, and the precepts of the Faith, storing these up in the coffer of his heart, that with these priceless treasures he might ransom his flock from slavery to heresy and error.

At Litiya, a Sticheron in Tone III

Thou didst hasten to the Lavra of Pochaev, fleeing the errors of the Latins as Lot fled Sodom; and in that tranquil monastic haven thou didst find the pearl of great price—the holy Orthodox Faith—which thou didst purchase with thy blood in martyrdom. Wherefore, O holy Maximus, the faithful honor thy holy memory with love.

Glory, in Tone IV

Having left the dark West of the setting sun, thou didst move toward the Sun of righteousness in the East; and having been illumined there by the never-waning radiance of light divine, which thou didst shine upon they much-suffering people, who had languished long in the darkness of Latin domination. Entreat Christ our God, that He enlighten and save our souls.

At the Aposticha, these stichera, in Tone IV:
Spec. Mel.: "Thou has given a sign..."

Merciful and all-loving is the good Shepherd, who left the flock and searched for thee, the lost sheep, in the mountains of Carpathia; and He brought thee back to the Orthodox Church, from whence thine ancestors were stolen away by false-shepherds and hirelings, betrayed to the ravening wolves of heresy.

Stichos: Returning to thy homeland after thy priestly ordination, thou didst lead thy people out of bondage to Latin error, as Moses led the children of Israel forth from Egyptian slavery; and they entered into the promised land of Holy Orthodoxy.

MATINS

Ode VI

Kontakion in Tone IV

Enlightened and moved by thy martyrdom, toward the Orthodox Faith, were our people. For giving up thy life for Christ God, thou didst endure tortures and sufferings in prison.

Ikos

In accordance with thy name, thou didst prove to be a champion most great, steadfast in thy confession of the triune God, faithfully opposing the errors of the Latin-minded.

Ode IX

All-holy is the Spirit Who proceedeth from the Father alone, and Who spake within thee when thou wast brought before the judges for the sake of Christ, having been delivered up by the enemies of the Holy Church, and hated unjustly for His name's sake. Yet thou didst endure to the end and wast saved, and at that same hour wast taught by the Spirit what to say, to confound the wicked plans of the ungodly. [515]

b. Twenty-Six Martyred Monks of Zographou

GREAT VESPERS

On the Aposticha, these Stichera, in Tone V

Rejoice, O divine regiment of the Monastery of Zographou, victorious company, pillars of piety, and steadfast, unyielding and undaunted contenders against the enemy, who, taking your stand upon the tower, did most boldly condemn the delusion of the Latins, of Michael, the vainglorious emperor of Byzantium, and with him the mindless Beccus, denouncing them all exceedingly, in that they had cast the flock of

---

515 *Menaion of the Orthodox Church, Volume XI, July*, "Commemoration of Saint Maximos Sandovich," trans. Reader Isaac E. Lambertsen (Liberty: Saint John of Kronstadt Press, 2011), 344-353.

Christ to the lions. Wherefore, entreat ye the Savior, that He grant us great mercy.

MATINS

Ode I

Through communion ye became sons of God, O steadfast venerable spiritual athletes, and having denounced the vile delusion of the heresy of the Latins and been reduced to ashes by the fire, ye have been crowned by Christ with a twofold wreath. Confessing with steadfastness of mind the Spirit Who proceedeth from the Father, as the Savior said, ye denounced and put the papists to shame as innovators, O wise ones.

Canon II of the venerable martyrs, in Tone IV

Let us praise today the assembly of the twenty-six venerable spiritual athletes, the steadfast diamonds who denounced the ungodliness of the Latins and endured an unjust death.

Ode III, Canon I

Showing forth a single patient endurance amid a multiplicity of bodies, the venerable fathers who suffered in the Monastery of Zographou put the cruel Latins to shame, and their heads have been crowned with wreaths of victory.

Canon II

Let the steadfast Paul and Sabbas be hymned, with Sergius, Simon and Dometian, and all the rest, for they denounced the mindlessness of the Latins.

Sessional Hymn, in Tone VIII

Taking the Cross of Christ upon your shoulders, O ye twenty-six blessed fathers, ye cleaved unto Him through ascetic endeavor; wherefore the enemy, hating your virtuous life, raised up against you the savage Latins, striving to weaken the steadfastness of your asceticism. Yet his machinations were set at naught when ye suffered most excellently. Pray ye to Christ God, that remission of transgressions be granted unto those who with love celebrate your holy memory.

Ode V, Canon I

With the power of the dogmas ye first cut down the heresy of the Latins, O wise ones; and were then murdered by them with fire. And having offered yourselves up fervently as sacrifices to the Lord, ye now join chorus with the angelic choirs, O ever memorable ones.

Ode VI, Canon I

That ye might receive everlasting life in the heavens, O most wise ones, ye gave your bodies over to temporal fire, denouncing the heresy of the Latins. Wherefore, rejoicing today, we celebrate your festival.

Kontakion, in Tone VIII

Let us praise the twenty-six sacred and venerable spiritual athletes, *the intercessors and protectors of Zographou, who cast down the pride of the Latins, and endured fiery immolation and were crowned as is meet; and let us cry: Rejoice, O venerable sufferers!

Ikos

The angels were amazed, looking down from heaven upon the ungodly assault of the Latins, how they burned in the fire the venerable ones who, for piety's sake, chose to die in piety. And having cast down the pride of the tyrants, they hear from us such things as these: Rejoice, O choir of venerable spiritual athletes; rejoice, steadfast regiment of those who suffered greatly. Rejoice, ye venerable ones, twenty-six in number; rejoice, O Thomas and the other martyrs! Rejoice, godly Barsanuphius and steadfast Micah; rejoice, Dometian, Menas and the radiant Paul! Rejoice with Anthony, O Euthymius and Hilarion; rejoice with Parthenius, O Simon and Joseph! Rejoice, ye two James's, together with Joannicius; rejoice, O Martinian, with Cosmas and Sergius! Rejoice, O glorious Cyprian, Cyril, Job and Sabbas; rejoice, O four glorious and unnamed radiant passion-bearers! Rejoice, O venerable sufferers!

Ode VII, Canon I

Consumed by the fire, ye burned up falsehood opposed to God, O venerable martyrs of Christ, denouncing the abominable addition of the Latins concerning the Spirit, and chanting: O God of our fathers, blessed art Thou!

Ode IX, Canon II, Exapostilarion

With splendor let us praise today the intercessors for the Monastery of Zographou, the venerable fathers who suffered, casting down the delusion of the Latins, the preachers of the Orthodox Faith who, consumed by fire, offered themselves to the Trinity as divine whole burnt sacrifices.

On the Aposticha, these Stichera, in Tone V

Rejoice, O divine regiment of the Monastery of Zographou, victorious company, pillars of piety, and steadfast, unyielding and undaunted contenders against the enemy, who, taking your stand upon the tower, did most boldly condemn the delusion of the Latins, of Michael, the vainglorious emperor of Byzantium, and with him the mindless Beccus, denouncing them all exceedingly, in that they had cast the flock of Christ to the lions. Wherefore, entreat ye the Savior, that He grant us great mercy.

Ode IV, Canon I

Forsaking corrupt glory and food, O fathers, ye struggled in the Monastery of Zographou, and steadfastly opposed the papists who strove to force you to embrace false Latin concepts of God; and ye offered yourselves unto God as sacrifices consumed by fire.

Ode IV, Canon II

Strengthened by courage and grace, the regiment of the venerable set at naught the wiles of the incorporeal foe and cast down the blasphemy of the papists which is full of impiety.[516]

---

516 *Menaion of the Orthodox Church, Volume 1, September,* "Commemoration of the Twenty-Six Martyred Monks of Zographou," trans. Reader Isaac E. Lambertsen (Liberty: Saint John of Kronstadt Press, 2011) 338-351.

c. Martyr St. Atanasie Todoran[517]

Ikos 1

Fighter for faith and nation, conqueror of Christ's opponents and fearless defender of Orthodoxy, you grew up in the Land of Năsăud, manfully receiving a martyr's death. For this, destroying the delusions of the oppressors, you won the unfading crown of holiness. Happy Athanasius, ask Christ God to have mercy and save our souls.

d. St. Gregory Palamas[518]

GREAT VESPERS

And 3 Stichera, Tone IV

Having adorned thy discourse with wisdom and blameless virtue, O most wise Gregory, in both thou wast wholly beautiful, noetically adorning and gladdening the people with thy God proclaiming words, extending to them the one Godhead of the Trinity; wherefore, having trampled alien heresy underfoot with Thine exceedingly glorious teachings, thou didst raise up the might of the Faith in the end. Standing before Christ with His immaterial ministers, ask thou peace and great mercy for our souls.

MATINS

Ode VI, Irmos

Having produced rules of precepts and brilliant discourses, whereby thou didst open the minds of the honored theologians to the Spirit, O Gregory, by thy supplications preserve the Church of Christ unshaken, and deliver it from all heresy.

517 "Akathist of the Holy Martyr Athanasius Todoran," Moldova & Bucovina, Romanian Orthodox Church Metropolia, accessed October 20th, 2022, https://doxologia.ro/ceaslov/acatiste/acatistul-sfantului-martir-atanasie-todoran

518 *Menaion of the Orthodox Church, Vol III, November*, "Commemoration of Our Father Among the Saints Gregory Palamas," trans. Reader Isaac Lambertsen (Liberty: St. John Press, 2008), 158-167.

Ode IX, On the Aposticha, four Stichera, in Tone I

O blessed saint, thou hast planted the dogmas of Orthodoxy * and cut down the thorns of heresy. * With thy words thou hast watered the seed of the Faith, * making it grow, * and as an active husbandman thou hast brought to God ** ears of wheat increased a hundredfold.

Ode IX, Tone IV

Having adorned thy discourse with wisdom and blameless virtue, O most wise Gregory, in both thou wast wholly beautiful, noetically adorning and gladdening the people with thy God proclaiming words, extending to them the (doctrine of the) one Godhead of the Trinity; wherefore, having trampled alien heresy underfoot with Thine exceedingly glorious teachings, thou didst raise up the might of the Faith in the end. Standing before Christ with His immaterial ministers, ask thou peace and great mercy for our souls.

e. Holy Hierarch, St. Dositheus, Metropolitan of Moldavia

Troparion, in Tone 8

Protector of Orthodoxy and teacher of holiness, shepherd gentle as a lamb, and great teacher of the Divine Liturgy, O Holy Hierarch Dositheus, entreat Christ God to save our souls!

f. Holy Hieromartyr St. Isidore of Yuryev and of His Seventy-Two Companions

VESPERS

What shall we name thee, O valiant Priest Isidore? For thou didst lead to Christ a regiment of martyrs, and with them hast glorified the Orthodox Faith of your fathers in the face of the vain-minded Latins, and didst cast down their strange doctrines and false persuasions by the power of Christ Who by His baptism hath crushed the heads of the serpents in the Jordan, that He might save us and wash away the multitude of our sins through the entreaties of His martyrs, in that He is compassionate and loveth mankind.

Rejoice, O Isidore, thou priest of God, valiant minister of the mysteries of Christ, having with thee the equally zealous assembly of seventy-two martyrs. For like a star of surpassing radiance thou hast shone forth in the firmament of the Church, didst manifestly preach the consubstantial and indivisible Trinity — the Father, the Son, and the Holy Spirit Who proceedeth from the Father — before the malicious Roman bishop and many people, denouncing the Latin belief. Wherefore your holy bodies were committed to the river's streams, O martyrs of Christ, yet were later cast up upon dry land by the providence of God, and Christ hath given rest to your spirits in the mansions of heaven. And now, O holy martyrs who died for the Orthodox Faith, entreat Christ God that our souls may be saved.

Great is the wonder! On the holy feast, the enemies of the Trinity prevent the wondrous Isidore and his flock from sanctifying the waters; yet having steadfastly resisted the persuasion of the heretics, the holy martyrs are thrust down through the ice by the ungodly, thereby sanctifying the river by their martyric death. O ye who love the saints of the Church, rejoice and be glad; for, having received their reward from Christ in the heavens, the martyrs pray fervently in behalf of those who honor their ineffable sacrifice.[519]

MATINS

Ode III

The evil-minded Roman bishop desired that ye cast off the Orthodox Faith, O saints, and espouse his false ideas and unleavened mass; but as valiant warriors ye defied him, O holy ones, and won victory over him by the power of Christ. [520]

---

519 *Menaion of the Orthodox Church, Volume V, January,* "Commemoration of Saint Isidore and the Seventy-Two Martyrs," trans. Reader Isaac E. Lambertsen (Liberty: Saint John of Kronstadt Press, 2012), 157-159.

520 Ibid., 162.

Ode V

Moved by great zeal, O divine martyrs, and strengthened by Christ, ye put the enemies of the Orthodox faith to shame and trampled the false doctrines and laws of the Latins underfoot, O Holy ones, regarding them as of no account. Through the entreaties of the martyrs, O Word of God, deliver from great tortures us who bless their holy torments with all our soul.[521]

Ode VII
Ikos

The all-wise Creator, the Master and Lord... hath shown forth hieromartyr Isidore and the company of seventy-two athletes with him, to be splendid martyrs and most excellent warriors. For, having trampled the traditions and laws of the Latins underfoot, O valiant ones, and by your mighty opposition and endurance having cast into confusion those who hate the Orthodox Faith, ye became like unto the ancient martyrs, O holy ones.[522]

g. Hieromartyr St. Hermogenes, Patriarch of Moscow and All Russia

MATINS

After Psalm 50, this sticheron, in Tone VI

O Hermogenes, thou wast shown to be a most fervent advocate for the Orthodox people, and, boldly rejecting heretical doctrine, didst show thyself to be a model of Orthodoxy for all, praying for all who follow thy divine teachings and instructions.

Sessional hymn, in Tone VIII, Special Melody: "Of the Wisdom"

Ascending to the summit of heaven, and having been illumined by an effulgence of miracles therefrom, O father, thou wast truly shown to be an all-radiant pastor for Orthodox Russia, and art for us an invincible intercessor amid perils. Wherefore, having all-gloriously vanquished our

---

521 Ibid., 163.

522 Ibid., 164.

enemies, thou didst drive away the falsehood of heresy and save thine Orthodox land from destruction. Entreat Christ God, O Hermogenes, that He grant remission of sins unto those who with love honor thy holy memory.

h. New Hieromartyr St. Bronko (Dobrosavljević) of Veljun

MATINS

Kontakion, Tone 4[523]

Unwilling to renounce Orthodoxy or abandon your people, you suffered a martyr's death with your son who was not afraid, the meaning of his name. As a shining follower of your Krsna Slava, George the Victorious One, you endured to the end, saving your soul from the demonic spirits of the enemies of Christ, O Holy Hieromartyr Branko; therefore, with Father Dmitar and all the martyred peasants who suffered with you, we glorify you: Rejoice, O Victors of Eternal Life.

i. St. Justin (Popović) of Tjelije

Apolytikion Mode 1[524]

Let us honor with splendor the divinely inspired theologian, the wise Serb Justin, who by the scythe of the Holy Spirit hath thrashed the error of atheism and the insolence of the Latins, being a mystic of the God-man and lover of piety, crying out: Glory to Christ Who hath glorified thee, glory to Him Who hath crowned thee, glory to Him Who hath rendered thee a luminary to those who are in a state of darkness.

---

523 Composed by Rev. Dr. Daniel M. Rogich, Ph.D. From: Fr. Daniel Rogich, *Serbian Patericon: Saints of the Serbian Orthodox Church – Volume One*, (Canton: Hesychia Press, 2023), 289.

524 Father (St.) Justin Popovich, *Orthodox Faith and Life in Christ*, trans. Fr. Asterios Gerostergios (Belmont: Institute for Byzantine and Modern Greek Studies, 2020), iii.

j. St. Raphael (Hawaweeny) of Brooklyn

VESPERS

Aposticha in the Sixth (Plagal of the Second) Tone[525]

Thou wast a guardian and a defender of the Church's teachings, thou didst protect thy flock from false doctrines and confirmed them in the true faith. O holy father Raphael, son of Syria and glory of North America, do thou now intercede that our souls may be saved.

MATINS

Ode 5 [526]

Through thy holy instructions, those who followed after the false gods of this world returned to worship the living and true God, and in recalling them thou hast become a worthy servant of God Almighty.

Ode 6 [527]

With the streams of thine admonitions thou didst stop the influx of wicked heresy, as a peaceful river, watering the flocks of the faithful with piety, O all-honored hierarch.

The Praises in the Fourth Tone [528]

As a worthy hierarch thou didst take upon thyself the needs and concerns of all thy flock. In towns and villages and farms thou didst gather them to thee. Thou didst keep thy sheep from straying into strange pastures; thy hand kept them safe from devouring wolves. Thy deeds of love grew brighter as the number of churches grew. Now standing at the throne of God, beseech Him to save our souls.

---

525 Antiochian Orthodox Christian Archdiocese of North America, *Our Father Among the Saints Raphael Bishop of Brooklyn* (Wichita: Antakya Press, 2000), 72.

526 Antiochian Orthodox Christian Archdiocese of North America, *Our Father Among the Saints Raphael Bishop of Brooklyn* (Wichita: Antakya Press, 2000), 89.

527 Ibid., 90.

528 Ibid., 97.

2. Selections from Akathist Hymns

a. Akathist Hymn to the Holy Photius, Patriarch of Constantinople, the Confessor, Great among Hierarchs and Equal of the Apostles (Unabridged)[529]

Whose Memory the Holy Church Doth Celebrate On the 6th of February

Kontakion I

We bless thee as a right flourishing meadow of wisdom and the unshakable foundation of the Church, O divinely inspired hierarch. As one who was filled with the enlightenment of the divine Spirit, enlighten the understanding of us who cry to thee:

Rejoice, O Photius most wise!

Ikos I

As a minister of wisdom, thou wast shown to be an angel of truth, O divinely revealed Photius, and with thine angelic voice thou proclaimest the beauties of Orthodoxy. Wherefore, marveling at thy brilliance, we cry aloud:

Rejoice, thou by whom the Trinity is hymned;
Rejoice, thou by whom the enemy is repelled!
Rejoice, great teacher of the Church;
Rejoice, most wise rhetor of piety!
Rejoice, God-proclaiming mouth of sacred doctrines;
Rejoice, lips of pious dogmas, filled with the thunder of the heavens!
    Rejoice, for thou dost mightily refute heresies;
Rejoice, for with divine wisdom thou didst endure persecution!
Rejoice, thou who didst share in the ways of the glorious martyrs;
Rejoice, dweller with pious and saintly monastics!
Rejoice, thou by whom falsehood is abolished;
Rejoice, thou through whom the Truth shineth forth!
Rejoice, O Photius most wise!

---

529 Holy Trinity Monastery, *Book of Akathists II* (Jordanville: Printshop of St. Job of Pochaev, 2021), 425-438.

Kontakion II

By apostolic zeal and all thy wisdom thou wast shown to be the foundation of the Church, O wondrous Photius, casting down the demonic thoughts of the heretics; for thou teachest all to chant unto the Holy Trinity: Alleluia!

Ikos II

By the will of the Lord thou didst sprout forth like a fruitful date palm from a noble family O most sacred father Photius, and with the fruits of thy virtues thou dost nurture the multitudes of the pious who cry out to thee with faith:

Rejoice, scion of a flourishing root;
Rejoice, cultivation of valuable fruit!
Rejoice, blossom put forth by holy parents;
Rejoice, acquisition of a divine lot!
Rejoice, height of abundant understanding, hard to discern;
Rejoice, most glorious depth of manifest grace!
Rejoice, for thou shinest with rays of the virtues;
Rejoice, for thou settest all creation afire with light!
Rejoice, most radiant lamp of faith;
Rejoice, unapproachable star of Him Who hath dominion over all!
Rejoice, abundance of all-wise teachings;
Rejoice, harp of precious gifts!
Rejoice, O Photius most wise!

Kontakion III

Abiding in imperial palaces, O wise one, as one full of understanding thou didst disdain earthly glory; and in every way looking to Christ, to Whom thou wast guided by light, O father Photius, thou didst cry out: Alleluia!

Ikos III

Thou wast resplendent in wisdom and a radiant way of life, and wast shown to be a rhetor of piety, for which cause we thus cry out to thee, as to the wise chief shepherd of the Church, who wast prophesied by divine benevolence:

Rejoice, rhetor of piety;
Rejoice, mouth of the Truth!
Rejoice, shepherd of the Church, appointed by God;
Rejoice, divinely inspired hierarch of Christ!
Rejoice, most wondrous name, beacon of the Orthodox;
Rejoice, report spread far and wide, confirmation of the pious!
Rejoice, for thou dost refute the errors of the iconoclasts;
Rejoice, for thou doest away with the harm of the Manichaeans!
Rejoice, thou who art wise in word and deed;
Rejoice, thou who art great in benefactions and good works!
Rejoice, thou who washest away the impurity of men's souls;
Rejoice, thou who dost manifest God's compassion toward us!
Rejoice, O Photius most wise!

Kontakion IV

Thou didst show thyself to be a zealot of the apostles of Christ in all things, O most sacred father. Wherefore, O father Photius, thou didst with faith preach the light of the Gospel among the Bulgars, whom thou didst bring to Christ, so that they chant: Alleluia!

Ikos IV

Thy radiant wisdom and the light of thy holy life have brought to Christ many who sit in the darkness of heresies, O divinely eloquent one. Wherefore, marveling at thy brilliance, we cry:

Rejoice, lamp for the benighted;
Rejoice, beacon for the lost!
Rejoice, great teacher of piety;
Rejoice, successor of the holy apostles!
Rejoice, mouth of the doctrine of salvation, moved by God;
Rejoice, untroubled eye of the luminous soul!

Rejoice, for thou pourest forth the sweetness of salvation;
Rejoice, for thou driest up the venom of evil!
Rejoice, divinely sculpted image of the shepherds;
Rejoice, rule of holy meekness!
Rejoice, lover and servant of Christ;
Rejoice, gazer upon the light of heaven!
Rejoice, O Photius most wise!

Kontakion V

With thy divinely eloquent tongue, O wise Photius, thou didst refute the error of Nicholas, the primate of Old Rome, and didst humble his pride down to the earth; for, mindless, he did not understand how rightly to cry unto the Trinity: Alleluia!

Ikos V

Directing the immaculate Church of Christ to the meadows of salvation in sacred manner, thou didst endure cruel persecutions, and wast separated from thy flock by force. Yet those faithful to thee, O holy one, did not cease to cry:

Rejoice, thou who art great among hierarchs;
Rejoice, thou who art divinely inspired among archpastors!
Rejoice, unshakable tower of patience;
Rejoice, thou who art unceasingly hymned by the devout!
Rejoice, sun of great splendor, illumining all the earth;
Rejoice, two-edged sword, cutting down the pride of the pope!
Rejoice, for thou didst endure persecution and afflictions;
Rejoice, for thou dost reprove the persecutors' ranks!
Rejoice, shepherd of all shepherds, chosen beforehand;
Rejoice, defender of all the faithful!
Rejoice, initiate of the mysteries of God;
Rejoice, our helper and our deliverer!
Rejoice, O Photius most wise!

Kontakion VI

As a proclaimer of piety, O father, thou preachest, in Orthodox manner, that the most Holy Spirit proceedeth from the Father, and thou didst denounce the erroneous faith of the Latins; but thou didst teach the faithful, O Photius, to chant to the Trinity: Alleluia!

Ikos VI

Having shone forth in the East like the radiant morning-star, thou castest light upon the whole world and the darkness of the West, O most wondrous hierarch, and winnest victory through thy luminous dogmas, hearing from us such things as these:

Rejoice, great luminary of the East;
Rejoice, thou who art revered by all the faithful!
Rejoice, denouncer of the darkness of the West;
Rejoice, thou who partakest of the effulgence of God!
Rejoice, burning coal, consuming all the falsehood of the Latins;
Rejoice, lamp illumining all with the grace of the Trinity!
Rejoice, for thou preachest the Holy Trinity;
Rejoice, for thou cuttest off the error of the Latins!
Rejoice, thou who art filled with immaterial light;
Rejoice, thou who aboundest with great grace!
Rejoice, thou who dost manifest divine gifts;
Rejoice, wise and glorious revealer of God!
Rejoice, O Photius most wise!

Kontakion VII

As a recorder of Orthodox dogmas, thou dost refute the error of the Manichaeans and the might of the iconoclasts, thundering forth in thy discourses, O Photius; and thou wast shown to be a divine revealer of sacred things, crying out: Alleluia!

Ikos VII

Wisely championing the canons of the Church and the rules of the saints, O divinely eloquent one, thou didst mightily withstand the attacks of the Latins, O Photius; wherefore, marveling at thy meekness, we cry out:

Rejoice, wounder of the Latins;
Rejoice, thou who dost lay delusion low!
Rejoice, thou who didst emulate the zeal of the apostles;
Rejoice, thou who didst repel the audacity of those whose faith is
    in error!
Rejoice, divinely inspired instrument of the wisdom of Rejoice,
    two-edged sword brandished against the falsehood of the
    enemy.
Rejoice, phial of heavenly virtues;
Rejoice, pillar recording holy battles!
Rejoice, well-spring of the waters of grace;
Rejoice, ray of heavenly brilliance!
Rejoice, thou who knewest the sacred life beforehand;
Rejoice, true instructor of the faithful!
Rejoice, O Photius most wise!

Kontakion VIII

The richness of thy great wisdom amazeth the hearts of the faithful,
O divinely eloquent one, for having passed through all that is good, thou
wast shown to be a receptacle of virtues, O Photius of great renown, who
guidest with light those who cry out: Alleluia!

Ikos VIII

Wholly at peace, and showing thyself to be a model of greatness
of soul, O father, thou didst stand before the company of persecutors
who assembled against thee, and by thy godly demeanor didst amaze the
faithful, who cried out:

Rejoice, arranger of grace;
Rejoice, most excellent theologian!
Rejoice, thou who didst endure most irrational rage;
Rejoice, thou who didst show forth invincible power!
Rejoice, treasury of meekness and love;
Rejoice, holiness of the Spirit and radiant guide for men's souls!
Rejoice, for thou didst confront the unjust assembly;
Rejoice, for thou dost teach with words of grace!
Rejoice, thou who wast undaunted by thine enemies' mindlessness;

Rejoice, thou who dost illumine the understanding of the faithful!
Rejoice, shaming of unjust judges;
Rejoice, our God-given victory!
Rejoice, O Photius most wise!

Kontakion IX

Guided through life by the Holy Spirit, thou didst manfully endure persecutions, O most sacred Photius; and having conformed thyself to the sufferings of Christ, thou didst come to share in His divine glory, crying: Alleluia!

Ikos IX

Being a divinely eloquent rhetor, as a wise chief shepherd thou didst set the words of salvation before thy reason-endowed flock and the whole Church, O Photius, and unto all thou didst show thyself to be a beacon illumining those who cry:

Rejoice, lamp of the entire Church;
Rejoice, consuming of soul-corrupting falsehood!
Rejoice, great and most wondrous Photius;
Rejoice, most sacred and glorious pastor!
Rejoice, torrent issuing forth from the mystic Eden;
Rejoice, impregnable rampart of the honored Church!
Rejoice, for thou shinest forth heavenly knowledge;
Rejoice, for thou givest health unto those who entreat thee!
Rejoice, sacred joy of the faithful;
Rejoice, utter wounding of enemies!
Rejoice, thou by whom the Latins are stricken mute;
Rejoice, thou to whom the faithful cry out!
Rejoice, O Photius most wise!

Kontakion X

In that He is good, the Saviour of all, the never-waning Effulgence, set thee again as a light for the Church, that by thy divinely wise discourse thou mightest illumine, guide and cultivate those who chant unto the Lord: Alleluia!

Ikos X

The wise men of the West, who spake against thee with blasphemous tongue, O father, were in nowise able to contradict thine all-wise words and the divine power of thy doctrines; and we cry out to thee with faith:

Rejoice, most radiant morning-star;
Rejoice, most magnificent and divine orator!
Rejoice, most fragrant meadow of wisdom;
Rejoice, denouncer of the use of painful torture!
Rejoice, treasury of divine gifts;
Rejoice, sacred phial of exalted thoughts!
Rejoice, for thou dost shepherd thy people most wisely;
Rejoice, for thou dost utterly consume the tinder of heresies!
Rejoice, for thou burnest with the divine fire;
Rejoice, thou who woundest the most wicked foe!
Rejoice, most sacred glory of the wise;
Rejoice, God-given strength of the faithful!
Rejoice, O Photius most wise!

Kontakion XI

As is meet, the entire Holy Church praiseth thee with sacred hymns, O wise hierarch Photius, for by thee hath it been delivered from most evil heresies through grace divine; and it chanteth to the Chief Shepherd: Alleluia!

Ikos XI

The prince of darkness trembleth before thy light, O father, and the horde of heresies vanisheth before thy light-bearing name, driven away as by fire, O Photius; and we cry out to thee with joy:

Rejoice, divinely inspired high priest;
Rejoice, our intercessor before the Lord!
Rejoice, thou who burnest up the tares of falsehood;
Rejoice, thou who reverseth demonic possession!
Rejoice, glittering fire of the Orthodox Faith;
Rejoice, luminous star of divine traditions!
Rejoice, reprover of the mindlessness of the popes;

Rejoice, bestower of mystic joy!
Rejoice, most fervent minister of Christ;
Rejoice, most wise pastor of pastors!
Rejoice, thou who illuminest the minds of the faithful;
Rejoice, thou who dost conquer the hordes of the enemy!
Rejoice, O Photius most wise!

Kontakion XII

Rejoicing, thou didst make thine abode in the mansions of heaven, O divinely inspired one, where thou dost gaze directly upon the effulgence of the most Holy Trinity, which passeth description; and, deified by communing therewith, Photius, thou dost unceasingly chant: Alleluia!

Ikos XII

Hymning thy struggles, O hierarch Photius, we fall down before thee with great compunction. O father, thou foundation of the fathers, grant me also a drop of thy wisdom, enlightening my heart, that I may continually cry to thee:

Rejoice, great primate;
Rejoice, intercessor for all the faithful!
Rejoice, enlightenment of Orthodox Christians;
Rejoice, adornment of the divinely eloquent fathers!
Rejoice, might and confirmation of the Church of Christ;
Rejoice, thou who with great power didst lay low the lies of the enemy!
Rejoice, thou who illuminest the beauty of Orthodoxy;
Rejoice, thou who dost cast down the errors of false religion!
Rejoice, thou by whom I am delivered from darkness;
Rejoice, thou through whom I am filled with light!
Rejoice, mediator between the faithful and Christ;
Rejoice, my deliverer, who bestowest light upon me!
Rejoice, O Photius most wise!

Kontakion XIII

O all-wondrous father, hierarch Photius, adornment of the whole Church! Mercifully accepting our chanted supplications, ask for us the divine and heavenly light, that we may sing unto the Holy Trinity: Alleluia! Alleluia! Alleluia!

This Kontakion is recited thrice, whereupon Ikos I and Kontakion I are repeated.

PRAYER TO THE HIERARCH PHOTIUS THE GREAT, PATRIARCH OF CONSTANTINOPLE, THE NEW ROME, CONFESSOR OF THE FAITH AND EQUAL OF THE APOSTLES

O all-wise and most excellent hierarch, equal of the apostles and enlightener of the land of Bulgaria, bright sounding harp of the divine Spirit, holy father Photius! Unto thee do we now hasten, and with compunction we offer thee this meager entreaty: Harken unto us, thy lowly children, and show forth thine intercession for us to the Most High, fervently beseeching Him to forgive us, His servants, and that He open unto us the gates of His lovingkindness. For we are not worthy, neither is it meet for us to gaze upon the heights of heaven, since we are bent over by the multitude of our sins. Yet even though we have sinned grievously and have in nowise done the will of our Creator, nor kept His commandments, yet have we not turned to any other god, nor have we stretched forth our hands to such. Kneeling before our Maker with contrite and humble hearts, we again ask thy paternal help: O Photius of who art gilded with light as with gold, intercede before Him for our land and Church of Bulgaria, which were once watered by the sweat of thy labors and is now eaten up by bitter temptations. Help us, O saint of God, lest we perish in our iniquities; deliver us from all evil and every contrary thing; direct our minds, and strengthen our hearts in the Orthodox Faith wherein, by thine intercession and mediation, let us not be separated from our Creator either by wounds, threats or any anger. We beseech thee, O good shepherd: Drive far from the flock of Christ the cruel wolves of the Latins' pride, both when it clotheth itself in humility and speaketh falsely of love, and when it riseth up with strength against the Church Universal; and cut it down as thou didst of old. Preserve us well from the machinations of the heretics, and instruct us how to speak the Truth with love. Teach us to do every good work, and even more to offer tearful repentance for our sins, that covered by the omophorion of thy supplications at the time of our departure for the life to come, and protected by the maternal aid of our all-blessed Mistress, we may be delivered from the aerial way-stations and from everlasting torment, that with thee and all the saints we may ever glorify the most hymned name of the Father, and the Son, and the Holy Spirit, now and ever, and for endless ages of ages. Amen.

b. Select Hymns to the Holy New Hieromartyr Maximus Sandovich, Protomartyr of the Lemko People[530]

Kontakion II

Entering a Roman Catholic monastery to receive religious instruction, thou wast repelled by the ungodliness of the monks and their contempt for thy people; wherefore, thou didst flee unto Mount Pochaev, to the safe haven of the Holy Lavra, where in purity and chastity thou didst study the truths of the Holy Orthodox Faith, that thou mightest pray aright unto God: Alleluia!

Ikos II

Rejoice, thou who helpest us to vanquish Satan;

Rejoice, thou who drivest away from us the soul-destroying
  demons, like as they were carrion fowl!

Rejoice, thou who teachest us to recognize the wiles of heretics,
  who are like jackals in the night;

Rejoice thou who repellest their bestial ravages upon our minds
  and hearts!

Rejoice thou who art a mighty ally against the prince of evil who
  assaileth this world!

Rejoice, sword of Spirit honed to sharpness to smite false belief;
  rejoice, dispeller of ungodliness!

Ikos III

Rejoice, thou whose precious body was felled by the weapons of
  the ungodly!

---

530 The Saint John of Kronstadt Press, *Holy New Hieromartyr Maximus Sandovich: Protomartyr of the Lemko People*, trans. Isaac E. Lambertsen (Liberty: The Saint John of Kronstadt Press, 1998), 37-47.

Ikos IV

Hearing of thy piety, the Orthodox people of Graba came to thee and besought thee to become the pastor of their right-believing flock; and taking up this ministry, thou didst not show thyself to be a hireling, but a true shepherd who laid down his life for his sheep. Wherefore, we rightly chant these praises unto thee, saying:

Rejoice, thou who instructest those in tribulations and sorrows to flee to the intercession of the saints;
Rejoice, thou who teachest us to turn to God in all our needs!

Kontakion V

Even those who are weak in faith and love are astonished by thy martyrdom, O hieromartyr, for as the holy children cast into the furnace of Babylon did not waiver in their confession of the true God, so thou didst not waiver in thy confession of Holy Orthodoxy, and for thy courage and endurance thou dost hear from us these hymns:

Ikos V

Rejoice thou who settest at nought the machinations of the devil and his angels;
Rejoice thou who castest down all their power!
Rejoice, forthright reprover of those in error!
Rejoice, thou who didst manifest complete self-denial when thou didst move Uniates to return to the Church of Christ;
Rejoice, thou who showest the heretics the paths of true repentance!

Kontakion VI

Right justly doth the Pope of Rome bear the blame for thine undeserved incarceration and martyrdom, O Maximus most great, for in the arrogance of his power he sought to enslave the Lemko people to his errors; but, led by thee to the true light of Orthodoxy, they eluded his wiles and machinations, and cleaved anew to the Faith of their fathers, crying out in joy: Alleluia!

Ikos VI

O the light which is poured forth upon the oppressed through thy brave sacrifice, O new martyr! For armed with the fiery sword of God's grace, thou didst dispel the darkness of falsehood from those who for long centuries had languished disconsolate in the shadow of the Latins' errors. Wherefore, praising God Who is wondrous in His saints, we cry out to thee:

Rejoice, thou who hast cast down the deception of the heretics;

Ikos VIII
Rejoice, for thou didst make no attempt to entreat the tyrant for thine earthly life;
Rejoice, for thou didst reject the errors of the Latins!

Ikos IX
Rejoice, thou who has uplifted all Orthodox Christians with thy mighty confession;
Rejoice, shaming of blasphemous heretics!
Rejoice, thou who hadst great desire to care for the souls of thy flock;
Rejoice, for thou didst hold the glory of this world to be foolishness.

Ikos XI
Every town and village of Lemkovina is filled with radiance, for the holy Maximus is set on high, like a splendid lamp, shining brightly with the light of grace, and guiding all along the straight and narrow path of Orthodoxy, which leadeth to the mansions of heaven. Wherefore, in compunction we cry unto him:

Rejoice, O wise one, who exchanged a transitory life for one that is eternal!
Rejoice, fearless preacher of truth;
Rejoice, thou who wast far wiser than the heretics who slew thee!

Kontakion XIII
Maximus, who confessed the Holy Spirit to proceed from the Father alone, who laid down his life for the Orthodox Faith, and was well-pleasing to his Lord and Master, standeth now amid the choir of the martyrs, arrayed in splendid vesture and wearing the crown which he received from Christ for his struggle; and with all the saints he joyously crieth aloud: Alleluia! Alleluia! Alleluia!

c. Select Hymns to St. Job of Pochaev[531]

Kontakion IV

Desiring to dispel the tempest of the assaults of the heretics, thou didst attend the sacred council of the Orthodox in the divinely saved city of Kiev, where thou didst boldly confess the unadulterated Faith and didst exhort all the people to cleave unto it; wherefore, thou didst not cease to commit sacred books to print in the Monastery of Pochaev, that all who read them might hold to the true Faith and chant unto God in Orthodox manner: Alleluia!

Ikos IV

Monks and layfolk beheld the abbot of the Monastery of Pochaev humbling himself by tilling the earth, planting trees, and gathering manure, and they marvelled at him as at a second Saint John of Damascus; and they came to despise all the pride of heresy and rendered their souls steadfast in Orthodoxy.

Ikos IX

Orthodox hierarchs and the whole sacred council were shown to be proclaimers of thy glory when thy relics, which had been hidden from the apostates from Orthodoxy, were again borne into the holy church, while the Christians bowed down and said in gladness:

Rejoice, ray of light which dispelled the darkness of heresy!
Rejoice, thou who didst thereby utterly denounce apostasy from
　　Orthodoxy!

Ikos XI

Thou wast a beacon of the Orthodox Faith and a pillar of piety, O Job our father, in word, life, love, faith, and purity; therein strengthen us by thy prayers and drive away from us all heresy and corrupt practices.

---

531 Saint Job of Pochaev. *St. Job of Pochaev: Life, Liturgical Service and Akathist Hymn*, trans. Reader Isaac E. Lambertsen (Liberty: St. John of Kronstadt Press, 1997), 86-88; 91; 93-94.

Kontakion XIII

O most blessed and venerable Job, great zealot of the Orthodox Faith and steadfast denouncer of heresy! Reject not this meager supplication, which is offered unto thee from the depths of our wretched hearts; but be thou for us a faithful guide in faith and repentance, a good helper amid struggles, and a never-tiring advocate before the Lord for the salvation of us who for thy sake chant unto God: Alleluia! Alleluia! Alleluia!

3. Excerpt from the the Office for the Reception of [Papist] Converts[532]

Introductory Note[533]: This excerpt is from the (Hapgood) Service Book of the Orthodox Church, for the Antiochian Archdiocese Orthodox Church of North America. It contains specific offices for the reception into Orthodoxy of a convert from another "Christian" confession. While the book's authority is small in scope, it is still an excellent example of this traditional practice of public repudiation. What follows are the texts that would be confessed by a convert from Catholicism during the service, renouncing the heresies of their former confession just before their baptism.

After the Prayer, the Bishop (or Priest) shall say to the convert:

Wherefore renounce now, with all thy heart, thine errors, and false doctrines, and mistakes of judgment, and confess the Orthodox-Catholic Faith.

And the Bishop questioneth the convert from the Roman-Latin Confession.

Bishop: Dost thou renounce the false doctrine that, for the expression of the dogma touching the Procession of the Holy Spirit, the declaration of our Saviour Christ himself: "who proceedeth from the Father": doth not suffice; and that the addition, of man's invention: "and from the Son": is required?

---

532 Isabel Florence Hapgood, *Service Book of the Orthodox Church* (Englewood: Antiochian Orthodox Christian Archdiocese, 1996), 455-456.

533 Introductory Note from The Orthodox Ethos team.

Answer. I do.

Bishop: Dost, thou renounce the erroneous belief that it doth not suffice to confess our Lord Jesus Christ as the head of the Universal Church; and that a man, to wit, the Bishop of Rome, can be the head of Christ's Body, that is to say, of the whole Church?

Answer. I do.

Bishop: Dost thou renounce the erroneous belief that the holy Apostles did not receive from our Lord equal spiritual power, but that the holy Apostle Peter was their Prince: And that the Bishop of Rome alone is his successor: And that the Bishops of Jerusalem, Antioch and others are not, equally with the Bishop of Rome, successors of the Apostles?

Answer. I do.

Bishop: Dost thou renounce the erroneous belief of those who think that the Pope of Rome is superior to the Ecumenical Councils, and infallible in faith, notwithstanding the fact that several of the Popes have been heretics, and condemned as such by the Councils?

Answer. I do.

Bishop: Dost thou renounce all the other doctrines of the Western Confession, both old and new, which are contrary to the Word of God, and to the true tradition of the Church, and to the decrees of the seven Ecumenical Councils?

Answer. I do.

The Crucifixion of the Lord
Greece, 14ᵀᴴ century

B. MAJOR ENCYCLICALS
AND RESOLUTIONS OF THE
MODERN PERIOD

1. Patriarchal Condemnation of Papalism
by Constantinople, Alexandria, Antioch, Jerusalem
(1848)[534]

Arianism was once one of these heresies that were spread to a large portion of the world, for reasons which the Lord knows. Such today is also Papism [the Filioque] is a heresy and those who believe it are heretics [...] For this reason also the one, Holy, Catholic, and Apostolic Church, following in the footsteps of the holy Fathers, eastern and western, declared both long ago in the days of our Fathers and rules once again today in council... that it is a heresy and its followers are heretics [...] Likewise, the congregations formed by them are heretical and every spiritual communion of the Orthodox children [...] with them is anticanonical, just as the 7th canon of the Third Ecumenical Council determines.

---

534 Koutloumousiou Monastery, Ὁ πειρασμὸς τῆς Ῥώμης [The Temptation of Rome], (Mt. Athos: price, 1992), 85-115. Quoted in Anastasios K. Gotsopoulos, On Common Prayer with the Heterodox, (Uncut Mountain Press, 2022), 19.

2. Encyclical of the Eastern Patriarchs, 1848
A Reply to the Epistle of Pope Pius IX,
"To the Easterns" [535, 536]

To All the Bishops Everywhere, Beloved in the Holy Ghost, Our Venerable, Most Dear Brethren; and to their Most Pious Clergy; and to All the Genuine Orthodox Sons of the One, Holy, Catholic and Apostolic Church: Brotherly Salutation in the Holy Spirit, and Every Good from God, and Salvation.

1. The holy, evangelical and divine Gospel of Salvation should be set forth by all in its original simplicity, and should evermore be believed in its unadulterated purity, even the same as it was revealed to His holy Apostles by our Savior, who for this very cause, descending from the bosom of God the Father, *made Himself of no reputation and took upon Him the form of a servant* (Phil. ii. 7); even the same, also, as those Apostles, who were ear and eye witnesses, sounded it forth, like clear-toned trumpets, to all that are under the sun (for *their sound is gone out into all lands, and their words into the ends of the world*); and, last of all, the very same as the many great and glorious Fathers of the Catholic Church in all parts of the earth, who heard those Apostolic voices, both by their synodical and their individual teachings handed it down to all everywhere, and even unto us. But the Prince of Evil, that spiritual enemy of man's salvation, as formerly in Eden, craftily assuming the pretext of profitable counsel, he made man to become a transgressor of the divinely-spoken command. So, in the spiritual Eden, the Church of God, he has from time to time beguiled many; and, mixing the deleterious drugs of heresy with the clear streams of orthodox doctrine, gives of the potion to drink to many of the innocent who live unguardedly, not

---

535 Original Greek Manuscript: Ἐγκύκλιος τῆς Μίας Ἁγίας Καθολικῆς καὶ Ἀποστολικῆς Ἐκκλησίας ἐπιστολὴ πρὸς τοὺς ἀπανταχοῦ ὀρθοδόξους (Κωνσταντινούπολη: Πατριαρχικὸ Εἶδος Τυπογραφεῖο, 1848), 1-50.

536 English taken from: "Encyclical of the Eastern Patriarchs, 1848 A Reply to the Epistle of Pope Pius IX, 'To the Easterns,'" Holy Synods of Constantinople, Antioch and Jerusalem, accessed October 16th, 2022, http://orthodoxinfo.com/ecumenism/encyc_1848.aspx

giving earnest heed to the things they have heard (Heb. ii. 10), *and to what they have been told by their fathers* (Deut. xxxii. 7), in accordance with the Gospel and in agreement with the ancient Doctors; and who, imagining that the preached and written Word of the LORD and the perpetual witness of His Church are not sufficient for their souls' salvation, impiously seek out novelties, as we change the fashion of our garments, embracing a counterfeit of the evangelical doctrine.

2. Hence have arisen manifold and monstrous heresies, which the Catholic Church, even from her infancy, *taking unto her the whole armor of God, and assuming the sword of the Spirit, which is the Word of God* (Eph. vi. 13-17), has been compelled to combat. She has triumphed over all unto this day, and she will triumph for ever, being manifested as mightier and more illustrious after each struggle.

3. Of these heresies, some already have entirely failed, some are in decay, some have wasted away, some yet flourish in a greater or less degree vigorous until the time of their return to the Faith, while others are reproduced to run their course from their birth to their destruction. For being the miserable cogitations and devices of miserable men, both one and the other, struck with the thunderbolt of the anathema of the seven Ecumenical Councils, shall vanish away, though they may last a thousand years; for the orthodoxy of the Catholic and Apostolic Church, by the living Word of God, alone endures for ever, according to the infallible promise of the LORD: *the gates of hell shall not prevail against it* (Matt. xviii. 18). Certainly, the mouths of ungodly and heretical men, however bold, however plausible and fair-speaking, however smooth they may be, will not prevail against the orthodox doctrine winning, its way silently and without noise. *But, wherefore doth the way of the wicked prosper?* (Jer. xii. 1.) *Why are the ungodly exalted and lifted up as the cedars of Lebanon* (Ps. xxxvii. 35), *to defile the peaceful worship of God?* The reason of this is mysterious, and the Church, though daily praying that this cross, this messenger of Satan, may depart from her, ever hears from the Lord: *My grace is sufficient for thee, my strength is made perfect in weakness* (2. Cor. xii. 9). *Wherefore she gladly glories*

in her infirmities, that the power of Christ may rest upon her, and that they which are approved may be made manifest (1. Cor. x. 19).

4. Of these heresies diffused, with what sufferings the LORD hath known, over a great part of the world, was formerly Arianism, and at present is the Papacy. This, too, as the former has become extinct, although now flourishing, shall not endure, but pass away and be cast down, and a great voice from heaven shall cry: *It is cast down* (Rev. xii. 10).

5. The new doctrine, that "the Holy Ghost proceedeth from the Father and the Son," is contrary to the memorable declaration of our LORD, emphatically made respecting it: *which proceedeth from the Father* (John xv. 26), and contrary to the universal Confession of the Catholic Church as witnessed by the seven Ecumenical Councils, uttering "which proceedeth from the Father." (Symbol of Faith).

    i.   This novel opinion destroys the oneness from the One cause, and the diverse origin of the Persons of the Blessed Trinity, both of which are witnessed to in the Gospel.

    ii. Even into the divine Hypostases or Persons of the Trinity, of equal power and equally to be adored, it introduces diverse and unequal relations, with a confusion or commingling of them.

    iii. It reproaches as imperfect, dark, and difficult to be understood, the previous Confession of the One Holy Catholic and Apostolic Church.

    iv   It censures the holy Fathers of the first Ecumenical Synod of Nicaea and of the second Ecumenical Synod at Constantinople, as imperfectly expressing what relates to the Son and Holy Ghost, as if they had been silent respecting the peculiar property of each Person of the Godhead, when it was necessary that all their divine properties should be expressed against the Arians and Macedonians.

    v.   It reproaches the Fathers of the third, fourth, fifth, sixth, and seventh Ecumenical Councils, which had published over the world a divine Creed, perfect and complete, and interdicted under dread anathemas and penalties not removed, all addition, or diminution, or alteration, or variation in the smallest particular of it, by themselves or any whomsoever. Yet was this quickly to be corrected and augmented, and consequently the whole theological doctrine of the Catholic Fathers was to be subjected to change, as if, forsooth, a new property even in regard to the three Persons of the Blessed Trinity had been revealed.

vi. It clandestinely found an entrance at first in the Churches of the West, "a wolf in sheep's clothing," that is, under the signification not of procession, according to the Greek meaning in the Gospel and the Creed, but under the signification of mission, as Pope Martin explained it to the Confessor Maximus, and as Anastasius the Librarian explained it to John VIII.

vii. It exhibits incomparable boldness, acting without authority, and forcibly puts a false stamp upon the Creed, which is the common inheritance of Christianity.

viii. It has introduced huge disturbances into the peaceful Church of God, and divided the nations.

ix. It was publicly proscribed, at its first promulgation, by two ever-to-be-remembered Popes, Leo III and John VIII, the latter of whom, in his epistle to the blessed Photius, classes with Judas those who first brought the interpolation into the Creed.

x. It has been condemned by many Holy Councils of the four Patriarchs of the East.

xi. It was subjected to anathema, as a novelty and augmentation of the Creed, by the eighth Ecumenical Council, congregated at Constantinople for the pacification of the Eastern and Western Churches.

xii. As soon as it was introduced into the Churches of the West it brought forth disgraceful fruits, bringing with it, little by little, other novelties, for the most part contrary to the express commands of our Savior in the Gospel — commands which till its entrance into the Churches were closely observed. Among these novelties may be numbered sprinkling instead of baptism, denial of the divine Cup to the Laity, elevation of one and the same bread broken, the use of wafers, unleavened instead of real bread, the disuse of the Benediction in the Liturgies, even of the sacred Invocation of the All-holy and Consecrating Spirit, the abandonment of the old Apostolic Mysteries of the Church, such as not anointing baptized infants, or their not receiving the Eucharist, the exclusion of married men from the Priesthood, the infallibility of the Pope and his claim as Vicar of Christ, and the like. Thus, it was that the interpolation led to the setting aside of the old Apostolic pattern of well-nigh all the Mysteries and all doctrine, a pattern which the ancient, holy, and orthodox Church of Rome kept, when she was the most honored part of the Holy, Catholic and Apostolic Church.

xiii. It drove the theologians of the West, as its defenders, since they had no ground either in Scripture or the Fathers to countenance heretical teachings, not only into misrepresentations of the Scriptures, such as are seen in none of the Fathers of the Holy Catholic Church, but also into adulterations of the sacred and pure writings of the Fathers alike of the East and West.

xiv. It seemed strange, unheard of, and blasphemous, even to those reputed Christian communions, which, before its origin, had been for other just causes for ages cut off from the Catholic fold.

xv. It has not yet been even plausibly defended out of the Scriptures, or with the least reason out of the Fathers, from the accusations brought against it, notwithstanding all the zeal and efforts of its supporters. The doctrine bears all the marks of error arising out of its nature and peculiarities. All erroneous doctrine touching the Catholic truth of the Blessed Trinity, and the origin of the divine Persons, and the subsistence of the Holy Ghost, is and is called heresy, and they who so hold are deemed heretics, according to the sentence of St. Damasus, Pope of Rome, who says: "If any one rightly holds concerning the Father and the Son, yet holds not rightly of the Holy Ghost, he is an heretic" (Cath. Conf. of Faith which Pope Damasus sent to Paulinus, Bishop of Thessalonica). Wherefore the One, Holy, Catholic, and Apostolic Church, following in the steps of the holy Fathers, both Eastern and Western, proclaimed of old to our progenitors and again teaches today synodically, that the said novel doctrine of the Holy Ghost proceeding from the Father and the Son is essentially heresy, and its maintainers, whoever they be, are heretics, according to the sentence of Pope St. Damasus, and that the congregations of such are also heretical, and that all spiritual communion in worship of the orthodox sons of the Catholic Church with such is unlawful. Such is the force of the seventh Canon of the third Ecumenical Council

6.   This heresy, which has united to itself many innovations, as has been said, appeared about the middle of the seventh century, at first and secretly, and then under various disguises, over the Western Provinces of Europe, until by degrees, creeping along for four or five centuries, it obtained precedence over the ancient orthodoxy of those parts, through the heedlessness of Pastors and the countenance of Princes. Little by little it overspread not only the hitherto orthodox Churches of Spain, but also the German, and French, and Italian Churches, whose orthodoxy at one time was sounded throughout the world, with whom our divine Fathers such as the great Athanasius and heavenly Basil conferred, and whose sympathy and fellowship with us until the seventh Ecumenical Council, preserved unharmed the doctrine of the Catholic and Apostolic Church. But in process of time, by envy of the devil, the novelties respecting the sound and orthodox doctrine of the Holy Ghost, the blasphemy of whom shall not be forgiven unto men either in this world or the next, according to the saying of our Lord (Matt. xii. 32), and others that succeeded respecting the divine Mysteries, particularly that of the world-saving Baptism, and the Holy Communion, and the Priesthood, like prodigious births, overspread even Old Rome; and thus sprung, by assumption of special distinctions in the Church as a badge and title, the Papacy. Some of the Bishops of that City, styled Popes, for example Leo III and John VIII, did indeed, as has been said, denounce the innovation, and published the denunciation to the world, the former by those silver plates, the latter by his letter to the holy Photius at the eighth Ecumenical Council, and another to Sphendopulcrus, by the hands of Methodius, Bishop of Moravia. The greater part, however, of their successors, the Popes of Rome, enticed by the anti-synodical privileges offered them for the oppres-

sion of the Churches of God, and finding in them much worldly advantage, and "much gain," and conceiving a Monarchy in the Catholic Church and a monopoly of the gifts of the Holy Ghost, changed the ancient worship at will, separating themselves by novelties from the old received Christian Polity. Nor did they cease their endeavors, by lawless projects (as veritable history assures us), to entice the other four Patriarchates into their apostasy from Orthodoxy, and so subject the Catholic Church to the whims and ordinances of men.

7. Our illustrious predecessors and fathers, with united labor and counsel, seeing the evangelical doctrine received from the Fathers to be trodden under foot, and the robe of our Savior woven from above to be torn by wicked hands, and stimulated by fatherly and brotherly love, wept for the desolation of so many Christians for whom Christ died. They exercised much zeal and ardor, both synodically and individually, in order that the orthodox doctrine of the Holy Catholic Church being saved, they might knit together as far as they were able that which had been rent; and like approved physicians they consulted together for the safety of the suffering member, enduring many tribulations, and contempts, and persecutions, if haply the Body of Christ might not be divided, or the definitions of the divine and august Synods be made of none effect. But veracious history has transmitted to us the relentlessness of the Western perseverance in error. These illustrious men proved indeed on this point the truth of the words of our holy father Basil the sublime, when he said, from experience, concerning the Bishops of the West, and particularly of the Pope: "They neither know the truth nor endure to learn it, striving against those who tell them the truth, and strengthening themselves in their heresy" (to Eusebius of Samosata). Thus, after a first and second brotherly admonition, knowing their impenitence, shaking them off and avoiding them, they gave them over to their reprobate mind. "War is better than peace, apart from God," as said our holy father Gregory, concerning the Arians. From that time there has been no spiritual communion between us and them; for they have with their own hands dug deep the chasm between themselves and Orthodoxy.

8. Yet the Papacy has not on this account ceased to annoy the peaceful Church of God, but sending out everywhere so-called missionaries, men of reprobate minds, it compasses land and sea to make one

proselyte, to deceive one of the Orthodox, to corrupt the doctrine of our LORD, to adulterate, by addition, the divine Creed of our holy Faith, to prove the Baptism which God gave us superfluous, the communion of the Cup void of sacred efficacy, and a thousand other things which the demon of novelty dictated to the all-daring Schoolmen of the Middle Ages and to the Bishops of the elder Rome, venturing all things through lust of power. Our blessed predecessors and fathers, in their piety, though tried and persecuted in many ways and means, within and without, directly and indirectly, "yet confident in the LORD," were able to save and transmit to us this inestimable inheritance of our fathers, which we too, by the help of God, will transmit as a rich treasure to the generations to come, even to the end of the world. But notwithstanding this, the Papists do not cease to this day, nor will cease, according to wont, to attack Orthodoxy — a daily living reproach which they have before their eyes, being deserters from the faith of their fathers. Would that they made these aggressions against the heresy which has overspread and mastered the West. For who doubts that had their zeal for the overthrow of Orthodoxy been employed for the overthrow of heresy and novelties, agreeable to the God-loving counsels of Leo III and John VIII, those glorious and last Orthodox Popes, not a trace of it, long ago, would have been remembered under the sun, and we should now be saying the same things, according to the Apostolic promise. But the zeal of those who succeeded them was not for the protection of the Orthodox Faith, in conformity with the zeal worthy of all remembrance which was in Leo III, now among the blessed.

9. In a measure the aggressions of the later Popes in their own persons had ceased, and were carried on only by means of missionaries. But lately, Pius IX, becoming Bishop of Rome and proclaimed Pope in 1847, published on the sixth of January, in this present year, an Encyclical Letter addressed to the Easterns, consisting of twelve pages in the Greek version, which his emissary has disseminated, like a plague coming from without, within our Orthodox Fold. In this Encyclical, he addresses those who at different times have gone over from different Christian Communions, and embraced the Papacy, and of course are favorable to him, extending his arguments also to the Orthodox, either particularly or without naming them; and, citing our divine and holy Fathers (p. 3, 1.14-18; p. 4, 1.19; p. 9, 1.6; and pp. 17, 23), he manifestly calumniates them and us their suc-

cessors and descendants: them, as if they admitted readily the Papal commands and rescripts without question because issuing from the Popes is undoubted arbiters of the Catholic Church; us, as unfaithful to their examples (for thus he trespasses on the Fold committed to us by God), as severed from our Fathers, as careless of our sacred trusts, and of the soul's salvation of our spiritual children. Usurping as his own possession the Catholic Church of Christ, by occupancy, as he boasts, of the Episcopal Throne of St. Peter, he desires to deceive the more simple into apostasy from Orthodoxy, choosing for the basis of all theological instruction these paradoxical words (p. 10, 1.29): "nor is there any reason why ye refuse a return to the true Church and Communion with this my holy Throne."

10. Each one of our brethren and sons in Christ who have been piously brought up and instructed, wisely regarding the wisdom given him from God, will decide that the words of the present Bishop of Rome, like those of his schismatical predecessors, are not words of peace, as he affirms (p. 7, 1.8), and of benevolence, but words of deceit and guile, tending to self-aggrandizement, agreeably to the practice of his anti-synodical predecessors. We are therefore sure, that even as heretofore, so hereafter the Orthodox will not be beguiled. For the word of our LORD is sure (John x. 5), *A stranger will they not follow, but flee from him, for they know not the voice of strangers.*

11. For all this we have esteemed it our paternal and brotherly need, and a sacred duty, by our present admonition to confirm you in the Orthodoxy you hold from your forefathers, and at the same time point out the emptiness of the syllogisms of the Bishop of Rome, of which he is manifestly himself aware. For not from his Apostolic Confession does he glorify his Throne, but from his Apostolic Throne seeks to establish his dignity, and from his dignity, his Confession. The truth is the other way. The Throne of Rome is esteemed that of St. Peter by a single tradition, but not from Holy Scripture, where the claim is in favor of Antioch, whose Church is therefore witnessed by the great Basil (Ep. 48 Athan.) to be "the most venerable of all the Churches in the world." Still more, the second Ecumenical Council, writing to a Council of the West (to the most honorable and religious brethren and fellow-servants, Damasus, Ambrose, Britto, Valerian, and others), witnesseth, saying: "The oldest and truly Apostolic Church of Antioch, in Syria, where first the honored name of

Christians was used." We say then that the Apostolic Church of Antioch had no right of exemption from being judged according to divine Scripture and synodical declarations, though truly venerated for the throne of St. Peter. But what do we say? The blessed Peter, even in his own person, was judged before all for the truth of the Gospel, and, as Scripture declares, was found blamable and not walking uprightly. What opinion is to be formed of those who glory and pride themselves solely in the possession of his Throne, so great in their eyes? Nay, the sublime Basil the great, the Ecumenical teacher of Orthodoxy in the Catholic Church, to whom the Bishops of Rome are obliged to refer us (p. 8, 1.31), has clearly and explicitly above (7) shown us what estimation we ought to have of the judgments of the inaccessible Vatican: — "They neither," he says, "know the truth, nor endure to learn it, striving against those who tell them the truth, and strengthening themselves in their heresy." So that these our holy Fathers whom his Holiness the Pope, worthily admiring as lights and teachers even of the West, accounts as belonging to us, and advises us (p. 8) to follow, teach us not to judge Orthodoxy from the holy Throne, but the Throne itself and him that is on the Throne by the sacred Scriptures, by Synodical decrees and limitations, and by the Faith which has been preached, even the Orthodoxy of continuous teaching. Thus did our Fathers judge and condemn Honorius, Pope of Rome, and Dioscorus, Pope of Alexandria, and Macedonius and Nestorius, Patriarchs of Constantinople, and Peter Gnapheus, Patriarch of Antioch, with others. For if *the abomination of desolation stood in the Holy Place*, why not innovation and heresy upon a holy Throne? Hence is exhibited in a brief compass the weakness and feebleness of the efforts in behalf of the despotism of the Pope of Rome. For, unless the Church of Christ was founded upon the immovable rock of St. Peter's Confession, *Thou art the Christ, the Son of the Living God* (which was the answer of the Apostles in common, when the question was put to them, *Whom say ye that I am?* (Matt. xvi. 15), as the Fathers, both Eastern and Western, interpret the passage to us), the Church was built upon a slippery foundation, even on Cephas himself, not to say on the Pope, who, after monopolizing the Keys of the Kingdom of Heaven, has made such an administration of them as is plain from history. But our divine Fathers, with one accord, teach that the sense of the thrice-repeated command, feed my sheep, implied no prerogative in St. Peter over the other Apostles, least of all in his successors. It was a simple restoration to his Apostleship, from which he had fallen by his thrice-repeated denial. St. Peter himself appears to have understood the intention of the thrice-repeated question of our Lord: *Lovest thou Me*, and *more*, and *than these?* (John xxi. 16); for, calling to mind the words, *Thou all shall be offended because of Thee, yet will I never be offended* (Matt. xxvi. 33), he *was grieved because He said unto him the third time, Lovest thou Me?* But his successors, from self-interest, understand the expression as indicative of St. Peter's more ready mind.

12. His Holiness the Pope says (p. viii. 1.12.) that our LORD said to Peter (Luke xxii. 32), *I have prayed for thee, that thy faith fail not: and when thou art converted, strengthen thy brethren.* Our LORD so prayed because Satan had sought to overthrow the faith of all the disciples, but the LORD allowed him Peter only, chiefly because he had uttered words of boasting, and justified himself above the rest (Matt. xxvi. 33): *Though all shall be offended, because of thee, yet will I never be offended. The permission to Satan was but temporary. He began to curse and to swear: I know not the man. So weak is human nature, left to itself. The spirit is willing, but the flesh is weak.* It was but temporary, that, coming again to himself by his return in tears of repentance, he might the rather strengthen his brethren who had neither perjured themselves nor denied. Oh! the wise judgment of the LORD! How divine and mysterious was the last night of our Savior upon earth! That sacred Supper is believed to be consecrated to this day in every Church: *This do in remembrance of me* (Luke xxii. 19), and *As often as ye eat this bread and drink this cup, ye do show the LORD's death till he come* (1 Cor. xi. 26). Of the brotherly love thus earnestly commended to us by the common Master, saying, *By this shall all men know that ye are my disciple, if ye have love one to another* (John xiii. 35), have the Popes first broken the stamp and seal, supporting and receiving heretical novelties, contrary to the things delivered to us and canonically confirmed by our Teachers and Fathers in common. This love acts at this day with power in the souls of Christian people, and particularly in their leaders. We boldly avow before God and men, that the prayer of our Savior (p. ix. l.43) to God and His Father for the common love and unity of Christians in the One Holy Catholic and Apostolic Church, in which we believe, *that they may be one, even as we are one* (John xvii. 22), worketh in us no less than in his Holiness. Our brotherly love and zeal meet that of his Holiness, with only this difference, that in us it worketh for

the covenanted preservation of the pure, undefiled, divine, spotless, and perfect Creed of the Christian Faith, in conformity to the voice of the Gospel and the decrees of the seven holy Ecumenical Synods and the teachings of the ever-existing Catholic Church: but worketh in his Holiness to prop and strengthen the authority and dignity of them that sit on the Apostolic Throne, and their new doctrine. Behold then, the head and front, so to speak, of all the differences and disagreements that have happened between us and them, and the middle wall of partition, which we hope will be taken away in the time of his Holiness, and by the aid of his renowned wisdom, according to the promise of God (St. John x. 16): "*Other sheep I have which are not of this fold: them also I must bring and they shall hear my voice* (Who proceedeth from the Father"). Let it be said then, in the third place, that if it be supposed, according to the words of his Holiness, that this prayer of our LORD for Peter when about to deny and perjure himself, remained attached and united to the Throne of Peter, and is transmitted with power to those who from time to time sit upon it, although, as has before been said, nothing contributes to confirm the opinion (as we are strikingly assured from the example of the blessed Peter himself, even after the descent of the Holy Ghost, yet are we convinced from the words of our LORD, that the time will come when that divine prayer concerning the denial of Peter, "that his faith might not fail for ever" will operate also in some one of the successors of his Throne, who will also weep, as he did, bitterly, and being sometime converted will strengthen us, his brethren, still more in the Orthodox Confession, which we hold from our forefathers; — and would that his Holiness might be this true successor of the blessed Peter! To this our humble prayer, what hinders that we should add our sincere and hearty Counsel in the name of the Holy Catholic Church? We dare not say, as does his Holiness (p. x. 1.22), that it should be done "without any delay;" but without haste, utter mature consideration, and also, if need be, after consultation with the more wise, religious, truth-loving, and prudent of the Bishops, Theologians, and Doctors, to be found at the present day, by God's good Providence, in every nation of the West.

13. His Holiness says that the Bishop of Lyons, St. Irenaeus, writes in praise of the Church of Rome: "That the whole Church, namely, the faithful from everywhere, must come together in that Church, because of its Primacy, in which Church the tradition, given by the

Apostles, has in all respects been observed by the faithful every-where." Although this saint says by no means what the followers of the Vatican would make out, yet even granting their interpretation, we reply: Who denies that the ancient Roman Church was Apos-tolic and Orthodox? None of us will question that it was a model of orthodoxy. We will specially add, for its greater praise, from the his-torian Sozomen (Hist. Eccl. lib. iii. cap. 12), the passage, which his Holiness has overlooked, respecting the mode by which for a time she was enabled to preserve the orthodoxy which we praise: — "For, as everywhere," saith Sozomen, "the Church throughout the West, being guided purely by the doctrines of the Fathers, was delivered from contention and deception concerning these things." Would any of the Fathers or ourselves deny her canonical privilege in the rank of the hierarchy, so long as she was guided purely by the doctrines of the Fathers, walking by the plain rule of Scripture and the holy Synods! But at present we do not find preserved in her the dogma of the Blessed Trinity according to the Creed of the holy Fathers as-sembled first in Nicea and afterwards in Constantinople, which the other five Ecumenical Councils confessed and confirmed with such anathemas on those who adulterated it in the smallest particular, as if they had thereby destroyed it. Nor do we find the Apostolical pat-tern of holy Baptism, nor the Invocation of the consecrating Spirit upon the holy elements: but we see in that Church the eucharistic Cup, heavenly drink, considered superfluous, (what profanity!) and very many other things, unknown not only to our holy Fathers, who were always entitled the catholic, clear rule and index of Orthodoxy, as his Holiness, revering the truth, himself teaches (p. vi), but also unknown to the ancient holy Fathers of the West. We see that very primacy, for which his Holiness now contends with all his might, as did his predecessors, transformed from a brotherly character and hierarchical privilege into a lordly superiority. What then is to be thought of his unwritten traditions, if the written have undergone such a change and alteration for the worse? Who is so bold and con-fident in the dignity of the Apostolic Throne, as to dare to say that if our holy Father, St. Irenaeus, were alive again, seeing it was fallen from the ancient and primitive teaching in so many most essential and catholic articles of Christianity, he would not be himself the first to oppose the novelties and self-sufficient constitutions of that Church which was lauded by him as guided purely by the doctrines of the Fathers? For instance, when he saw the Roman Church not only rejecting from her Liturgical Canon, according to the suggestion of the Schoolmen, the very ancient and Apostolic invocation of the Consecrating Spirit, and miserably mutilating the Sacrifice in its most essential part, but also urgently hastening to cut it out from the Liturgies of other Christian Communions also, — his Holiness slanderously asserting, in a manner so unworthy of the Apostolic Throne on which he boasts himself, that it "crept in after the division between the East and West" (p. xi. 1.11) — what would not the holy Father say respecting this novelty? Irenaeus assures us (lib. iv. c. 34) "that bread, from the ground, receiving the evocation of God, is no longer common bread," etc., meaning by "evocation" invocation: for that Irenaeus believed the Mystery of the Sacrifice to be consecrated by means of this invocation is especially remarked even by Franciscus Feu-Ardentius, of the order of popish monks called Minorites, who in 1639 edited the writings of that saint with comments, who says (lib. i. c. 18, p. 114,) that Irenaeus teaches "that the bread and mixed cup become the true Body and Blood of Christ by the words of invocation." Or, hearing of the vicarial and appellate jurisdiction of the Pope, what would not the Saint say, who, for a small and almost indifferent question concerning the celebration of Easter (Euseb. Eccl. Hist. v. 26), so boldly and victoriously opposed and defeated the violence of Pope Victor in the free Church of Christ? Thus he who is cited by his Holiness as a witness of the primacy of the Roman Church, shows that its dignity is not that of a lordship, nor even appellate, to which St. Peter himself was never ordained, but is a brotherly privilege in the Catholic Church, and an honor assigned the Popes on account of the greatness and privilege of the City. Thus, also, the fourth Ecumenical Council, for the preservation of the gradation in rank of Churches canonically established by the third Ecumenical Council (Canon 8), — following the second (Canon 3), as that again followed the first (Canon 6), which called the appellate jurisdiction of the Pope over the West a Custom, — thus uttered its determination: "On account of that City being the Imperial City, the Fathers have with reason given it prerogatives" (Canon 28). Here is nothing said of the Pope's special monopoly of the Apostolicity of St. Peter, still less of a vicarship in Rome's Bishops, and a universal Pastorate. This deep silence in regard to such great privileges — nor only so, but the reason assigned for the primacy, not "Feed my sheep," not "On this rock will I build my Church," but simply old Custom, and the City being the Imperial City; and these things, not from the LORD, but from the Fathers — will seem, we are sure, a great paradox to his Holiness entertaining other ideas of his prerogatives. The paradox will be the greater, since, as we shall see, he greatly honors the said fourth Ecumenical Synod as one to be found a witness for his Throne; and St. Gregory, the eloquent, called the Great (lib. i. Ep. 25), was wont to speak of the four Ecumenical Councils [not the Roman See] as the four Gospels, and the four-sided stone on which the Catholic Church is built.

14. His Holiness says (p. ix. 1.12) that the Corinthians, divided among themselves, referred the matter to Clement, Pope of Rome, who wrote to them his decision on the case; and they so prized his decision that they read it in the Churches. But this event is a very weak support for the Papal authority in the house of God. For Rome being then the center of the Imperial Province and the chief City, in which the Emperors lived, it was proper that any question of importance, as history shows that of the Corinthians to have been, should be decided there, especially if one of the contending parties ran thither for external aid: as is done even to this day. The Patriarchs of Alexandria, Antioch, and Jerusalem, when unexpected points of difficulty arise, write to the Patriarch of Constantinople, because of its being the seat of Empire, as also on account of its synodical privileges; and if this brotherly aid shall rectify that which should be rectified, it is well; but if not, the matter is reported to the province, according to the established system. But this brotherly agreement in Christian faith is not purchased by the servitude of the Churches of God. Let this be our answer also to the examples of a fraternal and proper championship of the privileges of Julius and Innocent Bishops of Rome, by St. Athanasius the Great and St. John Chrysostom, referred to by his Holiness (p. ix. 1. 6,17), for which their successors now seek to recompense us by adulterating the divine Creed. Yet was Julius himself indignant against some for "disturbing the Churches by not maintaining the doctrines of Nice" (Soz. Hist. Ec. lib. iii. c. 7), and threatening (id.) excommunication, "if they ceased not their innovations." In the case of the Corinthians, moreover, it is to be remarked that the Patriarchal Thrones being then but three, Rome was the nearer and more accessible to the Corinthians, to which, therefore, it was proper to have resort. In all this we see nothing extraordinary, nor any proof of the despotic power of the Pope in the free Church of God.

15. But, finally, his Holiness says (p. ix. l.12) that the fourth Ecumenical
Council (which by mistake he quite transfers from Chalcedon to
Carthage), when it read the epistle of Pope Leo I, cried out, "Peter
has thus spoken by Leo." It was so indeed. But his Holiness ought
not to overlook how, and after what examination, our fathers cried
out, as they did, in praise of Leo. Since however his Holiness, consulting brevity, appears to have omitted this most necessary point,
and the manifest proof that an Ecumenical Council is not only
above the Pope but above any Council of his, we will explain to
the public the matter as it really happened. Of more than six hundred fathers assembled in the Council of Chalcedon, about two
hundred of the wisest were appointed by the Council to examine
both as to language and sense the said epistle of Leo; nor only so,
but to give in writing and with their signatures their own judgment
upon it, whether it were Orthodox or not. These, about two hundred judgments and resolution on the epistle, as chiefly found in
the Fourth Session of the said holy Council in such terms as the
following: — "Maximus of Antioch in Syria said: 'The epistle of
the holy Leo, Archbishop of Imperial Rome, agrees with the decisions of the three hundred and eighteen holy fathers at Nice, and
the hundred and fifty at Constantinople, which is new Rome, and
with the faith expounded at Ephesus by the most holy Bishop Cyril: and I have subscribed it.'" And again, "Theodore the most religious Bishop of Cyrus: 'The epistle of the most holy Archbishop,
the lord Leo, agrees with the faith established at Nice by the holy
and blessed fathers, and with the symbol of faith expounded at Constantinople by the hundred and fifty, and with the epistles of the
blessed Cyril. And accepting it, I have subscribed the said epistle.'"

And thus, all in succession: "The epistle corresponds," "the epistle is
consonant," "the epistle agrees in sense," and the like. After such great
and very severe scrutiny in comparing it with former holy Councils,
and a full conviction of the correctness of the meaning, and not
merely because it was the epistle of the Pope, they cried aloud, un-
grudgingly, the exclamation on which his Holiness now vaunts himself: But if his Holiness had sent us statements concordant and in
unison with the seven holy Ecumenical Councils, instead of boasting of the piety of his predecessors lauded by our predecessors and
fathers in an Ecumenical Council, he might justly have gloried in
his own orthodoxy, declaring his own goodness instead of that of

his fathers. Therefore let his Holiness be assured, that if, even now, he will write us such things as two hundred fathers on investigation and inquiry shall find consonant and agreeing with the said former Councils, then, we say, he shall hear from us sinners today, not only, "Peter has so spoken," or anything of like honor, but this also, "Let the holy hand be kissed which has wiped away the tears of the Catholic Church."

16. And surely we have a right to expect from the prudent forethought of his Holiness, a work so worthy the true successor of St. Peter, of Leo I, and also of Leo III, who for security of the orthodox faith engraved the divine Creed unaltered upon imperishable plates — a work which will unite the churches of the West to the holy Catholic Church, in which the canonical chief seat of his Holiness, and the seats of all the Bishops of the West remain empty and ready to be occupied. For the Catholic Church, awaiting the conversion of the shepherds who have fallen off from her with their flocks, does not separate in name only, those who have been privily introduced to the rulership by the action of others, thus making little of the Priesthood. But we are expecting the "word of consolation," and hope that he, as wrote St. Basil to St. Ambrose, Bishop of Milan (Epis. b6), will "tread again the ancient footprints of the fathers." Not without great astonishment have we read the said Encyclical letter to the Easterns, in which we see with deep grief of soul his Holiness, famed for prudence, speaking like his predecessors in schism, words that urge upon us the adulteration of our pure holy Creed, on which the Ecumenical Councils have set their seal; and doing violence to the sacred Liturgies, whose heavenly structure alone, and the names of those who framed them, and their tone of reverend antiquity, and the stamp that was placed upon them by the Seventh Ecumenical Synod (Act vi.), should have paralyzed him, and made him to turn aside the sacrilegious and all-daring hand that has thus smitten the King of Glory. From these things we estimate into what an unspeakable labyrinth of wrong and incorrigible sin of revolution the papacy has thrown even the wiser and more godly Bishops of the Roman Church, so that, in order to preserve the innocent, and therefore valued vicarial dignity, as well as the despotic primacy and the things depending upon it, they know no other means shall to insult the most divine and sacred things, daring everything for that one end. Clothing themselves, in words, with pious reverence for "the most

venerable antiquity" (p. xi. 1.16), in reality there remains, within, the innovating temper; and yet his Holiness really hears hard upon himself when he says that we "must cast from us everything that has crept in among us since the Separation," (!) while he and his have spread the poison of their innovation even into the Supper of our LORD. His Holiness evidently takes it for granted that in the Orthodox Church the same thing has happened which he is conscious has happened in the Church of Rome since the rise of the Papacy: to wit, a sweeping change in all the Mysteries, and corruption from scholastic subtleties, a reliance on which must suffice as an equivalent for our sacred Liturgies and Mysteries and doctrines: yet all the while, forsooth, reverencing our "venerable antiquity," and all this by a condescension entirely Apostolic! — "without," as he says, "troubling us by any harsh conditions"! From such ignorance of the Apostolic and Catholic food on which we live emanates another sententious declaration of his (p. vii. 1. 22): "It is not possible that unity of doctrine and sacred observance should be preserved among you," paradoxically ascribing to us the very misfortune from which he suffers at home; just as Pope Leo IX wrote to the blessed Michael Cerularius, accusing the Greeks of changing the Creed of the Catholic Church, without blushing either for his own honor or for the truth of history. We are persuaded that if his Holiness will call to mind ecclesiastical archaeology and history, the doctrine of the holy Fathers and the old Liturgies of France and Spain, and the Sacramentary of the ancient Roman Church, he will be struck with surprise on finding how many other monstrous daughters, now living, the Papacy has brought forth in the West: while Orthodoxy, with us, has preserved the Catholic Church as an incorruptible bride for her Bridegroom, although we have no temporal power, nor, as his Holiness says, any sacred "observances," but by the sole tie of love and affection to a common Mother are bound together in the unity of a faith sealed with the seven seals of the Spirit (Rev. v. 1), and by the seven Ecumenical Councils, and in obedience to the Truth. He will find, also, flow many modern papistical doctrines and mysteries must be rejected as "commandments of men" in order that the Church of the West, which has introduced all sorts of novelties, may be changed back again to the immutable Catholic Orthodox faith of our common fathers. As his Holiness recognizes our common zeal in this faith, when he says (p. viii. l.30), "let us take heed to the doctrine preserved by our forefathers," so he does well in instructing us (l. 31) to follow the old pontiffs and the faithful of the Eastern Metropolitans. What these thought of the doctrinal fidelity of the Archbishops of the elder Rome, and what idea we ought to have of them in the Orthodox Church, and in what manner we ought to receive their teachings, they have synodically given us an example (15), and the sublime Basil has well interpreted it (7). As to the supremacy, since we are not setting forth a treatise, let the same great Basil present the matter in a few words, "I preferred to address myself to Him who is Head over them."

17. From all this, every one nourished in sound Catholic doctrine, particularly his Holiness, must draw the conclusion, how impious and anti-synodical it is to attempt the alteration of our doctrine and liturgies and other divine offices which are, and are proved to be, coeval with the preaching of Christianity: for which reason reverence was always bestowed on then, and they were confided in as pure even by the old orthodox Popes themselves, to whom these things were an inheritance in common with ourselves. How becoming and holy would be the mending of the innovations, the time of whose entrance in the Church of Rome we know in each case; for our illustrious fathers have testified from time to time against each novelty. But there are other reasons which should incline his Holiness to this change. First, because those things that are ours were once venerable to the Westerns, as having the same divine Offices and confessing the same Creed; but the novelties were not known to our Fathers, nor could they be shown in the writings of the orthodox Western Fathers, nor as having their origin either in antiquity or catholicity. Moreover, neither Patriarchs nor Councils could then have introduced novelties amongst us, because the protector of religion is the very body of the Church, even the people themselves, who desire their religious worship to be ever unchanged and of the same kind as that of their fathers: for as, after the Schism, many of the Popes and Latinizing Patriarchs made attempts that came to nothing even in the Western Church; and as, from time to time, either by fair means or foul, the Popes have commanded novelties for the sake of expediency (as they have explained to our fathers, although they were thus dismembering the Body of Christ): so now again the Pope, for the sake of a truly divine and most just expediency, forsooth (not mending the nets, but himself rending the garment of the Savior), dare to oppose the venerable things of antiquity, — things well fitted to

preserve religion, as his Holiness confesses (p. xi. l.16), and which he himself honors, as he says (lb. 1.16), together with his predecessors, for he repeats that memorable expression of one of those blessed predecessors (Celestine, writing to the third Ecumenical Council): "*Let novelty cease to attack antiquity.*" And let the Catholic Church enjoy this benefit from this so far blameless declaration of the Popes. It must by all means be confessed, that in such his attempt, even though Pius IX be eminent for wisdom and piety, and, as he says, for zeal after Christian unity in the Catholic Church, he will meet, within and without, with difficulties and toils. And here we must put his Holiness in mind, if he will excuse our boldness, of that portion of his letter (p. viii. L.32), "That in things which relate to the confession of our divine religion, nothing is to be feared, when we look to the glory of Christ, and the reward which awaits us in eternal life." It is incumbent on his Holiness to show before God and man, that, as prime mover of the counsel which pleases God, so is he a willing protector of the ill-treated evangelical and synodical truth, even to the sacrifice of his own interests, according to the Prophet (Is. lx. 17), *A ruler in peace and a bishop in righteousness.* So be it! But until there be this desired returning of the apostate Churches to the body of the One, Holy, Catholic, and Apostolic Church, of which *Christ is the Head* (Eph. iv. 15), and each of us "*members in particular,*" all advice proceeding from them, and every officious exhortation tending to the dissolution of our pure faith handed down from the Fathers is condemned, as it ought to be, synodically, not only as suspicious and to be eschewed, but as impious and soul-destroying: and in this category, among the first we place the said *Encyclical to the Easterns* from Pope Pius IX, Bishop of the elder Rome; and such we proclaim it to be in the Catholic Church.

18. Wherefore, beloved brethren and fellow-ministers of our mediocrity, as always, so also now, particularly on this occasion of the publication of the said Encyclical, we hold it to be our inexorable duty, in accordance with our patriarchal and synodical responsibility, in order that none may be lost to the divine fold of the Catholic Orthodox Church, the most holy Mother of us all, to encourage each other, and to urge you that, reminding one another of the words and exhortations of St. Paul to our holy predecessors when he summoned them to Ephesus, we reiterate to each other: *take heed, therefore, unto yourselves, and to all the flock, over which the Holy Ghost*

hath made you overseers, to feed the Church of God, which He hath purchased with His own Blood. For know this, that after my departing shall grievous wolves enter in among you not sparing the flock. Also, of your own selves shall men arise, speaking perverse things, to draw away disciples after them. Therefore, watch. (Acts xx.28-31.) Then our predecessors and Fathers, hearing this divine charge, wept sore, and falling upon his neck, kissed him. Come, then, and let us, brethren, hearing him admonishing us with tears, fall in spirit, lamenting, upon his neck, and, kissing him, comfort him by our own firm assurance, that no one shall separate us from the love of Christ, no one mislead us from evangelical doctrine, no one entice us from the safe path of our fathers, as none was able to deceive them, by any degree of zeal which they manifested, who from time to time were raised up for this purpose by the tempter: so that at last we shall hear from the Master: Well done, good and faithful servant, receiving the end of our faith, even the salvation of our souls, and of the reasonable flock over whom the Holy Ghost has made us shepherds.

19. This Apostolic charge and exhortation we have quoted for your sake, and address it to all the Orthodox congregation, wherever they be found settled on the earth, to the Priests and Abbots, to the Deacons and Monks, in a word, to all the Clergy and godly People, the rulers and the ruled, the rich and the poor, to parents and children, to teachers and scholars, to the educated and uneducated, to masters and servants, that we all, supporting and counseling each other, may be able to stand against the wiles of the devil. For thus St. Peter the Apostle exhorts us (1 Pet.): *Be sober, be vigilant because your adversary the devil, as a roaring lion walketh about, seeking whom he may devour. Whom resist, steadfast in the faith.*

20. For our faith, brethren, is not of men nor by man, but by revelation of Jesus Christ, which the divine Apostles preached, the holy Ecumenical Councils confirmed, the greatest and wisest teachers of the world handed down in succession, and the shed blood of the holy martyrs ratified. Let us hold fast to the confession which we have received unadulterated from such men, turning away from every novelty as a suggestion of the devil. He that accepts a novelty reproaches with deficiency the preached Orthodox Faith. But that Faith has long ago been sealed in completeness, not to admit of diminution or increase, or any change whatever; and he who dares to do, or advise,

or think of such a thing has already denied the faith of Christ, has already of his own accord been struck with an eternal anathema, for blaspheming the Holy Ghost as not having spoken fully in the Scriptures and through the Ecumenical Councils. This fearful anathema, brethren and sons beloved in Christ, we do not pronounce today, but our Savior first pronounced it (Matt. xii. 32): *Whosoever speaketh against the Holy Ghost, it shall not be forgiven him, neither in this world, neither in the world to come.* St. Paul pronounced the same anathema (Gal. i. 6): *I marvel that ye are so soon removed from Him that called you into the grace of Christ, unto another Gospel: which is not another; but there be some that trouble you, and would pervert the Gospel of Christ. But though we, or an angel from heaven, preach any other gospel unto you, than that which we have preached unto you, let him be accursed.* This same anathema the Seven Ecumenical Councils and the whole choir of God-serving fathers pronounced. All, therefore, innovating, either by heresy or schism, have voluntarily clothed themselves, according to the Psalm (cix. 18), (*"with a curse as with a garment,"*) whether they be Popes, or Patriarchs, or Clergy, or Laity; nay, if anyone, though an angel from heaven, preach any other Gospel unto you than that ye have received, let him be accursed. Thus, our wise fathers, obedient to the soul-saving words of St. Paul, were established firm and steadfast in the faith handed down unbrokenly to them, and preserved it unchanged and uncontaminated in the midst of so many heresies, and have delivered it to us pure and undefiled, as it came pure from the mouth of the first servants of the Word. Let us, too, thus wise, transmit it, pure as we have received it, to coming generations, altering nothing, that they may be, as we are, full of confidence, and with nothing to be ashamed of when speaking of the faith of their forefathers.

21. Therefore, brethren, and sons beloved in the LORD, *having purified your souls in obeying the truth* (1 Pet. i. 22), *let us give the more earnest heed to the things which we have heard, lest at any time we should let them slip.* (Heb. ii. 1.) The faith and confession we have received is not one to be ashamed of, being taught in the Gospel from the mouth of our LORD, witnessed by the holy Apostles, by the seven sacred Ecumenical Councils, preached throughout the world, witnessed to by its very enemies, who, before they apostatized from orthodoxy to heresies, themselves held this same faith, or at least their fathers and fathers' fathers thus held it. It is witnessed to by

continuous history, as triumphing over all the heresies which have persecuted or now persecute it, as ye see even to this day. The succession of our holy divine fathers and predecessors beginning from the Apostles, and those whom the Apostles appointed their successors, to this day, forming one unbroken chain, and joining hand to hand, keep fast the sacred enclosure of which the door is Christ, in which all the orthodox Flock is fed in the fertile pastures of the mystical Eden, and not in the pathless and rugged wilderness, as his Holiness supposes (p. 7.1.12). Our Church holds the infallible and genuine deposit of the Holy Scriptures, of the Old Testament a true and perfect version, of the New the divine original itself. The rites of the sacred Mysteries, and especially those of the divine Liturgy, are the same glorious and heart quickening rites, handed down from the Apostles. No nation, no Christian communion, can boast of such Liturgies as those of James, Basil, Chrysostom. The august Ecumenical Councils, those seven pillars of the house of Wisdom, were organized in it and among us. This, our Church, holds the originals of their sacred definitions. The Chief Pastors in it, and the honorable Presbytery, and the monastic Order, preserve the primitive and pure dignity of the first ages of Christianity, in opinions, in polity, and even in the simplicity of their vestments. Yes! verily, "grievous wolves" have constantly attacked this holy fold, and are attacking it now, as we see for ourselves, according to the prediction of the Apostle, which shows that the true lambs of the great Shepherd are folded in it; but that Church has sung and shall sing forever: "*They compassed me about; yea, they compassed me about: but in the name of the Lord I will destroy them*" (Ps. cxviii. 11). Let us add one reflection, a painful one indeed, but useful in order to manifest and confirm the truth of our words: — All Christian nations whatsoever that are today seen calling upon the Name of Christ (not excepting either the West generally, or Rome herself, as we prove by the catalogue of her earliest Popes), were taught the true faith in Christ by our holy predecessors and fathers; and yet afterwards deceitful men, many of whom were shepherds, and chief shepherds too, of those nations, by wretched sophistries and heretical opinions dared to defile, alas! the orthodoxy of those nations, as veracious history informs us, and as St. Paul predicted.

22. Therefore, brethren, and ye our spiritual children, we acknowledge how great the favor and grace which God has bestowed upon our

Orthodox Faith, and on His One, Holy, Catholic, and Apostolic Church, which, like a mother who is unsuspected of her husband, nourishes us as children of whom she is not ashamed, and who are excusable in our high-toned boldness concerning the hope that is in us. But what shall we sinners render to the LORD for all that He hath bestowed upon us? Our bounteous LORD and God, who hath redeemed us by his own Blood, requires nothing else of us but the devotion of our whole soul and heart to the blameless, holy faith of our fathers, and love and affection to the Orthodox Church, which has regenerated us not with a novel sprinkling, but with the divine washing of Apostolic Baptism. She it is that nourishes us, according to the eternal covenant of our Savior, with His own precious Body, and abundantly, as a true Mother, gives us to drink of that precious Blood poured out for us and for the salvation of the world. Let us then encompass her in spirit, as the young their parent bird, wherever on earth we find ourselves, in the north or south, or east, or west. Let us fix our eyes and thoughts upon her divine countenance and her most glorious beauty. Let us take hold with both our hands on her shining robe which the Bridegroom, "altogether lovely," has with His own undefiled hands thrown around her, when He redeemed her from the bondage of error, and adorned her as an eternal Bride for Himself. Let us feel in our own souls the mutual grief of the children-loving mother and the mother-loving children, when it is seen that men of wolfish minds and making gain of souls are zealous in plotting how they may lead her captive, or tear the lambs from their mothers. Let us, Clergy as well as Laity, cherish this feeling most intensely now, when the unseen adversary of our salvation, combining his fraudful arts (p. xi. 1.2-25), employs such powerful instrumentalities, and walketh about everywhere, as saith St. Peter, seeking whom he may devour; and when in this way, in which we walk peacefully and innocently, he sets his deceitful snares.

23. Now, the God of peace, "that brought again from the dead that great Shepherd of the sheep," "He that keepeth Israel," who "shall neither slumber nor sleep," "keep your hearts and minds," "and direct your ways to every good work."

Peace and joy be with you in the LORD.

May 1848, Indiction 6.

+ ANTHIMOS, by the Mercy of God, Archbishop of Constantinople, new Rome, and Ecumenical Patriarch, a beloved brother in Christ our God, and suppliant.

+ HIEROTHEUS, by the Mercy of God, Patriarch of Alexandria and of all Egypt, a beloved brother in Christ our God, and suppliant.

+ METHODIOS, by the Mercy of God, Patriarch of the great City of God, Antioch, and of all Anatolia, a beloved brother in Christ our God, and suppliant.

+ CYRIL, by the Mercy of God, Patriarch of Jerusalem and of all Palestine, a beloved brother in Christ our God, and suppliant.

The Holy Synod in Constantinople:
+ PAISIUS OF CAESAREA
+ ANTHIMUS OF EPHESUS
+ DIONYSIUS OF HERACLEA
+ JOACHIM OF CYZICUS
+ DIONYSIUS OF NICODEMIA
+ HIEROTHEUS OF CHALCEDON
+ NEOPHYTUS OF DERCI
+ GERASIMUS OF ADRIANOPLE
+ CYRIL OF NEOCAESAREA
+ THEOCLETUS OF BEREA
+ MELETIUS OF PISIDIA
+ ATHANASIUS OF SMYRNA
+ DIONYSIUS OF MELENICUS
+ PAISIUS OF SOPHIA
+ DANIEL OF LEMNOS
+ PANTELEIMON OF DRYINOPOLIS
+ JOSEPH OF ERSECIUM
+ ANTHIMUS OF BODENI

The Holy Synod in Antioch:
+ ZACHARIAS OF ARCADIA
+ METHODIOS OF EMESA
+ JOANNICIUS OF TRIPOLIS
+ ARTEMIUS OF LAODICEA

The Holy Synod in Jerusalem:
+ MELETIUS OF PETRA
+ DIONYSIUS OF BETHLEHEM
+ PHILEMON OF GAZA
+ SAMUEL OF NEAPOLIS
+ THADDEUS OF SEBASTE
+ JOANNICIUS OF PHILADELPHIA
+ HIEROTHEUS OF TABOR

3. The Patriarchal Encyclical of 1895: A Reply to the Papal Encyclical of Pope Leo XIII, On Reunion [537, 538]

To the most Sacred and Most Divinely-beloved Brethren in Christ the Metropolitans and Bishops, and their sacred and venerable Clergy, and all the godly and orthodox Laity of the Most Holy Apostolic and Patriarchal Throne of Constantinople.

"Remember them which have the rule over you, who have spoken unto you the word of God: whose faith follow, considering the end of their own conversation: Jesus Christ the same yesterday, and today, and forever. Be not carried about with divers and strange doctrines." (Hebrews 13:7-8).

I. Every godly and orthodox soul, which has a sincere zeal for the glory of God, is deeply afflicted and weighed down with great pain upon seeing that he, who detests that which is good and is a murderer from the

---

537 "The Patriarchal Encyclical of 1895, A Reply to the Papal Encyclical of Pope Leo XIII, on Reunion, Holy Synod of Constantinople," Orthodox Christian Information Center, accessed October 16th, 2022, http://orthodoxinfo.com/ecumenism/encyc_1895.aspx

538 Footnotes in the text are from the source.

beginning, impelled by envy of man's salvation, never ceases continually to sow divers tares in the field of the Lord, in order to sift the wheat. From this source indeed, even from the earliest times, there sprang up in the Church of God heretical tares, which have in many ways made havoc, and do still make havoc, of the salvation of mankind by Christ, which moreover, as bad seeds and corrupted members, are rightly cut off from the sound body of the orthodox catholic Church of Christ. But in these last times the evil one has rent from the orthodox Church of Christ even whole nations in the West, having inflated the bishops of Rome with thoughts of excessive arrogance, which has given birth to divers lawless and anti-evangelical innovations. And not only so, but furthermore the Popes of Rome from time to time, pursuing absolutely and without examination modes of union according to their own fancy, strive by every means to reduce to their own errors the catholic Church of Christ, which throughout the world walks unshaken in the orthodoxy of faith transmitted to her by the Fathers.

II. Accordingly the Pope of Rome, Leo XIII, on the occasion of his episcopal jubilee, published in the month of June of the year of grace 1895 an encyclical letter, addressed to the leaders and peoples of the world, by which he also at the same time invites our orthodox Catholic and Apostolic Church of Christ to unite with the papal throne, thinking that such union can only be obtained by acknowledging him as supreme pontiff and the highest spiritual and temporal ruler of the universal Church, as the only representative of Christ upon earth and the dispenser of all grace.

III. No doubt every Christian heart ought to be filled with longing for union of the Churches, and especially the whole orthodox world, being inspired by a true spirit of piety, according to the divine purpose of the establishment of the church by the God-man our Savior Christ, ardently longs for the unity of the Churches in the one rule of faith, and on the foundation of the apostolic doctrine handed down to us through the Fathers, "Jesus Christ Himself being the chief corner stone."[539] Wherefore she also every day, in her public prayers to the Lord, prays for the gathering together of the scattered and for the return of those who have gone astray to the right way of the truth, which alone leads to the Life of

---

539 Eph. 2:20.

all, the only-begotten Son and Word of God, our Lord Jesus Christ.[540] Agreeably, therefore, to this sacred longing, our orthodox Church of Christ is always ready to accept any proposal of union, if only the Bishop of Rome would shake off once for all the whole series of the many and divers anti-evangelical novelties that have been "privily brought in" to his Church, and have provoked the sad division of the Churches of the East and West, and would return to the basis of the seven holy Ecumenical Councils, which, having been assembled in the Holy Spirit, of representatives of all the holy Churches of God, for the determination of the right teaching of the faith against heretics, have a universal and perpetual supremacy in the Church of Christ. And this, both by her writings and encyclical letters, the Orthodox Church has never ceased to intimate to the Papal Church, having clearly and explicitly set forth that so long as the latter perseveres in her innovations, and the orthodox Church adheres to the divine and apostolic traditions of Christianity, during which the Western Churches were of the same mind and were united with the Churches of the East, so long is it a vain and empty thing to talk of union. For which cause we have remained silent until now, and have declined to take into consideration the papal encyclical in question, esteeming it unprofitable to speak to the ears of those who do not hear. Since, however, from a certain period the Papal Church, having abandoned the method of persuasion and discussion, began, to our general astonishment and perplexity, to lay traps for the conscience of the more simple orthodox Christians by means of deceitful workers transformed into apostles of Christ,[541] sending into the East clerics with the dress and headcovering of orthodox priests, inventing also divers and other artful means to obtain her proselytizing objects; for this reason, as in sacred duty bound, we issue this patriarchal and synodical encyclical, for a safeguard of the orthodox faith and piety, knowing "that the observance of the true canons is a duty for every good man, and much more for those who have been thought worthy by Providence to direct the affairs of others."[542]

---

540 John 14:6.

541 II Cor. 11:13.

542 Phot. Epist. iii. 10.

IV. The union of the separated Churches with herself in one rule of faith is, as has been said before, a sacred and inward desire of the holy, catholic and orthodox apostolic Church of Christ; but without such unity in the faith, the desired union of the Churches becomes impossible. This being the case, we wonder in truth how Pope Leo XIII, though he himself also acknowledges this truth, falls into a plain self-contradiction, declaring, on the one hand, that true union lies in the unity of faith, and, on the other hand, that every Church, even after the union, can hold her own dogmatic and canonical definitions, even when they differ from those of the Papal Church, as the Pope declares in a previous encyclical, dated November 30, 1894. For there is an evident contradiction when in one and the same Church one believes that the Holy Ghost proceeds from the Father, and another that He proceeds from the Father and the Son; when one sprinkles, and another baptizes (immerses) thrice in the water; one uses leavened bread in the sacrament of the Holy Eucharist, and another unleavened; one imparts to the people of the chalice as well as of the bread, and the other only of the holy bread; and other things like these. But what this contradiction signifies, whether respect for the evangelical truths of the holy Church of Christ and an indirect concession and acknowledgment of them, or something else, we cannot say.

V. But however that may be, for the practical realization of the pious longing for the union of the Churches, a common principle and basis must be settled first of all; and there can be no such safe common principle and basis other than the teaching of the Gospel and of the seven holy Ecumenical Councils. Reverting, then, to that teaching which was common to the Churches of the East and of the West until the separation, we ought, with a sincere desire to know the truth, to search what the one holy, catholic and orthodox apostolic Church of Christ, being then "of the same body," throughout the East and West believed, and to hold this fact, entire, and unaltered. But whatsoever has in later times been added or taken away, everyone has a sacred and indispensable duty, if he sincerely seeks for the glory of God more than for his own glory, that in a spirit of piety he should correct it, considering that by arrogantly continuing in the perversion of the truth he is liable to a heavy account before the impartial judgment-seat of Christ. In saying this we do not at all refer to the differences regarding the ritual of the sacred services and the hymns, or the sacred vestments, and the like, which matters, even though they still vary, as they did of old, do not in the least injure the substance and unity of the faith; but we refer to those essential differences which have reference to the divinely transmitted doctrines of the faith, and the divinely instituted canonical constitution of the administration of the Churches. "In cases where the thing disregarded is not the faith (says also the holy Photius),[543] and is no falling away from any general and catholic decree, different rites and customs being observed among different people, a man who knows how to judge rightly would decide that neither do those who observe them act wrongly, nor do those who have not received them break the law."[544]

VI. And indeed for the holy purpose of union, the Eastern orthodox and catholic Church of Christ is ready heartily to accept all that which both the Eastern and Western Churches unanimously professed before the ninth century, if she has perchance perverted or does not hold it. And if the Westerns prove from the teaching of the holy Fathers and the divinely assembled Ecumenical Councils that the then orthodox Roman Church, which was throughout the West, even before the ninth century read the Creed with the addition, or used unleavened bread, or accepted the doctrine of a purgatorial fire, or sprinkling instead of baptism, or the immaculate conception of the ever-Virgin, or the temporal power, or the infallibility and absolutism of the Bishop of Rome, we have no more to say. But if, on the contrary, it is plainly demonstrated, as those of the Latins themselves, who love the truth, also acknowledge, that the Eastern and orthodox catholic Church of Christ holds fast the anciently transmitted doctrines which were at that time professed in common both in the East and the West, and that the Western Church perverted them by divers innovations, then it is clear, even to children, that the more natural way to union is the return of the Western Church to the ancient doctrinal and administrative condition of things; for the faith does not change in any way with time or circumstances, but remains the same always and everywhere, for "there is one body and one Spirit," it is said, "*even as ye are called in one hope of your calling; one Lord, one faith,*

---

543 Patriarch of Constantinople; c. 800.

544 Phot. Epist. iii. 6.

one baptism, one God and Father of all, who is above all, and through all,
and in you all."[545]

VII. So then the one holy, catholic and apostolic Church of the seven Ecumenical Councils believed and taught in accordance with the words of the Gospel that the Holy Ghost proceeds from the Father; but in the West, even from the ninth century, the holy Creed, which was composed and sanctioned by Ecumenical Councils, began to be falsified, and the idea that the Holy Ghost proceeds "also from the Son" to be arbitrarily promulgated. And certainly Pope Leo XIII is not ignorant that his orthodox predecessor and namesake, the defender of orthodoxy, Leo III, in the year 809 denounced synodically this anti-evangelical and utterly lawless addition, "and from the Son" (*filioque*); and engraved on two silver plates, in Greek and Latin, the holy Creed of the first and second Ecumenical Councils, entire and without any addition; having written moreover, "These words I, Leo, have set down for love and as a safeguard of the orthodox faith" ("*Haec Leo posui amore et cautela fidei orthodoxa*"). [546]

---

545 Eph. 4:5-6.

546 See life of Leo III by Athanasius, presbyter and librarian at Rome, in his *Lives of the Popes*. The holy Photius also, making mention of this invective of the orthodox Pope of Rome, Leo III, against the holders of the erroneous doctrine, in his renowned letter to the Metropolitan of Acquileia, expresses himself as follows: "For (not to mention those who were before him) Leo the elder, prelate of Rome, as well as Leo the younger after him, shew themselves to be of the same mind with the catholic and apostolic Church, with the holy prelates their predecessors, and with the apostolic commands; the one having contributed much to the assembling of the fourth holy Ecumenical Council, both by the sacred men who were sent to represent him, and by his letter, through which both Nestorius and Eutyches were overthrown; by which letter he moreover, in accordance with previous synodical decrees, declared the Holy Ghost to proceed from the Father, but not also "from the Son." And in like manner Leo the younger, his counterpart in faith as well as in name. This latter indeed, who was ardently zealous for true piety, in order that the unspotted pattern of true piety might not in any way whatever be falsified by a barbarous language, published it in Greek, as has already been said in the beginning, to the people of the West, that they might thereby glorify and preach aright the Holy Trinity. And not only by word and command, but also, having inscribed and exposed it to the sight of all on certain shields specially made, as on certain monuments, he fixed it at the gates of the Church, in order that every person might easily learn the uncontaminated faith, and in order that no chance

Likewise he is by no means ignorant that during the tenth century, or at the beginning of the eleventh, this anti-evangelical and lawless addition was with difficulty inserted officially into the holy Creed at Rome also, and that consequently the Roman Church, in insisting on her innovations, and not coming back to the dogma of the Ecumenical Councils, renders herself fully responsible before the one holy, catholic and apostolic Church of Christ, which holds fast that which has been received from the Fathers, and keeps the deposit of the faith which was delivered to it unadulterated in all things, in obedience to the Apostolic injunction: "That good thing which was committed unto thee keep by the Holy Ghost which dwelleth in us"; *"avoiding profane and vain babblings, and oppositions of science falsely so called: which some professing have erred concerning the faith."* [547]

VIII. The one holy, catholic and apostolic Church of the first seven Ecumenical Councils baptized by three immersions in the water, and the Pope Pelagius speaks of the triple immersion as a command of the Lord, and in the thirteenth century baptism by immersions still prevailed in the West; and the sacred fonts themselves, preserved in the more ancient churches in Italy, are eloquent witnesses on this point; but in later times sprinkling or effusion, being privily brought in, came to be accepted by the Papal Church, which still holds fast the innovation, thus also widening the gulf which she has opened; but we Orthodox, remaining faithful to the apostolic tradition and the practice of the seven Ecumenical Councils, "stand fast, contending for the common profession, the paternal treasure of the sound faith."[548]

IX. The one holy, catholic and apostolic Church of the seven Ecumenical Councils, according to the example of our Savior, celebrated the divine Eucharist for more than a thousand years throughout the East

---

whatever might be left to secret forgers and innovators of adulterating the piety of us Christians, and of bringing in the Son besides the Father as a second cause of the Holy Spirit, who proceeds from the Father with honor equal to that of the begotten Son. And it was not these two holy men alone, who shone brightly in the West, who preserved the faith free from innovation; for the Church is not in such want as that of Western preachers; but there is also a host of them not easily counted who did likewise." — Epist. v. 53.

547 II Tim. 1:14; I Tim. 6:20-21.

548 St. Basil the Great, Ep. 243, To the Bishops of Italy and Gaul.

they already possess these blessings, and such as these, standing firm in the orthodoxy of their fathers and glorifying in it in Christ.

XXIII. These things being so, and being indisputably proved by ecclesiastical history, we, anxious as it is our duty to be, address ourselves to the peoples of the West, who through ignorance of the true and impartial history of ecclesiastical matters, being credulously led away, follow the anti-evangelical and utterly lawless innovations of the papacy, having been separated and continuing far from the one holy, catholic and apostolic orthodox Church of Christ, which is "the Church of the living God, the pillar and ground of the truth",[564] in which also their gracious ancestors and forefathers shone by their piety and orthodoxy of faith, having been faithful and precious members of it during nine whole centuries, obediently following and walking according to the decrees of the divinely assembled Ecumenical Councils.

XXIV. Christ-loving peoples of the glorious countries of the West! We rejoice on the one hand seeing that you have a zeal for Christ, being led by this right persuasion, "that without faith in Christ it is impossible to please God";[565] but on the other hand it is self-evident to every right-thinking person that the salutary faith in Christ ought by all means to be right in everything, and in agreement with the Holy Scripture and the apostolic traditions, upon which the teaching of the divine Fathers and the seven holy, divinely assembled Ecumenical Councils is based. It is moreover manifest that the universal Church of God, which holds fast in its bosom unique unadulterated and entire this salutary faith as a divine deposit, just as it was of old delivered and unfolded by the God-bearing Fathers moved by the Spirit, and formulated by them during the first nine centuries, is one and the same forever, and not manifold and varying with the process of time: because the gospel truths are never susceptible to alteration or progress in course of time, like the various philosophical systems; "for Jesus Christ is the same yesterday, and today, and forever."[566] Wherefore also the holy Vincent, who was brought up on the milk of the piety received from the fathers in the monastery of Lérins in Gaul, and flourished about the middle of the fifth century,

---

564 I Tim. 3:15

565 Heb. 11:6.

566 Heb. 13:8.

with great wisdom and orthodoxy characterizes the true catholicity of the faith and of the Church, saying: "In the catholic Church we must especially take heed to hold that which has been believed everywhere at all times, and by all. For this is truly and properly catholic, as the very force and meaning of the word signifies, which moreover comprehends almost everything universally. And that we shall do, if we walk following universality, antiquity, and consent."[567] But, as has been said before, the Western Church, from the tenth century downwards, has privily brought into herself through the papacy various and strange and heretical doctrines and innovations, and so she has been torn away and removed far from the true and orthodox Church of Christ. How necessary, then, it is for you to come back and return to the ancient and unadulterated doctrines of the Church in order to attain the salvation in Christ after which you press, you can easily understand if you intelligently consider the command of the heaven-ascended Apostle Paul to the Thessalonians, saying: "Therefore, brethren, stand fast, and hold the traditions which ye have been taught, whether by word, or our epistle";[568] and also what the same divine apostle writes to the Galatians saying: "I marvel that ye are so soon removed from him that called you into the grace of Christ unto another gospel: which is not another; but there be some that trouble you, and would pervert the gospel of Christ."[569] But avoid such perverters of the evangelical truth, "For they that are such serve not our Lord Jesus Christ, but their own belly; and by good words and fair speeches deceive the hearts of the simple";[570] and come back for the future into the bosom of the holy, catholic and apostolic Church of God, which consists of all the particular holy Churches of God, which being divinely planted, like luxuriant vines throughout the orthodox world, are inseparably united to each other in the unity of the one saving faith

---

567 *"In ipsa item Catholica Ecclesia magnopere curandum est, ut teneamus, quod ubique quod semper ab omnibus creditum est. Hoc est enim vere proprieque Catholicum (quod ipsa vis nominis ratioque declarat), quod omnia fere universaliter comprehendit. Sed hoc fiet si sequimur universalitatem, antiquitatem, consensionem"* (Vincentii Lirinensis Commonitorium pro CatholicEe fidei antiquitate et universalitate cap. iii, cf. cap. viii and xiv).

568 I Thess.2:15.

569 Gal. 1:6-7.

570 Rom. 16:18.

in Christ, and in the bond of peace and of the Spirit, that you may obtain the highly-to-be-praised and most glorious name of our Lord and God and Savior Jesus Christ, who suffered for the salvation of the world, may be glorified among you also.

XXV. But let us, who by the grace and goodwill of the most gracious God are precious members of the body of Christ, that is to say of His one holy, catholic and apostolic Church, hold fast to the piety of our fathers, handed down to us from the apostles. Let us all beware of false apostles, who, coming to us in sheep's clothing, attempt to entice the more simple among us by various deceptive promises, regarding all things as lawful and allowing them for the sake of union, provided only that the Pope of Rome be recognized as supreme and infallible ruler and absolute sovereign of the universal Church, and only representative of Christ on earth, and the source of all grace. And especially let us, who by the grace and mercy of God have been appointed bishops, pastors, and teachers of the holy Churches of God, "take heed unto ourselves — and to all the flock, over which the Holy Ghost hath made us overseers, to feed the Church of God, which He hath purchased with His own blood,"[571] as they that must give account. "Wherefore let us comfort ourselves together, and edify one another."[572] "And the God of all grace, who hath called us unto His eternal glory by Christ Jesus make us perfect, stablish, strengthen, settle us,"[573] and grant that all those who are without and far away from the one holy, catholic and orthodox fold of His reasonable sheep may be enlightened with the light of His grace and the acknowledging of the truth. To Him be glory and dominion for ever and ever.

Amen.

In the Patriarchal Palace of Constantinople,
in the Month of August of the Year of Grace MDCCCXCV.

+ ANTHIMOS of Constantinople, beloved brother and intercessor in Christ our God.

---

571 Acts 20:28.

572 I Thess. 5:11.

573 I Pet. 5:10.

+ NICODEMOS of Cyzicos, beloved brother and intercessor in Christ our God.

+ PHILOTHEOS of Nicomedia, beloved brother and intercessor in Christ our God.

+ JEROME of Nicea, beloved brother and intercessor in Christ our God.

+ NATHANAEL of Prusa, beloved brother and intercessor of Christ our God.

+ BASIL of Smyrna, beloved brother and intercessor in Christ our God.

+ STEPHEN of Philadelphia, beloved brother and intercessor in Christ our God.

+ ATHANASIOS of Lemnos, beloved brother and intercessor in Christ our God.

+ BESSARION of Dyrrachium, beloved brother and intercessor in Christ our God.

+ DOROTHEOS of Belgrade, beloved brother and intercessor in Christ our God.

+ NICODEMOS of Elasson, beloved brother and intercessor in Christ our God.

+ SOPHRONIOS of Carpathos and Cassos, beloved brother and intercessor in Christ our God.

+ DIONYSIOS of Eleutheropolis, beloved brother and intercessor in Christ our God.

4. Resolution of the Sobor of Bishops
of the Russian Orthodox Church Outside of Russia
Made on November 11/October 29, 1959,
With Regard to Questions Dealing with
the Roman Catholic Ecumenical Council
Being Convened by Pope John XXIII (1959) [574]

The Sobor of Bishops of the Russian Orthodox Church Outside of Russia considered questions received with regard to the stand to be maintained by the children of the Orthodox Church in connection with the Council projected by Pope John XXIII, which is called Ecumenical and is supposed to serve towards a unification of the Christian world. It is evident from the information pertaining to this matter, that the reports in the press, also including Roman Catholic, especially in the first months after the statement made by Pope John XXIII on January 25 of this year about his decision to call together an Ecumenical Council, created the impression in many that supposedly representatives of the Orthodox Church are to be invited to participate in the discussion of questions dealing with the unification of the whole Christian world. The danger of godless communism threatening this world made such a perspective of unification especially attractive. Indeed, what Christian heart does not grieve over the fact that Western Christians headed by Rome have been separated from us already for more than nine hundred years? And who would not rejoice if an end to this separation were to ensue? However, careful examination of responsible official statements originating in the Roman Catholic Church indicate that the original expression of a broad aimed projected Council does not correspond to present reality. The Encyclical of Pope John XXIII concerning the convening of the Council clearly testifies that the main task of the projected Council "will deal with the spread of the Catholic Faith and the rebirth of people based upon Christian principles, and the adjustment of Church disci-

---

574 Holy Trinity Monastery, "Resolution of the Sobor of Bishops of the Russian Orthodox Church Outside of Russia Dealing with the Roman Catholic Ecumenical Council Being Convened by Pope John XXIII," *Orthodox Life*, 61 no. 1 (January-February 1969): 3-5.

pline to the needs and conditions of present time." The Encyclical treats the union cherished by Rome in the form of a "return" of the Eastern Church to Rome, as to its "Father's home."

The character of the future Council is defined even more clearly by the state-secretary of the Vatican, Cardinal Tardini, who on October 30 of this year declared to the representatives of the press, that the imminent Council will be an "internal matter" of the Roman Catholic Church. Such an "internal matter" of Rome the Orthodox Church has no basis to discuss in its essence.

However, in so far as various opinions were expressed by the press concerning the Council of the Roman Church and a possible participation in it of the representatives of the Orthodox Church was mentioned, the Sobor of Bishops desires to make clear to its flock, that a common Sobor of Orthodox and Roman Catholics does not appear likely while the latter confess the dogma of the infallibility of the Pope in questions of Faith. This dogma, in placing the Pope above the Sobor and in making out of the latter, contrary to ancient doctrine of the Church, only a consultative body to the Pope as the Vicar of Christ, annuls the very conception of an Ecumenical Sobor as understood by the Orthodox Church. Independent of that, the Orthodox Church as a church accepting the Seven Ecumenical Sobors could not participate in any Sobor claiming to be Ecumenical, if it is called the twenty-first, since then merely such a name would signify its acceptance of all thirteen of the sobors considered to be ecumenical by the West as being authentically ecumenical, which would be identical to accepting their doctrines, which are rejected by the Orthodox Church, which considers them to be errors. The main obstacle to the participation of the Orthodox in a Roman Catholic Council is contained namely in this, and not in, as at times it was indicated in the press, that the Orthodox Church supposedly could not accept an invitation that simultaneously would not be extended to Protestant denominations, united in the World Council of Churches. Whatever encounters could take place between the Orthodox and the Protestants at so-called ecumenical gatherings, the Orthodox Church could not renounce its independence of the various other denominations remote to us in their doctrinal and liturgical life.

The Sobor of Bishops calls on the faithful children of the Russian Orthodox Church in exile to firmly follow the ancient traditions of our Fathers, without yielding to the externally enticing yet far removed from Orthodoxy perspectives of unification, connected both with doctrines of the prospective Rome Council and with the so-called Ecumenical Movement in which reigns the spirit of interconfessionalism, inescapably leading to indifference towards dogmatic truth.

The Orthodox Church, as the One, Holy, Catholic and Apostolic Church, from Which to their own misfortune and our sorrow the Western Confessions have been separated since 1054, will continue until the end of time to pursue its straight, royal way, firmly believing in the promise of our Saviour: "I will build My Church and the gates of hell shall not prevail against it." (Matth. 16, 18.).

5. Resolution of the ROCOR Synod of Bishops Concerning the Decision of the Moscow Synod Permitting Roman Catholics to Have Access to All Orthodox Sacraments (1970)[575]

The decision of the Moscow Synod permitting the administration of all the sacraments of our Church to Roman Catholics, which has been widely announced in the press, may bring confusion to the members of our Church and mislead the heterodox. Information has already reached the Synod of Bishops that some Roman Catholics have been asking for communion in Orthodox Churches.

The aforementioned decision of the Moscow Synod is clearly based not on canons, but on other considerations which are of neither a canonical nor a dogmatical nature. Any such action, connected as it is with the national and anti-religious policies of the Soviet Union, must inevitably depend upon the will of the Government and the Communist party, just as earlier political reasons lay behind the liquidation of the Uniate Church in the U.S.S.R. Inasmuch as a rapprochement is at present

---

575 Holy Trinity Monastery, "Resolution of the Synod of Bishops Concerning the Decision of the Moscow Synod Permitting Roman Catholics to Have Access to All Orthodox Sacraments," *Orthodox Life*, no. 3 (May-June 1970): 3-5.

taking place between Moscow and the Vatican, as may be inferred from the lively exchange of visits by high-standing hierarchs, one can presume that the permission to perform sacraments for Roman Catholics is an act that serves as compensation to the Vatican by lending support to its ecumenical policies. Nevertheless, leaving aside the true motives which may have prompted the decision of the Moscow Patriarchate, the necessity of a canonical appraisal remains. First of all, one must note that the present Moscow Patriarchate is not the authentic representative of the Church of Russia, since it has an atheistic Government as the source of its authority (Apostolic Canon XXX; Canon III of the Seventh Oecumenical Council). Therefore, its decision will not be binding on the Church of Russia in the future, when the Lord will deem fit to grant her freedom.

Aside from this consideration, the decision itself, which fully restores communion with Rome, whereas there would have been no changes in the latter's dogmatical doctrines which would make it Orthodox, constitutes a direct violation of the canonical norm and the relationship with the heterodox which is accepted by the whole Orthodox Church (Apostolic Canons X, XLV, XLVI; Canons VI and XXXIII of Laodicea; Canon IX of Timothy of Alexandria). According to certain sources, the Metropolitan of Leningrad, Nikodim, on being confronted with such indications during his recent stay in New York, made reference to a decision of the Most Holy Synod of the Russian Church in a decree dated February 25, 1870. According to that decree Orthodox priests were permitted to perform sacraments at the request of persons belonging to the Greek Uniate rite, if in that region there were no Uniate churches and clergy to perform all the sacraments for them.

This decision of the Synod, however — accepted a hundred years ago under the special conditions governing the existence of the Uniates in Russia at that time — is not relevant to contemporary Catholics or even to Uniates. It may not be taken out of the context of the specific situation that existed in Russia in the nineteenth century. When this decree was prepared, the process of the return of the Uniates to Orthodoxy was underway. Two years before the decree, the principal leader in that movement, Metropolitan Joseph Semashko, died with his life's work not yet accomplished. It was precisely in 1870 that the Uniates in the diocese of Kholm were reunited. The reunification was based on the assumption that Uniatism was forcibly introduced by the Polish authorities, and that the people who were drawn into it never actually accepted the errors of the Roman Catholic Church but remained inwardly as Orthodox as before. It was only under great pressure, against their will, that they outwardly obeyed the bishops appointed by Rome. Being liberated from Polish pressure, the Uniates soon began spontaneously to return to the fold of the Orthodox Church. In the reign of the Empress Catherine II the number of such persons rose to nearly two million. Under Emperor Nicholas I the process was continued with the active cooperation of Metropolitan Joseph Semashko of Lithuania. In 1839 the Tsar received a petition signed by 1305 clergymen with their flocks, requesting that they be reunited with the Orthodox Church.

In 1870 there took place a new conversion, this time in the Diocese of Kholm. There can be no doubt that the decision of the Synod to accord the sacraments in that year was taken in conjunction with this process to facilitate their reunion, just as, in 1836 (decree of August 17), when a mass reunion from Belorussia was being prepared, a decision was made that permitted the acceptance of Greek-Uniates for confession and communion — on condition, however, that they would never return to their former confession. That decree, as well as the decree of 1870, referred only to Uniates and not to Catholics in general, and was aimed at making it easier for them to be reunited with the Orthodox Church. The leniency in regard to them, which made it unnecessary for them to be subjected to special rites as converts, can be explained precisely by the fact that they continued to regard themselves as Orthodox who had been detached from the unity of the Church only under duress. Such Uniates in name but Orthodox in essence continued to exist in Austria — in Galicia and Carpatho-Russia. Whenever possible, they used to come as pilgrims to the Pochayev Monastery, and after the first World War many of them spontaneously returned to the Orthodox Church in Poland. In Carpathian Russia they formed a whole diocese.

Turning to the canons, we find such leniency in regard to those who are separated from the Church under duress approved in Canon II of St. Athanasius the Great and Canon II of Theophilus of Alexandria. These canons show leniency to priests who subordinated themselves to

Arians on the advice of their bishops. St. Athanasius calls them, "those who have withdrawn as a matter of necessity, but who have not been destroyed in bad faith." He says that Councils in Greece, Spain, Gaul, and Alexandria have determined that those "who have not disavowed the religion of piety, but have been dragged away as a result of necessity and violence, it has seemed best that they be given pardon and be allowed also to remain in the clergy, especially in view of the fact that they have presented a plausible apology. Accordingly, it has seemed right in this case that some concession should be made. For they have given assurances that they will not change over to the religion of impiety. But in order to prevent any who have become most impious from corrupting the Church they have preferred to go along with violence and carry the burden, rather than to let the people go to destruction." Therefore, the decision of the Most Holy Synod of 1870, referring as it did not to Roman Catholics in general but specifically to Russian Uniates alone, was of a pastoral and missionary nature, applying economy according to the aforementioned canons in order to help the Uniates in their return to the Orthodox Church, since they had never rejected her in their hearts.

The present decision of the Moscow Synod has a quite different meaning. It opens the doors to Roman Catholics generally, permitting them to receive all the sacraments of the Orthodox Church without those reasons of economy which the Most Holy Synod in the last century had. Here it is not a question of Uniates who regarded themselves as essentially Orthodox who wished to return to the fold of the Orthodox Church, but of Roman Catholics who maintain the errors of their confession. Therefore, the decision of the Moscow Synod for all practical purposes leads it into communion with the Roman Catholics, and thus represents a betrayal of Orthodoxy.

On the grounds of all the aforesaid, the Synod of Bishops rules:

1) To consider the decision of the Moscow Patriarchate granting Roman Catholics access to all the sacraments of the Orthodox Church as in violation of the holy canons and contrary to Orthodox dogmatical doctrines. Entering thus into communion with the heterodox, the Moscow Patriarchate estranges itself from the unity of the holy Fathers and Doctors of the Church. By its action it does not sanctify the heretics to whom it offers the sacraments, but it itself becomes part of their heresy.

2) To warn the rectors of churches that they should be on the alert so as not to give communion to Roman Catholics who might attempt to receive it, being misled by wrong information in the press.

3) To send a copy of this decision to the Heads of the Autocephalous Churches, to announce it by a circular decree to the clergy of the churches through their Diocesan Bishops, and to publish it in the press for the guidance of the flock.

Bishop Council of 1959 in the newly donated Synod of Bishops

Saints of Mount Athos
by the hand of Efstathios Christophorou
may his memory be eternal.

C. PUBLICATIONS
FROM THE HOLY MOUNTAIN

The Ninth Ecumenical Council gathered in the 14th century to defend the teachings of St. Gregory Palamas against the Latinized teachings of Barlaam and Akindynos. Against his detractors, St. Gregory Palamas defended the Athonite practice of hesychia and noetic prayer, the hesychastic experience of the Uncreated Light, and the necessity of the essence-energies distinction for understanding how the hesychasts come to know God empirically. St. Gregory defended the Church's teaching that the theologian is the hesychast, the man who comes to know God directly through ceaseless prayer and the purification of the heart. He rejected the Latin belief that philosophical study and books lead to the direct knowledge of God. For the triumph of his teachings at the Ninth Ecumenical Council, the Orthodox Church began to commemorate St. Gregory on the second Sunday of Great Lent, following the Sunday of Orthodoxy which celebrates the restoration of the holy icons and is referred to as the Sunday of the Triumph of Orthodoxy. In this way, the Ninth Ecumenical Council is seen by the Orthodox Church as a second Triumph of Orthodoxy. As Mt. Athos, both before and after St. Gregory Palamas, has served as the foundation for hesychastic experience, and has been the backbone of Orthodox monasticism more generally, it has been and continues to be "the voice" or "conscience" of Orthodoxy, confessing the truth of the Faith with a flame of spiritual zeal ignited from hesychia. As long as there are saints and holy elders who live as empirical theologians on Athos, the Holy Mountain will continue to be looked to as the spiritual center of the Orthodox Church and the conscience of the Church. For this reason, statements from Mt. Athos on dogmatic and other

601

matters must be received by the Church with great seriousness, particularly when signed by all of the representatives of the ruling monasteries, as seen with "The Announcement of the Extraordinary Joint Conference of the Sacred Community of the Holy Mount Athos," in Section 1, starting here.

1. The Announcement of the Extraordinary Joint Conference of the Sacred Community of the Holy Mount Athos[576]

The Extraordinary Joint Conference of the Sacred Community on Mount Athos, April 9/22, 1980, noting that the issue of the relations of our holy Orthodox Church with the heterodox has assumed a serious and resolute character, especially as it relates to the dialogue with Roman Catholics, has resolved publicly to state the opinion of the Athonite fathers on this subject for general consideration:

1. We believe that our holy Orthodox Church is the One, Holy, Catholic and Apostolic Church of Christ, which possesses the fulness of grace and truth and, in consequence thereof, unbroken apostolic succession.

On the contrary, the "churches" and "confessions" of the West, having in many ways perverted the Faith of the Gospel, the apostles and the fathers, are deprived of sanctifying grace, of real mysteries and apostolic succession. That this is correct, His Eminence, Metropolitan Maximos of Stavropolis stresses: "Orthodoxy is not one of the churches, but The Church herself. She has preserved precisely and authentically the teaching of Christ in its pristine splendor and in all its purity. Over and above a simple, unbroken historical continuity and consistency there exists in her a spiritual and ontological authenticity. The same Faith, the same Spirit, the same life. It is this which constitutes the distinguishing feature of Orthodoxy, and which justifies her claim that she is and remains The Church" (*Episkepsis*, #227, March 15, 1980).

---

576 Metropolitan Philaret (Voznesensky) of New York, "The Announcement of the Extraordinary Joint Conference of the Sacred Community of the Holy Mount Athos & An Epistle Response to Mount Athos," *Orthodox Life 30*, no. 3 (May-June 1980): 8-13.

2. Dialogue with the heterodox is not reprehensible from the Orthodox point of view if its goal is to inform them of the Orthodox Faith and, thus, make it possible for them thereby to return to Orthodoxy when they receive divine enlightenment, and their eyes are opened.

3. Theological dialogue must not in any way be linked with prayer in common, or by joint participation in any liturgical or worship services whatsoever; or in other activities which might create the impression that our Orthodox Church accepts, on the one hand, Roman Catholics as part of the fulness of the Church, or, on the other hand, the Pope as the canonical bishop of Rome. Activities such as these mislead both the fulness of the Orthodox people and the Roman Catholics themselves, fostering among them a mistaken notion as to what Orthodoxy thinks of their teaching.

The Holy Mountain is grievously disturbed by the tendency of certain Orthodox hierarchs who have been invited to participate in Roman Catholic services, celebrations and processions, especially on the occasion of the return of holy relics. Conversely, we congratulate those hierarchs who have publicly expressed their alarm for the fulness of Orthodoxy.

4. We express our complete approval of what His All-Holiness. the Ecumenical Patriarch said during the visit of the Pope to Constantinople, namely that there exist various impediments between Orthodox and Roman Catholics: "First of all, we have serious theological problems which concern fundamental principles of the Christian faith" (*Episkepsis*, #221, Dec. 1, 1979, p. 17). These divergences in the principles of the Christian faith requires that we do not advance to participation in common liturgies and worship services before oneness of faith is attained. The mystical character of the kiss of peace during the divine Eucharist always presupposes harmony of faith: "Let us love one another that with one mind we may confess ..." We cannot pray together, especially during the Divine Liturgy, when we do not believe in the same faith and are separated by fundamental questions of faith. Only an indifference to the faith could permit us to do so.

Moreover, the Holy Mountain cannot accept the opinion, expressed in the joint statement of the Patriarch and the Pope, concerning the "cleansing of the historical memory of our Churches" and the partial opening, by means of a dialogue of love, of the road towards "new movements in theological work and a new attitude to the past which is common to both

Churches" (*Episkepsis*, ibid., p. 19). Actually, the heretics must cleanse their own historical memory of all their own historically acknowledged deviations in faith and practice from the true, evangelical Orthodox Faith. On the contrary, the historical memory of the Orthodox, which is based on the inspiration of the Holy Spirit and on the constant experience of the apostolic faith of the God-bearing Fathers, must be lived by all of us in repentance and humility, and must instruct us both in the present and in the future life if we do not wish to fall from that faith. As Orthodox we must cleanse ourselves by means of the historical memory of the Church, but not "cleanse" her with an egotistical and anthropocentric spirit, setting ourselves up as judges of the Tradition of the Church.

5. The Holy Mountain is convinced, not without great anxiety, that although the Orthodox are making many concessions and compromises to the Roman Catholics, the latter antithetically continue to adhere to their own errors which have served as the cause of their schism from the Orthodox Church and later led to the Protestant split. Thus, the Pope, during his visit to the center of Orthodoxy in the patriarchal cathedral, did not in the least hesitate to proclaim that he was coming to Constantinople as the successor of Peter, "who as the ultimate authority has the responsibility of superintending the unity of all, to guarantee the agreement of the Church of God in fidelity and in the 'faith which was once delivered unto the saints' (Jude 3)" (*Episkepsis*, ibid., p. 9). In other words, the Pope defended (papal) infallibility and primacy; and there are many other actions and manifestations which the Pope has effected on behalf of *uniatism*. We remember the establishment of diplomatic relations between the Greek Government and the Vatican, which, even though it may justify papism, is unjust and strikes out at the Mother and Nourisher of our [Greek] nation, the Orthodox Church.

6. The Holy Mountain also expresses its anxiety over the constituency of the commission for the dialogue. Uniates comprise a portion of the Roman Catholic delegation, a fact which is a provocation for the Orthodox. The sensibilities and dignity of the Orthodox delegation demand the immediate substitution of others in place of the *uniates* in the membership. No Orthodox whose manner of thinking corresponds to this faith can agree to participate in a commission which includes *uniates*. Likewise, the Holy Mountain is disturbed by the great weakness and insufficiency

of the Orthodox delegation. The most remarkable Orthodox theologians are not participating. The Holy Mountain is also not represented, despite the fact that it is the sole monastic center which preserves the faith and the theology of the Fathers, and which is far removed from the influence of secularism and scholastic Western theology.

7. From the Orthodox point of view there is no justification for optimism in regard to the dialogue, and for this reason no haste should be exhibited concerning it. The Roman Catholics are pressing the dialogue, hoping to strengthen themselves by annexing Orthodoxy to themselves, for they are confronted by very powerful internal disturbances and crises, as is well known. The number of former Roman Catholics who have converted to Orthodoxy also disturbs them. But Orthodoxy has no reason to hasten towards dialogue since the papists remain so obdurate and immovable as regards infallibility, uniatism, and the rest of their pernicious teachings.

Hastening the dialogue under such conditions is equivalent to spiritual suicide for the Orthodox. Many facts give the impression that the Roman Catholics are preparing a union on the pattern of a unia. Can it be that the Orthodox who are hastening to the dialogue are unconscious of this? The Holy Mountain maintains that for it there can be no question of accepting a *fait accompli*, that, by the grace of God, it will remain faithful, as the Lord's Orthodox people, to the faith of the holy apostles and the holy Fathers, impelled to this also by love for the heterodox, to whom real help is given only when the Orthodox show them the vastness of their spiritual sickness and the means of its cure by maintaining a consistently Orthodox position.

The unsuccessful attempts in the past with regard to union must teach us that steadfast unity in the truth of the Church, in accordance with the will of God, presupposes a different preparation and a path distinct from that taken in the past and from that which, apparently, is now being taken.

Signed,
All of the Superiors and Representatives of the Twenty Sacred and Pious Monasteries of the Holy Mountain of Athos at the Extraordinary Joint Conference.

2. Letter to the Patriarch of Constantinople by the Sacred Community of Mount Athos Concerning the Balamand Agreement[577, 578]

December 8, 1993

To His Most Divine All Holiness, the Ecumenical Patriarch, our Father and Master, Kyr Kyr Bartholomew,

Most Holy Father and Master:

The union of the Churches or, to be precise, the union of the heterodox with our One, Holy, Catholic, and Apostolic Orthodox Church is desirable to us also so that the Lord's prayer may be fulfilled, ... *that they may be one* (John 17:21). At any rate, we understand and await according to the Orthodox interpretation. As Professor John Romanides reminds us, "Christ prays here that His disciples and their disciples may, in this life, become one in the vision of His glory (which He has by nature from the Father) when they become members of His Body, the Church..."[579]

For this reason, whenever heterodox Christians visit us, to whom we extend love and hospitality in Christ, we are painfully aware that we stand apart in faith and, because of this, we are not able to have ecclesiastical communion.

---

577 Holy Trinity Monastery, "Letter to the Patriarch of Constantinople by the Sacred Community of Mount Athos," *Orthodox Life 44*, no. 4 (July-August 1994): 27-39.

578 See page 861 for more information and a larger treatment of the Balamand Agreement.

579 To complete the thought of the author we continue the passage here: "which would be formed on Pentecost and whose members were to be illuminated and glorified in this life... This is how the Fathers understand this prayer... It is certainly not a prayer for the union of churches... which have not the slightest understanding of glorification (theosis) and how to arrive at it in this life." From a rebuttal to the Balamand Agreement by the renowned Orthodox theologian, Fr. John S. Romanides, Prof. of Theology, St. John Damascene (Antiochian) Orthodox Theological School, Balamand, Lebanon; Professor Emeritus, Univ. of Thessaloniki, Greece; former Professor of Orthodox Theology, Holy Cross Greek Orthodox Theological School, Brookline, MA.

Schism, the division between the Orthodox and the Non-Chalcedonians first and between the Orthodox and the Westerners later, truly amounts to a tragedy about which we must not become silent or complacent.

In this context, therefore, we appreciate efforts made with fear of God and in accordance with Orthodox Tradition that look to a union that cannot take place through the silencing or minimizing of Orthodox doctrines, or through toleration of the false doctrines of the heterodox, because it would not be a union in the Truth. And then in the end, it would not be accepted by the Church or blessed by God, because, according to the patristic saying, "A good thing is not good if it is not achieved in a good way."

On the contrary, it would bring about new schisms and new divisions and miseries to the already [dis]united[580] body of Orthodoxy. At this point, we would like to say that in the face of great changes taking place in lands that have an Orthodox presence, and before so many kinds of unstable conditions on a worldwide scale, the One, Holy, Catholic, and Apostolic, in other words Orthodox, Church should have strengthened the cohesion of the local Churches and given herself over to the care of her terror-stricken members and to their spiritual stabilization, on the one hand, and in her consciousness [as the One Holy Church], on the other, she should have sounded the trumpet of her unique redemptive power and Grace and manifested it before fallen humanity.

In this spirit, to the extent that our monastic office permits us, we closely follow developments in the so-called ecumenical movement and dialogues. We note that at times the word of Truth is rightly divided and, at times, compromises and concessions are made regarding fundamental matters of the Faith.

---

580 In the Greek text that appeared in *Orthodoxos Typos* there is an apparent typographical error and this word was simply "united," although the context of the complete sentence clearly implies the word "disunited."

I

Thus, actions and declarations which representatives of Orthodox Churches have engaged in, that were unheard of until today and are altogether contrary to our holy Faith, have caused us deep sorrow.

We shall cite first the case of His Beatitude [Parthenios], the Patriarch of Alexandria, who, on at least two occasions, has stated that we Christians ought to recognize Mohammed as a prophet. To this day, however, no one has called for him to step down, and this dreadfully heedless Patriarch continues to preside in the Church of Alexandria as if there were nothing wrong.

Second, we cite the case of the Patriarchate of Antioch, which, without a Pan-Orthodox decision, has proceeded to ecclesiastical communion with the Non-Chalcedonians [Monophysites]. This was done despite the fact that a most serious issue has not yet been resolved. It is the latter's non-acceptance of the Ecumenical Councils after the Third and, in particular, the Fourth, the Council of Chalcedon, which in fact constitutes an immovable basis of Orthodoxy. Unfortunately, in this case, too, we have not seen a single protest by other Orthodox Churches.

The gravest matter, however, is the unacceptable change in the position of the Orthodox that arises from the joint statement at the June 1993, Balamand Conference of the mixed commission for the dialogue between Roman Catholics and Orthodox. It adopted anti-Orthodox positions, and it is mainly to this that we call the attention of Your All Holiness.

First, we must confess that the statements which Your All Holiness has made from time to time that the Uniate movement is an insurmountable obstacle to the continuation of the dialogue between Orthodox and Roman Catholics until now put us at ease.

But the above document [of Balamand] gives the impression that your statements are being sidestepped. Furthermore, Unia is receiving amnesty and is invited to the table of theological dialogue despite the contrary decision of the Third Pan-Orthodox Conference in Rhodes requiring: "the complete withdrawal from Orthodox lands by the Uniate agents and propagandists of the Vatican; the incorporation of the so-called Uniate Churches and their subjection under the Church of Rome before the inauguration of the dialogue, because Unia and dialogue at the same time are irreconcilable."

II

Your All Holiness, the greatest scandal, however, is caused by the ecclesiological positions in the document. We shall refer here to fundamental deviations only.

In Paragraph 10 we read: "The Catholic Church... (which conducted missionary work against the Orthodox and) presented herself as the only one to whom salvation was entrusted. As a reaction, the Orthodox Church, in turn, came to accept the same vision according to which only in her could salvation be found. To assure the salvation of 'the separated brethren' it even happened that Christians were rebaptized and that certain requirements of the religious freedom of persons and of their act of faith were forgotten. This perspective was one to which that period showed little sensitivity."

As Orthodox, we cannot accept this view. It was not as a reaction against Unia that our Holy Orthodox Church began to believe that she exclusively possessed salvation, but She believed it before Unia existed, from the time of the Schism, which took place for reasons of dogma. The Orthodox Church did not await the coming of Unia in order to acquire the consciousness that she is the unadulterated continuation of the One, Holy, Catholic, and Apostolic Church of Christ, because she has always had this self-awareness just as she had the awareness that the Papacy was in heresy. If she did not use the term heresy frequently, it was because, according to Saint Mark of Ephesus, "The Latins are not only schismatics but heretics as well. However, the Church was silent on this because their race is large and more powerful than ours... and we wished not to fall into triumphalism over the Latins as heretics but to be accepting of their return and to cultivate brotherliness."

But when the Uniates and the agents of Rome were let loose on us in the East in order to proselytize the suffering Orthodox by mainly unlawful means, as they do even today, Orthodoxy was obliged to declare that truth, not for purposes of proselytism but in order to protect the flock.

Saint Photios repeatedly characterizes the *Filioque* as a heresy, and its believers as cacodox [wrongly believing].

Saint Gregory Palamas says of the westerner Barlaam, that when he came to Orthodoxy, "He did not accept sanctifying water from our Church... to wipe away [his] stains from the West." Saint Gregory obviously considers him a heretic in need of sanctifying grace in order to come into the Orthodox Church.

The statement in the paragraph in question unjustly heaps responsibility on the Orthodox Church in order to lessen the responsibilities of the Papists. When did the Orthodox trample upon the religious freedom of the Uniates and Roman Catholics by baptizing them against their will? And if there were some exceptions, the Orthodox who signed the Balamand document forget that those who were rebaptized against their wishes were descendants of the Orthodox who were forcibly made Uniates, as occurred in Poland, Ukraine, and Moldavia. (See Paragraph 11)

In Paragraph 13 we read: "In fact, especially since the Pan-Orthodox Conferences began and since the Second Vatican Council, the rediscovery and the giving of proper value to the Church as communion, both on the part of Orthodox and of Catholics, has radically altered perspectives and thus attitudes. On each side it is recognized that what Christ has entrusted to his Church — profession of apostolic faith, participation in the same sacraments, above all the one priesthood celebrating the one sacrifice of Christ, the apostolic succession of bishops — cannot be the exclusive property of one of our Churches. In this context, it is clear that every form of rebaptism must be avoided."

The new discovery of the Church as communion by Roman Catholics has, of course, some significance for them who had no way out of the dilemma of their totalitarian ecclesiology and, therefore, had to turn their system of thought to the communal character of the Church. Thus, alongside the one extreme of totalitarianism, they place the other of collegiality, always motivated on the same man-centered level. The Orthodox Church, however, has always had the consciousness that she is not a simple communion but a theanthropic communion or a "communion of theosis [deification]," as Saint Gregory Palamas says in his homily on the procession of the Holy Spirit. Moreover, the communion of theosis is not only unknown in but also irreconcilable with Roman Catholic theology, which rejects [the doctrine of] the uncreated energies of God that form and sustain this communion.

Given these truths, it was with deepest sadness that we confirmed that this paragraph [13] makes the Orthodox Church equal to the Roman Catholic Church which abides in cacodoxy [wrong belief].

Serious theological differences, such as the *Filioque*, Papal primacy and infallibility, created grace, etc., are receiving amnesty, and a union is being forged without agreement in dogma.

Thus, are verified the premonitions that the union designed by the Vatican, in which, as Saint Mark of Ephesus said, "the willing are unwittingly being manipulated," (i.e., the Orthodox, who also live under hostile circumstances ethnically and politically today and are captive to nations of other religions), is pushed to take place without agreement regarding doctrinal differences. The plan is for union to take place, despite the differences, through the mutual recognition of the Mysteries and apostolic succession of each Church, and the application of intercommunion, limited at first and broader later. After this, doctrinal differences can be discussed only as theological *opinions*.

But once union takes place, what sense is there in discussing theological differences? Rome knows that the Orthodox will never accept her alien teachings. Experience has proven this in the various attempts at union up to the present. Therefore, despite the differences, Rome is crafting a union and hoping, from a humanistic point of view (as her perspective always is), that, as the more powerful factor, in time she will absorb the weaker one, that is, Orthodoxy. Father John Romanides presaged this in his article "The Uniate Movement and Popular Ecumenism," in *The Orthodox Witness*, February 1966.

We would like to put these questions to the Orthodox who signed this document:

Do the *Filioque*, [Papal] primacy and infallibility, purgatory, the immaculate conception, and created grace constitute an apostolic confession? Despite all of this, is it possible for us Orthodox to recognize as *apostolic* the faith and confession of the Roman Catholics?

Do these serious theological deviations of Rome amount to heresies or not?

If they are, as they have been described by Orthodox Councils and fathers, do they not result in the invalidity of the Mysteries and the apostolic succession of heterodox and cacodox of this kind?

Is it possible for the fullness of grace to exist where there is not the fullness of truth?

Is it possible to distinguish Christ of the truth from Christ of the Mysteries and apostolic succession?

Apostolic succession was first set forth by the Church as a historic confirmation of the continuous preservation of her truth. But when the truth itself is distorted, what meaning can a formulistic preservation of apostolic succession have? Did not the great heresiarchs often have this kind of external succession? How can it be possible for them to also be regarded as bearers of Grace?

And how is it possible for two Churches to be considered "Sister Churches" not because of their pre-Schism common descent but because of their so-called common confession, sanctifying Grace, and priesthood *despite their great differences in dogmas?*

Who among the Orthodox can accept as the true successor to the Apostles the infallible one, the one with the primacy of authority to rule over the entire Church and to be the religious and secular leader of the Vatican State?

Would this not be a denial of Apostolic Faith and Tradition?

Or are the signers of this document unaware that many Roman Catholics today groan under the foot of the Pope (and his scholastic, man-centered ecclesiological system) and desire to come into Orthodoxy?

How can these people who are tormented spiritually and desire holy Baptism not be received into Orthodoxy because the same Grace is supposedly both here and there? Ought we not, at that point, to respect their religious freedom, as the Balamand declaration demands in another circumstance, and grant them Orthodox Baptism? What defense shall we present to the Lord if we withhold the fullness of Grace from them who, after years of agony and personal searching, desire the holy Baptism of our One, Holy, Catholic, and Apostolic Church?

Paragraph 14 of the document quotes Pope John Paul II: "The ecumenical endeavor of the Sister Churches of East and West, grounded in dialogue and prayer, is the search for perfect and total communion which is neither absorption nor fusion but a meeting in truth and love."

But how is a union in the truth possible when differences in dogmas are sidestepped and both Churches are described as sisters despite the differences?

The Truth of the Church is indivisible because it is Christ Himself. But when there are differences in dogmas there cannot be unity in Christ.

From what we know about Church History, Churches were called Sister Churches when they held the same faith. Never was the Orthodox Church called a sister of any heterodox churches, regardless of the degree of heterodoxy or cacodoxy they held.

We ask ourselves a basic question: have religious syncretism and doctrinal minimalism — the byproducts of secularization and humanism — perhaps influenced the Orthodox signers of the document?

It is apparent that the document adopts, perhaps for the first time by the Orthodox side, the position that two Churches, the Orthodox and Roman Catholic, together constitute the One Holy Church or are two legitimate expressions of her.

Unfortunately, it is the first time that Orthodox have officially accepted a form of the branch theory.

Permit us to express our deep sorrow over this in as much as this theory comes into screaming conflict with Orthodox Tradition and Consciousness until now.

We have many witnesses to the Orthodox Consciousness that our Church alone constitutes the One Holy Church, and they are recognized as pan-Orthodox in authority. They are the:

1. Council of Constantinople, 1722;

2. Council of Constantinople, 1727;

3. Council of Constantinople, 1838;

4. 1848 Encyclical of the Four Patriarchs of the East and their synods;

5. Council of Constantinople, 1895.

These decreed that only our Holy Orthodox Church constitutes the One Holy Church.

The 1895 Council of Constantinople summarizes all of the preceding Councils: Orthodoxy, that is, the Eastern Church, justly boasts in Christ that she is the Church of the Seven Ecumenical Councils and the first nine centuries of Christianity and is therefore the One, Holy, Catholic, and Apostolic Church of Christ, the 'pillar and bulwark of truth.' And the present Roman Church is the church of innovationism and adulteration of the writings of the Church Fathers and the distortion of the Holy Scriptures and the decrees of the Holy Councils. Justly and for good reason it was denounced and is denounced as long as it persists in its delusion. 'Better a praiseworthy war,' says Saint Gregory of Nazianzus, 'than a peace separated from God.' Representatives of the Orthodox Churches declared the same things at World Council of Churches conferences. Among them were distinguished Orthodox theologians, such as Father George Florovsky. Thus, at the Conference of Lund in 1952, it was declared: We came here not to judge other Churches but to help them see the truth, to enlighten their thought in a brotherly manner, informing them of the teachings of the One, Holy, Catholic and Apostolic Church, that is to say, the Greek Orthodox Church, which is unaltered from the apostolic period.

At Evanston in 1954: "In conclusion, we are obliged to declare our deep conviction that the Holy Orthodox Church alone has preserved 'the faith once delivered unto the saints' in all of its fullness and purity. And this is not because of any human merit of ours but because God is pleased to preserve His treasure in earthen vessels...

And at New Delhi in 1961: "Unity has been broken and it is necessary that it be won anew. For the Orthodox Church is not a Confession, not one of the many or one among the many. For the Orthodox, the Orthodox Church is the Church. The Orthodox Church has the perception and consciousness that her inner structure and teaching coincide with the apostolic kerygma and the tradition of the ancient, undivided Church. The Orthodox Church exists in the unbroken and continuous succession of the sacramental ministry, of the sacramental life, and of the faith. The apostolic succession of the episcopal office and the sacramental ministry, for the Orthodox, is truly a component of the essence and, for this reason, a necessary element in the existence of the whole Church. In accordance with her inner conviction and an awareness of the circumstances, the Orthodox Church occupies a special and extraordinary position in divided Christendom as the bearer and witness of the tradition of the ancient, undivided Church, from which the present Christian denominations originate by way of reduction and separation."

We could also set forth here the testimonies of the most distinguished and widely acknowledged Orthodox theologians. We shall limit ourselves to one, the late Father Demetrios Staniloae, a theologian distinguished not only for his wisdom but for the breadth and Orthodox mindset of ecumenical perspective.

In many places of his noteworthy book, *Towards an Orthodox Ecumenism*, he refers to themes that are relevant to the joint statement [being discussed here] and bears Orthodox witness. Through it, therefore, the disagreement between the positions taken in the document and the Orthodox faith shall be shown:

> "Without unity of faith and without communion in the same Body and Blood of the Incarnate Word, such a Church could not exist, nor could a Church in the full meaning of the word."

> "In the case of one who is entering into full communion of faith with the members of the Orthodox Church and is becoming a member, economia [dispensation] is understood to give validity to a Mystery previously performed outside of the Church."

> "In the Roman Catholic view, the Church is not so much a spiritual organism that is headed by Christ as it is a nomocanonical organization which, even in the best of circumstances, lives not in the divine but in the supernatural[581] level of created grace."

---

581 In the Western context here, the supernatural which man experiences or participated in, like created grace, refers to something that is not uncreated: "What is received in the creature must itself be created." *Catholic Encyclopedia*, Vol. 13, New York, 1967, 815.

"In the preservation of this unity, an indispensable role is played by the unity of faith because the latter wholly bonds the members with Christ and with one another."

"Those who confess not a whole and integral Christ but only certain parts of Him cannot achieve a complete communion either with the Church or with one another."

"How it is possible for the Catholics to unite with the Orthodox in a common eucharist when they believe that unity is derived more from the Pope than from the Holy Eucharist? Can love for the world spring forth from the Pope, that is, the love which springs from the Christ of the Holy Eucharist?"

"There is a growing recognition of the fact that Orthodoxy, as the complete body of Christ, reaches out in a concrete way to take in the parts that were separated."

It is self-evident that two complete bodies of Christ cannot exist.

III

Your All Holiness, one has to wonder why the Orthodox proceed to make these concessions while the Roman Catholics not only persist in but reinforce their pope-centered ecclesiology.

It is a fact that the Second Vatican Council [1963] not only neglected to minimize the primacy and infallibility [of the Pope], indeed, it magnified these. According to the late Professor John Karmiris, "Despite the fact that the Second Vatican Council covered over the familiar Latin claims about the Papacy's monarchical absolute rule with the mantle of the collegiality of the bishops, not only were those claims not diminished; on the contrary, they were reinforced by this Council. The present Pope [John XXIII] does not hesitate to promote them, even at inopportune times, with much emphasis."

And the Pope's Encyclical, "To the Bishops of the Catholic Church" (May 28, 1992), recognizes only Rome as the "catholic" church and the Pope as the only "catholic" bishop. The church of Rome and her bishop compose the "essence" of all other churches. Moreover, every local church and her bishop simply constitute expressions of the direct "presence" and "authority" of the bishop of Rome and his church, which determines from within every local church's ecclesial identity."

According to this papal document, since the Orthodox Churches refuse to submit to the Pope, they do not bear the character of the Church at all and are simply viewed as "partial churches." "*Verdienen der titer teilkirchen.*"

The same ecclesiology is expressed in *The Ecumenical Guide* ("a guide for the application of principles and agenda regarding ecumenism") of the Roman Catholic Church, presented by Cardinal Cassidy to the meeting of Roman Catholic bishops (May 10-15, 1993, one month before Balamand), with non-Catholics and indeed Orthodox in attendance.

The Ecumenical Guide stresses that Roman Catholics "maintain the firm conviction that the singular Church of Christ subsists in the Catholic Church, which is ruled by the successor to Peter and by bishops who are in communion with him," in as much as the "College of Bishops has as its head the Bishop of Rome, the successor to Peter."

In the same document, many nice-sounding things are said about the need to develop an ecumenical dialogue and ecumenical education — obviously to muddy the waters and draw away naive Orthodox by that effective, Vatican-designed method of unity, i.e., of submission to Rome.

The method, according to *The Ecumenical Guide*, is the following: The criteria that were established for ecumenical collaboration, on the one hand, are mutual recognition of baptism and the placement of the common symbols of faith in empirical liturgical life; and on the other, are collaboration in ecumenical education, joint prayer, and pastoral cooperation in order that we may be moved from conflict to coexistence, from coexistence to collaboration, from collaboration to sharing, from sharing to communion.

Such documents, however, that are full of hypocrisy are generally received as positive by the Orthodox.

We are saddened to ascertain that the joint declaration is founded upon the above Roman Catholic reasoning. Because of these recent developments under such terms, however, we begin to ask ourselves if those who claim that the various dialogues are detrimental to Orthodoxy might be justified after all.

Most Holy Father and Despota, in human terms, by means of that joint declaration Roman Catholics have succeeded in gaining from certain Orthodox recognition as the legitimate continuation of the One Holy Church with the fullness of Truth, Grace, Priesthood, Mysteries, and Apostolic Succession.

But that success is to their own detriment because it removes from them the possibility of acknowledging and repenting of their grave ecclesiology and doctrinal illness. For this reason, the concessions by Orthodox are not philanthropic. They are not for the good of either the Roman Catholics or the Orthodox. They jump from *the hope of the Gospel* (Col. 1:23) of Christ, the only God-Man, to the Pope, the man-god and idol of Western humanism.

For the sake of the Roman Catholics and the whole world, whose only hope is unadulterated Orthodoxy, we are obliged never to accept union or the description of the Roman Catholic Church as a "Sister Church," or the Pope as the canonical bishop of Rome, or the "Church" of Rome as having canonical Apostolic Succession, Priesthood, and Mysteries without their [the Papists'] expressly stated renunciation of the *Filioque*, the infallibility and primacy of the Pope, created grace, and the rest of their cacodoxies. For we shall never regard these as unimportant differences or mere theological opinions, but as differences that irrevocably debase the theanthropic character of the Church and introduce blasphemies.

The following decisions of Vatican II are typical:

> The Roman Pontiff, the successor to Peter, is the permanent and visible source and foundation of the unity of the bishops and of the multitude of the faithful.

> This religious submission of the will and mind must be manifested in a special way before the authentic teaching authority of the Roman Pontiff, even when he is not speaking *ex cathedra*.

> The Roman Pontiff, the head of the college of bishops, by virtue of his office, possesses infallibility when, strengthening his brethren (Luke 23:32) as the shepherd and highest teacher of all

the faithful, he declares a teaching through an act of definition regarding faith or morals. For this reason it is justly said that the decrees of the Pope are irreversible in nature and not subject to dispensation by the Church inasmuch as they were pronounced with the collaboration of the Holy Spirit... Consequently, the decrees of the Pope are subject to no other approval, to no other appeal, to no other judgment. For the Roman Pontiff does not express his opinion as a private person but as the highest teacher of the universal Church, upon whom personally rests the gift of the infallibility of the very Church herself and who sets forth and protects the teaching of the Catholic Faith.

In the course of his responsibility as the vicar of Christ and shepherd of the whole Church, the Roman Pontiff has the fullest, highest, and universal authority in the Church, which he is always empowered to exercise freely... There cannot exist an Ecumenical Council if it is not validated or at least accepted by the successor to Peter. The convocation, presidency, and approval of the decisions of the Councils are the prerogative of the Roman Pontiff.

Do all of these teachings, Your All Holiness, not fall upon Orthodox ears as blasphemy against the Holy Spirit and against the Divine Builder of the Church, Jesus Christ, the only eternal and infallible Head of the Church from Whom alone springs forth the unity of the Church? Do these not utterly contradict the Gospel-centered and God-Man-centered Orthodox Ecclesiology inspired by the Holy Spirit? Do they not subordinate the God-man to man?

How can we make concessions or co-exist with such a spirit without losing our faith and salvation? Remaining faithful to all that we have received from our Holy Fathers, we shall never accept the present Roman "Church" as co-representative with ours of the One, Holy, Catholic, and Apostolic Church of Christ.

We consider it necessary that among the theological differences the distinction between the essence and the energy of God, and the uncreatedness of the divine energies be noted, because if grace is created, as the Roman Catholics claim, salvation and the theosis of man is nullified, and the Church ceases to be a communion of theosis and degenerates into a nomocanonical institution.

Deeply pained in our soul because of all the above, we have recourse to you our Spiritual Father. And with deepest respect, we call upon you and implore you, in your characteristic pastoral understanding and sensitivity, to take this most grave matter in hand and not accept the [Balamand] document, and generally to take every possible action to stave off the undesirable consequences it will have for pan-Orthodox unity if by chance some Churches adopt it.

Moreover, we ask for your holy and God-obedient prayers so that we too who are lowly inhabitants and monastics of the Holy Mountain, in this time of spiritual confusion, compromise, secularization, and the dulling of our doctrinal acuity, may remain faithful unto death to that which was passed on to us by our Holy Fathers *as a form of doctrine* (Rom. 6:17), whatever that may cost us.

With deepest respect, we venerate your holy right hand.

Signed by:
All Representatives and Presidents of the Twenty Sacred Monasteries of the Holy Mountain of Athos

PS. Note that this letter was also sent to the Churches that participated in the theological dialogue and are, therefore, directly concerned, and to the remaining Churches to keep them informed.

3. An Open Letter to the Holy Abbots and the Holy Representatives of the Sacred Twenty Monasteries in the Holy Community of the Holy Mount Athos

*The So-Called Kelliotes Letter
to the Sacred Twenty Athonite Monasteries, 2006*[582]

Holy Abbots and Holy Fathers,
Bless!

We desire with this present letter to express our deepest concern and sadness for all that is happening to our Holy Orthodoxy for years now: things destructive to the teaching of the Holy Apostles and of the Holy Fathers and contrary to all the Sacred Canons enacted by the Oecumenical and local synods. We wonder if some Oecumenical synod has been assembled and has abolished the Canons which forbid joint prayer with heretics, or if the Pope has repented and renounced the heresies of the *Filioque*, of primacy, of infallibility, of unleavened bread, of the purifying fire [purgatory], of created grace, of the immaculate conception of the Most Holy Theotokos, and many others, most of which have been condemned and anathematized repeatedly by Orthodox synods and by the entirety of the Holy Fathers. Heaven was angered and the Holy Fathers exceedingly saddened by seeing and hearing all that took place at the Phanar at the feast of the Holy Apostle Andrew on the 30th of November of the current year — unprecedented and unheard of things in the two thousand year history of the Church: "The dogmas of the Fathers are held in contempt, the Apostolic traditions are disdained, the churches are subject to the novelties of innovators," as St. Basil the Great says, regarding the events of his own times.

Everything happened literally upside-down. Instead of the heretical Pope being placed below, as we see the heretics depicted in the icons of the Holy Synods, and being dismissed from the Divine Liturgy, on the

---

582 "An Open Letter to the Holy Abbots and the Holy Representatives of the Sacred Twenty Monasteries in the Holy Community of the Holy Mount Athos," Orthodox Christian Information Center, accessed March 26th, 2023, http:// orthodoxinfo.com/ecumenism/kelliotes.aspx

basis of the liturgical command, "the doors, the doors, in wisdom let us attend," we elevated him to a high throne, where he sat wearing an *omophorion*; the Orthodox deacons censed him; the Patriarch exchanged the kiss [of peace] with him at "let us love one another;" as the *proestos* [the one presiding] he proclaimed the "Our Father;" the choir of sacred cantors chanted "Many Years" to him, as well as a specially composed troparion from an Athonite hymnographer — Lord, have mercy! — if, of course, the news reports are true; he was [also] permitted to give the congregation his blessing [*evlogia*], or, rather, his folly [*alogia*] according to the Sacred Canons.

We allowed the Church militant on earth to be divided from the Church triumphant of the Saints in heaven, and to be united with churches and assemblies of the cunning heretics. We insulted all of the holy Martyrs and Confessors who struggled to the point of blood against the heresies, because we presented their struggles, their martyrdoms and their confessions as to no avail and unnecessary. Will not the blessed Hagiorite Fathers martyred under [Oecumenical Patriarch John] Vekkou, who refused to accept and to commemorate the Pope, lament, seeing that not only do we reject their example by our silence, but actually do the opposite? Why then did these and all of the previous Martyrs undergo martyrdom, and why did the Confessors stand fast in their profession of the Faith?

You know, Reverend Fathers, better than we do, the anti-Orthodox and blasphemous actions, declarations, and decisions of the Oecumenical Patriarch, and of the other Primates and Bishops who vociferously and visibly advocate bare-headed the acceptance and teaching of the chief heresy of Ecumenism, the greatest ecclesiological heresy of all the ages. This heretical teaching disavows the uniqueness of the One, Holy, Catholic, and Apostolic Church and equates it with the heresies, by accepting their sacraments as having and imparting sanctifying and saving grace. Besides recognition of the baptism of the followers of the Pope and of the Lutherans, we also have participation in the chalice with Monophysites, and in many cases with Papists in the Cyclades and in the Diaspora.

We take stock with much greater sadness that over the last few years the spiritual leadership of the Holy Mountain has not confronted these manifestations of apostasy with fortitude and the courage of confession, as did earlier Athonite Fathers. The Patriarch has gauged our responses, and because they are half-hearted, and many times non-existent, he proceeds without hindrance toward union with an unrepentant Pope, who remains enmeshed in heresies. He evaluated us and rejoiced greatly during his last visit to the Holy Mountain, as well, such that one would say that he came in order to take the consent and blessing of the Athonites for all that he had planned to do with the Pope a few days later.

We, lowly hieromonks and monks, confess to you that we have been scandalized by the silence and inaction of our spiritual leaders on Mount Athos, and together with us, the entire assembly of monastic-loving Orthodox Christians, both in Greece and throughout the world. They are all waiting to hear the voice of Mount Athos. From you, the wiser and more erudite, we learned that when the Faith is endangered, we are all held accountable if we are silent and shrink back, as St. Theodore the Studite says. A monk, in particular, must not allow the slightest innovation in matters of the Faith, according to the [aforementioned] Holy Father and great monastic leader, organizer of monastic life, and the Elder of us all. He did not fear the threats and the persecutions of the iconoclast emperors and patriarchs, but within Constantinople, within the enclosure of the Great Sacred Monastery of Stoudion, he organized a procession with a thousand torch-bearing monks, who held the forbidden Holy Icons in their hands.

Saints Sabbas the Sanctified and Theodosios the Cenobite, likewise great monastic leaders, assembled ten thousand monks of Palestine long before in Jerusalem, and saved Orthodoxy from the heresy of Monothelitism. Who will now save the Church from the most terrible heresy of Ecumenism and the deceit of Papism? The letters of protest, which the Holy Community [of Mount Athos] has sent at various times to the Oecumenical Patriarch, have not had any effect. It is no longer time for words, but for actions. We do not want to teach you, we the unlearned and wretched sinners, neither do we want to have ourselves appear as Confessors. Rather, we want to set at ease our monastic and Orthodox conscience; we want to honor and follow the conduct of the Holy Martyrs and Confessors, particularly those martyred under Vekkou. We do not want to shrink back, nor to place the monasteries and our brother-hoods above the purity of the Faith, above God and the Truth.

We believe that after so many written and oral protests and objections, back-peddling, retreats and compromises, the only thing that will gladden the Orthodox and shame the cacodox is to cease commemoration of the patriarch and of all the bishops agreeing with him or remaining in silence. Gather together, Holy Fathers, the monks of the coenobium, the sketes and the kellia into an all-monastic, fighting assembly — either within or outside of the Holy Mountain — and topple the towers of heresy, of Papism and of Ecumenism. Take up the good fight of the Faith. If you fail to act, we will prefer to do that which is God-pleasing, not man-appeasing.

May God enlighten all of us; may the Most Holy Theotokos shelter and bless her Garden; and may They protect the Orthodox Church from defamers of the Theotokos, and from heretics who fight against the Saints, as well as from faint-hearted pastors who leave the flock unprotected from attacks of the wolves.

Asking your prayers for all the foregoing, we, the undersigned, remain respectfully yours,

Hieromonk Ephraim, former abbot [of Philotheou], Elder of the Skete of Apostle Andrew ["Serrai", of the Holy Monastery of Vatopedi] and the brotherhood with me.

Elder Eustratios, Hieromonk, Holy Monastery of the Great Lavra
Elder Poimen, Hieromonk, Holy Monastery of Zographou
Elder Basileios, Hieromonk, Holy Monastery of Zographou
Elder Bessarion, Hieromonk, Holy Monastery of Zographou
Monk Nikodemos (Bilalis), Sacred Cell "of the Presentation" from Kapsala
Monk Artemios, Holy Monastery of the Great Lavra
Priestmonk Hilarion, Holy Monastery of the Great Lavra
Monk Paisios, Holy Monastery of the Great Lavra
Monk Savvas, Holy Monastery of the Great Lavra
Hierodeacon Chariton, Holy Monastery of the Great Lavra
Monk Chariton, Karoulia, Holy Monastery of the Great Lavra
Monk Athanasios, Karoulia, Holy Monastery of the Great Lavra
Elder Vlasios, Monk, Kserokalyvo Viglas, Holy Monastery of the Great Lavra
Monk Akakios, Sacred Kathisma of the Holy Trinity (Kyr Isaiah) Holy Monastery of the Great Lavra
Elder Isaiah, Monk, Kellion of the Birth of the Mother of God, Holy Monastery of the Great Lavra

Monk Cherubim, Sacred place of the Archangels,
Holy Monastery of the Great Lavra
Hieromonk Damaskinos, Kellion of Holy Trinity at Karyes,
Holy Monastery of the Great Lavra
Elder Nektarios, Monk, Kellion of Holy Trinity at Karyes,
Holy Monastery of the Great Lavra
Elder Theoklitos, Monk and the fathers with him; Kellion of the Sacred
Forerunner, St. Anne's Skete, Holy Monastery of the Great Lavra
Hieromonk Gabriel, Sacred Kellion of St. George (Kartsounaion) Sacred Skete
of St. Anne, Holy Monastery of the Great Lavra
Hieromonk Chrysostomos Kartsonas, Holy Monastery of the Great Lavra
Elder Kosmas Monk, Sacred Hut of St. Demetrios, Skete of Saint Anne,
Holy Monastery of the Great Lavra
Elder Panteleimon, Monk, Sacred Kellion of St. Panteleimon, Sacred Skete of
Holy Trinity, Holy Monastery of the Great Lavra
Elder Sophronios, Monk, Sacred Hut of Entrance of the Theotokos, Sacred
Skete of Holy Trinity, Holy Monastery of the Great Lavra
Monk Parthenios, Sacred Hut Entrance of Theotokos, Sacred Skete of Holy
Trinity, Holy Monastery of the Great Lavra
Monk Athanasios at Vouleutiria, Holy Monastery of the Great Lavra
Elder Serapheim, Hieromonk, Kellion of All Saints, Skete of Saint Anne, Holy
Monastery of the Great Lavra
Elder Daniel, Monk, Saint Anne's, Holy Monastery of the Great Lavra
Elder Gerasimos, Monk Sacred Hut of St. George, Katounakia,
Holy Monastery of the Great Lavra
Elder Benediktos, Hieromonk, Kellion of Ss. Konstantine and Eleni,
Holy Monastery of Vatopedi
Monk Paisios, Kellion of Archangels (Savvaion) Karyes,
Holy Monastery of Hilandar
Monk Silouanos, Sacred Hut of St. Nicholas, Nea Skete,
Holy Monastery of St. Paul
Monk Gabriel, Kellion of Koutloumousiou of Saint Christodoulos
Monk Dositheos, Koutloumousiou Monastery Kathisma
Elder Nektarios, Monk, Sacred Hut of Holy Trinity,
Skete of the Holy Monastery of Koutloumousiou
Monk Paisios, Kellion of Saint Barbara, Holy Monastery of Koutloumousiou
Elder Moses, Monk, Kellion St. John Chrysostomos,
Skete of St. Panteleimonos, Holy Monastery of Koutloumousiou
Elder Abraaham, Hieromonk, Sacred Hut of St. Gerasimos Kefalinias, Skete of
St. Panteleimonos, Holy Monastery of Koutloumousiou
Elder Spyridon, Monk, Kellion of St. Nicholas,
Holy Monastery of Koutloumousiou
Monk Theodoulos, formerly of the Holy Monastery of Koutloumousiou

Elder Chrysostom, Hieromonk, Kellion of St. Spyridon of Kerkyra, Holy Monastery of Koutloumousiou

Monk Hilarion, Sacred Kathisma of the Holy Monastery of Doheiariou (Platon area)

Elder Nikodemos, Monk, Kellion of St. Nektarios Kapsala, Holy Monastery of Pantokratoros

Hieromonk Gabriel, Kellion of Quick to Hear Mother of God, Holy Monastery of Pantokratoros

Monk Isaac, Kellion of Birth of Mother of God, Kapsala, Holy Monastery of Pantokratoros

Elder Athanasios, Monk, Kellion of St. Athanasios, Holy Monastery of Pantokratoros

Elder Meletios, Monk, Birth of Theotokos, Kapsala, Holy Monastery of Pantokratoros

Elder Gregory, Monk Kellion of St. Nicholas, Kapsala, Holy Monastery of Pantokratoros

Elder Onoufrios, Monk, Kellion Dormition of Theotokos, Karyes

Elder Nicholas, Monk, Kellion of St. Demetrios, Karyes

Hieromonk Gabriel, Kellion of Holy Archangels (Kombologas) Karyes

4. The Official Statement from Mt. Athos on the Pope's Visit to the Phanar[583]

KARYES, 30 DECEMBER 2006

The recent visit of Pope Benedict XVI to the Ecumenical Patriarchate on the occasion of the feast-day of Saint Andrew (30th November 2006) and thereafter the visit by His Beatitude the Archbishop of Athens Christodoulos (14th December 2006) gave rise to a multitude of impressions, evaluations and reactions. We shall bypass those things that the secular Press had evaluated as positive or negative, to focus on those things that pertain to our salvation, for the sake of which we abandoned the world to live in the barrenness of the Holy Mountain.

---

583 "The Official Statement from Mt. Athos on the Pope's Visit to the Phanar," Orthodox Christian Information Center, accessed March 26th, 2023, http://orthodoxinfo.com/ecumenism/athos_popevisit2006.aspx

As Monks of the Holy Mountain, we respect the Ecumenical Patriarchate, under whose jurisdiction we fall. We honor and venerate the Most Holy Ecumenical Patriarch Bartholomew and we rejoice in all that he has achieved and so diligently labored for, in his love of God, for the Church. We particularly commemorate the stolid and untiring defence of the Ecumenical Patriarchate, amid the many unfavorable conditions that exist, as well as the impoverished local Orthodox Churches and the care that is taken to project the message of the Orthodox Church throughout the world. Furthermore, we the Monks of the Holy Mountain honor the Most Holy Church of Greece, from which most of us originate, and we respect His Beatitude the Primate.

However, the events that took place during the recent visits of the Pope to Fanarion and of His Beatitude the Archbishop to the Vatican brought immense sorrow to our hearts. We desire and we struggle all of our life to safeguard the trust of the Holy Fathers, which was bequeathed to us by the holy Founders of our sacred Monasteries and the blessed reposed fathers before us. We strive to the best of our ability to live the sacrament of the Church and the unblemished Orthodox Faith, according to what we are daily taught by the divine Services, the sacred readings, and the teachings in general of the Holy Fathers which are set out in their writings and in the decisions of the Ecumenical Synods. We guard our dogmatic awareness "like the pupil of our eye," and we reinforce it, by applying ourselves to God-pleasing labours and the meticulous study of the achievements of the holy Confessor Fathers when they confronted the miscellaneous heresies, and especially of our father among the saints, Gregory of Palamas, the Holy Martyrs of the Holy Mountain and the Holy Martyr Kosmas the First, whose sacred relics we venerate with every honor and whose sacred memory we incessantly celebrate. We are afraid to remain silent, whenever issues arise that pertain to the trust that our Fathers left us. Our responsibility, towards the most venerable fathers and brothers of the overall brotherhood of the Holy Mountain and towards the pious faithful of the Church who regard Athonite Monasticism as their non-negotiable guardian of sacred Tradition, weighs heavily upon our conscience.

The visits of the Pope at Fanarion and the Archbishop's visit at the Vatican may have secured certain benefits of a secular nature, however, during those visits, various other events took place which were not according to the customs of Orthodox Ecclesiology, or commitments were made that would neither benefit the Orthodox Church, nor any other heterodox Christians.

First of all, the Pope was received as though he were a canonical (proper) bishop of Rome. During the service, the Pope wore an *omophorion*; he was addressed by the Ecumenical Patriarch with the greeting "blessed is the one who comes in the name of the Lord" as though it were Christ the Lord; he blessed the congregation, and he was commemorated as "most holy" and "His Beatitude the Bishop of Rome." Furthermore, all of the Pope's officiating clergy wore an *omophorion* during the Orthodox Divine Liturgy; also, the reciting of the Lord's Prayer, his liturgical embrace with the Patriarch, were displays of something more than common prayer. And all of this, when the papist institution has not budged at all from its heretical teachings and its policy; on the contrary, the Pope is in fact visibly promoting and trying to reinforce *Unia* along with the Papist dogmas on primacy and infallibility, and is going even further, with inter-faith common prayers and the pan-religious hegemony of the Pope of Rome that is discerned therein. As for the reception of the Pope in Fanarion, we are especially grieved by the fact that all of the Media kept repeating the same, incorrect information, that the psalms that were (unduly) sung at the time had been composed by Monks of the Holy Mountain. We take this opportunity to responsibly inform all pious Christians that their composer was not, and could never be, a monk of the Holy Mountain.

Then there is the matter of the attempt by His Beatitude the Archbishop of Athens to commence relations with the Vatican on social, cultural and bio-ethical issues, as well as the objective to mutually defend the Christian roots of Europe (positions which are also found in the Common Declaration of the Pope and the Patriarch in Fanarion), both of which may seem innocuous or even positive, given that their aim is to cultivate peaceful human relations. Nevertheless, it is important that all these do not give the impression that the West and Orthodoxy continue to have the same bases, or lead one into forgetting the distance that separates the Orthodox Tradition from that which is usually presented as the "European spirit." (Western) Europe is burdened with a series of anti-Christian institutions and acts, such as the Crusades, the "Holy" Inquisition, slave trading and colonization. It is burdened with the tragic division which took on the form of the schism of Protestantism; the devastating world wars, also the man-centered humanism and its atheist view. All of these are the consequence of Rome's theological deviations from Orthodoxy.

One after the other, the Papist and the Protestant heresies gradually removed the humble Christ of Orthodoxy and in His place, they enthroned haughty Man. The holy bishop Nicholas of Ochrid and Zitsa wrote the following from Dahau, "What, then, is Europe? The Pope and Luther [...] This is what Europe is, at its core, ontologically and historically." The blessed Elder Justin Popovich supplements the above, "The 2nd Vatican Synod comprises the rebirth of every kind of European humanism because the Synod persistently adhered to the dogma on the Pope's infallibility" and he surmises, "Undoubtedly, the authorities and the powers of (western) European culture and civilization are Christ-expellers." This is why it is so important to project the humble morality of Orthodoxy and to support the truly Christian roots of the united Europe; the roots that Europe had during the first Christian centuries, during the time of the catacombs and of the seven holy Ecumenical Synods. It is advisable for Orthodoxy to not tax itself with foreign sins, and furthermore, the impression should not be given to those who became de-Christianized in reaction to the sidetracking of Western-style Christianity, that Orthodoxy is related to it, thus ceasing to testify that it is the only authentic Faith in Christ, and the only hope of the peoples of Europe.

The Roman Catholics' inability to disentangle themselves from the decisions of their pursuant (and according to them, Ecumenical) Synods, which had legitimized the Filioque, the Primacy, the Infallibility, the secular authority of the Roman Pontiff, created Grace, the immaculate conception of the Holy Mother, *Unia*. Despite all these, we Orthodox continue the so-called traditional exchanges of visits, bestowing honors befitting an Orthodox Bishop on the Pope and totally disregarding a series of Sacred Canons which forbid common prayers, while the theological dialogue repeatedly flounders, and, after being dredged from the depths, it again sinks down.

All indications lead to the conclusion that the Vatican is not orienting itself to discard its heretical teachings, but only to "reinterpret" them — in other words, to veil them. Roman Catholic ecclesiology varies, from one circular to the other; from the so-called "open" ecclesiology of the Encyclical "*Ut Unum Sint*," to the ecclesiological exclusivity of the Encyclical "*Dominus Jesus*." It should be noted that both of the aforementioned views are contrary to Orthodox Ecclesiology. The self-awareness of the Holy Orthodox Church as the only One, Holy, Catholic and Apostolic Church does not allow for the recognition of other, heterodox churches and confessions as "sister churches." Sister Churches are only the local Orthodox Churches of the same faith. No other homonymous reference to "sister churches" other than the Orthodox one is theologically permissible.

The "*Filioque*" is promoted by the Roman Catholic side as yet another legal expression of the teaching regarding the procession of the Holy Spirit, and theologically equivalent to the Orthodox teaching that procession is "only from the Father" — a view that is unfortunately supported by some of our own theologians. Besides, the Pontiff is maintaining the Primacy as an inalienable privilege, as one can tell from the recent erasure of the title "Patriarch of the West" by the current Pope Benedict XVI; also from his reference to the worldwide mission of the Apostle Peter and his successors during his homily in the Patriarchal Temple, as well as from his also recent speech, which included the following, "within the society, with the Successors of the Apostles, whose visible unity is guaranteed by the Successor of the Apostle Peter, the Ukrainian Catholic Community managed to preserve the Sacred Tradition alive, in its integrity" (Catholic Newspaper, No.3046/18-4-2006).

Unia is being reinforced and reassured in many and various ways, despite the proclamations by the Pope to the contrary. This dishonest stance is witnessed, apart from other instances, by the provocative intervention of the previous Pope, John-Paul II, which led the Orthodox-Roman Catholic Dialogue in Baltimore into a disaster, as well as by the letter sent by the current Pope to the Cardinal Ljubomir Husar, the Uniate Archbishop of Ukraine. In this letter dated 22/2/2006, the following is emphatically stressed, "it is imperative to secure the presence of the two great carriers of the only Tradition (the Latin and the Eastern). The mission that the Greek Catholic Church has undertaken, being in full communion with the Successor of the Apostle Peter, is two-fold: on one side, it must visibly preserve the Eastern Tradition inside the Catholic Church; on the other, it must favour the merging of the two traditions, testifying that they not only can coordinate between themselves, but that they also constitute a profound union amid their variety."

Seen in this light, polite exchanges such as the visits of the Pope to Fanarion and the Archbishop of Athens to the Vatican, without the prerequisite of a unity in the Faith, may on the one hand create false impressions of unity and thus turn away the heterodox who could have looked towards Orthodoxy as being the true Church, and on the other hand, blunt the dogmatic sensor of many Orthodox. Even more, they may push some of the faithful and pious Orthodox, who are deeply concerned over what is taking place inopportunely and against the Sacred Canons, to detach themselves from the corpus of the Church and create new schisms.

Thus, out of love for our Orthodoxy, but with pain as regards the unity of the Church, and with a view to preserve the Orthodox Faith free of all innovations, we proclaim in every direction that which was proclaimed by the Extraordinary, Double, Holy Assembly of our Sacred Community of the Holy Mountain on the 9th/22nd of April 1980:

> We believe that our Holy Orthodox Church is the One, Holy, Catholic and Apostolic Church of Christ, having the fullness of Grace and the Truth, and for this reason, an uninterrupted Apostolic Succession. On the contrary, the "churches" and the "confessions" of the West, having distorted the faith of the Gospel, the Apostles and the Fathers on many points, are deprived of the hallowing Grace, the true Sacraments and the Apostolic Succession. Dialogues with the heterodox — if they are intended to inform them about the Orthodox Faith so that when they become receptive of divine enlightenment and their eyes are opened, they might return to the Orthodox Faith — are not condemned.

In no way should a theological dialogue be accompanied by common prayers, participation in liturgical assemblies and worship by either side and any other activities that might give the impression that our Orthodox Church acknowledges the Roman Catholics as a complete Church and the Pope as a canonical (proper) Bishop of Rome. Such acts mislead the Orthodox as well as the Roman Catholic faithful, who are given a false impression of what Orthodoxy thinks of them. With the Grace of God, the Holy Mountain remains faithful — as do the Orthodox people of the Lord — to the Faith of the Holy Apostles and the Holy Fathers, and also out of love for the heterodox, who are essentially helped, when the Orthodox with their steadfast Orthodox stance point out the extent of their spiritual ailment and the way they can be cured.

The failed attempts for union during the past teach us that for a permanent union, according to the will of God, within the Truth of the Church, the prerequisite is a different kind of preparation and course, than those which were followed in the past and appear to be followed to this day.

By all of the Representatives and Superiors of the Common Assembly of the Twenty Sacred Monasteries of the Holy Mountain Athos.

Christ Pantocrator, icon from Daphni, c. 1100

PART V

CONFESSING HIERARCHS & HOLY ELDERS

Metropolitan Philaret of New York

A. CONFESSING HIERARCHS

In addition to the saints already commemorated for their defense of Orthodoxy against Latin heresies, there are other hierarchs and holy elders which the Church has not (yet) glorified as saints but who have nevertheless been honored in the sacred histories and publications of the Church for their defense of the true Faith against Latin heresies.

1. Patriarch Michael Cerularius of Constantinople (1000-1056)

a. Letter to Patriarch Peter II of Antioch[584]

But you know very well that the Romans are not spitted on only one pike—the one regarding azymes [unleavened bread in the Eucharist] which is clearly known to all—but on many and various ones. On account of these it is necessary to avoid them. Their Judaizing practices are as follows: that same charge pending regarding azymes; eating strangled beasts; shaving; observing the Sabbath; eating unclean meats; monks eating pig's fat and all the skin right down to the meat; behaving in the same manner in the first week of Lent, Cheesefare Week, as in the week before; eating meat on Wednesday and cheese and eggs on Friday,

---

584 Patriarch Michael Keroularios, "Μιχαὴλ τοῦ ἁγιωτάτου ἀρχιεπισκόπου Κωνσταντινουπόλεως νέας ʽΡώμη καὶ οἰκουμενικοῦ τοῦ Κηρουλαρίου πρὸς Πέτρον τὸν ἁγιώτατον πατριάρχην Θεουπόλεως μεγάλας Ἀντιοχέιας." in *Patrologia Graeca, Vol. 120*, trans. Jacques Paul Migne (1857-1866) & Tia M. Kolbaba (2000) (Paris: Imprimerie Catholique, 1857), 789-792.

but fasting all day on the Sabbath. Beyond these [Judaizing practices] such things as the following are also true: reasoning badly and dangerously, they have made some sort of addition to the holy creed, so that it is as follows: ". . . and in the Holy Spirit, the Lord, the giver of life, who proceeds from the Father and the Son." And in the divine service they intone, "One holy, one Lord, Jesus Christ, in the glory of God the Father, with the Holy Spirit." They forbid the marriage of priests. That is, those who have wives cannot take up the dignity of the priesthood, but those who wish to be priests must be unyoked. Two brothers marry two sisters. During the liturgy, at the time for taking communion, one of the celebrants eats the unleavened bread [azyme] and then he kisses the others. Their bishops wear rings on their hands, as if, indeed, they took their churches as brides, and they say that they wear [the ring] as a pledge. Bishops, going forth to battle, stain their hands with blood, killing and being killed. As many have reported to us, they perform holy baptism by baptizing the candidates with only one immersion, invoking the name of the Father and of the Son and of the Holy Spirit. Also, they fill the mouths of the baptized with salt. Wrongly receiving the apostolic saying which reads, "A little leaven leavens the whole loaf," they have written it down thus: "A little leaven corrupts the whole loaf." Thus they try, through this little occasion of a word, to set aside the yeast which raises the leavened bread. They do not adore the relics of the saints. Some of them do not venerate icons, either. They accept neither our Fathers, teachers, and high priests—I mean Gregory the Theologian, Basil the Great, and the Divine Chrysostom, along with other saints whom they enumerate—nor any of their teaching. They do also other things which it would be a great work to enumerate one by one. Therefore, if they live in such a way and, enfeebled by such customs, dare these things which are obviously lawless, forbidden, and abominable, then will any right-thinking person consider that they are at all to be included in the category of the orthodox? I think not. But let those who declare that they think rightly while acting in this way take their part, but let us never envy them their concord and consent. Let us not be so insane. Let us not utterly take leave of our senses.

b. "The Pope is a Heretic"[585]

"O you who are Orthodox, flee the fellowship of those who have accepted the heretical Latins and who regard them as the first Christians in the Catholic and Holy Church of God!" For, as he said a little later, "The pope is a heretic."

2. Patriarch Theodore (Balsamon) of Antioch (1185-1195)[586]

QUESTIONS OF HIS HOLINESS PATRIARCH OF ALEXANDRIA,
KYRIOS MARKOS
AND RESPONSES OF HIS HOLINESS PATRIARCH OF ANTIOCH,
THEODORE BALSAMON

Question: Is there no danger in celebrating or praying alongside heretics, namely with Jacobites and Nestorians, in their churches or in ours? Or in partaking of a common table with them? Or in making them sponsors at Holy Baptism? Or in conducting memorials for their departed? For the narrowness of this land gives rise to many such cases, and I ask what we should do.

Answer: "Do not give holy things to the dogs," our Lord and God has said, nor "cast pearls before swine." Indeed, on this account canon 64 of the holy apostles, the heralds of God, also states, "If any clergyman or layman might enter an assembly of the Jews or heretics to pray, let him be defrocked and excommunicated." Canon 33 of the council of Laodicea, but indeed also 6 and 34, states the following concerning permitting heretics to enter into a house of God while they remain in heresy: "that one must not pray with a heretic or schismatic," "that a Christian must not abandon Christ's martyrs and depart for the false martyrs, namely,

---

585 Jaroslav Pelikan, *The Spirit of Eastern Christendom (600-1700)*, Vol 2 (Chicago: The University of Chicago Press, 1977), 171.

586 Patriarch Theodore Balsamon, "Questions of His Holiness Patriarch of Alexandria Kyrios Markos and Responses of His Holiness Patriarch of Antioch, Theodore Balsamon," in *Patrologia Graeca*, Vol. 138, ed. Jacques Paul Migne (1857-1866) & transl. into English by Gregory Heers (2022) (Paris: Imprimerie Catholique, 1857), 967-968.

heretical ones or those that the aforementioned heretics produced. For these are estranged from God. Therefore, let those departing for them be anathema." Indeed, for this reason, we also decide that both the laymen and the clergymen that pray in common with heretics within a church of the Orthodox or of heretics, or pray with them in any place in a priestly fashion, or even eat with them, be subjected not only to excommunication and deposition but also be punished in ways greater still, in accordance with the summary of the said divine canons. For the narrowness of these lands and the multiplication of the heretics has not changed the integrity of the Orthodox faith.

Question: Latin prisoners and others are present in our Catholic churches and seek to partake of the Divine Sanctified Elements. We seek to learn if this must indeed be permitted.

Answer: The Holy Gospel stated, "He who is not with me is against me, and he who does not gather with me scatters." Therefore, since many years ago the renowned assembly of the Western church (we speak of Rome) was cut off from the spiritual communion of the other four holy patriarchs, and was separated toward things alien to the customs and dogmas of the Catholic Church and the Orthodox, for this reason, the pope is not deemed worthy of the general commemoration of patriarchal names in the holy sacred rites. A member of the Latin nation ought not be sanctified by a priestly hand through the holy and undefiled Mysteries, unless he first promises to refrain from Latin dogmas and customs, and be catechized according to the canons, and be made equal to the Orthodox.

3. Patriarch Germanos II
of Constantinople (1222-1240)[587]

For this reason, do I adjure all the laity, as many of you as are genuine children of the [Orthodox] Catholic Church, to flee entirely from those priests that have fallen under the latin subjection and not even to congregate with them in church, nor to accept a chanced-upon blessing

---

587 Patriarch Germanos II of Constantinople, *Second Epistle to the Cypriots*, PG 140, 620A.

from their hands. For it is better to pray to God in your homes by yourselves than gather in churches with the latin-minded.

4. Cyril I (Lukaris), Patriarch of Constantinople (1572-1638)[588]

The venerable Hieromartyr Cyril Lukaris was born in Chandaka, Crete, on November 13th, 1572, and was named Constantine at his baptism. His father, Stephanos, was a priest, and his teacher was the Hieromonk Meletios Vlastos. After completing his initial education, Cyril traveled to Venice, Italy in 1584 to continue his education. There, he met a bishop named Maximus of Kythira, who took him under his protection and appointed him as his professor. In 1588 due to financial difficulties in his family he returned to Crete where he remained for a year before returning to Italy and enrolling in the University of Padua where he studied theology and philosophy. After his studies in Italy, Cyril returned to Crete in 1592 and became a monk at the Agarathos Monastery in central Crete. He remained there for a short time before being called to Egypt the following year by his relative, Saint Meletios (Pegas), the Patriarch of Alexandria. While in Egypt, he was ordained to the diaconate and to the priesthood by Saint Meletios and was eventually appointed as his Protosyncellus.

"In 1596 he was sent by the Patriarch of Alexandria to Poland to work against any Orthodox Union with Rome, and for six years served as professor of the Orthodox academy in Vilnius (in modern day Lithuania). He was a zealous opponent of the Latins, and particularly of the Jesuit effort to Romanize the Orthodox Churches. He became the Patriarch of Alexandria (as Cyrill III) from 1602-1620, and later the Patriarch of Constantinople. Patriarch Cyril Lucaris was revered by the Orthodox clergy and laity and is best known for his violent opposition to the *Unia*. As Patriarch of Constantinople, he was pressed between the

---

588 Cyril Lukaris was canonized by the Patriarch of Alexandria with a feast day of June 27th. Strong arguments can be made on either side of the questions whether he had Calvinist beliefs or not. In this section we offer information suggesting foul play by the Jesuits, but until a breakthrough discovery occurs, the issue remains unsettled.

Jesuits, who were constantly scheming against him, and the Protestant ambassadors, who wished to secure the endorsement of the Patriarch for their own purposes."[589]

After the repose of Saint Meletios on September 13th, 1601, Cyril was elected Patriarch of Alexandria at the age of twenty-nine years old. Upon becoming patriarch, Cyril convened "a local Synod in Cairo, [where] he condemned the Latin propaganda against the Christians of Egypt"[590] as the Latins had allied with the Coptic Monophysites in an attempt to destroy the canonical Patriarchate of Alexandria. In February 1612, while in Constantinople, he was elected as locum tenens of the Ecumenical Patriarchate for one year before resigning. However, Saint Cyril reigned on the throne of the Alexandrian Patriarchate for eighteen years. After the death of Patriarch Timothy II, the Synod of the Patriarchate of Constantinople elected Saint Cyril as Ecumenical Patriarch on November 4th, 1620. However, after two and a half years, he was removed from the ecumenical throne in April 1623, accused of plotting a revolution on the Greek islands. He was imprisoned and exiled to Rhodes. The new Patriarch, Anthimos, sent bishops to Rhodes to persuade him to submit a regular resignation. Nevertheless, he rejected the proposal and, by the order of the Grand Vizier, returned to Constantinople in September 1623, where he was triumphantly welcomed by the Orthodox Christians. Many people came to Galata where he resided to receive his blessing, and the Archbishops, dignitaries, and people earnestly sought his return to the throne. Patriarch Anthimos was forced to resign, and Cyril returned to the throne in October of 1623. His restoration was cause for general joy among the Orthodox, who saw in him their genuine and true shepherd and Patriarch. Saint Cyril would be "deposed and banished from his patriarchal throne only later to be restored

---

589 Fr. Josiah Trenham, *Rock and Sand: An Orthodox Appraisal of the Protestant Reformers and Their Teachings* (Columbia: Newrome Press, 2015), 156.

590 "Kyrillos III Loukaris (1601-1620)," Official Website of the Patriarchate of Alexandria and All Africa, accessed August 6th, 2023, https://www. patriarchateofalexandria.com/patriarch/kyrillos-iii-loukaris-1601-1620/?lang=en

six times, and, at the order of the Ottoman Sultan"[591] but largely through the influence of papist Jesuits and western governmental powers.

However, what is of major importance in the life of Saint Cyril besides his staunch confession of faith against the heretical Latin innovations, *uniatism*, and Jesuit proselytizing was that "in 1629 in Geneva, a *Confession of Faith* under his name was published, which was decidedly Calvinistic. In the same year it was published in two Latin editions, four French, one German, and one English. [...] Historians have differed on the authenticity of this confession, some affirming the authorship of Lucaris, and others noting that we have a large body of books and letters from the Patriarch in which he does not advocate Calvinist positions and is a defender of Holy Orthodoxy. There is no doubt that the Jesuits were seeking to undermine Lucaris and to brand him as a Calvinist and a betrayer to Holy Orthodoxy so that his valiant opposition to Latin"[592] proselytization and heretical innovations among the Orthodox faithful could be stopped.

While Lucaris knew Latin, when compared to his letters and writings, the polished Latin text of the *Confession* exceeds the level of his other Latin documents. Many Greek scholars assert that the Greek text which appeared with the Latin text four years later was the work of Calvin scholars with whom Lucaris communicated regularly and that they had combined many of his writings and letters into the *Confession*, but without having the grasp of Western (reformed) theology which he possessed.[593] The Protestants, fearful of a Latin unification with the Orthodox, had compelling reason to portray Lukaris as a "Protestant" Patriarch, while the Latins had equally compelling reason to portray Lukaris as betraying his own faith, due to his opposition to the Jesuits and Unia. The Latins, by the Jesuits and other anti-Orthodox factions in Constan-

---

591 Fr. Josiah Trenham, *Rock and Sand: An Orthodox Appraisal of the Protestant Reformers and Their Teachings* (Columbia: Newrome Press, 2015), 159.

592 Fr. Josiah Trenham, *Rock and Sand: An Orthodox Appraisal of the Protestant Reformers and Their Teachings* (Columbia: Newrome Press, 2015), 157.

593 Archbishop Chrysostomos (González de Iturriaga Alexopoulos) of Etna, "The Myth of the 'Calvinist Patriarch,'" Orthodox Christian Information Center, accessed August 7th, 2023, http://orthodoxinfo.com/inquirers/ca4_loukaris.aspx

tinople, working through the Austrian embassy succeeded in bribing the Turks to condemn and kill the patriarch.[594]

On June 22nd, 1638, Cyril was arrested by a detachment of guards and imprisoned in the fortress of Rumeli Hissar. On June 27th, 1638, fifteen Janissaries[595] and other high-ranking officials arrived, took him, boarded him on a ship where he was transported to the beach of Agios Stefanos and then strangled him to death. His body was hastily buried in the sand, but after three days, it was found by some fishermen. His martyred body was secretly transferred and buried in the Monastery of St. Andrew on the island of Agios Andreas in the Gulf of Nicomedia. In 1641, Ecumenical Patriarch Parthenios I the Elder (1639-1644) arranged for the relics of the new martyr to be moved and transferred to the Patriarchate. After the appropriate ceremonies, they were placed in the Holy Bema of the Monastery of Panagia Kamariotissa on Chalki Island. Later, they were moved to the Patriarchal Sacristy and, in 1975, were returned to the Holy Monastery of Agarathos, where they are kept today. Immediately after his martyrdom, Cyril was honored as a Saint and Martyr, and St. Eugene of Aitolia composed a service to commemorate him. His official canonization took place on October 6th, 2009, by the Holy Synod of the Patriarchate of Alexandria.[596]

5. Patriarch Silvester of Antioch 1724-1766[597]

On reference being made by the Christians of Damascus to Paisius then Ecumenical Patriarch and his synod concerning this succession, they sent for him from the Holy Mount, consecrated him Bishop, and

---

594 Ibid.

595 *Janissaries*: Members of an elite corps in the standing army of the Ottoman Empire from the late 14th century to 1826.

596 "Πρώτη ημέρα των εργασιών της Ιεράς Συνόδου του Πατριαρχείου Αλεξανδρείας," Επίσημη ιστοσελίδα του Πατριαρχείου Αλεξανδρείας και πάσης Αφρικής, accessed August 7th, 2023, https://web.archive.org/web/20110730164213/http://www.patriarchateofalexandria.com/index.php?module=news&action=details&id=373

597 John Mason Neale, *A History of the Holy Eastern Church: The Patriarchate of Antioch* (London: Rivington & Co., 1873), 185-187.

advanced him to the throne of Antioch, A.D. 1728. He was a man of virtuous life, having passed a considerable time in the hermitages on Mount Athos, and was in consequence unworldly, simple in his habits, easily cheated, severely persistent in the rules of the Sacred Canons, rigid and unbending. On this account he appeared unsuited for so high a spiritual rule in this world; for in addition to virtue, it is necessary that such as one should be a good manager, according to circumstances of the various human infirmities, performing the office of an evangelist with forbearance and patience, in meekness and condescension, shewing himself long suffering and full of endurance; that thus he may gain, if not all, at least many of those who are deceived and rebellious. But this blessed man on arriving at Aleppo from Constantinople on a Wednesday, and seeing fish on the table which had been prepared for his reception outside the city by the principal Christian inhabitants of Aleppo, in an ungovernable fit of passion, upset the table and violently reproved those leading Christians who had come out to meet him; paying not the slightest attention to their explanations, that in consequence of the lack of fast meats in those parts, the patriarchs his predecessors, had, by way of ecclesiastical condescension, granted this indulgence. On his entrance into Aleppo, he not only showed himself unbending to their earnest appeals on this subject, but excommunicated them in the churches as being guilty, through gluttony, of eating fish on fasting days.

Not satisfied with this, he further accused them to the pasha of Aleppo as Franks and infidels; on which some of the most distinguished among them were apprehended, imprisoned and punished: but the sufferers, burning with hatred and vengeance, turned the attack by bribing the pasha, who was about to apprehend Silvester and punish him.[598] When he had knowledge of this he fled to Laodicea, but after his secret retirement, all the Orthodox in Aleppo, with the exception of a very few, from their youth upwards have declared themselves papists, miserably withdrawing themselves from their mother, the Eastern Church, unto this day. After this, laboring and exerting himself much for the conversion of those Aleppines who had revolted from the pious doctrines of

---

598 The people who were breaking the fast were part of the Damascus party which were the severely Latinized Christians of the region who eventually became apostates from Holy Orthodoxy to the Pope, thus becoming the *Melkite Uniates*.

their fathers, and for others in Damascus, Beirut and elsewhere throughout Syria, who had been carried away, separated from the truth and miserably bowed down to western innovation and doctrine; and through the missionaries sent from Rome, with plenary papal indulgences and relaxations of fasts; and other irregularities forbidden by the Orthodox Eastern Church; and having used great exertions and gone to great expense in order to procure the expulsion of the false bishops, secretly brought into Aleppo by the Latinizers, and especially of one native agitator Seraphim, otherwise called Cyril, who became false patriarch and invaded for a time the throne by foreign intervention;[599] and having, for the purpose of meeting the great expenses which had reduced him to great poverty and distress, travelled through Wallachia, Moldavia and other parts, and endured much during the whole period of thirty-eight years of a patriarchate passed in the midst of so many toils and afflictions, distresses and dangers, labors and martyrdoms, he departed hence to the Lord, as having endured much, in the year 1776. After his death, as the bishops of the throne of Antioch could not agree concerning the election of a new patriarch from among themselves, they wrote to the Great Church, which took upon itself the government of the metropolitan see of Aleppo, so separating it from the patriarchate of Antioch, which was not able to rule it, owing to the inroads of the papists: and advanced to the patriarchate its metropolitan, whom thirteen years ago they had consecrated and sent; he was a native of Constantinople, and then residing in that city.

---

599 This man, being affected with papal doctrine, calling to his aid the violence and threats of a powerful chief of Mount Lebanon, was named Bishop in a certain cave, by Neophytus, Metropolitan of Beyrout (Beirut), and an Armeno-Catholic Bishop brought from Lebanon, cursing and excommunicating him — instead of prayers! After this comedy, the accursed man, aiming also at the patriarchal dignity, this too was accomplished in this still more ridiculous and horrible manner. A certain Capuchin friar, a Roman missionary in Syria, breathed on him thrice saying... "By the grace and power given me by the archbishop of Rome, I have this day appointed thee patriarch of Antioch." Thus, the lawless supremacy and insolence of the papal see unblushingly despises the divine laws and canons, shamelessly mocking at all that is sacred and holy for the sake of making one proselyte to Popery!

6. Patriarch Cyril V (Karakallos) of Constantinople (1748-1751 & 1752-1757)[600]

We command and order paternally and spiritually [...] from hence-forth do not dare at all to commune together with the aforementioned friars and francopriests and the rest of the Westerners in the sacred Mysteries of our Church and in the rest of the ecclesiastical rituals, prayers, and ceremonies, but to wholly preserve [...] your non-communion from them in all the sacred rituals and ceremonies. Should, however, after our patriarchal and synodal chastisement and this paternal and spiritual counsel and advice, any one of you dare to seem disobedient and opposed, or should one of the aforementioned priests dare and be caught praying together with the Latins or accepting their offerings or celebrating commemorations on their behalf [...] such a priest will be submitted to utter revocation of his priesthood.

7. Patriarch Gregory VI of Constantinople (1798-1881)

AN EXCERPT FROM THE ENCYCLICAL LETTER OF PATRIARCH GREGORY VI OF CONSTANTINOPLE, 1839: AN EXHORTATION FOR THE ORTHODOX FAITHFUL AGAINST LATIN INNOVATIONS[601]

Patriarchal and Conciliar Encyclical Epistle, Exhorting the Orthodox everywhere, and much more those in Egypt, Syria, and Palestine, that they may escape the prevalent Papal delusion.

---

600 Archimandrite Spyridon Bilalis, "Ὀρθοδοξία καὶ Παπισμός: Κριτικὴ τοῦ Παπισμοῦ [Orthodoxy and Papism: A Critique of Papism]" (Athens: Orthodoxos Typos, 2014), 367.

601 Patriarch Gregory VI (Fourtouniadis), *Patriarchal and Synodal Encyclical Letter, Exhorting the Orthodox Everywhere, and Especially those in Egypt, Syria and Palestine, to Avoid the Persistent Papal Fallacy* (Constantinople: Ecumenical Patriarchate, 1839), 1-8.

Proclaimed by the All-Holy Ecumenical Patriarch Sir Gregory
and the Sacred Council around him.

Now for the first time published in print at the own expense of His
most reverend All-Holiness.

Wherein is also appended in print an Epistle against the Latin
innovations,
A composition of the ever-memorable Eugene Boulgaris, as being very
necessary and beneficial.

It is distributed to the pious at no cost, unto their spiritual benefit.

In the Patriarchate 1839. Printed by A. and Th. Argyrammos.

GREGORY, BY THE MERCY OF GOD ARCHBISHOP OF CONSTANTINOPLE NEW ROME and ECUMENICAL PATRIARCH.

To the Orthodox Christians everywhere, beloved children in the
Lord of our Mediocrity: abundantly granting from the center of our
heart our fatherly prayers and blessings, we ask for enlightenment from
above and divine grace for all of you. Feeling it our duty, most sacred
of all duties, to preserve unharmed and unhurt Christ's rational sheep
that have been entrusted to our spiritual pastorship, that is, the spiritual
children of the Church, we have not ceased by the grace of God, ever
since we were raised by divine mercy to this patriarchal vantage point,
to keep vigil, as much as we have the strength, for the purpose of spiritually chasing away those who deceitfully enter the rational sheepfold,
the holy Church of Christ, and who multifariously plot against her,
the followers of Luther and of Calvin, the heretics. For the sake thereof
we had previously also published against them an Encyclical Conciliar
Epistle to the Orthodox everywhere, convicting their treacherous aims
and arguments, securing beforehand Christ's flock and calling those that
had been overthrown by them in any way back to the dogmas handed
down from our fathers. Since, however, the followers of the Pope have

now also appeared, shamelessly and recklessly attacking Christ's rational sheep, keeping with the ecclesiastical forethought that we owe to exhibit, we judged it necessary once again to raise the voice of the Church to the Orthodox everywhere and especially to the Orthodox peoples that lie under the three patriarchal thrones, of Alexandria, of Antioch, and of Jerusalem, where at present they [the heretics] have appeared to a higher degree and mightily prevail, devising all sorts of ways to overthrow the Orthodox that still survive there, endeavouring to make these, too, victims of their maniacal madness. And now, having published these days the Conciliar Encyclical Epistle regarding these matters, we thought to communicate it also in print, that it might be spread more easily to the Orthodox everywhere.

With it we judged it good also to append and to communicate to all in print a certain epistle, as being very beneficial, which came into our hands these days by divine providence, written against all Latin innovations, a genuine composition of that ever-memorable wise man, Eugene Boulgaris, which zealously and thoroughly examines the safeguarding of the Orthodox in Serbia at that time, against whom the Latins were plotting, and which was published in print for the first time in Constantinople in the year 1756, during the second patriarchate of Cyril V from Nicomedia. We hope that this epistle, having been written by such a man, will cause, with the help of God, especially in these times, great spiritual benefit, as fully as possible in all that it professes, unto all the Orthodox and particularly, as said, to the peoples of the forementioned patriarchal thrones, where such murky wanderers circulate [cf. Jude 13 —Transl.]. So, we have no doubt that you will receive with pleasure and willingly and diligently read [these texts] unto your souls' salvation, being thereby fortified and secured against the pernicious plots of these implacable enemies of Orthodoxy. Be well in the Lord in both the soul and body.

8. Metropolitan Antony (Khrapovitsky)
First Hierarch of the Russian Church Abroad
(1863-1936)

a. A Few More Words About Patriarch Tikhon[602]

May the late pastor's stand — bold, firm and abundant in love — serve as a guide for all of us, pastors and flock, to hold unswervingly to the Orthodox Faith and Church, to oppose inflexibly every heresy and schism, both those coming from abroad from the Latins and Protestants, and also the sects and all kinds of false teachings arising in Russia herself. Let us imprint in our hearts these divine words: "*If he neglects to hear the Church, let him be unto thee as a heathen and publican*" (Mt. 18,17); and the words of St. Cyprian of Carthage: "If the Church is not your mother, then God is not your Father." And may God give rest in the dwellings of the righteous to the teacher of this truth, His Holiness Patriarch Tikhon, that, following after Christ, in the words of Scripture, "*He shall see the travail of his soul and be satisfied*" (Is. 53, 11).

b. The Infallibility of the Pope According to Vladimir Soloviev[603]

Let us examine the very contents of the principle of the Papacy. First of all, we are told that in his edicts on faith the Pope is infallible; though leaving him a sinner in will and in life, God Himself speaks through him; there are two lives in him: one of them private, the other *ex cathedra*, and in the latter he is infallible. In itself, without any further deductions, this position is a great absurdity. God does not reveal His truth mechanically, when the human will is not identified with it: [...] to affirm that revelation can be transmitted through a will which still remains in its former sins, which is proud and wicked, amounts to saying that a wicked will has become good while remaining wicked. We have the direct word of the Scripture which confirms the absurdity of such a supposition: "God is found by those who do not try Him and does not appear to those who do not believe in Him. For unrighteous reasoning

---

602 Holy Trinity Monastery, "A Few More Words About Patriarch Tikhon," *Orthodox Life*, no. 2 (March-April 1975): 12.

603 Holy Trinity Monastery, "The Infallibility of the Pope According to Vladimir Soloviev," *Orthodox Life*, 37 no. 4 (July-August 1987): 36-43.

puts you far from God and the trying of His power will show up the foolish. Wisdom will not enter a crooked soul and it will not inhabit a body enslaved by sin. For the Holy Spirit of wisdom keeps away from crookedness, avoids foolish reasoning, and is ashamed of the approaching untruth." (Wisdom 1:2-6).

If a sinful man cannot be accepted as the supreme head of the Universal Church without this bride of Christ being completely dethroned, accepting the compatibility of the infallibility of religious edicts with a life of sin with a wicked will, would amount to blasphemy against the Holy Spirit of wisdom by admitting His compatibility with a sinful mind. Khomiakov very justly says that besides the holy inspiration of the apostles and prophets, Scripture tells us of only one inspiration — inspiration of the obsessed. But if this sort of inspiration was going on in Rome, the Church there would not be the Church of Christ, but the Church of His enemy. And this is exactly how Dostoevsky defines it in his "Grand Inquisitor" who says to Christ: "We are not with Thee, but with him."[...]

The triumph of the Christian is in this, that through Christ all men are his brothers, that he need not inquire of every passer-by whether he is of his people or of his party, he need not defend vital truth with worldly weapons, fencing it in with exterior securities. He knows that Christ is the head of everything, joining into one, with Christ he is as if he were with his father among his brothers, on earth he is like an inhabitant of heaven. And all of a sudden he is told: No, don't look up to Christ, do not gravitate towards Him with the desire of your conscience, but towards this sinful man who is endowed with political and clerical power; do not love men directly, do not recognize your unity with every Christian for this will only lead you away from the bodily unity represented by the chief of the Church, who is changed every ten or twenty years. If you act accordingly, in due time, after your death, you will enter the Kingdom of Christ. No, replies the Christian, I need no such kingdom, because everything that attracted me to the Kingdom of Christ as revealed in the New Testament was destroyed by you: in it I was promised a union with the Eternal and the Holy, and you impose on me an incomprehensible union with the temporary and the sinful; in it I rejoiced in the unity with numberless tribes and races, and you say that this union is no better than the union existing among soldiers, for it consists in the unity of the directing will, which belongs only to unworthy regiments, as a regiment possessed of true patriotism is also possessed of a better kind of unity — the unity of purpose. I do not want your rewards[...]

I want the union of faith in many things: I want the coming together of men in their sonship to God, which was promised to me in the New Testament; I want that union of the Greek and the Jew which, according to the word of the apostle, triumphs over the conditions of inborn antipathies; I want the constant miracle of the communion with God which the Lord promised to me at His Ascension. Do not dream of such an impossible union, remonstrates the author, saying: "When we insist that the specific principle of the social unity of the Church is neither directly in Jesus Christ, nor in the masses of the faithful but in the monarchical power of Peter, through whom Jesus Christ desired to unite with humanity as with a social and political being, — our feeling is confirmed by the remarkable fact that the property of being the stone of the Church has preserved the meaning of a proper name only for the prince of the apostles (Peter — a stone), which, in this wise, is the one stone of the Church in the special and accurate sense of the term that is the unifying foundation of the historical Christian community."[...] And so if the papists would only look closely into what wilderness of heathenry they were led by their principles of outer organization, instead of inner order, most certainly only a few of them would stand by their new self-made dogmas, but the majority would renounce them as ungodly.[...]

Yet, instead of Christ in Whom all are one, people offer us a sinful man; instead of the Holy Spirit, they offer us the oracles of the Pope, and comfort us with the promise that the reality of this bond is not going to be inferior to the reality of a political alliance! Then at least you ought not to give it the name of a religion! Do not call it a church either, but just a company formed of men and not distinguishable from any other worldly alliance, either in means or in essence: inquisitors and Jesuits are far too near such a definition of the church. It is true, though, that the author proudly points out that the Roman clergy, now at work on social reorganization, possess at present no state power and yet find it possible to act, because, in the West, the state professes no definite religion. But if, as he acknowledges, the Roman Catholic Church is deprived of the

help of the government, it must be that there also the Church is not complete, not altogether true? Then where is its difference from the Eastern
Church? The author does not help us to settle his self-contradiction, but
the general logic of things speaks for him. If the Roman Catholic clergy have lost their right of inquisition and execution, if the governments
of the West refuse to submit to them, still Soloviev's definition of the
Church as an institution which contains all forms of social life (not conscience only) is perfectly applicable to it. These clergy cannot use physical force, but the life of the old Adam, of the world which hates Christ,
does not consist of physical violence alone. However, the author ought
not to say that the governments of the world are a check on the Roman
Catholic clergy. On the contrary, when bound on some shady transaction, as, for instance, the smothering of the nascent national religious
self-consciousness of our brother Russians in Galicia and the destruction
of their sympathy for Russia, they call on the Jesuits, who are capable of
murdering a whole nation without either knife or rope, ad majorem Dei
gloriam, using all kinds of doubtful means, but chiefly lies and shameless
calumnies, as if to complete their league with the calumniating enemy
of Christ, the prince of this world. Yet all the horrifying doings of modern Jesuitism are merely the logical outcome of that worldly form of the
Christian religion, according to which the Gospel love of one's neighbor
is replaced by the love of the single sinful head of the Latin community.
Unlike their Protestant accusers, we do not want to discuss the vices of
the Roman Catholic clergy, which, after all, are personal sins, and are to
be judged by God alone, and in mentioning the events in Galicia, we do
not mean to reproach men, but to demonstrate the falseness of the faith
which prompts them, by having for its motive not the love of Christ, but
a loyalty towards a sinful man. Do they ever gather grapes from thorns
and figs from thistles? A bad tree cannot bring forth good fruit [...]

And if it is possible for the sons of the Orthodox Church to prefer
Latinism in the name of religious zeal, it only shows that our society
suffers from an interior alienation from the spirit of our Church. All the
reproaches which Soloviev heaps upon our Church, but to the religious
life of society people. Consequently, in order not to be responsible for
new apostasies of zealous but ill-advised people, our society ought to
come into a more profound and serious contact with the interior life

of our Church, it ought to read the Scriptures, the lives of saints, and the works of the Fathers of the Church, like [Saint] John Chrysostom or [Saint] Tikhon of Zadonsk; it ought to take part in the offices of the Church, in charitable and educational associations under the leadership of Church authorities, and so by creating an example of Orthodox Christianity in its social order, not only to make the apostasy of good people impossible, but also to attract towards the light of truth our erring Western brethren.[...]

Dostoevsky... in his "Grand Inquisitor," has characterized Papacy as a doctrine which is attractive exactly because of its worldly power, but devoid of the spirit of Christian communion with God and of contempt for the evil of the world. Having unmistakably foretold the birth of the present Latinophile tendencies, he, nevertheless, pointed out to us the "better faith" by disclosing, in his novel *The Brothers Karamazov* the positive aim Orthodox people must have in view in all their activities, and which begins with deeds of personal virtue, with the interior crucifixion of the old Adam and the interior union with the new and beneficial life of the Church.

9. Metropolitan Philaret (Voznesensky) First-Hierarch, Russian Church Abroad (1903-1985)

a. To Patriarch Athenagoras of Constantinople on the Lifting of Anathemas from 1054 against the Latin Papists (1965)[604]

AN APPEAL TO HIS HOLINESS ATHENAGORAS OF CONSTANTI-NOPLE, NEW ROME, AND ECUMENICAL PATRIARCH

Your Holiness:
From the Holy Fathers we have inherited the testament that in the Church of God all is done according to canonical order, in unity of

604 Metropolitan Philaret (Voznesensky) of New York, "An Appeal to His Holiness Athenagoras of Constantinople, New Rome, and Ecumenical Patriarch," Orthodox Word 2, no. 1 (January-March 1966): 27-30. As quoted in *Metropolitan Philaret of New York*, edited by Subdeacon Nektarios Harrison. (Florence: Uncut Mountain Press, 2022), 205-210.

mind and in agreement with ancient traditions. If, however, any from among the Bishops or even from among the representatives of auto-cephalous Churches should do anything not in agreement with what the whole Church teaches, each member of the Church may declare his protest. The 15th Rule of the Double Council of Constantinople in 861 acknowledges as worthy of "the honor befitting an Orthodox Christian" those Bishops or clergy who withdraw from communion even with their Patriarch, if he should publicly preach heresy or teach such openly in the Church. Thus, we are all guardians of the Church's truth, which has always been defended by concern that nothing possessing significance for the whole Church be done without the agreement of all. For this reason, our relation to various divisions which go beyond the bounds of separate local Churches has also been determined not otherwise than by the agreement of all these Churches. If our division with Rome was orig-inally determined in Constantinople, subsequently it was accepted by the whole Orthodox Church and became an act of the whole Orthodox world. No one local Church separately — and in particular the Church of Constantinople, long respected by all of us, from whom our Russian Church received the treasure of Orthodoxy — can change anything in the matter without the prior agreement of all.

Moreover, we, the presently ruling Bishops, cannot execute deci-sions which would be in disagreement with the teaching of the Holy Fathers who have lived before us — in particular, insofar as the matter concerns the West, Sts. Photios of Constantinople and Mark of Ephe-sus. In the light of these principals we, though we are the youngest of the representatives of the Church, yet as the head of the autonomous, free portion of the Russian Church, consider it our duty to declare a decisive protest against the act of Your Holiness concerning the solemn decla-ration, simultaneously with the Pope of Rome, of the removal of the excommunication proclaimed by Patriarch Michael Cerularius in 1054. We heard many expressions of dismay when Your Holiness, before the whole world, did something novel, unknown to Your predecessors and contrary to the tenth Apostolic rule, by meeting the Pope of Rome, Paul VI, in Jerusalem. We shall say frankly, without hesitation: the offense was great. We have heard that as a result of this many monasteries on the Holy Mountain of Athos ceased to mention the name of Your Holiness during Divine Services. Now, however, You go yet further when, by decree of Yourself and the Bishops only of Your Synod, You abrogate the decree of Patriarch Michael Cerularius, confirmed and accepted by the entire Orthodox East. Doing this, Your Holiness acts in disagreement with the relation toward Roman Catholicism that has been adopted by our whole Church. It is not a question of one or another valuation of the conduct of Cardinal Humbert; it is not a question of any personal falling out between Pope and Patriarch that could be easily healed by mutual Christian forgiveness; no —the essence of the question lies in those deviations from Orthodoxy which have become rooted in the Roman Church during the course of centuries, first of all the teaching of Papal Infallibility, definitively formulated at the First Vatican Council.

The declaration of Your Holiness and the Pope justly acknowledges the act of "mutual pardon" as insufficient for the cessation of former as well as of more recent divergences. But more than that, this act places a sign of equality between error and truth. During the course of centuries, the whole Orthodox Church has justly believed that she has departed in nothing from the teaching of the Holy Ecumenical Councils, while at the same time the Roman Church has accepted a series of novelties, discordant with Orthodoxy, in her dogmatic teaching. The more these novelties have been introduced, the deeper has the division become between East and West. The dogmatic deviations of the 11th century Rome did not yet contain such errors as were added later. Therefore, the revocation of the mutual interdictions of 1054 might have had a significance in that epoch, but now it serves only as a witness of neglect for the most important and essential, namely, the new teachings, unknown to the ancient Church, that were proclaimed after that, of which several, being indicted by St. Mark of Ephesus as a reason why the Union of Florence was rejected by the Holy Church. We declare decisively and categorically: No union of any sort of the Roman Church with us is possible until she renounces her new dogmas, and it is not possible to re-establish communion in prayer with her without the decree of all Churches — which, however, is not regarded by us as possible until the Russian Church, now compelled to live in the catacombs, becomes free. The hierarchy now headed by Patriarch Alexei cannot express the authentic voice of the

Russian Church, for it is completely subservient to the atheist authority, executing its will.

The representatives of several other Churches in Communist countries are also not free. Inasmuch as the Vatican is not only a religious center, but also a state, and one's relations to it — as the recent visit of the Pope to the United Nations clearly showed — have also a political significance, one cannot fail to reckon with the possible influence of the atheist powers upon the hierarchy of the captive Churches, on one side or the other, in the question of the Roman Church. History testifies that negotiations with those of different belief under the condition of pressure from political circumstances, have never brought the Church anything but disturbance and divisions. Therefore we consider it necessary to declare that our Russian Church Abroad, as undoubtedly also the Russian Church now in the "catacombs," will not consent to any "dialogues" whatever with other confessions concerning dogmas, and she rejects beforehand every agreement with them in this connection, acknowledging the possibility of restoration of unity with them only if they accept in full Orthodox doctrine in that form in which it has been preserved until now by the Holy Catholic and Apostolic Church. As long as this condition is unfulfilled, the interdictions of Patriarch Michael Cerularius maintain all their force, and their removal by Your Holiness is an act uncanonical and invalid. To be sure, we are not opposed to the well-wishing mutual relations with the representatives of other confessions, as long as Orthodox truth is not betrayed thereby. For this reason, our Church at one time accepted the kind of invitation to send observers to the Second Vatican Council, just as she had sent observers to the Protestant Conferences of the World Council of Churches, in order to have information from firsthand concerning the work of these meetings, without any participation in their decisions. We value a good relation to our observers and study with interest their detailed reports, which testify to the beginning of significant changes in the Roman Church. We shall thank God if these changes will serve the cause of her drawing near to Orthodoxy.

However, if Rome must change much in order to return to "the confession of the Apostolic faith," the Orthodox Church, which has preserved this faith until now uncorrupted, has nothing to change. Church tradition and the example of the Holy Fathers teach us that no dialogue is conducted with Churches that have fallen away from Orthodoxy. To them is always directed sooner the monologue of the Church's preaching, in which the Church calls them to return to her bosom through rejection of every teaching not in accord with her. A genuine dialogue supposes an exchange of opinions, admitting the possibility of the persuasion of the participants in it for the attainment of agreement. As is apparent from the encyclical Ecclesiam Suam, Pope Paul VI understands dialogue as a plan for our annexation to Rome, or for the restoration of communion with her with the aid of some kind of formula, which however leaves her doctrine totally unchanged, and in particular her dogmatic teaching on the position of the Pope in the Church. But any agreement with error is foreign to the whole history of the Orthodox Church and to her very being. It could lead, not to unanimous confession of the truth, but to a visionary external union similar to the agreement of the differently minded Protestant societies within the Ecumenical Movement. May such a betrayal of Orthodoxy not penetrate to our midst! We fervently beg Your Holiness to place a limit to the offense, for the path which You have chosen, if it should further bring You into union with the Roman Catholics, would call forth a division in the Orthodox world; for undoubtedly many of Your own spiritual children also will prefer faithfulness to Orthodoxy above the ecumenical idea of a compromising union with non-Orthodox without their full agreement in the truth.

Begging Your holy prayers I remain Your Holiness' obedient servant,

+ Metropolitan Philaret
Chairman of the Synod of Bishops of the Russian Orthodox
Church Outside of Russia

b. Excerpts from an Interview with His Eminence Metropolitan Philaret in the Roman Catholic weekly Publik (1971)[605]

Question: The Roman Catholic Church aspires toward fraternal dialog with the Russian Orthodox Church. Is it to be hoped that these contacts and collaboration will progress beyond purely formal relations, and if so, in what arenas?

Answer: The aspiration of the Orthodox Church is not defined by the word *dialog*, since dialog is usually perceived as a desire to reach certain compromises. In the spiritual arena compromises do not bring one closer to the Truth. Consequently, the Orthodox Church aspires not to "dialog," but to sincere Christian conversation — to mutually present our points of view to each other and to reach a proper understanding of them.

We aspire to live in Christian love, to respect the Christian soul in every baptized Christian, and to overcome those of our differences that do not pertain to confession of the faith, but which can be viewed as vestiges of historical misunderstandings.

Certain overly hasty actions, whether those of Moscow (for political reasons) or those of Constantinople (for different but also possibly political reasons), do not help to effectually overcome the schism: this is possible only through the mercy and grace of God in Spirit and in Truth.

Question: What is your appraisal of certain tendencies in the Roman Catholic Church that arose following the Second Vatican Council, concerning changes in relations between the Church and society?

Answer: We are wary of pursuing the sham popularity that results from employing unsuitable methods for church mission and preaching. We fear the pursuit of this age.

The Church is outside of time. The Church knows that there can be no paradise on earth, but that the Kingdom of God is a reality. And the sole task of the Church is to lead her children into that Kingdom.

---

605 Metropolitan Philaret (Voznesensky) of New York, "Interview with His Eminence Metropolitan Philaret in the Roman Catholic Weekly Publik," *Православная Русь (Orthodox Life)* 12, (Winter 1970): 9-12.

c. An Excerpt from the Second Sorrowful Epistle (1972)[606]

In a number of decisions of the Orthodox Church the Roman Catholics were regarded as heretics. Though from time to time they were accepted into the Church in a manner such as that applied to Arians, it is to be noted that for many centuries and even in our time the Greek Churches accepted them by Baptism. If after the centuries following 1054 the Latins were accepted into the Greek and Russian Churches by two rites, that of Baptism or of Chrismation, it was because although everyone recognized them to be heretics, a general rule for the entire Church was not yet established in regard to the means of their acceptance.

For instance, when in the beginning of the XII century the Serbian Prince and father of Stephan Nemania was forced into having his son baptized by the Latins upon his subsequent return later to Rasa, he baptized him in the Orthodox Church (*Short Outline of the Orthodox Churches, Bulgarian, Serbian and Rumanian*, E. E. Golubinsky, Moscow, 1871, p. 551). In another monumental work, *The History of the Russian Church* (Vols. I/II, Moscow, 1904, pp. 806-807), Professor Golubinsky, in describing the stand taken by the Russian Church in regard to the Latins, advances many facts indicating that in applying various ways in receiving the Latins into the fold of the Orthodox Church, at sometimes baptizing them and at others chrismating them, both the Greeks and Russian Churches assumed that they were heretics.

Therefore, the statement that during those centuries, "we did not cease to recognize in each other the validity of apostolic priesthood and the validity of the mystery of the Divine Eucharist" is absolutely inconsistent with historical fact. The separation between us and Rome existed and exists. Further, it is not illusory but actual. The separation appears illusory to those who give no weight to the words of the Savior spoken to His Holy Apostles and through them, to their successors, *"verily I say unto you, whatsoever ye shall bind on earth shall be bound in heaven;*

---

606 Metropolitan Philaret (Voznesensky) of New York, "The Second Sorrowful Epistle of Metropolitan Philaret," Orthodox Christian Information Center, accessed July 9, 2022, http://orthodoxinfo.com/ecumenism/sorrow2.aspx. As quoted in *Metropolitan Philaret of New York*, edited by Subdeacon Nektarios Harrison. (Florence: Uncut Mountain Press, 2022), 118-136.

and whatsoever ye shall loose on earth shall be loosed in heaven." (Matthew 18:18)

10. Bishop Gregory (Grabbe) of Washington and Florida (1902-1995)

a. Partnership — The Pope and an Atheist[607]

On March 9, 1992, *The New York Times*, one of the largest and most influential papers in the United States, ran an article entitled "My Partner the Pope," written by Mikhail Gorbachev. The very title of the article perplexes the reader. The Pope is the head of the Roman Catholic Church; Gorbachev, until recently, was the leader of the Communist government of the Soviet Union and consequently atheistic. Not long ago he defined his own personal position on religion as being atheistic. One would think that since the head of a "Christian Church" and the former leader of an atheistic government are in such diametrically opposed positions it would be impossible to speak of a close partnership between the two. St. Paul compares such a close relationship to the union of light with darkness. He asks, *what communion hath light with darkness?* And he continues on with other examples of contradiction: *And what concord hath Christ with Belial? Or what part hath he that believeth with an infidel? And what agreement hath the temple of God with idols?* (2 Corinthians 6:14-16). The closeness of the Pope of Rome, who aspires to head an entire Christian world, with an atheist politician forces one to question the nature of these two sides of the world, represented by the Pope and Gorbachev. Gorbachev writes, "It is very difficult to describe the relationship which took shape between the Pope and myself because the intuitive, personal element is always of great importance in such relationships. Simply put, when I was with him, I realized that the Pope had also played a role in what we came to call the *new political thinking*" (emphasis author's). In general, we Orthodox Christians could react disinterestedly to the growing closeness between the Pope of Rome and an atheist, who until recently headed a government located on Rus-

---

607 Holy Trinity Monastery, "Partnership—The Pope and an Atheist," *Orthodox Life* 42, no. 3, (May-June 1992): 15-17.

sian territory. At the same time, it is obvious from Gorbachev's essay that in certain matters he has remained very influential in the international political arena.

What direction does his interest and activity take and how is it connected with the Pope? In Gorbachev's essay we see that the Pope had a great influence on Church politics in Russia (perhaps through Gorbachev?). Gorbachev writes, "I think that the very significant steps we took in our country played a part in developing relations with the Vatican; in particular we understood the need for ties between the Russian Orthodox [i.e., the Moscow Patriarchate] and the Catholic Churches. This facilitated the establishment of relations between our country and the Vatican." Thus, an aspect of the "new political thinking" of Gorbachev and the Pope is their agreement on religious questions concerning the relations between Orthodoxy and Catholicism. Take note; questions involving religion are dealt with in the political sphere. The ancient Jesuit saying "the end justifies the means" is a fitting ruling principle for an atheist and a Catholic with a Jesuit mentality. What common purpose unites the Pope of Rome and his atheistic friend? The answer is clear; they both are intent on destroying Holy Russia, hateful to them both. This long-term goal is sought by both Catholic heretics and the Communist atheists, who spare no means to achieve it.

This explains why in 1985 the Vatican transferred all questions about interrelations with the Jews from the Secretariat of Relations with Non-Christians to the special "Commission for Union of Christians," headed by Cardinal Willebrands. The French journalist publicized the contents of the decisions of the Vatican Pontifical Commission in the conservative newspaper Presant in 1986. Especially significant was Point no. 12. The essence of this point is summed up in the title of the essay "Rome Calls on Catholics to Prepare with the Jews for the Coming of the Messiah." One of the major impulses in this direction is the ecumenical unification of all religions without concern for the preservation of Christian Truth. Gorbachev has also joined himself to this task of uniting Orthodox Christians with the Catholics. For him, as one who does not believe in God, this goal of unity is not religious, but only political.

We Orthodox Christians must recognize where the Pope of Rome and Gorbachev are leading us. We must understand where and caution believers about the danger of taking part in the joint labors of the Pope and Gorbachev. As they reach out to us, let us remember the words of the Apostle Paul, *what part do you want here?* (2 Corinthians 6:14).

b. The Decline of Roman Catholicism and Protestantism[608]

One can say that the contemporary errors regarding the Church arose above all from Papism. At the root of these errors is a loss of living faith in the both divine and human nature of the whole Church not only in heaven, but also on earth, and in the resolution of problems in the life of the Church without perception of this unity. In the effort to perfect and strengthen the Church organizationally according to the elements of this world, its earthly portion became almost self-sufficient in the Roman understanding. The authority to bind and loose, given to the holy Apostles by the Saviour, does to some extent extend the force of their decisions from earth to heaven, but by ascribing this authority primarily to the Bishop of Rome and by extending it, Roman Catholicism logically and, from an earthly standpoint, rationally was obliged to elevate the Pope to the position of Head of the Church and to endow him in this capacity with infallibility. The Pope's simultaneous role as a head of state led to a further secularization of the Roman Church. It became a religious empire instead of the Body of Christ. The bestowal of infallibility on the Pope at the First Vatican Council was the culmination of this process. From a practical standpoint the Latins considered it necessary to proclaim this right was a dogma to strengthen the Pope's authority in the fight with Protestantism and other anti-ecclesiastical tendencies. Whatever arguments Catholics might put forward to justify this dogma, nothing can change the fact that pride, legalism, and rationalism lie at the base of its definition.

In their Church Catholics merged the concept of the ecclesiastical society with that of the Pope as monarch, while Protestantism, on the other hand was a revolution in which the people rose up against that monarch. Protestantism opposes free individualism to the juridical unity of Rome. In it the personality and its opinions were placed above dog-

---

608 Protopresbyter George Grabbe, *The Dogma of the Church in the Modern World* (Jordanville: Holy Trinity Monastery, 1998), 18-19.

mas and the unity of the Church. Consequently, from its very beginning Protestantism was destined to a constant process of division.

After Rome fell away from Orthodoxy, the Western world long retained many Christian virtues and values through inertia, but it was on the way to obvious catastrophe. The strength of Khomyakov's works on the western confessions is found in the fact that he discovered and exposed this process. Roman Catholicism, eroded by waves of Protestantism and living by rationalism, is now itself becoming a Protestant religion. This process, which has long existed, although it was invisible to the superficial observer, began to develop with unbelievable speed after the Second Vatican Council.

c. Modernism[609]

Now what was written in refutation of Roman Catholicism fifty years ago is already out of date, not because it was incorrect, but because Roman Catholicism has changed so much. The waves of ecumenism, which long ago covered Protestantism, are now eroding even the stronghold of the Vatican. And they can threaten us too insofar as the Orthodox Churches have entered the ecumenical movement. This movement has less effect on Protestants, since it is an embodiment of their own teaching about the Church. It is difficult to express with sufficient strength the full depth of the dissolution which was introduced into the western world by the reforms of the Second Vatican Council. We might not have touched on this point if it were not for the fact that, because our flock lives in a western environment, it is involuntarily brought into contact with those who are being corrupted spiritually by these reforms. They are reducing to nothing the last remnants of the Church-consciousness which the western confession inherited from Orthodoxy. What has called forth this process at the present time?

Lack of faith in the power of grace and in one's own Church. The surrounding world seems so strong that it produces fear for the continued existence of one's Church organization by any other than earthly means. This is the one source of the desire for accommodation with the world even though one's basic principles suffer as a result. But the ac-

---

609 Protopresbyter George Grabbe, *The Dogma of the Church in the Modern World* (Jordanville: Holy Trinity Monastery, 1998), 19-20.

commodation of the Church to this world is unavoidably connected with a break with tradition and with doubts which undermine the stability of Church order.

Let me give you an example which confirms this general rule. When Pope Pius V issued a new missal on July 19, 1570, he issued a decree which was supposed to remain in force forever to the effect that nothing could ever be added to it, and nothing could be omitted from it. "At no time whatsoever in the future," wrote the Pope, "may any priest in the world or in a religious order be required to celebrate mass using any other form of service." He proclaimed that "by virtue of our Apostolic Authority we order and define that our present directive and decree must by observed unchangingly and may never lawfully be revoked or altered in the future." The Pope's decree was issued for all time and threatens anyone who might violate it with the anger of God and of the blessed Apostles Peter and Paul.

Let us imagine the reaction of a Catholic who knows this decree when he is now presented with a choice of several new "experimental" liturgies with the approval of the lawful successor of Pope Pius V. In the course of such experiments a Catholic will see a jazz mass, a mass in the kitchen, a mass for children with dolls and other toys. The credibility has been shattered. What is left?

In what name is this change, so destructive of the conscience of the faithful, made? — In the name of modernity. But this is not by any means the only reform which has shaken the foundation of contemporary Catholicism. It is now questioning everything. As a result, in the Catholic press priests deny the existence of the devil, write justifications of homosexuality, justify adultery and even cast doubts on the virginity of the Mother of God. Once having entered onto the way of modernism, Catholicism frequently surpasses Protestantism in this respect. Despite their close contact with this tendency in the ecumenical movement nowhere are the Orthodox Churches as yet accepting modernism in as pure a form as is the western world. But the example is infectious, and we already see signs of this infection in various places.

11. Patriarch Diodoros I (Karivalis) of Jerusalem (1980-2000)

FIRM DECLARATIONS OF PATRIARCH DIODOROS I OF JERUSALEM THAT STRENGTHEN THE FAITH OF THE ORTHODOX PEOPLE[610]

Most Blessed and Most Reverend Presidents of the Most Holy local Orthodox Patriarchates and Autocephalous and Autonomous Churches, Holy Brethren, beloved in the Lord:

We bless and glorify the God Who is worshipped in Trinity, Who in His Divine Providence arranged the present much-desired Consultation of the Most Reverend Presidents of the Patriarchates and of the Most Holy Autocephalous and Autonomous Orthodox Churches, for the fulfillment of our common yearning and our sacred desire to be face to face and to exchange thoughts on the contemporary problems of mankind and to deliberate about the topics that occupy our Holy Church.

Assuredly, after sending to all our beloved brethren, the Most Blessed Presiding Hierarchs, about three years ago our letter, numbered Protocol 395 and dated May 30 (Old Style), in which we emphasized the need for such a Summit Meeting of the Orthodox Presiding Hierarchs, we had in view that wherever this would take place, it would not be simply a conventional meeting, for the concelebration of the Liturgy and Communion from the same cup of life and for the projection of the love and unity that already exist among the Presiding Hierarchs, but that we would be given an opportunity to set before ourselves in common and at length many of the problems that seriously occupy our Holy Orthodox Church and to find their solutions, for the benefit of all the Orthodox.

This Assembly will constitute a truly historic landmark in the journey of our Orthodox Church. For this reason, we are summoned, so that united "in the bond of peace" and love in Christ, we might bear witness of this to the world, a witness of faith and truth, unity and peace, love

---

610 Constantine Cavarnos, "Firm Declarations of Patriarch Diodoros I of Jerusalem that Strengthen the Faith of the Orthodox People," in *The Question of Union: A Forthright Discussion of the Possibility of Union of the Eastern Orthodox Church and Roman Catholicism* (Etna: Center for Traditionalist Orthodox Studies, 2006), 41-50.

and righteousness, salvation and freedom in Christ. Hence, we departed in joy and exultation from the Holy City of Jerusalem, the earthly seat of the Heavenly King Christ, which was sanctified through His voluntary martyrdom on the Cross, and His glorious Resurrection from the dead, and blessed through the descent therein of the All-holy Spirit upon the Holy Disciples and Apostles, on the day of Pentecost, at the divine establishment of our Holy Church.

In ineffable gladness we are present in this Queen of Cities, which has played such an important role in the life of our Most Holy Church. And we come with the inward conviction that the Divine Builder of our Church, Jesus Christ, will lavish on all of us who have assembled "in the same place" His divine illumination, wisdom and power, so that we may address ourselves to the world, which awaits today the consoling voice of Orthodoxy. We firmly believe that in this sacred Assembly of ours, which culminates with a Pan-Orthodox liturgical concelebration on the day when we celebrate the triumph of Orthodoxy, the Spirit of God will preside, the unchanging voice of Orthodoxy will be proclaimed "with one mouth and one heart," the voice of the Lord "Who is the same yesterday, today, and forever." For this reason, we should reckon up the responsibilities which we shoulder as Presiding Hierarchs of our Churches, by the mercy of God, and spiritual guides of the flock that awaits blessings from us who stand "in the type of Christ." We have, therefore, an obligation imposed on us and a sacred duty to express our opinion in deepest faith, in truth and sincerity, fearing nobody and flinching under no adversary, for the Lord will give us "reason and wisdom, which all our enemies will be unable to gainsay or resist."

Following, then, the God-bearing Fathers and teachers, we consider it necessary to assure the present venerable and longed-for Assembly that our Holy Church of Jerusalem maintains without alteration the sacred Traditions and the order and practice of our Most Holy Church, which were consecrated by the Holy Ecumenical Synods, following faithfully what our Fathers taught. She repeats, therefore, that she adheres steadfastly to their definitions and decisions, accepting no innovation, but on the contrary, she rejects and condemns every attempt made from whatever source to create a new order in the Orthodox Church.

Thus, examining the proposed agenda, which is derived from the agreed Memoranda of our Most Blessed brethren, and having in hand the outline of the Message, which we are called upon to adopt, in order to give thereby to the world the witness of our Holy Orthodox Church, we have to remark on certain points and ask you, our Most Holy and beloved brethren, to take these into account and consider their importance, so that the text may truly be the voice of the united Orthodoxy which will find an echo not only in the ears, but also in the consciences of the Orthodox faithful. In the first place, the aim of the present sacred Assembly, as we have previously mentioned, is to formulate the opinion of the Church on the topics that occupy Holy Orthodoxy today. Our message, therefore, cannot have a standpoint unrelated to reality, but must express clearly and sincerely the position of Orthodoxy, re-echo her uneasiness, namely the evaluation of those things that are happening around her and often at her expense, stigmatize the bad and praise the good, and emphasize concretely what she feels, without hesitations and calculations inappropriate to the Church's manner of expression, and without considering any material advantages and promises.

A large part of our text, therefore, refers to the proselytizing of the Orthodox faithful practiced through the Unia in the countries which were under Communist regimes. The activities of the Uniates — to say nothing of the Roman Catholics in general — are clearly known, as are the methods through which they have been ceaselessly proselytizing the Orthodox faithful not only in Russia, Ukraine, Poland, Czechoslovakia, Romania and Serbia, but also in the Middle East, using all manner of means, such as education, employment, pressure, compulsion, violence and even crime, as the recent history of the Orthodox Church in Croatia, Ukraine, and elsewhere bears witness. We, as the spiritual leaders of the Orthodox Church, come together today in a historic Meeting. The Most Blessed Presiding Hierarchs of Russia, Serbia, Poland and Czechoslovakia, having received bitter experience of the persecutions against the Orthodox on the part of the Uniates and the Roman Catholics, recently sent to all of us precious letters, dramatizing the dreadful things that they, the Orthodox, are suffering within the bosom of their Orthodox Churches, requesting us to lend them moral support, but at the same time to condemn such actions, which not only constitute a flagrant

violation of basic human rights, but are also utterly opposed chiefly and
primarily to the spirit of Christian teaching.

It is natural, then, for this Assembly of ours not to be restricted only
to calling attention to and to ascertaining, but also to expressing its feelings sincerely — feelings of bitterness over the conduct of certain Christians, who have been given the opportunity and "have entered to spy
on the freedom which we have in Christ Jesus, in order to enslave us."
The offensive phrase of the Pope, the leader of the Roman Catholics,
speaking about the "re-evangelization of Europe," that the Orthodox
people who inhabit the Eastern states have not known Christ, must inspire all of us with serious thoughts and anxieties about the intentions
of the Roman Catholics against the Orthodox. We must not be asleep,
calming ourselves and each other about a supposed change of Rome's
intentions and her goodwill to continue the dialogue of love with the
Orthodox Church. The recent tragic events are unfortunately proof of
their hostile disposition. Our faithful Orthodox people do not accept
diplomatic solutions, nor do they compromise on matters of faith. For
this reason, they anxiously await the voice of Orthodoxy through us,
the voice of truth which boldly denounces evil, refutes falsehood, and
condemns plainly and directly every anti-Christian and anti-Orthodox
activity, from whatever source it proceeds. They await the condemnation of those who founded and support the Unia, and they await the
condemnation of the actions of the Roman Catholics in general and of
the Pope in particular, as inciting and encouraging the acts of violence
and other actions of the Unia at the expense of the Orthodox.

For this reason, it will be futile to continue the theological dialogues
with the Roman Catholics. Our Most Holy Church of Jerusalem has repeatedly begged them to end the proselytizing of the Orthodox faithful
by the Roman Catholics and the Unia — who have always used as many
artifices and ways as possible for this purpose — in the Middle East,
and especially in the Holy Land. Secondly, through her representatives
and written testimonies, our Church has complained to the bipartite
theological dialogue about what is being perpetrated against her. Finally, believing that She is laboring in vain in the dialogue with them, that
there is no purpose in continuing contacts with the unrepentant, in accordance with the injunction of the Apostle of the Nations, "Reject a

heretical man after the first and second admonition," She has broken off the Theological Dialogue, as the only correct response to the bleeding of our flock. Thus, She has made Her position clear.

Beyond the religious propaganda and the proselytizing of the Roman Catholics, however, our Patriarchate faces also their cunning attempts to outflank the Orthodox presence in the Most Holy Places of Pilgrimage and to increase their influence over the Holy Land, through the political diplomacy of the Vatican and the intervention of Catholic European forces into the international political scene. We therefore deem worthy of congratulations the decision of the Most Holy Church of Greece, which at the first regular Meeting of the Permanent Holy Synod in February denounced "the cunning policy of Rome," asked the Greek State "to break off diplomatic relations between the Vatican and Greece," and remarked that the dialogue with Rome "has proved neither sincere nor fraternal to the Orthodox world." We congratulate His Beatitude, Archbishop Seraphim of Athens and All Greece, for his courageous condemnation on television of the activities of the Vatican. The stopping of Theological Dialogues by our Church of Jerusalem, as much as the decision of the Church of Greece, has been praised by the Orthodox Faithful and appears to be a position imperative for all of us who are called to respond to the questions of the Orthodox people about how we should face the onslaughts of the Uniates and the Roman Catholics.

In the same spirit we think that theological dialogues with the heterodox have no positive outcome. Already some of the heterodox have diverged from their original position, adopting innovations alien to the spirit of the Church. Some of the Orthodox Bishops are engaging in dialogues with them, and worse than this, are praying with them, which causes scandal to the faithful and damage to their souls.

Likewise, optimism is expressed about the "positive"— as it is asserted — outcome of the dialogue with the Anti-Chalcedonians [the Monophysites], who have repeatedly been condemned for their persistence in heresy and false belief. Our Most Holy Church of Jerusalem abides steadfastly by the decisions of both the Holy Ecumenical Synod of Chalcedon and the subsequent Holy Ecumenical Synods, and neither setting aside any of the definitions nor subjecting them to fresh inquiry, she has broken off the theological dialogue with the non-Chalcedonians. She does not, however, exclude the possibility of their return and re-inclusion in the bosom of our Most Holy Orthodox Church. In what way the heterodox are received is known. They must fully accept — without any exception — the teaching of the One, Holy, Catholic and Apostolic Church, which is formulated in the definitions and decisions of the Ecumenical Synods.

The partial acceptance of the teaching of the Orthodox Church, that is, the exception of certain definitions of the Ecumenical Synods, as is being done by the heterodox according to what pleases them and serves their interests, as in this case by the Anti-Chalcedonians, cannot constitute a sign of their contact with our Most Holy Orthodox Church. On the contrary, it will entangle her in vicissitudes and divisions, which will weaken her healthy body. For this reason, we are bound to inform you, our Most Blessed brethren, in this fraternal Assembly, that our Most Holy Church is abstaining also from this dialogue. For, despite the positive estimate of its progress that it is going to develop further to the better, it will be of no benefit, unless it presupposes the full acceptance of the Orthodox Teaching. But if such is the progress of the Theological Dialogues with the heterodox, what are we to say about the active participation of the Orthodox Church in the World Council of Churches? The fact that this organization is composed of many "churches" of varied provenance — Protestant groups, Congregations and offshoots — means that it is not the ideal forum for us to present the spiritual wealth of our Most Holy Orthodox Church. Without doubt Orthodoxy is the diamond of the Christian faith and, as a precious stone, preserves its value, wherever it be found.

In this hodgepodge of Christian confessions, the voice of Orthodoxy is desperately raised, but disappears in the ocean of resolutions of the World Council of Churches, the style and content of which are far removed from true confession. With particular reference to the pitiful image — from an Orthodox perspective — evoked by the inaugural sessions, the festivals at the conclusion of the proceedings and its manifestations in general, which have a peculiar liturgical character and form a pandemonium of joint prayer and worship of anti-Orthodox syncretism, as they recently took place in Canberra, Australia, we note with sorrow the tragic participation of Orthodox Hierarchs in them, as applauding and blessing what happened.[611]

After we have all confirmed these points, there must be an international denunciation of the leading role of the Pope of Rome in the tragic actions against the Orthodox faithful and a condemnation of the acts of violence and of the proselytizing activities of the Roman Catholics and the Uniates incited and supported by them. Likewise, we must also make a decision about cutting off the Theological Dialogue with the Roman Catholics and the heterodox in general. Otherwise, the Orthodox people will have doubts about the assumptions and aims of the present Assembly. With good reason the Orthodox faithful will ask: Why do we condemn certain Orthodox groups[612] bluntly and make no mention at all of a dialogue of love with them, at the same time that the Orthodox Church engages in dialogues with heretics? How do we justify the expression that we must abstain from communion with such [Orthodox] groups, when we embrace the heterodox, whether this be opportunely or inopportunely?

Your Beatitudes and Your Eminences, Holy Brethren, in declaring hence, at this sacred Assembly, the position of our Most Holy Church of Jerusalem on the topics set before us today, in deepest realization of our calling and responsibility, not to mention our promise "rightly to teach the word of truth," we offer the following summary.

---

611 *Canberra, Australia:* This refers to the 7th Assembly of the World Council of Churches that took place in 1991 in which all religions were included and pagan ceremonies were conducted. Patriarch Diodoros is referring to the participation of certain Orthodox Bishops who were in attendance. For example, then Archbishop Kirill (Gundyayev) stated in an on-camera interview, "Orthodox people would like the World Council of Churches (WCC) to be the cradle of the one Church of the future."

612 Patriarch Diodoros is referring to Old Calendarists. The point being the canonical church will hypocritically and simultaneously condemn the Old Calendarists (who hold to Orthodox Christian dogmas) and strive for a false union with heretics found outside of the Holy Orthodox Church.

Our Most Holy Church of Jerusalem:

1. Accepts and preserves all the decisions and definitions of the Holy local and Ecumenical Synods, which our Holy Orthodox Church and her Sacred Tradition and practice dictate.

2. To remove all misunderstanding, recognizes all the prerogatives and rights of the Patriarchate of Constantinople and of the other Ancient Patriarchates, which the Holy Ecumenical Synods have bestowed upon them, and also that which the practice of our Holy Orthodox Church has lavished on them by way of privileges, and is opposed to any attempt at creating a new order in the Church.

3. Believes that, because our Most Holy Orthodox Church in general is the secure treasury of the Truth, the One, Holy, Catholic and Apostolic Church, for this reason the Theological Dialogue with the heterodox is turning out to her loss, to the extent that in the attempt to discover points that we can accept in common with them, the Orthodox Church places in doubt the truth that She possesses. For this reason, She:

4. Abides by Her decisions made in Sessions 65 (May 9/22, 1989) and 88 (February 23/March 7, 1992) of our Holy and Sacred Synod concerning the suspension of the Theological Dialogues with the heterodox in general, namely with the Roman Catholics, the Anglicans, the Anti-Chalcedonians, the Old Catholics, and the Reformed Churches.

5. Condemns forthrightly the proselytizing activities of the Vatican, as stirring up and strengthening its recent proselytizing and assaults on the Orthodox faithful in the countries of Eastern Europe and the Middle East, and denounces internationally its anti-Christian activity and behavior.

6. Abides steadfastly by her abstention from the theological Sessions of the World Council of Churches. We personally,

7. Abide by our previous recommendation concerning the meeting of the Presiding Hierarchs of the Most Holy Orthodox Churches for the scrutiny, study, and resolution of other varied problems that still exist and which seriously occupy our Holy Orthodox Church in her

totality, since, as is attested, the convocation of the Holy and Great Synod, is being delayed.

In making these suggestions to you, with much love, in this present sacred Assembly of Presiding Hierarchs, we entreat you to study the foregoing observations seriously, and we recommend that you make serious and definite decisions, such as are dictated by contemporary circumstances and the demands of the whole Orthodox Church.

In conclusion, we express our warm thanks to His All-Holiness, the Ecumenical Patriarch Bartholomew for his noble hospitality, and we wish him strength in the discharge of his Patriarchal and pastoral duties.

May our Lord be our helper, defender and inspirer, for the glory of the most praiseworthy name of the Supersubstantial Trinity and for the good of Holy Orthodoxy throughout the world.

DIODOROS I
Patriarch of Jerusalem

12. Bishop Augoustinos Kantiotes of Florina, Prespai, and Eordaia, Church of Greece (1907-2010)[613]

This was the beginning of the schism of the Churches. The Pope separated from Orthodoxy and continues to this day to be separated. Even though almost 1,150 years have passed, the Pope still does not recognize his mistakes and remains unrepentant; trying with various treacherous ways to mislead the Orthodox to his side. Unfortunately, there are Orthodox, clergymen and laymen, bishops and even Patriarchs who do not want to understand that Orthodoxy is in danger from such satanic efforts of the Pope. Even after this victory over the Pope, his enemies did not keep quiet; they dethroned him for a second time and sent him into

---

613 Bishop Augoustinos N. Kantiotes, *Fragrant Flowers: Orthodox Homilies on the Lives of the Saints,* trans. Asterios Gerostergios (Belmont: Institute for Byzantine and Modern Greek Studies, 2006), 18-20.

exile. He remained four years in exile. All the while he was studying and praying. Finally, on the 6th of February in 891 he passed away.

What did I say? Passed away? No, Photios did not die; he is living with all the martyrs and confessors and is waiting for the Second Coming of the Lord in order to receive the crown. Also, Saint Photios lives on in the Orthodox Church because whatever Saint Photios preached we also preach and teach to this day. As Saint Photios condemned the Pope, not only for his previous but also for his new heretical teachings, so too do we remain faithful to Orthodoxy. Orthodoxy is our priceless treasure. Imitators of Saint Photos let us preach Orthodoxy to East and West and let us be ready for its protection and spreading and endure every labor, sorrow, and sacrifice.

13. Metropolitans Seraphim of Piraeus & Faliro with Andrew of Dryinoupolis, Pogoniani & Konitsa[614]

An Excerpt of the Letter to Pope Francis Concerning His Past, the Abysmal State of Papism, and a Plea to Return to Holy Orthodoxy

THE HOLY METROPOLIS OF PIRAEUS AND FALIRO
Ἀκτή Θεμιστοκλέους 190, 18539 ΠΕΙΡΑΙΕΥΣ / 190 Themistokleous Coast, 18539 Piraeus,

April 10, 2014
Greece

To His Excellency, Francis,
Head of State of the Vatican City
Vatican City, Rome

Your Excellency,
With due respect and sincere love, we send you this Episcopal letter, the purpose of which doesn't come from any selfish motive, but from

---

614 "A Letter to Pope Francis Concerning His Past, the Abysmal State of Papism, and a Plea to Return to Holy Orthodoxy," Letter of Metropolitan Seraphim (Mentzelopoulos) of Piraeus to Pope Francis Bergoglio, accessed April 14th, 2023, http://orthodoxinfo.com/ecumenism/epistle-to-pope-francis.pdf

pure, sincere and selfless Christian love, from Christian duty, from an essential commandment of our Savior Christ, Who "desires all men to be saved and to come to a full knowledge of the truth," and finally from a warm and ardent desire for your salvation. Because of this we feel it to be our holy and mandatory duty, as the least of the members of the All-holy and All-pure Body of Christ, and especially as Orthodox Bishops, who belong as such to the Holy Synod of the Holy Autocephalous Church of Greece, which is our highest ecclesiastical authority, as to the whole and Undivided One, Holy, Catholic and Apostolic Orthodox Church, to endeavor with all our might to restore you to the Mother Orthodox Catholic Church, from which you left and from which you were cut off, a work which we hope, the Uncreated Divine Grace of the Lord cooperating, shall be achieved. This holy obligation of the return of heretics to the Orthodox Church has, of course, holy canonical grounds and basis and is supported by the 131st, 132nd, and 133rd holy Canons of the Local Council of Carthage (418 or 419 A.D.).

From the outset we must clarify that we Orthodox, not taking part in the politically correct spirit of western and especially ecumenist "Christianity," do not refer to those religious communities who have, sadly, been separated from the One, Holy, Catholic and Apostolic Orthodox Church as "Churches." But, following the example of our Holy Fathers throughout the ages, refer to them as heretics, and you, Your Excellency, and your followers, we denominate as "Papists" and your heresy as "Papism." These terms are, for us, not derogatory, neither are they slurs, but they are theological and even technical terms which best describe the spiritual and ecclesiastical delusion and error in which you find yourselves. We, in fact use them with love, for when one loves his brother, he tells him the truth hoping to bring him back to his senses.

It should also be made clear that the following words are written with pain of heart and not from some personal bitterness or hatred towards your respectable personage. Our purpose is not to offend you, but to reveal, rebuke, admonish and to refute your deluded and heretical ideas, theories and actions. Our basic rule is that we should love the heretics but rebuke and hate their heresy and delusions. Our only interest is our Holy Orthodoxy, the only place in which humans have salvation. We unceasingly pray that our Lord Jesus Christ gather together the deluded

"Pope" and his followers, through repentance and the renunciation of your delusion and heresy, into the One, Holy, Catholic and Apostolic, Orthodox Church and to assume as an Orthodox Pope, according to seniority of honor of the Pentarchy and in agreement with the Divine and Holy Canons, the Chairmanship of honor of the Autocephalous Orthodox Churches as *"primus inter pares."*

An additional reason, which shows the timeliness and importance of our present Episcopal epistle, are the intrigues in the realm of the modern heretical Ecumenical Movement with its ecumenist theological dialogues between Orthodox and Papists, where the representatives from the Orthodox side, animated unfortunately by the pan-heretical spirit of inter-Christian and inter-religious syncretistic ecumenism, and employing the false ecumenist love, a "love" without true love and unity in the Orthodox faith, deceive you, Your Excellency, claiming that Papism is a so called "Church," and moreover a "sister Church," with valid Mysteries (Sacraments), Baptism, the Priesthood and Grace, that Papism and Orthodoxy make up the so-called, "two lungs," with which the Church of Christ breathes, that you, the heretical "Pope," are a canonical bishop, successor of the Apostle Peter and Vicar of Christ on earth, who possess the Apostolically, Scripturally and Patristically groundless and non-existent "Petrine" primacy of power over all the Church, and the blasphemous "Papal Infallibility," instead of the true primacy of honor (διά τό είναι τήν Ρώμην πρωτεύουσα) as is commanded by the Holy Canons of the undivided Church of the first millennium to which the Orthodox Pope of Rome and Patriarch of the West is entitled, doctrines that are totally unknown and without foundation or witness in the general Tradition of the Catholic Orthodox Church of the first ten centuries and of the eight Holy Ecumenical Councils, doctrines which are a clear blasphemy against the All-Holy Spirit and which show your theological departure and the satanic pride of which you are possessed. Clear proof of the absurdity of the Orthodox Ecumenists is that, while they attribute to you ecclesiastical titles, you who are obviously heretical and erroneous in belief, they do not dare, even though it would be in keeping with their declarations, to come into sacramental communion with you, because they know from that moment, they will immediately lose their own ecclesiastical identity. Does this not make up the most blatant proof of the false doctrines of Ecumenism? If they indeed believe their unacceptable and provocative declarations, then let them dare to take the step into sacramental communion, because otherwise they prove by their actions the emptiness of the ecclesiastical titles which they give to you false bishops of the false believers. Clear confirmation of the above was the last-minute cancellation of your personal attendance at the celebrations of the 1700th anniversary of the Edict of Milan in Niš, Serbia, on June 10th, 2013, and the cancellation of your visit to the Holy Mountain of Athos the same month, as rumor has it.

In communicating with you through this present Episcopal letter, we desire that it be made known to you that, according to the diachronic Holy Scriptural, Canonical and Patristic Tradition and according to the infallible conscience of the fullness of the Eastern Orthodox Catholic Church, Papism, of which you are the leader, Your Excellency, is not a "Church," but a religious community, a parasynagogue, a heresy, an alteration, a demolishing and a total perversion of the Truth, namely, of the very God-man, Christ. Hosts of Orthodox Councils have condemned Papism as a heresy. We will cite some significant examples: The Council of 879-880 in Constantinople, under the Ecumenical Patriarch, Archbishop of Constantinople and New Rome, Saint Photios the Great, Equal to the Apostles, which condemned as heretical the teaching of the Filioque, and is considered by the consciousness of the Church to be the 8th Ecumenical Council, because in it were representatives of all the Patriarchates, including the then Orthodox Pope of Rome, John the 8th, and because the decisions of this council were universally accepted. Unfortunately, this heterodox belief has prevailed as your official teaching, from the beginning of the 11th century (1014) until today. Papism adopted after more than a millennium, a heretical teaching, which Rome had already condemned along with the other Orthodox Patriarchates, refuting and condemning itself as a heresy. Besides that, all the subsequent Orthodox Councils, like the Constantinopolitan Councils of 1170, 1341, 1450, 1722, 1838, and 1895 unequivocally condemned Papism as a heresy. What is more, all of the Saints who lived after the schism of 1054, such as St. Germanos Patriarch of Constantinople, St. Gregory Palamas, St. Mark of Ephesus, St. Simeon of Thessalonica, St. Nicodemus the Hagiorite, St. Cosmas of Aetolia, St. Nektarios of Pentapolis, St. Justin Popović and others, with one voice, condemn Papism as a heresy. Papism is not a "Church" but a State — the Vatican, a worldly organization, with a government, with you, the "Pope," as leader, with the Cardinals as Ministers and Secretaries and with the "Bank of the Holy Spirit." Neither is Papism a "Roman Catholic Church," because it is neither Roman, nor Catholic, nor a Church. It has no relation with Romiosini or with Romania. It isn't Catholic since it separated of its own will from the Catholic Orthodox Church in 1054 A.D. and since then it doesn't possess the fullness of the Orthodox Faith of our Holy Fathers, which you have distorted. You are not a Church, since you became a State, falling, instead, to the third temptation of Christ. You accepted the Devil's proposal to make you almighty earthly rulers in return for your allegiance to him. We Orthodox are the true Roman Catholic Church. We Orthodox are the Romans: to us belong Romania, Romiosini. Orthodoxy is the One Holy, CATHOLIC, and Apostolic Church, the true Roman Catholic Church, as we confess in the Nicene-Constantinopolitan Symbol of Faith.

The fact that Papism is a heresy is revealed by the appalling false doctrines which you confess. These are: I) the political existence and structure of the Vatican with ministries, bureaucracies and banks; II) the *Filioque* (the alleged procession of the Holy Spirit also from the Son); III) created Grace; IV) the primacy of power; V) the possession of worldly and spiritual power by the Pope; VI) Papal infallibility; VII) the theories that the Pope is the ultimate judge and Archpriest, the supreme authority and monarch of the Church; VIII) Baptism by sprinkling and the separation of it from the mystery of Chrismation; IX) the use of unleavened bread (Host); X) the transforming of the bread and wine into the Body and Blood of Christ with the words of institution rather than at the invocation of the Holy Spirit as well as the doctrine of transubstantiation; XI) the depriving of the Blood of Christ to the laity; XII) the depriving of Holy Communion to children; XIII) Mary worship; XIV) the dogma of the "immaculate conception" and the "bodily assumption" of the Mother of God; XV) purgatory; XVI) indulgences; XVII) the so-called "superabundant merits" of Christ; XVIII) the "superabundant merits" of the Saints; XIX) the merits of the works of man; XX) statuary and the secularization of religious art instead of Orthodox iconography; XXI) the mandatory celibacy of the clergy; XXII) the recognition of murderers (Stepinac) as "saints"; XXIII) the doctrine of the satisfaction of divine justice (the result of confusion regarding original sin and the legalism which is prevalent in Papism); XXIV) the rejection of Holy Tradition and the taking advantage of it as a tool for Papal claims (the Pope is Tradition); XXV) the belief that the "infallible Pope" is the only guardian, judge and interpreter of Divine Revelation; XXVI) the so-called "Church Suffering," which is allegedly made up of the faithful who are presently in purgatory; XXVII) the rejection of the equality of bishops; XXVIII) the Vatican's centralized and despotic administrative system where the "Pope" is absolute monarch, which introduced Caesaropapism; XXIX) the social/humanitarian character of the monastic orders; XXX) the impersonal and juridical character of the mystery of confession; XXXI) and, finally, the accursed Uniate, the Trojan horse of Papism [...].

We pray that the uncreated Grace of the All-Holy Spirit will enlighten your mind and strengthen you to shake off the slumber of delusion, heresy and sloth and to draw nigh to the open arms of the Orthodox Church.

Restore the abject and erstwhile senior and ancient Patriarchate of Old Rome and the West to the Body of Christ, to the Body of the Church. Take upon yourself your holy duties as the First Orthodox Primate of the Autocephalous Orthodox Churches with the true primacy of honor, which is your right as the Orthodox First Hierarch of the One, Holy, Catholic and Apostolic Church. Amen.[615]

With respect,
+ Andrew of Dryinoupolis, Pogoniani and Konitsa
+ Seraphim of Piraeus and Faliro

---

615 This lengthy eighty-seven-page letter was written by His Eminence, the Metropolitan of Piraeus, Seraphim, and His Eminence, the Metropolitan of Dryinoupolis, Andrew, both of the Holy Orthodox Church of Greece. It was sent to Pope Francis on April 10th, 2014. The original letter was edited into the English by the Orthodox Christian Information Center (OrthodoxInfo.com) and posted on Great and Holy Monday, April 14th, 2014. See previous footnote to read the entire published letter.

14. Bishop Luke (Murianka) of Syracuse, Abbot of Holy Trinity Monastery (1951-present)

YET ANOTHER STEP?[616]

The various Christian denominations and other world religions are obviously in movement towards union. One need only look at the various conferences, meetings, and prayer services reported in the news media over the last few years for proof that such a movement exists. What is the reason for all this activity? It seems to arise from disenchantment with the inadequacies that the participants see in their own denominations or faiths. They maintain that no single denomination represents the True Church. We have only to unite, they say, in order for the One Great Truth, heretofore hidden, to reveal itself to all. This movement gains momentum daily. The various meetings, joint international commissions, "concelebrations," dialogues, "final texts," and declarations are multiplying at a spectacular and, in the eyes of the discerning Orthodox Christian, an alarming rate.

One such joint international commission was the subject of an article in a Byzantine Catholic newspaper, *Horizons*, on 13 November 1988. The article quoted from a statement made by the Joint Committee of Orthodox and Roman Catholic Bishops (in the USA) concerning "the permanent character of priestly ordination in both the Orthodox and Roman Catholic Churches." The Orthodox and Roman Catholic bishops who signed the document agreed that "for both Orthodox Christians and Roman Catholics, when a member of the clergy who has been ordained, in a church that shared with them the understanding of the priesthood, by a bishop in an unquestionable apostolic succession, is received into either the Orthodox or Roman Catholic Church, his ordination should be recognized." The statement also contains an agreement that "the three sacred orders of diaconate, presbyterate, and episcopate have a sacramental nature" and that "these orders are exclusively conferred by bishops with unquestionable apostolic succession."

---

616 Holy Trinity Monastery, "Yet Another Step? By Hieromonk Luke (Murianka)," *Orthodox Life*, no 1 (January-February 1989): 24-29.

Had such statements been made solely by Roman Catholic bishops, they might be overlooked. But since the documents are also signed by Orthodox bishops, the average believer might very easily draw the conclusion that Orthodox and Roman Catholic clergy are both canonical, i.e., in layman's terms, that the Orthodox Church recognizes Roman Catholic clergy — and, by implication, the sacraments they perform — to be on an equal footing with Orthodox clergy and their sacraments. To draw such a conclusion, although understandable under the circumstances, does not reflect the teaching of the Orthodox Church.

The spiritual climate among the Orthodox Christians in Western countries has been to a large extent negatively affected by the mixed cultural and religious atmosphere that they live in. It is harmful for the average Orthodox believer to seek guidance or support from other groups that are not Orthodox and do not share our religious convictions. Answers to Orthodox questions come only from within Orthodox Tradition. This was first taught by St. Paul, who warned his spiritual children to distrust even an angel if he were to teach something contrary to the Gospel, he had delivered to them. The subtle deceptions and pitfalls which the contemporary Orthodox Christian must contend with should make us even more respectful of St. Paul's admonition. One such deception is contained in the statement made by the Joint Committee of Orthodox and Roman Catholic Bishops (in the USA) and reported in Horizons, in which they quote from the "Final Text" of the theological dialogue between the Roman Catholic Church and the Orthodox Church, which met in Uusi Valamo, Finland.

Before we can begin to examine the many confusing points found in this "Final Text," we must review the Orthodox Tradition on the subject of our relationship with the Roman Catholic Church and how this affects our attitude to their ordinations. The Latins have been "out of communion" with the Orthodox Church for nearly 1000 years. This situation is not accidental nor is it without great spiritual significance for Orthodoxy. Without even discussion the reasons for this division it is sufficient to recognize one fact. Orthodoxy has always viewed any separation from itself, for any reason, as a grave sin. In church terms this is called schism. St. John Chrysostom in his homilies on *St. Paul's Letter to the Ephesians* states, "Nothing is so offensive to God as division in the

Church. Even if we did thousands of good deeds, we will fall into no less condemnation as those who tore His body if we divide the body of the Church... I say and witness to the fact that to create a division in the Church is no less evil than to fall into heresy."

St. Cyprian in his letter 69 on the Baptismal controversy speaks out strongly against those who separate themselves from the Church, saying, "...The blessed Apostle John made no distinction between one form of heresy or schism and another, nor did he single out any special class of separatists. He called all who had gone out of the Church and worked against it Antichrists, saying, '...they went out from us, but they were not of us; for if they had been of us, they would have continued with us.'" St. Basil the Great in his *First Epistle to Amphilocus* discusses the spiritual state of schismatics (in this case the Cathari). He states, "...True enough, the separation resulted from a schism, but those who seceded from the Church had not the grace of the Holy Spirit upon them; for the impartation thereof *ceased with the interruption of (legal) canonical succession.* For although the ones who were the first to depart had been ordained by the Fathers, and with the imposition of their hands they had obtained the gracious gift of the Spirit, yet after breaking away they became laymen, and had no authority either to baptize or to ordain anyone, nor could they impart the grace of the Spirit to others..." St. Cyprian of Carthage in his stern address to those who had fallen away says, "...He who abandons the Church of Christ deprives himself of the rewards foreordained by Christ: he is a stranger, an outcast, he is her enemy. He cannot have God as a Father who does not have the Church as a Mother. He who is outside the Church might be able to be saved only if someone who was outside the ark of Noah was able to escape."

From these quotes we can see clearly how the Orthodox Fathers viewed separation from the Church. The dogma of the single unity of the Church was established by the Saviour, expanded by St. Paul, and confirmed by all the Ecumenical and Local Councils of the Orthodox Church up to the present day. A contemporary Holy Father, the New Martyr Archbishop Ilarion Troitsky also enlightens us with his thoughts. "Membership in the Church," he says, "is determined by unity with the Church... the Church is not only one body but also One Spirit... any separation from the Church will turn out to be incompatible with membership in the Church. *It is not the degree of the dogmatic dissent* on the part of the separated member *that is important*: what is significant in the extreme *is the fact of separation as such*, the cessation itself of the unity within the Church. Whether it be separation on the basis of an act of rebellion against the Church or simply a disciplinary insubordination without any dogmatic difference of opinion, separation form the Church will, for the one that has fallen away, have every sad consequence."

Returning again to the full text issued by the Joint International Commission for the theological dialogue between the Roman Catholic Church and the Orthodox Church, we meet many misleading statements which could well cause confusion in the minds of the Orthodox faithful. We read in paragraph 1: "...We rely on certitude that in our Churches apostolic succession is fundamental for the sanctification and the unity of the people of God." A true enough statement if it refers to the True Church and the True Apostolic Succession, bearing in mind what St. Basil says in his letter to Amphilocus where he states that True (Apostolic) Succession ceases where membership in the One, True Church is broken. We also read in paragraph 14 that "... The ecclesial ministry will be called apostolic because it is carried out in continuity with and in fidelity to what was given by Christ and handed on in his history by the Apostles..." The Orthodox Fathers have condemned the Latin Church precisely because it did not preserve "continuity and fidelity" with Tradition. Paragraph 22 emphasizes that "This is why the Church in which God's grace is at work is itself the Sacrament 'par excellence.'" But God's grace is *not* at work in the Church whose membership in the Body of Christ has been broken and therefore the separated Churches' 'Sacrament' is not effective. We see in paragraph 38 "...it also rests with him (the bishop) to see to it that there be given to his people by preaching and catechesis the authentic content of the Word of God given to the Apostles once and for all.'" But what if the bishop belongs to a Church that has been in separation and error for 1000 years? Can he really hope to pass on correct teaching?

There follow in Section IV of the Joint International Commission's "Final Text" many points concerning apostolic succession, all of which could cause much confusion for the average Orthodox believer if he has no answers from his own tradition. For example, in paragraph 46 we read: "...Apostolic succession, therefore, means something more than a mere transmission of powers. It is succession in a Church which witnesses to the apostolic faith in communion with other Churches, witnesses of the same apostolic faith..." The Orthodox Fathers would agree with such a statement to measure the truth of a given church body within Orthodoxy. But we ask, how can those outside Orthodoxy "witness to the apostolic faith" when they are not in any form of "communion with the other Churches"?

One of the most misleading and bold statements, paragraph 49, reads: "Through his ordination each bishop becomes successor of the apostles, whatever may be the Church over which he presides or the prerogatives of this Church among the other Churches." This statement reflects an attitude one meets in the writings of such early Fathers as Clement, Tertullian, and St. Basil. They also began to speak of all bishops as "successors of the Apostles." St. Basil even referred to such unlikely a place as Milan as "the see of the Apostles," although no Apostle ever had his see there. But, on the other hand, never did an Orthodox Father accept just any or all bishops as Apostles without the qualifications mentioned above. Such an indiscriminate acceptance would have created anarchy in Church life. And, furthermore, if we were to examine any standard text on dogmatic theology, we would discover those conditions necessary in order to qualify a clergyman as legal or canonical. One such text reads: "To be true Orthodox clergy you must, 1. receive the grace of the Holy Spirit through the descendants of the Apostles in unbroken succession; 2. perform the sacraments according to the forms handed down by Orthodox Tradition: 3. correctly confess the True Faith; 4. The clergy must rule their flocks according to the canons of the Holy Apostles, Ecumenical Councils, and other canons accepted by the whole Orthodox Church; 5. he must be in communion with the Orthodox Church in a spirit of peace and love. Those bishops, priests, and laymen who separate themselves from their spiritual leaders are cut off from the Church — according to the rules of the Apostles and Councils."

From the foregoing and what we have read from the Fathers we must surely dispute the validity of paragraph 49. But the confusion caused by statements like paragraph 49 is increased when we see that some Orthodox bishops have signed them. Even a superficial examination of our Tradition clearly illuminates the fundamental nature of the differences which separate us. How then can Orthodox bishops sign such documents? The tactic developed in the World Council of Churches and used extensively in negotiations between Anglicans, Roman Catholics, Lutherans, and other less reputable groups consists in burying differences and emphasizing similarities and points of agreement. This may achieve satisfactory results in settling Trades Union disputes and in Superpower negotiations, but it is also a primary reason why these institutions often do not even outlive the negotiators who participate in resolving their disputes. If the Early Fathers had employed this tactic, the Church would never have survived. Christianity, as the Apostles knew it would have quickly succumbed to the many heresies that assailed it. This did not happen because they saw the dangers, warning the faithful to avoid contact with those who had fallen away.

Let us examine some of the differences between Orthodoxy and Roman Catholicism which separate us. They include the way we understand the action of the Holy Spirit, the Virgin Mary, the position of the Pope and his authority, calendar usage, performance of the sacraments, the nature of grace, and the overall, most important stumbling block — the approach to the spiritual life. Where the Catholic Church recognizes sanctity and desirable spiritual manifestations, Orthodox Fathers see pride and deception — recent examples of this can be seen in the Charismatic movement. If the average Orthodox believer does not understand or see the dangers present in ecumenism, the points we have highlighted above should act as a warning.

Finally, it is interesting to note that in all of these ecumenical consultations it seems to be a foregone conclusion on the part of the participants that in any re-united Church Rome would resume her former role as "first among equals." But even if there were a sincere movement on the part of Rome to repent and rejoin the Orthodox Church, how could we then view her position? We acknowledge that God forgives and forgets the sins of the penitent as He did the Prodigal Son. On the other hand, after 1000 years of separation and the accumulation of many errors and attitudes foreign to Orthodoxy, such a repentant body could not hope to regain even equal, let alone a pre-eminent position among the Churches which have persevered in their Orthodoxy according to Apostolic and later traditions. Only after a period of carefully guided re-education in the principles of Orthodox practice and spiritual life could we begin to examine the possibility of the ancient position of honor, which, in any case, was conceded only where Orthodoxy was preserved in its purity. A true, sincere union, pleasing to God, can hardly be accomplished amid "dialogues," "joint commissions," and questionable ecumenical prayer meetings, followed by coffee and doughnuts and confirmed by handshakes.

We see serious repercussions in the fact that in articles like the one in *Horizons* and the documents that lie behind it the true teaching of the Orthodox Church and its attitude toward those groups which are separated from it are being misrepresented — and perhaps deliberately ignored — by Orthodox bishops. Furthermore, in many cases these bishops are pursuing their own desires for union regardless of the convictions of their flocks or the teachings of the very same Holy Fathers who have preserved and transmitted to them their Orthodox Faith.

Archimandrite Philotheos Zervakos

B. Holy Elders

Unique to Orthodoxy and not possible in heterodox communions is the role of the geronda or starets which have cleaned the house of their soul to such a state where God has come to dwell in them. They speak the word of the Holy Spirit in matters of salvation and this includes clarification on the Body of Christ: where it is and where it is not. Oftentimes, elders eventually become canonized as saints, so they exist in times contemporary or immediately proximate to our lives.

1. Elder Philotheos (Zervakos), Monastery of Longovarda, Greece (1884-1980)

a. Innovations are the Work of Heretics[617]

The Orthodox Church places under anathemas and excommunications the innovationists and reformers of the Apostolic and patristic traditions. Your friend falsely says that in the 9th and 10th century the Orthodox Church made reforms. Let his tongue cease from evil and his lips from speaking guile. The innovations are the work of the Catholics and the Protestants. The Eastern Orthodox Church does not have a habit of making innovations, but rather follows the teachings of the Apostles, the Teachers, the Holy Fathers and the seven Ecumenical Holy Synods, whose teachings the wise among the Latins and Protestants ought to also follow... so that they might be delivered from penances,

---

617 Father Philotheos Zervakos, *Paternal Counsels Vol. 2* (Thessalonika: Orthodox Kypseli Publications, 2005), 17-18.

the anathemas and excommunications of the holy Ecumenical Synods and of the Holy Fathers. We are obligated to pray for them so that God may return them from delusion to the straight path and so that we may all become one flock with the Ruler and founder of our true Orthodox faith as Leader, our Lord Jesus Christ and Savior the Deliverer and Liberator of our souls and bodies.

b. One Soul is Worth More Than the Whole World[618]

If God wills and I come, and I am able to grab away even one soul from sin, to bring it into repentance, from delusion to truth, from wickedness to virtue, from darkness to light, from the devil to Christ, this shall be the greatest fund drive for me and my Monastery, because one soul is worth more than the whole world [...] In one moment the truly great sacrament of Repentance and Confession makes the sinner righteous according to the witness of the second preacher of repentance Saint John Chrysostom. "As soon as the sinner confesses his sins and you make the subsequent safety, God declares him righteous."

The Jehovah's Witnesses, communists, evangelists, papists, masons, spiritualists and others with many different names and various ways being enemies, finding the sheep without good and true shepherds, enter in like wild wolves grabbing and scattering the sheep. The Church has need of many workers, because many are the opponents. It has need of workers who are not lukewarm, self-loving and flesh-loving, but of true workers with faith and zeal, with self-denial and wholehearted love for God and neighbor. Such as these do we wish and long to prepare even if few, but we have need of strengthening from both God and from men, as many as are able and wish to help. (From a letter to an Archbishop abroad.)

c. The Judgments of God are an Abyss[619]

Concerning the miracles which occur at the Virgin Mary at Lourdes and Francis of Assisi, know that miracles follow faith. The heretics whether Westerners, Protestants, or Ottomans, when they ask with faith for physical healings, receive indiscriminately, for He who receives their

---

618 Father Philotheos Zervakos, *Paternal Counsels Vol. 2* (Thessalonika: Orthodox Kypseli Publications, 2005), 25-26.

619 Ibid., 26.

request said: "*Ask and it shall be given, seek and ye shall find.*" The all-Good God, who wants all to be saved and to come to the realization, grants their request, so that through this He might draw them to the correct and true faith. If, however, they do not approach and die in heresy, in delusion, during the 2nd Coming He shall separate them from His kingdom. And then they shall tell Him: Lord did we not prophesy in your name, do powers, miracles! He shall tell them: Depart from me you workers of iniquity. With these things do not occupy yourself because they are mysteries and judgments of God which are an abyss and incomprehensible. You should be occupied with learning in a practical manner humility and love, and when you obtain them, and do not have a spirit of laziness, authority loving and vain talking you will be saved, you will go to Paradise, to the kingdom of the heavens, which may we all achieve. Amen.

d. The *Filioque* Resulted in Myriads of Cacodoxies and Heresies[620]

Rebelling against the Holy Spirit [...] darkened by the evil one, the Latins added the phrase "and from the Son". Subsequently the Pope-worshippers tumbled into myriads of cacodoxies and heresies [...] I pray that the Grace of God my preserve you from the wolves, the heretics.

e. Desperate Appeal to the Ecumenical Patriarch[621]

Translator's Preface: The author of this appeal is the best-known father-confessor and preacher of Greece — truly, a new St. Cosmas of Aitolia — who has traversed Greece on foot countless times in his 67 years of priesthood, being now in his 97th year. His spiritual children number in the thousands, not only in Greece, but in the United States, Australia, Europe, and other parts of the world as well. A truly apostolic man filled with the gifts of the Holy Spirit, he is known especially for exorcising demons and giving spiritual direction. According to the report, he has worked many miracles. He most vividly prophesied the destruction of Asia Minor in the early twenties, at a time when no one could

---

620 Anonymous, Ο Γέρων Φιλόθεος Ζερβάκος (ο Ουρανοδρόμος Οδοιπόρος), 565. Quoted in Protopresbyter Anastasios K. Gotsopoulos, *On Common Prayer with the Heterodox*, (Uncut Mountain Press, 2022), 17.

621 Orthodox Christian Books & Icons, "A Desperate Appeal to the Ecumenical Patriarch," *Orthodox Word 4*, no. 1 (January-February 1968): 11-20.

believe what he was saying. Therefore, the terribleness of his utterance in the present letter (p. 20), in which he foresees the terrible fall of the Ecumenical Patriarch if he does not repent...

THE LETTER

From some time past I had purposed to write to Your All Holiness because of Your hasty and unhesitating dealing toward a union of the Orthodox Eastern Church with the evil-doctrined Papacy. I did not write to You, because illustrious hierarchs, elect clerics, most pious professors and theologians, virtuous monks, learned, informed laymen have written clearly against this false union pursued in so hasty and servile a manner.[622]

I had hoped that the sufferings which have come from the sins of all us Greeks — both clergy and lay, men and women, small and great — would have brought You to Your senses, and that You would have diverted Your audacious and (to the Orthodox Church) most soul-harming resolution into an effort to unite the divided portions of the Orthodox Church in Greece. One would have expected that the Primate of Greek Orthodoxy would have first preached repentance to all of the Orthodox Church and to the sinful Greek people; that he would have given the sign for a return to the All-Ruler; and that he would call for a union and friendship with the most loving — but also most just — Heavenly Father, from Whom, as disobedient and ungrateful despisers of His Divine commandments and precepts, we have broken away and are become, instead of His friends, His enemies. Likewise, one would have expected that You would have taken care to restore the unity of our Church from the division and schism caused by that thoughtless, pointless, untimely and diabolical innovation — the introduction of the Gregorian (Papal) Calendar by Your Masonic predecessor, Meletios Metaxakis, who misled the then Archbishop of Athens, Chrysostom Papadopoulos.

---

622 See, for example, in *The Orthodox Word*, "The Ecumenical Patriarchate," by Theoklitos, Monk of Dionysiou (vol. 2, no. 1, 31 ff.); and "An Open Letter to the Ecumenical Patriarch'" by Archimandrite Epiphanios Theodoropoulos (vol. 2, no. 4, 141 ff.).

Unfortunately, not, however. Not only did You have no provision and no concern for the above-mentioned primary needs and similar urgent sacred matters that should take precedence over every other endeavor, but instead, to the strengthening and widening of the schism within the Church of Greece, You hasten with swift step and slavish mind to the fulfillment of Your first dubious decision — that is, toward false union with the falsely-infallible Pontiff who summoned You, as someone in error, to return to the Papal fold. It is precisely because I see that the Union above every other union — that is, the essential Union and Friendship with the Triune God — does not concern You (nor does the reestablishment of the unity of the divided and much-suffering Greek Orthodox Church) that I am obliged to write You, fearing lest I shall sin if I keep silent and do not profess the truth.

See, Your All-Holiness, how by means of dissension the wolf seizes and scatters the sheep of Your own flock which the Lord has entrusted unto You and for which He shed His Blood. And You have no concern for the sheep. You are only concerned at all cost to achieve union and friendship with — and Your own and Your flock's submission to — the Pope. But take care, Your All-Holiness, because the good and rational sheep of Christ's flock will not follow You, in accordance with the word of the Gospel: *And a stranger they will not follow, but will flee from him...* (St. John 10:5). Those that will follow You will be such as are outside of the fold of Christ, who are of Papal and Luthero-Calvinistic sheep pens, those whose minds are heterodox.

The first to speak already were the most righteous Fathers of the Holy Mountain, who gave the watchword, the good and honorable example, in imitation of their holy Orthodox Fathers who did not hearken to that other voice like Yours — that is, to the voice of the alien Latinizer, the Patriarch John Beccos.[623] Those Fathers preferred death to false union. And not only do the present Athonite Fathers not follow You, but they have also even ceased to commemorate You in the Divine services. You must know, Your All-Holiness, that there are not only the Holy Mountain Fathers, but also myriads of other Greek clergy and lay people, genuine Orthodox, some of whom have disavowed You and others who are ready to disavow You in so far as You persist in devious and

---

623 Who lived in the 13th century. See *The Orthodox Word*, vol. 3, no. 4, 138.

deliberate false union. By Your unconsidered and impatient endeavor, you have scandalized myriads of souls of elect Orthodox Christians. If it is better for him who has scandalized one of the least of these little ones to hang a millstone upon his neck and be sunk in the depths of the sea (St. Matthew 18:6), then what, Your All-Holiness, will be the punishment for Your sin? For You have scandalized not only one of the least, but myriads of the great — bishops, priests, priestmonks, monks, theologians, both men and women.

Understand this truth that others also have pointed out to You. Before anything else, it is Your job to bring peace and unity to the Orthodox Church, which has been literally shaken by the innovation [the Gregorian Calendar] which — in a manner that was anarchical and without the agreement of all Orthodox Churches — was introduced into the Church of Greece in the year 1924; an innovation that overturned the ecclesiastical order and Tradition established from ages past, that brought about dissensions and divisions, that destroyed unity of worship and created a religious schism among Orthodox everywhere. First take away this schism, and *then* turn toward the West. Then, and only then, open the portals of the Orthodox Church, and with pure and unfeigned love say unto the Pope and to the heretics, "You desire union? We also desire it and long for it ardently. Behold, we receive you gladly once you have previously cast off your evil doctrines and errors and cast away all that is against the sacred Canons and patristic Traditions of the seven Holy Ecumenical Councils."

But Your All-Holiness, nowhere do we have any indication that the Church of Rome has clarified her position regarding rapprochement with the Orthodox Church and the other Christian confessions. To the contrary, rather, we have occasion and cause to believe unwaveringly that the Papists persist stubbornly and unchangingly in their evil doctrines and arbitrariness. Even today they announce categorically and unblushingly preach that "Union of Christianity means nothing else but submission to Rome, to the sole Vicar of Christ on earth," and that "the Primacy and the Infallibility are not ecclesiological decrees which the Church can invalidate, but dogmas that no one can shake" (*Catholike*, the Roman Catholic newspaper of Athens, Oct. 16, 1963); and furthermore that "the Catholic Church is not about to sacrifice any of her truths"— say rather, *her errors*. To what end, therefore, is this ostentatious diligence on the part of the Orthodox? "The union pursued on both sides cannot be a true union, nor one that is permanent or stable, since it is not based upon unity of doctrine. It is quite clear that since inner union is impossible, external union is impossible also — that is, any rapprochement of the two churches without dogmatic unity in such a way that the followers of the one could partake of the mysteries from priests of the other without hesitation. This external union, which is based upon religious indifference, will have as its result not true union, but the confusion of the churches. The Eastern Church has never permitted, nor will it ever be able to permit her members to receive the pseudo-mysteries and the (supposed) grace of the Holy Spirit from the clerics of a heterodox church. Whoever thinks otherwise is assuredly not an Orthodox Christian."[624]

But the whole subject has been made marvelously and superbly clear, leaving no doubt whatever, by St. Nectarios of Pentapolis[625] in his God-enlightened book, *An Historical Study Concerning the Causes of the Schism [...] Concerning the Impossibility or Possibility of Union*. It would be most beneficial and to the enlightenment of the faithful if we quote the text verbatim. The Saint says on page 9: "The terms of union are such that they render the sought-for union impossible, because they have no point of contact. Each seeks from the other nothing more nor less than the denial of itself and the basic principles upon which the whole structure of the church is founded. For on the one hand, the Papal church is based on the primacy of the Pope according to their understanding of this point; and on the other, the Eastern Church is founded upon the Ecumenical Councils. Because of this, the terms of union brought forward by either side are impossible of acceptance since they overturn the churches from their very foundations. Hence the ineffectiveness of any concessions either side can make. The primacy of honor which is given by the Eastern Church to the Pope is a useless concession because it lacks the power to hold the fabric of the Western Church together.

---

624 K. Dyovouniotes (a theologian of the last century at the University of Athens).

625 Recently Patriarch Athenagoras designated St. Nectarios as "The Patron Saint of Union"! On the contrary; as the present quotation reveals, he was a champion of Orthodoxy.

The concessions given by the Pope to the Eastern Church — that is, her remaining in her own dogmas, customs and disciplines — are not in the least considered as "concessions" by her but as legitimate in themselves, since they are founded on the Canons of the Church, for which reason alone she abides in them. But she demands also that the Pope himself with all the Western Church return to her bosom, renouncing their former life, and come in repentance to her. Therefore, the apparent concessions have no meaning whatever, since they are not actually concessions. For union to come about, it is necessary that the concessions remove the main causes of separation. The concessions will truly be such when the Pope gives up his own ways, and not when he simply tolerates those things that have been well-established in the Church. Since the main causes of the separation remain as such, the churches persist in their own ways, and union is *impossible*. For union to be established, it must be made secure upon the same principle. Otherwise, every labor is vain."

Let there be union, Your All-Holiness, but in the way Christ wishes it: far from every worldly purpose and every compromise. Your desire regarding the evil-doctrined Papal church should be an Apostolic desire, a God-bearing and holy desire. Because, as the sacred Canons proclaim: "The things which have been transmitted in Orthodoxy are not 'Yea and Nay,' but they are 'Yea' in truth; and they remain unbroken and unshaken unto eternity." Concerning the middle way of compromise, St. Mark Evgenikos said that not even the idea of it should deceive anyone, because between two opposite doctrines a true middle way of compromise cannot exist. "For these reasons, those who proclaim the middle way of compromise and teach that there is nothing stable or definite and certain, but like hypocrites by means of concessions adapt and waver between each other's opinions, must be avoided." Neither say, Your All-Holiness, that we are pursuing merely an external rapprochement and unity for the formation of a united front of love against hunger, against misfortune, against atheism, against Communism, against war, *etc.*, since union must first be a triumph of truth, and then a triumph of love which springs forth from the unity of faith. And again, neither under the cover of achieving peace should You endeavor as You do, since as that great defender of Orthodoxy, St. Mark Evgenikos, says again, "It is impossible to restore peace if the cause of the schism is not previously removed, and the Pope, who is declared to be equal to God, does not come to self-realization."

Your All-Holiness, the whole history of the efforts for union, from 867 (and especially from 1054) and onward, assures us that the West has always offered to the East the longed-for union of the churches in order to pursue unadmitted Papal plans for the submission of the Orthodox Eastern Church. Furthermore, we are made even more hesitant by the lamentable fact that in our midst there exists — as there ought not — the Unia, which, according to the ever-memorable Chrysostom Papadopoulos, "craftily seeks to lead the people into Papism and gradually and imperceptibly to Latinize them." Since it is precisely because of their deceitful posture that the Uniates poison the relations between the two churches, You, Your All-Holiness, should have laid down as a primary condition for union the immediate disbanding of the Unia.

Of course, no true Orthodox Christian, cleric or layman, remains unmoved by the Christ-desired blessing of union as long as deceit and shameful enslavement are not hidden beneath its most sweet name. But a more serious study of the situation as it has taken shape during ten centuries of schism and complete separation, proves that matters are not so simple that with a mere dialogue in the hallways of the Lateran Palace we shall be able to achieve the longed-for union. And a dialogue on equal terms, at this moment being belied by the facts, is shown to be a utopian fantasy. The Western Church must take not merely steps, but giant leaps, in order to reach the place where it formerly stood as a sister to the Eastern Church. Otherwise, if the Church of Rome continues to persist in the principles of Papism and seeks through various means to extend her dominion over the whole *ecumene*, swallowing and assimilating all, it would be utter folly for us Orthodox to open discussions with men who have no intention of moving from their positions — not even in the slightest — but on the contrary show tendencies to swallow up all the other churches. The healthy and incorrupt conscience of the Orthodox rejects such purposeless and vain discussions.

Take heed, Your All-Holiness, lest with Your untimely endeavors You tear the Church asunder and divide the Orthodox even more than they are divided. Do You take the responsibility for breaking up the unity of the Greek people and shattering their spiritual bonds with the other Orthodox? Why should You force the Holy Mountain Fathers, or five to ten Metropolitans of Greece, to split the Church tomorrow in order to preserve her from an untimely "union"? What do You think You have achieved by Your "unique," but wholly uncanonical and unprecedented meeting with the Bishop of Rome? Most simply, You strengthened the Latin position on the schism. And what did Your melodramatic, far-fetched salutation, Your clinging embraces, and Your uncanonical exchange of gifts achieve? Precisely to increase the danger — the danger that the awareness the faithful now have that Papists are heretics will be blunted. Dialogue, prayers together, receiving of gifts, and "liberalizing" innovations are unforgivable according to Orthodox prescription, because they adulterate and change what has been transmitted through the holy Apostles, the holy Fathers, and the Ecumenical and Local Councils. You have infringed on those things "in which it is not permitted to add nor to subtract." And how is it that the contents of page 929 of the second volume of the Tome of Union escape Your attention and do not terrify You? — that is: *Unto those who disdain the sacred and divine Canons of our sacred Fathers who had the oversight of the Holy Church, which adorn the whole manner of Christian life and guide all to divine reverence: ANATHEMA.*

All Your endeavors (and especially chose inadmissible "encounters," which do not bear looking into, with the spiritual heads of the "churches"), bring only confusion and turmoil. No, Your All-Holiness; do not "lead us into an evil captivity, and do not aim to drag us down into the Babylon of Western customs and dogmas."[626] Do not, because You will meet resistance. Glory be to God, there exist in this land of martyrdom a love of Orthodoxy and a spirit of resistance. Like an ocean wave, Orthodox thought will overwhelm and sink Your skiff on its course toward a servile, anti-Christ union (submission) with the super heresy of Papism. Florence shall never live again in any form whatsoever. We will tolerate no kind of betrayal. The Greek people, a people who has once given birth to many like St. Photios, Patriarch Michael Cerularios, and St. Mark Evgenikos, will not tolerate betrayal. God has swept away the betrayers.

---

626 From the Encyclical of St. Mark of Ephesus to all pious Orthodox Christians after the Council of Florence; see *The Orthodox Word*, 1968, vol. 3, no. 2, 53ff.

Abide in the Apostolic decrees and patristic Traditions. Flee innovations as though they were dictated by the devil. Remain within the sacred Canons. *If you remain in them, you shall be saved and shall have peace, but if you disobey, you shall suffer torments and you [the bishops] shall have everlasting war with one another, receiving as reward a fitting judgment for heedlessness* (the Holy Apostles, Epilogue to the Sacred Canons). May You, Your Holiness, respond in such a manner and proclaim to all quarters, both by word and deed, that we also might rejoice and take courage: *We rejoice over them as he that has found great spoil, and press to our bosom with gladness the divine Canons, holding fast all the precepts of the same complete and without change, whether they have been set forth by the holy trumpets of the Spirit, the renowned Apostles, the six Ecumenical Councils, by councils locally assembled, or by our Holy Fathers. And those whom they placed under anathema we also anathematize; those whom they deposed, we also depose; those whom they excommunicated, we also excommunicate; and those whom they delivered over to punishment, we subject to the same penalty* (First Canon of the Seventh Ecumenical Council).

Your All-holiness, *The Lucifer of Rome having become exceedingly puffed up and having placed his throne above the stars*, be zealous and cry out: *Let us stand aright, let us stand in the venerable Traditions of the Fathers.*[627] Let us not be hasty to come to general and enthusiastic conclusions because of a few demonstrations. And especially, let us not deceive ourselves. Still distant — indeed very distant, unfortunately — is the union toward which all turn our hopes. All things, Your All-Holiness, proclaim the perils we undergo by dialogues with stubborn heretics. And all things oblige us to keep watchful vigil. By remaining rooted and immovable in our Orthodoxy we also give an opportunity to any of the heretics to awaken and to be incorporated into the One, Holy, Catholic, and Apostolic Church, so that they might find their salvation.

Do not flatter them, because by doing so You harm them. Let this be our primary and main concern: How we shall propitiate the Lord Who already is wrathful because of our sins; and how, with a pure repentance, we shall render Him kind and placable. Because, confessedly, I fear that concerning the unfortunate Ecumenical Patriarchate (and also in other

---

627 From the "Praises" of Orthros for the feast of St. Photios of Constantinople.

cases) the word of Scripture is repeated: the priests have set My law at naught and have defiled My sanctuary. Between the holy and the profane they have not discerned. It is terrible for me even to say it, but I see with the spiritual eyes of my soul, and I hear with the ears of my heart the angel of Revelation saying to the leader of Greek Orthodoxy: Bring to mind from whence thou hast fallen, and repent [...] but if not, I come unto thee quickly, and shall remove thy lamp from its place if thou repent not. What a fall! What a catastrophe!

Your All-Holiness, what has come to pass has come to pass. "To fall is human; to persist is satanic." Correct the wrong. Have pity on the wounded Christian faithful. Make steadfast and unite the Orthodox people, who are troubled and divided on each occasion — on one hand by the gross anti-canonical endeavors and acts of such-and-such a Patriarch or Archbishop who violates the calendar (and with it, ecclesiastical order and harmony), thus destroying the unity of the faithful in the matter of external worship; and on the other hand by rash and inadmissible meetings with heretics, and seeking an untimely and thoughtless union with them for the purpose of satisfying selfish desires and dark pursuits that do not look to the benefit of God's Church. We beseech You fervently: Put an end to scandal, "for the path which You have chosen, if it should further bring You into union with the Roman Catholics, would call forth a division in the Orthodox world; for undoubtedly many of Your own spiritual children too will prefer faithfulness to Orthodoxy above the ecumenical idea of a compromising union with non-Orthodox without their full agreement in the truth."[628]

---

628 Letter of Metropolitan Philaret to Patriarch Athenagoras (see *The Orthodox Word*, vol. 2 no. 1, January-March 1966, 30.) As the present citation indicates, this letter was very well received by pious Orthodox Greeks.

2. Elder Cleopa (Ilie) of Sihăstria Monastery, Romania (1912-1998)

a. All Confessions Outside of Orthodoxy are Enemies of the Cross of Christ[629]

Let us hold fast to our Faith, the same Faith that our earliest leaders held, the same Faith as our ancestors and all true Romanians. If you want to be a true son of Christ and of the Romanian country, then hold fast to the right Faith, Orthodoxy, which has been ours for two thousand years. If not, then you are neither a son of Christ's nor of the Church, and you are a foreigner to the Romanian people. You cannot be a citizen of Christ's and a Romanian if you do not have the right Faith in Christ. You are a foreigner. You are not a son of the country, for the true son of Romania is one who is Orthodox, since the Orthodox Church has prevailed in our land for two thousand years. Do not so much as receive these sectarians in your houses.

There are some confessions that are approved by the State, such as the Roman Catholics and a few others; that is their business. But they are also severed from the Orthodox Church and have become sectarians, no longer true sons of our country nor of the Church, and are the forerunners of satan. You need to know this. They are lying prophets who want to tear apart your faith and take our gentle people down into perdition. Hold fast to the right Faith and do not listen to them!

Our Romanian land has always been Orthodox, and we have to keep this line of Orthodoxy. We were born Orthodox from the beginning, from the colonization of Dacia; we have lived Orthodox for two thousand years, and we have to remain Orthodox until our death. This is the true Orthodox faith of Romania. Do not accept anything from outside, for they all want to tear apart the unity of our people, the Faith, and the Church. They are all enemies of the Cross of Christ.

---

629 Archimandrite Ioanichie Bălan, *Elder Cleopa of Sihastria; In the Tradition of St. Paisius Velichkovsky*, trans. Mother Cassiana (Lake Pueblo: New Varatec Publishing, 2001), 336-337.

b. Thoughts on a Union between Orthodoxy and the Roman Church[630]

"The ecumenical movement, and particularly the thrust for union between Orthodoxy and the Roman Church, was a topic of great discussion during Fr. Cleopa's later years. The Romanian Orthodox Church had been very active in the ecumenical movement. This was not necessarily the desire of the Church in Romania, but more at the instigation of the government which sought to convince the outside world that Romania was "modern" and in step with the times; it was also a ploy used by the communists to convince the western world that the Church was completely free in Romania. Yet, as we read the elder's words, we see that his mind was on his own approaching death as he encouraged the faithful to see more to their souls and not to force things that are not the Will of God.

"Father, do you see a union between the Churches?"

"Brothers, the union of the Churches is a divine matter, not a human one. It is not something within our power. This is how I see it: we need to fast and pray to God so that when the Holy Spirit comes, He will find us in a state like the holy apostles...."

3. Elder Athanasios Mitilinaios (1927-2006)[631]

This brings us to the Christian west, which is represented by the pope. The Christian West is the secularization of the Church, the worldly mindset resting within the Church. In fact, Father [Saint] Justin Popovich has stated that the anti-Christian order of historical figures is: Judas, Arius, the pope, and the Antichrist. So that you don't get the impression that Father [Saint] Justin is making this up, I will call upon Saint Kosmas the Aitoloian, who had said, "Curse the pope." But why? Christ had told us not to curse anyone. In what sense does the saint ask us to curse the pope? It is certain that we are not to curse the individ-

---

630 Archimandrite Ioanichie Bălan, *Elder Cleopa of Sihastria; In the Tradition of St. Paisius Velichkovsky*, trans. Mother Cassiana (Lake Pueblo: New Varatec Publishing, 2001), 331-332.

631 Archimandrite Athanasios Mitilinaios, *Revelation, Vol 3: The Seven Trumpets and the Antichrist*, trans. Constantine Zalalas (Dunlap: Zoe Press, 2015), 248-249.

ual person of each reigning pope. It is the office which the pope symbolizes that is to be cursed because it represents a secularized Church. In this sense, western thought can be a curse to Orthodox Christianity in that Orthodoxy can suffer terrible and deadly adulteration from the west which could result in the very elimination of salvation. A furious and relentless battle between eastern thought and lifestyle and western thought and lifestyle continues relentlessly throughout the centuries.

4. Elder Arsenie (Papacioc) of St. Mary Monastery, Romania (1914–2011)

a. On Catholics, Ecumenism and Sects[632]

Interviewer: Can you tell us about the sects and the Catholic church?

Elder Arsenie: I have written on this an entire book entitled "Solely, Orthodoxy." They are anathemized, that's the fact; "if one alters an iota from any word that our Savior said, let him be anathema," because he can no longer be saved. We ought to keep what all the Ecumenical Councils have decreed, because it wasn't you or I that have decided this way! Church dogma was decided in Councils that lasted hundreds of days, abounding with signs and wonders of the Holy Spirit. This is how the truth was established by the Seven Ecumenical Councils — starting with the first Council in 325 AD and ending with the last Council in 787 AD. They decided on all [Church] matters in unity. When the Catholics split [from the Orthodox] in 1054, all the Holy Councils were already completed. At the Sixth Ecumenical Council, Pope Martin was a martyr! Why do they betray him now? Why did they depart? And from here on, everything started... Luther began the protestant movement, the Anglicans other movement and so on. We do not guarantee that they will be saved. We cannot! The Holy fathers and all the Ecumenical Councils consider them heretics. We simply cannot consider an anathemized heretical teaching as salvific.

---

632 Archimandrite Arsenie (Papacioc), "On Ecumenism, Catholics and Sects," video interview by Unknown at Mănăstirea Cheia (Cheia Monastery), May 21st, 2005, translated by Ellaina Chiru, https://youtu.be/vhqJSLY0p_M

Interviewer: What about ecumenism?

Elder Arsenie: Well of course I'm against it. This is what I was talking about it — against it, as in a life and death struggle. And, what about ecumenism? What do you want to reconcile now? You know, they came and approached me with arrogance. So, the Pope didn't come to Romania to chat over a cup of coffee or to observe the true Christian life of our country and rejoice over the beauty of Church services during feast days, but he came and served a mass to prove something. He thought he will prevail with this. Look what he did with the Uniates (the Greek-Catholics in Transylvania). What did he do when he realized that he could in no way convince them? Because they initially worshipped in the Truth. So, he said to them "worship as you please but in regard to administration, you must belong to us. And look at them now; they are more catholic in custom than the Catholics. And this is what the Pope is trying to do now. True hegemony! They want to dominate regardless. May our good Lord forgive me, but I tell you "Woe to them all!" Look what they did recently in Rome (at the burial of Pope John Paul II); it was a nefarious demonstration with hidden motives. Do you believe that the Pope is just "a Pope"? No, he has many roles. God knows them all. My brothers, the smallest departure [from Truth] is a great fall! There is so much order and purity in Heavens, and we can certainly reach salvation, but without departure from the Truth. People are flabbergasted by the Catholic flamboyance and order but all of this is fake! It's false!

Interviewer: Like a show...

Elder Arsenie: A sickening show that suits their goal. In order to conquer. However, they have seriously wounded themselves spiritually in this self-destructive process. People are not that foolish! What the mob demands is irrelevant. What matters is the truth that comes out of the crowds! And the truth is only revealed in the illumined [holy] people. My beloved, God cannot be fooled by anyone. You can't mystify His word, one cannot add or distort His word, because these are transgressions against the Church dogma.

So, they say, the Pope is God's Vicar! But a vicar does not exist unless the master is dead! We Orthodox have a living Master, Christ! Our Christ is alive; why do I need a vicar? *"For lo, I am with you until the end of time."* We live through faith not eyesight! We have an order and a hierarchy. They too had this order during the first 1054 years. The patriarch of Rome was called *"primus inter pares"* or first among equals. He was the first to be consulted but only within a council. It was not one's own opinion that holds the way, but rather what the entire Council members held as the Truth.

The holy apostles immediately after the dormition of Theotokos — when they were brought together on the clouds of heaven — have held a council in Jerusalem but Peter was not the deciding apostle. The decisions were made by the entire Council; it was not something decreed from a position of power, as such thing cannot be when the Truth is at stake. Because God speaks through the majority. Thus, the Ecumenical Councils were established, starting with the first and the most important Council of 325 AD, where the Creed was revealed. And [continuing] at the Second Council with *"And in the Holy Spirit Who proceeds from the Father,"* and they [Catholics] added that *"it also proceeds from the Son!"* When Christ Himself says that *"it proceeds from the Father"* so why are you saying that it also proceeds from the Son?

Regarding the Papal Primacy and Pope infallibility, it was truly affirmed [St. Justin Popović] that three grave errors have been committed since the creation of the world: the fall of Adam, Christ's betrayal by Judas and Papal Infallibility. It's horrific my brothers. And then [they added] the Immaculate Conception, that the Mother of God was born without sin! It's a great error. We know who the Theotokos is. It's mind boggling just to think about her, but how are you comparing her to God? Do you make her identical with the Creator? She is still a servant; she is His handmaid. *"All nations shall call me blessed"* has a different meaning. Because she was born with the original sin that she inherited from Adam and only through the Holy Spirit shadowing her at Christ's conception she was cleansed of the original sin. And we are all cleansed from its bonds at our Baptism. In addition, they serve the liturgy with unleavened bread or azimes. The word [we use] is "arthos" or bread not "azimos". As in the new covenant, Christ gave us the whole bread [at the last supper] or arthos because the Truth is whole or leavened. And despite using the leavened bread [for communion] for 1054 years, they have changed the custom.

Then [the issue with] the Purgatory and the liturgy for the departed which they no longer have, because they no longer have the Proskomede [Prosphora]! In other words, the most important part of the liturgy when the priest prepares the gifts and commemorates names, and other things that the priest does which I have no time to explain now, they no longer have. At Proskomede, the priest commemorates the living and the dead. And towards the end of divine liturgy when the bread becomes the body and the wine becomes the blood of Christ, the discus is placed in the holy blood of Christ as the priest prays: "*Lord wash away the sins of those named here!*" But you see, they say that only God can forgive sins not us priests.

Later they added indulgences, so that they could finish building the great basilica of St. Peter in Rome, they call the people "*to sell [give] something that they may gain heaven.*" Be gone [away] with your interpretation of "heaven" as a business transaction. So terrible are these errors! One of the greatest errors in this battle is believing that "*the end justifies the means.*" In other words, I can murder someone because I'm justified by the church. It matters little if I murdered you, if the church supports me. And of course, you realize that there are many hard-headed people without sensibility, that can kill you because their religion justifies it. Like the [Judaic] Talmudic law that states: '*if you see a Christian on the edge of a precipice, push him over.*' And when this is considered a religious precept, one may think that he gives glory to God by doing such act. So that's what Catholics have done, they introduced the concept "*the end justifies the means*" thus during the battle one is allowed to bring you any type of harm because his end goal doesn't seem evil. This cannot be [and is not] the Truth but a grave error. But our Lord sees everything; thus, I have said that God tolerates and awaits but there will be a time of reckoning. And we await that time. May the Lord forgive me, if I speak as His priest, an ordinary but honest priest. I don't speak as one who is greatly advanced spiritually but as one in the Truth. And I say woe to them. It doesn't work to hide the Truth. The priesthood must be pure and blameless, Mr. Pope.

b. Catholicism Is Heresy: Excerpt from an Interview with Elder Arsenie[633]

Question: *What are the consequences of breaking off from the Church and the formation of schisms and heresies?*

Elder: God created man for Him alone, to be in the Kingdom together. For the perversion that Adam brought, Christ came and restored the human race. Christ did not come to annihilate, but to transfigure the human being, and He gave us more than Adam lost: *the power to be gods by Grace, to know how to love enemies, the power of discernment, the power to overcome evil and to accept and bear suffering.* The consequences are that they deviate from what the Savior said, it is not easy. Their salvation is at risk, this would be the biggest consequence. Apart from this, they encourage atheistic philosophy, because, they believe, "we have the freedom to interpret and do as we believe." The paths that lead to salvation have been interpreted endlessly and will always be interpreted, and in fact there is only one: the one that we keep without any change, and with zeal and passion even — the Orthodox Church. The Church is the one that leads the way to our salvation in any way, in the Orthodox style, as how it was fixed at the synods regarding the respective dogmas.

Question: *Your Holiness, what are the causes for schisms and heresies? Many times, are cited social, political, geographical and historical reasons, that they were not at the synods, etc.*

Elder: The main reason is this: the devil secretly marks the hearts of those who have mixed conceptions about the saving truth. Social and political reasons are invoked as bait, to say that we are not with history. It's about the Truth! It's not about time, or history. They broke off from the Church after 1054 years with this state of greatness, of the pride for Rome to be above Constantinople. The ultimate value is the Truth!

The encyclical of the Orthodox Patriarchs from 1848 — which is a response to the Pope's call for the Orthodox to come to the Catholic Church — condemns the papacy as a heresy especially because of the Filioque teaching. Father Justin Popović says about Roman Catholicism that it is a heresy, like Protestantism. Because they left the canonical, respectively dogmatic responsibility, they modified the Symbol of Faith

---

633 Archimandrite Arsenie (Papacioc), *Singur Ortodoxia* (Bucureşti: Editura Sophia, 2008), 31-36.

with the addition of the Filioque: they say that the Holy Spirit also proceeds from the Son.

Just the Savior Himself clearly says: *who proceeds from the Father;* He does not say: *and from Me.*[634] First of all, it is a matter of dogma, so how can I say otherwise, when the Truth has been established with great sacrifices? Then they started adding papal primacy, papal infallibility, indulgences, purgatory. They hold the Liturgy with ázymos (unleavened bread), not with leavened bread, which is the Savior's law. He made it with artos, He did not make it with ázymos. The Immaculate Conception is again a big mistake: The Mother of God born without sin.[635]

They also introduced something very serious from a strategic point of view and from the point of view of the fight for salvation: "The end justifies the means" — I kill you, because that's what my religion says (exactly as it says in the Talmud: "If you see a Christian on the edge of the precipice, push him to fall." It is a religious obligation among them). The Orthodox Church has the cult of the dead. Now what do we do with the dead? At the Proskomedia, we remember them with great reverence. Then we put in the Chalice, in the Blood of Christ: "[...] wash away, Lord, the sins of those mentioned here."

Christ forgives them through the Liturgies we hold — this is how the dead are saved. Sins can only be forgiven by Christ; He is the only one who can forgive sins. Roman Catholics do not have Proskomedia. In order to give an answer to the question: "What do we do with the dead?", they answer: "In a rational form, they burn there as much as they need for the sins they have committed, and they are automatically saved" — purgatory. Dogmatic error! Then they changed the Holy Cross, the form of the Holy Cross, which is motivated with regard to the Holy Trinity: Father, Son and Holy Spirit. They make the sign of the cross

---

634 Gospel of John 15:26.

635 It means that the renewal of humanity does not begin from the moment when the Son of God comes in the Virgin. The Virgin is placed above Christ and the beginning of salvation is made from her, not from the Son of God, who comes to her. That is why we cannot admit that she is the first to be cleansed of ancestral sin, because she is the first in which the Son of God comes, and He comes in a more complete way than He comes in other people, through Baptism. His coming is the decisive moment, not her. (Sorin Dumitrescu, *7 Dimineţi cu Părintele Stăniloae,* Publisher: Anastasia, 1992, p.180).

differently: with their whole hand and from left to right, just so it's different than it was. It means ambition and, from a strategic point of view, by bringing something new, they make proselytes faster.

The Cross has a meaning for us, the Holy Trinity: all the height, all the width and all the depth. There is nothing without significance in the Orthodox Church. The sad thing is that some time ago they started to claim that they are right and motivate themselves by mystifying historical truths. They also had martyred popes: Pope Martin at the Sixth Ecumenical Council and also Hippolytus, patriarch in Rome. So, they have reasons to return to Orthodoxy, to the initial Truth. Orthodoxy is not a title; it is a Truth!

4. Elder Justin (Pârvu) of Petru Voda Monastery, Romania (1919-2013)

a. There is No Salvation in the Heretical Catholic Creed[636]

The Catholic "Church" contains great heresies in its bosom. We have nothing to discuss with such hypocrites who invented their own "church" outside God's grace, [in order] to be independent and autonomous, just like Lucifer who wanted to set up another seat above the throne of God. The Papacy shut the gates of the Kingdom of Heaven to their faithful, so they may worship another throne, the Vatican. They tried to subjugate us too, throwing the lizard of Uniatism into our land, but the blood of our confessing martyrs drove them away by the power of the Holy Spirit.

I would accept their baptism if they renounced the papal primacy and infallibility, but as long as their Pope is considered Christ, pushing aside the Holy Trinity, what value does their baptism have? There is one Baptism in the name of the Holy Trinity which belongs to the Orthodox; while they have a baptism in the name of the Pope, even if they formally invoke the Holy Trinity. And thus, our Christianity was handed down to us so beautifully, but only through the labor and sacrifices of our [Orthodox Christian] mothers.

---

636 Archimandrite Justin (Pârvu), *Biserica Si Noile Erezii*, trans. Ellaina Chiru (Petru Vodă: Agathan Press, 2016), 1-20.

I remember a chapter from *Brothers Karamazov* [in Dostoevsky], where I was very amazed to see so many similarities in doctrines, how the Pope was represented as a grandiose Roman citizen, sitting up high in his balcony with all the pomp and down below, on a narrow street, our Savior Jesus Christ was barely walking carrying His weak and wounded legs. And the Pope shouted from his balcony: "Take Him away quickly and throw Him in prison! He no longer has a purpose because he interfered in our administration. We are the masters, we are the ones [giving] bread, justice, and happiness to the people." This is how Christ is seen in the papal conception. So, this is how their heretical dogmas about papal infallibility, *filioque* and other innovations of theirs appeared, in order to create an autonomous and dictatorial system in the Church, to the point where it removes God from the world. God is no longer present on earth, but a man, the superior man who is, of course, the Pope. Don't you see the striking similarity between the humanist, the nihilist, the papal and the communist doctrines?

This is how man, stripped of the luminous garment of God's grace, became empty, living in his worries and sins. He is not even naked like Adam in Heaven but has clothed himself with the dark garment of the false gods that I mentioned. Now that the pope is coming to Romania, I wonder what political goals he is coming with? This is how this history was played out, and nations divided, through visits and peace conferences. However, we are hoping to retain our whole Transylvania province. If so, many other popes failed to subjugate it, this one will not succeed either!

Salvation is therefore only in the Orthodox Church and not outside it, neither in any other pseudo-church. The only true Church remains the Orthodox Church. The good deeds of the non-Orthodox can help them to know the Orthodox Truth, but they are not enough for salvation. Without a Baptism in the name of the Holy Trinity, of a Trinity confessed in the Orthodox Creed, and not in the heretical catholic creed, there is no salvation. But there is still time for everyone to repent and to come to Holy Orthodoxy and we are awaiting all those who have lost their way with open arms.

b. The Greek-Catholics [*Uniates*] are Schismatics and Excommunicated by the Orthodox Church[637]

What is happening today in our Church life is not without importance, but it is a very serious matter. We must not ignore the problems facing our Church! The Holy Fathers teach us, that when our faith is endangered, the Lord's command is not to keep silent therefore no one is entitled to say, "You know, I am too small and unimportant, who am I to interfere in the Church's matters"? No, my dears, the Holy Fathers teach us that if we remain careless and silent, the very stones will cry out. It is necessary to know the Catechism, the Canons, and the teachings of our Church. [...] My beloved, you see how these times are so much more difficult, because they are now trying to deceive us through diplomatic and political means, in order to destroy our faith and to unite us like in a "union chorus" with all heretical beliefs. The poor Greek-Catholics [the Uniates], how they have fallen into the Papists' net, and became their slaves, even if they are not conscious of this! We have nothing against the poor Roman Catholic faithful, let them pray quietly in their churches, but they may not attempt to change our churches or to change our faith. We respect everyone and have never proselytized like the Catholic Church has done, and we have never imposed our faith on anyone.

We all know how much our Orthodox faithful from Transylvania had suffered under the Uniates and how much fraud and dishonesty they've been through! These have always been the methods that the Roman Catholics operated with. Therefore, what trust can we have in them? What union and mixture shall we have with them? Don't you see where all these ecumenical movements have led to? We ended up tarnishing the face of Orthodoxy through this non-canonical act of Metropolitan [Nicolae Corneanu of Banat]. The Papists brought only pain and suffering to our nation. The enemies of Truth want to compromise us at any cost. They no longer come to attack us directly, as in the past, but they come with cunning and deceptive pursuits.

That is why our Savior tells us to beware of wolves in sheep's clothing because "many false teachers will come into the world". What trust shall we have in this ecumenism, when as Father Dumitru Stăniloae says,

---

637 Archimandrite Justin (Pârvu), *Biserica Si Noile Erezii,* trans. Ellaina Chiru (Petru Vodă: Agathan Press, 2016),70-90.

"The Roman Catholics have made the problem of reuniting the churches an object of confessional bargaining". All they care about is the Pope's
supremacy and not [about] being in the Truth. All the unification attempts in church history did nothing but aggravate even more the fric-
tions between the West and the East; and have led to greater political,
economic, and military struggles. They constantly sought to expand
[over other nations] as they are accustomed to, because the papacy is
nothing but the crown of the great Roman Empire, just as they affirmed
that the Pope is the sun, and the emperor is the moon.

How much suffering and humiliation the poor Transylvanians have
endured, for not having been allowed to perform their worship, and
their liturgy in peace! But those Romanians have not remained in ignorance and silence and have confessed [their faith] alongside Saints Visar-
ion, Sophronie and [Nicolae] Oprea. Let them be an example for us! See
how much pain and at the same time courage they displayed in their requests to Queen Maria Tereza: "Here, we the peasants of the principality, namely from the county of Hunedoara, Alba, and Zarandului together with the most distant lands, make news to your Majesty, that from the
greatest to the least, we so desire to have... just like all nations have their
law [custom], and practice their law in peace, and as the prophet Moses
gave the law to the Jews, and they keep it in peace, while are we constantly persecuted for our law. Why don't you give us rest so we may live in
peace? Why should we give to the Uniates our churches that we poor
people have built, at our expense and with our own hands? We will never
obey this order as long as we're alive!" [...] "But let us be brief, honorable
gentlemen: when our bishop and father of our law will come, let him be
the judge of the matter whether any of our churches should be given to
the Uniates, but until then we will give up nothing. Because it is a great
sin for our churches to remain closed during this fast [Lent]. It is neither
pleasing to God nor that we'll allow it. That enough and in good faith
we have made this request to your Majesty, and received no answer, as if
we had never asked. We are not cattle either, as your Highnesses believe,
but we have our Church. And that's not why the churches are built, to
remain empty, and we will not worship in stables, but we will go to our
churches to pray, that they do not remain empty."

You see my dear, this is how our Orthodox faith has survived, only through the brave resistance of the people, the clergy, and the monks. From the beginning they appealed to the weak leaders, weak hierarchs, whom they lured with vain promises, but the faithful stood firm. And that you may see their cunning and perfidy, listen to what Gavril Kapy the superior of the "Propaganda Mission in Dacia" says in a letter dated March 11th, 1701, to Cardinal Leopold Kollonits,

> I think that it will be enough now to be satisfied with the acceptance of the union in principle, because it would be very dangerous, even impossible, to remove all the bad habits of the Romanians [from Transylvania]. That is why it will be enough for the bishop and those with him, when they make the confession of faith as Uniates in the future, to affirm that they want to depend on the Catholic faith and the substituted officiants, and that they want to live according to the Greek [Orthodox] rite approved by the Catholic Church like in the other countries. It will then be our duty in the future, to change little by little many of their customs, namely, to change even their liturgy and their form of divine worship, telling them that these customs were introduced to them by the stupidity and ignorance of their priests from these countries.

We see here what the true intentions of Jesuits were. At the synod of Ferrara Florence (1438 – 1439), many hierarchs have apostatized, but when they have repented, they saw their fall to be worse than any other fall. We are not to repeat their mistakes when we can learn from them. The Catholics [throughout history] appealed much to political means in their church's life. This is an unclean practice that uses dishonesty and political phariseeism. Because of this, we reached a certain moment in history when Transylvania fell into their hands without having any right to appeal, as such that today we are no longer able to rule over this county. They try to control us on all aspects of life: religiously, economically, financially, and linguistically. You can no longer find a sign [a banner] in the Romanian language, and large areas of Transylvania's lands, are now in their hands.

Let us remember the letter of Patriarch Dosoftei to Bishop Athanasius Anghel who had fallen into the temptation of Uniatism; who rebuked him as follows: "Chirr Athanasius, remember that you came to the Romanian Land and asked me to make you metropolitan in those lands [in Transylvania], also remember how I knew you to be a dishonest man, that your heart was not right with God and that so much time you wander from place to place, and then you came [to us] with promises and fearful oaths that you moved both me and the others [the synod of bishops] to elect you as a bishop and after all you were ordained with honor and you were considered by all to be higher than you really deserved. You confessed before the angels, the archangels and God, that you will have faith in the Holy Fathers and the Christ's only Church. Then a young man came here and told us that he saw you in Vienna as you celebrated mass with the cardinal and other Franciscan popes and twice in that Franciscan mass you renounced the holy Orthodox and Universal Church. You confessed the church of Rome [as the true church], that is schismatic and heretical.

Finally, I heard that you returned to Transylvania, on a chariot driven by six horses and torches were lit before you; that you gathered the priests from that country and promised them forgiveness from taxes and other worldly promises, only if they unite with Rome (that is, to unite with Papism), which is the same as being separated from God [...] And thus, you have become a wolf shepherd, because you snatched the sheep from the fold of Christ and threw them into the devil's mouth. I weep for you brother and hope that Christ may dwell in you; so, I say to you: "Son Athanasius come to your senses, don't be afraid of the vows you made at Vienna, but be afraid of the oaths you made when you were ordained as a bishop! You are not a child, but realize that the teachings of Latins are twisted, schismatic schemes, they are all deceptive lies, foreign to the Holy Gospel and the Holy Fathers." Therefore, let us not become partakers of heresy, for it's better to die as martyrs for the Church of Christ's Truth, as the troparion says: "Oh Thy holy martyrs, who through your sufferings have received the incorruptible crown, intercede to Christ our God to save our souls!" My Romanian brothers do not forget the martyrdom of our saints! Defend the True Faith so your soul and the soul of your children may be saved!

5. Elder Gabriel of Koutloumousiou Monastery, Mount Athos, Greece

On Recognizing the Sacramental Grace of the Latin Confession[638]

Geronda Gabriel: "If they believe that the Pope is a Church and has mysteries and [that] we have to unite, they are not shepherds but wolves in shepherds clothing. Whoever the Patriarch or the Archbishop is, who says something that the Fathers and the Gospel have not said when they say that the Pope [Latin Papism] is a Church and has mysteries and we have to unite...and even if he fasts, if he says this [or that] even if he fasts, even if he prophesies, and even if he practices virginity, does signs, does miracles, he's a wolf and not a shepherd [...] What does the Church say? The 45th Apostolic Canon [says], 'if a bishop, or a presbyter, or a deacon, while assembled with a heretic, jointly prays with heretics, he is excommunicated and deposed.'"

Cell Attendant: "If the Patriarch performs the liturgy [and] before him is [a] Cardinal, Papists, is this not joint Prayer?"

Geronda Gabriel: "Of course! They [the papists] need to leave the Church or we should not be there, we are jointly praying. We are excommunicated by the 45th [Apostolic] Canon. What do the saints say? Saint Gregory Palamas [says] there are three types of atheism. The first type of atheism, the atheists who say [that] God does not exist, the second type of atheism is the heretic, [the] third type of atheism is when the faith is in danger, and I am silent [and] I do not speak up. Saint Theodore the Studite says, 'It is a commandment from God to not be silent, do not stay silent when the faith is in danger. We should not be silent.'"

---

638 "Elder Gabriel [A Disciple of St. Paisios] On Patriarch Kirill," Gregory Decapolite, YouTube, accessed March 24th, 2023, https://www.youtube.com/watch?v=HXJ65qfUdGY

Hieromonk Seraphim Rose

PART VI

CLERICS, MONASTICS, & DISTINGUISHED LAY CONFESSORS

Commemorative medal depicting Eustratios Argenti

In the Orthodox Church, all are called to know the Faith and be prepared to confess the Faith whether in times of martyrdom or times of safety, following the words of the Lord, "Whosoever therefore shall confess Me before men, him will I confess also before My Father who is in Heaven" (Matthew 10:32) and St. Peter's instruction to "be ready always to give an answer to every man that asketh you a reason of the hope that is within you" (1 Peter 3:15). In every age there have been distinguished and revered teachers of the Faith from every part of the Church—laymen, lay monastics, deacons and priests as well as bishops and patriarchs. Often in the history of the Church, bishops attending Ecumenical Councils would be accompanied by those of lower ranks who could be trusted to advise them on theological matters. In addition to the witness of the Fathers, councils, hierarchs and elders already presented, this section includes the confessions of influential clerics, monastics, and laymen of recent centuries who clearly expressed the patristic witness concerning the Latins and their heresies.

A. IN HISTORY

1. Eustratios Argenti of Chios (1687-1757)

WHO IS EUSTRATIOS ARGENTI?

Eustratios Argenti of Chios, born in 1687, Eustratios Argenti was a prolific and extraordinarily gifted lay theologian, philosopher and medi-

cal doctor who made significant theological contributions to the Orthodox Church during the 18th century. He is primarily remembered as the
author of a lengthy and significant work concerning the Holy Eucharist.
Written against Latin Azymes, it is known to be the "most elaborate polemical work on this subject ever composed by an Orthodox writer."[639]
Argenti is also well known for his very important role and decisive written contributions during the so-called Baptismal Controversy that occurred during the reign of Patriarch Cyril V in the 1750's. It was during
this period that Patriarch Cyril V, a confessor of true Orthodoxy, was
involved in a raging theological war with his Latin-minded (*Latinoph-
roni*) Metropolitans on the Patriarchal Synod concerning the necessity
to baptize Latin Papists who were converting to Holy Orthodoxy. It was
this theological debate that caused Argenti to write his famous work on
Holy Baptism entitled *A Manual Regarding Baptism Called 'Guiding of
Those Who are Deluded,* in support of Patriarch Cyril V, which was first
published in Constantinople in 1756 and then in Leipzig, Germany in
1757.

THE PERSECUTION OF THE ORTHODOX BY THE LATIN PAPISTS[640]

So far as they are able, the Papists persecute and make war upon
the Orthodox. Without any fresh cause or open justification they have
seized the churches of Saint Anne at Ancona, of Saint Athanasius at
Rome, of the Panagia at Leghorn, three churches at Messina, and others
elsewhere in the west, which the Orthodox in their poverty had founded with great trouble and expense; they have seized the Holy Places at
Jerusalem; resorting sometimes to direct attacks and sometimes to deceit, they have utterly destroyed three of the Patriarchal Thrones; they
have compelled the Orthodox in Hungary and Poland to subscribe to

---

639 Kallistos Ware, *Eustratios Argenti: A Study of the Greek Church Under Turkish
Rule* (London: Oxford University Press, 1964), x.

640 Eustratios Argenti, Ἐγχειρίδιον περὶ Βαπείσματος, (Κωνσταντινούπολη: Οἰκουμενικὸ
Πατριαρχεῖο, 1756) 85-86. Quoted in Kallistos Ware, *Eustratios Argenti: A Study
of the Greek Church Under Turkish Rule* (London: Oxford University Press,
1964), 78-79.

Popery; and what further harm could they have done to the Orthodox, which they have not done.

THE LATIN PAPISTS ARE UNBAPTIZED[641]

Since, then, we have shown in the second chapter that westerners are unbaptized so far as the normal usage of the word "baptism" is concerned, so now we see that they are also unbaptized from the viewpoint of what is signified by the sacrament.

DEBATING A LATIN CONCERNING
RECEIVING THE EUCHARIST IN BOTH ELEMENTS[642]

We held a discussion in Egypt with two missionaries or false apostles of the Pope of Rome, Father Gabriel and Father Cyril, in the presence of many Arab and Syrian Christians who had been led astray, and of a few Orthodox. The subject changed to be the Holy Chalice. We proved clearly from Christ, from the Apostles, from the Councils and Fathers both eastern and western, and above all from the Holy and Orthodox Popes of Old Rome in the past, that the later Popes of Rome had acted unlawfully in depriving the laity of the Chalice. When this, I say, was clearly and plainly demonstrated, Father Cyril remained speechless, groaning and trembling in his perplexity; and being an ardent partisan of Popery, and feeling an excessive pride in his empty methods of scholastic reasoning, he could not endure his defeat; but he contracted an attack of asthma, which turned after not many days into consumption, accompanied by fever; and so, he died. At the time, both of them withdrew in shame and discouragement. Those of the deceived who were present gnashed their teeth; but the few Orthodox who were there sang a hymn of victory in Honour of Orthodoxy.

641 Εὐστράτιος Ἀργέντης, Ἐγχειρίδιον περὶ βαπτίσματος καλούμενον χειραγωγία πλανωμένων (Κωνσταντινούπολη: Οἰκουμενικὸ Πατριαρχεῖο, 1756), 89-90. Quoted in Kallistos Ware, *Eustratios Argenti: A Study of the Greek Church Under Turkish Rule* (London: Oxford University Press, 1964), 93.

642 Kallistos Ware, *Eustratios Argenti: A Study of the Greek Church Under Turkish Rule* (London: Oxford University Press, 1964), 55-56.

Against the Heretical Dogma of Papal Infallibility[643]

Concerning the False Infallibility of the Pope of Rome [...] in which it is clearly and plainly shown that it is possible for the Pope of Rome to become a heretic, and that many have actually become heretics, and that the Catholic Church teaches how it is possible for the Pope of Rome to become a heretic: which is also confirmed by the analogy of the faith [...]. Nevertheless, it is not our purpose here to reproach the Papists for the lawless and guilty actions of the Popes, nor for their schisms and anti-popes, nor for their simony, nor for their arbitrary and ungodly deeds. For these things are known to all, and the Papists themselves do not dare to deny them; and he who wishes can learn about them from ecclesiastical history.

Argenti Concerning Papist "Baptism"[644]

From what has been said throughout this short treatise, we conclude correctly that westerners who come to Orthodoxy require to be baptized. This practice is not called "rebaptism" (ἀναβαπτισμὸς), for we do not baptize them because we think that they have been badly baptized, but because they are entirely unbaptized. For what they call "baptism" is falsely so named, and is a false baptism.

Scholasticism of the Latin West[645]

More than a thousand years after the birth of Christ, there arose the heresy of the Scholastic Latin theologians, who wished to unite the philosophy of Aristotle with Christian theology. Nevertheless, they did not imitate the holy teachers of the early Church, who made philosophy fit theology; but the Scholastics did the opposite, making the Gospel and the holy Christian faith fit the doctrines of the philosopher Aristotle. From this source there arose in the Latin church so many heresies in the

---

643 Ibid., 161-162.

644 Ibid., 97.

645 Ibid., 110.

theology of the Holy Trinity, so many distortions of the words of the Gospels and the Apostles, so many violations of the Sacred Canons and the divine Councils, and finally so many corruptions and adulterations of the holy Sacraments.

CONCERNING THE TRUE ORTHODOX POPES OF OLD VERSUS THOSE NOW IN HERESY AND DELUSION CONCERNING THEIR ASSUMED UNIVERSAL AUTHORITY[646]

The Orthodox and Catholic Popes of Rome are praised, honoured, and seated in the first place and in the first rank among those who preside over the Church. They are called the successors of Peter, catholic teachers, fathers of fathers, ecumenical patriarchs, ecumenical popes, exarchs of the councils, canons of the faith, columns and pillars of Orthodoxy, heads of the Church, apostolical popes, judges of the bishops, supreme pontiffs, greatest pontiffs, guides of the truth, bishops of the Catholic Church, exponents of the Gospel. They are named chief, most blessed, most holy, best, lords, and masters. Other names and titles of honour may rightly be given to them; and these and similar titles of honour and praises are heaped upon their writings and their throne. But as soon as these same Popes begin to wander beyond the walls and frontiers of Orthodoxy, peace, and brotherly love; as soon as they also lay claim to a tyrannical monarchy and to an arbitrary position in the Councils, such as that which Dioscorus assumed; when they desire to be exalted over their brethren, and when they attempt to place their throne above the clouds of heaven: then, I say they are despised, they are set at naught, rebuked, excommunicated, deposed, condemned, persecuted, and anathematized.

---

646 Kallistos Ware, *Eustratios Argenti: A Study of the Greek Church Under Turkish Rule* (London: Oxford University Press, 1964), 168.

2. Christophoros the Aetolian (1755)

"No reproach is too bad for the Latins: they have the Devil for their father, and their Church is an adulteress to Satan; their baptism is not merely worthless but positively harmful, making those who receive it more filthy than before. 'Just as God gave the holy font that He might thereby wipe away original sin and lead up to heaven those who have been born again by Baptism; so too Satan invented satanical sprinkling, saliva, and salt, that through these things he might hinder the wiping away of original sin, and lead down to hell those who have been sprinkled, spat upon, and salted.'"[648]

"The Latin clergy shave — thus making clear to all that they do not possess the true priesthood—and they abstain from marriage that they may have the use of many mistresses."[649]

3. Alexei Stepanovich Khomiakov (1804-1860)

CONCERNING THE FILIOQUE[650]

I did not want to enter into the question of the *Filioque*. It is enough for me to have shown that the very act of altering the Symbol was a crime and a moral fratricide, and constituted a heresy against the Faith of the Church in its unity; but it is easy to see how absurd is the claim of the

---

647 Χριστόφορος ο Αιτωλός, Ραντισμού Στηλήτευσις (Κωνσταντινούπολις: χ.ε 1755), 15, 55, 67. Quoted in Ware, *Eustratios Argenti*, 100.

648 Χριστόφορος ο Αιτωλός, Ραντισμού Στηλήτευσις (Κωνσταντινούπολις: χ.ε 1755), 78. Quoted in Ware, *Eustratios Argenti*, 100.

649 Χριστόφορος ο Αιτωλός, Ραντισμού Στηλήτευσις (Κωνσταντινούπολις: χ.ε 1755), 137-138. Quoted in Ware, *Eustratios Argenti*, 100.

650 Alexei Stepanovich Khomiakov, *Encore Quelques Mots D'un Chretien Orthodoxe Sur Les Confessions Occidentales: A L'Occasion De Plusieurs Publications Religieuses, Latines Et Protestantes* (Leipzig: F.A. Brockhaus, 1858), 101.

pseudo-philosophers of Romanism when they attribute to the unity of substance what belongs to the character of the logical phase or moment. One could just as easily, as I have said, attribute the eternal generation of the Word to the Holy Spirit, given the unity of substance. The relationship between the two Hypostases was clearly understood by the great Damascene when he said that "the Spirit is the image (i.e., the reflection) of the Son." The principle, i.e., the procession, of knowledge is in the power of the first thought of the Father and of the Father alone, although the object of knowledge or the manifested Thought is the Son. The example of the Latins would show us, if it could be doubted, that in the Church the light of knowledge cannot be born of sin.

CONCERNING ROMANISM[651]

Among the points that distance the Russian Church from the Roman church, there are two that at first sight seems to enter in the category of dogmatic principles. These are: the Procession of the Holy Spirit [filioque] and the authority of the Pope on the Universal Church [...]. This man, former son of the Church, does he not know that the Church can never add anything to his dogmas, that the Church have never believed in something that has never been revealed to Her since the beginning, by the Holy Spirit, and that She will never believe more? Does he not know that this is a dogma, a fundamental dogma? But let's go further [...]. The Papal Infallibility wasn't known during the first centuries even according to the Romans; Saint Hippolyte could accuse the Pope Callixtus of Heresy. An Ecumenical Council could condemn the memory of Pope Honorius for an error in the dogma. On the other hand, the First Ecumenical Council took place only in the beginning of the 4th century.

The explanation of this fact is quite simple, as I have already shown in my first booklet. "The ancient heresies were errors in the revealed dogma, either of the intimate nature of God, or of his relations with human nature: but, while distorting the traditional doctrine, they claimed to

---

651 Alexei Stepanovich Khomiakov, *Encore Quelques Mots d'un Chretien Orthodoxe sur les Confessions Occidentales: A L'Occasion de Plusieurs Publications Religieuses, Latines et Protestantes* (Leipzig: F.A. Brockhaus, 1858), 18-22.

remain faithful to it. They were errors of varying degrees of guilt, but they were individual errors which did not attack the dogma of Ecclesiastical Universality, and which sought to prove their truth by the consent of all Christians. Romanism [i.e., papism], by replacing the unity of the Universal Faith by the independence of individual or diocesan opinion, was the first heresy against the dogma of the nature of the Church or of its faith in itself." The Romans [Latins] had decided without the consent of their brethren a matter of dogma: they had arrogated to themselves the monopoly of Grace. The Roman world had implicitly declared (and persists in this declaration), that the Eastern world was no more than a world of *helotes*[652] in Faith and doctrine. "It had committed moral fratricide."[653]

---

652 *Helots*: A state-owned serf population of the ancient Spartans. The helots were in a sense state slaves, bound to the soil and assigned to individual Spartans to till their holdings; their masters could neither free them nor sell them, and the helots had a limited right to accumulate property, after paying to their masters a fixed proportion of the produce of the holding.

653 The dogmas that Khomiakov is referring to that were innovated by the Latin Papists are that of the *Filioque* and the Papal Supremacy.

Alexei Stepanovich Khomiakov

Hieromonk Seraphim Rose

B. IN OUR DAYS

1. Hieromonk Seraphim (Rose) of St. Herman Orthodox Monastery

On October 4, 1965, Pope Paul VI gave an unprecedented address before the United Nations. This event corroborated exactly what Eugene had told Gleb about the United Nations back in 1961, on the day of their first meeting. "An examination of the Pope's address," Eugene wrote:

"[This speech] reveals a singular fact; the purpose of the Church of Christ is not mentioned, and the name of Christ appears in it only once, in an ambiguous final sentence. It is perhaps assumed that the audience knows for what the Pope stands; he said, indeed, 'You know our mission.' But later, when characterizing the 'aspiration' of the Church of Rome, he said only that she wished to be 'unique and universal — in the spiritual field!'

For a single moment only in his address did it seem that the Pope might be about to speak a word of genuine Christianity. Citing the com-

---

654 Hieromonk Damascene (Christensen), *Father Seraphim Rose; His Life and Works* (Platina: St. Herman of Alaska Brotherhood, 2010), 244-245.

mandment of our Lord to His Disciples to 'go and bring the good news to all peoples,' the Pope announced that he indeed had a 'happy message' for 'all peoples' represented at the United Nations. For Christians, this can only mean one thing; the good news of salvation, of eternal life in God. The Pope, however, had a different, an astonishing message: 'We might call our message a solemn moral ratification of this lofty institution.' This is what Rome offers today in place of the Christian Gospel!

The Pope's ideals come not from our Lord, not from the Apostles and Fathers of the Church of Christ, but rather from the rationalist dreamers of the modern age who have revived the ancient heresy of chiliasm — the dream of an earthly millennium. This heresy was explicit in the Pope's evocation of the 'new age' of humanity, and of a 'new history — peaceful, truly human history as promised by God to men of good will.' The Church of Christ has never taught this strange doctrine; it is, however, one of the cardinal doctrines of Freemasonry, of occultism and numerous related sects, and even (without mention of God) of Marxism. For adopting this sectarian fantasy into the body of Latin doctrine the Pope was acclaimed by the press as a 'prophet.'

Involuntarily one calls to mind the last work of the nineteenth century Russian philosopher, Vladimir Soloviev — the 'Short Story of Antichrist' (from *Three Conversations*) — in which, basing himself primarily on the Holy Fathers, he draws a chilling picture of Antichrist as a 'great humanitarian' and superman, accepted by the world as Messiah. Paul VI is not Antichrist; but the whole 'drama' in which he was the chief 'actor' something of the seductiveness of Antichrist is already present. To be sure, it is nothing original with him; it is rather the culmination of centuries of apostasy."

THE UNIVERSAL MONARCHY OF THE POPE & HOW THE UNIVERSAL MONARCH WILL BE THE ANTICHRIST[655]

Another underlying thread in this history of the apostasy is the search of universal monarchy. In his notes Fr. Seraphim wrote: "The thirteenth century saw the theory of the universal monarchy of the Pope

---

655 Hieromonk Damascene (Christensen), *Father Seraphim Rose; His Life and Works* (Platina: St. Herman of Alaska Brotherhood, 2010), 627.

— that all the land in the world belongs to the Pope as Christ's representative on earth, and he gives it to landholders. The climax of this point of view occurred at the jubilee of 1300 in Rome, when Pope Boniface VII seated himself on the throne of Constantine, arrayed himself in a sword, crown and scepter, and shouted aloud: 'I am Caesar — I am Emperor.' This was not just an act but an indication of something extremely deep in the whole of modern thought: the search for a universal monarch, which will be the Antichrist."

GRACE HAS BEEN LOST IN THE CHURCH OF ROME[656]

The Church of Christ is that which gives grace to people; and in the West, when Rome broke off from this Church, this grace was actually lost (maybe people incidentally found it here and there, but from their whole Church the grace was cut off). I look at modern Roman Catholicism as an attempt to substitute by human ingenuity, the grace which it lost. Therefore, it makes the Pope "infallible," having to give an answer to the question "where is truth?"

LET THE BETRAYERS OF ORTHODOXY UNITE WITH THE CATHOLICS BUT THEY DO NOT SPEAK FOR THE ENTIRE ORTHODOX CHURCH[657]

The deviations from Orthodoxy of the present Patriarch of Constantinople [Athenagoras] have reached a new peak in the recent "ecumenical" act of "mutual pardon" with the Pope of Rome (Dec. 7, 1965). It is more than time to bring up in the English language Orthodox press what has been long discussed in the Greek and Russian press. With the formal statement of Metropolitan Philaret, together with a similar one made by Archbishop Chrysostomos of Athens, the voices of protest

---

656 Fr. Seraphim Rose, *God's Revelation to the Human Heart* (Platina: St. Herman of Alaska Brotherhood, 2014), 47.

657 Orthodox Christian Books & Icons, "Orthodoxy in the Contemporary World; The Latest Step Toward 'Union'" *Orthodox Word* Vol 2, no. 1 (Jan-Feb-Mar1966): 37.

have now been joined by official declarations, and these have found responsive ears among the other Eastern Patriarchs.

The Orthodox world is lining up into two camps; if the new "union" with Rome is accomplished, the unionists will find themselves in schism, cut off from the Orthodox Church. As regards the Patriarch of Constantinople, a few basic facts should be kept in mind. First, he does not and cannot speak for the whole of the Orthodox Church; the present campaign of the unionists to make him the official spokesman for all of Orthodoxy has absolutely no foundation in Orthodox tradition; he is one bishop among many, enjoying a primacy only of honor among his fellow patriarchs and bishops.

Second, in the Orthodox Church no act or statement possesses validity merely because it comes from a bishop or patriarch; it can possess validity only if it is Orthodox. The actual statements and actions of Patriarch Athenagoras disqualify him to speak for any Orthodox Church, not even his own, since they represent, not Orthodoxy, but apostasy, — a departure from Orthodoxy which, if pursued further, will separate him entirely from the Church of Christ. The propagandists for "union" disdain such fact; for them, fidelity to Orthodox tradition is a small thing. Their campaign, rather, is waged on the most primitive level, that of pure publicity — empty words and gestures which, though condemned by a sound Orthodox consciousness, are capable of exerting an immense influence over those, even within the Church herself, who are ignorant of Orthodox tradition.

The act of "mutual pardon" was such an empty gesture. Possessing no canonical validity in itself, what it was in fact was merely a sign to the world that the "union" is close at hand, that the Patriarch of Constantinople is prepared to abandon the Church of Christ to join the universal pseudo-religious organization envisioned by the Vatican. Rather than anger, sorrow is perhaps the most appropriate response to such gestures — sorrow over the lack of love and understanding of their own tradition that such gestures reveal in the unionists. Anyone who actually believes that "nothing separates" Roman Catholicism from Orthodoxy, that they are but "two branches of the same Church," understands nothing whatever of genuine Orthodoxy. The unionists, apparently, are already Latins at heart, and the final act of union will only confirm their estrangement from the Church of Christ. Let the unionists, then, the betrayers of Orthodoxy, become Catholics if they will; but let them cease from pretending to speak for the Orthodox Church, which most emphatically rejects them.

2. Hieromonk Cosmas of Grigoriou Monastery, Mount Athos

Go to the True Church where the Priests have Beards and Cassocks[658]

One morning in May 1994, a middle-aged Zairian arrived at our Mission. I welcomed him and he told me his problem. He seemed troubled and uneasy and said the following: "Father, I am a worker at Jecamine. I fell seriously ill. As the doctors were unable to help me, I asked God to have mercy on me." I asked him to which church he belonged.

"I am a Roman Catholic," he replied. "One night I saw in a dream several priests like yourself wearing brilliant vestments and celebrating the Liturgy in a church like yours. One of the priests approached me and said: 'God has heard your prayer, but for your salvation you must join our Church, for it is the only true Church.' I do not know you or the name of your Church, but I have approached you because in my dream I saw priests like you, with beards, cassocks and brilliant vestments. I asked other people who told me that only Orthodox priests have beards and wear cassocks and other such clothing, and they also told me where to find your church."

I advised him and gave him a book, and suggested that he come to our church for catechism every Sunday. Since then, he has been a faithful member of our church, and has not perished from the grave illness, which so afflicted him.

---

658 Demetrios Aslanidis & Monk Damascene Grigoriatis, *Apostle to Zaire: The Life and Legacy of Blessed Father Cosmas of Grigoriou* (Florence: Uncut Mountain Press, 2022), 186-187.

A Roman Catholic is Led to the True Church[659]

In the month of March 1991, the priest in charge of the Orthodox Mission Center in Kolwezi, Archimandrite Meletios, had left for Likashi to celebrate the Forty Day Memorial service following the death of a Greek woman called Sophia. One evening, as he was walking along the street towards the church of St. John the Forerunner, he noticed that a Zairian woman was following him. She drew near him and asked his pardon, and then told him the following: Father, I am a Roman Catholic. Every day I ask God for guidance towards salvation. One night I had a dream. I saw a priest dressed as you are, with a cassock and a beard, and his face seemed to be full of light. He came up to me and spoke to me in Swahili, which amazed me, as this was the first time, I had seen him. He showed me a church and said: "since you plead with tears to be shown salvation, behold, here is the true church where you will find it. Go to this church and the priest will tell you what you must do to be baptized."

Go to the Orthodox Church[660]

In the middle of the month of September 1996, one of our priests accompanied the pregnant wife of one of our workers to the maternity clinic. There he met and spoke with the doctor and director of the clinic who was Roman Catholic. The clinic belongs to the Methodists. After a brief conversation with regard to the matter at hand, the priest, out of courtesy, invited the director, whose name was Mouagkala, to visit our Orthodox Church.

Before, however, he could arrange such a visit he was the recipient of a succession of mysterious night-time invitations and within three days had placed a call to the Mission Center. A meeting was arranged for the upcoming Sunday with the head of the Mission, Hieromonk Meletios. After their discussion Father Meletios sent him to me, telling me: "Talk a while with the good doctor and whatever he needs give it to him." Having greeted him, I asked him to tell me about himself and his

---

659 Ibid., 186-187.
660 Ibid., 211-212.

life. He told me the following: "I work as the director of the Methodist Maternity clinic. I am a Roman Catholic and I came here today to learn something about your Church. It is the first time I have ever entered an Orthodox Church." "How did you come to be interested in our Church?" I asked him.

"Father, the following incidents recently happened to me. For three con¬secutive days now, although asleep, I hear a voice that tells me repeatedly: 'Go to the Orthodox Church, go to the Orthodox Church.' I couldn't stand it any longer, so I called and came over to meet you." "God loves you," I told him, "and takes care for the salvation of your soul. Take these books and once you finish reading them come back to see me and we'll answer any further questions you might have. After¬wards, you can take other books as well."

He returned again and again, many times. That, however, which moved him the most and propelled him to decide to become a catechumen of the Church was the showing of videotapes of Litanies with the Incorrupt Relics of the Saints of our Church, such as Saint John the Russian, Saint Spyridon from Corfu, Saint Dyonisios of Zakinthos and others. He was amazed and greatly moved by this supernatural phenomenon of the incorrupt bodies of our Saints.

He was baptized, with his wife, who is also a doctor, and his six children on the Feast of Theophany of 1998. A friend of his, a professor of literature, together with his entire family followed him into the Church as well. May God bless them with eternal life.

3. Protopresbyter Theodore Zisis, Professor of the Theological School of the Aristotelian University of Thessaloniki[661]

The God-fearing members of the Church of Christ, full of bitterness and sadness followed the events that took place during the meeting of the

---

661 "Ecumenism and [the] Orthodox Church Meeting of Bartholomew and Benedict, Far From the Path of the Holy Fathers," Holy Monastery of Pantokrator (Melissochori), accessed March 26th, 2023, https://www.impantokratoros.gr/8AC792C1.en.aspx

Patriarch Bartholomew and Pope Benedict in Constantinople. Among the many phone calls the author received from many regions and metropolises, including the Holy Mountain, expressing this bitterness, special impression was made by the spiritual and most Reverend N. of Thessalonica together with a large number of his spiritual children, when he said that he cannot rest and he sorrows till death because they raped and dishonored our mother Orthodoxy. A married clergy and father of many children, of the Holy Metropolis of Demetriathos, who decided to discontinue commemorating his bishop who was in agreement with the Patriarch's actions, when I reminded him of the possible repercussions and punishments for doing so, he replied, "I prefer to till the fields as a simple farmer and hold onto my faith, than cooperate in its demolition and end up in hell together with the Patriarch and Bishops."

I do not know if this simple and not so literate priest had read the writings of the Holy Fathers. What he said though expresses the timeless conscience of the Church, in the stand of the faithful laity against the bishops and presbyters when they do not uphold the word of truth but instead strengthen heresy and deceit. In a number of specific confessions of the Fathers, there exists the saying, "Bad Obedience and Holy Disobedience." We are simply reminded of the indicative opinion of the great fighter of Orthodoxy, Great Athanasius against the Arian heresies. He writes that in situations where the bishop or presbyter, the eyes of the Church, behave badly and causes the people to become scandalized, they must be expelled, even if it risks for the faithful to be without a shepherd. It is better and advantageous to meet in the churches without bishops and priests, rather than the faithful be cast in hell together with the bishops and priests, where the Jews of Christ's period ended up with their Chief Priests Annas and Caiaphas. "It is better to meet with them in a blessed home, than to be cast out with them like Annas and Caiaphas, in the lake of fire." This is what Agiorite Hieromonk Gabriel did in our time when with his short and courageous Declaration and Confession ceased to commemorate the Ecumenical Patriarch Bartholomew after his co-worship and common declaration with the previous Pope, some two years ago, during the enthronement feast in Rome on 29 June 2004 and the inauguration of a Holy Orthodox church on July 1 of the same year. Following, he writes, "So that it may not appear that with my silence I condone what goes on. I shall not take part in the attendant commemorations of the name of the Ecumenical Patriarch, but I shall remain in my cell doing my normal and accepted monastic duties only to indicate my protest and until the holy community of the Holy Mountain take clear and appropriate position on the events happening these days."

THE NARCOTIC OF ECUMENISM AND OF ASSOCIATES IN INCREASING DOSES

There are many alert and sensitive consciences of the Orthodox people, who however, do not hear or see the voice or stand of the many different faithful. The clergy and theologian who sing praises and worship the beast of the Revelation, the religious band of the antichrist, the leveling of the religions and confessions, the multicultural and multi-religious model of the so-called New Age, that turns the world into darkness and the corruption of the pre-Christian era, that was aged and corrupted by the evil one, they now are shown as opposite of what they are and are magnified. With the same measure that Christ is persecuted, and people are de-Christianized, especially in the western and "civilized" world, under the responsibility of Papism and Protestantism, the devil progresses. The truth of God is modified, the true knowledge of God of the Gospel, with the lie of the new idolatry of multi-culturalism and syncretism (blending or fusion). The resultant slackening of the observance of the commandments, with the people ending up with the "untried mind" "paid by every evil" even in the perpetration of the most repugnant filth of Sodomy, that is praised and practiced by even homosexual clergy, as the Apostle Paul precisely presents in the pre-Christian era in the first chapter of his epistle to Romans that they wish to return to the so-called New Age of syncretism and pan-religion. No matter how many meetings occur between the Pope and the Orthodox Patriarchs, the only way of re-evangelization of the Christians is the return through repentance, in imitation of St. Peter's shedding of tears for denying Christ, now by the Pope for denying Holy Orthodoxy of the common Fathers and Saints of the first millennium. If he continues to selfishly insist on the so-called claim of Peter and the keys of the Kingdom as he does these days in

Constantinople in his secular ambitions and primacy, then the saying "shepherd my flock" does not apply but "go behind me Satan, for you do not mind the things of God but of the people."

In this climate therefore, of the so-called New Age that is cultivated by the Papist and Protestant Ecumenism, with further panorama of the pan-religion of the antichrist, Christ and the Church are not proclaimed as the unique light and the only road to salvation, unfortunately with the concurrence of most of the Orthodox Patriarchs, Archbishops and Bishops. We lie when we sing at the end of the Sacred Liturgy, that "We have seen the true light, we have received the Heavenly Spirit, we have received the true faith the indivisible Trinity we worship." Unfortunately the light that the patriarchal Holy Liturgy gave out at the Phanar, with the liturgical co-celebration with the Pope, was not the true light, the true faith but the darkness and the deceit of heresies, of the filioque, of the primacy, of the unleaven, of the purgatory, of the created grace, the distortion of all the mysteries, the worldly church of the Vatican that succumbed to the temptations of the devil to obtain wealth and power, to become a worldly state and in essence to stop having any relationship with Christ and Christianity, according to Dostoyevsky.

And the darkness was transmitted all the way to the Orthodox missionaries who were asked how could they now convince people to become Orthodox and not Roman Catholics or how could they empower those that had become Catholic, who are very numerous in the missionary countries, to come to Orthodoxy, when it was shown to the whole world pictures of co-worshipping and often co-celebrating of the presiding Pope and the 46th apostolic canon, which forbids us to recognize the baptism and the Sacred Eucharist of the heretics. Again unfortunately, they have been recognized by the Ecumenical Patriarchate and other Orthodox churches which quietly allow even the sharing of the chalice. Who turns the light of communion into darkness? Or the agreement with Christ to the agreement with Belial? Or who places the faithful with the unfaithful? How can we dare in a few days to address the born Christ and sing, "Your birth Christ our God, has brought forth to the world the light of knowledge" and like the magi so shall we worship "as the sun of justice" and receive our salvation in the "One, Holy, Catholic and Apostolic Church" the symbol of Faith, in the Orthodox Church?

How many Churches, how many faiths, how many baptisms exist, one, many, lots? If it is not one, the Orthodox and St. Paul err when they say, "One Lord, one faith and one baptism."

These questions though are now no more puzzling, even the meaning of heresy has become incomprehensible. People ceased to differentiate between correct and false, between truth and deceit. The narcotic of ecumenism, this new religion of the antichrist, the pan heresy according to the Elder Justin Popovich, given in small doses over many years and wrapped in Orthodox looking covering like the Unia, with falsely interpreted sections of the Holy Gospel and of the Church Fathers, has drugged the consciences of most people and even of many clergy and theologians. It has created an imaginary, false state of peace and union with the so-called dialogue of love, where the crowds rest blissfully, unsuspectingly taking free, through the media, the pill of ecumenical heroin. The doses continuously become stronger by the simple collaboration in both practical and secular topics, through the declarations of Orthodox representatives at the ecumenical conferences, that only the Orthodox Church is the true Church, we arrived at the complete destruction of the holy canons, with the openly obvious common prayers in the eyes of the angels and the people, to the horrible travesty on the mystery of the Holy Eucharist, mystery of total true union, with the liturgical embraces of the heretics and the supplications of the deacons for them and the singing of the "many years" by the chanter.

The Steps of Athenagoras Are Not the Steps of the Apostles and of the Fathers

Can one imagine the Great Athanasius, having Arius sitting across on the anti-throne, to pray together and embrace each other on the "let's love each other" and the chanters singing to Arius the "may you have many years" so that he may continue his heretical and destructive work? How does the icon that depicts St. Nicholas smacking and slapping Arius relate with the icon of the Patriarch embracing the pan-heretic Pope and believing his presence to be a blessing? Who is correct St. Kosmas Aitolos cursing the Pope, or the Patriarch praising and treating him like a brother? The desert monks of Palestine with their leader, who is also celebrated these days, St. Savva, who kept the Church unblemished from the heresy of "Single Will" or the wretched and poor monk from the Holy Mountain who composed hymns and troparia to honour the visit of the heretic Pope at Phanar? Do these Agiorites have anything in common with the holy martyr Agiorites who were martyred because they opposed the papist Patriarch John Vekkos?

It is certain that St. Efimia's incorrupt body that is in the patriarchal cathedral of St. George, who "praised the Orthodox and tore down the false believers" the Monophysites, she does not rejoice but sorrows with all these events and shrinks her grace. The same happens with St. Gregory the theologian and St. John Chrysostom, whose relics were venerated by both Patriarch and Pope, they did not rejoice but sorrowed. The apostolic succession is not only dependent on historical succession to the thrones, but it is also succession on process and teaching, and as the saying goes "on process participator and on the throne's successor." Succession ceases when the continuation of the truth of the Orthodox Faith, breaks down. The only truth in the addresses and speeches of the Patriarch is that he follows in the steps of his predecessors Athenagoras and Demetrius. However, the history of the Church does not start with Athenagoras but there is a history of over two thousand years of struggling Patriarchs and Confessors, archpriests, priests, monks, and lay people against Papism from Great Photius to the present. Of course, we the Orthodox follow those that are acknowledged by the time-tested conscience of the Church, Saints and Fathers and not those that are in heresy and Latin-leaning recent Patriarch, Archbishops and Bishops. The steps of Athenagoras and Demetrius are not the steps of the Apostles and the Fathers.

THE FENCE OF ORTHODOXY COLLAPSES, BISHOPS ARE NOT COMMUNED OR COMMEMORATED

These were written being fully conscious of the historical actual events we live in, of the negative and damaging actions and demonstrations against Orthodoxy. They were also written in full consciousness of the responsibilities and consequences of this, our stand. We prefer to be persecuted and despised, to remaining silent and less vocal than the fish, in front of the obvious assault on the Orthodox Faith, instead of cultivating the friendship and sympathy of the friends of the Papists and Latins. We wait and pray that the Orthodox camp becomes empowered with bishops and even the balking and wavering priests and monks. The truth though does not depend on numbers and money. The many have often strengthened the lie and deceit. We point out that the television pictures on the meeting of the Patriarch with the Pope, the liturgical embraces and well-wishing awakened the conscience of many, who ascertain that the integrity of the truth is compromised, that the bishops commemorated in the Sacred Liturgy, the guarantors of the union of faith, do not uphold the word of truth, are not in communion with the Saints in their presence but in essence they are uncommuned, since they are in communion with the uncommuned. The responsibility is great for anybody who stays silent when the Faith is endangered.

Saint Gregory Palamas who was criticized by his fellow monks because he left the agiorite hesychast monastery, the prayer and watchfulness, and went to Thessalonika to take on the struggle against the Papist Varlaam and sympathizers, characterizes it as "Unpious Piety" the abdication of presenting the dogmatic teaching of the Church and the checking of heresy and deceit as the Holy Fathers did for lesser evils. True piety is not to follow those that destroy the fences to allow the heretics to enter but the Godfearing Fathers. If one should overlook and underestimate the teaching of even one of the Fathers, he weakens the fence at that point, where a crowd of wicked heretics will soon find access. One sorrows and deeply wriggles, just considering the Patriarchal breach, that considers the Holy Fathers who have struggled against the Pope, as victims of the devil and worthy of the forgiveness and mercy of God. If, however Great Photius, Saint Gregory Palamas, Saint Mark the Courteous, Saint Kosmas Aitolos, Saint Nikodemus the Agiorite and many more fighters against the Papist heresies are members and victims of the devil, we should cross them out from the list of Saints, cancel the feasts and ceremonies and instead of calling for their intercession and their help, we should perform remembrance and thrice holy services that God may forgive them. However, St. Gregory Palamas says "It is true piety not to doubt the God bearing Fathers." Moreover, the theologies of the word spoken by the saints, provide the rules of true piety and

measure, each sealing and completing the enclosure of piety, without ne-
glecting any part, through which the wickedness of the heretics could
find great access. It likens those who keep silent and do not struggle
against the heresies as a third type of Godlessness, wherein the first two
types it ranks the unbelievers and the heretics. This assessment is blessed
when one reflects on the grave breach that silence means consent.

Ignoring the Sacred Canons.
"The guilty does not guilt make."

We shall not proceed further anymore. We had decided in view of
Christmas to postpone the struggles and wait. The situations, however, continue, piety is demolished, the understanding of divine incarnation is voided, and salvation is resisted. Christmas without true Christ,
without true faith, means absolutely nothing, results in a secular feast
of material wellbeing and bodily comforts. In a few days the scene will
be repeated in Rome on the visit of Archbishop Christodoulos. In the
future we shall present a shattering miracle of St. Spyridon who is feast-
ed, Patron Saint of Corfu, who expelled and sent far away from the Cathedral and consequently from the Orthodox Church, the Pope, as well
as the commentary on the miracle of St. Athanasius of Parou. In continuation and with the help of God and the intercessions of the strug-
glers against the Pope, the Saints who confessed and were martyred, we
shall comment on theological and ecclesiological basis, the events at the
Phanar "following the Holy Fathers" and not "the steps" of Athenagoras
and his predecessor Meletios Metaxakis. We shall show that apart from
the usual co-prayers, during co-liturgical services, the chalice is shared
in "ecumenical" liturgies and is simply hidden, and not shown officially
because the ecumenical heroin has not yet drugged all the conscience of
some "fanatics" who refuse to be drugged and react.

It is incomprehensible to pursue the union with the heretics and to
tear ourselves apart from our Orthodox brothers, those to embrace and
these to excommunicate and punish. We remain united with the established Church of the Saints, with the One, Holy, Catholic and Apostolic
Church, as her inmates and children. We accept all the dogmas, all her
sacred canons, all the ecumenical and local Synods and we resist and

renounce all the numerous heresies, old and new of the Papists and Protestants. Whoever justifies them as divinely inspired teachings, whoever
recognizes the mysteries and the grace of the so-called sister churches,
whoever has belittled and ridiculed the Church, by counting her with
the heresies of the so-called churches; they tear and divide the Orthodox faithful and come under the specific punishments of the holy canons that are not obsolete, nor voided but valid; valid and shall always be
valid. The new age, the new building started with the incarnation, with
the birth of Christ, and continues by the Apostles and the Fathers. The
Patriarchs and Bishops did not start it, by differentiating the ages and dividing the Church to evade the consequences of continuity and identity.

Whoever dares to use personally and according to their self-interests
some canons against the fighters and confessors of Orthodoxy, let them
think that firstly it is obvious and clear by everything they say and do
that they are themselves guilty of contravening a number of canons and a
part of the saying, "the guilty do not guilt make", they risk in cases of unjust decisions the danger of harming themselves in this life or after death.
We commemorate typically some canons that have been completely
shred apart by the transgressors. "A Bishop or Presbyter or Deacon who
just co-celebrates with the heretics will be excommunicated, but if he
permitted them to co-officiate as clerics shall be defrocked. A Bishop or
a Presbyter who accepts the baptism of the heretics will be defrocked,
for what accord could there be between Christ and Belial? Or what can
a believer share with an unbeliever? For the heretics should not be allowed to enter the house of God, if they persist in heresy. Nor should
anyone seek the blessing of the heretics and schismatics for it is nonsense
and not a blessing. Do not congregate with the heretics and schismatics."
"Espouse the sacred canons, heeding their full commandment and keep
them unblemished, as trumpeted by the Holy Spirit through the famous
Apostles, as well as the Holy Ecumenical Synods and those locally assembled to pronounce similar commandments, and those of our Holy
Fathers, for each and every one was pronounced by the Holy Spirit, setting the responsibilities. Those that they anathematize, we anathematize
too, and those they defrock we defrock too, and those they excommunicate, we excommunicate too, and those that they punish, we punish too."

4. Abbot Kosmas (Vasilopoulos) of the Orthodox Monastery of Archangel Michael

THE CATHOLIC CHURCH'S IDEA ABOUT SAINTS IS DISTORTED[662]

In the case of the Orthodox Church we continue that tradition for two thousand years and believe that without the Saints you cannot be sanctified, but they [Protestants] say you need Christ to be sanctified. Yes, that's correct, but the saints were sanctified by Christ and now Christ wants us in humility to also ask his mother for help, his angels for help, and his saints for help. And if we don't do that, we cannot become holy. That's the difference between the Protestant church and the Orthodox Church. As for the Orthodox Church and the Catholic church, that's another problem which I haven't got time to go into but their whole idea about saints is all distorted. See how the Church believed in the first thousand years before we split, we [the Orthodox Church] continued in the second thousand years. The Orthodox Church has not changed anything of how we believe and venerate saints. The [Roman] Catholic church has [changed] and now they're so distorted. I will read further on, and you will see what I mean of what they've done with regard to the saints.

THE CATHOLIC CHURCH DOESN'T VALUE PRE-SCHISM SAINTS ONLY RECENT ONES[663]

The saints of Trieste had largely been forgotten and it was St. John [Maximovitch] who restored their local veneration. The western [Catholic] church, even though they say they believe in saints like us, but they don't value them, they don't venerate them except the newer ones, the ones after the schism. Interesting. The ones before the schism who we

---

662 "Talk 79: Why Are the Lives of Saints Considered the Encyclopedia of Orthodoxy?" 3:37-4:44, Abbot Kosmas Vasilopoulos, Official Page of The Orthodox Monastery of the Archangel Michael, accessed February 1st, 2023, https://www.youtube.com/watch?v=p6Lqoxw1EvY

663 Ibid., Timestamp 33:48-35:37.

recognize, who we say are true saints, they're slowly forgetting about them but the new ones like John Paul II and all these new saints that they've got, them they venerate. Someone's behind that. Do you know who that someone is? Does anyone know? What's your name again? George. Do you know who it is? Starts with D or S. It's got two names. Do you know who it is?

George: I think I do.

Fr. Kosmas: Who?

George: Does he reside in the Vatican?

Fr. Kosmas: I think he lives there at times but who do you think it is? Ah, you're thinking of the pope. No, no, no, no. This one is higher than the pope.

George: Oh, really. He lives in a place that we don't want to go.

Fr. Kosmas: That's it. He lives in a place that we all don't want to go. He has a lot of control. This is what happens when we lose the traditions of the Church. When we lose our traditions, we're toast as they say in America. That's it, finished.

THE ORTHODOX CANNOT PRAY WITH CATHOLICS,
PARTICIPATE IN THEIR SERVICES[664]

Before doing any church services in Trieste, Fr. John [Maximovitch] took Fr. Spyridon to the relics of the saints, vested in an *epitrahili*, which is what I'm wearing and a small *omophorion* which is what the bishops wear.... With a censor and a cross in his hand, he would descend into the crypts, that's where the tombs were, under the cathedrals, where according to long lists of information, the saints had been buried according to his lists that he had, that Saint John [Maximovitch] had. He would sing their *troparia* and *kontakia* written on pieces of paper which he would pull out of his pockets, praying to the saints to intercede, in other words

---

664 Ibid., Timestamp 35:37-38:05.

to pray for the city and *only then* would he go to celebrate the services in Fr. Spyridon's Church. Like we say "St. Demetrios, the protector of Thessalonica." We have saints that are protectors of the city. I think St. Philothei, woman of Athens, and things like that but they've [the Roman Catholic church] lost a lot of that.

As Fr. Spyridon recalled, St. John acted as if the ancient local saints were present. Wherever he walked he had such faith in the saints that he was like that they were there next to him and he would pray to them and honor them. Before leaving Trieste, he contacted local Roman Catholic clergy acquiring from them various permits so that the Orthodox Church in Trieste would have free access to the relics and sites of the saints. Now some of you are strict on ecumenism and would say "Oh, he mixed with the Catholics. Saint John must be an ecumenist." But did he pray with them? No. So you can deal with them. You can talk to them. You can work together. *But you can't pray together. That's the difference.* Did Saint John pray with them? No. When he went into their churches, did he participate in their services? No. He went straight to where the relics of the Saints were, venerated the Saints and left. Don't get mixed up.

THE CATHOLIC CHURCH REMOVED NINETY-THREE SAINTS AND REVOKED THEIR FEAST DAYS[665]

Now I have to come to a very unfortunate part of the talk. I hope I don't contaminate you, but it has to be said. This is from *ABC News* April 26th, 2014. The Catholic church removed ninety-three saints from their universal calendar and revoked their feast days in 1969 when Pope Paul VI revised the canon of saints, that's the list of saints, and determined that some of the names had only ever been alive as legends or not enough was known about them to determine their status. Legends mean that they were made up. Like Mary Poppins or some other fairy tale or something like that.

There was another article written on it, and that was actually saying that they weren't even real, a lot of these saints. For example, this is who they've taken off the list; Saint Nicholas, Saint Barbara, Saint Chris-

---

665 Ibid., Timestamp 1:30:15 - 1:32:29.

topher, Saint George, Saint Catherine, Saint Marina, Saint Dionysius, Saint Vlasios, Saint Panteleimon, Saint Alexis the Man of God, Saint Estathios, Saint Veronica, and Saint Euphrosyne — this is some of them.

I don't know what the ninety-three are, but I wouldn't be surprised if they're all the pre-schism saints while the ones that came after, they don't get kicked off. Others say, you can still believe in them, but you don't have to. These are unheard of things in the Orthodox Church. So, after hearing that, you're going to have to, when you get home, have a spiritual bath. Got to wash yourselves. How do you wash yourselves? With prayer and ask God to help you to be cleaned from such blasphemy. It's actually blasphemy. But you expect it. I don't really get that offended because I would expect that. They've lost tradition.

CATHOLIC SAINTS DO NOT HAVE INCORRUPT RELICS[666]

Let's look at some of them [the saints] who lived close to our times. We should read the life of Saint John of Shanghai and San Francisco, 1966 he passed away. He was a Russian hierarch, ascetic and his relics are in USA, they're incorrupt. Do the Catholics have incorrupt relics? But they say they do but I think if you read closely, they're wax dummies, and they have some bones inside.

5. Protopresbyter John S. Romanides

A whole text has been prepared by Metropolitan Hierotheos (Vlachos) of Nafpaktos and Agios Vlasios on the teachings of Fr. John Romanides relating to the departure of the Western theological presuppositions from the Orthodox patristic foundations. The title is Patristic and Scholastic Theology in Perspective: Based on the Spoken Teaching of Father John Romanides.[667] For those interested in an in-depth intel-

---

666 Ibid., Timestamp 1:36:49 – 1:37:12.

667 Metropolitan Hierotheos (Vlachos) of Nafpaktos, *Patristic and Scholastic Theology in Perspective: Based on the Spoken Teaching of Father John Romanides* (Levadia: Birth of the Theotokos Monastery, 2023).

lectual history of the divergence made by the West in its pursuit of heresy, this is an extremely valuable resource.

CRITICAL EXAMINATION OF THE
APPLICATIONS OF THEOLOGY[668, 669]

The subject before us presupposes an interdependence between the theoretical aspects of any scientific discipline and its practical application either to the needs of man or to the testing and promoting of the theoretical aspects themselves of the science in question. We have here both research for the uncovering of knowledge for the sake of knowledge, which may in time prove useful, as well as research into a scientific discipline which has applicability to the needs of society in general and to man in particular already known.

Modern scientific method has developed a combination of imaginatively putting forth theoretical hypotheses and subjecting these to the critical test of repetitive experimentation to see under what combination of arrangements of elements and of their circumstances theoreti-

---

668 "Minutes of the Second Congress of Orthodox Theology," in Athens, August 19-29, 1976, published by Professor Savvas Agouridis, 413–441. Footnotes in the text are from the source.

669 The subject of this paper was not chosen by me but given to me. As will become clear from the study of this paper the critical examination of theology, is both presupposed by and identical with "the critical examination of the applications of theology." Testing the authenticity of theology and applying theology are two aspects of an identical process since only he who acquires and possesses the true application of theology acquires and possesses true and authentic theology. Purification, illumination and theoria are both the testing and the application of theology, i.e., 1) learning to distinguish between the energies of the Holy Spirit and of creatures, especially of demonic powers, and 2) participating in the former, too, and avoiding the third i.e, demonic or abnormal influences on one's personality and thought process. For documentation of the theses presented in this study I refer generally to the following selection of my studies: Τὸ Προπατορικὸν Ἁμάρημα, Athens 1957; Ἡ Δογματικὴ καὶ Συμβολικὴ Θεολογία τῆς Ὀρθοδόξου Καθολικῆς Ἐκκλησίας, Vol I. Thessaloniki 1973; Ρωμηοσύνη, Ρωμανία, Ρουμέλη, Thessaloniki 1975; The *Filioque*, in Κληρονομία, Thessaloniki vol. 7, no 2. July 1975, pp, 285-314; "The Christology of St. John of Damascus," in Papers, Dialogue Eastern and Oriental Churches, edited by Metropolitan Methodius of Aksum. Athens 1976, pp, 46-52.

cally predicted results arise. This in combination with the development of instruments capable of detecting, measuring, and analysing not only things before us, but also objects millions of miles away is staggering to those trying to keep informed.

However, the methods used so successfully in the realm of the physical and biological structure of the universe have not met with the same success in other research endeavors such as history, sociology, political science. Economics, psychology, paedagogy, religion and most theologies.

Almost all theologies have been swept away together with almost all philosophies by the modern critical mind which can no longer allow authority to speculation unless transformed into tested axioms which in turn are always left open to further testing and modification.

Even the very idea of unchanging and immutable truths supposedly hidden within, or underlying, or transcending the structure of observable and measurable or invisible and unmeasurable reality, so dear to philosophical and theological systems in the Latin and Protestant tradition, has been seriously weakened by the overwhelming evidence that all things, even though subject to a continuous and repetitive pattern, are in a steady state of change, development, and transformation.

There is a touch of humor in listening to those religious groups who formerly spoke so much about the value of those things which do not change and perish, now speak continuously of change and its wonders and value, even in bringing divided Christians into an always changing and developing unity.

We take up our subject having in mind the critical examination used in fields of research in general, the subject of this Conference and the title of this subsection, "Theology in the Renewal of the Life of the Church."[670]

In any case we cannot discuss our subject concerning applied theology unless we determine what the theology is that we are applying.

---

670 Strictly speaking we cannot talk of the renewal of the life of the Church, since 1) the Church is the Body of Christ in Whom and in Which the faithful dwell and by Whom and by Which the members of the Church are interpenetrated since Pentecost and since 2) the life of the Church is the glory of the Holy Spirit in this human nature of Christ the Logos. Therefore, neither the Church nor Her Life can be renewed. Only Her members are renewed.

Therefore a critical examination cannot be limited to the application, but must begin with the Theology itself which is being applied.

A. CRITICAL EXAMINATION

The first question one must ask is, *can any existing method of research and testing used in the scientific and sociological disciplines in use today be applied to Orthodox Theology and its applications?*

The answer to this question depends on what the subject matter and purpose of Orthodox Theology are and how they are applied.

Here we immediately meet with the question concerning the nature of theology and the application of criteria to test its authenticity.

1) Is Theology authoritatively revealed in such wise that it cannot be questioned and subjected to critical testing by methods in use in other disciplines?

2) Or is it a putting forth of speculative hypotheses which can be tested scientifically by methods in use and accepted as dogmatic axioms?

3) Or is Theology a combination of authoritatively revealed dogmatic axioms which can be searched out by reason for a progressively better and fuller understanding?

In all three possibilities the question of revelation itself presents serious problems for the application of research and testing methods known and used in research today. The reason for this is that whatever is accepted as revelation is itself the criterion and cannot itself be subject to critical examination and evaluation by methods in use for attaining to knowledge by means of research, unless what is finally known belongs to the same species of knowledge. Then what is considered by some as revealed dogmas and axioms in one age can be either rejected by critical examination in a subsequent age, whether the devotees of these dogmas like it or not, or else they finally end up supported by the result of research. The last presupposes that an item of revelatory experience has been found to be true by scientific or sociological research.

I

a. Since the critical examination of the applications of Theology is directly dependent on what one means by revelation, it may be useful to point out generally what has happened to those Latin and Protestant theological traditions which either identified the germ of revelation or the whole of revelation with the Bible.

It seems that it was inevitable that these Latin and Protestant traditions were destined to the rude awakening brought upon them by the whole development of their own Biblical criticism based on historical research 1) for the reconstruction of the life situation within which each part of the Bible was written, 2) for the examination of the literary and kerygmatic forms and methods used and their comparison with extra-biblical data, and 3) for the comparison of the Biblical ideas with extra thought patterns and beliefs in order to determine degrees of interdependence.

It is my personal opinion that the results, although devastating for the Latin and Protestant traditions have been a very valuable catharsis and should constitute a valuable lesson to those Orthodox who abandoned the Patristic tradition and either themselves have identified revelation with the Bible or believe that the Fathers identify revelation with the Bible.

To the first group belong the modern "Orthodox" fundamentalists who go by the name "conservatives" and to the second belong the modern "Orthodox" anti-fundamentalists who may go by the name "liberals." It is noteworthy that these distinctions are not founded on the Patristic tradition since the Fathers are not fundamentalists.

b. 1) The Latin and Protestant position that the Bible is the Word of God, or revelation, stems primarily from Augustine who believed that God appears to the prophets by means of creatures which God brings into existence in order that by means of them He may be seen and heard.[671]

Once He is thus seen and heard He then returns those created means of such revelation to non-existence. This revelation by means of seen and

---

671 *De Trinitate II.* 6 (11)-18(35).

heard symbols coming into and passing out of existence and reaching the intellect of the prophet and apostle by means of sense experience is the lowest form of revelation.[672]

2) The higher form of revelation is the direct injection into the prophetic and apostolic mind of the concept, idea, or teaching God wants revealed.[673]

3) Besides these two forms of revelation there is also vision or experience of the divine "essence"[674] by means of the soul's transcending all physical and sensory limitations of space and time by means of non-discursive ecstasy. Such an experience, however, does not necessarily identify itself with revelation unless ideas and concepts concerning God are conveyed to the intellect for passing on to others. However this is not what happens in such ecstasies which are associated usually with complete loss of contact with space and time and therefore the experiential contents of these. In any case this ecstatic intuition is supposedly an experience of the intellect aided by grace and liberated from space and time, to wit from physical and sensory limitations, and is from the Patristic viewpoint demonic.[675]

Latins and Protestants generally agreed on items 1) and 2) but not in every case on item 3) which was associated with monastic contemplation rejected generally by Protestantism and always by the Orthodox.

What is of immediate interest in regards to items 1) and 2) is that they trapped the Latin and Protestant traditions into the fundamentalistic positions which modern Protestant and Latin Biblical criticism has been busy for many years, testing and literally destroying.

There is no doubt but that the weakest part of Biblical fundamentalism is the idea that the Bible is not only divinely inspired, but also a book dictated by God in order to be His revelation to man.

---

672 See my study "Notes on the Palamite Controversy" in the *Greek Orthodox Theological Review,* VI, 2 (1960-61). IX, 2 (1963-64).

673 Ibid VI. 2(1960-61).

674 See chapter 2 of Fr. John Romanides' *The Ancestral Sin,* where he explains the patristic distinctions between essence and energy while criticizing the confusion between the two found in the history of Western metaphysics. See also the last paragraph of his "Notes on the Palamite Controversy and Related Topics, Part II."—Ed.

675 *Ibid* IX. 2(1963-64).

Thus the whole Bible became one big revealed axiom which was valid as criterion not only on questions concerning God and His relation to the world through Christ and the Holy Spirit but also on questions concerning the structure of the universe, the process of development in nature, and the history of man.

The amazing thing is that within the Latin and Protestant traditions the Bible is still equated with revelation by those who are still believers in a more or less traditional sense in spite of modern critical research. The reason for this is that the only understanding of revelation that the Latins and Protestants know is revelation of concepts which can be understood by a faithful and graced intellect.

c. In order to round out these observations concerning the use of critical examination within the Latin and Protestant traditions we should keep in mind the following general historical trends in the development of authoritative criteria for the interpretation of Scripture and the promulgation of credal, confessional and dogmatic formulas.

Once the equation of the Bible with revelation is accepted it becomes inevitable that an authority for the proper dogmatic or confessional interpretation of the Bible must be found to co-exist in history with the Bible.

The determination of the nature and limits of this authority is automatically governed by the fact that within this frame of reference revelation has already been identified or reduced to revelation of verbal and iconic symbols concerning God and His relation to the world and man through Christ and the Holy Spirit. The reason for this revelation of words and iconic symbols is unavoidably assumed to be both the duty and ability of man to understand by faith and grace the meaning of these words and images.

This means that revelation is directed at man's existing abilities to understand by means of faith and grace, but also that revelation itself is a given quantity in completed form which can be quantitatively possessed by both individual believers and the collective body of the Church and even by heretics and non-believers.

This is why the American and British Bible Societies are so intent on passing out a Bible to everyone in the world. They are actually disseminating God's revelation to man with the conviction that those who are predestined to salvation will be inspired by the Holy Spirit to read this revelation by means of faith and understand.

Until the time of the Protestant Reformation the Latins generally accepted Augustine's belief that the Church is a society of predestined faithful who have been given the gift of understanding revelation in the Bible, having accepted this revelation by faith. For Augustine the final authority for the interpretation of the given revelation is the Church.

However, the Church for Augustine does not have from the beginning a full understanding of the teachings of Christ. Just as the individual believers must first accept dogma by faith on the authority of the Church and then make an effort to build up an understanding of this faith, so in a similar manner the Church also increases Her own understanding of revelation with the passage of time.

Underlying this concept of revelation and its understanding by individual believers and the Church, which became the backbone of the Franco-Latin tradition, especially in support of the Filioque, is the belief that God gave the Bible and the Holy Spirit to the Church in such wise that the Church has revelation in a book and acquires understanding from the Holy Spirit Who teaches the Church and Her believers how to understand this Book.

Thus for Augustine Christ's promise that He will give to the Apostles the gift of the Holy Spirit Who proceeds from the Father and Who will guide the Apostles themselves into "all the truth" is transformed into a promise that the Holy Spirit will lead not only the faithful in general into all the truth, but also the Church Herself into all the truth.

Thus some 350 years after Pentecost, to wit in the year 393 Augustine makes the following remarkably naive statement in his lecture to the bishops of the Roman Province of Africa assembled at Carthage: "With respect to the Holy Spirit, however, there has not been yet, on the part of learned and distinguished investigators of the Scriptures, a discussion of the subject full enough or careful enough to make it possible for us to obtain an intelligent conception of what constitutes His special individuality (proprium)."[676]

---

676 *De Fide et Symbolo* 19.

For Augustine, as is well known, one first accepts the Bible and dogmas by faith and by the authority of the Church and then one makes every effort to understand intellectually.

But according to Augustine one who becomes reconciled with and a friend of God does not only come to know the acts and glory of God intellectually, but "all the secret things of God," including the very substance of God.

Augustine states his position very clearly, "And inasmuch as, being reconciled and called back into friendship through love, we shall be able to become acquainted with all the secret things of God, for this reason, it is said of the Holy Spirit that 'He shall lead you into all truth.'"[677]

What Augustine means by such language is made very clear by what he says elsewhere several years later. "I will not be slow to search out the substance of God, whether through His scripture or through the creature."[678] This searching out the substance of God by means of the Scriptures and philosophy remained Augustine's consistent theological method and became the central core of the Frankish theological tradition which is now commonly called scholastic theology.

The whole Augustinian approach to the Bible and theology presupposes the existence of uncreated universals and therefore a real similarity between God and His creatures or between the uncreated and the created, in such wise that both belong to a single system of truth which can be conceived by the human intellect, especially when receiving revelation, and which can therefore be adequately expressed in concept bearing words and images.

The first devastating blow against this approach was dealt by the new followers of Aristotle in the Frankish kingdom of the 13th century giving rise to the Thomistic synthesis between Plato, Aristotle, and Augustine to which was added a Frankish distortion of Dionysius the Areopagite and of John of Damascus.

The strange thing is that the Franks were not in a position to realise that both Dionysius the Areopagite and John of Damascus agree fully with the earlier Fathers that there are no uncreated universals of which creatures could be copies since there is no similarity whatever between

677 *Ibid* 19.

678 *De Trinitate II*, pref.

the created and the uncreated. The reason for this is that the Franks elevated Augustine to the position of the greatest Father of the Church and the best exponent of the Patristic tradition, whose theology is supposed to be not only the same as that of the other Fathers, but also the best example of Patristic Theology. This being so for the Frankish theological imagination, there can be no contradiction between Augustine and the other Fathers of the Church. Therefore, since Augustine accepts the Platonic universals, so must all the Fathers.

The next devastating attack on the Platonic basis of the Augustinian Frankish tradition came from the Nominalists, then from Martin Luther, and finally the complete destruction of this basis came about at the end of the last century with the collapse of traditional understandings of philosophy. The accumulation of so much evidence by modern science that there is no evidence for the existence of immutable and changeless natures and forms and species anywhere has left a tremendous doubt about the possibility of the existence of immutable archetypes of which the things of the universe are supposed to be copies. This in turn has led to a general collapse of the old Latin and Protestant belief in the existence of truth, law and moral norms in immutable forms which can act the part of criteria in the human thinking process. Even the old confidence of the Nominalists and of Luther that the Bible itself is the immutable truth, law and moral norm revealed by God has evaporated under the pressures of Biblical criticism.

d. Perhaps the most serious problem faced by the Latin and Protestant tradition is that the identification of revelation with the Bible set up the Bible not only as the criterion par excellence of the Church's teaching, but also put the Bible over and above the prophets and Apostles themselves. The prophets and Apostles are not themselves infallible teachers concerning God and His will and relation to the world in Christ by the Holy Spirit, but the means and instruments by which God Himself infallibly teaches what He wants in concept-bearing words and images. Inspiration is thus not a continuous spiritual state of the prophet and apostle, but a state limited in time to the duration of the event by which God passes on the concrete revelation of concepts and concept-bearing words and images to humanity by means of a prophet or Apostle. Thus the prophet and Apostle is inspired during the revelatory experience of receiving and writing down the word of God. It is even possible that the one receiving and writing does not fully understand exactly what he is receiving and writing and it is perhaps for this reason that Augustine and his followers seem to be actually saying that the Church understands better than the recipients of revelation themselves the meaning of Scripture with the passage of time.

In any case within the context of such presuppositions the prophet and Apostle can also be in a state of error or lack of correct or full understanding when not in the inspirational state of receiving and writing or conveying the word of God.

It is difficult to see how speculation over the meaning of revelation can be avoided within such context. One can imagine that a tradition of interpretation can be passed on from the prophets and Apostles together with the Bible. But unless this interpretative tradition had built into it some guarantee of infallible interpretative inspiration there would be no guarantee of correct understanding. Latin and Protestant traditions have understood such guarantee to be the Holy Spirit given to the Church by God through Christ, with the former ending up believing that the Latin Pope of Rome is the center of such guarantee and with the latter generally believing that the Holy Spirit inspires individuals and groups of individuals by more noninstitutionalized means than Popes and Councils of bishops.

At this point it should be pointed out that one finds difficulty differentiating Russian Orthodox deviations from the Patristic tradition since Peter the Great, if not earlier, from the above-described general Latin and Protestant approaches except that the Ecumenical Council was set up as the final and highest authority of Biblical dogmatic and moral teaching. Although the shape of such an approach is to be found in tradition, its Russian form is more similar to the fundamentalist Western Conciliar theories of the 14th–16th centuries.

It seems quite clear that the Latin and Protestant identification of revelation with the Bible invaded the Kingdom of Greece in the last century with the descent of Russian theology and thence found its way into the Four Patriarchates of the Romans of New Rome, Alexandria, Antioch and Jerusalem, because of the general weakening of Patristic monasticism brought about by the desire to imitate post Peter the Great

Czarist Russian Orthodoxy which became very European and therefore very modern, very rich, very powerful and very attractive.

e. In any case from the viewpoint of scientific research method the Latin and Protestant identification of revelation with the Bible can be tested and proven by observing repetitions in current human experience of men today receiving revelations in words and images from God. It is claimed by some that Mohammed was such an example and one may find others. But Latins and Protestants generally deny the possibility of such revelations claiming that the Bible is a unique and unrepeatable event.

This means that we have nothing to test and prove in terms of current religious or revelatory experience, unless the "Pentecostal" speaking in tongues now current in the Latin and Protestant Churches can be tested for similarity or identity with spiritual and revelatory experiences recorded within the Bible.

Given the uniqueness and unrepetitive nature claimed for the Bible by Latins and Protestants, there is also the approach of comparison of Biblical data with extra-Biblical and extra-Judaeo-Christian data to see how unique the Bible is and to see if perhaps the Biblical writers have been influenced by their environment rather than directly by God as claimed and to what degree.

It seems that this latter approach has been the dominant one in European and American Biblical studies, especially since the early part of the last century.

It is my personal opinion that the general results have been quite devastating for the Augustinian Frankish tradition whence both the Latin and Protestant traditions stem. On the one hand Augustine is no longer simply quoted in order to prove points, but is himself questioned. He is no longer regarded automatically as the one who understood the Bible better than all other Fathers. And not only has the scholastic tradition collapsed, but the authority of such Reformers as Martin Luther and John Calvin has been weakened also.

It seems almost as though the tradition of the Latin and Protestant systematic theologian giving guidelines has been replaced by a new tradition of the Protestant Biblical scholar giving guidelines with the Latin Biblical scholars now following from behind and some Orthodox Biblical scholars following rather by means of smell than by means of vision and understanding.

II

a. The very idea that the Bible can be identified with revelation is not only ridiculous from the Patristic viewpoint, but is clearly a heresy. The Bible is not revelation, but about revelation. The Bible is the unique criteria for authentic revelation but revelation is certainly not restricted even in time to the Bible. Pentecost is the final and highest form of revelation when the Holy Spirit led the Apostles into all the truth as promised by Christ, but Pentecost is not a once-in-history event, but an ongoing experience and sharing within the Church in the glorification of and by Christ bestowed as a gift upon those who have reached various levels of perfection, having passed from purification to illumination and culminating in the higher forms of *theoria*,[679] to wit *theosis* or glorification.

In other words the Pentecostal experience of the Apostles is handed down by Christ as the central core of tradition from one age to another in such wise that the Orthodox Church does have in her midst living witnesses to and of glorification in Christ who therefore have a full understanding of the revelation of the glory of God in Christ in both the Old and New Testament.

---

679 [*Theoria* (Gr. Θεωρία) or 'contemplation' is the perception or vision of the nous, through which one attains spiritual knowledge (γνῶσις—gnosis—or the immediate spiritual perception inspired by God. It may be contrasted with the practice of the virtues (πρακτική— praktiki) which designates the more external aspect of the ascetic life—purification and the keeping of the commandments—but which is an indispensable prerequisite of contemplation/*theoria*. Depending on the level of personal spiritual growth, contemplation/*theoria* has two main stages: it may be either of the inner essences or principles of created beings (of things as God sees them) (*theoria* physiki / θεωρία φυσική or 'natural contemplation') or, at a higher stage, of God Himself (*theoria* theologiki / θεωρία θεολογική or 'theological contemplation'). (The note and the one below on the term nous are adapted from the Glossary in GEH Palmer, Philip Sherrard, and Kallistos Ware (trs.), *The Philokalia, The Complete Text, Compiled by St Nikodimos of the Holy Mountain & St Markarios of Corinth* (Faber & Faber, London:4 vols, 1983-98).]

The Bible itself is not the uncreated glory of God in Christ nor His glorified humanity and therefore the Bible is not revelation. The Bible is not, for example, Pentecost, but about Pentecost. However, the glorification of the prophets, Apostles, and saints in the humanity of Christ is Pentecost at varying levels and therefore is revelation. Pentecost is for man the final form of glorification in Christ, but not only a past experience, but rather a continuing experience within the Church which includes words and images and, at the same time transcends words and images. To wit it includes the body, the intellect and the noetic faculty, but at the same time transcends these completely. This is why the aspect of the Pentecostal experience which transcends words, images, body, and intellect, cannot be either conceived or expressed in words. Therefore, the most important aspect of Pentecostal revelation cannot be identified with the Bible which is made up of concept-bearing words and images. This is why the Pentecostal experience itself is contained in the Bible, but at the same time transcends the Bible since the Bible is not itself the Pentecostal revelation of the glory of God in Christ by the Holy Spirit.

To put the subject in schematic form from the viewpoint of catechetical method found clearly in the Bible itself[680] and used till today in the Church, we would simply point out that concept-bearing words and images are used by the prophets, Apostles, and the incarnated Logos Himself for instructing those at the levels of purification and illumination. To those outside of the inner circle of those being illuminated, to wit to those being cleansed or in need of cleansing, Christ preaches the coming of the rule (Βασιλεία) of God in parables, since seeing they cannot yet see and hearing they cannot yet understand. This is so because the rule (Βασιλεία) of God takes over within the noetic faculty of man in the measure that the influence of the devil is being expelled.

As the influence of the devil is being expelled and the rule (Βασιλεία) or grace of Christ is taking over, the noetic faculty begins to become liberated from slavery to the intellect, the body, and the environment and thus one passes from the level of purification to that of illumination. At this level one attains to a clear understanding of what the concept-bear-

---

680 See my study "Justin Martyr and the Fourth Gospel," in *the Greek Orthodox Theological Review* IV, 2 (1958-59) 115-139.

ing words and images of the Bible are meant to convey and at the same time understands clearly what they are not meant to convey.

Concept-bearing words and images concerning God and His relation to the world in Christ and by the Holy Spirit are expressions of revelation which are intended for those who are passing through the stage of purification and are reaching into the higher stages of illumination. However, the revelation of the glory of God in Christ and the Holy Spirit transcends illumination which is knowledge about the Father, Son, and Holy Spirit, but not yet knowledge of the Holy Trinity in the ascended and glorified humanity of Christ in and after Pentecost.

The ascended and glorified humanity of the Logos dwelling in and bearing the Father and the Holy Spirit transcends the ability of concept-bearing words and images to convey. This is so because man can neither conceive nor express the Holy Trinity and the Incarnation of the Logos. But man glorified by and in the human nature of Christ can experience all the truth revealed in Pentecost with an experience above experience, a seeing above seeing, a hearing above hearing, a feeling above feeling, a tasting above tasting, a smelling above smelling, a knowledge above knowledge, and an understanding above understanding.

It is exactly because the Pentecostal revelation cannot be revealed in created words and images, or concepts that Christ told His Apostles, who had now become His friends by reaching the stage of illumination that "I have yet many things to say unto you, but you cannot bear them now. Howbeit when He, the Spirit of truth, is come, He shall guide you into all the truth: for He shall not speak from Himself; but what things soever He shall hear, these shall He speak: and shall declare unto you the things that are to come. He shall glorify me: for He shall take of mine, and shall declare it unto you. All things whatever the Father hath are mine: therefore said I, that He taketh of mine, and shall declare it unto you. A little while, and ye behold me no more; and again a little while, and ye shall see me." (John 16. 12-17).

In contrast to Augustine, the Fathers of the Church both inherited and witness to the tradition and present fact that Christ's promise that the Holy Spirit will lead the Apostles "into all the truth" was fulfilled on Pentecost.

b. It is important to keep in mind that unlike the Latin and Protestant traditions revelation is not itself the conveying of concept-bearing words and images which are the means used by the recipients of revelation for expressing God's actions and will to their followers not yet glorified. Biblical concepts, therefore, are the preparatory stage of revelation only. Even all the created words of Christ recorded in the Bible are such a preparatory stage of receiving the uncreated words of God which are unspoken words, ἄρρητα ῥήματα. That the Holy Spirit leads the Apostles into all the truth does not mean that some concepts about God and His relation to man and the world in Christ by the Holy Spirit had been revealed before Pentecost and that on Pentecost all concepts not yet revealed are now revealed. If this were the case then the theology of the Fathers and the Councils can be no more and no less than deviations from the complete truth revealed on Pentecost. As we have already seen, the Augustinian tradition (for which revelation is only the conveying of concepts and immutable ideas to the intellect) applies the promise of Christ in question to the Holy Spirit's supposed work of leading individuals and the Church to a better and fuller understanding of what has been revealed. In this way the work of the Fathers and Councils is somewhat justified. This is the line adopted by the Franks which continues to dominate Latin theological understanding till today.

From this viewpoint the Protestant *sola scriptura* tradition is more similar to the Patristic tradition, but differs radically from the Fathers in identifying this *scriptura* with the word of God and revelation, as we already indicated.

c. Since we have been developing our theme on the basis of the assumption that the Holy Spirit on Pentecost and in the continuing life of the Church reveals to the friends of Christ the uncreated glory and rule of God through the humanity of Christ dwelling within themselves, it may be appropriate to examine a classical example of the Patristic tradition in order to see clearly the relation between the continuing living tradition of personal experience of glorification and Orthodox dogma as well as how the key to opening the Bible's secrets works. It is obvious that without knowledge of this key and its proper use, the Bible remains a hidden mystery even to Biblical scholars who know and use every research device being used and tested by those outside the fold of spiritual life as experienced by the Fathers.

Even from a purely scientific research position, it stands to reason that the best way to understand revelations of the glory of God in the Bible is to find whether there continues to exist such a tradition today in order to compare the one with the other and perhaps thus uncover the meanings and purposes of terms used in expressing these revelations in the Bible, the Fathers, the Councils, and the lives of the Saints.

At this point one could use the official decisions and documents produced by the Councils of Constantinople / New Rome during the 14th century in order to point out the official teaching of the Church on the questions before us. I am sure that some would doubt whether this would be a very critical and scholarly approach to the subject in hand. Cultural inferiority complexes have led some Orthodox to believe that it is an act of humility to adopt Protestant and Latin research methods and an act of pride to follow only the Fathers in interpreting the Bible as required by the Orthodox tradition generally and the Councils especially.

Thus we would cite as a classical example of Patristic theological or Biblical method St. Gregory the Theologian who, when read within the context of the Orthodox tradition, is not at all speaking about a speculating systematic theologian who is trying to understand a revelation given in the distant past, but rather of revelation which is not different from but identical with understanding and not only in the distant past but a present reality, and not only the experience of others but also his own experience.

We quote the following: "Not to all, oh such ones, does it belong to philosophize about God, not to all; the matter is not thus cheap and low; And I will add, neither always, neither with everyone, neither about everything, but there is a when and a with whom, and an on what. Not to all, because it belongs to those who have been examined and have advanced to theoria, and before these, [who] have purified or are at the very least purifying the soul and body."[681]

So the theologian for St. Gregory is he who has reached *theoria*, a term which is dominant in the Gospel of John, and used by Christ in relation to the work of the Holy Spirit in leading the Apostles into all the

---

681 *Theological Orations* 1.3.

truth. "...He taketh of mine, and shall declare it unto you. A little while, and ye have *theoria* of me no more; and again a little while, and ye shall see me." On and after Pentecost the Holy Spirit reveals to the friends of God both what Christ has from the Father and also Christ the Logos Himself in and through His humanity. These friends of Christ are our theologians par excellence because they share in this Pentecostal experience in which revelation and understanding are identical.

However, it must also be pointed out that upon reaching this *theoria* the friends of God are not only united to the glory of the Holy Trinity in the humanity of the Logos, but also to each other. *Theoria* is therefore the highest form of unity in the glory of the humanity of Christ with each other. It is understood, therefore, that those who have this common experience have the same knowledge of God and therefore, the same theology about God. It goes without saying that only one who actually is graced with this revelation of God's glory in Christ by the Holy Spirit knows the identical or same experience of others and understands the linguistic and iconic symbols used by those glorified to express this glorification and uses these symbols himself.

This unity in the truth of the glory of the Holy Trinity with each other, to wit this unity in *theosis* or glorification in which those thus glorified have the same faith and understanding of faith based on the same experience of *theosis* or glorification, is the very core and summit of Christ's teaching and action brought to their highest consummation in Pentecost.

"Sanctify them in the truth. Thy word is truth. As Thou sent me into the world, so I sent them into the world: and on their behalf I sanctify myself, that they also may by sanctified in truth. I do not ask for them only, but also for those who believe in me by their word, that all may be one, as Thou, Father, in me and I in Thee, that they also may be in us, that the world may believe that Thou sent me. And I have given them the glory that Thou gavest me, that they may be one as We are one: I in them and Thou in me, that they may be perfected into one, that the world may know that Thou sent me and loved them as Thou loved me. Father I want that those whom Thou gavest me may be also with me where I am, that they may have *theoria* of my glory, which Thou gavest me, since Thou lovest me before the foundation of the world. Oh just Father, the world also did not know Thee, but I knew Thee, and these (disciples) have learned that Thou has sent me. And Ihave made known to them Thy name and I will make known, that the love with which Thou lovest me may be in them as I in them" (John 17:17-26).

This is obviously not a prayer for Church unity in the future, but the unity in the glory of Christ given to the Apostles and the faithful on Pentecost. The *theoria* or vision of the glory of the Father in Christ by the Holy Spirit is not only a futuristic promise but a present reality consummated in Pentecost and continued in the lives of the Saints. According to St. Gregory the Theologian it is this *theoria* which makes a person a theologian and causes identity in teaching among the theologians of the Church from the Prophets to the Apostles and Saints of the Church.

d. Having this in mind one begins to realize the unity and identity of spiritual experience and doctrine among the Prophets, Apostles, and Saints or to put it into terms used in today's dogmatic manuals, the unity and identity of revelation and dogma and their clear distinction from rational speculation.

Also one sees a clear distinction between the revelation of non-conceptual or supra-conceptual truth to those divinized or glorified in Christ and the formulation of this revelatory experience into dogmatic axioms or credal statements cast into terms made necessary not by speculative endeavor to understand intellectually the supra-rational mysteries revealed, but by a concrete heresy appearing in a concrete historical situation requiring the formulation of an expression of supra-rational truth in terms understandable within the life situation created by the heresy in question.

This clearly means that the formulation of doctrinal and creedal statements and the development of an adequate terminology into which these statements are cast are not a result of the Church's arriving at a better and more complete understanding of revelation by means of the efforts of speculating theologians intellectually investigating a supposedly deeper meaning of revelation not fully and completely understood by former theologians.

Also one sees clearly the identity of revelation and the ability to theologize correctly about revelation with the spiritual life and perfection in Christ since illumination presupposes purification, since *theoria* pre-supposes illumination, since *theoria* is revelation of the glory or truth in Christ, and since this is what constitutes the one able to philosophize correctly concerning God, according to St. Gregory the Theologian.

e. It cannot be overemphasised that both Orthodox and Arians fully agreed with the inherited Biblical and Patristic tradition that only God knows His own essence, to wit He Who knows the divine nature is Him-self God by nature, Thus, in order to prove that the Logos is a creature, the Arians argued that the Logos does not know the essence of the Fa-ther, nor for that matter His own essence. The Orthodox argued that the Logos does know the essence of the Father, which is His own, and therefore the Logos is uncreated.

The Eunomians threw a monkey wrench into the agreed rules for proving points with their shocking claim that not only does the Logos know the uncreated essence of God, but man also can know this essence. Therefore, the Logos does not have to be uncreated because He knows this uncreated essence.

Against the Arian and Orthodox position that creatures cannot know the divine uncreated essence, but may know the uncreated energy or will of God in its multiple but indivisible manifestations, the Euno-mians argued that the divine essence and uncreated energy are identical so that to know the one is to know the other.

Strangely, Augustine adopted these Eunomian positions, to wit that man can know the divine essence and that in God there can be no real distinction between uncreated substance and uncreated energy. There-fore when the Franks appeared in the East with these positions they were accused of being Eunomians.

These Augustinian positions in the hands of the Franks transformed the purpose of theology as a guide toward *theoria* of the glory of God in the humanity of Christ into a study or searching out of the divine substance and in this respect the scholastic tradition (in the minds of the Franks) far surpassed the tradition of the Latin-speaking and Greek-speaking Roman Fathers who, as we saw, consistently taught that not only man but even the angels neither know, nor will ever know the divine essence which is known only to the Holy Trinity.

f. In contrast to the Augustinian and Eunomian approach of the Franks to language and concepts concerning God, we have the patristic position expressed by St. Gregory the Theologian against the Eunomians.

Plato had claimed that it is difficult to conceive God, but to define or express Him in words is an impossibility.

St. Gregory disagrees with this and emphasizes that "it is impossible to express Him, and yet more impossible to conceive Him. For that which may be conceived may perhaps be made clear by language, if not fairly well, at any rate imperfectly..."[682]

The most important element in Patristic epistemology is that the partial knowability of the divine actions or energies and the absolute and radical unknowability and incommunicability of the divine essence is not a result of philosophical or theological speculation, as it is in Paul of Samosata, Arianism and Nestorianism, but of the personal experience of revelation or participation in the uncreated glory of God by means of illumination and *theoria*. Dialectical speculation can never become the source of authoritative teaching as though the Church, whether by means of a Pope, or Councils, or Protestant Biblical scholars, could transform research into dogma, as believed by the Franks and their successors.

The authority for Christian truth is not the written words of the Bible themselves, which cannot in themselves either express God or convey an adequate concept concerning God, but rather the individual Apostle, Prophet and Saint who is glorified in Christ and united in this experience of glory to all the friends of God of all ages.

Thus the Bible, the writings of the Fathers and the decisions of Councils are not revelation, but about revelation. Revelation itself transcends words and concepts although it inspires those participating in divine glory to express accurately and unerringly what is inexpressable in words and concepts. Suffice it that under the guidance of the Saints, who know by experience, the faithful know or should know that God is not to be identified with Biblical words and concepts which point to Him albeit infallibly when studied under the guidance of those having

---

682 *Ibid* 11.14.

reached *theoria*. The faithful know very well that it is a heresy to believe that Biblical concepts expressed in words could be penetrated by the believing intellect for the acquiring of an intellectual comprehension of God under the guidance of the Fathers. Biblical knowledge concerning God leads to supra-noetic, supra-intellectual, and supra-sentient knowledge of God which is both contained in the Bible, but at the same time is above the expressions concerning God in the Bible.

Having all that has been pointed out in this paper thus far in mind, we return to St. Gregory the Theologian in order to point out the fact that he does not only use Biblical texts to prove points, nor does he restrict himself to the revelatory experience of the Prophets, Apostles, and Saints in order to set out the theological foundations for confuting the Arians, Eunomians and Macedonians, but he also uses his own experience of this same revelation of divine glory in the humanity of the Logos, exactly as is done by other Fathers of the Church.

"What is this that has happened to me, O friends, and initiates, and fellow-lovers of the truth? I was running to lay hold of God, and thus I went up into the Mount, and passed through the Cloud, and was found within, away from matter and material things and as far as I could I withdrew within myself. And then when I looked I scarce saw the back parts of God; and this because I was sheltered by the Rock, the Word that was made flesh for us. And when I looked a little closer, I saw, not the first and unmingled nature, known to itself— to the Trinity I mean; not that which abideth within the first veil, and is hidden by the Cherubim; but only that (nature), which at last even reaches to us. And that is, as I know, the majesty ($\mu\varepsilon\gamma\alpha\lambda\varepsilon\iota\acute{o}\tau\eta\varsigma$) or as Holy David calls it, the magnitude ($\mu\varepsilon\gamma\alpha\lambda o\pi\rho\varepsilon\pi\varepsilon\acute{\iota}\alpha$) which is manifested in the creatures, which it has produced and governs, for these are the back parts of God, which are after Him, as tokens of Himself..."[683]

g. The tradition of this distinction between the first nature and the uncreated glory of God, the first known only to God and the other to those to whom God reveals Himself is to be found not only in the Bible and the Orthodox Fathers but also in Paul of Samosata, the Arians, and the Nestorians as already pointed out. These three have a common

---

683 *Ibid* 11.3.

philosophical approach according to which God is related to creatures only by will or energy and never by nature since natural relations mean necessary relations which would reduce God to a system of emanations. Paul of Samosata and the Nestorians argued that in Christ God is united to humanity not by nature, but by will. The Arians argued that God is related to the hypostatic Logos not by nature, but by will, whereas because the Logos derives His existence from non-being by the will of the father, and therefore is created, passible, and changeable in nature, He is united by nature, to wit by a necessity imposed by God, to His truncated human nature.

Against these positions the Orthodox Fathers argued that in Christ the Logos is united to His humanity by nature or hypostatically and the Father generates His Son by nature, the will not being in contradiction to what belongs to God by nature. Thus God generates the Logos and projects the Holy Spirit by nature from His own *hypostasis* and the Holy Trinity by will creates creatures from non-being and by will is related to creatures with the exception of the Logos who unites Himself hypostatically to His own humanity.[684]

h. At this point we must touch upon the most important and most central aspect of Biblical and Patristic Theology which since Augustine has been completely ignored by the Franco-Latin and Protestant traditions, and even by the modern Orthodox under the influence of post-medieval Russian theology.

Because Augustine transformed the doctrine of the Holy Trinity into a speculative exercise of philosophical and theological research in an attempt to understand this mystery rationally, the simplicity and schematic and Biblical nature of the doctrine was lost sight of by those just mentioned.

Thus the history of the doctrine of the Holy Trinity has been reduced to searching out the development of such concepts and terminology has led to phrases like Three Persons or Hypostases, one essence or

---

684 See my study "The Debate over the Christology of Theodore Mopsuestia and some suggestions for a fresh approach," in the *Greek Orthodox Theological Review*, V, 2 (1959-60) 140-185.

nature, *homoousios*, personal or hypostatic properties, manners of existence, one will, one energy, one divinity, etc.

For the Fathers, the Arians and the Eunomians, however, the doctrine of the Trinity and Christology is identical to the appearance of the Logos in His glory to the Prophets, Apostles, and Saints. The Logos is not an abstract concept conveyed by means of revealed words, created beings, or concepts, but is always identified with the concrete Angel of God, Lord of Glory, Angel of Great Council, Lord Sabaoth and Wisdom of God Who Himself appeared to the prophets of the Old Testament and became Christ by His own birth as man from the Virgin Theotokos. No one ever doubted and all firmly believed in this identity of the Logos with this concrete Individual who revealed in Himself the invisible God of the Old Testament to the Prophets with the peculiar exception of Augustine who in this regard is influenced by the gnostic and Manichaean traditions.

The controversy between the Orthodox and Arians/Eunomians was not about Who the Logos is in the Old and New Testament. They agreed that the Logos is He Who appeared to the Prophets and Who was born as man from the Virgin. They differed over what the Logos is and what His relation is to the Father.

The Orthodox insisted that the Prophets saw the Logos as uncreated, impassible and unchangeable having always existed from the Father Who by nature generates the Logos from Himself before the ages.

The Arians/Eunomians insisted that the Prophets saw the Logos as created, passible, and changeable deriving His existence from non-being before the ages by the will of God.

Thus the basic question between Orthodox and heretics was, did the Prophets and Apostles see in God's uncreated glory a created, passible, and changeable Logos or an uncreated, impassible, and unchangeable Logos, a Logos Who is God by nature and therefore has all the energies and powers of God by nature, or a God by grace, who has some but not all the energies of the Father and then only by grace and not by nature since he does not have the same essence or nature, but a different or created one.

Both Orthodox and Arians/Eunomians agreed in principle that if the Logos has every power and energy of the Father by nature then He is uncreated. If not He is a creature.

Since the Bible is a witness of Whom and What the Prophets and Apostles saw in the glory of the Father, the Bible itself, although itself not revelation, will reveal whether or not the Logos has all the energies and powers of the Father by nature. Thus we will know whether the Prophets and Apostles saw a created or an uncreated Logos, *homoousios* with the Father or not.

One can see clearly how for the Fathers the consubstantiality of the Logos with the Father is not only the experience of the Apostles and Saints, but also of the Prophets. The difference being that the Prophets in theoria saw God in the Logos or Angel without flesh by the Spirit, whereby the Apostles received the same revelation, but in and by the humanity of the Logos born as man from the Theotokos and having thus become consubstantial with us while being consubstantial with the Father.

It is very important to emphasise the fact that both Orthodox and Arians/Eunomians use both the Old and New Testaments indiscriminately. The argumentation is very simple. They make a list of all the powers and energies of the Father recorded in the Bible. They do the same for the Logos/Angel of Glory. Then they compare them to see if they are identical or not. The important thing is for them to be not similar, but identical.

Parallel to this, both Arians and Orthodox agree against the Sabellians and Samosatenes that the Father and Son have individual hypostatic properties and manners of existence which are not common, although they do not agree on what these are.

When the controversy is extended to the *Hypostasis* of the Holy Spirit the exact same method of theologizing is used.

Whatever powers and energies the Father and Son have in common the Holy Spirit must also have both in common and by nature in order to be God by nature.

Patristic theological method is clearly non-speculative, it is authoritatively experiential, it is not abstract, it is simple and schematic.

Stated simply the whole doctrine of the Holy Trinity may be reduced schematically to two simple statements:

> 1) What is common in the Holy Trinity, i.e. essence, will, energy and power, is common to and identical in all Three Hypostases.

> 2) What is Hypostatic, or hypostatic property, or manner of existence is radically individual and incommunicable and belongs to One Person or *Hypostasis* only.

Thus we have τὰ κοινά and τὰ ἀκοινώνητα, what is common and what is uncommunicably individual.

Having this in mind one realizes why the Romans did not take the Frankish *filioque* very seriously as a theological position, especially as one which was supposed to improve the Creed of the Second Ecumenical Council. [This is] why they made fun with syllogistic jokes until the Franks were able to conquer East Romania and back up their fantastic theological claims with an unbelievable self-confidence and a sharp sword.

i. In any case the argumentative process of Patristic theological method is always parallel to and checked by the experience of *theoria* of the glory of God in the humanity of Christ. This experience verifies and certifies the proper interpretation of the Bible's witness

> 1) to the revelatory encounter between the Logos and His friends the Prophets and Apostles in whom He comes and dwells with the Father in the Holy Spirit and reveals uncreated unspoken words which transcend concepts and

> 2) to the uncreatedness of the Logos and the Holy Spirit and Their oneness in nature with the Father and the identity of Their uncreated glory, rule, grace, will, etc., and

> 3) to the incommunicability of the hypostatic properties, including the incommunicability of the incarnation of the Logos, and the unending eternity of the humanity of the Logos, in which the Holy Spirit builds up the Church since Pentecost till the consummation.

The revelatory experience of the glory of God also certifies the Biblical teaching that there is absolutely no similarity between the uncreated and the created. This means that there can be no uncreated universals of which creatures are supposedly copies. Each individual creature is dependent upon the uncreated glory of God which is on the one hand absolutely simple yet is divided indivisibly among and within individual creatures and all of God is present in each and every energy simultaneously while God is also by will everywhere present and at the same time by nature everywhere absent, except for the Logos, hypostatic union with His human nature.

The Holy Spirit led the Prophets into the Truth and the Apostles into all the Truth on Pentecost, not by the revelation of concept-bearing rational truths not known before, but by the experience of the new presence of the humanity of Christ which, constituted and constitutes the Church victorious over death and the power of the devil that death may no longer prevail against the Church as was the case in the Old Testament. Thus all of Christ and not part of Him is present in each friend of God not only according to the uncreated rule ($\beta\alpha\sigma\iota\lambda\varepsilon\acute{\iota}\alpha$), glory or divinity, but also according to the created humanity of Christ.

From the viewpoint of the concept-transcending uncreated reality of God, the Prophets and Apostles experienced the same glorification in the Logos/Christ. It is, therefore, from the viewpoint of the Incarnation, the Death, the Resurrection, and the Ascension of Christ and His new presence in the Spirit on Pentecost establishing the Church as His Body that the Apostles and all those who after them share in *theoria* that all the Truth is revealed by the Holy Spirit. Since Pentecost every incident of the glorification of a Saint, in other words of a Saint having vision of God's uncreated glory in the humanity of Christ as Its source, is an extension of Pentecost at various levels of intensity.

This experience includes all of man, but at the same time transcends all of man including man's intellect. Thus the experience remains a mystery to the intellect having *theoria* and cannot be conveyed intellectually to another. Thus language can point to but cannot convey this experience. The spiritual father can guide to but cannot produce *theoria* which is a gift of the Holy Spirit.

When therefore the Fathers add terms to the Biblical language in use concerning God and His relation to the world, like *hypostasis, ousia, physis, homoousios*, union by nature, union by will, etc., they are not doing this because they are improving current understanding as over against a former age. Pentecost cannot be improved upon either as revelation or understanding which for the Fathers are the same, as we saw. All they are doing is defending the living tradition of Pentecostal experience which transcends words in the language of their time because a concrete heresy is leading the faithful away from and not to this experience which, means spiritual death to those led astray.

For the Fathers authority is not only the Bible, but the Bible plus those glorified, to wit the Prophets, Apostles, and Saints. The Bible as a book is not in itself either inspired or infallible. It becomes inspired and infallible within the communion of Saints who have the experience of divine glory described in, but not conveyed by, the Bible. To those outside of the living tradition of theoria the Bible is a Book which does not unlock its mysteries.

I cannot see how one can avoid the conclusion that this is in perfect accord with the understanding of the scientific methods in use today. Every science has its own language which can be understood only by those initiated into the speciality in question, by those who are already specialists. How can one begin understanding what *theoria* means if he is not in touch with the living tradition of *theoria*? And the living tradition of *theoria* is not made up of books about *theoria* only, but of those who have *theoria* and therefore know both what these books are about and how to teach others to read them. The Bible is such a book, the writings of the Fathers are such books, and the decisions of the Councils belong also to this class of documents since they are produced by the Fathers working collectively.

B. APPLICATIONS OF THEOLOGY

Having begun rather with a general examination of how an Orthodox may apply criteria for determining the nature of authentic theology, we can now make a general survey of the applications of this theology. This can be divided into two groups of applications, I) to the internal life of the Church and II) to the relations of the Church to society and the world at large. It must be born in mind that basically the *learning* and *application* of this *theoria*-based theology is identical.

I

a. The criteria for the application of theology are automatically determined by the nature and the purpose of theology as thus far explained. We should complete in as simple terms as possible what has thus far been said.

All men have been created and destined for the perfection associated with vision of the glory of God. In other words all will be saved, but not all will be glorified in *theoria*. This is so because there are those who will reach the perfection of eternal damnation and those who will eternally advance to higher stages of perfection in *theoria*. Those damned will see the uncreated glory of God as eternal fire and outer darkness, God Himself being a consuming fire to those who love not, and those eternally perfected will see the same glory of God as light. Within this context the whole structure of rewards and punishments as understood by Augustine and his followers in the Latin and Protestant tradition is unfounded and meaningless.

Thus one clearly understands that all men will come to know the truth in Christ, but not all will participate in the glory of God in Christ.

b. From the viewpoint of God there is no difference between eternal damnation and eternal glorification in the sense that God loves those in both categories equally.

Heaven and hell are on the one hand the same thing, but from the viewpoint of the creature, especially of man and angels, they are radically different. The difference is due to the creature's willingness or unwillingness to develop from lower to higher stages of love which seeks not its own. One can understand from this why the Augustinian doctrine of predestination and irresistible grace is nothing but childish nonsense.

It follows from this that any theology, philosophy and ideology which does not seek the transformation of self-centered, individualistic, and selfish love into the love which does not seek its own is a false guide and spiritually dangerous for those who believe in it.

It also follows that any theology, philosophy and ideology which only seeks such a transformation of selfish love into selfless love, but does not succeed in implanting this love in its adherents and does not know how to do so must also be judged as a fraud.

In contrast to this the Orthodox tradition not only seeks this transformation, but also both knows how to bring it about and does bring it about.

This also means that the Orthodox who are not aware of this do not belong to this Orthodox tradition by way of awareness and understanding, but rather follow from behind by way of smell, i.e., instinctively.

c. The pivotal point in Orthodox theology for the attainment of selfless love is the twofold struggle 1) to be united to each other in the uncreated glory of the humanity of the Logos in the state of *theoria* reached by passing the state of illumination and 2) to defeat the devil in all stages of perfection beginning with purification. The successful outcome of this struggle presupposes a willingness to learn to distinguish between the energies of the devil and the energies of the Holy Spirit from a spiritual father who has reached at least illumination if not *theoria* and thus has the gift of the discernment of spirits.

Since it is only the energies or the glory or the rule of God that man can come to know and since these can be discerned only by learning to distinguish them from the energies of creatures and especially of the devil, this means that an Orthodox theologian and spiritual father is the same thing. One cannot be a theologian without being a spiritual father and one cannot be a spiritual father without being a theologian.

d. However, when the Bible and the Tradition speak about illumination, what is being illumined and by what is it being illumined?

The Fathers speak about the darkening of the *nous*[685] of Adam and his descendants. Augustine and the Frankish tradition understood this

---

685 [The *nous* (Gr. νοῦς) is the highest faculty in a human being, through which— provided it is purified— s/he knows God and created things by means of direct apprehension or spiritual perception. Unlike the *dianoia* or reason, from which it must be carefully distinguished, the *nous* does not function by formulating abstract concepts and then arguing on this basis to a conclusion reached through deductive reasoning, but understands divine truth by means of immediate

to mean that the intellect of Adam had immediate vision of uncreated universals or ideas in the divine substance and therefore had all knowledge, meaning knowledge of all things in their essence and source. Thus by means of the fall man was cut off from this knowledge and became ignorant.

In view of the astounding advances of modern science it would be difficult to maintain such a viewpoint. Man's intellect seems unlimited in its capacity of uncovering and learning the mysteries of the universe, even when this ability seems to reveal continuously how much more there is to learn.

In any case it does not seem to be the intellect that was damaged by the fall.

For the Fathers of the Church the nous is not usually identified with the intellect, but is a distinct and separate faculty of the soul which has become in actuality inoperative by its confusion with the intellect and its enslavement to the intellect, the body, and the outside environment. Having lost its normal communion with God and thus being at varying degrees of abnormality, it has become a slave, whereas its purpose is 1) to be completely free in the Spirit from outside influences and 2) to influence the intellect, the body, and the environment without itself being influenced by anything but the grace or energy of God.[686]

experience, intuition or 'simple cognition' (the term used by St Isaac the Syrian). The *nous* dwells in the 'depths of the soul'; it constitutes the innermost aspect of the heart (St Diadochos). The nous is the organ of contemplation (*theoria*), the 'eye of the heart' (*Makarian Homilies*). Accordingly, its manner of knowing (noēsis/νόησις) is not by abstract concepts or visual images, but by the apprehension of spiritual realities in a direct manner. See note above on *theoria*. The reader should beware of a complication of terminology introduced by the fact that the English translators of the *Philokalia* have chosen 'intellect' to translate *nous* (following the intellectus of Scholastic usage), whereas by 'intellect', Romanides, who was writing before the *Philokalia* was translated means *dianoia* or 'reason'.]

686 See my studies "Notes on the Palamite Controversy and Related Topics, part I" in *The Greek Orthodox Theological Review*, IX, 2 (1963-1964) 225-236; "The Christological Teaching of St. John of Damascus," in Papers, Dialogue Eastern and Oriental Churches, edited by Metropolitan Methodius of Aksum. Athens 1976, pp, 46-52. It is important to point out that the terms are interchangeable and in themselves unimportant. The important thing is the process whereby unceasing prayer and the normal thinking functions operate simultaneously and that noetic prayer operates even during sleep. Failure to understand this

Illumination and the beginning of *theoria*, therefore, are the liberation of this noetic faculty from all outside influence by its occupying itself with the unceasing memory of God, or unceasing prayer. This state is a gift of God to which a spiritual father who has the gift is capable of leading his spiritual children. It is by the liberation of this noetic faculty by unceasing memory of God that self-love and pride are uprooted from the personality and replaced by humility and self-less love.

e. Those who belong to this tradition believe that these stages of illumination and *theoria* are the methods used by Christ in guiding not only the Apostles but also the prophets.

In any case it must be pointed out that a scientific research method in use today would require the verification of the existence of this noetic faculty in man and a determination of the conditions under which it operates as a distinct function distinguishable from the intellect.

Also one can suppose that this faculty can be set in some sort of operation by even a non-Christian or non-Orthodox spiritual exercise, in which case one would have to determine the differences. From the viewpoint of the tradition the noetic faculty may be set in motion or at least is kept inoperative by demonic influences.

However, when activated by the Holy Spirit the noetic faculty has unceasing memory of God in the Lord of Glory Who is Christ Incarnate. This is a state of liberation from demonic influences and unity in Christ in which the whole person, body and soul, is kept from error and gifted with inspiration in such wise that he does not confuse the energies of God with the energies of creatures and especially of the devil.

---

distinction between the intellect and the noetic faculty has led some to mistakenly propose the existence of two patristic spiritualities in Eastern Christendom, one based on the Platonic type ecstasy of the intellect and another based on the inclusion of discursive thought and the body in the highest form of spiritual life. What they do not realize is that when the Fathers speak of the noetic faculty as becoming completely disengaged from all influences from outside and emptied of all thoughts, ideas, etc., and as being occupied only with prayer, they are not speaking about the intellect at all, but about the noetic faculty. No Father, not even Dionysius the Areopagite, belongs to the Platonic tradition of spirituality. See my study mentioned at the beginning of this footnote.

To be kept from error and gifted with inspiration does not mean in this case that such a person attains to an unerring knowledge concerning created truth in its scientific details, but only in its relation of dependence to uncreated truth which is the glory of the humanity of Christ in the communion of saints.

A person in *theoria* and thus inspired does not become an unerring scientist, or scholar, but an unerring theologian. He does not make mistakes when speaking about God and His relations but this does not make him a scientist, or a historian, let alone an unerring one.

It is within such a context that we understand the inerrancy of the Bible, of the Fathers, and of the Councils of Fathers.

It stands to reason that a gathering of bishops some with noetic prayer (unceasing memory of God) and the rest struggling for noetic prayer, would certainly be a gathering of bishops who knew accurately the faith of the Church.

f. In any case, since 1) noetic prayer is a tradition to which one can belong only by having a spiritual father who has *theoria*, and since 2) this tradition of *theoria* produces not just words about piety but actual living examples of piety or love which does not seek its own, and since 3) the similarity if not identity of this living piety with that of the Bible is so obvious, it stands to reason that modern Orthodox Theologians (to use the title rather loosely from the patristic viewpoint) must study the theological method used in becoming a theologian in the traditional sense, in order to see whether the methods now in use to produce theologians are really effective or for that matter even relevant to any real need of man.

This would be the case not only in the production of an Orthodox theologian specializing in dogmatic theology, but especially in the field of Biblical interpretation.

It is obvious that the Church's injunction that the Bible should be studied and interpreted under the guidance of the Fathers of the Church is a very scientific approach since it is much more likely that the saints who have theoria understand the prophets and the Apostles who had and have *theoria*, where[as] Latins and Protestants, who have lost the tradition of *theoria*, do not understand *theoria* in the Bible and certainly mislead the Orthodox who have trust in them.

g. The alternative to tracing noetic prayer or unceasing memory of God as the culmination of illumination and as the beginnings of *theoria* to the apostolic and prophetic tradition is either to find another theological and spiritual method which can defeat the devil and produce *theoria* supposedly more like that of the Bible, or prove that there is no such tradition after Pentecost.

Another alternative to identifying noetic prayer with Biblical piety would be to prove that the noetic faculty must remain rather inoperative in the attainment of Christian perfection, supposedly because it has nothing to do with the teaching and practice of the Prophets, Apostles, and Christ.

Another alternative would be to prove that the noetic faculty does not exist as distinct from the intellect. However, the only way this can be proven is to demonstrate that noetic prayer both does not exist and is impossible.

But noetic prayer does exist and the noetic faculty is therefore a reality.

But certainly the noetic faculty is not an invention of the Fathers. It is part of human nature. All human beings have a noetic faculty, but not all are aware of its existence.

h. In the patristic tradition this unawareness of the existence of the noetic faculty is due to the fall and is participation in the fall of human nature.

Anyone with some feeling for modern scientific method can immediately recognize the tremendous power of this position. It explains why the Fathers of the Church never had the Augustinian and Franco-Latin obsession with the ridiculous myth of inherited guilt.

If the fall of man is the darkening of the noetic faculty, then liberation is its purification, illumination, and glorification, which is a transformation and change in the way man functions which can be tested and studied now. When comparing the state of darkness and slavery of the noetic faculty with its state of illumination and glorification one realizes why the Fathers never dealt with original sin within the Platonic framework of Augustine. According to the Fathers each person in imitation of Adam allows his noetic faculty to become confused with his intellect, passions and environment.

This understanding of the fall coupled with the Orthodox understanding of perfection in Christ by means of the illumination and glorification of the noetic faculty is a phenomenon observable not only by so-called theologians, but also by such scientists as psychologists and psychiatrists. However, neither the theologian, nor the psychologist, nor the psychiatrist can fully learn of the existence of the noetic faculty except from the tradition of Patristic theology and spiritual life.

Furthermore the only complete method by which a research scientist can put the noetic faculty into operation in order to observe its proper and natural function in the state of illumination and glorification is to get his own to function, but this he can do only by correct faith and submission to the spiritual guidance of a spiritual father who has the noetic prayer from his spiritual father.

i. However, here we come upon the most complex and difficult problem of modern Orthodox theology. Those Orthodox who are saturated with cultural inferiority complexes cannot learn patristic theology. This is so because patristic theology requires obedience to be learned since it is a tradition of a method of warfare against the devil for perfection. It can be learned only from those who are victorious by the grace of God.

Since a heretic is a person who does not possess this method it is impossible to learn it from a heretic.

When a person who calls himself Orthodox does not possess this method it is impossible to learn it from him either.

j. The works of the Fathers contain clear cut methods of testing the authenticity of spiritual experience at each level of perfection. These methods are not speculative. They are authoritative and one can see how they are at the same time dependent on Orthodox dogma and the basis of Orthodox dogma.

Vision of divine glory, for example, is tested by the fact that there is no similarity between the created and the uncreated. Therefore, if the light seen has colour, shape and dimension it is not [un]created since the uncreated glory of Christ can also be called by the opposite of light, i.e. darkness, not because it is darkness, but because it transcends both categories of light and darkness. Orthodox apophatic theology is not a philosophy, but a result of *theoria*. Because *theoria* exists in the Old Testament also, so this theology is already that of the Prophets.

When a vision contains the appearance of light or a being of light which has colour, shape, and dimension, then this being takes a position only outside, beside, and opposite the one aware of its presence. This is so because the devil cannot unite himself to man by κρᾶσις or saturation of interpenetration, but only by συζυγία or correlation or yoking.

In the experience of glorification one experiences himself and everything, around him interpenetrated and saturated by the uncreated glory emanating from the humanity of Christ dwelling in himself and others.

It is interesting that some psychiatrists have been recently studying the phenomenon of a being of light appearing to those passing to the state of death and medically being pronounced dead, but subsequently returning back to life.

k. We end this section by pointing out that all men regardless of nationality, race, and colour have the noetic faculty and therefore the possibility of reaching illumination by means of purification and then if God pleases they may experience glorification at its varying degrees.

In any case the varying levels of *theoria* are the highest experiences of Orthodox spiritual life and theology.

Such a spiritual life and theology is neither Greek, nor Russian, nor Bulgarian, nor Serbian, etc., but rather prophetic, apostolic, or simply christian.

In the light of this one may put the question, what is "Russian Spirituality," and why is it presented as something higher than or simply different from other Orthodox spiritualities?

II

It seems that once Orthodox theologians come to the realization that the highest form of theology is *theoria*, which is the ongoing tradition of Pentecost in history, then they can properly take up positions for examining this tradition in its historical setting in order to evaluate correctly the applications of this theology to the relations of the Church to society and the world at large.

a. The most powerful element in this understanding of theology before us is that its bearer is liberated from enslavement to his environment, not by means of escape from it, but by the liberation of the noetic faculty from influence and domination by the intellect, the passions and the environment in such wise that the intellect, the passions and the environment are transformed by those who have reached illumination and *theoria*. It is quite obvious that Christ prayed for the union of the Apostles and their followers in the vision of the glory of the Father in Himself by the Holy Spirit "in order that the world may believe" that the Father sent Him.

The world does not believe because of Christians in general, since they are many times no better and even worse than members of other religions. Because of such Christians many people cannot see the sense in taking Christianity seriously, even though they may accept Christ as a great religious leader and moral teacher. It is only because of Christians in the states of illumination and *theoria* that the world believes that the Father sent His Son. One can readily examine how those in *theoria* influence their environment by studying the cult of Saints especially centered in their icons and relics.

b. Having this tradition of *theoria* in mind one begins to realise that there are many idols and myths which have invaded modern Orthodox understanding of history by means of the official Russian tradition which after Peter the Great betrayed the Orthodox Civilization of New Rome and joined the Feudal Civilization of Frankish Europe. The unceasing tradition of *theoria* means that as long as this tradition continues the Patristic tradition continues, meaning simply that the central core of the Orthodox tradition continues.

At the time of the fall of New Rome this tradition was very strong among the Romans of the Patriarchates of New Rome, Alexandria, Antioch and Jerusalem.

However, soon after the foundation of the Patriarchate of Moscow, the Church of Moskovy officially condemned hesychasm, to wit the Trans-Volga Elders, known as Non-Possessors, and supported a type of monasticism which is foreign to the tradition of *theoria* and more like the feudal monastic establishments of feudal Europe.

Yet there is a tendency to picture the Roman Orthodox under Arabic and Turkish occupation as second-rate Orthodox Christians, and Russian Orthodoxy as the best example of everything Orthodox.

It seems rather that Churches with a strong tradition of *theoria* are no better or worse than the other Churches with a strong tradition of *theoria*. Since *theoria* is the same wherever it is found, so the piety, spiritual life and theology is the same also.

In any case it is clear that once the *Filioque* controversy broke out between Franks and Romans, the Franks automatically were forced to terminate the Patristic tradition since the Roman Fathers after St. John Damascus actively wrote against and condemned the Frankish *Filioque*.

It is necessary to study and get a clear picture of when and why the Russians followed the Franks in terminating the Patristic tradition. It is this Russian tradition which was taken to the new kingdom of Greece with the establishment of the Theological School of the University of Athens.

It is very significant that the Council of 1368 in Constantinople New Rome declared that St. Gregory Palamas is a Father of the Church like the other great Fathers and excommunicates all who disagree. What this Council was actually doing is condemning those who agreed with the Franks who believed that their scholastic theology is better than Patristic theology which for the Franks ended in the 8th century.

c. It is also very clear that the Orthodox tradition of *theoria* has no room whatsoever for the Latin distinction between the so-called active life and the so-called contemplative life. Both these parts of the life of celibacy of the Latin tradition of monasticism and orders are foreign to Orthodoxy.

The reason is obvious. When the noetic faculty attains to and contains the unceasing memory of God alone, the intellect, the memory, the body, and the passions continue to function, with the difference that instead of being dominated by the environment they are dominated by the noetic faculty which is completely liberated.

Because love in this state is not selfish but self-less the individual in this stage of perfection does not love God alone, but also all men and creation. He is even willing to forego his own salvation for that of others.

This means that true glorification extends from the noetic faculty and saturates the soul and body and sanctifies the environment, i.e., social and material creation.

The Orthodox warrior does not seek escape from the material world, but the sanctification of the material world by its liberation from the devil and his followers. However, he first learns how to win battles from those who have become experts in this warfare and then he teaches others.

This is what the Critical Examination of the Applications of Theology seems to be all about.

Do Forced Replacements of their Orthodox Predecessors have Apostolic Succession?[687, 688]

The question before us is quite simple. We are engaged in types of Ecumenical Movements whose end purpose is to reunite Christian Churches. However, certain historical facts have been swept under the carpet and out of sight which cause complications in this effort. Such invisible facts do not allow full treatment of the question of apostolic succession. Perhaps one of these facts swept under the carpet is that there are synods of bishops who derive their episcopal succession from bishops who caused the removal of synods of Orthodox bishops of the vanquished. We will deal briefly with specific instances whereby the Roman Orthodox bishops of the Papacy were forcefully replaced, first by turn-

---

687 Fr. John Romanides. "Do Forced Replacements of Their Orthodox Predecessors Have Apostolic Succession?" The ROMANS Ancient, Medieval, and Modern, 1992. http://romanity.org/htm/rom.26.en.apostolic_succession.htm.

688 Part of a presentation at the VIth Meeting of the Lutheran - Orthodox Joint Commission 31/5 - 8/6/1991 Moscow, USSR. Revised for Sub-commission Meeting, June 17-21,1992, Geneva and printed in "THEOLOGIA" Vol. 63 * Issue 3 * July -September 1992.

coat Roman lackeys of the Franks and then by the Franks themselves.[689] Then we will turn our attention to the orthodox bishops of the British Isles who were removed from their Churches at the instigation of the Frankish Papacy which had instigated the Norman invasion of England. These Norman conquerors and their allies condemned the Orthodox leadership of the British Isles as schismatics and heretics and imprisoned them for life and replacing them with themselves.

But this type of research may be applied also in such cases wherein the Orthodox themselves may have forcefully replaced non-Orthodox leaders with themselves. This had happened during the times of the Nine Roman Ecumenical Councils, whereby condemned heretics were replaced by the Orthodox according to Roman law. The theory behind this was strangely medical. In other words Orthodoxy is a cure of the sicknesses which stem from fantasies which are cured by the purification and illumination of the heart and glorification. The fantasies in question originate from an electrical short circuit between the spinal fluid and the blood fluid. These fantasies are the main tools by which humanity is ruled by either the devil or by mental sicknesses. This short circuit is repaired by the unceasing prayer in the heart called illumination which leads to illumination of the heart and perhaps to glorification which is ordination to prophethood in the Old and New Testament and within the Body of Christ since Pentecost. The lack of this tradition is the main cause of today's disunion among Christians because each group is ruled by their peculiar fantasies.

Roman Popes and Franco-Latin Popes

The key to the transition of the Orthodox Catholic Tradition from an illegal to a legal religion and then to an established Church lies in the fact that the Roman Empire realized that it was not confronted simply by another form of religion or philosophy, but by a well-organized society of psychiatric clinics which cured the happiness-seeking sickness of humanity and produced normal citizens with selfless love dedicated to the radical cure of personal and social ills. The relation between State

---

689 See John S. Romanides, "Franks, Romans, Feudalism and Doctrine, an interplay between theology and society", © Holy Cross Orthodox Press, 1981, Brookline, Mass.

and Church which developed was exactly parallel to that between the State and modern medicine.

The incorporation of the episcopate of Carolingian Francia into the Frankish army and its occupation by military officers whose duty was to pacify the revolutionary Gallo-Roman population is the key to understanding the so-called Great Schism between Roman and Latin Christendoms. These Frankish bishops and their successors never understood the meaning of Apostolic Tradition and succession which they reduced to episcopal power over a system of sacramental magic which sends people either to heaven or hell. This they transferred to the Papacy when they forcefully took it over during a struggle which reached its final stages between 983 and 1046.

This break in Apostolic Tradition and succession was provoked and sustained for centuries by military and political power as a normal function within Latin Christendom. Considered just as normal was the distortion of both the reality of the East Roman Empire and its Church and civilization which continues today under modified guise. This guise caked in "Byzantine" honey does not change distortion into truth.

Canon Law makes specific provisions for the regular convocation of the Synods of bishops presided over by a Metropolitan, Archbishop, or Patriarch at regular intervals for dealing with the proper execution of the Church's mission of cure within society. There are no such provisions for Ecumenical Councils.

The reason for this is that the local synods were part of the original structure of the Church, whereas the Ecumenical Synod was of an extra-ordinary and imperial nature. One may draw a parallel between Ecumenical Councils and the Apostolic Council convoked in Jerusalem (Acts 15, 6:6-29). Ecumenical Councils, however, were convoked by the Roman Emperor for the purpose of signing into Roman Law what the synods of Autocephalous and Autonomous Churches believed and practiced in common.

Arius, Nestorius and Eutyches were condemned by local Councils first and then by Ecumenical Councils. Paul of Samosata was condemned by a local council whose decision was accepted by all other synods. The same was the case with Sabellius. Even at Ecumenical Councils bishops participated as members of their own synods whose spokesmen were their Metropolitans, Archbishops, and Patriarchs, or their legates. It should be clear that neither can an Ecumenical Council become a substitute for local synods, nor can local synods take precedence over an Ecumenical Council, unless the one or the other strays from the faith. The reason for this is that authority resides neither in the Ecumenical nor Local Council, but in the glorified Prophets, Apostles and Fathers who participate in Councils or whose teachings the Councils follow.

Method

The method underlying this presentation is rather simple. The New Testament writers and the Fathers read back into history their own experience of purification and illumination of the heart and glorification which they identify with that of the Prophets of all ages beginning at least with Abraham. This is parallel to repetition of cure in medical science passed on from doctors to doctors, except that in this case Christ is the doctor Who personally cures and perfects His doctors in both the Old and New Testaments. This historical succession of cure and perfection in the Lord of Glory, both before and after His incarnation, is the heart and core of the Biblical and Patristic Tradition and the Synodical System.

Historical Context

Biblical Faith is one's co-operation with the Holy Spirit Who initiates the cure of the sickness of possessive love in the heart and transforms it into love which does not seek its own. This cure is consummated in glorification (theosis) and constitutes the heart of the Orthodox Catholic Church, which replaced paganism as the core of the Hellenic Civilization of the Roman Empire.

Political architects whose historians report history within the context of their plans for the future claim that the world is being Westernized by means of technology and economics. Orthodox Civilization is listed among those which are arrested.

Their claim that the Hellenic Civilization of the Roman Empire disappeared in the 8th century[690] and was replaced in the East by a "Byzantine" Civilization and Empire and in the West by a European Civilization is a modern modification of Charlemagne's theology of history.

---

690 The exact date has been shifting from time to time.

Charlemagne (768-814) fabricated this disappearance of the Roman Empire and its Civilization in order to solve a family problem. His grandfather, Charles Martel (715-741), had finally suppressed Gallo-Roman revolutions in the battles of Poitiers and Provence in 732 and 739, which were supported by Arabs and Numidian Romans who, together with the Spanish Romans, had recently overthrown the Goths in Spain (711-719). The Numidian Romans were under the command of Constantinople's governor of Mauritania in Ceuta. Another Gallo-Roman revolution was suppressed by Charlemagne's father and uncle in 742, the year he was born.

Charlemagne had to find a way to break the religious and cultural unity between his own enslaved Romans and the Roman Empire which now extended from parts of Italy to the frontiers of Persia. He devised a plan to convince his subjugated Romans that the Papal States, called Romania and Res Publica Romana, under his family's control since 756, was all that was left of the Roman Empire. The rest of the Empire would become "heretical" and therefore a hateful "Greece", inhabited not by Romans, but by "Greeks", and headed not by an Emperor of the Romans, but by an Emperor of "Greeks". The Franks called the Empire Roman for the last time in their *Libri Carolini* which attack the Empire as pagan and heretical. The Franks then decided by their Council of Frankfurt in 794 to give the names Graeci to the free Romans and Graecia to free Romania. This became Franco-Latin customary law.

Since the time of Roman Emperor Constantine the Great we have the beginning of a development which led to the Pentarchy of Roman Popes and Patriarchates: 1. Old Rome, 2. Constantinople New Rome, 3. Alexandria, 4. Antioch and 5. Jerusalem. The two Romes became equals as Capitals with Old Rome having precedence over New Rome. This arrangement remained intact until the Franks liberated the Roman Papacy from the Lombard threat. Then Charlemange decided to call the East Romans Greeks and heretics. The last time that Charlemange called the Eastern part of the Empire Roman and heretic was in his Libri Carolini. Thenceforth the Roman Empire in the East became for the Franks heretical and Greek and the Emperor a Greek heretic.

The modern guardians of this Carolingian law 1) replaced "Greek" with "Byzantine", and "heresy" with "change of Civilization". 2) Following Napoleon's plans for the dissolution of the Ottoman Empire and of the ecclesiastical remains of the Roman Empire within it, these same guardians destroyed the legal identity of the citizens of Greece with the Romans of Constantinople, by presenting them as having been under the yoke of this so-called "Byzantine Empire". 3) They have used this fabrication to Balkanize the "Roman Millet"[691] and dissolve its Ecumenical Patriarchate of New Rome Constantinople in the process.

Turning back to 8th century Western Europe we are indeed confronted by real and radical changes. Europe is dominated in its center by the Empire of Charlemagne. Gothic Spain is overrun by Arabs and Numidian Romans, who together had fought as liberators of the Spanish Romans but ended up as their masters. These Numidians were converted to Islam several times according to Ibn Khaldoun.

The birth of Frankish Civilization is described in a letter of St. Boniface to Pope Zacharias (natione Graecus[692] in 741. The Franks had rid the Church in Francia of all Roman bishops by 661 and had made themselves its bishops and clerical administrators. They had divided up the Church's property into fiefs which had been doled out as benefices according to rank within the pyramid of military vassalage. These Frankish bishops had no Archbishop and had not met in Synod for eighty years. They had been meeting as army officers with their fellow war-lords. They are, in the words of St. Boniface, "voracious laymen, adulterous clergy and drunkards, who fight in the army fully armed and who with their own hands kill both Christians and pagans".[693]

Fifty-three years later the successors to these illiterate barbarians condemned the East Roman Empire as "heretical" and "Greek" on Icons at their Council of Frankfurt in 794 and then on the Filioque at their Council of Aachen in 809. For 215 years the Roman Popes refused to conform to their Frankish masters on Icons and the Filioque.

These Frankish bishops were neither familiar with the Fathers of the Seven Ecumenical Councils, nor were they aware of, nor interested in learning anything about, illumination and glorification which were the

---

691 Islamic Law provided for the self-rule of each of the Jewish and Christian societies called a Millet.

692 i.e. a native of the Roman province, Magna Graecia, in Southern Italy.

693 Migne P. L. 89, 744; Mansi 12, 313-314.

presuppositions of these Councils. Between the end of the 8th and the 12th centuries the Franks were familiar only with St. Augustine, who was neither a Father of an Ecumenical Council, nor did he understand Biblical illumination and glorification, which he confounded with Neo-Platonic mysticism. He therefore did not understand the Apostolic Tradition and succession and deviated sharply from St. Ambrose who had baptized him. What the Franks finally accepted from the Eastern and Western Fathers they forced into Augustinian categories and so created the myth of Platonising Eastern Fathers, which is still dominant.

The Frankish bishops encountered by St. Boniface understood Apostolic succession as a magical power which allowed them to make it the property of their race and use it as the prime means of keeping their subjugated populations pacified by fear of their religious and military powers. Augustine's theories about original sin and predestination helped them in this direction.

This schism between Franks and Romans expanded into a schism between Franco-Latin and Roman Christendom with their diametrically opposed understandings of the mission of bishops and their synods within the Church and in society. The Franks literally captured a medical association and transformed it into a quack medical association. The East Franks completed the job when they took over the Papacy definitively between 1012-1046.

While the Norman Franks were in process of expelling the Roman army from Southern Italy and of helping the Italo-Franks wrest the Papacy from the Franconian emperors, their Duke William of Normandy invaded England with Pope Alexander's blessing in 1066. He had his Lombard friend, the "Blessed Saint" Lanfranc, the pope's teacher, installed as the first non-Roman /Saxon Archbishop of Canterbury in 1070, and together they replaced all native bishops with Franco-Latins. All Celtic and Saxon bishops and abbots were dismissed *en masse*[694] and sentenced

---

694 For documented sources of the details of the murder of the Celtic and Saxon Bishops and abbots and their replacement by nobles from the Frankish realms of Francia, i.e. Gallia, Germania and Italia see *Auguste Thierry, Histoire de la Conquête de l' Angleterre par les Normands*, Paris 1843, vol. 2, pp. 147 (1071-1072), 215-219 (1075-1076), 284, 313-314, 318 (1087-1094); vol. 3, pp. 35 (1110-1138), 214-215 (1203).

to prison to die premature deaths by torture and starvation.[695] The new noblemen bishops from the Frankish Empire were in turn killed by the people whenever opportunity presented itself.[696] Indeed the Saxons and Celts celebrated the death of Lanfranc in 1089 by launching their third and most severe revolt against the foreign intruders.[697] Such reforms by military might became crusades in both East and West. They ultimately provoked the Protestant Reformation and met with little success among the East Romans and some among the Slavs.

This tradition of killer bishops, clergy and monks was given its near final theological foundation by "Saint" Bernard of Clairvaux in his sermons "De Laude novae militiae ad milites Templi"[698] in which he argues that the religious Knight Templer "who kills for religion commits no evil but rather does good, for his people and himself. If he dies in battle, he gains heaven; if he kills his opponents, he avenges Christ. Either way, God is pleased".[699] Its final form was given by the Inquisition which condemned to death but usually turned executions over to laymen.

Orthodox Civilization may indeed become arrested, not, however, because of Westernisation; but because of strong doses of Franco-Latinisation introduced by Peter the Great (1682-1725), whose religious policies became the law of the Neo-Hellenic Nation in 1827.

Western Europe had been in a long process of De-Franco-Latinisation by means of powerful elements of Re-Greco-Romanisation, but not in its Apostolic form. Its embryo appeared in the 12th century with the rise of the middle class and went into labor during the Renaissance and the Protestant Reformation. It was born in the Enlightenment and

---

695 Ibid. vol. 2, pp. 55; 66 (1068) 111, 145, 184 (1070-1072), 215 (1075-1076), 240-242 (1082), 313-316 (1088-1089); vol. 3, pp. 35, 44, 47 (1110-1140).

696 Ibid.; vol. 2, pp. 232, 236 (1080); vol. 3; pp. 27, 36-37; 39 (1110-1138), 55 (1141-1142); vol. 4, 349 (1387).

697 Ibid., vol. 2, 315.

698 Migne, P. L.182, 921-940.

699 As summarized in *The History of Feudalism*, edited by David Herlihy, 1970, 282-283.

matured during the American and French Revolutions. American and French Democracies, based on human rights and the equality of all citizens, began the progressive destruction of the class distinctions which had been imposed by the Franks and their allies, who had brought Latin Christendom into existence on the ruins of those parts of Roman Christendom they conquered, including the Papacy. Franco-Latin metaphysics, cosmology and psychology were made past history by parallel developments in modern science.

But this has neither all happened everywhere, nor at the same time. Royalties, nobilities, the Papacy, and those Reformation Churches which still serve as props for the remnants of Teutonic royalty and nobility, badly need the identification of Franco-Latin Civilization and Western Civilizations for their own survival.

It is exactly this identity which parts of the Reformation and the American and French Revolutions had rejected. However, over a period of time seem to be now accepting.

Having the above background in mind the reader himself can study the question of such examples as the APOSTOLIC SUCCESSION OF THE NORMAN AND FRANCO-LATIN SUCCESSORS OF THEIR ORTHODOX PREDECESSORS or else leave it to God Himself to decide, which He may have already done. This may be so especially since the bishops and clergy in question probably do not know that apostolic succession depends on the cure of the purification and illumination of the heart which leads to glorification, i.e. to ordination to prophethood. These criteria probably are applicable for most churches and religions, including many individual Orthodox and their leaders today.

6. Protopresbyter George D. Metallinos

"Unia" [700]

When we say "Unia" we mean a religious-political formation that was fabricated by the Papacy for the Westernizing of the non-Latin East; its spiritual-political subjugation to the authority of the Pope. In other words, it is directly related to the Papacy's expansionist policy; it is the most consistent expression of European feudalism which continues to our day, through the State of the Vatican. Of course one needs to make a certain distinction between the various phases that the question of "Unia" presents historically. Because, precedent to the specific historical method was the idea and the plan involving the subjugation of the East—and indeed of the Orthodox—to the Pope; a permanent tendency of the Latin "Church" following its differentiation and its secession from the Orthodox East. Wherever Latinization proves difficult to impose directly, the Papacy implements the method of Unia, proving this to be a shrewd fabrication inasmuch as subjugation can be achieved, on the pretext of continuance and freedom.

This expansionist move by the Papal throne known as UNIA owes its name to the Latin word UNIO (=union), however it was only in 1596 in Poland that it officially obtained the name of UNIA (UNIJA in Slavic). The term was used at the time, not only to denote the move for unification with the Pope, but also the specific corpus (community) of the Orthodox who had synodically decided on their accession to the Papacy: not a full accession, but only in their recognition of the Pope as their spiritual head, otherwise preserving their worship rites and remaining customs so that "externally" they would give the impression of continuing and remaining in their national cadre.

The Uniates' retention of the "eastern" or "Byzantine" "rite" explains the various titles such as "Byzantine-rite," "Hellenic-rite," "Hellen-

---

700 Protopresbyter George D. Metallinos, *Unia: The Face and the Disguise*, trans. Ekaterina Nikolopoulou (Thessaloniki: Christian Orthodox Philanthropical Society of Friends of the Pantokrator Sacred Retreat of Melissohorion "Saint Gregory Palamas," 1992), 16-17.

ic-Catholic" e.a., with which they are usually characterized (in Greece). But the name that best corresponds to the facts is "Catholics of the East," given that Uniates are in essence Papists, who have accepted the Papist teaching overall (and in fact, the very dogmas that radically differentiate Papism from Orthodoxy) and who only externally and superficially— with the attire of their clergymen and their eastern customs ("rites") — give the false impression that they have remained Orthodox. This is also why they have correctly been named "United Roman Catholics" and "Unionates" (in Latin: UNITI/Uniates).

WHAT IS THE REAL DANGER?[701]

When observing the relatively small number of Uniates in Greece (a total of a mere few thousand), one is given the impression that the Nation is not exactly in any serious danger by Unia, which is the very same argument used by the Greek Uniates themselves and their supporters. However, events in countries of Eastern Europe (Ukraine, Czechoslovakia, Rumania) have proven how immense a threat the presence alone of Unia is, and to what extents it can go. Events have proven that in our Country also, the danger from Unia is inversely proportional to the number of its members.

In researching Unia's activity in the Orthodox East over time, we feel compelled to justify the Patriarchal Synod which in 1838 referred to the Uniates as "onerous wolves, corruptive, pernicious, in the form of sheep, devouring unsparingly and destroying those for whom Christ had died." It is a fact that—unfortunately—many unpleasant things have been committed, both visibly and secretly by the Uniate element—both to the detriment of Hellenism (also), but in general to Orthodoxy— on account of their blind obedience to and their collaboration with the Papacy. Whereas with the illusory peace in the relations between the Papacy and Orthodoxy during recent years many have come to believe that all the aforementioned events were simply an "unfortunate past,"

---

701 Protopresbyter George D. Metallinos, *Unia: The Face and the Disguise*, trans. Ekaterina Nikolopoulou (Thessaloniki: Christian Orthodox Philanthropical Society of Friends of the Pantokrator Sacred Retreat of Melissohorion "Saint Gregory Palamas," 1992), 47-56.

the new Uniate crimes in Eastern Europe—as well as the anti-Hellenic stance of the Vatican in the so-called "Macedonian" issue—have proven that NOTHING has changed in the Papacy's intentions towards the Orthodox East and Hellenism. The Vatican's medieval mentality continues to prevail, even today, simply because it has never changed. The Vatican functions as a secular power-State. Expansionism, as the incrementing of its influence, constitutes its permanent and immovable objective and to this end, insists on using Unia as its most obedient instrument.

The potential peril that Unia also presents in our land, becomes apparent in various directions:

(a)

Uniatism breeds a spirit and conscience of "janissarism"; in every generation it creates janissaries, who become the most formidable enemies of their fellow countrymen and capable of everything. During the prolonged enslavement of our Nation, it was not only the converts to Islam who were janissaries – that is, those who had aligned themselves with the conqueror from the East (the Turks)—but also the "Latinizers"—that is, those who had aligned themselves with a far more dangerous enemy of the Nation: the Pope (the Franks). Saint Kosmas of Aetolia had codified the relative teaching of our Saints (Photios the Great, Gregory Palamas, Mark of Ephesus and many others), by also interpreting the (historically justified) stance of the "anti-unionists," who had preferred the lesser of the two evils, i.e., the Ottoman domination. Being in the likeness of janissaries of the Franks, the Uniates are in an extremely difficult position and as such, are truly tragic existences! This is because they feel like ones who have no hearth or home, since they essentially do not belong anywhere as they are being utilized as pitiful instruments in the service and the reinforcement of the ruthless enemies of their own race. This is precisely what a Greek Uniate had tearfully admitted to me recently. Nevertheless, it is their janissary mentality that renders them a danger to their race, because at any given moment, they are willing (maybe even forced) to collaborate in every conspiracy against Greece. Regardless whether they claim that they feel they are Greeks. That is what the "Latin-minded" and the "janissaries" of the Turks also used to claim, and we are well aware today if they were telling the truth.

The Papist element, with which the Greeks have so unreservedly aligned themselves nowadays, has never been friendly towards Hellenism, nor has it ever supported the rightful Hellenic national interests. It has always sided with the will of its "headquarters"—the Vatican or Rome—and has always collaborated in favour of the miscarriage of Hellenic pursuits. In both the Venetian-occupied regions and Turkish-occupied Greece, the Papists had maintained the same, adamant stance. Not only were they opposed to the Hellenic Revolution of Independence of 1821; they in fact fought against it, by supporting the interests of the Turks. They did the same in 1920-1922, during the Asia Minor war. Afraid of a revival and strengthening of the Ecumenical Patriarchate, the Vatican had incited the French to assist the Turks. The Vatican had declared that it preferred "to have atop the dome of Haghia Sophia the crescent rather than the Greek Cross" and "the Muslim indifference rather than the Orthodox fanaticism." With their silence, the "Greek" Uniates were essentially approving this anti-Hellenic campaign.

Papists and Uniates had (and continue to have) the impression that they too are a "State within a State," and even more so, after the initiation of Greece's diplomatic relations with the Vatican (1979). This is why, both during the "inter-confessional" era and their protection by the French, as well as later on, they have never ceased to be on call, and ready to act as "fifth columnists": a direct threat to Greek national interests. That is why one can feel only sorrow and pity for those Greek Papists, and more so for Greek Uniates. When the files pertaining to the Cyprus issue (1974) are eventually opened, the continuing anti-Hellenic stance of the Papist element will emerge, albeit the existing data has already shed ample light on the matter.

I truly and sincerely desire that these views of mine regarding the "Hellenic" conscience of the Papists and the Uniates of our Country will be proven unrealistic, and attributable to mistaken evaluations. And I will be willing to recant every historically-based note that I have made, if the Papists (and Uniates) of Greece reply directly to the following questions:

1) Do the Greek Uniates possess the Greek bravery to demand from the Vatican to assimilate them immediately into the "Roman Catholic Church," thus putting an end to their hermaphrodite role? Let Greece

make the first move for the elimination of Unia, in order to truly pave the way to a new era in the relations between Orthodoxy and Roman Catholicism.

2) If the Vatican should reject such a proposal, would they be prepared to return to Orthodoxy through the proper procedure (libel, chrism, etc.)?

3) Bearing in mind the irregular situation in the Balkans and the Vatican's involvement in favour of the Papist forces (e.g. Croatia), are they willing, in case that—God forbid—the war is extended further, to fight at the side of Greece against the Papist forces?

(b)

An equally great danger lies in the permanent corruption that the Orthodox flock is exposed to, with the presence of Unia, because a specific model of union is being permanently projected, which in fact facilitates this movement immensely, and that model is Unia. The Vatican has every reason for Unia to continue to exist, both because it is able to use it for its political-economic objectives—as it is doing in the Countries of Eastern Europe—but mainly because there is a clearly visible model of union between Orthodox and Papists, which creates the impression that the union is taking place without the abandonment of Orthodoxy. This was proclaimed as early as the 1970's by Pope Paul VI, when projecting the model of the Ukraine and pronouncing as Cardinal its Uniate archbishop, Josyf Slipyj. At any rate, it has already been made clear how the Vatican envisages the union: The Vatican does not desire union "in the truth" of the Prophetic-Apostolic-Patristic tradition, but a "mutual recognition." By acting as a State, it has lost every trace of sensitivity in matters of the Faith, in spite of the promulgations to the contrary by its theologians.

(c)

There is yet another aspect—the most important—which however becomes obvious, only wherever the Orthodox conscience is healthy and robust. It is the spiritual-soteriological aspect. Unia exists, for the purpose of leading to the direct or indirect recognition and acceptance of the Papacy—the most serious estrangement from Christianity of all time (Protestantism had emanated later on from Papism, as did all other socio-political developments in the West). When the ever-memorable Fr. Justin Popovic linked the historical Fall of the Pope (Papism) to the Falls of Adam and of Judas, that was precisely the truth that he intended to stress: the complete de-Christianization by the Papacy as an awarding of absolutism and totalitarianism. It must furthermore be noted that the awarding of totalitarianism by the Papacy is diametrically different to related phenomena, which are observed from time to time in Orthodox environments. These perversions, which are incarnated through the Papist dogmas, will for us Orthodox forever remain blatant deviations from the salvatory Truth and as such are rejected and condemned as falls and sins. In Papism however, they have been rendered dogmas of faith; ones that are necessary for salvation (can a Latin Church exist without a Pope?). In the long run, this means that the incarnation of God the Logos took place in order for Papacy to be instated in the world, and totalitarianism (with all its consequences) be sanctified. Could there be a bigger blasphemy than this?

The recognition of Papism constitutes an abandonment of the in-Christ Truth, a denial of the in-Holy Spirit living (spirituality) and a reversal of Christianity into a secular ideology that is being drowned in everything endocosmic and in the thirst for power. Christianity however – as preserved in the persons of our Saints—comprises Man's therapy through the catharsis/cleansing of the heart from passions and of the 'nous' (mind) from reflections, so that he might attain the "visitation" (enlightenment) of the Holy Spirit and thus reach theosis (deification)—the "glorification" of his entire being within the uncreated, Holy Trinitarian Grace (the 'Kingdom'). Wherever this prospect is lost, and this objective is altered, Christianity-Orthodoxy does not exist! Because Man's course towards theosis simultaneously transforms Man's environment and it creates the potential to realize selfless love—which is the foundation of the authentic Christian society. And History teaches us that the slackening, or even the loss of this tradition, even in a section of us Orthodox, was reinforced or even provoked by the influence of that estranged Western Christianity in our lives during the previous centuries. The effect of the decadence in the West's civilization has, after all, always been catalytic among Orthodox peoples.

From the above, I believe one can understand just where the acceptance of Unia—as a method of unification with the Papacy - can lead. Every independence and freedom is lost for the Orthodox and consequently, so is the possibility to help Western Christianity through a Dialogue, in order for it to re-discover its forgotten Orthodox prerequisites and its Orthodox past. This alone can be the only purpose for a theological Dialogue from an Orthodox point of view, and never a "mutual recognition." Besides, what kind of recognition does Orthodoxy need to receive, from anti-Christian Papism? It would be like Christ asking for recognition from Belial! (2 Cor. 6:15) On the contrary, Unia contributes towards the preservation of Papist estrangement and the promotion of the Papacy as the authentic Church which we all supposedly need to be joined to, for our salvation. Thus, it becomes doubly harmful: firstly to non-Latin Christianity, because it leads it to a spiritual impasse; and secondly to Latin Christianity itself, because it impedes it from becoming aware of its downfall and thereafter from seeking—like the prodigal son—to return to the Truth.

7. Monk Gorazd of Holy Trinity Monastery, Jordanville, New York

VISIONS OUTSIDE THE CHURCH[702]

Many people have heard that the Mother of God has supposedly appeared to Roman Catholics in various places. They do not know what to think about these events. Some even go so far as to think that since the Mother of God appears to Roman Catholics, it follows that the Roman Catholic Church is a true, grace-filled church, especially since various miracles and healings take place at the locations of the visions. Fatima, in particular, has aroused much interest among Russians living abroad because the apparition allegedly speaks about Russia in strongly anti-communist terms, leading them to overlook the heretical and anti-Orthodox content of the message as a whole. What are we to make of these appear-

702 Monk Gorazd, *Visions Outside the Church* (Jordanville: Holy Trinity Monastery, 1990), 26-34.

ances and the claims made for them? What criterion should we use to guide us in testing the truth of visions outside of the Orthodox Church? Hopefully, what follows will help in understanding such phenomena.

The Holy Fathers, knowing that Satan can transform himself into an angel of light, advise us to be cautious and distrustful of all appearances in the visible world. "If you are silent in a good way, desiring to be with God," says St. Gregory the Sinaite, "never accept any physical or spiritual appearances, either outside or inside yourself, even if it might be an image of Christ, or an angel, or some Saint, or if light should appear, or imprint itself in the mind... Be attentive, that you may not come to believe something, even if it is something good, and be not captivated by it before consulting those who are experienced and are able to analyze the matter, so that you do not suffer harm...God is not displeased with the person who is attentive to himself, even if he, out of fear of deception, does not accept even that which is from Him, without consulting and testing." We might add that the Lord God could at all times give full assurance to a person, if He is pleased to do so, concerning the truth of a vision. If such caution is necessary concerning visions WITHIN the Orthodox Church, how much more circumspect should we be in relation to apparitions OUTSIDE the one, true Church! The sole criterion for examining these visions should be their Orthodoxy. If in any respect their Orthodoxy is lacking, then they must be rejected: even if 99% of the message is Orthodox and only 1% deviates from the doctrines laid down by the Church, then the whole must be rejected. God cannot deny Himself or preach untruth even in the smallest degree.

Let us examine three well-known cases which have occurred in our own century. First, we will deal with Fatima, which is of special interest, since the apparition there speaks about Russia and its role in the destiny of mankind. Towards the end of the First World War, at Fatima in Portugal, between May and October 1917, three shepherd children, two girls and a boy, had a series of visions of someone whom they said was our Lady, the Blessed Virgin. Throughout the six months of the apparitions, the messages which Lucia was told to make public, at that time or somewhat later, were largely concerned with the need to encourage devotion to the rosary and to our Lady's immaculate heart, and with the need for mankind to change the direction in which it was moving. Failure to make that change would bring down the wrath of God (from *Studies in Comparative Religion*, "A Question Concerning the Second Vatican Council," by Verak).

In December 1940 Sister Lucy (the only one of the three who remained alive and who is now a nun of the Carmelite order) wrote to Pope Pius XII saying, "In 1917 the Most Holy Mother prophesied to us the end of the war which at that darkened the face of Europe; she prophesied another war and said that she would come again. She insisted on the dedication of Russia to her most sacred heart, promising in return to hinder the spread of false teaching from Russia and to convert Russia." (from *News About Fatima, the Greatest Miracle of Our Time*, Brussels, 1962 p. 144). It is necessary to remember that Catholics understand "the conversion of Russia" to mean her conversion to Roman Catholicism. Again, we read in the journal *The Fatima Crusader* (issue #17, April-May 1985): "So it may well be that the conversion of a few Russians to Catholicism now is part of God's preparations for the conversion of Russia when the Pope and bishops finally obey the command of our Lady of Fatima to consecrate Russia in the manner prescribed by God. The reason why Jesus gave this specific command to the Pope and bishops is because he wants his whole church to recognize the consecration of Russia as a triumph of the immaculate heart of Mary. Sister Lucy records in a letter dated May 18, 1936: 'Intimately I have spoken to our Lord about the subject and not long ago, I asked Him why He would not convert Russia without the Holy Father making the consecration. He replied, 'Because I want My whole Church to acknowledge that consecration as a triumph of the immaculate heart of Mary so that it may extend its cult later on and put the devotion to the immaculate heart beside the devotion to My sacred heart.'"

Here something should be said about the un-Orthodox forms of devotion to the sacred heart of Jesus and the immaculate heart of Mary which the apparition advocates. A Roman Catholic nun, Mary Margaret Alacoque (who died in 1690), allegedly had a vision of Jesus Christ who showed her His heart, burning with love, and asked her to spread devotion to it. The revelations she received were first printed in the account of her life by the Jesuit bishop Lanje and caused such a scandal that the edition was destroyed. Due to the fact that these "revelations" were so exposed to the public eye, they were condemned by Pope Clement in 1772. Nonetheless, this cult continued to exist under the auspices of the Jesuits, and finally entered into the mainstream of Catholic religious life (*Pastoral Theology*, Part II, Archimandrite Constantine, Jordanville, 1961, p. 16). Sacred heart pictures and devotions became a major part of Catholic spirituality, and the popes added their endorsements in encyclicals, granting indulgences for the observance of the devotion. Not to be outdone, other groups, claiming to have seen apparitions of Mary, put forward the idea of devotion to "The Immaculate Heart of Mary."

The heart of Mary was sometimes depicted together with the sacred heart of Jesus motif: a picture with two hearts and later, the sorrowful heart of Mary, with five or seven swords piercing it became extremely popular. It would be difficult to accuse Roman Catholicism of denying the divinity of Christ, rather they have split the wholeness of Christ, emphasizing His human nature as a separate devotion, sometimes in a crudely biological way. This violates a central principle of the Councils, that devotion should be given to the devotion of Christ, and not to one of His natures, or parts of His body. Thus, by fragmenting the wholeness of the Son of God, a tendency develops to "Nestorianize." Parts of the body of Christ should not become parts of isolated objects of adoration, nor should they be pictorially depicted (i.e., a heart on fire, or a heart crowned with thorns surrounding it)" (from *Comparative Religion*, "Roman Catholicism: Some Devotional Practices," by Father George Mitchell). We mention these devotions here in order to illustrate the abyss which lies between Orthodox and Roman Catholic spirituality.

Yet another series of apparitions took place in a small mountain village called San Sebastian de Garabandal in the north of Spain. These apparitions took place between June 1961 and November 1965. The seers were four young girls. We repeat some of the messages given: "The Virgin also reminded us very often about visiting the blessed sacrament. As a matter of fact, even in her final apparition (November 13, 1965) the Virgin told me, 'Conchita, why do you not go more often to visit my Son in the tabernacle?' When I saw the Virgin I said to her, as if there were a spy in the village, 'You know, there are some Protestants here.' The Virgin replied, 'They are all my children.' The angel came and said, 'Many cardinals, many bishops and many priests are on the road to perdition and taking many souls with them. Less and less importance is given to the Eucharist.'"

It is interesting to note that in 1967 Conchita Gonzales (one of the seers) started to have doubts about the apparitions: "Yes, in 1967, sometime after the apparitions had taken place, I did have doubts. It happened suddenly on August 15. I will never forget it. There were many people around me and I was overwhelmed with the feeling that I was not honest. I felt I was deceiving all those people and that I ought to confess it. I went to a priest and told him that it was like an illusion or a dream or living a lie, that I had never seen the Virgin and that I had been deceiving everybody all the time...These doubts and denials of the Virgin's apparitions lasted five or six days. Since then, up to this time, I have confusion and doubt within me" (from *Miracle at Garabandal* by Conchita Gonzales with Harry Daley, Doubleday and Company, N.Y., 1983).

We mention this apparition here to show that even in a case where the seer herself is ultimately uncertain of the reality of what she saw, the story still seems to find apparently serious believers. They are not even discouraged by such disturbing facts as the following, reported by one of the seers: "After the apparitions started, we never missed a day of communion. When there wasn't a priest in town, an angel would come down to give us communion. At one point we were instructed by a priest to ask how it was that, since only a priest could consecrate the hosts, the angel was administering communion to us. We did ask, and the Virgin said that the angel would come down and take the already consecrated hosts from tabernacles on earth."

Can we not imagine the consternation this would cause in the church from which the hosts were taken! Can it be possible that angels need to take hosts from the tabernacles of churches? In the Orthodox life of St. Onuphrius an angel does, indeed, bring the Holy Communion, but it is quite unthinkable that an angel would need to take the Holy Gifts from an earthly tabernacle.

The third series of visions we will mention began on June 24, 1981, in the Yugoslavian town of Medjugorje, where a number of young children began to have visions of what they considered to be the Mother of God. The apparition has claimed that these revelations will be the last in the world. In November 1982 the apparition said, "After these

revelations finish there will be only some false revelations in the world."
People have flocked to Medjugorje from all over the world even though
the local Roman Catholic bishop of Mostar, Pavao Zanic, who denies
the verity of the apparitions, made a public declaration in the name of
the Yugoslavian Bishops' Conference to the effect that "It is not permitted for pilgrimages or for other manifestations to be organized which
are motivated by the supernatural character supposedly attributed to the
events of Medjugorje."

Already in 1981, the seers were saying: "There will be a visible and
lasting sign on the hill of the apparitions; it will come soon; you will see
it in a short time. Wait a little longer, be patient." And again: "The sign
will be on the feast of the Immaculate Conception, 1981, then at Christmas, then at New Year, etc." Needless to say, no sign has yet appeared on
the hill. For an Orthodox reader it is sufficient to know only some of the
ecumenical messages given by the apparition to be certain that it is not
the Mother of God who is appearing there. For instance: "All the religions are the same before God. God commands in all these religions as
a king in his realm." (*Counter-Reformation-Catholic*, 201 Eng. ed. Cf. Fr.
Blaise, 500 Messages a Vivre, p. 370, Montreal, 1986.) "In God neither
divisions or religions count. It is you in the world who have created the
divisions because believers have separated themselves from one another."
(*Apparition of the Virgin Mary at Medjugorje*, Jan Urban [in Czech]. The
Catholic Counter-Reformation in the XX Century, Sept/Oct. 1987;
Nov./Dec. 1985).

For the uninformed, this message has a seductive appeal and is in
keeping with the "one world" thinking. But as Orthodox Christians we
know that to say "all the religions are the same before God" is a denial of
Christ as the only Truth. Is it not He Himself who says, *I am the way, the
truth, and the life: no man cometh unto the Father, but by me* (John 14:6).
Therefore, to say that all religions are the same is a denial of Christ!

Without attempting to analyze too deeply the meaning of all the
messages it is sufficient enough to realize that each one of these apparitions, claiming to be the Mother of God, accepts the sacraments of the
Roman Catholic Church (Holy Communion, Priesthood, Confession)
as true, grace-filled Mysteries. This alone makes these apparitions totally
unacceptable for us since we know that grace-filled Mysteries can only

be found in the one, true Church of Christ. Since the Western Church separated itself from the one, true Church in the 11th century there can be no question about the existence of true Mysteries in the Roman Catholic Church. "The Church is one and only she has the fullness of the grace-filled gifts of the Holy Spirit. No matter who, or in what way one has fallen away from the Church, whether in heresy, schism, or in uncanonical gatherings, one loses the communion of the grace of God. Therefore, no sacraments performed outside the Church have any grace-filled power." (Archbishop Hilarion, *There Is No Christianity Without the Church*, p. 114, San Paulo, Brazil, 1954.) Even the presence of healings is not a proof of the truth of the appearances. Healings might be from God, from natural causes, or if God allows, from the evil one. Sozomen, in his *Ecclesiastical History* (Book II, #5) writes: "The temple of Aesculapius in Aegis, a city of Cilicia, and the temple of Venus at Aphaca, near Mt. Lebanon and the river Adonis, were undermined and entirely destroyed. Both of these temples were highly honored and revered by the ancients...because those among them who were infirm in body were delivered from diseases because the demon manifested himself by night and healed them." In the Vita Patrum of St. Gregory of Tours, we read in the life of St. Friardus the Recluse, "And as they courageously persevered in prayer, the tempter appeared at night to the deacon Secundellus, taking the form of the Lord and saying to him, 'I am Christ, to whom you pray every day. Already you are holy, and your name is written in the Book of Life. So go out from this island and perform healings among the people.' Secundellus, taken in by this deception, left the island...and even so as soon as he laid his hand upon the sick in the name of Jesus Christ, they were healed."

The words of Archpriest Boris Molchanov are very timely here: "It is very important to be aware of that little-known but remarkable spiritual law by which all false and hypocritical Christianity will inevitably lead its followers to acceptance of the Antichrist or to a movement which will prepare for his appearance. In every false teaching, like in the Pharisee's attitude towards truth, there is hidden the seeds of eternal damnation. Foolishly and in vain many people do not accept the importance of dogma. The close union between dogma of the faith, practical, moral activity, and the struggle for salvation has been expounded on by bishop Ignatius (Brianchaninov) and His Beatitude Metropolitan Anthony (Khrapovitsky). According to the teaching of the Church, there is nothing as import as confessing divinely-revealed Truth, in the work of salvation. The Word of God itself bears witness that God must be worshipped in Spirit and in Truth (John 4:23-24). Truth is not some kind of insignificant thing, which one could relate to as one wishes. In the truth, the Spirit of Truth, Who proceeds from the Father, is present in a real way. And correspondingly, in every lie, there is present the father of lies, the devil. Therefore, a person who confesses the truth receives the Spirit of Truth; and the one who confesses a lie will necessarily assimilate the spirit of lies, the fallen spirit. Outside the one, holy Orthodox Church there are not, and there will not appear the means for recognizing the Antichrist, nor is there any grace-filled power to resist him and all his temptations" (*Epoch of Apostasy*, Jordanville, 1976, p. 18).

We do not need heterodox apparitions to call us to repentance, prayer, and fasting. Further, these apparitions accept Roman Catholic sacraments, the papacy, encourage un-Orthodox forms of piety, and embrace false ecumenism. In our troubled times, times of subtle temptations and sublime deceptions, when false miracles, visions, and apparitions are on the increase, we Orthodox Christians should work out our salvation with fear and trembling, holding firm to our Holy Orthodox Faith and looking for guidance and inspiration to our Holy Orthodox Church alone.

WHO IS APPEARING IN MEDJUGORJE?[703]

But He answered and said unto them: An evil and adulterous generation seeketh after a sign... (Matt. 12:3)

There is certainly no lack of signs in our troubled times. One of them is the apparitions which are taking place in Medjugorje in Yugoslavia. The apparitions started on 24 June 1981. A number of young children belonging to the Roman Catholic Church began to have visions of what they consider to be the Mother of God. When the apparition was asked (on 26 June 1981) who she was, she said: "I am the Blessed Vir-

---

703 Monk Gorazd, "Who is Appearing in Medjugorje?" *Orthodox Life* 39, no. 1 (January-February 1989): 30-31.

gin Mary." Although these apparitions were not accepted as true by the local Roman Catholic Church authority, the bishop of Mostar, people from all over the world began to flock to Medjugorje. On 14 September 1985 alone, there were about 100,000 people there. On 9 January 1987, Cardinal Jranjo Koharic and Pauao Zanic, the Catholic bishop of Mostar, made a public declaration in the name of the Yugoslav Bishops' Conference saying: "Consequently, it is not permitted for pilgrimages to be organized or for other manifestations motivated by the supernatural character supposedly attributable to the events of Medjugorje." Nevertheless, people are still going to Medjugorje. The holy Fathers teach us that we must be extremely careful and cautious when dealing with any kind of revelation from the unseen world. So how much more prudent must we be when these apparitions involve members of the Roman Catholic Church.

We will allow the apparition to speak for itself, because if the words of the apparition are non-Orthodox, then it is not possible that the Mother of God is indeed appearing there. In 1981 someone handed to one of the children the following written question to be asked of the apparition: "Are all religions good?" The answer was: "All religions are the same before God. God commands in all religions, as a king does in his realm." In answer to the question: "What is the role of Jesus if the Muslim religion is good?" the child visionary Mirjana replied: "I have not spoken about this with the Virgin. She explained to me only what I have just said. She said 'Especially in the villages unity of religions is lacking. Each one's religion must be respected, while you preserve your religion for yourselves and for your children.'" Another declaration by the apparition was made concerning Protestants: "In God neither divisions nor religions count. It is you in the world who have created divisions. The sole mediator is Jesus Christ. There are divisions because believers have separated themselves from one another. Be no respecter of persons." If this is really what the apparition is saying, then the message is clear, and it is an ecumenical one. It is exactly in the spirit of false, syncretistic ecumenism which has to create the right atmosphere so that people will accept the one religion of the future — the Religion of Antichrist.

For there shall arise false Christs, and false prophets, and shall show great signs and wonders, insomuch that if it were possible, they shall deceive the very elect. (Matt. 24:24).

8. Father Daniel Sysoev

Life [704]

Father Daniel was born in Moscow on January 12, 1974. From early childhood he knew that one day he would serve the Church as a priest and would often pretend to give homilies. In his youth he read constantly and loved listening to the lives of the saints. Growing up during the Soviet period, he was often ridiculed by other children as well as teachers because of his deep faith, and was frequently pressured to renounce the Faith and embrace atheism and Marxism. Such trials gave him ample opportunity to learn to defend the Faith.

In 1991, Daniel entered the Moscow Theological Seminary where he would spend countless hours in the library reading and deepening his understanding of Orthodoxy far beyond what was required of him by his classes and instructors. On May 13, 1995, Daniel was ordained a deacon by His Eminence Bishop Evgeny of Verey. On July 14, 1995, he graduated from the Moscow Theological Seminary and began working at the missionary and educational center and in the rehabilitation center for victims of totalitarian cults and pseudo-religious movements in Moscow. In 1996 he was blessed by the patriarch to begin missionary Bible classes at the Krutitsy Patriarchal Metochian, for people who had suffered from the influence of sects and occultists. In 1997 he began giving regular talks on the Bible at the same metochion, which he continued to hold until his death. On May 24, 2000, Father Deacon Daniel was awarded a Letter of Commendation for his educational work by the Department of Religious Education and Catechesis.

In January of 2001, Father Deacon Daniel was ordained a priest and appointed to Saints Peter and Paul Church in Yasenevo. After ordina-

---

704 "Biography Fr. Daniel Sysoev," Orthodox Christian eBooks, accessed January 4th, 2024, https://danielsysoev.com/biografiya/

tion he traveled throughout Russia preaching fearlessly to Orthodox, Muslims, and others, and many of them turned to Christ in response to his preaching and teaching. Fr. Daniel became widely known for his ability to defend the Orthodox Faith and soon began having open discussions about the Faith in public, on TV, and on the radio with Muslims and members of various sectarian and pagan groups. Fr. Daniel also began to develop and lead missionary courses to train other Orthodox on how to discuss and defend the Orthodox Faith to people of other religious, sectarian, and atheistic backgrounds. Because of his success in leading people to the Orthodox Church, he would often face death threats, especially from Muslims.

On November 20, 2009, while Fr. Daniel was in the altar hearing a confession, a masked man entered the church where Fr. Daniel was, shouted "Where is Sysoev?" and began shooting. When Fr. Daniel heard this, he came out from the altar and said, "I am here," then walked fearlessly towards the killer and was mortally wounded. Afterwards, a militant Muslim group took credit for the killing. Fr. Daniel was 35 years old at the time of his repose and left behind a wife and three children. Since his death his writings have been translated into many languages and distributed throughout the world, and he has been venerated as a martyr who was killed for his defense of the Orthodox Faith and his success in leading to Orthodoxy Muslims, atheists, Latins, and people of all walks of life and beliefs.

THE FALLING AWAY OF THE ROMAN CHURCH[705]

The enemy of the human race, the devil, did not wish to watch as the Church of Christ rapidly crushed his power among the nations and overcame all heresies. He devised a plan to destroy the first among the world's churches in the same way that he, formerly the first among the angels, had himself fallen. For this purpose he incited a heresy in the West against the Holy Spirit, and thrust the bishop of Rome down into the abyss of pridefulness.

---

705 Priest Daniel Sysoev, *The Law of God: An Introduction to Orthodox Christianity*, trans. Deacon Nathan Williams (New Jersey: Daniel Sysoev Inc, 2016), 505-507.

In the 6th century in Spain, as a means of combating Arianism, an amendment was made to the Symbol of Faith ["We believe] in the Holy Spirit... Who proceedeth from the Father and the Son." This declaration, in Latin called the *Filioque* ("and from the Son"), added in violation of the conciliar prohibition against changing the Symbol of the Faith, became the chief reason for the falling away of the West.

Many theologians of the time understood these words in Orthodox manner—that the Holy Spirit has His existence solely from the Father, as the Lord Himself says (Jn. 15:26), and is sent into the world by the Son to sanctify all by grace. But in the ninth century there arose a significant school of theology that taught that the Holy Spirit has His existence from the Father and the Son as from a single Source. This debased the third Person of the Holy Trinity, confusing grace with the One Who bestows it. The heretics began to teach that God has no uncreated energies that are bestowed upon creation, and that grace itself is a sort of higher creation. This destroyed the hope of Christians for deification as a union with God Himself by grace, making man a being independent of the Creator.

The Ecumenical Church reacted swiftly to this delusion. Saint Photius of Constantinople condemned the heresy. And in 881 in the great cathedral of Hagia Sophia representatives of all the churches along with Pope John of Rome prohibited distorting the Symbol of Faith.

Until the eleventh century the churches preserved a unified teaching. But the heresy had not been crushed, and its supporters began planning a reformation of the Western Church. They taught that the pope had absolute authority over the Church, and altered the Liturgy. Under the influence of the reformers the emperor of Germany seized Rome and appointed a heretical pope, who in 1014 for the first time introduced the distorted Symbol of Faith in Rome. This marked the beginning of the separation of the churches. The western church began serving using unleavened (yeastless) bread, since the reformers did not believe that the Body of Christ remained life-giving after His death.

In 1054 a decisive schism occurred between the Ecumenical Church and the West. Acting for Pope Leo IX, Cardinal Humbert excommunicated Patriarch Michael of Constantinople. The Council of Constantinople then excommunicated the cardinal from the Church. Thus began the lamentable separation that continues to this day.

The Roman Church was reformed as the heretics had wished. The pope began to be revered as the head of the entire Church, and he demanded that he be given absolute civil authority, as well. Later the Roman Church declared the pope to be infallible in doctrinal matters of faith and morality when teaching *ex cathedra* ("from the chair"). Thus man declared himself to be equal to God. Pride had seized the first among the world's bishops.

Once they had begun changing Church Traditions, the Roman Catholics proved unable to stop. They introduced new dogmas: purgatory, in which a person allegedly pays for unredeemed sins; that the Theotokos was born without original sin; supererogation, or good works of the saints in excess of the amount required for salvation, which are transferred to the papal treasury and from there are distributed to those who lack sufficient good works (which gave rise to the practice of indulgences). The rites of the sacraments were also changed. Baptism began to be practiced by aspersion (sprinkling), and not by immersion, as the apostles had commanded. Chrismation began to be performed only after reaching adolescence, and thus children were deprived of the grace of the Holy Spirit and of Communion. The Liturgy began to be served using unleavened bread, and the laity were given Communion only in the form of bread, contrary to the Lord's words, *Drink ye all of it* (Mt. 26:27). Many other apostolic practices and dogmatic teachings were also distorted.

Since the existence of the Orthodox Church was a living rebuke to these innovations, the Roman Catholics began to treat their brethren with aggression. This included outright wars, when the Romans seized Constantinople and the greater part of Eastern Europe, forcing Orthodox to accept their heresy. It included attempts to join the Orthodox to themselves through false unions. Many martyrs, their blood shed not by pagans but by their former brethren, went to shine in the firmament of heaven.

May the Lord then grant repentance to the Roman Church, that she may return to the infallible apostolic faith from which she fell.

QUESTION: IN WHAT WAY ARE CATHOLICS HERETICAL?[706]

An unbaptized person will perish because the evil spirit has not been cast out of his heart. But if a person confesses the Roman Catholic heresy, i.e., the false teaching on the Holy Spirit and the false teaching on the Pope of Rome's place in the Church, then the sin of heresy will eat away at his soul. Will fornicators who are Orthodox be saved? Will murderers who are Orthodox be saved? If they do not repent, they will not be saved. If they repent, then they will. Will Catholics be saved? They will be saved if they repent, since in the apostle Paul's list of sins it clearly places murder, heresy, sorcery, and adultery in the same category. These are the deadliest sins, which destroy people. If a person repents of them then, by all means, all is well;[707] the Church recognizes Catholic baptism.[708] In the case of the Catholics it is a matter of perishing on account of heresy. They teach wrongly concerning the Holy Spirit. They teach that the Holy Spirit proceeds from the Father and the Son, as from a single source. According to their teaching the Holy Spirit is debased; it is played down before the other two Persons of the Holy Trinity. The Lord said that blasphemy against the Holy Ghost shall not be forgiven unto men... neither in this world, neither in the world to come (Mt. 12:31-32). Furthermore, according to the Roman Catholic teaching the

---

706 Priest Daniel Sysoev, *Questions to Priest Daniel Sysoev* (New Jersey: Daniel Sysoev Inc, 2016), 101-102.

707 For Catholics to repent of heresy requires that they reject the false teachings of the Pope, embrace the true dogmas of the Church, and be received into the Orthodox Church.

708 The Orthodox Church does not recognize sacraments of Roman Catholics or anyone else outside of the Orthodox Church as bestowing the grace of the Holy Spirit. Centuries ago, when the Latins performed the correct form of the baptism (three immersions in the name of the Holy Trinity) the Orthodox Church allowed the Latins to be received by chrismation under certain circumstances. However, once the Latins departed from the Apostolic form of baptism, the Church could not recognize single immersions, pouring, or sprinkling as "baptism" and it became necessary to insist that all Latins be received by baptism. For more on this topic, including Fr. Daniel's insistence that baptism must be done in three immersions in the name of the Holy Trinity, see *On the Reception of the Heterodox into the Orthodox Church: The Patristic Consensus and Criteria* published by Uncut Mountain Press.

grace of the Holy Spirit—this uncreated gift that we receive in the sacraments—is a sort of created reality. They say that we become united not with God but with a certain reality that was fashioned, created. This is a false teaching about God, which impedes salvation. Their attitude toward the Pope of Rome is a form of idolatry; that is, their treatment of the Roman bishop as the head of the entire Church, the infallible head of the Church. This is virtual deification of a person, imparting to a person divine qualities. This is inexcusable. This is idolatry.

QUESTION: HOW IS ROMAN CATHOLIC PRACTICE INCONSISTENT WITH THE TEACHINGS OF THE BIBLE?[709]

In many obvious ways. For instance, in Scripture it says concerning the Blood of the Lord: Drink ye all of it (Mt. 26:27), but from the 12th century on, Rome has rejected communion under both kinds. Following the Second Vatican Council the practice of communing under both kinds has been allowed in the Catholic Church but it is not observed everywhere.

TO ONE WHO ASKED ABOUT THE SOURCE OF DIVINE GRACE AND THE POSSIBILITY OF REUNION WITH THE CATHOLICS[710]

Every gift of God comes into the world from the Father, through the Son, in the Holy Spirit. All three Hypostases bestow one grace, though in diverse manner. As for whether the Son alone bestows the grace of the Holy Spirit, remember that in the Gospel of John (chapter 7) it is written that the Spirit was not yet upon them because Jesus had not yet been glorified. The condition for the bestowal of the gift of the Spirit is the death and resurrection of Christ. It is extremely important to emphasize this in our time, when many attempt to believe that the Spirit can act outside of Christ... and hence non-Christian mysticism can be perfectly acceptable.

---

709 Priest Daniel Sysoev, *Questions to Priest Daniel Sysoev* (New Jersey: Daniel Sysoev Inc, 2016), 192.

710 Priest Daniel Sysoev, *Letters*, trans. Deacon Nathan Williams (New Jersey: Daniel Sysoev Inc, 2022), 12-13.

But you are right that it is impermissible to mix the Hypostasis and the gift of the Holy Spirit. In this lies the chief error of Blessed Augustine.

As for the question of reunion with the Roman Catholics, I am for it, on Orthodox grounds. Let Rome acknowledge the Orthodox teaching concerning the Trinity and grace, the Church and salvation, and we will gladly be together. I think that Christ also desires precisely this. But union based on compromise in matters of faith (that is, based on an obvious double lie) is impermissible.

It is time for us to stop walling ourselves off from heretics, and instead to strive to return them to the embrace of the Church.

And another thing regarding "union," or rather, the reunion of Rome to the Church—I trust you do not think that I assert the existence of two Churches?

TO AN ORTHODOX CHRISTIAN ABOUT WHETHER CATHOLICS ARE CHRISTIANS IN THE FULL SENSE OF THE WORD[711]

Only members of the apostolic Church are Christians. Roman Catholics were our own until 1054. At present they are heretics, but if they return to the Church and confess the Orthodox faith they will become Christians again. One ought not to take the name given us by God Himself and give it to others, replacing it with one given by man.

TO A WOMAN LIVING IN SRI LANKA WHO MARRIED A BUDDHIST AND AFTERWARDS CONVERTED TO ORTHODOXY, WHO ASKED WHETHER, IN THE ABSENCE OF AN ORTHODOX CHURCH IN HER COUNTRY, SHE MIGHT GO TO A CATHOLIC CHURCH TO PRAY[712]

Regarding attending a Catholic church, I strongly advise you not to do so. The church canons forbid joining heretics for prayer—it is a grave sin, one that cuts a person off from the Church. And the reason here is not "prejudice," but the fact that false teaching engenders false spirituality. The very atmosphere of a Catholic church is completely different

---

711 Ibid., 86.
712 Ibid., 163-164.

from a house of God. It is not by accident that in your neighbor India there are Catholic monasteries that practice yoga. In the West the situation is the same. In general, Catholicism is wholly based on emotions and sentimentalism. Catholics often perceive prayer itself as meditation, and not as living communion with God. I think for you no good will come of attending a Catholic church.

It is another matter that with Catholics themselves we should have good personal relationships. We hate the sin of heresy, but we love the sinners and desire that they might return to God. A love that has forgotten the truth is not God's love.

View our situation as involuntary spiritual seclusion: pray to God more often (especially since you see the results of prayer), read the Bible each day, and always read the holy fathers' explanation of what you have read (all this is available online). Tell both the pagans and the Catholics about what you have heard. Exhort them to accept Orthodoxy.

Write to me. May God help you. And may God grant you wisdom.

9. A Confession of Faith Against Ecumenism: From a Convention of Orthodox Clergymen and Monks

GREECE, APRIL 2009[713]

Those of us who by the Grace of God have been raised with the dogmas of piety and who follow in everything the One, Holy, Catholic and Apostolic Church, believe that:

The sole path to salvation of mankind[714] is the faith in the Holy Trinity, the work and the teaching of our Lord Jesus Christ, and their continuance within His Body, the Holy Church. Christ is the only true

---

713 "A Confession Against Ecumenism: From a Convention of Orthodox Clergymen and Monks; Greece, April 2009," Holy Trinity Monastery (Jordanville, NY), accessed November 16th, 2022, https://www.jordanville.org/files/Articles/A-CONFESSION-OF-FAITH.pdf. Footnotes from the original.

714 See treatise by Gennadios II Scholarios, Patriarch of Constantinople: "Regarding the only way to the salvation of mankind," to George Scholarios "The complete extant works - Oevres Completes de Georges Scholarios," Volumes I-VII, Paris 1928-1936, publ. L. Petit - X. Siderides - M. Jugie, Vol. III, 434-452.

Light;[715] there are no other lights to illuminate us, nor any other names that can save us: "Neither is there salvation in any other: for there is none other name under heaven given among men, whereby we must be saved."[716]   All other beliefs, all religions that ignore and do not confess Christ "having come in the flesh,"[717] are human creations and works of the evil one,[718] which do not lead to the true knowledge of God and rebirth through divine Baptism, but instead, mislead men and lead them to perdition. As Christians who believe in the Holy Trinity, we do not have the same God as any of the religions, nor with the so-called monotheistic religions, Judaism and Mohammedanism, which do not believe in the Holy Trinity.

For two thousand years, the one Church which Christ founded, and the Holy Spirit has guided has remained stable and unshakeable in the salvific Truth that was taught by Christ, delivered by the Holy Apostles and preserved by the Holy Fathers. She did not buckle under the cruel persecutions by the Judeans initially or by idolaters later, during the first three centuries. She has brought forth a host of martyrs and emerged victorious, thus proving Her divine origin. As Saint John the Chrysostom beautifully expressed it: "Nothing is stronger than the Church... if you fight against a man, you either conquer or are conquered; but if you fight

---

715 John 8:12 "I am the light of the world - whosoever follows Me shall not walk in darkness, but shall have the light of life." John 3:19 "The light had come to the world and men loved the darkness rather than the light."

716 Book of Acts 4:12, KJV.

717 1 John 4:2-3: "Every spirit that confesses Jesus had cometh in the flesh, is from God; and every spirit that does not confess Jesus Christ had cometh in the flesh, is not from God. And this is what you have heard regarding the antichrist: that he cometh and is now already in the world."

718 See "Didaches" (Teachings) of St. Cosmas of Aetolia, of I. Menounos, "Cosmas of Aetolia teachings" (and biography), Tinos publications, Athens, Didache A1, 37, page 142: "All faiths are false, counterfeit, all of them the Devil's. This I realized as being true, divine, heavenly, correct, perfect, both by my word and by your word: that the faith of the pious and Orthodox Christians is good and holy, and that we must believe and be baptized in the name of the Father and the Son and the Holy Spirit."

against the Church, it is not possible for you to win, for God is the strongest of all."[719]

Following the cessation of the persecutions and the triumph of the Church over Her external enemies — in other words, the Judeans and the idolaters — the internal enemies of the Church began to multiply and strengthen. A variety of heresies began to appear, which endeavored to overthrow and adulterate the faith once delivered, such that the faithful became confused, and their trust in the truth of the Gospel and traditions was debilitated. In outlining the ecclesiastical state of affairs that was created by the dominance for over 40 years — even administratively — of the heresy of Arius, Saint Basil the Great says: "The dogmas of the Fathers have been entirely disregarded, the apostolic traditions withered, the inventions of the youth are observed in the Churches; people are now "logic-chopping" not theologizing; precedence is given to the wisdom of the world, pushing aside the boasting in the Cross. Shepherds are driven out, and in their place cruel wolves are ushered in, dispersing Christ's flock."[720]

That which happened because of external enemies — religions — also happened because of internal ones — heresies. The Church, through Her great and enlightened Holy Fathers, demarcated and marked the boundaries [perixarakose] of the Orthodox faith with decisions by Local and Ecumenical Synods in the cases of specific, dubious teachings, but also with the agreement of all the Fathers (Consensus Patrum), on all the matters of the Faith. We stand on sure ground when we follow the Holy Fathers and do not move the boundaries that they have set. The expressions "Following after our Holy Fathers" and "Not withdrawing the boundaries that our Fathers have set" are signposts for a steady course of spiritual advance and a guardrail for [remaining within] the Orthodox faith and way of life.

Consequently, the basic positions of our Confession are the following:

1. We maintain, irremovably and without alteration, everything that the Synods and the Fathers have instituted. We accept everything that they accept and condemn everything that they condemn; and we avoid

---

719 "Homily Prior to the Exile." ΕΠΕ 33, 186.

720 Epistle 90, "To the most holy brothers and bishops in the West" 2, ΕΠΕ 2, 20.

communication with those who innovate in matters of the Faith.[721] We neither add, nor remove, nor alter any teaching. Even from the apostolic era, the God-bearing Saint Ignatius of Antioch in his epistle to Saint Polycarp of Smyrna wrote: "Anyone who says contrary to what has been decreed — even if he is trustworthy, even if he fasts, even if he lives in virginity, even if he performs signs and prophesizes, let him appear to you as a wolf in a sheep's hide, aspiring to the corruption of the sheep." Saint John the Chrysostom, in interpreting the Apostle Paul's words "If any man preach any other gospel unto you than that ye have received, let him be anathema" (Gal. 1:9), observes that the Apostle "did not say if they should proclaim something contrary or if they should overturn everything, but that even if they should preach even the smallest thing that has not been delivered to you, even if they should simply provoke it, let them be anathema."[722] Upon announcing its decisions against the Iconoclasts to the clergy of Constantinople, the Seventh Ecumenical Synod wrote: "We have followed the tradition of the Catholic Church, neither loosening [the matters of faith] nor making any superfluous addition, but, having been taught in the apostolic manner, we maintain the traditions we have received, accepting and respecting everything that the Holy Catholic Church has received from the first years, unwritten and written... for the true and straightforward judgment of the Church does not make any allowance for innovations within Her, or for attempts to remove anything. We, therefore, by following the laws of our Fathers, having received Grace by the one Spirit, have duly safeguarded without any innovations and reductions, all the things of the Church."[723]

Along with the Holy Fathers and the Synods, we too reject and anathematize all the heresies that appeared during the historical course of the Church. Of the old heresies that have survived to this day, we condemn Arianism (still surviving, in the pseudo-Witnesses of Jehovah) and Monophysitism — the extreme form of Eutychius and the more

---

721 This refers to those who provoke and innovate with regard to the Faith. It does not mean that Orthodox Christians should have no contact with non-Orthodox in the context of missionary outreach and witness, which would mean the cessation of all evangelism, missionary work, sharing of our Faith, etc.

722 Galatians. 1, 9. To Gall. Homily chapt. 1, PG 61, 624.

723 Mansi, 13, 409-412.

moderate form of Severus and Dioscorus — according to the decisions of the 4th Ecumenical Synod of Chalcedon and the Christological teaching of the great Holy Fathers and Teachers such as Saints Maximus the Confessor, John of Damascus, Photios the Great and the hymns of our worship.

2. We proclaim that Roman Catholicism is a womb of heresies and fallacies.[724] The teaching of the "Filioque" — that is, the procession of the Holy Spirit AND from the Son — is contrary to everything that Christ Himself taught about the Holy Spirit. The entire chorus of Fathers, both in Synods and individually, regard Roman Catholicism as a heresy because apart from the Filioque, it produced a host of other fallacies, such as the primacy and the infallibility of the Pope, the unleavened

---

724 In our age of "political correctness" this statement may seem outrageous and unnecessarily inflammatory. It is, however, "soft" in comparison to the writings of the Holy Fathers (e.g., note the language of St. Photios the Great throughout his 10th-century treatise against the *filioque* clause, *On the Mystagogy of the Holy Spirit* – and this was long before many other heresies were introduced). The Holy Fathers have, for centuries, viewed the Roman Catholicism as a womb of heresies, beginning with the adoption and promulgation of the *filioque* clause. Consider the following statements from another *Confession of Faith* from modern times, the *Patriarchal Encyclical of 1848*: "As soon as [the *filioque*] was introduced into the Churches of the West it brought forth disgraceful fruits, bringing with it, little by little, other novelties, for the most part contrary to the express commands of our Savior in the Gospel — commands which till its entrance into the Churches were closely observed. It drove the theologians of the West, as its defenders, since they had no ground either in Scripture or the Fathers to countenance heretical teachings, not only into misrepresentations of the Scriptures, such as are seen in none of the Fathers of the Holy Catholic Church, but also into adulterations of the sacred and pure writings of the Fathers alike of the East and West." Similar language is found in the *Patriarchal Encyclical of 1895*: "[B]ut the present Roman Church is the Church of innovations, of the falsification of the writings of the Church Fathers, and of the misinterpretation of the Holy Scripture and of the decrees of the holy councils, for which she has reasonably and justly been disowned, and is still disowned, so far as she remains in her error... [A]s has been said before, the Western Church, from the tenth century downwards, has privily brought into herself through the papacy various and strange and heretical doctrines and innovations, and so she has been torn away and removed far from the true and orthodox Church of Christ." If some find the language of the "*Confession of Faith Against Ecumenism*" offensive, they might consider whether this is due to a lack of familiarity with the writings of the Holy Fathers, and past confessional statements of the Orthodox Church.

bread (host), the fires of Purgatory, the immaculate conception of the Theotokos, created Grace, the purchasing of absolution (indulgences)... it has altered nearly all of the teaching and the practice pertaining to Baptism, Chrismation, the Divine Eucharist and the other Sacraments, and has converted the Church to a secular State.[725]

Contemporary Roman Catholicism has deviated even further than the medieval Latins from the teaching of the Church to the extent that it no longer comprises a continuance of the ancient Church of the West. It has introduced a swarm of new exaggerations in its "Mariology," such as the teaching that the Theotokos is a parallel redeemer (co-redemptrix) of the human race. It has reinforced the "Charismatic Movement" of Pentecostal (supposedly Spirit-centered) groups. It has adopted eastern religious practices and methods of prayer and meditation. It has introduced additional innovations into Divine worship, such as dances and musical instruments. It has shortened and essentially ruined the Divine Liturgy. With respect to Ecumenism, it has set down the basis for a unification of all religions (*panthriskeia*) with its Second Vatican Council, by recognizing "spiritual life" in the people of other religions. Dogmatic minimalism has led it to a diminishing of moral requirements, on account of the bond between dogma and morality, resulting in the moral failures of leading clergymen and an increase in moral deviations such as homosexuality and pedophilia among clergymen.[726] By continuing to support "Uniatism" — that caricature of Orthodoxy with which it victimizes and proselytizes faithful — the Vatican is sabotaging the dialogue and is contradicting its supposedly sincere intentions for union.

---

725 Again, see the *Patriarchal Encyclicals* of 1848 and 1895, which lay this out in great detail.

726 The moral laxity and decadence, even among the clergy, had already been noted at the beginning of the 15th century, by Saint Simeon of Thessaloniki (see 'Dogmatic Epistle 16' in D. Balfour, by Simeon of Thessaloniki (1416/17-1429) "*Theological Works,*" Vlatades Gleanings 34, Thessaloniki 1981, page 218: "And furthermore, that they did not regard fornication at all entailing Hell, not even among their priests, but instead, they would unscrupulously have concubines and youths for fornication and would every day officiate." Ibid., 15, page 216: "They also do not follow an evangelical lifestyle; for, every kind of luxury and fornication to them is not a reprehensible matter, nor anything else that is forbidden for Christians." The moral decadence that is observed of late even among the Orthodox clergy is the result of liberalism, which accompanies ecumenism, and of secularism.

Generally speaking, after the Second Vatican Council there has been a radical change in Catholicism and a turn towards Protestantism, and even an adoption of various "spiritual" movements of the "New Age."

According to Saint Simeon of Thessaloniki, the Mystagogue, "Papism" caused more damage to the Church than all the heresies and schisms combined. We Orthodox have communion with the pre-Schism Popes and we commemorate many Popes as Saints. However, the post-Schism popes have all taught heresy; they have ceased to be successors to the throne of Rome; they no longer have Apostolic succession, because they no longer have the faith of the Apostles and the Fathers. It is for this reason that, as St. Symeon states, with each such pope, "Not only do we have no communion, but we also call him a heretic." On account of their blasphemy against the Holy Spirit with their teaching of the Filioque, they forfeited the presence of the Holy Spirit and therefore everything of theirs is deprived of Grace.[727] Not one of their Mysteries (Sacraments) is valid, according to Saint Simeon: "Therefore the innovators are blaspheming and are far away from the Spirit, by blaspheming against the Holy Spirit, hence everything of theirs is graceless, inasmuch as they have violated and have demoted the Grace of the Spirit... which is why the Holy Spirit is not among them, and there is nothing spiritual in them, as everything of theirs is new and altered and contrary to Divine tradition."[728]

---

727 The term "Grace" is often misunderstood today. The Patristic teaching on the subject was best expressed by our Venerable Father Diadochus the God-bearer, Bishop of Photike in Epirus. As he writes in his *Hundred Texts on Spiritual Knowledge and Discernment*: "Before holy baptism Grace encourages the soul towards good from the outside, while Satan lurks in its depths, trying to block all the intellect's ways of approach to the divine. But from the moment we are reborn through Baptism, the demon is outside, Grace is within." And, in our own days, Blessed Archbishop Seraphim of Sophia writes concerning the two forms of Grace: "According to the teaching of the Holy Fathers, the Grace of the Holy Spirit is manifest in two forms: firstly, as an external, providential Grace, which acts in and throughout the lives of everybody, enabling anyone to accept the True Faith; and, secondly, as an internal, salvific Grace, which revivifies, redeems, and functions solely in the Orthodox Church." Here the Confession refers to the latter form of Grace. The general operation of the Holy Spirit among all men is not in question.

728 Dialogue 23, PG 155, 120-121. Epistle regarding blessedness 5, in D. Balfour,

3. The same things apply to an even greater degree to Protestantism, which as the offspring of Papism has inherited many heresies, but has also added many more. It has rejected Tradition, accepting only Holy Scripture (Sola Scriptura), which it misinterprets; it has abolished the Priesthood as a unique Mystery (Sacrament), as well as the veneration of the Saints and of the holy Icons; it has failed to honor, or even, in some cases, slighted the person of the Most Holy Theotokos (Mother of God); it has discarded monasticism; among the Holy Mysteries, it accepts only Baptism and the Divine Eucharist, which are understood in a way that deviates sharply from the teaching and the practice of the Church; it teaches such things as absolute predestination (Calvinism) and justification through faith alone. Furthermore, its more "progressive" sector has introduced Priesthood for women and marriage between homosexuals — whom they even accept into the ranks of the clergy. But above all, it lacks a proper ecclesiology, because the Orthodox understanding of the nature of the Church does not exist among them.[729]

4. The only way that our communion with heretics can be restored is if they renounce their delusion (*plani*) and repent, so that there may be a true union and peace: a union with the Truth, and not with delusion and heresy. For the incorporation of heretics into the Church, canonical precision (*akriveia*) requires that they be accepted through Baptism.[730] Their previous "baptism," performed outside the Church (without the

---

Simeon Archbishop of Thessaloniki (1416/17-1429), *"Theological Works,"* Vlatades Gleanings 34, Thessaloniki 1981, page 226. These comments of Saint Simeon should be interpreted on the basis of the Patristic teaching on Grace, as referred to in note 14 above.

729 Here the Confession speaks generally of Protestant*ism*. Given that there are 26,000+ denominations, it is impossible to make a succinct statement about Protestant tenets that applies accurately to them all. The Confession is admittedly painting with a broad brush, but these are all aspects of Protestantism that apply more or less to all Protestant groups, unless otherwise specified as speaking to particular confessions (such as Calvinism).

730 "Canonical precision" or *akriveia*, is the norm, as it is most consistent with the theological principles under-girding the Canons concerning Holy Baptism. Nevertheless, the authors of the Confession would agree that, *when canonical presuppositions existed*, "canonical dispensation", or *oikonomia*, has been employed. It is also the case, however, that, in almost every case today, those presuppositions (such as triple immersion) do not exist.

triple immersion and emersion of the one being baptized in water sancti-fied by a particular prayer) is in no way a baptism.[731] All attempts at bap-tism outside the Church lack the Grace of the Holy Spirit (Who does not remain within schisms and heresies) and as such, we have nothing in common that unites us, as Basil the Great points out:

"those who had apostatized from the Church had no longer on them the Grace of the Holy Spirit, for it ceased to be imparted when the con-tinuity was broken...they who were broken off had become laymen, and, because they are no longer able to confer on others that Grace of the Holy Spirit from which they themselves are fallen away, they had no au-thority either to baptize or to ordain."[732]

That is why the new attempt by Ecumenists to push the idea that we have a common baptism with heretics is unfounded. Indeed, upon this nonexistent baptismal unity they want to base the unity of the Church, which supposedly exists wherever a baptism may exist.[733] One enters the

---

731 The reception of a convert into the Church by *oikonomia*, when indeed it is done within the canonical prescriptions and leads to the same end as *akriveia*, in no way can be interpreted as altering Orthodox ecclesiology. Employing *oikonomia* in the reception of non-Orthodox does not mean acceptance *per se* of non-Orthodox mysteries. The acceptance *per se* of non-Orthodox mysteries by some Orthodox representatives in the ecumenical movement is impossible to reconcile with Orthodox ecclesiology and is to be rejected as contrary to the Orthodox Dogma of the Church.

732 Canonical Epistle ʹΑ, *To Amphilochios of Iconion*, 1st Canon.

733 In the text of the 9th General Convention of the World Council of Churches in Porto Alegre, Brazil in 2006, which was accepted by the representatives of the Orthodox churches and was titled "Called to be the One Church," in paragraph 8 it states: "All those baptized in Christ are united in His name." In paragraph 9: "That we all belong in common to Christ through baptism in the name of the Father and the Son and the Holy Spirit, gives the churches the possibility and it invites them to walk together, even when they disagree. We assure that there is one baptism, exactly as there is one body and one Spirit, one hope in our calling, one Lord, one Faith, one God and Father to all of us (see Ephes.4:4-6)." The Metropolitan of Pergamos John (Zizioulas) in his work "Orthodox Ecclesiology and the Ecumenical Movement," *Sourozh Diocesan Magazine* (England, August 1985, vol.21, page 23), had paved the way for this position, by stating: "Within baptism, even if there is a break, a division, a schism, you can still speak of the Church... The Orthodox, in my understanding at least, participate in the ecumenical movement as a movement of baptized Christians, who are in a state of

Church, however, and becomes Her member, not with just any baptism, but only with the "one baptism," that uniformly performed baptism, officiated by Priests who have received the Priesthood of the Church.

5. As long as the heterodox continue to remain in their errors, we avoid communion with them, especially in common prayer. All those holy canons which address the matter of common prayer are unanimous in prohibiting not only common officiating and common prayer in the temple of God, but even ordinary prayers in private quarters. The Church's strict stance toward the heterodox springs from true love and sincere concern for their salvation, and out of Her pastoral care that the faithful be not carried away by heresy. Whosoever loves, reveals the truth and does not leave the other in falsehood; otherwise, any love and agreement with him would only be counterfeit and false. There is such a thing as a good war and a bad peace: "for a praiseworthy war is superior to a peace that separates one from God" says Saint Gregory the Theologian.[734] And Saint John the Chrysostom recommends: "If you should see devoutness infringed upon, do not prefer a oneness of mind to the truth, but stand fast until death... in no way betraying the truth". And elsewhere, he recommends with emphasis: "Do not accept any false dogma on the pretext of love."[735] This stance of the Fathers was also adopted by the great defender and confessor of the Orthodox faith against the Latins, Saint Mark of Ephesus, who concluded his own Confession of Faith in Florence with the following words: "All the teachers of the Church, all the Councils and all the divine Scriptures exhort us to avoid heretics, and to refrain from communion with them.

Therefore, am I to disregard them all, and follow those who under the pretense of a manufactured peace strive for union? Those who have counterfeited the sacred and divine Symbol of Faith (The Creed) and who introduced the Son as the second cause of the Holy Spirit? [...] May this never happen to us, benevolent Comforter (Paraclete), and may I never fall away from my own duteous thoughts, but by following Thy

---

division because they cannot express the same faith together. In the past this has happened because of a lack of love which is now, thank God, disappearing."

734 Apologetics on the flight to Pontus 82, ΕΠΕ 1, 176.

735 To Romans, Homily 22, 2, PG 60, 611. To Philippians, Homily 2.1, PG 62, 119.

teaching and the blessed men who were inspired by Thee, may I be added to my fathers, by bringing in, if nothing else, this: devoutness."[736]

6. Up until the beginning of the 20th century, the Church has steadfastly and immutably maintained a dismissive and condemnatory stance towards all heresies, as clearly formulated in the Synodicon of Orthodoxy which is recited on the Sunday of Orthodoxy. Heresies and heretics are anathematized, one by one; furthermore, in order to ensure that no heretics be left out of the anathema, there is a general anathema at the end of the text: "Let all heretics be anathematized." Unfortunately, this uniform, steady and unswerving stance of the Church up until the beginning of the 20th century has begun to be progressively abandoned, following the encyclical that was released by the Ecumenical Patriarchate in 1920, "Unto the Churches of Christ Everywhere," which for the first time officially characterized heresies as "churches"[737] that are not alienated from the Church, but are familiar and related to Her. It recommended that "the love between the Churches should above all be rekindled and reinforced, and they should no more consider one another as strangers and foreigners, but as relatives, and as being a part of the household of Christ and 'fellow heirs, members of the same body and partakers of the promise of God in Christ.'"[738]

The path is now open for the adoption, the shaping and the development of the heresy of Ecumenism within the sphere of the Orthodox Church — this "pan-heresy," initially of Protestant inspiration, now with Papal acceptance, which adopts and legalizes all heresies as 'churches' and assaults the dogma of the One, Holy, Catholic and Apostolic Church. This new dogma regarding the Church, this new ecclesiology, is now developed, taught and imposed by Patriarchs and bishops. According to this new teaching, no Church is entitled to demand for itself exclusively the designation of the catholic and true Church. Instead,

---

736 Confession of faith displayed in Florence, in Documents relatifs au Concile de Florence, II, Oeuvres anticonciliaires de Marc d'Ephèse, par L. Petit, *Patrologia Orientalis* 17, 442.

737 That is, "churches" in a more or less real, ecclesiological way, implying mystical union with the one, true Church of Christ, the Orthodox Church.

738 See I. Karmiris', *The Dogmatic and Symbolic Monuments of the Orthodox Catholic Church*, vol. 2, page 958.

each one of them is a piece, a part, and not the entire Church; they all together comprise the Church.[739]

All the boundaries set by the Fathers have fallen; there is no longer a dividing line between heresy and Church, between truth and delusion. Heresies are also 'churches' now; in fact, many of them — like the Papist one — are now regarded as 'sister churches' to which God has entrusted, jointly with us, the care for mankind's salvation.[740]

The Grace of the Holy Spirit now also exists within heresies, and therefore their baptisms are — like all the other mysteries — considered valid.[741] All who have been baptized into a heretical group are now considered members of Christ's Body, the Church.

The condemnations and the anathemas of the councils are no longer valid and should be stricken from liturgical books. We are now lodged in the "World Council of Churches" and have essentially betrayed — with

---

739 One recent example of this is found in the declaration of the 9th General Convention of the World Council of Churches in Porto Alegre, Brazil in 2006, which was accepted by the representatives of the Local Orthodox Churches and was entitled "Called to be the One Church." In section II, paragraph 6 of the document, which is a common declaration of Orthodox and heterodox, we read: "Each church is the Church catholic and not simply a part of it. Each church is the Church catholic, but not the whole of it. Each church fulfils its catholicity when it is in communion with the other churches." But, as it would be expected, this "new dogma" takes on a wide variety of expressions, from including only two churches, such as (in the "two lungs" theory) Roman Catholicism and the Orthodox Church, or three churches, as in the classic Branch Theory of the Anglicans, or including many churches, as has been expressed in the "invisible church" ecclesiology of the World Council of Churches and the "baptismal unity" theory. That which binds these various theories together is a rejection of "ecclesiological exclusivism" and an ecumenism "of return." A sentiment that is said often and by many, including Orthodox primates and hierarchs, is that "a Catholic will not become an Orthodox and vice versa, but we must approach the altar together" (Bishop Tichon, Diocese of Central and Western Europe of the Patriarchate of Bulgaria on his visit to the Pope, October 22nd, 2009.)

740 See joint statement by Pope John-Paul II and Patriarch Bartholomew during the latter's visit to Rome on the 29th of June 1995. The same had been proclaimed at an earlier date by the Combined Theological Committee for the Dialogue between Orthodox and Papists, in Balamand, Lebanon in 1993.

741 The term "valid" here means accepting heterodox baptism "per se", in and of itself, apart from the Church, and has ecclesiological implications which the *kat'oikonomia* reception of the non-Orthodox can never imply.

our membership alone[742] — our ecclesiastical self-awareness. We have removed the dogma regarding the One, Holy, Catholic and Apostolic Church — the dogma of "one Lord, one Faith, one Baptism."[743]

7. This inter-Christian syncretism has now expanded into an inter-religious syncretism, which equates all the religions with the unique knowledge of and reverence for God and a Christ-like way of life — all revealed from on high by Christ. Consequently, it is not only the dogma of the One, Holy, Catholic and Apostolic Church in relation to the various heresies that is being attacked, but also the foundational and unique dogma of revelation and salvation of mankind through Jesus Christ in relation to the religions of the world. It is the worst delusion, the greatest heresy of all ages.

8. We believe and confess that salvation is possible in Christ alone. The religions of the world, but also the various heresies do not lead man to salvation. The Orthodox Church is not merely the true Church; She is the only Church. She alone has remained faithful to the Gospel, the Synods and the Fathers, and consequently She alone represents the true catholic Church of Christ.

According to the blessed Elder Justin Popovich, Ecumenism is a common name for the pseudo-churches of Western Europe; their common name is "pan-heresy."[744]

This pan-heresy has been accepted by many Orthodox patriarchs, archbishops, bishops, clergymen, monks and laity. They teach it, "bareheaded," they apply it and impose it in practice, communing with heretics in every possible manner — with common prayers, with exchanges of visits, with pastoral collaborations — thus essentially placing them-

---

742 This is a question of methodology, the "essential betrayal" being an abandonment of the patristic methodology of witness, wherein the Scriptural command, "a man that is a heretic after the first and second admonition reject" (Tit. 3:10) is followed, if not in word than in spirit. Rather, we have "lodged" ourselves in the World Council of Churches as full organic members, even committing ourselves to dialogue without presuppositions or limits. This disregard for patristic and scriptural guidelines to proper witness inevitably has led to a betrayal of the Church's self-understanding.

743 Ephesians 4:5.

744 Archimandrite Justin Popović, *The Orthodox Church and Ecumenism*, Thessaloniki 1974, page 224.

selves outside the Church.[745] Our stance, per the Conciliar canonical decisions and per the example of the Saints, is obvious. Each one must now assume his responsibilities.

9. There are of course collective responsibilities also, and chiefly in the ecumenistic conscience of our hierarchs and theologians, towards the Orthodox people (pleroma) and their individual flocks. To them, we declare with a fear of God and with love that this stance of theirs and their involvement in ecumenistic activities are condemnable from every aspect, because:

a) they actively impugn our Orthodox-Patristic Tradition and Faith;

b) they are sowing doubt in the hearts of their flock and unsettle many, leading to division and schism, and

c) they are luring a portion of the flock into delusion, and thus, to spiritual disaster.

We, therefore, declare that, for the aforementioned reasons, those who endeavor within this ecumenist irresponsibility, whatever rank they may hold within the Church Body, contradict the tradition of our Saints and are thus standing in opposition to them. For this reason, their stance must be condemned and rejected by the entirety of the Hierarchy and Faithful.

---

745 What is not meant here is an institutional departure from the Church by excommunication or anathema. And this is clear by the use of the terms "essentially" and "placing themselves." Rather, what is meant is that by their actions and their words they have separated themselves in essence from the Church – from Her Fathers, Her Way and Her Life. They have essentially removed themselves from the Church by no longer following the Holy Fathers, no longer expressing the Orthodox Faith. The passage draws on the 15th canon of the 1st -2nd Synod. The understanding behind the phrase "essentially placing themselves outside the Church" is clearly implied in the canon when it states: "For not bishops, but false bishops and false teachers have they condemned..." The 15th canon, although praising those who cease commemoration of their bishop, who is teaching heresy "bareheaded", does not make ceasing commemoration a requirement. It leaves the particular course of action – based on the canons and councils and fathers – to the discretion of each. The Confession follows suit, clearly naming the heresy and calling all to appropriate response ("Our stance, per the Conciliar canonical decisions and per the example of the Saints, is obvious."), but leaving the particulars to each one's discretion ("Each one must now assume his responsibilities").

Metropolitan Panteleimon of Antinoes

Metropolitan Seraphim of Kythira and Antikythira

Metropolitan Kosmas of Etolia and Akarnania

Metropolitan Seraphim of Piraeus

Metropolitan Artemios of Raskas and Prizrenis, Kossovo and Metohia

Bishop George (Schaefer) of Mayfield, Abbot of Holy Cross Monastery, Wayne, West Virginia

Archim. Christodoulos, Abbot of the Holy Monastery of Koutloumousiou, Holy Mountain

Archim. Joseph, Abbot of the Holy Monastery of Xeropotamou, Holy Mountain

Archim. Philotheos, Abbot of the Holy Monastery of Karakalou, Holy Mountain

Archim. Agathon, Abbot of the Holy Monastery of Constamonitou, Holy Mountain

Archim. Nikodemos, Abbot of the Holy Monastery of Filotheou, Holy Mountain

Protopr. George Metallinos, Peer Professor, School of Theology, University of Athens

Protopr. Theodoros Zisis, Peer Professor, School of Theology, University of Thessaloniki

Archim. Markos Manolis, Spiritual Head of "Pan-Hellenic Orthodox Union"

Archim. Athanasios, Abbot of the Holy Monastery of Stavrovouniou, Cyprus

Archim. Timotheos Sakkas, Abbot of the Holy Monastery Paraklhtou, Oropos

Archim. Kyrill Kehagioglou, Abbot of the Holy Monastery of Pantokratoros Melissohoriou Langada

Archim. Sarantis Sarantos, Priest of the Dormition of the Theotokos, Amarousiou, Attica

Archim. Maximos Karavas, Abbot of the Holy Monastery of Saint Paraskevi, Milohoriou, Ptolemaidas

Archim. Gregory Hadjinikolaou, Abbot of the Holy Monastery of the Holy Trinity, Ano Gatzeas Volou

Archim. Athanasios Anastasiou, Abbot of the Holy Monastery of Great Meteorou

Archim. Theoklitos Bolkas, Abbot of Holy Isihastirio of Saint Arsenio the Kapadocian, Halkidiki

Archim. Chrysostomos, Abbot of the Holy Community of Saint Nikodemos, Pentalofos, Goumenitcha

Archim. Theodore Diamantis, Abbot of the Holy Monastery of the Theotokos, Molyskepastou, Konitsa

Archim. Palamas Kyrillidis, Abbot of the Holy Monastery of the Nativity of the Theotokos, Kallipetra, Veria

Archim. Eudokimos, Spiritual Father of the Holy Lavra of Savva the Sanctified, Jerusalem

Archim. Chrysostomos, Abbot of the Holy Monastery of Saint Gerasimos the Jordanian, Jerusalem

Archim. Laurentios Gratsias, Holy Metropolis of Florina, Prespon and Eordeas

Archim. Meletios Vadrahanis, Holy Metropolis of Florina, Prespon and Eordeas

Archim. Paul Demetracopoulos, Holy Monastery of the Transfiguration of the Lord, Moutsialis, Veria

Archim. Ignatios Kalaitzopoulos, Holy Monastery of Saint Paraskevi, Melohoriou, Ptolemaidas

Archim. Symeon Georgiadis, Holy Monastery of the Holy Trinity, Ano Gatzeas, Volos

Archim. Augustine Siarras, Holy Monastery of the Holy Trinity, Ano Gatzeas, Volos

Archim. Ambrosios Gionis, Holy Monastery of the Holy Trinity, Ano Gatzeas, Volos

Archim. Benedict, Abbot of the Holy Monastery of the Holy Archangels, Prizreni, with following

Archim. Gerasimos, Abbot of the Holy Monastery of Saint George, Jourgevi Stoupovi, with following

Archim. Nicholaos, Abbot of the Holy Monastery of the Holy Archangels, Mavropotami, with following

Archim. Romylos, Abbot of the Holy Monastery of the Entry of the Theotokos, Doumboki Potok, with following

Archim. Symeon, Abbot of the Holy Monastery of Saint Stephen, Baniska, with following

Archim. Stephanos, Abbot of the Holy Monastery of the Saints Anargyron Zotsitse, with following

Archim. Ioannikios Kotsonis, Abbot of the Holy Monastery of the Transfiguration of the Lord, Sohos, Thessaloniki

Archim. Paul Danas, Hieropreacher of the Holy Monastery of Etolias and Akarnanias

Archim. Constantine Paleologopoulos, retired priest of the Holy Monastery of Kalavriton and Egalias Egio

Archim. Paisios Papadopoulos, Abbot of the Holy Monastery of Saint Gregory Palamas, Filota, Metropolis of Florina

Archim. Epiphanios Hadjigiagou, Head Metropolitan of the Church of Florina, Florina

Archim. Athanasios Siamakis, Hieropreacher of the Holy Monastery of Florina

Archim. Anargyros Afthonidis, Military Priest, Florina

Archim. Augustine Andritsopoulos, Abbot of the Holy Monastery of Myrtias of the Holy Monastery of Etolia and Akarnania

Archim. Theodosis Kyprianou, Holy Monastery of Saint Filotheou, Skete Saint George, Karyes, Holy Mountain

Archim. Ignatios Kalaitzopoulos, Holy Monastery of Saint Paraskevi, Milohoriou, Ptolemaidas

Archim. Ierotheos Skiadas, Abbot of the Holy Monastery of the Dormition of the Theotokos, Vlohou, Agriniou

Archim. Ioasaph Makris, Holy Monastery of Meteora

Archim. Kosmas Paleogiannis, Cell of Saint John the Theologian of the Holy Monastery of Dohiariou, Holy Mountain

Archim. Sevastianos Amantidis, Abbot of the Holy Monastery of Saint Paraskevis Vasiliados, Kastoria

Archim. Christos Kyriazopoulos, past Educational Adviser, Thessaloniki

Archim. Nektarios Ziombolas, Military Priest

Archim. Joseph Aivazoglou, Holy Church of the Theotokos Ahiropiitou (not made by hand) Thessaloniki

Elder Gregory, Hieromonk, Holy Isyhastirion, Danieleon, Katounakia, Holy Mountain

Elder Efstratios, Hiermonk, Holy
Monastery of Great Lavvra, Holy
Mountain

Elder Fillipos, Hieromonk, Kalyvi of
Great Athanasiou, Mikra Agia Anna,
Holy Mountain

Hieromonk Athanasios, Holy
Isyhastirion Danieleon, Katounakia,
Holy Mountain

Hieromonk Nikodemos, Holy
Isyhastirion Danieleon, Katounakia,
Holy Mountain

Hieromonk Nephon, Holy Isyhastirion
Danieleon, Katounakia, Holy
Mountain

Hieromonk Chrysostom Kartsonas,
Kalyvi of Saint George, Holy Skete
of Saint Anna, Holy Mountain

Hieromonk Onoufrios, Kalyvi of the
Holy Forerunner, Holy Skete of
Saint Anna, Holy Mountain

Hieromonk Chrysanthos, Kalyvi of
the Holy Forerunner, Holy Skete of
Saint Anna , Holy Mountain

Hieromonk Azarias, Kalyvi of the Holy
Forerunner, Holy Skete of Saint
Anna, Holy Mountain

Hieromonk Gabriel, Holy Cell of the
Theotokos Gorgoepikoou, Holy
Monastery of Pantokratoros, Holy
Mountain

Hieromonk Panteleimon, Holy Cell of
Saint Panteleimon, Holy Monastery
of Saint Pantokratoros, Holy
Mountain

Hieromonk Basil, Abbot of the Holy
Monastery of Saints Anargyron,
Vratsevo, with following

Hieromonk Efthimios, Abbot of
the Holy Monastery of the Holy
Forerunner, Sotsanitsa, with
following

Hieromonk Theoktistos, Abbot of the
Holy Monastery of the Holy Trinity,
Sopotsani, with following

Hieromonk Tychon, Holy Isyhastirion
of Pantokratoros, Melissohorion

Hieromonk Chariton, Holy Cell of
Ascension, Karyes, Holy Mountain

Hieromonk Nestor

Hieromonk Augustine, Holy Monastery
of All Saints and Saint Savva the
Sanctified, Jerusalem

Hieromonk Modestos Diasakis, Holy
Monastery of Saint Paraskevi,
Kastoria

Hieromonk Raphael Kyriakou, Holy
Monastery of Saint Raphael-Marina,
Larnaka, Cyprus

Hieromonk Photios Georgiou, Holy
Monastery of Kastorias

Protopr. Lambros Photopoulos,
Officiating priest, Holy Church of
Saint Kosma Etolos, Amarousio,
Attica

Protopr. John Photopoulos, Officiating
priest, Holy Church of Saint
Paraskevi, Attica

Protopr. Athanasios Minas, Loutraki
Korinthias

Protopr. Eleftherios Palamas, Saints
Christophori (God-bearers)
Ptolemaid

Protopr. Constantine Mygdalis, In
Charge of the Holy Church of Saint
Constantine, Volos

Protopr. Photios Vezynias, Teacher, Holy
Metropolis of Langada

Protopr. Anthony Bousdekis, Abbot
of the Holy Monastery of Saint
Nicholas of Nicea

Protopr. Demetrios Vasiliadis, Holy
Metropolis of Maronia and
Komotini

Protopr. Vasilios E. Voloudakis,
Officiating priest, Holy Church of
Saint Nicholas Pefkakion, Athens

Protopr. Vasilios Gogidis, Officiating
priest, Holy Metropolitan Church of
Saint Nicholas, Megapoleos

Protopr. Nicholas Zaharopoulos,
Officiating priest of the Holy Church
of Saint Fanourios, Drapetsonas

Protopr. Haralambos Lalaitis,
Officiating priest, Holy Church of
the Theotokos Myrtidiotissis, Piraeus

Protopr. Chariton Pappas, Officiating
priest, Holy Church of Saint
Demetrios, Piraeus

Protopr. Panagiotis Sahtouris,
Officiating priest, Holy Church of
Saint Nilus, Pireaus

Protopr. Constantinos Tzafestas,
Officiating priest, Holy Metropolitan
Church of Kerkyra, Theologian,
retired Professor M.E., Kerkyra

Protopr. Christos Christodoulos,
Officiating priest, Holy Church
of Saint Constantine and Helen,
Piraeus

Protopr. Radoslav Jankovic, Secretary of
the Holy Metropolis of Raskas and
Prizrenis and Kossovo and Metohia

Protopr. Dimitrios Vasiliadis, Komotini

Protopr. Anastasios Semertzidis,
Hierarchal Commissioner of the
Kastoria eparchy

Protopr. George Kougioumtzoglou,
Thessaloniki

Protopr. Constantinos Andreopoulos,
Holy Monastery Florinis

Protopr. Vasilios Christidis, Holy
Monastery Attikis

Protopr. Haralambos Nalpadidis, Holy
Monastery Florinis

Protopr. Photios Bithas, Holy Monastery
of Saint Spyridon, Great Yarmouth,
England

Priest Dionysios tatsis, Educator,
Konitsa

Priest Demetrios Sarris, Officiating
priest, Holy Church of Pammegiston
Taksiarhon, Sesklou, Esonias

Priest Efthimios Antoniadis, Holy
Metropolis of Larisa

Priest Anastasios Gotsopoulos,
Officiating priest of the Holy
Church of Saint Nicholas, Patra

Priest George Papageorgiou, Holy
Metropolis Demetriados

Priest Peter Heers, Petrokerasa,
Halkidiki

Priest Theophanis Manouras, Officiating
priest, Holy Church of Saint
Athanasiou Valestinou, Magnesias

Priest Pashalis Ginoudis, Holy
Metropolis of Larisa

Priest George Diamantopoulos, Lavrio,
Holy Metropolis Mesogeas

Priest Vasilios Kokolakis, Officiating
priest, Holy Church of the Holy
Cross, Holargos

Priest Peter Pantazis, Officiating priest,
Holy Church of the Transfiguration,
Halandriou

Priest Anthony Valvis, Officiating priest,
Holy Church of Saint Nilus, Piraeus

Priest John Vernikos, Holy Church of
the Annunciation of the Theotokos,
Montgomery, Alabama

Priest Nicholas Gavalles, Holy Church
of the Holy Apostles, Psalidiou,
Amarousio

Priest Iraklis Drivas, Officiating Priest,
Holy Church of the Theotokos
Myrtidiotissa, Piraeus

Priest Demetrios Kalabounias,
Officiating priest, Holy Church of
Saint Nilus, Piraeus

Priest Demetrios Lambrou, clergy, Holy
Monastery Prevezis, Aneza-Artas

Priest Basilios Mouzelis, Officiating priest, Chapel of Saints Anargyron, Hospital of Halkidos

Priest Panagiotis Balis, Officiating priest, Holy Church of the Entry of the Theotokos, Imerovigliou, Thera

Priest Christopher Chronis, Holy Monastery Etolias and Akarnanias

Priest Sotirios Manolopoulos, Officiating priest, Holy Church of Saint Basil Vrahneika, Holy Monastery of Patra

Priest George Vasilakis, Lyon, France

Priest Theoharis Megas, Hieroteacher, Director of Plystylou, Kavalas

Priest Daniel de Oliveira Pinheiro, Ukrainian Orthodox Church in Brazil

Priest Demetrios Sykopoulos, Holy Monastery Kastorias

Priest Triantafyllos Xeros, Thessaloniki

Presvytera Maria Tsiplakaki, Vathilakkos, Kozani

Stewart Demetrios Papagiannis, Officiating priest, Holy Church of Saint Fanourios, Drapetsonas

Stewart John Psarras, Officiating priest, Holy Church of Saint George Mesoropis, Holy Monastery Eleftheroupoleos

Stewart John Kyprianou, Officiating priest, Holy Church of Saint Nicholas, Egomi-Lefkosia, Cyprus

Priest Miltiadis Karagiannis, Kefalohori Imathias

Hierodeacon Theologos Kostopoulos, Holy Monastery of the Holy Trinity, Ano Gazeas Volou

Hierodeacon Antonios, Holy Isyhastirion Pantokratoros, Melissohoriou

Hierodeacon George Theodoridis, Holy Metropolis of Lerou, Kalymnou and Astypaleas

Hierodeacon Iraklidios Kleanthous, Holy Metropolis Tamasou, Cyprus

Elder Theoliptos Monk, Hut of the Holy Forerunner, Holy Scete of Saint Anna, Holy Mountain

Elder Gabriel Monk, Cell of Saint Christodoulou, Karyes, Holy Mountain

Elder Ilarion Monk, near Arsana Constamonitou, Holy Mountain

Elder Daniel Monk, Holy Isyhastirion Danieleon, Katanoukia, Holy Mountain

Elder Akakios Monk, Holy Isyhastirion Danieleon, Katanoukia, Holy Mountain

Elder Stefanos Monk, Holy Isyhastirion Danieleon, Katanoukia, Holy Mountain

Elder Paul Monk, Holy Cell of the Holy Apostles, SceteXenofontos, Holy Mountain

Elder Onoufrios Monk, Holy Cell of the Nativity of the Theotokos, Holy Monastery Pantokratoros, Holy Mountain

Elder Nektarios Monk, Holy Cell of the Lifebearing Spring, Holy Monastery Koutloumousiou, Holy Mountain

Elder Isaak Monk, Holy Cell of the Nativity of the Theotokos, Holy Monastery Stavronikita, Holy Mountain

Elder Moses Monk, Holy Cell of Saint John Chrysostom, Scete of Saint Panteleimon, Holy Monastery Koutloumousiou, Holy Mountain

Elder Heruvim Monk, New Scete, Holy Mountain

Monk Arsenios Vliakoftis, Holy Isyhastirion of Saint Arsenios of Kappadocia, Halkidiki

Monk George, Holy Cell of the Nativity of the Theotokos, Holy Monastery of Pantokratoros, Holy Mountain

Monk Christopher, Holy Cell of the Apostles, Scete Xenofontos, Holy Mountain

Monk Maximos, Holy Isyhastirion Danieleon, Katanoukia, Holy Mountain

Monk Dositheos, Kathisma Holy Monastery of Koutloumousiou, Holy Mountain

Monk Spyridon, Cell of Saint Nicholas, Holy Monastery of Koutloumousiou, Holy Mountain

Monk Damaskinos Agiorite, Holy Cell of the Holy Forerunner, Holy Monastery of Karakallou

Monk Savvas Lavriotis, Holy Monastery of Great Lavra, Holy Mountain

Monk Theophilos Agiorite, Holy Cell Sanbri, Holy Mountain

Monk Paisios, Holy Cell of the Holy Archangels "Savveon", Holy Mountain

Monk Herouvim, Holy Cell of the Holy Archangels, Saint John Koukouzeli, Holy Mountain

Monk Nikodemos, Holy Cell of Saint Nektarios, Kapsala, Holy Mountain

Monk Disitheos, Holy Monastery of the Transfiguration of the Lord, Sohos, Langada

Monk Chariton, Hut of the Holy Forerunner, Holy Scete of Saint Anna, Holy Mountain

Monk Nikodemos, Hut of the Holy Forerunner, Holy Scete of Saint Anna, Holy Mountain

Monk Averkios, Hut of the Holy Forerunner, Holy Scete of Saint Anna, Holy Mountain

Monk Prodromos, Hut of the Holy Forerunner, Scete of Saint Anna, Holy Mountain

Monk Arsenios, Holy Hut of Saint Gerasimos, Scete of Saint Panteleimon, Holy Monastery Koutloumousiou, Holy Mountain

Monk Arsenios, Holy Isyhastirion Pantokratoros, Melissohoriou

Monk Demetrios, Holy Isyhastirion Pantokratoros, Melissohoriou

Monk Dionysios, Holy Isyhastiorion Pantokratoros, Melissohoriou

Monk Efstratios, Holy Isyhastirion Pantokratoros, Melissohoriou

Monk Ignatios, Holy Isyhastirion Pantokratoros, Melissohoriou

Monk Mardarios, Jerusalem

Monk Michael, Holy Isyhastirion Pantokratoros, Melissohoriou

Monk Nektarios, Holy Isyhastirion Pantokratoros, Melissohoriou

Monk Nicodemos Bilalis, Cell of the Visitation (Ypapanti) - Kapsala, Holy Mountain

Monk Pahomios, Holy Isyhastirion Pantokratoros, Melissohoriou

Monk Raphael, Holy Isyhastirion Pantokratoros, Melissohoriou

Monk Arkadios Sabbaite, Holy Lavra of Savva the Sanctified, Jerusalem

Monk Arsenios Kotzias, Holy Monastery of Saint Paraskevi, Kastoria

Monk George, New Scete, Holy Mountain

Monk Efraim Sabbaite, Holy Lavra of Savva the Sanctified, Jerusalem

Monk Zosimas Sabbaite, Holy Lavra of Savva the Sanctified, Jerusalem

Monk Ioannikos Sabbaite, Holy Lavra of Savva the Sanctified, Jerusalem

Monk Iosaph Sabbaite, Holy Lavra of Savva the Sanctified, Jerusalem

Monk Kallinikos Sabbaite, Holy Lavra
of Savva the Sanctified, Jerusalem

Monk Lazaros Sabbaite, Holy Lavra of
Savva the Sanctified, Jerusalem

Monk Merkourios Sabbaite, Holy Lavra
of Savva the Sanctified, Jerusalem

Monk Paisios Sabbaite, Holy Lavra of
Savva the Sanctified, Jerusalem

Monk Raphael Sabbaite, Holy Lavra of
Savva the Sanctified, Jerusalem

Monk Savvas Mousdikas, Holy
Monastery of Saint Paraskevi,
Kastoria

Monk Seraphim Sabbaite, Holy Lavra of
Savva the Sanctified, Jerusalem

Monk Philotheos Tzimoropoulos,
Holy Monastery of Saint Paraskevi,
Kastoria

Monk Herouvim Sabbaite, Holy
Lavra of Saint Savva the Sanctified,
Jerusalem

Nun Agathi Antoniou, Abbess, Holy
Monastery of Saint Stephen, Holy
Meteora

Nun Mariam, Abbess, Holy Monastery
of Saint Laurentios, Pilio

Nun Christonymphi, Holy Monastery
of Saint Laurentios, Pilio

Nun Laurentia, Holy Monastery of Saint
Laurentios, Pilio

Nun Agathinoi Antoniou, Holy
Monastery of Saint Stephen, Holy
Meteora

Nun Agathodouli Hondrou, Holy
Monastery of Saint Stephen, Holy
Meteora

Nun Agathokliti Athanatou, Holy
Monastery of Saint Stephen, Holy
Meteora

Nun Alexia Peppa, Holy Monastery of
Saint Stephen, Holy Meteora

Nun Vessaria Laskou, Holy Monastery
of Saint Stephen, Holy Meteora

Nun Eufimia Dionysopoulou, Holy
Monastery of Saint Stephen, Holy
Meteora

Nun Thekla Barka, Holy Monastery of
Saint Stephen, Holy Meteora

Nun Theodosia Bouba, Holy Monastery
of Saint Stephen, Holy Meteora

Nun Theoktisti Paila, Holy Monastery
of Saint Stephen, Holy Meteora

Nun Theologia Papadaki, Holy
Monastery of Saint Stephen, Holy
Meteora

Nun Theoproti Tzitzira, Holy
Monastery of Saint Stephen, Holy
Meteora

Nun Theotekni Mitsikosta, Holy
Monastery of Saint Stephen, Holy
Meteora

Nun Theophania Kyriazopoulou, Holy
Monastery of Saint Stephen, Holy
Meteora

Nun Justina Demetriou, Holy
Monastery of Saint Stephen, Holy
Meteora

Nun Magdalen Papadam, Holy
Monastery of Saint Stephen, Holy
Meteora

Nun Makrina Pappa, Holy Monastery of
Saint Stephen, Holy Meteora

Nun Mariam Kalogianni, Holy Shrine
of the Transfiguration of the Lord,
Holy Metropolis of Ierissou and of
the Holy Mountain

Nun Marina Famisi, Holy Monastery of
Saint Stephen, Holy Meteora

Nun Markella Gaki, Holy Monastery of
Saint Stephen, Holy Meteora

Nun Nektaria Bali, Holy Monastery of
Saint Stephen, Holy Meteora

Nun Nikodimi Siahouli, Holy
Monastery of Saint Stephen, Holy
Meteora

Nun Kseni Karamihou, Holy Monastery
of Saint Stephen, Holy Meteora

Nun Prodromi Kapeti, Holy Monastery
of Saint Stephen, Holy Meteora
Nun Sarra, Abbess, Holy Monastery
of Saint Nicholas, Kontsoul, with
following
Nun Silouani Phillips, Holy Monastery
of Saint Stephen, Holy Meteora
Nun Stephania Tesia, Holy Monastery
of Saint Stephen, Holy Meteora
Nun Synglitiki Rekata, Holy Monastery
of Saint Stephen, Holy Meteora
Nun Fevronia Dalla, Holy Monastery of
Saint Stephen, Holy Meteora
Nun Philothei Bali, Holy Monastery of
Saint Stephen, Holy Meteora
Nun Haralambia Mastoraki, Holy
Monastery of Saint Stephen, Holy
Meteora
Nun Christoniphi Bandeka, Holy
Monastery of Saint Stephen, Holy
Meteora
Nun Chrysostomi Polyzou, Holy
Monastery of Saint Stephen, Holy
Meteora
Nun Melani, Thessaloniki
Nun Christodouli, Thessaloniki
Archimandrite Philemon Castro, Los
Banos, Laguna, Philippines
Ieromonah Ioan Buliga, Manastirea
Jacul Romanesc
Ieromonah Leontios, Slobozia, Romania
Hieromonk Mark, Economos
Hieromonk Nicolas (Vera) Parish Priest
of the Parish of Saint Andrew and
Saint Nicolas Serbian Patriarchate,
Jeromonah Naum Mirkovic, Proiguman
Manastira Crna Reka Serbija
Hieromonk Nicolás (Vera), Parish Priest
of the Parish of Saint Andrew and
Saint Nicolás, Alicante (Spain),
Serbian Patriarchate
Jeromonah Irinej Ristic, iguman
manastira Bogorodia Brainska,

eparhija rasko prizrenska i kosovsko-
metohijska
Jeromonach Varnava Dimitrijevic,
manastir Crna Reka, eparhija rasko
prizrenskai kosovsko-metohijska
P. Protopresbitero Jorge (Georgios)
Faraj, Sacerdote Ortodoxo del
patriarcado de Antioquia en
Honduras, Centro America
Protopresbyter Roman Cheb, Russia
Siberia, sity Prokopyevsk, Paris
Priest, Sacred Temple of Saint
Nicholas
Pr. Constantin Diboş
Presbyter Sasha Petrovich, parish priest
of St. Nicholas Serbian Orthodox
Church, Omaha, Nebraska, USA
Priest Koniukhov Dimitry
Priest Toderita Rusu, the Ascension of
Lord, Bucharest Romania
Fr. Photios, Spiritual Director, St. James
the Just True Orthodox Center
website, Russian True Orthodox
Church
Pr. Paroh Mihai Solomon, Parohia Sf.
Ilie, Girona, Spania
Protodeacon Basil Alexandrovich
Yakimov, Russian Orthodox Church
Diacono Ignacio Miranda, Catedral
Ortodoxa Antioquena de San Pedro
Sula, Honduras, Centro America
Monah Hariton Vlajic, Manastir
Plocnik, eparhija rasko prizrenska i
kosovskometohijska
Monahia Eufimia, Mănăstirea Sfinţii
Arhangheli, Slobozia, România
Subdeacon Jorge Luiz Slobodaniuk,
Ukrainian Orthodox church in
Brazil (Ecumenical Patriarchate of
Constantinople)

Last update: 15 OCTOBER 2009

"Pope Paul VI of the Roman Catholic Church and bearded Orthodox Patriarch Athenagoras of Constantinople pose during a historic meeting on Jan. 8, 1964, on the Mount of Olives in a part of Jerusalem that was controlled by Jordan at the time. It was the first meeting between leaders of the split church since the East-West Schism of 1054" (From the Associated Press).

PART VII

ANALYSIS OF MAJOR
AND RECENT ERRORS

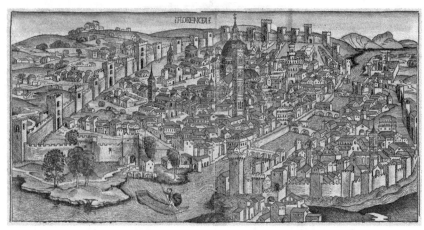

Florence in a 1493 woodcut from Hartmann Schedel's Nuremberg Chronicle

INTRODUCTION

This book demonstrates the Orthodox patristic witness concerning Catholicism and their heresies according to the saints, Fathers, and Councils of the Church. However, from the time of the Great Schism until today there have been many attempts to forge a false union between the Orthodox and the Latins without agreement in Faith, either through false councils or through theological agreements of academic committees intended to lead to such a union without the necessity of repentance and renunciation of heresy. The present section provides examples of such attempted false unions and theological agreements in the past so that the reader will understand that such attempts to unite Orthodoxy with heresy have occurred in the past and will likely continue to be made in the future. To walk according to the teachings of the God-inspired saints and councils of the Church concerning the Latins is essential so that we may arrive with the saints in Paradise and not be numbered among the heretics and apostates that have fallen into deception and abandoned the Orthodox faith for a false "unity".

The 1431-1435 false Council of Florence is presented here as an example of an attempted false union between the Orthodox and the Latins. Examples of more recent theological statements, also presented here, intended to help foster such a future false union include the 1975 Thyateira Confession, the 1993 Balamand Agreement, and the 1999 Orthodox-Catholic Agreed Statement on Baptism and "Sacramental Economy." While these 20th century Agreed Statements are shocking in their rejection of Orthodox patristic teaching, they have not been accepted as authoritative and binding on the Orthodox despite being endorsed by some bishops and synods. Below, these examples of false unions and agreements will be summarized with an introduction, then the texts or relevant excerpts presented, and then followed by Orthodox responses which defended the patristic witness concerning the Latins and their heresies.

A. THE FALSE COUNCIL OF FLORENCE (1431-1445)

The Council of Basel-Ferrara-Florence-Rome from 1431 to 1445 (commonly referred to simply as "The Council of Florence") was a false council convened in the Italian cities of Basel, Ferrara, Florence, and Rome and gathered representatives of the Pope along with those of the different Orthodox Patriarchates who signed the decree below, betraying Holy Orthodoxy, subjugating themselves to the Pope of Rome, and becoming Uniates. Subsequently, during the Orthodox Council of Constantinople in 1484, this entire false council was rejected, including the heretical doctrine of the Filioque, while the theological positions of Saint Photios the Great presented at the Eighth Ecumenical in 879 and the Council of Constantinople in 1282 were upheld. The Council of Florence is considered by the Latins to be their "17th Ecumenical Council." The decree below is just one of the many produced during multiple sessions which were held between 1431-1449 A.D. and demonstrates that the false union was predicated on the acceptance by the Orthodox of heretical Latin teachings concerning the procession of the Holy Spirit (the Filioque), purgatory, and papal primacy.[746]

---

746 "Council of Basel-Ferrara-Florence, 1431-49 A.D," Papal Encyclicals Online, accessed December 10th, 2022, https://www.papalencyclicals.net//councils/ecum17.htm. This online compendium of Papal Encyclicals contains all documented sessions of the heretical Council of Florence.

1. Decrees of Union[747]

*Eugenius, bishop, servant of the servants of God, for an everlasting re-
cord. With the agreement of our most dear son John Palaeologus, illustrious
emperor of the Romans, of the deputies of our venerable brothers the patriarchs and of other representatives of the eastern church, to the following.*

Let the heavens be glad and let the earth rejoice. For, the wall that
divided the western and the eastern church has been removed, peace and
harmony have returned, since the corner-stone, Christ, who made both
one, has joined both sides with a very strong bond of love and peace,
uniting and holding them together in a covenant of everlasting unity.
After a long haze of grief and a dark and unlovely gloom of long-endur-
ing strife, the radiance of hoped-for union has illuminated all.

Let the mother church also rejoice. For she now beholds her sons
hitherto in disagreement returned to unity and peace, and she who hitherto wept at their separation now gives thanks to God with inexpressible
joy at their truly marvellous harmony. Let all the faithful throughout
the world, and those who go by the name of Christian, be glad with the
mother catholic church.

For behold, western and eastern fathers after a very long period of
disagreement and discord, submitting themselves to the perils of sea and
land and having endured labours of all kinds, came together in this holy
ecumenical council, joyful and eager in their desire for this most holy
union and to restore intact the ancient love. In no way have they been
frustrated in their intent. After a long and very toilsome investigation,
at last by the clemency of the holy Spirit they have achieved this greatly
desired and most holy union. Who, then, can adequately thank God for
his gracious gifts? Who would not stand amazed at the riches of such
great divine mercy? Would not even an iron breast be softened by this
immensity of heavenly condescension?

These truly are works of God, not devices of human frailty. Hence,
they are to be accepted with extraordinary veneration and to be fur-

---

747 Council of Florence, "Decrees of Union of the Council of Basel-Ferrara-Florence-
Rome, 1431-1445," in *Creeds & Confessions of the Faith in the Christian Tradition*,
ed. Jaroslav Pelikan & Valerie Hotchkiss (New Haven: Yale University Press,
2003), 751-755.

thered with praises to God. To you praise, to you glory, to you thanks, O Christ, source of mercies, who have bestowed so much good on your spouse the catholic church and have manifested your miracles of mercy in our generation, so that all should proclaim your wonders. Great indeed and divine is the gift that God has bestowed on us. We have seen with our eyes what many before greatly desired yet could not behold.

For when Latins and Greeks came together in this holy synod, they all strove that, among other things, the article about the procession of the holy Spirit should be discussed with the utmost care and assiduous investigation.

Texts were produced from divine scriptures and many authorities of eastern and western holy doctors, some saying the holy Spirit proceeds from the Father and the Son, others saying the procession is from the Father through the Son. All were aiming at the same meaning in different words. The Greeks asserted that when they claim that the holy Spirit proceeds from the Father, they do not intend to exclude the Son; but because it seemed to them that the Latins assert that the holy Spirit proceeds from the Father and the Son as from two principles and two spirations, they refrained from saying that the holy Spirit proceeds from the Father and the Son. The Latins asserted that they say the holy Spirit proceeds from the Father and the Son not with the intention of excluding the Father from being the source and principle of all deity, that is of the Son and of the holy Spirit, nor to imply that the Son does not receive from the Father, because the holy Spirit proceeds from the Son, nor that they posit two principles or two spirations; but they assert that there is only one principle and a single spiration of the holy Spirit, as they have asserted hitherto. Since, then, one and the same meaning resulted from all this, they unanimously agreed and consented to the following holy and God-pleasing union, in the same sense and with one mind.

In the name of the holy Trinity, Father, Son and holy Spirit, we define, with the approval of this holy universal council of Florence, that the following truth of faith shall be believed and accepted by all Christians and thus shall all profess it: that the holy Spirit is eternally from the Father and the Son, and has his essence and his subsistent being from the Father together with the Son, and proceeds from both eternally as from one principle and a single spiration. We declare that when holy doctors and fathers say that the holy Spirit proceeds from the Father through the Son, this bears the sense that thereby also the Son should be signified, according to the Greeks indeed as cause, and according to the Latins as principle of the subsistence of the holy Spirit, just like the Father.

And since the Father gave to his only-begotten Son in begetting him everything the Father has, except to be the Father, so the Son has eternally from the Father, by whom he was eternally begotten, this also, namely that the holy Spirit proceeds from the Son.

We define also that the explanation of those words "and from the Son" was licitly and reasonably added to the creed for the sake of declaring the truth and from imminent need.

Also, the body of Christ is truly confected in both unleavened and leavened wheat bread, and priests should confect the body of Christ in either, that is, each priest according to the custom of his western or eastern church.

Also, if truly penitent people die in the love of God before they have made satisfaction for acts and omissions by worthy fruits of repentance, their souls are cleansed after death by cleansing pains; and the suffrages of the living faithful avail them in giving relief from such pains, that is, sacrifices of masses, prayers, almsgiving and other acts of devotion which have been customarily performed by some of the faithful for others of the faithful in accordance with the church's ordinances.

Also, the souls of those who have incurred no stain of sin whatsoever after baptism, as well as souls who after incurring the stain of sin have been cleansed whether in their bodies or outside their bodies, as was stated above, are straightaway received into heaven and clearly behold the triune God as he is, yet one person more perfectly than another according to the difference of their merits. But the souls of those who depart this life in actual mortal sin, or in original sin alone, go down straightaway to hell to be punished, but with unequal pains.

We also define that the holy apostolic see and the Roman pontiff holds the primacy over the whole world and the Roman pontiff is the successor of blessed Peter prince of the apostles, and that he is the true vicar of Christ, the head of the whole church and the father and teacher of all Christians, and to him was committed in blessed Peter the full power of tending, ruling and governing the whole church, as is contained also in the acts of ecumenical councils and in the sacred canons.

Also, renewing the order of the other patriarchs which has been handed down in the canons, the patriarch of Constantinople should be second after the most holy Roman pontiff, third should be the patriarch of Alexandria, fourth the patriarch of Antioch, and fifth the patriarch of Jerusalem, without prejudice to all their privileges and rights.

2. The Orthodox Response

The Orthodox patristic witness concerning the Council of Florence is found most notably in the words of St. Mark of Ephesus who attended the council, presented the Orthodox teaching in response to claims made by the Latins, and refused to sign the decree of union. See pages 95 and 366 concerning St. Mark of Ephesus and his defense of Orthodoxy against this false union.

For the synodal condemnation of the Council of Florence and vindication of St. Mark of Ephesus, see pages 843 regarding the councils held in Constantinople in 1450 and 1484.

B. THYATEIRA CONFESSION (1975)

Thyateira Confession: The Faith and Prayer of the People of God was a book published by Archbishop Athenagoras (Kokkinakis) of Thyateira and Great Britain (Ecumenical Patriarch 1948-1972) in 1975 with the blessing and authorization of the Synod of the Ecumenical Patriarchate.[748] This volume is a catechetical book produced in six different parts on various subjects with the second part consisting of the teachings of Archbishop Athenagoras and the Ecumenical Patriarchate on the subject of the heterodox. These teachings concerning the Latin Papists are some of the earliest and most egregious examples of anti-canonical and heretical ecumenism being officially endorsed and taught by one of the major Patriarchal Sees of the Holy Orthodox Church. This open betrayal of Holy Orthodoxy so shocked the Orthodox Christian world with its unequivocal teaching of heresy that it prompted a written response in the form of a third-sorrowful epistle from Metropolitan Philaret (Voznesensky) of New York from the Russian Orthodox Church Outside of Russia in December 6/19, 1975.[749] This work written by Archbishop Athenagoras and endorsed by the Ecumenical Patriarchate states that the schism that still exists between the Orthodox Church and the Latin Confession is no longer valid, that the Holy Mysteries such as Unction,

---

748 Archbishop Athenagoras (Kokkinakis), *The Thyateira Confession: The Faith and Prayer of the People of God* (Leighton Buzzard: The Faith Press, 1975), 1-2.

749 Metropolitan Philaret (Voznesensky) of New York, "The Third Sorrowful Epistle: On the Thyateira Confession (December 19, 1975)," in *Metropolitan Philaret of New York: Zealous Confessor for the Faith*, ed. Subdeacon Nektarios Harrison (Florence: Uncut Mountain Press, 2022), 136-142.

Marriage and the Holy Eucharist are open to papists who have not been received into the Orthodox Church, and that it is permissible for Orthodox Christians and papists to pray with each other and for them to use Orthodox Churches for their liturgical services and, in reciprocity, all is permitted for Orthodox Christians as well.

1. Excerpt from the Thyateira Confession: The Roman Catholics[750]

The Roman Catholics since 1054 when the Great Schism occurred, have added to the body of Christian doctrine elements which the Orthodox cannot accept. These additions are as follows:

1. The Sacrament of Chrismation is performed eight or ten years after Baptism. The Orthodox observe that this was not always the practice of the Church because Baptism and Chrismation or Confirmation were performed simultaneously. Perhaps for practical reasons the Roman Catholic Church has separated these two Sacraments. A similar separation of Baptism and Confirmation is also customary in the Anglican Church.

2. In the Mystery of Holy Communion, the Roman Catholics teach that "transubstantiation" takes place. This term taken from Scholastic Philosophy indicates that in every material object there are two things: the essence and the accidents. The essence of an object is not visible while the accidents are the characteristics which are visible. The characteristics are colour, taste, weight, shape, form, extension, etc. But how can we divide an object into essence and characteristics? If we detract from it its weight, colour, taste, extension, what is to remain? This philosophical theory maintains that the essence remains. However, such a thing is a concept only and not a reality.

On this reasoning, if we say that in the Holy Eucharist only the essence of the bread and of the wine is changed, we are in danger of placing

---

750 Archbishop Athenagoras (Kokkinakis), *The Thyateira Confession: The Faith and Prayer of the People of God* (Leighton Buzzard: The Faith Press, 1975), 63-69.

Christ on a non-existing level, because what makes the bread and wine are the characteristics that are experienced in their tastes, etc. When, therefore, in the Eucharist, it is said that only the essence is changed, the characteristics remaining unaffected, what then is the result? Is there not the danger of equating Christ with an abstract meaning and not with a reality, for the real things are the characteristics that exist, and these are said to remain unchanged while the non-existent essence alone is changed.

It is in fact, however, that the Roman Catholic Christians as the Orthodox do worship Christ in the Eucharist. They are not to be reproached simply because teachers and theologians of the Middle Ages being influenced by ancient philosophical theories and in trying to explain what is happening, have employed the term "transubstantiation." For the Christian the true interpretation is that we receive in the Eucharist the Very Body and the Very Blood of Christ. This is what Christ meant when He said: "This is My Body... This is My Blood."

The "transubstantiation theory" introduced by theologians became the foundation of the difference concerning the Holy Eucharist between Eastern and Western Christians. It is however enough for both to say that what we receive is the True Body and Blood of Christ. After the Prayer which the Priest and the people have offered (epiklesis), the Bread and the Wine both as essence and characteristics are changed by the operation of the Holy Spirit into Christ the God-Man, the Saviour of the world.

3.   Another point of disagreement is Purgatory, the place of fire where according to Roman Catholic teaching the souls of the dead are directed for their purification from venial or forgivable sins. This theory is not accepted by the Orthodox as it is not found either in the Holy Scriptures or in the teachings of the early Church and its Ecumenical Councils. This fact is recognised by the authors of the New Catechism of the Roman Catholic Church published by the Bishops of Holland. The Orthodox Christians believe that the souls of the dead receive a taste of what they will experience at the Last Judgement. This pre-taste is analogous with their faith and love and the fervour of the prayers offered privately and in

the Church on their behalf whenever memorial services are conducted.

It would be proper perhaps to add a few words in reference to the power of the Bishops of the Roman Catholic Church and especially of the Pope of Rome regarding the privilege to use the acts of supererogation — acta supererogandia — of the Saints and of the Virgin Mary and the Blood of Christ upon the Cross for the remission of the souls and their quick passage through Purgatory.

This power is unknown to the Church and the super-virtuous works of the Saints and of the Virgin Mary are not to be considered as constructing a spiritual bank out of which the Church through its Bishops may withdraw capital to pay the debts of others. For this reason, the Orthodox Church disagrees with such an idea which as it seems gives way to the usage of indulgences — a fact which hurt the Church everywhere — and this because it gave an opportunity to the atheistically-minded to mock the Church.

4. Another question which Orthodox and Roman Catholic Christians debate upon refers to the person of the All-Holy Mother of Christ, Mary Ever-Virgin. Roman Catholics since 1854 believe and teach that the Virgin Mary was born without the stigma or the guilt of original sin, the sin of Adam and Eve. The Orthodox hesitate to accept this new dogma and observe that though the Roman Catholic Christians love and honour and revere sincerely the Mother of Christ, with this new dogma they minimise or lessen the saving Mission of Christ, who came to save all. Before His coming, according to the Bible, none was born free of guilt and sin. For this reason, the Orthodox teach that St. Mary was born as all human beings are born and that She was cleansed at the Incarnation when the Holy Spirit overshadowed Her and when She received the Gospel in the Greeting: "Hail, Mary full of Grace the Lord is with thee."

At this point it is perhaps necessary to say something in reference to the pronouncement of new dogmas. The Church in its wisdom was always hesitant in defining dogmas, that is, infallible doctrines. The dogmas as such are binding and those who are unable for various reasons to accept them endanger their status in the Church, which means their membership in the Body of Christ. This is equivalent to forfeiting their salvation. For this reason, the Church since the beginning with great care and wisdom promulgated and defined dogmas which were always based upon the revealed teachings of Christ that are included in the New Testament.

For example, the new dogma of the Roman Catholic Church concerning the Assumption of the Virgin Mary is something which the Orthodox Church celebrates and believes but which it has never declared as a dogma and this because the Church does not want to endanger the salvation of those Christians who would find difficulty in accepting it. Generally speaking, Orthodox Christians do not adhere to the idea that there are unknown dogmas which the Church may find and promulgate because Christ Himself has revealed and His Church has already interpreted by the assistance of the Holy Spirit the totality of the saving Truth.

5.   Another problem which Orthodox and Roman Catholics debate upon at length is the position of the Bishop of Rome in the Church. The Pope of Rome has been declared by the First Council of the Vatican during the Nineteenth Century as infallible when he interprets the Christian Faith and Christian Morals. The Orthodox believe that only the Church is infallible when at an Ecumenical Council it defines and interprets the Christian Faith through the Bishops who seek the assistance of the Holy Spirit. Such an infallible doctrine is the Creed which the Bishops of the First and Second Ecumenical Councils issued in their efforts to define the Faith of the Church.

With this question the Primacy of the Pope is connected. According to history the Bishop of Rome little by little through the centuries exercised rights which even today he seems to practise, and which are unknown in the life of the early Church. For example, the Pope is considered as the Bishop of the Catholic Church. This prerogative means that he is the Bishop of the Bishops of the Church. This is something unknown in the history of the Church as no Apostle was considered as the Apostle of the Apostles. The Bishops as successors of the Apostles are equal among themselves. St. Peter was the representative of the Apostles so every Bishop being a successor of the Apostles is also a successor of St. Peter.

This distinction of Bishops into Pope and Patriarchs and Archbishops was made for practical reasons. Their dignity has no foundation in the Christian Revelation; it is not a revealed truth. It is necessary to have a presiding Bishop. This honour was at first accorded to the Bishop of Rome and then to the Bishop of Constantinople, not because they were successors of the two Brother-Apostles, Peter and Andrew, but because of the fact that Rome first and later Constantinople were the capital cities of the Roman Empire. Also, it is a fact that Rome besides its political significance was the only Apostolic See in the West and the place where St. Peter and St. Paul taught and were martyred.

Today this difficult anomaly appears to be in the process of correction. Wise Popes such as John XXIII and Paul VI regardless of the well-known reactions have tried to free their dignified position from the added prerogatives which had become a cause of friction and separation of the Christian people.

Thus, on account of the wisdom of Pope Paul VI and the inheritance of Pope John XXIII many things have been achieved in the rapprochement of the Churches and the renewal of love among the separated Christians.

We may observe the following:
1. The Schism of A.D. 1054 which has divided the Orthodox and Roman Catholic Churches is no longer valid. It has been erased from the history and life of the two Churches by the mutual agreement and signatures of the Patriarch of Constantinople, Athenagoras I; and the Patriarch of the West, Paul VI., in December A.D. 1967.

2. In the case of mixed Weddings, Roman Catholics and Orthodox Catholics can receive in both Churches the blessing of the Sacrament in order to keep their allegiance to the Church in which they have received the Seal of Christ. However, the directives of Rome (*Motu Proprio*, 1970) oppose this double wedding and blessing.

This attitude is one of the obstacles to unity, and causes many Christians to become disillusioned over founding their family upon the traditions of their Church, and discourages their participation in the Church's work for unity. (*The Orthodox Herald*, Vol. X, Nos. 111-112. Jan.-Feb., London 1974).

3. The Sacrament of Holy Unction is no longer performed only for those who are near to death. Today, any Roman Catholic Christian who desires this Sacrament for the health of his body and soul may receive it.

4. In the Sacrament of the Holy Eucharist, Christians often receive the Body and Blood of Christ, whereas previously only the clergy had the right to receive the Eucharist in Its two Species.

When they are not near a Roman Catholic Church, Roman Catholics are permitted to receive the Holy Communion in Orthodox Churches; and the same is also extended to Orthodox when they are not near an Orthodox Church.

5. It is now permissible for Orthodox and Roman Catholics to pray together, and for the Orthodox Liturgy to be offered in a Roman Catholic Church. Parallel permission is now granted by some Orthodox Churches for the celebration of the Catholic Mass in Orthodox churches. All these signs of mutual love and respect were not permitted a few years ago.

6. Every two years, a Synod of Bishops takes place in Rome, with the Pope himself presiding over it. This means that the Bishops' equality is recognised, and their participation in the administration of the Church is also emphasised. Thus, an Ecumenical Infallible Synod is gradually replacing the infallible decisions declared by the Pope himself.

7. Friendship, mutual visits, and all the other signs of love and co-operation indicated that the blessed hour is coming for the complete agreement and union of these two churches.

In this blessed moment, it is not to be expected that the Roman Catholics will come and say to the Orthodox Catholics that they have fallen into error, and seek forgiveness; neither will the Orthodox Catholics be expected to submit themselves to the jurisdiction of the Pope, or accept concepts, customs, and practices that are alien to them. The bond of love will guide both Churches in their procedure to meet Christ and keep the common Tradition which was honoured both in the East and in the West from the birth of Christianity until A.D. 1054.

2. The Orthodox Response:
The Third Sorrowful Epistle of Metropolitan
Philaret (Voznesensky) of New York[751]

December 6/19, 1975

AN EPISTLE TO THE PRIMATES
OF THE HOLY CHURCHES OF GOD
AND THE MOST REVEREND ORTHODOX BISHOPS
ON THE THYATEIRA CONFESSION

"BUT THOUGH WE, or an angel from Heaven, preach any other Gospel unto you than that which we have preached unto you, let him be accursed" (Galatians 1:8). With such firmness did St. Paul teach us to maintain the Orthodox Faith which had been delivered unto us. To his disciple Timothy he wrote, "But continue thou in the things which thou hast learned and hast been assured of, knowing of whom thou hast learned them" (2 Timothy 3:14). This is the instruction which should be followed by every Bishop of the Orthodox Church, which indeed he is obliged to keep according to the oath sworn at his consecration. The Apostle describes a Bishop as "holding fast the faithful word as he hath been taught, that he may be able by sound doctrine both to exhort and to convince gainsayers" (Titus 1:9).

In these days of vacillation, confusion of thought and corruption, we confess the true teaching of the Church regardless of the opinions held by those who might hear us and disregarding the skepticism and

---

751 Metropolitan Philaret (Voznesensky) of New York, "On the Thyateira Confession," *Orthodox Life 26*, no.2 (March-April 1976): 21-25.

faithlessness of our environment. If, for the sake of conforming to the errors of the times, we would suppress the truth or yet profess distorted doctrines to please the world, we would in fact be offering stones instead of bread. And the higher the position of one who would act in this way, the more profound the temptation and the more serious the consequences. It was for this reason that we felt great sorrow when we read the "Thyateira Confession" which was recently published in Europe with the blessing and authorization of the Patriarch and the Holy Synod of the Church of Constantinople.

We know that the author of this book, the Most Reverend Metropolitan Athenagoras of Thyateira, had in former times acted as a guardian of the Orthodox Faith. Therefore least of all did we expect from him a Confession of Faith which would be so far from Orthodoxy! Yet if it were only his own personal statement, we would write nothing about it. We are, however, forced to comment because this work bears the seal of approval of the Church of Constantinople in the persons of Patriarch Demetrios and the Synod of that Church. In a special letter addressed to Metropolitan Athenagoras by Patriarch Demetrios, it is stated that this work has been examined by a special Synodical Committee. After approval by that Committee, the Patriarch, in accordance with the decision of the Synod, extended his blessing for the publication of this, as he describes it, "excellent work." Therefore the responsibility for this work is transferred from Metropolitan Athenagoras alone to the entire hierarchy of the Church of Constantinople.

In our former "Sorrowful Epistles" we have already expressed the grief that we feel when from the See of St. John Chrysostom, Saints Proclos, Tarasios and Photios, the See of Fathers and Confessors of our Faith, we hear expressed doctrines which without doubt they would have anathematized. We are heart-struck as we write these words. How much would we rather hear the true doctrine of the Church expressed in the spirit of the blessed and great Hierarchs of the See of the Church of Constantinople which gave birth to our Russian Church! With what joy would we accept such a declaration and transmit it for the instruction of our pious flock! And conversely, how grieved we are when we are obliged to warn our people that from this former fountain of pure Orthodox confession, there now flow the putrid streams of error.

When we turn to the Thyateira Confession itself, alas, in it we find so many un-Orthodox thoughts and contradictions that to deal with all of them would require us to write volumes. But this is not necessary, for it is sufficient to point out the basis upon which all the un-Orthodoxy of the Confession is founded. On page 60, Metropolitan Athenagoras justly says that the Orthodox people believe that their Church is the One, Holy, Catholic and Apostolic Church, and that She teaches the true fullness of the Catholic Faith. He also recognizes that the other bodies have failed to maintain this fullness. But further on, he forgets that if a doctrine in some way deviates from the truth, it becomes in this regard false. By belonging to a religious association which professes this doctrine, one is already separated from the true Church. Metropolitan Athenagoras is prepared to accept this position in regard to some ancient heretics such as the Arians, but when he addresses contemporary heresies, he is not so inclined. In regard to them, he wishes to be guided not by the ancient Tradition, not by Sacred Canons, but by a "new understanding which prevails today among Christians" (p. 12), and by "the signs of our time" (p. 11).

But is this in agreement with the teachings of the Holy Fathers? Let us recall the first canon of the Seventh Ecumenical Council which gives us a very different criterion for the direction of our thoughts and for the regulation of the life of the Church. "For those who have been allotted the sacerdotal dignity, the representations of canonical ordinances amount to testimonies and directions." And further, "we welcome and embrace the divine canons, and we corroborate the entire and rigid fiat of them that have been set forth by renowned Apostles, who are the trumpets of the Holy Spirit, and those of the six holy Ecumenical Councils and of those of our Holy Fathers. For all those men, having been guided by the light dawning out of the same Spirit, prescribed rules that are in our best interest." But setting aside this principle, the Thyateira Confession constantly emphasizes the "new understanding." "Christian people," we read there, "now visit churches and pray with other Christians of various traditions with whom they were forbidden in the past to associate, for they were called heretics" (p. 12).

But what was it in the past which forbade such prayers? Was it not Holy Scripture, the Holy Fathers and the Ecumenical Councils? Are we perhaps speaking of those who were only called heretics but were not such in reality? Yet the first canon of St. Basil the Great gives a clear definition of those who are heretics, "Heresies is the name applied (by the Holy Fathers) to those who have broken entirely and have become alienated from the Faith itself." Does this not apply to those Western confessions which have fallen away from the Orthodox Church?

St. Paul teaches us, "A man that is a heretic, after the first and second admonition, reject" (Titus 3:10). But the Thyateira Confession would have us draw together with them and enter into communion of prayer. The 45th Canon of the Holy Apostles orders us, "Let any Bishop or Presbyter or Deacon that merely joins in prayer with heretics be suspended." We find the same injunction in the 65th Apostolic Canon and in the 33rd Canon of the Council of Laodicea. The 52nd Canon of the latter forbids us to accept even the blessing of a heretic. The Thyateira Confession, on the contrary, urges us to common prayer with them and goes so far as to permit the Orthodox to receive communion from them and to offer it to them!

Metropolitan Athenagoras himself informs us that among the Anglicans, many of their Bishops and laity accept neither the special grace of the priesthood, nor the infallibility of the decisions of the Ecumenical Councils, nor the Eucharistic Reality of the Holy Gifts in the Divine Liturgy, nor most of the other Mysteries, nor the veneration of the holy relics of saints. The author mentions the actual articles of their faith in which these views are expressed; yet putting all this aside, he finds it permissible for the Orthodox to receive communion from Anglicans and Roman Catholics and he finds it possible to administer communion to them in an Orthodox Church. And what is the foundation of such a practice? The teachings of the Holy Fathers? The canons? No. The grounds for such actions is the fact that such lawlessness has already occurred previously. And there exists "friendship" between Orthodox and Anglicans.

Yet, whatever might be the office of a person who commits a forbidden act, and whatever "friendship" might have served as the incentive, neither can serve as a justification for a practice which violates the Canons. What answer will justify a Bishop before the dread Throne of the Heavenly Judge when he must explain why he advised his spiritual children to accept, instead of True Communion, something which even those who give it do not believe that it is the very Flesh and Blood of Christ?

Such lawless actions ensue from the absolutely heretical, protestant or, in modern terminology, ecumenical doctrine of the Thyateira Confession in regard to the Holy Church. The Church is seen as without limits. "The Holy Spirit," we read there, "is active both within the Church and outside the Church. For this reason its limits are ever extended and its bounds are nowhere. The Church has a door but no walls" (p. 77). But if the Holy Spirit acts equally within the Church and outside Her, why, may we ask, was it necessary for our Savior to come to earth and establish Her? If we accept this doctrine of the Church, the legacy left us by our Lord, the Apostles and the Holy Fathers enjoining us to keep and confess true doctrine become unnecessary. Although the Confession says on page 60 "that the Orthodox Church can rightly claim at this moment of history to be the one true Church that Christ the Son of God founded upon earth," it does not see any need to keep the Faith of this Church unaltered thereby permitting the coexistence of truth and error.

In direct contradiction to the words of the Apostle that Christ presented Her to Himself "a glorious Church, not having spot, or wrinkle, or any such thing" (Ephesians 5:27); the Thyateira Confession presents the Church as combining the truth with what this confession recognizes as a deviation from it, in other words a heresy, though it refrains from using that description in this instance. The refutation of such a teaching is clearly expressed in the well-known Epistle of the Eastern Patriarchs (1848) concerning the Orthodox Faith, "We confess with no doubts, as a firm truth, that the Catholic Church cannot make mistakes or fall into error and express lies instead of truth; because the Holy Spirit, always acting through truly serving Fathers and Doctors of the Church, preserves Her from any error" (Article 12).

In submitting to the novel dogma of conforming and compromising with modern trends, the author of the Thyateira Confession seems to forget the Lord's command that if thy brother "neglect to hear the Church, let him be unto thee as a heathen man and a publican" (Matthew 8:17), and a similar instruction of the Apostle, "A man that is a heretic, after the first and second admonition, reject" (Titus 3:10). It is therefore with much grief that we must declare that in this Thyateira Confession, which comes to us from the Church of Constantinople, we hear not the voice of Orthodox Truth, but the voice of the ever-spreading heresy of Ecumenism. But what will follow on the part of those "whom the Holy Spirit hath made overseers, to feed the Church of God, which he hath purchased with His own Blood" (Acts 20:28)? Will this false doctrine, proclaimed officially in the name of the entire Church of Constantinople, be left with no protests on the part of the Bishops of the Churches of God? Will the Truth be betrayed by this very silence, in the words of St. Gregory the Theologian, by all?

Being the least of the Primates of the Churches, we would have rejoiced to have heard the voices of our Elders before we ourselves spoke out. But, alas, we have heard nothing. If it should be that they have not yet familiarized themselves with the content of this Confession, we ask that they do so without delay, so that it will not escape their condemnation. It is terrible to think that the words of the Lord addressed to the Angel of the Church of the Laodiceans might be applied to us, "I know thy works, that thou art neither cold or hot I would thou wert cold or hot. So then because thou art lukewarm, and neither cold nor hot, I will spew thee out of my mouth" (Apocalypse 3:15-16).

We now warn our flock and we appeal to our brothers, to their belief in the Church and to their understanding of our mutual responsibility for our flock to the Heavenly Archpastor. We beg them not to disregard the information that we herewith furnish them, thereby allowing the deliberate falsification of Orthodox Doctrine to remain covered and unconvicted, for the widespread propagation of this untruth has prompted us to make our sorrow known to the whole Church; we pray that our lament will be heard.

+ Metropolitan Philaret
Feast of St. Nicholas

C. THE BALAMAND
AGREEMENT (1993)

The Balamand Agreement: The Joint International Commission for the Theological Dialogue Between the Roman Catholic Church and the Orthodox Church, Seventh Plenary Session in 1993, titled as, *"Uniatism, Method of Union of the Past, and the Present Search for Full Communion"* was an event attended by nine Orthodox jurisdictions including Constantinople, Alexandria, Antioch, Russia, Romania, Cyprus, Poland, Albania, and Finland. The goal of this session was the overturning of Patristic Orthodox ecclesiology to help foster a false union between the Orthodox and the Latins. The joint statement sought:

1. Full ecclesiological recognition for herself, on the part of the Orthodox, as a "Sister Church"

2. Recognition on the part of the Orthodox of the right of the Uniate communities to exist

3. The maintenance in force of the decrees of the Second Vatican Council concerning the 'Eastern Churches;' or rather, to be precise, a passing beyond the limits of those decrees.[752]

In succinct terms this text approved by both Orthodox and Papist representatives in attendance served to give them recognition as "Sis-

---

752 Center for Traditionalist Orthodox Studies, *The Balamand Union: A Victory of Vatican Diplomacy*, trans. Holy Monastery Cyprian and Justina (Etna: St. Gregory Palamas Monastery, 1993), 4-5.

ter Churches" [to include the Uniates] without solving any theological divisions which are at the heart of the papist schism from the Eastern Orthodox Church, and created a mutual recognition of the "apostolic faith, participation in the same sacraments, [...] one priesthood celebrating the one sacrifice of Christ, the apostolic succession of bishops [that] cannot be considered the exclusive property of one of our Churches" thereby renouncing Orthodoxy's ecclesiological and soteriological exclusivity as the One Church of Christ.[753] This joint statement signed by representatives of nine Orthodox Churches represents one of the most historically significant betrayals of Orthodox patristic teaching by representatives of the Orthodox Church in the Ecumenical Movement. An Orthodox response to this false agreement was formulated by the respected professor of theology Fr. John Romanides.

1. Text: The Balamand Agreement[754]

JOINT INTERNATIONAL COMMISSION FOR THE THEOLOGICAL DIALOGUE BETWEEN THE ROMAN CATHOLIC CHURCH AND THE ORTHODOX CHURCH:

SEVENTH PLENARY SESSION

Balamand School of Theology (Lebanon) June 17-24, 1993

---

753 "Joint International Commission for the Theological Dialogue Between the Roman Catholic Church and The Orthodox Church: Seventh Plenary Session, Balamand School of Theology," The Vatican Holy See, accessed December 13th, 2022, https://web.archive.org/web/20031223144638/https://www.vatican.va/roman_curia/pontifical_councils/chrstuni/ch_orthodox_docs/rc_pc_chrstuni_doc_19930624_lebanon_en.html

754 "Joint International Commission for the Theological Dialogue Between the Roman Catholic Church and The Orthodox Church: Seventh Plenary Session, Balamand School of Theology," The Vatican Holy See, accessed December 13th, 2022, https://web.archive.org/web/20031223144638/https://www.vatican.va/roman_curia/pontifical_councils/chrstuni/ch_orthodox_docs/rc_pc_chrstuni_doc_19930624_lebanon_en.html

We publish here two items: 1) The Informative Communiqué from the meeting of the seventh plenary session of the joint international commission for theological dialogue between the Catholic Church and the Orthodox Church (Balamand, Lebanon, June 17-24, 1993); 2) the document of the joint dialogue commission on the theme: "Uniatism, method of union of the past, and the present search for full communion."

As with all the results of the joint dialogue commissions, this common document belongs to the responsibility of the Commission itself, until the competent organs of the Catholic Church and of the Orthodox Churches express their judgement in regard to it.

Communiqué

The seventh plenary session of the Joint International Commission for the Theological Dialogue between the Catholic Church and the Orthodox Church took place from June 17th to 24th, 1993, within the magnificent framework of Balamand, close to the monastery dating from the XIIth century and in the buildings of the School of Orthodox Theology "St. John Damascene" and of the new Orthodox University which is in full development. His Beatitude Ignatius IV Hazim by his personal presence was a living sign of the generous and cordial hospitality shown to all the participants by the Greek Orthodox Patriarchate of Antioch.

The Eucharist was celebrated by the Catholic delegation on Saturday afternoon and by the Orthodox delegation on Sunday morning, each ceremony taking place in the historic church of the monastery with the assistance of a great number of faithful. On Monday, June 21st, all the Patriarchs of the territory of Antioch, both Orthodox and Catholic, were guests of His Beatitude Ignatius IV for lunch. An official delegation representing the commission made a courtesy visit to Their Excellencies, the President of the Republic, Mr. Elias Hraoui, and the President of the Parliament, Mr. Nabeh Berri on Tuesday, June 22nd. The entire Commission then toured the historical centre of Beirut, and the members were guests at lunch hosted by the Orthodox Archbishop of the capital.

Representatives of nine autocephalous and autonomous Orthodox Churches were present for this plenary session of the Joint International Commission for dialogue. From the Catholic side, twenty-four members of the Commission took part in the meeting.

The theme of the seventh plenary session was entirely centered on the theological and practical questions presented by the existence and pastoral activity of the Oriental Catholic Churches. The profound changes which have taken place in Central and Eastern Europe, involving the rebirth of religious liberty and the resumption of open pastoral activity by the Oriental Catholic Churches, have made these questions the touchstone of the quality of the relations between the Catholic and the Orthodox Churches.

At Balamand, the Commission had before it a working paper, developed by the coordinating committee of the Commission during its meeting at Ariccia (Rome) in June 1991 which bears the title: "Uniatism, method of union of the past, and the present search for full communion". This text was studied and reworked in common, in a frank and brotherly spirit, accompanied by a deep concern for the continuation of the work of fostering the restoration of full communion between the Orthodox and Catholic Churches.

The text finally adopted at Balamand is composed of two parts: 1) Ecclesiological Principles and 2) Practical Rules. In the spirit of the ecclesiology of communion and because of the fact that the Catholic and Orthodox Churches recognize each other as Sister Churches, it was observed that, in the effort to re-establish unity, what is involved is achieving together the will of Christ for those who are His disciples and the design of God for His Church, by means of a common search for full agreement in faith. It is not a question of seeking the conversion of persons from one Church to the other. This latter type of missionary activity, which has been called "uniatism", cannot be accepted either as a method to follow or as a model for the unity which is being sought by our Churches.

Conscious of the fact that the history of divisions has deeply wounded the memories of the Churches, Catholics and Orthodox are determined to look to the future, with mutual recognition of the necessity for transparent consultation and cooperation at all levels of Church life.

The Joint International Commission for the Theological Dialogue will now submit the document adopted at Balamand to the authorities of the Catholic and Orthodox Churches for approval and application.

Balamand, June 23rd, 1993

TEXT: UNIATISM, METHOD OF UNION OF THE PAST, AND THE PRESENT SEARCH FOR FULL COMMUNION

Introduction

1. At the request of the Orthodox Churches, the normal progression of the theological dialogue with the Catholic Church has been set aside so that immediate attention might be given to the question which is called "uniatism."

2. With regard to the method which has been called "uniatism," it was stated at Freising (June 1990) that "we reject it as method for the search for unity because it is opposed to the common tradition of our Churches."

3. Concerning the Oriental Catholic Churches, it is clear that they, as part of the Catholic Communion, have the right to exist and to act in answer to the spiritual needs of their faithful.

4. The document prepared at Ariccia by the joint coordinating committee (June 1991) and finished at Balamand (June 1993) states what is our method in the present search for full communion, thus giving the reason for excluding "uniatism" as a method.

5. This document is composed of two parts:

    1) Ecclesiological principles and
    2) Practical rules.

Ecclesiological principles

6. The division between the Churches of the East and of the West has never quelled the desire for unity wished by Christ. Rather this situation, which is contrary to the nature of the Church, has often been for many the occasion to become more deeply conscious of the need to achieve this unity, so as to be faithful to the Lord's commandment.

7. In the course of the centuries various attempts were made to re-establish unity. They sought to achieve this end through different

ways, at times conciliar, according to the political, historical, theological and spiritual situation of each period. Unfortunately, none of these efforts succeeded in re-establishing full communion between the Church of the West and the Church of the East, and at times even made oppositions more acute.

8. In the course of the last four centuries, in various parts of the East, initiatives were taken within certain Churches and impelled by outside elements, to restore communion between the Church of the East and the Church of the West. These initiatives led to the union of certain communities with the See of Rome and brought with them, as a consequence, the breaking of communion with their Mother Churches of the East. This took place not without the interference of extraecclesial interests. In this way Oriental Catholic Churches came into being. And so a situation was created which has become a source of conflicts and of suffering in the first instance for the Orthodox but also for Catholics.

9. Whatever may have been the intention and the authenticity of the desire to be faithful to the commandment of Christ: "that all may be one" expressed in these partial unions with the See of Rome, it must be recognized that the reestablishment of unity between the Church of the East and the Church of the West was not achieved, and that the division remains, embittered by these attempts.

10. The situation thus created resulted in fact in tensions and oppositions.

Progressively, in the decades which followed these unions, missionary activity tended to include among its priorities the effort to convert other Christians, individually or in groups, so as "to bring them back" to one's own Church. In order to legitimize this tendency, a source of proselytism, the Catholic Church developed the theological vision according to which she presented herself as the only one to whom salvation was entrusted. As a reaction, the Orthodox Church, in turn, came to accept the same vision according to which only in her could salvation be found. To assure the salvation of "the separated brethren" it even happened that Christians were rebaptized and that certain requirements of the religious freedom of persons and of their act of faith were forgotten. This perspective was one to which that period showed little sensitivity.

11. On the other hand certain civil authorities made attempts to bring back Oriental Catholics to the Church of their Fathers. To achieve this end they did not hesitate, when the occasion was given, to use unacceptable means.

12. Because of the way in which Catholics and Orthodox once again consider each other in their relationship to the mystery of the Church and discover each other once again as Sister Churches, this form of "missionary apostolate" described above, and which has been called "uniatism," can no longer be accepted either as a method to be followed nor as a model of the unity our Churches are seeking.

13. In fact, especially since the pan-Orthodox Conferences and the Second Vatican Council, the re-discovery and the giving again of proper value to the Church as communion, both on the part of Orthodox and of Catholics, has radically altered perspectives and thus attitudes. On each side it is recognized that what Christ has entrusted to his Church — profession of apostolic faith, participation in the same sacraments, above all the one priesthood celebrating the one sacrifice of Christ, the apostolic succession of bishops — cannot be considered the exclusive property of one of our Churches.

14. It is in this perspective that the Catholic Churches and the Orthodox Churches recognize each other as Sister Churches, responsible together for maintaining the Church of God in fidelity to the divine purpose, most especially in what concerns unity. According to the words of Pope John Paul II, the ecumenical endeavour of the Sister Churches of East and West, grounded in dialogue and prayer, is the search for perfect and total communion which is neither absorption nor fusion but a meeting in truth and love (cf. Slavorum Apostoli, n. 27).

15. While the inviolable freedom of persons and their obligation to follow the requirements of their conscience remain secure, in the search for re-establishing unity there is no question of conversion of people from one Church to the other in order to ensure their sal-

vation. There is a question of achieving together the will of Christ for his own and the design of God for his Church by means of a common quest by the Churches for a full accord on the content of the faith and its implications. This effort is being carried on in the current theological dialogue. The present document is a necessary stage in this dialogue.

16. The Oriental Catholic Churches who have desired to re-establish full communion with the See of Rome and have remained faithful to it, have the rights and obligations which are connected with this communion. The principles determining their attitude towards Orthodox Churches are those which have been stated by the Second Vatican Council and have been put into practice by the Popes who have clarified the practical consequences flowing from these principles in various documents published since then. These Churches, then, should be inserted, on both local and universal levels, into the dialogue of love, in mutual respect and reciprocal trust found once again, and enter into the theological dialogue, with all its practical implications.

17. In this atmosphere, the considerations already presented and the practical guidelines which follow, insofar as they will be effectively received and faithfully observed, are such as to lead to a just and definitive solution to the difficulties which these Oriental Catholic Churches present to the Orthodox Church.

18. Towards this end, Pope Paul VI affirmed in his address at the Phanar in July 1967: "It is on the heads of the Churches, of their hierarchy, that the obligation rests to guide the Churches along the way that leads to finding full communion again. They ought to do this by recognizing and respecting each other as pastors of that part of the flock of Christ entrusted to them, by taking care for the cohesion and growth of the people of God, and avoiding everything that could scatter it or cause confusion in its ranks" (Tomos Agapis, n. 172). In this spirit Pope John Paul II and Ecumenical Patriarch Dimitrios I together stated clearly: "We reject every form of proselytism, every attitude which would be or could be perceived to be a lack of respect" (December 7th, 1987).

Practical Rules

19. Mutual respect between the Churches which find themselves in difficult situations will increase appreciably in the measure that they will observe the following practical rules.

20. These rules will not resolve the problems which are worrying us unless each of the parties concerned has a will to pardon, based on the Gospel and, within the context of a constant effort for renewal, accompanied by the unceasing desire to seek the full communion which existed for more than a thousand years between our Churches. It is here that the dialogue of love must be present with a continually renewed intensity and perseverance which alone can overcome reciprocal lack of understanding, and which is the necessary climate for deepening the theological dialogue that will permit arriving at full communion.

21. The first step to take is to put an end to everything that can foment division, contempt and hatred between the Churches. For this the authorities of the Catholic Church will assist the Oriental Catholic Churches and their communities so that they themselves may prepare full communion between Catholic and Orthodox Churches. The authorities of the Orthodox Church will act in a similar manner towards their faithful. In this way it will be possible to take care of the extremely complex situation that has been created in Eastern Europe, at the same time in charity and in justice, both as regards Catholics and Orthodox.

22. Pastoral activity in the Catholic Church, Latin as well as Oriental, no longer aims at having the faithful of one Church pass over to the other; that is to say, it no longer aims at proselytizing among the Orthodox. It aims at answering the spiritual needs of its own faithful and it has no desire for expansion at the expense of the Orthodox Church. Within these perspectives, so that there will be no longer place for mistrust and suspicion, it is necessary that there be reciprocal exchanges of information about various pastoral projects and that thus cooperation between bishops and all those with responsibilities in our Churches, can be set in motion and develop.

23. The history of the relations between the Orthodox Church and the Oriental Catholic Churches has been marked by persecutions and sufferings. Whatever may have been these sufferings and their causes, they do not justify any triumphalism; no one can glorify in them or draw an argument from them to accuse or disparage the other Church. God alone knows his own witnesses. Whatever may have been the past, it must be left to the mercy of God, and all the energies of the Churches should be directed towards obtaining that the present and the future conform better to the will of Christ for his own.

24. It will also be necessary — and this on the part of both Churches — that the bishops and all those with pastoral responsibilities in them scrupulously respect the religious liberty of the faithful. These, in turn, must be able to express freely their opinion by being consulted and by organizing themselves to this end. In fact, religious liberty requires that, particularly in situations of conflict, the faithful are able to express their opinion and to decide without pressure from outside if they wish to be in communion either with the Orthodox Church or with the Catholic Church. Religious freedom would be violated when, under the cover of financial assistance, the faithful of one Church would be attracted to the other by promises, for example, of education and material benefits that may be lacking in their own Church. In this context, it will be necessary that social assistance, as well as every form of philanthropic activity be organized with common agreement so as to avoid creating new suspicions.

25. Furthermore, the necessary respect for Christian freedom — one of the most precious gifts received from Christ — should not become an occasion for undertaking a pastoral project which may also involve the faithful of other Churches, without previous consultation with the pastors of these Churches. Not only should every form of pressure, of any kind whatsoever, be excluded, but respect for consciences, motivated by an authentic exigency of faith, is one of the principles guiding the pastoral concern of those responsible in the two Churches and should be the object of their common reflection (cf. Gal. 5, 13).

26. That is why it is necessary to seek and to engage in an open dialogue, which in the first place should be between those who have responsibilities for the Churches. Those in charge of the communities concerned should create joint local commissions or make effective those which already exist, for finding solutions to concrete problems and seeing that these solutions are applied in truth and love, in justice and peace. If agreement cannot be reached on the local level, the question should be brought to mixed commissions established by higher authorities.

27. Suspicion would disappear more easily if the two parties were to condemn violence wherever communities of one Church use it against communities of a Sister Church. As requested by His Holiness Pope John Paul II in his letter of May 31st, 1991, it is necessary that all violence and every kind of pressure be absolutely avoided in order that freedom of conscience be respected. It is the task of those in charge of communities to assist their faithful to deepen their loyalty towards their own Church and towards its traditions and to teach them to avoid not only violence, be that physical or verbal, but also all that could lead to contempt for other Christians and to a counter-witness, completely ignoring the work of salvation which is reconciliation in Christ.

28. Faith in sacramental reality implies a respect for the liturgical celebrations of the other Church. The use of violence to occupy a place of worship contradicts this conviction. On the contrary, this conviction sometimes requires that the celebration of other Churches should be made easier by putting at their disposal, by common agreement, one's own church for alternate celebration at different times in the same building. Still more, the evangelical ethos requires that statements or manifestations which are likely to perpetuate a state of conflict and hinder the dialogue be avoided. Does not St. Paul exhort us to welcome one another as Christ has welcomed us, for the glory of God (Rom. 15:7)?

29. Bishops and priests have the duty before God to respect the authority which the Holy Spirit has given to the bishops and priests of the other Church and for that reason to avoid interfering in

the spiritual life of the faithful of that Church. When cooperation becomes necessary for the good of the faithful, it is then required that those responsible to an agreement among themselves,
establish for this mutual assistance clear principles which are
known to all, and act subsequently with frankness, clarity, and
with respect for the sacramental discipline of the other Church.

In this context, to avoid all misunderstanding and to develop confidence between the two Churches, it is necessary that Catholic and
Orthodox bishops of the same territory consult with each other
before establishing Catholic pastoral projects which imply the creation of new structures in regions which traditionally form part of
the jurisdiction of the Orthodox Church, in view to avoid parallel
pastoral activities which would risk rapidly degenerating into rivalry
or even conflicts.

30. To pave the way for future relations between the two Churches,
passing beyond the outdated ecclesiology of return to the Catholic
Church connected with the problem, which is the object of this document, special attention will be given to the preparation of future
priests and of all those who, in any way, are involved in an apostolic
activity carried on in a place where the other Church traditionally
has its roots. Their education should be objectively positive with respect of the other Church. First of all, everyone should be informed
of the apostolic succession of the other Church and the authenticity
of its sacramental life. One should also offer all a correct and comprehensive knowledge of history aiming at a historiography of the
two Churches which is in agreement and even may be common. In
this way, the dissipation of prejudices will be helped, and the use of
history in a polemical manner will be avoided. This presentation will
lead to an awareness that faults leading to separation belong to both
sides, leaving deep wounds on each side.

31. The admonition of the Apostle Paul to the Corinthians (1 Cor. 6:1-
7) will be recalled. It recommends that Christians resolve their differences through fraternal dialogue, thus avoiding recourse to the
intervention of the civil authorities for a practical solution to the
problems which arise between Churches or local communities. This

applies particularly to the possession or return of ecclesiastical property. These solutions should not be based only on past situations or rely solely on general juridical principles, but they must also take into account the complexity of present realities and local circumstances.

32. It is in this spirit that it will be possible to meet in common the task of re-evangelization of our secularized world. Efforts will also be made to give objective news to the mass-media especially to the religious press, in order to avoid tendentious and misleading information.

33. It is necessary that the Churches come together in order to express gratitude and respect towards all, known and unknown — bishops, priests or faithful, Orthodox, Catholic whether Oriental or Latin — who suffered, confessed their faith, witnessed their fidelity to the Church, and, in general, towards all Christians, without discrimination, who underwent persecutions. Their sufferings call us to unity and, on our part, to give common witness in response to the prayer of Christ "that all may be one, so that the world may believe" (John 17, 21).

34. The International Joint Commission for Theological Dialogue between the Catholic Church and the Orthodox Church, at its plenary meeting in Balamand, strongly recommends that these practical rules be put into practice by our Churches, including the Oriental Catholic Churches who are called to take part in this dialogue which should be carried on in the serene atmosphere necessary for its progress, towards the re-establishment of full communion.

35. By excluding for the future all proselytism and all desire for expansion by Catholics at the expense of the Orthodox Church, the commission hopes that it has overcome the obstacles which impelled certain autocephalous Churches to suspend their participation in the theological dialogue and that the Orthodox Church will be able to find itself altogether again for continuing the theological work already so happily begun.

Balamand (Lebanon), June 23rd, 1993

The Thirteen Orthodox Members of the Joint International Commission on Orthodox-Catholic Dialogue who, as representatives of only nine Orthodox Churches, signed the "Balamand Union":[755]

1. **Patriarchate of Constantinople:** Archbishop Stylianos of Australia.
2. **Patriarchate of Alexandria:** Metropolitan Dionysios of Nubia, Professor Constantine Patelos.
3. **Patriarchate of Antioch:** Metropolitan Georges (Khodre) of Byblos, Archimandrite Youhanna.
4. **Patriarchate of Moscow:** Igumen Nestor (Iliayev).
5. **Patriarchate of Romania:** Metropolitan Antonie of Transylvania, Professor Dumitru Radu.
6. **Church of Cyprus:** Metropolitan Chrysanthos of Morphou, Professor Makarios Papachristophorou.
7. **Church of Poland:** Hieromonk Varsanufy (Doroszkiewicz).
8. **Church of Albania:** Professor Theodore Papapavli.
9. **Church of Finland:** Bishop Ambrose of Joensuu.

2. Orthodox Response: A Critique of the Balamand Agreement by Fr. John Romanides[756]

I. INTRODUCTION

1. Representatives of nine Orthodox Churches signed an agreement with representatives of the Vatican contained in a document entitled, "Uniatism, method of union of the past, and the present search for full communion." This was produced by members of the Orthodox-Vatican Dialogue at their VIIth Plenary Session 17-24 June 1993 at Balamand, Lebanon.

---

755 Center for Traditionalist Orthodox Studies, *The Balamand Union: A Victory of Vatican Diplomacy*, trans. Holy Monastery Cyprian and Justina (Etna: St Gregory Palamas Monastery, 1993), 28.

756 Fr. John Romanides, "A Critique of the Balamand Agreement," *Theologia*, Vol. VI, no. 4 (1993): 570-580. Quoted in http://orthodoxinfo.com/ecumenism/frjr_balamand.aspx. Footnotes in the text are from the source.

2. Six Orthodox Churches did not send representatives. Some boycotted this meeting in protest against the Vatican's anti-Orthodox and anti-Moslem responsibilities for the war in Bosnia, and other anti-Orthodox actions in parts of Eastern Europe and the Middle East. Some Orthodox Churches have come to realize the Vatican's centuries old "pattern" or "tactic" of "simultaneous war and dialogue" which it had transformed in the 1960s into "simultaneous attacks of Love and dialogue in public" and "underhanded activities in private."

3. The classic example of this earlier tactic was the dialogue between the Franco-Latins and the Roman Orthodox at Bari, Italy, in 1098. The Franco-Latins had just completed the expulsion of the Roman Orthodox from the Papacy in 1009/12-1046. This was followed up by William the Conqueror's capture of England in 1066 and by his appointment of the Lombard Lanfranc as the first Franco-Latin Archbishop of Canterbury with the blessings of the Lombard Pope Alexander II in 1070. Lanfranc and his Franco-Latin bishops got their apostolic succession by dismissing all their Celtic and Saxon predecessors *en masse*[757]. They condemned them as heretics and schismatics and sentenced them to prison for life where they were tortured and starved to death[758]. Lanfranc's successor in 1093 was the Lombard Anselm of Canterbury who was the chief exponent of the Franco-Latin positions at the above mentioned 1098 dialogue meeting at Bari.

4. No longer able to use this type of medieval military power, which it was still using openly up to the French Revolution, the Vatican learned by the middle of this century to attack in public by means of "love and dialogue" and "underhanded activities in reality." Thus the

---

757 For documented sources of the details of the murder of the Celtic and Saxon Bishops and abbots and their replacement by nobles from the Frankish realms of Francia, i.e. Gallia, Germania and Italia see Auguste Thierry, "Histoire de la Conqute de l'Angleterre par les Normands," Paris 1843, vol. 2. pp. 147 (1071-1072), 215-219 (1075-1076), 284, 313-314, 318 (1087-1094);vol. 3, pp. 35 (1110-1138), 214-215 (1203).

758 Ibid., vol. 2, pp.55, 66 (1068), 111, 145, 184 (1070-1072),215 (1075-1076), 240-242 (1082), 313-316 (1088-1089); vol. 3, pp. 35, 44, 47 (1110-1140). See also J. S. Romanides, "Church Synods and Civilization," in *Theologia*, Athens, vol. 63, issue 3, 1992,p. 427-428.

sincerity of the Vatican's public "love" and "dialogue," imposed upon it by the modern spread of democracy, is in need of much more substantiation to become convincing. Even the Bosnian Moslems have learned this by tragic experience after their prayer session with the Pope himself.

II. THE SO-CALLED SCHISM[759]

5. Behind this agreement are Latin specialists familiar with modern research on the military, political and social nature of the schism with the East Romans which the Franks and their allies deliberately provoked. Doctrine played the role of the chief Franco-Latin weapon against the East Romans who had provoked revolts among the West Romans against Teutonic oppression.[760] Of course the Balamand Latins had no need to touch upon this kind of research.

6. Ignoring the above, the Orthodox at Balamand accommodated the Latins by joining them in using the context of medieval Franco-Latin propaganda about the schism with a more or less Orthodox content, a combination which had been dominating Orthodox schools for a long time.

7. This agreement thus avoids the implications of the fact that since the 7th century the Franco-Latins usually received their apostolic succession by exterminating their West Roman, Celtic and Saxon predecessors having reduced the West Romans to serfs and villeins of Frankish Feudalism. This happened not only in Gaul, but also in North Italy, Germany, England, South Italy, Spain and Portugal.

8. The birth of Frankish Civilization is described in a letter of St. Boniface to Pope Zacharias (natione Graecus[761]) in 741. The Franks had rid the Church in Francia of all Roman bishops by 661 and had made themselves its bishops and clerical administrators. They had divided up the Church's property into fiefs which had been doled out as benefices according to rank within the pyramid of military

---

759 In addition to the work mentioned in note 1 see J. S. Romanides, "Franks, Romans, Feudalism and Doctrine: An Interplay Between Theology and Society," (Brookline: Holy Cross Orthodox Press, 1982)

760 Ibid., pp. 11-14.

761 I.e., a native of the Roman province Magna Graecia in Southern Italy

vassalage. These Frankish bishops had no Archbishop and had not met in Synod for eighty years. They had been meeting as army officers with their fellow war-lords. They are, in the words of St. Boniface, "voracious laymen, adulterous clergy and drunkards, who fight in the army fully armed and who with their own hands kill both Christians and pagans."[762]

9. Already in 794 and 809 the Franks had condemned the East Romans as "heretics" and "Greeks," at the councils of Frankfurt and Aachen, in other words some 260 years before the so-called schism of 1054. The Franks had begun calling the East Romans by the names "Greeks" and "heretics" in order that the enslaved West Romans may gradually forget their fellow-Romans in the East.

10. The Franks then also split the Greek speaking and Latin speaking Roman Fathers into so-called Latin and Greek Fathers and attached themselves to the so-called Latin ones. They thus created the illusion that their Franco-Latin tradition is part of an unbroken and continuous tradition with the Latin speaking Roman Fathers. Because the enslaved West Romans had become the serfs and villeins of Franco-Latin feudalism they stopped producing Church leaders and Fathers and all but a few recorded saints.

11. During 1009-1046 the Franco-Latins completed their expulsion of the Orthodox Romans from the Church of Old Rome and finally replaced them with themselves, thus inventing today's Papacy.

12. The 8th century Franks began their anti-Roman heresy hunting on the questions of Icons and the *Filioque* when they were illiterate barbarians. The then Roman popes protested. But they did not yet condemn the Franks. They imagined that they would eventually prevail upon the Franks like one does with stubborn children. Little did the Romans of Old and New Rome suspect that the Franks were deliberately provoking the schism between themselves and the free Romans as part of their permanent defensive strategy against the East Roman Empire and their own plans for world dominion.

13. The Roman popes had no choice but to tolerate Frankish tyranny in the interest of alleviating their enslaved fellow West Romans and of

---

762 Migne P L, 89, 744; Mansi 12, 313-314.

guaranteeing their own freedom and that of the Roman citizens of the Papal States.

14. But Roman Pope John VIII took part in the 8th Ecumenical Council of 879 in New Rome which condemned the Frankish heresies on icons and the Filioque, without however naming the heretics for fear of reprisals.[763]

15. With the appearance of the Pseudo-Isidorian Decretals by 850 the Roman Popes began to feel strong enough to aggressively demand that the Frankish leadership accept civilized standards of behavior. But these efforts finally backfired. The Franco-Latins reacted forcefully to the popularity of these Decretals by expelling the Romans from their political and Church leadership in Rome and the Papal States. The Franco-Latins began their final attack on the freedom and Romanity of the Papacy in 973-1003 and completed the subjugation of the Roman Papacy and the freedom of the Papal States between 1009 and 1046.[764] Thereafter the Popes are all members of the Franco-Latin nobility who use the name Roman Pope and Roman Papacy in order that the West Romans may continue to believe that they still had a Roman Pope.

16. From all the above it should be clear that the fixing of the date of the schism in 1054, within the fabricated distinction between "Greek East" and "Latin West," is not correct. The schism was between the Franco-Latins and the West and East Romans. 1054 was only one of the later manifestations of a schism which had already existed from the time the Franks decided in 794 to provoke the schism with the so-called "Greeks" for political reasons. The Church of Old Rome fought heroically to remain united to New Rome up to 1009.

17. From 809 onward the Franks never deviated from their position that the East Romans, i.e. their Greeks, are heretics. Up to 1009 the Church of Old Rome vigorously resisted this deliberate Frankish policy which was finally imposed by force.

---

763 J. S. Romanides, "Franks, Romans, Feudalism and Doctrine," 19-20.

764 Ibid., 20-38.

18. That this tradition continued into the middle of the 20th century was so evident during this writer's youth. In Latin books on Apologetics the Orthodox were vehemently described as heretics and without saints. Evidently this was due to the *Filioque* controversy which broke out in earnest prior to the Eight Ecumenical Council of 879. So supposedly the Orthodox had no Fathers of the Church after St. John of Damascus (circa 675-749) and St. Theodore of Studium (759-826).[765]

19. But the Franco-Latins and their Papacy continued their conquests accompanied by the extermination and/or expulsion of the Orthodox bishops and abbots and the reduction of the faithful to the status of serfs and villeins by completely taking over their properties. This the Moslem conquerors, neither Arab nor Turk, never did.

20. But even up to early part of this 20th century the Vatican was still doing its thing. In 1923 Italy took possession of the Dodecanese (The Twelve) Islands from Turkey. The Orthodox bishops were replaced by Tuscano-Frank and Lombard bishops, who since 1870 were posing as Italians. The Vatican hoped that the Orthodox faithful would accept clergy ordained by these Vatican bishops or else be left without sacraments. The situation changed when Greece took possession of these Islands. The exiled Orthodox bishops returned under the oversight of the Orthodox Patriarchate of Constantinople.

21. But then the Vatican made an about face and produced Vatican II's unilateral recognition of Orthodox sacraments. The question remains: Is this transformation from War to Love real? Or is it still the love of the wolf now dressed up in sheep's clothing out to catch its traditional prey? The Vatican's invasion of Orthodox countries with so many clerics hunting for prey seems to speak for itself.

---

765 See for example, F. Cayr, A. A. *Manual of Patrology and History of Theology* Vol. 2 (English version), (Tournai: Society of St. John the Evangelist, 1940) 314-349. Beginning from p. 351 of Vol. 2 and onward we are told about the Scholastic Successors of the Fathers and then the Great Successors of the Fathers and finally beginning on page 661 we are told about the "General Decadence of Scholasticism."

22. What the Vatican is doctrinally up to will depend on what it will do with all its Ecumenical Councils. At least on the primacy and the infallibility of the pope Vatican II continues to maintain that it is a matter of divine revelation and not of canon law.

III. ECCLESIOLOGY

23. Neither from the 7th century till 1054, nor since, have the Franco-Latin bishops and popes have had the slightest knowledge of, or interest in, the cure of the human personality via the purification and illumination of the heart and glorification (*theosis*). They still have a magical understanding of apostolic succession which many Orthodox have also have been accepting since the so-called reforms of Peter the Great.

24. The Balamand agreement is also based on an interpretation of our Lord's prayer in John 17 which is not part of the Patristic tradition. Christ prays here that His disciples and their disciples may in this life become one in the vision of His glory (which He has by nature from the Father) when they become members of His Body, the Church, which would be formed on Pentecost and whose members were to be the illuminated and glorified in this life. The Old Testament prophets saw in their own glorification the pre-incarnate Lord of Glory. Likewise the disciples had seen Christ's uncreated glory which He has by nature from His Father up to and before Pentecost, but not as members of His Body. Pentecostal glorification (*theosis*) was part of the Old and New Testament Church's becoming the Body of Christ. Thus this final form of glorification constitutes the core of the history of the Body of Christ which is the real core of Church history. Christ's prayer in John 17 is for the fulfillment of His Old and New Testament prophecies, teachings and promises, especially those recorded in John's Gospel and especially in 16:13. This final glorification is what is repeated in the life of each of the saints in history and which can neither be added to nor improved upon, especially since this experience transcends words and concepts, even those of the Bible. This is how the Fathers understand this prayer.

25. This prayer is not for the union of the members of the Body of Christ with those who are not in the states of purification, illumination and glorification (*theosis*). Of course this prayer implies the entry into these states of cure by non-members of the body of Christ, but it is certainly not a prayer for the union of churches. That John 17 can be applied to Churches which have not the slightest understanding of glorification (*theosis*) and how to arrive at this cure in this life is very interesting, to say the least.

26. This agreement takes advantage of those naive Orthodox who have been insisting that they are a "Sister" Church of a Vatican "Sister" Church, as though glorification (*theosis*) can have a sister otherwise than herself. The Orthodox at Balamand fell into their own trap since this presupposes the validity of Latin sacraments. This is a strange phenomenon indeed since the Latins never believed that glorification in this life is the foundation of apostolic succession and the mysteries (sacraments) of and within the Body of Christ. Even today the Latins and the Protestants translate 1 Cor. 12:26 as "honored" instead of "glorified."

27. But Vatican II had also set its trap of unilaterally recognizing Orthodox mysteries (sacraments) into which the Balamand Orthodox fell according to plan.

28. More important than the validity of mysteries is the question of who participates in them. Glorification is God's will for all, both in this life and in the next life. But God's glory in Christ is eternal life for those who are properly cured and prepared. But this same uncreated glory of Christ is eternal fire for those who refuse to be cured. The one group is glorified and the other becomes forever happy in their selfishness like the "*actus purus* god" they believe in. In other words everyone will be saved. Some will be saved by their participation in glorification and in all the Truth. The rest will be saved by knowledge of all the truth which for them will be the vision of Christ's uncreated glory as eternal fire and outer darkness. This is the state of *actus purus* happiness for which they strived for all their lives. In other words mysteries can be valid and not participated in at the same time. Thus, as important as valid mysteries are, one's *partic-*

ipation in these mysteries leading to purification and illumination of the heart, and glorification in this life—the central *reality* of the mysteries—is also essential. This holds true for non-Orthodox and Orthodox equally.

29. It would seem that the Orthodox may legitimately and dutifully wish and hope out of love that Latin and Protestant mysteries are indeed valid and efficacious, but leave the matter in the hands of God. But to pronounce them valid, 1) when the Latins do not accept glorification (*theosis*) in this life as the central core of apostolic tradition and succession and 2) when they believe instead that happiness is one's final end, is indeed strange. One does not need valid mysteries in order to become eternally happy.

30. Franco-Latin official teachings on the mysteries have been historically not only un-Orthodox, but anti-Orthodox. On this most Protestants agree in principle with the Orthodox, i.e. that communicated saving grace is uncreated. The Latin heresy that communicated grace is created has not yet been rejected by the Vatican.

IV. THE RAISON D'ETRE OF UNIATISM CEASES TO EXIST

31. The representatives of the Vatican proposed this captioned position and the Orthodox at Balamand accepted it. However, the Orthodox at Balamand were supposedly specialists who knew that this proposal was made within the context of both the Latin dogma about the pope and officially also within the context of all the Vatican's Ecumenical Councils. But an Orthodox position on this question is not evident from this agreement. Therefore, the impression is created that the Orthodox, at least implicitly, accepted the Latin dogma about the pope and that of all the Vatican's Ecumenical Councils.

32. At the time of Vatican II the *New York Times* had announced on its title page that the schism between the Orthodox and the Vatican had supposedly ended. This was due to the fact that the Latins understood the lifting of the anathemas of 1054 as a lifting of the excommunication. Constantinople lifted, as it seems, only anathemas. For the Latins this was in keeping with Vatican II on the validity of Orthodox mysteries. This made it possible for Latins to take com-

munion at Orthodox Churches and, according to the Latins, vice versa. The Orthodox had difficulties refusing communion to Latins and the Vatican temporarily suspended the practice.

33. This Balamand agreement has been accepted by the representatives of nine out of 14 Orthodox Churches but not yet by their Synods nor by a Pan-Orthodox Council. In the meantime the Vatican may once again encourage Latins and Uniates to take communion at Orthodox Churches while encouraging the Orthodox to do likewise. The very fact that the Orthodox at Balamand have extended full recognition to Latin mysteries means that the impression could be easily created that only bigotry could be the reason for refusing inter-communion and concelebration.

34. It is also possible that the pope at some point may desist from appointing a successor to at least one of his current Uniate Archbishops or even Patriarchs and put his local Uniate faithful under the spiritual leadership of the local Orthodox Archbishop or Patriarch as a trial test.

35. Since at least 1975 the WCC has been carefully and very successfully cultivating the image of the Orthodox as lacking Christian love for refusing communion to others. A likely refusal of the Orthodox to accept Uniates under one of their Archbishops or Patriarchs may become part of a similar practice of picturing the Orthodox as indeed bigots, especially since in this case they would be refusing communion to and concelebration with clergy whose mysteries they fully recognize.

36. Now that the Balamand agreement has become a candidate to become a sequel to Vatican II and in which case Uniatism will no longer have any reason for existing, the Orthodox will be faced with the consequences of their continued refusal of communion with the Latins and Uniates.

37. What is most interesting is the fact that according to the Balamand agreement mysteries are valid whether one accepts 7 or 22 Ecumenical Councils and their teachings and practices. The impression will be certainly created that only lack of love could be the reason why

the Orthodox may continue to refuse inter-communion and concelebration with the Vatican.

V. THE QUESTION

38. It seems that the Orthodox at Balamand are attempting to introduce an innovation in regards to Biblical mysteries. Up to now the Orthodox Churches usually accepted into their membership individuals or Churches by means of either exactitude (*akribeia*) or economy (*oikonomia*).

(a) By Exactitude one is accepted by baptism, chrismation and profession of the Orthodox Faith accompanied by rejection of former errors.

(b) By Economy one is accepted by chrismation and profession of the Orthodox faith and the rejection of former errors.

39. Neither of these two means of entry into the Church is in itself a judgment on the validity or non-validity of the sacraments of the Church of origin, since there are no mysteries outside of the Body of Christ. One is either a member of the Body of Christ by his baptism of the Spirit, i.e. illumination and/or glorification in Christ or one is still in the state of purification by his baptism by water unto forgiveness of sins and in the process of becoming a member of the Body of Christ and a temple of the Holy Spirit. One may be a believer in Christ without belonging to either of these categories. This holds true for nominal Orthodox also. It is up to each Synod of Orthodox bishops to decide the status of each group of those who are seeking communion within the Body of Christ.

40. In regard to the cure of purification, illumination and glorification there is no difference between Latins and most Protestants since, or if, they are not engaged in this cure which has nothing to do with mysticism*. This holds true for nominal Orthodox also. The reason for the increase of the numbers of the latter (especially since Peter the Great) is that professors of Orthodox faculties became no longer aware, and many are still not aware, of this Biblical/Patristic tradition of cure and are therefore prone to copy from non-patristic or non-Orthodox works to write their teaching manuals. The result has been the appearance of large groups of clergy who no longer see any

important difference between the Latin and Orthodox understandings of the Mysteries within the Body of Christ.

41. The basic question before us is clear: Is dogma 1) a protection from speculating quack doctors and 2) a guide to the cure of the purification and the illumination of the heart and glorification (*theosis*), or not?

42. "Let each person test himself, and thus eat of the bread and drink of the cup. For one who eats and drinks not discerning the Body eats and drinks his own judgment. For this reason many among you are weak and sick and many are dead" (1 Cor. 11:28-30). In other words one tests himself to see whether he is a member of the Body of Christ by being in the state of illumination, i.e. with at least kinds of tongues. Otherwise one shares in the bread and the cup "unworthily" (1 Cor. 11:27). In such a case one is still "weak" or "sick" and even spiritually "dead" (1 Cor. 11:30), i.e. not sharing in the resurrection of the inner person and so not yet communicating at the Eucharist unto life in Christ, but rather unto judgment. One should not use the Eucharistic gatherings as occasions to simply eat. This one does at home. "If we examine ourselves, we will not be judged. Being judged by the Lord we are instructed, so that we are not condemned with the world" (1 Cor. 11:31-32). In the states of illumination and glorification one is instructed in his spirit by Christ Himself. This is the cure which Paul explains in detail in 1 Cor. 12-15:11.[766]

VI. FORMULATIONS OF DOGMAS NOT TO BE CONFUSED WITH THE MYSTERY OF GOD

43. It was only to keep the faithful within this tradition of cure in Christ that heresies were condemned by the dogmatic formulations of Ecumenical and Local Councils. These formulations have nothing to do with the Augustinian and Franco-Latin *analogia fidei* and *analogia entis*, i.e. with theological and philosophical speculations based on a supposed similarity between the created and the uncreated. Belief in such a similarity was the basic characteristic of heresies and which has become common among some Orthodox also. The only purpose of dogmatic formulations is to serve as guides to the cure of the human spirit in and by Christ Himself.

---

766 See study referred to in the first note inside the text of this article.

VII. THE MYSTERIES

44. Franco-Latin doctrines on the sacraments and created grace are based on Augustine's Christology and his quest for Neo-Platonic happiness. He unknowingly rejected the First and Second Ecumenical Councils' identity of Christ with the Old Testament Angel of God, Him Who is, the God of Abraham, Isaac and Jacob Who appeared to Moses in the burning bush and the Lord of Glory, the Lord Sabbaoth, the Pantocrator, and the Angel of Great Council Who appeared to the Old Testament prophets. Augustine was misled into believing that this identity was the teaching of the heretical Arians alone. He did not know this was also the teaching of the Fathers of the First and Second Ecumenical Councils. Whereas the Arians and Eunomians believed that this Lord and Angel of Glory was created by God, the Orthodox Fathers knew from their own glorification in Christ and from the Bible that He is the uncreated Son of God and consubstantial with His Father. To his ignorance of this identity of Christ with the Old Testament Lord of Glory, Augustine also added his personal quest after Neo-Platonic happiness which has nothing to do with God's glorification of the apostles and prophets.

45. Augustine is the father of the strange teaching of the Franco-Latins whereby God brings into existence creatures to be seen and heard by the prophets and the apostles and which He passes back into non-existence after each specific revelation.[767] Thus the aforementioned Old Testament Angel of God and the fire in the burning bush, the pillar of fire and cloud, the bird at Christ's baptism, the glory and rule of God in both Testaments, and even the tongues of fire at Pentecost, are supposed to have been all brought into existence and then passed out of existence. In other words the linguistic symbols used by the writers of the Bible to indicate glorifications/revelations and the action of the grace of God are transformed into temporary creatures which pass into and out of existence. Indeed for the Franco-Latins this is supposed to be the lowest form of revelation which is superseded by God's revelations made directly to the intellect.

---

767 See for example his *De Trinitate* Books II and III.

46. This was the teaching of Barlaam the Calabrian who came from the West having become Orthodox not knowing the faith of the Church on these matters. After arguing with Orthodox monks and defending these Franco-Latin positions his teachings were condemned by the Ninth Ecumenical Council[768] of Constantinople of 1341. It became known a bit later that his teachings were the originalities of Augustine followed by the whole Franco-Latin Church. It was evidently for this reason, and not only for his *Filioque*, that Augustine was put on the sidelines of patristic authority. In contrast the Church celebrates the feast day of St. Gregory Palamas on the Second Sunday of Lent as a Second Sunday of Orthodoxy for the chief role he played against the Franco-Latin heresies of Barlaam and in order to protect the faithful on their road to uncreated grace by their purification, illumination and glorification in Christ. God makes Himself known to His saints by glorifying them. They thus become gods by grace and see God in his Logos made flesh and by the Holy Spirit.

---

768 According to Roman Law.

D. BAPTISM AND "SACRAMENTAL ECONOMY":

An Agreed Statement of the North American Orthodox-Catholic Theological Consultation

The document entitled "Baptism and 'Sacramental Economy' An Agreed Statement of the North American Orthodox-Catholic Theological Consultation, (Saint Vladimir's Orthodox Seminary, produced June 3rd, 1999), is another statement developed by Orthodox and Latin Ecumenists which undermines and contradicts Orthodox patristic teaching in the pursuit of a future false union. This Agreed Statement arrived at six conclusions: (1) the mutual recognition of Orthodox and papist baptism in both teaching and understanding of the mystery; (2) that baptism is a central element of both churches and that it is "not of us" therefore it belongs to both the Orthodox and papists equally; (3) that both the Orthodox and papists "practice this same faith and teaching" which then requires both the Orthodox and papists to recognize each other's baptism as equally acceptable; (4) that despite both the Orthodox Church and papist confession not being in ecclesiastical communion with one another there is no problem with a mutual recognition of baptism; an attempt is made here to use the Councils of Constantinople in 1484 and Moscow in 1667 as a validation for an the new ecumenist ecclesiology; (5) that the Orthodox *Rudder* produced by Saint Nikodemos of the Holy Mountain, which was approved by the Synod of the

Ecumenical Patriarchate is a recent innovation of the eighteenth century, that it is not taught in holy scripture, by the holy fathers, or the majority of the Orthodox Church; (6) that while modern-day Latins accuse the Orthodox Church of "sins against charity" when Orthodox who baptize converts from the Latins, historically the Latins have also received converts from Orthodoxy by baptism in some places even up to the present time. The problems with this Agreed Statement from the standpoint of the Orthodox patristic witness have been addressed in a brief response by Metropolitan Hierotheos of Nafpaktos[769] and are also critiqued in detail in the book *On the Reception of the Heterodox into the Orthodox Church: The Patristic Consensus and Criteria.*[770]

1. Text Excerpt: Baptism and "Sacramental Economy": An Agreed Statement of the North American Orthodox-Catholic Theological Consultation[771]

SAINT VLADIMIR'S ORTHODOX SEMINARY, JUNE 3, 1999.

For the past three years the North American Orthodox-Catholic Theological Consultation has directed its attention to the concluding section of the Nicene-Constantinopolitan Creed: in particular to the

---

769 Metropolitan Hierotheos (Vlachos) of Nafpaktos and Hagios Vlasios, "Baptismal Theology," *Ekklesiastike Parembase*, No. 71 (December 2001), 12, reprinted from Orthodox Tradition, Vol XX, No 2, 40-43.

770 An Orthodox Ethos Publication, *On the Reception of the Heterodox into the Orthodox Church: The Patristic Consensus and Criteria*, 1st ed. (Florence: Uncut Mountain Press, 2023), 377-381.

771 "Baptism and 'Sacramental Economy' An agreed Statement of the North American Orthodox-Catholic Theological Consultation Saint Vladimir's Orthodox Seminary, June 3, 1999," Assembly of Canonical Orthodox Bishops of the United States of America, accessed December 19th, 2022, https://www.assemblyofbishops.org/ministries/ecumenical-and-interfaith-dialogues/orthodox-catholic/baptism-and-sacramental-economy-an-agreed-statement-of-the-north-american-orthodox-catholictheological-consultation-saint-vladimirs-orthodox-seminary-june-3-1999

confession of "one baptism," and to the faith in one Holy Spirit and in "one holy, catholic, and apostolic Church" to which this single baptism is so closely related [...]

It is our common [Orthodox and Papist] teaching that baptism in water in the name of the Holy Trinity, as the Christian's new birth, is given once and once only. [...]

The Orthodox and Catholic members of our Consultation acknowledge, in both of our traditions, a common teaching and a common faith in one baptism, despite some variations in practice which, we believe, do not affect the substance of the mystery. We [...] declare that we also recognize each other's baptism as one and the same. This recognition has obvious ecclesiological consequences. The Church is itself both the milieu and the effect of baptism, and is not of our making. This recognition requires each side of our dialogue to acknowledge an ecclesial reality in the other, however much we may regard their way of living the Church's reality as flawed or incomplete. In our common reality of baptism, we discover the foundation of our dialogue, as well as the force and urgency of the Lord Jesus' prayer "that all may be one." Here, finally, is the certain basis for the modern use of the phrase, "sister churches." [...]

The centralized administration of the modern Catholic Church, and the absence of any office resembling the papacy in the modern Orthodox Church, helps to explain the contrast between the diversity in modes of reception of Catholics practiced by local Orthodox churches and the (relatively) unitary practice of the Catholic Church over the past five hundred years in receiving Orthodox. [...] Vatican II, however, was explicit in recognizing both the validity and the efficacy of Orthodox sacraments [...]

In the Orthodox Church, a consistent position on the reception of those baptized in other communions is much more difficult, though not impossible, to discern. [...] Both Cyprian and the Apostolic Canons, in any case, draw a sharp line between the authentic visible Church and every other group which exists outside its boundaries, and accords no value whatever to the rites of those "outside." [...] Basil of Caesarea's First Canonical Epistle (Ep. 188, dated 374) [...] distinguishes among three types of groups "outside" the Church: heretics, "who differ with regard to faith in God;" schismatics, who are separated from the body of the

Church "for some ecclesiastical reasons and differ from other [Christians] on questions that can be resolved;" and "parasynagogues," or dissidents who have formed rival communities simply in opposition to legitimate authority (Ep. 188.1). [...] This policy is also reflected in Canon 95 of the Council in Trullo [...] in spite of the solemn rulings of the Fifth and Sixth Ecumenical Councils against their Christological positions, "Severians" and Nestorians are clearly reckoned as still "of the Church," and seem to be understood in Basil's category of "parasynagogues;" their baptisms are thus understood — to use scholastic language — as valid, if perhaps illicit.

Relations between Catholics and Orthodox through the centuries have been, in consequence, highly varied, ranging from full communion, on occasion, well into the late Middle Ages (and, in certain areas, until later still), to a rejection so absolute that it seemed to demand the rebaptism of new communicants. There are, however, in the Orthodox tradition two important synodical rulings which represent the continuation of the policy articulated by Basil, and affirmed by the Synod in Trullo and later Byzantine canonists, rulings which we believe are to be accorded primary importance: those of the Synod of Constantinople in 1484, and of Moscow in 1667.[...] The [1484] rite therefore appears to have been understood as part of a process of reconciliation, rather than as a reiteration of post-baptismal chrismation. It is this provision of Constantinople in 1484, together with Canon 95 of the Synod in Trullo, which the Council of Moscow in 1667 invokes in its decree forbidding the rebaptism of Catholics, a decree that has remained authoritative in the East Slavic Orthodox churches to the present day.

Patriarch Cyril V issued a decree in 1755 requiring the baptism of Roman Catholics, Armenians, and all others presently outside the visible bounds of the Orthodox Church, when they seek full communion with it. This decree has never been formally rescinded, but subsequent rulings by the Patriarchate of Constantinople (e.g., in 1875, 1880, and 1888) did allow for the reception of new communicants by chrismation rather than baptism. Nevertheless, these rulings left rebaptism as an option subject to "pastoral discretion." In any case, by the late nineteenth century a comprehensive new sacramental theology had appeared in Greek-speaking Orthodoxy which provided a precise rationale for such pastoral discretion [...from] St. Nicodemus of the Holy Mountain (1748-1809).

The Ecumenical Patriarch Cyril V issued a decree in 1755 requiring the baptism of Roman Catholics, Armenians, and all others presently outside the visible bounds of the Orthodox Church, when they seek full communion with it. [...] Nicodemus gave form and substance to the requirement of rebaptism decreed by Cyril V.

Nicodemus inadvertently bestowed a new meaning on the term oikonomia... [and] the opposed principles of akriveia and oikonomia came to be accepted by much of Greek-speaking Orthodoxy as governing the application of canon law in such a way as to allow for either the rebaptism of Western Christians (kat'akriveian), or for their reception by chrismation or profession of faith (kat'oikonomian), without in either case attributing to their baptism any reality in its own right. [...] As a result, within world Orthodoxy, the issue of "sacramental economy" remains the subject of intense debate, but the Nicodemean interpretation is still promoted in important theological and monastic circles. Although these voices in the Orthodox world are significant ones, we do not believe that they represent the tradition and perennial teaching of the Orthodox Church on the subject of baptism. [...]

CONCLUSIONS

The "inconsistencies" to which we referred at the beginning of our second section turn out, on closer inspection, to be less significant than they might appear to be. Granted, a vocal minority in the Orthodox Church refuses to accord any validity to Catholic baptism, and thus continues to justify in theory (if less frequently in fact) the (re)baptism of converts from Catholicism. Against this one fact, however, we present the following considerations:

1. The Orthodox and Catholic churches both teach the same understanding of baptism. This identical teaching draws on the same sources in Scripture and Tradition, and it has not varied in any significant way from the very earliest witnesses to the faith up to the present day.

2. A central element in this single teaching is the conviction that baptism comes to us as God's gift in Christ, through the Holy Spirit. It is therefore not "of us," but from above. The Church does not simply require the practice of baptism; rather, baptism is the Church's foundation. It establishes the Church, which is also not "of us" but, as the body of Christ quickened by the Spirit, is the presence in this world of the world to come.

3. The fact that our churches share and practice this same faith and teaching requires that we recognize in each other the same baptism and thus also recognize in each other, however "imperfectly," the present reality of the same Church. By God's gift we are each, in St. Basil's words, "of the Church."

4. We find that this mutual recognition of the ecclesial reality of baptism, in spite of our divisions, is fully consistent with the perennial teaching of both churches. This teaching has been reaffirmed on many occasions. The formal expression of the recognition of Orthodox baptism has been constant in the teaching of the popes since the beginning of the sixteenth century, and was emphasized again at the Second Vatican Council. The Synods of Constantinople in 1484 and Moscow in 1667 testify to the implicit recognition of Catholic baptism by the Orthodox churches, and do so in a way fully in accord with the earlier teaching and practice of antiquity and the Byzantine era.

5. The influential theory of "sacramental economy" propounded in the Pedalion commentaries does not represent the tradition and perennial teaching of the Orthodox Church; it is rather an eighteenth-century innovation motivated by the particular historical circumstances operative in those times. It is not the teaching of scripture, of most of the Fathers, or of later Byzantine canonists, nor is it the majority position of the Orthodox churches today.

6. Catholics in the present day who tax the Orthodox with sins against charity, and even with sacrilege, because of the practice of rebaptism should bear in mind that, while the rebaptism of Orthodox Christians was officially repudiated by Rome five hundred years ago, it nonetheless continued in some places well into

the following century and occasionally was done, under the guise of "conditional baptism," up to our own times.

RECOMMENDATIONS

On the basis of these conclusions, we would like to offer to our churches the following suggestions:

1. That the International Commission begin anew where the Bari statement of 1987, "Faith, Sacraments, and the Unity of the Church," came to an abrupt conclusion, simply recognizing similarities and differences in our practice of Christian initiation, and that it proceeds to reaffirm explicitly and clearly, with full explanation, the theological grounds for mutual recognition by both churches of each other's baptism;

2. That our churches address openly the danger that some modern theories of "sacramental economy" pose, both for the continuation of ecumenical dialogue and for the perennial teaching of the Orthodox Church;

3. That the Patriarchate of Constantinople formally withdraw its decree on rebaptism of 1755;

4. That the Orthodox churches declare that the Orthodox reception of Catholics by chrismation does not constitute a repetition of any part of their sacramental initiation; and

5. That our churches make clear that the mutual recognition of baptism does not of itself resolve the issues that divide us, or reestablish full ecclesial communion between the Orthodox and Catholic Churches, but that it does remove a fundamental obstacle on our path towards full communion.

2. Orthodox Response: Baptismal Theology by Metropolitan Hierotheos (Vlachos) of Nafpaktos and Hagios Vlasios[772]

THERE HAS BEEN in the past, and there is in our own day, a good deal of discussion about the Baptism of heretics (the heterodox [1]); that is, whether heretics who have deviated from the Orthodox Faith and who seek to return to it should be Baptized anew or simply Chrismated after making a profession of faith. Decisions have been issued on this matter by both local and Œcumenical Synods.

In the text that follows, I should like to discuss, by way of example, the agreement reached between the Standing Conference of Canonical Orthodox Bishops of America and the National Conference of Catholic Bishops in America [2] on June 3, 1999. The Greek translation of the original text was made by Protopresbyter George Dragas, a professor at the Holy Cross Greek Orthodox School of Theology in Boston [Brookline—*Trans.*], who also provided a summary and critique of this agreed statement between Orthodox and Roman Catholics in America.

The basis of this document is the Balamand Agreement of 1993, "Uniatism, Method of Union of the Past and the Present Search for Full Communion," which it evidently wishes to uphold.

The text on which we are commenting, that is, the agreement signed by Orthodox and Roman Catholics in America and entitled "Baptism and 'Sacramental Economy,'" is based on several points, in my observation, that are very typical of the contemporary ecumenical movement and indicative of its entire substance.

The first point is that "Baptism rests upon and derives its reality from the faith of Christ Himself, the faith of the Church, and the faith of the believer" (p. 13). At first sight, one is struck by the absence, here, of *any reference to the Triune God*—perhaps in order to justify this flexible interpretation of Baptism. Faith, then, becomes the fundamental mark and element of Baptism.

---

772 Metropolitan Hierotheos (Vlachos) of Nafpaktos and Hagios Vlasios, "Baptismal Theology," *Ekklesiastike Parembase*, No. 71 (December 2001), 12, reprinted from *Orthodox Tradition*, Vol XX, No 2, 40-43.

The second point is that Baptism is not a practice *required by the Church*, but is, "rather, the Church's foundation. It establishes the Church" (p. 26). Here, the notion that Baptism is not the "initiatory" Mystery whereby we are introduced into the Church, but the foundation of the Church, is presented as the truth.

The third point is that "Baptism was never understood as a private ceremony, but rather *as a corporate event*" (p. 13). This means that the Baptism of catechumens was "the occasion for the whole community's repentance and renewal" (p. 13). One who is Baptized "is obliged to make his own the community's common faith in the Savior's person and promises" (p. 14).

The fourth point is a continuation and consequence of the foregoing points. Since Baptism rests upon faith in Christ, since it is the basis of the Church, and since, moreover, it is the work of the community, this means that any recognition of Baptism entails recognition of the Church in which the Baptism is performed. In the Agreed Statement we read: "The Orthodox and Catholic members of our Consultation acknowledge, in both of our traditions, a common teaching and a common faith in one baptism, despite some variations in practice which, we believe, do not affect the substance of the mystery" (p. 17).

According to this text, there is a common faith and teaching concerning Baptism in the two "Churches," and the differences that exist do not affect the substance of the Mystery. The two sides each acknowledge an ecclesial reality "in the other, however much they may regard their way of living the Church's reality as flawed or incomplete" (p. 17). "The certain basis for the modern use of the phrase 'sister churches'" (p. 17) is to be found in this point. The Orthodox Church and the Latin Church are these two "sister Churches," because they have *the same Tradition, the same Faith, and the same Baptism*, even though there are certain differences between them. Hence, the following opinion is repeatedly affirmed in the text: "We find that this mutual recognition of the ecclesial reality of baptism, in spite of our divisions, is fully consistent with the perennial teaching of both churches" (p. 26). Misinterpreting the teaching of St. Basil the Great, the signers of this document aver that the two "Churches," in spite of the "imperfections" that exist, constitute the same ecclesial reality: "By God's gift we are each, in St. Basil's words, 'of the Church'" (p. 26).

The fifth point is that the authors of the Agreed Statement *find fault with St. Nicodemos the Hagiorite*, who, in interpreting the views of St. Cyprian of Carthage, St. Basil the Great, and the Second Œcumenical Synod, talks—as do all of the *Kollyvades* Fathers of the eighteenth century—about exactitude (*akribia*) and economy (*oikonomia*) with regard to the way in which heretics are received into the Orthodox Church. That is to say, the Fathers have at times received heretics by exactitude—namely, by Baptism—and at times by economy—namely, by Chrismation. However, even when the Church does receive someone by economy, this means that She effects the mystery of salvation at that very time, precisely because the Church is superior to the Canons, and not the Canons to the Church, and because the Church is the source of the Mysteries and, *eo ipso*, of Baptism, whereas Baptism is not the basis of the Church. The Church can receive this or that heretic by the principle of economy, without any implication that She recognizes as a Church the community that previously baptized him. This is the context within which St. Nicodemos interprets the relevant decision of the Second Œcumenical Synod.

Confusion is certainly heightened by the fact that one of the recommendations of the Agreed Statement is subject to many different interpretations. According to this recommendation, the two Churches should make it clear that "the mutual recognition of baptism does not of itself resolve the issues that divide them, or reëstablish full ecclesial communion between the Orthodox and Catholic Churches, but that it does remove a fundamental obstacle on the path towards full communion" (p. 28).

From this brief analysis, it is obvious how much confusion prevails in ecumenist circles regarding these issues. It is also obvious that [Orthodox] ecumenists understand the acceptance of the baptism of heretics (Catholics and Protestants, who have altered the dogma of the Holy Trinity and other dogmas) to mean accepting the ecclesial status of heretical bodies and, worse still, that the two "Churches," Latin and Orthodox, are united in spite of "small" differences, or that we derive from

898   The Orthodox Patristic Witness Concerning Catholicism

the same Church and should seek to return to it, thereby forming the one and only Church. This is a blatant expression of the branch theory.

When there is such confusion, it is necessary to adopt an attitude of strictness, which preserves the truth: that all who fall into heresy are outside the Church and that the Holy Spirit does not work to bring about their deification.

In any event, baptismal theology creates immense problems for the Orthodox. From the standpoint of ecclesiology, the text under consideration is riddled with errors. The Patristic Orthodox teaching on this subject is that the Church is the Theanthropic Body of Christ, in which revealed truth—the Orthodox Faith—is preserved and the mystery of deification is accomplished through the Mysteries of the Church (Baptism, Chrismation, and the Divine Eucharist). The essential precondition for this is that we participate in the purifying, illuminating, and deifying energy of God. Baptism is the initiatory Mystery of the Church. The Church does not rest upon the Mystery of Baptism; rather, the Baptism of water, in conjunction with the Baptism of the Spirit, operates within the Church and makes one a member of the Body of Christ. There are no Mysteries outside the Church, the living Body of Christ, just as there are no senses outside the human body.

In closing, I should like to cite the conclusion of Father George Dragas, which he appends to his "Summary and Critique":

These recommendations will not win the agreement of all Orthodox, and certainly not of those who are Greek-speaking (or Greek-minded), and consequently they are, by their very nature, divisive. My primary reason for coming to such a negative conclusion is that this inquiry into sacramental theology is devoid of any ecclesiological basis and that it onesidedly interprets—or rather, misinterprets—the facts of Orthodox sacramental practice, and particularly vis-à-vis the heterodox at different periods in the history of the Church. These recommendations and conclusions and, indeed, the entire Agreed Statement are the epitome of Western skepticism. Their acceptance by Orthodox theologians signals a deliberate betrayal of Orthodox views and a capitulation to the outlook of Western ecumenism. This is something that we should reject.

The Baptism of Christ

Saint Gregory Palamas

APPENDIX

Two Tomes from the Ninth Ecumenical Council

The Synodal Tome of 1341[773]

1. Truly praiseworthy is he who said that humility is the acquisition of truth; for humility is the recognition of our own limits, through which we gather peace towards God and towards our neighbor. By this peace in turn, we obtain rest in the present and the future age, according to that divine saying of the Lord which is so instructive in this regard, "Learn from me because I am gentle and lowly in heart, and you will find rest for your souls". Humility persuades him who has obtained it to take heed to himself and rely on God, avoiding all evil by the fear of the Lord, according to the word of the wise Solomon. It teaches him to practice reverence and moderation concerning what is beyond him, respecting the eternal boundaries of the fathers and avoiding deviations on both sides (I mean excesses and deficiencies) and to travel that royal road of moderation which leads towards the heavens and God without error or accident.

2. But the monk Barlaam embarking from Calabria, with insane self-reliance set forth onto the sea of personal opinion. Confident in his knowledge of secular philosophy, attacking the teaching of the Spirit in opposition to the supernatural true philosophy, he adopted instead the unacceptable natural philosophy, which is completely incapable of receiving the things of the Spirit. In the guise of a disciple this man once deceitfully approached some of our monks, those who have chosen the silent life, who have said farewell to everything else and attend only to God. He went on purpose not to any of the better-educated monks, but to the simpler, doubtless fearing to be detected. A little later, moreover, after leaving them, he accused them in writing of an abominable doctrine, which he claimed was advocated by them. For after he had heard them saying, as receiving it from the tradition of the holy fathers, that those who are purified in heart through God's commandments receive divine illumination occurring mystically and ineffably within them, he accused them

---

773 Holy Synod of Constantinople, "Synodical Tome of 1341," in *Creeds & Confessions of Faith in the Christian Tradition*, ed. Jaroslav Pelikan & Valerie Hotchkiss (New Haven: Yale University Press 2003), 320-333.

of asserting that it was possible to participate in the very essence of God.

3. When they replied, "Not in the essence but in the uncreated and deifying grace of the Spirit," he presumed to lay on them the charge of ditheism. Not only so, but addressing the Church of God and reporting these matters to Our Modesty, accusing especially the most honored among hieromonks, Lord Gregory Palamas, he sought that they should be summoned into our holy and divine synod.

4. When they were summoned, Barlaam reversed himself. He fled and did not submit to meet with the council. He would not debate with the monks whom he had accused or let them confront him in regard to what he had written against them. He presented as the excuse for his flight the emperor's absence at that time, but in truth he was aware of his own guilt and feared examination.

5. Then when the council was assembled in the renowned temple of the Wisdom of God the Word, in the presence of the illustrious and blessed emperor from God, the senate, not a few of the most honorable archimandrites and abbots, and the representatives of the state, Barlaam himself was summoned and bidden to speak and show if he had anything to say against the monks who lived the life of stillness. While they were already present at the council, he himself, as if suffering forgetfulness of the issue but actually trying to confuse the subject, proceeded to dogmatic questions and puzzles and sought resolution of his theoretical problems. He persisted in this and insisted that he would say nothing before he obtained answer and resolution for these questions. Even when he had been rebuffed with severity once and twice, he did not yield from this insistence nor was he persuaded to speak concerning the investigation of the issue, namely, his written accusation against the monks.

6. Our Modesty ordered the sacred and divine canons to be read in the hearing of the council, through which it is forbidden and altogether prohibited not only for those like him but also for anyone else to raise any dogmatic issues, to create a necessity for others in consequence to defend themselves concerning these matters, and assuming the teaching authority to hold forth on any ecclesiastical

subjects; for this is granted only to bishops by the grace from above. For the sixty-fourth canon of the sixth ecumenical council says, "It is not right for a layman to speak in public or to teach, assuming the teaching authority, but he must submit to the authority appointed by the Lord, open his ears to those who have received the grace of instructive discourse, and learn divine matters from them. For in the one Church God has made different members, according to the saying of the apostle, which Gregory the Theologian interprets, clearly establishing the proper order in these matters: 'Let us respect this order, brethren, let us keep this; let one be the hearing, another the tongue, another the hand, another some other member. Let one teach, the other learn; the learner in obedience, the leader with cheerfulness, and the worker with eagerness; let us not all be tongue, the most active member. We shall not all be apostles; we shall not all be prophets. We shall not all interpret.' And a little later: 'Why do you make yourself a shepherd, when you are a sheep? Why do you become a head, when you are a foot? Why do you try to be a general, when you are enrolled among the soldiers?' And elsewhere Wisdom exhorts: 'Do not be swift in words, do not compete as a poor man with the rich, do not seek to be wiser than the wise.' But if anyone is found weakening the present canon, let him be excommunicated for forty days." And again, the nineteenth canon of the Council of Chalcedon: "Every day, especially on the Lord's Day, those who preside in the Church must teach all the clergy and the people with pious discourses, gathering from the Divine Scripture the ideas and expressions of the truth, and not transgressing the boundaries already set or the tradition of the inspired fathers. But if a controversy regarding Scripture should be stirred up, let them not interpret this otherwise than as the illuminators and teachers of the Church have set down in their own writings. Let them find approval with these rather than compose their own discourses, lest sometimes through lack of skill they may depart from what is proper. For through the teaching of the aforementioned fathers the people will come to know what should be desired and chosen and what should be rejected as disadvantageous, and will redirect their lives for the better. They will not remain in a condition of ignorance, but by attending to instruction they will motivate themselves to avoid evil and to work out their salvation in fear of the impending punishments."

7. After the reading of the same sacred and divine canons, there were brought into the midst the reports which Barlaam earlier had made against the monks. And when these reports had been read, the distinguished priest-monk Lord Gregory Palamas was entrusted with making the defense in regard to them, since they especially concerned him. As a prologue to his speech, he made such defense as was fitting, then narrated how their conflict developed: first the same Barlaam made written accusations against the stated above, setting out propositions opposed (as has been shown) to the divine words of the fathers; and then he himself was impelled by necessity to defense and rebuttal.

8. Then the decision was made to bring in the writings of Barlaam which he misleadingly entitled "Against the Messalians". In these writings, concerning the unapproachable light of the transfiguration of the Lord our Savior Jesus Christ and concerning his preeminent disciples and apostles who were found worthy to behold this light, he said in these exact words: "That which shone on Tabor was not the unapproachable light of Godhead, nor in truth did there exist a light of Godhead nor any light more sacred or more divine than the angels, but it was a light even inferior to and lower than our own intellectual activity. For all the concepts and objects of thought are nobler than that light, because it comes to the sight through the atmosphere and is subject to the power of sensory perception, and shows only perceptible things to those who see it. It is material and has shape; it appears in a place and a time, and colors the air. At one time it holds together and appears; then it dissolves and yields to nonexistence, because it acts on the imagination, is divisible, and has boundaries. Therefore, also it was seen by those who suffered deprivation of their intellectual energies, or rather had not yet fully acquired them and were not yet purified, but were imperfectly prepared even for that very sight on the mountain, since they had not yet been granted the godlike intellectual power. We are led upward from this kind of light to objects of intellectual contemplation, which are incomparably superior to that light. Therefore, those who

say that it is 'beyond thought' and 'true' and 'unapproachable' and the like are absolutely in error. They have seen nothing more sublime than perceptible beauty, and because of this they introduce impious and deadly teachings into the Church." Barlaam wrote these words, clearly heterodox and opposed to what the saints have said about that divine light.

9. Insisting that they were believing and speaking in conformity with the saints' teachings, the monks cited the passages which follow. The divine John of Damascus says, "Today the abyss of unapproachable light, today the infinite outpouring of divine brilliance shines on the apostles on Mount Tabor. Now appears what is invisible to human eyes, an earthly body radiates divine luminance, a mortal body pours out the glory of divinity. For the Word became flesh, and the flesh became Word, although each did not depart from its own nature —what a marvel! Not from outside did the glory come upon the body, but from inside, from the supremely divine Godhead ineffably united to it in the hypostasis of God the Word.

10. "The angels cannot rest their eye on him without bending, yet the foremost of the apostles see him shining forth with the glory of his own kingdom.

11. "Therefore, he takes the leaders of the apostles as witnesses of his own glory and divinity, and he reveals to them his own divinity. Surely those men are perfect who behold the divine glory, which is beyond all things, which alone is beyond perfection and more than perfect.

12. "The truly divine mastery, Dionysius, who speaks of God, says this: 'He will be seen by his perfect servants, as on Mount Tabor he appears to the apostles. He takes John with him, as the pure virgin mouthpiece of theology, so that after beholding the timeless glory of the Son, he may proclaim in a voice of thunder, "In the beginning was the Word, and the Word was with God, and the Word was God."'

13. "Silence is the mother of prayer, and prayer is the revelation of divine glory. For when we close our senses and stay with ourselves and

God, and freed from the outer distraction of the world stay inside ourselves, then within ourselves we will clearly see the kingdom of God. The kingdom of the heavens, which is the kingdom of God, is within us, Jesus our God announced.

14. "In the presence of the disciples he is transfigured who is always thus glorified and shines with the lightning of divinity.

15. "Begotten from the Father without beginning, he has obtained the natural unoriginate radiance of Godhead, and the glory of the God-head becomes also the glory of his body.

16. "But his glory, not appearing in his visible body, was called invisible for those bound by the bonds of flesh, for those who cannot receive what even angels cannot contemplate. He is transfigured, however, not taking on what he was not, nor being changed into what he was not, but revealing to his own disciples what he was, opening their eyes and making them sighted instead of blind. This is what is meant by 'He was transfigured before them'. For although he remained identically the same, his disciples saw him appearing differently from how he appeared before. And it says he shone like the sun, not because he did not shine brighter than the sun (for it is impossible to represent the uncreated perfectly in the creation), but because he shone as brightly as those who saw were able to behold.

17. "No one has seen God at any time, as he is by nature; whatever any-one has seen, he has beheld in the Spirit. This is the change of the right hand of the Most High; this is what eye has not seen and ear has not heard and has never entered into the heart of man. Just so in the age to come we will be always with the Lord, seeing Christ flash-ing in the light of his divinity. This light surpasses every nature; this is the life which has overcome the world. But Peter said, 'It is good for us to be here'; and then a cloud, not of gloom, but of light over-shadowed them. The mystery which was hidden from the ages and from the generations is revealed. The voice of the Father issues from a cloud of the Spirit, and glory perpetual and everlasting is revealed."

18. The prophetic Andrew of Crete says: "The Savior leads his disciples up to the high mountain, to do what or to teach what? To show

them the glory and brightness of his own divinity, which is more brilliant than lightning.

19. "This is what we celebrate today, the deification of our nature, the change into something better, the ecstasy and ascent to what is beyond nature, by which we achieve the conquest of the better, or to speak more properly, the ineffable deification.

20. "At this the angels marvel. At this the archangels give glory.

21. "At this all the spiritual rank of the celestial ones, feasting at the immaterial banquet, make the clearest and most infallible witness of the Word's love for us.

22. "Nothing of what appears in the creation can contain the excess of this brightness. For he who is beyond essence truly entered into essence. In a manner beyond essence, he assumed our essence. He became a citizen with us in the flesh, and yet he also shone out surpassingly on the mountain.

23. "He did not then become more radiant or more sublime than himself (far from it!), but what he was before he appeared in truth to those of his disciples who were perfected and initiated in the more sublime mysteries. For departing from the flesh and the world, as far as is possible, there they learned already from their own experience the conditions of the coming dispensation.

24. "For although the good is imparted in some degree to everyone, it becomes accessible not as it is but to the extent and in the manner, it is possible for the participants. And this is true because of the high goodness which proceeds to everyone and pours forth with infinitely munificent illumination. This is demonstrated by the blessed and renowned experience itself, which the apostles underwent on the mountain, when the unapproachable and timeless light transfiguring its own flesh shone supernaturally with the excess of its own outpouring of light — what a marvel! In the perfect ecstasy of their nature, they fall into deep sleep, and overcome by fear, they close their senses, completely drawing back all their intellectual movement and apprehension. Thus, they came to be with God in that divine invisible darkness beyond light. By seeing nothing they received

the capacity to see truly, and by incomprehensible experience they obtained the supreme ignorance. They were initiated by sleep into the wakefulness which is higher than all intellectual authority. They went outside of everything seen and thought, and even of themselves, so that through unknowing and unseeing, by the appearance of the Word and the overshadowing of the Spirit and the voice of the Father brought from on high out of the cloud, they might be taught the supremely supernatural mystery which goes beyond all ignorance and negation."

25. Concerning this divine light, the great Gregory the Theologian says, "The Godhead which was revealed to the disciples on the mountain is light a little too strong to see"; and again, "He will come according to my word, but such as he was seen by the disciples or was revealed when divinity overcame the flesh."

26. The holy Maximus says: "The Gospel of God is this, the intercession with God and the assistance to mankind through the Son who was made flesh and bestowed on those who believe in him the unbegotten deification as a reward of reconciliation with the Father; I call unbegotten deification the individually realized illumination which does not have a beginning, but incomprehensible revelation in those who are worthy."

27. And again, he says: "Not always with glory does the Lord appear to all his adherents: to those who are being instructed he comes in the form of a servant, but to those who are able to follow him as he ascends to the high mountain of his transfiguration he appears in the form of God, in which he was before the world existed".

28. And again, the same saint says: "The light of the face of the Lord, which exceeds the capacity of human perception, formed for the blessed disciples the model of mystical theology by negation, according to which the blessed and holy Godhead in its essence is beyond ineffable and beyond unknowable and infinitely removed from all unlimitedness. It leaves no track at all of comprehension however slight afterwards for those who have experienced it.

29. "He who is not participable by beings according to his essence," says the same saint, "but who wishes to participate in another manner with those who are able, does not entirely depart from his essential hiddenness. Even the very manner in which he willingly participates remains perpetually unrevealed to everyone."

30. And the great Basil says: "The Holy Spirit is unapproachable by nature, but accessible because of his goodness. He fills everything by his power, but can be shared only by those who are worthy. He is not shared in the same measure by all, but distributed his energy in proportion to the faith of the recipient. He is simple in his essence, manifold in his powers.

31. "He is present as a whole to each one and everywhere. He is distributed without suffering injury, and is shared as a whole, like a ray of the sun. While he is present to each recipient as if he were present to him alone, he sends his grace sufficient and complete to all."

32. And again, St Basil says: "The energies of God are diverse, but his essence is simple. We say that we know God from his energies, but we do not pretend to approach his essence. For his energies descend to us, but his essence remains unapproachable."

33. For this is what the great Athanasius also says that no human being is able to see the naked essence of God in any way. From this it is clear that the saints behold not the essence of God, but his glory. It is also written concerning the apostles, that Peter and his companions saw his glory when they awoke.

34. And again, the same saint says: "Christ is free from suffering even in the sufferings of his flesh, since as God he overcame death and rose on the third day and ascended into heaven, in natural glory and not in grace. He will come in his own divinity, clearly radiating his ineffable glory from the holy body which he received from Mary, as also on the mountain he partially revealed, teaching us that both before and now he is the same, being unchangeable always and having no alteration affecting his divinity."

35. The great Dionysius also says this: "When we become incorruptible and immortal, and we arrive at the most blessed and Christlike

condition, we will be always with the Lord according to the saying. In pure contemplation we will be filled with his visible revelation, which will envelop us with exceedingly brilliant radiance, as it enveloped the disciples in that most divine transfiguration. When our minds become impassible and immaterial, we will participate in his spiritual illumination and in the union beyond understanding, by the unknowable and blessed reception of the rays which surpass appearance, in a more divine imitation of the celestial intelligences."

36. And the great Basil says: "The reward of virtue is to become God and to receive the lightning flash of the most pure light, becoming a sun of that day which is not cut off by darkness. For a different sun makes this day, the sun which flashes with the true light. When once this sun shines on us, it is no longer hidden in gloom, but enfolds everything in its illuminating power. It continuously and perpetually enlightens those who are worthy and even makes those who participate in that light into other suns. 'Then', it says, 'the righteous shall shine like the sun.'"

37. The divine Maximus says: "The soul becomes God by the participation of divine grace. It both desists from all the activities of the mind and perception and at the same time stops the natural activities of the body. The body is deified along with the soul in proportion to its participation in deification, so that God alone then appears through both the soul and the body, as their natural characteristics are overcome by the excess of glory."

38. The great Dionysius says: "We do not see any deification or life which accurately resembles the cause which is situated above all."

39. The same saint was asked how he who is beyond all things is also beyond the source of God and beyond the source of good. He says: "If you would understand Godhead and goodness, it is the very substance of the good-creating gift and the inimitable imitation of the supremely divine and supremely good, by which we are made god and made good. For if this becomes the source of deification and perfection for those who are becoming gods and becoming good, the supreme source of every source is both beyond what we call

Godhead and goodness and beyond the source of Godhead and the source of goodness."

40. The divine Gregory of Nyssa says: "If his judgments cannot be examined, and his ways cannot be tracked down, and the promise to the good surpasses all conjecture from guesswork, how much more in its ineffability and unapproachability the divine itself is also higher and more sublime than what we understand about it."

41. The divine John of Damascus also writes in his sacred songs: "So that thou mayest show clearly how at thy ineffable second coming thou wilt be seen standing as the most high God in the midst of gods, as thou didst shine ineffably to the apostles on Tabor, and to Moses with Elijah."

42. And in another song, he writes: "And briefly hiding the outer garment of flesh he was transfigured before them, revealing the comeliness of the archetypal beauty, though not in full. He satisfied them and spared them at the same time, lest with the vision they lose their life, but he appeared as they were able to endure, using their bodily eyes."

43. The great Dionysius again says: "The divine darkness is the unapproachable light, in which God is said to dwell. It is both invisible, because of its supreme brightness, and unapproachable, because of the excess of its supernatural effusion of light."

44. "Not God, however", says our father Chrysostom, "but grace is poured out."

45. In addition, Barlaam disparaged the fear which came upon the apostles at that most divine sight, alleging that the apostles' fear showed that they were imperfectly prepared even for that very sight, and indicated that the light which they saw at that time was of an earthly nature. Then, undoubtedly enlightened in mind by this same light, the most divine and renowned emperor said, "There is also a fear not of beginners but of the perfect, concerning which the prophet says, 'The fear of the Lord is clean, enduring forever'; and again elsewhere, 'Fear the Lord all you, his saints.' Proof that the apostles then experienced the fear not of beginners but of the perfect: they sought

to remain always with that ineffable vision. 'Let us make here', Peter says, 'three tents', and 'It is good for us to be here.' One who has the other kind of fear desires to escape from that which he fears. Peter, the summit of the apostles, thinking that this age of dimensions and limits had passed away, but that the dimensionless and unceasing age of light had been revealed, said prophetically from the state of his soul, 'It is good for us to be here'. For he evidently saw that which human nature would surely be unable to see if it were not permeated with the grace of the Holy Spirit. Those men were then found worthy of such sight as human nature would receive only if assisted by the Spirit."

46. Again, the emperor spoke, wise in divine matters as is to be expected among those who praise that most divine light: "Let none of us who hears suppose that we are saying that the nature of God is visible; for even though the apostles had ascended to such a height of contemplation, they saw divine grace and glory but not the nature itself which produces this grace. For we know, being initiated by the Divine Scriptures, that that nature is imparticipable, incomprehensible, invisible, even to the celestial and sublime powers, leaving not the slightest trace of comprehension afterward to those who have experienced it. Likewise, the most theological of Gregories, after discussing the prophets' visions, in continuing immediately added, 'But neither these prophets, about whom we are speaking, nor anyone else like them, stood in the council and essence of the Lord, as it is written, nor saw or taught the nature of God.'" By these words and arguments, Barlaam was being refuted and put to shame for sacrilegiously and erroneously attacking what is sacred.

47. Furthermore, Barlaam was found to have made many misrepresentations and accusations in writing against the practitioners of the silent life. At the same time, he attacked the prayer customary with them, or rather with all Christians, the "Lord Jesus Christ, Son of God, have mercy on me." For he made this statement also concerning the prayer in these very words: "While there are many charges which one could justifiably make against the promulgator of this kind of doctrine, second to none I consider this, that trying to overturn the mysteries of Christians through his breathing exercises, he calumni-

ates even the fathers, claiming that what he now teaches, these men also thought before. You crazy and wretched man, by which of them was such monstrosity as you teach ever called 'watchfulness' and 'guarding of the heart' and 'attention'? They say that this man made it a rule for his initiates to use this prayer continually, 'Lord Jesus Christ, Son of God, have mercy on me.' From this therefore we can understand what kind of man he was who invented these breathing exercises. For on one hand the 'Our Father', which the Bogomils use differently, he does not prescribe, for he supposed that, if he did, his heresy would be obvious; nevertheless, for those whom he directs to attend throughout life to this one small prayer, he leaves all the other prayers to be considered merely foolish babble. Furthermore, while all Christians call in this prayer our Lord Jesus Christ also 'our God', this man changed the 'our God' into 'Son of God'. By this change he revealed to us the whole of his own heresy. For it is to follow the doctrine of the Bogomils that this man changes in the aforementioned prayer the 'our God' into 'Son of God', since no one could give any other reason why he would have made such a change." These things that most godless Barlaam said.

48. These allegations contradict both the blessed utterances of that foundation of the faith, Peter, the leader of the disciples, and the Lord's blessing on his words. For Peter said to him, "Thou art the Christ, the Son of the living God"; and the Lord replied, "Blessed are you, Simon son of Jonah, because flesh and blood did not reveal this to you, but my Father in heaven." Besides, in the creed we say, "We believe in one God, the Father, the Almighty, and in the only-begotten Son of God, begotten of the Father before all ages." So, do we not glorify Christ as God, when we say that we believe in the Son of God? And about this sacred prayer also the divine teacher John with golden words says, instructing the monastics: "Devote yourself always to the Lord and persist in supplicating him until he has mercy on us. Seek nothing else but only mercy from the Lord of glory. Seeking mercy, seek with a humble and merciful heart, and cry out from morning to evening, and if possible, all night, 'Lord Jesus Christ, Son of God, have mercy on us.' I beseech you, force your mind to this work until death. For this work requires much force, because narrow is the gate and hard is the way which leads

to life, and men of force go in by it. For the kingdom of heaven belongs to men of force. I beseech you, do not separate your heart from God, but persist and guard it with the recollection of our Lord Jesus Christ always, until the name of the Lord takes root within your heart, and think of nothing else but that Christ might be magnified in you. I beseech you, therefore, never desist or despise the rule of this prayer, but whether you eat or drink or travel or do anything, unceasingly cry out, 'Lord Jesus Christ, Son of God, have mercy on us.' For 'pray without ceasing', the divine apostle says, without anger and speculation."

49. But also, the divine Diadochus says: "When we close every outlet to the mind by the recollection of God, it imperiously demands something to satisfy its need of activity. We must then give it the Lord Jesus, as the sole occupation that fully answers its need. For 'no-one', it is written, 'calls Jesus Lord, except by the Holy Spirit.'" Those who repeat this holy and glorious name in the depth of their heart unceasingly can sometimes see the light of their own intellect. For then we grow fully conscious that the name is burning up all the filth which covers the surface of the soul. For "our God", it is written, "is a consuming fire". Therefore, finally the Lord summons the whole soul to love of his glory. For when the intellect with fervor of heart maintains persistently its remembrance of the glorious and desirable name, then that name undoubtedly implants in us a disposition to love his goodness. For this is the pearl of great price, which one can find by selling all its possessions and have unspeakable joy in finding it. And it would take too long to tell how the God-bearing fathers explain this and exhort us to it. The monks maintained persistently that this prayer is a thoroughly divine and delightful occupation according to the understanding of the God-bearers, inspired by the Spirit. At the same time, they desired to continue telling how much the saints have set down in their writings, for example what was said by that John who constructed in words the ladder of the spiritual ascent; for he says, "May the memory of Jesus be united with your breath, and then you will know the value of quietness.'"

50. As the monks were desiring to continue saying such things, the emperor, marvelous in all respects, who has now closed his life with a

blessed end, as the Lord's anointed took up speech again on behalf of Christ who anointed him. He said, "So be it. Let us grant that one of the heretics was the first to say this. It is no crime in us if we use well what they invented badly. For just because the Persians call Abraham the God of heaven, it does not follow that it is wrong for us to say, 'I reverence the God of heaven'. Nor, because the pagan Greeks say that god is a mind which creates the universe, will we refrain from saying that he is the maker of the universe; neither would we be justly accused of thinking like them when we say this. For when the Greeks said that matter was unbegotten and coeternal with God, even if they said that God is the maker of the universe, they called him this not as one who produces what previously did not yet exist at all, but as one who arranges what already exists, merely giving form and harmonious arrangement to existing matter, with a small skill like man's. They attributed nothing more than this to the power of God. For our part, just as we believe that everything has received from God its progress from nonbeing into existence and thus we know him accurately as maker of heaven and earth and everything in between, so also when we say that our Lord Jesus Christ is the Son of God, we praise and proclaim him as true God from true God, both confessing the divinity of the Son and bearing witness to the source of the Son's divinity. But they say that the Messalians and Bogomils pray the prayer which was transmitted by the Lord to his holy disciples and apostles. So, what? Shall we therefore abstain from this prayer and abandon what is ours to those who have stolen it, and we ourselves avoid the truly pious expression because of those who imitate piety in words? Away with such shameful evil counsel! But since 'we have an advocate with the Father, Jesus Christ the righteous, and he himself is the expiation for our sins', with hope we will call on his name, and obtain salvation from such supplication, according to what was said by the prophet, 'and everyone who calls on the name of the Lord will be saved'. And since 'there is no other name given among men, by which we must be saved', and 'no one is able to say "Jesus is Lord" except by the Holy Spirit', and 'in the name of Jesus Christ every knee shall bow of things in heaven and on earth and under the earth', blessed is he who through continual repetition of this much-praised name has God dwelling within him."

51. So, by these words Barlaam was revealed and refuted as speaking blasphemously and heretically both about the divine light on Tabor and in his allegations against the monks concerning the sacred prayer which they practice and recite repeatedly. But the monks were demonstrated superior to his accusation. They were proved to be accepting and abiding by the explanations and traditions of the holy fathers concerning these matters, just as they themselves clearly confessed and insisted. Therefore, the same Barlaam, convicted (as has been said) by a common vote of the council for treating divine subjects wrongly and erroneously, sought indeed to be forgiven for these actions. And therefore, we declare that if, on the one hand, he shows true repentance and corrects himself, and is no longer found speaking and shows true repentance and corrects himself, and is no longer found speaking and writing concerning such matters, it is well; but if not, he shall be excommunicated and cut off from the holy, catholic and apostolic Church of Christ and from the orthodox community of Christians.

52. Furthermore, if anyone else should appear again repeating any of his blasphemous and heretical spoken or written accusations against the monks or in any way harassing them in such matters, he will be subject to the same condemnation from Our Modesty; he also shall be excommunicated and cut off from the holy, catholic and apostolic Church of Christ and from the orthodox community of Christians.

53. With severity therefore and spiritual austerity and censure we say: No longer from now on and hereafter shall anyone at all make dogmatic discourses concerning these and other doctrinal issues (that is, either in writing or unwritten), since no small scandals spring up from such activity in the Church of God. Confusion and disturbance, earthquakes and tidal waves assail the souls of the listeners, especially of the simpler people. Undoubtedly indeed it was for this reason that the God-bearing and holy fathers established the previously cited canons. Exercising foresight that no one hereafter may fall into similar errors, and publishing the present document as security, we have subscribed with our own signature, in the month of August of the ninth indiction. It was also subscribed by the divine

and patriarchal hand: John by the mercy of God archbishop of Constantinople New Rome and Ecumenical Patriarch.

The Synodal Tome of 1351[774]

1. We do not think that anyone is unaware of the madness of the Church's common enemy, or of the Savior's victory. Although innumerable troubles have flowed over the Church, through this victory she has not only survived his assaults but even shines more brilliantly. The blood of God and the voluntary passion and the cross demonstrate the enemy's madness; of God's assistance the persecutors of the Church provide an accurate testimony. Some of them were transformed into evangelists, others were proclaimed a monument of God's power not by their elevation but by their fall. So, it was, and the common enemy could not keep still; but as if blaming himself for inadequate strategy, he undertook the war against the Church, not with a small nation as of old with the Jews, but bitterly arming the whole inhabited world against her. His generals were the associates of Diocletian and Maximian and Decius and anyone like them, who perished as shamefully as they had known how to fight. Their memorial has gone like an echo, but of God's Church the sound has gone out into all the earth; the most reliable testimony of her power is the bodies of the martyrs which drive out all demons. Thus, the power of God is proved extraordinary even through her misfortunes. But the evil one did not learn even when he suffered, fool that he is. He reversed his tactics for attacking the Church, for he very much despaired of openly fighting, disliking public shame. Instead, he entered into those around Sabellius and Arius and their followers. Purporting to be getting rid of polytheism, he persuaded the mindless fools by the pretext of honour to one God not to believe at all in the true God. But he himself turned out to be plotting against himself, because the Church of God won as booty of this

---

774 Holy Synod of Constantinople, "Synodical Tome of 1351," in *Creeds & Confessions of Faith in the Christian Tradition*, ed. Jaroslav Pelikan & Valerie Hotchkiss (New Haven: Yale University Press 2003), 334-374.

war the doctrine that the three persons of the Trinity have equality in honour.

2. This evil one laid many other sieges against the Church; and now yielding, now advancing, at one time with unhealthy doctrines, at another time with pleasures, in which he is accustomed to delight, of which the end is separation from God, at last he put on the person of Barlaam, to wage war against the truth. This man, a monk of Calabrian origin who had advanced far in the learning of the pagan Greeks and relied entirely on this, proceeded against the truth and those sacredly adhering to it. He accused of ditheism those who call uncreated not only the trihypostatic essence of God, in which no one can participate, but also the grace of the Spirit, which is eternal and deifying, in which the worthy participate. When a divine synod was assembled on these issues, he was refuted and excommunicated by the holy, catholic and apostolic Church of Christ through the theological writings of the holy fathers. The advocates of the word of truth were Palamas, who is now the most reverent metropolitan of Thessalonica, and the monks. But a little later Akindynos, adhering to his evil opinion, not at all chastened or improved by the condemnation of his teacher, undertook to accuse the same men again on the same issues. He deceitfully denied his teacher and invoked terrible curses upon him, insisting that he had never believed or spoken the same as Barlaam, in order that he would be thus permitted to speak; but to those to whom he spoke, he showed the hidden Barlaam, believing, speaking, and writing the same evil opinion as his.

3. For this heresy, then, when a second synod had been assembled, under the presidency of our present mighty and holy autocrat, the lord John Cantacuzenus, Akindynos was proved to be holding and teaching the same beliefs as Barlaam and making the same accusations against the monks. Because of this he drew on himself the same condemnation as Barlaam, from the preceding synodical tome against the blasphemies of that Barlaam. He was cut off from the whole Christian community, as this very synodical tome recites, for many other reasons and especially because he undertook to demonstrate that the light of the Lord's transfiguration, seen by the blessed disciples and apostles who went up with them, is created and cir-

cumscribed and is nothing more than a perceptible light. The synodical tome did not excommunicate this Barlaam alone, but anyone who, following his example, makes war on the monks and the Church of God and thereby subjects himself to the same penalties. For it says, word for word: "Furthermore, if anyone else should appear again repeating any of his blasphemous and heretical spoken or written accusations against the monks or in any way harassing them in such matters, he will be subject to the same condemnation from our Modesty; he also shall be excommunicated and cut off from the holy, catholic and apostolic Church of Christ and from the orthodox community of Christians."

4.   But he who works in the sons of disobedience, as it is written, the wicked serpent, source of evil, saw that when he attacked the true faith and those who held firmly to it, using men not commended by their rank, because of this he was unable to reach those whom he wished. Therefore, he entered into John, who was then counted among the patriarchs, a vessel openly receptive of his evil intention. This man held the same beliefs as Akindynos, and had done and written and plotted many things against the true faith and those who adhered to it, or rather himself against himself (for he was the one who in writing had brought the condemnation on that Barlaam who was excommunicated), besides seizing the civil war as a golden opportunity. This man also found the worthy recompense for his own zeal and his wicked plots. For having been refuted, he was deposed; and when he also had been excommunicated and that by synodical judgment, a sacred tome was published by the synod, declaring both his attachment to Akindynos' heresy and at the same time his unjustified rage towards the Orthodox. But the tome, confirmed by the signature of thirty hierarchs, and later approved and signed also by the most holy patriarch of Jerusalem, expels from the catholic Church and cuts off from the community of Christians not only Akindynos and the holder of the patriarchate, "But also", it says, "if anyone else at all is ever caught believing or saying or writing the same things against the aforesaid most honourable priest-monk Lord Gregory Palamas and the monks with him, or rather against the venerable theologians and the Church itself, we both make the same decree against him and subject him to the same condemna-

tion, whether he be one of the ordained or of the laity. Lord Gregory Palamas himself, the oft-mentioned most honourable priest-monk and the monks who agree with him, who have written and believed nothing contrary to the divine sayings, but have understood with accurate examination, or rather have defended the divine sayings and our common faith and tradition in all ways as is fitting, we do not only judge higher in every respect than the disputes against them or rather against the Church of God, as also the earlier synodical tome declares, but also we declare them most reliable defenders and champions and helpers of the Church and of the true faith. For thus also the preceding tome of those councils will hold, just as indeed it holds, that which is reliable and secure."

5. But he who always rejoices at our calamities did not even thus know how to keep peace, nor did he go around seeking to remedy a lack of agents. He still had some who had kept company with Barlaam and that Akindynos, and were fatally ill with their disease. Through them he subjected to himself the one who is called bishop of Ephesus and the bishop of Gannos, Gregory and Decius. These men formed a society and collected other persons as companions, never thinking up anything healthy at any time, stirring up dissension against the Church of God, zealously striving to lead the many astray and to cut them off pitiably from the Church, supposing that they would obtain glory from this for themselves. So, it was necessary because of this to assemble a great council, as our most clement emperor took pity on the souls which were perishing. Therefore his mighty and holy majesty from God and the most holy ecumenical patriarch, Lord Kallistos, summoned the most reverend and honourable hierarchs of Herakleia, Thessalonica, Cyzicus, Philadelphia, Chalcedon, Melenikos, Amasea, Pontoerakleia, Pegae, Berroia, Trebizond, Trajanoupolis, Selivria, Apro, Amastris, Ainos, Sogdaia, Brysa, Madutoi, Bizue, Grevella, Medea, Tenedos, Kallioupolis, Hexamilios; the hierarchs of Adrianopolis, Christoupolis and Didymoteichon being also in agreement. Also present were the God-beloved bishops of Panion, Charioupolis, Pamphylos, Athyra, Campania, Sinaon, Eleutheroupolis. Our most clement mighty and holy sovereign and emperor Lord John Cantacuzenus presided in the hall which is called Alexiakon of the sacred palace of Blachernae. Seated together

with his holy majesty was also the most holy ecumenical patriarch Lord Kallistos, as well as the much-desired brother of his holy majesty the most fortunate Augustus, Lord Manuel Asen, and also the much-desired nephew of his holy majesty the extremely august Lord Andronikos Asen. The senate also sat beside them with the archbishops and rulers of the Church, and gathered together the abbots and archimandrites in this blessed city, and in addition not a few priest-monks and priests and monks. The rulers of the state were not unrepresented, as well as many bystanders who were avid listeners in these matters. These men who were causing disruption and dissension in the Church were also summoned and were asked why, while an emperor was living piously, they dared such things against the true faith. They alleged as cause that some addition had been made in the confession of the appointed hierarchs. They blamed also the metropolitan of Thessalonica, since they said they were scandalised by some of his writings in controversy with Barlaam and Akindynos.

6.   The metropolitan of Thessalonica said: "Well then, you yourselves believe these doctrines". But just as Akindynos denied Barlaam, the leader of his error, so they denied both Barlaam and Akindynos. The metropolitan of Thessalonica in reply said: "Indeed most of those who, as we previously said, were speaking in opposition to us and openly defending the heresy of Barlaam and Akindynos have continued unrepentant even until now. The rest of you are undoubtedly clearly aligned with them, because you are closely following the example of their doctrines. On these issues", he said, "the addition by the divine synod, which you say you dislike (which would not justly be called an addition, since it merely interprets the sixth holy ecumenical council), is nothing other than an excommunication of Barlaam and Akindynos. It is obvious to everyone with any understanding at all that those who blame this are defending Barlaam and Akindynos." They again denied following those two; but as they began to say in what matters they were scandalised, they cited as cause in the very words what both Barlaam and Akindynos before recited against the metropolitan of Thessalonica and the monks. As it became obvious in consequence that they were incurably ill with those men's disease, the most glorious and holy emperor decided with the agreement of the most holy ecumenical patriarch and all the sacred

synod that the truth in these matters should be determined by an enquiry concerning the doctrines in question, examining them from the beginning to the end. When the metropolitan of Thessalonica joined in praise of this decision, they utterly disagreed. But being requested to set forth openly their own opinion concerning the issues, they were altogether unwilling, citing the previously mentioned grounds of offence. After many speeches had been exchanged during this first session, the discussion of this disagreement was adjourned; but it was ratified in writing that in the second session these men who differ from the Church shall begin wherever they wish and say as much as they want, and that then after them the metropolitan of Thessalonica beginning wherever he wishes shall say everything according to his judgment.

7. When the second session was assembled, those men also presented themselves. To begin with they spoke against the metropolitan of Thessalonica as much as they wished. When he in turn began to respond point by point to what they had said, they confused the words and set out to flee. After making many vehement arguments, they refused to remain. Although they gave promises to stay in the city again for another session, they fled, with no one pursuing, before the appointed time. But the metropolitan of Thessalonica, exhorted by our emperor from God and the holy Church of God, made a fuller discourse, speaking freely to all concerning the doctrines set before the Church for investigation. He added this also: "Defence of Orthodoxy is one thing and confession of faith is another. In a controversy it is not necessary for the defender to speak with great accuracy in his expression, as the great Basil says; but in a confession accuracy in all respects is preserved and required. Because of this I added to my adversarial speech against Barlaam and Akindynos also a confession of the faith which I received from the saints, so that those who happened on our words might learn from the confession the significance of the controversy." When he said this, our mighty and holy sovereign and emperor asked for this confession of his, and when it was provided, he commanded that it should be read. When this was done, each was asked to say what his judgment was concerning it. There was no one who did not make mention of praise in declaring his opinion of that statement, both admiring

the metropolitan of Thessalonica and praying that he himself might depart with the doctrines of that confession and appear with them before the Judge of the living and the dead on the day when all must make their defence.

8. The session after this was also assembled. Coming forward, the dissenters also asked for their own confession to be read. When this was done, at the end they added this also: "As for Barlaam and Akindynos, we hold our judgment concerning them as the holy Church of God believes concerning men like them". After many intervening speeches had been exchanged, the opponents began their accusation against the metropolitan of Thessalonica. It was like this: "That indeed in some of his compositions he often writes about two and many divinities, some superior and some inferior." When they made this argument often and rattled it around and kept criticizing these expressions, the most pious emperor commanded us to clarify these matters: "Are you making an issue of the very words of what has been said, of the reality revealed through the words, or both? If on one hand the war is over the reality, why do you do battle with the shadow of the reality, holding fast to the words? We must examine the bare reality, and the theologians must seek the truth in this. But if on the other hand you have been in agreement all along on the reality, why do you blame the words? We for our part have not come together here for the sake of words, nor will we join battle, as the Theologian says, over names. We know no danger in the words as long as the mind appears to be healthy."

9. In reality to this the metropolitan of Thessalonica said, "I have little to say about words, for our truth and our piety does not lie in expressions but in reality, as Gregory the Theologian says. I make my struggle for doctrines and reality. And if anyone agrees in the reality, I do not quarrel over the words. But in regard to the accusation brought forward by my opponents, I say this. I have not believed, I do not believe, nor by the grace of Christ will I believe in two or many or different divinities in the Holy Trinity, so that there would be one of the Father, another of the Son, and another of the Spirit. Those who believe this I subject to anathema. But neither do I say that anything else is divinity outside of the trihypostatic Godhead. I have called

by the name of divinity not a divine or angelic essence or hypostasis (as the great Dionysius says) but divine energies and emanations (so to speak) proceeding by nature and from eternity for God. In this I judge that I am speaking in agreement with the saints. But I would not have said even this, if I had not been compelled by my opponent to reply and to strive with him, when he said that the essence of God alone is uncreated, but reduced all divine power and energy to the status of creature, differing from the essence. In particular I said this without inferring many divinities in consequence, as they falsely allege; and this is clear both from my other writings and from the confession. For in all of them this is attributed to me, being said by my opponents, but not accepted by me; for I know one Godhead, the same trihypostatic and omnipotent and active. Except neither then was my purpose concerning words, but the whole contest was concerning reality, nor now do I differ over names and syllables. If the reality is correctly proclaimed by the grace of Christ, I am ready to embrace and accept everything which the divine synod decides concerning the words." At this the most pious and clement emperor and the divine synod, fully approving the metropolitan of Thessalonica for his pious attitude, which he continued using in divine matters, and especially praising him for his right judgment, defined securely that two or many or any number of divinities should not be spoken or even thought (for this had explicitly not been said by the theologians); but the distinction of divine essence and divine energy or divine energies they bade very much to be thought and spoken, since this teaching had been expressly preached by the Church, as will be demonstrated below. The metropolitan of Thessalonica willingly and eagerly received this. And the third session concluded with this.

10. When the fourth session took place, the dissenters began again to criticize certain expressions occurring in the writings of the metropolitan of Thessalonica, paying no attention to the reality. But as the most glorious emperor and the synod were examining the reality, and from the theologians of the church were seeking the demonstrations of the problem, the synodical tome published against Barlaam was brought forth. When this had been read by the divine command of our most clement emperor, it demonstrated that the dissenters shared in all respects in the heresy of Barlaam. But they refused not

to keep on opposing what was written there, especially concerning the most divine light of the Lord's transfiguration. Not only so, but when the metropolitan of Thessalonica and those who differed from the Church were asked what opinion they held about the most divine light, the one through what he said and read from his writings in the hearing of all, consistently proved that he was conformed unfailingly with the thought of the theologians; but the others, through what they said and were found writing, were proved to be separating into created and uncreated the one Godhead of the Father and the Son and the Holy Spirit, by calling the essence of God uncreated divinity, deprived of all divine power and energy, but rejecting and denying all divine power and energy and simply all his omnipotence, and reducing God to a created being, and calling him two divinities, uncreated and created, superior and truly inferior. They said at one time that the light of divinity which shone on Tabor is the essence of God, but at another time they called it appearance and veil and image and creature, so that the same light was according to them both created thing and essence of God. The metropolitan of Thessalonica brought forward writings of theirs written in their own hands, in which they accused him of saying that the most divine light and radiance was uncreated but not the essence of God. They also accused the metropolitan of Thessalonica of saying that there are many divinities, since indeed he insists that all the divine powers and energies common to the three hypostases are uncreated. By this accusation they made it clear that their war was not over expressions, but that they acknowledged neither the distinction of divine essence and divine energy nor that the divine and omnipotent energy is uncreated.

11. In this regard as the theologians of the Church were being brought forward as evidence from the great Basil many other passages were read and in particular this: "For if Eunomius applies no concept to God, so that he may not seem to reverence God with human titles, he will confess that all the attributes of God are equally essence; how therefore would it not be ridiculous to say that the creative power is essence, the providential power is also essence, the power of foresight likewise, and simply every energy is reckoned as essence?"

12. A passage was read from the theologian of Damascus, in what he teaches concerning the two energies in our Lord Jesus Christ, saying, "It must be known that energy is one thing and energetic faculty is another, and action is another and the actor is another; for the active and essential impulse of the nature is energy, but the nature from which the energy proceeds is the energetic faculty. The accomplishment of the energy is action, but the one who uses the energy is the actor, that is the hypostasis."

The glorious Maximus, in the chapter entitled "From the Secret Discourse" says: "Undoubtedly it is necessary to say that Christ has wills and energies, and entirely necessary; for none of existing beings subsists without a natural energy. The holy fathers say clearly that no nature whatever exists or is known without its essential energy."

In what the dissenters said, they were not only continuing to fight against the saints individually, but already were attempting to overthrow and dissolve the holy sixth ecumenical council itself. That council had no other purpose; its whole subject concerned the two natural wills and the two natural energies in our Lord Jesus Christ. Because of this it was necessary to bring in the Acts of the council and to read them, and from these to proclaim the true faith; so, they were set out in the midst. But as soon as they were brought forth the dissenters at once cried out, "Not the Acts of the council, but read the definition only." But while the divine synod was uncertain what this outcry meant, and why they rejected and did not accept the Acts, those men still did not depart in any degree from the same futile evil opinion and their twisted attitude, not at all accepting the reading of the Acts.

At this, by the glorious command of our most clement emperor, a passage was read from the Synodikon which is customarily read on the ambo on the Sunday of Orthodoxy, which word for word is this: "On those who reject the words of the holy fathers, which were expressed at the confirmation of the correct doctrine of the Church of God, of Athanasius, Cyril, Ambrose, Amphilochius who spoke God's words, Leo the most holy bishop of the elder Rome, and the rest, and in addition on those who did not embrace the Acts of the ecumenical councils, the fourth, that is, and the sixth, anathema."

On this subject a passage from the Acts was also read, containing these words: "For who, even if he is slow in understanding, will not see, what is evident to all, that it is impossible and contrary to the order of nature for a nature to be able to exist and not to have a natural energy? Not even the heretics ever thought fit to say this, although they invented all the human villainies and crooked controversies against the uprightness of the faith and assemblies suitable to their wickedness. How therefore can it be rashly asserted at the present time, what neither the holy fathers ever spoke, nor the impure heretics dared to invent, that the two natures of Christ, namely the divine and the human, of which the properties are known to be unconfused in Christ, have one energy? What man who thinks logically will ever be able to demonstrate, when they say it is one, whether they can say it is temporal or eternal, divine or human, uncreated or created, the same as the Father's or different from the Father's? If (you see) it is one and the same, it is one and common to the divinity and humanity of Christ, which is absurd to say. Therefore, since the Son of God is himself God and man, performing human actions on earth, the Father also has acted equally with him by nature, since whatever the Father does, the Son also does equally. As the truth provides, insofar as Christ performed certain human acts, it is attributed only to his person as Son; these acts are therefore not the same as those of the Father. And obviously Christ performed one kind of action and another, so that according to his divinity, whatever the Father does, the Son also does equally; and according to his humanity, this same one performed as man the actions which are proper to man, since he is true God and true man. Whence we truly believe that this same, being one, has natural energies, namely the divine and the human, the uncreated and the created, as true and perfect God and true and perfect man, one and the same, mediator between God and man, the Lord Jesus Christ."

And again, from the same Acts another passage was presented; containing these words: "We know that there is an energy of each nature, I mean what is essential and natural and corresponding, inseparably proceeding from each essence and nature, according to its inherent natural and essential equality and the accompanying indivisible and at the same time unconfused energy of each essence. For this makes the difference of the energies in Christ, just as the being of each nature gives it its nature."

13. Moreover, the definition which they sought, when it was read, had this word for word: "The present holy ecumenical council faithfully receiving and with uplifted hands embracing the offering made of the most holy and blessed pope of the elder Rome Agathon to our most pious emperor"; and after an interval: "following both the five holy ecumenical councils and the holy and select fathers and defining in agreement with them, confesses our Lord Jesus Christ, our true God, one of the holy and consubstantial and life-giving Trinity, perfect in divinity and the same perfect in humanity, and like us in every respect except sin. Before the ages he was begotten of the Father according to divinity, but in the last days the same for our sake and for our salvation from the Holy Spirit and the Virgin Mary (she who is properly and in truth called Theotokos) according to humanity; one and the same Christ, Son, Lord, only-begotten. He is made known in two natures without confusion, without change, indivisibly, inseparably. The difference of the natures is not at all removed because of the union, but rather the property of each nature is preserved. The two natures come together in one person and one hypostasis, not divided or separated into two persons, but one and the same Son only-begotten, God the Word, Lord Jesus Christ, just as of old concerning him the prophets and Jesus Christ himself taught us and handed over the creed of the holy fathers to us. And likewise, we proclaim two natural wills or volitions in him, and two natural energies inseparably, unchangeably, indivisibly, unconfusedly, according to the teaching of the holy fathers, and two natural wills not opposed (far from it) as the impious heretics said, but his human will following and not conflicting or contrary, rather indeed even subjecting itself to his omnipotent divine will."

14. When these had been read, the leaders of the heresy were like deaf men, crying out and insisting that the divine and uncreated essence and its divine and uncreated energy are one and altogether indistin-

guishable. They also brought forward statements, one from the holy confessor Maximus, the other from the confessor among the saints Theodore the Branded, twisting and misinterpreting these towards their own impiety. For how would the glorious Maximus have made war on the energy of God, he who on behalf of the two energies in Christ, namely the divine and the human, was driven such a course, was deprived of his godly tongue, had his hand cut off, and finally, condemned to perpetual exile, nobly embraced the death of a martyr? But as they still opposed and reproached the metropolitan of Thessalonica for saying that the divine energy is Godhead, passages of the saints were read, first of all Basil the Great in what he wrote to Eustathius the physician: "I do not know how those who fabricate everything cite the designation of divinity to prove the nature, as if they had not heard from the Scripture that there is no such thing as an appointed nature. Moses was appointed god of the Egyptians, when he who called him, this said to him, 'I gave you as God to Pharaoh'. Therefore, the designation signifies some power, either of vision or of action. But the divine nature, as it is, remains inexpressible in all the conceptual names, as we say."

15. When Gregory of Nyssa in his Oration concerning the Deity of the Son and the Spirit says, "The Spirit-fighters say that divinity signifies nature ... but we say that the divine nature either does not have a signifying name or does not have one for us. But if it is called something either from human custom or from the divine Scripture, it is one of the things which are indicated around it. But the divine nature itself remains ineffable and inexpressible, surpassing every signification by the voice. Let them recognise also the serpent as an accuser of their foolish blasphemy, for he shows that the name of Godhead has the signification of visionary power ... for advising to touch what was forbidden, he promises this, that 'your eyes will be opened, and you will be like gods'. Do you see that he confirms the power of sight by the mention of divinity? For it is not possible to see anything unless the eyes are opened. Therefore, the designation of divinity indicates not nature but the power of sight." Again, the same saint writing to Ablabius says, "'God' signifies the energizer, but 'divinity' signifies energy. None of the three is energy, but rather each of them is energizer."

16. When these men had been altogether refuted in this way, they were summoned by the Church to repentance. First our most clement emperor with attractive and appealing words exhorted them vehemently not to turn away from the good medicine of repentance. But they did not accept, saying openly, "I do not wish to know your ways". For they persisted in what they understood badly from the beginning. Therefore, by the glorious command of our mighty emperor and the most holy ecumenical patriarch a tome was read which had been decided a little time before for deposition of the bishops of Ephesus and Gannos and others, on the grounds that they had caught the disease of Barlaam and Akindynos. It had not yet taken effect, because they were waiting for their change of heart and repentance, and were trying by every manner and means to elicit this with all eagerness and zeal. And when it had been read, the most honourable great chartophylax and chief of the philosophers, according to the ecclesiastical custom, began to ask each one what opinion he held concerning the dogmatic topics which had been individually discussed and examined. And all with one mouth and moved by one Spirit confessed openly, along with the union, also the theologically appropriate distinction and difference between the divine essence and energy, following the theologians. They acknowledge that the divine energy is uncreated, just as indeed the essence is also; and willingly they heard and accepted that this divine energy is also named divinity by the same theologians.

17. When the most holy ecumenical patriarch was asked himself also to express his own opinion on these questions, he first went through a full discussion of the difference between divine essence and energy, examining thoroughly and individually the kinds of difference discussed by the saints. In addition, he demonstrated the inseparable union of the energy and the divine essence. He also showed that the divine energy was called "uncreated" and "divinity" by the saints. Accordingly, he thus threw himself wholly into counsel to those who differed, exhorting, advising, rebuking, in every way with the greatest eagerness and zeal out of love for God summoning them to repentance and urging them to agreement with the saints and the holy synod. But as he saw that even so these men were incurably ill, holding once and for all to the former blasphemies and altogether

rejecting repentance, taking up zeal worthy not only of himself and his virtue since childhood, but worthy also of his patriarchal throne, he stripped the bishops of Ephesus and Gannos of their episcopal insignia and of all priestly functions, with the agreement of the holy synod; but the others with them, the leaders of the heresy and those who followed them in wickedness and were subject to condemnation with them, were dismissed. Some of them sought forgiveness and obtained this through repentance. And so, this session ended.

18. From that time a few days passed, as our most clement and holy emperor had commanded, wisely keeping open the door of repentance for the dissenters. But as they still were incurable, he decided to gather another synod again, so that through examination the truth of Orthodoxy concerning the problems raised would become more evident from the theological writings of the saints. And when this came about, as the heterodox were not willing to meet, but refused this once and for call, the most pious emperor gave the following instructions: "Many dogmatic topics have been raised. First, is there in regard to God a theologically appropriate distinction between essence and energy? Then, if the distinction is affirmed, is this energy created or uncreated? Third, if this divine energy is shown to be uncreated, how would one avoid supposing that God is therefore composite, for which the heterodox dare to reproach the Church of God? Fourth, is the name of divinity used by the theologians not only in reference to the essence but also in reference to the divine energy (for from this the enemies of the Church spew out that ugly charge of ditheism on the Church of God)? Fifth, do the theologians say that the essence is superior in some respect to the energy, since this also incurs blame from the opposition? And finally, still, if it is possible to participate in God, is the participation according to the essence or according to the energy? Since so many subjects of enquiry have just now been set before us, we should not discuss all of them at once for thus we would not grasp the subject at all accurately, nor as we proposed. Let us instead determine concerning each question individually and then go on to another, using as unerring guides the venerable theologians.

19. "And first, if it is agreed, let us discuss the first question. Is there a theologically appropriate distinction in regard to God between essence and energy (which is denied by the dissenters, who suppose that they can infer many other absurd things from this and polytheism in particular), or are they altogether the same and indistinguishable?" When the mighty emperor had given these instructions and the divine synod had attended to what he said, "We know no other road", they said, "O most pious emperor, which more easily leads to the truth than this which you have indicated to us just now". And when the theologians had been read in the hearing of all, to determine what opinion they held concerning these issues, it became clear that those who do not teach the distinction of the divine essence and energy, as well as their union, are godless and surround themselves with many other absurdities. For according to the great Dionysius, "That which has no power or energy neither exists nor is anything nor can anything at all be affirmed or denied of it". But that which has something differs undoubtedly in some respect from what it has. Therefore, if there is not a difference between the divine essence and the divine energy, the essence of God cannot have energy. But that which does not have energy is not energised, and that which is not energised is nonexistent.

20. The inspired John of Damascus writes, "The eternal generation is the work of the divine nature, but the creation is the work of the divine will"; and St Cyril writes, "Making is from the energy, but begetting is from the nature, and nature and energy are not the same". As for those who say that the divine essence and the divine energy are indistinguishable, since according to St Cyril begetting is from the nature, but according to them the energy is indistinguishable from the nature, then according to them begetting will also be from the energy, and thus the things made will be things eternally begotten, because they are from the divine nature. But since on the other hand making is from the energy, but the nature is indistinguishable from the energy according to them, then making will be from the nature. And thus, according to them what is from the nature will be created things. Likewise, when the same saint writes in the second of the dialogues to Hermias, "Besides all this we say that the burning fire has been made from the energy of God, and indeed also water whose

character is to chill", those who say that essence and energy are the same and indistinguishable will be forced to say that fire and water are from the essence of God. And thus, the heresy now has become worse than the error of the pagan Greeks, if indeed those men believed that only the rational soul was from the essence of God, but these men think that even these material perceptible bodies are from God's essence.

21. Furthermore, in the Gospel according to John the Lord our God said, "I and the Father are one". The glorious Chrysostom in the sixtieth homily of the interpretation of this gospel, elucidating this expression, says that this assertion is made in reference to power, and his whole discourse was about this. "But if the power is the same, evidently the essence is also." And a little later he says, "For it is not possible to learn anything from something different, whether it be essence or power". And again, on the same Gospel, when the apostle Philip says, "Lord, show us the Father, and it will suffice for us," this glorious Chrysostom in the same series of homilies says, "Let us see what it is that Philip seeks to see – is it the wisdom of the Father? Is it the goodness? No, but the very 'what God is' – the essence itself". Again, the same saint interprets the apostolic saying of the epistle to the Romans, which says, "For the mind of the flesh is dead, but the mind of the Spirit is life and peace". He says, "By mind of the flesh he means evil, and by mind of the Spirit he means the grace given and the energy joined to the good choice. He is not at all speaking here about hypostasis and essence". Again, the same Chrysostom, in the discourse here he interprets, "Put your hand under my thigh and swear", says this word for word: "The Lord's flesh was the true candle stand which showed the illumination of the Holy Spirit with sevenfold grace. For Isaiah says, 'A rod shall come forth from the root of Jesse, and a blossom will come up from it, and the Spirit of God will rest on it'. What kind of spirit? The Spirit of God which is manifold in energies and great in nature will rest on it (here he interprets the essence, he means that which brings the energies of the Spirit), the Spirit of wisdom and understanding, the Spirit of counsel and might, the Spirit of judgment and piety, the Spirit of the fear of God". By the symbol of a seven-branched candle stand he represents the seven graces of the Holy Spirit which have rested on

the Lord's body. And again, the same glorious Chrysostom in the treatise concerning the Holy Spirit says, "One does not receive all the gracious gifts, lest anyone think that grace is nature."

22. Moreover, since the holy martyr and philosopher Justin writes, "As, therefore, God has essence on the one hand in order to exist, but will in order to create", he who rejects the distinction of essence and will rejects both the existence of God and his creativity. Whoever rejects the distinction, is he not clearly proved to be both denying God and glorifying what happens by accident? For according to the glorious John from Damascus, "The will is also energy", as he makes clear in the thirty-sixth of the dogmatic chapters concerning energy. After speaking first concerning other matters and especially about human and divine will, he adds in the beginning of the next chapter these words: "One must know that all the aforesaid powers, those of learning, of life, and of nature and of skill are called energies. For the natural power and motion of each essence is energy, of which only the nonexistent is deprived."

23. When these topics had been altogether thoroughly examined, it was very clearly proved that the distinction was valid and could not be otherwise, not in persuasive words of human wisdom, as the inspired Paul says, but in words taught by the Holy Spirit, that is by the divinely inspired theological writings of the fathers. The divine synod said that those who had tried to differ in any way at all on this issue, even if they had not done so before, should now at least piously expel the disease of contentiousness from their minds, and be readily willing to be convinced by our common leaders and teachers of the true faith, who send forth voices all but more brilliant than any trumpet concerning the distinction of divine essence and energy. They should no longer attempt to oppose them in any way or try to meddle any further with what energy is and what kind of the distinction there is and how this might come about.

24. As it seems, they have not heard Father Chrysostom, where he explains the Divine Gospel according to John, teaching that the divine energy is inexplicable and incomprehensible and beyond the laws of nature. For he says, "If you do not know how to interpret this wind, of

which you receive perception by hearing and touch, nor its way, how do you concern yourself with the energy of the divine Spirit, when you do not understand the energy of the wind, although you hear its sound? 'It blows where it wishes' is said to exhibit the power of the Paraclete. If no one grasps the wind, but it goes where it wishes, much less can the energy of the Spirit be grasped by the laws of nature, or the boundaries of corporeal generation, or anything else of this kind."

Neither have they listened to the great Basil, when he makes a theological reply to Eunomius: "So therefore if we were going to measure everything by comprehension, and to suppose that what cannot be grasped by reasoning does not even exist at all, the reward of faith will vanish, the reward of hope will vanish." How would we still be worthy of the blessings which are stored up for faith in things not seen, if we believed only those things which are apparent according to reason? Whence were the Gentiles subjected to vanity and their foolish heart darkened? Was it not because following those things which appear to reasoning, they disbelieved the preaching of the Spirit? Whose destruction does Isaiah mourn: "Woe to those who are wise in their own sight and understanding before themselves"? Is it not people like these?

25. They should have heard these things from the saints who wrote theology, and indeed they should at once have listened willingly. Most pleasantly they would have attended to those and would have submitted painlessly to their glorious voices indicating this distinction, with pious silence embracing and accepting it. They would have added the "how" either not all or at least not in an attempt to refute the distinction, if indeed they expected to gather themselves with those counted in any way among the pious. But since they reached such a height of arrogance and shamelessness, or rather of insanity, as to rage against the very saints and the ecumenical councils and all (so to speak) the sacred theologians, and to dare to bring even these into public examination, and to say that some of them gave off a smell of pagan Greek and similar doctrines, and that others are indicated for the greatest ignorance although they were a complete synod. They also asserted that some have been brought to this theology by force, even though they willingly chose a martyr's death on

its behalf, and that others have written this as encomium and not as truth (O, how would one endure to tell their blasphemies individually?) — come now, because they do not accept the obedience of the lovers of Christ, as somewhere someone of the fathers rejected by them said. Whatever at any time is said by the saints concerning the divine doctrine, even if it is not very much fitted out with truth and theological precision, we rely on the God whom they teach. Whenever we try to explain briefly the manner of union and distinction of divine essence and energy, we do not attempt to invent reasons of our own to support the theology which has been piously stated by them long ago, but we keep the law which we have zealously kept everywhere, to confirm the doctrines of the Church by the teachers of the Church, and never from ourselves to put forward or to take away any part of the doctrines they have taught. Using this principle here also, when we have heard the saints explicitly proclaiming that the divine energy is from the divine essence, we do not think that this energy is from God in the same way that everything is, as the dissenters suppose along with many other absurdities. For "from God" is said also in regard to created things, but "from the essence of God" is never said in regard to any of the creatures; especially indeed the saints deny this altogether.

26. For the great Basil says, "What is made is not from the essence of the maker." The glorious Damascene also says, "The creation, even if it has taken place after this, yet is not from the essence of God"; and "Creation and making is altogether different: the thing created and made comes to be from the outside and not from the essence of the Creator and Maker". No indeed, but we did not suppose that the energy is from the divine essence as being outside of the divine essence, as it came into the opposition's head to say nonsensically, not so much impiously as ignorantly (may no one ever be so far out of his mind). Rather, knowing that this energy is an essential and natural activity of God according to the theologians, we say that it proceeds and flows from the divine essence as from an ever-flowing spring, and never appears without this. It always remains inseparable from the divine essence, and from eternity exists along with it, and is indivisibly united, because it cannot be separated from the divine essence by any age or temporal or spatial interval, but timelessly and

eternally proceeds from it and inseparably exists together with it. For the great Athanasius says, "When all things are activated by God through Christ in the Holy Spirit, we see that the energy is indivisible of the Father and the Son and the Holy Spirit". And Athanasius, marvelous among the saints, who also taught the holy ecumenical council to call this man great, in his second treatise concerning the uncircumscribed, says, "Let us see what the heretics presume to say about God. They say God is in everything by energy, but by essence nowhere, calling energy the result coming forth from the energy; but I would say for my part that the energy of God is inseparable from his nature". And a little later he says: "Where the energy appears, the essence from which it proceeds is contemplated along with this, for each is uncircumscribed, and because of this they are altogether inseparable from each other; for the energy proclaims the hidden essence, and it is contemplated as being present along with the energy, since it cannot exist without this." And again, he says, "The energy is in everything, but the essence is inseparable from this."

27. Indeed, just as we proclaim the divine and eternal union not only with the word "inseparable" but especially with the communion of the uncreated and uncircumscribed according to the theology of the saints, so also again we have learned to glorify the distinction and difference which according to them is theologically appropriate. We do not draw them apart into complete division and separation, nor imagine that this distinction is something foreign and a natural alienation, nor do we separate these from each other by intervals (far from it). We are taught by the saints to accept the causes and effects according to nature, distinguishing only in theologically appropriate thought what are united and inseparable by nature. For the great Athanasius in his fifth treatise against the Arians says that whatever is "from something" is one thing, and that "from which it is" is another thing; therefore, according to this saint they are two. But if they were not two, but were said of the same one, the cause and the effect will be the same, the begetter and the begotten, which has been shown absurd in the case of Sabellius. Therefore, since it has been convincingly demonstrated according to all the theologians that the energy is from the essence, it has clearly appeared that they are one thing and another, that they are two, and therefore that

they differ from one another, as they are "that from which" and "that which is from something", that is the cause and the effect, as this great theologian teaches the divine matters. And a little later he says: "Let a human illustration be the fire and the radiance from it: they are two in existing and in being seen, but one in that the radiance is from the fire and inseparable". So just as in the case of fire and the light from it, the one being nature and cause, the other natural and effect, he has said "one" because of inseparability and again "different" because of cause and effect, so also in the case of the divine nature and the energy from it, we must understand the identity and the different — the one according to the inseparable union, the other according to the cause and what results from it as cause. For neither does the sameness drive out the different, nor indeed does the difference at all overthrow the oneness; but we have contemplated each piously according to the saints, nor will each at all be turned aside by the other.

28. The glorious Gregory of Nyssa also knew full well that this distinction of the causes and effects is attached to truth and does not at all injure the identity of nature. In writing to Ablabius he said: "When we confess the indistinguishability of the nature, we also do not deny the difference according to cause and effect, by which alone we understand that the one is distinguished from the other, in that we believe the one to be cause, the other to be from the cause". But his brother, Basil the truly great, obviously provides once and for all the difference for these causes and effects, as he states dogmatically their order from natural succession. He thus explicitly names the first and the second in the case of the cause and the effect, and judges that not to confess this, but to try to deny these things, is absurd and irrational. He said that Eunomius either did not comprehend this distinction or hid it intentionally, when he wrote: "But that Eunomius either does not know or intentionally hid; because there is a kind of order not arising from our arbitrary stipulation, but occurring in the very succession according to nature, as the 'from it' is for fire in relation to light. In these cases, we name first the cause, second what is from it, not separating by an interval these things from each other, but by reckoning from the effect inferring the cause. So how is it reasonable to deny the order, in the case of things which have a first and

a second, not according to our arbitrary choice but from the succession which is inherent in them according to nature?" Anyone who is able to reason at all can therefore understand accurately how the saint was concerned equally with truth and with piety. For by saying, "not arising from our arbitrary stipulation but occurring in the succession according to nature", they showed that the distinction in this order of effects and causes is from an inescapable and great and natural necessity, and brilliant truth, and never admits of being otherwise, but always appears in these; but by adding "separating these not by an interval but by thought, and contemplating the distinction of first and second only by the mind", the fact of union appears thoroughly piously confirmed. He adds no harm to the union from this distinction, but theologically states that the union itself is unconfused, and teaches that the difference is altogether inseparable. So again, when Eunomius tried to remove this distinction completely, this great saint said, "How do you leave no difference, not even that existing between the causes and what comes from them?" Thus, to opine that there is no difference in the case of causes and effects clearly springs from the madness of Arius and Eunomius. For as they were striving to remove the "consubstantial" in every way, they had heard in the Gospel the Lord saying that the Father is greater than he, and they had taken this saying to imply a difference. From there they dared at once to introduce impiously the difference in nature; but the difference of cause and effect they denied once and for all, because they knew that it could not introduce any natural change or separation anywhere, but would always keep the union of nature indivisible. Against them these three saints nobly took up the struggle on behalf of the Trinity; and because those men's heresy eliminated the great and supernatural mystery of the Trinity, they expelled it from the Church as far as possible.

29. Therefore, with good reason those who now reject this distinction are found to have shared in that heresy. Those, however, who confess, accept and embrace it willingly are still adhering to the piety and theology of these saints, or rather of the party of Christ, distinguishing the divine things in union and unifying them in distinction. One would first and properly name one kind of distinction of the divine essence and energy. They differ from each other in that

the divine energy is participated and divided indivisibly and named and conceived in some way (even if obscurely) from its results, but the essence is imparticipable and indivisible and nameless, because it is obviously beyond naming and altogether inconceivable.

30. After this we sought to have it demonstrated from the writings of the saints, whether this energy (which is inseparable but distinguished from the divine nature) is uncreated, which those who oppose the Church by no means accept. This also was demonstrated to be proclaimed clearly by the saints. The chief evidence comes from the sixth holy ecumenical council, as has been demonstrated very sufficiently above through its statements severally set forth. At the same time, it was proved that those who do not accept that the inseparable and natural energy of the divine essence is uncreated but differs from this essence, as has been said, make also the very essence of God a created thing. For according to the holy Maximus, "the nature of each thing is characterised by its energy", the uncreated energy showing an uncreated nature, but the created energy showing a created nature. Besides, the glorious John the Damascene says: "The created energy will reveal a nature also created, but the uncreated energy characterises an uncreated essence". So those who say that the divine energy is created make also the divine nature to be created, since it is characterised by the divine energy.

31. Not only so, but also, they are Monothelites, worse and more absurd that those at any time, and they believe that some eternal things are created. For since we confess two natures in our Lord Jesus Christ, the one uncreated but the other created, those who do not say that the divine nature has an uncreated will and energy acknowledge only one will and one energy in Christ, which the sixth council rejected and anathematised. And thus, they themselves are clearly proved Monothelites, but far worse than those earlier, inasmuch as those said that there are one will and one energy in Christ, but uncreated (that is to say, they removed the created); but they say that there are one will and one energy, but created, evidently not accepting the uncreated.

32. Furthermore, the great Basil writes in his treatise to Amphilochi-us: "Such names of the Spirit are supernatural and great, yet they do not have any excess in regard to glory, but the energies are what? Ineffable because of their greatness, innumerable because of their multitude; for how shall we imagine those things which are beyond the ages? What were his energies before the intellec-tual creation?" Those who say that the divine energies are created obviously believe that there are created things from beyond the ages. This also was proved, not through two or three witnesses, but through the whole Divine Scripture, that the common and natural divine energies of the trihypostatic nature are uncreated.

After this we sought from the saints' writings whether one could not imagine that God is in any way composite because of the dis-tinction of the divine essence and energy. For the opposition insist on this also. It was demonstrated that all the saints proclaim that we cannot believe that there is any synthesis in God because of this. For the glorious Maximus, in his disputation with Pyrrhus, shows most clearly that no synthesis comes about because of energy: "You see," he says to Pyrrhus, "that you are in error because of this, because you are altogether unaware that the syntheses are of things which are in the same hypostasis and not of things which appear in different en-tities. This is the common understanding of all, both of the outside philosophers and of the mystagogues of the Church who have the wisdom of God. But if you say that there is a synthesis of the wills, you will be forced to say that there is also a synthesis of other natu-ral properties." Moreover, Gregory of Nyssa in the sixth chapter of his Exposition of the Hexaemeron explains thus word for word: "If therefore in man, although different organs for perception happen to have been arranged by our nature, nevertheless the mind, activat-ing and moved throughout and using each appropriately for its pur-pose, is one and the same, not changing its nature with the different energies, how would one suppose that the essence of God has many parts because of the variety of his powers?"

33. At the same time, it was also proven that those who really make God composite are those who follow the opposition in not accepting the distinction of the divine essence and the energy, and simply every-

thing which appears naturally around the divine essence. The great Basil clearly says: "If we posit all the divine names as referring to the essence, we will not only show God composite, but composed of unlike parts, because each of the names signifies something different". And the great Gregory the Theologian writes: "Or also the immortality and the goodness and the unchangeability are essence of God; but if this is so, there are many essences of God, and not just one, or the Godhead is composed of these; for these are not without composition, if indeed they are essences". And also, the glorious Cyril says: "For neither the unbegottenness nor the incorruptibility nor the immortality nor the invisibility is essence. If each of these signifies an essence, from so many essences God is composed, as properties belonging to him by nature appear; for there are many properties which belong to him alone, and to no other of all beings". And the glorious Chrysostom says: "The Scripture calls the grace of the Spirit at one time fire, at another time water, showing that these are not names of essence but of energy; for the Spirit does not consist of different essences, being invisible and of one form". And Gregory of Nyssa to Eunomius says: "Who is there who says that God has two natures except you, who attach every named concept to the essence of the Father, and who say nothing from outside belongs to him, but who graft each of the names associated with divinity onto the essence of God?"

34. After this it was asked whether indeed the divine and uncreated energy is called Godhead by the saints, because those who now dissent did not accept this either. And this also was clearly proclaimed by the holy theologians. For example, the great Basil in his books against Eunomius says, "And the very name of divinity, whether it signifies the power of vision or the power of foresight, was properly applied to the human". And again, the same saint in his epistle to Eustathius the physician says, "Therefore the identity of energy in the case of the Father and the Son and the Holy Spirit shows plainly the identity of the nature. So that even if the name of divinity signifies nature, the community of essence allows this designation to be applied properly also to the Holy Spirit. But I do not know how those who fabricate everything cite the designation of divinity to prove the nature". And a little later he says: "Therefore the designation signifies some power,

either of vision or of action. But the divine nature, as it is, remains inexpressible in all the conceptual names, as we say. For when we learned 'benefactor' and 'judge', 'good' and 'just', and whatever else is similar, we were taught the differences of energies. But we are none the more able to learn the nature of the energizer through our recognition of the energies. For when one gives a definition of each of these names, and of the nature itself, with which the names are associated, he will not give the same definition of both. But whatever has a different definition has also a different nature. Therefore, essence is one thing, and no informative definition has yet been found, but the signification of the names associated with it is something else; they are named from some energy or dignity". And again the same great Basil writes in the same epistle: "Whether Godhead is a name of energy (as when we say there is one energy of Father and Son and Holy Spirit, so we say the Godhead also is one), or according to the opinion of the many the name of Godhead is indicative of nature (because no difference is found in the nature), not unreasonably we define the Holy Trinity as having one Godhead".

35. Saint Athanasius says, "The designation 'God' obviously refers to energy. It does not represent the very essence of God; for it is impossible to know this; but 'God' represents and reveals his theoretic energy to us". And again, the same saint says: "The name 'God' does not signify the essence of the Godhead, for this is incomprehensible and nameless; but from his theoretic energy he is called 'God', as the great Dionysius says, either from θεειν, that is, 'to run', or from αἰθειν, which is 'to burn'". But the great Dionysius says, "If we should name the supersubstantial hiddenness 'God' or 'life' or 'essence' or 'light' or 'word', we do not have in mind anything other than the powers brought forth from it to us, which are deifying or essence-making or life-generating or wisdom-giving. But we apply those names to it as all the intellectual energies are overcome, since we see no deification or life or essence which resembles the cause which more than all transcends all." And again, the same saint says, "The providence which sees [θεωμένη] all is Godhead [Θεότης]." But we know that that providence is an energy especially from what the great Athanasius writes: "The Father and the Son do not work according to different providences, but according to one and the same essential

energy of Godhead." The great Dionysius also says again in the second epistle to Gaius, that the reality of the deifying gift is Godhead, and "the inimitable imitation of what is beyond God and beyond goodness, by which we are deified and perfected."

36. Besides this, the great gift and energy of the Spirit, namely deification, according to which the saints are deified, is called "Godhead" by the saints, but the opponents of the metropolitan of Thessalonica say it is created Godhead. They evidently construct this belief from the fact that the great Dionysius calls God the "giver of the substance" of deification. The sacred synod decreed that in calling this "imitation" and "relationship" of the partakers they spoke impiously. Nevertheless, when the divine synod had also enquired whether any one of the saints said that deification was uncreated, and whether "relationship" and "imitation" and "gave substance" are said also about uncreated things, sayings of the saints were provided, making clear that these expressions are not always used in regard to created things. For the great Basil in his Antirrheticus says, "He who has formed drops of dew has not given substance in the same manner to the drops and to the Son". And in the first homily on the Hexaemeron he says: "In order to show that the cosmos is a production of skill, set before all for contemplation, so that through it the wisdom of him who made it may be recognised, the wise Moses used no other expression about it but said, 'In the beginning he made' — not 'he energised', nor 'he gave substance', but 'he made'; just as many of those who imagine that the cosmos exists from eternity along with God did not grant that it had come into being from him". It was proved at the same time by this saint that "energising" and "being energised" can be said not only in regard to created things but also in regard to eternal and uncreated things (since the dissenters when they hear that grace is energised think at once that it is created). For Gregory the great theologian says: "Let it be also from energy, if you wish; not even thus will you remove us; for he would have energised this consubstantiality itself."

37. And also, the glorious Gregory of Nyssa says: "We cannot name three gods, activating the divine and visionary energy together and indistinguishably from each other in regard to us and all the cre-

ation." But concerning "imitation" the metropolitan of Thessalonica said that the great Dionysius attributed inimitability to the imitation, so that the deifying gift is not rather imitation than imitability. Gregory the Theologian says that the Son is also an imitation of the Father, writing in his second treatise concerning the Son: "The Son is an image of the Father as consubstantial, and because he is from the Father, but not the Father from the Son. For this is the nature of an image, to be an imitation of the archetype and of that which it is called." So, the word "imitation" does not hinder the deification from being uncreated. Moreover, the providence of God in regard to what is foreseen is a relationship, and so is his foreknowledge in regard to what is foreknown, and the eternal decrees of God in regard to what is predestined. For each of these the fact of being a relationship does not hinder being uncreated. After all, the deifying gift of the Spirit (deification itself) is not a created thing just because it is a relationship in regard to what is deified. For that it is uncreated, the glorious Maximus will establish securely and concisely, writing: "The divine grace, although it gives enjoyment to those who participate according to grace, yet it does not give comprehension. For it remains incomprehensible even in the participation of those who enjoy it, because according to its unoriginate nature it is unlimited." And again, "This is the gospel of God, the dispensation of God toward mankind through the Son, who was made flesh and granted the reward to those who believe in him, the unoriginate deification."

38. After it appeared that the divine energy truly is named Godhead, we sought to discover from the theologians whether God is according to essence superior to the divine energy and those things which are essentially associated with him. This also was clearly proclaimed by all the saints. At the same time, it was proved also that those who do not accept this are really polytheists. They say there are many origins, because they do not refer to one cause and one origin those things which are essentially associated with God. For the great Basil in his Antirrheticus says: "There is a kind of order not arising from our arbitrary stipulation, but occurring in the very succession according to nature, as the 'from it' is for fire in relation to light. For these we name first the cause, second what is from it, not separating by an interval these things from each other, but by reckoning from the

effect inferring the cause. So how is it reasonable to deny the order, in the case of things which have a first and a second, not according to our arbitrary choice but from the succession which is inherent in them according to nature?" But also, in his books to Amphilochius he writes: "But what are the energies of the Spirit? Ineffable because of their greatness, innumerable because of their multitude; for how shall we imagine those things which are beyond the ages? What were his energies before the intellectual creation? How great were his graces around the creation? What is his power in regard to the ages to come? For he existed and preexisted and coexisted with the Son and the Father before the ages. So even if you imagine something of what is beyond the ages, even this is more recent than the Spirit, proving that the eternal energies of the Spirit rank below the Spirit himself." But in his treatise concerning the divinity of the Son and the Spirit, the glorious Gregory of Nyssa says: "The divine nature remains ineffable and unutterable, surpassing all representation by voice". Therefore, the designation of divinity indicates not nature but the visionary power of the Spirit. Moreover, the great Athanasius in his second treatise against the Arian heretics (who said that the Son was from the will but not from the nature of the Father) says, "If they grant to God the power of willing concerning what does not exist, why do they not recognise what surpasses God's power of willing?" In the third treatise against the same heretics, he writes: "The heretics have seen what is opposed to the will, but what is greater and surpasses it they have not contemplated. For just as that which is contrary to the intention is opposed to the will, so that which is according to nature surpasses and precedes the willing". And the same saint writing against Macedonius says, "Know that being God is secondary in relation to the nature; for we ourselves, if we become imitators of God, according to Paul, become gods; but we cannot become of the same nature". Moreover, the glorious Maximus says, "God is exceedingly far removed, infinitely in number and in degree, from all things which exist, from all things which participate or are participated in."

39. Furthermore, the great Dionysius in the twelfth chapter of the Divine Names says: "The things which are holy or divine or lordly or royal surpass the things which do not exist; the things which par-

ticipate only in themselves surpass those which participate in other things. In the same manner he who is above all existing things transcends all existing things, and the unparticipated cause transcends all participation and everything which participates." And in his second epistle to Gaius, he says: "How is he who is beyond all things above the source of Godhead and above the source of good? If you would imagine Godhead and goodness, it is the very reality of the gift which makes good and makes God, and the inimitable imitation of what is beyond God and beyond goodness, by which we are deified and perfected: for if this becomes the source of being made God and made good for those who are being deified and perfected, he who is above the cause of every cause, is also above the so-called Godhead and goodness, as he is beyond the source of God and the source of good." And again the same saint says: "Now we must go on to that which is truly the theological essential name of that which truly is; but only this will we mention, that the aim of the discourse is not to reveal the superessential essence, insofar as it is superessential; for this is ineffable and unknowable and altogether impossible to reveal, and transcends the oneness itself; but to praise the procession of the divinely originated source of being which gives essence to all beings." But the glorious Maximus in his Scholia says: "By procession here he means the divine energy, which has created every essence."

Moreover, the glorious Chrysostom in his first treatise concerning the incomprehensible says, "Not only are the prophets evidently ignorant of what God is essentially, but also, they do not know how great his wisdom itself is. For the essence does not come from the wisdom, but the wisdom from the essence. But when they cannot comprehend even this with accuracy, how great madness it would be to think one could subject the essence itself to one's own processes of reasoning!" And on the Gospel according to John again the same saint says, "God 'does not give the Spirit by measure.' For we all received the energy of the Spirit in a measure. For here he calls the energy 'Spirit', for energy is what is divided; but the Spirit has the whole energy without measure and complete. But if his energy is without measure, how much more his essence!"

40. Those who attack the Church say that all things participate in the essence of God because the divine essence and the divine energy are indistinguishable, and they call nothing else God except the essence alone. We, however, have been taught by the Holy Scriptures that God has not only essence but also power and energy (or rather powers and energies), which are distinct from the divine essence; for thus he will be not only trihypostatic but also omnipotent. So, we asked what it is in which all things share, in the divine essence or in the divine energy of God. But the divine synod said this: We know on one hand that the divine essence and the energy of the divine nature are inseparable; for there would not be an energy without its own essence. But concerning those things which have been created from the beginning by God, who does not know, they said, unless he is delirious like those who oppose the Church, that every creation received a share of its Creator's energy but not of his essence? For the house has obtained a share not of the essence of the builder, nor the ship of the essence of the shipwright, but of the skill and energy, according to the theologian of Nyssa. But that even the saints who are deified by union with God participate not in the divine essence but in his divine energy, Gregory the great theologian indicates, writing about our Lord Jesus Christ: "He is called Christ because of his divinity; but this is the anointing of his humanity, not sanctifying anointed things by energy like the others, but by the presence of the whole anointer". And the great Basil says: "the Holy Spirit fills everything by his power, but can be shared only by those who are worthy. He is not shared in the same measure by all, but distributes his energy in proportion to the faith of the recipient." And again, elsewhere he says: "Just as the reflections of the faces are not made in every material, but in those which have smoothness and transparency, so not in every soul is the energy of the Spirit reflected, but in those which have nothing crooked or twisted." Saint Maximus says: "Everything which God is he also will be who is deified through grace, except the identity in essence." The great Dionysius says: "The divine thoughts are moved in a circle, united to the radiances without beginning or end of the good and beautiful". By referring to them in the plural, he showed that they are not the essence of God; for the essence is never mentioned in the plural, but by calling

them "radiances", and adding both "without beginning" and "without end", he showed that they are divine and uncreated energies.

Our Lord and God in the Holy Gospel according to John says, "He who believes in me, as the Scripture said, rivers of living water will flow from his bosom". This he said about the Spirit, of which they were going to partake who believed in him. For the Holy Spirit was not yet, because Jesus was not yet glorified. Interpreting this the glorious Chrysostom says: "'Rivers from his bosom will flow', hinting at the abundance and bounty of his grace (as elsewhere he says, 'A fountain of water springing up for life eternal') that is, he will have much grace. Moreover, elsewhere he says, 'eternal life' but here 'living water'. By 'living' he means that which is always acting. For the grace of the Spirit, when it comes into the thought and settles there, bubbles up more than any spring, and does not cease periodically nor is emptied nor stops. Revealing at the same time the inexhaustibility of the expenditure and the ineffability of the energy, he called it a fountain and a river — not just one river but innumerable; and there he represented the flood through the phrase 'springing up.'" And a little later the same saint says: "No longer was there a prophet among them, nor did grace reveal to them the holy things; since the Holy Spirit had hitherto been held back, but was going to be poured out abundantly. But the beginning of this distribution happened after the cross, not only of abundance, but also of greater gifts — for the gift was more marvelous, as when it was written, 'You do not know of what Spirit you are', and again, 'For you did not receive a Spirit of slavery, but you received a Spirit of adoption'. For the ancient people of God themselves had the Spirit but did not provide it to others; but the apostles filled multitudes. So, since they were going to receive this grace, but it had not yet been given, because of this he says, 'The Holy Spirit was not yet' (that is, not yet given) 'since Jesus was not yet glorified', calling the cross 'glory'. For we were enemies and sinners, lacking the gift of God and hateful to God, but the grace was the proof of reconciliation. But since a gift is given not to enemies or those who are hated but to friends and those who are well pleasing, the sacrifice first had to be offered on our behalf, and the enmity in the flesh had to be resolved, and we had to become friends of God and then receive the gift. For if this happened in the case of the promise to Abraham, much more in the case of grace."

41. Furthermore, the same Chrysostom in his thirty-sixth homily on the same subject says: "And in our case the water does not operate in a simple manner, but when it receives the grace of the Spirit, then it releases all our sins". And a little later: "But even if the whole world comes, the grace is not used up, nor is the energy consumed, but it remains the same and such as it was even before this. And just as the sun's rays give light every day and are not consumed, nor does their light become less because of so much expenditure, so also and much more the energy of the Spirit is not diminished from those who are enjoying it." And again, the same saint in his fifth homily on the same subject, explaining the saying, "Everything came into being through him", says, "Speaking about the creation John brings in also a word on providence, saying, 'In him was life'. For indeed lest anyone doubt how many and so great things came to be through him, he added that in him was life. So just as in the case of the spring which gives birth to abysses, no matter how much you take away, you have not reduced the spring at all, so also in the case of the energy of the Only-begotten, however many things you believe have been created and made through it, the energy has not become at all less." And again, when the Gospel has said, "From his fulness we all have received", the same glorious Chrysostom in his fourteenth homily explaining this says: "And whatever does it mean that 'Of his fulness we all have received'? For we must direct our discourse to this. He does not merely participate in the gift, but he is the very fountain and very root of excellent things — life itself and light itself and truth itself — not keeping the wealth of good things to himself, but pouring out to all others also, and after the outpouring remaining full. He is not at all diminished by providing to others, but always wells up; and giving a share of these excellent things to all, he remains in the same perfection. But what I bring can be shared, for I received it from another. It is a small part of the whole, like a paltry drop compared to the inexpressible abyss and the infinite ocean. Or rather not even this comparison would be able to represent what we are trying to say. For if you take a drop out of the ocean, you have diminished the sea itself, even if the diminution is undetectable; but

in the case of that fountain, this cannot be said, but however much one draws, it remains not at all diminished. For this reason, especially, we must turn to another comparison, itself weak and unable to represent what we are seeking, but serving more than the first to lead us towards the notion which now lies before us. For let us suppose that there is a fountain of fire, then from that fountain ten thousand lamps are lit, and twice as many and three times and many times. Does not the fire remain of the same fullness even after sharing its energy with so many? It is obvious to everyone. But if in the case of bodies which are divisible, of those which are diminished by having something taken away, some such object was found, which even after providing to others something of itself is not at all harmed, much more in the case of that incorporeal and inviolate power will this happen. For if where that which is shared is corporeal essence, it is both divided and not divided, much more will division be unlikely when the discourse concerns energy, and the energy from the incorporeal essence. For this reason, also John said, 'From his fulness we all have received'. We, all of us — the twelve, the three hundred, the five hundred, the three thousand, and the five thousand, the many myriads of the Jews, the whole community of the faithful, those then and those now and those who will be in the future, from his fulness we have received — but what have we received? 'Grace instead of grace,' he says."

42. The great Basil, explaining the forty-eighth Psalm, says, "God made man from the earth and his ministers a flame of fire; nevertheless, men also have the power of conceiving and understanding their Creator and Demiurge. For 'he breathed into his face', that is he put some part of his own grace into man, so that by like he should recognize like." And again, the same saint in his treatise to Amphilochius concerning the Holy Spirit says: "The Lord, renewing mankind, and giving back again the grace of the Lord's breath which, he had lost, breathed into the face of the disciples, and said what? 'Receive the Holy Spirit.'" The glorious John the Damascene in the section concerning the foreknowledge and foreordination of his theological chapters says: "This man the Creator made male, giving to him a share of his divine grace and making him to be in fellowship with himself through this grace of his". And again, the glorious Basil in

his treatise to Amphilochius says: "Who is so ignorant of the good things which God has prepared for the worthy as not to know that the crown of the righteous is the grace of the Spirit, which then will be more generously and more perfectly granted?"

43. Furthermore, in St Cyril's third book to Hermias, this very Hermias asks about the divine indwelling in us and participation, and says: "Except now I am most eager to learn from you how the fulness of the Father and the Son would be conceived and accomplished in us, if their fulness is one and not different." Answering this the holy Cyril says, "Indeed in this there is nothing difficult or hard to understand; for how otherwise could it be than through the Holy Spirit filling us with divine gifts through himself and revealing us as partakers of the ineffable nature?" And again, the same saint in his Thesaurus says, "But if the Holy Spirit were really a created being, according to the madness of the heterodox, how does he have the whole energy of God? For no one, I suppose, will rightly cry out that he thinks so strange a thing as this, that he dares even only to say that the divine essence is provided with energy through some organs brought into being from outside, the energy from it going through naturally to some who are ready to receive it."

44. And the great Athanasius in his epistle to Serapion says, "All that belongs to the Father belongs to the Son; therefore, also whatever has been given from the Son in the Spirit is a gift of the Father. And because the Spirit is in us, the Word also, who gives us the Spirit, is in us, and the Father is in the Word. Thus 'I and the Father will come, and we will make our dwelling with him', as it is written. For where the light is, there its radiance is also, and where the radiance is, there also are its energy and radiant grace. Paul taught this writing again to the Corinthians in his second epistle, saying, 'The grace of our Lord Jesus Christ and the love of God and the communion of the Holy Spirit be with you all'. For the grace and gift given in the Trinity is given from the Father through the Son in the Holy Spirit. For just as the grace which is given comes from the Father through the Son, so also there would not be communion of the giving in us, if it were not in the Holy Spirit. For partaking in this, we have the love of

the Father and the grace of the Son and the communion of the Spirit himself. So, from these the energy of the Trinity is shown to be one."

45. Moreover, St. Athanasius in his treatise on the Spirit says, "This agrees with what the inspired Paul says concerning the Spirit. For he called the believers temples of God, which had obtained the indwelling grace of the Spirit: 'Do you not know that you are the temple of God, and the Spirit of God dwells in you?' and again, 'Do you not know that your bodies are a temple of the Holy Spirit, which is in you, which you have from God?' These passages teach directly that the Holy Spirit is of the divine nature. For if those who have believed are called temple of God, because they have received the grace of the Spirit, then the Holy Spirit must be from God. For having obtained the indwelling grace of the Spirit, they are called temples of God." And the glorious Chrysostom in the fourth of his commentaries on Acts, explaining the saying, "And tongues were seen on them divided as of fire", says: "He said well, 'divided', for they were of one root, so that you may learn that it is an energy sent from the Comforter." And again, the same saint in the same work says: "And they were all filled; they did not simply receive the grace of the Spirit, but they were filled." Furthermore, when the Messalians said that those who have been purified among them are established in participation of the essence of God, and brought forth that Gospel saying, "I and the Father will come, and we will make our home with him," and twisted this foolishly towards their own heresy, the council convening against these very Messalians, beating back their evil doctrine, said: "There comes an abiding of the Comforter, and God dwells in the worthy, but not as Godhead is by nature."

46. After this it was sought to be proved from the saints' writings, both that the light of the Lord's transfiguration is uncreated, and that this is not the essence of God. And nearly all said that this was proved according to the fourth session. At that session those who opposed the Church were present. At one time they said, clearly blaspheming, that this was created and appearance and veil and image; at another time they impiously asserted that this was uncreated and the essence of God. For in that session Gregory named for his theology was cited, he who wrote: "No one is in the substance and essence of the

Lord, as it is written, nor has he seen or spoken the nature of God." And the glorious Maximus wrote in the seventh chapter of the third century of his theological works, "He in whom existing beings cannot participate according to his essence, but who wishes those who are able to participate in another manner, altogether maintains the hiddenness of his essence." And the glorious Chrysostom writing for the same feast says: "Transfigured on the mountain, the Saviour briefly somehow as master showed to his disciples the glory of his invisible divine kingdom, but straightaway they will say who use an unrestrained and insolent tongue: 'And if his divine glory is invisible, how did he show it to his apostles? For if it could be seen, it was not invisible; but if it is invisible, it could not be seen'. Therefore, listen intelligently. Christ the Master here showed to his disciples the glory of his invisible kingdom, and did not reveal it; that is, he disclosed his divinity a little but not perfectly, satisfying them but sparing them. He satisfied them by showing them the divine glory of his invisible kingdom, not as much as it was, but as much as they were able to see with their bodily eyes; but out of desire to spare them, not because he grudged it, he did not show them his whole glory of his invisible kingdom, lest along with the sight they should lose their life." Moreover, all the saints call that light "illumination" and "brightness" and "grace" and "deification" and "Godhead revealed a little too hard to see" and "light unapproachable" and "natural unoriginate ray of the Son," "missile of divinity," "lightning-flash of Godhead," and so on.

In that session the first conciliar tome on this subject was also brought forth, which securely and with love of the true faith revealed this light to be uncreated but not essence both through many testimonies from the Divine Scripture and the word and pious declaration of our thrice-blessed and renowned emperor, the Lord Andronicus Palaeologus, in accordance with the saints. Seeing that those who opposed the most reverend metropolitan of Thessalonica were also opposing and speaking against this sacred and divine tome at that time, we expelled them for the following reasons: because they at one time held that the light of the Lord's transfiguration is created, but at another time too inconsistently held that it is essence of God; and because they did not accept that the essence of God has an uncreated power and energy, but they reduced all the common powers and energies of the Father and the Son and the Holy Spirit illogically to the status of created things; and they called polytheists those who confess God to be uncreated, not in essence only, but also in the hypostases and in the common divine power and energies of the three hypostases.

47. On these topics Akindynos' books were brought into the midst and read, in which he was obviously teaching other old and new heresies, and especially insisted that there is no uncreated energy common to the trihypostatic Godhead, except only the Son and the Holy Spirit. But the divine synod, recognizing well and with the love of God that this was the impiety of Marcellus and Photinus and Sophronius the earlier heretics, at once summoned the glorious Chrysostom against this heresy, sending him from heaven like a thunderstorm to burn up the undergrowth of Akindynos' nonsense. In explaining the epistle to the Philippians Chrysostom says, "Marcellus and Photinus and Sophronius say that the Word is energy, and that this energy (not an essence in a hypostasis) came to dwell in the one from David's seed. Arius confesses the Son, but in word only; he says that he is a creation, and far lower than the Father. But others say he does not have a soul. Did you see their chariot stopped? See then also how they fall, how St. Paul overturns and throws all of them down at once, at one blow all together. So how does he overthrow them? 'Let this mind be in you', he says, 'which was in Christ Jesus, who being in the form of God did not consider it robbery to be equal to God'. Because of this Paul of Samosata fell, and Marcellus and Sabellius. 'Being in the form of God', he says. How do you say, wretched man, he began from Mary, and before this he was not? How do you say he is energy? The form of God, he says, took the form of a servant. Is the form of the servant energy of a servant or nature of a servant? Undoubtedly indeed the nature of a servant. Therefore, also the form of God is the nature of God; therefore, it is not energy."

48. Furthermore, the glorious Gregory of Nyssa in his discourse to Ablabius says: "'God' signifies the energiser, but 'Godhead' the energy. None of the three is energy, but rather each of them is energiser." "From this indeed", the divine synod says, "it has been clearly proved

that he who says only the Son and the Holy Spirit are uncreated energies of God, not glorifying the common natural energy of the three hypostases (which Akindynos rejects), dares to reintroduce into the Church of God the heresy of Marcellus and Photinus and Sophronius, long ago dead and abolished. But if some of the saints call the Son or the Holy Spirit 'power' or 'energy', they call them the power or energy of the Father — and accordingly each of them, as a perfect hypostasis, has energy and power." And this is a common name, according to the glorious Dionysius, of the Godhead, all-perfect and more than full; by this designation even the Father is called 'power'. But just now we were not discussing this energy and power, but that which is common to the trihypostatic Godhead (the Godhead which is not a hypostasis but a nature) and supernaturally belongs to each of the hypostases originating in God, according to the tradition of the theologians. For, according to the great Athanasius, we confess one God in three hypostases which have one essence and power and energy, and whatever else is attributed to the essence in theological writings or hymns. And so that we may give a seal to the discourse and may have a full collection according to theology, let us hear in order that when he is called uncreated, bodiless, timeless, unoriginate, eternal, endless, unlimited, unknowable, shapeless, inexplicable, untraceable, God of gods, Lord of lords, King of kings, All-Ruler, Creator, Demiurge, Light, holy, life, good, mighty, All-Powerful, and whatever else indicates superiority and causation, each of these is not called essence, but they are attributed to the essence. They are called both a collection and a fulness of Godhead according to the Scripture, appearing in and theologically attributed equally to each of the three holy hypostases. "For whatever the Father has is mine, and I am glorified in them." The Son is called the power of the Father, and so is the Holy Spirit, for various reasons, which the theologians have handed down, but especially because the Father's whole power lies on the Son, as the great Basil writes explicitly in dispute with Eunomius. So how is it right to remove the natural and common power of the trihypostatic Godhead, through which the theologians praise both the Son and the Holy Spirit as power of the Father?

49. In these matters by the decree of our mighty and holy sovereign and emperor, the great chartophylax and consul asked each of the wisdom-loving hierarchs and the senatorial and ecclesiastical leaders what opinion he held concerning all these issues which had been discussed and examined now at the divine and sacred synod. And each of them individually declared that he had no doubts concerning these matters. They all expressed gratitude to the most reverend metropolitan of Thessalonica, because he had spoken and written in accord with all the saints and had striven so zealously to defend the truth of orthodoxy, and had endured such insolence and slander and other abuse in order to refute that Barlaam and Akindynos and those who appeared afterward up to the present time in agreement with them, who were striving to move the Church of Christ away from the faith and piety towards God received from the fathers. But finally after all the others, as all rose from their seats, the most illustrious senators and the most reverend hierarchs, as it is customary at such times, a declaration was also made by the truly most sublime and wise in divine matters, most clement, mighty and holy autocrat and emperor, Lord John Cantacuzenus, stating: "Unrighteousness is a great evil even for those beings which creep on the earth, because it is able to corrupt and divide a whole nation, since also its opposite, righteousness, elevates a nation, as it is written. But if, in the case of things below, unrighteousness is so great an evil, how much more when it is spoken in regard to the divine height by those who think wrongly, and the very truth of God is wronged by those who reject it. But those who accept and proclaim this, and defend it as far as they are able, are abused and falsely accursed and slandered by those attempting to lead the multitude astray with a deviant intention! I for my part see so much harmony with the saints in what has been spoken by the most reverend metropolitan of Thessalonica and has just now been read from his compositions for defense of the true faith, and I see the saints making so much zeal in their own compositions on behalf of the divine doctrines which have recently been at issue, that no one who wishes to live with prudence would desire further investigation. Concerning the theological statements which have been made by the blessed disciples and apostles of Christ and by the saints and the ecumenical councils and the holy fathers,

I have so much eagerness because of the grace of Christ in me, that I would be ready, if I had only one cup of blood left, to shed even this willingly on their behalf. But I am grateful to the one God of all, our Master and Lord Jesus Christ, that he granted his great mercy to us, being well pleased that the truth of piety should be revealed and confirmed today, and not permitting any part of this to be turned aside and shaken by those who have been undertaking with many attempts and deceits and devious machinations over fourteen years already to turn this aside and shake it down." So, this is what the most glorious emperor said.

50. When his divine and venerable command was delivered also to the Holy Mountain, so that those from there excelling in understanding and virtue might stay for the synod assembled in this blessed great city, but because of the length of the road and the harshness of the weather they were not able to stay, they sent two of the priest-monks to our mighty and holy sovereign and emperor, informing him that they had sent their own written opinion to the synod. So those priest-monks who had been sent stood up and gave their speeches to the synod on behalf of the whole Holy Mountain. These speeches were composed by the most sacred metropolitan of Herakleia Lord Philotheos while he still remained there with them. They brought forward also the written opinion of all which had recently been sent from there. When this had been read in the hearing of all, their opinion continued to agree and bear witness together with the most sacred metropolitan of Thessalonica in all respects in regard to the truth of piety. This is what the whole Holy Mountain said.

51. As the whole divine and sacred synod gathered by the grace of Christ in the hall which is called Alexiakon of the sacred Blachernae palace, and now fighting on behalf of the true faith, and having made an accurate and suitable investigation and examination concerning the matters set before us, and ratifying the earlier synodical tomes on these issues as most pious (or rather also following these), we justly subject that Barlaam and Akindynos to the anathema from Christ because they behaved insolently in the very crisis of the true faith and did not at all repent while still alive. And whoever now has been revealed and refuted by the synod as agreeing with these men, and

simply as many as are of their faction, we hold them excommunicated and expelled from the catholic and apostolic Church of Christ, unless they repent, and we subject them to the anathema from Christ. Those who keep fellowship with them in knowledge we hold deprived of fellowship, and those who are ordained we strip of every priestly ministry. Those who have been carried away and dragged into error by these men and are not leaders of the heresy, if they remain unrepentant, we subject to similar condemnation. But if they sincerely repent and abandon their evil opinion and those who persist in it, we gladly admit them not only into the communion of piety but also into the sacred ministry, not at all reducing them in rank, according to the judgment and proclamation for such cases of the seventh holy ecumenical council, which defined: "We absolutely do not recognize the originators and leaders and champions of the heresy, even if they repent, into the sacred ministry; but those who were forced or carried away and dragged into error, if they repent truly and sincerely, we receive into sacred ministry each according to his proper rank." But also, if anyone else at all is ever caught believing or saying or writing the same things against the most reverend metropolitan of Thessalonica, or rather against the venerable theologians and the Church itself, we will make the same decree against him and subject him to the same condemnation, whether he be one of the ordained or of the laity. As for the oft-mentioned most reverent metropolitan of Thessalonica, who has written and believed nothing contrary to the divine sayings, but has understood with accurate examination, or rather has defended the divine sayings and our common faith and tradition in all ways as is fitting, we do not only judge him higher in every respect than the disputes against him or rather against the Church of God, as also the earlier synodical tomes declare, but also we declare him a most reliable defender and champion and helper of the Church and of the true faith. For thus also the preceding tomes of those synods will hold, just as indeed they hold, that which is reliable and secure.

52. As these matters turned out thus, obviously not without the cooperation and grace of the good Spirit, it remained still for those of good will to remove every cause from those who wished consume, and not to pass by without examination what the enemies of the

Church blamed in the writings of the most reverent Metropolitan of Thessalonica, even if all these were also included in what was then examined in the divine synod. So, when our mighty and holy sovereign and emperor found these written down in part by their hands and gave them to us, we read and examined each of these in the book of the most reverend metropolitan of Thessalonica, meeting in the Great Church and passing the whole day together not once but twice and three times and many times. And we found the most reverent metropolitan of Thessalonica in agreement in these writings also with the sacred theologians and a defender by the grace of Christ of the truth of Orthodoxy; but as for them, from the written distortions and accusations which they tried to make, we found that they were falling into many great heresies. For they continued to oppose openly what the theologians have said explicitly, and dared to say that the deification of the Lord's assumed humanity is created; and because the essence of God is called by the saints unapproachable and imparticipable, they declared impiously that those who think in this way about it consider it corruptible (what audacity!) — even though God said to Moses, "No one will see my face and life." But also, the seven spirits which rested on the flower from the root of Jesse, namely our Lord Jesus Christ (that is, the energies of the Holy Spirit, according to the sacred theologians), which the venerable Zacharias praised as seven eyes of Christ looking down on the whole earth. But the glorious Maximus stated theologically that these belonged by nature to the Son of God, they reckoned with created things. It is not easy to number their other assertions which tend no less to heresy. Therefore, from these also their condemnation was ratified, if they should not repent. What was explained and decided just now by us in this synod with the royalty from God will bring security and certainty among all, as it is undoubtedly in agreement with what the Church and all the holy fathers and the sacred and divine councils had earlier for their purpose and the conciliar tomes of these councils. And the entirely lawful and synodical tome, written and subscribed just now, will be preserved immovable for the whole age, by the all-powerful energy and grace of our almighty and great God and Savior, on behalf of which and because of which we have completed that present struggle.

JOHN Cantacuzenus in Christ our God Faithful Emperor and Autocrat of the Romans.

JOHN Palaeologus in Christ our God Faithful Emperor and Autocrat of the Romans.

By the Reverend and Patriarchal Hand:
KALLISTOS
by the Mercy of God Archbishop of Constantinople, New Rome, and Ecumenical Patriarch

The Unworthy Metropolitan of Herakleia, President of the Most Honorable and Exarch of all Thrace and Macedonia,
PHILOTHEOS

The Unworthy Metropolitan of Thessalonica, Most Honorable and Exarch of all Thessaly,
GREGORY

The Unworthy Metropolitan of Cyzicus and Exarch of all the Hellespont,
ARSENIOS

My Royalty being about to subscribe to the present tome, made earlier by the might and holy sole autocrat and emperor, the father of My Royalty, and the divine and sacred synod for confirmation of the holy catholic and apostolic church of Christ, for removal of the godless heresy of Barlaam and Akindynos, orders and declares that this is accepted unchangeable and immovable, without compulsion or pressure of any kind, as written by God through the saints who speak inspired by him. My Royalty receives and embraces what the present tome accepts, and hands over to anathema, whatever it hands over to anathema. In regard to those who oppose this divine and sacred tome, my Royalty orders them to be rejected in words and deeds and to be rejected as common enemies of the church; but those who adhere to this shall be deemed worthy of acceptance and imperial favour. My Royalty declares this, as established by God through his grace as defender and vindicator of the Church. This decree of my Royalty shall remain firm and immovable from age to age. It is signed by My Royalty, and I have offered it, bringing it as a sacred offering in my own hands to the holy altar, in the presence of my mighty and holy autocrat and emperor, the father of My Royalty, and of my most holy master the ecumenical patriarch Lord Philotheos, and of the divine and sacred council around him. In the month of February of the seventh indication. Matthew Asen Cantacuzenus in Christ our God faithful emperor and autocrat of the Romans.

BIBLIOGRAPHY

Alexandria, Saint Athanasius. "Four Discourses Against the Arians, Discourse II." In *Nicene and Post-Nicene Fathers, Athanasius: Selected Works and Letters, Vol 4*, edited by Philip Schaff & Henry Wace. Peabody: Hendrickson Publishers, 1999.

An Orthodox Ethos Publication. *On the Reception of the Heterodox into the Orthodox Church: The Patristic Consensus and Criteria*. 1st ed. Florence: Uncut Mountain Press, 2023.

Antiochian Orthodox Christian Archdiocese of North America. *Our Father Among the Saints Raphael Bishop of Brooklyn*. Wichita: Antakya Press, 2000.

Ἀγατιανός, Θεόδωρος. "Ὁ Βυζαντινὸς ἡσυχασμὸς σὲ ἀντιπαράθεση μὲ τὴν θεολογία τῆς Δύσης. Ἅγιος Γρηγόριος Παλαμᾶς - ἀντιησυχαστές." Μ.Α. διατριβή, Ἀριστοτέλειο Πανεπιστήμιο Θεσσαλονίκης, 2015.

Apostolopoulou, Machi Paizi. "Concilum Constantinopolitanum 1484." In the *Great Councils of the Orthodox Churches Decisions and Synodika: From Constantinople 861 to Constantinople 1872, Vol 1*, edited by Giuseppe Alberigo & Alberto Melloni. Translated by Gregory Heers (2022). Bologna: Brepols Publishers, 2016.

Ἀργέντης, Εὐστράτιος. *Ἐγχειρίδιον περὶ βαπτίσματος καλούμενον χειραγωγία πλανωμένων*. Κωνσταντινούπολη: Οἰκουμενικὸ Πατριαρχεῖο, 1756.

Arkas, Archimandrite Nicholas. "Saint Athanasios Parios (1722-1813)." Translated by Hugh Cyril Donohoe. Accessed November 5th, 2023, https://www.johnsanidopoulos.com/2013/06/saint-athanasios-parios-1722-1813.html

Aslanidis, Demetrios & Grigoriatis, Monk Damascene. *Apostle to Zaire: The Life and Legacy of Blessed Father Cosmas of Grigoriou*. Florence: Uncut Mountain Press, 2022.

Assembly of Canonical Orthodox Bishops of the United States of America. "Baptism and 'Sacramental Economy' An agreed Statement of the North American Orthodox-Catholic Theological Consultation Saint Vladimir's Orthodox Seminary, June 3, 1999." Accessed December 19th, 2022. https://www.assemblyofbishops.org/ministries/ecumenical-and-interfaith-dialogues/orthodox-catholic/baptism-and-sacramental-economy-an-agreed-statement-of-the-north-american-orthodox-catholictheological-consultation-saint-vladimirs-orthodox-seminary-june-3-1999

Assembly of Canonical Orthodox Bishops of the United States. "The Filioque: A Church-Dividing Issue? An Ageed Statement of the North American Orthodox-Catholic Theological Consultation Saint Paul's College, October 2003." Accessed August 9th, 2023. https://www.assemblyofbishops.org/ministries/ecumenical-and-interfaith-dialogues/orthodox-catholic/filioque-a-church-dividing-issue

Atallah, Hieromonk Isaac. *Saint Paisios of Mount Athos.* Translated by Hieromonk Alexis (Trader) & Father Peter Heers. Chalkidiki: Holy Monastery of Saint Arsenios the Cappadocian, 2009.

Bălan, Archimandrite Ioanichie. *Elder Cleopa of Sihastria; In the Tradition of St. Paisius Velichkovsky.* Translated by Mother Cassiana. Lake Pueblo: New Varatec Publishing, 2001.

Bălan, Archimandrite Ioanichie. *Patericul Românesc.* Sihăstria: Mănăstirea Editura, 2005.

Baldimtsis, Nicholas. *Life and Witness of St. Iakovos of Evia.* Florence: Uncut Mountain Press, 2023.

Balsamon, Patriarch Theodore. "Questions of His Holiness Patriarch of Alexandria Kyrios Markos and Responses of His Holiness Patriarch of Antioch, Theodore Balsamon." In Patrologia

Graeca, Vol. 138. Translated by Jacques Paul Migne (1857-1866) & Gregory Heers (2022) Paris: Imprimerie Catholique, 1857.

Bilalis, Archimandrite Spyridon. *Ορθοδοξία και Παπισμός: Κριτική τοῦ Παπισμού*. Ἀθήναι: Ὀρθόδοξος Τύπος Ἐκδόσεις, 2014).

"Biography Fr. Daniel Sysoev." Orthodox Christian eBooks. Accessed January 4th, 2024. https://danielsysoev.com/biografiya/

Брянчанинов, Святой Игнатий. *Полное собрание творений святителя Игнатия рянчанинова. Том 4*. Эдитед бы Александр Николаевич Стрижев. Москва: Издательство Паломник, 2001.

Brianchaninov, Bishop Ignatius. *The Arena*. Translated by Archimandrite Lazarus. Jordanville: Printshop of St. Job of Pochaev, 1997.

Brianchaninov, Bishop Ignatius, The Area. Translated by Archimandrite Lazarus. Jordanville: Holy Trinity Monastery, 2012.

Cabasilas, St. Nicholas. *A Commentary on the Divine Liturgy*. Translated by J.M. Hussey and P.A. McNulty. London: SPCK, 1983.

Cabasilas, St. Nicholas. *The Life in Christ*, Translated by Carmino J. DeCatanzaro. Crestwood: St. Vladimir's Seminary Press, 1974.

Cavarnos, Fr. Constantine. "Life of Saint Nectarios." In *The Modern Orthodox Saints*. Belmont: Institute for Byzantine Studies, 1981.

Cavarnos, Fr. Constantine. *The Question of Union: A Forthright Discussion of the Possibility of Union of the Eastern Orthodox Church and Roman Catholicism*. Translated by Hieromonk Patapios. Etna: Center for Traditionalist Studies, 2006.

Center for Traditionalist Orthodox Studies. *The Balamand Union: A Victory of Vatican Diplomacy.* Translated by Holy Monastery of Cyprian and Justina. Etna: St. Gregory Palamas Monastery, 1993.

Cherniavsky, Michael. "The Reception of the Council of Florence in Church History." *Church History: Studies in Christianity and Culture,* 24, no. 4. (December 1955): 347-359.

Chrysostomos, Metropolitan of Etna. "The Myth of the 'Calvinist Patriarch'". Orthodox Christian Information Center. Accessed August 7th, 2023, http://orthodoxinfo.com/inquirers/ca4_loukaris.aspx

Christensen, Hieromonk Damascene. *Father Seraphim Rose; His Life and Works.* Platina: St. Herman of Alaska Brotherhood, 2010.

Coleman, Heather, J. *Russian Baptists and Spiritual Revolution,* 1905-1929. Indianapolis: Indiana University Press, 2005.

Constantinople, Holy Synod. "Synodical Tome of 1341." In *Creeds & Confessions of the Faith in the Christian Tradition,* edited by Jaroslav Pelikan & Valerie Hotchkiss. New Haven: Yale University Press, 2003.

Constantinople, Holy Synod. "Synodical Tome of 1351." In *Creeds & Confessions of the Faith in the Christian Tradition,* edited by Jaroslav Pelikan & Valerie Hotchkiss. New Haven: Yale University Press, 2003.

Damascus, Saint John of. *De fide orthodoxa,* in Kotter, Die Schriften des Johannes von Damaskos II, 36 (= PG 94.849B).

Decapolite, Gregory. "Elder Gabriel [A Disciple of St Paisios] On Patriarch Kirill." YouTube. Accessed March 24th, 2023. https://www.youtube.com/watch?v=HXJ65qfUdGY

Demetracopoulos, Archim. Andronicus. Ἱστορία τοῦ Σχίσματος τῆς Λατινικῆς Ἐκκλησίας Ἀπὸ τῆς Ὀρθοδόξου Ἑλληνικῆς [A History of the Schism of the Latin Church from the Greek Orthodox Church]. Leipzig: Otto Wigand, 1867.

Dionysiates, Monk Lazarus. "Ἡ ἑνωτικὴ κίνησις καὶ τὸ Ἅγιον Ὄρος: Λατινόφρονες ἐπὶ αἰῶνος τυμπανιαῖοι [The Unionist Movement and the Holy Mountain: Latin-Minded Bloated for Centuries]." (December 1963).

Dionysiates, Monk Lazarus. "On the Union of the Churches and on the Excommunicated." In Hagiorite Library, 5, no. 325-326, edited by Sotirios N. Skhinas. Translated by Gregory Heers (September-October 1963): 21-24.

Dionysius, Saint, The Areopagite. "On Mystical Theology." In Patrologia Graeca, Vol. 3. Translated by Jacques Paul Migne (1857-1866) & Gregory Heers (2022) Paris: Imprimerie Catholique, 1857.

Dositheos of Jerusalem, Δωδεκάβιβλος (Thessalonike: Ekdoseis Bas. Regopoulou, 1983).

Dragas, Father George. "The Eighth Ecumenical Council: Constantinople IV (879/880) and the Condemnation of the Filioque Addition and Doctrine" (The Greek Orthodox Theological Review, Vol. 44, Nos. 1-4, 1999), 357-369. In https://web.archive.org/web/20050817074822/http://www.geocities.com/trvalentine/orthodox/dragas_eighth.html

Επίσημη ιστοσελίδα του Πατριαρχείου Αλεξανδρείας και πάσης Αφρικής. "Πρώτη ημέρα των εργασιών της Ιεράς Συνόδου του Πατριαρχείου Αλεξανδρείας." Accessed August 7th, 2023, https://web.archive.org/web/20110730164213/http://www.patriarchateofalexandria.com/index.php?module=news&action=details&id=373

Ἐγκύκλιος τῆς Μίας Ἁγίας Καθολικῆς καὶ Ἀποστολικῆς Ἐκκλησίας ἐπιστολὴ πρὸς τοὺς ἀπανταχοῦ ὀρθοδόξους. Κωνσταντινούπολη: Πατριαρχικὸ Εἶδος Τυπογραφεῖο, 1848.

Ἐφέσου, Ἅγιος Μάρκος. «Ἐπιστολὴ πρὸς Ἱερομόναχο Θεοφάνη.» Στὸ Ὀρθόδοξος Ἑλλάς, ἤτοι, περὶ τῶν Ἑλλήνων τῶν γραψάντων κατὰ Λατίνων καὶ περὶ τῶν συγγραμμάτων αὐτῶν. Λειψία: Τύποις Μέτζγερ καὶ Βίττιγ, 1872.

Ezepnidis, Saint Paisios. *Spiritual Counsels: Volume I, With Pain and Love for Contemporary Man.* Translated by Cornelia A. Tsakiridou & Maria Spanou. Souriouti: Holy Monastery Evangelist John the Theologian, 2011.

Florence, Council. "Decrees of Union of the Council of Basel-Ferrara-Florence-Rome, 1431-1445." In *Creeds & Confessions of the Faith in the Christian Tradition*, edited by Jaroslav Pelikan & Valerie Hotchkiss. New Haven: Yale University Press, 2003.

Florovsky, Georges. "Review of 'Studies and Documents Relating to the History of the Greek Church and People Under Turkish Domination' by Theodore H. Papadopoulos, M. A.," *Church History* 23, no. 1 (March 1954), 90-92.

Fourtouniadis, Patriarch Gregory VI. *Patriarchal and Synodal Encyclical Letter, Exhorting the Orthodox Everywhere, and Especially those in Egypt, Syria and Palestine, to Avoid the Persistent Papal Fallacy.* Constantinople: Ecumenical Patriarchate, 1839.

González de Iturriaga Alexopoulos, Archbishop Chrysostomos of Etna. *Orthodox and Roman Catholic Relations.* Etna: Center for Traditionalist Studies, 2001.

González de Iturriaga Alexopoulos, Archbishop Chrysostomos of Etna. "The Myth of the 'Calvinist Patriarch.'" Orthodox Christian

Information Center. Accessed August 7th, 2023. http://orthodoxinfo.com/inquirers/ca4_loukaris.aspx

Gorazd, Monk. "Who is Appearing in Medjugorje?" *Orthodox Life* 39, no. 1 (January-February 1989): 30-31.

Gorazd, Monk. *Visions Outside the Church*. Jordanville: Holy Trinity Monastery, 1990.

Gotsopoulos, Protopresbyter Anastasios K. *On Common Prayer with the Heterodox*. Florence: Uncut Mountain Press, 2022.

Grabbe, Protopresbyter George. *The Dogma of the Church in the Modern World*. Jordanville: Holy Trinity Monastery, 1998.

Gregory, Saint of Nyssa. "That When We Speak of Three Person in the Godhead We Do Not Speak of Three Gods: To the Greeks, from the Common Notions." In *Patrologia Graeca*. Vol. 45. Translated by Jacques Paul Migne (1857-1866). Paris: Imprimerie Catholique, 1857.

Hawaweeny, Saint Raphael. *The True Significance of Sacred Tradition and Its Great Worth*. Translated by Fr. Patrick Demetrios Viscuso, PhD. DeKalb: Northern Illinois University Press, 2016.

Hapgood, Isabel Florence. *Service Book of the Orthodox Church*. Englewood: Antiochian Orthodox Christian Archdiocese, 1996.

Heier, Edmund. "A Note on the Pashkovites and L. N. Tolstoy." Canadian Slavonic Papers / Revue Canadienne Des Slavistes 5 (1961): 114–21.

Heppell, Muriel. *The Paterik of the Kievan Caves Monastery*. Translated by Muriel Heppell. Cambridge: Harvard University Press, 1989.

"Hieromartyr Hermogenes, Patriarch of Moscow and All Rus." Russian Orthodox Church Official Website of the Moscow Patriarchate. Accessed November 11th, 2022. http://www.patriarchia.ru/db/text/909261.html

Holy Apostles Convent & Dormition Skete. *The Great Synaxaristes of the Orthodox Church, May* Translated by Holy Apostles Convent and Dormition Skete. Buena Vista: Holy Apostles Convent & Dormition Skete, 2003.

Holy Apostles Convent & Dormition Skete. *The Great Synaxaristes of the Orthodox Church, September*. Translated by Holy Apostles Convent and Dormition Skete. Buena Vista: Holy Apostles Convent & Dormition Skete, 2003.

Holy Apostles Convent & Dormition Skete. *The Great Synaxaristes of the Orthodox Church, January*. Translated by Holy Apostles Convent and Dormition Skete. Buena Vista: Holy Apostles Convent & Dormition Skete, 2003.

Holy Apostles Convent & Dormition Skete. *The Great Synaxaristes of the Orthodox Church, April*. Translated by Holy Apostles Convent and Dormition Skete. Buena Vista: Holy Apostles Convent & Dormition Skete, 2003.

Holy Apostles Convent & Dormition Skete. *The Great Synaxaristes of the Orthodox Church, May*. Translated by Holy Apostles Convent and Dormition Skete. Buena Vista: Holy Apostles Convent & Dormition Skete, 2003.

Holy Monastery of Pantokrator (Melissochori). "Ecumenism and [the] Orthodox Church Meeting of Bartholomew and Benedict, far from the Path of the Holy Fathers." Accessed March 26th, 2023. https://www.impantokratoros.gr/8AC792C1.en.aspx

Holy Monastery of Pantokrator (Melissochori). "Why Christianity Should Not Change with the Times." Accessed October 19th, 2022. https://www.impantokratoros.gr/saint_theophan_christianity.en.aspx

Holy Transfiguration Monastery. *The Great Horologion*. Boston: Holy Transfiguration Monastery, 1997.

Holy Trinity Monastery. "A Confession Against Ecumenism: From a Convention of Orthodox Clergymen and Monks; Greece, April 2009." Accessed November 16th, 2022. https://www.jordanville.org/files/Articles/A-CONFESSION-OF-FAITH.pdf

Holy Trinity Monastery. "A Few More Words About Metropolitan Tikhon." *Orthodox Life*, no. 2 (March-April 1975): 12.

Holy Trinity Monastery. *Book of Akathists II*. Jordanville: Printshop of St. Job of Pochaev, 2008.

Holy Trinity Monastery, "Concerning the Impossibility of Salvation for the Heterodox and Heretics," *Orthodox Life* 41, no. 1 (January-February 1991): 12-14.

Holy Trinity Monastery. "Letter to the Patriarch of Constantinople from the Sacred Community of Mount Athos." *Orthodox Life* 44, no. 4 (July-August 1994): 27-39.

Holy Trinity Monastery. "On the Serbian Orthodox New Martyrs of the Second World War." *Orthodox Life* 33, no. 1 (January-February 1983): 15-22.

Holy Trinity Monastery, "Orthodox/Episcopal Relations and Ministrations in America [Issued in 1912]," *Orthodox Life*, no. 6 (November-December 1993): 22-26.

Holy Trinity Monastery. "Partnership —The Pope and an Atheist." *Orthodox Life* 42, no. 3, (May-June 1992): 15-17.

Holy Trinity Monastery. "Resolution of the Sobor of Bishops of the Russian Orthodox Church Outside of Russia Dealing with the Roman Catholic Ecumenical Council Being Convened by Pope John XXIII." *Orthodox Life*, 61 no. 1 (January-February 1969): 3-5.

Holy Trinity Monastery. "Resolution of the Synod of Bishops Concerning the Decision of the   Moscow   Synod Permitting Roman Catholics to Have Access to All Orthodox Sacraments." *Orthodox Life*, no. 3 (May-June 1970): 3-5.

Holy Trinity Monastery. "Schemamonk John of Moldavia." *Orthodox Life* 29, no. 6 (November-December 1979): Not Known.

Holy Trinity Monastery. "The Church — The Treasury of Salvation." *Orthodox Life*, no. 4 (July-August 1970): 14-29.

Holy Trinity Monastery. "The Historical Background of the Martyrdom of St. Peter the Aleut." *Orthodox Life*, no. 1 (January-February 1981): 12-22.

Holy Trinity Monastery. "The Holy and Glorious Greatmartyr Phanourios the Newly-manifest." *Orthodox Life*, no. 3 (May-June 1981): 36.

Holy Trinity Monastery, "The Holy New Martyr, St. Athanasius of Brest," *Orthodox Life* 23, no. 4 (Jul-Aug 1973): 6, 8-10.

Holy Trinity Monastery. "The Infallibility of the Pope According to Vladimir Soloviev." *Orthodox Life*, 37 no. 4 (July-August 1987): 36-43.

Holy Trinity Monastery. "The Life of Our Holy Father Theodosius, Archbishop of Chernigov." *Orthodox Life*, no. 1 (January-February 1979): 2-13.

Holy Trinity Monastery. "The Suffering of The Holy Hieromartyr Isidore The Priest and The Seventy-Two Martyred with Him in Yuriev of Livonia." *Orthodox Life*, 28, no. 1 (January-February 1978): 3-7.

Holy Trinity Monastery. "Yet another Step? By Hieromonk Luke (Murianka)." *Orthodox Life*, no. 1 (January-February 1989): 24-29.

Holy Trinity Russian Orthodox Church. "St. Theophan the Recluse, Bishop of Tambov (1894)." Accessed November 5th, 2023, https://www.holytrinityorthodox.com/htc/orthodox-calendar/?year=2023&today=23&month=1&trp=0

Hypselantes, Athanasios Comnenos. *Τὰ Μετὰ τὴν Ἅλωσιν [The Aftermath of the Fall of Constantinople]*. Constantinople: 1870.

Ivanon-Treednadzaty, Herman Father Deacon. *The Vatican & Russia*. Jordanville: Holy Trinity Monastery, 1990.

Kantiotes, Bishop Augoustinos N. *Fragrant Flowers: Orthodox Homilies on the Lives of the Saints*. Translated by Asterios Gerostergios. Belmont: Institute for Byzantine and Modern Greek Studies, 2006.

Kantiotes, Metropolitan Augustinos. *St. Kosmas of Aetolia*. Athens: Orthodox Missionary Brotherhood, 2014.

Karmiris, I.N. *Τὰ Δογματικά καί Συμβολικά Μνημεῖα τῆς Ὀρθοδόξου Ἐκκλησίας*. Athens: 1953. [In Greek].

Kazhdan, Alexander, Talbot Mary, Alice. "Council of 879-80." In *The Oxford Dictionary of Byzantium*, edited by Alexander Kazhdan & Alice Mary Talbot. Oxford: The Oxford University Press, 1991.

Κεφαλᾶ, Νεκταρίου, Μητροπολίτου Πενταπόλεως. *Μελέτη Ἱστορικὴ περὶ τῶν Αἰτιῶν τοῦ Σχίσματος, περὶ τῆς Διαιωνήσεως αὐτοῦ καὶ περὶ τοῦ Δυνατοῦ ἢ Ἀδυνάτου τῆς Ἑνώσεως τῶν Δύο Ἐκκλησιῶν, τῆς Ἀνατολικῆς καὶ Δυτικῆς*, Τόμος Α΄. Ἀθήναις: Ἐκ τοῦ Τυπογραφείου Παρασκευᾶ Λεώνη, 1911.

Kefalas, Saint Nectarios, of Pentapolis. *Historical Studies on the Causes of the Schism*, Vol. 1, 2nd edition. Athens: 2000.

Kefalas, St. Nectarios of Pentapolis, *The Seven Oecumenical Synods* [in Greek]. Athens: 1892.

Kefalas, Saint Nektarios, *The Priesthood, Volume 4*. Translated by Nun Christina & Anna Skoubourdis. Jerusalem: Virgin Mary of Australia and Oceania, 2021.

Keroularios, Patriarch Michael. "Μιχαὴλ τοῦ ἁγιωτάτου ἀρχιεπισκόπου Κωνσταντινουπόλεως νέας ʿΡώμη καὶ οἰκουμενικοῦ τοῦ Κηρουλαρίου πρὸς Πέτρον τὸν ἁγιώτατον πατριάρχην Θεουπόλεως μεγάλας Ἀντιοχείας." In Patrologia Graeca, Vol. 120, trans. Jacques Paul Migne (1857-1866) & Tia M. Kolbaba (2000) (Paris: Imprimerie Catholique, 1857).

Khomiakov, Alexei Stepanovich. *Encore Quelques Mots D'un Chretien Orthodoxe Sur Les Confessions Occidentales: A L'Occasion De Plusieurs Publications Religieuses, Latines Et Protestantes*. Leipzig: F.A. Brockhaus, 1858.

Kokkinakis, Athenagoras Archbishop. *The Thyateira Confession: The Faith and Prayer of the People of God*. Leighton Buzzard: The Faith Press, 1975.

Kolbaba, Tia. *The Byzantine Lists: Errors of the Latins.* Chicago: University of Illinois Press, 2000.

Kolbaba, Tia M. "Meletios Homologetes on the Customs of the Italians." *Revue es études Byzantines*, tome 55, (1997): 137-168.

Kontouma, Vassa. "Concilum Constantinopolitanum 1755-1756." *The Great Councils of the Orthodox Churches Decisions and Synodika: From Constantinople 861 to Constantinople 1872,* Vol 1, edited by Giuseppe Alberigo & Alberto Melloni. Bologna: Brepols Publishers, 2016.

Koutloumousiou Monastery. Ὁ πειρασμὸς τῆς Ῥώμης *[The Temptation of Rome].* Mt. Athos: Koutloumousiou, 1992.

Lidbetter, Sebastian, "Hadrian IV (1154-1159) and the 'Bull' Laudabiliter: A Historiographical Review." Wilfrid Laurier University, 2019. Accessed August 24th, 2023. https://scholars.wlu.ca/etd/2221.

Machitadze, Archpriest Zakaria. *Lives of the Georgian Saints.* Translated by David Ninoshvili, Lauren Elizabeth Ninoshvili. Platina: Saint Herman of Alaska Brotherhood, 2006.

Makarios, Hieromonk of Simonos Petra. "St. Nicodemus of the Holy Mountain – Bright Star of the Church." Adapted by Sretensky Monastery Press, translated by Maria Stepanova. Accessed November 5th, 2023. https://orthochristian.com/155098.html

Makarios, Hieromonk of Simonos Petra. *The Synaxarion: The Lives of the Saints of the Orthodox Church, Volume Five, May—June.* Translated by Christopher Hookway. Ormylia: Holy Convent of the Annunciation of Our Lady, 2005.

Makarios, Hieromonk of Simonos Petra. *The Synaxarion: The Lives of the Saints of the Orthodox Church, Volume One, September— October.* Translated by Christopher Hookway. Ormylia: Holy Convent of the Annunciation of Our Lady, 1999.

Makarios, Hieromonk of Simonos Petra. *The Synaxarion: The Lives of the Saints of the Orthodox Church, Volume Seven, Appendix— General Index.* Translated by Mother Maria (Rule). Thessaloniki: Indiktos Publishing Company, 2008.

Makarios, Hieromonk of Simonos Petra. T*he Synaxarion: The Lives of the Saints of the Orthodox Church, Volume Six, July—August.* Translated by Mother Maria (Rule) and Mother Joanna (Burton). Ormylia: Holy Convent of the Annunciation of Our Lady, 2008.

Makarios, Hieromonk of Simonos Petra. *The Synaxarion: The Lives of the Saints of the Orthodox Church, Volume Three, January— February.* Translated by Christopher   Hookway.   Ormylia: Holy Convent of the Annunciation of Our Lady, 2001.

Makarios, Hieromonk of Simonos Petra. *The Synaxarion: The Lives of the Saints of the Orthodox Church, Volume Two, November— December.* Translated by Christopher Hookway. Ormylia: Holy Convent of the Annunciation of Our Lady, 1999.

Mark of Ephesus, Saint. "Confession of Faith: Letter of Lord Mark of Ephesus to Lord George Scholarius." In *Patrologia Graeca*, Vol. 160. Translated by Jacques Paul Migne (1857-1866) & Gregory Heers (2023). Paris: Imprimerie Catholique, 1857.

Maximovich, Saint John. "The Faithfulness to the Russian Path of Righteousness." *Pravoslavnaja Rus,* no. 11. (June: 1994): 1-3.

Maximovitch, Saint John. *The Orthodox Veneration of the Mother of God.* Platina: Saint Herman of Alaska Brotherhood, 1975.

Meletios of Athens, Metropolitan. Ἐκκλησιαστικὴ Ἱστορία [Church History], Vol. III, §9. Vienna: 1784.

Menaion of the Orthodox Church, Volume I, September. "Commemoration of the Twenty-Six Martyred Monks of Zographou." Translated by Reader Isaac E. Lambertsen. Liberty: Saint John of Kronstadt Press, 2011.

Menaion of the Orthodox Church, Volume III, November. "Commemoration of Our Father Among the Saints Gregory Palamas." Translated by Reader Isaac Lambertsen. Liberty: St. John Press, 2008.

Menaion of the Orthodox Church, Volume V, January, "Commemoration of Saint Isidore and the Seventy-Two Martyrs." Translated by Reader Isaac E. Lambertsen. Liberty: Saint John of Kronstadt Press, 2012.

Menaion of the Orthodox Church, Volume XI, July. "Commemoration of Saint Maximos Sandovich." Translated by Reader Isaac E. Lambertsen. Liberty: Saint John of Kronstadt Press, 2011.

Mentzelopoulos, Metropolitan Seraphim. "A Letter to Pope Francis Concerning His Past, the Abysmal State of Papism, and a Plea to Return to Holy Orthodoxy." Accessed April 14th, 2023. http:// orthodoxinfo.com/ecumenism/epistle-to-pope-francis.pdf

Mesaritēs, Nikolaos. Nicholas Mesarites: His Life and Works (in translation). Edited by Michael Angold. Liverpool: Liverpool University Press, 2017.

Metallinos, George D., Protopresbyter. I Confess One Baptism. Translated by Hieromonk Seraphim. Daphne: Saint Paul's Monastery, 1994.

Metallinos, George D., Protopresbyter. *Unia: The Face and the Disguise.* Translated by Ekaterina Nikolopoulou. Thessaloniki: Christian Orthodox Philanthropical Society of Friends of the Pantokrator Sacred Retreat of Melissohorion "Saint Gregory Palamas", 1992.

Metrophanes, Schema-monk. *Blessed Paisius Velichkovsky: The Man Behind the Philokalia.* Platina: St. Herman of Alaska Brotherhood, 1994.

Mitilinaios, Archimandrite Athanasios. *Revelation, Vol. 3: The Seven Trumpets and the Antichrist.* Translated by Constantine Zalalas. Dunlap: Zoe Press, 2015.

Moldova & Bucovina, Romanian Orthodox Church Metropolia. "Akathist of the Holy Martyr Athanasius Todoran." Accessed October 20th, 2022. https://doxologia.ro/ceaslov/acatiste/acatistul-sfantului-martir-atanasie-todoran

Moldova & Bucovina, Romanian Orthodox Church Metropolia. "Hieromonk Paisios Defender of Orthodoxy in Northern Bucovina." Accessed October 20th, 2022. https://doxologia.ro/pateric/ieroschimonahul-paisie-aparatorul-ortodoxiei-bucovina-de-nord

Moldova & Bucovina, Romanian Orthodox Church Metropolia. "The Lives of the Holy Martyrs and Confessors of Năsăud." Accessed October 20th, 2022. https://doxologia.ro/liturgica/vietile-sfintilor/viata-sfintilor-martiri-marturisitori-nasaudeni

Moldpres News Agency. "Metropolitan Varlaam, great scholar, theologist, architect of Moldova's national Church," Moldpres, accessed November 17th, 2023, https://www.moldpres.md/en/news/2021/01/22/21000425

Moses the Athonite, Monk. "Hieromartyr Kosmas the Aitolos (+1779)." Translated by John Sanidopoulos. Accessed November

5th, 2023, https://www.johnsanidopoulos.com/2014/08/hieromartyr-kosmas-aitolos-1779-1-of-2.html

Moses the Athonite, Monk. Μέγα Γεροντικὸ ἐναρέτων Ἁγιορειτῶν τοῦ Εἰκοστοῦ Αἰῶνος [Great Gerontikon of Virtuous Athonites of the Twentieth Century], Vol. 2: 1956-1983. Mygdonia: Thessaloniki, 2011.

Moss, Vladimir. *The Fall of Orthodox England.* Mayford, Woking, Surrey, United Kingdom: OrthodoxChristianBooks.com, 2011. Accessed November 3rd, 2021. https://www.orthodoxchristianbooks.com/downloads/910_THE_FALL_OF_ORTHODOX_ENGLAND.pdf

Mouravieff, Boris. *A History of the Church of Russia.* Translated by R.W. Blackmore. London: Rivington & Co., 1842.

Neale, John Mason. *A History of the Holy Eastern Church: The Patriarchate of Antioch.* London: Rivington & Co., 1873.

Nikodemus the Hagiorite, Saint. Ἑορτοδρόμιον, ἤτοι Ἑρμηνεία εἰς τοὺς ἀσματικοὺς κανόνας τῶν Δεσποτικῶν καὶ Θεομητορικῶν ἑορτῶν [Heortodromion: Interpretation of the Canons of the Feasts of our Lord and of our Lady]. Venice: Nicholas Glykys, 1836 [In Greek].

Nikodemos, Saint of the Holy Mountain and St. Makarios of Corinth. *The Philokalia: The Complete Text Volume IV.* Translated by G.E.H. Palmer, Phillip Sherrard and Kallistos Ware. London: Faber and Faber Ltd., 1995.

Nikodemos, Saint, and Agapios, Hieromonk. *The Rudder (Pedalion): Of the Metaphorical Ship of the One Holy, Catholic, and Apostolic Church of Orthodox Christians.* Translated by D. Cummings. Athens: Kesisoglou the Caesarian, 1908.

Nikon, Bishop. "The Life of the Pastor of Kronstadt." Accessed November 7th, 2023, https://orthochristian.com/43914.html

Νοταρᾶς, Πατριάρχης Ἱεροσολύμων Δοσίθεος Β΄. "Πρακτικὰ τῆς Συνελθούσης ἐν Κωνσταντινουπόλι Συνόδου τοῦ Φωτίου, Γράφει ὁ Ἰγνάτιος ἀπὸ τὸ Πατριαρχείο," στὸν Τόμο Χαρᾶς. Μεταφρασμένο ἀπὸ τὸν Ἱερομόναχο Πολύκαρπο (Strosnider). Ἐπεξεργασία ἀπὸ τὸν Κωνσταντῖνο Σιαμάκη καὶ τὸν Γρηγόριο Χῖρς. Θεσσαλονίκη: Ρηγοπούλου, 1985.

Official News Agency, Basilica.ro, The Romanian Orthodox Church. "Holy Hierarch Dositheus, Metropolitan of Moldavia; Martyrs Eustratius, Auxentius, Euguene, Mardarius and Orestes at Sebaste; Virgin-Martyr Lucy of Syracuse." Accessed October 20th, 2022. https://basilica.ro/en/%E2%80%A0-holy-hierarch-dositheus-metropolitan-of-moldavia-%E2%80%A0-martyrs-eustratius-auxentius-eugene-mardarius-and-orestes-at-sebaste-virgin-martyr-lucy-of-syracuse/

Official News Agency, Basilica.ro, The Romanian Orthodox Church. "St. John the Merciful, Patriarch of Alexandria; Martyrs and Confessors of Nasaud: Athanasius, Basil, Gregory and Basil; St. Nilus the Faster of Sinai." Accessed October 20th, 2022. https://basilica.ro/en/st-john-the-merciful-patriarch-of-alexandria-martyrs-and-confessors-of-nasaud-athanasius-basil-gregory-and-basil-st-nilus-the-faster-of-sinai/

Official News Agency, Basilica.ro, The Romanian Orthodox Church. "Venerable Theodore the Sanctified: Ven. Silas, Paisios and Nathan from Sihastria Putnei." Accessed October 20th, 2022. https://basilica.ro/en/venerable-theodore-the-sanctified-%E2%80%A0-ven-silas-paisios-and-nathan-from-sihastria-putnei/

Orthodox Christian Books & Icons. "A Desperate Appeal to the Ecumenical Patriarchate by Elder Philotheos Zervakos." *Orthodox Word 4*, no. 1 (January-February 1968): 11-20.

Orthodox Christian Books & Icons. "Address of St. Mark of Ephesus on the Day of His Death." *Orthodox Word 3*, no. 3 (June-July 1967): 89-106.

Orthodox Christian Books & Icons. "Encyclical Letter of St. Mark of Ephesus." *Orthodox Word 3*, no. 2 (March-April-May 1967): 53-59.

Orthodox Christian Books & Icons. "On the Writings of Saint Nektarios." *Orthodox Word 2*, no. 2 (April-May-June 1966): 59-61.

Orthodox Christian Books & Icons. "Orthodoxy in the Contemporary World; The Latest Step Toward 'Union.'" *Orthodox Word Vol 2*, no. 1 (Jan-Feb-Mar1966): 37.

Orthodox Christian Books & Icons. "St. Mark of Ephesus and the False Union of Florence." *Orthodox Word 3*, no. 1 (January-February 1967): 2.

Orthodox Christian Books & Icons. "The Life and Ascetic Labors of Elder Paisius Velichkovsky Part Fifteen: The Letters of Elder Paisius from Niamets." *Orthodox Word 11*, no. 5 (September-October 1975): 202-203, 210.

Orthodox Christian Books & Icons. "The Meaning of the Russian Diaspora." *Orthodox Word 9*, no. 3 (May-June 1973): 93.

Orthodox Christian Books & Icons. "The True Church of Christ." *Orthodox Word 1*, no. 5 (September-October 1965): 184-187.

Orthodox Christian Information Center. "An Open Letter to the Holy Abbots and the Holy Representatives of the Sacred Twenty Monasteries in the Holy Community of the Holy Mount Athos." Accessed March 26th, 2023. http://orthodoxinfo.com/ecumenism/kelliotes.aspx

Orthodox Christian Information Center. "Encyclical of the Eastern Patriarchs, 1848 A Reply to the Epistle of Pope Pius IX, 'to the Easterns.'" Holy Synods of Constantinople, Antioch and Jerusalem. Accessed October 16, 2022. http://orthodoxinfo.com/ecumenism/encyc_1848.aspx

Orthodox Christian Information Center. "The Official Statement from Mt. Athos on the Pope's Visit to the Phanar." Accessed March 26th, 2023. http://orthodoxinfo.com/ecumenism/athos_popevisit2006.aspx

Orthodox Christian Information Center. "The Patriarchal Encyclical of 1895, A Reply to the Papal Encyclical of Pope Leo XIII, on Reunion, Holy Synod of Constantinople." Accessed October 16th, 2022. http://orthodoxinfo.com/ecumenism/encyc_1895.aspx

Orthodox Times. "Memory of Saint Justin Popović." Accessed November 5th, 2023, https://orthodoxtimes.com/memory-of-saint-justin-popovic-2/

Ostroumoff, Ivan N. *The History of the Council of Florence.* Translated by Basil Popoff. Boston: Holy Transfiguration Monastery, 1971.

Parios, St. Athanasios. *Epitome or Collection of the Divine Dogmas of the Faith* [in Greek]. Leipzig: 1806.

Palamas, Saint Gregory. *Apodictic Treatises on the Procession of the Holy Spirit.* Translated by Fr. Christopher C. Moody and Gregory Heers. Florence: Uncut Mountain Press, 2022.

Papacioc, Archimandrite Arsenie. "On Ecumenism, Catholics and Sects." Video Interview by Unknown at Mănăstirea Cheia (Cheia Monastery). Translated by Ellaina Chiru. May 21st, 2005. https://youtu.be/vhqJSLY0p_M

Papacioc, Archimandrite Arsenie. *Singur Ortodoxia*. Bucureşti: Editura Sophia, 2008.

Papadakis, Aristeides. *The Christian East and the Rise of the Papacy*. Crestwood: St. Vladimir Seminary Press, 1994.

Papadakis, Aristeides. *Crisis in Byzantium: The Filioque Controversy in the Patriarchate of Gregory II of Cyprus (1283-1289)*. New York: Fordham University Press, 1983.

Papal Encyclicals Online. "Council of Basel-Ferrara-Florence, 1431-49 A.D." Accessed December 10th, 2022. https://www.papalencyclicals.net//councils/ecum17.htm

Papal Encyclicals Online. "Fourth Lateran Council: 1215, 4th Constitution, On the Pride of the Greeks Towards the Latins." Accessed December 16th, 2022. https://www.papalencyclicals.net/councils/ecum12-2.htm#4

Paris, Edmond. *Genocide in Satellite Croatia, 1941-1945: A Record of Racial and Religious Persecutions and Massacres*. Chicago: The American Institute for Balkan Affairs, 1961.

Paros, Saint Athanasios of, *"That the Holy Spirit Proceeds from the Father Alone."* In Compendium or Collection of the Divine Doctrines of the Faith (Ἐπιτομὴ εἴτε Συλλογὴ τῶν Θείων τῆς Πίστεως Δογμάτων). Translated by Gregory Heers (2022). Leipzig: Breitkopf & Härtel, 1806.

Pârvu, Elder Justin. *Biserica Si Noile Erezii.* Translated by Ellaina Chiru. Petru Vodă: Fundatia Justin Pârvu, 2014.

Pavlov, Andrei Nikolaevich. *Kriticeskie Opyty Po Istopie Drevnejse Greko-Russkoj polemiki protev Patenjan.* Translated by Nicholas Nelson. St. Petersburg, 1878.

Paschalidis, Symeon. "Concilum Constantinopolitanum 1484." In *The Great Councils of the Orthodox Churches Decisions and Synodika: From Constantinople 861 to Constantinople 1872, Vol 1*, edited by Giuseppe Alberigo & Alberto Melloni. Bologna: Brepols Publishers, 2016.

Patriarchae Constantinopolitani, S. Athanasii I. Epistulae CXV Ad Imperatorem Andronicum II, Eiusque Propinquos Necnon Officiales Missae, translata per Alice-Mary Maffry Talbot. Washingtoniae, D.C.: Dumbarton Oaks, 1975.

Πατριαρχείο Αλεξανδρείας και πάσης Αφρικής, ο επίσημος ιστότοπος. "Πρώτη ημέρα των εργασιών της Ιεράς Συνόδου του Πατριαρχείου Αλεξανδρείας". Πρόσβαση στις 7 Αυγούστου 2023. https://web.archive.org/web/20110730164213/http://www.patriarchateofalexandria.com/index.php?module=news&action=details&id=373

Patriarchate of Alexandria and All Africa, The Official Website. "Kyrillos III Loukaris (1601-1620)." Accessed August 7th, 2023. https://www.patriarchateofalexandria.com/patriarch/kyrillos-iii-loukaris-1601-1620/?lang=en

Pelikan, Jaroslav. *The Spirit of Eastern Christendom (600-1700), Vol 2.* Chicago: The University of Chicago Press, 1977.

Photios, Saint. "The Encyclical Letter to the Bishops of the East in 866 by St. Photios the Great." *In Creeds & Confessions of the Faith in the Christian Tradition*, edited by Jaroslav Pelikan & Valerie Hotchkiss. New Haven: Yale University Press, 2003.

Photios, Saint. *The Mystagogy of the Holy Spirit.* Translated by Joseph P. Farrell. Brookline: Holy Cross Orthodox Press, 1987.

Pochaev, Saint Job. *St. Job of Pochaev: Life, Liturgical Service and Akathist Hymn.* Translated by Reader Isaac E. Lambertsen. Liberty: St. John of Kronstadt Press, 1997.

Popović, Saint Justin. *The Life and Writings of Blessed Justin Popovich: The Conscience of the Serbian Church.* New South Wales: Holy Dormition Sisterhood, 2003.

Popović, Saint Justin. *The Orthodox Church and Ecumenism.* Translated by Benjamin Emmanuel Stanley. Birmingham: Lazarica Press, 2000.

Popovich, Father Justin. *Orthodox Faith and Life in Christ.* Translated by Asterios Gerostergios Belmont: Institute for Byzantine and Modern Greek Studies, 2020.

"Previous Patriarchs Archives - Page 3 of 7." Πατριαρχείο Αλεξανδρείας. Accessed January 21st, 2024. https://www.patriarchateofalexandria.com/patriarch_category/previous-patriarchs/page/3/?lang=en

Rogich, Fr. Daniel. *Serbian Patericon: Saints of the Serbian Orthodox Church – Volume One.* Canton: Hesychia Press, 2023.

Romanides, Father John. "A Critique of the Balamand Agreement." Theologia, Vol. VI, 1993, Issue no. 4, pages 570-580. Quoted in http://orthodoxinfo.com/ecumenism/frjr_balamand.aspx

Romanides, Father John. "Do Forced Replacements of Their Orthodox Predecessors Have Apostolic Succession?" Romanity.org.

Accessed August 24, 2023. http://romanity.org/htm/rom.26.
en.apostolic_succession.htm#k8

Romanides, Father John. "Examples of the Science of the Ethnic
Cleaning of Roman History and a Vision of the Future United
States of Franco-Romania," Romanity.org, Accessed January 31,
2024. http://www.romanity.org/htm/rom.21.en.the_ethnic_
cleaning_of_roman_history.01.htm#s6

Romanides, Father John. "Some Underlying Positions of this Website"
Part V, Romanity.org. Accessed August 24th, 2023. http://www.
romanity.org/htm/rom.00.en.some_underlying_positions_of_
this_website.htm

Rose, Father Seraphim. *God's Revelation to the Human Heart.* Platina:
St. Herman of Alaska Brotherhood, 2014.

Runciman, Steven. *The Great Church in Captivity: A Study of The
Patriarchate of Constantinople from the Eve of the Turkish
Conquest to the Greek War of Independence.* 1st ed., Cambridge:
University Printing Press, 1968.

Russian Orthodox Church. "Hieromartyr Hermogenes, Patriarch
of Moscow and All Rus." Official Website of the Moscow
Patriarchate. Accessed November 11th, 2022. http://www.
patriarchia.ru/db/text/909261.html

Russian Orthodox Church. "Martyr Macarius of Kanevsky." Official
Website of the Moscow Patriarchate. Accessed November 11th,
2022. http://www.patriarchia.ru/db/text/913570.html

Saint Anthony's Greek Orthodox Monastery. *Monastic Wisdom: The
Letters of Elder Joseph the Hesychast.* Florence: Saint Anthony's
Greek Orthodox Monastery, 1998.

Saint John of Kronstadt Press. *Holy New Hieromartyr Maximus Sandovich: Protomartyr of the Lemko People.* Translated by Isaac E. Lambertsen. Liberty: The Saint John of Kronstadt Press, 1998.

Saint Paisius Monastery. "St. Paisius (Velichkovsky): A Brief Summary of His Life, Compiled by the Sisters of St. Paisius Monastery." Accessed November 1st, 2023, https://stpaisiusmonastery.org/about-the-monastery/life-of-st-paisius/a-brief-life/a-brief-life-english/. See also his life translated by Fr. Seraphim Rose from St. Herman of Alaska Press.

Sakharov, Saint Sophrony. *Striving for Knowledge of God.* Essex: Stavropegic Monastery of St. John the Baptist, 2016.

Savas, Hieromonk of the Holy Mountain. *Healing the Soul: Saint Porphyrios of Kafsokalyvia as a Model for Our Lives.* Translated by Sisterhood of the Saint John Chrysostomos Greek Orthodox Monastery. Pleasant Prairie: St. John Chrysostomos Monastery, 2021.

Scholarios, Saint Gennadios II. *From Ashes and Ruin: Selection from the Writings of St. Gennadios Scholarios.* Translated by Dr John Palmer. Columbia: Newrome Press, 2022.

Second Ecumenical Council. "Canons of the One Hundred and Fifty Fathers who assembled at Constantinople, Canon I." In *Nicene and Post-Nicene Fathers, The Seven Ecumenical Councils, Vol. 14,* edited by Philip Schaff & Henry Wace. Peabody: Hendrickson Publishers, 1999.

Simpson, Alicia. *Niketas Choniates: A Historiographical Study.* Oxford: Oxford University Press, 2013.

Snychev, Metropolitan John of St. Petersburg and Ladoga. "The Life of Holy Hieromartyr Hilarion (Troitsky), Archbishop of Verey."

Translated by Nun Cornelia. The *Orthodox Word*, Issue #264-265, Jan.-Apr. 2009, Vol. 45, Nos. 1-2.

St. Anthony's Greek Orthodox Monastery. "St. Joseph the Hesychast (1897-1959)." Accessed November 7th, 2023, https://stanthonysmonastery.org/pages/st-joseph-the-hesychast

"St. John, Metropolitan of Kiev (1089)." Today's Scripture Readings. Accessed December 9th, 2023, https://www.holytrinityorthodox.com/calendar/los/August/31-04.htm

Svetosavlje Orthodox Christianity of Serbian Style and Experience. "Saint Vasilije Ostroski."Accessed March 26th, 2023. https://svetosavlje.org/sveti-vasilije-ostroski/

Symeon, Saint, Archbishop of Thessaloniki. "Against All Heresies." In *Patrologia Graeca, Vol. 155*. Translated by Jacques Paul Migne (1857-1866) & Gregory Heers (2022). Paris: Imprimerie Catholique, 1857.

Symeon, Saint, Archbishop of Thessalonica. "On the Sacred Liturgy." In *The Liturgical Commentaries*. Translated by Steven Hawkes-Teeples. Toronto: Pontifical Institute of Mediaeval Studies, 2011.

Sysoev, Priest Daniel. *The Law of God: An Introduction to Orthodox Christianity*. Translated by Deacon Nathan Williams. New Jersey: Daniel Sysoev Inc, 2016.

Sysoev, Priest Daniel. *Letters*. Translated by Deacon Nathan Williams. New Jersey: Daniel Sysoev Inc, 2022.

Sysoev, Priest Daniel. *Questions to Priest Daniel Sysoev*. New Jersey: Daniel Sysoev Inc, 2016.

Talbot Maffry, Alice-Mary. "Patriarch Athanasius (1289-1293; 1303-1309) and the Church." In *Dumbarton Oak Papers*, 27 (1973), 11-28.

Telepneff, Fr. Gregory. *The Egyptian Desert in the Irish Bogs.* Etna, CA: Center for Traditionalist Orthodox Studies, 2001.

Theophylact, Saint of Ohrid. "Concerning Those Who Accuse the Latins." In *Patrologia Graeca,* Vol. 126. Translated by Jacques Paul Migne (1857-1866) & Bogomil Sabtchev (2020). Paris: Imprimerie Catholique, 1857.

Third Ecumenical Council. "The Canons of the Two Hundred Holy and Blessed Fathers Who Met at Ephesus: Canon VII" In *Nicene and Post-Nicene Fathers: The Seven Ecumenical Councils, Vol.14,* edited by Philip Schaff & Henry Wace. Peabody: Hendrickson Publicatons, 1999.

Thornton, Protopresbyter James. *Pious Kings and Right-Believing Queens: An Encyclopedia of the Royal and Imperial Saints of the Orthodox Church.* Belmont: Institute for Byzantine and Modern Greek Studies, 2013.

Three Hierarchs Publishing. "A Life of Saint Porphyrios of Kavsokalyvia." *God is Wonderful in His Saints: Book of Akathists.* Wenatchee: Three Hierarchs Publishing, 2015.

Trenham, Fr. Josiah. *Rock and Sand: An Orthodox Appraisal of the Protestant Reformers and Their Teachings.* Columbia: Newrome Press, 2015.

Troitsky, Saint Hilarion. *The Church on Unity & the World Conference of Christian Communities.* Translated by Margaret Jerinec Acton. Montreal: Monastery Press, 1975.

Union of Orthodox Journalists. "Athonite Geronda to Phanar Head: Repent and Leave a Slippery Slope." Accessed March 24th, 2023. https://spzh.news/en/news/66195-afonskij-starec--glave-fanara-pokajtesy-i-sojdite-so-skolyzkogo-puti

University of Pennsylvania Press. "The Sack of Constantinople: Accounts of the Sack by Niketas Choniates." In *Translations and Reprints from the Original Sources of European History, Volume III.* Philadelphia: University of Pennsylvania Press, 1912.

Vasilopoulos, Abbot Kosmas. "Why Are the Lives of Saints Considered the Encyclopedia of Orthodoxy?" Abbot Kosmas, Official Page of The Orthodox Monastery of the Archangel Michael. Accessed February 1st, 2023. https://www.youtube.com/watch?v=p6Lqoxw1EvY

Vatican, Holy See. "Joint International Commission for the Theological Dialogue Between the Roman Catholic Church and The Orthodox Church: Seventh Plenary Session, Balamand School of Theology." The Vatican Holy See. Accessed December 13th, 2022. https://web.archive.org/web/20031223144638/https://www.vatican.va/roman_curia/pontifical_councils/chrstuni/ch_orthodox_docs/rc_pc_chrstuni_doc_19930624_lebanon_en.html

Velichkovsky, St. Paisius. "A Young Orthodox Martyr." In *The Life of Paisij Velyčkovs'kj.* Translated by J.M.E. Featherstone. Cambridge: Harvard University Press, 1989.

Velimirovich, Bishop Nikolai, Saint. *A Treasury of Serbian Orthodox Spirituality.* Translated by Fr. Theodore Micka and Fr. Steven Scott. Grayslake: The Free Serbian Orthodox Diocese of the United States of America and Canada, 1988.

Velimirovich, Saint Nikolai. *Missionary Letters of Saint Nikolai Velimirovich – Volume 1.* Translated by Hierodeacon Serafim

(Baltic). Grayslake: Joe Buley Memorial Library/New Gracanica Monastery, 2008.

Velimirović, Saint Nikolai. *The Prologue of Ohrid: July to December, Volume II.* Translated by Father T. Timothy Tepsić. Vrnjačka: Interklima-Grafika, 2008.

Velimirovich, St. Nikolai. "Woman as a Symbol of Christ." *Orthodox Life,* 1951, Nos. 5 and 6.

Vlachos, Metropolitan Hierotheos, *Patristic and Scholastic Theology in Perspective.* Translated by Sister Pelagia Selfie. Levadia: Birth of the Theotokos Monastery, 2023.

Vlachos, Metropolitan Hierotheos of Navpaktos and Hagios Vlasios. "Baptismal Theology." Ekklesiastike Parembase, No. 71 (December 2001), 12, reprinted from Orthodox Tradition, Vol XX, No 2, 40-43.

Voznesensky, Metropolitan Philaret of New York. "An Appeal to His Holiness Athenagoras of Constantinople, New Rome, and Ecumenical Patriarch." *Orthodox Word* 2, no. 1 (January-March 1966): 27-30.

Voznesensky, Metropolitan Philaret of New York. "Interview with His Eminence Metropolitan Philaret in the Roman Catholic Weekly Publik." *Православная Русь (Orthodox Life)* 12, (Winter 1970): 9-12.

Voznesensky, Metropolitan Philaret of New York. "On the Thyateira Confession." Orthodox Life 26, no.2 (March-April 1976): 21-25.

Voznesensky, Metropolitan Philaret of New York. "The Announcement of the Extraordinary Joint Conference of the Sacred Community of the Holy Mount Athos & An Epistle Response to Mount

Athos." In *Metropolitan Philaret of New York: Zealous Confessor for the Faith*, edited by Subdeacon Nektarios Harrison. Florence: Uncut Mountain Press, 2022.

Voznesensky, Metropolitan Philaret of New York. "To Patriarch Athenagoras of Constantinople on the Lifting of Anathemas from 1054 against the Latin Papists (1965); A Statement by the Head of the Free Russian Church on the Orthodox Relation to the Church of Rome." In *Metropolitan Philaret of New York: Zealous Confessor for the Faith*, edited by Subdeacon Nektarios Harrison. Florence: Uncut Mountain Press, 2022.

Voznesensky, Metropolitan Philaret of New York. "The Second Sorrowful Epistle (First Sunday in Lent 1972)." In *Metropolitan Philaret of New York: Zealous Confessor for the Faith*, edited by Subdeacon Nektarios Harrison. Florence: Uncut Mountain Press, 2022.

Voznesensky, Metropolitan Philaret of New York. "The Third Sorrowful Epistle: On the Thyateira Confession (December 19, 1975)." In *Metropolitan Philaret of New York: Zealous Confessor for the Faith*, edited by Subdeacon Nektarios Harrison. Florence: Uncut Mountain Press, 2022.

Ware, Kallistos. *Eustratios Argenti: A Study of the Greek Church Under Turkish Rule*. London: Oxford University Press, 1964.

Ware, Timothy. *The Orthodox Church*. Penguin Books, 1997.

White, Despina Stratoudaki. *Patriarch Photios of Constantinople: His Life, Scholarly Contributions, and Correspondence Together with a Translation of Fifty-Two of His Letters*. Boston: Holy Cross Press, 1981.

Wright, Thomas, *The Historical Works of Giraldus Cambrensis*. London, UK: George Bell & Sons, 1905.

Χριστόφορος ὁ Αἰτωλός. *Ραντισμού Στηλήτευσις.* Κωνσταντινούπολις: χ.ε
     1755.

Zervakos, Geronda Philotheos. *Paternal Counsels Vol. 2.* Thessalonika:
     Orthodox Kypseli Publications, 2005.

Zisis, Protopresbyter Theodore. *Following the Holy Fathers: Essays on the
     Timeless Guides of Authentic Christianity.* Columbia: Newrome
     Press, 2017.

INDEX

A

Abbot John (Kantara Monastery), Saint, 137

Affusion, 399, 409

Akriveia or *akribia*, 273, 823-824, 892, 897

Alexander II, Pope, 155

Alexander Nevsky, Grand Prince, Saint, 469-470

Alexandria, 20, 50, 51, 95, 168-169, 180, 191, 242, 244, 252, 264, 266, 270, 276-277, 279, 287, 307, 370, 443-444, 547, 557, 562, 572, 595-597, 608, 639, 641-642, 644, 649, 757, 783, 789, 847, 861, 874

Alexei Stepanovich Khomiakov, 651, 718, 724-726

Alexis Toth of Wilkes-Barre (Pennsylvania), Saint, 132, 457

Anathema, 27, 29, 39, 62, 107, 109, 134, 184-185, 226-227, 229-233, 235-236, 244, 246, 262, 268-269, 271, 275-276, 287, 296, 303-304, 309, 314, 316, 330-331, 339-342, 366, 370, 382, 418, 440, 549-551, 560, 569, 621, 640, 654, 689-690, 698-699, 703, 723, 743, 819, 826-827, 829, 856, 882, 924, 928, 941, 959-960, 962

Anglo-Saxon, 203

Anglo-Saxon Chronicle, 155

Antichrist or anti-christ, 40, 172, 388, 497, 683, 698, 702, 730-731, 738-739, 806-808, 817

Antioch, 20, 95, 168-169, 180, 191, 242, 264, 271, 276, 287, 307, 370, 434-435, 445, 456, 544-545, 547, 556-557, 562-563, 572-573, 606, 608, 637, 639, 644-646, 649, 757, 783, 789, 819, 847, 861, 863, 874

Antony (Khrapovitsky), Metropolitan, 30, 650, 807

Apostolic Canons. See Canons, Apostolic.

Apostolic Succession, 499, 602, 610-612, 615, 631, 681, 684-685, 740, 785, 791, 793, 822, 862, 867, 872, 875, 876, 880-881

Aquinas, Thomas. See Thomas Aquinas.

Argenti, Eustratios of Chios. See Eustratios Argenti of Chios.

Aristotle or Aristotelian philosophy, 488, 722, 735, 755

Arius (heretic), 185, 295, 335, 412-413, 416, 702, 739, 787, 818, 918, 940, 956

Arsenie (Papacioc) of St. Mary Monastery, Elder, 703, 704, 707

Assumption of the Virgin Mary, 679, 852

Atanasie Todoran of Bichigiu, Saint, 66, 68-70, 524

Athanasios I, Patriarch of Constantinople, Saint, 55, 57, 346

Athanasios Mitilinaios, Elder, 702

Athanasios of Paros, Saint, 407

Athenagoras (Kokkinakis) of Thyateira, Archbishop, 848

995

F

G

I

Iakovos of Evia, Saint, 501,
Idolatry, 297, 412, 415, 488-489, 491, 737, 814
Ignatius Brianchaninov, Saint, 411, 476, 807
Ilie, Cleopa of Sihăstria Monastery, Elder. See Cleopa (Ilie) of Sihăstria Monastery, Elder.
Immaculate Conception, 293, 470-472, 474-475, 481, 577, 581, 611, 621, 629, 679, 705, 708, 805, 821
Immersion (Baptismal),
    Single, 288
    Triple, 367, 440, 579, 823-824
Indulgences, 245, 424, 432, 455, 483, 488, 493, 646, 679, 706, 708, 803, 812, 821, 851
Infallibility, 225, 280, 293, 446-448, 483-485, 487-493, 496, 505-506, 552, 577, 586, 593, 604-605, 611, 616, 618-619, 621, 628-629, 650-651, 656, 663, 677, 679, 694, 705, 708-710, 722, 725, 820, 858, 880
Innocent III, Pope, 86, 163, 166, 168, 359, 449-451
Intercommunion, 91, 494, 611
Iosif (Joseph) Muşat, Metropolitan, First Hierarch of Moldavia, Saint, 149
Ireland, 154, 156-157
Irinej (Ćirić) the Confessor, Bishop of Bačka, Saint, 118
Isidore of Yuryev, Saint, 81, 525
Iviron (Iveron) Monastery, Monks and Martyrs Cast into the Sea by the Latinizers, 133-134

J

Jakšić, Danilo. See Danilo (Jakšić) the Confessor, Bishop of Upper Karlovac and Plaški, Saint,
Jeremiah (Kantara Monastery), Saint, 137
Jerusalem, 20, 65, 95, 134-135, 160, 168-169, 179-180, 242, 264, 266, 270-272, 276-277, 279, 307, 327, 367, 415, 456, 465, 545, 547, 562, 572-573, 581, 623, 649, 655, 666-667, 669-670, 673-674, 705, 720, 757, 783, 787, 789, 830, 832, 835-836, 838, 847, 920
Jesuits (Society of Jesus), 19, 28, 43, 45, 51, 58-63, 102, 124, 207, 384, 641-643, 652-653, 713, 803
Job of Pochaev, Saint, 58, 62, 543
John II, Metropolitan of Kiev, 287, 292, 310
John III Doukas Vatatzes the Merciful, Saint, 65, 162
John XXIII, Pope, 592, 616, 853
John Bekkos (Vekkos or Beccus), Patriarch, 36, 43, 56, 64, 79, 90-91, 94, 216-217, 219-220, 245-246-248, 250-251, 253-255, 260-262, 268, 349, 520, 523, 740

P

R

S

UNCUT MOUNTAIN PRESS TITLES

Books by Archpriest Peter Heers

Fr. Peter Heers, *The Ecclesiological Renovation of Vatican II: An Orthodox Examination of Rome's Ecumenical Theology Regarding Baptism and the Church*, 2015

Fr. Peter Heers, *The Missionary Origins of Modern Ecumenism: Milestones Leading up to 1920*, 2007

The Works of our Father Among the Saints, Nikodemos the Hagiorite

Vol. 1: *Exomologetarion: A Manual of Confession*
Vol. 2: *Concerning Frequent Communion of the Immaculate Mysteries of Christ*
Vol. 3: *Confession of Faith*

Other Available Titles

Elder Cleopa of Romania, *The Truth of our Faith*
Elder Cleopa of Romania, *The Truth of our Faith, Vol. II*
Fr. John Romanides, *Patristic Theology: The University Lectures of Fr. John Romanides*
Demetrios Aslanidis and Monk Damascene Grigoriatis, *Apostle to Zaire: The Life and Legacy of Blessed Father Cosmas of Grigoriou*
Protopresbyter Anastasios Gotsopoulos, *On Common Prayer with the Heterodox According to the Canons of the Church*
Robert Spencer, *The Church and the Pope*
G. M. Davis, *Antichrist: The Fulfillment of Globalization*
Athonite Fathers of the 20th Century, Vol. I
St. Gregory Palamas, *Apodictic Treatises on the Procession of the Holy Spirit*
St. Hilarion (Troitsky), *On the Dogma of the Church: An Historical Overview of the Sources of Ecclesiology*
Fr. Alexander Webster and Fr. Peter Heers, Editors, *Let No One Fear Death*
Subdeacon Nektarios Harrison, *Metropolitan Philaret of New York*
Elder George of Grigoriou, *Catholicism in the Light of Orthodoxy*
Archimandrite Ephraim Triandaphillopoulos, *Noetic Prayer as the Basis of Mission and the Struggle Against Heresy*
Dr. Nicholas Baldimtsis, *Life and Witness of St. Iakovos of Evia*
On the Reception of the Heterodox into the Orthodox Church: The Patristic Consensus and Criteria
Patrick (Craig) Truglia, *The Rise and Fall of the Papacy*
St. Raphael of Brooklyn, *In Defense of St. Cyprian*
The Divine Service of the Eighth Œcumenical Council
Hieromartyr Seraphim Zvezdenskiy, *Homilies on the Divine Liturgy*

Select Forthcoming Titles

This 1ˢᵗ Edition of

THE ORTHODOX PATRISTIC WITNESS CONCERNING CATHOLICISM

written by The Orthodox Ethos team, typeset in Garamond Premier Pro, and printed in this two thousand and twenty-fourth year of our Lord's Holy Incarnation is one of the many fine titles available from Uncut Mountain Press, translators and publishers of Orthodox Christian theological and spiritual literature. Find the book you are looking for at

uncutmountainpress.com

**GLORY BE TO GOD
FOR ALL THINGS**

AMEN.

Printed in the USA
CPSIA information can be obtained
at www.ICGtesting.com
LVHW051337070324
773415LV00003B/3